T0318483

THE ROUTLEDGE HANDBOOK OF FINANCIAL GEOGRAPHY

This handbook is a comprehensive and up-to-date reference work that offers a survey of the state of financial geography. With Brexit, a global recession triggered by the COVID-19 pandemic, and new financial technology threatening and promising to revolutionize finance, the map of the financial world is in a state of transformation, with major implications for development.

With these developments in the background, this handbook builds on this unprecedented momentum and responds to these epochal challenges, offering a comprehensive guide to financial geography. Financial geography is concerned with the study of money and finance in space and time, and their impacts on economy, society, and nature. The book consists of 29 chapters organized in six sections: theoretical perspectives in financial geography; financial assets and markets; investors; intermediation; regulation and governance; and finance, development, and the environment. Each chapter provides a balanced overview of current knowledge, identifying issues and discussing relevant debates. Written from a wide range of disciplines in an analytical and engaging style by authors based on six continents, the work also offers reflections on the direction in which the research agenda is likely to advance in the future.

The book's key audience will primarily be students and researchers in geography, urban studies, global studies, and planning who are more or less familiar with financial geography and who seek access to a state-of-the art survey of this area. It will also be useful for students and researchers in other disciplines, such as finance and economics, history, sociology, anthropology, politics, business studies, environmental studies, and other social sciences, who seek convenient access to financial geography as a new and relatively unfamiliar area. Finally, it will be a valuable resource for practitioners in the public and private sector, including business consultants and policy-makers, who look for alternative approaches to understanding money and finance.

Janelle Knox-Hayes is an Associate Professor of Economic Geography and Planning and Head of the Environmental Policy and Planning Group in the Department of Urban Studies and Planning, MIT.

Dariusz Wójcik is a Professor of Economic Geography at the School of Geography and the Environment, Oxford University, and Fellow of St Peter's College, Oxford.

ROUTLEDGE COMPANIONS IN BUSINESS, MANAGEMENT AND MARKETING

Routledge Companions are prestige volumes that provide an overview of a research field or topic. Surveying the business disciplines, the books in this series incorporate both established and emerging research themes. Compiled and edited by an array of highly regarded scholars, these volumes also benefit from global teams of contributors reflecting disciplinary diversity.

Individually, *Routledge Companions in Business, Management and Marketing* provide impactful one-stop-shop publications. Collectively, they represent a comprehensive learning and research resource for researchers, postgraduate students, and practitioners.

Published titles in this series include:

THE ROUTLEDGE COMPANION TO HAPPINESS AT WORK
Edited by Joan Marques

THE ROUTLEDGE COMPANION TO ANTHROPOLOGY AND BUSINESS
Edited by Raza Mir and Anne-Laure Fayard

THE ROUTLEDGE COMPANION TO INTERNATIONAL HOSPITALITY MANAGEMENT
Edited by Marco A. Gardini, Michael C. Ottenbacher and Markus Schuckert

THE ROUTLEDGE HANDBOOK OF CRITICAL FINANCE STUDIES
Edited by Christian Borch and Robert Wosnitzer

THE ROUTLEDGE HANDBOOK OF FINANCIAL GEOGRAPHY
Edited by Janelle Knox-Hayes and Dariusz Wójcik

For more information about this series, please visit: www.routledge.com/Routledge-Companions-in-Business-Management-and-Marketing/book-series/RCBUS

THE ROUTLEDGE HANDBOOK OF FINANCIAL GEOGRAPHY

Edited by

Janelle Knox-Hayes and Dariusz Wójcik

NEW YORK AND LONDON

First published 2021
by Routledge
52 Vanderbilt Avenue, New York, NY 10017

and by Routledge
2 Park Square, Milton Park, Abingdon, Oxon, OX14 4RN

Routledge is an imprint of the Taylor & Francis Group, an informa business

Library of Congress Cataloging-in-Publication Data
Names: Knox, Janelle Kallie, 1983- editor. | Wójcik, Dariusz, 1972- editor.
Title: The Routledge handbook of financial geography / edited by Janelle Knox-Hayes and Dariusz Wójcik.
Description: 1 Edition. | New York : Routledge, 2020. | Series: Routledge companions in business, management & marketing | Includes bibliographical references and index.
Identifiers: LCCN 2020029022 (print) | LCCN 2020029023 (ebook) | ISBN 9780815369738 (hardback) | ISBN 9781351119061 (ebook)
Subjects: LCSH: International finance--Handbooks, manuals, etc. | Banks and banking--Handbooks, manuals, etc. | Foreign exchange rates--Handbooks, manuals, etc. | Investments--Handbooks, manuals, etc.
Classification: LCC HG3881 .R688 2020 (print) | LCC HG3881 (ebook) | DDC 332/.042--dc23
LC record available at https://lccn.loc.gov/2020029022
LC ebook record available at https://lccn.loc.gov/2020029023

ISBN: 978-0-8153-6973-8 (hbk)
ISBN: 978-1-351-11906-1 (ebk)

Typeset in Bembo
by SPi Global, India

To Gordon L Clark, our mentor, our partners Jarrod and Ania, and Janelle and Jarrod's daughters Isabelle and Mackenzie

CONTENTS

FIGURES

TABLES

Tables

CONTRIBUTORS

Lindsey Appleyard is an economic geographer with research interests around financial geographies, specializing in financial inclusion and inclusive economies. Lindsey's recent research has focused on responsible lending and borrowing, subprime credit, financial capability, and financial citizenship. Her research makes an academic contribution by providing nuanced understandings of the 'lived experience' of financialization. Through Lindsey's networks and collaborations, her body of research aims to make a significant impact on the economy and society by influencing policy and practice.

David S. Bieri is Associate Professor of Urban Affairs and Associate Professor of Economics at Virginia Tech. Bieri's current research examines 'money and the metropolis', focusing on the joint evolutionary dynamics of urbanization and the development of the monetary–financial system. His other research examines regulatory aspects of international finance and global monetary governance. He also writes about the history of economic thought. Prior to his work in the academy, Bieri held various senior positions at the Bank for International Settlements (BIS) in Basel, Switzerland, including as the Adviser to the CEO. Bieri also worked as a high-yield analyst at Bankers Trust in London and in fixed-income syndication at UBS in Zürich. Bieri received his Ph.D. from the School of Public & International Affairs at Virginia Tech. He holds an M.Sc. in corporate and international finance from the University of Durham and a B.Sc. (hons) in economics from the London School of Economics.

Patrick Bigger is a lecturer in Economic Geography at the Lancaster Environment Centre. His work looks at a range of financial–environmental entanglements and their governance, including carbon trading, green bonds, for-profit biodiversity conservation, and environmental impact investing, with field sites spanning California, London, and Kenya. He holds a Ph.D. in

Economic Geography from the University of Kentucky, and previously worked as a Marie Curie Post-Doctoral Fellow at the University of Manchester and as Senior Research Associate at the Pentland Centre for Sustainability in Business at the Lancaster University Management School.

Patrick Bond is Professor at the University of the Western Cape School of Government in Cape Town. He began his career at the US Federal Reserve Bank (1983–85) while studying at the Wharton School of Finance, and then pursued doctoral studies in economic geography at Johns Hopkins University in Baltimore. After moving to Southern Africa in 1989, he served urban social movements working on financial justice based at the NGO Planact in Johannesburg. In 1994 and 1996, he worked in the Reconstruction and Development Ministry in President Nelson Mandela's office. His best-known work is *Elite Transition: From Apartheid to Neoliberalism in South Africa*, and other critical analyses can be found in the books *Politics of Climate Justice*, *Against Global Apartheid*, *Talk Left Walk Right*, *Looting Africa*, *The Accumulation of Capital in Southern Africa*, *Zimbabwe's Plunge*, *Uneven Zimbabwe,* and *Cities of Gold, Townships of Coal.*

Kate Booth is Senior Lecturer in Human Geography at the University of Tasmania. Her research is motivated by an interest in place and places, and the possibility of political dissent. She is particularly interested in the co-production of financial and economic processes and urban places and life, and currently leads the ARC Discovery Project When Disaster Strikes: Geographies of house and contents under-insurance (DP170100096). Kate also leads the Geography and Spatial Sciences postgraduate teaching program and coordinates the professionally accredited Master of Planning course. She teaches regional and urban planning. In the face of climate catastrophe, Kate is an active participant in Extinction Rebellion.

Gabriella Y. Carolini is an Associate Professor of urban planning at the Massachusetts Institute of Technology (MIT). Her research examines the governance and evaluation of urban infrastructure development across cities in sub-Saharan Africa, Latin America, and North America, with a focus on the financial architecture of water and sanitation projects. Gabriella has advised and worked with several international organizations, including the UN Economic Commission for Africa, UN-Habitat, UN Economic Commission for Latin America and the Caribbean, and the Japanese International Cooperation Agency. Her work is published in a broad range of academic journals, including the *International Journal of Urban and Regional Research*, *Urban Studies*, *Environment and Planning C*, *The Lancet*, and the *American Journal of Public Health.*

Wim Carton has a Ph.D. in Human Geography and a background in Development Studies, International Relations, and History. He is currently Assistant Professor at the Lund University Center for Sustainability Studies, Sweden. His primary research focus is on the political ecology and political economy of climate change mitigation, with a particular emphasis on questions of carbon removal. He has previously worked on the political economy of market-based mechanisms for climate and energy policy, on the politics of carbon offsetting in the forestry sector, and on radical agricultural alternatives.

Jungwoo Chun is a Ph.D. candidate at the Department of Urban Studies & Planning at MIT, where he studies public policy and urban sustainability. He is a graduate instructor of a variety of negotiation courses, environmental policy and planning, and water diplomacy. He is a lecturer and an organizing committee member of the BLOXHUB Summer School on Urban Resilience.

Gordon L. Clark, D.Sc., FBA, is Professorial Fellow at St Edmund Hall, Oxford and Halford Mackinder Professor of Geography Emeritus, and Director Emeritus of the Smith School of Enterprise and the Environment at Oxford University. With expertise in organization theory, finance, and decision-making, he has held appointments at Harvard's John F. Kennedy School of Government, Harvard Law School, the University of Chicago, Carnegie Mellon University, and Monash University (Australia). He has also been a Mellon Fellow at the US National Academy of Sciences. Recent papers on human behavior, financial literacy, and advice-seeking have been published in major geography, economics, and finance journals. Related research on organizations and decision-making can be found in academic journals and his co-authored *Institutional Investors in Global Markets* (with Ashby Monk). Gordon has also been an employer-nominated trustee on the Oxford Staff Pension Scheme's for 10 years and has interests in a number of US start-up tech and finance companies. He is also on the advisory boards of a number of investment companies.

Isadora Cruxên is a Ph.D. candidate in International Development at MIT's Department of Urban Studies and Planning. Her current research interests focus on interactions between state and financial actors, and the ways in which they influence urban development and access to public services in cities in Latin America. Isadora holds a Bachelor's degree in Political Science from the University of Brasília, Brazil, and a Master's in City Planning from MIT. She previously worked as a research fellow at the Institute for Applied Economic Research in Brazil on projects concerning public participation in policy development.

Priyanka deSouza is a Ph.D. candidate on a Presidential fellowship at the Department of Urban Studies and Planning. She has Bachelor's and Master's degrees of Technology in Energy Engineering and a minor in physics from the Indian Institute Technology of Bombay (2013), an M.Sc. in Environmental Change and Management (2014) and an MBA (2015) from the University of Oxford, where she studied as a Rhodes Scholar. Priyanka worked as a consultant for UN Environment in Nairobi (2015–16), where she was responsible for working on developing an air quality monitoring system for the city of Nairobi. She has also worked as a Drawdown Fellow (2016–17) and was a contributing author to the NYTimes Bestseller *Drawdown: The Most Comprehensive Plan Ever Proposed to Reverse Global Warming.*

Gary Dymski is Professor of Applied Economics at the Leeds University Business School, a position he took up in 2012 after 22 years in the University of California system. Gary's research focuses on discrimination and redlining in credit markets, urban economic development, financial crisis, the subprime and Eurozone crises, banking and financial regulation, and urban development. His research projects at Leeds include one on inequality and finance in Europe, and another on the challenge of inequality and the robotic transition. He coordinates the institutions research hub for the ESRC Rebuilding Macroeconomics project and is a co-investigator on the ESRC Productivity Insights Network. Both projects are seeking to introduce new approaches to policy-making that build in considerations of regional-rebalancing, inequality, and ecological and social sustainability. Gary is also a member of the UK Commission on a Gender-Equal Economy.

Daniel Haberly is a Senior Lecturer in Human Geography in the School of Global Studies at the University of Sussex. His research examines the political and institutional geography of global finance, with areas of emphasis including sovereign wealth fund investment and asset management, and the architecture, regulation, and politics of the global offshore financial network. He is currently leading a UK Department for International Development-funded project, in collaboration with the Tax Justice Network, that seeks to understand how historical changes in the international regulatory landscape have impacted the use of shell companies for corruption-linked and other illicit financial activities.

Sarah Hall is Professor of Economic Geography, at the University of Nottingham. Supported by funding from the Economic and Social Research Council, the British Academy, and the Leverhulme Trust, her research centers on London's international financial district and its relations with North America, Europe, and China. She is the author of *Global Finance* (Sage, 2017) and *Respatialising Finance* (Wiley 2020). Her work has been published in a number of leading academic journals and the media. She is joint Editor-in-Chief of the journal *Geoforum* and held a British Academy Mid-Career Fellowship (2015–17). She is currently a Senior Fellow at the UK in a Changing Europe, working on the impacts of Brexit on financial services.

Christopher Harker's research examines spatial practices of debt and finance in Palestine and the UK. He is interested in everyday practices of politics and agency, and developing alternatives that allow people both to manage existing debt problems and to create new forms of flourishing beyond debt. His published work advances a spatial conceptualization of debt, drawing primarily on a decade-long ethnographic engagement with the Palestinian city of Ramallah. His work analyses the role debt plays amidst a broader range of socio-cultural and economic practices to create new modes of living in the face of ongoing colonial occupation. These ideas are explored most extensively in his forthcoming monograph *Spacing Debt: Obligations, Endurance and Impasse in Ramallah, Palestine* (Duke University Press).

Stefanos Ioannou is a Postdoctoral Research Associate in Finance and Geography, University of Oxford. He obtained his Ph.D. in Economics from the University of Leeds in 2016. Prior to his doctoral studies, he completed an M.Phil. in Economics at the University of Athens (2012) and an M.Sc. in Finance at Newcastle University (2009). His research interests include fiscal and monetary policy, financial macroeconomics, and economic geography. His peer reviewed articles have been published in *Urban Studies*, the *Review of Political Economy*, and *Environment and Planning A: Economy and Space*, among other outlets. Stefanos has also lectured in Economics (University College Cork, 2016–17), teaching advanced macroeconomics and finance.

Britta Klagge is a Full Professor of Geography and Head of the Department of Geosciences at the University of Bonn, Germany. Her current research focuses on economic geography with a special interest in renewable energies, finance, globalization, and governance. She obtained a Master's degree in Geography from the University of Wisconsin-Madison and a Doctorate in Geography from the University of Vienna, prior to which she obtained a diploma in mathematics at the University of Bonn. Britta has many years of experience in both quantitative and qualitative methods, and has directed various research projects, most of them with an international perspective and comparative approach. Her international partners include colleagues from China, Kenya, Poland, Switzerland, and the UK.

Jana M. Kleibert leads the Leibniz-Junior Research Group Constructing Transnational Spaces of Higher Education at the Institute for Research on Society and Space (IRS) in Erkner, Germany, and at the Humboldt University of Berlin. She is an economic geographer with a keen interest in the geographies of globalization, the internationalization of service industries, the networks and spaces of global production, and the re-making of global cities. She received her Ph.D. in Human Geography from the University of Amsterdam with a dissertation on the offshoring of information technology-enabled service employment to the Global South. Jana Kleibert has held visiting appointments at the Goethe University of Frankfurt/Main, at the University of Manchester, and at the National University of Singapore.

Tobias J. Klinge is a Ph.D. candidate at the Division of Geography and Tourism, KU Leuven, Belgium, where he currently researches economic geographies of corporate financialization processes. Departing from an interest in geographies of globalization, his previous work investigated agricultural investments and urban land prices.

Janelle Knox-Hayes is an Associate Professor of Economic Geography and Planning, and Head of the Environmental Policy and Planning Group in the Department of Urban Studies and Planning, MIT. She directs the Resilient Communities Lab, which seeks to help communities integrate their core values into decision-making and planning across a variety of scales. Her research focuses on the ways in which social and environmental systems are governed under changing temporal and spatial scales as a consequence of globalization. Her latest projects examine how social values shape sustainable development in the Arctic, and how communities in Southern Louisiana are managing coastal retreat. Her publications include multiple peer reviewed articles and two books, *Saving for Retirement* and *The Culture of Markets: The Political Economy of Climate Governance.*

Karen P.Y. Lai is Associate Professor at the Department of Geography, Durham University. Her research areas cover geographies of money and finance, market formation, service sectors, global city networks, and financial center development. Her recent project examines everyday financialization through the knowledge networks of financial advisors and consumers. She is currently working on two projects regarding the global financial networks of investment banks and law firms in Asia, and how FinTech could be reshaping the roles of financial centers. She is on the Executive Committees of the Global Network on Financial Geography (FinGeo) and the Economic Geography Research Group of the Royal Geographical Society (with the Institute of British Geographers). She also serves on the journal editorial board of *Geoforum* and *Geography Compass* (Economic section).

Paul Langley is Professor of Economic Geography at Durham University. Paul's research interests focus on geographies of money, finance, and financialization. His publications include *The Everyday Life of Global Finance* (Oxford University Press, 2008) and *Liquidity Lost* (Oxford University Press, 2015). Paul is presently researching a number of new and emerging spaces of money and finance, including social finance, green finance, and digital finance.

Andrew Leyshon is Professor of Economic Geography at the University of Nottingham. His work has mainly focused on financial and musical economies, and the impact of digital technology on both. He has authored and edited various books that reflect these interests. They include *Reformatted: Code, Networks and the Transformation of the Music Industry* (Oxford University Press, 2014), which explores how P2P networks and MP3 software helped re-make the musical economy, and *Money/Space: Geographies of Monetary Transformation* (with Nigel Thrift, Routledge, 1997), which argued that not only does money have a geography, but that it is also inherently geographical. He is currently investigating the implications of the rise of the digital platform business model.

Ashby H.B. Monk is the Executive and Research Director of the Stanford Global Projects Center. His current research focus is on the design and governance of institutional investors, with particular specialization on pension and sovereign wealth funds. Outside Stanford, he is the co-founder of Long Game Savings, a personal finance application that uses gamification and behavioral finance to encourage positive financial behaviors. He is also the co-founder and President of Real Capital Innovation, a software company that facilitates dynamic portfolio construction and management for long-term investors. He received his Doctorate in Economic Geography at Oxford University and holds a Master's in International Economics from the Université de Paris I—Pantheon Sorbonne and a Bachelor's in Economics from Princeton University.

Johnna Montgomerie is Head of Department in European and International Studies at King's College London. Her research on financialization, debt, and households explores the many facets of inequality created by debt-driven growth and austerity. Her most recent book, *Should We Abolish Household Debt?*, was published in 2019 by Polity, and she is Principle Investigator for the ESRC Rebuilding Macro framework Opening the Black-Box of the Household.

Susan Newman is a Professor of Economics at the Open University, UK. She is interested in investigating the relationship between developments in finance and the restructuring of production, with particular focus on the Global South. Her work takes a historical and interdisciplinary approach that is rooted in political economy. Susan has published works on the financialization of agri-food commodity chains, the political economy of post-apartheid South Africa, and the relationship between finance and industrial policy. She is a member of Reteaching Economics and the International Initiative for Promoting Political Economy, and is committed to the promotion of political economy in economics education.

Stefan Ouma is the Chair of Economic Geography in the Department of Geography at the University of Bayreuth. His research is primarily concerned with the economic geographies of globalization, drawing on insights from political economy/ecology, socio-economics, and poststructuralist and practice oriented theories. His overriding research goal is to rematerialize 'the economy' in times of seemingly unbounded economic relations, and to open it up for political debate regarding the more sustainable and just pathways and forms of economy-making. His current research on the themes 'global commodity chains and critical geographies of logistics', 'industrial work in the digital age', and 'agricultural transformations in the context of financialization and digitization' reflects this concern.

Fenghua Pan is Associate Professor of Economic Geography at the School of Geography in Beijing Normal University. He holds a Ph.D. degree in human geography from Peking University and was a research associate at University College London and visiting scholar at the University of California, Los Angeles, and the University of Hong Kong. He is the founding member and executive committee member of the global network on financial geography

(FinGeo). He organized the 1st FinGeo Global Conference in Beijing in September 2019. His current research interests are the global financial network, financialization, Fintech, venture capital and the capital market, and urban and regional development in China. His recent papers have been published in lead journals including *Regional Studies*, *Urban Studies*, *Geoforum*, *Urban Geography*.

Katharina Pistor is the Edwin B. Parker Professor of Comparative Law at Columbia Law School and director of the Law School's Center on Global Legal Transformation. Her research and teaching spans corporate law, corporate governance, money and finance, property rights, comparative law, and law and development. She has published widely in legal and interdisciplinary journals and is the author and co-author of several books. She is the recipient of the Max Planck Research Award (2012) and of several grants, including from the Institute for New Economic Thinking and the National Science Foundation. She is a member of the Berlin-Brandenburg Academy of Science and a Fellow of the European Corporate Governance Institute. Her most recent book is *The Code of Capital: How the Law Creates Wealth and Inequality* (Princeton University Press, 2019).

Shaina Potts is an Assistant Professor in the Departments of Geography and Global Studies at the University of California, Los Angeles. Her interests lie at the intersection of political and economic geography, international political economy, and critical legal studies. Her research has applied this interdisciplinary approach to a range of topics including cross-border financial geographies, post-colonial sovereign debt relations, and the politics of territory. Her current project examines the linked roles of US domestic law in producing both global capitalism and US hegemony.

Raquel Rolnik is a professor at the Faculty of Architecture and Urban Planning of the University of São Paulo. Architect and urban planner, with over 35 years of scholarship, activism, and practical experience in planning, urban land policy, and housing issues, she has held various government positions including Director of the Planning Department of the city of São Paulo (1989–92) and National Secretary for Urban Programs of the Brazilian Ministry of Cities (2003–07), as well as working with an NGO and in consultancy at national and international levels. From 2008 to 2014, Raquel Rolnik was UN Special Rapporteur on adequate housing. She is author of several books and articles on financialization of housing and urban policies, including *Urban Warfare: Housing in the Age of Finance* published by Verso.

Aniket Shah is a Senior Fellow at Columbia University's Center on Sustainable Investment (CCSI). He has spent his career at the intersection of international finance and sustainable development. Previously, Aniket was the Head of Sustainable Investing at Oppenheimer Funds, a global investment manager, and prior to that he was the Head of Finance for Sustainable Development at the UN Sustainable Development Solutions Networks. Aniket has a Ph.D.

in Economic Geography from the University of Oxford and a B.A. from Yale University. Aniket is a member of the Economic Club of New York and the Bretton Woods Committee, and serves on the International Board of Amnesty International.

Dariusz Wójcik is a Professor of Economic Geography at the School of Geography and the Environment, Oxford University, and Fellow of St Peters College Oxford. His research focuses on finance and globalization, and their impacts on urban and regional development. He serves on the editorial board of *Economic Geography*, the *Journal of Economic Geography*, *Environment and Planning A*, *Growth and Change*, *Sustainability*, and *GeoJournal*. His books include *The Geography of Finance: Corporate Governance in a Global Marketplace* (2007, OUP) and *The Global Stock Market: Issuers, Investors and Intermediaries in an Uneven World* (2011, OUP). He is the co-editor of the *New Oxford Handbook of Economic Geography* (2018, OUP) and *International Financial Centres after the Global Financial Crisis and Brexit* (2018, OUP). He co-founded and chairs the Global Network on Financial Geography (www.fingeo.net) and leads the European Research Council-funded project on Cities in Global Financial Networks: Financial and Business Services and Development in the 21st Century (www.citynet21.org).

Matthew Zook is a University Research Professor in the Department of Geography at the University of Kentucky. His research centers on evolving economic and social practices afforded by information technology and big data. This includes studying how code, algorithms, space, and place interact as people increasingly use mobile, digital technologies to navigate through their everyday, lived geographies. His most recent project focuses on how blockchain cryptocurrencies reshape the spaces and practices of valuation and financing, particularly within tech-based startup firms. He is currently the managing editor of the open access Sage journal *Big Data & Society*.

ACKNOWLEDGMENTS

The editors are grateful to Brianna Ascher, Naomi Round Cahalin, Mary Del Plato, Megan Smith, and David Varley from Routledge, New York, and Natalie Hamil at SPi Global, for their encouragement, advice and assistance. We are deeply appreciative of our two editorial assistants and collaborators Jungwoo Chun and Priyanka deSouza who dedicated many hours to the preparation of the manuscript.

Janelle Knox-Hayes would like to acknowledge funding from the MIT Humanities and Social Science, and Bemis Funds.

Dariusz Wójcik would like to acknowledge funding from the European Research Council (ERC) under the European Union Horizon 2020 Research and Innovation programme (Grant Agreement Number 681337).

Obviously, the book reflects only the authors' views and those listed above are not responsible for any use that may be made of the information it contains.

1

INTRODUCTION

Janelle Knox-Hayes and Dariusz Wójcik

Introduction: Background and Objectives

Financial geography is concerned with the study of money and finance in space and time, and their impacts on economy, society, and nature. Geography is fundamental to understanding finance and vice versa. Finance is one of the most globalized and networked of human activities. Financial centers as nodes in these networks epitomize modern capitalism. Money penetrates every nook and cranny of the global economy, changing social and political relations and cultures in the process, as well as the natural environment. Though rooted in geography, financial geography is more than its subdiscipline. It is an interdisciplinary perspective informed by research in finance and economics, history, sociology, anthropology, politics, business studies, environmental studies and other social sciences, in addition to geography. While the terms 'financial geography' and 'geography of finance' are mostly used interchangeably, we make deliberate use of the former term. For us, the difference is more than one of syntax, and is underpinned not only by studying the impacts of money and finance on economy, society, and nature, but also by recognizing that understanding money and finance is fundamental to understanding geographical phenomena beyond money and finance. Put differently: in financial geography, finance is also 'a lens through which one can look at other issues' (Aalbers, 2018: 916). This highlights the open-ended, inclusive, and interdisciplinary character of financial geography.

As such, financial geography has a rich tradition that goes back to at least the 1980s. This tradition has been revitalized and financial geography made more interdisciplinary than ever in the wake of the global financial crisis, which laid bare the inadequacies of the mainstream approaches to money and finance in economics. This momentum is exemplified by the creation of the

Global Network on Financial Geography (www.fingeo.net), with hundreds of members worldwide and the first working paper series dedicated to financial geography. With Brexit, the continued rise of Asian financial centers, new digital currencies, the cybersecurity risks facing financial firms, and new financial technology threatening and promising to revolutionize finance, the map of the financial world is in a state of transformation, with major implications for development. With these developments in the background, we have realized that the time is ripe to build on this unprecedented momentum and respond to these epochal challenges with a handbook that offers a comprehensive guide to financial geography.

We started the *Handbook* project in mid-2017, our aim being to create a comprehensive and up-to-date reference work that offers students, researchers, and practitioners a survey of the state of financial geography—one that could be cited as an authoritative source on this burgeoning subject and that included emerging and cutting-edge areas. Our key audiences are students and researchers in geography, urban studies, global studies, planning, and other disciplines closely related to geography; audiences that are more or less familiar with financial geography who seek access to a state-of-the art survey of this area. In addition, we would like the *Handbook* to be used by students and researchers in other disciplines, such as finance and economics, history, sociology, anthropology, politics, business studies, environmental studies, and other social sciences, who seek convenient access to financial geography as a new and relatively unfamiliar area. Finally, we want to reach out to practitioners in the public and private sectors, including business consultants and policy-makers, who look for alternative approaches to understanding money and finance.

Of course, ours is not the first handbook or handbook-style text on financial geography. In 1994, Stuart Corbridge, Ron Martin, and Nigel Thrift edited *Money, Power and Space*, which focused on the geopolitics of money, relationships between money, states and markets, and 'money politics'. That influential volume took what could be described as a political economic geography approach to finance, discussing among other topics competition among currencies, the rise and fall of Japanese financial power, offshore finance, European monetary integration, and the restructuring of pension provision. In 1998, we saw the publication of Risto Laulajainen's *Financial Geography: A Banker's View* by the Gothenburg School of Economics and Commercial Law (republished in 2003 by Routledge). The book is, indeed, structured as though it were designed by a financial industry insider, starting with a discussion on assets, institutional investors, regulators and rating agencies, and legal issues, moving on to mapping and charting the evolution of various financial markets, exchanges, banking, and insurance, and finishing with a section on finance centers, from the leading global centers through to those offshore. The book explains with exceptional clarity how the different parts of finance work. It is illustrated with a wealth of data on trends and patterns that is, arguably, unprecedented and still unmatched in the area of financial geography. In 1999, came *Money and the*

Space Economy edited by Ron Martin, complementing and updating the contribution of *Money, Power and Space* (1994). It could be said that the volume was more economic geographical in approach than its 1994 predecessor, with greater emphasis on the spatiality of banking, financial center development, and the impacts of finance on local development. In the introduction, Ron Martin talks about the emergence of the 'geography of money' as a new subdiscipline, stressing its close relationship to economic geography. The vitality of financial geography in the mid- and late 1990s is also reflected in the publication of the first progress reports on the topic written by Andrew Leyshon for *Progress in Human Geography* (1995, 1997, 1998).

The late 1990s and the early and mid-2000s brought a considerable number of major financial developments: the Asian financial crisis, the creation of the Eurozone, the dot.com bubble and burst, corporate governance scandals with Enron leading the fray, and the build-up of the housing price bubble, to name just a few. While these events stimulated the publication of many papers and some research monographs (see, e.g., Clark and Wójcik, 2007, a book focusing on corporate governance), it took the global financial crisis for *Progress in Human Geography* to commit to more reports on finance—in fact, a whole series of them (Hall, 2010, 2011, 2012; Christophers, 2014, 2015, 2016; Aalbers, 2018, 2019a, 2019b; Wójcik, 2020, 2020b). It was a long time before anyone attempted another handbook-style project. The latter was undertaken once more by Ron Martin, who teamed up with Jane Pollard. Their *Handbook on the Geographies of Money and Finance* (2017) is a 26-chapter tour de force of the field, remaking the case for geographies of finance, discussing the spatial organization of the financial system, spaces of financial and monetary regulation, as well as new and emerging money spaces, such as environmental finance, community currencies, migrant remittances, Islamic finance, crowdfunding, and Bitcoin. The following year brought the single-authored *Global Finance* by Sarah Hall (2018), a textbook-like exposition of the subject, focusing on financial centers, financialization, financial elites, and financial exclusion, and advancing a case for cultural and political geographies of finance. Another sign of the revitalization of financial geography in recent years is the fact that the *New Oxford Handbook of Economic Geography* published in 2018 (edited by Clark, Feldman, Gertler, and Wójcik) devotes an entire section comprising six chapters to finance, compared to two chapters in a section on global economic integration found in the original 2000 edition of the *Handbook* (edited by Clark, Feldman, and Gertler).

In the above discussion, we cover only English language publications, so it is possible that we are overlooking works in other languages. In 2014, for example, Hans-Martin Zademach published the textbook-style *Finanzgeographie*, which outlines the development of the discipline and its methodological foundations; explains the global financial system, and financial flows, and their impacts on development; and ends with chapters on financial centers and financialization. Of course, there have also been many edited works on financial geography with some handbook features, but with a narrower focus. One example here is *Money and Finance After the Crisis: Critical Thinking for Uncertain Times* (2017) edited by Brett Christophers, Andrew Leyshon, and Geoff Mann, which focuses on financial imaginaries, practices, and financialization. Another is *Geofinance between Political and Financial Geography: A Focus on the Semi-Periphery of the Global Financial System* (2020) edited by Silvia Grandi, Christina Sellar, and Juvaria Jafri.

Tracking the evolution of financial geography as a field of research is not straightforward, since it is a tricky topic on which to conduct a bibliometric analysis. One the one hand, a Web of Science search for works that contain the terms 'financial geography', 'geography of finance', or 'geography of money' in the title, abstract, or keywords yields only 120 publications, starting in 1995. On the other hand, a search that uses terms 'geograph*' AND ('financ*' OR 'money' OR 'monetary') brings up 8,900 records going back to the 1960s. Neither should be used as a reliable estimate of the size of financial geographical scholarship. The former set is certainly too restrictive, and the latter contains many works that do not really focus on financial geography while, at the same time, excluding many that focus on financial issues such as pensions or real estate, but do not use the terms 'financ*', 'money' or 'monetary' in the title, abstract, or keywords. What this simple exercise nevertheless shows is that, although research that involves a combination of finance and geography is sizeable, only a fraction of this scholarship promotes the identity of financial geography directly. For comparison, according to Web of Science, the number of works that use the term 'economic geography' in the title, abstract, or keywords is close to 5,000. This, in our view, clearly highlights the need for reference works that present financial geography as a diverse but coherent area of research.

Financial Transformations and Geographical Questions

The coevolution of finance and information technology throughout the twentieth and twenty-first centuries deepened and expanded the interaction capacity of human geographies. However, the growth of interaction *capacity* between spatially situated social, political, and economic systems does not necessarily result in the greater interaction and integration of societies. The disaggregation of the interactive capacity of human geographies allows analysts to engage in the fruitful parsing of contemporary events. For example, the reemergence of populist nationalism such as the Brexit campaign is a product of the disjuncture between political integration and economic integration. While some of the underlying political and social infrastructure has been damaged through events such as Brexit (i.e., the separation of markets), many of the ties that bind remain (the connection of borders, the similarity of social institutions such as those of education, and the integration of financial exchange). Disaggregating interaction capacity allows analysts to distinguish more carefully between the sectors that suffer change or damage and those that do not, as well as to assess the consequences.

While the processes of human interaction continue to evolve in different ways, with respect to finance, the interaction capacity and processes of human geographies continue to grow. As the Asian financial crisis in the late 1990s and the 2007–8 global financial crisis originating in the United States demonstrate, financial processes and practices in one geography can, through contagion effects, profoundly impact polities and societies far removed from the epicenters of crisis. From the Society for Worldwide Interbank Financial Telecommunication (SWIFT) banking network through interdependent currency valuations to the potential of a global (or at least regional) financialized system for regulating carbon emissions, finance has harnessed together peoples across vast scales and made them mutually vulnerable to economic policy—though, in practice, the vulnerability falls disproportionately on small and poor states. Yet, as this volume demonstrates, the impacts of financial integration have varied considerably across geographic regions. Finance-driven growth looks considerably different in Bangkok or Reykjavik, for example, than it does in Beijing or Washington. This suggests a set of profoundly geographic questions: How does finance-driven interaction capacity vary across space (and time)? How does sensitivity to finance shift across space? How do polities and societies confront these sensitivities?

The deepening and widening of interaction capacity underpinned by finance also has profound structural effects. Capital generated in one geography can be accumulated in another and invested in material outcomes in a third. Thus, the expansion of geographic interaction through financialization has the potential, through the globalized flow of capital, to redistribute wealth through investment rematerialization. As wealth generated in one geography seeks advantageous returns, underdeveloped economic geographies where growth potentials are greatest should benefit. In practice, however, scholarship indicates that relationship between finance, geography, and development functions in reverse. As finance-driven interaction capacity has grown, it has functioned to a substantial degree to siphon wealth from underdeveloped geographies to existing centers of capital accumulation across scales—national, regional, and global (Godechot, 2016). As with acute crises, geographers are well-positioned to tackle crucial questions regarding the spatial flows of wealth, how it (re)materializes, and the ways polities and societies adapt to and seek to alter these structural flows.

The specific form(s) of financial interaction capacity also interact with geographic effects. Evidence suggests the digitization of finance produces divergent effects across various economic sectors and their socio-economic outcomes (Sabbagh et al., 2013). The 2007–8 financial crisis owed as much to the complex interconnections of digitized finance—for example, complex algorithmic valuations of packaged mortgage products, increased speed and volume of transactions—as to poor economic behavior at the point of origin of mortgages in the United States. The concentration of wealth (and socialization of costs when costs were materialized) facilitated by these digitized processes can be understood as a key contributor to a backlash against globalization. Some have argued that, in the wake of the crisis, we have even witnessed 'slowbalisation' (*The Economist*, 2019). A cyclical downturn has been followed by the rise of nationalist policies. Finance-driven growth has generated 'slowbalisation' as politicians across the 'West' have promulgated nationalist policies, erected new barriers to migration (particularly low-skilled), and fomented trade tensions, if not wars, with US–China relations at the epicenter.

Here, the analytic disaggregation of interaction capacity and process is helpful. While nationalist politicians have impeded some of the processes of globalized finance, interaction capacity remains relatively unscathed. The digitization of finance has proceeded largely unhindered. The emergence of new regulations (i.e., political processes)—the relatively easily manipulated interbank interest rate benchmark LIBOR is to be replaced, the general move away from over-the-counter securities trading, new transparency rules for debt, and country-by-country reporting rules for multinational firms—as well as the rise in the power of central banks suggest that the interaction capacity underpinning globalization remains strong and is, perhaps, even growing. But this capacity is not equal in effect; the processes built on it benefit a select few central nodes in the network. The largest central bank, with the US Federal Reserve in the lead, has grown in its extraterritorial influence. The IMF and World Bank continue to exercise substantial systemic power, in contrast to the relatively slow growth of the New Development Bank (formerly known as the BRICS Development Bank) and the Asian Infrastructure Investment Bank.

In the twenty-first century, climate change and other global environmental processes also deepen and broaden the interaction capacity of dispersed human geographies. Decisions regarding economic and energy policy in the United States, now as in the past, reverberate around the world, jeopardizing the lives and livelihoods of people thousands of miles away as climate change reshapes rainfall patterns, sea levels, land use, flora and fauna distribution, freshwater reserves, and so on (Davies et al., 2020). Environmental processes and practices once independent are now harnessed together through rising atmospheric concentrations of carbon dioxide. The conjunction of finance and climate change raises a myriad of questions: How are financial flows shaping the prevalence and success of development investments (e.g., the nature and scope of China's massive Belt and Road Initiative)? How is finance responding to climate risks (the need for cities and municipalities around the globe to mitigate greenhouse gas emissions while adapting infrastructure and other critical human systems to the adverse effects of climate change)? How is finance reifying climate risks? How is finance shaping perceptions of financial risk? What are the spatial and economic consequences of the interaction between finance and climate processes? These general questions suggest a vast research enterprise, and economic and financial geographers are poised to rise to the challenge.

Outline of the Structure

Our *Handbook* consists of 29 chapters, including this Introduction. This size presented us with the opportunity and the challenge of making the book diverse and comprehensive in coverage. Our contributors are based in nine countries on six continents, with the largest numbers based in the United Kingdom and the United States. While nearly half our contributors work in geography departments, others work in departments of urban studies, European and international studies, economics, management, law, sociology and government, and sustainability. There are nearly as many female as male contributors. There are baby boomers, generation X as well millennials among them. Three of our authors (Patrick Bond, Gordon L. Clark, and Andrew Leyshon) actually wrote chapters for the 1994 classic volume discussed above.

The structure of the *Handbook* is based on six parts. Part I deals with theoretical perspectives on finance from the concept of financial and business services, through Marxian approaches, the cultural economy of finance, and the role of law in the production of financial geography, to the notions of financial ecosystems and ecologies. Part II is devoted to major types of financial assets: currencies, stocks, housing, commodities, and infrastructure. Part III looks at investors and their behavior, with chapters on long-term investment management, financial decision-making, household finance, impact investors, and development banks—the latter two of which have recently become prominent players in global finance.

Part IV focuses on intermediation, covering banks and credit, insurance, the process of unbundling value chains in finance, and the impacts of financial technology (FinTech) on intermediation. Part V moves to regulation and governance, starting with the legal foundations of finance, through central banking, integrated reporting, credit rating agencies, to the question of offshore finance. Part VI is concerned with the relationship between finance and various dimensions of development. Here, we start with a regional focus on sub-Saharan Africa, followed by a chapter on financial imbalances and crises. Chapters 27, 28 and 29 focus on environmental aspects: finance for renewable energy, finance and climate change, and a financial geographical take on environmental sustainability in general.

Part I opens with Chapter 2, by Dariusz Wójcik, and examines financial and business services (FABS). FABS are key to understanding finance and the global economy, but there is much diversity, if not outright confusion, concerning the use of the term and its relationship with such categories as professional services, business services, producer services, or knowledge-intensive business services. In this context, the goal of the chapter is to: (i) clarify terms related to FABS by explaining their origin, evolution, and relationships with statistical classifications; (ii) showcase the variety of data available on FABS, and highlight some important patterns and trends in FABS development; and (iii) suggest some directions for future research on FABS. The key trends on

FABS discussed in this chapter include growth over recent decades, their urban character, and increasingly close relationships between FABS and information technology (IT) in the form of FinTech—a development that may challenge existing statistical classifications. The author argues that studying FABS, rather than just a narrowly defined financial sector, is important, having the potential for theoretical, methodological, and empirical development of financial and economic geography, and beyond.

In Chapter 3, Patrick Bond focuses on the foundations of Marxist financial geography. The chapter considers the diverse roles played by money and credit in capital accumulation, and investigates the emergence of 'overaccumulation of capital' in the economy's productive sector, involving falling rates of profits and a shift of capital to speculative activities. The author discusses the footprint of this crisis tendency of capitalism, with uneven geographical development logically amplified within the shifting circuits of capital, as finance roams through space and across scale in search of restored profitability. The chapter reminds us that the nature and success of financial-system reform depends both upon the degree to which the underlying dynamics have been properly analysed, and the political narratives of resistance that correspond to the theoretical challenge of accurate diagnosis. It concludes with a call for more research, stating that the Marxist foundations of financial geography nevertheless require a far stronger response by those aiming for genuine change: a probe into why the *mode of production itself is to blame* for the depravity so much of the world faces at the hands of finance.

Chapter 4, by Sarah Hall, brings interdisciplinary dialogue and collaboration to the study of financial geography with an examination of the evolution of the cultural economy of finance. Drawing on the heterodox social scientific literature on finance within economic geography, she outlines a cultural economy approach to money and finance: market making relies on the purposive activities of financiers alongside a range of non-human elements, known as market devices, including computer screens, financial formulae, regulatory interventions and market infrastructures such as high speed computer cabling. Hall argues that, by incorporating a greater attention to the micro processes and practices that make up economies, cultural economy approaches to the study of finance provide a scalar counterpoint to earlier work within the geography and wider social science that conventionally emphasize the macro, and political economy foundations of global finance. Hall expands the micro approach to show the continued uneven trajectories of regional and urban development in the most advanced economies. Finally, she extends the analysis beyond traditional studies of finance in North America and Western Europe to consider the conclusions cultural economy of finance might suggest for cases beyond the Global North.

Shaina Potts, in Chapter 5, synthesizes her approach to law, finance, and geography with three propositions. First, law is more than context in which finance occurs; it is constitutive of finance. Put differently: all financial markets, instruments, and practices are legally constructed. Bonds, derivatives, and stocks are legal constructs. Second, law is always spatial. It is not only always produced in, but is co-produced with space. Put together with the first assertion, this means that legal geographies are constitutive of financial geographies. Third, law is always connected to the state and, hence, so is finance. The connection can be quite complex, with law operating both within and beyond national borders. The core of the chapter reviews literature that examines and illustrates the three propositions. In doing so, the chapter goes beyond a conventional treatment of law in financial and economic geography, which tends to focus on (de)regulation. In addition, it advances claims of the relative autonomy of law within capitalism, whereby law cannot be reduced to an instrument of capitalist interests but, rather, has to be understood through its own traditions, practices, and discourses.

Metaphors are common in research, and geography is no exception in this regard. The nineteenth century saw economics borrow ideas predominantly from physics, a trend that was followed by geography in the middle of the twentieth century, with concepts such as the gravity model. In contrast, in the late twentieth and early twenty-first centuries, biology—with its emphasis on evolution and competition—became a more popular source of metaphors, and so it was for geography. In this vein, Andrew Leyshon, in Chapter 6, explores the notions of financial ecologies and financial ecosystems. In his view, the former represents a bottom-up approach linked closely to the treatment of finance as comprising networks of relationships, such as those present, for example, in subprime lending—a financial ecology that, despite its relatively small size, proved to have grave consequences for the global financial system. Financial ecosystems, in contrast, according to Leyshon, are grounded in complexity theory, viewing finance as a complex adaptive system, and focus on systemic issues of financial risk and crises. The chapter draws attention to the fact that the way these concepts are used is often shaped by consulting firms, key agents in what Nigel Thrift called the 'cultural circuit of capital', or what Wójcik called the 'financial and business services' (FABS) complex. Leyshon highlights the potential of both concepts for research at the intersection of financial and environmental geographies.

Matt Zook opens Part II, on the investable world, with Chapter 7, on currencies. He traces the evolution of money and currency from pre-modern forms such as shells to coins, money of account, and state credit money. He argues that all forms of money and currency are inherently cultural and geographical, as they emerge at particular moments in time and space and are designed to solve particular problems such as trade, exercising cultural or political power, or the inclusion or avoidance of particular actors. At the same time, the history of money is the history of technological change, whether it concerns the metallurgical technologies of minting coins, accounting practices of recording assets and liabilities, or programming languages used to write code. The decade to 2020 appears particularly eventful in terms of technologies influencing the development of money, with the emergence of cryptocurrencies. The chapter explains the roots of cryptocurrencies and the blockchain technology supporting them, and discusses different types of cryptocurrencies including bitcoin, digital currencies promoted by central banks, and Facebook's Libra. Finally, the chapter considers the potential of cryptocurrencies to challenge state-backed fiat currencies, and calls for more research on the topic as 'currency is much too important to leave it uncontested and undebated' (163).

Chapter 8, by Fenghua Pan, explains the geography of global stock markets. Stock markets sit at the heart of the modern economy. Pan argues that economic geographers are well-placed to offer a new analytical perspective on the activities of stock markets that is attentive to socio-spatial relations, and to unpack the spatialities of finance while considering the traditional influence of firms, labor, and states. Pan provides an analysis of internationalized firms and the choices they make with respect to listing on domestic or foreign stock exchanges. He argues that capital mobility has accelerated the virtualization of stock exchanges by allowing anytime-anywhere access for investors and the growing competition between international exchanges for firm listings. Using stock exchange data from the World Federation of Exchanges, Pan provides insights into the evolution of the geography of stock markets at the global scale and an overview of the most internationalized exchanges, and discusses the behavior of Chinese firms, which are increasingly choosing to list on the NYSE and Nasdaq.

Raquel Rolnik, in Chapter 9, describes housing as one of the most powerful frontiers of financialization since the 1970s, with global finance gradually taking over the housing sector for the purposes of capital accumulation. As a result, we have seen an erosion of the meaning of housing as a social good. The chapter charts the development of four key models for the financialization of housing: mortgage markets, government subsidies for the purchase of private housing, housing micro-finance used mainly for home improvements, and the emergence of global corporate landlords in the residential rental market. The last model has developed particularly swiftly since 2008, with private equity funds, hedge funds, and other investors seizing the opportunity to invest in cheap property directly or indirectly; for example, by funding companies such as Airbnb. The chapter emphasizes the negative social and economic effects of these trends, including housing price bubbles and the dispossession of poor communities. Some optimism is offered through examples on how citizens can resist housing financialization; for example, through non-governmental organizations, social movements, or tenants' unions. The author, however, has little hope that such resistance can reverse the process of financialization.

Chapter 10 on commodities, by Stefan Ouma and Tobias Klinge, suggests that, in the world of global finance, commodities are less straightforward than they may initially appear. Large institutional investors—such as pension funds, for example—make portfolio allocations based on the specific risk–return and liquidity characteristics of certain asset classes. The process of guaranteeing that the harvested returns allow firms to meet their liabilities is both a discursive and socio-technical activity. *Discursive*, because such boundaries become established via acts of speech and representation in the everyday craft of finance, rendering what lies 'within' a legitimate investment opportunity. *Sociotechnical*, because new material infrastructures, standards, and eventually often laws—phenomena that are as much social as they are technical—underpin the consolidation of a new asset class. When considering the world of agriculture, the classification of domains from the direct commodification of assets (farmland) to trading rights (i.e., water or emissions rights) introduces additional complexity. Ouma and Klinge argue that geographers have made important contributions to studying these fields and the diverse ways in which finance penetrates these various resource-based domains in different geographical contexts. In particular, they show the degree to which investments in commodities such as agriculture—and, even more so, land—have been politicized to an extent not seen with any other asset class. They argue that finance's increasingly complex relationship with nature in the form of land and commodities entails significant socio-economic transformations that need critical investigation by scholars, as they reshape large parts of the agricultural commodity chain.

Chapter 11 on infrastructure, by Gabriela Carolini and Isadora Cruxên, examines macro trends in infrastructure investment at a global scale, paying particular attention to basic service infrastructures within the urban environment. The rise of new agents of development assistance, the growth of dedicated infrastructure funds within the private investment community, and the impact of decades of efforts to devolve financial responsibility—particularly for basic services—to local governments means that some cities are well-positioned to leverage increased demands for infrastructure investment vehicles, but also that cities are more vulnerable to the whims and priorities of this widening portfolio of actors in infrastructure finance. Their analysis provides broad insights into sectoral preferences according to actor classes across global regions, such as preferences for infrastructure, as well as the financial mechanisms through which investment influences urban development within cities of the Global South. They address important questions: Who gains and who loses when infrastructure is the new asset class of choice for highly mobile capital? What are the implications for governance when financial actors involved in infrastructure development are divorced from local accountability and infrastructure sustainability? Leveraging datasets on infrastructure finance from the private sector and a meta-analysis of literatures on urban infrastructure in the Global South, Carolini and Cruxên provide a thorough review of the current landscape of infrastructure investment and related research across Southern geographies. They conclude with an exploration of the implications of recent developments for local governance in cities situated within lower- and middle-income contexts.

Part III opens with Chapter 12, on assessing long-term investor performance, by Ashby Monk and Gordon Clark. This chapter situates its arguments within the growing literature on corporate governance in the social sciences. While much of the research on financial market stability and performance focuses on the trading strategies of investment managers, more often than not investment managers are employees of large, complex financial institutions (Clark, 2016). How these organizations are managed, how they deploy human resources, how they reward and sanction certain types of behavior, and how they integrate the activities of separate departments and employees into the performance of the organization as a whole, all matter when it comes to these institutions achieving their long-term goals. Clark and Monk set out an analytical model that conceptualizes the management of financial institutions via a set of building blocks—namely, the internal systems and processes that encourage employees to focus on the organization's goals and objectives, rather than on their separate and, sometimes, competing interests. Working through concepts including governance, institutional investment, and performance management, Clark and Monk show that long-term investors succeed when they take greater responsibility for the end-to-end management of their assets.

Chapter 13 on financial decision-making, by Gordon Clark, maps twenty-first-century capitalism by focusing on the knowledge economy. 'Silicon Valley was made and is reproduced time and again by agents and organizations seeking to take advantage of their proximity to local knowledge. At one level, knowledge can be prosaic or sophisticated: it is often difficult, if not impossible, to separate one from the other. At another level, knowledge is both a stock and a flow. If knowledge can be commodified and sold, being close to centers of innovation is likely less important than the *process* of making knowledge at the interface between experience, organizations, and markets' (286). Clark, in particular, distinguishes between tacit knowledge, which cannot be easily acquired and transferred over space and time, and codified knowledge, which can be formalized and communicated through organizations, norms, conventions, and routines. He argues that people use knowledge to make informed decisions for themselves and their households. It is often assumed that financial literacy (codified knowledge) is preferred as a means of bypassing everyday practice (tacit knowledge) in favor of informed and more rational consumption of financial products and services. Clark demystifies these assumptions, explaining the costs and benefits of formal conceptions of financial literacy. Being an effective financial decision-maker can have immediate and long-term payoffs for those seeking to enhance their earned incomes and long-term welfare. The chapter brings a behavioral psychology and cognitive science perspective with which to better understand the role of rationality and context in financial decision-making.

Johnna Montgomerie and Christopher Harker, in Chapter 14, show that the household is crucial for understanding finance and financialization. The chapter focuses on three ways of approaching households in financial geography: household as a scale of analysis, as a node in financial networks, and as a place of and for lived experience. The use of the three approaches is illustrated with the example of austerity policies in the United Kingdom in 2010–20. In conclusion, the authors posit that 'financial geographies of the household provide a specific way of framing socio-economic changes that, in turn, provides crucial insights about the ways in which incorporation/exclusion, power/resistance, and divergence/difference operate to produce and reproduce the global financial system. Geographical approaches to household finance make visible new hierarchies and inequalities in the distribution and redistribution of gains and losses from financialization' (308).

When the US subprime crisis was unravelling in 2007–8, the Rockefeller Foundation organized meetings at its Bellagio Center on Lake Como to explore with leaders in finance, philanthropy, and development the need for, and ways of, developing a worldwide industry that would focus on investing for social and environmental impact. This is the starting point for Chapter 15 by Paul Langley, on impact investing. The author dissects the term, showing a large diversity of investors, assets, and types involved in impact investing, and its relatively modest—at least, thus far—financial scale. It illustrates the concentration of the 'industry', with most investors located in Western Europe and North America, and investments in the Global South. Langley reviews literature on the topic, examining impact investing in relation to research on the 'financialization of development', 'financialization of nature', 'poverty finance', and 'green finance'. Taking a cultural economy perspective, Langley argues that 'The impact investor is shown to be figured in ways that are consistent with and run counter to the making of the mainstream investor: investors are financial subjects that act as the authoritative arbiters of capital allocation in return for legitimate returns, but the impact investor is also an ethical agent of change who has the potential to address global challenges through their distinctive financial techniques and practices' (331).

Chapter 16, by Aniket Shah, presents a critical review of the topic of development banking. In particular, Shah analyses the conceptual underpinnings of development banking so as to afford a more critical assessment of the form, function, and effectiveness of development banks in their respective domains. 'The combined assets of the world's development banks are well over $5 trillion dollars…Despite the persistence and prevalence of development banks, there is little academic or policy knowledge about how these organizations operate and what their impacts are on economic and sustainable development outcomes' (352). Shah provides an overview of the constitution and evolution of development banks, and examines the conceptual underpinnings of development banks. In particular, he investigates the theoretical and empirical debates surrounding the development, economic affairs, institutions, and markets of development banking. He argues that financial geographer's have important insights to offer due to their capacity to examine the interaction of finance with social outcomes.

Lindsey Appleyard opens Part IV, which concerns intermediaries, with Chapter 17, on banks and credit. Access to banking services is an essential part of everyday life, helping people secure needs such as housing and employment. The chapter focuses on consumer credit guided by questions relating to who banks are for and the nature of their role in society. The chapter starts by outlining the contribution of economic geography to studying banking and credit, and their spatial constitution and impacts on communities. The author explains how bank–consumer relations have evolved as a result of banking liberalization, securitization, deregulation, and restructuring in the context of financialization and neoliberalization. In particular, the chapter explores the creation of prime, near prime, and subprime market segments, and the role of credit scoring in the process. The implications of these processes for financial inclusion and exclusion are discussed using the concept of financial ecologies.

As Kate Booth states in Chapter 18: 'Insurance is commonly assumed to be a benign financial tool in the distribution and management of risk, premised on a singular and universal logic' (400). As she demonstrates, geographers have been influential in challenging such assumptions and unpacking the complexities of insurance. The key concept used in the chapter is that of insurability, framed through calculations of risk and uncertainty. The chapter reviews three categories of insurance: self-insurance (e.g., life, health, and retirement), property (e.g., home, contents, and government assets), and climate (e.g., weather, crop yield). The author explains how, in each of these categories, insurability creates non-insurability, and how excess of insurability is mobilized by the industry to build dependence on and enthusiasm for insurance. At the same time, however, she believes that 'the excess of insurability also creates spaces of contestation or resistance to these power structures and dynamics' (415).

Jana Kleibert, in Chapter 19, reviews literature on global value chains in finance by focusing on the geographies of offshoring. The chapter starts by explaining the relationships between outsourcing, back sourcing, offshoring, and reshoring, and how these processes evolved over time, as unbundling of the financial services value chain took place alongside increasing spatial specialization. As a result, we have seen the emergence and growth of financial industry in places that are neither conventional financial centers, nor offshore jurisdictions but, rather, are places that concentrate labor—and, increasingly, also technology-intensive parts of the financial value chain. Deutsche Bank, for example, employs 11,000 staff in India in Pune, Mumbai, Bangalore, and Jaipur; 2,000 people in Manila (Philippines); and 2,000 in Birmingham (the United Kingdom). In Kraków (Poland), the offshore services sector (including, but not limited to, financial services) became the largest economic sector of the city in terms of employment and value added. The chapter describes these case studies and examples, and ends by discussing the potential futures of offshoring in finance, including the impacts of FinTech and Brexit.

Chapter 20, by Karen Lai, states that FinTech encompasses a new wave of companies developing new products and platforms to change the way businesses and consumers make payments, lend, borrow, and invest. Lai examines the ways in which FinTech products and services are reshaping the intermediation function of banks, and how financial institutions have engaged with FinTech firms in different ways, resulting in variegated forms of organizational change, inter-firm relationships, and changing production and financial networks. 'Operating at the intersections of financial services and technology sectors, technology-focused startups and new market entrants are creating new products and services that are currently provided by the traditional financial services industry. In doing so, FinTech is gaining significant momentum and causing disruption to the traditional value chain and roles of conventional financial institutions' (440). Lai suggests that it is not sufficient to understand banks and technology firms as direct competitors in the FinTech ecosystem. Instead, it is important to consider their respective positions and power in different product segments, geographical markets, and industry networks. Lai uses a financial ecologies approach to study the shifting configurations of economic actors across banking and FinTech sectors, and provides important implications for how we understand the nature of financial/non-financial firms. In particular, Lai comments on the changing roles of international financial centers, and the nature of inter-firm and inter-industry networks in global finance.

Chapter 21, by Katharina Pistor, opens Part V by examining the legal foundations of finance. 'Finance is about making investments in an unknown future in the hope and expectation of making some return on that investment. Financial assets are specific manifestations of a claim to receive some payoff at a future date, whether it is a debt instrument, or an 'I owe you' (IOU), or a share that promises participation in any profit the project generates' (461). Pistor explains the complexities of moving from debt relations in relatively small, homogeneous settings, in which people know and trust each other, to financial systems in which assets worth trillions of dollars are traded on a daily basis. Pistor argues that the leap to a financialized economy reflects the transformation of simple agreements into binding contracts that are enforceable in a court of law, as well assets that have strong self-executing features. She shows that the basic 'tool kit' for transforming simple assets into financial assets that are fit for a huge, anonymous marketplace consists of contract, collateral, property, trust, corporate, and bankruptcy law. Even the most sophisticated derivative instruments today can be broken down into these basic legal modules. She argues that large-scale, complex financial systems are coded in law, even in the absence of regulation. Deregulation, or the scaling back of public law interventions, therefore does not create a space devoid of law. Instead, deregulation merely expands the scope for private actors to shape financial markets with the private law tools at their disposal. 'In short, law is *in* finance' (462).

The global financial crisis has clearly underlined the key role of central banks in the global financial system. Admittedly, however, research on and attention paid to central banking by financial geographers has been quite sparse. One reason for this is that the spatiality of central banks is not easy to capture. Central banks do not have extensive branch networks and employ relatively few people. To highlight and address this gap, Chapter 22, by

David Bieri, explores the evolving position of central banks in the post-crisis geography of money. It explains how central bank balance sheets are connected with the rest of the economy, and why they sit at the top of the 'hierarchy of money'. To analyse monetary spaces, Bieri proposes Perroux's theorization of economic space as a set of 'economic plans', 'field forces', and 'homogeneous aggregates', rather than the conventional notion of 'spaces of places'. Applying these ideas to finance, Bieri develops and illustrates the concepts of 'policy space', 'regulatory space', and 'currency space'. He also explains how the emergence of digital currencies poses challenges in all of these spaces. The chapter ends with a provocative call: 'Instead of being shackled by a singularly faithful focus on locational and agglomerational aspects that operate within the limiting confines of 'banal economic space', the future potential of financial geography would be well-served were it to be infused with a healthy dose of abstract economic spaces that de-localize economic units and economic relations' (505).

Chapter 23, by Gary Dymski, seeks to find the 'space' of financial geography by exploring alternative approaches to cross-border financial imbalances and crises in the global economy. Dymski argues that the first step to building a field of financial geography is to avoid the practice of discussing events distributed across space and time without confronting the fundamental challenges posed by space for social analysis. The second step is to recognize that hierarchical power is implicitly or explicitly an inescapable component of financial relations that unfold across spatial boundaries. From the 1980s onward, the US current account deficit grew, and the capital account surplus with it. The Federal Reserve encouraged global markets to hold dollars. This provided financing for the growing federal government deficit. Financial globalization creates a global pyramid, under the terms of which only the country at the top can stop panic when financial crises occur. Dymski (2018) has shown that, in the post-crisis period, austerity macroeconomic policies have had the effect of reversing the overall current and capital account positions of advanced and developing nations: so, whereas before the crisis the developing nations had a current account surplus with advanced nations, in the post-crisis period these positions have reversed. In the absence of an effective counter-narrative, the consequences of global financial power go unremarked, even unseen. Financial geography can fill this gap.

Chapter 24, by Stefanos Ioannou, is devoted to credit rating agencies. These are organizations that exercise power out of proportion to their size as companies. They rate hundreds of national and subnational governments, and thousands of companies, affecting their cost of debt, impacting public policies, and influencing—rather than simply reflecting—the stability of the global financial system. The market for credit rating is dominated by three agencies (S&P, Moody's, and Fitch), whose combined worldwide market share exceeds 90%. The chapter outlines the history of credit rating agencies, and presents the overview of their current geographies, including office networks. It introduces the readers to the rating methodology, and presents an up-to-date picture of sovereign ratings and their recent changes. The core of the chapter critically analyses the role of the agencies from a political economy perspective, focusing on the issues of moral hazard, conflicts of interest, and their role in aggravating the global financial crisis and in promoting austerity policies in the wake of the crisis. The chapter also discusses cultural biases displayed in the work of the agencies; for example, higher ratings granted to entities from the agencies' home economies. It ends by discussing why, despite expectations, the credit rating industry has hardly changed since the crisis. The potential of technology to transform the industry in the near future is treated with much skepticism.

While Katharina Pistor's chapter explains the legal foundations of finance, Chapter 25, by Daniel Haberly, elucidates how, in addition to political geography, legal geography is necessary in combination with financial geography in order to understand offshore finance. In his view 'rather than being regarded as some veil of illusions that obscures our view of the economy, the offshore system needs to be regarded as an integral and critical component of its operational fabric' (553). The chapter starts by explaining the concepts of offshore jurisdictions, facilities, and states. The discussion is grounded in the theory of the state as a 'protection racket' and Polanyian 'double movement'. The chapter maps the evolution of offshore finance, from the City of London Corporation, through medieval fairs and cities, Geneva, Caribbean island states, and the British Second Empire, through to Delaware, Hong Kong, and Ireland. It explains why offshore jurisdictions tend to be small. Onshore and offshore, according to Haberly, are two faces of the state in capitalism, coexisting and coevolving in a dialectical relationship.

Susan Newman opens Part VI on finance and development by exploring these topics in the context of sub-Saharan Africa, in Chapter 26. The region has seen a major shift in the relationship between finance and development. While the emphasis between the 1950s and the 1970s was on financing development, with a focus on funding indigenous industry, from the 1980s—and, particularly, the 1990s—it has shifted to financial development, with the growth of the private financial sector and credit, a reflection of broader international trends of financialization and neoliberalization. The chapter describes changes in the role of finance in development policies, practices, and processes in sub-Saharan Africa. It charts the trajectory of external debt and financial flows in the region. The chapter presents two extensive case studies of Tanzania and South Africa; these studies show that 'The concrete forms taken by financial development and financialization are shaped by historical developments in capitalism from colonialism into independence' (615). Looking ahead, Newman argues 'finance for development policies needs to be informed by detailed historical analysis of the development of finance in particular space and time, as it is related to the processes and patterns of accumulation in specific locations and is in relation to regional and global dynamics' (616).

Chapter 27, by Britta Klagge, examines the evolving landscape of investment into renewable energy, with particular attention to the cases of Germany and Kenya. Klagge argues that 'Both solar PV and wind have developed dynamically in recent decades, not only in terms of investment and technology, but also regarding ownership and financing structures. Starting from small-scale, owner- and bank-financed operations, renewable power generation from wind and solar has become a large-scale business with access to capital market finance' (621). The transition to renewable energies has been accompanied by great public and academic attention and support for the implementation of renewable energy, as well as comparative analysis of the impacts of renewable energy across geographies. Financial geographers can lend considerable expertise to the study of renewable energy investment. Klagge argues that public actors and policies are vitally important for the transition to renewable energies. First, national government agencies have a profound impact through regulation and support schemes. Second, especially in the Global South, public investment into renewable energy projects is important not only in its own right, but also by facilitating and leveraging private investment, thereby playing a decisive role in globalizing the renewable energy revolution. Klagge uses case studies from Germany and Kenya to exemplify the twofold argument: the German case shows how strong public support policies can trigger a national renewable energy revolution, while Kenya illustrates the importance of the national state for the development of renewable energy facilities, and also the key role of international development finance institutions as (co-)investors in a Global South context.

Chapter 28, by Patrick Bigger and Wim Carton, examines the linkages between global finance and anthropogenic climate change. Bigger and Carton state that 'There has been wide spread experimentation for climate governance in both the private and public sector since the late 1990s, but even as these experiments dabbled at the edges of the carbon economy, global emissions and proven fossil fuel reserves continued to grow' (646). They interject that, since the 1990s, a critical trend has been neoliberalization. Mechanisms for regulating greenhouse gas emissions such as emissions trading markets, feed-in tariffs, and renewable energy credits mostly cleaved to prevailing elite attitudes that markets were the most efficient mechanism for achieving desirable outcomes. Nevertheless, brown finance (involving fossil fuels) has dwarfed carbon economy, with the market capitalization of Exxon Mobile alone five times the value of all greenhouse gas emission markets in 2016. Bigger and Carton examine the entanglements of finance and climate change, as both causes and responses to crisis. They argue that we need a robust political response to the staggering inequities bound up in the conjunction of global warming and financialization. Economic geographers, with their study of economies in space and time, are well-suited to lending insight to the ongoing impediments to the meaningful decarbonization or transformative adaptation of the global economy. Assigning monetary values to economies and associated determents are not sufficient.

A meaningful engagement with the broader operation of economies, the latent inequities within, and nodes of power and decision-making are necessary.

Chapter 29, on finance and environmental sustainability, by Janelle Knox-Hayes, Jungwoo Chun, and Priyanka deSouza, argues that to engage with sustainability financial geography must engage with the question of how value is created within and around resource-based economies. The authors suggest that the resource curse—that regions with an abundance of natural resources tend to have less economic growth, less democracy, and worse development outcomes than countries with fewer natural resources—can be understood from the standpoint of resource value. 'Capital is not just a process of value creation or representative of the nature of the resource, but also the means through which resources create value in conjunction with social and environmental space and time' (669). They illustrate their argument through the examination of the divergent cases of Louisiana and Norway. Despite having a plethora of natural resources, Louisiana has suffered numerous social and ecological crises as a consequence of extractive industries that have destroyed marshland, reengineered riparian dynamics, and generated land subsidence and a rise in sea level. In contrast, Norway has diversified the value and built incredible present and long-term social and economic value from its petroleum resources, as exemplified by its trillion dollar public pension fund. Despite its success, there is still lingering doubt about the Norwegian model due to its being built, at best, on weak sustainability, since the petroleum resource at is heart is generating anthropogenic climate change. The authors conclude that sustainable finance requires that governments pursue economies that are beneficial not only in the distribution of the wealth they create, but also in the nature of the resources they harness.

We believe that the *Handbook* offers a comprehensive and up-to-date review of state-of-the-art research on financial geography. Of course, due to the physical limitations of scope and the availability of contributors, we were unable to cover every possible topic. Perhaps to the surprise of some readers, we do not have a chapter dedicated specifically to financial centers, although many chapters touch on this topic. As we finish writing this Introduction, much of the world is in lockdown due to coronavirus. The outbreak of the pandemic is a powerful reminder of the lethal dangers of globalization. Direct human interaction is minimized to slow down the spread of the virus but, at the same time, a concerted collective action at local, national, and global scales is absolutely vital to avert the worst human and economic consequences of the pandemic. In the midst of the crisis, many of us predict that the world will never be the same. Most likely, finance will not be the same either (Wójcik and Ioannou, 2020). Governments have offered fiscal stimulus packages unprecedented in type and scale. Central banks are cutting interest rates to the bone (again). There is flight from many currencies to the US$. Financial and business services firms, as well as their clients, are learning how to continue their business, with all employees working remotely from home. A major recession looms large. Infrastructure investment will surely need to be rethought to address the risk of pandemics. These are just few of the themes with which financial geographers will need to engage in the near future.

References

Aalbers, M. (2018). Financial geography I: Geographies of tax. *Progress in Human Geography*, 42(6), pp. 916–927.

Aalbers, M. (2019a). Financial geography II: Financial geographies of housing and real estate. *Progress in Human Geography*, https://journals.sagepub.com/doi/full/10.1177/0309132518819503.

Aalbers, M. (2019b). Financial geography III: The financialization of the city. *Progress in Human Geography*, https://journals.sagepub.com/doi/10.1177/0309132519853922.

Christophers, B. (2014). Geographies of finance I: Historical geographies of the crisis-ridden past. *Progress in Human Geography*, 38(2), pp. 285–293.

Christophers, B. (2015). Geographies of finance II: Crisis, space and political-economic transformation. *Progress in Human Geography*, 39(2), pp. 205–213.

Christophers, B. (2016). Geographies of finance III: Regulation and 'after-crisis' financial futures. *Progress in Human Geography*, 40(1), pp. 138–148.

Christophers, B., Leyshon, A., and Mann, G. (2017). *Money and Finance After the Crisis: Critical Thinking for Uncertain Times*. Hoboken, NJ/Chichester, UK: John Wiley & Sons.

Clark, G.L., Feldman, M., and Gertler, M.S. (2000). *The Oxford Handbook of Economic Geography*. Oxford: Oxford University Press.

Clark, G.L., Feldman, M., Gertler, M.S., and Wójcik, D. (2018). *The New Oxford Handbook of Economic Geography*. Oxford: Oxford University Press.

Clark, G.L. and Wójcik, D. (2007). *Geography of Finance: Corporate Governance in a Global Marketplace*. Oxford: Oxford University Press.

Corbridge, S., Martin, R., and Thrift, N. (1994). *Money, Power and Space*. Oxford: Basil Blackwell.

Davies, Anna, Gregory, H., Janelle, K.-H., and Raoul, S.L. (2020). "Riskscapes and the socio-spatial challenges of climate change". *Cambridge Journal of Regions, Economy and Society*.

Godechot, O. (2016). Financialization is marketization! A study of the respective impacts of various dimensions of financialization on the increase in global inequality. *Sociological Science*, 3, pp. 495–519.

Grandi, S., Sellar, C. and Jafri, J. (2020). *Geofinance between Political and Financial Geography: A Focus on the Semi-Periphery of the Global Financial System*. Cheltenham, UK: Edward Elgar.

Hall, S. (2010). Geographies of money and finance I: Cultural economy, politics and place. *Progress in Human Geography*, 35(2), pp. 234–245.

Hall, S. (2011). Geographies of money and finance II: Financialization and financial subjects. *Progress in Human Geography*, 36(3), pp. 403–411.

Hall, S. (2012). Geographies of money and finance III: Financial circuits and the 'real economy'. *Progress in Human Geography*, 37(2), pp. 285–292.

Hall, S. (2018). *Global Finance: Places, Spaces and People*. London: Sage.

Laulajainen, R. (1998). *Financial Geography: A Banker's View*. Gothenburg: Gothenburg School of Economic and Commercial Law (also published in 2003 by Routledge).

Leyshon, A. (1995). Geographies of money and finance I. *Progress in Human Geography*, 19(4), pp. 531–543.

Leyshon, A. (1997). Geographies of money and finance II. *Progress in Human Geography*, 21(3), pp. 381–392.

Leyshon, A. (1998). Geographies of money and finance III. *Progress in Human Geography*, 22(3), pp. 433–446.

Martin, R. (1999). *Money and the Space Economy*. New York/Chichester, UK: John Wiley & Sons.

Martin, R. and Pollard, J. (2017). *Handbook on the Geographies of Money and Finance*. Cheltenham, UK: Edward Elgar.

Sabbagh, K., Friedrich, R., El-Darwiche, B., and Koster, A. (2013). Digitization for economic growth and job creation: Regional and industry perspective. The global information technology report 2013, pp. 35–42.

The Economist. (2019). A new pattern of world commerce is becoming clearer—as are its costs. 24 January. https://www.economist.com/leaders/2019/01/24/the-steam-has-gone-out-of-globalisation.

Zademach, H.M. (2014). *Finanzgeographie*. Darmstadt: WGB.

Wójcik, D. (2020). Financial Geography I: Exploring FinTech - Maps and concepts. *Progress in Human Geography*. https://journals.sagepub.com/doi/full/10.1177/0309132520952865.

Wójcik, D. (2020b). Financial Geography II: The impacts of FinTech - Financial sector and centres, regualtion and stability, inclusion and governance. *Progress in Human Geography*, https://journals.sagepub.com/doi/full/10.1177/0309132520959825.

Wójcik, D. and Ioannou, S. (2020). COVID-19 and Finance: Market Developments So Far and Potential Impacts on the Financial Sector and Centres. *Tijdschrift voor economische en sociale geografie*, 111(3), pp. 387–400.

PART I

Theoretical Perspectives in Financial Geography

2

FINANCIAL AND BUSINESS SERVICES

A Guide for the Perplexed

Dariusz Wójcik

Financial and business services (FABS), including accounting, law, and business consulting, are crucial for understanding the world economy. In addition to bankers, large financial transactions such as new equity, debt issuance, or mergers and acquisitions involve accountants, lawyers, and business consultants. FABS epitomize globalization, as they include some of the most globalized companies in the world, such as JPMorgan, McKinsey, and PwC. They help other companies internationalize and globalize. FABS are key agents of financialization, providing companies, governments, and other organizations with capital and financial advice. FABS are key to understanding urban development. They concentrate in cities, create financial centers, and connect them through flows of money, information, and professionals. In short, we have to understand FABS in order to understand globalization, financialization, and the map of the world.

Considering their significance, it is not surprising that a considerable amount of interdisciplinary literature on FABS has accumulated over a long period of time. Within this literature, however, there is a panoply of concepts that can easily perplex readers, particularly those new to this field of enquiry. Professional services, business services, producer services, advanced producer services, and knowledge-intensive business services are just examples of terms used in addition to FABS. What do they mean? Where do they come from? How do they relate to each other? How are they measured? Even though a review of selected works was conducted in preparation for this chapter, its goal is not to offer a comprehensive review of literature. The objective is rather: (a) to clarify terms related to FABS by explaining their origin, evolution, and relationships with statistical classifications; (b) to showcase the variety of data available on FABS, and highlight some important patterns and trends in FABS development; and (c) to suggest some directions for future research on FABS.

While the focus is on clarification and guidance, the chapter also contains an argument—and, in doing so, reflects my perspective and research on global financial networks (GFNs). The latter are defined as networks of FABS, the world's leading governments, financial centers, and offshore jurisdictions, all closely interlinked with each other at the heart of the world economy, and holding financial, economic, political, and cultural power. By the end of this chapter, I hope to convince the reader of the importance of studying FABS, rather than just a narrowly defined financial sector, an approach that affords the potential for theoretical, methodological, and empirical development of financial and economic geography, and beyond.

Evolution of FABS-Related Concepts

The concept of FABS in GFNs emerged only several years ago, and builds on a long history of related concepts (see Figure 2.1). The figure shows the time of origin of these concepts, the extent to which they focus on finance, the number of scholarly works focusing on each concept, and the share of geographical works in this number. Geography is defined here broadly, and includes urban

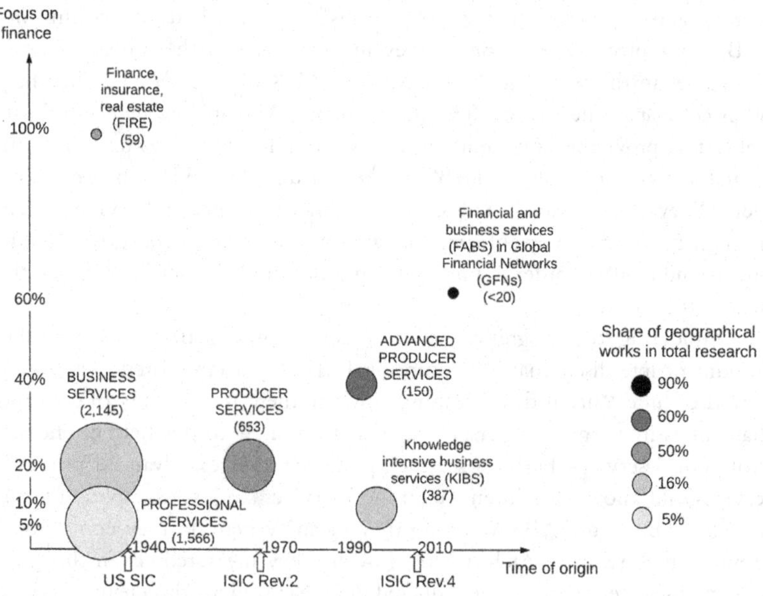

Figure 2.1 A stylized map of FABS-related concepts

Notes: Figures in parentheses under each concept represent the number of works that include this concept in the title, abstract, or keywords, published before the end of 2018, according to Web of Science.

Source: Author and Web of Science.

and regional studies. Figure 2.1 also indicates major milestones in the history of industrial classifications that have been instrumental to the evolution of FABS related concepts and research.

Given that the bibliometric analysis here uses Web of Science, the results are based on English-language terms and biased towards English-language scholarship. A multilingual analysis of FABS related concepts is certainly in order, but beyond the scope of this chapter. In what follows, we present an intellectual history of FABS related concepts, but one with a small i and a small h, with the goal of introducing and clarifying these terms, rather than presenting an in-depth, comprehensive account of debates and controversies surrounding each concept (see Christophers, 2013, for an example). Most of the section will be devoted to discussing each term in turn, in a more or less chronological order.

FIRE, Business, and Professional Services

Finance, insurance, and real estate (FIRE), business, and professional services appear to be the first generation of FABS related terms, the great-grandparents in our scheme. Finance, insurance, and real estate were put together in the first US Standard Industrial Classification (SIC) developed in the 1930s (Pearce, 1957). The US SIC also had a category for business and repair services, which included: automobile storage, rental and repair, advertising, and other business services. Legal, engineering, and miscellaneous professional services were lumped together with medical, health, and educational services in the category of professional and related services (US Census Bureau, 1940). As such, financial, business, and professional services were separated from each other and, in the case of professional services, mixed with what today we would consider personal and social services, rather than business services. International statistics paid much less attention to business and professional services. The original International Standard Industrial Classification (ISIC) of 1948–9 distinguished banking, insurance, and real estate as a category, while legal and related business services were lumped together with religious organizations, welfare institutions, and trade associations in a residual subcategory of services (UN, 1953). The treatment of FABS related services in ISIC did not change substantially until the second ISIC revision in 1968. The relative distinction of FABS related services in the US SIC in contrast to the ISIC may reflect a higher level of FABS development in the United States compared with the rest of the world.

Despite its long heritage, FIRE—F representing mainly banking—appears in our figure as a relatively unpopular concept. This is, however, influenced by the complications of bibliometric analysis available in Web of Science. We could not search for works using the term 'FIRE', as Web of Science search function is not case sensitive, so most results would have nothing to do with finance. In this situation, we searched for works using the term 'finance, insurance and real estate' (with and without 'and', and various combinations of commas) in the title, abstract, or keywords. This is bound to underestimate the real number of works on FIRE. Just for comparison, the total number of works focused on 'financial services' is over 5,000. Interestingly, about half of all the works on FIRE that we were able to identify come from geography.

Business services is the most popular of all terms considered in our review, with about one-sixth of all contributions coming from geography. About half of all works on the topic come from broadly defined business studies and economics. In geography, the term has been applied alongside the term 'producer services', introduced in the 1960s, and often these two terms have been used interchangeably. One of the leading geographers in this area, Peter Wood, defined business services as those where 'clients are found in other organizations, including private sector extractive, manufacturing and service enterprises, and the public sector. Business services therefore serve what is conventionally regarded as 'intermediate' business and public sector demand, rather than consumers final demand' (Wood, 1991: 162). As a result, a substantive part of research on business services covers some or all financial services.

'Professional services' is also a very popular term in research, building on a long tradition of interest in professions. With the preponderance of works in business studies, public administration, law, and economics, the share of geographical works on the topic is low, close to 5%, though their contribution is not to be underestimated (e.g., Beaverstock, 2004; Faulconbridge, 2006). In one of the most cited works in this area, von Nordenflycht (2010) shows that by far the most popular examples of professional services firms in management related literature come from accounting, law, and management consulting. He also proposes three distinctive characteristics that help to identify professional services: knowledge-intensity, low capital intensity, and professionalized workforce (with a high degree of autonomy and self-regulation). Low capital intensity stands out here as the feature that distinguishes professional services from financial services. Note, however, that core financial services such as conventional investment banking (including M&A advisory) require little capital, while the capital-intensity of some professional service firms has increased due to globalization (Faulconbridge and Muzio, 2009). Real estate could also, at least partly, be included in professional services, as it broadly satisfies the criteria set by van Nordenflycht; for example, by being anchored in statutory provisions for property surveying (Wood and Wójcik, 2010).

Producer Services

While our story of FIRE, business and professional services started with industrial classifications, the genesis of the producer services concept goes back to a particular individual and his work. In 1966, Harry I. Greenfield, an economist at Columbia University, published *Manpower and the Growth of Producer Services*, based on a project contracted by the US Department of Labor. Greenfield admits that he started his investigation with the notion of business services, but then found it a misnomer, given that these services can be sold to or performed by the government. Instead, drawing on the distinction between producer and consumer goods, he proposes the term 'producer services', defined as 'services which business firms, nonprofit institutions, and governments provide and usually sell to the producer rather than to the consumer' (1966: 1). Greenfield credits Stigler, the 1982 Nobel Prize winner, for recognizing the difficulty of separating consumer and intermediate services. To estimate employment in producer services, he uses shortcuts, by including fractions of some service categories; for example, 50% of employment in FIRE and legal services, and 90% of accounting (1966: 22). According to his estimates, in 1960 producer services represented 13.2% of total US employment.

The notion of producer services has been very prolific, particularly in geography, contributing about half of all works focusing on the concept, followed by economics and business studies. In the mid-1980s, the Institute of British Geographers established a working party on producer services chaired by Peter Daniels. As many as eight reports on producer services were published in the *Progress in Human Geography* between 1985 and 1993 (Daniels, 1985, 1986, 1987, 1988, 1989, 1991; Beyers, 1992, 1993).

Definitions of producer services used in geography vary significantly in terms of scope and structure, but they all include at least part of financial services. For example, Nigel Thrift, writing in *The Dictionary of Human Geography* (2000: 640), defines producer services as 'services supplied to businesses and governments, rather than directly to individual (or 'end') consumers. Such services, often characterized as those which provide 'intermediate' inputs into the process of production, include economic activities as diverse as financial services, research and development, computer services, marketing and advertising, and certain kinds of transport and communication.' Coffey (2000), reviewing research on producer services in Urban Geography, highlights definitional differences in this field. Some research equates producer services with business services. For others, producer services are the sum of business services and FIRE. Yet others include in producer services what many would consider distribution services, including transportation, storage, and communications.

Not surprisingly, the use of the term 'producer services' has attracted criticism. Allen (1988) called it a chaotic concept. First, financial, accounting, and legal services, often put at the center of producer services, are dominated by firms that serve both producers and consumers, a problem that we have already discussed above. Second, according to Marxian tradition, financial services should be considered as circulation services, as they mediate and abbreviate the exchange processes within the economy, and are concerned mainly with the velocity of turnover of commodities, money, and capital. As such, Allen argues, they are neither producer nor consumer services.

Notwithstanding such critiques, the joint consideration of financial and related services continued in research under the label of 'producer services', and was reflected and reinforced in 1968 with ISIC Revision 2, which created a new division 8 called 'financing, insurance, real estate and business services', split into three groups: financial institutions, insurance, and real estate and business services. The latter included rental and leasing, as well as computer and related services, in addition to legal, accounting, and consulting services. This marks a major milestone in international statistics. Business services have been elevated from being a part of residual services to being placed in a category of their own, and their close relationship to finance has been highlighted. Interestingly, while definitely influenced by Greenfield and related work on producer services, ISIC has not adopted the term 'producer services' but, rather, continued to use the established notion of business services. Conversely, despite the ISIC terminology, research using the term 'producer services' proliferated alongside that applying the notion of business services. As we shall see, the former became the grandfather of FABS related concepts in our scheme, even if it had not been recognized literally in official international statistics.

Advanced Producer Services

About 25 years after the concept of producer services arose its offspring arrived: the concept of advanced producer services, popularized primarily through research on global and world cities, with the majority of contributions coming from geography—particularly urban geography and urban studies. While the term 'advanced producer services' does not appear in Saskia Sassen's book *The Global City* (1991, 2000), the very idea of the global city rests on identifying a subset of producer services. Sassen defines global cities as those that have 'the bundle of specialized services and professionals that can handle the needs of global firms and markets' (2000: 360). Two elements of this definition are worth highlighting. First, it includes professionals, which raises the question of including professionals that work within non-FABS firms (i.e., internalized producer services) in FABS related concepts. Second, it mentions the bundle, elsewhere in her book also referred to as 'producer services complex'. At the same time as stressing their close relationships, however, Sassen emphasized what she saw as the growing divergence between financial and other producer services, with the rise of securitization spawning new financial instruments and regulation in finance, going beyond professional standards present in law and accounting.

The world city concept goes back to seminal papers by Friedmann and Wolff (1982) and Friedmann (1986). The earlier paper talks about high-level business services, including management, banking and finance, law, and accounting, but excluding real estate. Friedmann (1986) describes world cities as 'basing points of capital' and defines them as concentrations of corporate headquarters, international finance, global transport and communications, and high-level business services, such as advertising, accounting, insurance, and legal services. The world city concept has obviously had a major impact on the global city idea.

Starting in the early 1990s, scholars building on global and world city concepts began using the notion of advanced producer services explicitly, sometimes interchangeably with advanced business services, while the terms 'specialized producer' or 'high-level business services' did not gain popularity. The scope of the definition of advanced business services varies between studies, with some including and others excluding services such IT, transport, and logistics. The Global and World Cities dataset (GaWC, 2019), and the related World City Network literature, afford the prime example of a narrower focus, and cover banking, insurance, accountancy, law, management consultancy, and advertising (Beaverstock, Taylor, and Smith, 1999; Taylor, 2004). The size of the circle representing the number of scholarly works focusing on advanced producer services underestimates its significance, since many works use the term 'producer services' without the adjective 'advanced' while effectively being concerned with advanced services only.

Knowledge-Intensive Business Services

Social sciences in the early 1990s popularized the notion of knowledge economy, based on claims that knowledge, including information and technology, were increasingly more important to economic development. This discourse has also influenced thinking about business services, leading to the concept of knowledge-intensive business services (KIBS). A report by Ian Miles et al. (1995), based on a project for the European Commission, defines KIBS as a subset of producer services that are knowledge intensive; that is, they (a) rely heavily on professional knowledge; (b) either supply products that are themselves sources of information and knowledge (such as reports, measurements, training, consultancy), or use their knowledge to produce services that are intermediate inputs to their clients' knowledge (e.g., communication and computer services); (c) have as their main clients other businesses (or government). The report distinguishes between two groups of KIBS: traditional professional services liable to be intensive users of new technology, and new technology-based KIBS. Traditional professional services include marketing and advertising, training, design, some financial services (e.g., securities and stock market related activities), office services, building services, management consultancy (unless it involves new technology), accounting and bookkeeping, legal services, and environmental services. New technology-based KIBS focus on software, telecoms, computer networks, technical engineering, R&D, and management consultancy involving new technology.

The literature on KIBS is large, dominated by business studies and economics, with about one-sixth of works coming from geography. The range of definitions used is somewhat broad. While some follow the report by Miles et al. (1995), others include all of FIRE in KIBS, bringing KIBS close to the concept of APS. Others go in the opposite direction, excluding both FIRE and professional services in order to focus on 'pure' KIBS, such as telecoms, information services, and data processing (e.g., Shearmur and Doloreux, 2008).

The ongoing growth, globalization, and differentiation of business services—which concepts, such as world and global cities, APS and KIBS were trying to capture—took a very long time to influence international statistics. Only in 2008, with ISIC Revision 4, computer and related services were taken out of a general category of business services and placed in a separate category of information and communication (section J). Finance and insurance were put in section K, real estate in L, while business services (now excluding computer and related services) were divided into sections M and N. As the European NACE Revision 1.1 (equivalent to ISIC Revision 4) document explains 'The NACE Rev 1.1 section for real estate, renting and business activities has been split up into three sections in NACE Rev. 2. Real estate is now represented as a stand-alone section (section L) due to its size and importance in the System of National Accounts. The remaining activities have been separated into section M (Professional, scientific and technical activities), covering activities that require a high degree of training and make specialized knowledge and skills available to users, and section N (Administrative and support service activities), covering activities that support general business operations and do not focus on the transfer of specialized knowledge' (Eurostat, 2008). For further details of ISIC Revision 4, see Table 2.1. Without using the term 'APS', ISIC has thus facilitated research on, broadly speaking, higher-skilled versus lower-skilled producer services. Considering the timing of the revision, it is also symbolic that the revision recognized the importance of real estate. The global financial crisis that originated in the US subprime market was around the corner.

Financial and Business Services in Global Financial Networks

The increasing role of finance in the world economy, including the process of securitization, highlighted by Sassen in the global city hypothesis in the early 1990s, has accelerated ever since. This phenomenon has been captured in the notion of financialization, with hundreds of studies devoted to the topic across social sciences (Ioannou and Wójcik, 2019). FABS related research in geography and beyond has been influenced accordingly.

There is a sense and evidence that business services have become financialized. The expansion of financial markets has made financial firms a rapidly growing part of the FABS complex. International expansion has made firms in other parts of FABS more capital-intensive. Their interactions with financial firms and involvement in financial transactions have become more frequent, as the volume of financial transactions worldwide has grown. Big four firms, for example, not only offer financial advisory services, but have even started underwriting securities issues. The financialization of FABS is reflected in research. In the 2012 GaWC data collection, banks and financial firms account for as many as 75 out of 175 APS firms under consideration (Taylor and Derudder, 2016). Dicken defines advanced business services as 'providers of highly specialized knowledge which facilitates the increasingly complex configuration and operation of global production networks' (2011: 370), and divides them into: (a)

Table 2.1 Key FABS-related categories in the main contemporary international statistical classifications

Classification and source	*High-level FABS related categories*	*Comments*
CPC 2.1 (UN, 2015)	Section 7: Financial and related services Section 8: Business and production services, including the following divisions: 81: R&D 82: Legal and accounting 83: Professional, technical, and business services 84: Telecommunications, broadcasting, and information supply services 85: Support services	Bike and video rental are included in section 7, but credit rating services are in group 859. Investment banking and asset management are difficult to distinguish, scattered across categories and aggregated with loosely related services. Public sector financial and fiscal services are in a section 9, subclass 91112.
ISIC Rev. 4 (UN, 2008)	Section K: Financial and insurance activities, with the following divisions: 64: Financial service activities, except insurance and pension funding 65: Insurance, reinsurance, and pension funding 66: Activities auxiliary to financial service and insurance activities Section L: Real estate activities Section M: Professional, scientific, and technical activities 69: Legal and accounting 70: Activities of head offices and management consultancy activities 71: Architectural and engineering activities; technical testing and analysis 72: Scientific research and development 73: Advertising and market research 74: Other 75: Veterinary activities Section N: Administrative and support services activities 77: Rental and leasing activities 78: Employment activities 79: Travel agency and reservation	Asset management is difficult to identify, with fund management in division 66, while funds and trusts as investment vehicles are in division 64. Investment banking is not mentioned at all, although division 66 includes securities brokerage. Head office activities (class 701) are covered only if an enterprise has a separate establishment whose principal function is head office activity. Consequently, head office activities of single-establishment enterprises are not classified as part of 701.

(*Continued*)

Table 2.1 (Continued)

Classification and source	*High-level FABS related categories*	*Comments*
	80: Security and investigation activities 81: Services to building and landscape 82: Office administrative, office support and other business support activities	
NACE Rev.2 (Eurostat, 2008)	Based on ISIC Rev. 4 and adapted to the European circumstances. No significant differences for FABS related categories.	
NAICS Revision 2017 (OMB, 2017)	Sector 52: Finance and insurance Sector 53: Real estate, rental, and leasing Sector 54: Professional, scientific, and technical services Sector 55: Management of companies and enterprises Sector 56: Administrative and support, and waste management and remediation services	Credit rating agencies are included in 5614 together with call centers. In analogy with ISIC Rev. 4, management of companies and enterprises (55) is covered only if an enterprise has a separate establishment whose principal function is such management.
ISCO (ILO, 2012)	In major group 1: Managers: Sub-major group 112: Managing directors and chief executives 121: Business services and administration managers Minor group 1346: Financial and insurance services branch managers In major group 2: Professionals 241: Finance professionals 242: Administration professionals Major group 3: Technicians and associated professionals 331: Financial and mathematical associate professionals Major group 4: Clerical support workers, including: 421: Tellers, money collectors, and related clerks	Accountants and financial analysts are included in 241 as professionals, but securities dealers (often very highly paid) are part of 331 as associate professionals only, together with real estate agents.

(*Continued*)

Table 2.1 (Continued)

Classification and source	*High-level FABS related categories*	*Comments*
BPM6 (IMF, 2009)	1.A.b.6 Insurance and pension services 1.A.b.7 Financial services 1.A.b.10 Other business services, consisting of: 1.A.b.10.1 Research and development services 1.A.b.10.2 Professional and management consulting services 1.A.b.10.3 Technical, trade related, and other business services	Financial services includes financial intermediation services indirectly measured, in addition to those charged explicitly. This is a method applied in the System of National Accounts to capture the difference between rates paid by borrowers and those paid to savers (for details, see SNA, 2008).

Notes:
CPC—Central Product Classification.
ISIC—International Standard Industrial Classification.
NACE—Nomenclature statistique des Activités économiques dans la Communauté Européenne.
NAICS—North American Industry Classification System.
ISCO—International Standard Classification of Occupations.
BPM—Balance of Payments Manuals.

financial services, which include finance, insurance, and accounting, but not real estate; and (b) professional business services made of law, business consultancy, advertising, and executive recruitment. French, Lai, and Leyshon (2010) use a definition of financial services encompassing finance, insurance, legal activities, and accounting (excluding real estate). As French, Lai, and Leyshon argue (2010: 64): 'This is for two reasons: first, much of the commercial activity conducted by legal and accounting firms complements and overlaps with the services offered by financial services companies; second, previous analyses have made clear the significant role played by these in the development of provincial financial centers over the past two decades.' After a decade-long series of progress reports focused on producer services, in 1995 *Progress in Human Geography* published its first progress report devoted to finance (Leyshon, 1995), followed by many more (Leyshon, 1997, 1998; Hall, 2010, 2011, 2012; Christophers, 2014, 2015, 2016; Aalbers, 2018, 2019). Not a single progress report on producer services has appeared in *Progress in Human Geography* since the 1993 report by Beyers. This does not mean, however, that research on producer and business services has not advanced. In fact, it has developed prolifically, but mainly through research using global and world city approaches, including the world city network project. Put differently, research on these services has been financialized and urbanized at the same time (Coffey, 2000).

It would seem that, after over 25 years since the emergence of the term 'advanced producer services', the time has come for a new generation of concepts. My recent research, conducted solo and collectively, reflects such a search, focused on capturing the continuing globalization and financialization of financial and business services. In undertaking my research, I have been trying to recognize their growth and centrality in the world economy in a way grounded not only in urban geography and studies, but also across economic, political, and cultural geography. In the first in a series of works, I reflected on the relationship between advanced business services and offshore finance, coining the term 'ABS-offshore nexus', by arguing that 'advanced business services hold considerable power, which they exercise by operating legal and financial vehicles designed to escape the control of governmental or intergovernmental organizations through the use of offshore jurisdictions' (Wójcik, 2013: 330). The paper defined ABS as 'a broad category which, beyond financial services, law and accountancy, includes advertising, human resources consultancy and management consultancy' (Wójcik, 2013: 335). In a subsequent piece, co-authored with Neil Coe and Karen Lai, we coined the phrase Global Financial Networks, comprising ABS, world cities, and offshore jurisdictions, and mention finance, law, accountancy, and business consultancy as key ingredients of ABS (2014). Wójcik (2018) further modifies the idea of GFNs, rebranding ABS as financial and business services (FABS), and world cities as financial centers, to clarify the financial focus of the GFN concept. This version stresses the hierarchical nature of FABS, with investment banks acting as its elite, occupying this position since more or less the late 1980s, and probably reaching its peak of influence in the mid-2000s, before the 2008 crash. It also uses the term 'FABS complex' to emphasize close relationships between finance and other parts of FABS. In Figure 2.1, to distinguish the general term 'financial and business services' from the FABS concept discussed above, I use the term FABS in GFNs, and highlight finance as its overarching focus.

GFN is a work in progress, being modified further; for example, in my joint work with Daniel Haberly and others (Haberly et al., 2019). Of course, there are other scholars searching for new related concepts. David Bassens and Michiel van Meeteren, for example, revisit Sassen's APS complex to propose an augmented world city hypothesis. As they argue: 'By incorporating financialization processes in Friedmann's (1986) world city hypothesis, we hypothesize that the world city archipelago remains an obligatory passage point for the relatively assured realization of capital. The advanced producer services complex appropriates superprofits as producers of co-constitutive knowledge on operational and financial firm restructuring, the creation of new circuits of value, and capital switching.' (Bassens and van Meeteren, 2015: 752). As with FABS in GFNs, their idea is also firmly focused on finance.

In summary, FABS related concepts have come a long way. The story that emerged from my research into these concepts starts in the late 1930s with professional and, particularly, business services somewhat marginalized in statistical classifications in relation to finance. This probably reflects the fact that business services were relatively small and underdeveloped, while professional services were rendered mainly for consumers rather than businesses. Strong growth of FABS related sectors, however, led to the elevation of business services (including some professional services) in international statistics, culminating in the ISIC Revision 2 of 1968, and in research (mainly under the guise of producer services). What followed were decades of further growth, internationalization (or even globalization), financialization, and internal differentiation of FABS. This resulted in a twofold conceptual development. On the one hand, APS research, developed primarily through global and world city approaches, focused on the urban dimensions of FABS, paying much attention to finance. On the other hand, KIBS focused on the influence of new information and communication technologies from a sectoral perspective, with much less emphasis on finance. Finally, research in the last decade, significantly motivated by the experience of the global financial crisis, draws financial and business services closer together, looking at the processes and impacts of continued financialization through the lens of concepts such as FABS and GFNs.

Data, Trends and Patterns

The story just told highlights close relationships between the evolution of FABS related concepts in academic research, on one hand, and national and international statistics, on the other. This is unsurprising, as any economic and social research relies for data on the apparatus of the state, intergovernmental organizations, and, as sometimes is the case, private business. To offer a practical research guide, in Table 2.1, I present a summary of key FABS related categories in the main contemporary international statistical classifications. Presenting and comparing national classifications would be a large project in its own right and is beyond the scope of this chapter. In addition to ISIC, the leading international industry classification, and its equivalents in the EU (NACE) and North America/NAFTA (NAICS), Table 2.1 covers CPC, as the most comprehensive international classification of products and services; ISCO, the major classification of occupations; and BPM, used in international trade statistics. As such, these classifications approach FABS from different perspectives and allow research into various dimensions of FABS. As the last column of Table 2.1 shows, each of these classifications comes with warning signs for researchers, including cases of problematic classification of some activities.

The existence of statistical classifications does not necessarily mean that data are actually collected and made available to researchers. Thus, to help readers further, Table 2.2 summarizes the key sources of international data on FABS. All sources, with one exception, are publicly available. Oxford Economics is included, despite offering only proprietary data on subscription, as the scope of their data is unique, and significantly complements other sources. Of course, there are probably other rich proprietary sources of international data on FABS of which I am unaware.

Table 2.2 Summary of selected key sources of international data on FABS

Source	*Main features and link (valid as of January 15, 2019)*
GGDC	10-sector database, including FABS as a broad category, on employment and value added for over 40 countries, with coverage for 1950–2013 for some countries, based on ISIC Rev. 3.1. https://www.rug.nl/ggdc/productivity/10-sector/
	WIOD database on employment, value added, and other characteristics for over 50 sectors based on ISIC Rev. 4 in over 40 countries, 2000–14. Data is drawn partly from OECD STAN database. http://www.wiod.org/database/seas16
	World Input-Output Tables, covering 43 countries, and a model for the rest of the world for the period 2000–14. Data for 56 sectors are classified according to ISIC Rev. 4. http://www.wiod.org/release16
	World Input-Output Tables and underlying data, covering 40 countries, and a model for the rest of the world for the period 1995–2011. Data for 35 sectors are classified according to ISIC Rev. 3. http://www.wiod.org/release13
OECD	STAN database, covering employment and value added in over 30 countries, based on ISIC Rev. 4, with finer sectoral detail than GGDC WIOD, for the period 2005–15. http://www.oecd.org/industry/ind/stanstructuralanalysis database.htm
	OECD Regional Database, covering employment and value added in subnational regions in over 30 countries, based on ISIC Rev. 4, for the period 2004–15. http://www.oecd.org/cfe/regional-policy/regionalstatistics andindicators.htm
Oxford Economics	Proprietary data, covering over 7,000 cities and regions across the world, with figures on variables including employment and value added in a broad FABS category since 2000, with forecast until 2035. https://www.oxfordeconomics.com/cities-and-regions
ILO	Data on sex and employment by economic sector and occupation for most countries since 2000. https://www.ilo.org/ilostat/
WTO	Breakdown of exports and imports for finance, insurance and categories of business services for 2005–17 based on BPM6, and 1980–2013 based on BPM5. http://data.wto.org/inventory/en

Note: The selection includes the best sources available according to the author. Eurostat, for example, is not included, since it offers little in terms of FABS coverage that would be additional to the above.

To give readers a taste of the various types of data, the rest of this section shows some general trends and patterns in FABS development. This is important, since FABS related concepts evolved primarily in (a delayed) response to these developments, and so painting these trends with a broad brush will help us contextualize the historical trajectory of these concepts. In addition, an overview of data-based trends and patterns will help us reflect on the future directions for FABS research. What is referred to as FABS in this section may vary depending on the data source used, and is explained in notes accompanying each figure.

In FABS, I focus on employment, rather than value added, since the interpretation of value added in FABS is fraught with difficulty. Most calculations for value added in real estate include, and in terms of magnitude are dominated by, the imputed value of rents in owner-occupied properties (see UN, 2008, for details). Value added in the whole financial sector can be significantly inflated through the impact of asset price bubbles, including credit bubbles, which can lead to crises and reflect problems rather than the health of the sector. This issue relates to the controversial topic of measuring productivity in banking and the financial sector, which is important but beyond our consideration here (see Christophers, 2013).

In 2010, 39 countries for which data were available had 109 million people employed in FABS, defined on the basis of ISIC Revision 3.1 (consisting of financial intermediation, real estate, renting, and business services), representing 5% of total employment. This was up from 29 million people (2.6% of total employment) in 1975. As Figure 2.2 shows, the sector exhibits a steady growth since at least 1950. It accelerated in the USA between the late 1970s and 2000, and in Europe since the late 1960s. This suggests that although FABS grew in the Fordist era of the 1950s and 1960s, their boom came with post-Fordist flexible accumulation—this echoes arguments made, inter alia, by Wood (1991), re-emphasized recently by Wójcik (2018), linking the rise of FABS in recent decades with globalization and financialization.

Low growth of FABS in Latin America since the late 1970s until the early 1990s may be due to the Latin American debt crisis and relatively low economic growth of this period. The FABS share in employment in Africa and Asia started from a very low level, and has grown surprisingly slowly, particularly in Asia. It is also hard to explain why, by 2010, the share of FABS in employment in Asia was comparable with that of Latin America in 1950. This contrast between Asia and Latin America is striking, and may have to do with the intricacies of ISIC application in some Asian countries, particularly China, to which we will return later.

GGDC used as a source in Figure 2.2 does not offer up-to-date data. Thus, to present more recent trends, and some predictions, in Figure 2.3 we switch to Oxford Economics, using data for the same 39 countries as in Figure 2.2, plus Germany. Oxford Economics data is based on ISIC Revision 4, and goes back to 2000, but I use 2010 as a starting point just to reflect briefly on the

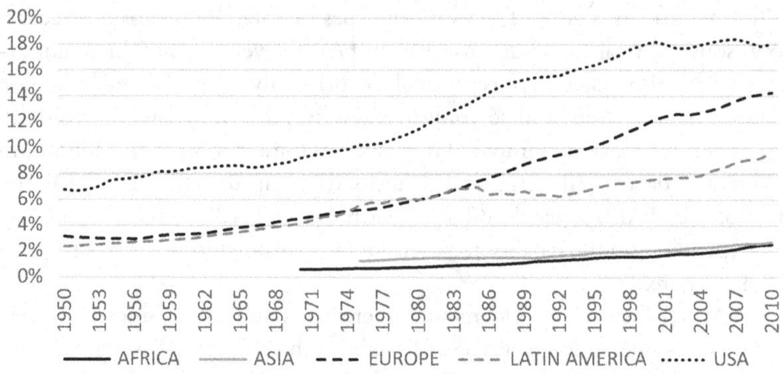

Figure 2.2 Share of FABS in total employment, 1950–2010

Notes: FABS are defined as sections J + K of ISIC Rev. 3.1; The sample covers 39 countries: Botswana, Ethiopia, Ghana, Kenya, Malawi, Mauritius, Nigeria, Senegal, South Africa, Tanzania, Zambia, Morocco, Egypt in Africa; China (inc. Hong Kong), India, Indonesia, Japan, South Korea, Malaysia, Philippines, Singapore, Taiwan, Thailand in Asia; Argentina, Bolivia, Brazil, Chile, Colombia, Costa Rica, Mexico, Venezuela in Latin America; Denmark, Spain, France, the United Kingdom, Italy, Netherlands, Sweden in Europe; and the United States in North America. Two countries from the full GGDC sample are not included: Germany, due to incomparability of data before and after reunification, and Peru, due to lack of data prior to 1960.

Source: GGDC, https://www.rug.nl/ggdc/productivity/10-sector/.

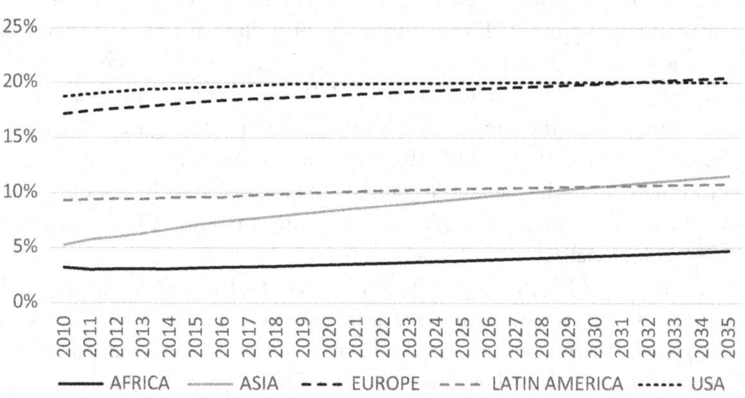

Figure 2.3 Share of FABS in total employment, 2010–17, and forecast until 2035

Notes: FABS are defined as sections KLMN of ISIC Rev. 4. The sample covers the same countries as Figure 2.2 plus Germany.

Source: Oxford Economics Global Cities Database.

relationship between the two datasets, without going into too much detail. For 2010, Oxford Economics FABS employment figures are slightly lower than those from GGDC for Latin America, slightly higher for the United States and Africa, significantly higher for Europe, and much higher for Asia.

With computer services included in section K of ISIC Revision 3.1 but not included in KLMN under ISIC Revision 4, it may be surprising to see Oxford Economics reporting larger FABS employment. On the other hand, however, ISIC Revision 4 includes a few categories not included in FABS by ISIC Revision 3.1: travel agencies and ticket reservation and booking (included previously under transport services); veterinary activities (which used to be part of health and social work); installation of fire and burglar alarms; supporting services for the government (including the operation of government buildings); vehicle licensing; landscaping; and sweeping and watering of streets. In general, the definition of lower-skilled business services (N) under ISIC Revision 4 is quite broad. This inclusion of many lower-skilled services may contribute to explaining the big jump in the share of FABS in total employment in Asia, from 2.7% in 2010, according to GGDC, to 5.2%, according to Oxford Economics. This can, however, be only a partial explanation. The difference is simply too great to be driven solely by ISIC revision, particularly in Asia in comparison to other parts of the world. It is also difficult to explain the drop in the Latin American figure, as we move from GGDC to Oxford Economics, considering that the continent does not host a large computer services sector. In sum, this serves as a warning against making far-flung observations based on direct comparisons between GGDC and Oxford Economics data, and implies that really long-term international analysis of FABS employment (not to mention value added) is a tricky business.

Notwithstanding the above warning, Figure 2.3 shows some clear, broad trends. Between 2010 and 2017, FABS continued to increase its share in total employment worldwide, with particularly rapid growth in Asia. The pace of growth was faster in Europe than in the United States, with the old continent catching up with the United States. According to the Oxford Economics forecast, the FABS share in total employment in the United States and Europe would level off just above 20% in 10–20 years; exceed 10% in Asia, thus overtaking Latin America in about 10 years; and reach 5% in about 20 years in Africa. According to Oxford Economics, in the sample countries FABS employed 213 million people in 2017, up from 157 million in 2010, and up from 7% to 9% of total employment. Globally, according to Oxford Economics, and given that the sample covers approximately two-thirds of the world population and employment, we can estimate that in 2017, broadly defined, FABS employed approximately 300 million people, with expected average growth in the 2010–35 period of 10 million additional workplaces a year.

Figures 2.4 and 2.5 make further use of Oxford Economics data. Figure 2.4 shows a strong positive relationship between the share of FABS in total employment and GDP per capita by country. The relationship holds for the sample as a whole and for each of the four continental subsets. This is consistent with literature on finance and development, which, for the most part, shows that financial development is strongly and positively related to economic development, as well as contributing to it. A recent generation of this literature,

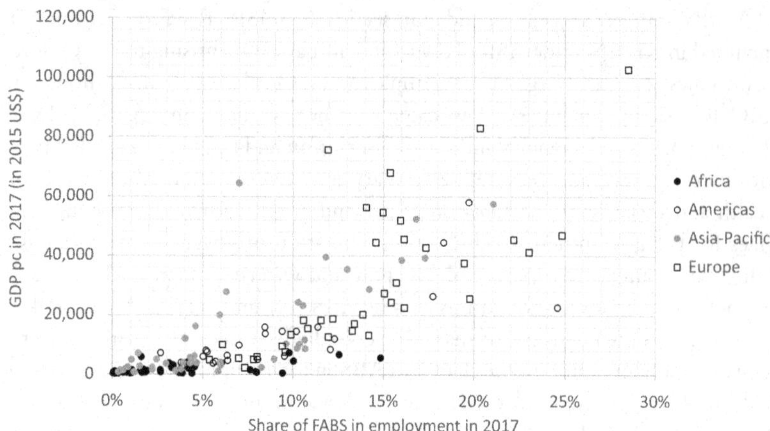

Figure 2.4 FABS employment share and GDP pc by country in 2017

Notes: Data covers 155 countries, all for which OE data was available. Africa's border with Asia-Pacific is defined as the North-Eastern border of Egypt; Russia is included in Europe; Turkey, Caucasus, Australia and Oceania in Asia-Pacific.

Source: Oxford Economics Global Cities Database.

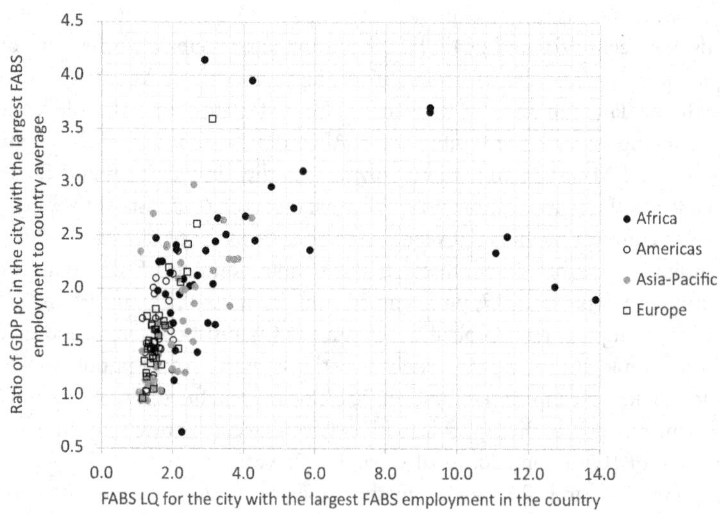

Figure 2.5 Specialization and GDP pc of the largest national FABS centers

Note: FABS LQ—share of FABS in the total employment of the city with the largest FABS employment in the country divided by the share of FABs in the total national employment.

Source: Oxford Economics Global Cities Database.

however, shows that financial development, measured most commonly as a ratio of credit to GDP, has a positive effect on economic growth only up to a point, with very high levels of financial development having a negative impact. This new research is in tune with literature on the negative effects of financialization.

While there is rich literature on the finance and growth nexus, Figure 2.4 underscores the need for more research on FABS and the growth nexus. One exception here is a study by Ioannou and Wójcik (2020) showing that the relationship between the FABS employment share and GDP growth also follows an inverted U-shape pattern, with very high levels of FABS intensity associated with lower economic growth, after controlling for other factors, such as the starting level of GDP per capita. Moreover, this result holds when the relationship is analysed at the city level. To be sure, the relationship between FABS and economic development operates in both directions, and it is always going to be difficult to establish causality, particularly considering the limits of internationally comparable long-term data.

As well-established in literature, FABS have a distinctly urban character. This is highlighted in Figure 2.5. Of a total of 155 countries captured in the data, there is no country in which the largest FABS center (in terms of total FABS employment) does not have a location quotient larger than 1, calculated as the share of FABS in total employment of the city divided by the FABS share in the total national employment. The median quotient is a high 1.8. All countries where the leading national center has a quotient above 5 are in Africa; all those with a quotient between 3 and 5 are in Africa or the Asia-Pacific, with the exception of Ukraine. This, in itself, suggests that FABS tend to develop disproportionately in leading urban centers before they become more dispersed. The dispersion, however, in an important contrast to manufacturing, has its limits. Leading centers remain highly specialized in FABS, even while they may shed some lower-value added FABS to other places.

Another important message of Figure 2.5 is the positive relationship between the degree to which the largest national FABS center specializes in FABS and its advantage over the rest of the country in terms of GDP per capita. The positive relationship holds for every continent, a group of African outliers notwithstanding. This observation reinforces the message from Figure 2.4, on the positive relationship between FABS and economic development, this time at the level of cities. The only leading national FABS centers that had GDP per capita below the country average (and only slightly below) in 2017 were Reykjavik, Dubai, Manama, Riyadh, and Monrovia. The median GDP per capita advantage of the largest national FABS center was as high as 1.7. Of course, there are many factors behind spatial income inequalities, and the relationship between the latter and FABS concentration operates in both directions, but Figure 2.5 is a good reminder that FABS and their geography have to be investigated as one of the factors behind spatial income and wealth disparities.

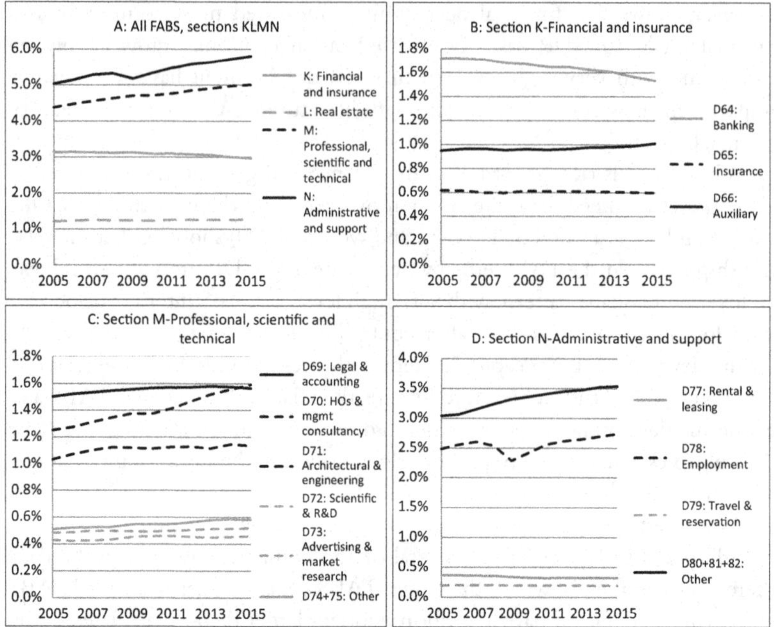

Figure 2.6 Share of FABS categories in total employment

Notes: Based on ISIC Rev. 4. Letter D followed by a number stands for a division of ISIC classification. OECD data covers 36 OECD member states plus Costa Rica (undergoing accession), though data availability varies across countries. As a result, the size of the sample for various time series varies from 36 to 30. For each time series, only countries for which data was available for the whole period were included.

Source: OECD STAN database.

The sheer size of the FABS sector makes it crucial to investigate its structure. The OECD offers data that allows such analysis for over 30 OECD countries for the period 2005–15. In Figure 2.6, we use this data to reflect on the changing structure of FABS, by focusing on figures showing the share of various FABS subsectors in total employment. First, as panel A shows, professional, scientific, and technical service activities (ISIC Revision 4, section M) are larger than FIRE (K + L combined), and administrative and support service activities (N) are still larger. It also shows that while FIRE has only just maintained its share in total employment, the absolute majority of employment growth in FABS in 2005–15 was generated in FABS other than FIRE. In 2005, in OECD countries, FIRE, M and N accounted for about one-third of total FABS employment each, but since then M and N have outgrown FIRE.

Figure 2.7 complements Figure 2.6 to zoom in on FABS employment since the global financial crisis. Not surprisingly, given that the crisis originated in the housing market, it had the fastest impact on the real estate industry, which experienced a drop in absolute employment in 2008. Declines in all

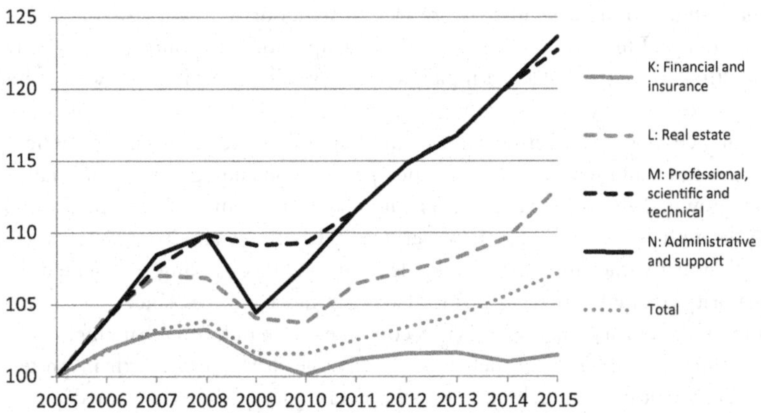

Figure 2.7 Growth of FABS and total employment, 2005–15

Source: OECD STAN database.

other FABS subsectors and the economy as a whole followed in 2009. The patterns of decline and recovery, however, differ significantly across FABS. Professional, scientific, and technical services declined least and recovered quickly. Administrative and support services declined most but also recovered quickly. The decline in FIRE lasted the longest but, while real estate bounced back to employment levels much above the 2007 pre-crisis peak, recovery in financial and insurance services has been fragile, with these subsectors not having reached the pre-crisis employment peak by 2015. These contrasting patterns lead to hypotheses that warrant further research. The resilience of the professional, scientific, and technical services may be due to the fact that this subsector includes services that actually have the capacity to grow during a crisis, such as legal services growing in response to changes in regulation, or management consulting offering services to help companies and government organizations to restructure. In contrast, the vulnerability of the administrative and support services during the crisis may be due to the lower-skilled character of the subsector, with more precarious jobs, leading to more layoffs during the crisis and rehiring when economic growth resumes. Finally, the pattern of employment in financial and insurance services points to the possibility of a secular long-term downward trend. Notice in Figure 2.7 that, even during the roaring mid-2000s, financial and insurance services lagged behind growth in other FABS, and barely matched growth in total employment.

Panels B, C, and D of Figure 2.6 delve into sections K, M, and N. Panel B shows that relative decline in financial and insurance services employment is driven by a significant decline in banking, from 1.7% to 1.5% of total employment. In 2015, banking in OECD countries employed approximately 6% fewer people than a decade earlier, being the only subcategory of FABS that registered an absolute decline in employment. Importantly, this decline pre-dates 2008, again highlighting a secular nature to this trend, driven by factors including technology. Employment in insurance kept up with the economy as a whole, resulting in a stable share. Employment in auxiliary services grew by 13%. While technology affects both insurance and auxiliary financial services, the insurance industry experienced no equivalent of the credit boom experienced by banking, and demand for insurance products, including pension insurance, has grown. Related to that, growth in auxiliary finance may be explained partly by growth in fund management services (Haberly et al., 2019). It is worth noting that while, until 2010 (and at least since 2005), banking represented the majority of employment in financial and insurance services, since 2011 insurance and auxiliary financial services combined have outgrown banking.

Panel C of Figure 2.6 helps us identify the drivers of growth in professional, scientific and technical services. Every part of this subsector depicted in Figure 2.6 has outperformed the economy as a whole in terms of employment growth, with an absolute growth of at least 10% over the decade. The champion of growth in this section, however, is not law and accounting but, decidedly, head office and management consultancy services. Employment in this division grew by nearly 35%, with the trend showing no signs of weakening. Unfortunately, the OECD does not offer data on the composition of this division. For that, we are left with national sources. Based on US data, I estimate that about one-third of employment in this division is in management consulting and two-thirds in head offices. Thus, growth in the division is likely to come from both parts, though the question requires further investigation.

Finally, in panel D of Figure 2.6, we see within administrative and support services that travel and reservation services, and rental and leasing have declined in relative terms. The impressive growth of the section as a whole has been sustained by employment services (despite a major decline in 2008–9) and, above all, by other services, which have kept growing throughout the decade. The latter is made of three divisions: security and investigation activities; services to buildings and landscape activities; and office administrative, office support, and other business support activities. Though further investigation is necessary, we suspect that most growth has come from the last division, which includes the activities of call centers. A simultaneous fast growth in head offices employment and in specialized support services establishments is an intriguing observation that calls for further analysis. Consider, one of the premises of the global city hypothesis was that with globalization companies increasingly outsource financial and other coordinating functions to specialized service providers, rather than concentrate them in their own head offices. The data are suggesting that both head offices and specialized FABS have been growing simultaneously.

When we reflect on Figures 2.6 and 2.7, we should keep in mind that jobs move between different parts of FABS, and between FABS and the rest of the economy, as well as between the OECD and the rest of the world. For example, banking may be shrinking as some jobs move to call and support services centers within the OECD. Rising head office employment may be

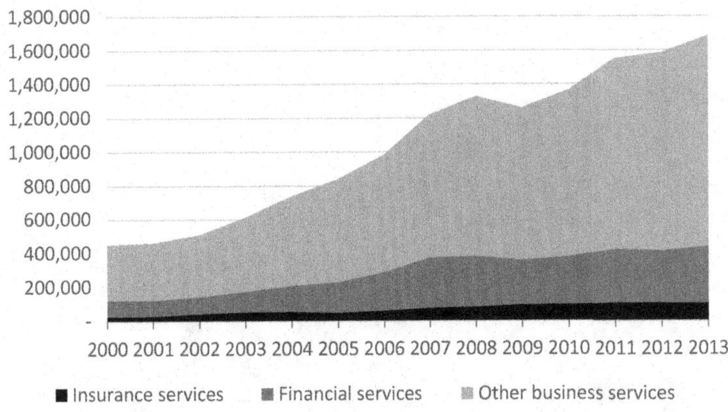

Figure 2.8 Global exports of FABS (US$ million)

Note: Categories based on BOP5.

Source: Author based on data.wto.org.

the result of international companies centralizing their headquarters functions and moving related jobs from non-OECD to OECD countries. It is intriguing to see a rapid rise of other administrative and support services in the OECD, while many would associate such activities with non-OECD countries, such as India and the Philippines. We should add that all the broad trends illustrated in Figures 2.6 and 2.7, and discussed above, are quite consistent across countries.

Figures 2.8 and 2.9 show trade in FABS. Since 2000, global exports of FABS nearly quadrupled and, by 2018, they were considered likely to reach US$2 trillion per year. Absolute majority of trade in FABS was in other business services, approximately three times more than in financial and insurance services, though trade in the latter has increased at a similar rate as that of other business services. Overall trade in FABS increased its share in total merchandise and services trade from 7% in 2000 to 9% by 2013.

Figure 2.9 complements the picture by showing the largest exporters and importers of FABS in 2017. Exports of financial services appear much more concentrated than imports, but this pattern does not apply to insurance or other business services. This reflects a much more concentrated geography of tradeable financial services compared to a more dispersed geography of insurance and other business services as a whole. The United States and the United Kingdom are leading exporters and importers, with the United Kingdom as the largest net exporter of FABS in 2017. Luxembourg features as a major exporter of financial services, but is also the largest importer, reflecting the offshore character of Luxembourg as a financial center, with transactions passing through, in, and out of the country. Countries outside Europe and the United States feature rarely, with Singapore as a leading exporter of financial services, and United Arab Emirates and China as major importers of insurance services.

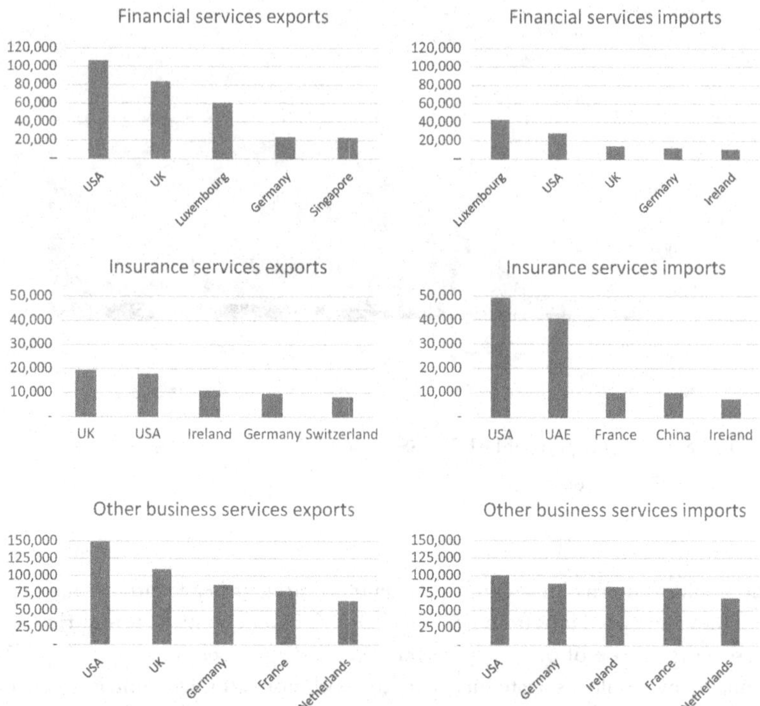

Figure 2.9 Top trading countries in FABS in 2017 (US$ million)

Note: Categories based on BOP6.

Source: Author based on data.wto.org.

A closer inspection of World Trade Organization (WTO) data reveals the rise of non-European countries in FABS trade, with countries such as India in the lead.

To illustrate the potential of input–output data, in Table 2.3 we used 2014 data for the United States, the world's largest producer, consumer, exporter, and importer of FABS. The selected data sheds light on the concept of FABS as a complex. First, defined broadly under ISIC Revision 4 as KLMN, FABS buy the majority of their intermediate input from other FABS, ranging from 93% for insurance and over 70% for the rest of finance, through over 60% for professional, scientific, and technical services, to over 50% for real estate, and administrative and support services. For every FABS category for which data are available, the biggest input came from one of the FABS categories. Each of the four parts of FIRE, as well as legal, accounting, head offices, and management consulting services, actually sourced the biggest part of intermediate input from itself! In this context, it is important to note that the FABS concept I proposed in work on GFNs focuses exactly on these sectors.

Table 2.3 Input–Output use table for FABS, USA 2014 (US$ billion)

	K64	*K65*	*K66*	*L68*	*M69+ M70*	*M71*	*M72*	*M73*	*M74+ M75*	*N77*	*N78*	*N79*	*N80 to N82*	*FABS as % of Total Intermediate Use*	*Biggest Use outside of FABS*		*Share of Households in Total Use*	*Total Use at Producer Prices*
K64	59	13	20	43	20	5	3	3	1	16	2	0	4	58%	23	PA	39%	615
K65	9	300	14	22	9	4	2	2	1	5	3	1	5	67%	82	Health	45%	1,068
K66	43	100	36	2	8	1	1	1	0	1	1	0	1	67%	32	PA	32%	503
L68	4	8	18	146	42	17	9	9	3	9	6	1	10	33%	119	Health	65%	2,805
M69+M70	17	18	26	15	50	21	11	11	4	13	11	2	20	22%	95	W.Trade	9%	1,223
M71	8	8	10	8	39	18	10	10	3	8	4	1	8	35%	40	PA	4%	641
M72	4	4	6	5	21	10	5	5	2	4	2	0	4	35%	21	PA	4%	346
M73	4	4	6	5	21	10	5	5	2	4	2	0	4	35%	22	PA	4%	348
M74+M75	1	1	2	1	7	3	2	2	1	1	1	0	1	35%	7	PA	4%	114
N77	3	5	25	7	35	6	3	3	1	7	3	1	5	26%	26	PA	15%	553
N78	3	4	4	54	10	6	3	3	1	6	3	1	6	46%	19	PA	7%	246
N79	1	1	1	11	2	1	1	1	0	1	1	0	1	46%	4	PA	7%	51
N80 to N82	6	8	6	99	19	11	6	6	2	12	6	1	11	46%	35	PA	7%	452
FABS as % of total intermediate input	75%	93%	73%	58%	64%	60%	60%	60%	60%	58%	52%	52%	52%					
Biggest input outside of FABS	15 A&F	9 A&F	26 Com	125 Con	41 Com	8 A&F	4 A&F	4 A&F	1 A&F	11 Com	6 Com	1 Com	11 Com					
Intermediate inputs	217	507	235	719	443	186	100	101	33	150	87	18	160					

Source: GGDC at http://www.wiod.org/database/nat_suts16

Notes: Based on ISIC Rev.4, see other figures and tables for the explanation of FABS codes.

A&F-accommodation and food services; Com- Computer programming, consultancy and related services; information services; Con-Construction; PA- Public administration and defence; compulsory social security; Health- Human health activities; W.Trade- Wholesale trade, except of motor vehicles and motorcycles.

There were only three sectors that featured as the largest input providers other than FABS. Of 13 FABS subsectors, accommodation and food services feature six times, in finance and insurance and most professional services, showing how important business travel is in finance and professional services. Computer and information services also feature six times, for auxiliary finance (not surprisingly, since this category includes very computer-savvy securities firms and exchanges), and all administrative and support services (which often rely on processing information and connectivity with customers). For real estate, the biggest input provider other than itself is the construction industry.

FABS are also very important users of their own services. In each of the FIRE and administrative and support services, the biggest user of services is found within FABS. In professional, scientific, and technical services, the biggest user is outside FABS, with public administration, defense, and compulsory social security in the lead, followed by human health. This reminds us of strong links and mutual dependence between FABS and the public sector. Certainly, many FABS services are used directly by households, representing final consumption rather than intermediate use. The share of households varies significantly between subsectors, ranging from 65% for real estate, 45% for insurance, and 39% for banking, through 32% for auxiliary financial services, down to only 6% for professional, scientific, and technical services, and 10% for administrative and support services. These figures remind us of claims that the notion of producer services is a misnomer. They also lend support to the use of the term 'FABS'. Note that business services defined most broadly as professional, scientific, and technical services (M, according to ISIC Revision 4), and administrative and support services (N), are, indeed, in their absolute majority sold to other businesses.

Opportunities and Challenges for Future Research

While painting a picture of general trends and patterns in FABS development, we have already indicated some possible directions for future research. In terms of opportunities created by data, one could add to the list the potential use of transactional data. As mentioned at the start of the chapter, not only major financial and corporate transactions, but also some major public sector transactions, such as bond issuance, involve all kinds of FABS firms simultaneously. This creates opportunities for more research on relationships among FABS and between FABS and their clients, using network and other types of analysis. Admittedly, this kind of data is not publicly available, and has to be purchased from companies such as Thomson Reuters or Dealogic. Nevertheless, such data is crucial in order to move beyond research that relies on data on FABS office networks (Pažitka, Wójcik, and Knight, 2019).

On a related note, we need more research that investigates power relations within the FABS complex, which, in turn, influence their relations with other actors in the world economy. In my previous research, I coined the phrase 'investment bank capitalism' to highlight the power of investment banks as the key movers and shakers within FABS (Wójcik, 2012). But this has not always been that the case. From my conversations with FABS leaders, I would suggest that in the 1960s and 1970s management consultants were probably more influential than investment bankers. There was a great deal of corporate restructuring that involved consulting, but it was not dominated by the logic of financial deals to the extent we have witnessed since the early 1990s. Consequently, the primacy of investment banks at the pinnacle of FABS is not guaranteed for the future, particularly not since the global financial crisis. Much new research documents the rising significance of institutional investors and asset managers (Clark and Monk, 2017), and I would argue that this involves a slow shift of power away from investment banks (Wójcik and Cojoianu, 2018b; Wójcik, 2019). One difficulty with research investigating this important shift will be the fact that existing statistical classifications do a poor job to identify investment banking or asset management as industries (see issues described in Table 2.1). As such, researchers will need to rely on more qualitative research, including close-dialogue interviews (Clark, 1998), corporate documents, and corporate biographies.

Another major conceptual and methodological challenge facing research on FABS is whether to treat FABS as a sector (i.e., a set of firms), or a set of occupations or functions. This question is present throughout the evolution of FABS related concepts, but has never been conclusively resolved, not least due to problems with data availability. Daniels (1985: 447) stressed 'the emergence of corporate complexes which are composed of an interlocking set of head office, business and financial service activities'. In his world city hypothesis, Friedmann (1986) focuses on the concentrations of professionals specialized in control functions, including those working in corporate headquarters. Sassen, in her global city hypothesis (1991, 2000), pays much attention to internalization versus externalization of producer services functions. The rise in head office employment illustrated in the preceding question as a major driver of recent FABS growth is a powerful reminder of the significance of this issue. People working in FABS firms and those performing FABS functions in the headquarters of non-FABS firms form pretty much the same segment of the labor market. From a social and cultural perspective, FABS professionals working in head offices should be considered a part of the FABS social elite.

The challenge and opportunity that may look most exciting from the perspective of the time when this chapter is being written concerns the relationship between FABS and technology. This is epitomized in the boom of FinTech, a fascinating convergence of financial and technology industries involving new generations of mobile banking, blockchain, cryptocurrencies, robo-advisors and other innovations (Wójcik, 2020; Wójcik and Cojoianu, 2018a). Many predict that FinTech will decimate employment in the financial sector and reshape the geography of it, perhaps even making financial centers redundant (Wójcik, 2020b). Others, including myself, are skeptical about the impacts.

In our review of trends, we have already seen a long-term stagnation, if not decline, of employment in banking, but nothing close to a revolution. The hype surrounding the influence of FinTech on finance notwithstanding, an important related question is the potential impact of FinTech on business services beyond finance, including accounting, law, consulting, and administrative and support services. Will FinTech make production chains and networks in FABS longer and more expansive, or will it simplify the configuration of FABS by connecting service providers directly with consumers through digital platforms? What will be the geographical footprint of these processes?

There is a degree of irony in FinTech development in relation to international statistics. Recall that, as part of ISIC Revision 4, information technology was not separated from FABS until 2008. Arguably, this was exactly the time when the 'FinTech revolution' bringing technology and finance closer to each other in novel ways started (Arner et al., 2015). Even the recently revised NAICS 2017 does not mention financial technology. This is a classic case of economic reality catching industrial statistics completely by surprise, and will surely represent a major challenge for future revisions of statistical classifications. It is already a significant challenge for researchers grappling with the questions of defining and measuring FinTech. In any case, FinTech is definitely a likely addition to Figure 2.1, as a concept attracting a great deal of FABS related research, much of it hopefully coming from geography (Knight and Wójcik, 2020).

Elsewhere in the industry, there is increasing use of the term 'global business services'. Manning et al. (2017) define them as firms providing services to globally distributed business clients. In Poland, for example, the sector is estimated to employ over 200,000 people (Hashimoto and Wójcik, 2020; ABSL, 2017). This group of firms lies at the center of the process of outsourcing and offshoring in FABS, but there is no easy way to capture them through existing industrial classifications. As with FinTech, this is another example of the constantly changing configuration of FABS, evolving in interaction with other sectors under the influence of technology.

References

Aalbers, M. (2018). Financial geography I: Geographies of tax. *Progress in Human Geography*, 42(6), pp. 916–927.

Aalbers, M. (2019). Financial geography II: Financial geographies of housing and real estate. *Progress in Human Geography*, https://journals.sagepub.com/doi/full/10.1177/0309132518819503.

ABSL. (2017). *Sektor nowoczesnych usług biznesowych w Polsce (Modern Business Services Sector in Poland)*. Warsaw: Association of Business Services Leaders (ABSL).

Allen, J. (1988). Service industries: Uneven development and uneven knowledge. *Area*, 20(1), pp. 15–22.

Arner, D.W., Barberis, J., and Buckley, B.P. (2015). The evolution of fintech: A new post-crisis paradigm? Univ. Hong Kong Fac. Law Res. Pap. 2015/047, pp. 1689–1699.

Bassens, D. and van Meeteren, M. (2015). World cities under conditions of financialized globalization: Towards an augmented world city hypothesis. *Progress in Human Geography*, 39(6), pp. 752–775.

Beaverstock, J.V. (2004). 'Managing across borders': Knowledge management and expatriation in professional service legal firms. *Journal of Economic Geography*, 4(2), pp. 157–179.

Beaverstock, J.V., Taylor, P.J., and Smith, R.G. (1999). A roster of world cities. *Cities*, 16(6), pp. 445–458.

Beyers, W.B. (1992). Producer services. *Progress in Human Geography*, 16(4), pp. 573–583.

Beyers, W.B. (1993). Producer services. *Progress in Human Geography*, 17(2), pp. 221–231.

Christophers, B. (2013). *Banking Across Boundaries: Placing Finance in Capitalism*. Chichester, UK: Wiley-Blackwell.

Christophers, B. (2014). Geographies of finance I: Historical geographies of the crisis-ridden past. *Progress in Human Geography*, 38(2), pp. 285–293.

Christophers, B. (2015). Geographies of finance II: Crisis, space and political-economic transformation. *Progress in Human Geography*, 39(2), pp. 205–213.

Christophers, B. (2016). Geographies of finance III: Regulation and 'after-crisis' financial futures. *Progress in Human Geography*, 40(1), pp. 138–148.

Clark, G.L. (1998). Stylized facts and close dialogue: Methodology in economic geography. *Annals of the Association of American Geographers*, 88(1), pp. 73–87.

Clark, G.L. and Monk, A.H.B. (2017). *Institutional Investors in Global Markets*. Oxford: Oxford University Press.

Coe, N., Lai, K., and Wójcik, D. (2014). Integrating finance into global production networks. *Regional Studies*, 48(5), pp. 761–777.

Coffey, W.J. (2000). The geographies of producer services. *Urban Geography*, 21(2), pp. 170–183.

Daniels, P.W. (1985). The geography of services. *Progress in Human Geography*, 9(3), pp. 443–451.

Daniels, P.W. (1986). The geography of services. *Progress in Human Geography*, 10(3), pp. 436–444.

Daniels, P.W. (1987). The geography of services. *Progress in Human Geography*, 11(3), pp. 433–447.

Daniels, P.W. (1988). Some perspectives on the geography of services. *Progress in Human Geography*, 12(3), pp. 431–440.

Daniels, P.W. (1989). Some perspectives on the geography of services. *Progress in Human Geography*, 13(3), pp. 427–437.

Daniels, P.W. (1991). Some perspectives on the geography of services. *Progress in Human Geography*, 15(1), pp. 37–46.

Dicken, P. (2011). *Global Shift. Mapping the Changing Contours of the World Economy*. New York and London: Guilford Press.

Eurostat. (2008). NACE Rev. 2 Statistical classification of economic activities in the European Community. Eurostat Methodologies and Working Papers. Luxembourg: Eurostat.

Faulconbridge, J. (2006). Stretching tacit knowledge beyond a local fix? Global spaces of learning in advertising professional service firms. *Journal of Economic Geography*, 6(4), pp. 517–540.

Faulconbridge, J. and Muzio, D. (2009). The financialization of large law firms: Situated discourses and practices of reorganization. *Journal of Economic Geography*, 9(5), pp. 641–661.

Friedmann, J. (1986). The world city hypothesis. *Development and Change*, 17(1), pp. 69–83.

Friedmann, J. and Wolff, G. (1982). World city formation: An agenda for research and action. *International Journal for Urban and Regional Research*, 6(3), pp. 309–344.

GaWC. (2019). *World city relational data. Global and World Cities Research Network*. https://www.lboro.ac.uk/gawc/data.html.

Greenfield, H.I. (1966). *Manpower and the Growth of Producer Services*. New York and London: Columbia University Press.

Haberly, D., MacDonald-Korth, D., Urban, M., and Wójcik, D. (2019). Asset management as a digital platform industry: a global financial network perspective, *Geoforum*, 106, pp. 167–181.

Hall, S. (2010). Geographies of money and finance I: Cultural economy, politics and place. *Progress in Human Geography*, 35(2), pp. 234–245.

Hall, S. (2011). Geographies of money and finance II: Financialization and financial subjects. *Progress in Human Geography*, 36(3), pp. 403–411.

Hall, S. (2012). Geographies of money and finance III: Financial circuits and the 'real economy'. *Progress in Human Geography*, 37(2), pp. 285–292.

Hashimoto, T. and Wójcik, D. (2020). The geography of financial and business services in Poland: Stable concentration. *European Urban and Regional Studies*, https://journals.sagepub.com/doi/full/10.1177/0969776420943664.

ILO. (2012). *International Standard Classification of Occupations*. Geneva: International Labour Office.

IMF. (2009). *Balance of Payments and International Investment Position Manual*. Washington, DC: International Monetary Fund.

Ioannou, S. and Wójcik, D. (2019). On financialization and its future. *Environment and Planning A: Economy and Space*, https://journals.sagepub.com/doi/pdf/10.1177/0308518X18820912.

Ioannou, S. and Wójcik, D. (2020). Finance and growth nexus: an international analysis across cities and regions. *Urban Studies*, https://journals.sagepub.com/doi/pdf/10.1177/0042098019889244.

Knight, E. and Wójcik, D. (2020). FinTech, Economy and Space: Introduction to the Special Issue. *EPA: Economy and Space*, https://journals.sagepub.com/doi/full/10.1177/0308518X20946334.

Leyshon, A. (1995). Geographies of money and finance I. *Progress in Human Geography*, 19(4), pp. 531–543.

Leyshon, A. (1997). Geographies of money and finance II. *Progress in Human Geography*, 21(3), pp. 381–392.

Leyshon, A. (1998). Geographies of money and finance III. *Progress in Human Geography*, 22(3), pp. 433–446.

Manning, S., Kannothra, C.G., and Wissman-Weber, N.K. (2017). The strategic potential of community-based hybrid models: The case of global business services in Africa. *Global Strategy Journal*, 7, pp. 125–149.

Miles, I., Kastrinos, N., Flanagan, K., Bilderbeek, R., den Hertog, P., Huntink, W., and Bouman, M. (1995). Knowledge-intensive business services. Users, carriers and sources of information. A report to DG13 SPRINT-EIMS. Manchester: University of Manchester.

OMB. (2017). North American industry classification system. Washington, DC: Executive Office of the President, Office of Management and Budget (OMB).

Pažitka, V., Wójcik, D., and Knight, E. (2019). Construct validity in world city network research: From office location networks to inter-organisational projects in the analysis of intercity business flows. *Geographical Analysis*, https://onlinelibrary.wiley.com/doi/epdf/10.1111/gean.12226.

Pearce, E. (1957). History of the standard industrial classification. Washington, DC: Executive Office of the President, Bureau of the Budget, Office for Statistical Standards.

Sassen, S. (1991, 2000). *The Global City: New York, London, Tokyo.* Princeton, NJ: Princeton University Press.

Shearmur, R. and Doloreux, D. (2008). Urban hierarchy or local buzz? High-order producer service and (or) knowledge-intensive business service location in Canada, 1991–2001. *The Professional Geographer*, 60(3), pp. 333–355.

Taylor, P.J. (2004). *World City Network: A Global Urban Analysis.* New York and London: Routledge.

Taylor, P.J. and Derudder, B. (2016). *World City Network: A Global Urban Analysis.* London: Routledge.

Thrift, N.J. (2000). Producer services. In: R.J. Johnston, D. Gregory, G. Pratt, and M. Watts (eds), *The Dictionary of Human Geography*. Oxford: Blackwell, pp. 640–641.

UN. (1953). A system of national accounts and supporting tables. Studies and Methods No. 2. New York: United Nations, Department of Economic Affairs, Statistical Office.

UN. (2008). International Standard Industrial Classification of All Economic Activities (ISIC), Rev. 4. New York: United Nations.

UN. (2015). Central Product Classification (CPC) Version 2.1. Statistical Papers Series M No. 77, Ver. 2.1. New York: Department of Economic and Social Affairs, Statistics Division, United Nations.

US Census Bureau. (1940). Comparative occupation and industry statistics 1930 and 1940. Washington, DC: US Census Bureau.

Von Nordenflycht, A. (2010). What is a professional service firm? Toward a theory and taxonomy of knowledge-intensive firms. *The Academy of Management Review*, 35(1), pp. 155–174.

Wójcik, D. (2020). Financial Geography I: Exploring FinTech - Maps and concepts. *Progress in Human Geography.* https://journals.sagepub.com/doi/full/10.1177/0309132520952865.

Wójcik, D. (2020b). Financial Geography II: The impacts of FinTech - Financial sector and centres, regualtion and stability, inclusion and governance. *Progress in Human Geography*, https://journals.sagepub.com/doi/full/10.1177/0309132520959825.

Wójcik, D. (2012). The end of investment bank capitalism? An economic geography of financial jobs and power. *Economic Geography*, 88(4), pp. 345–368.

Wójcik, D. (2013). Where governance fails: Advanced business services and the offshore world. *Progress in Human Geography*, 37(3), pp. 330–347.

Wójcik, D. (2017). The global financial networks. In: G.L. Clark, M. Feldman, M.S. Gertler, and D. Wójcik (eds), *The New Oxford Handbook of Economic Geography.* Oxford: Oxford University Press, pp. 557–574.

Wójcik, D. and Cojoianu, T. (2018a). Conclusions: A global overview from a geographical perspective. In: Y. Cassis and D. Wójcik (eds), *International Financial Centers after the Global Financial Crisis and Brexit.* Oxford: Oxford University Press, pp. 207–231.

Wójcik, D. and Cojoianu, T. (2018b). Resilience of the US securities industry to the global financial crisis. *Geoforum*, 91, pp. 182–194.

Wójcik, D., Knight, E., O'Neill, P., and Pažitka, V. (2019). Economic geography of investment banking since 2008: The geography of shrinkage and shift. *Economic Geography*, 94(4), pp. 376–399.

Wood, P. and Wójcik, D. (2010). A dominant node of service innovation: London's financial, professional and consultancy services. In: F. Gallouj and F. Djellal (eds), *The Handbook of Innovation and Services.* Cheltenham: Edward Elgar, pp. 589–620.

Wood, P.A. (1991). Flexible accumulation and the rise of business services. *Transactions of the Institute of British Geographers*, 16, pp. 160–172.

3

FOUNDATIONS OF MARXIST FINANCIAL GEOGRAPHY

Patrick Bond

Introduction

Since David Harvey's *Limits to Capital* set out the first clear understandings of financial geography within Marxism in 1982, there have been rich explorations of *Das Kapital*'s spatial perspectives, several of which have been centered on the contradictory role of money within capitalist crisis. Nevertheless, major controversies remain because, when interpreting the spatial, power, and speculative dynamics of capitalism, the financial circuit has often confounded Marxist scholars and geographers alike.[1]

After fast-reviving US banking power was flagged during the late 1960s, a vast literature soon emerged.[2] From the early 1980s, Harry Magdoff and Paul Sweezy (1987) regularly alerted scholarly and popular critics to the 'financial explosion' gathering pace in the wake of the 'Volcker Shock'. That was U.S. Federal Reserve chair Paul Volcker's 1979 decision to raise interest rates dramatically, imposing a severe recession to fight inflation and restore the dollar's strength, thereby shifting unprecedented amounts of capital from productive investment into the financial markets. By 1993, 'a long-term shift from production to finance within the overall economy' was unmistakable, according to *Monthly Review* (2019) editors, and the term 'financialization' was coined by 'conservative political-analyst-turned-critic (and former advisor to Richard Nixon) Kevin Phillips, and was adopted not long after by left theorists'. After the turn of the twenty-first century—especially when a 2008–09 world economic meltdown was catalyzed by banks' abuse of real estate credit—the question emerged again: Was it *capitalist*—and not just financial-deregulatory—crisis tendencies that required critique? With the short-lived Occupy movement three years later, radical critics identified not only a regulatory reform agenda (such as the U.S. Dodd-Frank legislation), but also proposals for mass debt repudiation, inspired by leading anarchist strategist David Graeber (2012).

Indeed, depending on whether the banks' power or vulnerability is stressed by scholars and movement strategists, a profound divide between reformist and transformative perspectives exists within the financialization literature. This alone merits a return to the somewhat wobbly foundations of Marxist financial geography. After all, Marxists interested in money and credit were initially frustrated by *Das Kapital*'s third volume (completed by Friedrich Engels in 1894 from loose notes) as part of a general demolition of the mode of production's laws of motion, including the tendency to crisis (Bond, 2018). But, soon thereafter, an excessively institutionalist, reformist grounding of Marxist finance was provided by Rudolf Hilferding (1981), whose 1910 book *Finanz Kapital* stressed the power and economic control functions of finance (Bond, 2020).

In reality, numerous instances of far-reaching capitalist crisis before and after Hilferding's major work revealed how *systemic fragility* was a central problem for financial markets. Amelioration of credit and speculative bubbles certainly was possible, but financial crisis contagion prevailed at key moments—such as in the 1870s–80s, 1929–33, 1979–81, 1989–91, 1995–98 in the middle-income countries; 2001–02 in the dot.com sector; and 2008–09, 2009–13 in Europe and the early 2020s. Hence, the ideas of another original writer in the German political economy tradition, Henryk Grossman, are worthy of consideration in any search for Marxian geographical foundations. Six months before the world's worst banking and stock market collapse, in October 1929, Grossman (1992) published a provocative book about capitalist 'breakdown': *Das Akkumulations- und Zusammenbruchsgesetz des Kapitalistischen Systems: Zugleich eine Krisentheorie* (Kuhn, 2007).

But neither Hilferding nor Grossman provided the spatial elements needed to fill out a theory of geographical political economy, as was attempted by Harvey (1982). There, the critical question posed—and extended in this chapter—is how capitalist crisis tendencies are *displaced* through time and through space, using financial markets; and later, Harvey (2003) added the 'accumulation by dispossession' process, which includes usury, foreclosures, and repossessions, and other financial depravities. In the process, uneven geographical development is amplified, reflecting the ways the contradiction-prone characteristics of finance feed back into the rest of the economy, society, environment, and geopolitical terrain. This is a very different way to frame the underlying tendencies within financial geography than typically occurs within the discipline and, as a result, a more robust anti-capitalist politics with internationalist features can be envisaged, in contrast to a largely regulatory reform agenda.

Xiaoyang Wang (2017: 13) remarks: 'Economic geographers have often ignored the spatialities of finance. Rare studies on financial geography published in the 1970s and 1980s hardly added up to a substantial or coherent body of theoretical or empirical research.' When, in the 1990s, the field of financial geography began to develop, attention turned mainly to 'financialization, promoted by a series of books and papers by economists and geographers', in which the latter 'argued that location and place remain of crucial importance' (Wang, 2017: 13). For example, within 'a quicksilver global economy' of the twenty-first century, the major financial centers were, Wang (2017: 14) notes, 'increasingly fulfilling gateway functions for spatial circuits of national and foreign capitals' thanks to 'a particular set of locational determinants, and local characteristics and localized information' that 'jointly define the advantages of a given location as a financial center'.

In this body of work, the task for financial–geographical research appears mainly to explore spatial and locational features of financial systems as they evolve (sometimes offering constructive reform suggestions where irrationalities are obvious), rather than to probe deeper-rooted contradictions and especially tendencies to crisis (not to mention suggesting much more revolutionary solutions).[3] This leads, Ewa Karwowski and Marcos Centurion-Vicencio (2018: 4) confirm, to a quasi-positivist agenda: 'Three research strands can be distinguished within the financialization literature: (1) approaches addressing shifts in accumulation regimes, (2) approaches based on shareholder value and (3) approaches focusing on the financialization of everyday life.'

In contrast, Marxist economists Stavros Mavroudeas and Demophanes Papadatos (2018: 451) argue that 'the financialization hypothesis is a theoretical blind alley' because '[t]he spectacular ballooning of the financial system during the recent decades of weak profitability and accumulation does not constitute a new epoch, let alone a new capitalism. Instead, it represents a familiar capitalist response to periods of weak profitability.' The same point was made by *Monthly Review* (2019) editors, in worrying that the term financialization 'is reduced to a cyclical process based on shifts in regulation and nonregulation, downplaying the underlying trends and the stagnation-financialization trap. What distinguishes Marxian theory in that regard, in contrast, is precisely the analysis of the relation of financialization to the stagnation of investment/accumulation.' For Mavroudeas and Papadatos (2018: 451), 'The Marxist theory of crisis and fictitious capital offers an analytically and empirically superior understanding of this process.' Moreover, adds Michael Roberts (2019), use of the term financialization 'leads to the abandonment of the labor theory of value, an erroneous understanding of modern capitalism's *modus operandi* and, I think, eventually to reformist politics.

To consider how such conflicts persist in relation to the geography of financialization and whether Marxian theory sheds light on their spatial character, this chapter considers, first, how money and credit play diverse, changing roles within capital accumulation. We then investigate how the 'overaccumulation of capital' emerges as a core crisis tendency within the economy's productive sector, leading to falling rates of profits and then a shift of capital to speculative activities, as well as to new geographical outlets ranging from local to global. Uneven geographical development is logically amplified within the shifting circuits of capital, as finance roams through space and across scale in search of restored profitability, all the while exacerbating the problem with capital flows that Neil Smith (1990) termed a 'plague of locusts' —a metaphor capturing the profit system's essential geographical characteristic. The chapter concludes by giving a reminder that the nature and success of financial-system reform depends both on the degree to which the underlying dynamics have been properly analysed, and the political narratives of resistance that correspond to the theoretical challenge of accurate diagnosis.

The Roles of Finance in Capitalism: Accommodation, Control, Speculation

By way of definition, first, 'finance' is a term considered to encompass *external sources of funding* beyond the normal revenue streams that generally consist of company profits, state tax receipts, the wages and salaries of households, and the revenues of other institutions. It thus includes myriad forms of debt, as well as corporate equity (shares) issued on stock markets. *Financial capital* refers to the totality of financial institutions and instruments that advance money (and credit and other financial paper) for the purpose of gaining a return (interest, dividends, increases in share value, and so on). But, like capital itself, financial capital is not a mere thing *per se*, but encompasses social processes as well. Also, by way of definition, 'finance capital' in Hilferding's formulation was the merger of several branches of capital—financial, industrial, and commercial—under the guiding hand of the banks. And 'fictitious capital' is a way of referring to paper representations of capital such as records of equity ownership, securities, real estate titles, and the like.

It is important to clarify core economic processes. Under capitalism, money plays three well-known roles: it is (i) a medium of exchange and payment, (ii) a measure of value, and (iii) a store of wealth. Consider money as medium exchange. Marx termed credit 'interest-bearing money capital' and showed how it lubricates capitalist production and commerce in three ways. First, the smooth operation of markets depends on firms moving resources to where profits can be found, which has the effect of equalizing the rate of profit between firms. A well-functioning financial system is critical, both because credit is an extremely fluid means of allocating capital to where it is most highly rewarded, and because new investments (which add to competition and, hence, profit equalization) normally occur through borrowing.

Second, also lubricating exchange, the credit system allows more efficient forms of money (such as bills of exchange) to replace physical money handling. Hence, as Marx (1967: 436) put it, 'credit accelerates the velocity of the metamorphosis of commodities, and with this the velocity of monetary circulation'. In the process, the turnover time of capital is shortened and profits are realized more rapidly. In the *Grundrisse*, Marx (1973: 359) argues that 'the necessary tendency of capital is therefore circulation without circulation time, and this tendency is the fundamental determinant of credit and of capital's credit contrivances'.

Third, credit also allows for greater centralization of capital. This is a precondition for large firms to become publicly traded on the stock market and, hence, to raise further investment funds easily. Moreover, with credit, the individual capitalist acquires 'disposal over social capital, rather than his own, that gives him command over social labor. The actual capital that someone possesses, or is taken to possess by public opinion, now becomes simply the basis for a superstructure of credit' (Marx, 1967).

These three *accommodating* characteristics of finance—providing lubrication to the payments system, speeding the velocity of capitalist production and centralization, and centralizing funds for investment or hiring large numbers of workers—are not the only characteristics to consider. With the movement of capital into more concentrated and centralized form over time, there also emerge *controlling* characteristics of finance. Then, there also arises another characteristic of finance: *speculation*. This function increases in importance as capitalist crises appear and intensify, once investment funds are drawn into financial assets that lose their grounding in the productive assets they are meant to represent (as securities, shares of stock, real estate titles, and the like). Securitization, derivatives, cryptocurrencies, and other exotic products are examples of financial innovations to this end. In short, the shifting emphasis on different characteristics and roles of financial capital reflect how a maturing economy evolves from using money merely to accommodate the real sector, to a controlling function when finance works to centralize capital, to a state in which greater profits are made within financial speculation than in production.

Hyman Minsky (1977) described the inevitable devolution of credit quality, from the 'hedge' stage (where repayment of a loan from future revenues is assured), to the 'speculative' stage (whereby repayment is a gamble, and principal must often be repaid from sale of assets), to a 'Ponzi scheme' (whereby new loans are advanced simply so the borrower can pay interest on old). Harvey (2003: 75–6) worried that the latter stage is now a general condition, as part of a renewed 'accumulation by dispossession' accompanying capitalist crisis:

> The credit system and finance capital have, as Lenin, Hilferding and Luxemburg all remarked, been major levers of predation, fraud and thievery. Stock promotions, Ponzi schemes, structured asset destruction through inflation, asset stripping through mergers and acquisitions, the promotion of levels of debt encumbrancy that reduce whole populations, even in the advanced capitalist countries, to debt peonage, to say nothing of corporate fraud, dispossession of assets (the raiding of pension funds and their decimation by stock and corporate collapses) by credit and stock manipulations—all of these are central features of what contemporary capitalism is about.

The effect, in sum, is that as money and credit emerged from their most basic roles in the hoarding of wealth and early commerce to develop more fully as financial capital (i.e., money extended for the purpose of making more money), they also evolved from lubricating early capitalist relations to exhibiting controlling and speculative characteristics. But, as we consider next, the ultimate determinant over which of these characteristics emerges and dominates at any given point in time and space is the capital accumulation process, which gives meaning to the discrete acts of production, commerce, and value realization that money and credit were ostensibly developed under capitalism primarily to serve (not undermine).

Capital Accumulation, the Tendency towards Overaccumulation and the Rise of Finance

Capital accumulation refers to the generation of wealth in the form of 'capital'. It is capital because it is employed by capitalists not to produce with specific social *uses* in mind but, instead, to produce *commodities* for the purpose of *exchange*, for profit, and, hence, for the self-expansion of capital. Such an emphasis by individual capitalists on continually expanding the 'exchange-value' of output, with secondary concern for the social and physical limits of expansion (size of the market, environmental, political and labor problems, etc.), gives rise to profound contradictions. These are built into the very laws of motion of the system.

The most serious of capitalist self-contradictions, the most thoroughly embedded within the capital accumulation process, is the general tendency towards an increased capital–labor ratio in production—more machines in relation to workers—which is fueled by the combination of technological change and inter-capitalist competition, and is made possible by the concentration and centralization of capital. Individual capitalists cannot afford to fall behind the industry norm, technologically, without risking their price or quality competitiveness such that their products are not sold. This situation creates a continual drive in capitalist firms towards the introduction of state-of-the-art production processes, especially labor-saving machinery.

With intensified automation, the rate of profit tends to fall. Profit correlates to 'surplus value' that is generated through the exploitation of labor in production. Labor is paid only a proportion of the value produced, with a surplus going to capital. Since capitalists cannot 'cheat in exchange'—buy other inputs, especially machines that make other machines, from each other at a cost less than their value—the increases in value that are the prerequisite for production and exchange of commodities must emanate from workers. This means, in class terms, that capitalists do not and cannot systematically exploit other capitalists, but they can systematically exploit workers. This is the source of the central contradiction: with automation (which Marx conceived as 'congealed labor' reflecting past eras of exploitation), the living labor input from which surplus value is drawn becomes an ever-smaller component of the total inputs into production. And, as the labor content diminishes, so too do the opportunities for exploitation, for surplus value extraction, and, ultimately, for profits.

This situation exacerbates what becomes a self-perpetuating vicious spiral. Inter-capitalist competition intensifies within increasingly tight markets, as fewer workers can buy the results of their increased production. In turn, this results in a still greater need for individual capitalists to cut costs. A given firm's excess profits are but only temporarily achieved through the productivity gains that automation typically provides, since every capitalist in a particular industry or branch of production is compelled to adopt state-of-the-art technologies just to maintain competitiveness. This leads to growth in productive capacity far beyond an expansion in what consumer markets can bear.

Countervailing tendencies to this process emerge, such as an increased turnover of capital, automation so as to raise productivity, and the speeding up of work, as well as expansion of the credit system to enhance demand. But these rarely overwhelm the underlying dynamic for long. The inexorable consequence, a continuously worsening problem under capitalism, is termed the *overaccumulation* of capital. Overaccumulation refers to a situation in which excessive investment has occurred and, hence, goods cannot be brought to market profitably, leaving capital to pile up in sectoral bottlenecks or speculative outlets without being put back into new productive investment. Other symptoms include unused plant and equipment, huge gluts of unsold commodities, an unusually large number of unemployed workers, and the inordinate rise of financial markets. When an economy reaches a decisive stage of overaccumulation, then it becomes difficult to bring together all these resources in a profitable way to meet social needs.

There are many ways to move an overaccumulation crisis around through time and space, but the only real 'solution' to overaccumulation—the only response to the crisis capable of reestablishing the conditions for a new round of accumulation—is widespread *devaluation*. Devaluation entails the scrapping of the economic deadwood, which takes forms as diverse as depressions, banking crashes, inflation, plant shutdowns, and, as Schumpeter called it, the sometimes 'creative destruction' of physical and human capital (though sometimes the uncreative solution of war). The process of devaluation happens continuously, as outmoded machines and superfluous workers are made redundant, as waste (including state expenditure on armaments) becomes an acceptable form of mopping up overaccumulation, and as inflation eats away at buying power. This continual, incremental devaluation does not, however, mean capitalism has learned to 'equilibrate', thus avoiding more serious, system-threatening crises. Devaluation of a more cathartic nature—the Great Depression and World War II were the most spectacular examples—is periodically required to destroy sufficient economic deadwood so as to permit a new process of accumulation to begin.

When overaccumulation becomes widespread, extreme forms of devaluation are invariably resisted (or deflected) by whatever local, regional, national, or international alliances exist or are formed in specific areas under pressure. This was observed by Tony Smith (2006: 141):

> When overaccumulation crises break out, those who control capital mobilize their vast economic, political, and ideological weapons in the attempt to shift as many of the costs of the downturn as possible onto wage-laborers, through increased unemployment, lower wages, and worsened work conditions. Each unit of capital, each network of capitals, and governments of each region, will attempt to shift the costs of devaluing excess fixed capital onto other units, networks, and regions.

Hence, overaccumulation has very important geographical and geopolitical implications in the uneven development of capitalism, as attempts are made to transfer the costs and burden of devaluation to different regions and nations, or to push overaccumulated capital into the buildings (especially commercial real estate), infrastructure, and other features of the built environment as a last-ditch speculative venture. Moreover, the implications of overaccumulation for balance in different sectors of the economy—between branches of production (mining, agriculture, manufacturing, finance, etc.), between consumers and producers, and between capital goods (the means of production) and consumer goods (whether luxuries or necessities)—can become ominous. Indeed, because the rhythm of overaccumulation varies across the economy, severe imbalances between the different sectors and 'departments' of production (sometimes termed 'disproportionalities' or 'disarticulations') emerge and introduce threatening bottlenecks in the production and realization of value, which further exacerbate the crisis. This 'uneven sectoral development' is most acute between finance and other circuits of capital.

These processes enhance the control and speculative functions of finance. As overaccumulation begins to set in, as structural bottlenecks emerge, and as profit rates fall in the productive sectors of an economy, *capitalists begin to shift their investable funds out of reinvestment in plant, equipment, and labor power, and, instead, seek refuge in financial assets.* To fulfil their new role as not only a store of value, but as an investment outlet for overaccumulated capital, those financial assets must be increasingly capable of generating their own self-expansion, and also be protected (at least temporarily) against devaluation in the form of both financial crashes and inflation. Such emerging needs mean that financiers, who are competing against other profit-seeking capitalists for resources, induce a shift in the function of finance away from merely accommodating the circulation of capital through production.

Increasingly, finance takes on both speculative and control functions. The speculative function attracts further flows of productive capital, and the control function expands to ensure the protection and the reproduction of financial markets. For example, where consumer price inflation may be a threat, the control functions of finance often result in high real interest rates and a reduction in the value of labor-power (and, hence, lower effective demand). Where bankruptcies threaten to spread as a result of overenthusiastic speculation, the control functions of finance attempt to shift those costs elsewhere, especially in terms of using geography to displace the overaccumulation crisis, in what Marx termed the 'annihilation of space by time'.

From Evidence to Retheorization of Overaccumulation and Rising Finance

Capitalist crises reflecting overaccumulation tendencies occurred during the periods 1825–45, 1872–92, 1929–48, and in the era that began around 1973 (Kondratieff, 1979; Mandel, 1980). These 'long waves' can be measured in various ways but, from a Marxist perspective, the crucial variables include capital intensity ('the organic composition of capital'), surplus value rates, the velocity of circulation of capital, the geographical expansion of capitalist relations, capacity utilization, and inventory build-up. Within the long wave of accumulation, at a subnational scale, there are even more obvious 'Kuznets cycles' of durations ranging from15 years to three decades (Kuznets, 1930). These are witnessed in labor migration patterns and investment in buildings, infrastructure, and other facets of the built environment (Thomas, 1972). Harvey used empirical evidence of Kuznets cycles to reflect on the Marxist theory of overaccumulation, followed by devaluation (Harvey, 1989: 77).

The rise and fall of finance inevitably occur during the course of accumulation cycles, especially at the global level. To illustrate with international financial flows, during four particular periods—the late 1820s, the 1870s, the 1930s, and the 1980s—at least one-third of all national states fell into default on their external debt, following an unsustainable upswing of borrowing at a time of declining foreign-sourced productive sector investment. Another such debt crisis episode appears imminent, as even the World Bank and International Monetary Fund have remarked on how the 2008–09 global economic meltdown failed to clear away debt and financial bubbling, but simply added more, deflecting the crisis until a later date using bank bailouts, extremely low interest rates, and quantitative easing (which, together, inflated the price of financial assets). In their World Bank publication *Global Waves of Debt*, Ayhan Kose et al. (2020: 41–2) remark on the particular problem of emerging markets and developing economies (EMDEs):

> Debt sustainability has deteriorated since the global financial crisis both in advanced economies and in EMDEs...EMDE borrowing costs have tended to rise sharply during episodes of financial stress, and higher debt servicing costs can cause debt dynamics to deteriorate and rollover risk to rise. A recent example is Argentina, where five-year U.S. dollar-denominated sovereign bond yields more than doubled during 2018, to over 11 percent by early September. Indeed,

every decade since the 1970s has witnessed debt crises in EMDEs, often combined with banking or currency crises.

Christian Suter (1992) explained the 'global debt cycle' by way of stages in the long wave, beginning with technological innovation and utilizing international product cycle theory. At the upswing of a Kondratieff cycle, as basic technological innovations are introduced in a labor-intensive and unstandardized manner, both the demand for and supply of external financing are typically low; in any case, the residue of financial crisis in the previous long cycle does not permit rapid expansion of credit or other financial assets into high-risk investments. As innovations are spatially diffused, however, peripheral geographical areas become more tightly integrated into the world economy, supported by international financial networks. Moreover, as the power of innovation led growth subsides, and as the consumer markets of the advanced capitalist countries become saturated, profit rates decline in the core.

In turn, this process pulls and pushes waves of financial capital into peripheral areas where, instead of achieving balanced accumulation and growth, low returns on investment plus a variety of other political and economic constraints inexorably lead to sovereign default. In sum, at the global scale there is a three-stage process characterized by, as Suter (1992: 41) puts it, 'first, intense core capital exports and corresponding booms in credit raising activity of peripheries; second, the occurrence of debt service incapacity among peripheral countries; and third, the negotiation of debt settlement agreements between debtors and creditors'.

Evidence is compelling at one level: the international scale. But, in transcending the world systems approach, a foundational Marxist theory of financial geography would seek to accomplish at least five other tasks on other terrains, as well:

- More closely integrate trends in the productive circuits of capital with the dynamics of finance;
- Incorporate evidence of financialization at global, national, regional, local, and household scales;
- Encompass the speculative and control features of finance as integral—albeit often rapidly-shifting—features across scales and spaces;
- Explain other forms of financial ascendance that occur during periods of crisis, including financial product innovation, volatile and unevenly-applied interest rates, explosions in speculative stock market and real estate prices followed by their inevitable devalorization, untenable consumer (and currently student) debts, the interplay of corporate and government exposure to credit markets (especially when bailouts occur due to systemic fragility), and a qualitative increase or decrease in the political clout of financiers; and
- Interrogate the uneven successes of social protest and state-regulatory resistance to financial power.

However, one debilitating factor that partially explains the lack of synthetic study of financial geography from a Marxian perspective is that, for nearly a century following Hilferding's defining work, most inquiries into money and credit were sidetracked by the presumption that finance capital continually concentrates, centralizes, and collects socio-political power, without facing debilitating contradictions (Bond, 2020). The roots of this mismeasurement in Hilferding (1981: 368) are illustrated in his claim that 'taking possession of six large Berlin banks would mean taking possession of the most important spheres of large scale industry, and would greatly facilitate the initial phases of socialist policy during the transition period, when capitalist accounting might still prove useful'.

Grossman (1992: 200) rebutted this in 1929: 'The historical tendency of capital is not the creation of a central bank which dominates the whole economy through a general cartel, but industrial concentration and growing accumulation of capital leading to the final breakdown due to overaccumulation.' These two differing perspectives on finance—one highlighting power, the other vulnerability—allow a dialectical perspective in which, from opposite stances, there emerges a new synthesis, itself ripe with contradictions. It is here that the spatial processes of uneven development become critical subjects of study.

Space, Time and the Displacement of Overaccumulation

What is required to transcend this divide is an investigation into the *limits of finance capital power*, and the *displacement of capitalist crisis* (across space and time). Together, these are vital components in explaining the financial system's failure to achieve a harmonious relationship by lubricating accumulation. Harvey (1982: 285) assists us by more clearly specifying 'the contradiction between the financial system and its monetary basis', in part because of a set of countervailing tendencies to capitalist crisis hitherto unexplored within the Marxist tradition: 'Absorption of capital (and labor) surpluses through temporal and geographic displacement played key roles in the history of crisis resolution.' For Harvey, credit serves a temporal displacement function—a so-called 'temporal fix' to overaccumulation—since finance not only accelerates the turnover time of capital, as Marx observed, but also sends surplus capital into 'the production of goods that have long term future uses in production or consumption'. This helps to displace crisis in the short term, but exacerbates the overaccumulation problem down the road.

There is also a 'spatial fix' to overaccumulation. In serving a geographical displacement function (such as through foreign lending), finance sends surplus money elsewhere, according to Harvey (1982: 434): 'The implication is that overaccumulation at home can be relieved only if surplus money capital (or its equivalent in commodities) is sent abroad to create fresh productive forces in new regions on a continuously accelerating basis.' This amounts to a short-term solution to overaccumulation that comes back to haunt the lending country when, in order to pay off the debt, the borrower must cut imports from, and increase exports to, the lender. The same principle works at other geographical scales. In sum, the tensions and contradictions in value production and realization can only be resolved, says Harvey (1982: xvi), 'at the price of internalizing the contradictions within itself. Massive concentration of financial power, accompanied by the machinations of finance capital, can as easily destabilize as stabilize capitalism.' Harvey (1982: 283) thus highlights the constraints on the power of finance imposed by the full logic of the accumulation process, and 'finance capital' is therefore seen, far more usefully, in terms of 'the countervailing forces that simultaneously create and undermine the formation of coherent power blocs within the bourgeoisie'.

The main geographical concept that arises from this theoretical explanation, then, is the financial system's amplification of *uneven development.* There are three aspects: first, underlying dynamics of sectoral unevenness between and within the spheres of production, reproduction, and finance; followed, second, by uneven geographical development; and, third, by some considerations on the problem of scale in the relations between finance and uneven development.

The Uneven Development of Sectors

The issue, simply, is whether the power of finance is asserted through an *intensification* of processes of uneven development, as opposed to *diminishing* (or leveling) such processes (in part through the imposition of universalizing standards). Although Marx also used phrases such as 'great leveller and cynic' to describe money, the Marxist approach accepts this thesis only up to a point. Marx (1967) commented on uneven development as a necessary process under capitalism:

> In the same relations in which wealth is produced, poverty is produced also; that in the same relations in which there is a development of the forces of production, there is also the development of a repressive force; that these relations produce bourgeois wealth, i.e. the wealth of the bourgeois class, only by continually annihilating the wealth of the individual members of this class and by producing an ever growing proletariat.

This 'absolute general law of capitalist accumulation' is a useful grounding for a theory of uneven development associated with financial systems. Whereas Neil Smith (1990), in his seminal study of *Uneven Development*, roots the equalization and differentiation of capital (the fundamental motions of uneven development) in the emergence of a division of labor, Ernest Mandel (1968: 210) searched even further back, to 'private production' among different producers within the same community. He insisted that 'differences of aptitude between individuals, the differences of fertility between animals or soils, innumerable accidents of human life or the cycle of nature' (Mandel, 1968: 210) were responsible for uneven development in production.

As a result, societies faced a choice: either engage in mutual aid (usually feasible in a society based on cooperation) to ensure the subsistence of an entire community, or *save* and *lend money to those who need it* (eventually gaining some rate of interest). The latter route led to the historical development of money and credit, which, in turn, paved the way for fully fledged commerce and, ultimately, for capitalist relations of production and distribution. In this abstract version of the capitalist development process, finance as an accommodating feature of early stages of economic growth had the effect of ameliorating uneven development, particularly in equalizing the rate of profit across firms and sectors.

This could also, presumably, be the case in the sphere of *social reproduction*, where the development of consumer and government credit markets offered finance the means to level certain reproductive relations. This phenomenon has been most important, of course, in advanced capitalist societies. When an overaccumulation crisis is absent as a factor, then the inherent unevenness of the reproductive sphere—'disarticulated' development, as Alain de Janvry (1982) called the differential production and consumption of durable goods along class lines—tends to be diminished by the role of credit in establishing what Michel Aglietta (1979: 232) termed a 'consumption norm'. This sort of finance also serves to level the unevenness of productive–reproductive processes because it 'absorbs the divergence between the rhythm at which income is received and the rhythm at which it is spent, given the lumpiness of durable goods', according to Aglietta (1979: 232).

At the same time, the steady evolution of consumer savings and non-corporate contractual savings (pension and insurance funds), much of which is used to fund production, led finance 'irrevocably into direct participation in determining the general strategy of accumulation' (Aglietta 1979: 143). Astronomic growth in consumer credit—hire purchase, home mortgage bonds, car loans, credit for consumer durables, credit cards, and the like—after World War II reflected the mass consumption orientation of 'Fordism' and the 'intensive regime of accumulation'. All this implies that, under relatively good economic conditions, unevenness in the reproductive sphere can be ameliorated by finance, but the cost of this is growing indebtedness that, in turn, leaves the sphere of reproduction increasingly subject to the power of finance. In these theoretical arguments, in sum, the basis of finance–production–reproduction relations is one of amelioration; credit levels natural differences.

Finance has the opposite effect on uneven development under other conditions, however. It is only when we look beyond accommodating features of finance, and look instead to the *control* and *speculative* functions, that we can clearly see the roles of finance (as both cause and effect) in the uneven development of capitalism. To some degree, uneven sectoral development is most directly a function of imbalances in production between capital goods and consumer goods, and here the role of finance is by no means ameliorative. Such problems have 'all kinds of manifestations in shifting investment flows from productive to speculative outlets', according to Aglietta (1979: 359). For example, the increased turnover of short-term stocks of capital goods during the boom phase leads to ever-shorter terms for credit. More generally, Aglietta argued: 'Uneven development creates artificial differences in the apparent financial results of firms, which are realized only on credit. These differences favour speculative gains on the financial market.'

Aglietta (1979) documented how, in the United States, uneven sectoral development reached crisis proportions in the 1920s, leading to financial chaos during 1929–33 and the Great Depression. However, in considering the post-war era, Aglietta (1979: 378) invoked Hilferding in suggesting that finance can stabilize itself. The devaluation of money (inflation) and deflation of debt (write-downs in selected sectors) together permit a 'threshold of resistance' to crisis: 'What is important to note here is that the entire structure of modern capitalism functions in such a way as to avoid this phase degenerating into financial panic.' The overall message from Aglietta's 'Regulation School' of political economy is that the development of a 'mode of regulation' to serve particular 'regimes of accumulation' makes finance and uneven development a much less explosive combination.

But, if the intrinsic unevenness within and between finance, production, and reproduction may be temporarily muted due to successful strategies of regulation, that does not mean that an overaccumulation crisis has been resolved; neither does it mean that we can dismiss theoretically derived tendencies towards sectoral unevenness that ultimately manifest themselves in financial crisis. As discussed above, the role of finance in accommodating production evolves into a much more contradictory function under conditions of overaccumulation crisis. It is here that finance *accentuates* other processes of uneven development in the productive circuit of capital. Consider, especially, the phenomenon of speculation. According to Harvey (1982: 326), financial speculation has the effect, at times, of restructuring productive capital, since it:

> allows individualized and private experimentation with new products, new technologies (including organizational forms), new physical and social infrastructures, even whole new cultures, class configurations, and forms of class organization and struggle. It is this aspect to speculation that Marx ignores. The crash rationalizes and restructures production so as to eliminate extraneous elements—both old and new alike. It also disciplines all other aspects of social life to capitalist *class* requirements and hence typically sparks some kind of organized or unorganized response, not only on the part of labor (which goes without saying) but also from various affected factions within the bourgeoisie.

Consider, also, the damage to the productive sector wrought by speculation, unmitigated by any meaningful role in restructuring production to support renewed accumulation. Indeed, much of the displacement of capitalist crisis into speculative outlets, today and historically, is not merely unsustainable as the basis for regenerating productive development, it is also plainly self-destructive. For capital, the challenge at this stage becomes undergirding unproductive financial assets with productive assets. This was vividly expressed by Thomas Johnson, a leading US banker, in considering the potential implications of the Third World debt crisis during the 1980s: 'There is a possibility of a nightmarish domino effect, as every creditor ransacks the globe attempting to locate his collateral' (Smith, 1990: 161). This is the point at which the dynamic of uneven development reaches the brink. Expressed here is the transition from finance as an accommodating agent in the development of the productive forces of capitalism, to finance as both a controlling power and a speculative vehicle gone awry.

The Uneven Development of Space

It is by considering the process of spatial development during financial ascendance, that we can link analyses of unevenness more generally, between and within advanced capitalist settings and poorer countries. Ironically, while spatial metaphors are often easy for visionary bankers such as Thomas Johnson under conditions combining overaccumulation crisis and financial power, until Harvey, geographers wrote very little about finance in economic development. This was a serious oversight for, as Harvey (1989: 176) put it: 'Money creates an enormous capacity to concentrate social power in space, for unlike other use values it can be accumulated at a particular place without restraint. And these immense concentrations of social power can be put to work to realize massive but localized transformations of nature, the construction of built environments, and the like.'

Mainstream economic geography has treated finance as a service enterprise with specific locational and employment features that can be incorporated into pre-existing models of the space-economy. The location of financial institutions and the distribution of their physical lending and deposit-taking functions are considered effective barometers of economic vitality, or of other productive sector activities less easily traced. The limits of such an approach, though, is that it assumes, rather than questions, the underlying rationality of the spatiality of finance. In the context of speculative financial markets and the rise of financial power, this assumption is immediately suspect. Yet, the spatial structure of financial organization has all manner of contingent features that flow from institutional and historical accidents. As a result, it is crucial to distinguish between the *necessary* and the *contingent institutional* features of a financial system in geographical terms. The financial penetration of space has, it seems, enormous implications for the nature of territorial divisions of production and reproduction, as well as for the operation of financial power across different scales.

Smith (1990: 150) situates the origins of uneven development in 'the constant necessary movement from fixed to circulating capital and back to fixed. At an even more basic level, it is the geographical manifestation of the equally constant and necessary movement from use-value to exchange-value and back to use-value.' The movement from exchange-value to use-value and back, after all, *depends on money as a medium of exchange and store of value.* (Later, credit amplifies these roles.) As a consequence, the dynamism of uneven development relates at least to some degree to the exercise of financial power. The abstract notion of money as a means of verifying trade and commerce takes on added meaning in practice, particularly when considered in relation to the actual development of capitalism. For example, during the epoch of imperialism, entire currency blocs battled each other for trading dominance. This sort of totalizing process was one through which finance *seemed to* level local dynamics of uneven development, in the course of imposing similar conditions drawing closer the various components of the global space economy into a universal law of value.

In moments such as these, it may well appear that financial power overwhelms nations, regions, cities, and suburbs—or, at least, compels them to operate under a substantially similar global logic of credit-based expansion or contraction. Yet, while finance levels certain local processes, this by no means implies the transcendence of uneven spatial development. To the contrary, there is growing evidence that under particular conditions—an overaccumulation crisis, financial ascendance, and, in turn, financial crashes—the application of financial power *exacerbates* processes of uneven development.

This would appear to be the case particularly if frictional constraints to the movement of financial capital across space diminish over time. Such friction takes the form of technological–logistical, political–economic, or natural geographical barriers to the free flow of capital, commodities, or labor power. To the degree that these constraints are gradually removed, finance will 'sharpen differences in the territorial division of labor because small advantages will be easier to capitalize upon', Harvey (1992: 2) remarks. As overaccumulation sets in, as the power of money tends to increase, and as financial markets are consequently liberalized, there is then less scope for the ameliorative capacity of finance to level territorial differentials (as Mandel suggested was the historical basis for money). The reverse is also true, in that the existence of such friction—especially in impeding the geographical shift of funds to where they are most needed—constrains the power of money. In other words, as finance exacerbates uneven development, geography simultaneously sharpens the contradictions within finance.

The depth of historical evidence for such phenomena varies depending on the contingencies of different national financial institutions and systems. Simon Clarke (1988: 110) assessed historical processes in Britain that suggest the role of friction in financial crashes:

> In the initial phase of development of the credit system accumulation was frequently disrupted at an early stage by the failure of local banks. Although this was often put down to unsound banking practices, it was primarily a result of the geographical unevenness of accumulation which led to imbalances in the inter-regional flows of commodities and of capital, which resulted in an inflow of money into some regions and an outflow from others. Banks in some regions accumulated ample reserves of the money commodity, while banks elsewhere found themselves under increasing pressure.

Indeed, the process seems to unfold in two directions, both extremely sensitive to issues of scale. On the one hand, geographically uneven development prevents locally oriented banks from adapting to spatial changes in the productive circuits of capital. The solution to this problem is to permit banks to 'jump scale', such that highly concentrated national banking systems have emerged to level out such differentiations of scale. On the other hand, though, the effect of overaccumulation on the rise and fall of financial power is most spectacular precisely because it is during these moments that *geographical differentiation* is most ambitiously generated. Space becomes a much more crucial 'means of production' (Smith, 1990: 85–7) when the circulation of capital in productive sectors is overshadowed by increasingly futile attempts to *realize* surplus value through commerce or financial speculation, regardless of where (and whether) it is being created.

It is at this point that speculation takes on crucial geographical characteristics, especially when land titles become the preferred form of fictitious capital, because planting the seeds of future accumulation is often impossible. As Harvey (1982: 349) acknowledges, 'monopoly control guarantees that the problem of land speculation will acquire deep significance within the overall unstable dynamic of capitalism'. Speculation is both cause and effect in this respect. As Harvey (1982: 397) continues: 'The whole system of relations upon which the production of spatial configurations in the build environment is based, tends to facilitate and, on occasion, to exacerbate the insane bouts of speculation to which the credit system is any case prone.' Examples of the insanity of financial speculation abound, including the 'reckless overbuilding of commercial space that has taken place since 1974, continuing frenetically even through the trough of the severe 1981–82 recession', argues Mike Davis about the United States (1985: 112):

> This hypertrophic expansion of the financial service sector is not a new, higher stage of capitalism—even in America speculators cannot go on endlessly building postmodernist skyscrapers for other speculators to buy—but a morbid symptom of the financial overaccumulation prolonged by the weakness of the US labor movement and productive capital's fears of a general collapse.

Moreover, overaccumulation and financial speculation in the built environment together generate spatial bottlenecks, just as the productive sector suffers from uneven development and periodic bottlenecks in production and commerce. Harvey (1982: 398) suggests that, in generating 'the chaotic ferment out of which new spatial configurations can grow', speculative tendencies in the built environment 'are as vital to the survival of capitalism as other forms of speculation'. However, 'Too much speculation, to be sure, diverts capital away from real production and meets its fate of devaluation as a consequence.' The trick, Harvey (1982: 398) posits, is to calculate 'how much appropriation is appropriate. To that there is no clear answer and even if there were there is no guarantee that the forces at work under capitalism could ever achieve it.'

Hence, at the local level, primarily through zoning decisions, the state attempts to work out the equilibrium of land as use-value and as exchange-value. That is sometimes helped, more often hindered though, by central bank decisions regarding credit supply, and by national housing and housing finance programs that set out to achieve broad macroeconomic goals.

We have traced the contradictory route of speculation through space, and thus turn next to the control function of finance, where there are any number of spatial implications. Consider some examples of manipulative corporate decision-making of various types that have generated publicity in recent years: the provision of funds to corporations for overseas expansion ('loan-pushing', especially to dictatorial regimes), the forced termination of the pension funds of overindebted companies (to speed loan repayments), wage takebacks imposed under similar circumstances, or the closing of factories deemed necessary by the financiers who pull industrialists' strings (Bond, 1990).

The urban, regional, and national—and, increasingly, global—implications of these financial control functions are legion. Indeed, the reach of financial power extends beyond the corporation and into other arenas of production and reproduction where space is actively constructed. Various examples epitomize uneven geographical development. During the 1980s, financiers began to use 'debt-for-nature swaps' to force overindebted nation states to drop their sovereignty over tracts of land now slated for environmental conservation (having for prior years encouraged the degradation of such lands in order merely to record higher returns on Third World loans) (Potter, 1988). By the 2000s, financiers at the World Bank, Deutsche Bank, and various New York and London financial institutions drove the 'neoliberal nature' process, especially with (generally unsuccessful) strategies for carbon trading and 'Payment for Ecosystem Services' (Bond, 2012). The geographical impact of such forms of 'structural adjustment' imposed by international financial power is vast. At a local scale, Harvey (1985: 88) argues that over time *urbanism* itself has 'been transformed from an expression of the production needs of the industrialist to an expression of the controlled power of finance capital, backed by the power of the state, over the totality of the production process'.

Across a variety of scales, uneven development is generally accentuated during those periods when financial institutions increase their range of movement, the velocity and intensity of their operations, and, simultaneously, their power over debtors (whether companies, consumers, or governments). But specifying the control function of finance, within a multi-faceted relationship between financial power and uneven spatial development, is not uncontroversial. To illustrate, the legacy of the notion of 'finance capital' can be seen in the work of Edward Soja. 'Finance capital', in Soja's periodized account, was initially 'relatively unimportant' in structuring urban space at the turn of the twentieth century (this was still the turf of productive capital). Later, with intensified concentration of capital and greater demands on the built environment for 'expanded reproduction', Soja (1989: 101) attributed to finance a primary role in the planning of cities. But there is no need to periodize in this manner to capture the *underlying dynamic* of financial circuits in uneven urban development. Finance-driven spatial changes (especially speculative land and investment booms) are typical outcomes of overaccumulation in the productive sectors. They do therefore supplant the circuit of industrial capital. And they occur according to a transhistorical rhythm that does not seem to respect as much as *determine* the evolving role of the city in the reproduction of the capitalist system.

Still invoking periodization, Soja (1989: 101) attributed to a post-Depression 'coalition of capital and the state' factors such as the 'intensified residential segregation, social fragmentation and the occupational segmentation of the working class'. To the degree, however, that these factors did actually *reflect* an inner logic of urban capitalism (rather than being necessarily *functional* to the urban 'consumption machine', as Soja seemed to imply), this is surely not a logic constrained by the parameters of the institutional prerequisite that Soja identifies: the supposed planning power of 'finance capital'. In short, Soja demonstrated a focus on institutional form, to the neglect of process.

The contemporary manifestations of this lesson are crucial for, just as in the earlier period, financial power arises in ways that overwhelm built environment investment that came before it. The dynamic here, however, is not primarily a new urban form that an omnipotent 'finance capital' has appended to the existing socio-spatial landscape (though it may have that *appearance*) but, in contrast, a profoundly vulnerable reaction to a sustained crisis of overaccumulation that plays itself out increasingly in the financial circuit of capital. As in the speculative booms of the nineteenth century or the 1920s, the contemporary situation cannot continue in this state of displaced tension indefinitely. The search for surplus value realization in space becomes ever more fruitless, as the restructuring of the space economy becomes, concomitantly, more frenetically finance-driven. The power of finance over the course of uneven development is, then, at its most self-contradictory, and the spatial and socio-economic landscapes left in the wake of the inevitable collapse of financial power bear clearest witness to the fallibilities of the system. Hence, the need is clear to investigate the spatial dimensions of the *non-accommodating* roles of finance: the speculation and the control functions.

There is yet another concern, however: how to demonstrate the applicability of levers of financial speculation and power at different *scales*. Given the omnipresent dynamic of development and underdevelopment across scale, and the need to trace its well-spring to the operation of the laws of motion of capitalism at various scales, these challenges are central to the task ahead.

The Uneven Development of Scale

The issue of scale, Smith (1990: 134) insists, provides a 'crucial window on the uneven development of capital, because it is difficult to comprehend the real meaning of 'dispersal,' 'decentralization,' 'spatial restructuring' and so forth, without a clear understanding of geographical scale'. In this section, financial and monetary aspects of the integration of capitalist circuits at various scales are briefly considered, mainly with a view to establishing the theoretical basis for the power of international money in relation to economic processes determined at national and subnational levels. But even power established and exercised at the highest scales is subject to challenge and to decay, depending on whether that power is geared to the accommodating, control, or speculative functions of finance at particular moments.

Smith, relying on *production-bound* understandings of scale derived from the division of labor, apparently considers the uneven power of finance at different scales a contingent (and relatively unimportant) feature of capitalist development. For Smith (1990: 123), the key to uneven development was found in the changing basis of the centralization and dispersal of productive capital across international, national, and urban scales, with finance subordinate: 'Certainly the spatial centralization of money capital can be considerably enhanced by the centralization of social capital as a whole, but in itself the spatial centralization of money capital is of little significance.'

Here, Smith referred to the accommodating function of finance. But in the 1970s, for instance, as overaccumulation became generalized and financial power was ascendant, it was precisely the spatial centralization of money capital from petroleum consumers to the New York bank accounts of Middle East rulers that represented the most proximate catalyst and facilitator for the flood of Petrodollars to the Third World, with all that implied for the restructuring of the international division of labor and dependency relations of peripheral regions. After all, in contemporary times, the main way in which spatially centralized financial power is experienced is through the determination of national-level policies by the international financial institutions based in Washington, DC.

Smith's (1990) *Uneven Development* is vital for advancing the theory of the geographical expansion of trade and investment beyond the limits of Lenin's *Imperialism* and other period works. But, in concluding that point-of-production relations are definitive in a contemporary understanding of the national state, he appeared to err. In contrast, Suzanne de Brunhoff (1978: 61) drew out the regulatory functions of both labor and money into the ambit of state policy:

> Public management of labor-power contributes to the reproduction of its value, which is something required by capital, but not guaranteed by capital itself. As for the reproduction of money as a general equivalent, this calls for state management of central bank money as the national currency lying 'between' private bank money and international money. The circuit M-C-M', which represents the valorization of money capital, M, in circulation, cannot reproduce itself without these non-capitalist supports.

Indeed, while the national state ultimately acts to implement the workings of the law of value, such 'political' functionality assumes vastly different forms under a system in which national accumulation is oriented to (domestic) production, as opposed to (international) finance. Somewhere intermediate between national and international determinations are super-regional currency blocs, such as that of the European Union. Just such variability—whether in the past (such as the reign of import-substitution industrialization from the 1930s to the 1960s), or, as Samir Amin (1990) advocated, through the future 'delinking' of the Third World from the most destructive global circuits of trade, investment, and finance (e.g., the successful AIDS medicines struggle of the early 2000s that allowed for local generic manufacturers to violate Northern firms' intellectual property rights)—inspires the need for concrete investigations. The most obvious hypothesis is that while jumping scales to higher levels of determination occurs under conditions of ascendant financial power, the subsequent collapse of finance allows the issue of financial power to be broached, again, at lower levels.

It is useful, therefore, to revisit de Brunhoff's (1978: 40–3) typology of money according to three different scales: deposits in local banks, national currency, and international money. The dominant role of money during a particular stage of the accumulation process (whether accommodating, controlling, and/or speculative) and in different institutional settings make a great deal of difference to the exercise of financial power at these various scales. At the lowest scale, the mobilization of deposits in local banks was central to early capitalist development. In contrast, in tightly concentrated national banking systems characterized by high levels of financial power, local differentiation of scale can be washed away. Moreover, under certain institutional circumstances that tend to exist at the national scale, and during times when the tendency to overaccumulation is muted (such as the period from the mid-1940s to the 1960s in most of the world), national state-level policies emerge whereby control over financial power is quite feasible (a situation often described as 'financial repression') (Burkett, 1987). Indeed, there are many historical examples of the repression of finance (and likewise financial power) by those states that are temporarily prejudiced by the dictates of national productive capital, or that are influenced, electorally, by populist sentiments.

From the standpoints of monetary policy and financial regulatory policy, the issue of scale returns again and again. All the levers that concretize the uses and limits of financial power can, at times, be subsumed by the power of the national state (however that may be constituted at different stages)—and yet, at other times, when applied by the IMF or World Bank from above (or from below, by financiers within the national state), they overwhelm state bureaucrats. Are these different power relations reflective of changing aspects of the necessary functions of money management in the reproduction of capitalism as an international system, or are they contingent? A sensitivity to scale is crucial to working out the modalities of financial power, as the geopolitics of international financial power demonstrate.

A starting position is that *uneven hierarchies of scale are exacerbated during times of financial ascendance*; at the same time, unevenness in sectoral and spatial patterns of development is being generated. While the national scale of capitalist development usually occupies financial economists to the neglect of the subnational, it is the international scale of financial power that, since the late 1970s, turns the heads and quickens the pulse of analysts and practitioners alike. Enormous evidence has accumulated since the turn of the millennium to support the vivid claim of Hillel Ticktin (1986: 37), that international financiers 'have knowledge, global forms of action and speed on their side. Against them social democracy appears as clumsy peasants attached to one nation and with the horizon of village idiots.' The power of international money over development strategies at the national scale is today reflected across the Third World, as well as in many advanced capitalist countries.

Subnationally, the ramifications of international financial power are increasingly evident. For smaller, home-bound manufacturing industries not well-located near air or shipping lanes to serve global markets, the fluctuating interest rates and national currency values dictated from Washington (DC), New York, London, Tokyo, Frankfurt, and other sites of international financial control can be debilitating. The size of the national market, which was typically the key consideration in the expansion and contraction of production, has given way to trade liberalization enforced by the major financial institutions. Not just national states, but also cities and regions are increasingly caught up in the vortex of the international law of value, as more direct—often municipal-level—strategies of restructuring production and reproduction are brought into play, often at the behest of global financiers and aid agencies (Bond, 2000). In effect, the national state gives way to the city as a new unit of analysis, implementation and control, and as a means of enhancing the international competitiveness of production, via structural adjustment policies.

Other aspects of the determination of scale occur not by productive relations but, rather, by financial power. Uneven development of the built environment at the urban scale, for example, intensifies principally because the land rent structure becomes one in a set of portfolio options for financiers. 'Rent', Harvey (1982: 396) explains, 'is assimilated as a form of interest identified specifically with locational attributes.' Smith (1990: 148) confirms that: 'To the extent that ground rent becomes an expression of the interest rate with the historical development of capital, the ground rent structure is tied to the determination of value in the system as a whole.' Rent as an integrative lever—in this case, a means of universalizing capitalist space relations—is, hence, integrated into the broader capitalist economy by another lever of financial power: interest. The rate of interest, in turn, reflects a combination of factors, of which the most important are the demand for money and the concomitant balance of power relations between creditors and debtors of various sorts.

It is at this stage that Harvey (1982: 396) asserts the 'hegemonic role' of finance:

> The power of money capital is continuously exerted over all facets of production and realization at the same time as spatial allocations are brought within its orbit. The credit system affects land and property markets and the circulation of state debt. Pressure is thereby brought to bear on landowners, developers, buildings, the state and users. The formation of fictitious capital, furthermore, permits interest-bearing money capital to flow on a continuous basis in relation to the daily use of fixed, long-lived and immobile use values. The titles to such revenues can even circulate on the world market though the assets themselves are immobile.

Harvey (1982: 396–7) shows how the exercise of financial power includes the vision to monitor the markets in various types of financial capital—land, shares, debt instruments—so as to receive 'elaborate signals for investment and disinvestment from one place to another...The effect is to reduce time and space to a common socially determined metric—the rate of interest, itself a representation of value in motion.' Moreover, financial power imparts the capacity to avoid 'one-shot devaluations' through their socialization, and the strength to occasionally absorb localized devaluations.

It appears, now, that, at its peak, financial power—specifically, the interest rate, which becomes the main weapon in the battle between productive and financial circuits—has the capacity to level differences of scale altogether. As Dick Bryan (1995: 41) insisted, 'the money form of capital most readily converts distinct and spatially diverse activities into a common unit of measurement'. But contradictions are manifest, particularly in relating financial capital to surplus value extraction, and this means that, returning to Grossman (1992), the levelling process could equally as well represent a tendency to breakdown, rather than to renewed accumulation.

Conclusion: Finance, Uneven Development and Public Policy

The hypothesis is clear: in the context of overaccumulation tendencies and especially full-blown capitalist crisis, the rise of finance *intensifies the amplitude* of uneven geographical and sectoral development at crucial moments, accompanying a shift in the role of finance from accommodation towards speculation and control, and across a variety of scales. Conversely, when finance experiences conclusive devaluation, this can be the signal for a revived accumulation process that is locally determined, more proportional, and tightly-articulated between sectors, and better-balanced geographically. It would be a time to restore the role of finance as hand-maiden not master within capitalism.

There is not sufficient space to spell out how that might occur in different settings.[4] The most important question to pose is whether the return to the *foundations* of Marxist financial-geographical theory in the pages above can add to the insights being developed in other branches of financial geography and political economy. If the arguments above drawn from *Das Kapital* are less attractive to explore than a post-Keynesian version of the financialization hypothesis—as appears to be the case, given how few geographers have taken up these conceptual challenges—it may be, too, that the preferred politics of financial reform will differ markedly.

The degenerate forms of financialization so often railed against by scholars and activists alike—for example, in the 'IMF Riots' of the 1980s–1990s, the 2011 Occupy movement, and subsequent mass protests such as against financial power in 2019–20 stretching from Chile and Argentina to Ecuador and Haiti to Lebanon and Indonesia—are to some extent capable of regulation. For example, after the US financial meltdown in 2008–09 there was a Dodd-Frank Act; after China's 2015–16 stock market crashes, exchange controls were re-imposed; after South African university student protesters opposed adding further debt to their post-graduation burden, free tuition was introduced in 2017. The sense in many of these struggles is that the central task is to restore financial capital to an accommodating mode and, in the process, to regulate away its control and speculative roles. Regulations are welcome, to be sure, since the pain of financial violence can be so acute. But the Marxist foundations of financial geography nevertheless require a far stronger response by those aiming for genuine change: a probe into why the *mode of production itself is to blame* for the depravity so much of the world faces at the hands of finance.

Notes

1 To illustrate, even prior to Harvey's (1973) explorations of local financial market power over urban development, a major post-war US study, *Empire of High Finance* by Victor Perlo (1957), was rebutted in Paul Baran and Paul Sweezy's (1966: 15) *Monopoly Capital* on grounds that the modern corporation had achieved 'financial independence…and hence is able to avoid the kind of subjection to financial control

which was so common in the world of Big Business fifty years ago'. Nevertheless, concern about growing bank power was soon revived in the 1968 Wright Patman Report of the U.S. Congress' House of Representatives Banking Committee, in a 1969 critique of US capitalism by Stanislav Menshikov (1969), and in a fierce early-1970s debate within the US Left about financial control that revealed diverse ways of understanding capitalist dynamics. Robert Fitch and Mary Oppenheimer (1970) argued that financial institutions' interlocking directorships, trust department shareholder voting weight, and debt financing gave bankers the upper hand, but they were scolded by Paul Sweezy (1972) for mistaking superficial institutional characteristics for underlying dynamics of accumulation.

2 Numerous Marxist, post-Keynesian, or otherwise radical scholars pursued crucial research into financialization's processes or episodes in this period, in the process shedding light on the uneven geographic development of capitalism, especially at specific historical junctures of financial ascendance or collapse. Even if synthetic, theoretically grounded work such as Harvey's is rare, political economists committed to radical critique of financial power and speculation since the 1970s have included Rawi Abdeal (2007), Suzanne de Brunhoff (1976), François Chesnais (2013), James Crotty (1985), Judith Dellheim (2018), Gerald Epstein (2005), Trevor Evans (2004), Ben Fine (2013), Susan George (1988), Ilene Grabel (2017), Laurence Goodwyn (1978), Gary Green (1987), William Greider (1987), Edward Herman (1981), Geoffrey Ingham (2004), Makoto Itoh (1978), David Kotz (1978), Jan Kregel (1998), Greta Krippner (2005), Costas Lapavitsas (2013), Alain Lipietz (1988), Hyman Minsky (1977), Beth Mintz and Michael Schwartz (1985), Fred Mosely (2004), Robin Murray (1988), Dani Nabudere (1990), R.T. Naylor (1985), Chris Niggle (1986), Henk Overbeek (1980), Cheryl Payer (1991), Robert Pollin (1987), GeorgeAnn Potter (1988), Howard Sherman (1991), Jan Toporowsky (2002), and Howard Wachtel (1986).

3 Of course, many scholars who pursue geographically informed financial theorizing and interpretation have also provided engaged critiques of underlying capitalist dynamics. Multiple works from the early 1990s onwards could be cited by authors including Manuel Aalbers, John Agnew, Charles Barthold, Sarah Bracking, Brett Christophers, Gordon Clark, Stuart Corbridge, Gerald Davis, Gary Dymski, Rodrigo Fernandez, Andrew Leyshon, Philip Mader, Thomas Marois, Daniel Mertens, Nigel Thrift, Natascha van der Zwan, Till van Treeck, and Dariusz Wójcik.

4 I have explored anti-neoliberal resistance strategies at various scales; for example, in the world financial system in Bond (2014), the United States in Bond (1990), the African continent in Bond (2004, 2006, 2019), Zimbabwe in Bond and Manyanya (2003), and South Africa in Bond (2013a, 2013b, 2015).

References

Abdeal, R. (2007). *Capital Rules: The Construction of Global Finance*. Cambridge: Harvard University Press.

Aglietta, M. (1979). *The Theory of Capitalist Regulation*. London: Verso.

Amin, S. (1990). *Delinking*. London: Zed Press.

Baran, P. and P. Sweezy (1966). *Monopoly Capital*. New York: Monthly Review Press.

Bond, P. (1990). The New US Class Struggle: Financial Industry Power vs. Grassroots Populism. *Capital and Class*, 40, Spring, pp. 150–181.

Bond, P. (2000). *Cities of Gold, Townships of Coal*. Trenton: Africa World Press.

Bond, P. (2004). Bankrupt Africa: Imperialism, Subimperialism and Financial Politics. *Historical Materialism*, 12, 4, pp. 145–172.

Bond, P. (2006). *Looting Africa*. London: Zed Books

Bond, P. (2012). *The Politics of Climate Justice*. Pietermaritzburg: University of KwaZulu-Natal Press.

Bond, P. (2013a). Historical Varieties of Space, Scale and Speculation in South Africa: The Uneven and Combined Geographical Development of Financialised Capitalism. *Transformation*, 81–82, pp. 179–207.

Bond, P. (2013b). Debt, Uneven Development and Capitalist Crisis in South Africa. *Third World Quarterly*, 34, 4, pp. 569–592.

Bond, P. (2014). Global Economic Volatility and Slap-Dash Repairs to the International Financial Architecture. In: G. Epstein, T. Schlesinger, and M. Vernengo (eds), *Banking, Monetary Policy and the Political Economy of Financial Regulation*. Cheltenham: Edward Elgar, pp. 225–258.

Bond, P. (2015). Contradictions in Consumer Credit: Innovations in South African Super-Exploitation. *Critical Arts*, 29, 2, pp. 218–239.

Bond, P. (2018). Capital Volume Three Gaps Seen from South Africa. In J. Dellheim and F. Wolf (eds), *The Unfinished System of Karl Marx. Critically Reading Capital as a Challenge for Our Times*. New York: Springer, pp. 299–330.

Bond, P. (2019). Neoliberal Liberalism → African Authoritarianism → Disorganized Dissent. *Research in Political Economy*, 35, 2019, pp. 89–116.

Bond, P. (2020). Contradictions in Hilferding's Finance Capital. In: J. Dellheim (ed), *Hilferding's Critical Political Economy*. New York: Springer.

Bond, P. and M. Manyanya (2003). *Zimbabwe's Plunge: Exhausted Nationalism, Neoliberalism and the Search for Social Justice*. London: Merlin Press.

Bryan, D. (1995). *The Chase across the Globe: International Accumulation and the Contradictions for Nation States*. Boulder: Westview Press.

Burkett, P. (1987). Financial 'Repression' and Financial 'Liberalization' in the Third World. *Review of Radical Political Economics*, 19, 1, pp. 1–21.

Chesnais, F. (2013). *La Finance Mondialisée: Racines Sociales et Politiques, Configuration, Conséquences*. Paris: La Découverte.

Clarke, S. (1988). *Keynesianism, Monetarism and the Crisis of the State*. Aldershot: Edward Elgar.

Crotty, J. (1985). The Centrality of Money, Credit, and Financial Intermediation in Marx's Crisis Theory. In: S. Resnick and R. Wolff (eds), *Rethinking Marxism*. New York: Autonomedia, pp. 45–81.

Davis, M. (1985). Urban Renaissance and the Spirit of Postmodernism. *New Left Review*, 151, pp. 106–113.

de Brunhoff, S. (1976). *Marx on Money*. New York: Urizen Books.

de Brunhoff, S. (1978). *The State, Capital and Economic Policy*. London: Pluto Press.

de Janvry, A. (1982). *The Agrarian Question and Reformism in Latin America*. Baltimore: Johns Hopkins University Press.

Dellheim, J. (2018). 'Joint-Stock Company' and 'Share Capital' as Economic Categories of Critical Political Economy. In: J. Dellheim and F. Wolf (eds), *The Unfinished System of Karl Marx. Critically Reading Capital as a Challenge for our Times*. New York: Springer, pp. 265–298.

Epstein, G. (2005). *Financialization and the World Economy*. Cheltenham: Edward Elgar.

Evans, T. (2004). Marxian and Post-Keynesian Theories of Finance and the Business Cycle. *Capital and Class*, 83, 47–100.

Fitch, R. and M. Oppenheimer (1970). Who Rules the Corporations? *Socialist Revolution*, 1, 1, pp. 73–107.

Fine, B. (2013). Financialization from a Marxist Perspective. *International Journal of Political Economy*, 42, 4, pp. 47–66.

George, S. (1988). *A Fate Worse than Debt*. Harmondsworth: Penguin.

Goodwyn, L. (1978). *The Populist Moment: A Short History of the Agrarian Revolt in America*. New York: Oxford University Press.

Grabel, I. (2017). *When Things Don't Fall Apart: Global Financial Governance and Developmental Finance in an Age of Productive Incoherence*. Cambridge: Massachusetts Institute of Technology Press.
Graeber, D. (2012). *Debt: The First 5000 Years*. London: Penguin.
Green, G. (1987). *Finance Capital and Uneven Development*, Boulder: Westview Press.
Grossman, H. (1992). *The Law of Accumulation and Breakdown of the Capitalist System*. London: Pluto Press.
Greider, W. (1987). *Secrets of the Temple*, New York: Simon and Schuster.
Harvey, D. (1973). *Social Justice and the City*. Baltimore: Johns Hopkins University Press.
Harvey, D. (1982). *The Limits to Capital*. Oxford: Basil Blackwell.
Harvey, D. (1985). *The Urbanization of Capital*. Baltimore: Johns Hopkins University Press.
Harvey, D. (1989). *The Condition of Postmodernity*. Oxford: Basil Blackwell.
Harvey, D. (1992). *Personal Correspondence with Patrick Bond*. Oxford, July 5 (in author's possession).
Harvey, D. (2003). *The New Imperialism*. Oxford: Oxford University Press.
Herman, E. (1981). *Corporate Power, Corporate Control*. New York: Cambridge University Press.
Hilferding, R. (1981). *Finance Capital*. London: Routledge & Kegan Paul.
Ingham, G. (2004). *The Nature of Money*. Cambridge: Polity Press.
Itoh, M. (1978). The Formation of Marx's Theory of Crisis. *Science and Society*, 42, 2, pp. 129–155.
Karwowski, E. and M. Centurion-Vicencio (2018). Financialising the State. FinGeo Network, February 6. http://www.fingeo.net/financialising-the-state-recent-developments-in-fiscal-and-monetary-policy/
Kondratieff, N. (1979). The Long Waves of Economic Life. *Review*, 2, 4, pp. 519–562.
Kose, M.A., P. Nagle, F. Ohnsorge, and N. Sugawara (2020). *Global Waves of Debt: Causes and Consequences*. Washington, DC: World Bank.
Kotz, D. (1978). *Bank Control of Large Corporations in the United States*. Berkeley: University of California Press.
Kregel, J. (1998). Yes, 'It' Did Happen Again. Working Paper 234, Levy Economics Institute of Bard College, Annandale-on-Hudson, NY.
Krippner, G. (2005). The Financialization of the American Economy. *Socio-Economic Review*, 3, 2, pp. 173–208.
Kuhn, R. (2007). *Henryk Grossman and the Recovery of Marxism*. Champaign: University of Illinois Press.
Kuznets, S. (1930). *Secular Movements in Production and Prices*. New York: Houghton Mifflin.
Lapavitsas, C. (2013). *Profiting Without Producing: How Finance Exploits Us All*. London: Verso.
Lipietz, A. (1988). The Limits of Bank Nationalisation in France. In: Harris, L., J. Coakley, M. Croasdale and T. Evans eds., *New Perspectives on the Financial System*. Beckenham, Kent: Croom Helm.
Magdoff, H. and P. Sweezy (1987). *Stagnation and the Financial Explosion*. New York: Monthly Review Press.
Mandel, E. (1968). *Marxist Economic Theory*. London: Merlin Press.
Mandel, E. (1980). *Long Waves of Capitalist Development*. Cambridge: Cambridge University Press.
Marx, K. (1967). *Capital*. New York: International Publishers.
Marx, K. (1973). *Grundrisse*. Harmondsworth: Penguin.
Mavroudeas, S. and D. Papadatos (2018). Financialization Hypothesis: A Creative Contribution or a Theoretical Blind Alley? *World Review of Political Economy*, 9, 4, pp. 451–476.

Menshikov, S. (1969). *Millionaires and Managers: Structure of U.S. Financial Oligarchy*. Moscow: Progress Publishers.

Minsky, H. (1977). A Theory of Systematic Fragility. In: Altman, E. and A.W. Sametz eds., *Financial Crises*. New York: Wiley & Sons.

Mintz, B. and M. Schwartz (1985). *The Power Structure of American Business*. Chicago: University of Chicago Press.

Monthly Review. (2019). The Critique of Financialization. *Monthly Review*, April. https://monthlyreview.org/2019/04/01/the-critique-of-financialization/

Mosely, F. (2004). *Marx's Theory of Money*. London: Palgrave Macmillan.

Murray, R. (1988). Pension Funds and Local Authority Investment. In: Harris, L., J. Coakley, M. Croasdale, and T. Evans eds., *New Perspectives on the Financial System*. Beckenham, Kent: Croom Helm.

Nabudere, D. (1990). *The Rise and Fall of Money Capital*. London: Africa in Transition Trust.

Naylor, R.T. (1985). *The Domain of Debt*. Montreal: Black Rose.

Niggle, C. (1986). Financial Innovation and the Distinction between Financial and Industrial Capital. *Journal of Economic Issues*, 20, 2, pp. 375–382.

Overbeek, H. (1980). Finance Capital and the Crisis in Britain. *Capital and Class*, 4, 2, pp. 99–120.

Payer, C. (1991). *Lent and Lost*. London: Zed Books.

Perlo, V. (1957). *Empire of High Finance*. New York: International Publishers.

Pollin, R. (1987). Structural Change and Increasing Fragility in the US Financial System. In Robert D. Cherry, Christine D'Onofrio, Cigdem Kurdas, Thomas R. Michl, Fred Moseley, Michele I. Naples (eds), *The Imperiled Economy*. New York: Union for Radical Political Economics.

Potter, G. (1988). *Dialogue on Debt*, Washington, DC: Center of Concern.

Roberts, M. (2019). Owning Financialization. *Monthly Review*, April. https://monthlyreview.org/2019/04/01/owning-financialization/

Sherman, H. (1991). *The Business Cycle*. Princeton: Princeton University Press.

Smith, N. (1990). *Uneven Development*. Oxford: Basil Blackwell.

Smith, T. (2006). *Globalization: A Systematic Marxian Account*. Amsterdam: Brill.

Soja, E. (1989). *Postmodern Geographies*. London: Verso.

Suter, C. (1992). *Debt Cycles in the World Economy*. Boulder: Westview Press.

Sweezy, P. (1972). The Resurgence of Financial Control: Fact or Fancy? *Socialist Revolution*, 2, pp. 235–283.

Thomas, B. (1972). *Migration and Urban Development*. London: Methuen.

Ticktin, H. (1986). The Transitional Epoch, Finance Capital and Britain. *Critique*, 16, pp. 23–42.

Toporowsky, J. (2002). *The End of Finance*. London: Routledge.

Wachtel, H. (1986). *The Money Mandarins*, New York: Pantheon.

Wang, X. (2017). Financial Centre Development in Mainland China: A Financial Geography Perspective. PhD thesis, School of Geography and the Environment, University of Oxford, Oxford.

4
CULTURAL ECONOMY OF FINANCE

Sarah Hall

Introduction

One of the most exciting aspects of studying the geographies of finance is the opportunities it brings for interdisciplinary dialogue and collaboration. Indeed, this is seen in the early work on the geographies of finance. For example, in the 1990s, in order to understand the formation of what is commonly understood as the international financial system, geographers drew on work in political economy and international political economy in particular (see, e.g., Strange, 1986) following the collapse of Bretton Woods and the US dollar gold standard in the 1970s (Leyshon and Thrift, 1997). In many ways, this interdisciplinary collaboration should not be surprising. Finance and financial markets themselves constantly overflow the financial sector itself as work on financialization and finance-led capitalism has so clearly showed us (French et al., 2011; Froud et al., 2006). For example, finance is increasingly influential in activities relating to corporate decision-making (Froud et al. 2006), environmental governance (Knox-Hayes, 2009), as well as household decision-making and the role of finance in shaping everyday life (Langley, 2008).

Drawing on this history of heterodox social scientific collaboration, from the early 2000s, economic geographers have contributed to the development of an interdisciplinary body of work commonly termed a 'cultural economy approach' to money and finance. This literature draws on insights from sociology, anthropology, political science, and critical accounting to draw attention to the process of (financial) market-making. A central insight of this literature is that market-making relies on the purposive activities of financiers alongside a range of non-human elements, known as 'market devices', including computer screens, financial formulae, regulatory interventions, and market infrastructures such as high-speed computer cabling (see, e.g., MacKenzie, 2003a, 2003b;

Muniesa et al., 2007). In so doing, this work draws on three broader theoretical provocations in the social sciences more generally. The first is an heightened appreciation of the role of non-human actors in socio-economic life as developed within an actor-network theory approach (on which see Callon, 1984; McFall, 2009). The second is the wider cultural turn within the social sciences from the 1990s onwards through which researchers have drawn attention to the ways in which the economy is thoroughly shot through with cultural elements, while culture itself has increasingly been understood as a potential economic resource (for one of the earliest interventions in this field, see Lash and Urry (1993). Third, work in a cultural economy tradition studying contemporary financial markets also reflects the growing interest in attending to the everyday practices that constitute economic life within and beyond financial markets (see Jones and Murphy, 2010). More recently, the second and third of these strands have been brought together in an important literature that seeks to explore the lived experience of households under conditions of austerity particularly in the post-financial crisis United Kingdom. By focusing on the social and cultural practices associated with everyday economic lives, this literature reveals a myriad of coping strategies and relations that are used by households often positioned as either marginal to mainstream economic activity, or reliant on an ever-decreasing neoliberal welfare state (Hall, 2016).

By incorporating a greater attention to the micro processes and practices that make up economies, cultural economy approaches to the study of finance provide a scalar counterpoint to earlier work within geography on the wider social sciences that emphasized the macro, political economy foundations of global finance (Hall, 2011). In so doing, this work has been vital in opening the black box of global finance as MacKenzie (2005) put it (see also Leyshon, 1995). This is important because it emphasizes the process by which global financial markets are produced, transformed, and reproduced, thereby opening up space to ask critical questions about how such financial markets may be made in more economically, socially, and environmentally sustainable ways (Hall, 2012).

In this chapter, I explore how the potential of cultural economy approaches could be maximized by responding to two critiques that have been made of the approach. The first critique focuses on the extent to which the focus on micro scale processes and practices allows cultural economy to reflect critically on the wider politics and power relations at work in global finance (Hall, 2018a). This issue has become increasingly important given the ways in which the fallout from the financial crisis of 2007–8 continues to shape uneven economic development in a number of profound ways—including, for example, the continued and in many ways uneven trajectories of regional and urban development in most advanced economies (see, e.g., Martin, 2011; Martin et al., 2015). Second, the cultural economy literature has its own geographically specific genealogy. In this respect, it has been developed in the heartlands of global finance in North America and Western Europe, particularly in London, New York, and

Chicago (Ho, 2009; MacKenzie, 2003b; Zaloom, 2006) during the so called NICE decade of No Inflation Constant Expansion in which finance-led capitalism flourished in the 2000s. Therefore, important questions remain concerning how the approach could be developed and applied to finance beyond the Global North and the critical insights that might be developed in doing this.

By exploring these critiques, the chapter aims to demonstrate how a sympathetic critique of the cultural economy of finance literature, one that takes seriously the geographies of cultural economy knowledge production, offers the potential to develop meso-level approaches with flatter ontologies to the geographies of finance. This means exploring how both micro elements of financial markets (such as pricing theories and recent technological developments) are entwined with what are typically assumed to be macro elements of finance (such as national and international regulation, and financial policy) to be grounded and instituted in particular places, notably international financial centres, at particular times. I argue that these approaches have the potential to attend to the micro processes and practices of financial market-making while also speaking to wider questions, often conceived of at the macro level, concerning the politics and power of the international financial system. In particular, I suggest that using the financial centre as a concrete entry point into analysis provides a potentially valuable way of operationalizing such an approach that draws together both micro and macro considerations in its analysis. This argument is developed over three further sections. First, I set out the main parameters of cultural economy approaches to money and finance before, second, exploring some of cultural economy's silences and blind spots. In the third substantive section, I explore how these could be productively addressed by developing the geographical imaginations of cultural economy research more fully through a substantive focus on financial centres. I conclude by reflecting on the wider contribution of such an approach to interdisciplinary work on the geographies of finance more widely.

Placing the Cultural Economy of Finance

Since the early 2000s, cultural economy has developed into a diverse literature not only in terms of its disciplinary foundations, as noted above, but also in terms of its topics of enquiry. These range from studies of the financial theories that underpin option pricing that was central to the development of securitized finance in the 2000s (MacKenzie, 2003a), through work on the material technologies that have underpinned financial markets historically (Preda, 2006), to detailed examinations of more recent technologies, notably the interaction between traders and their computer screens within face-to-screen trading environments (Knorr Cetina and Bruegger, 2002) and the materiality of recent development in high frequency algorithmic trading (MacKenzie, 2018). However, within this diversity, a commonality can be found in a shared, and distinctive, epistemological and associated methodological approach to the study of finance that is heavily influenced by post-structural thinking. Drawing on the work of authors such as J.K. Gibson-Graham (2006) and Judith Butler (1993a), this approach emphasizes the social construction of economic and financial life, paying greater attention than political economy approaches to micro practices and processes, relations between human and non-human actors and the place of culture, particularly gender and corporality, in the making of financial markets. While earlier relational approaches within economic geography draw attention to the distanciated networks that make up economic life (Bathelt and Gluckler, 2003), the approach advocated here places greater emphasis on the range of actors and networks involved, including financial and foreign policy and regulatory devices and interventions. In so doing, more emphasis is placed on the discursive foundations of finance and the ways in which discourses are enrolled in the (re)production of financial markets (see De Goede, 2005; MacKenzie et al., 2007).

A key concept that has been widely used, sometimes explicitly and sometimes implicitly, within the cultural economy approach is that of performativity (MacKenzie, 2005, 2018). This strand of thinking can be traced back to the work of Butler (1993b: 2), who understands performativity as 'the reiterative and citational practice through which discourse produces the effects that it names'. This means that meaning is made and remade through practices and performances, providing the grounding and rationale for the focus on the practice of financiers in making financial markets within much of the cultural economy literature on finance. However, it is important to note that what are commonly understood as cultural economy approaches are by no means the only literatures in which such an approach has been deployed. For example, working at the intersection between post-structuralist approaches to performativity, feminist geography, and studies of the changing nature of work, McDowell (1997) provided a highly influential study of the changing gendered nature of financial work in London's financial district in the late 1990s following the introduction of increasing numbers of US and European investment banks and the associated decline of the British merchant banking business model. Merchant banking was historically predominately relationship-based, with clients using one bank for their financial services; investment banking is typically more transaction-based with banks competing with each other to secure client business, often drawing attention to their technical expertise alongside their relationship management (Kynaston, 2002) While clearly drawing heavily on post-structuralist thinking, this study comes before a cultural economy literature of finance could be readily identified.

Drawing on post-structuralist thinking on performativity as well as broader post-structuralist writing on actor-network theory and economic life (Çalışkan and Callon, 2009, 2010), cultural economy approaches to finance are characterized by their commitment to understanding financial markets as the dynamic ensembles of networks, bodies, machines, concepts, discursive interpretation, knowledge, and information that are constantly in the process of being brought together in new formations as financial markets are developed, reproduced, and changed over time. The growth and development of such an approach to finance is reflected in the publication of several notable key edited collections and monographs in the field (see, e.g., Knorr Cetina and Preda, 2005; MacKenzie, 2006; MacKenzie et al., 2007; Muniesa et al., 2007). While this approach has been particularly influential in terms of work on finance, it is important to note that it has also extended to a wider body of work on market-making and marketization more broadly demonstrating the wider growth of post-structuralist thinking in studies of the contemporary global economy (see, e.g., Berndt, 2015; Berndt and Boeckler, 2009).

Within this broad post-structuralist approach, three key areas of focus within cultural economy approaches to finance can be identified. First, work has revealed the ways in which technologies are entangled with other actors in the making of financial markets (Muniesa et al., 2007). Importantly, this insight goes beyond simply identifying a list of the material components of markets, such as computers, prices recording technologies, and consumer credit scoring techniques that facilitate market relations. Rather, the term 'market device' is used to signify the ways in which markets rely upon and are based on the dynamic entanglement between human and non-human financial market actors. As Muniesa et al. (2007) argue, the term 'market device' is a 'simple way of referring to the material and discursive assemblages that intervene in the construction of markets'. One of the most significant ways in which this approach has been utilized is through work on the role of computer screens in the framing of global foreign exchange markets for traders (Knorr Cetina and Bruegger, 2002), and through more recent work on the role of computers and associated technology in the development of high frequency and algorithmic trading (MacKenzie, 2018; Zook and Grote, 2016). In this work, the relationship between a trader and their screen is understood as an example of a global 'microstructure' such that the transnational nature of foreign exchange trading across time zones is enacted through the micro relationship between traders and their screens. For Knorr Cetina and Bruegger (2002), the importance of this approach lies in the ways in which market sociality that is frequently associated with face-to-face trading occurs in these face-to-screen trading environments through the entanglement of traders with their computer screens.

The second area of focus within cultural economy research on finance takes this work on market devices and applies it to another non-human actor within finance: economic theory. As the title of MacKenzie's (2006) book suggests, in a similar vein to work on market devices more generally, this work goes beyond arguing that financial theory is simply used within financial markets to explore how the use of financial theory changes the operation of markets themselves. In other words, and as the title of MacKenzie's (2006) book signals, financial theory is more than simply a camera being used to take pictures of pre-existing financial markets; rather, it acts as a central engine, performing these markets in important ways. Work in this area has been developed most fully through a focus on option pricing theory and, particularly, the Nobel Prize winning Black Scholes option pricing theory. As MacKenzie (2003a: 852) reveals, the use of this model was performative of financial markets because it 'altered patterns of pricing in a way that increased the validity of the model's predictions, in particular helping the model to pass its key econometric test: that the implied volatility of all options on the same stock with the expiration should be identical'. More recently, this approach to focusing on the role of financial theory in making financial markets has been applied to a range of other financial markets, including automated high-frequency trading (MacKenzie, 2018) and green finance (Bracking, 2015).

In revealing the power of financial theory within option pricing in derivative markets that were so central to the financialized boom in North America and Western Europe, particularly in the 2000s, MacKenzie's (2006) work also provides a sociology of the rise and transformation of financial theory and financial economics itself. This history traces its transition from the margins of economic thought in the 1950s to being at the centre of neo-classical economics. This history can be traced back to the 1950s, when mathematical models of investment strategies were beginning to be developed, linked to the wider rise of econometrics as a sub-discipline within mainstream economics (Dezalay and Garth, 2002). However, at least initially, this was seen as a marginal activity within economics and was not widely used to support financial market-making. As a result, the boundary between gambling and what counted as legitimate investment activity was not clear. However, the rise of financial theory and its legitimation within economics started from the 1970s onwards, associated with the rise of key business school sights—notably that of Chicago and MIT—such that financial economics and financial theory became a highly legitimate area of economics and was subsequently used to emphasize the technical and professional prowess of financial investment decision-making, as opposed to the unscientific risk-taking associated with gambling. It is useful to be reminded of this history, given the ways in which, in many senses the 2007–8 crisis triggered a return to debates about the separation, or not, of financial investment and gambling.

The third area of focus within cultural economy research on finance is characterized by its methodologies of choice, which emphasize in-depth, qualitative research techniques with key informants. This often involves ethnographies within the heartlands of global finance, including work on the labour market practices within investment banks on Wall Street within New York's financial district (Ho, 2009) and Zaloom's (2006) detailed treatment of the comparison between open out-cry (face-to-face) trading in the pit of the Chicago Board of Trade (CBOT) with electronic trading (face-to-screen) trading in a London futures dealing firm. Reflecting the wider interest in the socio-economic dimensions of financial markets, she was particularly interested in exploring how the rise of electronic trading technologies—termed in this literature market devices—change the nature of financial market sociality. In particular she wanted to demonstrate how such sociality is just as critical in a face-to-screen environment as it is in face-to-face trading, such that electronic trading cannot be described as rational and asocial. Clearly, pit-based trading is a highly corporeal and social activity. As Zaloom (2003: 262) writes:

> Standing on the trading floor of the CBOT, noise and color engulf the senses. A roar from inside the raised octagonal pits follows the electronic screech of the opening bell. Traders stand in tiered pits, each one dedicated to a single contract, some based on the U.S. Treasury bond complex, others on the Dow Jones Industrial Average or other indexes. Individual voices pierce the din, shouting '50 at 3' or '5 for 100,' indicating the quantity and price they are selling 'at' or paying 'for' futures contracts. Each call indicates how many contracts the individual trader is willing to buy or sell at their price.

In particular, she draws attention to the highly embodied nature of such trading through bodily gestures, comportment, and vocal tone. She goes on:

> Voice is number one. [. . .] You have to be a controlled loud. You can't be like a panic loud because once the panic comes out of your mouth you're pretty much admitting to whoever wants to assume the other side of the trade with you that that's not a good trade [...]. Tones of your voice are very important. A lot of guys have higher voices [. . .] and they can really be heard throughout the pit....

Zaloom goes on to explain that tones of voice are important because having distinctive voices that can be easily heard are beneficial to attracting trade, but that voices that are too loud can seem stressed or uncertain which, in turn, makes completing a trade less certain. When undertaking work in London, Zaloom uncovered how, although at first sight screen may seem to represent a straightforward numerical representation of financial markets, in fact social relations were equally present in these markets, albeit in different ways, thereby challenging assumptions that have been taken for granted that these markets are somehow rational. As she writes:

> A close examination of traders' practices and information technologies can break down the analytical complicity with native discourses of rationalization, illustrating instead how technologies and forms of creative action animate economic life.... Traders who use financial technologies do not take up numbers as objective descriptions of supply and demand. In the context of both open-outcry and screen-based technologies, traders seek out non-quantitative information that is located within the market numbers. They find and exploit the social where there seem to be only non-interpretive facts. Traders

> prosper from constructing knowledge strategies at the junction of market numbers and their material presentation [such as using interpersonal networks and trust based relations with other traders in order to make trading decisions].
>
> (Zaloom, 2003: 269)

Taken together, these three strands of focus (non-human market actors, financial theory, and in-depth, often ethnographic qualitative research) have allowed the cultural economy literature on finance to reveal the dynamic combination of human and non-human actors that are constantly being brought together in the production and reproduction of financial markets, thereby providing a useful corrective to macro political economy accounts that have typically overlooked these more micro and socio-cultural dimensions of everyday life within the international financial system. However, the development of this approach over the last twenty years has also come with a number of critiques and silences of its own, and it is to these that I now turn.

The Geographies of Cultural Economy Approaches to Finance

While cultural economy approaches to finance have been highly influential in opening the black box of global finance to reveal the range of bodies, technologies, discourses, and sources of knowledge and information that are central to its operation, they have faced criticism for lacking the political sensitivity and critical engagement with questions concerning the power of global finance that were central problematics of the political economy tradition of work that predates the cultural economy literature (Hall, 2011, 2018a). This critique is important because some of the key concepts and insights from cultural economy research are themselves intimately bound up with the uneven power relations and economic outcomes that characterize global finance. For example, financial markets are not always performed in ways that were anticipated or predicted. A clear example of this comes from the growth of securitized mortgage finance and the growth of the sub-prime mortgage market in the United States in the 2000s. In making sub-prime loans, lenders in this market were reliant on homeowners acting as responsible 'investor subjects' (Langley, 2008) who would maintain their repayments. As interest rates rose, this became impossible for borrowers with profound and uneven outcomes for homeowners in particular parts of the United States (on which see Aalbers, 2009a, 2009b; Dymski et al. 2013).

In some ways, the lack of attention to critical questions of power and politics within the cultural economy literature reflects the geographies and temporalities of its own development. Here, it is instructive to note that the cultural economy of finance literature developed predominately in the 2000s during a period of rapid finance-led economic growth in much of North America and Western Europe. Indeed, with some notable exceptions (see, e.g., Hertz, 1998), the majority of the case study locations used to explore the theoretical developments advanced within the literature were also the heartlands of the international financial system, notably financial districts in London, New York, and Chicago. Acknowledging the situated nature of the knowledge production process within cultural economy research is important because it has shaped the questions and foci of cultural economy research on finance, seeking as it does to advance understanding of the operation of globally powerful financial markets.

However, this means that there are a number of theoretical and empirical blind spots within cultural economy approaches to money and finance. For example, cultural economy research has paid much less attention to the role of regional financial centres (French et al., 2011). It has also paid less attention to processes of monetary change and transformation beyond Europe and North America. As heterodox macro-economic research beyond the case of cultural economy research shows, this neglect of finance beyond the Global North is not limited to work in a cultural economy tradition. For example, there is a growing literature that explores the different experiences and trajectories of countries that are positioned lower down the currency hierarchy within international finance, particularly emerging capitalist economies in South American, which is challenging some of the assumptions made in the extant financialization literature (see, e.g. Kaltenbrunner, 2015; Kaltenbrunner and Painceira, 2018). This work suggests that there is considerable opportunity not only to apply cultural economy insights to cases beyond the Global North, but also to theorize back and across from less well-studied researched sites in order to advance cultural economy theory more generally (see Comaroff and Comaroff, 2012).

The need to diversify the research sites within cultural economy research on finance can be located within a wider need to develop the geographical imaginations of this literature more carefully (Hall, 2011). This is not to say that geography, and questions of space and place, have been entirely absent from the development of the literature to date. Indeed, an appreciation of the importance of context in shaping processes of marketization and financial performativity are thoroughly embedded within the literature. For example, the title of one of the seminal papers in the field by Donald MacKenzie (2003a), 'An equation and its world', signals the importance of attending to where financial formulae are utilized, and the associated importance of geographical and institutional context in shaping performativity. Moreover, in work that explores the rise and legitimation of financial economics, the importance of the institutional setting in Chicago has been widely emphasized, revealing how place matters in the (re)production of financial markets (MacKenzie, 2005).

However, in much of this work, places act as a relative inert backdrop that shapes the nature of financial market-making but remains relatively unchanged itself within this process. In contrast to this approach, recent work has utilized a renewed interest in territory within human geography to examine how places are enrolled in processes of (financial) market-making and, in so doing, are changed themselves through the process (see Elden, 2010, for broader discussions of territory). One particularly fruitful approach to territory that is highly relevant for work on the geographies of finance comes from the discussion in Christophers (2014) of how space can act as a territorial fix, developing more widely known work on how spatial fixes are used to expand geographical markets in order to respond to the inherently crisis prone nature of capitalism. As Christophers (2014: 755) writes:

> modern capitalism is constantly in the process of enacting territorial fixes: constituting, segmenting, differentiating and extracting value from actively territorialized markets at a range of geographical scales

This argument is important for two reasons in the context of this chapter. First, it draws attention to how places are actively enrolled in processes of market-making and are potentially changed in the process. Second, and following on, it signals how questions of power and politics are central to understanding how and why particular places serve to be important within the making of (financial) markets. Inspired by this work, in the rest of this chapter I explore how such a heightened and more sensitive geographical imagination may be productively put to work in order to produce more geographically and politically sensitive cultural economy approaches to money and finance through the case of the making of new international markets for the Chinese currency, the Renminbi (RMB). In particular, in this case, I suggest that using financial centres as a concrete entry point into research might be instructive in developing geographically and politically engaged cultural economies of finance.

Geographically and Politically Sensitive Cultural Economies of Finance

The internationalization of the RMB has been identified as one of the 'most significant global financial markets developments since the formation of the Euro' (Deutsche Bank, 2014: 2). Indeed, the growing use of the RMB offshore (i.e., beyond the boundaries of mainland China) is a rapid and recent change in global financial relations. The currency has changed from one that was prohibited from being used outside mainland China until the early 2010s to one of the 10 most used currencies for making trade-based payments (Hall, 2017). This clearly reflects the wider internationalization and 'going out' strategy of the Chinese economy more generally under President Xi Jinping (Walter and Howie, 2011). However, what is of particular importance for the arguments being made here is the fact that new RMB markets are being made in a small number of offshore RMB centres that can be defined as financial centres 'outside [mainland] China that conduct a wide variety of financial services denominated in RMB' (ASIFMA, 2014: 20).

A cultural economy approach is instructive in terms of understanding the market devices (Muniesa et al., 2007) that have been central to the creation of these offshore RMB markets. Of particular importance in this respect are regulatory devices such as the Renminbi Qualified Foreign Institutional Investor (RQFII) initiative that allows foreign investors who hold an RMB denominated RQFII quota in certain offshore RMB centres to use this quota to invest directly into mainland China's bond and equity markets (Hall, 2018a; Töpfer and Hall, 2018). It also includes the designation of RMB clearing banks within offshore RMB centres, the holding of RMB deposits outside of mainland China (Hall, 2017), as well as the knowledge and expertise of both Chinese and non-Chinese nationals who work in RMB denominated finance outside mainland China (Hall, 2019). However, to date, much of the work on RMB internationalization has not taken place within a cultural economy framework. Rather, extant understandings are typically grounded in an international political economy (IPE) framework. This work draws on longstanding interests in the relationship between nation state power and international currency power to focus on the potential for the RMB to challenge the US dollar as the global reserve currency as part of wider debates concerning the potential for China to become the world's next global superpower (see, e.g., Cohen, 2015; Kirschner, 2014).

However, by focusing on the potential endpoint of the RMB becoming a global reserve currency, this literature has overlooked some of the micro and meso practices associated with the transformation and internationalization of the RMB itself—practices that are central to a cultural economy approach. Advancing understandings of these practices is important because it is through such a focus that the power relations and political dynamics at the heart of RMB internationalization come to the fore. This suggests that understanding these details will be critical if we are to assess the likely future development of the RMB. Moreover, such an approach reveals how, by attending to the geographies of market-making, a politically sensitive cultural economy approach can be developed. In what follows, I examine two elements associated with London's development as a leading Western offshore RMB centre in order to explore how financial centres may be an instructive scale of analysis in addressing these critiques.

The first example comes for the case of Chinese commercial banks and their operations in London. As Table 4.1 shows, Chinese state-owned commercial banks are now very significant players within the international banking system, with the top four banks ranked by tier 1 capital globally all being Chinese. However, prior to 2013, Chinese banks were not eligible to obtain a wholesale banking licence to operate within the United Kingdom. This reflected the relatively cautious approach of the UK financial regulators at the time, who did not want to expose the United Kingdom's banking system to what was

Table 4.1 Top 10 world banks by Tier 1 capital (US$ billion), 2018

Rank	*2017 Ranking*	*Bank*	*Country*	*Tier 1 Capital (US$ billion)*
1	1	ICBC	China	324
2	2	China Construction Bank	China	272
3	4	Bank of China	China	224
4	6	Agricultural Bank of China	China	218
5	3	JP Morgan Chase	US	209
6	5	Bank of America	US	191
7	8	Wells Fargo	US	178
8	7	Citigroup	US	165
9	10	Mitsubishi UFJ	Japan	153
10	9	HSBC	UK	151

Source: The Banker (2018).

assumed to be potentially greater overseas risks following the 2007–8 financial crisis. However, Chinese banks, alongside other overseas banks, lobbied hard to change this regulation (Hall, 2018b). This approach began to yield change, particularly at the 2013 bilateral meeting between UK and Chinese finance ministers (such bilateral meetings have been an essential mechanism through which London has developed its position as a leading offshore RMB centre). In the minutes from that meeting, at which a currency swap line between China and the UK was agreed, there is a statement that notes that the United Kingdom would be interested in granting Chinese banks wholesale banking licenses. This did, indeed, happen and by the end of 2015, just two years later, the four leading Chinese state-owned banks all held UK bank branch licences, which allows them to undertake a wider range of tasks as compared with operating as a subsidiary only. This occurred because the UK financial authorities recognized that providing a clear and positive response to China's needs in relation to facilitating RMB internationalization through London would be important in facilitating the ongoing central role of London within the wider RMB internationalization.

The implications of these policy changes have been marked. As Figure 4.1 shows, from a situation in the early 2010s, when Chinese state-owned banks could not secure a wholesale banking licence in the United Kingdom, by the late 2010s, a nascent Chinese financial and related professional services cluster can be identified within London's historic financial district. Indeed, this location is noteworthy in itself. The majority of international investment banks operating in London do so to the east of the historic financial district in Canary Wharf. They are located here to take advantage of the more flexible

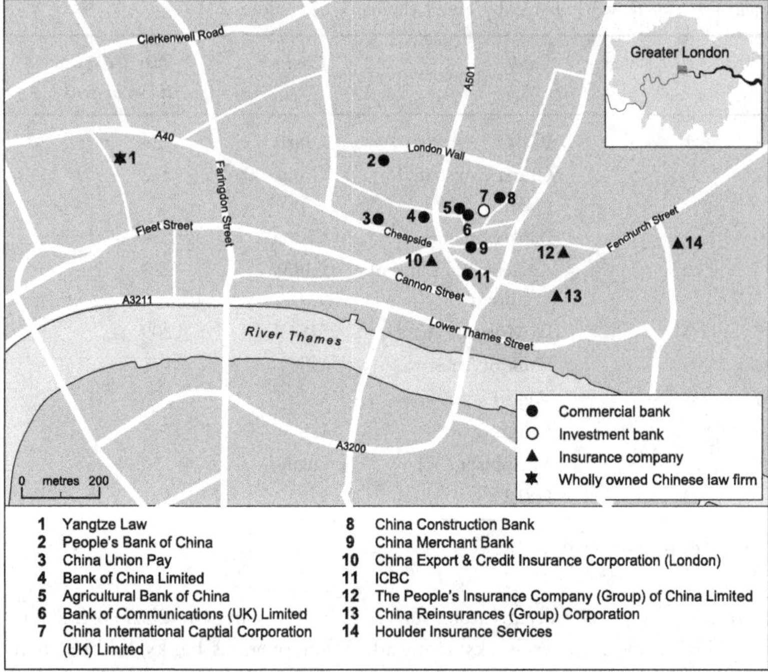

Figure 4.1 Location of main Chinese financial institutions operating in London

Source: Hall, 2019: 707.

and open plan office space that is used in other financial districts, facilitating frequent face-to-face interaction between financiers. In contrast, Chinese banks have located very closely around the Bank of England. This reflects their locational strategies in Beijing, where being located close to their regulator is important. Therefore, this seemingly simple map points to the ways in which the internationalization of Chinese finance in London is not following the same trajectory as other waves of internationalization, notably that of European and American investment banks.

The value of a cultural economy perspective here is that it draws attention to the micro scale devices (including swap line agreement meeting notes and regulatory changes) that, in turn, shape the marking, or performativity, of RMB markets in London's financial district, which, in turn, provide important signals as to the changing power relations within global finance associated with the growing international outlook of Chinese financial institutions. These details and the subtle changes in the way in which Chinese finance was understood in London would be missed if the focus were on the macro scale more typical of IPE work on RMB internationalization. Moreover, by changing the regulatory make-up of London's financial district to allow Chinese bank branches, London essentially served as a territorial fix, altering its own regulatory make-up to facilitate a Chinese financial policy objective of operating international bank branch networks. This points to the need to understand London's financial district not as an inert obligatory passage point (Van Meeteren and Bassens, 2016) within RMB internationalization but, rather, as a place that was changed in order to attract Chinese finance to London in the hope of cementing London's position as a leading international financial centre and, in particular ways, within the wider RMB internationalization project.

The second example within the wider RMB internationalization project that reveals the importance of adopting a geographically and politically sensitive cultural economy reading of financial market-making at the scale of the financial centre relates to London's awarding of an RQFII quota in 2013. Echoing the importance of bilateral meetings between Chinese and UK financial policy-makers, the awarding of this quota was the most significant outcome of two days of talks between the then Chancellor of the Exchequer, George Osborne, and his Chinese counterpart, Vice Premier Ma Kai, within the wider framework of Economic and Financial Dialogues between Britain and China. The initial quota was set at RMB 80 billion and allowed investors in London to apply for a licence that would allow them to invest RMB directly into China. This development was heralded as a major landmark in the development of London as a leading global offshore RMB centre, and reflected the commitment of George Osborne, in particular, to utilizing stronger economic and financial relations with China to facilitate the continued development of the United Kingdom's economy based around financial services in London's financial district. As he put it, in 2014:

> Connecting Britain to the fastest growing parts of the world is central to our [the UK Government's] economic plan. It's why I've put such government effort over the last three years into making sure we're the leading western centre for trading in the Chinese currency, the renminbi. That effort has paid off [...] London now has the critical mass of infrastructure helpful to put Britain at the front of the global race [to develop denser and deeper economic relations with China]. This means jobs and investment in the future.
>
> (George Osborne, 25 March 2014)

However, an examination of the use of the RQFII quota in London reveals a rather different story, with the quota not being fully utilized. As the *Financial Times* noted:

> while it is widely expected that Singaporean fund managers will rapidly take up their [RQFII] allocation, there is little evidence that fund managers in London are as enthused by this opportunity as the UK

> Chancellor obviously was. Indeed, the possibility of Singapore's managers using up their allocation quicker than those in London is likely.
> (Financial Times, 2013)

While this outcome is not necessarily surprising, given the close economic and financial relations between mainland China and Singapore (Lai, 2012), this example is empirically important because it points to the ongoing uncertainty surrounding RMB internationalization. However, it is also important conceptually for the focus on the cultural economy approaches being advocated for in this chapter. By examining how one particular market device, the RQFII quota, operates in practice in the making of RMB markets, it becomes possible to examine how the culturally and geographically specific ways in which financial markets are expected to perform shape the wider global outcomes of RMB internationalization. In this sense, it was expected that the RQFII quota would be used to shape or perform, in the language of cultural economy, a more globally integrated RMB market. However, a lack of private sector appetite for such an investment opportunity in London's financial district has revealed how the quota has not performed as anticipated by policy-makers, thereby signalling some of the potential limitations to RMB internationalization which, again, would be overlooked if we did not attend to this micro and meso scale analysis within and between financial centres.

Conclusions

In this chapter, I have offered a sympathetic critique of cultural economy approaches to finance. This interdisciplinary body of work draws on approaches from geography, sociology, anthropology, political science, and critical accounting studies to draw attention to the range of human and non-human actors that are central to the making and performing of financial markets. In so doing, it is clear that the rapid growth of this literature from the early 2000s onwards has done much to address concerns that earlier heterodox approaches to money and finance, particularly within economic geography, paid insufficient attention to the detailed micro scale practice of finance. However, while cultural economy approaches have signalled the importance of context in shaping the operation of financial markets, the geographical imaginations of work within this literature remain relatively limited in two senses. First, the empirical focus of the literature has largely been advanced capitalist markets in the Global North. This means that important questions about how financial markets might be made, or performed differently elsewhere in the world, remain largely unanswered from a cultural economy perspective. Second, when space and place are considered from a cultural economy standpoint, they are typically viewed as providing specific institutional, regulatory, and cultural contexts for the practice of market-making.

While it is undoubtedly true that financial markets are shaped by these contexts, in this chapter I have called for cultural economy research to expand its geographical imaginations by working with a more dynamic understanding of space and place at the scale of the financial centre or district that attends to how the geographies of financial markets are constantly being remade. Here, recent work on territory and territorial fixes provides a valuable theoretical vocabulary, because it draws attention to the intimate connection between the spaces in which financial markets are made, and the power relations and politics that surround them. Inspired by this approach, the final section of the chapter explored the value of thinking territorially about financial market-making through the case of RMB market-making in London's financial district.

However, there is scope to develop this analysis further. For example, following recent work on global currency relations (Alami, 2018; Kaltenbrunner, 2015; Kaltenbrunner and Painceira, 2018), there is considerable need to explore how the key concepts of cultural economy such as performativity, market-making, and market devices travel when we explore financial markets beyond the Global North. Moreover, there is scope to develop cultural economy analyses at a range of scales, alongside my focus here on the financial centre—particularly that of the firm and the household, which have received less attention to date. Undertaking such a task that uses a detailed reading of space, place, and territory to think critically about financial market-making is urgent, given the considerable transformations and uncertainties associated with the future development of global finance from innovations such as FinTech and high-frequency trading through the challenge to open trade globally, as seen in the United Kingdom's decision to leave the EU, as well as changing everyday conditions of financial life, which are increasingly shaped by austerity. Indeed, the importance of adopting a geographical imagination is increasingly being identified beyond academia to include policy-makers and regulators. For example, in a speech in 2017, this position was articulated by the Deputy Governor of the Bank of England, Sam Woods, when he argued that 'geofinance' is 'the defining challenge of the next few years', understood as 'the impact of geography on the geometry of finance in terms of the impact of borders, location and distance on the shape of banks, insurers and financial regulation' (Woods, 2017). A geographically and politically sensitive cultural economy reading of finance provides one valuable way of responding to such a challenge.

Acknowledgments

The research presented in this paper was supported by a British Academy Mid-Career Fellowship (MD130065).

References

Aalbers, M. (2009a). Geographies of the financial crisis. *Area* 41, 34–42. https://doi.org/10.1111/j.1475-4762.2008.00877.x

Aalbers, M. (2009b). The financialization of home and the mortgage market crisis. *Compet. Change* 12, 148–166. https://doi.org/10.1179/102452908X289802

Alami, I. (2018). On the terrorism of money and national policy-making in emerging capitalist economies. *Geoforum* 96, 21–31. https://doi.org/10.1016/j.geoforum.2018.07.012

ASIFMA. (2014). *RMB Roadmap*. Asian Securities Industry and Financial Markets Association, Hong Kong.

Bathelt, H., Gluckler, J. (2003). Toward a relational economic geography. *J. Econ. Geogr.* 3, 117–144. https://doi.org/10.1093/jeg/3.2.117

Berndt, C. (2015). Ruling markets: the marketization of social and economic policy. *Environ. Plan. A* 47, 1866–1872. https://doi.org/10.1177/10.1177_0308518X15598324

Berndt, C., Boeckler, M. (2009). Geographies of circulation and exchange: constructions of markets. *Prog. Hum. Geogr.* 33, 535–551. https://doi.org/10.1177/0309132509104805

Bracking, S. (2015). The anti-politics of climate finance: the creation of performativity of the green climate fund. *Antipode* 47, 281–302.

Butler, J. (1993a). *Bodies that Matter: On the Discursive Limits of 'Sex'*. Routledge, London.

Butler, J. (1993b). *Bodies that Matter*. Routledge, London.

Çalışkan, K., Callon, M. (2009). Economization, part 1: shifting attention from the economy towards processes of economization. *Econ. Soc.* 38, 369–398. https://doi.org/10.1080/03085140903020580

Çalışkan, K., Callon, M. (2010). Economization, part 2: a research programme for the study of markets. *Econ. Soc.* 39, 1–32.

Callon, M. (1984). Some elements of a sociology of translation: domestication of the scallops and the fishermen of St Brieuc Bay. *Sociol. Rev.*, 32, 196–233.

Christophers, B. (2014). The territorial fix: price, power and profit in the geographies of markets. *Prog. Hum. Geogr.* 38, 754–770. https://doi.org/10.1177/0309132513516176

Cohen, B.J. (2015). *Currency Power: Understanding Monetary Rivalry*. Princeton University Press, Princeton.

Comaroff, J., Comaroff, J. (2012). *Theory from the South: or How Euro-America is Evolving toward Africa*. Routledge, London.

De Goede, M. (2005). *Virtue, Fortune, and Faith*. University of Minnesota Press.

Deutsche Bank. (2014). *At the Centre of RMB Internationalisation: A Brief Guide to Offshore RMB*. https://www.db.com/en/media/At-the-centre-of-Renminbi-internationalisation–A-brief-guide-to-offshore-RMB.pdf, last accessed 20/8/14.

Dezalay, Y. and Garth, B. (2002). *The Internationalization of Palace Wars: Lawyers, Economists and the Contest to Transform Latin American States*. University of Chicago Press, Chicago.

Dymski, G., Hernandez, J., Mohanty, L. (2013). Race, gender, power, and the US subprime mortgage and foreclosure crisis: a meso analysis. *Feminist Econ.* 19(3), 124–151.

Elden, S. (2010). Land, terrain, territory. *Prog. Hum. Geogr.* 34, 799–817. https://doi.org/10.1177/0309132510362603

Financial Times. (2013). London plays it cool on Chinese RGQFII investment. *The Financial Times*, 24 November 2013. Available from: https://www.ft.com/content/df147354-5145-11e3-9651-00144feabdc0

French, S., Leyshon, A., Wainwright, T. (2011). Financializing space, spacing financialization. *Prog. Hum. Geogr.* 35, 798–819. https://doi.org/10.1177/0309132510396749

Froud, J., Johal, S., Leaver, A., Williams, K. (2006). *Financialization and Strategy: Narrative and Numbers*. Routledge, London and New York.

Gibson-Graham, J.K. (2006). *A Post Capitalist Politics*. University of Minnesota Press, Minnesota.

Hall, S. (2011). Geographies of money and finance I: cultural economy, politics and place. *Prog. Hum. Geogr.* 35, 234–245. https://doi.org/10.1177/0309132510370277

Hall, S. (2012). Making space for markets in economic geography. *Dialogues Hum. Geogr.* 2, 142–145. https://doi.org/10.1177/2043820612449311

Hall, S. (2015). Everyday family experiences of the financial crisis: getting by in the recent economic recession. *J. Econ. Geogr.*, 16, 305–330.
Hall, S. (2017). Rethinking international financial centres through the politics of territory: renminbi internationalisation in London's financial district. *Trans. Inst. Br. Geogr.* 42, 489–502. https://doi.org/10.1111/tran.12172
Hall, S. (2018a). Regulating the geographies of market making: offshore Renminbi markets in London's International Financial District. *Econ. Geogr* 94, 259–278. https://doi.org/10.1080/00130095.2017.1304806
Hall, S. (2018b). *Global Finance:Places, Spaces and People.* Sage, London.
Hall, S. (2019). Reframing labour market mobility in global finance: Chinese elites in London's financial district. *Urban Geogr.* 40, 699–718. https://doi.org/10.1080/02723638.2018.1472442
Hertz, E. (1998). *The Trading Crowd: An Ethnography of the Shanghai Stock Market.* Cambridge University Press, Cambridge.
Osborne, G. (2014). Chancellor welcomes landmark agreement on London renminbi clearing and settlement arrangements. Available from: https://www.gov.uk/government/news/chancellor-welcomes-landmark-agreement-on-london-renminbi-clearing-and-settlement-arrangements
Ho, K. (2009). *Liquidated: An Ethnography of Wall Street.* Duke University Press, Durham and London.
Jones, A., Murphy, J.T. (2010). Theorizing practice in economic geography: foundations, challenges, and possibilities. *Prog. Hum. Geogr.* 35, 366–392. https://doi.org/10.1177/0309132510375585
Kaltenbrunner, A. (2015). A post Keynesian framework of exchange rate determination: a Minskyan approach. *J. Post Keynes. Econ.* 38, 426–448. https://doi.org/10.1080/01603477.2015.1065678
Kaltenbrunner, A., Painceira, J.P. (2018). Subordinated financial integration and financialisation in emerging capitalist economies: the Brazilian experience. *New Polit. Econ.* 23, 290–313. https://doi.org/10.1080/13563467.2017.1349089
Kirschner, J. (2014). Regional Hegemony and an emerging RMB zone, in: *The great wall of money*, E. Helleiner and J. Kirshner (eds). Cornell University Press, Ithaca, NY, 213–240.
Knorr Cetina, K., Bruegger, U. (2002). Global microstructures: the virtual societies of financial markets. *Am. J. Sociol.* 107, 905–950.
Knorr Cetina, K., Preda, A. (2005). *The Sociology of Financial Markets.* Oxford University Press, Oxford.
Knox-Hayes, J. (2009). The developing carbon financial service industry: expertise, adaptation and complementarity in London and New York. *J. Econ. Geogr.* 9, 749–777. https://doi.org/10.1093/jeg/lbp004
Kynaston, D. (2002). *The City of London, Vol. 4: A Club No More 1945–2000.* Pimlico, London.
Lai, K. (2012). Differentiated markets: Shanghai, Beijing and Hong Kong in China's Financial Centre Network. *Urban Stud.* 49, 1275–1296. https://doi.org/10.1177/0042098011408143
Langley, P. (2008). *The Everyday Life of Global Finance Saving and Borrowing in Anglo-America.* Oxford University Press, Oxford.
Lash, S., Urry, J. (1993). *Economies of Signs and Space.* Sage, London.
Leyshon, A. (1995). Geographies of money and finance I. *Prog. Hum. Geogr.* 19, 531–543.
Leyshon, A., Thrift, N. (1997). *Money/Space: Geographies of Monetary Transformation.* Routledge, London.
MacKenzie, D. (2003a). An equation and its worlds. *Soc. Stud. Sci.* 33(6), 831–868.
MacKenzie, D. (2003b). Long-term capital management and the sociology of arbitrage. *Econ. Soc.* 32(2), 349–380.

MacKenzie, D. (2005). Opening the black boxes of global finance. *Rev. Int. Polit. Econ.* 12(4), 555–576.

MacKenzie, D. (2006). *An Engine, Not a Camera: How Financial Models Shape Markets.* MIT Press, Cambridge, MA.

MacKenzie, D. (2018). Material signals: a historical sociology of high-frequency trading. *Am. J. Sociol.* 123, 1635–1683. https://doi.org/10.1086/697318

MacKenzie, D., Muniesa, F., Sui, L. (2007). *Do Economists Make Markets? On the Performativity of Economics.* Princeton University Press, Princeton.

Martin, R. (2011). The local geographies of the financial crisis: from the housing bubble to Economic recession. *J. Econ. Geogr.* 11, 587–618.

Martin, R., Pike, A., Tyler, P., Gardiner, B. (2015). Spatially rebalancing the UK Economy: the need for a new policy model. *Reg. Stud.* 3404. https://doi.org/10.1080/00343404.2015.1118450

McDowell, L. (1997). *Capital Cultures: Gender at Work in the City of London.* Blackwell, Oxford.

McFall, L. (2009). Devices and desires: how useful is the 'new' new economic sociology of understanding market attachment. *Sociol. Compass* 3, 267–282.

Muniesa, F., Millo, Y., Callon, M. (2007). An introduction to market devices. *Sociol. Rev.* 55, 1–12. https://doi.org/10.1111/j.1467-954X.2007.00727.x

Preda, A. (2006). Socio-technical agency in financial markets: the case of the stock ticker. *Soc. Stud. Sci.* 36, 753–782.

Strange, S. (1986). *Casino Capitalism.* Blackwell, Oxford.

The Banker (2018). *Top 1000 World Banks 2018*, available from https://www.thebanker.com/Top-1000-World-Banks/Top-1000-World-Banks-2018?ct=true

Töpfer, L.-M., Hall, S. (2018). London's rise as an offshore RMB financial centre: state–finance relations and selective institutional adaptation. *Reg. Stud.* 52, 1053–1064. https://doi.org/10.1080/00343404.2016.1275538

Van Meeteren, M., Bassens, D. (2016). World cities and the uneven geographies of financialization: unveiling stratification and hierarchy in the World City Archipelago. *Int. J. Urban Reg. Res.* 40, 62–81. https://doi.org/10.1111/1468-2427.12344

Walter, E.C., Howie, F. (2011). *Red Capitalism: The Fragile Financial Foundation of China's Extraordinary Rise.* John Wiley & Sons, Singapore.

Woods, S. (2017). Speech: Geofinance. Speech given by Sam Woods, Deputy Governor Prudential Regulation and Chief Executive Officer, Prudential Regulation Authority, Mansion House City Banquet, London, 4 October 2017, available from https://www.bankofengland.co.uk/-/media/boe/files/speech/2017/geofinance---speech-by-sam-woods.pdf?la=en&hash=1B7B8C099846ED4D305128BBB265F7BB71A354BA

Zaloom, C. (2003). Ambiguous numbers: trading technologies and interpretation in financial markets. *Am. Ethnol.* 30, 258–272.

Zaloom, C. (2006). *Out of the Pits: Traders and Technology from Chicago to London.* Chicago University Press, Chicago, IL.

Zook, M., Grote, M.H. (2016). The microgeographies of global finance: high-frequency trading and the construction of information inequality. *Environ. Plan. Econ. Space* 49, 121–140. https://doi.org/10.1177/0308518X16667298

5

BEYOND (DE)REGULATION

Law and the Production of Financial Geographies

Shaina Potts

Introduction

Law runs through much existing work in financial geography and related fields. From regulation theory, to the varieties of capitalism literature, to the variegated capitalism literature, path-dependent institutional and regulatory change is seen as central to explaining spatial variation in economic relations. Beyond this, financial geography contains innumerable references to and studies of particular laws. The most common topic for geographical analyses of the law–finance nexus has been financial (de)regulation—that is, laws understood as either prohibiting or permitting particular financial practices. Yet, law does far more than prohibit or permit. This chapter makes no attempt to provide an exhaustive overview of all the ways law is addressed in financial geography. Rather, it reviews a small, but growing body of work that has begun to move beyond large-scale institutional analyses and (de)regulation to focus on the legal geographies of finance *per se*. It situates this work in relation to longer-standing conversations in critical legal geography and economic geography, and extrapolates key insights that emerge from considering this work as a whole. In doing so, it aims not simply to summarize existing work, but also to contribute further to the theorization of the law–finance–space dynamic, responding to calls from within and beyond economic geography for more attention to the details of legal practices (Riles, 2005; Valverde, 2009; Barkan, 2011; Poon, Pollard, and Chow, 2018).

Although law is fundamental for economic geography more generally, it is worth noting at the start that the relative intangibility of finance makes the law–finance relation especially distinctive. Economic processes are always shaped by more than their physical components. Conversely, most financial assets are ultimately dependent on physical things such as houses or agricultural yields, and all finance is rooted in tangible people, places, and fiber optic cables. Nevertheless, compared to the production of iPhones or the transport of oil, financial instruments are far less tangible than most other objects of accumulation. This contributes to common descriptions of finance as placeless and frictionless. Geographers have done significant work pushing back against these metaphors to ground finance in material geographical relations. Yet, it is true that, since the 1970s, increasingly trans- and multi-jurisdictional financial flows, along with sophisticated financial instruments, have complicated obsolete categories of national financial space and made it 'difficult to know how to assign a spatial dimension to financial transactions' (Bryan, Rafferty, and Wigan, 2017: 49).

One contention of this chapter is that, in practice, law *does* assign spatial dimensions to financial processes—however complicated and contested that spatiality may be. Its relative intangibility means that finance is especially strongly determined by legal practices. Indeed, a bond or derivative is little more than a legal construct. This has major implications not only for the technical functioning of financial markets, but for the distribution of power and resources within and beyond them. As Riles (2014: 98–9) puts it:

> The point is that in the absence of clear scientific answers to epistemological questions like 'where is a security?' lawyers have been busy inventing creative answers rooted in the pragmatics of the implications of those answers for their clients, and for the most part, these are answers that serve the interests of the financial industry.

Investors and their lawyers are not the only ones engaged in this process. So are subnational, national, and international politicians and regulators, as well as judges, legal scholars, and those who attempt to resist certain financial practices in court. In short, legal geographies of finance are an important site of construction, conflict, and contestation among a wide variety of actors and interests. Many of these struggles revolve around legal definitions of the spatiality of finance.

Three fundamental assertions form the explicit or implicit basis for the emerging literature on law, finance, and geography. First, law is constitutive of finance. Finance does not simply occur in the context of law. Rather, all financial markets, instruments, and practices are legally constructed. Without law, there is no finance. On this point, the legal geographies of finance scholarship is in agreement with a small body of research in legal studies, most notably that of law professor Katharina Pistor (2013), whose article, 'A legal theory of finance', examines the paradoxical role of law in ensuring financial value, and mediating the essential instability and hierarchical nature of financial systems. Theorizing the constitutive role of law in finance means attending to a wide variety of legal practices, from contracts to litigation, to legal discourses.

Second, law is always spatial. Financial geography is defined by taking seriously the fact that finance not only occurs in, but is also co-produced with, space. Geographers investigate and conceptualize this relationship, exploring the always uneven spatial and temporal development of financial processes. Recent efforts to conceptualize the law–finance–space nexus take a similar approach to law. These analyses draw on a rich body of work in critical legal geography focused on non-financial and often non-economic topics (e.g., Blomley, 1994; Delaney, Ford, and Blomley, 2001). Most importantly, legal geographers have shown that law is always spatially defined, and that legal practices and decisions, in turn, produce space. More specifically, boundary-making is a fundamental function of law. This includes not only jurisdictional boundaries, but also legally constituted conceptual boundaries, both of which, as we will see below, have important implications for finance. Finally, both law and geography are simultaneously discursive and material. Legal ideas are not inscribed on material space. Rather, society is constituted in important ways through spatio-legal discursive practices. The co-production of law and space, together with the constitutive role of law in finance, means that it is not only law, but also legal geographies that are constitutive of financial geographies.

Third, law is always connected to the state. Here, financial geographers focusing on law are, again, in agreement with Pistor and her colleagues, who have suggested that this is what distinguishes law from a broader category of rules or norms. Law often has a hybrid character between state and non-state, but it is always at root 'an expression of state power' (Deakin et al., 2017: 190). Together with the constitutive role of law in finance, this means that state and finance are always entangled. Despite neoliberal rhetoric to the contrary, this entanglement has intensified since the 1970s—neoliberalism has meant restructuring the state, not destroying it (Peck and Tickell, 2002; Mansfield, 2005; Barkan, 2011; Bryan, Rafferty, and Wigan, 2017). Furthermore, while law has always been constitutive of capitalist economic relations, Foucault (2008) argued in the 1970s, and Harvey (2007) more recently, that neoliberalism increases the emphasis on contract rights and legal mediation. Legal anthropologist Annelise Riles (2011) likewise suggests that international neoliberal market projects often work through and alter legal forms. In the context of simultaneous processes of neoliberalization and financialization within and across national borders, the changing relationship between law and finance has been a major axis of this reconfiguration.

In the rest of this chapter, I examine recent work on law and financial geography. I arrange the chapter in terms of three major themes that emerge, explicitly or implicitly, from this work, and that illustrate the relevance of such analyses for financial geography more broadly. In the first section, I turn to the constitutive role of law in producing all financial contracts, and in mediating the distribution of risk and value. In the following section, I focus on the role of the classic spatio-legal functions of bounding and articulation in both constituting particular financial markets and in connecting diverse markets and legal spaces across multiple scales. The examples examined point to the difficulty of clearly separating legal governance or regulation from the legal constitution of financial geographies more broadly, and to the need to consider both processes of legal harmonization and strategic differentiation. In the third section, I turn to the ways that legal geographies of finance complicate our conceptions of state spatiality and state power. Drawing on a variety of empirical examples, I discuss how law both mediates state authority within national borders and how it operates beyond the political borders we see on maps. In the Conclusion, I briefly summarize the most important takeaways and identify several pressing areas for further research.

One major gap in the existing literature should be mentioned at the outset. The work reviewed here is skewed towards Anglo-American law, especially US law, although offshore financial spaces beyond these jurisdictions are also considered, as well as fascinating work on law and Islamic finance. Although the global importance of Anglo-American legal and financial spaces means they have import far beyond their borders, this is still a major lacuna in existing work on the legal geographies of finance, at least in the English-language scholarship to which the present discussion is limited. My hope is that many of the insights emerging from the work considered here will be of service to scholars engaging these questions from other places and perspectives.

All the papers discussed deepen our understanding of many processes of general interest to financial geographers, from the distribution of losses during financial crises, to tax havens and regulatory arbitrage, to the development of derivatives. They also contribute to at least two important conversations in economic geography beyond finance. First, the concept of economic performativity is now widespread in economic geography and cognate disciplines. A central insight of the performativity literature is that calculative practices and formulas that purport only to describe the economy actually produce it (MacKenzie, 2006; Callon, Millo, and Muniesa, 2007). Although these authors often include law and law firms on lists of those things that constitute the economy, however, this has been done largely in passing. The work reviewed here has begun to change that, exploring how legal technologies and discourses about markets constitute financial practices from contracts to transnational markets.

Second, the law–finance–space dynamic should be seen as central to broader projects of mapping the variegated, non-monolithic capitalist system within which we live (Brenner, Peck, and Theodore, 2010). While the varieties of capitalism scholarship emphasizes ideal-type and usually national models of capitalist regulation, the variegated capitalism perspective advocates for a relational approach to the always uneven development of differentiated but interconnected global capitalism across borders and scales. More specifically, Brenner et al. argue that neoliberalization has not meant the homogenization or convergence of all rules but, rather, the intensification of 'the uneven development of regulatory forms across places, territories, and scales', and they call for careful empirical investigation of 'nationally and subnationally scaled processes of regulatory restructuring' as active producers of *global* neoliberal processes (Brenner, Peck, and Theodore, 2010: 184, 194). As their own language suggests, law (although law that should be understood as much more than regulation) is central to this. The growing body of work on law and financial geography contributes to theorizing the 'constitutively uneven...spatially heterogenous and temporally discontinuous' spread of market rule in an age of neoliberalization, and helps connect work on the geographies of capitalism across micro-, meso-, and macro-scales (Brenner, Peck, and Theodore, 2010: 188).

The Legal Constitution of Financial Value

The role of the state in, at least potentially, enforcing all contracts and thus allowing markets to function is commonly noted. Financial geographers have recently gone further, showing how law is central to constituting markets and financial value in more specific ways. Not only is law an explicit focus of many financial accumulation strategies, it also mediates how much value gets realized, when, and for whom. This becomes especially apparent during crises.

First, law itself has increasingly become a focus of financial accumulation strategies. Most obviously, investors make strategic choices about which laws and jurisdictions to use—this process of legal arbitrage will be discussed in the following section. In the past few decades, financiers have also begun to use law strategically in more complicated ways. For instance, some sovereign debt traders now buy highly discounted debt from countries in economic crisis in order to sue those countries for recovery of the full face-value of the debt—usually in New York courts (Potts, 2017a). This strategy relies not only on significant resources and time, but also on lawyers-turned-financiers who know the ins and outs of relevant statutes and case law. More generally, legal scholars have examined how 'activist' hedge funds now search government and corporate bond contracts in order to find potential contract violations, buy up those bonds, and then enforce those contacts through legal means (Kahan and Rock, 2009). Other forms of legal experimentation proliferate as well. Knuth (2018: 225) shows how companies have learned to profit from solar energy financing by buying and securitizing Obama-era renewable energy tax credits: 'They achieve this cheap financing by experimenting with how renewable energy infrastructures might be legally owned (often in highly complex ownership structures), and what types of specially tailored financial benefits investors might derive from their development.' In short, complex legal technicalities are increasingly being incorporated into financial investment, requiring extensive overlap between financiers and lawyers, and between financial and legal strategies.

Yet, the connection between law and financial value goes deeper, to the way law mediates the distribution of all financial value. Law, backed by the state, does more than simply ensure the enforcement of contracts when one party reneges. How jurisdictions define and judges interpret a range of laws determines how contracts are written, and which contracts are and which are not enforced. The interpretation and application of legal rules on interest rates, for instance, determines whether loan contracts at 30% interest will be upheld in one legal space but not another. Definitions of contract fraud also vary by jurisdiction. New York requires a much higher bar for demonstrating fraudulence than California, which contributes to New York's pro-business appeal (Miller, 2009).

Drawing on the work of John R. Commons, Ashton (2014) examines an even more fundamental aspect of law, finance, and value, rooted in the necessary link between finance and uncertainty. Law is central to shaping the 'intangible and temporal dimensions' of producing economic value (Ashton, 2014: 962), and the state mediates the relationship between value and the future: 'Thus, for an economy to expand, the state must be omnipresent in transactions even where it is seemingly invisible, as the promise of state action—at some point in the future—is what makes possible the regulation of uncertainty in pursuit of investment and growth. The futurity of value and the futurity of state action are always intertwined' (Ashton, 2014: 963). This process becomes more complicated, but does not disappear, at the transnational scale, and it is never static. Christophers, Leyshon, and Mann (2017) argue that, since the 2008 crisis, major transnational banks have restructured their risk profiles, partly in response to post-crisis regulatory changes, bolstering equity and interest-bearing assets, and cutting illiquid, long-term assets such as subprime mortgages and small business loans. Much of this financing has since been taken up by 'shadow banks' and bond markets. What this transformation means for the law–finance–futurity relation requires further investigation.

The role of law in mediating risk and value is clearest precisely when the 'unexpected' actually happens. During economic crises, the reality is that not all contracts can be fulfilled, and that fulfilling certain contracts will mean not fulfilling others. Law plays a direct role in determining the hierarchy of contract fulfillment and in mediating the distribution of the realization, or not, of value in such situations. It does so, for instance, by ranking various investor claims to the assets of a bankrupt business, or by legally putting the claims of a city's or country's creditors before those of its pensioners. During the 2008 subprime crisis, the legal mediation of the distribution of value occurred most famously through the United States' Troubled Asset Relief Program, which used federal legislative power to socialize the losses of major banks, transferring the costs to taxpayers but protecting the value of those companies.

Law mediated the distribution of value after the crisis in more complicated ways, as well. The gap between the pace of financial innovation and legislators' ability to respond to it has meant regulatory agencies have increasingly relied on adjudication techniques such as arbitration, settlement, and deferred prosecution agreements, which are faster, more flexible, and more customizable than passing new laws or undertaking formal litigation (Ashton, 2014). After the financial crisis, Ashton argues, regulators pursued high-profile settlements with subprime lenders not so much in order to compensate victims of subprime loans (when measured on a per capita basis, payouts were quite small) but, rather, as a way to perform a type of symbolic punishment while simultaneously helping stabilize the very institutions being prosecuted. Sweeping loan contract modifications in some settlements, for example, restructured subprime mortgages, ostensibly to help borrowers remain in their homes, but simultaneously ensuring banks would preserve the value of those loans over the long term. More generally, settlements enable firms to pay damages without formally admitting guilt, and they create no binding legal precedents on other institutions or future lending practices.

Christophers and Niedt (2016) consider very different attempts to use law to soften the impact of the subprime crisis on homeowners. A handful of cities across the United States developed plans to use the legal practice of eminent domain to force lenders to sell underwater mortgages to cities at market rates (well below the amounts still owed by homeowners), in order to enable people to remain in their homes. The plans, which presented a serious challenge to dominant practices of urban financial capitalism (and law's usual role in underwriting it), were immediately challenged by Wall Street. Although the plans were ultimately unsuccessful, the authors draw important conclusions for conceptualizing the relationship between law and financial value: 'The law figures in this political-economic drama as a crucial field where value and risk outcomes are rendered negotiable and are, accordingly, contested and (re)produced' (Christophers and Niedt, 2016: 487). The plan would, indeed have run counter to financiers' interests: 'if eminent domain would not actually—physically—cause losses per se, it would do more than *just* reveal them: it would cause losses *to be realized*' (emphases in original) (Christophers and Niedt, 2016: 492).

In short, law constitutes and mediates the distribution of risk and value, during both normal economic times and crises. It does so by serving as the basis of explicit financial strategies, by interpreting and adjudicating contracts, and by enabling financial investment in the face of an uncertain future. This makes law central to all financial transactions. But the constitutive role of law in finance goes still further. Law not only mediates the realization, or not, of value for particular investments; it also constitutes the markets within and across which they operate.

Making and Articulating Financial Geographies

Law plays a constitutive role in making financial geographies, from bounding particular financial markets, to defining the (sub)national legal spaces within which major financial transactions take place. Law both produces legal–financial space at multiple scales and coordinates the articulation of financial processes across these spaces. Considering the multiple ways in which law does this makes the line between the legal regulation or governance of finance and the legal constitution of finance especially blurry. It also raises questions about tensions between homogenizing and heterogenizing factors in shaping 'globalizing' finance.

Christophers' work on the performative role of law in bounding markets for particular kinds of economic activity is especially innovative (Christophers, 2014, 2015, 2016). Focusing on competition and anti-trust law, he uses the concept of the 'law's markets' to examine how, in attempting to describe and represent the scope of economic markets, law actually defines and enacts them for the purposes of competition and regulation. In doing so, legal decisions shape actually existing markets, determining which firms, whether in insurance or banking, are allowed to merge, establish prices, and so on. For instance, legal decisions to define US commercial banking competition at a relatively local scale actually enabled larger-scale mergers to escape anti-trust oversight—eventually contributing to the rise of the 'too big to fail' banks at the center of the 2008 financial crisis (Christophers, 2014). The fact that law constitutes these markets, however, does not mean it does so in any simple way. Real world competition is always messier than the law's markets reflect, while law nevertheless constrains and enables certain forms of market behavior:

> This, ultimately, has been the main contention of the present article: that in its struggle to re-present markets that do not exist, the law, ironically, produces and reproduces *real* markets; not the precise markets envisioned by the law, but markets nonetheless.
>
> (Christophers, 2015: 140)

Resonant analyses of the constitutive role of law in producing markets have perhaps been most closely explored by political ecologists in relation to the ongoing commodification of nature and production of new forms of property (see summary in Kay, 2016). Similar analyses are still required for different sorts of financial transactions, as well as for transnational markets.

Law's role in the production of financial centers is equally important and more widely studied. Some of the most developed work on law and financial geography comes from geographers and other social scientists working on offshore finance (Maurer, 1997; Palan, Murphy, and Chavagneux, 2010; Shaxson, 2012; Haberly and Wójcik, 2017). Although tax havens or offshore financial centers are often presented as beyond the law, they are, in fact, constituted precisely by law and sovereignty. Whether literally islands such as the Caymans, or onshore 'offshore' spaces such as Delaware or the City of London, these spaces are useful to finance insofar as they establish jurisdictional boundaries that separate them from other financial spaces. They attract capital not only by a lack of stricter 'onshore' regulation, but by offering a host of *useful* laws on taxes, fees, and secrecy that benefit mobile capital. Which precise laws are offered varies by jurisdiction, creating an interconnected array of differentiated legal spaces, of which transnational corporations and wealthy individuals often use more than one.

Law also plays a major role in producing onshore financial centers. The importance of law in making global cities includes the agglomeration of lawyers and legal services firms whose job is to assist banks and other investors (Sassen, 2001), but goes well beyond this. These cities themselves, or rather the jurisdictions within which they operate, design their own laws so as to be more favorable to finance. New York state and national English law have been designed to support New York City and the City of London, respectively, and legislators, officials, and judges understand these cities as competing to attract not only financial business, but also legal business (Potts, 2016).

Another example of the role of law in producing financial space comes from fascinating work on changing dynamics of finance and Shariah law. This work examines, for instance, overlapping geographies of English and Islamic law within Malaysia, and how they are changing as Malaysia positions itself as a growing, global center for Islamic finance, though in ways that are still thoroughly neoliberal (Poon, Pollard, and Chow, 2018). These sorts of overlapping legal genealogies, which continue to shape complicated regulatory and jurisdictional questions around the world, need more study, especially in post-colonial spaces.

Law, then, is central to producing the boundaries and character of financial geographies, from individual markets to financial hubs. It plays an equally critical role in articulating financial markets within and across these spaces. It does so most obviously through international agreements, which may be more or less formally ratified, from the Basel Accords to the World Trade Organization. Such institutions are well-recognized as harmonizing legal rules in ways that enable firms to engage more easily in transnational investment. The LIBOR rate, for instance—which Ashton and Christophers (2015) define as a semi-public, semi-private legal technology—facilitates interconnection across global financial markets by establishing a benchmark figure for international interbank interest rates and by creating comparability across otherwise disconnected financial assets. As in the law's markets described by Christophers in relation to competition law, while LIBOR purports simply to describe existing financial markets, it actually mediates and makes them.

Law also articulates markets across jurisdictional boundaries within particular investments or financial transactions. A dramatic example of this concerns the legal geographies structuring transnational payment flows. These flows, which can occur in microseconds, are usually assumed to be smooth and frictionless. In fact, legal geographies of financial payment are not continuous at all but are, rather, structured in discrete (if not entirely stable) spatial segments, organized, variously, by jurisdiction, ownership, liability, and agency. A huge amount of effort goes into writing contracts and planning investments with these legal borders in mind. When things run smoothly, this may go largely unnoticed but, when problems arise, these legal distinctions can become the focus of intense legal contestation (Potts, 2020).

Law enables finance to engage across national borders and markets in other ways, as well. Geographers have examined the role of derivatives in complicating financial geographies, including by divorcing geographies of assets from geographies of exposure to those assets (Bryan and Rafferty, 2006; Bryan, Rafferty, and Wigan, 2017). Derivatives play an important commensuration function in the global economy, allowing diverse kinds of assets in different places to be turned into financial commodities that can be priced against and traded with one another. Yet, this important process is itself legally constituted.

As Wójcik (2013a) has shown, in order to be traded, assets, securities, and derivatives must all be assembled into legal entities called 'investment vehicles' (IVs). These IVs themselves are combined 'legal, accounting and financial abstractions,' and law firms are closely involved in their production (Wójcik, 2013b: 333). IVs, often registered in offshore financial centers, are especially important for articulating financial investment across national jurisdictional borders, playing a nodal role in connecting world cities and a variety of offshore spaces. Indeed, Haberly and Wójcik (2014, 2017) have demonstrated the centrality of multi-jurisdictional legal practices more generally for articulating onshore and offshore finance. These insights contribute to increasing recognition among geographers and other scholars that offshore financial centers are neither simply marginal within the global economy, nor 'beyond' onshore finance—rather, offshore and onshore financial geographies are closely integrated, with the connections between them structuring major transnational financial geographies.

Considering the relation between onshore and offshore finance immediately raises the question of financial regulation. There is no denying the importance of what we commonly call 'deregulation' in this era of neoliberalization and financialization. Nevertheless, understanding that law is always constitutive of finance pushes us to reframe the concept. There is no outside the legal in contemporary capitalism, especially for finance, which is in large part a legal construct. What there are, rather, are strategic political decisions about what kinds of legal spaces exist where. De-regulation—or, more usefully, re-regulation—involves the creation of legal infrastructures that tend to favor private, especially financial, interests over public ones, and often creditors over debtors, in particular. This means regulatory arbitrage is not about choosing the least regulated but, rather, the most usefully regulated legal spaces, and about making use of differences among them, as, for instance, between the differentiated offshore spaces just discussed. New York and London, likewise, offer distinct and complementary financial advantages (Gowan, 1999; Wójcik, 2013a). It is not simply a matter of finance-friendly and finance-unfriendly jurisdictions. Rather, there is a huge range of legal spaces that are more or less useful for particular kinds of financial transactions. At a systemic level, variation in legal space, then, in part reflects the usefulness of legal specialization for finance.

Of course, there are real tensions between those who (at some times and in some ways) want to rein in financial power and those who want to unleash it: in other words, there are struggles over what form a particular legal space should take, and the regulatory 'race to the bottom' is significant. Law, it turns out, is equally involved on all sides of these struggles. For one thing, 'Lawyers play a dual role in international regulation, advising governments on how to build it and businesses on how to circumvent it' (Wójcik, 2013b: 339). Pistor (2013: 324) points out a deeper ambiguity in the role of law when she notes that law, backed by state power, ensures the enforcement of contracts, but that 'to the extent that financial instruments are designed to weaken regulatory costs it [this enforcement] effectively sanctions regulatory arbitrage and the erosion of formal law'. In other words, even getting around the law is a legal practice.

In short, legal geographies and financial geographies are co-constituted at every scale. Law not only produces financial instruments and market boundaries, but also coordinates across them. This has important implications for how we understand 'global' finance. First, no matter how quickly financial processes occur once the institutional, including legal, infrastructure through which they operate is established, it takes massive amounts of time and effort to create and maintain that infrastructure. This is an important challenge to dominant narratives portraying globalization as an inevitable, technologically-driven process in which capital bursts all regulatory bounds. Second, the kinds of coordination across markets that law enables are sometimes based on legal harmonization—that is, on making rules more similar across jurisdictions. Often, however, as in the case of legal differentiation within payment flows, or the proliferation of niche offshore spaces, the legal articulation of diverse financial geographies is not about homogenization at all. It is about the maintenance and strategic use of legal difference.

In other words, there is a dialectical tension between the international harmonization (usually Americanization) of financial law, on the one hand, and the erection of legal barriers and differences that are useful to finance, on the other. Barkan (2011: 7) hints at the implications of this for understanding capitalist variegation:

> The recognition that the legal landscape is both conceptually and geographically variegated offers an opening for geographic analysis. Given the extensive geographic research into inequality and uneven spatial development, we might inquire into whether or not the fragmented and uneven landscape of global legal systems represents a failure of a truly globalizing legal process, or is part and parcel of how global law operates.

Finance, Law, and Geographies of State Power

The previous two sections have considered the lessons of recent work on legal geographies of finance for understanding how law, always imbricated with state power, produces financial geographies. In this final section, I consider the flipside of this relationship: the ways finance and law are constitutive of state authority and spatiality. I focus on two important dimensions of this. First, the role of discursive legal borders in mediating the state–finance relationship within particular political territories, and, second, the way legal spaces of finance often extend beyond official political boundaries.

Law is an important mediator of finance–state relations within a given legal space. It performs this function in important ways through producing conceptual boundaries between, on the one hand, law, economy, and politics, and, on the other, public and private. In the context of the neoliberal obsession with private autonomy and a sharply bounded economy, these conceptual borders have been both constantly transgressed and defended all the more fiercely. These fictions of legal closure, in which law is presented as separate from both the state (equated here with politics) and society, have bolstered law's self-representation as objective, formal, and neutral. The critical legal studies project, conversely, has traditionally been about 'opening' the law and exposing law's embeddedness in socio-political relations of all kinds (Blomley, 1994). Legal geographers of finance have begun to engage this critical project, as well.

Ashton and Christophers (2015), for example, uncover the work that goes into making LIBOR appear as a neutral benchmark, influenced by neither governments nor market power. Although LIBOR actively shapes the financial markets it purports to represent, this market-making work depends on LIBOR being *seen as* a neutral mechanism external to markets. LIBOR is 'a calculative legal technology required to perform 'neutral' benchmarking work, but nonetheless rooted in the reality of concentrated market power' (Ashton and Christophers, 2015: 197). In the wake of the 2012 LIBOR scandal, furthermore, although US and UK regulators brought charges against Barclays and other banks, the settlements reached were not designed to punish these banks so much as to restore the image of neutrality disrupted by the scandal. The goal was to restore the appearance of a sharp separation between rules and markets, and between these private rule-makers and governments. Christophers and Niedt (2016) similarly show how discourses of legal closure framed in terms of the sanctity of contract were deployed by financiers opposing municipal eminent domain plans. One could find many other examples. In all these cases, despite the constitutive relation between law and the state and between law and finance, the operative fiction is that law is separate from both, and that, because of this, law can be a neutral force, devoid of power relations.

The public/private distinction is closely related to the law/politics and law/economics distinctions. In relation to economic questions, public/private is generally understood in US law as mapping onto state/non-state. The neoliberal natures scholarship has extensively analysed the reconfiguration of public and private in relation to the privatization of conservation and related questions (Heynen et al., 2007; Mansfield, 2009). Niedt (2013) analyses the complexity of the public/private distinction in mediating the use of US eminent domain law, which is designed to allow states to seize private property in order to put it to public use. Further research on how the public/private distinction operates in finance specifically is needed, but preliminary work shows that it suffuses the relevant legal discourses. Governing law clauses, for instance, which are discussed further below, allow contracting parties to select which laws and which courts will govern their own transactions. They were once rejected as improperly giving legislative power to individuals. Pro-private, anti-state discourses emerging from the neoliberal turn in legal theory after World War II, however, eventually cleared the way for the widespread use of these 'private' legal mechanisms, and they are now found in all major financial contracts (Potts, 2016). To take another example, beginning with the eventual response to the massive debt crises of the 1980s, the United States, the International Monetary Fund, and others have pushed for *ad hoc* debt restructuring practices, in which creditors can choose whether or not to participate. Despite massive intervention from the US Treasury and other governments, these restructurings are framed as voluntary, private, and market-based, and defended in these terms against the possibility of a 'mandatory' debt restructuring program that could be organized by the United Nations or some other international body and enshrined in international law (Potts, 2017b).

All these examples show that although, in practice, states, laws, and markets are always entangled, these conceptual divisions are not mere pretense. The continual reconfiguration of the public/private and law/politics/economy distinctions shapes shifting boundaries of what is considered legitimate state versus non-state behavior, as well as what *type* of state power (e.g., executive, legislative, or judicial) is exercised where, over what kinds of economic transactions (Potts, 2017b). These distinctions are part of law's performative production of markets and states. In other words, an important insight from emerging work on law, finance, and geography is that law plays a key role in constituting the broader distinction between the economic and the political—a distinction extensively studied by social science scholars from a variety of theoretical perspectives (e.g., Polanyi, 2001; Mitchell, 2002; Krippner, 2011).

The law–finance relation mediates state authority and spatiality in other ways, as well. Although law is always rooted in state space, this does not mean legal space coincides in any simple way with the political borders drawn on maps. More nuanced analyses of the relation between legal and state space are particularly important for ongoing debates about the reconfiguration of nation-states and national space in the context of increasingly transnational financial processes. Economic geographers have eschewed methodological nationalism and the reification of any neatly nested scalar model of economic relations, and they have worked to denaturalize the idea of a 'national economy' (Peck and Theodore, 2007; Glassman, 2012; Christophers, Leyshon, and Mann, 2017). Yet, when it comes to law, usually equated with regulation, there is still a widespread tendency to assume a coincidence of political borders and legal reach. This, in turn, supports the common narrative of innovative global finance outrunning slow and clunky national attempts at regulation. Even sophisticated work on the path-dependent nature of regulatory change and the ways that regulators are sometimes working against, and sometimes in collaboration with finance can fall into this trap. Yet, while it is true that there are important limits on the ability of regulators to rein in global finance, the relationship between law, finance, and states is far more complicated. Closer attention to law and financial geography shows that the overlapping, trans-scalar, messy spatiality of law is just as complex as that of finance. Law is not national because it is confined within, or coterminous with national borders, but because it is anchored in them.

In practice, subnational and national domestic laws frequently operate beyond the official borders of the states on which their power is based. These transnational extensions of domestic legal–financial space do not simply exceed state spatiality, moreover, but reshape it. The ability to project law transnationally is not evenly distributed. It is concentrated, for now, in a few Western countries, mostly in the United States. Transnational commercial law is widely studied by law professors, although almost always in terms of what are seen as apolitical market forces (e.g., Whytock, 2009; Gerber, 2012). A separate literature on the 'extraterritorial' extension of US law (focused mostly on statutes) does recognize this ability as rooted in US economic and political dominance (e.g., Putnam, 2009; Raustiala, 2011; Colangelo, 2013). Both literatures provide a trove of useful and largely untapped empirical details that deserve to be mined by social scientists, although both have tended to ignore, or pay limited attention to power, geopolitics, and geography, and to explain the expansion of transnational or extraterritorial law through a simplistic and naturalizing narrative about globalization.

Social scientists outside law and business studies have recently begun turning more critical attention to this phenomenon. Sassen (2008) considers the increasing role of national courts in hearing multi-national cases as an example of emerging forms of transnational power, while Gowan (2010) notes recent attempts to extend US jurisdiction internationally in the context of US hegemony. A handful of financial geographers have begun to investigate these processes more substantially, analysing the transnational extension of US law with detailed attention to its spatial and political implications. Haberly and Wójcik (2017) analyse the projection of significant US regulatory power offshore, including Securities and Exchange Commission anti-fraud regulation and US bankruptcy court jurisdiction. The United States has also extended its jurisdictional power abroad to police terrorist financing (de Goede, 2017), and to issue injunctions over and demand discovery from financial institutions in Europe in the context of sovereign debt litigation (Potts, 2020).

Governing law clauses—by which large-scale commercial parties are allowed to select, via contract, which laws and which courts will govern many aspects of their transactions—are a further important mechanism by which legal authority is extended transnationally (Potts, 2016). New York state law and English national law are by far the most common jurisdictions selected through such clauses, even for many transactions with little or no connection to those places. Governing law clauses add another dimension to geographies of arbitrage, enabling major commercial actors to select the most strategic legal space without having to alter their transactions at all. These clauses not only select jurisdictions, but also enlarge them and, with them, the scope of New York or English state authority.

Although legal space does not exhaust state space, the fundamental relationship between law and state power means that the former is an important part of the latter. As critical legal geographers and legal studies scholars have explored at more local scales (Delaney, Ford, and Blomley, 2001; Valverde, 2008), the transnational legal spaces of finance are overlapping, fragmented, and interpenetrating. They vary not just by jurisdiction, but also by the particular kinds of financial transaction and the modality of legal power in question. Together with the performative work carried out through law's conceptual distinctions between law, state, and economy, the legal geographies of finance are a central site for analysing the changing role of nation-states today. Finance and law shape geographies of the state. Financial power and state power, furthermore, are linked in important ways. The financial power of both world cities and offshore financial spaces are inseparable from their state-backed legal qualities. At the same time, the transnational legal power of major financial centers such as New York City or London is predicated on their financial power. US courts, of which New York courts are the most important, are able to claim extensive extraterritorial authority, while many other countries are not, because people all over the world want to retain access to New York's commercial space.

Conclusion

Together, the constitutive roles of law in finance and of space in law, and the fundamental connection between law and state power make conceptualizing the legal geographies of finance an important task for financial geography as a whole. Questions about improving financial regulation to limit financial instability and inequality remain of paramount analytical and political importance. Emerging work on law and financial geography both benefits from and contributes to studies of de/re-regulation. Yet, the law–finance nexus is about far more than whether and how nation-states should regulate finance. This chapter has considered some of the many ways that more-than-national, but still nationally rooted legal practices do, in fact, already constitute all financial geographies.

More specifically, law is a necessary element of financial accumulation, from legal interpretations and enforcement of contracts, to the increasing use of complex legal strategies in financial investment, to the way the promise of state-backed enforcement makes investments in an uncertain future viable. Law mediates how much value is realized, when, and by whom, in ways that are especially noticeable during crises.

At a larger scale, law constitutes financial markets, from defining the boundaries of banking competition, to making offshore financial centers strategically useful, to shaping global cities in which legal and financial power are co-constituted. In these ways, law both produces and maintains the borders between different kinds of financial spaces and provides opportunities for legal arbitrage. It also, however, manages the articulation of financial transactions across these borders, from establishing transnational market rules, to giving legal meaning to transnational payments, to establishing multi-jurisdictional financial instruments and investment vehicles. A synthetic assessment of diverse examples of these processes begins to illuminate the larger implications of a focus on the legal geographies of finance for conceptualizing global capitalism: even globalizing finance has not meant the homogenization of financial spaces, or the breakdown of all financial barriers. Rather, there has been a simultaneous process of the harmonization of certain legal rules, on the one hand, and the erection and maintenance of legally constituted financial borders and distinctions, on the other.

At the same time—and not surprisingly, given the fundamental connection between law and the state—legal geographies of finance are relevant for understanding the dynamic relationship between states and markets. Taken together, we can see how the continual (re)definition of the law/politics, law/economy, and public/private distinctions is part of larger processes of mediating the relationship between finance and the state. Moreover, the law's spatiality is not simply contained within official political borders. Rather, in its constitution of transnational financial processes, domestic laws themselves reconfigure geographies of state power. This is especially so for the world's most powerful financial centers. Further analysis of such processes is needed to make our understanding of legal geographies and their imbrications with state power as nuanced as our analyses of transnational finance.

All the work considered in this chapter speaks to the relative autonomy of law within capitalism. Although law has always been internal to capitalism, legal developments cannot be neatly subsumed within more commonly discussed logics of credit creation, capital concentration, or profit-seeking. Legal practices have their own genealogies, and legal changes must be justified according to always shifting legal traditions, decisions, and discourses. This suggests that, while law in capitalist societies has worked hand-in-hand with the interests of business overall, law is never reducible to an instrument of capital, and has itself shaped the trajectories of capitalist development. The performative role of law in making markets, often as it purports merely to describe them, must be understood alongside developments in economic models, accounting practices, and telecommunications technologies as reshaping political economic relations.

Finally, attending to the legal geographies of finance contributes to the broader project of investigating global capitalism as an interconnected but variegated system. It does so by adding empirical detail to our understanding of diverse financial spaces from New York to Malaysia. Just as significantly, law makes certain places more alike, but also differentiates many economic spaces and manages cross-border relationships among them. Brenner, Peck, and Theodore (2010) themselves suggest that variation in regulatory forms is constitutive of variegated capitalism. The research considered here lends weight to this view, while also broadening the category of 'regulatory form' to include a much wider variety of legal practices and processes than the term usually implies.

Explicit attention to law in financial geography is still rare, and there is a huge amount of research to be done. Work on each of the topics considered above remains relatively isolated, and further analyses of related examples or other contexts would go a long way to fleshing out and nuancing these arguments. Perhaps most simply, far more work on the legal constitution of many of the financial instruments we study the most is required, from collateralized debt obligations, to municipal bonds, to interest swaps. More glaringly, there is a serious lack of regional coverage in existing work on legal geographies of finance. While many of the insights here will likely be useful for analysing the law–finance nexus in other parts of the world, some will not. Conversely, having a better understanding of how law functions differently in different places will make the significance of law for constituting financial geographies of all kinds clearer. Ideally, such comparative work will go beyond simply noting similarities and differences, to investigating the divergent but interconnected genealogies of law around the world.

References

Ashton, P. (2014) 'The evolving juridical space of harm/value: remedial powers in the subprime mortgage crisis', *Journal of Economic Issues*, 48(4), pp. 959–979.

Ashton, P. and Christophers, B. (2015) 'On arbitration, arbitrage and arbitrariness in financial markets and their governance: unpacking LIBOR and the LIBOR scandal', *Economy and Society*, 44(2), pp. 188–217.

Barkan, J. (2011) 'Law and the geographic analysis of economic globalization', *Progress in Human Geography*, 35, pp. 589–607.

Blomley, N. K. (1994) *Law, Space, and the Geographies of Power*. New York: Guilford Press.

Brenner, N., Peck, J. and Theodore, N. (2010) 'Variegated neoliberalization: geographies, modalities, pathways', *Global Networks*, 10(2), pp. 182–222.

Bryan, D. and Rafferty, M. (2006) *Capitalism with Derivatives: A Political Economy of Financial Derivatives, Capital and Class*. New York: Palgrave Macmillan.

Bryan, D., Rafferty, M. and Wigan, D. (2017) 'From time–space compression to spatial spreads: situating nationality in global financial liquidity', in Christophers, B., Leyshon, A., and Mann, G. (eds) *Money and Finance After the Crisis: Critical Thinking for Uncertain Times*. John Wiley & Sons.

Callon, M., Millo, Y. and Muniesa, F. (eds) (2007) *Market Devices*. 1st edn. Wiley-Blackwell.

Christophers, B. (2014) 'Competition, law, and the power of (imagined) geography: market definition and the emergence of too-big-to-fail banking in the United States', *Economic Geography*, 90(4), pp. 429–450.

Christophers, B. (2015) 'The law's markets', *Journal of Cultural Economy*, 8(2), pp. 125–143.

Christophers, B. (2016) *The Great Leveler: Capitalism and Competition in the Court of Law*. Harvard University Press.

Christophers, B., Leyshon, A. and Mann, G. (eds) (2017) *Money and Finance After the Crisis: Critical Thinking for Uncertain Times*. John Wiley & Sons.

Christophers, B. and Niedt, C. (2016) 'Resisting devaluation: foreclosure, eminent domain law, and the geographical political economy of risk', *Environment and Planning A*, 48(3), pp. 485–503.

Colangelo, A. J. (2013) 'What is extraterritorial jurisdiction', *Cornell Law Review*, 99, p. 1303.

Deakin, S. et al. (2017) 'Legal institutionalism: capitalism and the constitutive role of law', *Journal of Comparative Economics*, 45(1), pp. 188–200.

Delaney, D., Ford, R. T. and Blomley, N. K. (eds) (2001) *The legal geographies reader: law, power and space*. Blackwell Publishers.

Foucault, M. (2008) *The Birth of Biopolitics: Lectures at the Collège De France, 1978–79*. Basingstoke [England]; New York: Palgrave Macmillan.

Gerber, D. (2012) *Global Competition: Law, Markets, and Globalization*. OUP Oxford.

Glassman, J. (2012) 'The global economy', in Barnes, T. J., Peck, J., and Sheppard, E. S. (eds) *The Wiley-Blackwell Companion to Economic Geography*. Blackwell Publishing.

de Goede, M. (2017) 'Banks in the frontline: assembling space/time in financial warfare', in Christophers, B., Leyshon, A., and Mann, G. (eds) *Money and finance after the crisis: critical thinking for uncertain times*. John Wiley & Sons, pp. 119–144.

Gowan, P. (1999) *The Global Gamble: Washington's Faustian Bid for World Dominance*. London: Verso.

Gowan, P. (2010) *A Calculus of Power: Grand Strategy in the Twenty-First Century*. London: Verso.

Haberly, D. and Wójcik, D. (2014) 'Tax havens and the production of offshore FDI: an empirical analysis', *Journal of Economic Geography*, 15(1), pp. 75–101.

Haberly, D. and Wójcik, D. (2017) 'Culprits or bystanders? Offshore jurisdictions and the global financial crisis', *Journal of Financial Regulation*, 3(2), pp. 233–261.

Harvey, D. (2007) *A Brief History of Neoliberalism*. Oxford: Oxford University Press.

Heynen, N. et al. (2007) *Neoliberal Environments: False Promises and Unnatural Consequences*. Routledge.

Kahan, M. and Rock, E. (2009) 'Hedge fund activism in the enforcement of bondholder rights', *Nw. UL Rev.*, 103, p. 281.

Kay, K. (2016) 'Breaking the bundle of rights: conservation easements and the legal geographies of individuating nature', *Environment and Planning A*, 48(3), pp. 504–522.

Knuth, S. (2018) ''Breakthroughs' for a green economy? Financialization and clean energy transition', *Energy Research & Social Science*, 41, pp. 220–229.

Krippner, G. R. (2011) *Capitalizing on Crisis: The Political Origins of the Rise of Finance*. Cambridge, MA: Harvard University Press.

MacKenzie, D. (2006) *An Engine, Not a Camera: How Financial Models Shape Markets*. Cambridge, MA: MIT Press.

Mansfield, B. (2005) 'Beyond rescaling: reintegrating the 'national' as a dimension of scalar relations', *Progress in Human Geography*, 29(4), pp. 458–473.

Mansfield, B. (2009) *Privatization: Property and the Remaking of Nature-Society Relations*. John Wiley & Sons.

Maurer, B. (1997) 'Creolization redux: the plural society thesis and offshore financial services in the British Caribbean', *NWIG: New West Indian Guide/Nieuwe West-Indische Gids*, pp. 249–264.

Miller, G. P. (2009) 'Bargains bicoastal: new light on contract theory', *Cardozo Law Review*, 31, p. 1475.

Mitchell, T. (2002) *Rule of Experts: Egypt, Techno-politics, Modernity*. Berkeley: University of California Press.

Niedt, C. (2013) 'The politics of eminent domain: from false choices to community benefits', *Urban Geography*, 34(8), pp. 1047–1069.

Palan, R., Murphy, R. and Chavagneux, C. (2010) *Tax Havens: How Globalization Really Works*. Ithaca, NY: Cornell University Press.

Peck, J. and Theodore, N. (2007) 'Variegated capitalism', *Progress in Human Geography*, 31(6), pp. 731–772.

Peck, J. and Tickell, A. (2002) 'Neoliberalizing space', *Antipode*, 34(3), pp. 380–404.

Pistor, K. (2013) 'A legal theory of finance', *Journal of Comparative Economics*, 41(2), pp. 315–330.

Polanyi, K. (2001) *The Great Transformation: The Political and Economic Origins of Our Time*. 2nd edn. Beacon Press.

Poon, J. P., Pollard, J. and Chow, Y. W. (2018) 'Resetting neoliberal values: lawmaking in Malaysia's Islamic finance', *Annals of the American Association of Geographers*, 108(5), pp. 1442–1456.

Potts, S. (2016) 'Reterritorializing economic governance: contracts, space, and law in transborder economic geographies', *Environment and Planning A*, 48(3), pp. 523–539.

Potts, S. (2017a) 'Deep finance: sovereign debt crises and the secondary market 'fix'', *Economy and Society*, 46(3–4), pp. 452–475.

Potts, S. (2017b) *Displaced Sovereignty: U.S. law and the Transformation of International Financial Space* (dissertation). University of California at Berkeley.

Potts, S. (2020) '(Re-)writing markets: law and contested payment geographies', *Environment and Planning A: Economy and Space*, 52(1), pp. 46–65.

Putnam, T. L. (2009) 'Courts without borders: domestic sources of US extraterritoriality in the regulatory sphere', *International Organization*, 63(3), pp. 459–490.

Raustiala, K. (2011) *Does the Constitution Follow the Flag?: The Evolution of Territoriality in American Law*. Oxford University Press.

Riles, A. (2005) 'A new agenda for the cultural study of law: taking on the technicalities', *Buffalo Law Review*, 53, pp. 973–1033.

Riles, A. (2011) *Collateral Knowledge: Legal Reasoning in the Global Financial Markets*. University of Chicago Press.

Riles, A. (2014) 'Managing regulatory arbitrage: a conflict of laws approach', *Cornell International Law Journal*, 47, p. 63.

Sassen, S. (2001) *The Global City: New York, London, Tokyo*. 2nd edn. Princeton, NJ: Princeton University Press.

Sassen, S. (2008) 'Neither global nor national: novel assemblages of territory, authority and rights', *Ethics & Global Politics*, 1(1–2), pp. 61–79.

Shaxson, N. (2012) *Treasure Islands: Uncovering the Damage of Offshore Banking and Tax Havens*. New York: Palgrave Macmillan.

Valverde, M. (2008) 'Analyzing the governance of security: jurisdiction and scale', *Behemoth A Journal on Civilisation*, 1(1), pp. 3–15.

Valverde, M. (2009) 'Jurisdiction and scale: legal 'technicalities' as resources for theory', *Social & Legal Studies*, 18(2), pp. 139–157.

Whytock, C. A. (2009) 'Domestic courts and global governance', *Tulane Law Review*, 84, p. 67.

Wójcik, D. (2013a) 'The dark side of NY–LON: financial centres and the global financial crisis', *Urban Studies*, 50(13), pp. 2736–2752.

Wójcik, D. (2013b) 'Where governance fails: advanced business services and the offshore world', *Progress in Human Geography*, 37(3), pp. 330–347.

6

FINANCIAL ECOSYSTEMS AND ECOLOGIES

Andrew Leyshon

Introduction

This chapter discusses the rise of two related but distinct concepts about the organization of the financial system that each take their inspiration from ideas developed within the natural sciences: financial ecologies and financial ecosystems. Both of these concepts were developed in the early twenty-first century to create new understandings of endemic problems within the contemporary financial system: the uneven geographies of financial exclusion and precarity, on the one hand, and tendencies towards regular and destabilizing systemic crises, on the other. The chapter outlines the development of these concepts, and presents a critical review of their relative effectiveness in producing new insights into the workings of the contemporary financial system.

Borrowing concepts from science to use as heuristic tools to help explain social processes is not new; it has a long history in both the social sciences and the humanities more generally. This process, often described as 'metaphorical redescription' (Barnes, 1992; Bradie, 1998; Hatch, 1999), involves taking an idea from one field, where it is more or less established and understood, and then applying it within another field in an attempt to provide new insights and understandings. Lakoff and Johnson argues that the 'primary function of metaphor is to provide a partial understanding of one kind of experience in terms of another kind of experience' (1980: 153). By 'drawing similarities between something that is known and something that is not' (Barnes, 1996: 116), metaphorical redescription can help make sense of hitherto misunderstood processes, and/or destabilize and problematize seemingly established understandings of phenomena. These disruptive interpretative acts have been described by anthropologists and ethnologists as the process of 'making the familiar strange, and the strange familiar' (Comaroff and Comaroff, 1992: 6; Moore, 1998: 42).

Within studies of the economy, the process of appropriating and redeploying metaphors to facilitate understanding is both widespread and of long-standing. For example, early economic and political economy thinking was strongly influenced by metaphors imported from medicine (Clément and Desmedt, 2009), which partly explains the persistence of the notion of an economic *crisis*. Derived from medical Latin, a crisis denotes a decisive point in the progress of a disease or an affliction. When in a *critical* condition, patients are between recovery and death, and it is this medical tipping point that is evoked in an economic crisis. As political economy evolved into neoclassical economics during the late nineteenth century, it did so by borrowing heavily from the scientific discipline of physics and, in particular, understandings of the dynamic force of energy, for which it substituted the notion of utility. This explains the importance within economics of the notion of equilibrium, as well as the use of mathematical methods, also borrowed from physics, which brought both prestige and scientific respectability to the discipline (Mirowski, 1989). Meanwhile, during its quantitative turn in the 1960s geography rather belatedly followed the path of economics by also borrowing from physics. Geography developed concepts such as the gravity model, where distance and associated transport costs are seen to act as a friction to movement, to explain the geography of settlements and of economic activity. In doing so, the quantitative turn developed a repertoire of mathematical methods and modelling techniques (Barnes, 1996), until they were more or less abandoned in the 1970s in a turn towards political economy and social theory (Thrift, 1999). Meanwhile, in the cognate discipline of management and business studies (Wells, 2006), scientific metaphors have tended to be borrowed from the fields of biology, evolution, and ecology. The reasons for this, Wells suggests, is what he claims is an 'affinity between the evolutionary principle of the survival of the fittest, and the process of competition in which the most efficient firm prevails over all others' (Wells, 2006: 115). A similar neo-Darwinian perspective has also informed recent thinking in economics, where evolutionary approaches have emerged to challenge the primacy of the physics inspired equilibrium approaches of the mainstream discipline (Arthur, 1989, 1999; Hodgson, 1999). These, in turn, have influenced and intermingled with management studies and economic geography research that have been inspired by an evolutionary perspective (Blauwhof, 1994; Boschma and Martin, 2007; Grabher and Stark, 1997; Grabher, 2009; Martin and Sunley, 2007; Morgan and Murdoch, 2000).

The concepts of financial ecosystems and financial ecologies, which are the focus of this chapter, take their inspiration from ideas first developed in this latter domain; that is, of biology, evolution, and ecology. Moreover, participants from the three main academic disciplines referred to above have influenced thinking around financial ecosystems and financial ecologies: economics, geography, and business/management. In addition, both concepts have been appropriated and developed by that layer of academically informed but typically practically oriented research and opinion produced by what Thrift describes as the 'cultural circuit of capital'; namely, management consultants and think tanks seeking to inform and influence corporate executives and managers, and public policy-makers (Leyshon et al., 2005; Thrift, 2001, 2005). This has ensured that the concepts have gained traction as modes of explanation and justification within the very industries that they purport to describe and explain.

The remainder of this chapter is organized as follows. The next section looks at the development of the concepts of ecosystems and ecologies, and the ways in which they have been used more broadly within the social science literature, with a particular focus on business and management research. The chapter goes on to look at the concept of the financial ecology that took inspiration from the rise of network approaches in a range of disciplines and is distinctly bottom-up in its approach, drawing inspiration from actor-network theory and directing attention to presences and absences in financial networks. The subsequent section looks at the rise of the concept of financial ecosystems, an integrative top down approach that has its roots in complexity theory and has been used to draw attention to the systemic problems of financial risk and crisis. The chapter concludes with suggestions for a possible way forward.

Ecology and Economy

The concept of ecology has been defined as a scientific endeavour 'primarily concerned with the non-human world and, more specifically, with the complex relations between organisms and their environment' (Prudham, 2009: 175), and often understood as 'the science of environment' (Prudham, 2009: 176). The origins of ecological thinking have been traced back as far as Ancient Greece, although the modern concept is usually dated to the mid-nineteenth century and the coining of the neologism 'oecologie' by biologist and Darwin acolyte Ernst Haecker (Benton, 1994; Prudham, 2009). A core ecological focus is on the interconnections and arrangements of often distinctive flora and fauna, located within specific environmental contextual conditions—such as climate, geology, topography, etc.—that can be stable over time, but that can also be subject to occasional disruption and change. It is this idea—a stable system liable to disruptive change—that has appeal in narratives of the economy. In acts of metaphorical redescription, firms, institutions, and other economic actors take the place of flora and fauna, while variations in culture, regulation, and infrastructure form an 'economic environment' within which such interconnections and interactions take place. Acts of metaphorical redescription between ecology and economy were relatively straightforward, partly because of the historical circulation of ideas between these disciplines; the development of ecology itself was influenced strongly by eighteenth- and nineteenth-century concepts of an 'economy of nature' and the ways in which energy was seen to flow and recycle through an ecological system.

Ecology also shared a common foundation with economics in the notion of equilibrium and stasis, although by the twentieth century factors such as dynamism, fragility, and change had begun to be considered, following the introduction of the concept of the 'ecosystem' (Adams, 2009; Tansley, 1935). An ecosystem was taken to represent 'the sum total of the physical, chemical and biological entities and processes in a given place, with emphasis on the interactions between the physio-chemical and biological components' (Cooper, 2003: 63). The genesis of the ecosystem concept was strongly influenced by physics, not least because Tansey, based at the University of Cambridge, had been influenced by the 'brilliant progress' that physics had made in the University's Cavendish Laboratory, and that influenced his interpretation of ecological evolution as a machine-like process (Keller and Golley, 2000: 26). This influence can be seen in Tansley's foundational contribution, where he voices concerns about 'the relative instability of the ecosystem', which he considers to be a result of 'the imperfections of its equilibrium, is of all degrees of magnitude, and our means of appreciating and measuring it are still very rudimentary' (1935: 302).

While the ecosystem concept has proved contentious within ecology—Keller and Golley argue that it is doubtful whether any other recent ecological concept had attracted such widespread and vituperative comment (2000: 27)—it has proved highly influential and productive elsewhere, not least in the disciplines of economics, geography, and business (Adams, 2009). Moreover, it is deployed routinely in language beyond the academy as a handy heuristic device, and currently has significant traction within everyday accounts of the economic world. Indeed, searching for the term in leading economic and financial newspapers reveals the ubiquity of the concept, due to its being a taken-for-granted organizational concept within the modern economy. A search for 'ecosystem' on the website of the *Financial Times* in the summer of 2019 produced over 3,000 hits. While the articles include a few items on subjects that would be of direct interest to ecologists, most of the reports referred to ecosystems as economic entities, in ways that seem a long way from their ecological roots. For example, there are articles about ecosystems in the realms of, *inter alia*, artificial intelligence, banking, brewing, digital and platform businesses, drug development, global brands, mobile phones, technology, and tourism. The ecosystem has become a ubiquitous term in descriptions of contemporary business arrangements, often used in an aspirational way, as a form of organization and a geography *to be achieved* that, if manifested, may deliver competitive advantages to companies and business. How has this come to be?

One attempt to answer this question has been made by Zoltan Acs and others (Acs et al., 2017) in contributions to a themed issue of the journal *Small Business Economics*. Across several articles, the contributors focus on the rise of what they describe as the rise of an *entrepreneurial ecosystems approach*. They draw attention to the ways an ecological and ecosystem approach is advocated as a means of incubating and accelerating new business ideas and ventures (e.g., see Acs et al., 2017; Brown and Mason, 2017; Bruns et al., 2017; Sussan and Acs, 2017). In this work, the link to the ecological origins of the ecosystem concept is justified as follows:

> an ecosystem is about performance and performance is what economics is about. The more nuanced answer is that economics has always been about the systems that explain differential output (economic behavior) and outcomes (aggregate welfare). Entrepreneurship is an important output of such systems—it is both enabled and constrained by its context and an important mechanism to explain the outcome of economic systems.
>
> (Acs et al., 2017; 2)

The power of the ecosystem as a concept for both describing and explaining contemporary business practices is its perceived flexibility, which is most often used to express both 'a spatial logic and a level of relational interactivity' (Brown and Mason, 2017: 22). Thus, the term 'ecosystem' is sometimes used to describe innovations around technological platforms, based on particular kinds of operating systems, which are proliferative of related hardware and software applications and which can capture large shares of the markets in which they operate (Andersson Schwarz, 2017; Bratton, 2015; Gillespie, 2017; Langley and Leyshon, 2017; McAfee and Brynjolfsson, 2017; Srnicek, 2016). These platform ecosystems *may* have a geography, associated with key centres of technological innovation, but a spatial expression of these arrangements is not critical to the use in this context. This flexible use—being both spatial and organizational—has contributed greatly to its circulation within debates about the contemporary economy due to the interest in the apparent 'winner takes all logic' of platform forms of organization (Kenney and Zysman, 2016, 2018).

This non-spatial use of ecosystems both supplements and complements the use of the concept to refer to particular geographical arrangements, which Brown and Mason identify as merely the 'latest conceptual tool designed to shed light on…centripetal agglomerative forces' (2017: 13) that help to produce uneven economic geographies. Ecosystems here build on the work that began in the late 1970s and early 1980s on identifying Marshallian Industrial Districts in the Third Italy. This research mapped broader clusters of leading-edge economic activity, regional innovation systems and more recently 'technological competence blocs' (Brown and Mason, 2017: 13). In common with these longer-standing concepts, the more novel idea of *entrepreneurial ecosystems* has been developed by the cultural circuit of capital, shaped within public policy recommendations and traded in consultancy reports. The description of these ecosystems makes them appear very much like the earlier agglomerations that have circulated through the academic, consultancy and policy literature since the 1980s:

> The concept of ecosystems is an inherently dynamic one which acknowledges the importance of entrepreneurial processes and cognitive belief systems which underpin interactions within an economy…

> The crucial aspects of ecosystems are the actors, processes and institutions [including] start-ups…large firms, universities, public sector bodies, health care systems, banks and stock markets.
>
> (Brown and Mason, 2017: 15)

Thus, a concept that helps to explain the instability of the economy over time has itself now become stabilized within the academic and cultural circuit of capital accounts of economic change. But, although the ecosystem metaphor draws attention to instability, it does so in a broadly positive way, as disruption is seen as temporary with the system, only changing in appropriate ways in response to broader environmental conditions, with arrangements of actors and institutions that emerge to prominence that are better suited to the imperatives of the time. Indeed, work of this kind is, for the most part, focused on growth, seeking to identify and explain new and dynamic parts of the economy. In this sense, it carries further similarities with the academic literature that sought to identify and name the dynamic agglomerations and clusters that appeared amid the wider problems of economic structural decline in the 1970 and 1980s, because these new economic spaces offered economic growth and expansion in a wider environment of structural decline (see Henry and Dawley, 2011).

However, the 1970s was also the period in which ecological theory took a theoretical turn that moved it away from the mechanistic assumptions of equilibrium borrowed from nineteenth-century physics, incorporating instead ideas from complexity theory that undermined ideas of a self-correcting 'balance of nature'. Rather, it saw the natural world not only as being more than merely unstable, but also as highly fragile—a world that was precarious with non-linear trajectories. These ideas would, in turn, also be appropriated and then incorporated in economic accounts that would lead to the development of the concept of financial ecosystems, which emanated initially from a key node of the financial regulatory system: the Bank of England. Contemporary ecological ideas were retooled to help rethink the relative precarity of the financial system that had hitherto been seen as robust, adaptable, and self-healing, but which needed urgent and significant intervention from governments and taxpayers to prevent its total collapse.

But, before addressing this work, we turn first to a less heralded body of work that emerged from economic geography and which sought to explain the spatial variability of the financial system in ecological terms, but did so from a different perspective. Rather than focus on the dynamics of the system in its *totality*, the financial ecology approach looked at the formation of distinctive arrangements of institutions, markets, and economic actors in particular configurations of geographical space. Significantly, the initial focus was on an ecology that was a significant point of weakness within the global financial system: the ecology of the sub-prime market.

Financial Ecologies: The Material Consequences of Networks

The financial ecology concept is inherently relational and seeks to emphasize the ways in which the workings of the financial system generate outcomes that are uneven in their connectivity and constitutive properties, which, in turn, produces distinctive socio-spatial inequalities. The ways in which different people, places, and institutions are connected to the financial system matters, and produces material outcomes in the form of ecologies that can vary markedly in scope, form, and levels of resilience. The concept apprehends the financial system as being made up of a constellation of distinctive and dynamic constitutive ecologies that are, in turn, made up of varying levels of financial knowledge, by different modes of financial intermediation, and variable subjectivities, which unfold across space and evolve in relation to geographical differences. According to Karen Lai (2016, 30), 'the ecologies concept can offer…topological finesse around questions of why particular sets of relations are more durable or porous, allowing for a more precise consideration of power in relational thinking'.

The concept of financial ecology was first developed as part of ongoing research into the geographies of financial exclusion (Leyshon et al., 2004, 2006). The work was seeking to explore an idea linked to a notion of 'financial citizenship', whereby some individuals may be located firmly 'inside' the financial system. They enjoy the privileges of citizenship by having access to financial services at competitive market rates that provide credit and debt at affordable levels, and assist with income smoothing and with the purchase and accumulation of assets over time. However, others may be denied such privileges, existing either outside the mainstream financial system, or only partially connected to it. Thus, the spatial arrangement of the financial system may resemble a network that connects to some places better than others and that is disconnected from, or only partially connected to, other places. The variegated engagement of these networks over geographical spaces is the process that carves out different kinds of financial ecologies.

The concept was clearly influenced by ecological thinking, although it was one step removed, not imported directly from natural science but, rather, from its previous appropriation by research in science and technology studies and actor-network theory, which viewed the development of society as the evolution of various kinds of socio-technical network. The financial ecology concept was influenced by earlier attempts to use an ecological approach to understand technological systems that argued that systems are no more and no less than a combination of myriad interrelated technological and informational ecologies. Viewing systems in this way is an overtly political strategy; by decomposing systems to the level of the different ecologies that constitute them, it becomes possible 'to find individual points of leverage, ways into the system, and avenues of intervention' (Nardi and O'Day, 1999: 50). Such a strategy is important when confronted with a system that seems to be an opaque 'black box' that would otherwise resist attempts to understand it and limit critique of its operating logics (MacKenzie, 2010).

The concept of the financial ecology seeks to draw an analogy between the organization of retail financial services and ecosystems, whereby certain arrangements emerge that are reproducible over time. These processes unfold across space and evolve in relation to geographical difference so that distinctive ecologies of financial knowledge and practice emerge in different places. This approach is focused particularly on the interrelationship between institutions and actors in space, and the ways in which different competences and practices evolve to enable these ecologies to reproduce themselves (or not). For heuristic purposes, two idealized financial ecologies were theorized. The first ecology is that of the middle-class suburb, probably the most important site in the everyday reproduction of the mainstream financial system. This ecology contains what is described as the 'prime' market of retail financial consumers, made up of individuals and households that generate the feedstock of the global financial system in the form of regular savings and investments, on the one hand, and payments for debt products such as mortgages and loans, on the other. Thus, the 'prime' financial ecology is one with high levels of competition between retail financial services providers and, as a result, offers a relatively wide product choice for its inhabitants, based on their levels of income, the value of their existing assets, and anticipated linear and progressive subjectivities. At an aggregate level, such ecologies would also possess relatively high levels of financial knowledge or financial literacy (Finlayson, 2009; Leyshon, Thrift, and Pratt, 1998), with strong and frequent connections to the financial services industry as a whole.

The second ecology was that of 'sub-prime'. This was an ecology that had largely been ignored or downgraded by the mainstream financial services industry, ensuring that very different arrangements of institutions, customers, and financial services emerged. In the United Kingdom, these ecologies included areas that scored highly on indices of multiple deprivation (Leyshon et al., 2006) and suffered higher than average closures of bank and building society branches during the 1990s (Leyshon, French, and Signoretta, 2008). This was despite these closures taking place against an already low base, as these areas were never particularly important to the mainstream industry and had attracted few branches. In the United States, sub-prime financial ecologies tended to be inner city areas, where the majority of sub-prime mortgages were issued, mostly to African-American and Hispanic borrowers (Langley, 2008; Newman and Wainwright, 2009; Newman and Wyly, 2004; Wyly et al., 2006, 2009).

Cash preferences and the riskiness posed by the non-linear subjectivities of people living at the economic margins meant that the financial services firms that saw market opportunities in these spaces were different to those in the prime ecology, with distinctive products and distribution networks.

These products and distribution networks were not new; indeed, in the United Kingdom, such spaces could be described as possessing 'relic' financial ecologies because, in the twenty-first century, they were still being served by door-to-door delivery systems first developed in the nineteenth century that had long been abandoned by most mainstream firms. The purpose of framing the spatial manifestation of relations between financial institutions, markets, and economic agents in place as ecologies was not only to help promote a developmental understanding of such arrangements, but also to consider the wider sustainability and desirability of different ecologies within the context of normative evaluations about social justice, 'the injuries of class and race', and uneven economic development.

Over time, the concept was taken up and developed in related studies of geographies of money. It enabled economic geographers to explore the relationship between space, financial institutions, and the socio-economic status of financial subjects in a range of different contexts. This research ranged from attempts to recognize the significance of space and place within studies of financialization (French, Leyshon, and Wainwright, 2011), and included detailed studies of the impact of financialization on lived experience in deprived rural areas (Coppock, 2013), as well as depictions of the emergence of financial ecologies even more privileged than the prime market; namely, the coalescence of private wealth management and independent financial advice services in key financial centres serving 'high net worth individuals' and families (Beaverstock, Hall, and Wainwright, 2013; Lai, 2016). The concept has also circulated within cognate disciplines, such as anthropology, where Maurer (2015, loc. 528) has drawn attention to 'the complex money ecologies of people around the world, and people's elaborate and diverse repertoires for using money as they navigate and add to those ecologies', and in public policy research (see, e.g., Ossandón et al., 2011).

The identification of sub-prime ecologies in the earliest incarnation of this concept was perhaps prescient, for it was in such spaces in the United States that the debt problems that led to the global financial crisis of 2008 first manifested. The development of financial products targeted at low-income consumers with erratic credit histories were initially heralded as a device that could break the barriers of financial inclusion and exclusion, by using credit scoring algorithms to unearth 'good' credit risks at a distance in ways that were unavailable to financial institutions using more traditional methods of credit evaluation (MacDonald, 1996). Customers with non-linear subjectivities that may, after all, be 'good for their debt' could now perhaps be identified with just a little more careful analysis and an appropriate risk-pricing strategy (Burton et al., 2004; Marron, 2007). At least, that is what the advocates of such techniques claimed, who had been persuaded to believe this, given the profitability of 'sub-prime loans'. These profits, and the growth of the Originate to Redistribute model in banking, saw the issuers of these loans quickly repackage the repayments they received into tradeable securities such as Collateral Debt

Obligations. The initial returns on these investments fuelled the market still further, as did the demand from borrowers who, until this point, been denied access to such easy credit by the mainstream financial system.

The collapse of the sub-prime market triggered the global financial crisis. One of the puzzles of the crisis was precisely why the financial system failed so catastrophically, given that the bad debt was generated in a financial ecology that made up a relatively small part of the wider financial ecosystem (Haldane, 2009), and was of a level that, on its own, should have generated asymmetric outcomes where harm was concentrated most heavily among defaulting borrowers and the banks most involved in this market. That the crisis was so widespread encouraged some key actors in the global financial regulatory arena to turn back to ecological thinking both for clues and for new forms of interpretive inspiration.

Financial Ecosystems: Finance as a Complex Adaptive System

In retrospect, it seems strange that the warning signals that indicated that a crisis was building in the United States residential mortgage market were ignored for so long. One reason was the widespread belief in public policy circles that processes of financial innovation and reregulation had evolved in lockstep over time to produce an efficient and largely self-regulating system. This system appeared to work effectively to evaluate and price risks, and to ensure that capital was allocated to its best and most productive use. The power and influence of neoliberal ideology, and the apparent victory of neoclassical theory and what Mirowski (2013) describes as a broader 'Neoliberal Thought Collective', encouraged submission to the logic of the market. In doing so, it drew from the ideas of Hayek, who harboured a distrust of experts, whom he 'accused of essentially serving as little more than apologists for whomever employs them', and promoted, instead, 'a core conviction that the market really does know better than any one of us what is good for ourselves and for society, and that includes the optimal allocation of ignorance within the populace' (Mirowski, 2013, loc. 1608). But while Hayek's ideas may be implicated in fomenting the crisis, as work by Melinda Cooper and Jeremy Walker reveals (Cooper, 2011; Walker and Cooper, 2011), his ideas also bear a similarity to a radical rethinking of ecological theory that began in the early 1970s—a rethinking that rejected equilibrium in nature and helped develop new responses to crisis.

The origins of this rethinking were the work of ecologist Crawford Hollings. He sought to move his field 'away from the mechanistic assertions of equilibrium typical of postwar cybernetics and towards the contemporary 'complexity science' view of ecosystems' (Walker and Cooper, 2011: 145). This was to have profound impacts on the understanding of concepts of resilience and sustainability across a range of subjects and domains:

> The key image of science that propelled the formalization of economics (in the 1870s) and ecology (in the 1950s) was one of smooth and continuous returns to equilibrium after shock, an image derived from different vintages of classical mechanics and thermodynamics. Holling's (1973) widely cited paper 'Resilience and Stability of Ecological Systems' represents the destabilization of the notion of 'equilibrium' as the core of the ecosystem concept and the normal terminus of ecosystem trajectory, and the beginning of a major shift among ecologists away from the notion that there exists a 'balance of nature' to which life will return if left to self-repair.
>
> (ibid.)

The radical message of Holling's work was not just that systems may be inherently unstable, but also that a belief that systems would automatically stabilize was in itself *inherently destabilizing*. It inculcated undue faith in the ability of systems to right themselves over the long term. In other words, 'the equilibrium approach was dangerous in its abstraction: glossing over the unknowing complex interdependencies of specific landscapes pressed into the conditions of maximum yield, it accelerated the process of fragilization, potentially leading to the irreversible loss of biodiversity' (Walker and Cooper, 2011: 146). Moreover, while Hollings did not argue that ecosystems could not stabilize over the long term, his work and that of his followers later introduced the possibility of a new phase, *collapse*, which introduced a new kind of jeopardy and risk:

> all ecosystem and all socio-ecological system dynamics can be approached heuristically as non-linear iterations of an 'adaptive cycle', in which four distinct phases can be identified. Where classical systems ecology focused only on the phases of rapid successional growth (*r*) followed by the conservation phase of stable development (K)…[Hollings] argues that these phases are inevitably followed by collapse (Ω), and then a spontaneous reorganization that leads to a new growth phase (α).
>
> (Walker and Cooper, 2011: 147)

Cooper and Walker argue that while Hollings did not directly cite Hayek, the latter's ideas on the futility of planning and regulation, and the impossibility of intervening positively in highly complex systems, meant that there was greater willingness to adopt a non-equilibrating approach. Hayek's work about the problem of establishing *ex ante* systems of coordination, where there are myriad actors and points of contact, gained traction across the political divide, based on the problems faced by large coordination problems, such as in central planning and other forms of bureaucracy within an extended division of labour (Sayer, 1995: 55–63).

By the 1990s, these ideas had encouraged a proliferation of work that could be captured under the broader title of 'complexity theory', which constituted a collective set of related concepts including 'non-linearity, self-organization, emergent order and complex adaptive systems' (Thrift, 1999: 34):

> Most of the many writers on complexity theory...usually lay claim to a whole series of fields of study which they assert are a part of this impulse, including chaos theory, fractal modelling, artificial life, cellular automata, neural nets and the like, and to a companion vocabulary which has become both technical and metaphorical—chaos, attractors, fractals, emergent orders, self-organization, implicate order, autopoiesis, life at the edge of chaos, and so on.
>
> (Thrift, 1999: 34)

These ideas gradually gained recognition and credibility across a range of scientific disciplines, helped by key nodes of knowledge creation and dissemination such as the Santa Fe Institute in New Mexico and the Cato Institute in Washington, DC. Significantly for the argument in this chapter, complexity theory also gained purchase within business circles through its promulgation by the cultural circuit of capital, a heterodox group of actors that includes business school academics, consultants, journalists, and practitioners that develop abstract and practical theories about the working of the contemporary economy (Leyshon et al. 2005; Thrift, 2001, 2002, 2005). The cultural circuit of capital was attracted to the ideas within complexity theory because it provided a way to explain to managers that they should embrace and accept the levels of anxiety they faced in their jobs by the need to comprehend and react to a fast-moving dynamic economy. Complexity began to circulate as a business idea because of its links to cybernetics and systems theory, which had a long history in management science. Reimagining the economy as a complex adaptive system gave greater authority to the use of metaphors that became guides to practical action within organizations facing volatile and unpredictable changes in the business environment, and already routinely using terms and practices such as 'flexibility', 're-engineering', 'downsizing', and 'outsourcing', for example.

By the mid-2000s, these ideas had captured the attention of central bankers, and paved the way for the development of a concept that saw finance as a complex adaptive system, a *financial ecosystem*. Walker and Cooper (2011: 151) reveal that, as early as 2006, the Federal Reserve Bank of New York had organized a conference to explore the utility of using complexity models developed within ecological studies as a means of understanding contemporary financial markets. At the conclusion of the conference, it was pronounced that 'systemic risk' in the financial system bears a strong resemblance to the dynamics of many complex adaptive systems in the physical worlds, so that it may be possible to import risk management techniques from natural and physical systems into attempts to improve the regulation and management of financial risk.

However, there was insufficient time to put these ideas into practice before the global financial crisis became manifest from 2007 onwards. Founded originally in sub-prime housing debt in the United States, but amplified through complex derivatives, the depth and severity of the crisis necessitated significant and expensive government interventions in financial markets, including expensive rounds of nationalization and bailouts. In its wake, policy-makers and regulators embarked on a rethink as to how to regulate financial systems to prevent the necessity for such radical interventions in the future (Christophers, Leyshon, and Mann, 2017).

One central banker went further than most in exploring how to reimagine the financial system as a complex adaptive ecosystem: Andrew Haldane, currently Deputy Governor of the Bank of England. In 2009, when he was Executive Director of Financial Stability at the Bank, Haldane addressed the Financial Student Association in Amsterdam, setting out an argument for considering the financial system as a complex adaptive system (Haldane, 2009). He argued that, in the build up to the crisis, the financial system could be characterized as a network that was not only increasingly complex, but also increasingly homogeneous—qualities in environmental systems that would point to considerable systemic risk. By the middle of the first decade of the twenty-first century, the financial system was 'both robust and fragile—a property exhibited by other complex adaptive networks, such as tropical rainforests' (Haldane, 2009: 3). In other words, while the process of financial innovation appeared to have introduced a healthy level of diversity and robustness into the financial system, as many new products were brought into being to aid risk management, these products also increased complexity and uncertainty. Meanwhile, diversity was 'gradually eroded by institutions' business and risk management strategies, making the whole system less resistant to disturbance—mirroring the futures of marine ecosystems whose diversity has been steadily eroded and whose susceptibility to collapse has thereby increased' (Haldane, 2009: 4).

Haldane thanked the biologist Robert May for his support in his acknowledgements to the above paper, and later co-authored a paper with him that sought to develop a scientifically robust model for the original argument set out in 2009 (Haldane and May, 2011). In so doing, Haldane and May refer directly to the transformation in ecological thinking in the 1970s that moved ecology away from a faith in a naturally equilibrating system:

> In the wake of the global financial crisis that began in 2007, there is increasing recognition of the need to address risk at the systemic level, as distinct from focusing on individual banks.This quest to understand the network dynamics of what might be called 'financial ecosystems' has interesting parallels with ecology in the 1970s. Implicit in much economic thinking in general, and financial mathematics in particular, is the notion of a 'general equilibrium'. Elements of this belief underpin, for example, the pricing of complex derivatives. But, as shown below, deeper analysis of such systems reveals explicit analogies with

> the concept that too much complexity implies instability, which was found earlier in model ecosystems.
>
> (2011: 351)

Given the similarities of the systems, Haldane and May advocate that financial regulation should also draw public policy lessons from the ecological sphere, by ensuring that future regulation needs to have a system-wide perspective to promote and manage 'resilience'. Thus, past regulatory interventions to limit risk exposure, such as the stipulations laid down by the Basel Committee on Bank Supervision (Basel I, and Basel II), which require cash reserves to be set in relation to the accumulation of assets, are based on individual institutional risk, not systemic risk. This was clearly inadequate. Regulation should be 'operated countercyclically, with buffers rising in booms and falling in recessions' because 'increasing insurance in a boom would increase system-wide resilience against the subsequent bust, as well as providing an incentive for banks to curb risk-taking during a boom' (Haldane and May, 2011: 354).

This new way of viewing the financial system has led to changes in ways in which regulators approach the financial system, and introduced a new vocabulary of intervention and surveillance, one that moves away from a blind faith in the logic of the market and a sense that things will equilibrate over time. Hence, this kind of radical thinking has encouraged 'new methods of futurology, contingency planning and crisis response onto the [financial] policy reform agenda' (Walker and Cooper, 2011: 152).

While Haldane's contributions here, and his writings elsewhere on the consequences of the financial crisis (e.g., Haldane, 2012, 2014, 2015), represent an important and significant intervention—not least, because of where he is located, at the heart of the global financial network—the mobilization of the concept of the financial ecosystem has not escaped criticism. For example, while Erturk et al. (2011) applaud Haldane's effort to bring new ways of apprehending the financial system to bear in service of better ways of regulating and controlling it in order to prevent a future financial cataclysm, they argue that his vision of imposing regulatory order is limited by the metaphors of redescription that he chooses to employ. Seeking to impose regulation at a systemic level to prevent reckless risk-taking underestimates the ability of individual institutions to respond reflexively to new regulations to ensure that they are always one step ahead of the game. Drawing on their substantial body of work on the financial crisis (Engelen et al., 2010, 2011; Erturk et al., 2010), Erturk et al. argue that the capacity for financial innovation escapes the framing of the financial system in network and/or ecological terms due to the importance of reflexivity in the operation of financial system (Dodd, 1994):

> financial innovation takes the form of bricolage which builds structures from events…so that regulatory change is often not a constraint on innovation but an input for the next phase, as was the case

> with derivatives after the Basel II regulations on capital adequacy... Mapping the financial network in an attempt to identify and vaccinate the superspreaders would therefore probably encourage the development of different kinds of securities or a reshaping of markets to frustrate or game the controlling intervention. Once financial actors learn that regulators are using particular measures to assess risk based on a particular model of network, they will move to areas not visible on the map, or find ways of making money by a kind of arbitrage on mapping rules and procedures.
>
> (Erturk, et al., 2011: 401)

Moreover, notwithstanding such concerns, there has, in any case, been very little attempt to put much new regulatory thinking in place. Mervyn King—who, as governor of the Bank of England, signed off on the engagement between natural scientists and employees such as Andrew Haldane—argued in a speech to the International Monetary Fund that a decade on from the crisis that there has been a systemic failure to recognize the radical uncertainty that faces actors within the financial system, and the dangers of a pervasive faith in equilibrium and the rectifying power of markets:

> a market economy, although by far the best means we have discovered for promoting prosperity, does not have self-stabilising properties... The failure of conventional models to capture the reasons for weak growth of the world economy, and the failure to establish a proper *ex ante* framework for the provision of central bank liquidity in a crisis, reflect an intellectual and political unwillingness to challenge the conventional wisdom. 75 years ago, the IMF was borne out of a commitment to radical reforms to the international financial system. At Bretton Woods, half a century of global conflict was a powerful incentive to contemplate something new. Is not a global financial crisis followed by more than a decade of secular stagnation sufficient to persuade economists and politicians to be equally radical?
>
> *(King, 2019: 16)*

Conclusions

This chapter has considered the development of financial ecologies and financial ecosystems. Although the concepts share a source of inspiration in ideas first developed in ecological thinking, they are also markedly different in their scope and approach. The idea of the financial ecology was inspired by the deployment of network approaches across a range of disciplines and was seen to be distinctly bottom-up in its approach, focusing attention on presences and absences in financial networks. It focused on the sub-prime ecology, which was later revealed as a key site of weakness in the global financial system leading up to the global financial crisis. The concept of financial ecosystems, in contrast, was an integrative top-down approach with its roots in complexity theory, and was used to draw attention to the systemic problems of financial risk and crisis.

Perhaps one way forward would be for work to explore links between these concepts, bridging the gaps between the scale and scope of financial ecologies and financial ecosystems, to show how engagement with the uneven material geographies of the financial system can create further new ways of thinking about the hidden dangers in abstracted financial products. However, given the inability of these ideas to do much to shift current thinking about the inherent risk that the financial system poses to the future viability of the economic system, perhaps advocates of financial reform should learn lessons from those protesting the dangers of an imminent global ecological disaster in the form of climate change. This action does seem to have moved the dangers of an imminent climate crisis up the policy agenda. Perhaps making efforts to link ideas of financial ecologies and ecosystems to research that is already beginning to explore the links between financial markets and the ecosystems and environments (see, e.g., Bridge et al., 2019; Leichenko, O'Brien, and Solecki, 2010) would be the next logical step forward.

Acknowledgements

I would like to thank Janelle Knox-Hayes and Dariusz Wójcik not only for inviting me to contribute to this volume, but also for their considerable patience as the time taken for me to complete the chapter kept extending. I am also grateful to Adam Algar, for kindly lending me some books on ecology that helped establish the origins of work in this tradition, and to Paul Langley for alerting me to the important work of Melinda Cooper and Jeremy Walker on financial ecosystems.

References

Acs, Z. J., E. Stam, D. B. Audretsch, and A. O'Connor. (2017). The lineages of the entrepreneurial ecosystem approach. *Small Business Economics* 49 (1):1–10.

Adams, B. (2009). Ecosystem. In *The Dictionary of Human Geography*, eds. D. Gregory, R. Johnston, G. Pratt, M. J. Watts, and S. Whatmore, 185–186. Oxford: Blackwell.

Andersson Schwarz, J. (2017). Platform logic: An interdisciplinary approach to the platform-based economy. *Policy & Internet* 9 (4):374–394.

Arthur, B. W. (1989). Competing technologies, increasing returns, and lock-in by historical events. *The Economic Journal* 99:116–131.

———. (1999). The end of economic certainty. In *The Biology of Business: Decoding the Natural Laws of Enterprise*, ed. J. H. Clippinger, 31–47. San Francisco, CA: Jossey-Bass.

Barnes, T. J. (1992). Reading the texts of theoretical economic geography. In *Writing Worlds*, eds. T. J. Barnes and J. Duncan, 118–135. London: Routledge.

Barnes, T. J. (1996). *Logics of Dislocation: Models, Metaphors, and Meanings of Economic Space*. New York: Guilford Press.

Beaverstock, J. V., S. Hall, and T. Wainwright. (2013). Servicing the super-rich: New financial elites and the rise of the private wealth management retail ecology. *Regional Studies* 47 (6):834–849.

Benton, T. (1994). Ecology. In *The Blackwell Dictionary of Twentieth Century Social Thought*, eds. W. Outhwaite and T. Bottomore, 173–174. Oxford: Blackwell.

Blauwhof, G. (1994). Non-equilibria and the sociology of technology. In *Evolutionary Economics and Chaos Theory*, eds. L. Leydesdorff and P. V. D. Desselaar, 152–166. London: Pinter.

Boschma, R., and R. Martin. (2007). Editorial: Constructing an evolutionary economic geography. *Journal of Economic Geography* 7 (5):537–548.

Bradie, M. (1998). Explanation as metaphorical redescription. *Metaphor and Symbol* 13 (2):125–139.

Bratton, B. H. (2015). *The Stack: On Software and Sovereignty/Benjamin H. Bratton*. Cambridge, MA; London: MIT Press.

Bridge, G., H. Bulkeley, P. Langley, and B. van Veelen. Pluralizing and problematizing carbon finance.(2019). *Progress in Human Geography* 0 (0):0309132519856260.

Brown, R., and C. Mason. (2017). Looking inside the spiky bits: A critical review and conceptualisation of entrepreneurial ecosystems. *Small Business Economics* 49 (1):11–30.

Bruns, K., N. Bosma, M. Sanders, and M. Schramm. (2017). Searching for the existence of entrepreneurial ecosystems: A regional cross-section growth regression approach. *Small Business Economics* 49 (1):31–54.

Burton, D., D. Knights, A. Leyshon, C. Alferoff, and P. Signoretta. (2004). Making a market: The UK retail financial services industry and the rise of the complex sub-prime credit market. *Competition & Change* 8 (1):3–25.

Christophers, B., A. Leyshon, and G. Mann. (2017). Money and finance after the crisis: Taking critical stock. In *Money and Finance after the Crisis: Critical Thinking for Uncertain Times*, eds. B. Christophers, A. Leyshon, and G. Mann, 1–40. New York: Wiley.

Clément, A., and L. Desmedt. (2009). Medicine and economics in pre-classical economics. In *Open Economics: Economics in Relation to Other Dsisciplines*, eds. R. Arena, S. Dow, and M. Klaes. London: Routledge.

Comaroff, J., and J. Comaroff. (1992). *Ethnography and the Historical Imagination*. Boulder, CO: Westview Press.

Cooper, G. J. (2003). *The Science of the Struggle for Existence: On the Foundations of Ecology*. Cambridge: Cambridge University Press.

Cooper, M. (2011). Complexity theory after the financial crisis. *Journal of Cultural Economy* 4 (4):371–385.

Coppock, S. (2013). The everyday geographies of financialisation: Impacts, subjects and alternatives. *Cambridge Journal of Regions, Economy and Society* 6 (3):479–500.

Dodd, N. (1994). *The Sociology of Money: Economics, Reason and Contemporary Society*. Cambridge: Polity.

Engelen, E., I. Erturk, J. Froud, A. Leaver, and K. Williams. (2010). Reconceptualizing financial innovation: Frame, conjuncture and bricolage. *Economy and Society* 39 (1):33–63.

Engelen, E., I. Erturk, J. Froud, S. Johal, A. Leaver, M. Moran, A. Nilsson, and K. Williams. (2011). *After the Great Complacence: Financial Crisis and the Politics of Reform*. Oxford: Oxford University Press.

Erturk, I., J. Froud, S. Johal, A. Leaver, and K. Williams. (2010). Ownership matters: Private equity and the political division of ownership. *Organization* 17 (5):543–561.

Erturk, I., J. Froud, A. Leaver, M. Moran, and K. Williams. (2011). Haldene's gambit. *Journal of Cultural Economy* 4 (4):387–404.

Finlayson, A. (2009). Financialisation, financial literacy and asset-based welfare. *British Journal of Politics & International Relations* 11 (3):400–421.

French, S., A. Leyshon, and T. Wainwright. (2011). Financializing space, spacing financialization. *Progress in Human Geography* 35 (6):798–819.

Gillespie, T. (2017). Is "platform" the right metaphor for the technology companies that dominate digital media? In *NiemanLab*, available at https://www.niemanlab.org/2017/08/is-platform-the-right-metaphor-for-the-technology-companies-that-dominate-digital-media/

Grabher, G. (2009). Yet another turn? The evolutionary project in economic geography. *Economic Geography* 85 (2):119–127.

Grabher, G., and D. Stark. (1997). Organizing diversity: Evolutionary theory, networks analysis and postsocialism. *Regional Studies* 31 (5):533–544.

Haldane, A. (April 2009). Rethinking the financial network. Speech delivered at the Financial Student Association, Amsterdam. Available at: http://tinyurl.com/396ybql.

———. (2012). The doom loop. *London Review of Books* 34 (5):21–22. https://www.lrb.co.uk/v34/n04/andrew-haldane/the-doom-loop.

———. (April 4, 2014). The age of asset management? Speech given by Andrew G Haldane, Executive Director, Financial Stability and member of the Financial Policy Committee. Available at: http://www.bankofengland.co.uk/publications/Documents/speeches/ 2014/speech723.pdf.

———. (June 30, 2015). Stuck. Speech given by Andrew G Haldane, Chief Economist, Bank of England. Availabe at: http://www.bankofengland.co.uk/publications/Documents/speeches/2015/speech828.pdf.

Haldane, A. G., and R. M. May. (2011). Systemic risk in banking ecosystems. *Nature* 469 (7330):351–355.

Hatch, M. J. (1999). Exploring the empty spaces of organizing: How improvisational Jazz helps redescribe organizational structure. *Organization Studies* 20 (1):75–100.

Henry, N., and S. Dawley. (2011). Geographies of economic growth 1: Industrial and technology regions. In *The SAGE Handbook of Economic Geography*, eds. A. Leyshon, R. Lee, L. McDowell, and P. Sunley, 273–285. London: SAGE.

Hodgson, G. M. (1999). *Economics and Utopia: Why the Learning Economy is Not the End of History*. London: Routledge.

Keller, D. R., and F. B. Golley. (2000). Entities and process in ecology. In *The Philosophy of Ecology: From Science to Synthesis*, eds. D. R. Keller and F. B. Golley, 21–33. Athens, GO: University of Georgia Press.

Kenney, M., and J. Zysman. (2016.) The rise of the platform economy. *Issues in Science and Technology* 32 (3).

———. (2018). Unicorns, cheshire cats, and the new dilemmas of entrepreneurial finance? Available at SSRN: https://papers.ssrn.com/sol3/papers.cfm?abstract_id=3220780.

King, M. (October 19, 2019). The world turned upside down: Economic policy turbulent times. The Per Jacobsson Lecture, Internationbal Monetary Fund. Available at: https://meetings.imf.org.

Lai, K. P. Y. (2016). Financial advisors, financial ecologies and the variegated financialisation of everyday investors. *Transactions of the Institute of British Geographers* 41 (1):27–40.

Lakoff, G., and M. Johnson. (1980). *Metaphors We Live By*. Chicago, IL: University of Chicago Press.

Langley, P. (2008). Sub-prime mortgage lending: A cultural economy. *Economy and Society* 37 (4):469–494.

Langley, P., and A. Leyshon. (2017). Platform capitalism: The intermediation and capitalisation of digital economic circulation. *Finance and Society* 3 (1):11–31.

Leichenko, R. M., K. L. O'Brien, and W. D. Solecki. (2010). Climate change and the global financial crisis: A case of double exposure. *Annals of the Association of American Geographers* 100 (4):963–972.

Leyshon, A., D. Burton, D. Knights, C. Alferoff, and P. Signoretta. (2004). Towards an ecology of retail financial services: Understanding the persistence of door-to-door credit and insurance providers. *Environment and Planning A* 36:625–645.

Leyshon, A., S. French, and P. Signoretta. (2008). Financial exclusion and the geography of bank and building society branch closure in Britain. *Transactions of the Institute of British Geographers* 33 (4):447–465.

Leyshon, A., S. French, N. Thrift, L. Crewe, and P. Webb. (2005). Accounting for e-commerce: Abstractions, virtualism and the cultural circuit of capital. *Economy and Society* 34 (3):428–450.

Leyshon, A., P. Signoretta, D. Knights, C. Alferoff, and D. Burton. (2006). Walking with moneylenders: The ecology of the UK home-collected credit industry. *Urban Studies* 43 (1):161–186.

Leyshon, A., N. Thrift, and J. Pratt. (1998). Reading financial services: Texts, consumers, and financial literacy. *Environment and Planning D-Society & Space* 16 (1):29–55.

MacDonald, H. (1996). The rise of mortgage-backed securities: Struggles to reshape access to credit in the USA. *Environment and Planning A* 28 (7):1179–1198.

MacKenzie, D. (2010). Opening the black boxes of global finance. In *Financial Markets and Organizational Technologies: System Architectures, Practices and Risks in the Era of Deregulation*, ed. A.-A. Kyrtsis, 92–116. London: Palgrave Macmillan UK.

Marron, D. (2007). 'Lending by numbers': Credit scoring and the constitution of risk within American consumer credit. *Economy and Society* 36 (1):103–133.

Martin, R., and P. Sunley. (2007). Complexity thinking and evolutionary economic geography. *Journal of Economic Geography* 7 (5):573–601.

Maurer, B. (2015). *How Would You Like to Pay? How Technology is Changing the Future of Money*. Durham, NC: Duke University Press.

McAfee, A., and E. Brynjolfsson. (2017). *Machine, Platform, Crowd: Harnessing Our Digital Future* New York: W. W. Norton & Company.

Mirowski, P. (1989). *More Heat Than Light : Economics as Social Physics, Physics as Nature's Economics*. Cambridge: Cambridge University Press.

———. (2013). *Never Let a Serious Crisis Go To Waste: How Neoliberalism Survived the Financial Meltdown*. London: Verso.

Moore, A. (1998). *Cultural Anthroplogy: The Field Study of Human Beings*. New York: Rowman & Littlefield.

Morgan, K., and J. Murdoch. (2000). Organic vs. conventional agriculture: Knowledge, power and innovation in the food chain. *Geoforum* 31 (2):159–173.

Nardi, B. A., and V. L. O'Day. (1999). *Informational Ecologies: Using Technology with Heart*. Cambridge, MA.: MIT Press.

Newman, K., and E. K. Wyly. (2004). Geographies of mortgage market segmentation: The case of Essex County, New Jersey. *Housing Studies* 19 (1):53–83.

Ossandón, J., T. Ariztía, M. Barros, and C. Peralta. (2011). *The Financial Ecologies and Circuits of Commerce of Retail Credit Cards in Santiago de Chile*. Santiago, Chile: Instituto de Investigación en Ciencias Sociales (ICSO) Universidad Diego Portales.

Prudham, S. (2009). Ecology. In *The Dictionary of Human Geography*, 5th Edition, eds. D. Gregory, R. Johnston, G. Pratt, M. J. Watts, and S. Whatmore, 175–177. Chichester: Wiley-Blackwell.

Sayer, A. (1995). *Radical Political Economy: A Critique*. Oxford: Blackwell.

Srnicek, N. (2016). *Platform Capitalism*. Cambridge: Polity.

Sussan, F., and Z. J. Acs. (2017). The digital entrepreneurial ecosystem. *Small Business Economics* 49 (1):55–73.

Tansley, A. J. (1935). The use and abuse of vegetational concepts and terms. *Ecology* 16:284–307.

Thrift, N. (1999). The place of complexity. *Theory Culture & Society* 16 (3):31–69.

———. (2001). 'It's the romance, not the finance, that makes the business worth pursuing': Disclosing a new market culture. *Economy and Society* 30 (4):412–432.

———. (2002). 'Think and act like revolutionaries': Episodes from the global triumph of management discourse. *Critical Quarterly* 44 (3):19–26.

———. (2005). *Knowing Capitalism*. London: Sage.

Wainwright, T. (2009). Laying the foundations for a crisis: Mapping the historico-geographical construction of residential mortgage backed securitization in the UK. *International Journal of Urban and Regional Research* 33 (2):372–388.

Walker, J., and M. Cooper. (2011). Genealogies of resilience: From systems ecology to the political economy of crisis adaptation. *Security Dialogue* 42 (2):143–160.

Wells, P. E. (2006). Re-writing the ecological metaphor: Part 1. *Progress in Industrial Ecology: An International Journal* 3 (1–2):114–128.

Wyly, E., M. Moos, D. Hammel, and E. Kabahizi. (2009). Cartographies of race and class: Mapping the class-monopoly rents of American Subprime Mortgage Capital. *International Journal of Urban and Regional Research* 33 (2):332–354.

Wyly, E. K., M. Atia, H. Foxcroft, D. J. Hammel, and K. Phillips-Watts. (2006). American home: Predatory mortgage capital and neighbourhood spaces of race and class exploitation in the United States. *Geografiska Annaler Series B-Human Geography* 88B (1):105–132.

PART II

Financial Assets and Markets

7

FROM COWRY SHELLS TO CRYPTOS

Evolving Geographies of Currency

Matthew Zook

While systems of money and currency are often couched as 'natural' solutions to the cumbersome requirements of barter, this understanding is fundamentally misleading. Far from a generalizable solution readily applied to all societies and spaces, the practices of money and forms of currency are inherently cultural and geographical. They emerge at particular moments in time and space, and are designed to solve particular problems, such as trade, exercising cultural or political power, or the inclusion or avoidance of particular actors. In short, money and currency are tied to the socially embedded process of technological change—be it metallurgical, mechanical, communicative, or encryption-based—shaped by cultural drivers and political ideologies (Leyshon and Thrift, 1997; Zelizer, 1997; Golumbia, 2016).

The early twentieth-first century represents a particularly dynamic time, as existing systems of state-based fiat currencies face a range of alternatives complicating the modern expectation of a single legal tender within a territory. While single territorial currencies have never been truly universal, the current era of digital technology and growing corporate power over platforms have produced new currency-like systems. To be clear, many of these do not (and likely will not) act as 'fully-equipped' substitutes to state fiat currencies (Halaburda and Sarvary, 2016: 53) as their designers' goals are much more modest—promoting local economies, or incentivizing customer loyalty. At the same time, other currencies—most notably blockchain-backed cryptocurrencies—are designed with the explicit goal of competing with state-backed fiat and existing banking systems, representing the most recent chapter in the complicated history of money and currency.

Understanding Money

Before focusing on currency—the medium of exchange used in trade, production, and consumption, it is necessary to outline a brief but working understanding of money. An important goal of this section is to counter the idea of money 'as something that is inert, sterile and boring' (Orrell and Chlupatý, 2016: 30) and, instead, highlight its dynamism and embeddedness in society and geography.

Functions of Money

An important role of money is facilitating trade by lowering transaction costs ranging from replacing barter to standardizing units of exchange, to creating forms of currency that are easier to transport. In addition, money is generally characterized by three main functions:[1] a medium of exchange, a store of value, and a unit of accounting. Acting as a *medium of exchange* facilitates trade by creating fungible and standardized units that are easy to move across space, scarce,[2] and hard to counterfeit. While money need not meet all these criteria well, those that do are generally more successful than those that fall short. The second function of money is acting as a *store of value* in which to place assets for retrieval later, making stability and predictability key to this function. While money's function as a medium of exchange prioritizes liquidity, the store of value function is often associated with more illiquid forms: real estate, ownership of companies, and so on (Dodd, 1994). The third function of money—*a unit of accounting*—is used to determine the worth of goods and services, particularly relative to others. This function is particularly important in accounting and contracts where the current and future worth of items are enumerated.

Not all types of money are equally adept at fulfilling each of these functions. For example, houses in the United States are increasingly important to many people as a store of value (in addition to acting as a dwelling), but houses are not useful as daily means of exchange. The importance placed on the balance between circulation and value contributes to attitudes towards desirable monetary policy. For example, many fringe right-wing theories of money have long complained about central banks 'needlessly' increasing monetary supplies and have advocated returning to the gold standard (or currencies such as Bitcoin designed with a strict supply limit) to 'protect' the store of value aspect of money (Golumbia, 2016). These three functions of money (and attitudes towards desirability) are constrained to particular moments in time and space. After all, a bill of exchange that worked as money in medieval Italy is a historical curiosity today, and Hong Kong dollars are not accepted in Berlin grocery stores. In short, the ability for money to function as money is dependent on the material spaces and social networks in which it operates.

Embedding Money

To better understand this connection, one must look beyond money's three functions and build what Zelizer (1997: 24) calls a 'fully sociological model of money'. In other words, the embedding of money in society and space is absolutely fundamental to its ability to function as money. While this grounding comes in any number of forms—images printed and stamped on money; the dimensions of wallets to fit certain sized notes; and even the terms we use, wooden nickels and brass farthings—the connection to the state is a particularly important way in which money is embedded. While money and currencies need not be state issued, rulers of territories—ranging from absolute monarchies to democracies—have long been intertwined with monetary practices and are an important factor in their success or failure.

While, often, the state's role is based on the power of the mint, it also connects to more intangible factors representing the overall idea of the state, nation, or community. As Orrell and Chlupatý (2016: 117) argue, an important part of state-backed currencies:

> is the story that surrounds them. The US dollar, the British pound, the euro, the yuan, all carry with them, and are supported by, associations about their countries and their economic systems. And as always, power is at the heart of the matter, because money's validity—which is always fragile and liable to evaporate—relies on the authority of its issuers.

A striking example of the power and momentum of the 'story' supporting currency is the Somalia shilling. Although the country's civil war rendered unified state control unworkable and destroyed the centralized monetary authority, the Somalia shilling continued to act as money and currency within the Somalia territory. The continued function of the shilling was, in part, due to the lack of an alternative for small-scale everyday exchange but also was 'underpinned by a strong social glue', which meant that an 'individual who flouts the system risks jeopardizing trust in both himself [sic] and his clan' (*The Economist*, 2012: 79). In short, while the state apparatus originally behind it had diminished, the social embeddedness of the Somalian shilling allowed it to continue to act as money.

Considering Currency

Currency, the specific instruments of money used as a medium of exchange, has come in many forms—grain, beads, cowry shells, peppercorns, cigarettes, cans of mackerel, potatoes, and so on. Forms of currency that are highly portable, uniform but divisible into smaller units, of limited supply and hard to counterfeit are generally preferred and, as a result, coins have long existed, although they have been supplemented (albeit still not entirely replaced) by paper and digital forms (Davies, 2010). Indeed, the currencies most commonly encountered today—Euros, Dollars, Yuan, Yen, Pounds—come in coin, paper, and digital forms.

Currencies are generally divided into two types: commodity and fiat. Commodity currencies are where the material used has an intrinsic value of its own. Gold and silver could be fashioned into objects or jewelry, food stuffs and spices could be consumed, and cigarettes could be smoked. Thus, an important aspect of commodity currencies is that users are in direct contact with the material of value. A closely related form of currency is representative forms of money acting as tokens that are not valuable in themselves but can be exchanged for a commodity; for example, gold-backed certificate notes. In contrast, fiat currencies are supported by government backing, private means, or the agreement among market actors of its worth but having no material value. State-backed fiat currencies act as the prime medium of exchange for people living in the territory of the issuing state and are generally exchangeable for other state-backed fiat currencies. There are approximately 180 state currencies recognized by the Swiss Association of Standardization (2018); the vast majority have floating exchange rates and about one-quarter of them are pegged to a fixed exchange rate to another currency, most often the US dollar.

Fraud is a concern for both commodity and fiat currencies, and efforts to prevent it have shaped the design and materiality of currencies and the technologies used to produce them. For example, coin edges are were rimmed originally so as to make it obvious when coins were clipped (i.e., small pieces of precious metal removed) and the intricate engravings, special papers and watermarks on paper bills seek to confound counterfeiting. It is important, however, to recognize that currency need not have a material basis, and even state-backed currencies often only exist as data entries. Moreover, while national state-backed currencies have been the norm for the modern era, currencies are not limited to state-backing. A number of other entities—companies, localities, cooperatives—also maintain currencies or currency-like systems. The intent of these systems varies—encouraging consumer loyalty (frequent flyer points), or replacing state fiat currency (cryptocurrencies)—depending on the goals and ideology of the central issuer. A key question, taken up later in the chapter, is the extent to which these currency-like systems can be considered 'real currencies', or what Halaburda and Sarvary (2016: 53) call 'fully equipped currencies'.

Evolution of Currency

Before exploring, the 'reality' of currencies, it is important to review the history of their development. Leyshon and Thrift (1997) distinguish five broad stages in the evolution of money and currencies: (i) pre-modern money, (ii) commodity money, (iii) money of account, (iv) state credit money, and (v) virtual money (which I rename 'digital money' in this chapter). Stressing the importance of social embeddedness and geography, Leyshon and Thrift (1997: 3) associate each of the five stages with 'a particular set of formal instruments of money [or currencies], a particular set of financial institutions and practices, and a broadly conceived set of interpretations of what money is and what it does'.

In tracing this history,[3] I highlight how changes in the form, function, and practices associated with currency make it an *inherently geographical phenomenon*. For example, the increasing dematerialization of currency over history has contributed to the time space compression of money and currency (Leyshon and Thrift, 1997: 22). Dematerialization comes about via specific technological innovations ranging from double-entry bookkeeping, to telegraphy, to blockchain backed cryptocurrencies. Innovations in communications are particularly important as they allow for an increase in the speed of money circulation, as well as a need for new systems to trust and verify exchange at a distance. As Giddens (1990: 24) argues:

> Money, we can say, is a means of bracketing time and so of lifting transactions out of particular milieux of exchange. More accurately put … money is a means of time-space distanciation. Money provides for the enactment of transactions between agents widely separated in time and space.
>
> In short, the history and practice of money, '*is itself a geography.*'
>
> (Leyshon and Thrift, 1997: 3)

From Pre-modern to Commodity Money

An oft-repeated trope is that money arose to replace a more cumbersome bartering process. Scholars of the history of money, however, emphasize a more complex and less instrumental process.

> Objects originally accepted for one purpose [ornamental, religious, ceremonial] were often found to be useful for other noneconomic purposes…[and] because of their growing acceptability, began to be used for general trading also. We face considerable difficulty in trying to span the chronological gap which separates us from a true understanding of the attitudes of ancient man [sic] towards religious, social and economic life.
>
> (Davies, 2010: 24)

Thus, rather than a rational decision made by *homo economicus*, the history of exchange is deeply embedded in society and culture.

Building on Polanyi's distinction between 'primitive' and 'modern' money, Leyshon and Thrift (1997: 5) emphasize the cultural nature of pre-modern money, the multiplicity of forms (or currencies) used, and the complicated and often non-economic motives to which it was put. In short, they argue that:

> the origins of money are cultural, inasmuch as the use of money arose in processes of exchange that were firmly non-economic in their orientation….in other words, money evolved from relatively narrow, culturally specific uses, to take on later a much broader range of social and economic functions commonly associated with money.

Moreover, each form and practice of pre-modern money was associated with its own restricted geography that struggled to survive when encountering a 'more powerful cultural form' of money (Leyshon and Thrift, 1997: 23). While there are few (if any) groups remaining isolated from modern money, this does not mean that money and currency is disembedded from its cultural context. After all, people still make distinctions between different kinds of money—an allowance, a bribe, a salary, a windfall—even if it comes in the same form of currency. As Zelizer (1997: 25) argues, 'Detached from its qualitative distinctions, the world of money becomes indecipherable.'

Thus, as pre-modern money systems shifted to commodity money, where the material used has an intrinsic value, it remained culturally embedded. Beginning with 'large silver blobs or 'dumps'' (Davies, 2010: 62), commodity money evolved into standardized shapes, weights, and stampings, eventually emerging as coinage[4]—a currency form that survives today. This also brought about the need for more precious metals, driving advances in mining technologies to increase supply, as well as debasement of coinage; that is, reducing the weight or percentage of precious metals in coins, while asserting that they were of equal value of previous versions (Davies, 2010: 111). Control over minting coins also provided an important economic and political advantage to rulers of a territory, as they could ensure 'the value of the revenue received…in the form of tribute and taxation', and even increase their own wealth by 'altering the physical make-up of money, while prohibiting their subjects from doing the same' (Leyshon and Thrift, 1997: 10–11).

Money of Account and State Credit Money

Eventually, the constraints of a monetary supply limited by the availability of precious metals resulted in alternative systems in which money and currency were represented not in coins, but in accounting practices (Davies, 2010: 150). This new form of money—money of account—originated within the taxation practices of royal treasuries making the political power of the state a key factor in producing the conditions for this form of money to operate. Ingham (2013) argues that the authority of the state to determine the money of account is fundamental to its operation and value as a form of government obligation. Because the state possessed the power of coercion, it was assured revenue via taxation—thus making political power the ultimate foundation for the value of money.

Taxation by the state relied on wooden sticks with marks (known as 'tallies') recording payments and acting as receipts. The use of these records of debts and payments evolved to allow the transfer of debts between parties, thus creating an alternative system of money circulation that did not require coins (Leyshon and Thrift, 1997 12). As this form of currency was not restricted by supplies of gold and silver, the Treasury became 'more and more a clearing house for writes and tallies of assignment and less and less the scene of cash transactions' (Davies, 2010: 151). Despite the advantages of tallies used in this way—that is, increasing monetary supply and a form of credit—the need for debtor and creditor both to be physically present to process payments limited its function. To address this problem of time–space coordination, markets emerged for buying and selling tallies (representing the debt of others) at a discount, thus saving the holder of a debt the trouble of visiting each debtor. Moreover, because these markets were private, rather than part of the royal Treasury, they also represent a shift in power, as monarchies no longer had absolute control over the monetary system (Davies, 2010: 69).

Paralleling the uses of accounting for taxes were similar practices, driven by the needs of merchants facing the difficulty and danger of transporting large amounts of coinage. Instead, merchants developed bills of exchange—a document guaranteeing payment at a set time or on, demand often backed by kinship ties of scattered populations—that allowed trade in goods to be displaced in time and space from the exchange of currency (Leyshon and Thrift, 1997: 13–15). These bills of exchange evolved from specific trades (money for commodities) to generalized debt (money for debt) and developed in specific locations (most notably Venice and Florence), creating new international capital markets (Ingham, 2013). From their origin, bills of exchange were inherently spatial, as they were conveyed by mail (taking weeks or months to arrive). Also, they relied on the idea of usance to function—usance being the length time between when a bill was written and when it matured for redemption. These instruments—technological innovations in their own right—also depended heavily on communications and record-keeping, not only to track debt and payments, but also for information about trade and other conditions. In short, information and communication have long been central to practices of currency and, as Leyshon and Thrift (1997: 28) argue: 'money has never been able to be separated from the discourse about money'. Although bills of exchange challenged the absolute power of the state or monarch over money, the state largely remained the producer of the most visible manifestation of money: coins. Moreover, beginning in the eighteenth century, states reasserted themselves, taking advantage of increased monetary supply to create national debt, as well as starting national banks to oversee currency regulation. This eventually led to central state banks acting as lenders of last resort and a codification of the modern monetary system in the Bretton Woods agreement with state-backed currencies the norm.

This process, however, was far from simple or uniform in its development, as the example of the United States shows. From the formation of the country in the late eighteenth century to the Civil War beginning in 1860, the federal government was relatively uninvolved in currency, issuing some gold and silver coins but no bills, a reaction to the counterfeiting and depreciation suffered by paper currency issued during the Revolutionary War (Greenberg, 2020). Instead, private banks issued a wide variety of bills—estimated at over 8,000 different currencies issued by up to 1,500 banks (Halaburda and Sarvary, 2016: 35)—that were used as mediums of exchange. This large number of currencies created a number of problems in determining value, and exchange rates posing particular issues for trade and travelers. One traveler's account from the 1830s notes:

> Started from Virginia with Virginia money—reached the Ohio River—exchanged $20 Virginia note for shin-plasters [a term meaning worthless currency] and a $3 note of the Bank of West Union—paid away the $3 note for breakfast—reached Tennessee—received a $100 Tennessee note—went back to Kentucky-forced there to exchange the Tennessee note for $88 of Kentucky money—started home with Kentucky money. ... At Maysville, wanted Virginia money—couldn't get it. At Wheeling, exchanged $50 note, Kentucky money, for notes of the North Western Bank of Virginia—reached Fredericktown—there neither Virginia nor Kentucky money current—paid a $5 Wheeling note for breakfast and dinner—received in change two one dollar notes of some Pennsylvania bank, one dollar Baltimore and Ohio Rail Road...one hundred yards from tavern door, all the notes refused except the Baltimore and Ohio Rail Road.
>
> (Dillistin, 1949: 44–5)

In response, this era had regular printings of 'bank books' detailing current discount rates for various banks based on the perception of the bank, known counterfeit notes, and the distance between the printer and the bank in question (Weber, 2015). As Halaburda and Sarvary (2016: 37) note 'ultimately it contributed to people's general aversion to less popular banknotes or banknotes from geographically distant locales'. This situation finally ended around the Civil War, when the federal government, needing additional money for the war effort, printed notes in green ink that became known as greenbacks. This eventually coalesced into a system of national banks (private banks but chartered by the federal government) issuing insured notes of a standard design. Even with these advantages, however, state bank notes continued to circulate until federal tax policy de-incentivized their use (Halaburda and Sarvary, 2016: 45).

Digital Money and New Compressions of Time Space

Leyshon and Thrift (1997: 20) refer to the last stage of money as 'virtual money' or, when money 'becomes an activated double book entry, a spontaneous acknowledgement of debt that is no longer a commodity'. While agreeing with the definition, I prefer the term 'digital money' to emphasize not only its reality in action, but also the socio-materiality in which it operates. Rather than circulating as precious metal or paper and readily seen, it exists as data manifesting as 1s and 0s in the circuit boards and memories of digital technology. This emphasis on its materiality also serves to bolster Leyshon and Thrift's (1997: 21) assertion that, despite the difficult of perceiving it physically, digital money remains embedded in society: '*It consists of a set of social practices just like any other*. It is not just a ghost in the machine.'

While digital money comes in many forms—bank account records, foreign exchange, commercial currencies run by platform companies, cryptocurrencies—they share the common characteristic of compressing time-space through technologies. This compression, however, is not fundamentally new. Postal service, carrier pigeons, the telegraph, and telephone have long been used to transmit information about prices and exchange rates. As early as 1845, merchant banks in London and Hamburg were regularly communicating by telegraph, followed shortly thereafter with trans-Atlantic telegraphy between New York and London (Leyshon and Thrift, 1997: 29). Thus, while the scale and speed of time-space compression has increased dramatically today (Zook and Grote, 2017), this represents the continuation of a trend, rather than a new phenomenon.

The ability of technology to compress time-space, however, brings with it new challenges, particularly regarding trusting the accuracy and reliability of transactions with spatially or socially distant counterparts (Leyshon and Thrift, 1997: 30). Historically, kinship or social ties ameliorated this trust at a distance. The need for trust is arguably even more pronounced with digital money and currencies, since actors in an exchange are often unknown to each other. This gives rise to what Giddens (1990: 28) calls "expert systems' tasked with providing "guarantees' of expectations across distanciated time-space. This 'stretching' of social systems is achieved via the impersonal nature of tests applied to evaluate technical knowledge and by public critique.' Distantiated trust comes in many forms, including regulation, media reports, and reputational systems (such as those pioneered by the online marketplace eBay). Perhaps the most widespread example is credit and debit cards: consumers trust that merchants will not alter the bill, and merchants trust that obligations will be paid. While these exchanges are backed by verification technology—PIN codes, anti-fraud alerts, and legal sanctions—trust remains consequential; for example, we expect customer service from reputable brands such as Visa when mistakes arise. As Ferguson (2008: 30) argues:

> ...money is a matter of belief, even faith: belief in the person paying us; belief in the person issuing the money he uses or the institution that honours his cheques or transfers. Money is not metal. It is trust inscribed.

Current Currency Ecosystem

The history of money and currency demonstrates the variability in currency forms and backings. Turning to review currency and currency-like systems that are currently active, I use Halaburda and Sarvary's (2016: 53–4) requirements for a currency to be considered 'fully-equipped' as a means for comparison. These requirements consist of three attributes—*acquirability* (how a currency is obtained), *transferability* (to whom can it be given and under what conditions), and *redeemability* (what can it buy)—to evaluate the ability of currencies to serve as a medium of exchange. Systems in which it is possible to acquire the currency easily—that is, one need not complete specific tasks or have special status, freely transfer it to others, and redeem it for things generally (including state-backed fiat currencies)—are 'fully equipped.'

Not surprisingly, most state-backed fiat currencies—that is, those without monetary and exchange controls—easily meet the definition of 'fully equipped currencies', as they are designed for that purpose. It is useful to note, however, that even state fiat currencies fulfill these three functions differently depending on form; that is, coins, notes, or assistance voucher. One would expect difficulty in using sacks of pennies to buy a car, and depositing US$100,000 in cash is likely to trigger inquiry by the state. Moreover, states also produce currencies that are much more restricted in acquirability, transferability, and redeemability. For example, the Supplemental Nutrition Assistance Program (SNAP) in the United States provides poor families and individuals with a limited currency (first, paper food stamps and, more recently, cards similar to those used in ATMs) that can only be used to purchase food items, specifically prohibiting the purchase of alcohol or soap (Halaburda and Sarvary, 2016: 55–6).

Local Currencies

National governments, however, are not the only possible issuers of currencies. Indeed, the scholar of cities, Jane Jacobs (1969), argues that cities are a much more appropriate scale than countries because city-based currencies would act as a feedback mechanism about the competitive and innovative success of cities. In contrast, cities using national currency receive 'flawed and inappropriate feedback' (Jacobs, 1969: 58) and, rather than reflecting the local situation, provide the less meaningful average for all cities in a country. Other arguments for local currencies focus on the importance of local consumption or social ties (North, 2005) and, thus, issuers of these currencies focus on 'building community spirit and social capital', and design systems whose 'use is associated with an increase in reported well-being' (Orrell and Chlupatý, 2016: 189). Examples of purposeful local currencies include Ithaca Hours in upstate New York, created in 1992 and accepted at over 900 local business (Fortier, 1996), or Berkshares based in Western Massachusetts, introduced in 2006 as a means to offset increases in costs of living caused by tourism.

In contrast to the functional definitions of currency introduced earlier in the chapter, these local currencies are often associated with particular progressive (or even utopian) politics, making the intertwining of currency and society explicit in their design. These currencies often come into being during moments of crises—such as the emergence of Red Global de Trueque in Argentina—when stated-back fiat is no longer working well, or unemployment is high (North, 2007). Almost all of these local alternative currencies operate as a resisting (or, at least, an alternative) force to capitalism and, as such, embody key elements of a 'fully equipped' currency, including acquirability and transferability. However, because these currencies are designed for local use, redeemability becomes an issue, particularly when purchasing outside goods or services. In short, local currencies face difficulties when moving beyond the local sphere, an issue contributing to the downfall of the Red Global de Trueque when it attempted to scale up its networks (North, 2005: 229).

Commercial Currencies

In addition to fiat backed by states, there are a number of commercially backed systems exhibiting some of the attributes of currencies. Casino chips, Chuck E. Cheese gaming tokens, and buy one, get one free (BOGO) coupons all represent mediums of exchange, but fall short of 'fully equipped' by design. While these examples are freely acquired and readily transferred between people, their redemption is limited, as they are primarily only usable for goods and services offered by the companies that issue them. Nevertheless, these systems are popular among businesses and consumers: 'The latest loyalty card from the UK chemist Boots has space on it for more than 20 different loyalty currencies' (Boyle, 2015: 6). Despite this popularity, however, loyalty points are more akin to company scripts or credit than currencies. For example, frequent flyer miles offered by airlines are held by hundreds of millions of people and number in the trillions (*The Economist*, 2005). Originating in the 1970s as a means to promote customer loyalty:

> programs come with defined terms and conditions written in the interest of the airline. Among other things, these terms specify that miles are *not* the property of the member (a point held up by case law), are subject to confiscation for misuse (such as selling a reward seat) and the terms for earning and redeeming are subject to change at any time.
>
> (Zook and Graham, 2018, p.394)

Other commercial currencies, such as Facebook credits (2009) or Amazon coins (2013), restricted transferability and redeemability to build customer lock-in and brand loyalty, and to limit consumer choice. Despite concerns voiced at the time that these currencies would compete with state fiat (Marketwatch, 2013), these examples of commercial currencies were not strong challenges to state fiat currencies, 'because platforms issuing them go to great pains to disable the main functions that are necessary for a widely adopted currency' (Halaburda and Sarvary, 2016: 8).

In other words, it is the design, rather than the issuer of the currency, that makes these systems less than fully equipped. Facebook credits, introduced in 2009 and retired in 2013, could neither be transferred between users nor be exchanged for state currencies, and simply were means to encourage purchases on the platform. It is possible to imagine systems—such as Facebook's newly announced Libra currency discussed at the end of the chapter—that more closely correspond to fully equipped currencies. As Birch and McAvoy (1996) argue:

> if a consortium comprising Norwich Union and Marks & Spencer began issuing transferable loyalty points for cross-accepting within their consortium (the currency *keiretsu*) they could provide an acceptable currency for transaction and lock consumers into their group... If you believe that Marks and Spencer will always redeem your points and that points will keep their value then you're happy to accept them in payment.

Indeed, some commercial currencies, particularly game currencies such as World of Warcraft gold and Second Life Linden dollars, were widely used as mediums of exchange to purchase virtual objects and land within these games. While the rules of World of Warcraft disallowed the direct purchase of World of Warcraft gold with state-based fiat currencies, online markets appeared elsewhere (such as eBay) in which players could purchase World of Warcraft currency and other game items on the sly with state-based fiat. In contrast to this more restrictive system, the virtual world of Second Life depended on players building things to populate the game, therefore making it easy for people to sell virtual items (especially digital real estate) to others. To help facilitate these exchanges, the company actively promoted the exchange of Linden dollars for state-fiat currencies. While this made Linden dollars a fully equipped currency by Halaburda and Sarvary's (2016: 77) standards, Linden dollars had little impact beyond the game itself as the active community and exchange amounts never became particularly large.

Nonetheless, World of Warcraft gold and Linden dollars illustrate how commercially based currency systems can have an impact beyond their original scope, even if a company tries to restrict use. For example, the Chinese social media platform Tencent introduced Q-coins that were designed for purchasing digital enhancements of online experience. Tencent users, however, also started using the currency for peer-to-peer exchange, ultimately leading the Chinese government to regulate and subsequently ban its use (Halaburda and Sarvary, 2016: 85). In short, commercially backed currency can work as currencies, although their ability to do so depends on both the intent of the company, and the attitude and actions of the state.

New Challenges from Cryptocurrencies

The final type of currency reviewed in this chapter—cryptocurrency—is also the newest. Cryptocurrencies are designed around a technology known as 'blockchain', a decentralized database where security, record-keeping, and validation is distributed, rather than dependent on centralized institutions. Given the experience of currencies thus far—backed by centralized private or state institutions and embedded in society—the idea of a currency with 'no centralized entity to keep track of the transactions' is quite novel (Halaburda and Sarvary, 2016: 102). Also referred to as a distributed ledger, a blockchain tracks ownership and exchange of a cryptocurrency (which has no physical form, existing *only* as database entries) in order to guard against anyone using currency to which they have no right. The creator of the first and largest blockchain cryptocurrency, Bitcoin, focused on the desirability of decentralization: 'We don't have to worry about a chain of custody of communication. It doesn't matter who tells you a longest chain, the proof-of-work speaks for itself' (Nakamoto, 2010). In other words, blockchain replaces trust with evidence, such as the longest chain and a testable proof. Thus, blockchain-based cryptocurrencies are fundamentally predicated on a logic of algorithmic proofs, rather than centralized human governance. However, despite the rhetoric of separation, human actions are deeply intertwined with all cryptocurrencies through the actual everyday economic practices that perform and sustain them (MacKenzie, 2006).

To achieve workable decentralized systems, cryptocurrencies rely on three key technologies: *distributed databases*, for recording interactions; *networks of computer nodes*; and *encryption protocols* (see Zook and Blankenship, 2018, for a more detailed review). The distributed database is a permanent record of exchanges of a cryptocurrency stored in sequential elements called blocks that are linked (or chained) together. A key discursive point of blockchain is that no centralized entity can alter the data by itself. In practice, however, these unalterable databases have been manually altered by humans multiple times due to coding errors (Shubber, 2014), or hacks (Madeira, 2018). The second element of cryptocurrencies is a *network of computers called miners*, used to verify which blocks are legitimate. The most common technique used by blockchain miners to verify (or achieve consensus) is called 'proof-of-work' and requires miners competitively to solve a computational problem known as a 'hash'. The first miner to solve the hash receives a reward in cryptocurrency, and when 51% of the miners agree on the solution, a new block (containing records of exchanges) is added to the blockchain. This system architecture is designed to prevent people from adding blocks with false records of exchanges. This algorithmic governance via proof of work (rather than a centralized authority) is likewise a key rhetorical point, but is also deeply imbricated with human decision-making, such as the choice of which cryptocurrency to mine (Zook and Blankenship, 2018). The third and final part of blockchain technologies is *encryption* to establish identity and run the proof-of-work consensus used by miners, as outlined above. All interactions and exchanges are based on public addresses (known as 'wallets') that record cryptocurrency transfers and other transactions. Using encryption to establish identity provides some anonymity to users (a useful discursive argument for proponents), although this is far from foolproof (Bohr and Bashir, 2014; Bohannon, 2016).

Embeddedness of Cryptocurrencies

While the design of open blockchain-backed cryptocurrencies has a number of geographic manifestations—where its developers live, how different state regulations shape its use and popularity—the clearest tie is via energy consumption. Because miners running proof-of-work algorithms rely on computational power to solve hash encryptions (de Vries, 2018) a hardware-driven, energy intensive arms race emerged as cryptocurrencies gained exchange value. According to some estimates Bitcoin mining alone may have represented as much as 0.5% of the world's total electricity consumption by the end of 2018 (de Vries, 2018). The key role of electricity results in geographies based on energy costs, manifesting in massive Chinese computer networks organized around state-subsidized power (Fairley, 2017), pop-up mining networks in regions such as Venezuela (*The Economist*, 2018) and Iran (BBC, 2019) with heavily subsidized electricity.

While the technology and geographies of blockchain are complex, the practices of cryptocurrencies meet Halaburda and Sarvary's (2016) requirements for a fully equipped currency. Cryptocurrencies can be readily acquired (by participating in mining or purchase), they are fully transferable (via encrypted digital wallets), and are generally redeemable for state fiat currencies at multiple online exchanges. Although their use as a means of exchange is problematic—due to volatile exchange rates and limited vendors accepting cryptocurrencies directly—the ability to exchange them for dollars or euros is well-established. Moreover, cryptocurrencies have the standard characteristics expected from currency—readily divisible into smaller parts, easily transportable—and offer some new protections against fraud, counterfeiting, or seizure by a centralized authority. Whether these attributes lead to a widespread adoption among consumers and companies depends on the preferences of actors and use cases that are attractive. Although these questions remain to be answered, states and their regulatory bodies are certainly paying attention.

Since the launch of Bitcoin in 2009, over 2,000 cryptocurrencies have appeared and, as of July 2019, these currencies had a combined market capitalization of a US$288 billion. This capitalization, however, is concentrated in just a few currencies, with Bitcoin representing 65% of this total and the next four largest currencies accounting for approximately another 20%. The sheer size of cryptocurrencies means that they represent a much more compelling competitor to state fiat and banking systems than other commercial currencies, such as Linden dollars. As the European Union's Blockchain Observatory and Forum (2018: 6) argues:

> the success of Bitcoin and other crypto assets shows, blockchain offers a relatively easy technological means for individuals or organisations to issue their own tokens, thereby challenging the traditional authority of governments to assume this role. Blockchains allow for viable, direct transactions between parties, challenging the authority of banks who today hold a virtual monopoly in the safeguarding and exchange of value.

This sentiment is echoed by Dowd (2014: 88) who notes that blockchain:

> opens up almost unimaginable possibilities for private parties to free themselves from state control—to buy illegal drugs, engage in illegal forms of gambling, evade taxes, protect their wealth from the government, and so on. This, in turn, raises profound issues of an emerging spontaneous social order, in particular, the prospect of a crypto-anarchic society in which there is no longer any government role in the monetary system and, potentially, no government at all.

Ideologies of Cryptocurrencies

Given these ideas of a changing power balance (readily expressed within by cryptocurrency activists, as well), it is important to review the motivations behind cryptocurrencies. Why were they designed to be decentralized and how do they interact with states? The motivations for blockchain and cryptocurrencies come in two main streams, one largely practical and one highly ideological. The practical case focuses on the transaction costs of exchange including currency exchange, as well as the settlement and oversight of business contracts and payments. Arguments made for blockchain use cases in these situations highlight the inefficiency of current systems and the number of 'middle-men' who could be replaced with an automated and algorithmically verified blockchain system. The second set of motivations turns on distrust of the state and a corresponding desire to avoid state fiat currencies, particularly the tracking and surveillance associated with their use. While the advantages this brings to criminal economies is self-evident, the arguments advanced do not foreground this. Instead, the ideological motivations are couched in libertarian and right-wing concerns ranging from fixations on 'debasements of currency' by central banks, to attitudes towards the state as fundamentally broken and the source of problems, rather than solutions.

These views are often generalized as cyberlibertarianism, an ideology promoting market-based solutions and minimal state roles, particularly regulating digital technologies—which are seen as inherently liberating. While cyberlibertarianism emerged from the Californian tech culture of the 1980s (particularly via the Cypherpunk movement; May (1992), Golumbia (2016) traces the genealogy of ideas back to Hayek and the Austrian school of Economics, as well as more fringe groups, such as the John Birch Society. In particular, Golumbia (2016) argues that extremely pernicious right-wing ideas—government power is inherently evil, gold is the only trustworthy backing for currencies, central banks needlessly devalue fiat currencies through inflation, central intermediaries should be avoided at all costs—have been central to Bitcoin and the larger cryptocurrency project since inception. As a result, Bitcoin proponents 'incorporate critical parts of a right-wing worldview even as they manifest a surface rhetorical commitment to values [such as freedom or civil rights] that do not appear to come from the right' (Golumbia, 2016: 4).

Thus, the goal of decentralization cannot simply be limited to removing intermediaries but, instead, is deeply intertwined with a political project focused on reducing state regulation in the favor of markets. Cloaked in the rhetoric of neutral algorithmic governance being superior and desirable (Zook and Blankenship, 2018), cryptocurrencies such as Bitcoin characterize any central authority as inherently bad. While it is clear that the design of blockchain is socially embedded, like any other technology, its developers—largely coming from the computer science and mathematics communities—are often unwilling to acknowledge this. Instead, they view computer expertise as knowledge that trumps 'all other forms of expertise' (Golumbia, 2016: 22) and follow 'a dream of using software to dismantle the very project of representative governance, at the bidding of nobody but technologists and in particular technologists who loathe the political apparatus others have developed' (Golumbia, 2016: 33). In short, the design of Bitcoin and subsequent cryptocurrencies emerges from, and is embedded in, a particular segment of society working to mainstream some rather fringe ideas about money and currency.

While decentralization is often couched in terms of freedom and preventing central powers from controlling or stealing wealth (e.g., inflating away a currency's value or taxation), there are clearly important reasons for regulating exchange and currencies. The 2007 global financial crisis illustrates the dangers of under-regulated finance at the macro level, while the ability to intervene and fix an incorrect charge on a credit card highlights the usefulness of central authority in everyday life. Indeed, the much-vaulted irreversibility of Bitcoin transactions offers cold comfort when fraud or theft occurs (Shubber, 2014). Moreover, Bitcoin's decentralization is in many ways more rhetoric than real. While the architecture of the system creates no central node(s) to control, a number of large mining pools with hundreds of dedicated machines have recentralized mining power within the Bitcoin system. This concentration raises real concerns that a few large mining pools could collude and gain control of 51% of all miners, allowing them to rewrite the blockchain and fraudulently transfer coins. Because mining pools cluster in certain places with low-cost electricity—Kaiser *et al.* (2018) estimate that mining pools within China represent 60–80% of Bitcoin miners—an agreement within a regional cartel or state action could result in the takeover of the Bitcoin blockchain. Ownership of Bitcoin is likewise highly concentrated, with over 40% of all Bitcoin held in just 1,000 wallets (Kharif, 2017).

One Blockchain to Rule Them All?

While Bitcoin brings with it the possibility of a new kind of currency, its model of a decentralized authority and ledger is far from the only way to implement a digital currency. For example, many central banks and settlement companies are exploring the use of blockchain not as a currency but, rather, as a back-end technology to lower transaction costs. These systems vary in a number of ways from Bitcoin including the most important difference of operating as permissioned blockchains, rather than open blockchains. This means that rather than having a network of miners verifying and adding new blocks by proof-of-work consensus, permissioned blockchains only allow certain trusted parties to add blocks. In short, permissioned systems reintroduce centralization to the blockchain. These kinds of systems require much less electricity to operate (because miners are not competing), and are generally considered to be more scalable and faster than systems like Bitcoin.

One example of a permissioned blockchain that stands out is Facebook's proposed currency, the Libra, announced in June 2019 and reported to become operational sometime in 2020. While Libra uses blockchain as its backend, it is a permissioned system overseen by a consortium including companies such as Uber, Visa, and Paypal. Facebook emphasizes—in media and congressional testimony—that Libra is designed as a cross-border payment system for its 2.4 billion users rather than a bank (which would trigger stringent regulations), and will maintain a reserve of state fiat currencies in order to maintain a stable value for the currency (Libra, 2019). The Libra proposal, however, has been met with considerable skepticism, given the numerous Facebook scandals around the misuse of users' data and concerns that Libra will simple solidify Facebook's already considerable power as an economic platform.

Other concerns involve the proper regulation of Libra. While Facebook insists that it is merely a way to speed up transactions and reduce costs, a similar proposal for an internal payment system proposed by Walmart in 1998 was met with strong resistance from trade groups and skepticism from Congress. This ultimately resulted in the abandonment of these plans by Walmart. A particular issue was a single corporation offering both banking and retail services, and possibly treating retail competitors unfairly, such as refusing to extend loans or requiring them to use a particular payment system. This is likely why the Libra currency is nominally operated by a consortium, rather than just Facebook. In addition to possible conflicts of interest, there are also questions of what Libra may mean for the international banking system. As Inman and Monaghan (2019) argue, Libra 'could speed up transactions and cut costs, especially in developing world countries, it could also undermine the stability of a banking system that has only just recovered from the crash of 2008'. More specifically, Dayen (2019) worries that 'In the name of making it easier for users to transfer cash to friends or make purchases, Facebook means to shift control over money from central banks and regulators to a private consortium of for-profit companies, which are mainly buying in because of the self-enrichment possibilities [and] exacerbate national financial crises, expose billions to privacy abuses, and shift too much power away from democratic structures...If Libra gets to scale, you could easily see it wiping away sovereign capacity to stop capital flight.' In short, while the proposed vision for Libra seems possible both technically and commercially, if it is implemented as initially outlined, the currency could operate at a scale and scope on par with major state-backed fiat currencies, which is something novel.

Conclusion

Currencies have long played a vital role in trade, wealth accumulation, and the development and integration of a global economy. This chapter reviews some of the key aspects of currency not only in terms of its history, but also its form, function, and geography leading to this summation, which highlights three central lessons. First is the important role played by technological innovation. From the first minting of commodity currencies to the creation of cryptocurrencies, technologies have enabled the dematerialization of currency, making it easier to transport and use in trade. Advances in communications technology are particularly effective in allowing for new systems of verifying trust at a distance (Giddens, 1990), as well as increasing the rate at which currency circulates. In short, the geographies of money and currencies advanced hand-in-hand with technology, affording advantages to certain actors and places, and providing the means to disrupt previous systems.

Second, there has never been a single manifestation of currency: coins and notes circulate alongside barter and social exchange even as accounting systems are in effect. As Leyshon and Thrift (1997, p.190) argue:

> money *in use* can never be identified as one money, but only as a set of overlapping monetary networks which have profound effects on flow and liquidity. These 'special' or, more accurately, 'multiple' monies can never be reduced to one money … A process of social earmarking is always at work which is based on the location of particularly monetary forms with defined monetary networks.

Moreover, each of these overlapping monetary networks comes with, and creates, their own geographies, sometimes co-habiting in territories and places, while other times actively competing for dominance. As Zelizer (1997: 24–5) argues:

> even in the heartland of capitalism, different networks of social relations and systems of meaning mark modern money, introducing controls, restrictions, and distinctions that are as influential as the rationing of primitive money. Multiple monies in the modern world may not be as visibly identifiable as the shells, coins, brass rods, or stones of primitive communities, but their invisible boundaries work just as well. How else, for instance, do we distinguish a bribe from a tribute or a donation, a wage from an honorarium, or an allowance from a salary? How do we identify ransom, bonuses, tips, damages, or premiums? True, there are quantitative differences between these

various payments. But surely the special vocabulary conveys much more than different amounts. Detached from its qualitative distinctions, the world of money becomes indecipherable.

Third, currency is fundamentally embedded in society and space. Monarchs organized currency systems in order to ensure tax revenue for themselves. Medieval merchants developed bills of exchange to solve their problems in transporting and securing currency for trading. Cryptocurrencies were designed as decentralized systems to address concerns about centralized control and surveillance, and then subsequently re-designed by Facebook to accrue more power for its platform. None of these designs are 'natural' and as new currencies based on decentralized algorithmic control emerge, it is important to recognize these new loci and avenues of power; especially the ways in which code transforms ideologies into software and is made law (Lessig, 2009).

In closing, I borrow from Orrell and Chlupatý (2016: 227) the provocation that if 'money is a way of stamping numbers onto the world, … what do we do when the numbers look wrong?' Because the definition of 'wrong' is a political choice—for example, inflation, or imposed austerity, or a moribund local economy, and so on: the answer necessarily lies in society and politics, rather than a blind faith in technology. Questions of currency design are fundamental to our future as they shape our economies and retreating from the political conversations surrounding them abdicates responsibility. As Golumbia (2016: 76) argues, 'What is required to combat that power is not more wars between algorithmic platforms and individuals who see themselves as above politics but a reassertion of the political power that the blockchain is specifically constructed to dismantle.' In short, currency is much too important to leave it uncontested and undebated.

Notes

1 Although most functional definitions of money are limited to these three tasks, money certainly does other work, such as unifying territories (e.g., the Euro-zone, or projecting the power of its issuer over space).

2 The importance of scarcity is colorfully demonstrated in Douglas Adams' (1989) fictional depiction of a society emerging from a spaceship wreck that adopts the leaf as its currency and subsequently encounters a serious inflationary problem. Sadly, Adams never detailed how efforts to revalue the leaf through massive defoliation worked out.

3 For reasons of space, I focus primarily on European experiences.

4 The origin of coinage depends on definitions, but Chinese and Mediterranean cultures were using coin-like objects as early as 2000 BCE (Davies, 2010: 56–8).

References

Adams, D. (1989). *The Restaurant at the End of the Universe*. New York City: Tor.

BBC (2019). Iran seizes 1,000 Bitcoin mining machines after power spike. [online]. *BBC.com*, June 28. Available at: https://www.bbc.com/news/technology-48799155 [Accessed July 15, 2019].

Birch, D. and McAvoy, N. (1996). *Downloadsamoney. Demos Quarterly*, 8. Cited in Boyle, D. (2015). *The Money Changers: Currency Reform from Aristotle to E-Cash*. New York: Routledge.

Bohannon, J. (2016). Why criminals can't hide behind Bitcoin. [online]. *Science*. Available at: http://www.sciencemag.org/news/2016/03/why-criminals-cant-hide-behind-bitcoin [Accessed July 15, 2019].

Bohr, J. and Bashir, M. (2014). Who uses Bitcoin? An exploration of the Bitcoin community. *Twelfth Annual Conference on Privacy, Security and Trust (PST) IEEE*. Available at: http://ieeexplore.ieee.org/abstract/document/6890928/ [Accessed July 15, 2019].

Boyle, D. (2015). *The Money Changers: Currency Reform from Aristotle to E-Cash*. New York: Routledge.

Davies, G. (2010). *History of Money*. Cardiff: University of Wales Press.

Dayen, D. (2019). Facebook wants to become the world's banker—and Congress isn't paying enough attention. [online]. *The American Prospect*. Available at: https://prospect.org/article/facebook-wants-become-worlds-banker-and-congress-isnt-paying-enough-attention [Accessed July 17, 2019].

de Vries, A. (2018). Bitcoin's growing energy problem. *Joule*, Vol. 2 (5), pp. 801–805.

Dillistin, W. H. (1949). *Bank Note Reporters and Counterfeit Detectors, 1826–1866*. New York: American Numismatic Society.

Dodd, N. (1994). *The Sociology of Money: Economics, Reason & Contemporary Society*. New York: Continuum Intl Pub Group.

Dowd, K. (2014). *New Private Monies*. London: Institute of Economic Affairs.

The Economist. (2005). Frequent-flyer miles in terminal decline? *The Economist*. January 6. Available at: http://www.economist.com/node/3536178 [Accessed January 27, 2016].

The Economist. (2012). Somalia's might shilling. Hard to kill. *The Economist*. March 31. p. 79.

The Economist. (2018). Why are Venezuelans mining so much Bitcoin? April 3. Available at: https://www.economist.com/the-economist-explains/2018/04/03/why-are-venezuelans-mining-so-much-bitcoin [Accessed July 15, 2019].

EU Blockchain Observatory and Forum. (2018). *Blockchain innovation in Europe*. Available at: https://www.eublockchainforum.eu/sites/default/files/reports/20180727_report_innovation_in_europe_light.pdf [Accessed July 5, 2019].

Fairley, P. (2017). Feeding the blockchain beast: If Bitcoin ever does go mainstream, the electricity needed to sustain it will be enormous. *IEEE Spectrum*, Vol. 54 (10), pp. 36–59.

Ferguson, N. (2008). *The Ascent of Money: A Financial History of the World*. New York: Penguin.

Fortier, J. (1996). Underthrowing the system: How low finance undermines corporate culture. *Conscious Choice: Journal of Ecology and Healthy Living*, Vol. 9 (5), pp. 61–63.

Giddens, A. (1990). *The Consequences of Modernity*. New York: John Wiley & Sons.

Golumbia, D. (2016). *The Politics of Bitcoin: Software as Right-Wing Extremism*. Minneapolis: University of Minnesota Press.

Greenberg, J. R. (2020). *Bank Notes and Shinplasters: The Rage for Paper Money in the Early Republic*. University of Pennsylvania Press.

Halaburda, H. and Sarvary, M. (2016). *Beyond Bitcoin: The Economics of Digital Currencies*. New York: Palgrave.

Ingham, G. (2013). *The Nature of Money*. John Wiley & Sons.

Inman, P. and Monaghan, A. (2019). Facebook's Libra cryptocurrency 'poses risks to global banking'. *Guardian Newspaper*. June 23. Available at: https://www.theguardian.com/technology/2019/jun/23/facebook-libra-cryptocurrency-poses-risks-to-global-banking [Accessed July 15, 2019].

Jacobs, J. (1969). *The Economy of Cities*. New York: Vintage.

Kaiser, B., Jurado, M., and Ledger, A. (2018). The looming threat of China: An analysis of Chinese influence on Bitcoin. arXiv preprint. Available at: https://arxiv.org/abs/1810.02466 [Accessed July 15, 2019].

Kharif, O. (2017). The Bitcoin whales: 1,000 people who own 40 percent of the market. *Bloomberg*. Available at: https://www.bloomberg.com/news/articles/2017-12-08/the-bitcoin-whales-1-000-people-who-own-40-percent-of-the-market [Accessed July 13, 2019].

Lessig, L. (2009). *Code: And Other Laws of Cyberspace*. New York: Basic Books.

Leyshon, A. and Thrift, N. (1997). *Money/Space: Geographies of Monetary Transformation*. New York: Routledge.

Libra. (2019). The Libra White Paper. Available at: https://libra.org/en-US/white-paper/?noredirect=en-USintroduction [Accessed July 14, 2019].

MacKenzie, D. (2006). *An Engine, Not a Camera: How Financial Models Shape Markets*. Cambridge: MIT Press.

Madeira, A. (2018). The DAO, the hack, the soft fork, and the hard fork. *CryptoCompare*. Available at: https://www.cryptocompare.com/coins/guides/the-dao-the-hack-the-soft-fork-and-the-hard-fork/ [Accessed July 17, 2019].

Marketwatch. (2013). With Amazon minting currency, fed at risk. Available at: https://www.marketwatch.com/story/could-amazon-run-central-banks-out-of-business-2013-02-13 [Accessed July 15, 2019].

May, T. (1992). The Crypto Anarchist Manifesto. Available at: https://www.activism.net/cypherpunk/crypto-anarchy.html [Accessed June 16, 2019].

Nakamoto, S. (2010). Bitcoin minting is thermodynamically perverse. Bitcointalk.org. Available at: https://bitcointalk.org/index.php?topic=721.msg8114msg8114 [Accessed July 17, 2019].

North, P. (2005). Scaling alternative economic practices? Some lessons from alternative currencies. *Transactions of the Institute of British Geographers*, Vol. 30 (2), pp. 221–233.

North, P. (2007). *Money and Liberation: The Micropolitics of Alternative Currency Movements*. Minneapolis: University of Minnesota Press.

Orrell, D. and Chlupatý, R. (2016). *The Evolution of Money*. New York: Columbia University Press.

Shubber, K. (2014). The 9 biggest screwups in Bitcoin history. *Coindesk*. Available at: https://www.coindesk.com/9-biggest-screwups-bitcoin-history/ [Accessed July 17, 2019].

Swiss Association of Standardization. (2018). Current currency & funds code list. Available at https://www.currency-iso.org/en/home/tables/table-a1.html [Accessed June 29, 2019].

Weber, W. (2015). The efficiency of private E-money-like systems: The U.S. experience with National Bank Notes (March). FRB Atlanta CenFIS Working Paper No. 15-2. Available at: http://dx.doi.org/10.2139/ssrn.2586211 [Accessed July 17, 2019].

Zelizer, V. (1997). *The Social Meaning of Money*. Princeton, NJ: Princeton University Press.

Zook, M. and Grote, M. H. (2017). The microgeographies of global finance: High-frequency trading and the construction of information inequality. *Environment and Planning A: Economy and Space*, Vol. 49 (1), pp. 121–140.

Zook, M. and Graham, M. (2018). Hacking code/space: Confounding the code of global capitalism. *Transactions of the Institute of British Geographers*, Vol. 43 (3), pp. 390–404.

Zook, M. and Blankenship, J. (2018). New spaces of disruption? The failures of Bitcoin and the rhetorical power of algorithmic governance. *Geoforum*, Vol. 96, pp. 248–255.

8

THE GEOGRAPHY OF GLOBAL STOCK MARKETS AND OVERSEAS LISTINGS

Fenghua Pan

Introduction

Stock exchanges are the marketplaces for trading equity instruments and provide one of the most important ways for firms to raise money. By selling company shares in stock exchanges, firms can raise financial capital for further expansion. Investors can easily buy or sell stocks in the stock markets. In addition, stock markets provide divestment opportunities for venture capital and private equity investments, which is critical for the cultivation of high-tech industries. The proper interactions between stock exchanges and venture capital markets are crucial to the booming of high-tech industries in the United States (Zook, 2002). Thus, a stock market that operates well is of great value to economic development.

Stock markets are at the center of modern economies (Wójcik, 2009, 2011). In fact, most large multinational enterprises are publicly listed on stock exchanges. The more developed economies usually have very competitive stock markets. An absence of proper stock markets would inhibit the growth of companies and economic development. In addition, the international financial centers (IFCs) usually house well-known stock exchanges. For example, New York has the NYSE and Nasdaq, and London has the London Stock Exchange. Many more stock exchanges have been set up in less-developed economies and some have grown rapidly. Not every economy has an efficient stock market, and there is an uneven geography of equity markets (Wójcik, 2011).

In the context of financialization, stock exchanges have played an increasingly important role in the global economy. A nascent focus within the widely defined geographies of finance and financialization has been to understand the pervasive influence of stock markets and their geographies in a variety of contexts (Clark, Wójcik, and Bauer, 2006; Clark and Wójcik, 2007; Sarre, 2007; Wójcik, 2009, 2011, 2012). The growth in size and visibility, and the sheer power of stock markets means that studies into the nature of stock markets are timely and much warranted. With widening financial globalization according to measures such as gross capital flows, stocks of foreign assets and liabilities, and the degree of co-movement of asset returns, the impact of stock market activity will only increase in volume and scope in the future (Claessens and Schmukler, 2007). Economic geographers are well-placed to offer a new analytical perspective on the activities of stock markets that is attentive to socio-spatial relations and unpacks the spatialities of finance, as well considering the traditional influence of the firm, labor, and the state (Barnes and Sheppard, 2000).

In terms of stock market activity, it is most common for firms in any country to choose to list their shares on their domestic stock exchange. A growing trend is that, alternatively, firms may choose to bypass or supplement domestic listing by listing firm shares on a foreign stock exchange. This process of foreign listing is defined by Wójcik and Burger (2010: 276) as 'the listing and trading of corporate shares on stock markets outside of the home country of the issuer'. Listing on a foreign exchange can occur either as the first point of entry for a firm into the public equity market, or after having listed on their domestic exchange.

Firms came to realize that the best means of raising equity financing was through the direct listing of shares on the most competitive exchanges, so as to yield optimum returns (Clark and Wójcik, 2007). Growing internationalization of firms has coupled with proliferation of individuals and investors investing funds in foreign equity markets to diversify their portfolios and to earn higher yields than would be possible through their domestic market. In particular, institutional investors (e.g., pension funds) have developed a huge demand to diversify their portfolios internationally with accessibility to stock markets (Clark, 1998, 2000; Toporowski, 1999). Such capital mobility has been accelerated by the virtualization of stock exchanges allowing anytime-anywhere access for investors and the growing competition between international exchanges for firm listings (Pagano, Röell, and Zechner, 2002).

According to the World Federation of Exchanges (WFE), there are 80 stock exchanges in 69 economies. There are 52,209 firms listed on these stock exchanges and the total market capitalization of the 80 stock exchanges was US$76.72 trillion as at the end of 2018. In the meantime, many firms are listed on overseas stock exchanges, especially those from emerging economies (Wójcik and Burger, 2010). Drawing on the latest information for all stock exchanges from the WFE,[1] this study seeks to address the following questions: What is the geography of stock markets at the global scale? How has it evolved over time? Which are the most internationalized stock exchanges as destinations for overseas listings? In addition, this study will utilize the case of Chinese firms listing on the NYSE and Nasdaq to illustrate the process of overseas listings.

The Stock Market in Financial Geography Research

Stock Market in Financialization Era

Recent years have seen growing attention to the manifold processes of financialization as they take shape at different geographical scales. Research has sought to unpack a range of issues from the global financial crisis and economic globalization, to the role of finance in regional development, to the impacts of financial systems on individuals and households (Clark and Wójcik, 2007; Lee et al., 2009; Pike and Pollard, 2010; Weber, 2010; French, Leyshon, and Wainwright, 2011). This exciting new area of research has brought a new vigor for examining the processes of financialization, defined loosely as the 'the growing influence of capital markets, their intermediaries, and processes in contemporary economic and political life' (Pike and Pollard, 2010: 30). The process of financialization is increasingly becoming a spatial phenomenon and is becoming increasingly engrained in the economic geographies of our personal, working, and public lives through our access to and use of bank accounts, mortgages, pensions, and savings; employers' ownership; access to capital and financing; and public infrastructure and services (O'Neill, 2001). As such, it is becoming increasingly important to understand processes of financialization across scales and via multiple geographical contexts, and to interrogate the varied social and economic impacts brought about by such processes. Such impetus will only increase as the integral and negative role of finance in the unfolding global economic crisis is brought to the fore (French and Leyshon, 2010).

One of the major empirical thrusts within geographies of finance has been to understand the pervasive influence of financial markets penetrating economic processes across a number of scales. Following this, in new studies of financialization the role, processes, and impacts of financial and stock markets are increasingly of interest. Wójcik (2009) identifies three reasons why stock markets should be at the vanguard of research on financialization. First, because stock markets are important for the sheer scale and size of economic activity that they encompass, manage, and circulate. Second, stock markets produce interesting geographies that are bound up with the multiple and complex processes entwined with economic globalization. Third, as has long been recognized, in a rejection of overly technologically deterministic accounts about the 'new economy', stock markets are both physical and virtual spaces. For Wójcik, the growth and expansion of the stock market is reflective of the unprecedented influence of financialization on the affairs of firms, public organizations, and the livelihoods of ordinary people.

Furthermore, stock markets are interesting because they embody important human geographical phenomena and are the results of the interplay between place, space, and scale. In this sense, stock markets provide an interesting rebuttal to debates concerning the perceived 'flattening' effects of economic globalization (O' Brien, 1992; Freidman, 2005). In such debates, financial integration is characterized by the 'end of geography' or the 'death of distance' reducing the importance of physical proximity, or the influence of unique place-based characteristics on economic processes. As Wójcik (2009) argues, stock markets construct and embed new financial and economic geographies rooted in very material places and performed out of a constellation of numerous economic, political, cultural processes.

Geographers can offer a new analytical perspective on the activities of stock markets that is attentive to socio-spatial relations and construction, and that unpacks the spatiality of finance as well as considering the traditional influence of the firm, labor, and the state (Barnes and Sheppard, 2000). As French et al. note (2011), research thus far has tended to focus on processes of financialization at three particular spatial scales: the nation state; the firm or corporation; and the household and individual. Specifically, there has been a lack of attention to other spaces, such as the region and the international financial system. It is therefore the assertion of this chapter that the role of geographers should be to dissect how financialization broadens the role and influence of stock markets across multiple scales, and then to explore the dynamic between territorial and relational spatialities of geographic differentiation and uneven development.

Overseas Listings in the Context of Financial Globalization

The overseas listing is characterized by several trends explored in the literature (Saudagaran and Biddle, 1992; Karolyi, 1998, 2006; Pagano et al., 2002; Sarkissian and Schill, 2004). First, as firms globalize their markets and production chains, direct access to foreign capital markets via an equity listing can yield important benefits. There has, therefore, been a growing trend of firms, particularly those from developing economies, listing overseas in order to access a range of benefits including increased visibility, lower cost capital, better governance structures, diversified risk, and so on. Second, the international integration of capital markets has led to unprecedented levels of competition among stock exchanges. In this competitive struggle, the winners are the exchanges that manage to attract more foreign listings, and the attendant trading volume and business opportunities. Third, with financial globalization reaching unprecedented levels and increasingly rapidly according to measures such as gross capital flows, stocks of foreign assets and liabilities, and degree of co-movement of asset returns, the listing of firms beyond their home market will only increase in volume and scope in the future (Claessens and Schmukler, 2007). As such, the geography of the stock market requires further analytical attention in order to understand the processes and outcomes of international competition between exchanges, and the benefits and disadvantages experienced by firms listing overseas.

Overseas listing has a long history dating back to the very emergence of stock markets themselves in the seventeenth and eighteenth centuries (Braithwaite and Drahos, 2000). Through time, overseas listing has been cyclical in nature and reflective of wider macro-economic trends and conditions. Evidence suggests that, during periods of economic prosperity, the process of overseas and cross-listing is more likely due to the fact stocks can yield more on markets, and also that it is easier to raise capital from would-be investors (Pagano et al., 2001; Edison and Warnock, 2008). Sarkissian and Schill (2011) have provided a comprehensive analysis of global listing activity. They observe that, in the 1950s, the hosting of foreign equity by stock exchanges was largely a European phenomenon. The leading source of these listings comprised American and South African stocks. By the 1980s, Tokyo became a dominant destination for foreign listings, followed by a strong reversal of foreign listings from Tokyo in the 1990s. By the 2000s, Canadian and Indian firms were the primary source of overseas listings, and the United States became the dominant host for markets, attracting more than 50% of all new foreign-placed shares, followed by Luxembourg and the United Kingdom.

Since the turn of the millennium, two important trends have been impacting on what we could term the 'geography of overseas listings'. First, since 2000 there has been a rapid expansion in the number of host markets for overseas listing, with a number of smaller and emerging markets joining the ranks of more established markets such as those in New York, London, and Hong Kong. New markets have included the likes of Argentina, Finland, Israel, Mexico, Poland, Portugal, Taiwan, and the United Arab Emirates (UAE) (Sarkissian and Schill, 2011). Second, there has been a growth in the number of firms from emerging economies seeking to list overseas. Notably, the growing number of firms from the so-called BRICs emerging economies of Brazil, Russia, India, and China seeking to internationalize is now attracting popular and academic interest (Karolyi, 2004; Karmel, 2006; Wójcik and Burger, 2010; Zhang and King, 2010; Economist, 2011).

Studies have explored the types of firm who list overseas, the motivations for doing so, and discussions about the impacts on the firms and the market. As Karolyi observes (2006: 100), much of the early research on overseas listing emphasized 'the importance of the benefits of a lower cost of capital, an expanded global shareholder base, greater liquidity in the trading of shares, prestige, and publicity over the costs of having to reconcile financial statements with home and foreign standards, direct listing costs, exposure to legal liabilities, taxes and various trading frictions'. New approaches have identified varied reasons from access to new markets and capital to regulatory advantages such as investor protection and greater corporate transparency. Listing on foreign markets presents firms from emerging markets with multiple opportunities: lower transaction costs for investors; more informative financial reporting; more accurate analyst forecasts; and, ultimately, better access to capital (Edison and Warnock, 2008).

Despite assumptions about the economic gains of overseas listing in a globalized world, the various theorizations about why and how firms internationalize lacks sensitivity to geographical factors. When examining the motivations for overseas listing, theoretical and conceptual approaches need to be sensitive to the nuances of place, space, and scale. There is strong evidence to suggest that geographical, cultural, economic, and industrial proximity have a strong influence on where firms choose to list overseas. In their seminal study of global overseas listing activity since 1998, Sarkissian and Schill (2004) show clear evidence of how proximity influences firm decisions regarding where to list and investor decisions concerning in which firms to invest. Their analysis demonstrates strong evidence of regional clustering and proximity preferences between neighbouring markets. Moreover, when choosing to list overseas, firms do not appear to be driven purely by economic gain.

The Uneven Geography of Stock Markets in the Globe

Lead Stock Exchanges in the World

A number of lead stock exchanges dominate the markets. Table 8.1 lists the top 20 stock exchanges by market capitalization at the end of 2018. The top 16 stock exchanges, each with a total market capitalization over US$1 trillion, account for 86.70% of global market capitalization. In North America, the lead stock markets are the NYSE (US$20,679.48 billion), Nasdaq-US (US$9,756.84 billion), and the TMX Group (US$1,937.90 billion). In Asia, the Japan Exchange Group has the largest market capitalization at US$5,296.81 billion as at the end of 2018. China's capital markets have developed markedly. In 2018, the market capitalization of the Shanghai Stock Exchange, Hong Kong Exchanges and Clearing, and the Shenzhen Stock Exchange was US$3,919.42 billion, US$3,819.22 billion, and US$2,405.46 billion, respectively. Other relatively large stock markets in Asia include BSE India Limited (US$2,083.48 billion), National Stock Exchange of India Limited (US$2,056.34 billion), Korea Exchange (US$1,413.72 billion), and Australian Securities Exchange (US$1,262.80 billion). In Europe, the five largest stock exchanges measured by market capitalization are Euronext (US$3,730.40 billion), the London Stock Exchange (LSE) Group (US$3,638.00 billion), Deutsche Börse AG (US$1,755.17 billion), SIX Swiss Exchange (US$1,441.16 billion), and Nasdaq Nordic Exchanges (US$1,322.82 billion).

The top five stock exchanges with the largest market capitalization are the NYSE, Nasdaq-US, Japan Exchange Group, Shanghai Stock Exchange, and Hong Kong Exchanges and Clearing which are located in the well-known financial centers of New York, Tokyo, Osaka, Shanghai, and Hong Kong. The top five stock exchanges account for 56.66% of global market capitalization.

The NYSE, the world's largest stock exchange, accounts for 26.95% of global market capitalization, with a market capitalization of US$20,679.48 billion. The NYSE itself is bigger than the world's 70 smallest major stock exchanges, which together only account for 25.20% of global market capitalization.

Table 8.1 Top 20 stock exchanges by market capitalization at the end of 2018

	Stock exchange	*City*	*Market capitalization (US$ billion)*	*Share to global total (%)*	*Number of listed companies*	*Value of share trading (US$ billion)*
1	NYSE	New York	20,679.48	26.95	2,285	22,940.79
2	Nasdaq-US	New York	9,756.84	12.72	3,058	43,656.06
3	Japan Exchange Group Inc.	Tokyo	5,296.81	6.90	3,657	7,207.44
4	Shanghai Stock Exchange	Shanghai	3,919.42	5.11	1,450	6,140.33
5	Hong Kong Exchanges and Clearing	Hong Kong	3,819.22	4.98	2,315	2,483.00
6	Euronext	Amsterdam	3,730.40	4.86	1,208	2,263.20
7	LSE Group	London	3,638.00	4.74	2,479	4,767.73
8	Shenzhen Stock Exchange	Shenzhen	2,405.46	3.14	2,134	7,600.36
9	BSE India Limited	Bombay	2,083.48	2.72	5,066	121.17
10	National Stock Exchange of India Limited	Bombay	2,056.34	2.68	1,923	1,165.83
11	TMX Group	Toronto	1,937.90	2.53	3,383	1,447.56
12	Deutsche Börse AG	Frankfurt am Main	1,755.17	2.29	514	2,348.70
13	SIX Swiss Exchange	Zürich	1,441.16	1.88	270	1,100.08
14	Korea Exchange	Seoul	1,413.72	1.84	2,207	2,559.16
15	Nasdaq Nordic Exchanges	Stockholm	1,322.82	1.72	1,019	920.75
16	Australian Securities Exchange	Sydney	1,262.80	1.65	2,146	982.03
17	Taiwan Stock Exchange	Taipei	959.22	1.25	945	982.90
18	BM&FBOVESPA S.A.	São Paulo	916.82	1.20	339	816.90
19	Johannesburg Stock Exchange	Johannesburg	865.33	1.13	360	422.26
20	BME Spanish Exchanges	Madrid	723.69	0.94	3,006	691.88

Nasdaq-US is the world's second-largest stock exchange, with a market capitalization of US$9,756.84 billion. The combined market capitalization of the two stock exchanges in the United States is US$30,436.32 billion, accounting for 39.67% of global market capitalization.

Overall, those stock exchanges located in Western Europe and the United States have a longer history. For instance, in Europe, the Deutsche Börse AG in Germany was established in 1585, the LSE Group in 1698, the Wiener Börse in 1771, the NYSE in 1792, and the Irish Stock Exchange in 1793. Stock exchanges in other parts of the world are quite young. For instance, two Chinese stock exchanges, the Shanghai Stock Exchange and the Shenzhen Stock Exchange, were set up in 1990.

The number of listed firms on each major stock exchange varies a great deal, from several hundred to several thousand. For instance, BSE India Limited, founded in 1875, has the largest number of listed companies at 5,066. It is also the first stock exchange in Asia. Despite the largest number of listed firms, the average market capitalization of each listed company on this stock exchange is small, only US$0.41 billion. The stock exchanges with a relatively large number of listed firms are the Japan Exchange Group, TMX Group, Nasdaq-US, and BME Spanish Exchanges. The listed companies of the top five stock exchanges account for 34.83% of the total number of listed firms.

The top five stock exchanges measured by share trading value are Nasdaq-US, the NYSE, Shenzhen Stock Exchange, Japan Exchange Group, and Shanghai Stock Exchange. Although the market capitalization of Nasdaq-US is smaller than that of the NYSE, the number of listed companies and the value of stock trading of Nasdaq-US are greater than those of the NYSE, reflecting that Nasdaq-US is a highly dynamic market for investors. Similarly, the Shenzhen Stock Exchange in China ranks 8th by market capitalization, but its share of trading value puts it in 3rd place, coming after Nasdaq-US and the NYSE. The market capitalization of the Shanghai Stock Exchange is 1.6 times that of the Shenzhen Stock Exchange. However, the number of listed companies and share of trading value of the Shenzhen Stock Exchange are larger than those of the Shanghai Stock Exchange.

Overall, the market capitalization of all stock exchanges has grown over time, but the rankings of the stock exchanges have been relatively stable since the mid-2000s. Figure 8.1 shows the changes in market capitalization of the 10 lead stock exchanges from 2003 to 2018. During this period, the market capitalization of the NYSE had been the highest in the world, far higher than any other exchange. From 2011, Nasdaq took second place, which it has since maintained. The two Chinese stock markets, the Shenzhen Stock Exchange and the Shanghai Stock Exchange, have made rapid growth both in the number of listed firms and the amount of market capitalization.

The rise of Nasdaq-US is significant. Nasdaq-US is a young stock exchange, only established in 1971. However, the market capitalization of Nasdaq has grown rapidly. The gap in market capitalization between Nasdaq-US and the NYSE has been closing since the end of the 2000s. It is now the major

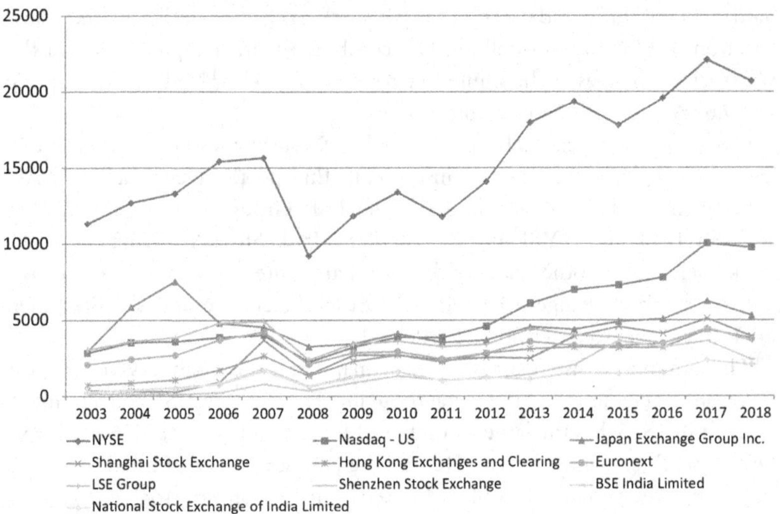

Figure 8.1 Market capitalization of 10 lead stock exchanges, 2003–2018 (US$ billion)
Source: Author's creation.

destination for initial public offerings (IPOs) of high-tech firms. For instance, Alphabet (Google), Microsoft, and Facebook are all listed on Nasdaq-US. In addition, Nasdaq is attractive not only to American firms, but also to high-tech firms worldwide (Pan and Brooker, 2014).

Due to the financial crisis of 2008–09, the market capitalization of all stock exchanges dropped dramatically; however, as the two lead stock markets, the NYSE and Nasdaq-US recovered from the financial crisis more quickly than others. In 2013, the NYSE's market capitalization surpassed the pre-crisis level, and Nasdaq recovered even more quickly, surpassing its pre-crisis level one year earlier than the NYSE. In contrast, recovery for other stock exchanges took longer. The market capitalization of the Japan Exchange Group and LSE Group was still smaller than these exchanges' pre-crisis peak. In fact, the gap between the top two stock exchanges, the NYSE and Nasdaq, and the other lead stock exchanges has increased significantly since the mid-2000s. Consequently, as a financial center, New York has strengthened its position due to the performance of the two lead stock markets.

Interestingly, the number of listed firms on these lead stock exchanges is relatively stable. Even the financial crisis did not impact the number of listed firms in most stock exchanges to any appreciable degree. Figure 8.2 shows the top 10 stock exchanges by number of listed companies for the period 2003–18. Most stock exchanges have experienced a slow growth in the number of listed firms; the TMX Group and LSE Group are exceptional in their performance. BSE India Limited have had the largest number of listed companies since the mid-2000s. During the period 2004–15, the number of listed firms on BSE

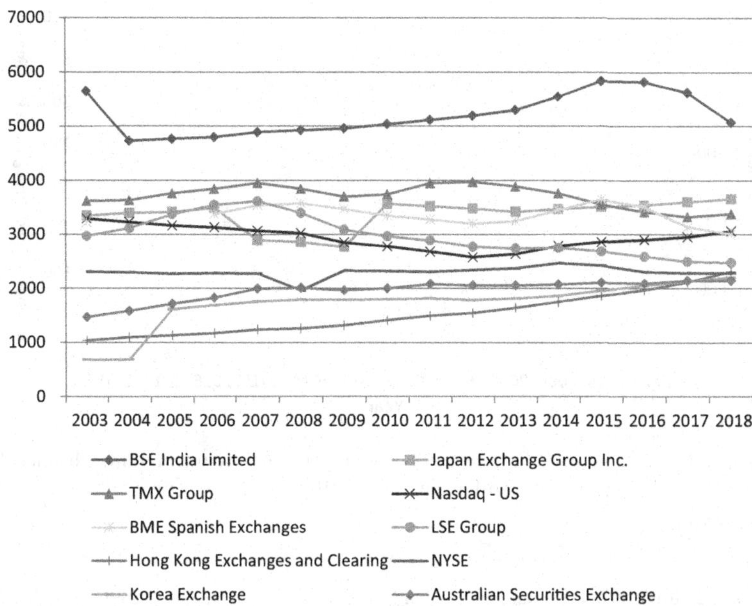

Figure 8.2 Top 10 stock exchanges by number of listed companies, 2003–2018
Source: Author's creation.

India Limited grew slowly and have only recently begun to decline slightly. In contrast, the number of firms listed on Hong Kong Exchanges and Clearing has grown steadily. The key reason for this may be that many firms from mainland China have sought listing in Hong Kong market.

IPOs in Major Markets

Most firms go public through making IPOs on a stock exchange. The number and size of IPO deals a stock exchange handles can offer a relatively clear picture of its dynamics. Figure 8.3 shows the number of new IPOs and investment flows during 2007–18. Overall, the figures are quite stable.

In 2009–18, certain stock exchanges have handled more new IPOs than others. As shown in Table 8.2, the Shenzhen Stock Exchange in China has dealt with the largest number of new IPOs, followed by the TMX Group, Hong Kong Exchanges and Clearing, the LSE Group, and Nasdaq-US. In addition to those stock exchanges from developed economies, stock exchanges from India and Poland have good records of new IPOs.

Table 8.3 shows top 10 stock exchanges with the largest number of new IPOs and largest investment flows through IPOs in 2018. Due to the IPOs of firms from mainland China (Pan and Brooker, 2014), Hong Kong Exchanges and Clearing ranked the first in both indicators. In addition, Nasdaq-US, the LSE Group, Japan

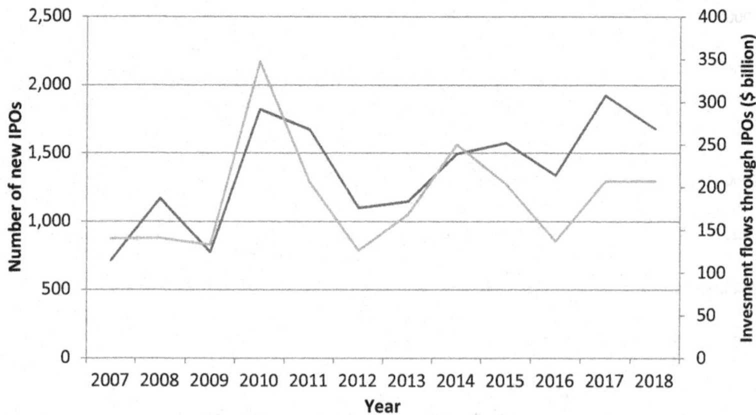

Figure 8.3 Total number of new companies listed and investment flows channeled through an IPO worldwide, 2007–2018

Source: Author's creation.

Table 8.2 Top10 stock exchanges by total number of new companies listed through an IPO, 2009–2018

	Stock exchange	*Number of new IPOs*
1	Shenzhen Stock Exchange	1,363
2	TMX Group	1,212
3	Hong Kong Exchanges and Clearing	1,093
4	LSE Group	1,026
5	Nasdaq-US	985
6	Korea Exchange	856
7	Australian Securities Exchange	826
8	NYSE	735
9	BSE India Limited	698
10	Warsaw Stock Exchange	630

Exchange Group, and NYSE are all main destinations of new IPOs, reflecting the important roles of New York, London, and Tokyo as international financial centers. The high ranking of the Shenzhen Stock Exchange, Shanghai Stock Exchange, and Indonesia Stock Exchange indicates the rise of developing economies.

Uneven Geography of the Stock Markets

The number of stock exchanges rose from 45 in 2003 to 80 in 2018, while uneven geographies of stock markets exist globally (see Figure 8.4). Most stock exchanges

Table 8.3 Top 10 stock exchanges by number of new IPOs and investment flows through IPOs in 2018

	Stock exchange	*Number of new IPOs in the year*	*Stock exchange*	*Investment flows through IPOs (US$ million)*
1	Hong Kong Exchanges and Clearing	205	Hong Kong Exchanges and Clearing	36,736.20
2	Nasdaq-US	150	Japan Exchange Group Inc.	28,431.76
3	TMX Group	127	NYSE	26,253.00
4	LSE Group	119	Nasdaq-US	22,300.80
5	BSE India Limited	97	Shanghai Stock Exchange	13,147.58
6	National Stock Exchange of India Limited	97	LSE Group	11,179.08
7	Korea Exchange	97	Shenzhen Stock Exchange	7,766.08
8	Australian Securities Exchange	94	Deutsche Börse AG	7,167.75
9	Japan Exchange Group Inc.	89	Indonesia Stock Exchange	6,586.85
10	NYSE	65	Australian Securities Exchange	6,285.05

are located in Europe, North America, and the Asian countries. The 80 major exchanges are distributed in 69 countries (regions) and 75 cities. In addition, as at the end of 2018, the stock exchanges with the largest market capitalization (represented by the size of circle in Figure 8.4) are located in a small number of international financial centers, such as New York, London, Tokyo, and Hong Kong.

Since the mid-2000s, more stock markets have been established in less-developed economies; in particular, in African and Asian countries. Moreover, some stock exchanges in less-developed economies have become very influential, such as the Shanghai Stock Exchange, Shenzhen Stock Exchange, and Indonesia Stock Exchange. Conversely, the number of stock markets in developed countries has decreased, due to mergers and acquisitions. The market capitalization of stock exchanges in some second-tier financial centers in developed economies—for example, Brussels, Amsterdam, Frankfurt, and Paris—have stagnated, or even declined.

Overall, developed economies have relatively higher ratio of total market value to GDP, while less-developed economies have lower ratio of total market value to GDP. China and India are the two exceptions. Table 8.2 shows the top

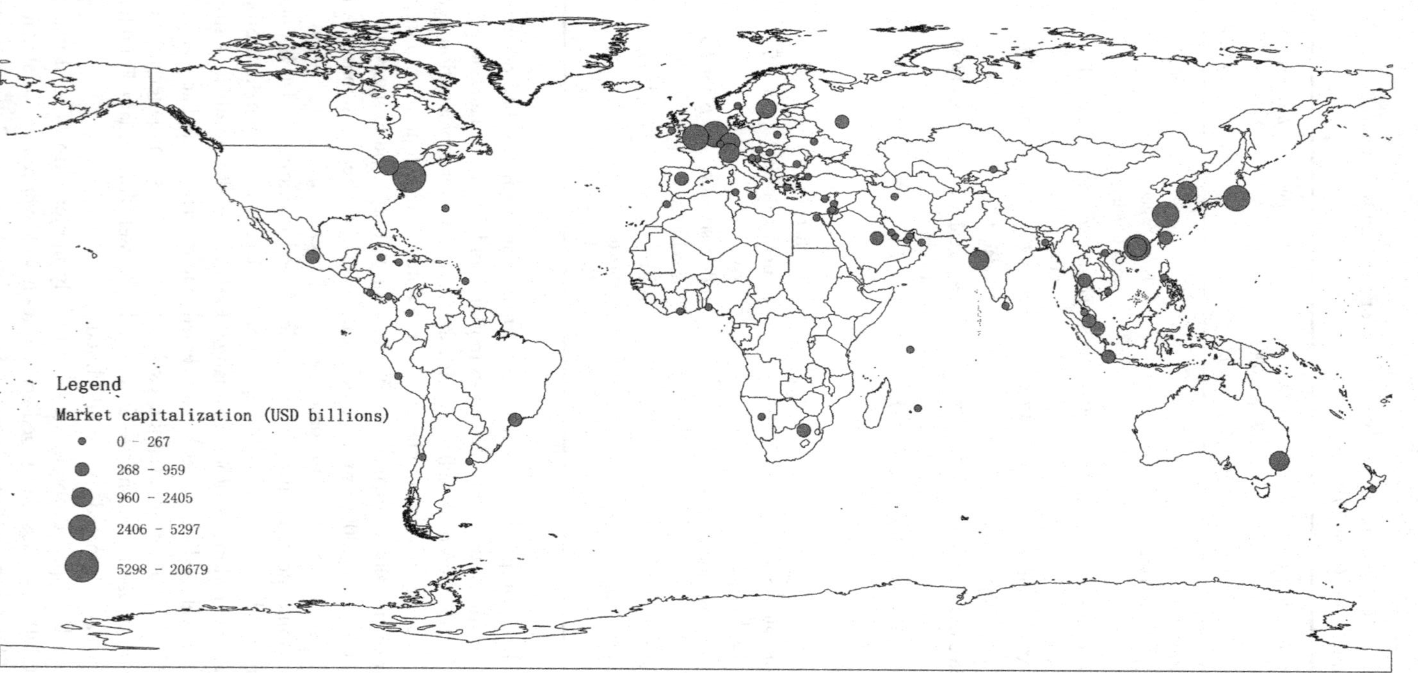

Figure 8.4 Distribution of stock exchanges in the world

Source: Author's creation.

Table 8.4 Top 10 countries (regions) by total market capitalization at the end of 2018

	Country	*Number of exchanges*	*Market capitalization in 2018 (US$ billion)*	*Share to the global total market capitalization (%)*	*Market capitalization in 2017 (US$ billion)/ Country's GDP in 2017 (US$ billion) (%)*	*Country's GDP in 2017/ World GDP in 2017 (US$80,935 billion) (%)*
1	United States	2	30,436.31	39.67	165.65	23.96
2	China (mainland)	2	6,324.88	8.24	71.18	15.12
3	Japan	1	5,296.81	6.90	127.72	6.02
4	India	2	4,139.82	5.40	180.06	3.21
5	Hong Kong SAR, China	1	3,819.22	4.98	1,274.13	0.42
6	Netherlands	1	3,730.40	4.86	531.71	1.02
7	United Kingdom	1	3,638.00	4.74	169.90	3.24
8	Canada	1	1,937.90	2.53	143.19	2.04
9	Germany	1	1,755.17	2.29	61.52	4.54
10	Switzerland	1	1,441.16	1.88	248.42	0.84

10 economies with the largest market capitalization of the stock markets as at the end of 2018. In most of the 10 economies, the ratio of market value to GDP is higher than 100%, except for China and Germany. Hong Kong has the highest ratio, at 1,274.13%, which is followed by the Netherlands, Switzerland, and India.

As a superpower, the United States accounted for 23.96% of the world's GDP in 2018 and 39.67% of the world's stock market value in 2017, both ranking the first in the world. The US stock market capitalization was 165.65% of GDP in 2017. China is the second-largest economy in the world. Its GDP accounts for 15.12% of the world's total, and its stock market value accounts for 8.24% of the world's total, both ranking in second place in the world. China's ratio of stock market capitalization to its GDP is only 71.18%, much lower than that of the United States.

Overseas Listings as a Global Trend

Overseas Listings on International Stock Exchanges

Overseas listings have become a global trend. Table 8.5 lists the top 10 stock exchanges with the largest number of foreign listing companies by the end of 2018. The Wiener Börse in Vienna, NYSE, Nasdaq-US, and the LSE Group have the largest numbers of foreign listings. However, the most internationalized stock exchanges are the smaller ones. For instance, the Wiener Börse in Vienna in Austria has 610 foreign listed companies, accounting for 90.10% of the total. Similarly, the Luxembourg Stock Exchange is also highly internationalized, as the foreign listing firms account for 83.33% of the total.

Figure 8.5 shows the number of foreign companies listed on the NYSE, Nasdaq-US, and the LSE. Overall, the number of foreign firms on the NYSE was quite stable during 2003–18. Following the financial crisis of 2008–09, the number of foreign firms increased slightly. The number of foreign listings on Nasdaq-US increased more significantly than that on the NYSE, particularly after 2012. In contrast, the number of foreign companies listed on the LSE Group decreased quickly following the financial crisis, and the trend continues.

The transaction volumes of foreign firms' shares in some international stock exchanges—in particular, Nasdaq-US, the NYSE, and the LSE Group—are quite large. As shown in Table 8.6, the share trading value of foreign shares on Nasdaq-US was US$4,903.61 billion in 2018, ranking first in the world and accounting for 11.23% of the total trading value in this market. The share trading values of foreign firms listed on the LSE Group and the NYSE in 2018 were US$1,589.36 billion and US$1,299 billion, respectively. The rate of the share trading value of foreign shares to the market total in the LSE Group was 33.34%, which is much higher than that of Nasdaq-US and the NYSE.

Table 8.5 Top 10 stock exchanges by number of foreign listed companies at the end of 2018

	Stock exchange	*Total*	*Domestic*	*Domestic/ total (%)*	*Foreign*	*Foreign/ total (%)*
1	Wiener Börse	677	67	9.90	610	90.10
2	NYSE	2,285	1,775	77.68	510	22.32
3	Nasdaq-US	3,058	2,622	85.74	436	14.26
4	LSE Group	2,479	2,061	83.14	418	16.86
5	Singapore Exchange	741	482	65.05	259	34.95
6	Hong Kong Exchanges and Clearing	2,315	2,161	93.35	154	6.65
7	Euronext	1,208	1,059	87.67	149	12.33
8	Australian Securities Exchange	2,146	2,004	93.38	142	6.62
9	Luxembourg Stock Exchange	162	27	16.67	135	83.33
10	Taiwan Stock Exchange	945	855	90.48	90	9.52

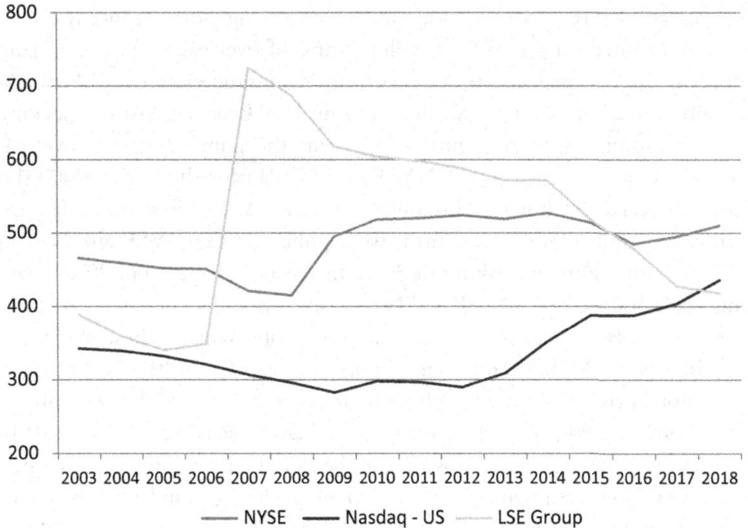

Figure 8.5 The number of foreign listed companies of the three lead stock exchanges, 2003–2018

Source: Author's creation.

Table 8.6 Top 10 stock exchanges by share trading value of foreign shares (US$ billion) at the end of 2018

	Stock exchange	*Value of share trading (US$ billion)*	*Share trading value of foreign shares (US$ billion)*	*Share to total (%)*
1	Nasdaq-US	43,656.06	4,903.61	11.23
2	LSE Group	4,767.73	1,589.36	33.34
3	NYSE	22,940.79	1,299.00	5.66
4	Deutsche Börse AG	2,348.70	578.25	24.62
5	SIX Swiss Exchange	1,100.08	88.03	8.00
6	Hong Kong Exchanges and Clearing	2,483.00	84.02	3.38
7	Johannesburg Stock Exchange	422.26	78.49	18.59
8	Taiwan Stock Exchange	982.90	64.32	6.54
9	Australian Securities Exchange	982.03	50.41	5.13
10	Nasdaq Nordic Exchanges	920.75	36.54	3.97

Chinese Companies Listed on Stock Markets in the US

As the largest BRICs economy and the fastest growing global economy, China provides an interesting case for the illustration of overseas listings. As Zhang and King (2010) argue, due to the significant economic growth in China and the ambitions of growing firms, Chinese firms have been aggressive in seeking capital via foreign listings. Figure 8.6 presents the number of new overseas listings of Chinese firms on the NYSE and Nasdaq for the period 2000–17. There are over 300 Chinese firms listed on the two American stock exchanges. A growing number of Chinese firms went public on the NYSE and Nasdaq from 2000, the number peaking in 2010. In recent years, around 20 Chinese firms made IPOs on the NYSE and Nasdaq each year.

In the 1990s and early 2000s, some large state-owned Chinese firms—including China Mobile, and Petro China—made IPOs on the NYSE. After 2000, more privately owned high-tech firms—for example, Baidu, Alibaba, and JD—listed publicly on the two stock exchanges (Pan and Brooker, 2014). Most Chinese firms listed on Nasdaq and the NYSE are from more developed regions in China. As shown in Figure 8.7, Beijing, Shanghai, and Shenzhen have the largest number of overseas listings on the two American stock exchanges. Not surprisingly, the large state-owned firms and high-tech firms are mostly concentrated in a small number of cities.

There are strict regulations on overseas listings in China, while the attitude of the Chinese central government to overseas listings has been ambiguous.

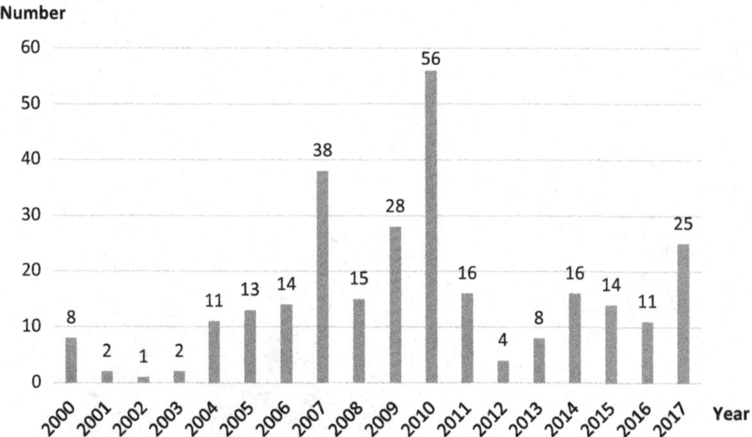

Figure 8.6 Number of new overseas listings of Chinese companies on NYSE and Nasdaq, 2000–2017

Source: Author's creation.

On the one hand, it has long been considered an important channel through which China can attract foreign investment. Moreover, overseas listings have been considered a way to boost reform on state-owned firms. For these large firms, listing on foreign exchanges represents a good way to raise capital, and flagship state-owned firms are more likely to gain such opportunities (Green, 2004; Du and Xu, 2009). Listing on foreign exchanges requires firms to comply with strict corporate governance and accounting standards that can help reform state-owned firms; there is also a wider argument that entering foreign markets will encourage state firms to compete with multinational corporations abroad and encourage broader internationalization.[2]

However, on the other hand, the government is keen to develop China's domestic bourses by encouraging companies to list locally. As a consequence, the government approach to overseas listings has varied depending on the ownership of firms with generally central government encouraging state-owned firms to list overseas.[3] The overseas listings of state-owned firms are under the direction from the central government. In the meantime, the regulation on privately owned firms' overseas listings has been strict. Firms that turned to overseas capital markets needed approval to do so from the China Securities Regulatory Commission and other ministers. In light of this, a large number of private Chinese firms have sought to change their incorporation so as to be offshore firms, and then seek to go public on a foreign stock market without approval from the government.[4]

The government has influence regarding the choice of location Chinese firms may make for overseas listing—especially for state-owned firms. Of all the destinations, Hong Kong, the NYSE and LSE main board are particularly

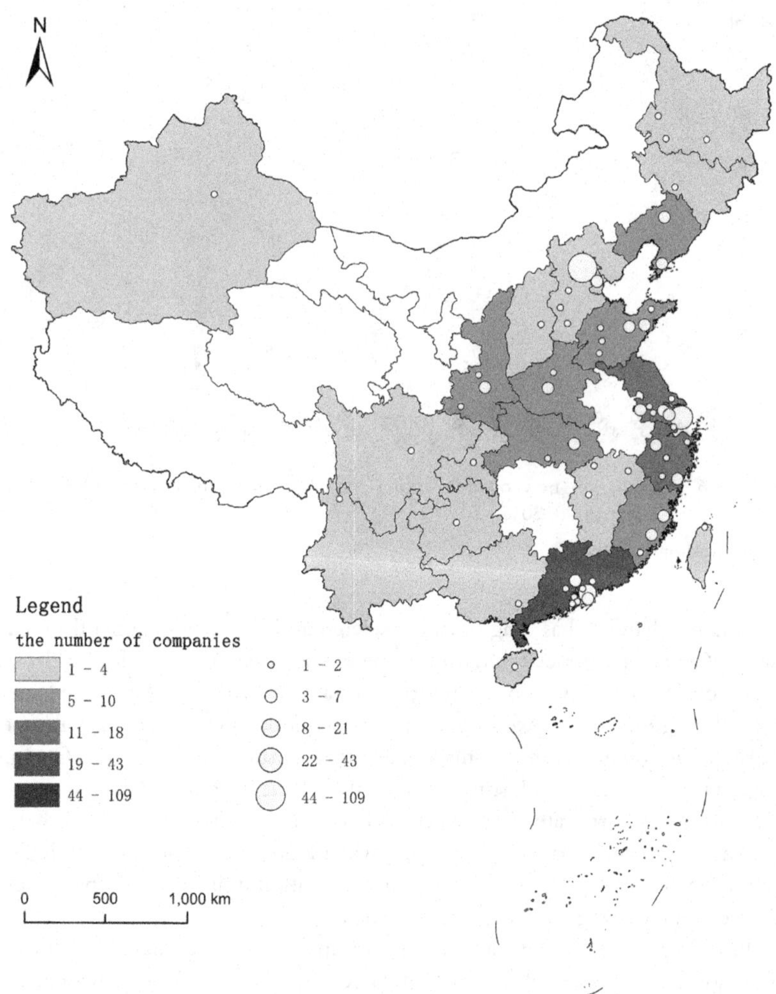

Figure 8.7 Geography of overseas listings of Chinese companies on NYSE and Nasdaq in the end of 2018

Source: Author's creation.

favored by central government. Hong Kong was returned to China in 1997 and has been the most important destination for Chinese firms from early on (Karreman and Van der Knaap, 2012).[5] The NYSE was favored by the central government of China as it is one of the most well-known stock exchanges in the world. The Chinese government aims to improve corporate governance for state-owned firms and, in an effort to make them more competitive in the global market, puts them in direct competition with large multinational corporations. Thus, many state-owned firms went public on the NYSE.[6]

Since listing on domestic stock exchanges in China for private firms is an uncertain and time-consuming procedure (Pan and Brooker, 2014; Pan and Xia, 2014), many private companies turn to overseas stock markets. To do this, many private Chinese firms first change their incorporation to that of offshore firms and then seek to go public in the foreign stock markets without approval from the Chinese government. By adopting the well-known Variable Interest Entity structure, a large number of Chinese private companiesare listed on Nasdaq—particularly companies from the high-tech sector, such as Baidu and Sina.

Chinese firms listing in the US markets have obtained certain benefits (Luo, Fang, and Esqueda, 2012). It seems that these overseas listed firms have improved corporate governance and operating performance, and also enjoyed other benefits (Luo et al., 2012). The empirical enquiry of Baker et al. (2002) asserts that the greatest visibility can be obtained by listing on the NYSE or the LSE. Similarly, Chinese firms could enhance visibility and improve their reputation by listing on overseas stock exchanges (Busaba et al., 2015; Pan et al., 2020).

The listing of many Chinese firms on the NSYE and Nasdaq has strengthened the competiveness of the American stock markets, which is also beneficial to New York as an international financial center. Conversely, the Chinese capital market has lost many good companies. In response, the policy-makers in the finance sector in China have made many reforms and set up many new boards. For instance, the Small and Medium-Sized Board and the Growth Enterprise Market were set up in the Shenzhen Stock Exchange in 2004 and 2009, respectively, with the purpose of providing platforms for startups in the high-tech sector to raise capital via IPOs. In 2013, the National Equities Exchange and Quotations (NEEQ) was established in Beijing as a new national platform for startups. More recently, the Sci-Tech Innovation Board (STAR Market) in the Shanghai Stock Exchange was set up in 2019 with the aim of attracting high-tech startups. The financial and other requirements for domestic listing have been relaxed over time and Chinese firms have more options for domestic listings. Overall, the capital market in mainland China has made significant progress, partly due to the competition from the global markets.

Summary

The ever-changing global financial landscape has been partly shaped by the rise and fall of stock exchanges. This study has presented the uneven geographies of stock exchanges. Overall, the lead global stock exchanges are located in a small number of international financial centers; for example, New York, London, Tokyo, Hong Kong. Some stock exchanges in second-place financial centers have either declined, or merged with other lead global stock exchanges. In the meantime, some emerging stock exchanges, such as the Shanghai Stock Exchange and the Shenzhen Stock Exchange in China, have been catching up rapidly. However, many newly established stock exchanges in less-developed economies are in a very marginal position when measured by market capitalization and their trading value of shares. Moreover, many economies have no stock market.

Given the uneven geographies of stock market activity, there has been an increasing trend for overseas listings. A large number of firms worldwide have chosen to list on the lead global stock exchanges for a variety of reasons. In this manner, the NYSE, Nasdaq, and the LSE Group are the most favored destinations for overseas listings. In addition, there are also some regional hubs attracting firms from neighboring economies to list their shares. For instance, a very large proportion of foreign firms are listed on Wiener Börse, the Singapore Exchange, and Luxembourg Stock Exchange. Drawing on the case of Chinese firms listing overseas on Nasdaq and the NYSE, this study illistrates the motivations and impacts of the process. Overseas listings can bring significant benefits, including financial capital, reputation, improvement of corporate governance among others. In addition, the host stock exchange may strengthen their global influence by attracting more foreign listings, which could underpin the international financial center in which the stock exchanges are located.

The global financing activities of corporations have been heavily reliant on the function of stock exchanges. More research is required on the role of stock exchanges in this era of financialization. What is the role of the lead stock exchanges in shaping the global financial landscape? To what extent will the continuing trend for mergers and acquisitions between stock exchanges affect the global markets? Is there any stock exchange emerging from China or India that could fundamentally reshape the current orders of global stock exchanges? Overseas listings have been considered a typical way of integrating into global financial networks (Coe, Lai, and Wójcik, 2014; Pan et al., 2020), what is the role of the stock exchange in a burgeoning research area of global financial networks? How have stock exchanges interacted with the firms that list, with other financially advanced business service firms, and with national and local governments in the formation of global financial networks? The studies on the geography of stock markets and overseas listings could shed light on the debates on financial centers, the geopolitics of finance, and how global financing may influence regional development.

Notes

1 All data are collected from the World Federation of Exchanges (WFE) for the period December 2003–December 2018. The LSE Group data for 2003–08 used the combined data of the London Stock Exchange and Borsa Italiana. The Japan Exchange Group Inc. data for 2003–3 used combined data from the Japan Exchange Group, the Tokyo and Japan Exchange Group, and Osaka.

2 http://stock.sohu.com/20080825/n259192491.shtml

3 http://news.xinhuanet.com/fortune/2010-02/08/content_12950524.htm

4 http://www.forbes.com/sites/richardpearson/2012/10/18/looking-at-chinese-vies/

5 http://www.chinadaily.com.cn/epaper/html/cd/2002/200210/20021007/20021007011_1.html

6 http://stock.sohu.com/20080825/n259192491.shtml

References

Barnes, T. J. and E. Sheppard (2000). *A Companion to Economic Geography*. Oxford: Blackwell.

Braithwaite, J. and P. Drahos (2000). *Global Business Regulation*. Cambridge: Cambridge University Press.

Busaba, W.Y., L. Guo, Z. Sun and T. Yu (2015). The dark side of cross-listing: a new perspective from China. *Journal of Banking & Finance*, 57, 1–16.

Claessens, S. and S. L. Schmukler (2007). International financial integration through equity markets: which firms from which countries go global? *Journal of International Money and Finance*, 26, 788–813.

Clark, G. (1998). Pension fund capitalism: a causal analysis. *Geografiska Annaler: Series B, Human Geography*, 80, 139–157.

Clark, G. and A. Wójcik (2007). *The Geography of Finance: Corporate Governance in the Global Marketplace*. Oxford: Oxford University Press.

Clark, G. L. (2000). *Pension Fund Capitalism*. Oxford: Oxford University Press.

Clark, G. L., D. Wójcik and R. Bauer. (2006). Geographically dispersed ownership and inter-market stock price arbitrage – Ahold's crisis of corporate governance and its implications for global standards. *Journal of Economic Geography*, 6, 303–322.

Coe, N. M., K. P. Lai and D. Wójcik (2014). Integrating finance into global production networks. *Regional Studies*, 48, 761–777.

Du, J. and C. Xu. (2009). Which firms went public in China? A study of financial market regulation. *World Development*, 37, 812–824.

Economist. (2011). *Red Alert*.

Edison, H. and F. Warnock. (2008). Cross-border listings, capital controls, and equity flows to emerging markets. *Journal of International Money and Finance*, 27, 1013–1027.

Freidman, T. (2005). *The World Is Flat: A Brief History of the Twenty-First Century*. New York: Farrar.

French, S. and A. Leyshon. (2010). 'These f@#king guys': the terrible waste of a good crisis. *Environment and Planning A*, 42, 2549–2559.

French, S., A. Leyshon and T. Wainwright. (2011). Financializing space, spacing financialization. *Progress in Human Geography*, 35, 789–819.

Green, S. (2004). *The Development of China's Stockmarket, 1984–2002: Equity Politics and Market Institutions*. London: RoutledgeCurzon.

Karmel, R. S. (2006). The Brazilian securities market: Brazil finds favour among foreign securities investors. *New Jersey Law Journal*, 13, 23.

Karolyi, G. A. (1998). Why do companies list shares abroad? A survey of evidence and its managerial implications. *Financial Markets, Institutions and Instruments*, 7, 1–60.

Karolyi, G. A. (2004). The role of American depositary receipts in the development of emerging equity markets. *Review of Economics and Statistics*, 86, 670–690.

Karolyi, G. A. (2006). The world of cross-listings and cross-listings of the world: challenging conventional wisdom. *Review of Finance*, 10, 99–152.

Karreman, B. and G. A. Van der Knaap (2012). The geography of equity listing and financial centre competition in mainland China and Hong Kong. *Journal of Economic Geography*, 12, 899–922.

Lee, R., G. Clark, J. Pollard and A. Leyshon (2009). The remit of financial geography – before and after the crisis. *Journal of Economic Geography*, 9, 723–747.

Luo, Y., F. Fang and O. A. Esqueda (2012). The overseas listing puzzle: post-IPO performance of Chinese stocks and ADRs in the US market. *Journal of Multinational Financial Management*, 22, 193–211.

O'Brien, R. (1992). *Global Financial Integration: The End of Geography*. New York: Council on Foreign Relations.

O'Neill, P. (2001). Financial narratives of the modern corporation. *Journal of Economic Geography*, 1, 181–199.

Pagano, M., O. Randl, A. Roell and J. Zechner (2001). What makes stock exchanges succeed? Evidence from cross-listing decisions. *European Economic Review*, 45, 770–782.
Pagano, M., A. Röell and J. Zechner (2002). The geography of equity listing: why do companies list abroad? *Journal of Finance*, 57, 2651–2694.
Pan, F. and D. Brooker (2014). Going global? Examining the geography of Chinese firms' overseas listings on international stock exchanges. *Geoforum*, 52, 1–11.
Pan, F. and Y. Xia (2014). Location and agglomeration of headquarters of publicly listed firms within China's urban system. *Urban Geography*, 35, 757–779.
Pan, F., C. Yang, H. Wang and D. Wójcik. (2020). Linking global financial networks with regional development: a case study of Linyi, China. *Regional Studies*, 54, 187–197.
Pike, A. and J. Pollard. (2010). Economic geographies of financialization. *Economic Geography*, 86, 29–51.
Sarkissian, S. and M. Schill. (2004). The overseas listing decision: new evidence of proximity preference. *The Review of Financial Studies*, 17, 769–809.
Sarkissian, S. and M. Schill. (2011). *Cross-Listing Waves*. SSRN. http://papers.ssrn.com/sol3/papers.cfm?abstract_id=1244042 (last accessed 8 May 2012).
Sarre, P. (2007). Understanding the geography of international finance. *Geography Compass*, 1/2, 1076–1096.
Saudagaran, S. and G. Biddle. (1992). Foreign listing location: a study of MNCs and stock listing locations in eight countries. *Journal of International Business Studies*, 26, 319–341.
Toporowski, J. (1999). *The End of Finance: Capital Market Inflation, Financial Derivatives and Pension Fund Capitalism*. London: Routledge.
Wójcik, D. (2009). Geography of stock markets. *Geography Compass*, 3/4, 1451–1499.
Wójcik, D. (2011). *The Global Stock Market: Issuers, Investors and Intermediaries in an Eneven World*. Oxford: Oxford University Press.
Wójcik, D. (2012). *The Global Stock Market: Issuers, Investors, and Intermediaries in an Uneven World*. Cheltenham: Prior Books.
Wójcik, D. and C. Burger (2010). Listing BRICs: stock issuers from Brazil, Russia, India, and China in New York, London, and Luxembourg. *Economic Geography*, 86, 275–296.
Weber, R. (2010). Selling city futures: the financialization of urban redevelopment policy. *Economic Geography*, 86, 251–274.
Zhang, C. X. and T. H. D. King (2010). The decision to list abroad: the case of ADRs and foreign IPOs by Chinese companies. *Journal of Multinational Financial Management*, 20, 71–92.
Zook, M. A. (2002). Grounded capital: venture financing and the geography of the Internet industry, 1994–2000. *Journal of Economic Geography*, 2, 151–177.

9

HOUSING UNDER THE EMPIRE OF FINANCE[1]

Raquel Rolnik

Introduction

Millions of indebted or foreclosed homeowners, subprime victims of a decade of credit booms; empty neighborhoods, towns, and bankrupted new developments, protesters occupying streets and public spaces for months, a hunger strike of owners deprived from their promised apartments—scenes of different cities and regions at the end of the first decade of the twenty-first century.[2] A new financial crisis: starting in the US mortgage market, and turning into a credit crunch that spread rapidly over cities and regions, gaining considerable size and outreach. Not surprisingly, the first sector to be deeply hit was housing. Fed by pension funds, private equities, hedge funds, and other 'fictitious commodities', housing became a fictitious commodity itself when it was taken over by finance. Housing has been one of the most powerful new frontiers of financialization during the decades of economic boom and was converted, from the beginning of the crisis, into one of the main strategies to recover from it. At the end of the second decade of the new millennium, the global housing crisis is far from being overcome, and has gained a new face, at least in some European and US cities: the financialization of rental units.

Backed initially by the political force of homeownership ideology Ronald (2008) and property-owning democracy, deeply rooted in some societies and recently adopted in others, and by the 'socialization of credit'—the inclusion of middle- and low-income consumers into financial circuits, the takeover of the housing sector by global finance opened a new frontier for capital accumulation, allowing the free circulation of financial capital over almost all urban land. The movement I have just described has been a path dependent shift of housing policy paradigms in almost every state; initiated by Wall Street and neoliberal US and UK politicians, the change of meaning and economic role of housing gained *momentum* with the fall of the Berlin Wall in 1989 and the subsequent hegemony of free market ideology. Whether freely decided by governments or imposed by international financial institutions and other actors as loan conditions, the new paradigm was mainly based in the implementation of policies designed to create stronger and larger residential financial markets, including for middle- and low-income consumers. In 1993, a World Bank influential report 'Housing: enabling markets to work', summarized the new thinking: the report contained not only extensive arguments on how potent the housing sector could be for the economy, but also guidelines for governments on how best to design policies to achieve this goal (World Bank, 1993). Since the 1990s, housing finance has increased dramatically in developed economies. In the United States, United Kingdom, Denmark, Australia, and Canada, among other countries, residential mortgage markets represent 50–100% of the gross domestic product (GDP) (Schwartz and Seabrooke, 2009: 16). From former Soviet countries in Central Asia and Eastern Europe (Kazakhstan, Ukraine) to Latin America (Chile, Mexico, Peru, and Brazil), and from Africa (South Africa) to Asia (India, Thailand, China), the takeover of the housing sector by finance has been a massive and prevalent trend in such a way that another World Bank report issued in 2006 defined the conjunction with the words 'the housing finance genie is out of the bottle' (Buckley and Kalarickal, 2006).

In the history of cities, cycles of production, destruction, and devaluation of built space generating new expansion fronts for surplus capital are not new. However, there are some novelties now: the huge scale of this process, proportionate to the massive concentration and availability of global financial capital today, which can circulate freely around the planet; the velocity, directly derived from the technological revolution of value representation, in online and real-time transactions, in increasingly abstract circuits that no longer have any connection to the social work embedded into built space, let alone to its inhabitants (Harvey, 2014: 241).

The commodification of housing, as well as the increased use of housing as an investment asset, integrated in a speculative globalized financial market, has deeply impacted the enjoyment of the right to adequate housing in the world. The belief that markets could regulate the allocation of housing as the most rational means of resource distribution, combined with experiments with 'creative' financial products related to housing, has led public policies towards the abandonment of the conceptual meaning of housing as a social good, part of the commonalities a society agrees to share or to provide to those with fewer resources, a means to redistribute wealth. Housing, as other sectors, was affected by a wave of dismantling basic institutional welfare and the mobilization of a range of policies intended to extend market discipline, competition, and commodification (Brenner and Theodore, 2002).

In each country, the new ideas confronted existing national welfare systems and housing policy coalitions, so that financialization of housing can assume different forms that differ from each other not only in their origin, but also in the kind of impact they have on economies, cities, and people's lives. I will focus here on four 'models': mortgage-based systems; systems based on the association of financial credit with direct governmental subsidies linked to the purchase of market-produced units; micro-finance schemes; and, more recently, the emergence of global corporate landlords in residential rental markets (Fields and Uffer, 2014).

Mortgage Markets

The 1970s economic financial crisis caused the longest international recession since the 1930s. From that moment on, a transformation of the government's role was mooted in both theoretical and practical terms: from housing providers, governments became 'facilitators' whose mission was to make way for and support the expansion of private markets. The 1993 World Bank report 'Housing: enabling markets to work' summarizes this thinking: 'Governments should be encouraged to adopt policies that enable housing markets to work…and [to] avoid distorting [them]' (World Bank, 1993: 6). Their role was thenceforth to create the conditions, institutions, and regulatory models that would promote housing financial systems capable of enabling homeownership (Doherty et al., 2005).

In some countries, this happened through the sale of public social housing, generally subsidized rental stock to their residents—boosting homeownership and reducing state expenditure (UN-Habitat, 2011a: 9). This privatization process was further encouraged by the stigmatization and residualization of social housing, which started to be identified with poverty and marginality (Rolnik, 2013). In Europe and North America, the privatization of public housing stocks occurred in various forms: the sale of units to long-term tenants through the Right to Buy in the United Kingdom (Priemus and Dieleman, 2002); the transfer of properties to not-for-profit organizations in the Netherlands (Czischke and Pittini, 2007: 49); and, in some cases, the transfer of properties to for-profit companies, as in the United States. In various countries, such as Spain, the 'advantages' of the creation of a home-purchase market also included the reform of rental legislation, reducing protection and increasing insecurity of tenure for tenants. In almost every country—mainly via tax exemptions and subsidized interest—housing commodification was promoted through the adoption of incentives to purchase.

The role of states went beyond that of a mere 'facilitator'. States actively deconstructed social housing and the urban policies that supported it, and deregulated monetary and financial markets, in order to promote the new alternatives. The United Kingdom and the United States were the two epicenters of this theoretical and practical model.

In the UK, housing was one of the pillars of the welfare state after World War II. Local authorities were instructed to house those who could not provide for themselves. More than one million new homes, half of which were council houses, were constructed within five years after World War II. This rhythm was sustained during the following two decades, with peaks of more than 300,000 units per year in the early 1950s and late 1960s (Griffith and Jefferys, 2013: 13). By the end of the 1970s and beginning of the 1980s, with Margaret Thatcher's reforms, there was a considerable change of paradigm. Policies and institutions were created in order to deregulate housing finance systems, privatize council housing, and reduce public expenditures—except those related to fiscal benefits and other forms of subsidy for homeownership. The Housing Act passed in 1980, aiming 'to provide security of tenure', introduced the Right to Buy as a central element of this new approach (United Kingdom, 1980). Essentially, the Right to Buy system gave to long-standing tenants the opportunity to buy their council house at a large discount. Around 2 million social housing units were sold between 1980 and 2013—most of them in the 1980s. Of those, 1.8 million were council housing units (DCLG, 2012a, table 678). The reliance of the economy on private housing debt, rather than public debt—'privatized Keynesianism' (Crouch, 2011) has been a key element of the new regime. Considering the political economy of housing, the Right to Buy—with its large discounts for sitting tenants—has helped to enable the Conservative party to enlarge its constituency.

An 'asset-based welfare' model—with housing property becoming an ATM machine from which people could extract wealth by refinancing their mortgages—has then put down roots, acting as an incentive to keep prices high (Matthew Watson cited in Robertson, 2013). In this context, homeowners rely on the valorization of their homes and support policies that promote it. With sales exceeding new construction, the structural composition of housing tenure forms has changed: in 1971, owner-occupiers represented 52% of England's housing stock; in 2007, this rate was close to 70% (DCLG, 2012a, table 104). The private rental sector has been growing continuously: between 1981 and 2012, the number of households in this sector doubled—from 1.9 to 3.8 million (DCLG, 2013: II, image I.I). Social rental housing corresponded to around 30% of the housing stock in 1970; in 2007, it was less than 18%.

The British experience epitomizes the political, ideological, and economic dismantling of social housing and its takeover by the sphere of finance. It also shows how this shift led to the reduction of the right to housing for the poorest and most vulnerable, and to the regression of housing conditions for current generations. Comprehension of the US trajectory, however, is fundamental to understand the origin—theoretical and practical—of one of the most powerful models of housing financialization: the mortgage.

In the United States, the 1930s Housing Acts (1934 and 1937) inaugurated a dual housing system: on the one hand, the construction of public rental housing projects, with direct aid for low-income families; on the other, subsidized credit—mainly via tax exemptions—to promote homeownership among middle-class families. This dual housing policy was also responsible for creating a new urban landscape: the housing projects were largely located in inner-city areas, while the majority of the private houses built via Federal Housing Agency credit were concentrated in exclusively residential suburbs with low population densities.

The US public housing stock numbered 1.4 million units at the end of the 1970s. The program had been implemented by the federal government in order to provide decent and safe rentals to low-income families, elderly people, and individuals with special needs. However, the model of housing projects came under scrutiny as they were increasingly stigmatized as sites of extreme poverty, crime, and social marginalization. The perception of a decline in the quality of public housing came both from the buildings' physical deterioration—due to their age and lack of maintenance—and from the wider issue of racial and economic urban segregation, since housing projects are desproportionally inhabited by the non-white population (Smith, 2006: 30). The Housing and Community Act of 1974 decreed the end of federal funding for the construction of public housing projects. It also introduced the Housing Choice Voucher Program (HCVP, commonly known as Section 8), granting subsidies to private sector tenants and to real estate developers who agreed to reserve some of their units for rent-controlled contracts. The HCVP marked an important change in public housing policy, as it moved funds from public housing authorities—historically in charge of building and managing housing projects—to the private sector.

Therefore, since the 1970s, public resources earmarked for the construction and maintenance of public housing stocks have been progressively reduced. This process was aggravated by President Reagan's fiscal restructuring measures. Concurrently, public subsidies for home-purchase grew, as well as programs supporting private rental, such as Section 8 and Project-Based Assistance, subsidized fiscal credit certificates directed to builders to increase the local supply of rental housing at prices slightly below market rate. In the 1980s, budget cuts resulted in the gradual erosion and lack of maintenance of the public housing system. In the 2000s, deterioration brought about the loss of 170,000 public housing units. Today, most of the stock stands in need of substantial repair and restoration. On the one hand, this federal housing policy resulted in an even higher number of homeowners; on the other, it reduced the supply of public housing (which numbered 1 million units in 2010) through demolishing or closing more than 300,000 units without replacing them.

In terms of homeownership promotion, important changes also occurred in the domain of housing finance. A movement to incorporate lower-income sectors was accompanied by the amplification of ties to the financial market *sensu stricto*. These changes resulted from two interconnected processes: first, the Community Reinvestment Act of 1977; second, the growth of securitization. The 1977 Act required banks to allocate part of their mortgage portfolios to the neighbourhoods from which their depositors came. Banks had therefore to modify their usual risk definitions, transforming what was, until then, 'redline' into a specific mortgage product: *subprime*—or very high-cost credit certificates, offered mainly to families composed of minorities or other groups who, historically, had no access to credit, as they were considered high-risk.[3]

The federal government did everything it could to encourage the subprime secondary market, which became one of the biggest sources of credit leverage—also for the financing of home-purchase. Securitization also included subprime loans. In 2007, the subprime business accounted for US$1.5 trillion of outstanding loans within the global financial market. Wall Street banks and investment funds created special divisions to operate in the subprime mortgage market and earned high commissions for every transaction in the global market.

The growth of available resources for residential real estate financing and the development of 'innovative' mortgage products allowed buyers to acquire more expensive properties, which also contributed to the elevation of real estate prices. So long as prices kept growing, buyers with any kind of difficulty in paying installments could refinance their homes through new loans. But, when the real estate bubble burst, prices leveled out or dropped, and larger installments began to be billed. And so the debacle began: debts piled up, leading to foreclosures, loss of homes, and a rise in homelessness. In the United States, over the course of the five years between 2008 and 2013, over 13 million foreclosures resulted in more than 9 million households being evicted (Sassen, 2014: 5–6).

The subprime mortgage crisis in 2008 was not the product of an unsuccessful attempt to amplify the private housing market to embrace the poorest, reducing their dependency on public funds and on the state. Instead, it resulted from a clear and aggressive policy of destruction of the existing alternatives of housing access for the poorest, pushing them towards aggressive indebtedness. Such a policy intended to facilitate, precisely within the lower-income housing sector, a new form of income extraction: income moved from mortgage markets and indebted homeowners to financial investors (Aalbers, 2008).

The subprime crisis did not affect only Europe and the United States. Emerging mortgage markets that have made heaviest use of global securitization (e.g., the Russian Federation, Kazakhstan, and the Republic of Korea) were most affected (Chiquier and Lea, 2009: xxxvii). In Kazakhstan in 2010, more than 40,000 borrowers were waiting for their apartments to be finished while construction companies went bankrupt (Rolnik, 2012).

Despite its failure to provide adequate housing for all, the model has become global: market-based housing finance has spread throughout the world at an unprecedented rate. In the United States, European countries, Australia, and Japan, two years after the subprime crisis, residential mortgage markets represented between 50% and 100% of gross domestic product (GDP) (IMF, 2011: 133–4). By 2009, the ratio of mortgage debt to GDP had reached more than 100% in Denmark and the Netherlands (IMF, 2011: 133–4). Although mortgage markets were not so prevalent in emergent economies until the subprime crisis, they have grown since the 2000s. For example, the Chinese mortgage market, which only started in the early 1990s, has been growing at more than 40% annually since 2000, reaching 11% of GDP in 2010s (Stephens, 2010).

Similarly, the Indian market grew in this period at 30% per year (Chiquier and Lea, 2009: xxxi). In the same decade, South Africa housing loans experienced the highest percentage growth among all asset classes, with the ratio of mortgage debt to GDP doubling from 20% in 2001 to 42.3% in 2007 (Center For Affordable Housing Finance in Africa, 2016). According to IMF data, residential loans and housing prices increased significantly in Turkey, the Philippines, China, Colombia, Indonesia, Mexico, Ukraine, Malaysia, Brazil, Russia, and Thailand during the 2010s (Zhu, 2014).

The onset of the burst of the housing bubble, and the subsequent global financial and economic crises, has yet not resulted in a paradigm shift. Recovery measures based on austerity (i.e., cuts in public spending) led in some instances to additional curtailment of social housing programs, as was the case of the OEK (Workers' Housing Organization) scheme in Greece, and the privatization of social housing in Germany, while huge public resources were allocated to 'bailouts' of financial institutions. Hedge funds and private equity companies bought up foreclosed housing at fire-sale prices and started an aggressive lucrative rental market. This has resulted in increased evictions, homelessness, indebtedness of families, and worsening housing conditions, as we are currently witnessing in Germany, England, Belgium, Spain, and other countries (Feantsa, 2018).

Demand Subsidies

A major component of the shift from supply-side to demand-side housing policies has been the promotion of demand subsidies as a means of enlarging the market for privately produced residential units, mobilizing public resources and directing them to potential buyers. The rationale behind demand-subsidy programs is that low-income households will be able to finance their housing through the free market, with their own savings, assisted by a down-payment subsidy or a subsidized loan provided by the state (Rolnik, 2012). A central component of this policy is the internationally funded massive production of standardized units promoted by a small number of developers.

Chile under the Pinochet dictatorship (1973–90) was the main laboratory for this model and influenced other countries, particularly in Latin America and Africa, in countries where most of housing production has been built by the people themselves in irregular allotments or on squatter land (Gilbert, 2002: 305–24). The model emphasizes the shift of responsibility for housing provision from the state to the private sector and mobilizes public budgets to provide one-time grants for home purchase while curtailing all indirect subsidies, also promoting household savings as part of the total investment. Since cash subsidies cover part of the purchase price of a formally constructed dwelling offered for sale in the market by private developers, the sale of their products is assured by the state. Subsidies may be combined with mortgage or micro-finance loans and/or household savings. Capital grants are perceived to encourage the integration of lower-income households into conventional housing markets, leading to financial market expansion (Mitlin, 2007: 151–79, 163). The Chilean model has been widely replicated in Latin America (Brazil, Colombia, Costa Rica, Ecuador, El Salvador, Guatemala, Mexico, Panama, Peru, and Venezuela). Outside Latin America, the capital-grant approach has been implemented on a large scale in South Africa since 1994 (South Africa Financial and Fiscal Commission, 2012).

Although the rationale for the implementation of subsidized mortgage markets is supposedly to reduce state intervention in the housing sector, support for savings banks, interest rate subsidies, and tax allowances mobilize a large amount of public money. On other hand, as most of the less-developed countries where housing finance schemes of this type were implemented, the program was supposed to reach out the poorest, as they—even with subsidies—are unable to pay back the cost of their homes, particularly any interest. However, in the absence of land management policies, a large amount in subsidies available in the housing market has led to significant increases in land and housing prices—a general problem of affordability for low-income households—and long waiting lists. The combination of land shortages and irregular budgetary expenditure, high housing deficits, and fast population growth (characteristics of most ot the developing countries that implemented capital subsidies) has led to limited coverage of subsidy programs in the face of growing demand.[4] In Brazil, 'the largest homeownership and construction/mortgage subsidy scheme ever launched in the world' (Aalbers, 2019: 4)—the Minha Casa Minha Vida Program (MCMV)—was unable to reduce the country's housing deficit. Between 2009 and 2015, the program contracted some 2.6 million housing units, while the housing deficit in the same period rose from 6 million to 6.35 million housing units. Although the number of houses has increased, a boom in housing prices, including rent, made access to housing less affordable for the poor, increasing the housing deficit (FJP, 2015).

Problems also soon emerged with regard to the location of the housing projects. In Chile, planning regulations were loosened and city limits expanded under the premise that a freely operating land market would automatically contribute to providing access to adequate housing through the market (Pablo Trivelli and Company, 2010: 18). Unlike in the case of housing markets for higher-income families, in which suppliers have to be sensitive to demand requirements—and, therefore, to the product–price–location nexus, as they operate in a competitive context—operators that supply social housing have a captive demand, particularly when it is subsidized. In the context of a housing deficit, beneficiaries of housing subsidies, without any other option, will simply 'buy' what is available for them at the moment (Pablo Trivelli and Company, 2010: 18).

It is therefore not surprising that subsidized housing developments have been built primarily in the urban periphery, where land costs are lowest. In México, Brazil, and Chile, among others, massive construction of housing occurred in peripheral locations that lacked enough or adequate infrastructure, schools, health facilities, and employment opportunities. Poor public transport and road quality further impairs residents' ability to access services and employment (Pablo Trivelli and Company, 2010: 18; Rodríguez and Sugranyes, 2005: 61). Subsidy programs in South Africa, Mexico, and Brazil have also been criticized for replacing widespread informal housing with low-standard and stigmatized market-based housing typologies concentrating low income families (Amore et al., 2015; Jiménez-Cavieres, 2006). The result is greater urban and social segregation, an increase in the disparity in access to urban services, a worsening of local living conditions, increased environmental damage, and urban security problems. In many countries, the promotion of those massive housing developments outside urbanized cities was also a means to displace consolidated informal settlements in prime locations.

Increased segregation and evictions were not only the result of financialized housing policies in countries of the Global South. These circumstances have also been the case in European cities, where massive production of new developments in peripheral locations was also part of a dispossession machinery in which, in order to fill the gap between current real estate value and the value under the highest and best use, renters were either displaced, or had to pay much higher rents in order to stay put. The result is a current housing affordability crisis in several European cities, with households overburdened with housing costs (Feantsa, 2018).

Housing Micro-finance

In the 1980s, a new finance paradigm emerged, one that appeared to be able to address poverty through the expansion of small, informal sector income-generating credit: micro-finance. Private financial investors became convinced of the profitability of micro-finance and came to regard the poor as 'bankable' (Johnston and Morduch, 2008: 517–37). The result has been a dramatic rise in the flow of private investment capital (supported by donors, multilateral banks, and international organizations) into the micro-finance sector and, more recently, into housing financial services adapted to support incremental building processes (Ferguson and Smets, 2010: 288–99; Chiquier and Lea, 2009: 395). The growing commercial presence of major Western banking groups in developing countries and their interest in micro-finance (including for housing) has been based on the idea that the 'bottom of the pyramid' represents a large untapped market (Prahalad and Hart, 2002: 1–14).

Since the end of the 2000s,[5] a growing number of housing micro-finance programs have been initiated, offering loans to homeowners ranging from US$300 to US$5,000, frequently with repeating lending opportunities and repayment terms of 1–15 years. In comparison with enterprise micro-finance, housing micro-finance loans are generally larger and given for longer periods, and are also much smaller than mortgage loans, typically granted for shorter terms; their target population is that not served by formal private or public financial institutions (Center for Urban Development Studies, 2000). Owing to their limited scope, housing micro-finance loans are used mainly to finance improvements to housing (e.g., building sanitary amenities) and expansions to an existing dwelling, or for the incremental construction of a home (Chiquier and Lea, 2009: 399; Ferguson, 2003: 21–31).

Housing micro-finance institutions employ diversified and more relaxed collateral strategies compared with traditional mortgage collateral, including co-signers, assignment of future income, payroll deduction, other financial assets such as life insurance, and the so-called 'social collateral', mostly the social networks to which they belong (UN-Habitat, 2008: 20; Merrill, 2009: 4). Many home micro-finance agencies, particularly in Asia and Africa, have savings requirements, which serve both as an assessment of the borrower's repayment capacity and as a means to acquire funds (UN-Habitat, 2005: 114).

Although micro-finance agencies' interest rates are typically lower than those of informal moneylenders, they are much higher than those charged by formal financial institutions and have much shorter maturities. In most cases, the interest rates range between 20% and 50% per year (UN-Habitat, 2008: 19). For example, MiBanco in Peru charges a 37% annual rate (Chiquier and Lea, 2009: 410) and Compartamosbanco in Mexico charges almost 70% interest on its housing micro-finance program.[6] The poorer the client, the more likely the housing micro-finance agency will attempt to manage default risk by reducing the time over which the client must repay the loan, increasing the interest rate, and reducing the size of the loan (UN-Habitat, 2008: 24–5). In some cases, the small loan amount is not sufficient and needs to be supplemented by additional borrowing from external sources, which carry very high interest rates and expose the household to increased risk (Manoj, 2010: 190). High interest rates increase clients' indebtedness and reinforce a vicious cycle of poverty and the likelihood of default. In some cases, long-held family assets (such as equipment or land) need to be sold, or other income flows (remittances, pensions) need to be diverted into repayment. These 'fall back' strategies account for the generally high repayment rates of housing micro-finance, but reduce household equity, economic resilience' and housing affordability. As is often the case in subprime mortgage lending, housing micro-finance clients have been penalized for their 'low profitability' by being forced to pay higher prices for access to housing finance. Therefore, despite the fact that housing micro-finance loans are seemingly more accessible and affordable to the poor, they are, in effect, extremely discriminatory and remain highly unaffordable.[7]

The Rental Housing Boom: New Frontiers of Housing Financialization

A new type of institutional, corporate landlord, usually linked to transnational financial assets management companies, has begun to control a great number of rental houses and apartments in many cities. This landlord's entry into the housing market was combined—in some global cities and in tourist destinations such as London, New York, and Barcelona—with other dimensions of the residential real estate–financial complex to produce this new and toxic trend, unleashing massive processes of dispossession.

Broadly speaking, large financial investors entered the rental housing market after the bursting of the real estate bubble of 2008, seizing the opportunity to buy those so-called toxic assets on the cheap. Sometimes referred to as vulture investors, global financial conglomerates bought devalued assets in order to transform them into a new market frontier, infiltrating territories that had been neglected by them—or protected from them. By mobilizing an enormous amount of capital via private equity funds, hedge funds, real estate investment trusts (REITs) and other financial instruments, or capital obtained through shareholders or directly from loans, they were able to buy up deeply undervalued 'housing stocks' available in cities.

These funds first entered the market by purchasing real estate—a 'stock' of toxic assets composed of foreclosed or defaulting mortgages—directly from banks. Another way in for the funds was the acquisition of companies created after the crisis in order to 'clean' the banks' portfolios. Many funds also bought directly from indebted and desperate homeowners. But these funds have also captured part of the controlled and regulated public housing stock, buying many social housing units from indebted cities asphyxiated by fiscal austerity measures.

Once the phase of wholesale buying of 'toxic' or 'rotten' stocks was over, these global corporate landlords (Beswick et al., 2016: 321–41) had become deeply rooted in local residential markets, controlling hundreds—sometimes thousands—of units in single districts or counties. From that point on, they started to behave like monopolies, pressing for a general increase in rents, indexing those markets towards a higher price.

The financial crisis itself ended up creating the demand for this new product:rental housing. The increased demand has been fueled both by the expulsion of dwellers from their mortgaged houses and by the end of easy access to loans, creating a situation in which many people could no longer afford homeownership. Without access to social housing provision—destroyed in the previous cycle—and unable to become homeowners, people's only available option in residential markets is to rent.

Since 2008, in the United States, private equity funds have bought foreclosed homes repossessed from indebted families. But it was only in 2011 that some of the biggest private equity funds that invest in real estate—such as Blackstone, or Colony Capital—decisively entered the business. They set up affiliates that have accumulated thousands of housing units, especially in the cities most devastated by the mortgage collapse (Beswick et al., 2016: 324; Call and Heck, 2014). For instance, today Blackstone owns 82,000 units in 17 US markets.[8] According to a report on the subject in Atlanta, the housing stock owned by private equity funds in the United States amounted to 200,000 units in 2013 (Call and Heck, 2014: 6; Rahmanai et al., 2013).

At first, the purchase of toxic assets that were by-products of the financial crisis was a short-term move. The idea was to buy real estate units at extremely low prices and sell them on: quick profits were made as a result of the difference between capital costs and the yields obtained through letting or resale. Later, there was a process of consolidation of those companies, accompanied by mergers and acquisitions. They have also entered the stock market, investing in real estate investment funds (Goldstein, 2017). These asset management funds operate in the United States and elsewhere. Blackstone, for example, has picked up Catalunya Caixa's bankrupt estate stock in Spain, paying €3.6 billion for a stock valued at the time at €6.5 billion (Beswick et al., 2016: 325).

The entry of financial funds into collapsing housing markets was eagerly promoted by national and local governments, which have regulated and fostered the operation of these funds as a part of their post-financial crisis measures. In addition, as part of bailout policies, asset management companies were created to segregate the toxic assets—those with little or no possibility of repayment—from the banks' portfolios. This was the case, for instance, of Ireland's National Asset Management Agency (NAMA), the UK Asset Resolution (UKAR), and the Spanish Sociedad de Gestión de Activos Procedentes de la Reestructuración Bancaria (Sareb) (Byrne, 2015).

But, in Spain and in other European countries, the formation of large, institutional landlords also took place through the acquisition of public social housing, sold by municipalities and governments directly to funds and REITs. In Spain, the first Sociedad Anonima Cotizada de Inversión Imobiliária (SOCIMI) owned by Blackstone is called Fidere. Fidere bought 1,860 public housing units in 2013 from the city of Madrid's Empresa Municipal de la Vivienda (EMV). Though this transaction created great controversy and was taken to court, the units remain with the American fund to this day (Ruiz, 2017).

Like the other processes described in this article, the financialization of rental housing has been a result of public policies. States promote a 'regulated deregulation' (Aalbers, 2016: 117) that enables and supports the pervasive expansion of this new urban business, strengthening a financial asset-based housing and urban policy (Byrne, 2016: 31–45).

Even though the actual percentage of units controlled by these financialized landlords is only a minor proportion of local rental housing markets, the impacts of this process on tenants' living and housing conditions have been significant. First, this housing stock is not geographically distributed in a random or scattered manner. Whole districts collapsed with the financial and mortgage crisis, especially in the suburbs and city outskirts. There have also been radical changes in downtown areas where it was once possible to find affordable lets. Amid intense and conflictive processes of gentrification and resistance, corporate landlords owned by affiliates of globalized investment companies have now captured those units.

From the investors' viewpoint, it is necessary to maximize the profitability of the invested capital, unlocking the wealth embedded in residential built spaces. In the words of a World Bank study aiming to persuade governments of the advantages of this new frontier: 'Rental markets also play a key role in enhancing the market value of housing assets and in generating revenues from an unlocked housing wealth' (Peppercorn and Taffin, 2013: x). 'Unlocking' means liberating these assets from any constraints that could block their immediate disposal. One way is the eviction of dwellers who can no longer afford the prices determined by funds.

The capacity to set prices is directly linked to the number of units controlled by these funds and their concentration in certain areas. But it also derives from the practices adopted by financialized landlords in order to 'unlock' those assets. Coercion and intimidation are the words most often heard in the stories told by evictees and tenants who experienced pressure to leave their homes. In Spain, Germany and the United States, the same tactics are being used by banks and funds to get rid of tenants: from imposed agreements to free the housing units from indebted tenants, to assaults on people living in old public rental units with stabilized rent in New York and Berlin, especially in gentrifying neighbourhoods (Fields, 2014; Fields and Uffer, 2014; Soederburg, 2017). Cutting off essential services or lowering the quality of buildings maintenance are other common tricks: winters without heating, buildings under endless repair with the tenants inside, threats to call immigration services, monthly rent cheques systematically returned, offers of cash to quit the building or not renew the contract.

In addition to those strategies, some countries and municipalities are working to facilitate evictions by making the rules more flexible.[9] In the United Kingdom, the government commissioned the Montague Report, a study to examine the obstacles and to propose measures for attracting large-scale institutional investment in new homes for private rent—such as student housing (DCLG, 2012b). And, despite the fact that this new wave has been detected in European and American cities, there are signs that it also impacts cities of the so-called Global South.[10]

The rental housing market, though, has not been restructured solely by the presence of corporate landlords. If the housing crisis has been especially acute in New York, London, and Barcelona, this is also down to the tourism industry and to a global market of second homes that removes housing units from the long-term rental market.

Buying high-end houses and apartments in global, cultural, or tourist cities has become a safe-deposit box for the transnational wealthy elite. It functions as a stable store of value for part of their capital, with great scope for appreciation. Many of these transactions are made via offshore tax havens, below the radars of national and local governments (Fernández et al., 2016). London, New York, and Miami are cities in which this phenomenon is conspicuous. Over the last few years, Barcelona has also become a valued target for foreign investors.

One of the factors that has contributed to launching Barcelona as a target was Spain's promotion of the 'Golden Visa' as one of its post-crisis recovery measures. Golden Visas are nothing less than the gift of citizenship in exchange for investments in real estate. Cyprus, Greece, and Portugal, among others, have also offered permanent residence or even citizenship in exchange for a minimum amount of investment in property.

Furthermore, in the cases of Barcelona and New York, the popularity of sharing-economy platforms that connect people seeking to let their apartments—or apartment fractions—to people hoping to pay less than hotel rates on their next trip is another element that affects rental housing markets. Airbnb is the most notorious example of such platforms.

Although Airbnb presents itself as a 'community market', the company is, in fact, a very profitable startup. Airbnb's market price exceeds US$1 billion and the company has not yet floated its capital on the stock market. The maths behind its profitability are very simple: the website charges a 10% commission for each reservation and another 3% commission for processing the payment. The 'host' pays these, but the 'guest' also pays a 6–12% fee for the service. We are talking about a two-sided market that manages to make a profit from both sides. The platform's appeal is confirmed by its list of investors. They include venture capital companies such as Mighty Capital, Sequoia Capital, Bracket Capital; global financial services firms such as Morgan Stanley and JP Morgan Chase & Co.; banks such as Citigroup, and private equity companies such as China Broadband Capital.[11]

Resistances

The creation and expansion of housing financialization do not proceed without resistance, especially in cities where the upheaval has been particularly intense and where there is a history of organized social movements. The victims of dispossession, together with activists for the right to housing and to the city, are challenged to develop new forms of resistance in order to confront the opacity and abstraction that are intrinsic to the world of finance (Fields, 2014).

In New York, resistance originated from a network of community organizations, non-governmental organizations and legal advisory groups that had existed since the struggles for adequate housing in the 1960s. Stabilized rent was one of their conquests. This network was revived in order to confront the city's urban crisis at the end of the 1970s. Rooted in the poorest communities, mainly home to African-Americans and Hispanics, they were able to reactivate their capacities for mobilization and struggle, reinventing strategies as soon as they began to detect the ominous signs of the entrance of private equity funds into the stabilized-rent housing stock in those neighborhoods. Local coalitions, such as the Association for Neighborhood and Housing Development, along with neighborhood organizations such as the Northwest Bronx Community and Clergy Coalition, committed to developing a critical narrative about what was going on. They mapped and developed social indicators; they engaged in advocacy, provided legal advice to tenants, and designed eye-catching actions with the media.

With all these tactics, they managed to change public opinion in the city about what could be considered 'predatory equity'. In a positive reaction, the municipality began to intervene in the most egregious cases and has, more recently, started to offer free legal counseling—and other services and measures—to those threatened with eviction (Teresa, 2016: 472; Fields, 2014).

In the case of Barcelona, despite the emergence of a new social housing movement in 2005, Plataforma por la vivienda digna (Platform for decent housing), it was only after the outbreak of the financial and mortgage crisis that the tenants' defense bureau Plataforma de Afectados por la Hipoteca (PAH) (Platform for People Affected by Mortgages) was formed, organizing those affected by foreclosures side-by-side with activists, housing rights campaigners, and lawyers. Thanks to its wide-ranging advisory services for victims, information campaigns, proposal of legal bills, and direct action—whether to stop evictions, or to find shelter for those in urgent need—PAH has amplified its social base and political influence to the point that one of its leaders and founders, Ada Colau, was elected Barcelona's mayor in 2015.

Besides PAH, several organizations in the districts affected by speculation have come together in a 'tenants' union'. Their agenda includes measures to introduce rent control and collective forms of negotiation of those prices, in favor of social housing and for the protection of tenants threatened with eviction.[12] Initiatives to de-commodify housing are also springing up. Examples are social cooperatives, community land trusts, and squatting in empty housing units. Under pressure from—and committed to—those social movements, Barcelona's new city government has attempted to promote social housing, adopting measures such as the introduction of rent control caps for units renovated using municipal loans. The city has also embarked on building a new stock of public housing. It has confronted predatory tourism by controlling the number of housing units rented for short-term periods through online platforms. The municipality is also keeping an eye on accommodation listed on Airbnb and similar platforms that are not registered with the municipality, or that violate zoning laws, fining Airbnb and HomeAway directly (Tavolari, 2017: 269). Given its financial and jurisdictional limitations in this matter, the local government has acted in concert with other cities to influence national housing policies, to reform rental housing legislation, and to abolish the benefits and tax incentives given for real estate funds and REITs, and through Golden Visas (Burgen, 2017).

New York and Barcelona are not the only cities in which new social movements and activism around housing are taking place. Squatting and resisting evictions are becoming common practices in cities around the globe. Although those political actions are not able to reverse the financialization of housing, their practices build a link between the materiality of the victims' concrete lives—and the privations to which they are subjected—and the abstraction of transnational financial flows, advancing towards a more multi-dimensional comprehension of the phenomenon. These struggles have begun to delineate the political confrontation between territories understood as spaces for life and territories understood as playgrounds for finance capital, uprooted and disconnected from human needs and desires. This aspect provides the connecting point between the movements around housing and the more general, anti-speculative, and rentist faces of capital.

Notes

1 This chapter is based on my book *Urban Warfare: Housing under the Empire of Finance* (Rolnik, 2019), where more detailed information on the examples used here can be found.

2 The scenes just described correspond, respectively, to the United States, Spain, Mexico, and Kazakhstan, all of which I visited as UN Special Rapporteur on the right to adequate housing (2008–14) in official missions or working visits during the period 2009–11.

3 For more data on the extent to which banks were forced to offer 'risky' loans, see Marcuse (1979).

4 In Chile, in 1998, the estimated waiting time for a housing subsidy was over 20 years (UN-Habitat, 2011b: 55).

5 Although micro-finance institutions such as Grameen Bank have had housing loan programs since the 1980s, housing micro-finance has only begun to attract significant attention since the end of the 2000s.

6 See Gentera, www.compartamos.com (last accessed 07 March 2019).

7 A more recent form of housing micro-finance, developed mainly in Africa and Asia, is community funds. These funds work with group loans and/or savings in order to assist communities to finance land regularization and acquisition, infrastructure and service provision, and home improvements (UN-Habitat, 2005: 120). For more detail, see Rolnik (2019: 98–9).

8 See invitationhomes.com (last accessed 30 January 2018).

9 The Spanish rental law and the revision of stabilized rents in public housing units in Berlin and New York are some examples (Rolnik, 2019).

10 Santiago de Chile and São Paulo (Brazil) are examples (Rolnik, 2019).

11 For the complete list of investor companies, see crunchbase.com/organisation/airbnb (accessed 18 January 2017).

12 See sindicatdellogateres.org (last accessed 23 January 2018).

References

Aalbers, M. (2008). The Financialization of Home and the Mortgage Market Crisis. *Competition & Change*, 12 (2).

Aalbers, M. (2016). *The Financialization of Housing: A Political Economy Approach.* New York: Routledge.

Aalbers, M. (2019). Financial Geographies of Real Estate and the City: A Literature Review. *Financial Geography Working Paper Series*, 21 (Jan.)

Amore, C. S., Shimbo, L. Z. and Rufino, M. B. C. (2015). *Minha casa… e a cidade? Avaliação do programa minha casa minha vida em seis estados brasileiros.* Rio de Janeiro: Letra Capital.

Beswick, J., Alexandri, G., Byrne, M., Vives-Miró, S., Fields, D., Hodgkinson, S. and Janoschka, M. (2016). Speculating on London's Housing Future. *City*, 20 (2).

Brenner, N. and Theodore, N. (2002). *Spaces of Neoliberalism: Urban Restructuring in North America and Western Europe*. Oxford: Blackwell.

Buckley, R. M. and Kalarickal, J. (eds.). (2006). *Thirty Years of World Bank Shelter Lending: What Have We Learned?* Washington, DC: World Bank.

Burgen, S. (2017). Airbnb Faces Crackdown on Illegal Apartment Rentals in Barcelona. *The Guardian*, 2 June. Available at: theguardian.com [Accessed 23 Jan. 2018].

Byrne, M. (2015). Bad Banks: The Urban Implications of Asset Management Companies. *Urban Research and Practice*, 8 (2).

Byrne, M. (2016). 'Asset Price Urbanism' and Financialization after the Crisis: Ireland's National Asset Management Agency. *International Journal of Urban and Regional Research*, 40 (1).

Call, D. P. and Heck, S. (2014). Blackstone: Atlanta's Newest Landlord – The New Face of Rental Market. *Homes for All*. Available at: homesforall.org [Accessed 22 Jan. 2018].

Center for Affordable Housing Finance in Africa. (2016). *Housing Finance in Africa: A Review of Some of Africa's Housing Finance Markets*. Parkview, South Africa: CAHF.

Center for Urban Development Studies, Harvard University Graduate School of Design. (2000). *Housing Micro-finance Initiatives: Synthesis and Regional Summary: Asia, Latin America and Sub-Saharan Africa with Selected Case Studies*. Bethesda, MD: Microenterprise Best Practices, Development Alternatives, Inc.

Chiquier, L. and Lea, M. (eds). (2009). *Housing Finance Policy in Emerging Markets*. Washington, DC: World Bank.

Crouch, C. (2011). *The Strange Non-death of Neo-liberalism*. Cambridge: Polity Press.

Czischke, D. and Pittini, A. (2007). *Housing Europe 2007: Review of Social, Co-operative and Public Housing in the 27 EU Member States*. Brussels: Cecodhas European Social Housing Observatory.

DCLG (Department of Communities and Local Government). (2012a). *Live Tables on Social Housing Sales*. London: DCLG. Available at: gov.uk [Accessed 12 Jan. 2015].

DCLG. (2012b). *Review of the Barriers to Institutional Investment in Private Rented Homes*. London: DCLG. Available at: gov.uk [Accessed 12 Jan. 2015].

DCLG. (2013). *English Housing Survey: Households 2011–2012*. London: DCLG. Available at: gov.uk [Accessed 15 Nov. 2014].

Doherty, J. et al. (2005). *The Changing Role of the State: Welfare Delivery in the Neoliberal Era*. Brussels: Feantsa.

Feantsa. (2018). *Third Overview of Housing Exclusion in Europe 2018*. Brussels/Paris: Feantsa/Fondation Abbé Pierre. Available at: www.feantsa.org/download/full-re-port-en1029873431323901915.pdf [Accessed 7 Mar. 2019].

Ferguson B. and Smets, P. (2010). Finance for Incremental Housing: Current Status and Prospects for Expansion. *Habitat International*, 34.

Ferguson, B. (2003). Housing Micro-finance: A Key to Improving Habitat and the Sustainability of Micro-finance Institutions. *Small Enterprise Development*, 14.

Fernández, R., Hofman, A. and Aalbers, M. (2016). London and New York as a Safe Deposit Box for the Transnational Wealth Elite. *Environment and Planning A*, 48 (12).

Fields, D. (2014). Contesting the Financialization of Urban Space: Community Organizations and the Struggle to Preserve Affordable Rental Housing in New York City. *Journal of Urban Affairs*, 37 (2).

Fields, D. and Uffer, S. (2014). The Financialisation of Rental Housing: A Comparative Analysis of New York City and Berlin. *Urban Studies*, 53 (7).

FJP (Fundação João Pinheiro). (2015). *FJP Dados: Déficit Habitacional No Brasil*. Available at: fjpdados.fjp.mg.gov.br/deficit/ [Accessed 21 Jan. 2019].

Gilbert, A. (2002). Power, Ideology and the Washington Consensus: The Development and Spread of Chilean Housing Policy. *Housing Studies*, 17 (2).

Goldstein, M. (2017). Major Rental-Home Companies Set to Merge as U.S. House Prices Recover. *New York Times*, 10 Aug. Available at: nytimes.com [Accessed 22 Jan. 2018].

Griffith, M. and Jefferys, P. (2013). *Solutions for the Housing Shortage*. London: Shelter.

Harvey, D. (2014). *Seventeen Contradictions and the End of Capitalism*. Oxford: Oxford University Press.

IMF (International Monetary Fund). (2011). *Global Financial Stability Report: Durable Financial Stability: Getting There from Here*. Washington, DC: IMF.

Jiménez-Cavieres, F. (2006). *Chilean Housing Policy: A Case of Social and Spatial Exclusion?* Doctoral dissertation, Technical University of Berlin.

Johnston, D. and Morduch, J. (2008). The Unbanked: Evidence from Indonesia. *The World Bank Economic Review*, 22 (3).

Manoj, P. K. (2010). Prospects and Problems of Housing Micro-finance in India: Evidence from 'Bhavanashree' Project in Kerala State. *European Journal of Economics, Finance and Administrative Sciences*, 19.

Marcuse, P. (1979). The Deceptive Consensus on Redlining: Definitions Do Matter. *Journal of the American Planning Association*, 45 (4) (Oct.).

Merrill, S. R. (2009). *Micro-finance for Housing: Assisting the 'Bottom Billion' and the 'Missing Middle'*. IDG Working Paper, No. 2009-5, June. Urban Institute Center on International Development and Governance.

Mitlin, D. (2007). New Directions in Housing Policy. In: A. M. Garland, M. Massoumi and B. A. Ruble (eds.), *Global Urban Poverty: Setting the Agenda*. Washington, DC: Woodrow Wilson International Center for Scholars.

Pablo Trivelli and Company, Ltd. (2010). *Urban Structure, Land Markets and Social Housing in Santiago, Chile*.

Peppercorn, I. G. and Taffin, C. (2013). *Rental Housing: Lessons from International Experience and Policies for Emerging Market*. Washington, DC: World Bank. Available at: documents. worldbank.org [Accessed 22 Jan. 2018].

Prahalad, C. K. and Hart, S. L. (2002). The Fortune at the Bottom of the Pyramid. *Strategy and Business*, 26.

Priemus, H. and Dieleman, F. (2002). Social Housing Policy in the European Union: Past, Present and Perspectives. *Urban Studies*, 39 (2).

Rahmanai, J., George, B. and O'Steen, R. (2013). *Single - Family REO: An Emerging Asset Class* (3rd ed.). New York: Keefe, Bruyette & Woods, Inc.

Robertson, M. (2013). *What Goes Up Mustn't Come Down: The Contradictions of the Government's Response to the UK Housing Crisis*. RC43 Pre-conference PhD Workshop, Mimeo. Available at: academia.edu [Accessed 6 Jan. 2015].

Rodríguez, A. and Sugranyes, A. (2005). l problema de vivienda de los 'con techo'. In: A. Rodríguez and A. Sugranyes (eds.), *Los Con Techo: Un Desafio para la Pol í tica de Vivienda Social* (1st ed.). Santiago: Ediciones SUR.

Rolnik, R. (2012). *Thematic Report about the Impact of Financialization on the Right to Adequate Housing*. UN-Doc., A/67/286.

Rolnik, R. (2013). Late Neoliberalism: The Financialization of Homeownership and Housing Rights. *International Journal of Urban and Regional Research*, 37 (3).

Rolnik, R. (2019). *Urban Warfare: Housing under the Empire of Finance*. London and New York: Verso.

Ronald, R. (2008). *The Ideology of Home Ownership: Homeowner Societies and the Role of Housing*. New York: Palgrave Macmillan.

Ruiz, A. S. (2017). Blackstone construye un gigante de viviendas para el alquiler en España. *Cinco Días*. Available at: cincodias.elpais.com [Accessed 22 Jan. 2018].

Sassen, S. (2014). Finance as Capability: Good, Bad, Dangerous. *Arcade (Stanford)*. Available at: arcade.stanford.edu/occasion/finance-capability-good-bad-dangerous [Accessed 2 Mar. 2019].

Schwartz, H. and Seabrooke L. (2009). *The Politics of Housing Booms and Busts*. Basingstoke: Palgrave Macmillan.

Smith, J. L. (2006). Public Housing Transformation: Evolving National Policy. In: L. Bennett, J. L. Smith and P. A. Wright (eds), *Where Are Poor People to Live? Transforming Public Housing Communities*, Armonk, NY: M. E. Sharpe.

Soederburg, S. (2017). The Rental Housing Question: Exploitation, Eviction and Erasures. *Geoforum*, 89, 114–123.

South Africa Financial and Fiscal Commission. (2012). *Building an Inclusionary Housing Market: Shifting the Paradigm for Housing Delivery in South Africa*. Presentation to the FinMark Forum.

Stephens, M. (2010). Locating Chinese Urban Housing Policy in an International Context. *Urban Studies*, 47 (14) (Dec.).

Tavolari, B. (2017). AirBnB e os impasses regulatórios do compartilhamento de moradia. In: A. F. Rafael Zanatta, P. de Paula and C. B. Beatriz Kira (eds.), *Economias do compartilhamento e o direito*, Curitiba: Juruá. Available at: internetlab.org.br [Accessed 30 Jan. 2018].

Teresa, B. F. (2016). Managing Fictitious Capital: The Legal Geography of Investment and Political Struggle in Rental Housing in New York City. *Environment and Planning A*, 48 (3).

UN-Habitat. (2005). *Financing Urban Shelter: Global Report on Human Settlements*. Nairobi: UN-Habitat.

UN-Habitat. (2008). *Housing for All: The Challenges of Affordability, Accessibility and Sustainability – The Experiences and Instruments from the Developing and Developed Worlds*. Nairobi: UN-Habitat.

UN-Habitat. (2011a). *Affordable Land and Housing in Europe and North America*. Nairobi: UN-Habitat.

UN-Habitat. (2011b). *Affordable Land and Housing in Latin America and the Caribbean*. Nairobi: UN-Habitat.

United Kingdom. (1980). *Housing Act 1980*. London: HMSO. Available at: legislation.gov.uk [Accessed 12 Jan. 2015].

World Bank. (1993). *Housing: Enabling Markets to Work*. Washington, DC: World Bank.

Zhu, M. (2014). Managing House Price Booms in Emerging Markets. *IMF Blog*. Available at: blogs.imf.org/2014/12/10/managing-house-price-booms-in-emerging-markets/ [Accessed 20 Feb. 2019].

10
COMMODITIES

Stefan Ouma and Tobias J. Klinge

Introduction

When talking about commodities in the world of global finance, matters are less clear than they first appear. While usually associated with investments into hard and soft commodities,[1] other 'investment plays' involving farmland, or different stages of commodity production and natural resource extraction are often also categorized as commodities.

In the realm of finance, such ambiguities are no trivial matter. Large institutional investors such as pension funds—the driving forces in the world of money management—usually make portfolio allocations based on the specific risk–return and liquidity[2] characteristics of certain asset classes (Arjaliès et al., 2017; Clark and Monk, 2017). This, in turn, is supposed to guarantee that the investors' harvested returns allow them to meet their own liabilities, hence ensuring solvency. For doing this efficiently, the boundaries of such classes need to be clearly demarcated. This is, itself, a discursive and socio-technical activity that evolves dynamically: *discursive*, because such boundaries become established via acts of speech and representation in the everyday craft of finance, rendering what lies 'within' a legitimate investment opportunity; *socio-technical*, because new material infrastructures, standards, and eventually often laws—phenomena that are as much social as they are technical—underpin the consolidation of a new asset class. For instance, something institutional investors were somewhat shy of targeting—farmland—has recently been heralded as a new alternative asset class (Fairbairn, 2014, 2020; Ouma, 2020a). Further complexity results when we include domains where the investment activity is about the prevention of the direct commodification of resources, such as investments in carbon credit schemes. Here, financial investments are made in the non-extraction of resources (preventing their direct destruction, but trading the emission rights associated with them and thus adding a new layer of derivative commodification). Similar complexity exists in domains such as trade in water rights, where the user-rights, rather than the underlying commodity itself, are being traded. Finance thus has multiple entry points for permeating the world of natural resource extraction and trade, including investments in the very infrastructures that help mobilize such resources. Some of these investment products are public and thus accessible to a broader group of investors (such as retail investors investing in an exchange-traded farmland fund, or a commodity index fund), usually attracting stronger public scrutiny and regulation. Other such investment products are part of the private or grey capital market—such as private equity-style investments in agribusiness companies, or 'over-the-counter' commodity investments.

Geographers have made important contributions to studying these fields and the diverse ways in which finance penetrates various resource-based domains in different geographical contexts (Asiyanbi, 2018; Bargawi and Newman, 2017; De Los Reyes, 2017; Knox-Hayes, 2013; Labban, 2010; McGill, 2018; Muellerleile, 2015; Ouma, 2016; Purcell, 2018). These contributions have variously excavated the regulatory shifts, discursive framings, actor landscapes, or the new socio-spatial relations and practices that have shaped the transformation of resources with a use-value into objects of financial value. Furthermore, they have often problematized the impacts of these processes on communities, resource markets, agricultural producers, and nature.

This chapter focuses on farmland, and the trade in non-agricultural and agricultural commodities as two major commodity domains—one considered to be a somewhat illiquid asset class with specific material and political properties, the other more liquid and less vulnerable to direct political contestation and regulation. For both domains, similar arguments have been made as to why investors should recognize their potential. Besides their attractive physical properties (high demand meeting limited supply), their price movements are said to be uncorrelated with the movements of other major asset classes, such as stocks and bonds. For institutional investors who are keen on diversifying their portfolios and insulating them against external shocks, such counter-cyclical assets are particularly attractive. Finally, both farmland and commodity prices 'tend to rise as inflation rises, offering a natural form of protection against downside risk' (Black Rock, 2019). In other words, while other asset values may wither away during times of inflation, commodities are said to preserve their value.

This chapter is structured as follows. First, we briefly characterize what 'commodities as an investment case' means in practice. In accordance with Zeller (2010: 106), who builds on Robinson (1971 [1956]), we mobilize the term 'financial placements', rather than investments in relation to the commodity space, as the latter term usually describes the utilization of financial resources in order to produce capital goods. Financial placements, on the other hand, correspond to the acquisition of rights, shares, or debts, which are either financed from savings or from the sale of other assets. Therefore, placements can be considered a specific mode of rent-seeking. We then excavate the trends that have led to investors' rising interest in commodities, before situating the contemporary run on commodities historically in order to arrive at a more nuanced assessment of what is actually new about this and what has, in fact, a longer history. The notion of an 'asset' as an object of financial desire plays a central role in this analysis. Afterwards, we show how financial investments into soft commodities—and, even more so, into land—have been politicized to an extent not seen with any other asset class. In this regard, the quality of land and food as the bare sources of life plays a crucial role. In the final section, we discuss some of the regional impacts of the rising financial interest in both farmland and commodity trade by using empirical research results from New Zealand and Tanzania. By way of conclusion, we argue that scholars need to critically investigate significant socio-economic transformations entailed in finance's increasingly complex relationship with nature in the form of land and commodities because they reshape large parts of the agricultural commodity chain.

Commodities as an Investment Case

In May 2012, the Teachers Insurance and Annuity Association (TIAA), the leading retirement provider in the United States of America (USA) for people working in the fields of academic, medical, cultural, government, and research, launched its new investment vehicle: Global Agriculture LLC. The pension fund was ready to invest US$2 billion in farmland in Brazil, Australia, Eastern Europe, and the USA itself. The fund also opened this vehicle to other institutional investors, such as the Swedish pension fund AP2 and the British Columbia Investment Management Corporation. In 2013, TIAA took its interest in farmland one step further and began to sponsor the Farmland Research Institute at the University of Illinois, home to one of the most prestigious agricultural economics departments in the United States. In August 2014, it announced that it had raised another US$1.4 billion for its second farmland co-investment platform: Global Agriculture II. This time, 20 more investors were on board.

The 'pension fund-gone-farming' espouses a phenomenon that has been making headlines for some time: the large-scale acquisition of agricultural land (via purchase, lease, or concession) by global financial investors to grow food, forests (as timber, or as carbon sinks), or agrofuels. Since the financial crisis of 2007–08, institutional investors in particular have been looking for new, safe investment havens. This supply side dynamic met a range of demand side dynamics that financial investors found particularly appealing. Most notably, this was the dramatic rise of world food prices in 2007–08, a 'food crisis' that had been in the making for some time, but that only erupted at a global scale around the same time as the financial crisis. A sudden hike in prices led to 'food riots in countries as far apart as Haiti, Guinea, Mauritania, Mexico, Morocco, Egypt, Senegal, Uzbekistan, Yemen, Bangladesh, Philippines and Indonesia', and many other 'countries were threatened by social unrest, as rising food prices caused not merely dissatisfaction but even the spread of hunger among social groups who were not inured to it' (Gosh, 2010: 80–1). A growing world population; changing diets in Asian emerging markets; a rising demand for arable land for agrofuels and carbon sinks in the context of peak oil and climate change; stagnating or declining yields in core production regions—all served to remind investors that 'no matter how bad things get, we all need to eat' (*The Economist*, 2009). This seemed to make farmland and agriculture a safe bet, even more so since land is a limited resource and, compared to other financial products, appears as something tangible with relatively little complexity. This was exactly what was needed after the world had been hit by complex and risky real estate investment products blowing up. The low interest rate environment created by quantitative easing policies pursued by several central banks meant that the financial sector 'had a lot of easy money to burn' (Foroohar, 2016: 183). Some of that ended up in farmland and, more significantly, in more liquid commodity markets.

Accordingly, the number of funds that, in one way or another, targeted agricultural commodities or businesses involved either in commodity production, or in servicing it (e.g., agricultural technology companies) rose from 38 in 2005 to 523 by mid-2018, with 161 of these funds having direct exposure to farmland. By 2018, US$83 billion had been invested in the agricultural investment space.[3] Behind these numbers lies a rising demand for farmland in major crop-producing regions such as North America, South America, Australia, New Zealand, different parts of Europe, and Russia (de Lapérouse and Vitón, 2017). Even though these investment volumes may seem rather small compared to other investment spaces such as real estate, investments into the different stages of agricultural production are steadily expanding, with noticeable consequences for land markets, as well as agricultural production and trade worldwide.

When it comes to capital placements in the farmland investment space, institutional investors—not just pension funds, but also insurance companies—are the most important players. In addition to these, investment banks, university endowments, family offices, sovereign wealth funds, large agribusiness corporations, high-net worth individuals, and, to a lesser extent, even retail investors[4] have gained 'exposure' to farmland and agricultural production. Many of these players, such as family offices and high-net worth individuals, have different 'risk appetites' than pension funds or insurance companies. Investors use a variety of investment vehicles—such as private equity fund structures, joint-ventures, or co-investment platforms—to channel capital into agriculture, as well as different operational models on the ground in order to extract value from agriculture (Ouma, 2020a).

These sophisticated investors, defined by their professional knowledge of financial markets, can be contrasted with retail investors, who are a product of the massification of financial investment among middle classes over recent decades (French et al., 2011: 801). While these may already obtain exposure to farmland through mutual funds, or through the acquisition of shares in listed agribusiness companies, they cannot yet enter the farmland space directly due to the inaccessibility of more sophisticated investment vehicles to the general (non-specialist) public. This has changed with the rise of exchange-traded farmland funds such as Bonnefield in Canada, and Gladstone and Farmland Partners in the USA. As Fairbairn (2020: 100) demonstrates, these investment structures represent a first attempt at securitizing farmland, because they bundle income streams from the leasing out of several individual farm properties into a single vehicle that can be listed publicly (see also Stevenson, 2014). This makes them tradable on stock exchanges and accessible to the masses, thereby fostering liquidity. The recent rise of 'fractional farmland ownership' platforms such as FarmFundr and AcreTrader complements retail investor-focused capital placement structures in agriculture (Fairbairn, 2020: 101). Finally, development finance institutions are also playing an increasing role for agricultural investments, by providing risk insurance and/or equity capital. These are also increasingly being called on by industry players to provide 'patient capital' in order to fund agricultural infrastructure in regions where it is not well-developed (Brooks, 2016).

The rising interest in farming by financial investors is also mirrored in the evolution of the Global Farmland Index, launched by the UK real estate firm Savills in 2012 (Ouma, 2020a). It shows a significant upwards movement for the regions of South America, North America, Western Europe, Australasia, and Central Europe since 2002, even though several key regions have experienced (commodity) market-induced volatilities, or even declines in values, since 2012. The 'green gold rush' is also reflected in the performance of the US-focused Farmland Income Index issued by the National Council of Real Estate Investment Fiduciaries (NCREIF), one of the few sources of institutional farmland returns. This index increased dramatically from US$1.1 billion to US$8.1 billion (= values of property) between 2008 and 2017 (Conrad, 2018) (see Figure 10.1).

Despite having an original quality as so-called direct investments, financial placements in farmland (and along the agricultural commodity chain) can be read as an extension of global finance trying to capitalize on the commodities boom that set in from the early 2000s onwards. Since then, we have seen a steep increase in the involvement of financial investors in the trade of both agricultural and non-agricultural commodities, accompanied by increasing market volatility (Ederer et al., 2016). This boom was disrupted by the financial crisis in 2008, only to rebound until 2012, when investors started to look for safe investment underpinned by strong market fundamentals (McGill, 2018). The increasing entanglement of financial institutions with liquid commodity trading markets is also reflected in a bewildering array of financial products through which purely financial investors can obtain exposure to the world of commodities.

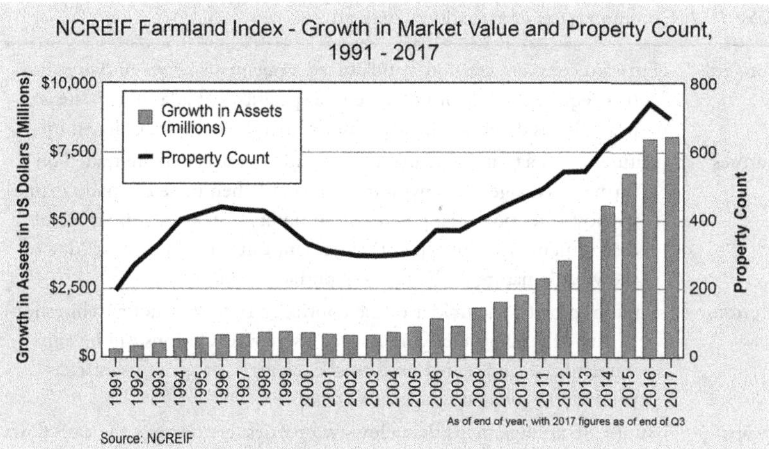

Figure 10.1 NCREIF Farmland Index: Growth in Market Value and Property Count, 1991–2017

Source: Redrawn from Conrad (2018); reprinted with permission.

Of the diverse group of investors targeting farmland and the agricultural commodity chain more broadly, it is particularly pension funds, hedge funds, and investment banks that have placed capital into the trade with hard and soft commodities (Ederer et al., 2016). The investment structures used include commodity index funds (CIFs), an investment structure we will discuss in detail further below. Index funds, also known as 'exchange-traded commodity funds', can also be traded like a stock on public exchanges. The commodity investment space further comprises 'true' commodity funds, which invest directly in the underlying commodity asset or company; for example, a fund that holds a direct position in publicly listed seed, gold, oil, or grains trading companies (Clapp, 2019). Finally, it includes investment products built around some form of agricultural derivative, so called because its value is derived from the price of an underlying commodity. Forward contracts are the most basic form of an agricultural derivative, with a history dating back centuries. A *forward contract* enables the seller (e.g., a farmer) to lock in a price for a specific quantity of commodities with a specific buyer (and vice versa) at a set date in the future, thus insulating them from the price volatilities of supply and demand (Clapp and Isakson, 2018: 33). These relatively simple products have been complemented by a variety of more complex products such as *futures*, *swaps*, or *options* (Table 10.1).

All these funds may also involve giving investors exposure to livestock such as cattle or pigs (Geman, 2015).[5] While derivatives in principle allow for market participants to insure themselves against future volatility related to commodity-related transactions, especially those variants that can be settled in cash—such as futures—may well enable distinct speculation and hence produce additional price volatility instead (Clapp 2011; Schumann 2011).

Table 10.1 Common types of agricultural derivatives

Forwards	Forward contracts are non-standardized agreements between two parties that require the sale or purchase of a specific asset at a future date at a price that is determined at the time when the contract is drawn up
Futures	Futures contracts are standardized forward contracts that are traded on formal exchanges ('anonymous markets'). When these contracts expire, in most cases no actual physical commodity is delivered in favour of cash settlements. This type of investment can carry higher risk due to the volatile nature of the futures contracts market.
Options	Options provide the holder of the contract a right (but not an obligation) to buy or sell an underlying asset at a set price. Options can be either standardized, and traded on formal exchanges, or specific contracts privately negotiated between two parties.
Swaps	Swaps are arrangements that allow two parties to exchange the cash flows (e.g., fixed versus floating prices) over a specified period of time.

Source: Adapted from Clapp and Isakson (2018: 34); reprinted with permission.

These developments are an expression of the increasing 'financialization' of liquid commodity markets (UNCTAD, 2011). Clapp and Isakson (2018: 42) provide some stunning data: investments in these commodities rose from US$10 billion in 2000 to US$450 billion in 2011, the peak of the commodity bonanza before the super-cycle ended in 2012. Trade in commodity futures doubled between 2004 and 2007, and investments in exchange-traded CIFs climbed from US$10 billion in 2006 to US$200 billion in 2012. Financial institutions increasingly became shapers of commodity derivative markets (Foroohar, 2016). The post-2000 entry of finance into commodity markets was fuelled by a number of developments, including regulatory changes (e.g., the Commodity Modernization Act passed in the USA in 2000), advances in trading technologies, and the bust of the dot-com bubble, which released capital for new investment rounds.

At the same time—analogous to processes in industry or retailing—commodity traders themselves have become active in financial markets. Traders such as Vitol, Glencore, Cargill, or ADM have formed investment companies that offer exposure to both agricultural derivatives and trade in the underlying commodities (or even farmland) themselves, thus capitalizing on their insider knowledge (Salerno, 2014). The global commodity trading oligopoly's profitability is estimated to surpass even that of the investment banking sector, but most operations are hidden from view (Chesnais, 2016: 115–17). For instance, even though in 2016 five of the ten largest firms in Switzerland, known for its pro-business environment, were involved in commodity trade, it was not even clear how many people worked in that sector, or what turnovers, profits, and taxes accrued in the sector to companies (Kesselring et al., 2018: 11). Even commercial players who do not pursue a financial market agenda themselves are increasingly orienting their business practices towards the prices that financial forces help to shape via futures markets (Newman, 2009; Staritz et al., 2018); for example, by engaging in more sophisticated forms of price–risk management.

With some background on the more recent relationship between commodities and finance, it is now crucial to take a step back and re-evaluate what changes were truly novel this time around.

Finance and Commodities: Re-placing History in Financialization Research

The rise of financial interests in the commodity space is often associated with broader financialization trends in the global economy since the late 1970s (Chesnais, 2016; Lapavitsas, 2013). Indeed, many of the regulatory shifts that allowed finance to move into resource-based domains beyond ordinary public stocks happened fairly recently. For instance, US and UK pension funds—now major players in the global farmland race—were only allowed to invest in agricultural properties from the mid-1950s onwards, when restrictions on riskier real asset allocations were lifted (Ouma, 2020b). Commodity markets in the USA became heavily regulated in the 1920s, seriously constraining purely speculative behaviour and the engagement of non-commercial traders. This situation lasted until the 1980s, when the first banks began to sell agricultural derivatives 'over-the-counter', bypassing the regulations of public commodity futures exchanges.

In the 1990s, they also started to offer CIFs. These 'bundle futures contracts for a range of commodities, including oil and minerals, as well as agricultural commodities, into a single financial instrument based on a commodity price index' (Clapp, 2011: 140). Investors thus no longer required specific knowledge of commodity markets, and were able to 'bet on market price movements, rather than the purchase and sale of the commodity itself' (Clapp, 2011: 140). A landmark here was the launch of the Goldman Sachs Commodity Index in 1991 (GSCI, now the S&P GSCI). According to Schumann (2011: 26):

> [the] index reflected the development of futures prices for 25 different commodities, ranging from aluminium to sugar, and included only those raw materials for which there was liquid futures trading on the exchange. The index was calculated on the basis of the most recent prices for the next futures contracts to expire in the relevant commodity group.

These trends were buttressed by changing regulation in the 1990s—most importantly, the replacement of the Glass-Steagall Act from 1933 with the Gramm-Leach-Bliley Act in 1999 and the passing of the Commodity Futures Modernization Act 2000. The Gramm-Leach-Bliley Act lowered the barriers for financial institutions to engage with real assets such as physical commodity trade, mining and oil. The Commodity Futures Modernization Act 2000 'exempted financial derivatives traded over the counter or off regulated changes from CFTC [Commodity Futures Trading Commission] or SEC [Securities and Exchange Commission] oversight' (Foroohar, 2016: 192). These cumulative events, combined with the boom in commodities from the early 2000s onwards, led to the increasing influence of speculators and index funds compared to the traditional hedgers, who would use financial products to aid their physical trading business (see Figure 10.2). Between 2006 and 2008, the financial behemoth Goldman Sachs made between US$3 billion and US$4 billion per year on both the ownership of commodities and the trading of their derivatives. In other words, this supposed investment banking firm, like the aforementioned traders, was both trading in the market and shaping its dynamics, and providing risk management services to other firms by selling the derivatives (Foroohar, 2016: 192).

While both trends outlined here seem stunning, these more recent moments of financial expansion must not let us lose sight of the long-standing historical entanglements between commodity production, trade, and finance. A *longue dureé* perspective reveals that both private and public forms of finance played a crucial role in the production of capitalist agricultural landscapes since at least the late eighteenth and early nineteenth centuries in different parts of the world (Byerlee, 2013; Weaver, 2003).

As shown by Ouma (2020a), even the entry of institutional investors into commodity production itself is not a thing of the recent past. Munton (1985) noted that, between 1966 and 1982, finance-driven investments in British farmland saw a significant expansion. By the end of 1984, financial institutions in Great Britain owned some 290,000 hectares of lease land and a further of

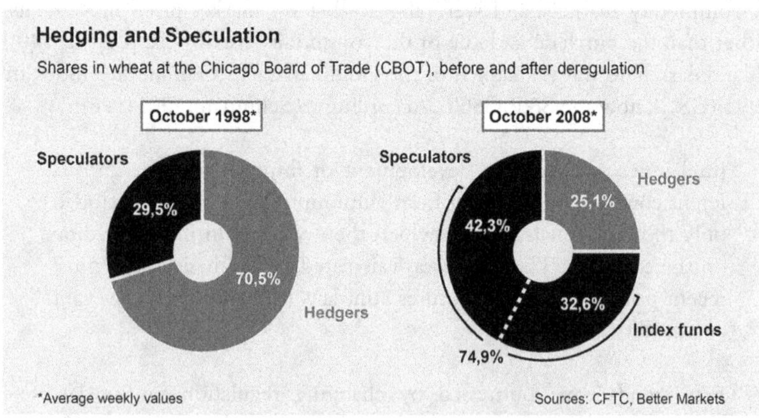

Figure 10.2 Share in wheat at the Chicago Board of Trade (CBOT), before and after deregulation

Source: Redrawn from Schumann (2011: 41); reprinted with permission.

50,000 hectares with vacant possession. This was 'equivalent to 1.9% of the total agricultural area and 3.0% of the area of crops and grass in Great Britain' around that time (Munton, 1985: 160). In the USA (with its particular institutional environment and agrarian structures) pension funds, university endowments, and wealthy families have been targeting timber and farmland more systematically since at least the late 1980s (Gunnoe and Gellert, 2011), the latter becoming a popular object of investment in the wake of the great farming crisis that left many owner-operated farms bankrupt (Fairbairn, 2014, 2020; Koeninger, 2018).

Equally, the development of future contracts and options, as well as the development of early stock exchanges such as the Chicago Board of Trade, in 1865, and the Amsterdam Stock Exchange, in 1602, can be historically linked to trade in agriculture (Bernstein, 1998; Clapp, 2011). Since the end of the nineteenth century, producers and agricultural traders have hedged against future price fluctuations—first, in Great Britain and, later, in the USA—by means of futures contracts (Clapp, 2011). For a long time, trading in agricultural futures contracts concentrated on a few exchanges, including the Chicago Board of Trade, the New York Board of Trade (NYBOT), and the London International Financial Futures and Options Exchange, now part of the London Commodity Exchange (Newman, 2009). Cronon (1992) demonstrated in great detail how the rise of the financial centre of Chicago was tightly entangled with what would be called the financialization of the Midwest Prairies.

These examples show that we must carefully examine how current phases of 'financialization' compare to earlier periods, as Christophers (2015: 23–4) rightly points out (see also Ouma, 2015). We find that finance has had a long (but by no means easy) entanglement with agriculture, but this does not mean that there is nothing novel about finance's contemporary run on all things agricultural. As Fairbairn (2015: 212) puts it:

> the expanded size and clout of institutional investors...the increasing prioritization of financial profits over productive profits among both financial and nonfinancial companies...and the growing acceptance of financial investment as a morally legitimate activity...can probably all help to explain why the historically recurring demand for land as a financial asset has taken a novel form over the last few years.

Having established the (dis)continuities of the current version of finance's coupling with commodities, it is furthermore important to revisit briefly the broad strands of critique associated with it.

Commodities as Controversial Investments

As should have become clear so far, the activities in global commodity markets, including those for land, can no longer be imagined today without the influence of both public and private capital markets. This growing influence has not been without its critics across the 'commodity spectrum', but criticism has been particularly pronounced for the incorporation of agricultural commodities and land into global financial networks.

For both agricultural soft commodities and land, similar lines of criticism have emerged. First, the incorporation of these domains is often cited as yet another case of relentless financialization through which the rule of global financial markets over the bare source of life itself—*resources*—is being expanded. This critique has also been extended to firms that have strong ties to capital markets and are involved in resource extraction. They have been repeatedly put under critical scrutiny for the short-termism and extraordinary profit-orientation induced by the shareholder value gaze (Bowman, 2018; De Los Reyes, 2017), with often stark consequences for labour, the environment, adjacent communities, and state coffers. For soft commodities, it has frequently been argued that financialization has led to a considerable decoupling of market prices and the goods actually being traded, as well as to increased price volatility (for pro-arguments, see Clapp, 2011; Gosh, 2010; Kesselring et al., 2018; Schumann, 2011; for counter-arguments, see, e.g., Bohl and Sulewski, 2019; Irwin and Sanders, 2011; see also the summary in McGill 2018).[6] In the course of the food price crisis of 2007–08, the implications of these processes were discussed primarily for consumers from the countries of the Global South, who were suddenly forced to spend more of their income on food procurement due to abrupt price increases for many staple commodities. The impact of financialized commodity markets on producers are less widely documented, but, by some accounts, are assumed to be significant (Bargawi and Newman, 2017; Breger Bush, 2012; Staritz et al., 2018). Since the deregulation and liberalization of global agricultural markets, which began in the early 1990s, has led to market concentration along the food supply chains, while protective mechanisms for small players and state support structures have been dismantled in many countries, this has also led to an uneven exposure to commodity market risks. In financialized commodity chains, larger companies are presumably much better able to protect themselves against price volatility than smaller players; for instance, through accessing hedging mechanisms.

For the land domain, a similar argument has been mobilized. The increasing financial demand for land is said to have led to price hikes, whereby the financial value of land no longer reflects the present or even projected productive capacity. According to critics, this would also be accompanied by increasing concentration of land in corporate hands; the promotion of industrial-scale agriculture suitable for large-scale institutional investments; globalized forms of absentee land ownership; and lock-outs of less capitalized farmers from land markets, if not their outright dispossession (in places where 'investment' implies more violent dynamics) (Clapp, 2014; Isakson, 2014; Romero, 2015).

Furthermore, critics have warned that the financialization of both land and agricultural commodities implies the 'the one-sided and dominant transfer of economic value to land [and food] as [...] resource[s]' (Herre, 2013: 8). This critique in the tradition of free markets critic Karl Polanyi (2001 [1944]), lambasts the expansion of the commodity form into those domains that sustain human life. The quest for 'fictitious commodities', as Polanyi calls such real abstractions, is taken to its extreme with some derivative investment products in liquid commodity markets, where exchange opportunities have been created that no longer depend on or reflect the physical demand for food or other resources.

Lastly, it is often argued that the financialization of commodities, as in other domains, is a process detached from the real economy through which profits are generated speculatively or virtually, be it through commodity futures markets, or through direct investments in farmland. The assertion that the financial sector does not generate any real value, but only lives from betting on the price development of an object's value and by trading the rights to the revenues from this development, has a long tradition dating back to Marx (Huber, 2018).

While these critiques raise a range of significant issues, some of the assumptions underlying these criticisms are problematic in themselves. For instance, financialization is not simply about turning something into a commodity, as is often suggested; rather, it is about *assetization*. Assets are domains of life that have been turned into property and generate a stream of income (Ouma, 2020a). In contrast to most goods, assets do not become cheaper when demand rises; rather, they become more expensive with increasing demand because they are constructed in such a way that their reproducibility is limited (e.g., by private property rights). Only when assets can be converted into a liquid form—in the case of real estate, for example, via securitization, or in the case of a soft commodity via derivativization—do they become tradable as commodities on secondary markets (Langley, 2020). The true character of assetization needs to be unveiled before we can engage in meaningful critique.

Impacts on the Ground

Illiquid Commodity Markets: The Case of Farmland in New Zealand

Due to exceptional data availability, the most detailed insights into the local impact of the financialization of farmland can be made in New Zealand (Klinge, 2020, Ouma, 2020a). New Zealand has been one of the main destinations of finance-driven investments in farmland since 2010, yet remains suspiciously absent in most accounts of the global land rush (which usually focus on the economies of the Global South). New Zealand's history is firmly entangled with overseas investment. Just as the general structure of agriculture was modelled by the state in favour of family farming, foreign ownership of farmland was restricted until 1984. In the following years, the country underwent a fundamental restructuring as part of wider neoliberal reforms (Kelsey, 1995). The sizeable and culturally significant agricultural sector was rapidly overhauled from a model of state-led agricultural expansion that assisted farmers to bolster their exports, to a model of turbulent markets in which farmers found themselves responsible for survival in a situation of dwindling prices, rising costs, and diminished export opportunities (Cloke, 1989). As a result, the farming sector changed its focus from sheep and beef to dairy, horticulture, and viticulture, because new export markets promised stabler returns. Higher competitive pressures entailed concentration and consolidation of agricultural activity and the emergence of larger agribusinesses. These were then mainly funded by private finance, rather than state subsidies and loans, and increasingly leveraged to afford productivity investments needed to compete in the world market (Le Heron and Roche, 1999; Roche et al., 1992).

Furthermore, rural land was opened up to a new wave of investment, at first largely via the privatization of state forests (Le Heron, 1991; Wallace, 2016). With more liberalization ensuing from 1995 (Rolleston, 2016), foreign investments into dairy, horticulture, viticulture, and fruit orchards increased. Effectively, the transformative processes resulted in a twofold 'structural dependence' (Le Heron, 1993: 152) of New Zealand's agricultural sector on specific commodities and export markets, as well as on private—and often overseas—capital (Kalderimis, 2011; Rosenberg, 1997). It is important to note that the regulatory environment supported these developments with a legislation that, in theory, applied high thresholds to overseas land investments but, in practice, proved largely open to the decisions by the respective ministers (Klinge, 2020). The regulatory set-up thus served to deflect public controversy away from the respective government to the underlying bureaucracies, and made the contested land acquisitions manageable (Kalderimis 2013).

A new wave of agricultural land purchases began from 2009 onwards, with an increasing number of agribusiness multinationals and institutional investors entering primary production (dairy, sheep, beef, and viticulture). While some of the agribusiness multinationals arguably had the intention of securing food supplies for sizable and/or net food-importing overseas populations (e.g., China, which signed a bilateral trade agreement with New Zealand in 2007), institutional investors were seeking greener pastures in the wake of the financial crisis. New Zealand provided compelling market fundamentals, as it offered a welcoming regulatory environment built around the hegemonic notion of the importance of 'overseas capital' to the domestic economy, and promises of significant capital gains as land prices had already been rising rapidly for some time, particularly in the dairy industry. Its reputation as a 'rock-star economy', far away from the turmoil of Anglo-Atlantic capitalism but close to the rising economies of Asia, also attracted investors' interests.

The analysis presented here is based on a unique set of secondary data that covers most investments into land and agriculture between 2001 and 2017.[7] What becomes clear is that, first, between 2001 and 2017, a total of 800,000 hectares (net, meaning it was sold from a 'domestic' to a 'foreign' party) of rural land (forestry and farmland) changed hands, accounting for about 6% of New Zealand's productive land (13.9 million hectares in 2016; Stats NZ, 2018)[8]. Much of this, however, was forestry, which has been traded among a small number of large global investors since the 1990s. Between 2001 and 2017, some 146,000 net hectares of freehold and 138,000 net hectares of leasehold farmland were transferred to foreign investors from New Zealand parties, with 45% of these areas being transferred in the period from 2011 to 2015. Although comparisons with earlier years are difficult, as existing studies seldom single out farmland acquisitions, or highlight net transactions separately (e.g., Rosenberg, 1997), these figures suggest that global interest in New Zealand farmland has received a significant boost with the financial and food price crisis of 2007–08. This interest, especially around peak years such as 2013, often materialized itself as a small number of sizable transactions by large players.[9] At the same time, it seems as though the wave identified has largely run out of steam. The reasons for this, however, are hard to pin down, as they potentially range from a general realization of land price bubbles, to a shortage of buyable properties suitable for the specific demands of investors, to the recent shift in government which took a less benign approach to overseas land ownership.

Second, another noteworthy trend is the increasing presence of institutional investors, as opposed to classic agrobusiness interests, timber companies, or individuals. In the sample period, these players have acquired 79,700 net hectares, of which some 64,000 net hectares were freehold. While prices were disclosed for only around 92% of all transactions involving these investors, they stood at an impressive total of NZ$1.31 billion. Unlike in the forestry sector, financial actors had been largely absent from the 'farmland scene' until 2009, yet quickly came to dominate overseas investments into rural resources between 2013 and 2015 (see Figure 10.3).

Third, despite an unprecedented boom of overseas investment into farmland used or intended to be used for dairying between 2010 and 2016, there are two trends of overseas investment into farmland regarding their targeted sectors. Sheep and beef, the historical base of New Zealand's agriculture from the late nineteenth century onwards, remained surprisingly popular among overseas investors throughout most of the years analysed, notwithstanding the fact that there has been a general decline since the 1980s, with many of those farms in the South Island being converted to parcels of 'white gold', entailing severe dangers of environmental degradation. This shift from sheep and beef to dairy farms has undoubtedly been 'the most dramatic shift in pastoral use' (Smith and Montgomery, 2004: 113) in the country's recent history, driven by strong export growth to primarily Asian markets—in particular, Chinese markets. Consequently, for many years, involvement in the dairy industry was a favourite occupation among both domestic (family and corporate) farmers and overseas investors alike, due to its potential to generate a strong cash-flow, global competitiveness (due to a largely grass-fed system), and promise of asset price appreciation. The 'white gold fever'—by no means being limited

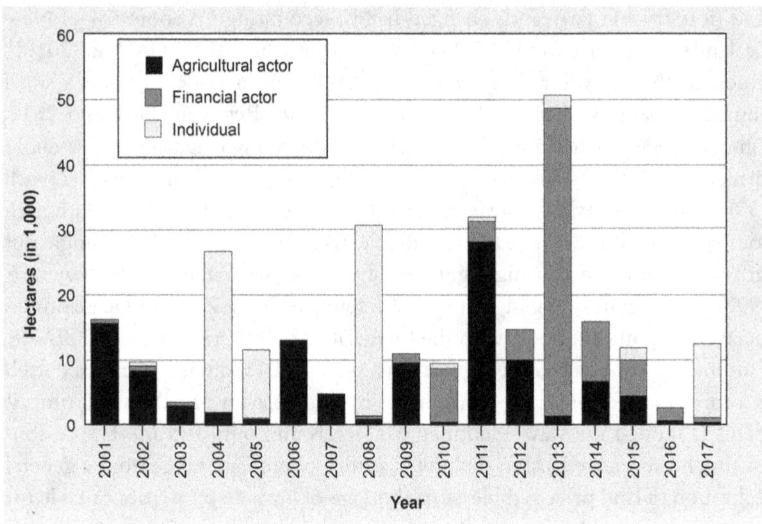

Figure 10.3 Investors in New Zealand farmland, 2001–17. Net hectares of approved applications concerning the acquisition of agricultural land classified by type of investor (n = 565)

Source: The authors; see also footnote 7.

to overseas investors, but also including domestic farmers—is also reflected in the geographical patterns found in the investment data, where the four regions of Nelson/Marlborough, Canterbury, Otago, and Southland account for at least 75% of all agricultural land sold or leased out during 2001 and 2017, but only for about 46% of New Zealand's total agricultural land in 2016 (Stats NZ, 2018). These regions have also been hotspots for dairy farm conversions. However, the persisting popularity of sheep/beef farming among foreign institutional investors can be explained by the fact that, even though these sectors have a lower cash flow than the recent 'investment favourite' of dairy, they are also less intensive and more stable in terms of market demand, and thus less risky.

Liquid Commodity Markets: The Case of Coffee in Tanzania

The financialization of liquid commodity markets has also significantly impacted the organization, geography, and dynamics of (global) food chains. This can be effectively demonstrated with the example of coffee markets, where prices at the level of commodity exchanges have been increasingly shaped by financial interests (see Figure 10.4). An growing number of studies also demonstrate how these prices are increasingly being transmitted along commodity value chains, and thereby shape the formation of farm-gate

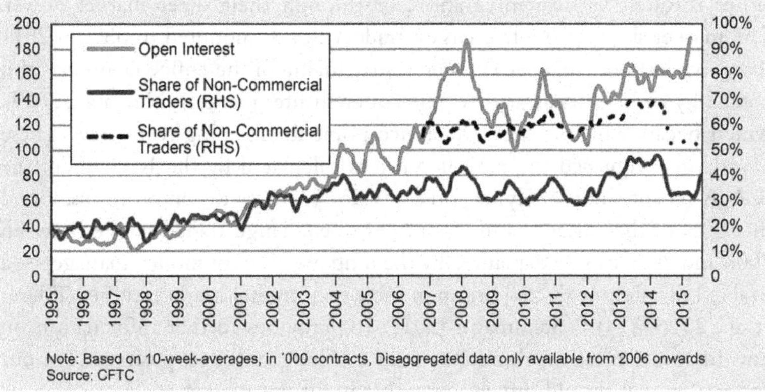

Figure 10.4 Open positions and share of financial investors in coffee futures transactions (based on Intercontinental Exchange data), C coffee.

Notes: Open positions in 1995–2015. Up to 2006 data on commercial and non-commercial traders were reported with the large share of index investors/swap dealers being part of the commercial trader category. Hence, the share of non-commercials underrepresents the share of financial investors. From 2006 onwards, swap dealers and money managers have been reported separately, but are jointly shown in the financial investor category.

Source: Redrawn from Tröster and Staritz (2015: 12); reprinted with permission.

market prices and demand dynamics in producer countries (Staritz et al., 2018). It now becomes increasingly evident that 'financial instruments play a critical role in determining commodity prices at all points in the supply chain' (Kesselring et al., 2018: 7). However, other examples from liquid commodity markets such as wheat or cotton (Staritz et al., 2018) could also be cited to demonstrate the transformative power of financialization processes in global commodity chains.

For decades, the global coffee market was framed by state-supported international agreements and marketing systems in the coffee-growing countries of the tropics. The International Coffee Agreement (ICA) and the International Coffee Organization (ICO) ensured stable world market prices through price calculations and quotas, while national marketing systems often strengthened the power of local producers—often organized in cooperatives—over traders. In 1989, this system of stabilized world market prices collapsed due to conflicts between members (Daviron and Ponte 2005). As a result, new players, such as Vietnam, massively conquered market shares in the global coffee market. Other countries, such as Tanzania, which had long been an important player in the market, rapidly lost market share. When the World Bank and IMF pushed many Southern economies into structural adjustment in the 1980s and 1990s, many coffee markets were opened up to private traders. In this environment, large coffee exporters, traders, and roasters were often able to exert massive influence on producer prices, partly either through vertical integration, or through their sheer market power. The market share of the five largest traders alone amounted to 55% in 2011 (Bargawi and Newman, 2017). The restructuring of the coffee chain was also fuelled by the financialization of the coffee futures markets (Newman, 2009), which became an important reference point for forming real prices. These have largely replaced the indicator prices calculated by the ICO under the ICA. A recent study, applying forecast error variance decompositions, found that 50% of the variations in real prices in exchange-traded coffee between 2006 and 2016 can be explained by the long positions of money managers—a sizable but often neglected group in most commodity market studies (Ederer et al., 2016: 474).[10] Schumann (2011: 18) provides further information on how futures markets work, and the nature of long and short positions. For our context here, it should suffice to say that in futures markets:

> [b]uying positions are referred to as long positions, and selling positions as short. Contracts don't become valid until there is a buyer for a seller, and vice versa. Thus there are always just as many long as short positions in futures trading. The sum of all current contracts is referred to in exchange statistics as open interest. Futures contracts have to be closed out at the latest during the month of their due date, shortly before they expire. This is often done via the neutralization of existing positions and the financial settlement of the price difference between long and short positions.
>
> (Schumann, 2011: 24)

How the transmission of futures prices at a global level to local settings takes place depends on the local institutional setting, and the organization and governance of commodity chains (Figure 10.5). The example of Tanzania illustrates this (for a recent assessment, see Kessy, 2020). While the country today accounts for only a small share of global coffee trade, its coffee is in strong demand due to its high quality and is often used for blending with other varieties. After the end of the colonial era in 1961, the coffee sector in Tanzania was supported by a state-organized marketing system in accordance with a socialist economic doctrine, in which cooperatives played an important role. The coffee was sold to exporters at an auction in the city of Moshi, at the foot of Mt. Kilimanjaro. At the beginning of the 1990s, private traders were also admitted to the auctions as part of a neoliberal structural adjustment (Ponte 2002), leading to the emergence of various marketing and export channels. However, the auction remains an important marketing channel. Many of the bidders are subcontractors of multinational companies, and their bidding strategies are, in turn, influenced by commodity futures transactions in New York and London. While producer prices in Tanzania rose slowly after liberalization in the early 1990s, they had fallen to an all-time low by

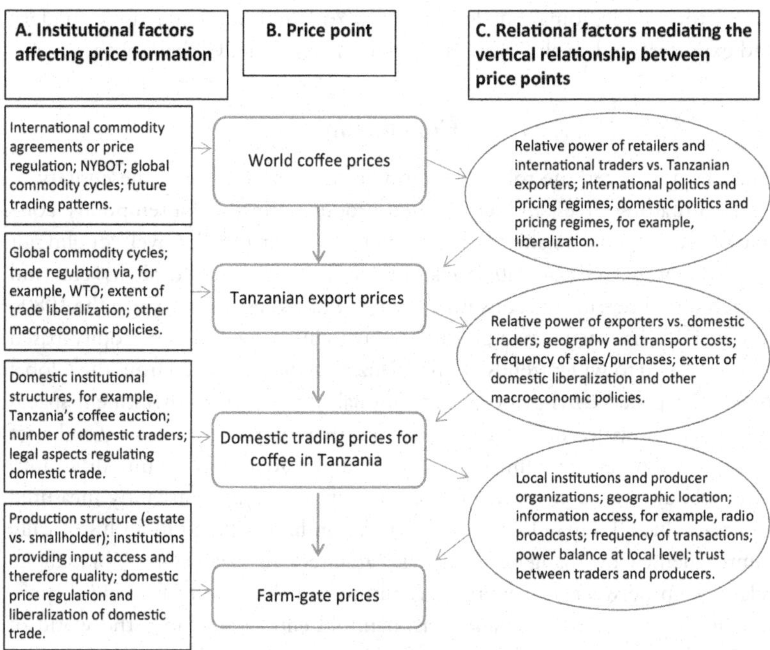

Figure 10.5 Institutional and relational factors affecting the formation of spot market prices in the coffee sector in Tanzania

Source: Adapted from Bargawi and Newman (2017: 166).

2001–2002. They then rose until 2005, before volatility intensified again until 2011. During this time, the prices had been increasingly diverging from the auction and export prices and from the global reference value (the ICO indicator price). This had to do not only with the market power of traders and roasters, but also with the financialization of commodity futures markets, which, in turn, led to a decoupling of price movements and the actual physical market needs for coffee. For many local farmers, this divergence and the processes behind it remained invisible. What they did feel, however, was that coffee revenues were unable to keep pace with rising prices for consumer goods and agricultural input. This disconnect between global market forces and local dynamics has destabilized the livelihood systems of Tanzanian coffee farmers (Bargawi and Newman, 2017; Newman, 2009), with many of them opting out of the coffee trade.

When consumers finally sip their coffee at home, or at some posh coffee shop, they are unlikely tos suspect that financial markets are an essential part of the product they consume. Not only in the conventional sense as a provider of credit, but as a disciplining force that redistributes value and risk. The financialized coffee chain is a clear example of the conflict-laden relationship between speculators and legitimate hedgers in New York and London; roasters, traders, and exporters; and small farmers in the countries of the Global South.

Conclusion

This chapter placed the role of commodities—conceived of as the entirety of land, natural resources, and agricultural products—in the contemporary configuration of global finance. Far from being an 'unnatural', novel coupling, it showed that this relation dates back historically to immature capitalist eras, and that commodities, in fact, constituted one of the earliest 'assets'. Since the 1980s, however, we have witnessed profound structural changes in commodity-based sectors related to wider trends of financialization that emanated from the Global North. Propelled by the rise of institutional investors, new investment spaces have been constructed. Financial networks between investors, money and asset managers, and various vehicles on the ground now render commodities into investible objects of financial value extraction, which are constantly measured and re-evaluated. These logics of accumulation have resulted in an historically unprecedented overhang of a financial architecture that has recalibrated the relationship between real-world agriculture and the world of financial speculation. At this juncture, finance has manifold entry points into the world of commodities: from outright ownership over private equity forms, commodity index funds, and exchange-traded funds to a variety of derivative products. In a climate of economic uncertainty following the global financial turmoil, commodities became even more appealing in their function as a safe operating space for global capital, all the more so after the earlier commodities boom of the 2000s, and especially under the new impact of low interest rate policies and the further growth of private wealth. Undergoing new rounds of discursive and socio-technical formation, commodities spawned new institutional and geographic degrees of proximity and distance that have enabled finance to propel processes of 'assetization'. These reformat both local and global relations between commodity producers (e.g., farmers, agribusiness companies, mining firms, and oil companies), investors, consumers, and the state. Furthermore, processes of this nature may introduce the additional volatility characteristic of lightly regulated financial markets into commodity-based sectors already under growing pressures. 'Assetization' thus enforces a new hierarchy of interests between investors, asset managers, or traders, on the one hand, and farmers, rural communities, and food-dependent households, on the other. These processes are necessarily and fundamentally contested because they are as much about food and land as a means of life as they are about social norms and values. Illustrative evidence from institutional investment landscapes in New Zealand and coffee production under the influence of new financial instruments in Tanzania were used to exemplify the local articulations of global financial networks. In the case of New Zealand, an agricultural sector extremely dependent on commodity exports and capital imports has become a widely hailed recipient for capital placements by large institutional investors from the Global North, who seek to capitalize on globally growing demands for particular status commodities and intensifying agricultural reorientation and the growth of large-scale agribusiness. In the case of Tanzanian coffee producers, the growing presence of financial actors in commodity derivatives markets exacerbated market unpredictability stemming from liberalized production and trade relations. Thus, an established pillar of the locally embedded, but globally shaped, economic fabric was disrupted. We conclude that future research in financial geography should be aware of these financially disrupted socio-spatial connections. Researchers should furthermore place the workings of finance in liquid and illiquid commodity markets centre-stage, in order to shed light on how novel forms of financial value are being created from natural resources. This would help to better inform public debate, as well as to give voice to those personal destinies hidden behind the barcodes of the final products and the returns harvested from them.

Notes

1 These are normally categorized as follows: agricultural products, sometimes also called 'soft commodities' (e.g., grains, cattle, sugar, soybeans, cacao, coffee); energy (e.g., crude oil, natural gas, nuclear energy, hydro energy) and metals (e.g., iron, copper, aluminium, nickel, lead) (Kesselring et al., 2018).

2 The degree of liquidity describes how quickly something can be turned into ready cash. 'Rather than a natural property of financial instruments' (Orléan 2014: 208), it is a 'social institution' (ibid.).

3 As high as this may appear, this was only about half the value of all global timber investments at that time, and a tiny fraction of the US$533 billion invested in natural resources in 2017 (Preqin, 2018: 56). Together, both farmland/agriculture and timberland represented 2.2% of all alternative assets (such as private equity, hedge funds, real estate, infrastructure, and commodity funds) under management in 2016, or 0.3% of all global assets (= US$69 trillion) under management (Valoral Advisors 2018: 8).

4 Inexperienced 'mom-and pop investors' are often called 'retail investors'.

5 For an excellent explanation and visualization of how both CIFs and futures contracts work in detail, see Schumann (2011).

6 The most comprehensive study so far has been that of Ederer et al. (2016: 479) who largely confirm 'that the controversially discussed hypothesis of financialization of commodity derivatives markets can be supported'. The influence is direct (financial interest shapes food trade) and indirect (speculation on oil commodity products led to price hikes in agricultural commodities, since many of them depend on oil-based inputs for their production).

7 This data is derived from the Overseas Investment Office (OIO) website, the main regulatory body related to foreign investments in New Zealand. It documents all approved and declined investments and some background details. The dataset also includes information gathered by the non-governmental organization Campaign against Foreign Control of Aotearoa (CAFCA) from the organization pre-dating the OIO (which was only established in 2005), the Overseas Investment Commission (OIC), stretching back to 2001. Unfortunately, the OIO does not classify investors by type, which is why we relied on the company's description as provided by the

OIO, as well as on publicly available information from company websites and the media to distinguish different types of investor. As a 'soft' classification, the conclusions derived from it need to be treated with caution. For further details, see Klinge (2020).

8 In 2013, for example, only two financial investors—a US-based investment group targeting dairy, and a Dutch pension fund targeting sheep and beef land—accounted for more than 75% of all net transactions.

9 The gross figure stood at 1.9 million hectares.

10 They furthermore found that this applies to 45% of all hard red winter (HRW) wheat, 40% of all soft red winter (SRW) wheat, 15% of all cotton and 10% of all Brent crude oil traded (ibid.). The US Commodity Futures Trading Commission, which provides regular market reports on the size of traders' positions in US commodity futures markets, classifies financial investors into 'swap dealers', 'money managers' (hedge funds, commodity trading advisors (CTAs) or commodity pool operators (CPOs), and index traders (ibid.: 467).

References

Arjaliès, D.L., Grant, P.C., Hardie, I., MacKenzie, D., and Svetlova E. (2017). *Chains of Finance: How Investment Management Is Shaped*. Oxford, UK: Oxford University Press.

Asiyanbi, A.P. (2018). Financialisation in the green economy: Material connections, markets-in-the-making and Foucauldian organising actions. *Environment and Planning A: Economy and Space* 50(3): 531–548.

Bargawi, H.K., and Newman, S.A. (2017). From futures markets to the farm gate: A study of price formation along Tanzania's coffee commodity chain. *Economic Geography* 93(2): 162–184.

Bernstein, P.L. (1998). *Against the Gods: The Remarkable Story of Risk*. New York: Wiley.

Black Rock. (2019). *What are Commodity Funds?* Available at: https://www.blackrock.com/us/individual/products/commodity-funds (accessed 12 March 2019)

Bohl, M.T., and Sulewski, C. (2019). The impact of long-short speculators on the volatility of agricultural commodity futures prices. *Journal of Commodity Markets*. 51(5): 1545–1574, Online first. https://doi.org/10.1016/j.jcomm.2019.01.001.

Bowman, A. (2018). Financialization and the extractive industries: The case of South African platinum mining. *Competition & Change* 22(4): 388–412.

Breger Bush, S. (2012). *Derivates and Development: A political Economy of Global Finance, Farming and Poverty*. New York: Palgrave MacMillan.

Brooks, S. (2016). Inducing food insecurity: Financialisation and development in the post-2015 era. *Third World Quarterly* 37(5): 768–780.

Byerlee, D. (2013). Are we learning from history? In: Levenstein SL and Kugelman M (eds.), *The Global Farms Race: Land Grabs, Agricultural Investment, and the Scramble for Food Secuirty*. Washington, DC: Island Press, 21–43.

Christophers, B. (2015). The limits to financialization. *Dialogues in Human Geography* 5(2): 183–200.

Chesnais, F. (2016). *Finance Capital Today: Corporations and Banks in the Lasting Global Slump*. Leiden, Boston: Brill.

Clapp, J. (2011). *Food*. Oxford: Polity Press.

Clapp, J. (2014). Financialization, distance and global food politics. *Journal of Peasant Studies* 41(5): 797–814.

Clapp, J. (2019). The rise of financial investment and common ownership in global agrifood firms. *Review of International Political Economy* 28(3): 1–26. 10.1080/09692290.2019.1597755.

Clapp, J., and Isakson, R. (2018). *Speculative Harvests: Financialization, Food and Agriculture*. Black Point: Fernwood Publishing.

Clark, G.L., and Monk, A.H.B. (2017). *Institutional Investors in Global Markets*. Oxford, UK: Oxford University Press.

Cloke, P. (1989). State deregulation and new Zealand's agricultural sector. *Sociologica Ruralis* 29(1): 34–48.

Conrad, J. (2018). *Expert commentary: A decade in the farmland asset class evolution*. Available at: http://www.globalaginvesting.com/decade-farmland-asset-class-evolution/ (accessed 17 June 2018).

Cronon, W. (1992). *Nature's Metropolis: Chicago and the Great West*. New York: W.W. Norton.

Daviron, B., and Ponte, S. (2005). *The Coffee Paradox: Global Markets, Commodity Trade and the Elusive Promise of Development*. London/New York: Zed Books.

De Los Reyes, J.A. (2017). Mining shareholder value: Institutional shareholders, transnational corporations and the geography of gold mining. *Geoforum* 84: 251–264.

Ederer, S., Heumesser, C., and Staritz, C. (2016). Financialization and commodity prices–An empirical analysis for coffee, cotton, wheat and oil. *International Review of Applied Economics* 30(4): 462–487.

Fairbairn, M. (2014). 'Like gold with yield': evolving intersections between farmland and finance. *Journal of Peasant Studies* 41(5): 777–795.

Fairbairn, M. (2015). Reinventing the wheel? Or adding new air to old tires? *Dialogues in Human Geography* 5(2): 210–213.

Fairbairn, M. (2020). *Fields of Gold. Financing the Global Land Rush*. Ithaca, NY: Cornell University Press.

Foroohar, R. (2016). *Makers and Takers: The Rise of Finance and the Fall of American Business*. New York: Crown Business.

French, S., Leyshon, A., and Wainwright, T. (2011). Financializing space, spacing financialization. *Progress in Human Geography* 35(6): 798–819.

Geman, H. (2015). *Agricultural Finance: From Crops to Land, Water and Infrastructure*, Chichester, West Sussex, United Kingdom: John Wiley and Sons Inc.

Gosh, J. (2010). The unnatural coupling: Food and global finance. *Journal of Agrarian Change* 10(1): 72–86.

Gunnoe, A., and Gellert, P.K. (2011). Financialization, shareholder value, and the transformation of Timberland Ownership in the US. *Critical Sociology* 37(3): 265–284.

Herre, R. (2013). *Agribusiness-Expansion, Land Grabbing und die Rolle europäischer privater und öffentlicher Gelder in Sambia: Eine Bewertung basierend auf dem Recht auf Nahrung*. Cologne: FIAN.

Huber, M. (2018). Resource geographies I: Valuing nature. *Progress in Human Geography* 42(1): 148–159.

Irwin, S.H., and Sanders, D.R. (2011). Index funds, financialization, and commodity futures markets. *Applied Economic Perspectives and Policy* 33(1): 1–31.

Isakson, S.R. (2014). Food and finance: the financial transformation of agro-food supply chains. *Journal of Peasant Studies* 41(5): 749–775.

Kalderimis, D. (2011). Regulating foreign direct investment in New Zealand. In: Frankel S (ed.): *Learning from the Past, Adapting to the Future: Regulatory Reform in New Zealand*. Wellington: LexisNexis NZ Limited, 445–488.

Kalderimis, D. (2013). Regulating foreign direct investment in New Zealand – Further analysis. In: Frankel, S. and Ryder, D. (eds.), *Recalibrating Behaviour: Smarter Regulation in a Global World*. Wellington: LexisNexis NZ Limited, 63–100.

Kelsey, J. (1995). *The New Zealand Experiment: A World Model for Structural Adjustment?* Auckland: Auckland University Press.

Kessy, A.T. (2020). Neoliberalism, economic crisis, and domestic coffee marketing in Tanzania. In: Samuel Ojo Oloruntoba and Toyin Falola (eds), *Palgrave Handbook of African Political Economy*. Springer Nature, 399–412.

Kesselring, R., Leins, S., and Schulz, Y. (2018). *Valueworks: Effects of Financialization along the Copper Value Chain*. Working Paper, University of Basel: Basel.

Klinge, T.J. (2020). Foreign investments in New Zealand's agricultural sector and their regulation, 2001–2017. *Globalizations*: 1–18, 10.1080/14747731.2020.1795427.

Knox-Hayes, J. (2013). The spatial and temporal dynamics of value in financialization: Analysis of the infrastructure of carbon markets. *Geoforum* 50: 117–128.

Koeninger, J. (2018). *History of Institutional Investment in Farmland*. Available at: http://www.globalaginvesting.com/institutional-farmland/ (accessed 17 June 2018).

Labban, M. (2010). Oil in parallax: Scarcity, markets, and the financialization of accumulation. *Geoforum* 41(4): 541–552.

Langley, P. (2020). The folds of social finance. Making markets, remaking the social. *Environment and Planning A: Economy and Space* 51(1): 140–157.

Lapavitsas, C. (2013). *Profiting without Producing: How Finance Exploits Us All*. London, New York: Verso.

de Lapérouse, P., and Vitón, R. (2017). Trends in allocations to farmland investing: A global perspective. *GAI Gazette* 4(4): 1–16.

Le Heron, R. (1991). New Zealand agriculture and changes in the agriculture-finance relation during the 1980s. *Environment and Planning A* 23: 1653–1670.

Le Heron, R. (1993). *Globalized Agriculture: Political Choice*. Oxford, UK: Pergamom.

Le Heron, R., and Roche, M. (1999). Rapid reregulation, agricultural restructuring, and the reimaging of agriculture in New Zealand. *Rural Sociology* 64(2): 203–218.

McGill, S. (2018). The financialization thesis revisited: Commodities as an asset class. In: Clark, G.L., Feldman, M.P., Gertler, M.S., and Wójcik, D. (eds.), *The New Oxford Handbook of Economic Geography*. Oxford, UK: Oxford University Press, 645–664.

Muellerleile, C. (2015). Speculative boundaries: Chicago and the regulatory history of US financial derivative markets. *Environment and Planning A: Economy and Space* 47(9): 1805–1823.

Munton, R. (1985). Investment in British Agriculture by the financial institutions. *Sociologia Ruralis* 25(2): 155–173.

Newman, S.A. (2009). Financialization and changes in the social relations along commodity chains: The case of coffee. *Review of Radical Political Economics* 41(4): 539–559.

Stats, N.Z. (2018). *Agricultural and horticultural land use*. Available at: http://archive.stats.govt.nz/browse_for_stats/environment/environmental-reporting-series/environmental-indicators/Home/Land/land-use.aspx (accessed 30 April 2020).

Orléan, A. (2014). *The Empire of Value. A New Foundation for Economics*. Cambridge, MA: MIT Press.

Ouma, S. (2015). Getting in between M and M' or: How farmland further debunks financialization. *Dialogues in Human Geography* 5(2): 225–228.

Ouma, S. (2016). From financialization to operations of capital: Historicizing and disentangling the finance–farmland-nexus. *Geoforum* 72: 82–93.

Ouma, S. (2020a). *Farming as Financial Asset. Global Money and the Making of Institutional Landscapes*. Newcastle: Agenda.

Ouma, S. (2020b). This can('t) be an asset class: The world of money management, 'society', and the contested morality of farmland investments. *Environment and Planning A: Economy and Space* 52(1): 66–87.

Polanyi, K. (2001 [1944]). *The Great Transformation: The Political and Economic Origins of our Time*. Boston, MA: Beacon Press.

Ponte, S. (2002). *Farmers & Markets in Tanzania: How Policy Reforms Affect Rural Livelihoods in Africa*. Oxford, Portsmouth, NH: J. Curry Heinemann.

Preqin. (2018). *2018 Preqin Global Natural Resources Report*. London: Preqin.

Purcell, T.F. (2018). 'Hot chocolate': financialized global value chains and cocoa production in Ecuador. *The Journal of Peasant Studies* 45(5–6), S. 904–926. 10.1080/03066150.2018.1446000.

Robinson, J. (1971 [1956]). *The Accumulation of Capital*, Third Edition. London/ Basingstoke: Macmillan.

Roche, M., Johnston, T., and Le Heron, R. (1992). Farmers' interest groups and agricultural policy in New Zealand during the 1980s. *Environment and Planning A* 24: 1749–1767.

Rolleston, W. (2016). Tenants in our own country. Why foreign investment can't be avoided. In: Massey C. (ed.), *The New Zealand Land & Food Annual: Why Waste a Good Crisis? The End of 'White Gold Fever', and Rethinking Agribusiness*. North Shore: Massey University Press, 95–114.

Romero, S. (November 16, 2015). TIAA-CREF, U.S. Investment Giant, Accused of Land Grabs in Brazil. *New York Times*.

Rosenberg, B. (1997). *Foreign Investment in New Zealand: The Current Position*. Available at: canterbury.cyberplace.org.nz/community/CAFCA/publications/Backgrounders/ Chapter1.pdf (accessed 14 July 2019).

Salerno, T. (2014). Capitalising on the financialisation of agriculture: Cargill's private equity-driven land acquisition in the Philippines. *Third World Quarterly* 35(9): 1709–1727.

Schumann, H. (2011). *The Hunger Makers. How Deutsche Bank, Goldman Sachs and Other Financial Institutions Are Speculating with Food at the Expense of the Poorest*. Berlin: Food Watch.

Smith, W., and Montgomery, H. (2004). Revolution or evolution? New Zealand agriculture since 1984. *Geojournal* 59(2): 107–118.

Staritz, C., Newman, S., and Tröster, B. (2018). Financialization and global commodity chains: Distributional implications for cotton in Sub-Saharan Africa. *Development and Change* 49(3): 815–842.

Stevenson, A. (July 21, 2014). Cash crops with dividends: Financiers transforming strawberries into securities. *The New York Times*. Available at: http://dealbook.nytimes.com/2014/07/21/cash-crops-with-dividends-fi (accessed 21 June 2014).

The Economist. (2009). *Green shoots*. Available at: http://www.economist.com/node/13331189 (accessed 18 September 2012).

Tröster, B., and Staritz, C. (2015). *Global commodity chains, financial markets, and local market structures: Price risks in the coffee sector in Ethiopia*, Working Paper, Austrian Foundation for Development Research (ÖFSE), Vienna.

United Nations Conference on Trade and Development (UNCTAD). (2011). *Price Formation in Financialized Commodity Markets: The Role of Information*. Geneva: UNCTAD.

Valoral Advisors. (2018). *2018 Global Food & Agriculture Investment Outlook*. Luxembourg: Valoral Advisors.

Wallace, N. (2016). *When the Farm Gates Opened: The Impact of Rogernomics on Rural New Zealand*. Dunedin: Otago University Press; meBooks.

Weaver, J.C. (2003). *The Great Land Rush and the Making of the Modern World, 1650–1900*. Montreal: McGill-Queen's University Press.

Zeller, C. (2010). Die Natur als Anlagefeld des konzentrierten Finanzkapitals. In: Schmieder, F. (ed.), *Die Krise der Nachhaltigkeit: Zur Kritik der politischen Ökologie*. Frankfurt am Main: Peter Lang, 103–136.

11

INFRASTRUCTURE

The Harmonization of an Asset Class and Implications for Local Governance

Gabriella Y. Carolini and Isadora Cruxên

Introduction

Infrastructure investment levels across diverse political economies and national income environments represent a sort of bellwether for how well public and private sector interests align. Given the persistence of major infrastructure investment gaps in the Global South and the need to update aging infrastructure in higher-income environments across the Global North, that alignment will presumably strengthen in the twenty-first century. Investments in infrastructure today represent an annual US$2.5 trillion industry (McKinsey & Company, 2016). However, the implications of this relationship for societies present many questions—particularly in highly unequal and lower-income contexts where basic infrastructures represent a literal lifeline. Which infrastructures get funded, how equitably infrastructure investments' benefits are shared, and how well their costs are distributed all depend on several structural and contextual factors. These factors include both the financial and environmental regulatory landscape for domestic and foreign investments in place, the transparency and accountability of government to its local residents, competence in monitoring and maintaining major projects, wider regional and global infrastructure market trends, and civic organizational and participatory decision-making, to name a few.

In relating the state of infrastructure as an investment asset class today, this chapter's objective is twofold. First, we aim to identify broad macro trends in infrastructural investments at a global scale—focusing on lower- and middle-income countries in the regions of East Asia and the Pacific, Latin America and the Caribbean, and the Middle East and North Africa, South Asia, and sub-Saharan Africa within the Global South. What sectoral preferences are there within infrastructure investment portfolios across these regions? What investment vehicles are used? What type of investors are interested? To answer these questions, we leveraged our access to the Preqin database, a leading privately managed database on finance that offers comprehensive data on infrastructure (among other) investment activities and investors. We were able to study 6,221 infrastructure investment activities in lower through upper-middle-income countries of the aforementioned regions between 2000 and 2018, providing a strong picture of infrastructure investment growth in the Global South.

Second, our intention is to analyse the collective knowledge gathered about infrastructure investments in the Global South, particularly in cities, given the urbanization of the global population and of poverty since the turn of the millennium. To this end, we conducted a meta-analysis of two aggregated literatures—one in business sciences and the other in social sciences—to understand what researchers in each identify as major questions, issues, and concerns about infrastructure projects and investments in cities within the Global South over the same period of time as the investments we studied in the Preqin database. More specifically, we explored leading peer reviewed articles in the business and organizational management field to grasp how researchers engaged in studying private sector activities perceived and analysed substantive concerns, and presented empirical evidence in their examinations of infrastructure investment related activities within the Global South. We also conducted a review of infrastructure related articles in top-ranked peer reviewed journals in planning and development, and more broadly within their social science publication platforms, to gain an understanding of how social scientists were positioning research concerns about infrastructure in the same geographies.

Before presenting the results of our analyses, the chapter begins with a brief review of the demands for infrastructure investments to situate the current trends in the global infrastructure market. We then present a detailed account of the organizational boom that has accompanied the rise of infrastructure as an asset class at the global scale, describing both investor and investment vehicle diversification therein. After presenting sectoral trends across geographies, highlighting how different infrastructure assets have dominated investment markets within regions of the Global South, we provide a meta-analysis of how researchers situate these trends within diverse literatures. More specifically, we pull out from these literatures themes that capture the governance concerns typically addressed in research as a means of providing empirical contexts to the rich narrative growing across literatures about infrastructure and the financialization of basic needs such as water, energy, and transport. Finally, we conclude with a consideration of the concerns that arise about local governance within the diverse cities of the Global South impacted by the growth of the global infrastructure investment industry.

Infrastructure Investments: A Brief History of Gaps and Aspirations

Infrastructure has long been recognized as an essential driver of economic growth and development. Its particular role in the growth and productivity of urban centers is well-cemented in the histories of capitals, economic centers, and regional hubs across the globe. If cities are engines of national economic growth, infrastructure systems are their fuel. However, it is the quality of infrastructure, its reach, affordability, and sustainability that broadly determine how well societies are served by infrastructure projects across sectors such as energy, transportation, water and sanitation, and telecommunications.

In low- and middle-income countries, the demand for basic infrastructure investments in water, sanitation, energy, transport, and telecom is pervasive, if not always prioritized by governments or by the private sector. Estimates indicate that lower- and middle-income countries would need anywhere between 2% and 8% of their GDP per year dedicated to addressing infrastructure deficits if they are to be met by 2030 (Rozenberg and Fay, 2019). Urbanization plays no small role in this. The oft cited reference to the unprecedented rapidity of urban population growth in the small- and medium-sized cities of Africa and Asia helps explain why the infrastructure gap across so many low-income contexts is so daunting.[1] Here, among low-income countries, the annual rate of change in the urban population is the global high, sitting at 3.68% between 1995 and 2015 (UN-Habitat, 2016). Cities across lower- and middle-income countries experiencing such growth today are often characterized by the advance of neighborhoods lacking in basic services such as potable water, sanitation systems, energy connections, and public transit. The absolute number of urban residents living in such substandard conditions—or slums—grew between 1990 and 2014 by 28%—with conservative estimates sitting at 880 million people (UN-Habitat, 2016).

Within this landscape, economic development aspirations, the acceleration of climate change, and environmental vulnerabilities complicate efforts to address current infrastructure gaps across the diverse cities of the Global South. Some of the challenges posed by climate change, for example, are evident in the context of multi-locational household survival strategies feeding labor migration, as well as in adaptation challenges across coastal urban environments. With regard to the latter, a study of the impacts of climate change on 136 major coastal cities found that cities would need to invest an additional US$50 billion in flood defenses to offset the impacts of climate change (Hallegatte et al., 2013). The goals set forth by the Millennium Development Goals (MDGs), followed by the Sustainable Development Goals (SDGs), since the turn of the millennium—which increased the urgency attributed to investing in quality infrastructure—add to the costs of addressing infrastructure gaps in the midst of increasing social and environmental vulnerability to climate change. A report by the United Nations Secretariat estimates that closing the financing gap to achieve the SDGs in developing countries would require between US$2.5 trillion and US$3 trillion in investments per year (United Nations, 2019).

Stepping up investments in infrastructures to increase resilience and economic growth, while also serving the basic needs of poor populations (as well as the demands of a growing middle class) represents a bill that most national and sub-national governments in lower- and middle-income countries are struggling to pay. Own-source revenues are delimited by weakly functioning taxation systems (Bird & Slack, 2014; Franzsen & McCluskey, 2017). Lending windows from multi-lateral development banks, while expanding with the introduction of new organizations such the Asian Infrastructure Investment Bank, are insufficient to address estimated infrastructure investment gaps. Importantly, increasing environmental vulnerabilities—particularly those associated with climate change—are likely to scale the cost of capital for developing countries upwards. A 2018 report commissioned by the UN Environment Programme finds that, in the previous decade, 'climate vulnerability has cost V20 [Vulnerable 20] countries an additional US$62 billion in interest payments, including US$40 billion in additional interest payments on government debt alone' (Fishman, 2018).

Unsurprisingly, enticing private sector investments has become de rigor.[2] The aforementioned United Nations Secretariat report on closing the financing gap for SDGs notes that money is to be found in 'the global financial system—with gross world product and global gross financial assets estimated at over US$80 trillion and US$200 trillion respectively' (United Nations, 2019: 1). Institutional investors such banks, pensions funds, insurance companies, sovereign wealth funds, and private equity funds are often cited as key infrastructure partners, partially because of the aggregate volume of assets they manage—in the vicinity of US$120 trillion (McKinsey & Company, 2016). Other rationales behind the suiting of institutional investors include those that evoke (some) institutional investors' public sector base—if they are managing public monies, their investments should support projects that serve the public, such as infrastructure. In addition, institutional investors' investment strategies, as well as their fiduciary responsibilities, can situate them in a market for relatively higher-grade, stable investment vehicles. In short, the golden formula behind the aspiration of filling the infrastructure investment gap is to couple the relatively long-term investments in infrastructure with large-volume investors from the buy-and-hold investment community seeking long-term investment vehicles with stable cash flows.

This formula, however, has been complicated by a few factors in the context of urban infrastructure needs in parts of the Global South, including the lack of risk data and historical financial records from public sector partners, and the variation in contracts and financial regulation across geographies. In addition, perceived political and economic instabilities, coupled with recent research (Flyvbjerg et al., 2009) highlighting the global trend in the underestimation of infrastructure project costs and the overestimation of benefits, further hinder the appeal of infrastructure investments, damaging the potentiality of the asset class's rise within contexts where the demand for such investments is greatest: parts of Asia, Africa, and Latin America. It is the response to these challenges by the international community of stakeholders—including international organizations, development banks, and investors themselves—that the next section highlights.

The 21st Century's Renewed Infrastructure Passion

Organizational Explosion

International advocacy around strengthening how well infrastructure projects—particularly in the Global South—translate into a recognizable and bankable asset class has exploded into numerous efforts from a diverse, but single-minded group of stakeholders. Their efforts center on the harmonization and standardization across geographies of infrastructure project data, project development, contracts, and financial regulations.

One of the longest standing efforts to attract infrastructure investment to lower- and middle-income countries is housed in the World Bank and supported by 11 different multi-lateral and bi-lateral donors—the Public-Private Infrastructure Advisory Facility (PPIAF). Established at the cusp of the new century in 1999, the PPIAF remains a central advocacy tool behind building the institutional environment to support investment in infrastructure outside high-income countries. Its sectoral focus is on information and communications technology (ICT), water and sanitation, energy, and transport. Critically, since 2008 it supports the Sub-National Technical Assistance (SNTA) program—focusing entirely on aiding sub-national entities, including municipalities, state-owned enterprises, and utilities, to secure funding for water and sanitation, energy, and transport systems (PPIAF, 2019). The SNTA aims to help improve subnational entities' creditworthiness and thus enhance their access to private financing for infrastructure investments. In 2018 alone, it approved 10 new grants toward this end, the majority of which were for entities within sub-Saharan Africa, while also working with another 66 ongoing low- and middle-income clients from across multiple regions (PPIAF, 2019).

Several other initiatives by international organizations with country membership have emerged since the PPIAF and its SNTA initiative launched, particularly in the aftermath of the 2008 financial crisis. Chief protagonists to this end are the Organization for Economic Cooperation and Development (OECD) as well as the Group of Twenty (G20), the international forum for economic policy negotiations between governments and central bank governors from the European Union and 19 countries across high- and lower-middle income contexts. For example, the G20 started the Global Infrastructure Initiative and Hub in 2014—a staffed organization based in a mandate to work with both the private sector and public sectors in high-income and emerging economies to strengthen the quality and increase the quantity of infrastructure projects in development and investments therein. Four years later, under the Argentine presidency of the G20, the group also produced a 'Roadmap' to further developing infrastructure as an asset class to promote institutional investment therein. This Roadmap identifies standardization as the greatest overall challenge that the international community needs to collaborate around and address; namely, through advancing improvements in project development (e.g., standardizing contracts, financial statements, improving data and project preparation) and creating a stronger enabling environment for investments (e.g., through regulatory frameworks and financial engineering for risk mitigation or allocation) (G20/OECD/WB, 2018).

The OECD also hosts a Program on Long-term Investment, launched in 2012, which involves several initiatives. These include an annual survey of large pension funds around their interests and perceived obstacles to long-term investments, as well as the maintenance of a network of investors with whom the OECD seeks to engage in consultation around the issue of long-term investments (LTI). The OECD-LTI network includes over 3,000 contacts that are regularly invited to OECD fora on enhancing infrastructure as an asset class. In addition, the OECD joined the G20 on a Task Force on Long-Term Investment Financing by Institutional Investors, which meets regularly to advance this issue and promote discussion of next steps around data standardization. The latest move therein involves the creation of the Infrastructure Data Initiative to enhance data and analysis of infrastructure investments, bringing together the G20 with the OECD, multilateral development banks, the G20's own Global Infrastructure Hub, and the Long-term Infrastructure Investment Association (LTIIA).

The LTIIA itself represents one of the many private sector efforts to advocate and build cooperation around strengthening the infrastructure asset class globally. While some private sector efforts are centered around information packaging, others such as the LTIIA are focused on networking and advocacy around improving opportunities and market depth in the infrastructure investment space. The LTIIA was founded in 2014 by investors who collectively boast more than US$10 trillion of assets under management. It acts as an advocate for investors across infrastructure sectors by sponsoring research and engaging in international fora, such as those hosted by the OECD and G20.

The International Project Finance Association is another private membership association. Established in 1998, it comprises an international network of more than 650 public and private institutional members for whom it hosts webinars, training sessions, and events to bring interested stakeholders together. Finally, the Global Listed Infrastructure Organization is a group whose existence represents the diversification of the infrastructure investment market. It started in 2016 to advance the promotion of listed infrastructure investment vehicles (as opposed to unlisted infrastructure projects in which investors directly invest in projects). Listed infrastructure allow investors to buy shares into a portfolio of several infrastructure assets with particular risk and return profiles, much as a mutual fund works.

In the data production and management arena, several private efforts have similarly emerged since the 2000s to gather infrastructure investment data and produce related analytical products. The EDHEC Infrastructure Institute-Singapore (EDHECinfra), for example, is a private research firm that specializes in measuring the risk-adjusted performance of unlisted infrastructure investments and creating investment indices against which investors can track their performance. EDHECinfra, like Preqin, also hosts a historical database on infrastructure investment data. Inframation is yet another online information platform, providing access to infrastructure deal news, profiles of different stakeholders in the industry (e.g., lenders, investors, advisors) and historical transaction data on infrastructure projects.

Investor Diversification and Vehicle Innovation

The risks affiliated with infrastructure investments from an investor standpoint range from project-specific risks (e.g., construction delays and quality, operational risks, market demand) to more structural risks (e.g., political change, corruption, regulatory change, interest rate movements). Given the stability and cash-flow public institutional investors such as pensions funds typically require, the consensus around advancing institutional investment in infrastructure has targeted isolating and packaging risks into investment vehicles that help investors manage their exposure (Inderst and Stewart, 2014). One of the most promising vehicles to emerge to this end has been the growth of infrastructure funds. Rather than investing in several relatively small infrastructure projects, such funds allow institutional investors to invest in shares of an aggregated infrastructure portfolio—both spreading risks and the research costs of investment strategies across projects.

Nonetheless, even with the advent of infrastructure funds, institutional investors predominantly invest in higher income countries. As such, several efforts have been launched by international organizations and governments to help diversify investors' portfolios toward lower-income countries and infrastructure therein. For example, in 2013, the International Financial Corporation—the private-lending arm of the World Bank Group—established a Managed Co-Lending Portfolio Program (MCPP), including a specific infrastructure initiative. The MCPP infrastructure initiative's appeal centers on providing institutional investors with a predictable revenue stream. It does so by accompanying investors' capital advances with the IFC's own investment through a syndication structure—in short, it creates a diversified loan portfolio for institutional investors that reflects the IFC's own portfolio of infrastructure investments much as an index fund would. In the initiative's first phase, the Swedish International Development Cooperation Agency (SIDA) partnered with the IFC with the purpose of also providing credit enhancements for participating institutional investors in the MCPP—creating for such investors a less risky investment-grade portion—or senior tranche—of the infrastructure investments (Mapila et al., 2017).

National governments in higher-income countries are also pursuing the spread of infrastructure investments in the Global South—eyeing such as opportunities for the expansion of businesses in their own country. In 2014, Japan established the Japan Overseas Infrastructure Investment Corporation for Transport & Urban Development (JOIN) which, as of March 2018, managed

JP¥46.45 billion in capital. JOIN's central aim is to promote Japan's infrastructure systems (and the Japanese businesses that produce them) in overseas markets including, thus far, investments in Myanmar, Indonesia, and Brazil. More significant in the infrastructure space in lower- and middle-income countries, however, is China. Over 50% of China's overseas investments on the African continent between 2000 and 2013, for instance, targeted infrastructure projects (AidData, N.D.).

Infrastructure Investment Trends across Geographies

Given the organizational architecture and emergence of data and investment vehicles centering on spreading the wealth of institutional investments into infrastructure in the Global South, one may expect to begin witnessing a degree of distribution among investments across sectors and geographies. Instead, infrastructure investment interests from the private sector are growing, but continue to demonstrate sectoral and contextual preferences, concentrating in the energy arena and spreading from the usual suspects in the Global North toward the usual suspects—namely, leading regional economies—in the Global South. Over almost two decades, the private sector's participation in infrastructure projects has grown from a low of 70 projects in 2002 to a high of 832 projects in 2016 (see Figure 11.1). The energy sector, however, has been consistent in its domination over the same period of time, as shown in Figure 11.2.

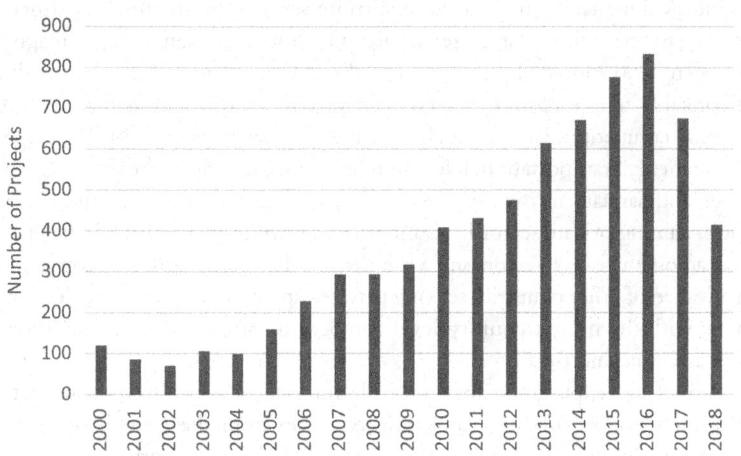

Figure 11.1 Infrastructure projects with private sector participation in the Global South (2000–18)

Source: Authors' calculations based on data from Preqin.

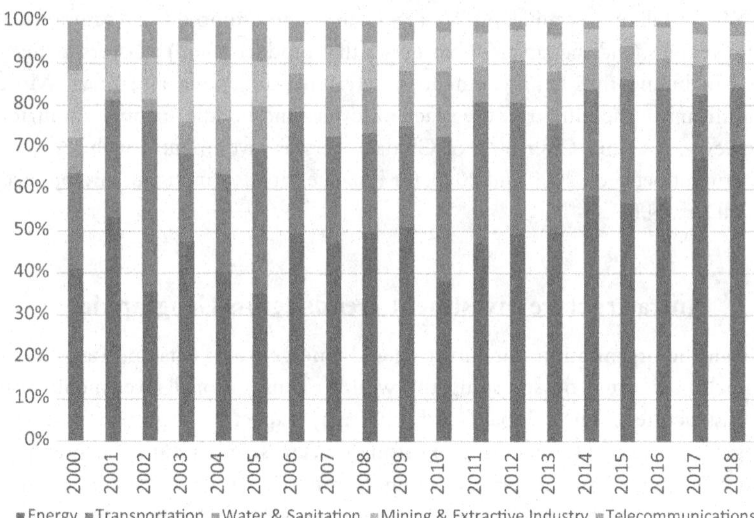

Figure 11.2 Infrastructure projects with private sector participation in the Global South by sector (2000–18)

Source: Authors' calculations based on data from Preqin.

Within the energy arena, the largest number of projects with private sector participation between 2000 and 2018 were located within India (with 856 projects), followed by China and Brazil, and, from further afield, by South Africa and Peru, as demonstrated in the map presented in Figure 11.3.

India's dominance in the race for private sector infrastructure investments extends to the transportation sector, for which it is an even stronger magnet. Between 2000 and 2018, India developed 992 projects, four times the number of bankable transportation projects with private sector interests than its next national competitor, Brazil, which hosted 245 projects (Preqin, N.D.). Indeed, across energy, transportation, telecommunications, mining and extractives, and water and sanitation, India is the stand-out among countries in the Global South gaining private sector investments. As shown in Figure 11.4, India's projects across these five sectors since the turn of the millennium position it well in advance of other countries seeking private capital for infrastructure development, with the nearest country-level competition again from regional leaders such as China and Brazil.

Part of the explanation for India's dominance in attracting private sector investment for its infrastructure projects comes from the growth of private sector investors in the infrastructure space over the same period of time. As shown in Figure 11.5, the number of unique private sector investors in the infrastructure arena—for most regions in the Global South—has grown since 2000. This is especially the case for the South Asian region, where the number

Figure 11.3 Energy projects in the Global South with private sector participation (2000–18)

Source: Authors' calculations based on data from Preqin.

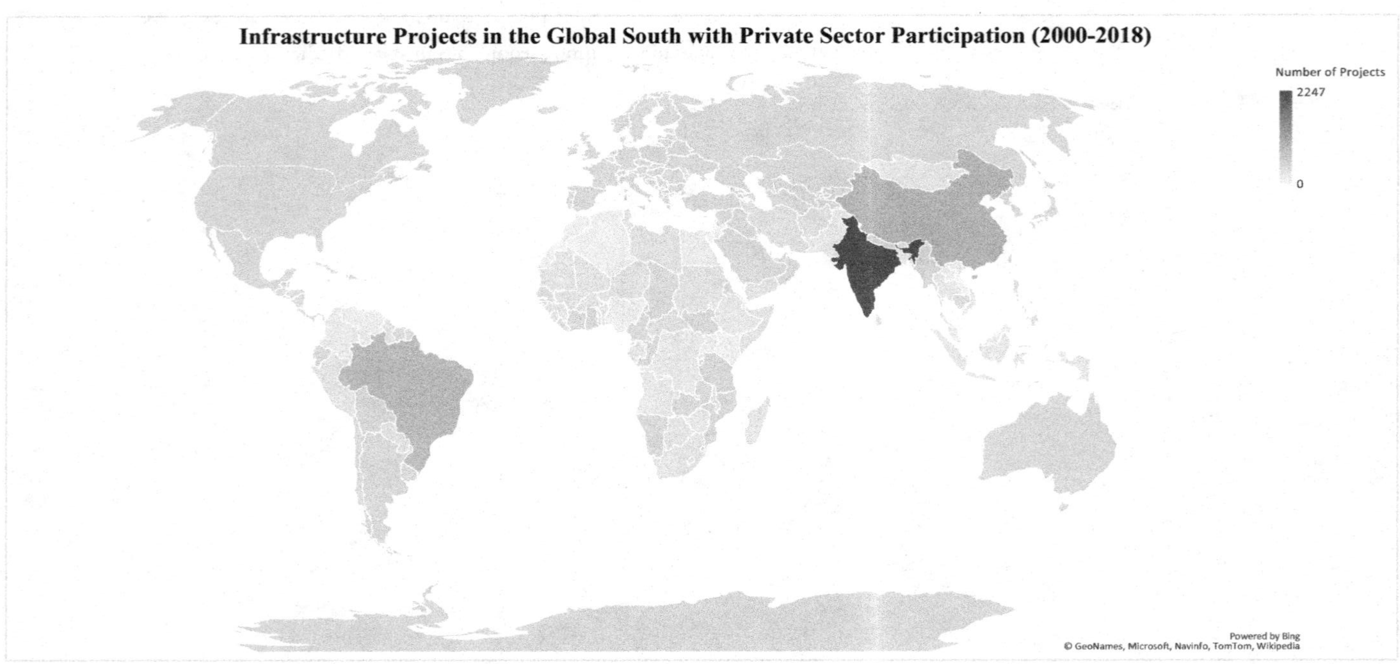

Figure 11.4 Infrastructure projects in the Global south with private sector participation (2000–18)

Source: Authors' calculations based on data from Preqin. Infrastructure projects included here are from the economic infrastructure sectors, including energy, transport, telecommunications, mining and extractives, and water and sanitation.

of unique private sector players went from a low of 21 investors in 2002 to a high of 182 investors in 2015.

However, contrary to expectation, we find that the relevant investor pool is less diversified than recent discourse suggests. Among investors across the Global South with profiles on the online database publicly available through

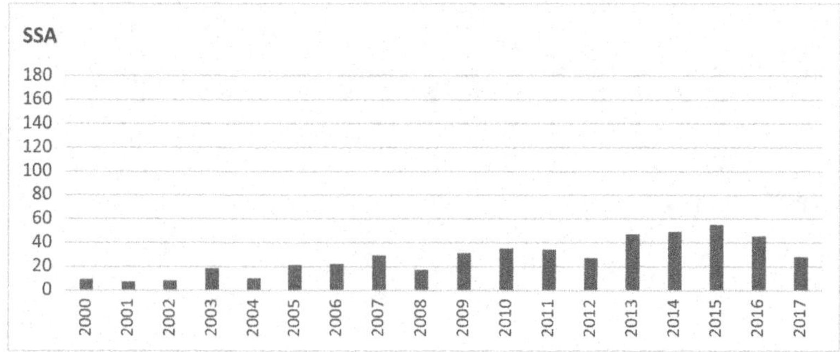

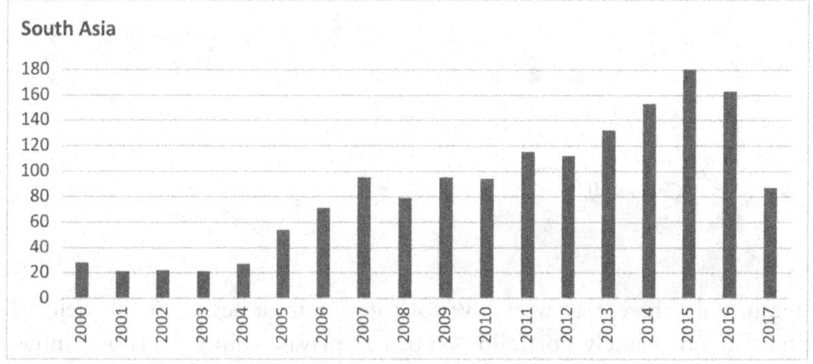

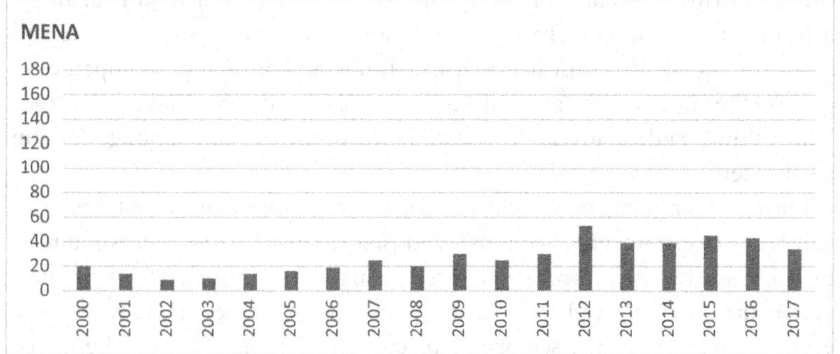

Figure 11.5 Unique private sector investors active in infrastructure projects in the Global South

Note: Regions noted above represent World Bank Classifications: East Asia and Pacific (EAP), Latin America and the Caribbean (LAC), Middle East and North Africa (MENA), South Asia, sub-Saharan Africa (SSA).

Source: Authors' calculations based on data from Preqin.

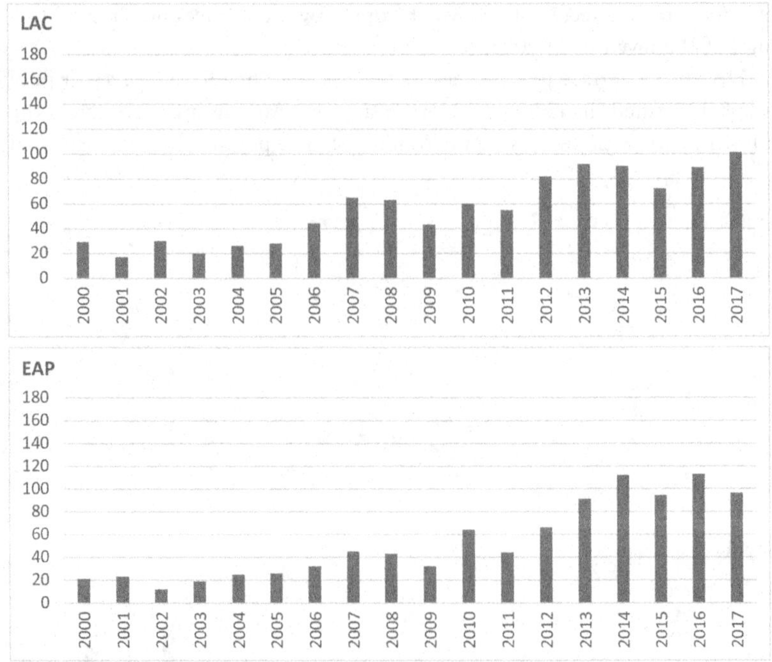

Figure 11.5 (*Continued*)

Preqin, only three classes of investors appear most active in the field of infrastructure; namely, portfolio companies, private equity firms, and infrastructure firms (see Table 11.1). In sum, while the investor field is growing in terms of the number of players, only a few investor classes or types still dominate the field. Critically, pension funds and insurance companies—perhaps the most sought after of buy-and-hold institutional investors, given their volume and relatively low trading volumes, are not among the top stakeholders.

Finally, in projects for which data on the type of private investment was available, concession contracts dominated (see Figure 11.6). In concession relationships, such as build-operate-transfer arrangements, private sector partners receive the exclusive rights to operate, maintain, or invest in infrastructure services, while the public sector retains ownership rights. This highlights the importance of global advocacy—from both private investors and international organizations—around improving the standardization of contracting across regions, with the objective of diminishing perceived or actual risks of investments in infrastructure projects across—for institutional investors—what may be new geographies of interest.

Table 11.1 Investor class active in infrastructure projects in the Global South (2000–17)

Region/investor type	*Portfolio company*	*Private equity firm*	*Infrastructure firm*	*Corporate investor*	*Private sector pension fund*	*Hedge fund manager*	*Private Equity fund of funds manager*	*Real estate firm*	*Others*
East Asia & Pacific	52	50	22	14	3	3	1	1	5
Latin America & Caribbean	48	24	13	11	4	2	1	2	10
Middle East & North Africa	15	13	16	2			1	1	2
South Asia	109	42	17	14	3	2	5	5	9
Sub-Saharan Africa	44	14	21	5	3		2	1	10

Source: Authors' calculations based on data from Preqin. The category of 'Others' in the table includes natural resource firms, government agencies, insurance companies, and wealth managers.

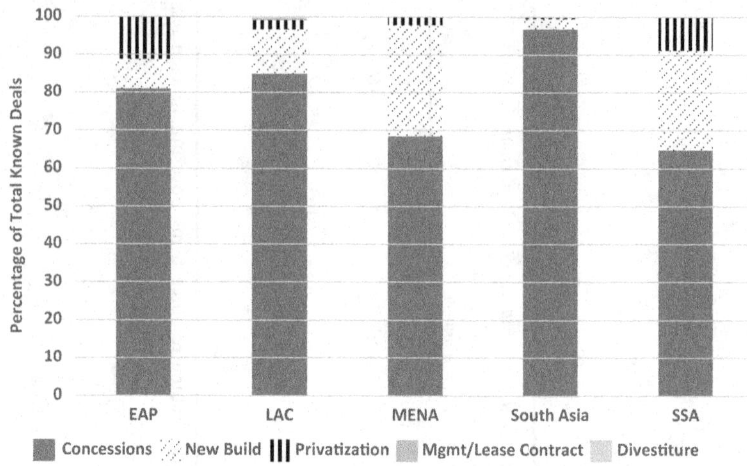

Figure 11.6 Private participation levels in infrastructure projects in Global South (2000–18)

Note: Most project transactions studied between 2000 and 2008 did not indicate the level of private participation. More specifically, for EAP, the data represents 27% of project data (or 439 deals); for LAC, the data represents 18% (or 212 deals); for MENA, the data represents 41% (or 95 deals); for South Asia, the data represents 31% (or 1523 deals); and for SSA, the data represents 22% (or 125 deals).

Source: Authors' calculations based on data from Preqin.

The Place for Local Governance in the Infrastructure Rush

While the preceding sections provide a snapshot of the growing institutional landscape for investment in infrastructure projects within the Global South, that institutional landscape does little to provide a specific accounting of the types of grounded risks and opportunities of investments—for the investment community but, most critically, also for the public sector entities and societies those infrastructures serve. Two directions of research—one aspirational and the other cautionary—provide much of those missing details in the wider narrative about the deepening financialization of infrastructure.

The following section directs us toward answering the crucial question behind recent infrastructure investment trends: What are the implications of these financial arrangements and the participation they bring from an evolving set of private actors—particularly for local governance and for urban development in countries of the Global South. To explore this question, we sought to identify the core debates and concerns driving analyses of infrastructure finance in the Global South, and to examine whether and how they addressed governance issues. We conducted an extensive review of abstracts of research articles published in relevant journals across two main domains: finance, business, and international management; and urban planning and international development. Our aim was to gain a broad understanding of the discourses around infrastructure financing across a spectrum of literatures in the social sciences and management sciences.

For our review, we focused on research articles that articulated, in their abstracts, an explicit focus or direct linkage to market reforms, private financing, and governance of urban infrastructure in the Global South. For business and management, we used the Scimago Journal & Country Rank[3] as the basis for identifying relevant journals. We focused on the top five journals listed under the subcategory 'Business and International Management', which appeared more relevant, given our focus on infrastructure projects in the Global South.[4] We also examined articles published in some of the specialized journals on infrastructure development, public works, and utilities.[5] For planning and development, we found that the most productive approach was to search through publishing platforms such as Elsevier and Sage, which provided a more expansive view of potentially relevant articles from the social sciences. In our search, we used keywords such as 'infrastructure', 'infrastructure finance', 'energy', 'water', 'telecommunications', and 'transport'. We also considered more specific keywords such as 'project finance' and 'public-private partnerships', as well as geographical markers such as 'developing country', 'emerging markets', 'Latin America', 'South Asia', 'Southeast Asia', and 'sub-Saharan Africa'. The temporal range for the searches included the years 2000–19, a time range that matches the reviewed data on private sector participation in infrastructure projects. We examined a total of 256 article abstracts.[6] In what follows, we begin by situating the core concerns we identified in articles published in finance, business, and international management journals, as well as in specialized journals. We subsequently discuss how these compare with concerns identified in social science publications more broadly, particularly those related to urban planning and international development.

Management Sciences

To start, we note that our search returned very few relevant articles in the top finance and business journals. The articles from these journals that appeared most relevant typically referred to countries in the Global North and therefore were not included in our discussion. This does not necessarily mean, of course, that these disciplines are silent on the topic of infrastructure financing. Rather, based on our analysis, it is more likely that scholars from these fields who study infrastructure tend to publish in specialized journals, or in other development and planning-related journals.

We find, somewhat unsurprisingly, that the mainstream political economy, business, and management scholarship on the financing of infrastructure tends to overlook questions of local governance and equity, and to prioritize concerns with efficiency and productivity. Where governance does come into the picture, it is primarily from the standpoint of setting up an institutional and regulatory environment that is more conducive to efficiency gains, or to increased private participation in the financing of infrastructure projects. We organized the core concerns identified in this literature into four overarching themes: performance, contractual design and implementation, regulatory environment, and financing instruments and investment trends.

First, a majority of the articles surveyed were concerned with the economic and operational performance of different forms of infrastructure provision or financing arrangements, focusing mainly on issues such as cost-effectiveness and relative economic efficiency (Boubakri and Cosset, 1998; Sabbioni, 2008; Wang et al., 2011; Perelman & Serebrisky, 2012; Ferro et al., 2014; Ferro & Mercadier, 2016; Loch et al., 2018).[7] For example, in the water and sanitation sector, Wang et al. (2011) use econometric tools to explore the impact of private sector participation in urban water supply in 35 major Chinese cities between 1998 and 2008. They find that private participation improved service coverage and production, but not investments in fixed assets. In the electricity sector, Loch et al. (2018) examine how the government—acting either as a shareholder or regulator—affects the financial performance of utility companies in Brazil. They observe that returns on assets were lower, on average, in firms in which the government was a shareholder. An important subset of studies in this vein focuses specifically on the performance of public-private partnerships (PPPs) for infrastructure provision, exploring metrics such as cost-effectiveness, technical efficiency, and productivity (Gangakhedkar and Mishra, 2012; Tsukada, 2013; Vadali et al., 2014; Gopalkrishna and Karnam, 2016). In the transport sector, for example, Gopalkrishna and Karnam (2016) deploy data envelopment analysis to estimate efficiency scores for highway PPPs in India compared to non-PPP projects. They find that PPP projects have a higher mean technical efficiency. Tsukada (2013) offers an example of a study that attempts to relate performance to issues of local governance in India, tying poor performance and delays in highway PPP projects to problems of inter-agency coordination and policy design.

The issue of policy design brings forth a second set of concerns emerging from this literature: contractual issues, and the design and implementation of collaborative arrangements for the provision of infrastructure. In this vein, some studies explore, for example, the problem of incomplete contracts for the provision of public goods (Besley and Ghatak, 2001), or the effects of the unbundling of public procurement on bidding behavior (Estache and Iimi, 2011). However, contractual choices related to infrastructure PPP projects and privatization receive the bulk of attention, driven by concerns with aspects such as risk mitigation (Mahalingam et al., 2011; Chambouleyron, 2014; Marzouk and Ali, 2018), opportunities for corruption and rent-seeking (Auriol and Blanc, 2009; Guasch and Straub, 2009; Takano, 2017), and policy requirements for effective PPPs (Jamali, 2004; Mahalingam et al., 2011; Biygautane, 2017).

Some studies have also examined what shapes public and private decision-making in the structuring of contracts. On the public side, for example, a recent study of 65 PPP contracts in the telecommunication, energy, and transport sectors in Peru argues that factors such as demand risks, sources of financing, and the scale of projects influenced the government's decision to include economic regulation in PPP contracts (Ruiz Diaz, 2017). On the private side, Vedachalam et al. (2016) have sought to explain variation in levels of private participation by examining 163 water and wastewater PPP contracts initiated between 1999–2012 in India. They observe that the scope of private participation is greater when projects are located 'in cities with larger populations, better PPP regulatory environments, regional party rule, and lower sanitation scores' (Vedachalam et al., 2016: 71). These studies point to the need for expanding the scope of analysis to situate the design and effectiveness of financing arrangements within the broader socio-political and institutional context in which infrastructures are located.

A third important concern relates to the regulation of infrastructure provision. Analyses in this vein have examined how the regulatory environment affects the ability to attract private financing (Bertoméu-Sánchez et al., 2018), what shapes regulatory capacity and decision-making (Stern, 2000; González, 2017), and why countries pursue different pathways for regulatory reform (Arango et al., 2006). In line with the dominant concern with performance, several studies also attempt to establish the effects of regulation on the provision of infrastructure services and utility efficiency (Seroa da Motta and Moreira, 2006; Cheng and Hebenton, 2008; Ferro et al., 2011; Thamae et al., 2015; Pinto and Reis, 2017).

Finally, some studies concentrate on understanding financing instruments and investment trends (Ruet, 2006; Satyanand, 2011; Da Silva et al., 2006; Maniar, 2013; Gemson & Rajan, 2016; Peng & Poudineh, 2017). Da Silva et al. (2006), for example, study a sample of 121 utilities in the water and transport sectors across 16 countries to examine how the financing structure of regulated privatized utilities has evolved. They note that debt has become increasingly more important than equity as a financing instrument. With regard to private equity (PE) investments, Gemson et al.'s (2012) analysis of 2,821 infrastructure projects indicates that where PE investments occur in developing countries, the number of private sponsors tends to be higher, as a way to share risk. In line with the growing importance of multilateral organizations in supporting infrastructure investments—as discussed earlier in this chapter—the business literature community has also dedicated attention to the impact of multilateral organizations and international financing institutions (Mutambatsere et al., 2013; Hausman et al., 2014; Basílio, 2014).

As noted earlier, very few articles published in finance, business, and management fields articulated an explicit interest in the implications of market reforms or financing arrangements for local governance and the issue of equitable infrastructure provision. Haselip et al.'s (2005) attention to the distributive outcomes of market reforms in the Argentine electricity sector is one exception. They note that local actors questioned the legitimacy of these reforms and pointed to their disproportionate impact on costs for low-income consumers. The analysis by Wright-Contreras (2018) of urban water supply in Hanoi, Vietnam, is also worthy of mention. The author attempts to understand the financing of urban water supply in relation to local urban development patterns, socio-ecological issues, and the power relations involving multiple actors such as private firms, multilateral organizations, and government agencies.

Social Sciences

While encompassing a rather broad set of literatures, we identified three general themes in social science research on infrastructure-related topics in planning and development journals:

(i) governance (broadly construed) of infrastructure sectors (including the political power, coordination, and administrative capacities across actors and levels of government involved in infrastructure planning and delivery);
(ii) critical analyses of the financing of infrastructure projects (e.g., public-private partnerships and the role of private actors such as multinational corporations, foreign investors, and construction companies in infrastructure development); and
(iii) infrastructure services for the poor (e.g., how access to infrastructure and the landscape of service provision, particularly for poorer households, is (or is not) being addressed and shaped, and by whom).

The governance of urban infrastructure systems is perhaps the broadest theme in the social science research we encountered in our survey. Prevalent governance themes emerged in studies of megaprojects, perhaps unsurprisingly given the number of mega-events such as the Olympics and World Cups staged within cities in countries such as South Africa and Brazil. Beyond critical examinations of infrastructures for sporting events, research around megaprojects tended to look critically at how major investments in infrastructure systems were prioritized around building cities' reputations, perhaps more so than actually responding to the infrastructural needs of marginalized communities (Watson, 2014; Hannan and Sutherland, 2015; Kennedy, 2015; Sutherland et al., 2015; Dogan and Stupar, 2017). Power, politics, and local capacities in the administration and planning of infrastructure systems and/or regulatory affairs therein also occupy a central research concern in literatures we examined (Fuseini and Kemp, 2016; Bunte and Kim, 2017; Berrisford et al., 2018; Yates and Harris, 2018; Acey, 2019). Finally, the positive and negative implications for local ownership and control of infrastructures marries explorations of privatization or private (often foreign) participation in financing local public infrastructure systems in the period of time we studied (Kassim and Ali, 2006; Tan, 2012; Gasmi et al., 2013; Chin and Gallagher, 2019; Gregory and Sovacool, 2019; Kennedy and Sood, 2019). China's particular strength and interest as an infrastructure investor is especially pronounced as a research subject in this regard, particularly given the country's projects throughout Asia and Africa, and its launch of the Asian Infrastructure Investment Bank (Alemu and Scoones, 2013; Alves, 2013; Mohan, 2013; Onjala, 2018; Wang, 2019).

Critical analyses of how infrastructure gaps are being financed also occupy social science research agendas, even if the angle of inquiry is centered more on the public sector's and/or civil society's concerns and interests, and the role of development aid, rather than the private sector's interests or challenges in securing bankable infrastructure investments. For example, a number of scholars study how economic growth agendas and the domination of neoliberal reforms are shaping financing packages for infrastructure, who benefits from financed infrastructure projects, and/or the role of development aid for such projects (Awortwi, 2004; K'Akumu, 2004; Collier and Cust, 2015; Herbert and Murray, 2015; Huynh, 2015; Jacobs, 2016; Carolini, 2017; Berrisford et al., 2018; Husain, 2018; Kennedy and Sood, 2019).

The potential of new technologies to enhance the provision of infrastructure to the urban poor is one of the few positively situated subjects in which social scientists have explored the infrastructure domain. This is especially true in the energy sector, where several scholars analysed renewable energy developments in regions such as sub-Saharan Africa (Alemu and Scoones, 2013; Amsterdam and Thopil, 2017; Sudmant et al., 2017; Pueyo, 2018). In particular, researchers studied the benefits of off-grid solutions, and the governing arrangements around such new 'micro' infrastructures (Jacobson, 2007; Kirubi et al., 2009; Gollwitzer et al., 2018).

Nonetheless, the introduction of investments in infrastructure spaces, historically ignored by governments and investors alike, also raises concerns. Researchers have long highlighted the inequalities in access to infrastructure services, and how this often gives rise to what are deemed 'informal' small-scale providers to fill public infrastructure gaps (K'Akumu, 2004; Bartlett et al., 2012). Our survey of literatures, however, shows that social science research is also now outlining the financial and social shocks that marginalized and informal workers absorb with new efforts to regulate or replace their small-scale or unregulated service provision systems (Allen et al., 2006; Agbiboa, 2016; Hooper, 2019). Displacement, of course extends beyond labor, too. Scholars cite concerns with unfavorable compensation terms, poor public participation, and scant communication around community displacement on physical sites where infrastructure investments are planned (Donaldson and Du Plessis, 2013; Jordhus-Lier, 2015; Carolini, 2017), underscoring the precarity of the poor in the face of development projects perversely meant to improve urban quality of life and community well-being.

Implications and Conclusion

While tremendous energy is currently directed toward channeling the institutional investment community toward infrastructure investment opportunities within countries of the Global South, the fruits of that labor are being harvested unevenly thus far. That unevenness is apparent not only across (and within) geographies and sectors, but also across stakeholders involved in terms of preparation, advocacy, and capacities.

The dominant private sector players within the Global South are not pension funds or insurance companies, but portfolio companies, private equity firms, and infrastructure firms. Furthermore, the herd mentality of the investment community appears just as prevalent in the Global South as it is in the Global North. Private sector participation in infrastructure projects is concentrating in just three leading economies of the South—India, China, and Brazil—as opposed to the many other lower- and middle-income countries with infrastructure needs. Part of the explanation for this concentration may reflect investors' preferences for geographies with ample investment opportunities in the infrastructure domain, thereby reducing their 'per deal' research costs in terms of their knowledge of the local political economy, legislative rules, and regulations shaping investments. Relatedly, mega-cities and urban populations therein—along with their growing demand for infrastructures—mean that countries such as India are likely to be in the infrastructure building mode for quite some time. As Corria da Silva et al. (2006) found in their study of a sample of 121 utilities in the water and transport sectors across 16 countries, and of 23 transport infrastructure operators and 23 transport services operators distributed over 23 countries, debt is increasingly more important than equity as a financing instrument in such contexts. Furthermore, among the deals with publicly known details, concession contracts are the vehicle of choice for private sector participation. In sum, we see a flocking of infrastructure investors in just a few larger economies of the Global South, using debt instruments and concession contracts to manage their risk exposure.

Especially with all the growth in private sector investment in energy and transportation, for example, we could expect that public sector funds would thus be freed up to concentrate on investments in sectors such as water and sanitation, where private investments tread more lightly than in other sectors. However, such an assumption ignores the transaction and financial costs of luring private investment into public infrastructure projects—the costs, staff capacity, and the time put toward project preparation; data production and analytics; and standardization in public sector administrations that much of the international organizational advocacy has promoted.

In Mozambique, for example, the national government has long participated in efforts to build up its financial attractiveness and transparency through public financial management reforms and aid provided by the international donor community (Warren-Rodríguez, 2008). It also introduced a law governing public-private partnerships in 2011, and actively participated in PPIAF programming—including building up its financial management capacities among municipalities. Authorities in the same national government that have been forwarding these public financial management initiatives, however, were also behind a recently revealed scheme for the illegal provision of national government guarantees for loans from European and Russian banks. Those loans were meant to support the construction of a fleet for coastal security and related infrastructures to improve the productivity and stability of private sector investments in energy—specifically, natural gas extraction in the country's north by firms such as Exxon and Anadarko. Ironically, the type of coastal 'security' the country desperately required became clear in the terrible aftermath of Cyclones Idai and Kenneth, which devastated the country in 2019. However, such infrastructures were not prioritized over investments secured to create a better investment environment for the Exxons and Anadarkos of the world. In short, there is little reason to believe that private investor activity in some sectors, such as energy, will translate into public sector investment in other sectors in other countries similarly faced with unequal infrastructures, on the one hand, and opportunities to partner with private investors to develop long evasive infrastructures, on the other.

If the cost of luring in private sector investment is largely covered by public monies, more must be done to support public sector work—to improve public sector investment in infrastructures with relatively less lucrative returns, such as basic water and sanitation; to elevate public sector efforts to ensure those infrastructures are designed with climate resilience in mind; and to improve the public sectors' negotiating skills at the contract and project design level. An organizational advocacy boom, akin to that supporting the global institutional investment community, will be required. Here, we are not simply referring to the technical capacity-building efforts and training opportunities that organizations such as the World Bank and OECD already host for public sector entities from the Global South. Public sector authorities do not simply need to know how to valuate project risks and returns. Rather, public sector entities—particularly at the subnational level where there is relatively less experience in financing infrastructure than at national levels—will need support in building up the kind of tacit knowledge and strategic thinking that are typically advanced and shared among peers in networking events (formal and informal) within the private sector.

It is tacit knowledge—of banks, advisors, lawyers, and investors—coupled with the formal training already available to public authorities from the South that can make a difference to how well public sector entities are equipped to secure the best arrangement for their publics. Networking events and workshops provide these types of opportunities, as outlined earlier, and their numbers have exploded for the private sector in an effort to steer their direction toward the Global South. Yet, public sector entities—particularly those lacking the funding to travel, industry insights, or training typical among authorities from larger economies—will also need their own advocacy networks and organizations working to diminish information asymmetries in dealing with the financial sector, and to help them meet with one another and share their own strategies, insights, and experiences in negotiating infrastructure investment partnerships with private sector stakeholders.

Notes

1 The popular reference is to the Population Division of the Department of Economic and Social Affairs of the United Nations' World Urbanization Prospects estimates on urban growth which, in 2007, situated the world population as a majority urban population for the first time, and has since predicted major urban growth in Asia and Africa. especially.

2 Though it is worth noting that some sectoral controversies about private sector participation in public infrastructures such as water and sanitation provision remain fresh (Bakker, 2010).

3 Accessed at: https://www.scimagojr.com/journalrank.php (February 26, 2019).

4 The core journals surveyed based on the ranking were: the *Quarterly Journal of Economics*, *The Journal of Finance*, *Journal of Financial Economics*, *Econometrica*, the *Journal of Political Economy*, *Academy of Management Annals*, *Academy of Management Journal*, and the *Strategic Management Journal*. *The Journal of Marketing* and the *Journal of Marketing Research* were in the top five journals for the subcategory 'Business and International Management' within Scimago Journal & Country Rank, but were not considered relevant for the purposes of the analysis.

5 The specialized journals included *Utilities Policy*, *Journal of Infrastructure Development*, and *Public Works Management and Policy*.

6 A few clarifying notes on the search process: (1) Geographical descriptors such as 'global South' or 'developing country' may not capture articles that made specific references to certain countries (as opposed to a region). For instance, 'India' might have been a more accurate keyword to search for than 'South Asia' but our aim was not to search all relevant countries in the South; (2) It is worth noting that the search functions of the journal platforms were very limited so we might not have captured the full range of relevant articles given the selected keywords.

7 One exception here is Galiani et al.'s (2005) analysis of the effect of water privatization in Argentina on health outcomes (specifically, on child mortality). They find that child mortality rates associated with water-related diseases decreased faster in provinces that privatized than in those that did not. Additionally, in the telecommunications sector, El-Haddad (2017) considered the effects of liberalizing market reforms on service quality, access, and prices in Egypt. The author finds that reforms generated welfare gains such as improved quality, greater access, and lower prices.

References

Acey, C. S. (2019). Silence and voice in Nigeria's hybrid urban water markets: Implications for local governance of public goods. *International Journal of Urban and Regional Research*, *43*(2), 313–336

Agbiboa, D. E. (2016). 'No condition is permanent': Informal transport workers and labour precarity in Africa's largest city. *International Journal of Urban and Regional Research*, *40*(5), 936–957. https://doi.org/10.1111/1468-2427.12440

Alemu, D., & Scoones, I. (2013). Negotiating new relationships: How the ethiopian state is involving china and brazil in agriculture and rural development. *IDS Bulletin*, *44*(4), 91–100. https://doi.org/10.1111/1759-5436.12045

Allen, A., Dávila, J. D., & Hofmann, P. (2006). The peri-urban water poor: Citizens or consumers? *Environment and Urbanization*, *18*(2), 333–351. https://doi.org/10.1177/0956247806069608

Alves, A. C. (2013). China's 'win-win' cooperation: Unpacking the impact of infrastructure for-resources deals in Africa. *South African Journal of International Affairs*, *20*(2), 207–226. https://doi.org/10.1080/10220461.2013.811337

Amsterdam, H., & Thopil, G. A. (2017). Enablers towards establishing and growing South Africa's waste to electricity industry. *Waste Management*, *68*, 774–785. https://doi.org/10.1016/j.wasman.2017.06.051

Arango, S., Dyner, I., & Larsen, E. R. (2006). Lessons from deregulation: Understanding electricity markets in South America. *Utilities Policy*, *14*(3), 196–207. https://doi.org/10.1016/J.JUP.2006.02.001

Auriol, E., & Blanc, A. (2009). Capture and corruption in public utilities: The cases of water and electricity in Sub-Saharan Africa. *Utilities Policy*, *17*(2), 203–216. https://doi.org/10.1016/J.JUP.2008.07.005

Awortwi, N. (2004). Getting the fundamentals wrong: Woes of public-private partnerships in solid waste collection in three Ghanaian cities. *Public Administration and Development*, *24*(3), 213–224. https://doi.org/10.1002/pad.301

Bakker, K. (2010). *Privatizing Water: Governance Failure and the World's Urban Water Crisis*. Ithaca: Cornell University Press.

Bartlett, A., Alix-Garcia, J., & Saah, D. S. (2012). City growth under conflict conditions: The view from Nyala, Darfur. *City and Community*, *11*(2), 151–170. https://doi.org/10.1111/j.1540-6040.2012.01396.x

Basílio, M. S. (2014). The determinants of multilateral development banks' participation in infrastructure projects. *Journal of Infrastructure Development*, *6*(2), 83–110. https://doi.org/10.1177/0974930614564991

Berrisford, S., Cirolia, L. R., & Palmer, I. (2018). Land-based financing in sub-Saharan African cities. *Environment and Urbanization*, *30*(1), 35–52. https://doi.org/10.1177/0956247817753525

Bertoméu-Sánchez, S., Camos, D., & Estache, A. (2018). Do economic regulatory agencies matter to private-sector involvement in water utilities in developing countries? *Utilities Policy*, *50*, 153–163. https://doi.org/10.1016/J.JUP.2018.01.001

Besley, T., & Ghatak, M. (2001). Government versus private ownership of public goods. *The Quarterly Journal of Economics*, *116*(4), 1343–1372. https://doi.org/10.1162/003355301753265598

Bird, R., & Slack, E. (2014). Local taxes and local expenditures in developing countries: Strengthening the Wicksellian connection. *Public Administration and Development*, *34*, 359–369.

Biygautane, M. (2017). Infrastructure public–private partnerships in Kuwait, Saudi Arabia, and Qatar. *Public Works Management & Policy*, *22*(2), 85–118. https://doi.org/10.1177/1087724X16671719

Boubakri, N., & Cosset, J.-C. (1998). The financial and operating performance of newly privatized firms: Evidence from developing countries. *The Journal of Finance*, *53*(3), 1081–1110. https://doi.org/10.1111/0022-1082.00044

Bunte, J. B., & Kim, A. A. (2017). Citizens' preferences and the portfolio of public goods: Evidence from Nigeria. *World Development*, *92*, 28–39. https://doi.org/10.1016/j.worlddev.2016.11.008

Carolini, G. Y. (2017). Sisyphean dilemmas of development: Contrasting urban infrastructure and fiscal policy trends in Maputo, Mozambique. *International Journal of Urban and Regional Research*, *41*(1), 126–144. https://doi.org/10.1111/1468-2427.12500

Chambouleyron, A. (2014). Mitigating expropriation risk through vertical separation of public utilities: The case of Argentina. *Utilities Policy*, *30*, 41–52. https://doi.org/10.1016/J.JUP.2014.07.002

Cheng, K.-T., & Hebenton, B. (2008). Regulatory governance of telecommunications liberalisation in Taiwan. *Utilities Policy*, *16*(4), 292–306. https://doi.org/10.1016/J.JUP.2008.01.003

Chin, G. T., & Gallagher, K. P. (2019). Coordinated credit spaces: The globalization of Chinese development finance. *Development and Change*, *50*(1), 245–274. https://doi.org/10.1111/dech.12470

Collier, P., & Cust, J. (2015). Investing in Africa's infrastructure: Financing and policy options. *SSRN*, 7(1), 473–493. https://doi.org/10.1146/annurev-resource-100814-124926

Corria da Silva, L., Estache, A., & Järvelä, S. (2006). Is debt replacing equity in regulated privatised infrastructure in LDCs? *Utilities Policy*, *14*(2), 90–102. https://doi.org/10.1016/J.JUP.2005.03.001

Dogan, E., & Stupar, A. (2017). The limits of growth: A case study of three mega-projects in Istanbul. *Cities*, *60*, 281–288. https://doi.org/10.1016/j.cities.2016.09.013

Donaldson, R., & Du Plessis, D. (2013). The urban renewal programme as an area-based approach to renew townships: The experience from Khayelitsha's Central Business District, Cape Town. *Habitat International*, *39*, 295–301. https://doi.org/10.1016/j.habitatint.2012.10.012

El-Haddad, A. (2017). Welfare gains from utility reforms in Egyptian telecommunications. *Utilities Policy*, *45*, 1–26. https://doi.org/10.1016/J.JUP.2016.10.003

Estache, A., & Iimi, A. (2011). (Un)bundling infrastructure procurement: Evidence from water supply and sewage projects. *Utilities Policy*, *19*(2), 104–114. https://doi.org/10.1016/J.JUP.2010.12.003

Ferro, G., & Mercadier, A. C. (2016). Technical efficiency in Chile's water and sanitation providers. *Utilities Policy*, *43*, 97–106. https://doi.org/10.1016/J.JUP.2016.04.016

Ferro, G., Lentini, E. J., Mercadier, A. C., & Romero, C. A. (2014). Efficiency in Brazil's water and sanitation sector and its relationship with regional provision, property and the independence of operators. *Utilities Policy*, *28*, 42–51. https://doi.org/10.1016/J.JUP.2013.12.001

Ferro, G., Romero, C. A., & Covelli, M. P. (2011). Regulation and performance: A production frontier estimate for the Latin American water and sanitation sector. *Utilities Policy*, *19*(4), 211–217. https://doi.org/10.1016/J.JUP.2011.08.003

Fishman, A. 2018. Report finds increasing cost of capital in developing countries due to climate change. Available at: http://sdg.iisd.org/news/report-finds-increasing-cost-of-capital-in-developing-countries-due-to-climate-change/. Accessed October 9, 2019.

Flyvbjerg, B., Garbuio, M., & Lovallo, D. (2009). Delusion and deception in large infrastructure projects. *California Management Review*, *51*(2), 170–193.

Franzsen, R., & McCluskey, W. (2017). *Property Tax of Africa: Status, Challenges, and Prospects*. Lincoln Institute of Land Policy: Cambridge, MA

Fuseini, I., & Kemp, J. (2016). Characterising urban growth in Tamale, Ghana: An analysis of urban governance response in infrastructure and service provision. *Habitat International*, *56*, 109–123. https://doi.org/10.1016/j.habitatint.2016.05.002

G20/OECD/WB. (2018). Stocktake of tools and instruments related to infrastructure as an asset class—Progress report. Retrieved from http://www.oecd.org/g20/G20_OECD_WB_Stocktake-Progress Report.pdf

Galiani, S., Gertler, P., & Schargrodsky, E. (2005). Water for life: The impact of the privatization of water services on child mortality. *Journal of Political Economy*, *113*(1), 83–120. https://doi.org/0022-3808/2005/11301-0006$10.00

Gangakhedkar, R., & Mishra, R. K. (2012). Public–private partnership in power sector: A focus on ultra mega power projects. *Journal of Infrastructure Development*, *4*(1), 27–39. https://doi.org/10.1177/0974930612449535

Gasmi, F., Maingard, A., Noumba, P., & Recuero Virto, L. (2013). The privatization of the fixed-line telecommunications operator in OECD, Latin America, Asia, and Africa: One size does not fit all. *World Development*, *45*, 189–208. https://doi.org/10.1016/j.worlddev.2012.11.005

Gemson, J., & Rajan, A. T. (2016). What do PE investors seek from syndication partners? Evidence from the infrastructure sector. *Public Works Management & Policy*, *21*(3), 231–262. https://doi.org/10.1177/1087724X15613095

Gemson, J., Gautami, K.V., & Thillai Rajan, A. (2012). Impact of private equity investments in infrastructure projects. *Utilities Policy, 21*, 59–65. https://doi.org/10.1016/J.JUP.2011.12.001

Gollwitzer, L., Ockwell, D., Muok, B., Ely, A., & Ahlborg, H. (2018). Rethinking the sustainability and institutional governance of electricity access and mini-grids: Electricity as a common pool resource. *Energy Research and Social Science, 39*, 152–161. https://doi.org/10.1016/j.erss.2017.10.033

González, C. I. (2017). Measuring and comparing the distribution of decision-making power in regulatory arrangements of the telecommunication sector in Latin America. *Utilities Policy, 49*, 145–155. https://doi.org/10.1016/J.JUP.2017.04.002

Gopalkrishna, N., & Karnam, G. (2016). Are the Indian National Highway PPPs more efficient than non-PPPs? An empirical analysis through data envelopment analysis. *Journal of Infrastructure Development, 8*(1), 27–35. https://doi.org/10.1177/0974930616648819

Gregory, J., & Sovacool, B. K. (2019). The financial risks and barriers to electricity infrastructure in Kenya, Tanzania, and Mozambique: A critical and systematic review of the academic literature. *Energy Policy, 125*, 145–153. https://doi.org/10.1016/j.enpol.2018.10.026

Guasch, J., & Straub, S. (2009). Corruption and concession renegotiations: Evidence from the water and transport sectors in Latin America. *Utilities Policy, 17*(2), 185–190. https://doi.org/10.1016/J.JUP.2008.07.003

Hallegatte, S. et al. (2013). Future flood losses in major coastal cities. *Nature Climate Change, 3*, 802–806. http://dx.doi.org/10.1038/NCLIMATE1979

Hannan, S., & Sutherland, C. (2015). Mega-projects and sustainability in Durban, South Africa: Convergent or divergent agendas? *Habitat International, 45*(P3), 205–212. https://doi.org/10.1016/j.habitatint.2014.02.002

Haselip, J., Dyner, I., & Cherni, J. (2005). Electricity market reform in Argentina: Assessing the impact for the poor in Buenos Aires. *Utilities Policy, 13*(1), 1–14. https://doi.org/10.1016/J.JUP.2004.03.001

Hausman, W. J., Neufeld, J. L., & Schreiber, T. (2014). Multilateral and bilateral aid policies and trends in the allocation of electrification aid, 1970–2001. *Utilities Policy, 29*, 54–62. https://doi.org/10.1016/J.JUP.2013.12.004

Herbert, C. W., & Murray, M. J. (2015). Building from scratch: New cities, privatized urbanism and the spatial restructuring of Johannesburg after Apartheid. *International Journal of Urban and Regional Research, 39*(3), 471–494. https://doi.org/10.1111/1468-2427.12180

Hooper, M. (2019). When diverse norms meet weak plans: The organizational dynamics of urban rubble clearance in post-earthquake Haiti. *International Journal of Urban and Regional Research, 43*(2), 292–312. https://doi.org/10.1111/1468-2427.12696

Husain, M. (2018). Dichotomy of development aid's ambition and neoliberal imperatives: A case-study of private-sector development in Bangladesh. *Development Policy Review, 36*, O803–O814. https://doi.org/10.1111/dpr.12366

Huynh, D. (2015). The misuse of urban planning in Ho Chi Minh City. *Habitat International, 48*, 11–19. https://doi.org/10.1016/j.habitatint.2015.03.007

Inderst, G., & Stewart, F. (2014). Institutional investment in infrastructure in emerging markets and developing economies. Washington, DC. https://doi.org/10.2139/ssrn.2494261

Jacobs, B. (2016). Can the addis ababa action agenda bring about a more integrated blend? Facilitating African infrastructure development through institutionalized portfolio approaches. *Forum for Development Studies, 43*(3), 385–413. https://doi.org/10.1080/08039410.2016.1164236

Jacobson, A. (2007). Connective power: Solar electrification and social change in Kenya. *World Development, 35*(1), 144–162. https://doi.org/10.1016/j.worlddev.2006.10.001

Jamali, D. (2004). A public-private partnership in the Lebanese telecommunications industry. *Public Works Management & Policy*, *9*(2), 103–119. https://doi.org/10.1177/1087724X04268365

Jordhus-Lier, D. (2015). Community resistance to megaprojects: The case of the N2 Gateway project in Joe Slovo informal settlement, Cape Town. *Habitat International*, *45*(P3), 169–176. https://doi.org/10.1016/j.habitatint.2014.02.006

K'Akumu, O. A. (2004). Privatization of the urban water supply in Kenya: Policy options for the poor. *Environment and Urbanization*, *16*(2), 213–222. https://doi.org/10.1630/0956247042310025

Kassim, S. M., & Ali, M. (2006). Solid waste collection by the private sector: Households' perspective-findings from a study in Dar es Salaam city, Tanzania. *Habitat International*, *30*(4), 769–780. https://doi.org/10.1016/j.habitatint.2005.09.003

Kennedy, L. (2015). The politics and changing paradigm of megaproject development in metropolitan cities. *Habitat International*, *45*(P3), 163–168. https://doi.org/10.1016/j.habitatint.2014.07.001

Kennedy, L., & Sood, A. (2019). Outsourced urban governance as a state rescaling strategy in Hyderabad, India. *Cities*, *85*, 130–139. https://doi.org/10.1016/j.cities.2018.09.001

Kirubi, C., Jacobson, A., Kammen, D. M., & Mills, A. (2009). Community-based electric micro-grids can contribute to rural development: Evidence from Kenya. *World Development*, *37*(7), 1208–1221. https://doi.org/10.1016/j.worlddev.2008.11.005

Mapila, K., Lauridsen, M., and Chastenay, C. (2017). Mobilizing institutional investments into emerging market infrastructure, World Bank Other Operational Studies 30362. Washington, DC: World Bank.

Loch, M., Marcon, R., Pruner da Silva, A. L., & Xavier, W. G. (2018). Government's impact on the financial performance of electric service providers as both regulator and shareholder. *Utilities Policy*, *55*, 142–150. https://doi.org/10.1016/J.JUP.2018.09.007

Mahalingam, A., Devkar, G. A., & Kalidindi, S. N. (2011). A comparative analysis of public-private partnership (PPP) coordination agencies in India. *Public Works Management & Policy*, *16*(4), 341–372. https://doi.org/10.1177/1087724X11409215

Maniar, H. (2013). Scenario of viability gap funding (VGF) concept in Indian infrastructure projects. *Journal of Infrastructure Development*, *5*(1), 33–65. https://doi.org/10.1177/0974930613488295

Marzouk, M., & Ali, M. (2018). Mitigating risks in wastewater treatment plant PPPs using minimum revenue guarantee and real options. *Utilities Policy*, *53*, 121–133. https://doi.org/10.1016/J.JUP.2018.06.012

McKinsey & Company. (2016). Bridging global infrastrucutre gaps. Retrieved from https://www.mckinsey.com/industries/capital-projects-and-infrastructure/our-insights/bridging-global-infrastructure-gaps

Mohan, G. (2013). Beyond the enclave: Towards a critical political economy of China and Africa. *Development and Change*, *44*(6), 1255–1272. https://doi.org/10.1111/dech.12061

Mutambatsere, E., Nalikka, A., Pal, M., & Vencatachellum, D. (2013). What role for multilateral development banks in project finance? Some thoughts from the rift valley railways in Kenya and Uganda. *Journal of Infrastructure Development*, *5*(1), 1–20. https://doi.org/10.1177/0974930613488291

Onjala, J. (2018). China's development loans and the threat of debt crisis in Kenya. *Development Policy Review*, *36*, O710–O728. https://doi.org/10.1111/dpr.12328

Peng, D., & Poudineh, R. (2017). An appraisal of investment vehicles in the Tanzania's electricity sector. *Utilities Policy*, *48*, 51–68. https://doi.org/10.1016/J.JUP.2017.09.002

Perelman, S., & Serebrisky, T. (2012). Measuring the technical efficiency of airports in Latin America. *Utilities Policy*, *22*, 1–7. https://doi.org/10.1016/J.JUP.2012.02.001

Pinto, L., & Reis, M. (2017). *The new Brazilian economy*, 151–176. https://doi.org/10.1057/978-1-137-46297-8

PPIAF (2019). Public–private infrastructure advisory facility annual report 2019. https://ppiaf.org/documents/5799/download?otp=b3RwIzE1OTc5MjgwMTk=. Accessed August 20, 2020.

Pueyo, A. (2018). What constrains renewable energy investment in Sub-Saharan Africa? A comparison of Kenya and Ghana. *World Development*, *109*, 85–100. https://doi.org/10.1016/j.worlddev.2018.04.008

Rozenberg, J., & Fay, M. (2019). *Beyond the Gap: How Countries Can Afford the Infrastructure They Need while Protecting the Planet.* Washington, DC: World Bank. https://openknowledge.worldbank.org/handle/10986/31291

Ruet, J. (2006). Cost-effectiveness of alternative investment strategies for the power sector in India: A retrospective account of the period 1997–2002. *Utilities Policy*, *14*(2), 114–125. https://doi.org/10.1016/J.JUP.2005.06.001

Ruiz Diaz, G. (2017). The contractual and administrative regulation of public-private partnership. *Utilities Policy*, *48*, 109–121. https://doi.org/10.1016/J.JUP.2016.04.011

Sabbioni, G. (2008). Efficiency in the Brazilian sanitation sector. *Utilities Policy*, *16*(1), 11–20. https://doi.org/10.1016/J.JUP.2007.06.003

Satyanand, P. N. (2011). Foreign direct investment in India's power sector. *Journal of Infrastructure Development*, *3*(1), 65–89. https://doi.org/10.1177/097493061100300103

Seroa da Motta, R., & Moreira, A. (2006). Efficiency and regulation in the sanitation sector in Brazil. *Utilities Policy*, *14*(3), 185–195. https://doi.org/10.1016/J.JUP.2006.03.002

Stern, J. (2000). Electricity and telecommunications regulatory institutions in small and developing countries. *Utilities Policy*, *9*(3), 131–157. https://doi.org/10.1016/S0957-1787(01)00011-X

Sudmant, A., Colenbrander, S., Gouldson, A., & Chilundika, N. (2017). Private opportunities, public benefits? The scope for private finance to deliver low-carbon transport systems in Kigali, Rwanda. *Urban Climate*, *20*, 59–74. https://doi.org/10.1016/j.uclim.2017.02.011

Sutherland, C., Sim, V., & Scott, D. (2015). Contested discourses of a mixed-use megaproject: Cornubia, Durban. *Habitat International*, *45*(P3), 185–195. https://doi.org/10.1016/j.habitatint.2014.06.009

Takano, G. (2017). Public-Private Partnerships as rent-seeking opportunities: A case study on an unsolicited proposal in Lima, Peru. *Utilities Policy*, *48*, 184–194. https://doi.org/10.1016/J.JUP.2017.08.005

Tan, J. (2012). The pitfalls of water privatization: Failure and reform in Malaysia. *World Development*, *40*(12), 2552–2563. https://doi.org/10.1016/j.worlddev.2012.05.012

Thamae, L. Z., Thamae, R. I., & Thamae, T. M. (2015). Assessing a decade of regulatory performance for the Lesotho electricity industry. *Utilities Policy*, *35*, 91–101. https://doi.org/10.1016/J.JUP.2015.07.006

Tsukada, S. (2013). Potential pitfalls in PPP policy application: Lessons learned from National Highway Development Programmes in India. *Journal of Infrastructure Development*, *5*(1), 87–102. https://doi.org/10.1177/0974930613488298

United Nations. (2019). Roadmap for financing the 2030 agenda for sustainable development 2019–2021. United Nations Secretariat. Available at: https://www.un.org/sustainabledevelopment/wp-content/uploads/2019/07/UN-SG-Roadmap-Financing-the-SDGs-July-2019.pdf. Accessed October 9, 2019.

UN-Habitat. (2016). Urbanization and development: Emerging futures. Urban development in the Muslim world. Nairobi, Kenya: UN Human Settlements Programme. https://doi.org/10.4324/9781351318204-5

Vadali, N., Tiwari, A. P., & Rajan, A. T. (2014). Effect of the political environment on public private partnership projects. *Journal of Infrastructure Development*, *6*(2), 145–165. https://doi.org/10.1177/0974930614564651

Vedachalam, S., Geddes, R. R., & Riha, S. J. (2016). Public–private partnerships and contract choice in India's water and wastewater sectors. *Public Works Management & Policy*, *21*(1), 71–96. https://doi.org/10.1177/1087724X15596171

Wang, H., Wu, W., & Zheng, S. (2011). An econometric analysis of private sector participation in China's urban water supply. *Utilities Policy*, *19*(3), 134–141. https://doi.org/10.1016/J.JUP.2011.01.004

Wang, H. (2019). The new development bank and the Asian infrastructure investment bank: China's ambiguous approach to global financial governance. *Development and Change*, *50*(1), 221–244. https://doi.org/10.1111/dech.12473

Warren-Rodríguez, A. (2008). Putting aid on budget: A case study of Mozambique. A study for the Collaborative Africa Budget Reform Initiative (CABRI) and the Strategic Partnership with Africa (SPA). Retrieved from http://mokoro.co.uk/wp-content/uploads/AOB-MozambiqueReportApril08final.pdf

Watson, V. (2014). African urban fantasies: Dreams or nightmares. *Environment and Urbanization*, *26*(2), 561–567.

Wright-Contreras, L. (2018). A transnational urban political ecology of water infrastructures: Global water policies and water management in Hanoi. *Public Works Management & Policy*, *24*(2), 195–212. https://doi.org/10.1177/1087724X18780045

Yates, J. S., & Harris, L. M. (2018). Hybrid regulatory landscapes: The human right to water, variegated neoliberal water governance, and policy transfer in Cape Town, South Africa, and Accra, Ghana. *World Development*, *110*, 75–87. https://doi.org/10.1016/j.worlddev.2018.05.021

PART III

Investors

12

LONG-TERM INVESTMENT MANAGEMENT

The Principal–Agent Problem and Metrics of Performance

Gordon L. Clark and Ashby H.B. Monk

There is a large and growing literature on corporate governance in the social sciences (Spulber, 2009). Compendiums abound with theories, research programmes, critical studies of the impact of globalization on regimes of corporate governance, as well as claims and counterclaims over the link between regimes of corporate governance, and the economic performances of nations and groups of nations (Helpman, 2008; Hopt et al., 1998; Williams and Zumbansen, 2011). For economic geographers, any regime of corporate governance is necessarily embedded in a complex web of country-specific rules, regulations, social norms, and conventions (Bathelt and Glückler, 2011; Gertler, 2010). Nonetheless, there remains an overarching interest in best practice—that is, modes of organization and management that are more effective than others in realizing common objectives.

Much of the literature on corporate governance can trace its roots to Berle and Means (1933) and their study of the early-twentieth century US industrial corporation, and the relationship between owners and managers in the context of anti-trust policy and the like. It held the attention of scholars for much of the twentieth century and continues to be of relevance because it conceptualized one of the core problems in the field—that is, the proper roles and responsibilities of managers and owners, as well as the accountability of the former to the latter. So, for example, this issue goes to the heart of research by Michael Jensen (1993, 2000) on the 'failings' of US industrial corporations. His treatise on the principles and policies underpinning models of management sought a more effective relationship between managers, owners, and stakeholders.

This logic has found favour around the world in MBA programmes, multilateral organizations such as the OECD, and in the development policies of nation-states seeking to join the global economy. Whereas much of the focus has been on global corporations, increasing attention has been paid to the organization and management of investors in general and, more particularly, long-term institutional investment organizations such as endowments, family offices, insurance companies, pension funds, and sovereign wealth funds (for an early intervention, see Morrison and Wilhelm, 2007). If somewhat neglected, their enormous growth over the past 50 years or so, along with their evident importance for the governance of public and private corporations (Kay, 2012), has prompted research designed to shed light on the challenges inherent in managing investment organizations that hold billions, tens of billions, hundreds of billions, even trillions of US dollars (Monk et al., 2017).

The problematic nature of these investment organizations was hardly noticed through the golden era of global financial markets stretching from the 1960s through to the global financial crisis of 2007/08 (Litterman, 2004). Thereafter, how these organizations invest, in what they invest, their time horizons, and their geographical reach have all become important topics for research and public policy, which recognize that the costs and consequences of financial instability are rarely isolated to one jurisdiction at the margins of the global economy (Barro, 2006). In fact, Haldane and May (2011), among others, have noted that the organization and management of these investors can have profound effects on the stability of global financial markets.

While much of the research on financial market stability and performance focuses on the trading strategies of investment managers, more often than not investment managers are employees of large, complex financial institutions (Clark, 2016). How these organizations are managed, how they deploy human resources, how they reward and sanction certain types of behaviour, and how they integrate the activities of separate departments and employees into the performance of the organization as a whole, all matter when it comes to these institutions achieving their long-term goals. How they are organized and managed is the topic of this chapter, for which we have drawn on our research on the organization and management of large asset owners (Clark and Monk, 2017, 2019), rather than on asset manager and intermediaries such as BlackRock or Fidelity.

Specifically, in this chapter we set out an analytical model that conceptualizes the management of financial institutions via a set of building blocks—namely, the internal systems and processes that encourage employees to focus on the organization's goals and objectives, rather than on their separate and, sometimes, competing interests. At one level, our model of management is an analytical statement of what we have observed in the industry. At another level, however, it is a normative framework that provides a means by which financial institutions may better align internal interests with external constituencies. As such, there is an element of idealism inherent in this chapter in that we do not measure or estimate the likely performance of organizations that would follow our framework—any management framework is necessarily embedded in a much broader regulatory and social context (Gertler, 2003).

The model of management presented along with the related metrics of performance should also be seen as a deliberate attempt to engage the industry as a whole, while recognizing that its implementation is necessarily subject to the conditions obtaining in markets and countries. Functional performance matters (Merton and Bodie, 2004). The model of management presented here can be seen as a research framework in which customary practice is interrogated for its efficacy (see Davis, 2015).

Governance: Theory and Practice

The standard treatment of corporate governance is through the principal–agent 'problem'—see Pratt and Zeckhauser (1985), for the seminal statement. In sum, it can be described as follows: the owners of a corporation are deemed to be separately and collectively the 'principal', and those employed to make good on the goals and objectives of the corporation are deemed 'agents'. The principal can be a single entity or person; equally, it can be many people and/or investors. In the first instance, a single entity or person can have a direct relationship with the agent, making it relatively simple to translate goals and objectives into actions. Where there are many people and/or investors with the status of 'principal', however, governance becomes a collective problem and thus more or less difficult to resolve (Williamson, 1996).

Theory has it that the principal delegates to the agent responsibility for realizing the goals and objectives of the corporation and are subject to the supervision of a board of directors (Bolton and Dewatripont, 2005). A board normally has two functions—it represents the interests of various classes of investors, and it holds managers to account for realizing the corporation's goals and objectives. Inevitably, the principal defers to the expertise of managers; to do otherwise would be to intervene directly in the management process, thereby incurring significant transaction costs, as well as the likelihood of making poor decisions on issues that are large and small in scope and significance (Clark, 2004). Whereas this is a plausible account of the public corporation, private equity groups have sought to narrow the gap between principals and agents using incentives that enhance collaboration and the alignment of interests.

This governance model has been deployed by academics and policy-makers interested in the Anglo-American corporation with applications to corporate governance in countries such as Germany, France, and Japan (Dore, 2000). It has also been used to assess the integrity of corporate governance in China, including analysis of the relationships between the party, government, and corporations, as well as the status of third-party investors such as the major investment groups from the West. When used to assess the performance of Anglo-American corporations, its shortcomings are often explained by the following: (i) the inability of principals to solve collective action problems; (ii) lack of clarity on the goals and objectives of corporations; and (iii) the inability of principals to observe directly the intentions and actions of their agents (Hart, 2011).

As noted above, one solution has been to take corporations private, thereby better aligning the interests of principals with those of principals and agents.[1] Another solution has been to simplify the goals and objectives of the corporation, eschewing complex mission statements for a simple formula, such as maximizing the rate of return. One solution to the problem of observing the actions and intentions of agents has been to dissemble the corporation into its parts, thus rendering the management process and its results in those parts more transparent. Each solution has brought with it unintended consequences—for example, maximizing the rate of return has encouraged short-termism, has raised questions about the legitimacy of the corporation despite standard metrics of performance, and has brought about a failure to invest in long-term value compared with competitors from different regimes of corporate governance (Kay, 2012).

Asset owner-investors face similar issues. Large pension funds typically act on behalf of two types of principal—the entities that offer pension benefits to their employees, and the employees themselves. In some cases, sponsors and employees are relatively homogeneous, in that they come from a certain industry with a particular type of employee. For example, there are pension funds that act on behalf of certain types of public employee, such as teachers, police, and firefighters. Even here, it may be difficult to organize sponsors into coherent groups, just as it may be difficult to identify and monitor the interests of employees who have different concerns by virtue of their age, gender, years of service, and family circumstances. Sponsors and participants typically delegate the task of articulating and representing their interests to board members. This may or may not be effective[2] (Clark and Urwin, 2008).

It is reasonable to assume that the purpose of a pension fund is clear cut: it is responsible for the retirement welfare of plan participants, given their current circumstances and likely needs in the longer term. This is, however, a rather abstract idea, in that it could provide little guidance on the management of the investment process over the short to medium terms. Furthermore, in the absence of some entity that guarantees the pension benefits of participants, the future retirement well-being of the latter is contingent on investment performance, which is, itself, contingent on the performance of public and private financial markets. There is a significant stochastic element in investment management that derives from the imperfect nature of financial markets, as well as the problematic behaviour of market traders and institutions (Weitzman, 2007).

Often, pension funds outsource the production of investment returns according to different types of investment strategy and asset class. In these cases, the pension fund is the principal, and the service provider is the agent. In doing so, the pension fund acts on behalf of the board of directors, which is, in theory, the representative of the immediate principal (the sponsor) and the ultimate principal (beneficiaries). In some cases, pension funds may invest directly, using their own professionals and the fund's investment organization. Here, though, the investment process is rarely a unitary system; more often than not, it is segmented by asset class and mandate, thus mimicking the production of investment returns by market players (Clark, 2016). Here, too, there are significant coordination problems internal to these organizations. Just as public corporations, notwithstanding the seemingly simple objective functions of these organizations and their networks of providers, this is a complex process (Arjaliès et al., 2017).

In this chapter, we deal with the governance of the investment management process in relation to the production of pension benefits paid now and in the future, matching our larger concern about the governance of beneficial financial institutions (Clark and Monk, 2017). Throughout, we focus on the alignment of the interests of the various agents and principals embedded in these types of organizations, paying particular attention to their ultimate purpose. Whereas 'golden rules' are sometimes invoked to give coherence to these organizations, it is apparent that a golden rule such as 'maximizing the rate of return' is an inadequate means of governing the principal–agent problem. Our framework, along with its measures and metrics of management, has implications for beneficial financial institutions and for long-term investors (LTIs) in general.

Enhancing the ways in which LTIs access markets and produce returns may create better outcomes through a more aligned and often shorter chain of financial intermediaries. However, this can create a set of new challenges. For example, it is increasingly difficult to capture or quantify the underlying drivers of performance of these new and innovative activities. In part, this is because LTIs are often quite different, one from the other. Even within the same type of institution (pension fund, endowment, foundation), jurisdiction (the United States, Canada, Netherlands, Australia), and time horizon over which the purpose of the institution is to be judged (distant commitments and/or investment in perpetuity), it can be difficult to identify peers or direct comparators against which to judge a fund's performance. While benchmarking is common practice in the industry, it can also have pernicious effects, as in managing towards benchmarks, rather than total returns (see Shiller, 2005; Shleifer, 1985). As such, boards of directors, and the senior managers they hold accountable, require new measures and metrics to assess the performance of these types of organizational strategies.

A Model of Institutional Investment

The global community of LTIs includes pension funds, superannuation funds, sovereign wealth funds, endowments, foundations, family offices, and insurance companies. These organizations account for approximately US$40–50 trillion in assets and sustain the global asset management industry, which holds perhaps a further US$30 trillion in assets. In recent years, however, it has been acknowledged that intermediation involves significant costs, and a pernicious and systematic misalignment of the incentives that connect asset owners with the asset management industry (Ambachtsheer, 2016; Monk and Sharma, 2018).

As a result, LTIs have sought to take greater responsibility for the production of their own investment returns, manifest either as a reduction in their reliance on external asset managers or, for those unable to internalize investment management, as a reduction in their reliance on consultants and external agents (see Arjaliès et al., 2017). Whatever their specific circumstances, LTIs have sought to reduce principal–agent costs, minimize the erosion of returns from fees paid to external managers, and improve the alignment of interests between those investing capital and those reliant on capital accumulation (Monk et al., 2017). These organizations have sought to enhance their governance, culture, and technology to improve the process through which investment returns are generated.

Organizational Enablers

The quality of any organization's investment performance can be traced, in part, to its organizational enablers—that is, the untraded or intangible advantages that derive from its organizational context; for example, its sponsor, location, and/or place in the industry (Helfat et al., 2007: 86). We define these enablers as governance, culture, and technology. Whereas these enablers are often treated as passive (i.e., inherited), LTIs can, in fact, cultivate and develop their enablers, thereby sustaining innovation and investment performance in ways not immediately available to other similar organizations.

Governance is a form of meta-process management for organizations. It represents the formal and informal processes whereby an organization manages itself in relation to its goals and objectives. More prosaically, LTIs' boards set and oversee the delegation of roles and responsibilities, as they receive and respond to information on the separate and collective performance of the organization. In general, boards represent the resources and management capacity of their organizations, cultivating capabilities in relation to goals and objectives. For example, boards typically approve the building and maintenance of information and risk management systems that communicate pertinent information to boards and related decision-makers. Boards can also experiment with arm's length governance structures to bring more capital behind a strategy, or change the constraints and encumbrances binding the organization to existing systems of management.

Culture represents the beliefs, assumptions, values, and modes of operating that give investment organizations their distinctive, and even unique, characteristics (Dalio, 2017). More often than not, the culture of an organization is to be found in its norms and conventions, not just its governance structures (Brennan et al., 2014; Clark, 2018). For example, a culture of knowledge-sharing can improve the flow of information and build trust between boards and staff. A culture of risk-taking and accountability can empower professionals to take on new investment opportunities, while linking their initiatives to the overarching purpose of the organization. And a 'member-first' culture can ensure that the time horizon over which investments are framed and implemented is consistent with members' interests. Finally, culture is also a form of effective communication, helping to create consistent interpretations of information and data.

Technology is an 'asset' that expands capabilities and enhances efficiency. It is the medium through which organizations transfer and communicate decision-critical information to decision-makers, such as boards and/or investment committees. These systems can serve to empower professionals and streamline investment processes, including risk management. Whereas data and information systems are typically counted as costs to any organization and, at times, discounted accordingly, effective and timely information systems can reinforce an organization's comparative advantage, build or reinforce the legitimacy of an investment team and its board, and thereby distinguish an LTI from other competing organizations.

If an investment organization is to improve the way it invests, it will rely on these enablers to do so.[3] It can use its governance, culture, and technology to alter the quality and combination of its production inputs, which we focus on in the next section, to create better outputs. It can also seek to change its enablers, such as improving technology or governance, so as to enhance performance.

Factors of Production

The production of investment returns relies on four key factors or inputs—capital, people, process, and information (Clark and Monk, 2013; Clark and Urwin, 2008). Investors combine these inputs internally, externally, or in some hybrid manner to generate a desired risk-adjusted rate of return. The stock of financial assets is the medium through which investment strategy is conceived and implemented, while the flow of returns sustains both the stock of financial assets and the ultimate objectives of the organization. Given the enablers of an investment organization, it is the combination of the four production inputs that produces, at any point in time, the measured risk-adjusted rate of return.

Capital: The size of a fund's capital stock matters when framing and setting investment strategy. Moreover, the owner of capital, and the ways in which the investor may return it to beneficiaries, matter for how an investor produces returns. Long-term investors with a large stock of capital and no explicit liabilities invest differently from investors holding a relatively small stock of capital and are preoccupied with short-term returns in relation to well-defined liabilities.

People: The professionals who generate returns may be developed internally, as in Canada's pension funds, or they may be sourced from the market via asset managers. For example, US endowment funds tend to source the professionals on whom they rely to make investment decisions. The location of a fund may help to determine the quality of people available (e.g., New York, NY, versus Juneau, Alaska), while the sponsor may have an edge in recruiting talent through privileged contacts and networks (as is the case with university endowments). Whatever the source, investment professionals with high-quality skills and expertise are a scarce resource, command a premium in the marketplace, and require sophisticated recruitment strategies (Clark, 2016).

Process: The organizational mechanisms by which investment decisions are made and implemented are, quite obviously, key to the production of investment returns. These processes are often complex, multi-layered, and subject to oversight. Indeed, blueprints or manuals describing these processes are significant and complex documents. Embedded in the process of investment decision-making are delegation frameworks; risk management systems; and systems of accountability, such as reference portfolios and benchmarks. When reliant on external providers, the larger the number of service providers in an investment chain, the more complex the oversight of the investment process (Clark and Monk, 2019).

Information: The investment management industry is fundamentally about information processing. Whereas market information is typically collected and disseminated by intermediaries, the quality and quantity of information management and dissemination are the lifeblood of any investment organization's investment performance. In this respect, the measurement and metrics of performance are key inputs/outputs of the production process.

Smart people can create smart processes that, in turn, can improve the reliability of information. Nonetheless, LTIs are often rich in one or two of these inputs and must adapt their operating models to compensate for shortcomings in other inputs. Likewise, some institutions are rich in enablers, whereas others may face shortfalls in these resources. In part, these variations can be sheeted-back to the sponsors of investment institutions where, for example, endowment funds may have certain advantages over public sector pension funds, while sovereign wealth funds may face significant shortfalls in their enablers but can marshal high-quality factors of production.

The capacity to bring together high-quality factors of production depends on these enablers. For example, if a fund would benefit from recruiting high-quality professionals, giving effect to this ambition could depend on the governance of the fund (the respect and compensation accorded senior managers by the board), the cultural fit between the fund and its target employees (which translates into commitment), and the technological sophistication of the organization relative to its peers and the competing asset management industry. Alternatively, if senior managers aim to improve the process of setting investment strategy, then its implementation depends on the governance of the fund (delegated powers), the culture of the organization (accountability), and the effectiveness of knowledge management (information collection and distribution).

Performance Management and Measurement

The theory of corporate governance would have it that organizations should be managed against a simple, well-specified, objective function (Jensen, 2000). For many years, this was conceived in terms of profit maximization. In part, this goal was justified by reference to a distinction made by Milton Friedman, amongst others, between capitalism and socialism, wherein the role of the corporation in liberal democracies is to maximize profit, leaving social and environmental concerns (for example) to government and the democratic process. While this golden rule is now subject to debate and dissent, it remains an important reference point in contemporary debate of corporate governance and regulation (see Davis, 2015).

A simple well-defined objective function has three virtues. First, it provides in unambiguous terms the ultimate goal of the management function, whether short-term, medium-term, or long-term, thereby leaving any other issues subservient to the golden rule. Second, it is a reference point against which competing claims over the allocation of resources, management time and effort, and the distribution of authority and responsibility in an organization are resolved. Third, it provides a reference point for employee-related rewards and sanctions—to the extent to which executive compensation is tied to performance against the golden rule, there is an 'objective' basis for justifying variable levels of compensation.

As such, profit maximization provides a reference point for behaviour within the corporation and an unambiguous rationale for the purpose of the corporation. Many public corporations proclaim adherence to this golden rule, albeit modified or reframed in accordance with the conditions obtaining in their industry, jurisdiction, or competitive context. But, it has also attracted many critics, especially those concerned about the wider responsibilities of the corporation on matters such as environmental sustainability and social responsibility; on its own, profit maximization legitimates corporations that produce armaments, cigarettes, asbestos, and other products of a similar nature. Also, for investors concerned about reconciling profit maximization with long-term performance, this rule may well result in the destruction of value over the long term.

Other theorists have taken a more nuanced approach. For example, early work by March and Simon (1958) and Cyert and March (1993) on organizational structure and performance and, especially, the nexus between organizational structure and individual behaviour, has developed over the years into research and policy programmes aimed at mobilizing internal resources and constituencies around multifunctional conceptions of corporate purpose and results (Helfat et al., 2007). To take one example, the balanced scorecard approach to organizational management recognizes that individual employees and their teams are embedded in a set of related activities and functions that require (separately and together) motivation and coordination so as to achieve their immediate objectives and the objectives of the organization (Kaplan and Norton, 1996).

In a related fashion, successful investment management organizations are typically described by their reported rates of return over well-defined time periods (such as monthly, quarterly, or yearly). Not surprisingly, this has proven to be an incomplete way of measuring the success of an LTI. While measures of performance that focus on investment performance allow for comparison among peers, they tend to ignore the risks (internal and external) used to generate returns and the long-term liabilities that chosen investment strategies are meant to cover. Moreover, given the existence of significant context-dependent differences among institutional investors, including organizational enablers and factors of production, it is often difficult to find standardized measures of investment performance that provide meaningful comparisons.

In addition to the unique features of investment organizations, it is also difficult to compare performance over time, especially when, for some organizations, the relevant time horizon is the short term, while for others it is the long term (however defined). Developing measures of performance that offer reliable insights into the short-term progress towards a long-term goal is also challenging. In these cases, the construction and deployment of effective measures of performance is about choosing the appropriate metrics that bear on and reinforce the investment 'journey' of the organization. Too often, despite their commitment to long-term performance, the boards of LTIs over-emphasize short-term performance because of shortfalls in governance—that is, in the absence of effective governance procedures, they fall-back on short-term investment performance oversight.

Recognizing that the long-term risk-adjusted rate of return is important to LTIs, whatever their type and whoever their sponsor, the integration of the short-term with a long-term goal depends on measuring in some acceptable way the onward 'journey' to that goal. In this respect, we rely on insights from our research programme, as well as on lessons learned from related case studies underpinning this chapter, to identify three 'intermediate' outputs of the onward journey to the long-term goal. As shown below, these measures are indicators of organizational performance—key outputs of the combination of organizational enablers and the factors of production.

Commitment: The support of internal or external investment professionals to the long-term mission of the LTI is a key measure of performance, in that many LTIs view it as a 'signal' of positive investment results to come. This is about the 'effort' of investment professionals as much as it is about their 'belief' in the investment organization and its goals (Clark and Monk, 2019).

Alignment: The long-term financial performance of an LTI depends on linking compensation and professional advancement to each step in the journey. External asset managers often generate high fees and performance-related bonuses over the short term, even when client performance fails to keep pace with industry peers or relevant benchmarks over the long term. As such, the virtues of alignment are often invoked as the basis for insourcing or re-intermediation of the investment process. While compensation is an important motivating factor in any organization, LTIs who rely on their own teams can design compensation regimes that make explicit the alignment of interests over the relevant time horizons.

Knowledge management: As suggested above, LTIs are in the business of developing and sustaining the flow of information about investment opportunities, and absolute and comparative performance. These insights can be about managers, competing institutions, currencies, and the many variables related to investment performance. This information may come through deep networks of peers and professionals that long-term investors tap to generate insight. Or it can be based on digital networks, via computers, databases, algorithms, and the like. Keeping count of the flow of information and knowledge is a key measure of performance (Clark, 2018).

By this account, the long-term performance of an investment organization is the product of its enablers and factors of production, managed in ways that mobilize the commitment of investment professionals by ensuring that the alignment of interests and the sharing of information and knowledge are consistent with its comparative advantages and the organization's long-term goals. As such, the investment 'journey' is sustained by ensuring transparency on matters such as commitment and the alignment of interests, punctuated by checks on short-term performance on the journey towards long-term goals and objectives.

Measures and Metrics

Any measure of performance requires a metric or set of metrics that is accepted across the organization and that represents, department by department and function by function, the contributions made by employees and management to realizing the long-term goals of the organization.[4] In research, we have found that the explicit identification and measurement of performance against these types of indicators can facilitate the reconciliation of the short term with the long term. In addition, the widespread acceptance of these measures of performance can sustain an investment organization, even in the face of market risk and uncertainty.

Note, however, there are critics of metrics of performance and the related attempts to articulate the link between 'effort' and 'outcomes' through measurement. Muller (2018: 18) argued that a 'fixation' with metrics is often destructive of shared beliefs and the commitment to the organization as a social entity, not just a set of functions. He contended that 'not everything that is important is measurable, and much that is measurable is unimportant'. He also claimed that those caught up in systems of measurement and metrics become adept at manipulating those metrics, thereby sacrificing time and effort to subverting the purpose of the organization. He then suggested that an obsession with metrics discounts professional integrity, and the discretion and respect owed to many employees by virtue of their skills and expertise. In this respect, measurement and metrics can become a prison in which inspiration and innovation are stifled (along with the long-term performance of the organization).

These criticisms are well-meant and, in some organizations, describe the costs and consequences of measurement and metrics systems that impose on organizations and their employees' frameworks that are self-defeating. It should also be acknowledged that senior managers can introduce top-down models of oversight and accountability through measures of performance so as to sustain their power in circumstances where their organization is failing. Many years ago, Arrow (1974: 72–3) argued that 'control mechanisms are, after all, costly' for organizational efficiency and resource allocation. Indeed, it is arguable that organizations that are able to maintain a level of ambiguity or ambidexterity as to their form and functions are those that are better able to adapt to changing market conditions, and shifts and changes in the underlying parameters that frame market expectations (Lo, 2012).

It is also the case that some industries more than others, and some professions more than others, are not only accustomed to measurement and metrics, but have also inculcated these aspects of their working lives into the culture of the industry and into its participating organizations and institutions. This is particularly relevant to the finance industry, which is dominated by metrics of performance—witness the pervasive influence of third-party information systems that communicate metrics of performance to the industry 24/7 and 365 days a year (Clark et al., 2004). At this level, measures and metrics of performance are literally the lifeblood of the industry. At another level, however, the premium on quantitative skill and expertise is such that investment professionals understand their place in the industry by virtue of accepted measures and metrics of performance. In the organizations that have been the basis of our research, measures and metrics of performance are more often demanded by investment professionals, rather than imposed by their institutions.

On this basis, we would argue that metrics and measures of performance are cultural attributes of the industry as much as mechanisms of oversight and management. In this regard, it is accepted that the most relevant (and controversial) metric of LTI performance is the long-term risk-adjusted rate of net return as realized in the pension benefits paid to participants, whether on an accumulation basis (defined contribution), or against a pension promise (defined benefit). It should be acknowledged that sponsors and governments have had important roles in specifying and legitimating this metric. For example, in the defined contribution universe, governments are increasingly concerned about pension 'adequacy', not just the conversion of accumulated account balances into a monthly and/or yearly pension payment. Likewise, governments are increasingly concerned about the sustainability or persistence of defined benefit pension institutions, both at the fund level and across relevant jurisdictions.

Here, we provide a set of measures and metrics of organizational performance following, in order, the building blocks underpinning our model. This framework and its building blocks are an analytical lens through which to identify key points of intervention in the management of long-term investments. At the same time, it is apparent that the building blocks making up this framework overlap and, in high-performing organizations, cohere with one another to drive superior performance. Nonetheless, some building blocks and their particular elements may be more relevant than others, depending on the type of long-term investor and its jurisdiction. As such, we offer a stylized framework, informed by our knowledge of the industry, of relevant and generalizable metrics of performance.

Care should be taken in selecting measures and associated metrics of performance, as academic evidence suggests that these data points can profoundly affect organizational behaviour. The academic and related business literature has shown that managers prioritize measures of performance that can be quantified, with significance assigned to those measures that have status across whole organizations (Lowenstein, 1996). More specifically, the relevant research on measures and metrics suggest that 'effective' metrics can sustain an organization's mission, whereas 'ineffective' metrics can deflect an organization from its purpose, or worse. Drawing on our research findings, including the particularities of the investment management industry (see also Blake and Timmerman, 2002), the venture capital industry (Doerr, 2017), and Kaplan and Norton's (1996) attempt to map the scope and complexity of large organizations via performance measures and management, we would argue that effective metrics take advantage of the following attributes of effective LTIs.

Elsewhere, we have been shown that short-term efficiency and long-term innovation are difficult to reconcile in any organization, and especially in investment organizations that are simultaneously short-term and long-term oriented (Clark and Monk, 2017). As such, chosen metrics must ensure a balance between efficiency and the never-ending search for innovation. In these ways, effective metrics for LTIs have the following attributes:

- Effective metrics are *consistent* (not in conflict) across the organization, so that the performance of the entire organization can be understood through the sum of its parts. Ineffective metrics are inconsistent, being in conflict with other parts of the organization or, indeed, in conflict with the stated goals of the organization.
- Effective metrics are *function and/or task relevant*, in that they are framed with respect to organizations' goals, objectives, and constituent functions. Ineffective metrics lack specificity, in that they empower neither the organization nor its departments.
- Effective metrics are *parsimonious and transparent*, erring on the side of simplicity and clarity, so that debate over their applicability, meaning, and relevance is minimal. Ineffective metrics are overly complex and require

interpretation both by those who perform against the metrics and those who interpret their added value.

- Effective metrics are *mutually exclusive but collectively exhaustive*, in that they are focused on key activities and resources to ensure that overlaps are minimized, and responsibilities reinforced. Ineffective metrics confuse, rather than motivate—pulling in different directions, rather than ensuring focus and accountability.
- Effective metrics are, given market risk and uncertainty, *flexible and/or adaptive*. That is, there is a process whereby metrics are adapted and revised in relation to investment experience. Ineffective metrics imprison organizations in past imperatives and missed opportunities (Clark, 2018).
- Effective metrics are *aspirational*, not just performance focused, thereby promoting the realization of long-term objectives which, in the short term, are not wholly integrated into management functions. Ineffective metrics tend to reward incremental adaptation, rather than set goals and objectives that may facilitate organizational innovation.

These types of metrics are consistent with the interests of those who directly benefit from the performance of LTIs, including beneficiaries, stakeholders, and regulators. Ineffective metrics do not connect functional or task-specific activities to the overarching purpose of an organization, and, for example, tend to prioritize current investment performance, rather than focusing on future funding levels.

Enablers, Factors, and Outputs

High-performing investment organizations are self-conscious about the value of their 'untraded and intangible assets' and seek, wherever possible, to sustain those advantages over time and space with respect to the activities that underpin long-term performance. Recognizing the distinctive properties of LTIs and financial markets, we argue the measures and metrics provided below should incorporate the distinctive advantages of LTIs over the asset management industry. These are threefold.

Time Horizon: A long-term time horizon is a key comparative advantage that LTIs have over market-based asset managers. As this implies, the metrics selected should not directly or indirectly push LTIs into a short-term posture, or force them to give up their long-term perspective. A useful metric should thus reveal the direction of travel (towards or away from a goal or objective), rather than signal that a goal or set of goals has been achieved outright (once and for all).

Idiosyncratic Advantages: Chosen metrics should not diminish investors' ability to cultivate their own unique comparative advantages. With insourcing and re-intermediation, LTIs may develop entirely new and different capabilities and resources that reflect, in part, their origins and their distinctive goals and objectives. As a result, the measures and metrics chosen by an LTI should be sensitive to their circumstances and discount the temptations of common practice. While valuable for benchmarking purposes, for asset owners to succeed they must cultivate their own comparative advantage, as is the case in many industries marked by innovation (Gertler, 2003).

Organizational Ambidexterity: Given their time horizons, LTIs need to cultivate organizational innovation and dexterity to be effective; they must avoid becoming imprisoned by the past, and learn to adapt to changing markets and the global economy (Lo, 2012). Too often, LTIs prioritize internal cost-efficiency, but ignore the unintended consequences of such an approach in terms of discounting or restricting the pace of innovation.

To be more specific, we set-out below relevant measures and metrics of performance providing a detailed account, rather than a summary or overview of topics. In doing so, we acknowledge that LTIs will likely 'pick-and-mix' from the headline issues and the specific metrics relevant to those issues. So, in a larger sense, what follows is a 'map' of options emphasizing depth as well as scope.

Organizational Enablers

METRIC 1: BOARD ENGAGEMENT: A high performing board is important to the success of an LTI. In principle, best practice boards focus on strategic issues and avoid tactical or deal-specific matters. The challenge is to ensure that the risks taken are consistent with the governance budget of an organization. This is not only an issue of the number of risk-related decisions taken over time; it is also an issue of the size and significance of those decisions, and where the board stands on these issues. Here, it is about strategy, not tactics. There are two specific ways of measuring board engagement and effectiveness:

- *Opportunities Reviewed*: It is useful to keep count of the percentage of opportunities brought to a board for review and whether or not the board can handle the complexity of the organization.
- *Delegations Utilized*: Alternatively, the focus of the board can be assessed by reviewing its delegation policy and the utilization of that policy.

METRIC 2: CULTURE: Our research indicates that LTIs measure their culture in a variety of ways, including employee surveys and focus groups. These types of qualitative assessments are important in many sectors, although employee commitment to an organization seems to vary across sectors and countries. These surveys can be used to measure the culture of investment organizations. Here are three possible measures:

- *Net Promotor Rankings*: How employees think about their organization can be assessed by asking 'Would you recommend our company to a friend or colleague?'[5]
- *Success Focused*: Through an annual survey of staff, management, and the board, an LTI can assess whether stakeholders understand what success means for the organization, for their teams, and for themselves.

- *Investment Beliefs*: Many LTIs have developed investment beliefs that seek to anchor staff thinking in a longer-term logic.

METRIC 3: TECHNOLOGY: The overwhelming view of our case study participants is that technology will play a bigger role in institutional investment in the future. As such, our respondents indicated a commitment to understanding better, and investing in, technology relevant to their organizations. In terms of measuring the perceived value of technology, there are two likely metrics:

- *Percentage of Budget*: An organization measures the percentage of resources spent on internal technology versus the fees paid to external providers.
- *Technology Satisfaction*: Similar to culture surveys, staff surveys of an LTI's technology and its utility can be very revealing.

Factors of Production

As noted above, long-term investors produce investment returns by combining enablers with capital, people, process, and information. Whereas an organization's enablers are embedded and require cultivation over the longer term, senior managers can often directly affect both the quality and the combination of the factors of production (e.g., internal versus external) in ways that enhance the performance of the organization.

METRIC 4: CAPITAL LEVERAGE: It has been shown that the size and characteristics of an organization's capital base can affect the success of its investment strategy. A larger capital base can mean advantageous fees, and contractual terms and conditions, together with the close alignment of interests with investment partners. It can also mean constraints when placing large tranches of assets. The relevant measure and metric can be summarized in the following statement:

- *Capitalizing on Capital*: At issue is the extent to which LTIs utilize their capital bases and can overcome their weaknesses related to capital base and sources. Senior managers may emphasize some issues over others in terms of asset-specific investment performance and the performance of the whole organization.

METRIC 5: PEOPLE and ORGANIZATION: Many investment organizations track human resource data to identify emerging issues with their employees in a timely fashion. Indicators include absenteeism, illness, turnover, and requests for consultation, together with anything out of the ordinary compared with normal practice.

METRIC 6: PROCESS: Successful investors align their governance budgets with their risk budgets (Clark and Urwin, 2008). Governance is a finite resource: senior managers and board members have limited time, expertise, and commitment when assessing competing issues. We suggest the following metrics on risk-governance come close to the mark:

- *In the first instance,* by reviewing the minutes of board meetings and investment committees, the amount of time used to assess and oversee investment risks (and opportunities) can be measured against the total time devoted to other agenda items.
- *In the second instance,* the resources used to oversee investment risks, including data systems, risk systems, and human resources, can be monitored against competing claims for the use of these resources. Collecting the numbers on these issues can be challenging but the process can impose discipline and focus for the Board.

METRIC 7: INFORMATION: Having the requisite information is a vital ingredient in the governance of financial institutions, enabling oversight and control of portfolio managers either internal or external to the institution. It is also critical in ensuring that technology is utilized to the fullest extent. Given Metric 4, the following issues are significant:

- Senior managers can assess data integrity by using a series of 'yes–no' questions with a higher number of 'yes' responses indicating higher data integrity. For example, is there a data governance policy in place? Is there a data sub-committee on the Board and/or investment committee? Is there a dedicated team on staff focused on data management? Is there an ethics policy as it pertains to data use, yours and others? Is there a cost–benefit framework in place for judging the value of additional data and whether it is mission critical? Each question could be equally weighted. But, strategically, senior managers could emphasize some issues in terms of the priorities of the LTI.

Intermediate Outputs

The production of a target long-term risk-adjusted rate of return also depends on the *production* and *reproduction* of an organization whose employees and modes of decision-making are consistent with realizing those return objectives. That is, the production process is based on producing and reproducing the organization *and* the rate of return simultaneously. In this section, we focus on commitment, alignment, and knowledge management.

METRIC 8: COMMITMENT: Being an LTI is a comparative advantage that most pension and sovereign funds utilize in their investing. Here, it is important to measure the extent to which the internal investment organization is committed to the long term. To summarize, consider the following metric:

- *Time Horizons*: To illustrate, we would add the 'length' of executive compensation, in years, as shown in all employees' compensation agreements and divide it by the number of employees. If employees' average compensation extends over four, or even five, years, it is reasonable to expect that the fund is taking a longer-term view. The higher the number, the more likely it is that staff members are focused on long-term goals.

METRIC 9: ALIGNMENT: Just as important is the alignment of interests between employees and their investment institution. Time serving can result in a divided and contested investment management process wherein individuals' goals and objectives trump those of the organization. Here, then, are two related metrics (see also Metric 2):

- *Goal Focused*: Survey employees to determine whether they can make a clear link between the goals of their particular department or team in relation to the over-arching goals of the organization.
- *Goal Consistency*: Using this kind of survey, senior managers could also test whether employees believe that their personal career objectives and the objectives of the organization are mutually dependent.

METRIC 10: KNOWLEDGE MANAGEMENT: Information is the lifeblood of investment management. However, information must be converted into knowledge to ensure that knowledge of specific domains and across the organization feed into the process whereby the risk-adjusted rate of return of the fund is the realization of these separate and compatible functions. Here, then, are two related metrics:

- *Knowledge Sharing*: A long-term investor is only as good as its capacity to bring together insights across different investment functions and asset classes in ways that promote a 'whole fund' perspective. The effectiveness of this process can be measured by attendance at weekly callout sessions on current issues *and* the volume of posts by employees on intranet investment forums (Clark, 2018).
- *Knowledge Quality*: A second metric could involve surveying the fund's investment professionals so as to ascertain the sources of investment insights, scoring internal sources over close relationships with external colleagues and public sources of investment news and insights.

Final Outputs

Ultimately, investors, whether short-term or long-term, are judged in terms of their investment performance. However, care should be taken not to reduce performance measures to one number. While this is commonplace in the asset management industry, LTIs often have a range of commitments that can be recognized.

METRIC 11: INVESTMENT PERFORMANCE: Here are two metrics of final performance:

- *Portfolio Health*: Some of our exemplars have indicated that they see the discount rate (or expected return target) of a pension fund as the best heuristic for understanding the health of a pension promise and the quality of the investment organization. This indicator is useful when combined with the funding ratio.
- *Cost Efficiency*: The long-term direct and indirect costs of the investment department being measured in terms of staff costs, infrastructure costs, space and running costs, and the costs of shared services (within the organization) relative to performance (as above) *and* the observed and imputed costs of outsourcing these services.

Implications and Conclusions

Long-term investors have taken greater responsibility for the end-to-end management of their assets. These funds take a long-term view and embrace their distinctive characteristics by cultivating comparative advantage in creative ways. Nonetheless, there remain challenges, including the development of relevant measures and metrics that bring together information on the performance of the elements making up the production process and the realization of long-term goals. Our objective in this chapter has been to introduce the reader to the significance of principal–agent problems in the finance industry and to provide an organizational framework for realizing these problems in ways that enhance social welfare.

To explain our framework, we have provided a stylized account of an LTI's operating model, one that is appropriate to the globally diverse community of asset owners. We have also provided a conceptualization of the inputs that LTIs utilize to achieve their (various) desired outputs, as well as the organizational enablers that allow investors to augment inputs and the ways in which they are combined. This has meant that we have reduced the complex set of industry forms and functions apparent in the investment world to a standardized production function. Based on this simple model of production, we set out quantitative ways of measuring these activities, inputs, and outputs, and offered a set of related metrics of management that capture the investment industry.

At one level, the production of investment returns is a complex and often institution-specific process embedded in the regulatory environment of specific jurisdictions. Rules and regulations matter. Nonetheless, whatever the differences among LTIs in terms of how they arrange these building blocks in accordance with local circumstances and their regulatory environment, the model presented provides a reference point applicable across a range of long-term investors, including pension funds, endowment funds, sovereign wealth funds, and the like. This model draws on insights from our research reported here and elsewhere (Clark and Monk, 2017).

The focus of this chapter has been on the mission-critical inputs and outputs identified in the model of investment management, while recognizing the effects on investment performance when LTIs manage themselves against relevant measures and metrics. Throughout, we have identified metrics that can stand the test of time: that is, measures and metrics that can be as relevant now as in five or even ten years' time, thereby providing the logic required to focus on the key building blocks of performance. Separately and together, the measures and metrics require coordination and integration with the units and systems of management that underpin LTIs. In this regard, we have sought to shape how to understand the principal–agent problems that bedevil the global financial services industry and to suggest ways in which LTIs could circumvent those problems through the effective management of their own organizations.

We have ignored metrics that are commonplace and/or pose serious problems for any LTI. For example, we have discounted return metrics such as the Sharpe Ratio and the Information Ratio. These metrics, while useful, have many problems and can be 'gamed' by smart investors using private markets or hedge funds. As such, we sought to focus our metrics on meaningful and useful predictors of long-term performance, rather than performance itself. Fundamental to this chapter and the metrics agenda is the intelligent use of measures and metrics in ways consistent with the long-term interests of institutional investors.

Whatever the metrics chosen by LTIs, successful investors spend more time thinking about what success means for their organizations and how they mobilize their factors of production to meet those success goals. Before making major investment decisions, including the framing of investment strategy for entire organizations, boards and senior managers often ask what success looks like for a decision and for their fund. They ask about the metrics that will be used to measure success, including the relevant time horizon that will be used in the measurement process. Being accountable in these ways is a necessary condition for realizing the benefits of metrics and measures of performance.

Acknowledgments

The authors wish to thank Janelle Knox-Hayes, Dane Rook, Rajiv Sharma, Roger Urwin, and Dariusz Wójcik for their continuing interest in our research programme and comments on previous drafts of this chapter. The authors are pleased to acknowledge the support of Stanford University, and members of the research consortium on financial institutions, coordinated by the Global Projects Center of the Faculty of Civil and Environmental Engineering. Support for our research on the management of investment institutions has been provided, in part, by members of the Stanford Research Consortium.

The authors remain wholly responsible for the content of this chapter and the implications drawn therefrom.

Notes

1 This comes with plenty of costs as well; see https://blog.ltse.com/the-cost-of-companies-staying-private-hits-all-of-us-f7622d1e9643
2 It is important not to exaggerate the uniqueness of an organization's heritage and to recognize that best-practice plans are about mobilizing an organization's capabilities and resources in ways that seek to transcend its past (Gans, 2016).
3 In our experience, governance and culture are relatively fixed, which means that they can become 'disablers' of innovation. Conversely, technology is changing so fast that there is a sense of inevitability to technological innovation. Many investors have turned to technology to enable innovation within their production systems not otherwise available in their management systems.
4 By way of definition, a measurement is some observable 'fact' at a given point in time, while a metric is that fact put into a specific context. In other words, measurements are data, while metrics are information. Metrics rely on measurement, just as information relies on data (Rook and Monk, 2018; van Gelderen and Monk, 2016).
5 In a similar fashion, the UK government recently (15 August 2018) required banks to publish data on the likelihood that customers would recommend their bank to"friends, relatives or other businesses'. For details, see www.gov.uk/government/news/banks-scored-on-quality-of-service

References

Ambachtsheer, K.P. (2016). *The Future of Pension Management: Integration Design, Governance, and Investing*, Hoboken, NJ: John Wiley and Sons.

Arjaliès, D-L., Grant, P., Hardie, I., MacKenzie, D. and Svetlova, E. (2017). *Chains of Finance: How Investment Management Is Shaped*, Oxford: Oxford University Press.

Arrow, K.J. (1974). *The Limits of Organization*, New York: Norton.

Barro, R.J. (2006). 'Rare disasters and asset markets in the twentieth century', *Quarterly Journal of Economics*, 121 (3): 823–866.

Bathelt, H. and Glückler, J. (2011). *The Relational Economy: Geographies of Knowing and Learning*, Oxford: Oxford University Press.

Berle, A.A. and Means, G.C. (1933). *The Modern Corporation and Private Property*, New York: Macmillan.

Blake, D. and Timmerman, A. (2002). 'Performance benchmarks for institutional investors: measuring, monitoring and modifying investment behavior'. In Knight, J. and Satchill, S. (eds) *Performance Measurement in Finance: Firms, Funds, and Managers*, Oxford: Elsevier, pp. 108–141.

Bolton, P. and Dewatripont, M. (2005). *Contract Theory*, Cambridge, MA: MIT Press.

Brennan, G., Eriksson, L., Goodin, R.E. and Southwood, N. (2014) *Explaining Norms*, Cambridge: Cambridge University Press.

Clark, G.L. (2004). 'Pension fund governance: expertise and organizational form', *Journal of Pension Economics and Finance*, 3 (2): 233–253.

Clark, G.L. (2016). 'The components of talent: company size and financial centres in the European investment management industry', *Regional Studies*, 50 (1): 168–181.

Clark, G.L. (2018). 'The culture of finance'. In Beaverstock, J., Cook, G., Johns, J., McDonald, F., and Pandit, N. (eds) *The Routledge Companion to the Geography of International Business*, London: Routledge, pp. 513–534.

Clark, G.L. and Monk, A.H.B. (2013). 'Principles and policies for in-house asset management', *Journal of Financial Perspectives*, 1 (3): 39–47

Clark, G.L. and Monk, A.H.B. (2017). *Institutional Investors in Global Markets*, Oxford: Oxford University Press.

Clark, G.L. and Monk, A.H.B. (2019). 'Asset owners, investment, and commitment: an organizational framework', *Journal of Retirement*, 6 (3): 9–22.

Clark, G.L., Thrift, N. and Tickell, A. (2004). 'Performing finance: the industry, the media, and its image', *Review of International Political Economy*, 11: 289–310.

Clark, G.L. and Urwin, R. (2008). 'Best-practice pension fund governance', *Journal of Asset Management*, 9 (1): 2–21.

Cyert, R.M. and March, J.G. (1993). *A Behavioral Theory of the Firm*, Englewood Cliffs, NJ: Wiley.

Dalio, R. (2017). *Principles: Life and Work*, New York: Simon & Schuster.

Davis, G.F. (2015). 'Editorial essay: what is organizational research for?' *Administrative Science Quarterly*, 60 (2): 179–188.

Doerr, J. (2017). *Measure What Matters*, New York: Penguin.

Dore, R. (2000). *Stock Market Capitalism: Welfare Capitalism. Japan and Germany versus the Anglo-Saxons*, Oxford: Oxford University Press.

Gans, J. (2016). *The Disruption Dilemma*, Cambridge, MA: MIT Press.

Gertler, M.S. (2003). 'Tacit knowledge and the economic geography of context or the undefinable tacitness of being (there)', *Journal of Economic Geography*, 3 (1): 75–99.

Gertler, M.S. (2010). 'Rules of the game: the place of institutions in regional economic change', *Regional Studies*, 44 (1): 1–15.

Haldane, A. and May, R.M. (2011). 'Systemic risk in banking ecosystems', *Nature*, 469 (7330): 351–355.

Hart, O. (2011). 'Thinking about the firm: a review of Daniel Spulber's The Theory of the Firm', *Journal of Economic Literature*, 49 (1): 101–113.

Helfat, C.E., Finkelstein, S., Mitchell, W., Peteraf, M.A., Singh, H., Teece, D.J. and Winter, S. (2007). *Dynamic Capabilities: Understanding Strategic Change in Organizations*, Oxford: Blackwell.

Helpman, E. (ed.) (2008). *Institutions and Economic Performance*, Cambridge, MA: Harvard University Press.

Hopt, K.J., Kanda, M., Roe, M.J., Wymeersch, E. and Prigge, S. (eds) (1998). *Comparative Corporate Governance: The State of the Art and Emerging Research*, Oxford: Oxford University Press.

Jensen, M.C. (1993). 'The modern industrial revolution, exit, and the failure of internal control systems', *Journal of Finance*, 48 (3): 831–880.

Jensen, M.C. (2000). *A Theory of the Firm: Governance, Residual Claims, and Organizational Forms*, Cambridge, MA: Harvard University Press.

Kaplan R.S. and Norton, D.P. (1996). 'Using the balanced scorecard as a strategic management system', *Harvard Business Review*, 74 (1): 75–85.

Kay, J. (2012). *The Kay Review of UK Equity Markets and Long-term Decision Making*, London: HM Government, Department for Business, Innovation and Skills.

Litterman, B. (2004). *Modern Investment Management*, New York: John Wiley.

Lowenstein, L. (1996). 'Financial transparency and corporate governance: you manage what you measure', *Columbia Law Review*, 96 (5): 1335–1362.

Lo, A. (2012). 'Adaptive markets and the new world order', *Financial Analysts Journal*, 68 (2): 18–29.

March, J. and Simon, H.A. (1958). *Organizations*, New York: John Wiley.

Merton, R.C. and Bodie, Z. (2004). 'The design of financial systems: towards a synthesis of function and structure', *Journal of Investment Management*, 3 (1): 1–23.

Monk, A.H.B. and Sharma, R. (2018). 'Organic finance: the incentives in our investment products'. In Clark, G.L., Feldman, M.P., Gertler, M.S. and Wójcik, D. (eds) *The New Oxford Handbook of Economic Geography*, Oxford: Oxford University Press.

Monk, A.H.B., Sharma, R. and Sinclair, D.L. (2017). *Reframing Finance: New Models of Long-Term Investment Management*, Stanford: Stanford University Press.

Morrison, A.D. and Wilhelm, W.J. (2007). *Investment Banking: Institutions, Politics, and Law*, Oxford: Oxford University Press.

Muller, J. Z. (2018). *The Tyranny of Metrics*, Princeton, NJ: Princeton University Press.

Pratt, J. and Zeckhauser, R. (eds) (1985). *Principals and Agents: The Structure of Business*, Boston: Harvard Business School Press.

Rook, D. and Monk, A. (2018). 'Managing knowledge management: towards an operating system for institutional investment (3 November 2018)'. Available at SSRN: https://ssrn.com/abstract=3277989 or http://dx.doi.org/10.2139/ssrn.3277989

Shiller, R.J. (2005). *Irrational Exuberance* (2nd edn), Princeton, NJ: Princeton University Press.

Shleifer, A. (1985). 'A theory of yardstick competition', *Rand Journal of Economics*, 16 (3): 319–327.

Spulber, D. (2009). *The Theory of the Firm: Microeconomics with Endogenous Entrepreneurs, Firms, Markets, and Organizations*, Cambridge: Cambridge University Press.

van Gelderen, E. and Monk, A.H.B. (2016). 'Knowledge management in asset management'. Available at http://dx.doi.org/10.2139/ssrn.2642467

Weitzman, M. (2007). 'Subjective expectations and asset-return puzzles', *American Economic Review*, 97 (4): 1102–1130.

Williams, C. and Zumbansen, P. (eds) (2011). *The Embedded Firm: Corporate Governance, Labor, and Finance Capitalism*, Cambridge: Cambridge University Press.

Williamson, O.E. (1996). *The Mechanisms of Governance*, Oxford: Oxford University Press.

13

KNOWLEDGE, EXPERIENCE, AND FINANCIAL DECISION-MAKING

Gordon L. Clark

One way of mapping twenty-first-century capitalism is to focus on the knowledge economy (Stiglitz and Greenwald, 2014). Since knowledge has value when it is 'sticky', economists and geographers have sought to understand the evolution of the economic landscape by reference to the spatial differentiation and concentration of knowledge. So, for example, it is arguable that Silicon Valley was made and is reproduced time and again by agents and organizations seeking to take advantage of their proximity to local knowledge. At one level, knowledge can be prosaic or sophisticated: it is often difficult, if not impossible, to separate one from the other. At another level, knowledge is both a stock and a flow. If knowledge can be commodified and sold, being close to centres of innovation is likely to be less important than the *process* of making knowledge at the interface between experience, organizations, and markets (see Clark (2018), on the governance and regulation of financial management).

In his seminal contribution to the economic geography of the knowledge economy, Gertler (2003), drawing on Polanyi (1944), and Nelson and Winter (1982), among others, distinguished between codified and tacit knowledge. In brief, he suggested that knowledge can be formalized and communicated through organizations, norms, and conventions, and/or routines. As such, codified knowledge can be transferred to others within a locality and across localities in ways that reap the benefits of common access, although the 'transfer rate' is fundamentally affected by the social context in which knowledge is produced. This issue has received considerable attention in economics and geography (see, e.g., Levitt and List, 2013). Gertler (2001) also argues that tacit knowledge is, by definition, not easily acquired or transferred over space and time; there is a premium to be had in managing the production and distribution of tacit knowledge in time and space.

These issues are important for this chapter, even if its focus is on individual financial decision-making rather than groups of people in organizations and/or industry and regional complexes. Here, I consider how people use knowledge to make informed decisions for themselves and their households, *and* the relationship between codified and tacit knowledge as found in experience and learning by doing. So far, this sounds familiar. However, the import of the distinction between codified and tacit knowledge has not always been recognized in other fields of scholarship. For example, the financial literacy movement relies on a set of questions designed to test whether respondents, whatever their region or nation of residence, have a level of financial literacy consistent with effective decision-making in financial markets and about financial products (Lusardi and Mitchell, 2011, 2014). Often missing in this account is appropriate recognition of the ways in which people actually make decisions when reliant on everyday practice. In fact, financial literacy (codified knowledge) is proffered as a means of bypassing everyday practice (tacit knowledge) in favour of an informed and (more) rational consumer of financial products and services.

It is commonly assumed that a high level of financial literacy allows agents to discount the pernicious effects of experience—that is, the rules of thumb or heuristics that agents develop over time in response to their particular circumstances and the exigencies of the moment.[1] In the next section of this chapter, I explain the costs and benefits of formal conceptions of financial literacy, as well as the assumptions made about the stability of the concepts found in test regimes. Note, however, that I do not dispute the importance of financial literacy. Being an effective financial decision-maker can have immediate and long-term pay-offs for those seeking to enhance their earned incomes and long-term welfare (Clark et al., 2012). To think otherwise would be to miss one of the defining characteristics of lived-life in Western economies. At issue is whether the test regime and what it represents is fit for purpose.

Economic geographers often dispute the relevance of universal conceptions of knowledge, as opposed to embodied and/or embedded conceptions of knowledge (Bathelt and Glückler, 2011; Grabher, 1993). This is an attractive way of representing the issue. Even so, little attention has been devoted to competence—not so much about *what* individuals know as it is about *how* they make decisions in the context of risk and uncertainty. This argument is developed in the section 'Decision-Making in Financial Markets' of this chapter, in which I focus on the process of decision-making. In the section 'Experience and Behavior', the issue of experience and behaviour is considered, bringing to bear the lessons of the behavioural revolution for understanding the virtues or otherwise of learning by doing. These threads are brought together in the section 'Mapping Financial Risk', which deals with the governance and regulation of financial risk across different segments of society. In conclusion, implications are drawn for the status of experience and learning by doing.

There is a long tradition in economic geography of a concern for behavioural issues, especially with regard to how people cope with and adapt to various kinds of risk—see, for example, Golledge et al. (1972), Webber (1972), and Wolpert (1980). Here, my argument is informed by research on financial decision-making that intersects with contemporary behavioural psychology and cognitive science (see Clark et al., 2012). Behavioural psychology and cognitive science have raised profound issues about how to understand rationality and the role that context plays in decision-making (Henrich et al., 2005). These issues are of concern to the human sciences, and for economics and human geography, in particular (Ainslie, 2001; Strauss, 2008, 2009). We should acknowledge, however, a rising tide of criticism about the use of behaviouralism informed by cognitive science and its methods of research in economics and geography (see Levitt and List, 2007; Pykett, 2013).

Financial Services and Financial Literacy

The growth of the global financial services industry is the subject of academic research inside and outside economic geography (see, e.g., Wójcik, 2013). For some analysts, it is, first and foremost, an Anglo-American phenomenon (Boyer, 2000). For others, it is the product of globalization and economic growth, together with the search for value in even remote corners of the world (Bernanke et al., 2011). In this respect, the global financial services industry is the intermediary between the growing volume of savings around the world, and the deployment of those assets for productive and not-so-productive uses. There is a lively debate about the value of intermediation in general and with respect to consumer welfare (see Diamond, 1984; Judge, 2015).

Financial Services and Consumers

The global financial services industry consists of more than banking institutions and financial markets linked together in spatially extensive networks of transactions. It is also an industry that reaches through to the consumer, although the extent to which individual consumers are caught up in financial intermediation depends on national institutions and regulation (Preda, 2009). In the Anglo-American world, three interlocking forces have conspired to insert 'financialization' into everyday life (Langley, 2008). Here, these forces are briefly described, recognizing that there is a significant body of literature on each within and without economic geography.[2]

Deregulation. The rationale behind the deregulation of financial markets in the 1980s and 1990s has been widely documented (Morrison and Wilhelm, 2007). Closely connected was the deregulation of financial service providers and products, especially banking services, credit, home mortgages, insurance, mutual funds, and pension saving and retirement products. The extension of credit has been especially significant, taking in areas such as the purchase of consumer products, as well as short-term loans designed to bridge shortfalls in income with consumer spending. Increased competition and innovation through deregulation were expected to spread financial products and services to so-called 'underserved' communities. Nonetheless, consumers have struggled to distinguish between cost-effective products and 'lemons', in part because providers often seek to conceal the negative attributes of products (Akerlof, 1970; Gabaix and Laibson, 2006).

Rational self-interest. Underpinning the deregulation of financial markets was an assumption that rational self-interest was sufficient to justify light-touch regulation. Some critics argue that this was a 'cover' allowing for exploitative practices to flourish on both sides of the market. Even so, it was given legitimacy by theoretical developments in the social sciences that presupposed that any assumption other than a strong version of rational self-interest would be a mistake in theory and practice. Game theory, rational expectations, and efficient markets were bound together in a compelling intellectual agenda (Axelrod, 1984). Counterclaims developed in behavioural psychology and cognitive science (Kahneman and Tversky, 1979; Tversky and Kahneman, 1974) gained little traction until waves of 'irrational exuberance' prompted re-evaluation of their plausibility (Shiller, 2005).

Debt and leverage. One result of deregulation and the presumption in favour of agent rationality was the extension of credit and related financial products to segments of society that had previously found it difficult to access these facilities. On one side of the market, consumers were encouraged to take on debt despite the increasing volatility in capital and labour markets. On the other side of the market, consumer debt was commodified by aggregating consumers' forward commitments into bundles of traded securities. In effect, consumers were subject to less scrutiny of their forward commitments, while institutions holding consumer commitments were able to pass through these commitments to the market. Risk-sharing between institutions discounted the need to monitor consumer commitments and allowed market participants to leverage their positions until the system failed (Clark, 2011).

Financial Literacy

In the aftermath of the global financial crisis, each element or factor underpinning the spread of financial services has been subject to close scrutiny. For example, the virtues of deregulation have been counter-posed by the apparent welfare costs of market failure. Likewise, the idea that risk-sharing between financial institutions would be sufficient to cover the higher frequency of consumer default in some segments of the population was found wanting when these risks morphed into systemic threats to the integrity of the financial system (Haldane and May, 2011). Various solutions have been proffered, including tighter regulation of financial institutions with regard to their capacity to weather systemic shocks.

It has also been suggested that knowledgeable consumers—combined with greater scrutiny by lending organizations of the capacity of consumers to deal with the volatility of financial and labour markets—could help rein-in indebtedness and leverage. Here, though, two issues have had to be confronted. The first concerns what counts as financial literacy, which has obvious implications for the design of programmes and policies relevant to those most at risk of taking on unsustainable financial debt and leverage. The second issue is just as obvious—identifying patterns of financial literacy within and across societies, thereby providing policy-makers with the means to target financial literacy programmes to those who need this type of knowledge so as to be more effective participants in the financial services industry.

In its simplest form, financial literacy was conceived in terms of individuals' understanding of a select group of fundamental financial concepts. These concepts are important in their own right and are representative of a broad set of financial concepts which, taken together, could improve financial decision-making across a set of topics and issues relevant to many individuals and their households whatever their incomes (Hung et al., 2009). These concepts have been taken up by multilateral organizations such as the OECD, and there have been extensive surveys done within and across countries in terms of their applicability (Lusardi and Mitchel, 2011; Lusardi et al., 2011).

The financial literacy programme can be summarized in three test questions. The first tests whether respondents understand the benefits of compounding; the second tests whether respondents understand the difference between the real and nominal value of money; and the third tests whether respondents understand the concept of diversification. These questions have a number of virtues. Respondents either know or do not know the answer. The first two questions are amenable to a quick back-of-the envelope calculation using simple arithmetic. And, these questions can be translated into different languages, making appropriate adjustments for local currencies.

Question 1 goes as follows: 'Suppose you had US$100 in a savings account and the interest rate was 2% per year. After five years, how much do you think you would have in the account if you left the money to grow?' The answer options provided to the respondents include: 'More than US$102', 'Exactly US$102', 'Less than US$102', or 'Not sure/don't know'. The correct answer is 'More than US$102'. The second question goes as follows: 'Imagine that the interest rate on your savings account was 1% per year and inflation was 2% per year. After one year, how much would you be able to buy with the money in this account?' The answer options provided to respondents include 'More than today', 'The same as today', 'Less than today', or 'Not sure/don't know'. The correct answer is 'Less than today'. The third question is: 'Do you think that the following statement is true or false? 'Buying a single company stock usually provides a safer return than an investment fund containing multiple stocks." The answer options provided include 'True', 'False', or 'Not sure/don't know'. The answer is 'False'.

Survey results based on these questions are revealing (Lusardi and Mitchell, 2011). Country of residence matters, reflecting differences between countries in terms of their levels of economic development, the exposure of residents to financial institutions and markets for relevant financial products and services, and the mix of public and private responsibility for social welfare. In some countries, there are regional variations in survey results distinguishing, for example, between southern Italy and the Third Italy, between eastern and western Germany, and between southern and northern England. Likewise, there are differences between respondents located in major metropolitan regions, as opposed to provincial cities, and there are differences between individuals taking into account their age, family circumstances, gender, income, and experience (Innocenti et al., 2019).

Decision-Making in Financial Markets

Tests of financial literacy presuppose that financial decision-making involves the application of well-defined rules to the world at large. As such, each rule or principle provides an off-the-shelf solution to a related problem. Together, these rules and the related rulebooks of financial decision-making are deemed applicable across a broad range of topics in consumer finance.

Financial Markets and Products

Consumers go to financial markets and purchase financial products for many reasons. Relevant to this discussion, the global financial services industry provides three interrelated functions. Note, there are various ways of explaining the significance of these functions and/or products, including those that link functions to institutions (Crane et al., 1995), and those that situate functions within theories of financial market performance (Merton and Bodie, 2004). To simplify, assume our representative agent would like to purchase a home by means of a down-payment and mortgage. This 'simple case' entails significant issues related to the governance and regulation of consumer welfare:

- In the first instance, a mortgage is a means of making a forward commitment to purchase an asset through current and expected earned income. In effect, the mortgage issuer provides the needed capital at the time the house is purchased in exchange for the consumer's commitment to pay off the loan in regular instalments at a set or variable price over time.
- In the second instance, a mortgage contract is a means of allocating risk between the consumer and the provider of finance. In some countries, consumers can obtain a mortgage at a fixed interest rate over a set period of time. In these circumstances, the provider bears the risks associated with unexpected changes (increases) in interest rates—not surprisingly, the provider may well offset those risks by selling on the mortgage contract to other parties more willing and/or able to bear the risk. In other countries, the consumer bears the interest rate risk—therefore, the consumer must

make forward estimates of their ability to cope with increased interest rates given expected commitments. On the other side of the market, the provider assesses the risk of default should the consumer be unable to cope with unanticipated increases in mortgage costs.

- In the third instance, financial markets provide participants with opportunities to adapt or adjust to changing circumstances, so that neither party is locked into a commitment that turns out to be inconsistent with future circumstances. So, for example, the sale of a house normally involves the completion of a mortgage contract subject to certain conditions regarding the costs of pay-off and/or transfer of the obligation. At issue is the degree to which consumers can adapt to changing circumstances against commitments, and the degree to which the providers of credit are able to accommodate changes in the consumers' circumstances.

Risk and uncertainty can be tamed through the convergence of individuals and institutions on best practice with regard to the optimal allocation of roles and responsibilities. However, financial markets are subject to exogenous shocks that disturb behavioural norms and conventions in unanticipated ways (Weitzman, 2007). As such, learning by doing can be misleading, inconsistent in effect, and produce winners and losers when one side dominates the other. Whereas 'light-touch' regulation was the operative logic underpinning government regulation of financial markets and products leading up to the global financial crisis of 2007–8, reform has sought to rebalance the governance and regulation of the allocation of financial risk in the United States and in other OECD countries.

Making Financial Decisions

A book of decision rules or financial principles may be insufficient for the average consumer as an effective guide for purchasing financial products. In that regard, Elizabeth Warren's Consumer Finance Protection Bureau was a step towards regulating risk and governing the relationship between product producers and consumers. However, behavioural psychologists and cognitive scientists would go further and argue that *how* people make decisions is just as important as the substance of those decisions. Specifically, and with respect to the types of decision consumers take in relation to the purchase of financial products, three issues affect individual and collective welfare—how people make decisions in time, how they assess risk, and how they adapt to changing circumstances.

These types of issues are at the core of the judgement and decision-making paradigm (Lewis, 2017). Initiated by Simon (1956), Tversky and Kahneman (1974), and Kahneman and Tversky (1979), it has been shown that people tend to discount the future and attribute more value to the immediate future and much less to the distant future. Put slightly differently, many people give precedence to options that have an immediate or slightly delayed pay-off over those that would have pay-offs distributed far into the future (Ainslie, 2001). At the same time, when comparing the discount functions of younger people with older people who have experience in financial markets, it has been shown that younger people not only discount the future, but also often have incoherent conceptions of time. By contrast, those with relevant experience tend to have shallower discount functions and give more weight to the distant future relative to the short and medium terms (Clark et al., 2007).[3]

Just as significant have been experimental findings to the effect that many people are risk averse and make financial decisions that overweight the costs of risk-taking in relation to the benefits of risk-taking in relation to long-term welfare. The implications are twofold. First, being risk averse can result in consumers making suboptimal decisions by paying a premium for the non-risk option, despite a low likelihood of a negative result. Second, being risk averse can encourage consumers to switch commitments as they encounter new options (not previously available) at a lower risk. Having encountered outcomes where taking a risk incurs a penalty, consumers may switch to other options that promise a certain, but lower, return. Either way, the transaction costs involved in switching and re-switching may be so significant that long-term welfare is adversely affected.

The behavioural programme has also shown that many people have difficulty making forward estimates of the likelihood of certain events.[4] Their understanding of the principles of probability is often poor; they have little understanding of different kinds of probability distributions; and they tend to over-value the significance of current events in relation to the distribution of past events. Whereas standard decision theory assumes that individuals use Bayes' rule when attributing value to the current manifestation of a larger process, many people over emphasize the present, ignore instances of the past that are inconsistent with current preferences, and attribute to themselves a level of control over the outcomes of past decisions not justified by the evidence (Jones and Love, 2011; Oaksford and Chater, 2009).

These behavioural biases are representative of a much broader set of behavioural anomalies (Kahneman, 2003; Krueger and Funder, 2004). As such, the findings of the behavioural revolution have reinforced the importance of *how* people make financial decisions as against focusing on the rules of modern financial theory and practice. Financial literacy is, for many people, less important than how they cope with a changing world using heuristics that can be self-defeating, or prone to error. Whereas it could be argued that financial literacy is less about the substance of decision-making and more about promoting disciplined and informed decision-making, in these circumstances it is reasonable to ask whether most people, most of the time, simply should not carry these responsibilities.

Experience and Behaviour

It has been suggested that the rules that embody codified knowledge are insufficient for effective financial decision-making. It has also been argued that behavioural traits affect the process of financial decision-making especially in the context of risk and uncertainty. In these ways, my argument joins cognition (the acquisition and application of knowledge) and context (the setting in which decisions are framed and implemented). These two issues are often treated separately; however, they are fundamentally entwined in the sense that cognition is always embedded in context (Simon, 1956).

Experience: Learning by Doing

The financial literacy programme is also a recipe for public policy in that, if individuals' knowledge can be deepened in relation to a broad class of financial issues, then social welfare will (presumably) be advanced. As is the case across the social sciences, it is assumed that education contributes to the formation of human capital which, itself, is a prerequisite for long-term economic development (Lucas, 2009). Nonetheless, there remains debate about whether education drives economic development, or is the product of economic development.

On the other side of the argument is the notion that knowledge is a dynamic process in which the stock of knowledge is forever being applied and re-conceived through experience. Put slightly differently, at any point in time the stock of knowledge summarizes what has been inherited from the past and adapted to the present in relation to the future. So, for example, the notion that financial risk is best managed through a diversified portfolio of investments reflects the principles of modern portfolio theory (Markowitz, 1952) and the experience of many investors over the period leading up to the global financial crisis (French et al., 2010). Through the financial crisis, however, it became apparent that these principles were ineffective because the risks of different asset classes became highly correlated, thus discounting the benefits of diversification.

The importance attributed to experience is owed to economic and social theorists, including Arrow (1962) and Polanyi (1944), and has become one of the foundations of contemporary economic geography (Bathelt and Glückler, 2011; Gertler, 2003). Given the importance attributed to experience, it is reasonable to suggest that the ontological status of the discipline is owed, in part, to its focus on geographically anchored learning by doing. To illustrate, in Clark (2014) it is shown that the principles of financial literacy are only given life when implemented at the local level, thereby demonstrating the relevance or otherwise of certain principles, as well as the ways in which these principles are adapted in the light of experience. Experience suggests that, notwithstanding the three principles that dominate the test regime, other principles may be important, including having a viable set of options given the shifting boundary between noise and signal in financial markets (Scheinkman, 2014).

Experience and learning by doing at the local level are nested in processes and institutions found at the local, regional, national, and international scales. For example, the current and expected value of a house and the value of a mortgage are determined, in part, by the demand and supply of housing at the regional and national levels. While we do not directly experience the national market for housing, many people attribute to the local level the largest portion of house value (Clark, 2012). The rules governing individuals' eligibility for a mortgage are typically set by provincial, national, and even supra-national regulatory institutions. The effects of these rules can be observed directly, but not the process through which the rules are set, implemented, and changed. As the global financial crisis demonstrated, the process determining the value of housing and the price of a mortgage can be global in scope.

Two implications ensue: first, experience can be direct and indirect. Being direct, experience can involve making an estimate of the current and expected price of a house and a mortgage (subject to repayment schedules and termination conditions) given local conditions. As people buy and sell houses, as they search for and switch between providers of credit, and as they experience changes in the current and expected price of the houses they purchase, they may well become adept at finding value and reaping the benefits of their decision-making. Equally, people may over-estimate the significance of experience, given the importance of financial markets and processes operating 'above' local experience. At best, many people have only indirect 'experience' of these types of processes.

Second, as a result, experience and learning by doing may be reinforced or confounded by unobserved processes operating at higher tiers of the economy.[5] People may not always appreciate, until an event takes place, the connection between the value of their house and the cost of the mortgage they have assumed in relation to the performance of global financial markets. Inevitably, learning by doing lags behind events and forces individuals to react against past decisions, often reinforcing status quo bias (Samuelson and Zeckhauser, 1988).

Limits of Learning by Doing

The simplest stylized model of learning by doing goes as follows: a plan is made to realize an intended outcome sometime in the future; past experience and current circumstances inform the design of the plan and the likelihood of realizing the intended outcome; and, as new information is received, expectations are revised and the plan and/or the intended outcome are revised accordingly. If the environment is unstable, is subject to stochastic shocks that disturb the underlying distribution of the costs and benefits of alternatives courses of action, and always goes forward rather than repeating events and outcomes time and again, then risk and uncertainty become endemic to the planning process.[6]

One response may be to shorten the planning horizon. Another may be to limit commitments to the future so as not to impair people's options should events conspire to derail the best-laid plans. The focus of the behavioural psychology and cognitive science literature is on the adverse effects of risk and uncertainty on decision-making, thus demonstrating, for example, that people may systematically exclude options that are accompanied by possible losses should plans not be realized (Kahneman and Tversky, 1979). Should decision rules fail, procrastination is a likely result (O'Donoghue and Rabin, 1999).

Heuristics enable agents to 'tame,' if not 'neutralize', the effects of cognitive biases and anomalies. Baron (2008: 53) cites Polya (1945) in suggesting that heuristics are a form of reasoning that is partial and provisional, used to 'discover' what works and what does not work when solving a particular problem. Gigerenzer et al. (1999: 30) go further to suggest that heuristics are devices designed to deal with new issues and/or shifts in the underlying structure of the environment. For Gigerenzer and his colleagues (1999: 30), heuristics rely on inference to produce 'fast and frugal' solutions to problems. In a similar manner, Stanovich (2010: 128) refers to heuristics as a form of cognitive processing that 'is fast, automatic, computationally inexpensive, and that does not engage in extensive analysis of all possibilities'.

By this account, learning by doing has virtue, even if it is unlikely to result in optimal outcomes. It is, by definition, partial and incremental and, as such, likely to result in solutions that are 'good enough' for the moment (Tversky and Kahneman, 1974). However, heuristic reasoning has shortcomings. First, by imposing limits on the relevant options, individuals can reinforce the status quo (Samuelson and Zeckhauser, 1988). Second, when people select options close at hand, they are likely to reinforce past commitments and make decisions anchored in commitments.[7] Third, being a recursive process, there is no stopping rule other than the cognitive resources of the individual (Baron, 2008).

Mapping Financial Risk

Individual decision-making in the context of financial risk and uncertainty has implications for how behaviour is conceptualized and modelled in economics and in economic geography (Clark et al., 2012; Laibson, 1997). However, this is not the complete story, in that the social sciences are also concerned with the relationship between individuals and institutions, and the ways in which those relationships result in variable maps of behaviour and social welfare.

Financial Literacy (again)

When tests of financial literacy are applied around the world, it is apparent that there are considerable variations between and within countries in terms of respondent performance. For example, there are striking differences between the performances of respondents from southern Italy and the Third Italy. Likewise, there are significant differences between Germany, the United Kingdom and the United States, despite the heterogeneity of the US test results, which take respondents' age, gender, race, earned income, and educational attainment into account (Lusardi and Mitchell, 2011). Importantly, it has been shown that test scores are higher in major metropolitan regions than they are in provincial cities.

Moreover, there are differences between and within countries in the use and relevance of financial instruments and products such as credit cards, home mortgages, retail investment products such as mutual funds, and various kinds of insurance. In this regard, when comparing Germany with other European countries, particularly the United Kingdom, it has been noted that the average German household is less involved in the financial services industry. Many German households do not hold credit cards and have few ways of accessing short-term credit. Furthermore, it is quite remarkable that, until recently, holders of workplace sponsored Reister pension funds were guaranteed a minimum rate of return on their defined contribution pension accounts. Whether because of public policy, cultural attitudes to risk, and/or relationships between social partners, there is a highly differentiated map of risk exposure.

As such, observed patterns of financial literacy could be the result of: (i) the level of economic and financial development of the jurisdiction, and/or (ii) the exposure of residents to financial products and services. To the extent that the sophistication of a country's financial system is a prerequisite for economic development and that the financial sectors of most countries are concentrated in major metropolitan regions, it follows that residents' financial literacy reflect these processes. On the other hand, it could be that variable rates of financial literacy within and between countries reflect the options that are and are not available to residents. For example, in some countries, residents' pension funds are protected from the costs of financial turmoil, whereas in other countries this is not the case.

One implication is that German households have *not* had to acquire the same level of financial literacy as Anglo-American households. Another is that, because high-earning Anglo-American households often hold large defined contribution account balances, it makes sense that their risk exposure is matched by higher than average rates of financial literacy. Yet another implication is that sub-cultures of risk-avoidance and risk-taking exist in many OECD countries, which means that people's economic statuses and prospects reinforce their behavioural predispositions and preferences. This works to the detriment of those who are only 'just coping', as opposed to those who are willing and able to take advantage of the benefits accruing to their place in society (Payne, 2017).

Institutions and Individual Choice

The implication is that public and private institutions set the nature and scope of the risks that individuals face when seeking access to certain kinds of financial services *and* that they frame the desirability of the options available within and between different types of financial services. Put slightly differently, institutions can affect behaviour by virtue of the risks associated with various types of financial services, and the advantages and disadvantages of the choices available to market participants. Inevitably, there is an intimate relationship between financial literacy and institutional structure. To illustrate, consider how various countries deliver certain functions—in the simplest, case credit facilities, and, in the more complex case, retirement income.

Consumer credit. In some countries, those in the lowest one-third of earned income have difficulty accessing short-term credit. As a consequence, they are vulnerable to companies that provide short-term credit in advance of wages on an extortionate basis. There are various explanations for this phenomenon. In some cases, lower-income earners are excluded from the formal banking system by virtue of the multiple forms of identity required to open a bank account, required minimum account balances, and harsh penalties for being overdrawn. In other cases, where residents are able to establish their legal status, they are entitled to a bank account by virtue of government regulation. Here, however, establishing a line of credit can be difficult, given requirements to maintain a minimum account balance. Illegal immigrants, limited-term residents, and residents with poor language skills can be excluded from these types of credit facilities.

For the sake of simplicity, let us assume two types of people: one type that can meet the terms required for a bank account and credit, and the other that cannot. It is obvious that the former faces lower costs when accessing credit facilities and has a broader set of options than the latter. Those excluded from the formal banking system by virtue of their identity and/or status also face much higher risks in the labour market, both in terms of the volatility of employment and the probability of being systematically exploited (McDowell et al., 2008, 2009). These patterns illustrate the argument that the design of institutions and the regulation of financial service providers can systematically discount risks, and reinforce economic and social advantage for certain types of people while disadvantaging others. The evidence suggests that the first group scores well on financial literacy and the second group does not.

Saving for retirement. Lessons drawn from the behavioural revolution have been applied to the design and management of countries' pension systems (Cronqvist and Thaler, 2004; Thaler and Benartzi, 2005). Consider the following issues. First, because many people tend to discount the future, they may simply ignore the importance of the topic. Second, because many people are myopic, they may overweight current consumption as opposed to future consumption. Third, because some people are confident of their capacity to adapt to future circumstances, they may simply put off planning for the future, assuming that when they 'get there' adjustments can be made to secure an adequate retirement income. As a result, individuals and their dependants face significant long-term risks to their economic well-being. Insofar as some people are effective long-term planners and others are not, the inevitable result is increasing income inequality.

Many nation-states once offered retirement income guarantees through their own schemes and/or private arrangements. Few countries now willingly assume such long-term risks. Employers have likewise sought to avoid these risks. One response has been to encourage people to save for the future through tax concessions and benefits. Another has been to require employers to provide retirement savings vehicles *and* to require employees to participate in them. Yet another response has been to set mandatory contribution rates *and* to regulate the costs and benefits of retirement savings instruments. Notice, however, that the long-term risks associated with saving for retirement are systematically and unevenly distributed. To the extent that these schemes are tied to current and future earned income, those at risk of periods of unemployment, of variable earned incomes, and of early retirement are likely to have much lower retirement incomes than those already well-positioned in the labour market (Weil, 2014).

These risks are well-known. At the same time, there is little research into the systematic processes that, in effect, allocate more risk to some types of people than to others. A lack of knowledge about the issues, an inability to make effective financial decisions over the long term, and an inability to affect the design and incentive structure underpinning a country's pension system reinforce the risks borne by some people more than others while privileging some groups over others. Ironically, those who score well in financial literacy tests are privileged groups of retirement planners, whereas those who do not are those exposed to high levels of risk in terms of their future welfare. The allocation of risk, and its imposition through public policy and market processes, is as much a moral as a political issue, albeit hidden behind the rhetoric of choice and self-actualization (Oberdiek, 2017).

Economic geographers are keenly aware of these issues; witness research on the demand for credit in poorer UK metropolitan neighbourhoods, and the ways in which residents' beliefs and expectations frame their responsiveness to loan sharks (Leyshon et al., 2004, 2006). Nonetheless, it has taken a Nobel Prize winner in finance to state the obvious:

> investors differ in geographic location, homeownership, profession, and so forth. We term these aspects an individual's *position*. If two people have different positions, they may wish to hold different portfolios. Similarly, people may have different feelings about risk, present versus future gratification, and so on. We term these an individual's *preferences*. Differences in preferences will lead investors to choose different portfolios
>
> (Sharpe, 2007: 11).

Implications and Conclusions

The field of economic geography brings together a variety of disciplines, with each seeking, in its own terms, a mode of explanation that can make sense of spatial diversity in the face of the processes driving spatial homogeneity. One response to reconciling diversity with higher levels of abstraction has been to invoke a set of economic principles that stand for laws or regularities that operate everywhere and at every time. As described, this appears a grandiose and empirically unjustified analytical move, implausible because of its breadth and unifying logic. Sophisticated analysts are conscious of 'difference' whether found in cultural, institutional, and/or socio-political systems (Rodrik, 2013). Furthermore, at every turn, economic development is path-dependent, rather than driven by universal axioms that are expressed the same way in every place.

Nonetheless, this approach can be found in standard treatments of regional economic growth. For example, there is an argument to the effect that, in a world of integrated capital and labour markets, the demand and supply of both factors of production will equilibrate in such a way that the economic landscape that emerges is an optimal surface of economic activity and social welfare (Barro and Sala-I-Martin, 1995). Here is both a macroeconomic and a microeconomic logic. The macroeconomics are obvious. Perhaps less obvious are the microeconomic assumptions, notably that agents' beliefs and expectations about how the world works and their place in it knit together knowledge of the principles of market structure and performance (at one scale) and their own experience (at another scale). In other words, this is a world of rational expectations.

Various objections have been made to this argument. Some analysts cut against assumptions made about the spatial efficiency of capital and labour markets. Some analysts invoke an uneven surface of information and the costs involved in searching for information consistent with realizing optimal outcomes. Some foreground institutional variety, suggesting that any presumption in favour of spatial economic homogeneity flies in the face of institutional difference and the long-term evolution of economic systems (Boschma and Martin, 2010). More specifically, economic geographers have focused on the geographical foundations of economic growth and development, emphasizing the acquisition and deployment of knowledge and, hence, the differentiation of the economic landscape. The microeconomics of spatial heterogeneity are expressed in experience and learning by doing, and sustain the argument that spatial differentiation is produced and reproduced across the world.

Here, I have suggested a rather different approach to the issue. I began with the principles of financial literacy, which were used to represent axioms or statements about how financial markets work and the appropriate behavioural responses. Although we can debate whether these principles are an adequate empirical representation of the contemporary world, we can also juxtapose their abstract nature with the agents' decision-making competence. As such, we are able to focus on the causes of observed mismatches between principles and practice, and can interrogate arguments to the effect that the implementation of abstract principles, such as financial literacy, depends on acquiring and utilizing the appropriate information to bridge the gulf between the local and the global.

It is also noted that behavioural research suggests that people are selective in terms of their use of past experience in relation to current circumstances and expectations of the future. Fiedler and Juslin (2012, 8) note that 'the information provided by the social and physical environment can be highly selective as a function of spatial and temporal constraints, social distance, control restrictions, or variable density of stimulus events'. They also go on to observe that '(n)ot only does environmental input vary quantitatively in terms of the density or amount of detail; it is also biased toward cultural habits, conversational norms, redundancy, and specific physical stimulus properties'.

This is obvious in the urban realm of many developed economies, as evident in the spatial segmentation of living and working, and is expressed in various ways—for example, a significant portion of the working population is excluded from well-regulated banking and related credit organizations (Leyshon et al., 2006). Many people are taken advantage of by well-placed individuals and organizations using the asymmetrical distribution of information in time and space to garner rents from their actions. At the heart of this chapter, moreover, is an argument to the effect that, for many people, experience and learning by doing produces beliefs and expectations that are either self-defeating, or are so imperfect when measured against the principles of effective decision-making that their long-term welfare is adversely affected.

One way of explaining the adverse consequences of experience and learning by doing is to suggest that people, if left to themselves, either collect the wrong kind of information, are excluded from information relevant to their interests, or are unable to collect the type of information needed to make effective financial decisions. This is either because they lack the sophistication and/or the appropriate third-party reference points that could help in matching experience and learning by doing with how the world works. At this level, it is an issue of sampling—that is, individuals are 'partial' in terms of the nature and scope of information they select from the environment. For some theorists, this is not particularly problematic, in that there may be 'solutions' at hand, including the provision of information from a third party and the institutional interventions that, at a local level, mediate the relationship between the producers and consumers of financial information.

It is apparent that financial literacy programmes designed for middle-class consumers with access to banking institutions and consumer credit do not resonate with those at the margins of labour markets and housing markets (Clark, 2014). More problematic is the fact that behavioural psychologists and cognitive scientists show that selection is not (just) an issue of circumstances, but is a profoundly important human trait in that people *always* sample their action-spaces. Some circumstances may be sufficiently rich in the pre-processing and organization of information that the costs and consequences of sampling are discounted in favour of the average consumer. In other circumstances, not so rich in social resources, the average financial consumer is left to his or her own devices.

The contrast to be drawn is between a vision of strong rationality, which underpins universal conceptions of financial literacy *across* time and space, and the circumstantial logic underpinning the observed behaviour of people *in* time and space. On one hand, it is assumed that, given appropriate knowledge of financial principles, people can make sense of their own circumstances and select the information needed to make informed decisions consistent with their welfare and the welfare of others. On the other hand, it is believed that people begin from their own circumstances, and select information from what is immediately available and consistent with their beliefs and expectations, even if inconsistent with their notional long-term best interests. The contrast to be drawn is between so-called rational expectations and bounded rationality, wherein the latter is understood as an issue of cognition and behavioural predisposition, not just limited information (Doherty, 2003).

Whereas behavioural research in economics has focused on the inconsistency of preferences over time, the discounting of future commitments and the apparent inability of many people to place themselves and their interests into the future, the economic geography implicit in the behavioural revolution has been largely ignored. And yet, embedded in many tests of reasoning and the formation of beliefs and expectations is a presumption, which many behavioural psychologists and cognitive scientists share, that experience and learning by doing are almost always local. Bringing these issues to the front and centre through the medium of economic geography is one way of understanding behaviour in context.

Acknowledgements

This work was supported by Zürich Insurance and the Oxford research programme on financial literacy and insurance. In that respect, I have benefited from the insights and expertise of my colleagues, including Stefania Innocenti, Sarah McGill, and Noel Whiteside. I am also pleased to acknowledge the support of colleagues—notably, Harald Bathelt, Meric Gertler, Maryann Feldman—and Dariusz Wójcik and Janelle Knox-Hayes, for comments on previous drafts of this chapter. The late John C. Marshall gave generously his knowledge of behavioural psychology and cognitive science. None of the above should be held responsible for the views and opinions expressed herein.

Notes

1 A generation ago, there was considerable debate over the presumption in favour of a strong version agent rationality wherein analysts sought to show that supposed instances of irrationality were, in fact, expressions of a certain kind of rationality (Becker and Murphy, 1988). Following Simon (1956), in this chapter it is assumed that agents are intentionally rational, albeit subject to behavioural traits that may discount their interests in certain circumstances.

2 Analysts tend to wrap these forces together with other expressions of what is termed 'neoliberalism' (see Springer et al., 2016). Whether this is justified by the evidence is subject to dispute; see Rodrik (2013), on the continuing significance of the nation-state, and Storper (2016) and Weller and O'Neill (2014), on the challenges involved in demonstrating the significance of the concept.

3 There are few studies of adults with roles and responsibilities demanding a level of expertise consistent with the domain in which they make decisions. In part, lack of research on these issues reflects academics' ease of access to students. It also reflects an interest in sustaining a common research programme across the behavioural sciences via the test of 'universal' subjects (Fiedler and Juslin, 2012).

4 Throughout, I refer to the average person, rather than all people—or, for that matter, those with relevant skills and expertise. It is the 'average' person who is the object of public policy (Atkinson, 2008), initiatives such as 'nudge' (Thaler and Sunstein, 2008), and attempts to equip people with better financial advice (Thoresen Review, 2008).

5 The problem of spatial scale is twofold. When people look beyond the local to the global, they must select and assimilate yet more information. At the same time, there is an issue of salience: deciding what is relevant given a lack of knowledge and understanding of higher-scale economic and political processes (Bordalo et al., 2012). With cognitive and resource constraints, people tend to overweight the local over the global. See Schneider and Barnes (2003) and, on the issue of framing inflation expectations, see Shafir et al. (1997).

6 The importance or otherwise of events in people's lives for decision-making deserves greater attention. Elsewhere, we show that certain types of events that have the potential to affect individuals' long-term health and welfare, and trump all other considerations, including their knowledge and understanding of financial concepts and modes of reasoning (see Clark et al., 2012).

7 Faced with a volume of relevant information larger than their capacity to assimilate and process, people use various strategies, including sampling, to select information that approximates to their needs. See Caplin et al. (2011), who take insights developed by Spence (1976) and others on the economics of information, and adapt the underlying logic of this school of thought to the contingent nature of reasoning favoured by behavioural theorists.

References

Ainslie, G. (2001). *Breakdown of Will*, Cambridge: Cambridge University Press.

Akerlof, M. (1970). 'The market for lemons: quality uncertainty and market mechanisms', *Quarterly Journal of Economics*, 84: 488–500.

Aragones, E., Gilboa, I., Postlewaite, A., and Schmeidler, D. (2005). 'Fact-free learning', *American Economic Review*, 95: 1355–1368.

Arrow, K.J. (1962). 'The economic implications of learning by doing', *Review of Economic Studies*, 29.3: 155–173.

Atkinson, A. (2008). *Evidence of Impact: An Overview of Financial Education Evaluations*, Consumer Research Report 68. London: Financial Services Authority.

Axelrod, R. (1984). *The Evolution of Cooperation*, New York: Basic Books.

Baron, J. (2008). *Thinking and Deciding*, 4th edn, Cambridge: Cambridge University Press.

Barro, R., and Sala-I-Martin, X. (1995). *Economic Growth*, New York: McGraw-Hill.

Bathelt, H., and Glückler, J. (2011). *The Relational Economy: Geographies of Knowing and Learning*, Oxford: Oxford University Press.

Bathelt, H., and Glückler, J. (2014). 'Institutional change in economic geography', *Progress in Human Geography*, 38.3: 340–363.

Becker, G.S., and Murphy, K.M. (1988). 'A theory of rational addiction', *Journal of Political Economy*, 96.4: 675–700.

Bernanke, B.S., Bertaut, C., DeMarco, L.P., and Kamin, S. (2011). 'International Capital Flows and the Returns to Safe Assets in the United States, 2003–2007', International Finance Discussion Papers 1014. Washington, DC: Board of Governors of the Federal Reserve System.

Boschma, R., and Martin, R. (eds.) (2010). *The Handbook of Evolutionary Economic Geography*, Cheltenham: Edward Elgar.

Bordalo, P., Gennaioli, N., and Shleifer, A. (2012). 'Salience theory of choice under risk', *Quarterly Journal of Economics*, 126.3: 1243–1285.

Boyer, R. (2000). 'Is a finance-led growth regime a viable alternative to Fordism? A preliminary analysis', *Economy and Society*, 29.1: 111–145.

Brennan, G., Eriksson, L., Goodin, R.E., and Southwood, N. (2014). *Explaining Norms*, Oxford: Oxford University Press.

Caplin, A., Dean, M., and Martin, D. (2011). 'Search and satisficing', *American Economic Review*, 101.7: 2899–2922.

Clark, G.L. (2011). 'Myopia and the global financial crisis: context-specific reasoning, market structure, and institutional governance', *Dialogues in Human Geography*, 1.1: 4–25.

Clark, G.L. (2012). 'Property or pensions?' *Environment and Planning A*, 44.5: 1185–1199.

Clark, G.L. (2013). 'Mapping financial literacy: cognition and the environment', *Geografiska Annaler B: Human Geograph*, 95.2: 131–145.

Clark, G.L. (2014). 'Roepke Lecture in Economic Geography: financial literacy in context', *Economic Geography*, 90.1: 1–23.

Clark, G.L., Strauss, K., and Knox-Hayes, J. (2012). *Saving for Retirement: Intention, Context, and Behaviour*, Oxford: Oxford University Press.

Crane, D.B., Froot, K.A., Mason, S.P., Perold, A.A., Merton, R.C., Bodie, Z., Sirri, E.R., and Tufano, P. (eds.) (1995). *The Global Financial System: A Functional Perspective*, Boston: Harvard Business School.

Cronqvist, H., and Thaler, R. (2004). 'Design choices in privatized social-security systems: learning from the Swedish experience', *American Economic Review*, 94.2: 424–428.

Diamond, D. (1984). 'Financial intermediation and delegated monitoring', *Review of Economic Studies*, 51.3: 393–414.

Doherty, M.E. (2003). 'Optimists, pessimists, and realists', in *Emerging Perspectives on Judgement and Decision Research*, edited by Schneider, S.L. and Shanteau, J. (pp. 643–679), Cambridge: Cambridge University Press.

Fiedler, K., and Juslin, P. (2012). 'Taking the interface between mind and environment seriously', in *Information Sampling and Adaptive Cognition*, edited by Fiedler, K. and Juslin, P. (pp. 3–29), Cambridge: Cambridge University Press.

French, K.R., Baily, M.N., Campbell, J.Y., Cochrane, J.H., Diamond, D.W., Duffie, D., Kashyap, A.K., Mishkin, F.S., Rajan, R.G., Scharfstein, D.S., Shiller, R.J., Shin, H.S., Slaughter, M.J., Stein, J.C., and Stulz, R.M. (2010). *The Squam Lake Report: Fixing the Financial System*, Princeton: Princeton University Press.

Gabaix, X., and Laibson, D. (2006). 'Shrouded attributes, consumer myopia, and information suppression in competitive markets', *Quarterly Journal of Economics*, 121.2: 505–540.

Gertler, M.S. (2001). 'Best practice? Geography, learning and the institutional limits to strong convergence', *Journal of Economic Geography*, 1.1: 5–26.

Gertler, M.S. (2003). 'Tacit knowledge and the economic geography of context, or the undefinable tacitness of being (there)', *Journal of Economic Geography*, 3.1: 75–99.

Gigerenzer, G., Todd, P.M., and the ABC Research Group. (1999). *Simple Heuristics that Make Us Smart*, New York: Oxford University Press.

Golledge, R., Brown, L.A., and Williamson, F. (1972). 'Behavioural approaches in geography: an overview', *Australian Geographer*, 12.1: 59–79.

Grabher, G. ed. (1993). *The Embedded Firm: On the Socioeconomics of Industrial Networks*, London: Routledge.

Greif, A. (2006). *Institutions and the Path to the Modern Economy: Lessons from Medieval Trade*, Cambridge: Cambridge University Press.

Haldane, A., and May, R. (2011). 'Systemic risk in banking systems', *Nature*, 469.7330: 351–355.

Henrich, J., Boyd, R., Bowles, S., Camerer, C., Fehr, E., Gintis, H., McElreath, R., Alvard, M., Barr, A., Ensminger, J., Smith Henrich, N., Hill, K., Gil-White, F., Gurven, M., Marlowe, F.W., Patton, J.Q., and Tracer, D. (2005). "Economic man' in a cross-cultural perspective: behavioural experiments in 15 small-scale societies', *Behavioral and Brain Sciences*, 28.6: 795–815.

Hogarth, R.M. (2001). *Educating Intuition*, Chicago: University of Chicago Press.

Hung, A.A., Meijer, E., Mihaly, K., and Yoong, J.K. (2009). '*Building Up, Speeding Down: Financial Literacy, Retirement Savings Management, and Decumulation*, Working Paper WR-712. Los Angeles: Rand Corporation.

Innocenti, S., Clark, G.L., McGill, S., and Cuñado, J. (2019). 'The effect of past health events on intentions to purchase insurance: Evidence from 11 countries', *Journal of Economic Psychology*, 74: 102204.

Jones, M., and Love, B.C. (2011). 'Bayesian fundamentalism or enlightenment? On the explanatory status and theoretical contributions of Bayesian models of cognition', *Behavioural and Brain Sciences*, 34.4: 169–187; 215–231.

Judge, K. (2015). 'Intermediary influence', *University of Chicago Law Review*, 82:573–642.

Kahneman, D. (2003). 'Maps of bounded rationality: psychology for behavioural economics', *American Economic Review*, 93(5): 1449–1475.

Kahneman, D., and Tversky, A. (1979). 'Prospect theory: an analysis of decision under risk', *Econometrica*, 47.2: 263–291.

Krueger, J.I., and Funder, D.C. (2004). 'Towards a balanced social psychology: causes, consequences, and cures for the problem-seeking approach to social behavior and cognition', *Behavioral and Brain Sciences*, 27.3: 313–328.

Laibson, D. (1997). 'Golden eggs and hyperbolic discounting', *Quarterly Journal of Economics*, 62: 443–477.

Langley, P. (2008). *The Everyday Life of Global Finance: Saving and Borrowing in Anglo-America*, Oxford: Oxford University Press.

Levitt, S.D., and List, J.A. (2013). 'Toward an understanding of learning by doing: evidence from an automobile assembly plant', *Journal of Political Economy*, 121.4: 643–681.

Leyshon, A., Burton, D., Knights, D., Alferoff, C., and Signoretta, P. (2004). 'Towards an ecology of retail financial services: understanding the persistence of door-to-door credit and insurance providers', *Environment and Planning A*, 36.4: 625–645.

Leyshon, A., Burton, D., Knights, D., Alferoff, C., and Signoretta, P. (2006). 'Walking with moneylenders: the ecology of the UK home-collected credit industry', *Urban Studies*, 43.1: 161–186.

Lucas, R.E. (2009). 'Ideas and growth', *Economica*, 76.4: 1–19.

Lusardi, A., and Mitchell, O.S. (2011). 'Financial literacy around the world: an overview', *Journal of Pension Economics and Finance*, 10.4: 497–508.

Lusardi, A., and Mitchell, O.S. (2014). 'The economic importance of financial literacy: theory and evidence', *Journal of Economic Literature*, 52.1: 5–44.

Lusardi, A., Schneider, D.J., and Tufano, P. (2011). *Financially Fragile Households: Evidence and Implications*, WPG 17072, Cambridge, MA: National Bureau of Economic Research.

McDowell, L., Batnitzky, A., and Dyer, S. (2008). 'Internationalization and the spaces of temporary labour: the global assembly of a local workforce', *British Journal of Industrial Relations*, 46.4: 750–770.

McDowell, L., Batnitzky, A., and Dyer, S. (2009). 'Precarious work and economic migration: emerging immigrant divisions of labour in Greater London's service sector', *International Journal of Urban and Regional Research*, 33.1: 3–25.

Markowitz, H. (1952). 'Portfolio selection', *Journal of Finance*, 7.1: 77–91.

Merton, R.C., and Bodie, Z. (2004). 'The design of financial systems: towards a synthesis of function and structure', *Journal of Investment Management*, 3.1: 1–23.

Morrison, A.D., and Wilhelm, W.J. (2007). *Investment Banking: Institutions, Politics, and Law*, Oxford: Oxford University Press.

Nelson, R.R., and Winter, S. (1982). *An Evolutionary Theory of Economic Change*, Cambridge, MA: Harvard University Press.

O'Donoghue, T., and Rabin, M. (1999). 'Doing it now or later', *American Economic Review*, 89.1: 103–124.

Oaksford, M., and Chater, N. (2009). 'Précis of Bayesian rationality: the probabilistic approach to human reasoning', *Behavioural and Brain Sciences*, 32.1: 69–84.

Oberdiek, J. (2017). *Imposing Risk: A Normative Framework*, Oxford: Oxford University Press.

Payne, K. (2017). *The Broken Ladder*, New York: Viking.

Polanyi, K. (1944). *The Great Transformation*, New York: Farrar & Rinehart.

Polya, G. (1945). *How to Solve It: A New Aspect of Mathematical Method*, Princeton: Princeton University Press.

Preda, A. (2009). *Framing Finance: The Boundaries of Markets and Modern Capitalism*, Chicago: University of Chicago Press.

Pykett, J. (2013). 'Neurocapitalism and the new neuros: using neuroeconomics, behavioural economics and picoeconomics for public policy', *Journal of Economic Geography*, 13.5: 845–869.

Rodrik, D. (2013). 'Roepke Lecture in Economic Geography: who needs the nation-state?' *Economic Geography*, 89.1: 1–19.

Samuelson, W.A., and Zeckhauser, R. (1988). 'Status quo bias in decision making', *Journal of Risk and Uncertainty*, 1.1: 7–59.

Schneider, S.L., and Barnes, M.D. (2003). 'What do people really want? Goals and context in decision making', in *Emerging Perspectives on Judgment and Decision Research*, edited by Scheider, S.L. and Shanteau, J. (pp. 394–427), Cambridge: Cambridge University Press.

Schick, F. (1997). *Making Choices: A Recasting of Decision Theory*, Cambridge: Cambridge University Press.

Sedlmeier, P., and Gigerenzer, G. (2001). 'Teaching Bayesian reasoning in less than two hours', *Journal of Experimental Psychology: General*, 130.3: 380–400.

Shafir, E., Diamond, P., and Tversky, A. (1997). 'Money illusion', *Quarterly Journal of Economics*, 112.2: 341–374.

Sharpe, W.F. (2007). *Investors and Markets: Portfolio Choices, Asset Prices, and Investment Advice*, Princeton: Princeton University Press.

Scheinkman, J.A. (2014). *Speculation, Trading, and Bubbles*, New York: Columbia University Press.

Shiller, R. (2005). *Irrational Exuberance*, 2nd edn, Princeton: Princeton University Press.

Simon, H.A. (1956). 'Rational choice and the structure of the environment', *Psychological Review*, 63.2: 129–138.

Spence, A.M. (1976). 'Symposium: the economics of information', *Quarterly Journal of Economics*, 90.4: 591–597.

Springer, S., Birch, K., and MacLeavy, J. (2016). 'An introduction to neoliberalism', in *The Handbook of Neoliberalism*, edited by Springer, S., Birch, K., and MacLeavy, J. (pp. 1–14), London: Routledge.

Stanovich, K.E. (2010). *Decision Making and Rationality in the Modern World*, Oxford: Oxford University Press.

Stiglitz, J.E., and Greenwald, B.C. (2014). *Creating a Learning Society*, New York: Columbia University Press.

Storper, M.J. (1993). *The Geography of Conventions: Territorial Proximity, Frameworks of Action, and Economic Competitiveness*, Los Angeles: University of California.

Storper, M.J. (2016). 'The neoliberal city as idea and reality', *Territory, Politics, Governance*, 4.2: 241–263.

Strauss, K. (2008). 'Re-engaging with rationality in economic geography: behavioural approaches and the importance of context in decision-making', *Journal of Economic Geography*, 8: 137–156.

Strauss, K. (2009). 'Cognition, context, and multi-method approaches to economic decision making', *Environment and Planning A*, 41.2: 302–317.

Thaler, R.H., and Benartzi, S. (2005). 'Save more tomorrow: using behavioral economics to increase employee savings', *Journal of Political Economy*, 112.1: 164–187.

Thaler, R., and Sunstein, C. (2008). *Nudge: Improving Decisions about Health, Wealth and Happiness*, New Haven, CT: Yale University Press.

Thoresen Review (2008). *Generic Financial Advice*, Final Report, London: HM Treasury.

Tversky, A., and Kahneman, D. (1974). 'Judgement under uncertainty: heuristics and biases', *Science*, 185.4157: 1124–1131.

Webber, M.J. (1972). *Impact of Uncertainty on Location*, Canberra: Australian National University Press.

Weil, D. (2014). *The Fissured Workplace: Why Work Became So Bad for So Many and What Can Be Done to Improve It*, Cambridge, MA: Harvard University Press.

Weitzman, M. (2007). 'Subjective expectations and asset-return puzzles', *American Economic Review*, 97.4: 1102–1130.

Weller, S., and O'Neill, P. (2014). 'An argument with neoliberalism: Australia's place in a global imaginary', *Dialogues in Human Geography*, 4.2: 105–130.

Wójcik, D. (2013). 'Where governance fails: advanced business services and the offshore world', *Progress in Human Geography*, 37.3: 330–347.

Wolpert, J. (1980). 'The dignity of risk', *Transactions, Institute of British Geographers*, 5.4: 391–401.

14
HOUSEHOLD FINANCE

Christopher Harker and Johnna Montgomerie

Introduction

In this chapter, we argue that geographical approaches make clear how crucial the household is for understanding finance and financialization. We outline how geographical approaches have positioned households as distinct but interconnected financial spaces. In so doing, we argue that the household has been understood in three overlapping ways. The first is the household as a scale; the second is the household as a node in networked relations; third, the household as a place of and for lived experience. Many geographies of household finance cited in this chapter advance multiple spatial perspectives at once, sharing concerns about agency and power. They demonstrate that households and household finances vary geographically and historically. They also understand the household as a space through and in which political, economic, social, cultural, and ecological power relations become knotted and potentially transformed. In other words, the household can become a location or a conceptual lens through which to critically understand and change geographies of finance. We show how such a lens works in relation to austerity in Anglo-America. We argue in conclusion that financial geographies of the household provide a specific way of framing socio-economic changes that, in turn, provides crucial insights about the ways in which incorporation/exclusion, power/resistance, and divergence/difference operate to produce and reproduce the global financial system. Geographical approaches to household finance make visible new hierarchies and inequalities in the distribution and redistribution of gains and losses from financialization.

The Household and Finance: Bridging the Divide

Finance has long been something associated with particular spaces of global capitalism, the steel and glass of global financial centres connected in a web of what become 'global' cities (Sassen, 1991; Graham and Marvin, 2001). As the economic centre of gravity has shifted from the postwar Keynesian 'productive economy' to the present-day financial economy (Froud and Williams, 2002; Krippner, 2005), financial geographies have foregrounded the spatial dynamics constituted by flows of money, people, and goods that make up the global political economy, and the places that co-constitute these flows. A critical geographical perspective further explores how the inequalities that emerge from such circulations lead to the active exclusion of particular people (e.g., women, indigenous peoples: see de Goede, 2005; Bourne et al., 2018) and places (e.g., Greece, Hungary: see Blyth, 2013; Pósfai et al., 2017). This is a double exclusion, both from the wealth created by global financialization, and from many academic accounts of finance and financialization. Financialization is used in this chapter 'to describe a host of structural changes in the advanced political economies' that share a common evaluation of how global finance has altered the underlying logics of economic activity, as well as the workings of democratic society (Van der Zwan, 2014: 99). However, accounts of financialization that focus on markets, cities, and states often exclude the household. In doing so, they miss how power and agency operate in the context of 'the financialization of everyday life' (Van der Zwan, 2014: 100). The household is key for many capitalist processes and the political, economic, and social struggles that surround them. Consequently, it is a crucial site for doing critical geographies of finance, not least because geographies of household finance are never just limited to the household.

How can we begin to account for the space of the household in finance? French et al. (2011) argue that the household is not simply a spatial container of financialized capitalism but, rather, a site that participates in the growing integration of the international and domestic financial systems, retail, and global financial markets. Finance connects everyday life and global financial markets through specific apertures of integration. 'Constitutive ecologies' of financial regulation, practices, and knowledges that produce subjectivities in different places, result in uneven geographies of connection and disparate material outcomes (French et al., 2011: 812). While the architecture of global finance works towards homogenous structures, institutions, and norms, everyday life unfolds in idiosyncratic and heterogenous ways. This, in turn, presents challenges for processes of financial connection and integration.

Methodologically, we can begin to approach the architecture of integration through a basic accounting framework: credits and debits, assets and liabilities. The balance sheet is a specific social technology (de Goede, 2005). Methods of accounting standardize economic activity (Joseph, 2014). Modes of accounting create, sustain, or transform the social relations of everyday life.

Thus, the balance sheet is a powerful tool because it is a common register for making visible the household, the firm, the nation-state to be valued and evaluated. Feminist economics provides a rich empirical basis for understanding how methods of counting and accounting are foundational to understanding gendered forms of economic inequality. *If Women Counted*, Marilyn Waring's (1989) ground-breaking critique of the system of national accounts, details how the processes of measurement and valuation of work that takes place in households, such as women's unpaid work and care responsibilities, remain invisible in the current system of calculating national wealth. Domestic work conducted by women is classified as 'non-producer' and, as such, cannot expect to gain from the distribution of benefits that flow from economic production. Therefore, public policy derived from the national accounts framework will tend to ignore over half the population (Waring, 2015: 12) because it is blind to economic activities of the household that occur beyond the production boundary. Economic analyses remain blind to the household as the 'domestic sphere' for reasons that are 'partly substantive ('no exchange takes place'), ('there is no value attached'), and partly technical ('how could it be measured?')' (Hoskyns and Rai, 2007: 301). The exclusion of the domestic sphere has enabled understandings of finance as a practice associated primarily with markets, corporations, and states. However, accounts that treat the household as a sphere of non-economic activity cannot explain why financialization as a macroeconomic regime is so dependent on residential mortgages and consumer demand (e.g., household consumption is 70% of GDP in financialized economies). Conceptual and methodological exclusions of the household map onto, and are produced through, clear conceptual boundaries between the public and private spheres, between production (where paid labour produces things) and consumption (where wages buy goods and services), and between a monetary economy and a non-monetary economy.

Geographical thinking transgresses the conceptual boundaries imposed by conventional economic approaches. Drawing on the feminist literature on 'the household', which is too extensive to be fully summarized in this short chapter, we build a picture of household finances in relation to unfolding financialization. Informed by feminist economists' engagement with women's unpaid (and uncounted) work in the home and low-paid work in labour markets (Waring, 1989; Elson and Cagatay, 2000; Himmelweit, 2002), feminist political economy's articulation of the unvalued labour of social reproduction (Bakker, 2007; Steans and Tepe, 2010; Elias and Rai, 2019), and feminist geographers' conceptualization of the unseen power relations in the political construction of scale/space where the household is the sphere of social reproduction and consumption (Katz, 2001; Marston, 2008; Massey, 2013), we argue that the household is a key conceptual lens for financial geography.

The household makes visible how daily life constitutes financialization as a macroeconomic regime. The heterogeneity of socio-cultural dynamics therein is relevant for understanding how and why different groups within society can participate in and benefit from financialization, and others cannot. The household foregrounds relationality (not the rationality of the unitary economic actor) between its members. It is not simply a decision-making unit. The actions, reactions, and inactions of different subjects within the household inform the distribution of resources and, thus, enactments of financialization. We understand the household as a conceptually complex, empirically heterogeneous, and politically contested space. Building on critical geographical scholarship in this area, this chapter argues that there are three geographical concepts through which household finance can be understood: *scale, networked relation*, and *place*. When deployed, these concepts often overlap. Collectively, they position the household as a key lens for analysing the inequalities and power hierarchies at play in the unfolding of financialization. Making visible the mundane everyday activities of financial management and paying attention to the complexity of socio-cultural dynamics within the household fuels a critical geographical approach to finance that seeks not only to understand the world, but also to change it. It draws our attention to the power and agency of households themselves, how they shape their financial lives (albeit not under conditions of their own choosing), and the potential for alternative practices. In developing our argument, we acknowledge the close association between household, house, home, and family. There are important differences between these concepts, and occasionally we overstep the boundaries between them in ways that may make some readers uncomfortable. We do so in order to build an expansive case for the importance of feminist and post-colonial approaches to studying geographies of finance.

Household as Scale

Geographers have argued for a number of decades that scale is not 'a pre-ordained hierarchical framework for ordering the world—local, regional, national and global. It is instead a contingent outcome of the tensions that exist between structural forces and the practices of human agents' (Marston, 2000: 220). This understanding of space has been very useful not only because it connects the household—thought about as local, in scalar terms—with financial practices operating at other scales, but also because it helps foreground the power relations through which households are positioned (i.e., marginalized) with hierarchical geographies of finance. A scalar perspective demonstrates how intersections between the household and the monetary economy can be observed in geographies of money (income/savings, wealth/capital, credit/debt), people (urbanization and migration), and goods and services (monetary circuits of production and consumption) within the global political economy. The household becomes, at once, the localized site for capitalist accumulation and, simultaneously, a space that impacts regional, national, and global processes.

In Anglo-American contexts, scale makes visible how financialization has been built on debt burdens accumulated by residential mortgages to access housing, student loans to access education, lines of credit (or payday loans) as a safety net, and a plethora of bank and non-bank consumer credit products for consumption and automobile purchases. These debts are the feedstock for global financial markets, as interest revenue is securitized to become a long chain of ownership claims on interest income from household debt (Leyshon and Thrift, 2007; Montgomerie, 2009). These interest payments, in turn, represent income claims by pension funds and institutional investors in search of yield from debt-based products (see Fichtner, 2019). Fixed-income debt securities that originate as loans to households are a lucrative profit centre for the financial sector precisely because of the extent to which household finance has become integrated into global finance. In other words, the household produces finance at a global scale. It is also produced as a local scale by finance, as the structuring forces of debt within global markets bear down on the contingent and heterogenous practices of the human agency collectivized in the household.

The household is also produced by and productive of national scales, as financialized processes are intimately connected with state policies that have supported social (asset-based) welfare. Financial geographies of welfare capitalism draw on a multi-scalar frame to explain the ways in which global finance markets integrate into public policy efforts to retrench social security provision by dismantling the 'welfare state' (Montgomerie, 2013; Soederberg, 2014). In Anglo-America, public policy supports a debt-led macroeconomic growth regime, as financial market de-regulation has supported credit-fuelled asset appreciation. For households, these changes have materialized as residential housing booms and busts, as households desire secure shelter and a long-term, low-risk savings vehicle. While residential mortgages bolster aggregate demand as house prices increase, homeowners have used mortgages to convert equity into cash to fuel consumption and national economic growth. Debt-led growth has also opened up the possibility for households to engage credit-leveraged investments. A central example is home-equity loans (HELs), as households extract future anticipated asset gains or collateral from their home. This is another way in which the heterogenous and hierarchical processes of the household are integrated into global financial circuits. As such, common-sense understandings of residential housing as a safe asset ('safe as houses') is contingent on the swings and roundabouts of global financial markets (Doling and Ronald, 2010). Some households will benefit from asset-based welfare ('my house is my pension'), but others will lose out, or be excluded all together. Housing-based welfare has become a dominant source of long-term savings for households in Anglo-America, but also a source of cash to fuel consumption that shores up aggregate demand. Consequently, property prices become the bellwether of personal/household financial well-being and national economic vitality. The mutual dependence of people on secure housing and shelter, of banks on securing profit by issuing mortgage loans, and of national governments on privatizing welfare costs has created a situation where indebtedness is the root of savings, investment, and growth, connecting the national aggregate to the local scale and practices of everyday life.

As financialization makes global markets more vulnerable to the losses incurred from flash-crashes, downturns, and corporate scandals, market crises and systemic crises are simply 'downloaded' onto the average retail investor, or the household (Bryan, 2010; Engelen et al., 2011). Since the 1990s, a clear pattern has emerged in economies of the Global North. As financialization has intensified, it has brought a boom, bust, bail-out, austerity cycle. Policy responses have evolved from targeted bail-outs (Brady Bonds) in the early 1980s, to interest rate cuts as a whole market bail-out (2001), to unconventional monetary policy (quantitative easing) in Japan in the late 1990s and in Anglo-America and Europe since 2008. This culminates in the present-day afterlife of the global financial crisis—negative real interest rates and unconventional monetary policy have intensified inequality and secular stagnation (the long-term condition of negligible or no growth). At the scale of the household, secular stagnation becomes a product of vulnerability to financial markets volatility. Mian and Sufi (2014) explain how residential mortgages create systemic financial risks, and Green and Lavery (2015) detail how a 'regressive recovery' led by quantitative easing monetary measures translates into wealth gains only for the top 5% of households. It is thus a driver of inequality that underpins stagnation. The capacity of most households to use financial markets for wealth gains has become increasingly constrained. Initially, interest bearing savings accounts were decimated by low interest rates (cutting off a source of risk-free liquid savings for households), at the same time quantitative easing contributes to the declining long-term profitability of pension investments (due to downward pressure on government bond yields). Thus, scale makes visible the structural forces that act on the household. This opens up a space to consider how stratification and hierarchies within and across households produce clear patterns of wealth gains at the top end of the distribution, variability in middle-income groups, and losses for households at the bottom of the income and wealth distribution.

Scalar approaches thus make visible how financialization has perpetuated long-standing structural inequalities between social classes and genders, and along racial and ethnic lines (Roberts, 2013; Fields, 2015; García-Lamarca and Kaika, 2016). For example, recent mapping of household debt in Canada by Simone and Walks (2019) makes a compelling argument that the urban geographies of housing in Canada's three largest cities can be explained through the differential access recent transnational migrants have to debt. Such households can purchase housing through easy access to credit, something enabled and justified through nation-building federalist policies. This results in those households shouldering disproportionately high levels of private debt, which the authors suggest underpins an asset-based welfare system supporting predominantly older, white Canadians. The household scale is something that is produced differently in particular times and places. Thus, in the detailed study by

Stenning et al. (2010) of two neighbourhoods in Kraków, Poland, and Bratislava, Slovakia, the post-socialist transition provides the most important frame for understanding everyday household financial practices. The move from a socialist economy to a market economy after 1989 resulted in widespread changes to work, housing and property, and family life, manifesting increases in poverty and inequality. The authors argue that access to international banking and financial services must be seen alongside a multiplicity of practices of lending and borrowing, that combine the old and the new, the formal and the informal, the global and the local (c.f. Durst, 2016). Scalar perspectives foreground the difference that geography makes to thinking household finance.

Scalar geographies of household finance beyond Euro-America also show how finance itself differs geographically. Most notable in this regard is the extensive work on microfinance, a means through which millions of households in the Global South are connected to increasingly global forms of capital (Roy, 2012; Kar, 2018). As a popular panacea for development and poverty reduction—particularly for women—state and international institutions have promoted the growth of this industry globally. This is underpinned by a belief that entrepreneurial subjects will create their own forms of economic development, although in practice such finance is often used for building and reproducing households (Rankin, 2001; Elyachar, 2002). Given the global and national legibility of microfinance projects, comparison across scales has become part of the practices of microfinance itself (Roy, 2012). Lenders compare the riskiness of borrowers in different countries, while borrowers compare different loans as part of a wider repertoire of financial strategies to make do (Kar and Schuster, 2016: 348). Such studies also articulate with research on consumer credit in Anglo-American contexts, which has argued that households lower down the income distribution use small-scale consumer debts to participate in economic life (Montgomerie, 2009; Gibbons, 2014). While a small market by relative size, consumer credit is important because it integrates households that are not portfolio investors or homeowners directly into the global financial system. As microfinance has been swept up, and, to a certain extent, superseded by broader financial inclusion initiatives that promote new forms of financial technology (FinTech) as a development panacea (Gabor and Brooks, 2017; Mader, 2018), new methods of linking local households and global markets are proliferating across the Global South.

The Household as Networked Relation

Building on arguments for a non-scalar geography (Marston et al., 2005), there have been growing numbers of studies that examine households as a node or point in the broader relational network of finance. Such an approach seeks to challenge the hierarchies of scale and advance a flat ontological approach. Households are positioned—ontologically—alongside other spaces of finance, rather than 'below', or at the margins. Crucially, such an approach does not, and should not, be understood as ignoring hierarchies of power. One of the leading proponents of this perspective, Doreen Massey (2005), suggests that all flat ontologies are premised on differential politics of connectivity. In other words, the relationship between what we think of as the local and the global are premised on 'power geometries', in which some spaces are better connected (and thus global), while others are less connected and even abandoned. Crucially, relations constitute nodal points or places in the network as much as those sites, in turn, construct the relations between them.

Households, understood as a networked geography, are highly differentiated places through which the global political economy is produced. The practices within and relations between and across households, in turn, constitute the very stuff of finance. The work by Langley (2006, 2008a) on everyday borrowing and saving in Anglo-America provides one of the most authoritative examples of this approach. Using Actor Network Theory, he demonstrates how 'global' finance is a distributed network of practices that largely relies on household practices of middle-class subjects. In his account, pensions, ISAs, and mortgages are not simply disembodied economic objects, but everyday practices located in suburban spaces. 'Homeowners' and 'savers'—subjects that are, in turn, produced through a more extensive set of discursive practices—become the key means through which financial products and markets are, quite literally, constituted (see also Lai, 2017). Such work very much prefigured the subprime crisis, in which the failure of borrowers to repay debts resulted in a global financial crisis—thought about as a rippling of failure through spatially distributed networks of finance (Langley, 2008b).

Approaches to finance as networked geographies have also demonstrated how households themselves are refigured through their broader relational ties. The household has become a space of financial calculation and speculation that requires new kinds of domestic labour tied to practices such as credit scoring. There are clear gender dimensions to such processes, or what Allon (2014) terms the 'feminisation of finance', as women are folded into financial markets through increased access to mortgage credit and positioned as autonomous, entrepreneurial subjects. The study of digital debt management by Stanley et al. (2016) demonstrates how networked relations between household debtors are increasingly important means for debtors to cope with the practices of credit collection.

Allen and Pryke's (2013) important work on the financialization of water infrastructure in the United Kingdom also shows how the materiality of the household (and the necessity for humans to have access to water) becomes a key site for financial profit generation. This work not only foregrounds how the household is co-constituted through the non-human, but also introduces the spatial figure of topology (see also Langley, forthcoming). Building on the flat ontological assumptions underpinning networked conceptions of finance, topology seeks to understand spatial relations beyond those that have presence in geometric (topographic) space. In their account of water, the investment firm Macquarie—ostensibly an Australian investment firm—become proximate to, and even part of, millions of households in Southern England who pay their bills to Thames Water. Harker's (2017) ethnography of debt in Ramallah deploys a topological approach to show how households fold family and social relations elsewhere into the growth of finance under Israeli Occupation. Topological spacings of debt are co-constituted by particular topographies (or networks) of mobility, bounding, place, and distribution (Harker, 2017: 601). Thus, the household is an intensive site in which relations between bodies, institutions, and colonial practices co-constitute practices of debt and indebtedness. This approach draws on Allen's (2011: 284) argument that:

> [p]ower relationships are not so much positioned in space or extended across it, as compose the spaces of which they are a part. Distanciated ties and real-time connections are not understood as lines on a map which cut across territories, but rather as intensive relationships which create the distances between powerful and not so powerful actors.

The stretching of the household finance beyond the material confines of its physical form is a key geographical insight emerging from networked and topological approaches. For instance, Kirwan (2019) uses topology to understand how household finances expand to, and enfold, the space of the debt advice office. Moodie's (2013) study of Kiva.org demonstrates how this lending platform creates virtual (colonial) forms of kinship between households in the Global North and South. The stretching of the household has particularly been emphasized in relation to mobile practices. For instance, practices of migration stretch everyday financial practices across nation-state borders, through both debts owed in multiple locations and remittances sent back to points of origin (Pratt, 2004; Datta and Aznar, 2019). These geographies build on the concept of global householding, Peterson's (2010: 271) account of how many households transgress national boundaries 'through transborder marriages, overseas education, labor migration, and war displacements'. If the household has 'gone global' (Elias and Gunawardana, 2013), then it is often relationships of care that connect households across borders (Pratt, 2004). Once again, gender is crucial in understanding such geographies, since it is largely women from the Global South who migrate to perform acts of care for households predominantly in the Global North (Ehrenreich and Hochschild, 2003), creating remittance economies that are distinctly colonial (Guermond and Samba, 2018). The act of embodied care provided by transnational migrants to wealthy and middle-class citizens of nation-states in the Global North enables acts of financial care for households in the Global South. However, such practices often rely on the unpaid labour of other household members in the Global South, such as grandparents caring for their grandchildren. Such arrangements often undermine the (global) migrant household, as absence and the tensions of working across vast differences are barely mitigated by technologies of connection, leading to family breakdown (Pratt, 2012). Montgomerie and Tepe-Belfrage's (2017) study of care in Anglo-American households 'stretches' finance in a slightly different way by interrogating how unpaid work within homes 'cares for debts' (i.e., ensures their repayment). This approach links intimate relationships and the work of social reproduction with financialization and indebtedness from the position of the household, while also foregrounding how households can resist the encroachment of financial power into everyday life by not caring for/about their debts.

Household as Place

The household as a particular kind of place of, and for, finance foregrounds lived experiences and their co-constitution through uneven power relations. This frame builds on Massey's (2005: 131) understanding of place as a spatio-temporal event. '[P]lace—as open ('a global sense of place'), as woven together out of ongoing stories, as a moment within power-geometries, as a particular constellation within the wider topographies of space, and as in process, as unfinished business.' Thinking about the household as a place situates financialization within specific spaces-times, which maps onto the complexity and heterogeneity of the household as its defining conceptual feature. This, in turn, troubles dominant registers that conjure the monetary economy as a national economic entity, or a global economic system. For instance, economic understandings of the household as an agent take Becker (1981) at face-value; 'intra-household bargaining' involves the allocation of time or money as scarce resources in household production, where the altruism of the (male) household head ensures that bargaining decisions produce an optional allocation of contractual and non-contractual obligations (Becker, 1981). In such approaches, the household is a unitary actor with a unitary will that will maximize utility and has a set of preferences to achieve that goal. The complexity of the household is assumed away by such rational expectations and agent-based modelling, which seeks only to make causal claims. Nancy Folbre's (1986) critique of Becker explains the fallacy of treating the household as an undifferentiated unit of analysis and ignoring the significant differences between the economic position of men, women, and children within broader patriarchal relations. '[The] analysis of the household must be situated within a larger structural analysis of gender and age-based inequalities and their interaction with class structure and national position within the world capitalist system' (Folbre, 1986: 6). Put simply, the individuals who make up the family have competing (or non-cooperative) desires and wants, culture shapes how households manage their resources, and political economy shapes household finances. Thinking the household as place recognizes the systematic redistributive (gender, race, and age-based) power relations that intertwine with other power relations to shape internal household distributions (Katz, 1997; Iversen, 2003). Methodologically, conceptualizing the household as place is an ongoing project to push at the boundaries imposed on it. This conceptual frame ensures the household is not reduced and confined to decision-making preferences, naturalized as the domestic sphere, or generalized into a meaningless level of analysis or sphere of activity, wholly separate and subordinate to the state and the market. Like the other approaches discussed in this chapter, this approach also foregrounds geographical difference.

Sociological and ethnographic approaches to household finance have done most to unsettle and open up the household as a place of spatio-temporal difference. As Zelizer (1997: 33) notes, 'which family members (are) entitled or competent to control, manage and spend family funds is of crucial importance when assessing the relative power structures within the family'. Power in the home is not reducible to money, but money can reflect power relations within the home. In other words, household finances are differentially entangled in power relations that may be gendered, patriarchal, and heteronormative across time-space (Ruwanpura, 2007; de Henau and Himmelweit, 2013). Resources may not be equally distributed and norms of equality may not exist in many households, but they do in some. Inequalities are, in turn, created and amplified through practices of household finance. Schuster's (2014) ethnography in Ciudad del Este, Paraguay, demonstrates how practices of lending and borrowing create what she terms 'the social unit of debt'. Assumptions about gendered sociality are folded into credit extension practices, in ways that lead to these financial practices re-creating households and communities as places of gender difference, where women are marginalized while men are empowered. In Ramallah, Palestine, Harker et al. (2019) trace the ways in which assumptions about gender and labour, which map on to the external/internal boundary of the house, shape how living with debt is differentially distributed and experienced within households. Masculinity is (re)made as the practice of dealing with household finances outside the home, while femininity is defined as the often-invisible labour of making do within the home. Crucially, such practices need to be understood in relation to the powerful impact Israeli settler colonialism has on co-constituting Ramallah as a particular type of place (see also Harker, forthcoming).

Place-based approaches to household finance also show how intimate forms of harm link bodies and everyday experience with household/community dynamics and global finance. Harm is understood as not only embodied physically and/or psychologically, but also encoded in the norms and processes (or mechanisms) of the political economy. Global and state financial practices can be read through acts of physical violence and deprivation (where bodily integrity is compromised through hunger, malnourishment, or the withdrawal of health care), psychological harm, emotional stress, and hardship, as well as the loss of freedom or liberty of the person (Stanley et al., 2016). Han's (2013a) ethnography of health and care in Santiago, Chile, is exemplary in this regard. Her account of how health policies and the expansion of consumer credit become embodied in and as everyday household practices can be read as a detailed portrait of ways in which violence produced by state institutions and market forces is downloaded onto, and becomes part of, the intimate everyday (see also Han, 2013b). These forms of harm are distributed within and across domestic relations at the neighbourhood scale in ways that both mitigate and intensify violence. Placed-based approaches to understanding financial harm overlap with both scalar and networked approaches. However, they are arguably more powerful because they foreground the body and lived experience, and thus the visceral nature of financial harm.

Conceptualizing the household as a place also means it is a situated perspective from and through which to think about finance and its impacts through and across time and space. Such work is well-placed to contribute to efforts to decolonize (geographies of) finance (Harker, 2017; Bourne et al., 2018). This burgeoning scholarship takes issue with the ways in which many knowledge claims are embedded in, and reproduce Euro-America as the implicit spatial context for a series of general claims. Reproducing Euro-America particularly as 'global' not only continues to marginalize knowledges made beyond Euro-America, but also risks missing: (i) the diversity of experiences of household finance (including within Europe and America), and (ii) the connections between different contexts through which particular forms and experiences of household finance become more extensive. De- and post-colonial approaches do not deny the usefulness of Northern theory, but rather seek a 'recalibration of the geographies of authoritative knowledge' (Roy, 2009: 820) that opens up theory to other places, voices, and practices. In other words, household finances that are often ignored must become part of the map. Like the feminist perspectives discussed earlier in this chapter, de- and post-colonial approaches foreground difference and inequality. Post-colonial worlds are literally indebted to, and thus connected and divided from, their former colonial sovereigns in historically and geographically specific and asymmetric ways (Blyth, 2013). Transformations in household finances and socio-cultural practices therefore graft onto existing power relations, but also create new forms of power (Guérin, 2015). For example, James' (2015) ethnography of financialization in South Africa shows that financial processes must be understood through the lens of the post-Apartheid transition. In particular, the commitment to provide previously disenfranchized black people with housing and undo the effects of credit apartheid shape a national economic system in which generating profit has become based on consumption and rent-seeking, rather than production. However, there are also considerable differences between (urban and rural) places within South Africa itself, which can also be traced to Apartheid and its legacies.

Geographies of the Household Finance and Austerity

Geographies of household finance, whether understood through the concepts of scale, network, or place, make visible the everyday practices through which financialized capitalism is constituted. Household finance foregrounds how socio-cultural dynamics shape the ways in which different subjects and groups can participate in and benefit from financialization. Making visible the mundane everyday activities of households therefore creates a new intellectual space for analysing the inequalities and power hierarchies at play in the geographies of finance. Moving deeper into the material reality of everyday life points to the stratified costs of accessing debt, and the unequal distribution of income and wealth gains. Socio-cultural perspectives explain how access to credit works together with entrepreneurial forms of citizenship to condition how individuals participate, or are valued as participants, in a financialized economy. It also enables a critical response to the pervasive morality of finance (Lazzarato, 2012), in which debt-fuelled investment in housing or higher education is 'good'; while borrowing for consumerism or any reason that results in an inability to manage debt is 'bad.'

While the three geographical lenses discussed in this chapter come with their own conceptual commitments, in practice they are often deployed to similar ends. Many analyses of household finance will draw on all three perspectives—sometimes simultaneously—to pursue a critical exploration of political and intellectual challenges. In this section, we demonstrate how this works in relation to austerity, which has become a key focus in UK studies of finance in the decade following the 2008 financial crisis. However, it is important to recognize the coherence across spatially different forms of post-crisis austerity: in Greece and the Eurozone, but also in America. There has been a successive ratcheting up of the financialized business cycle of boom, bust, bail-out for lenders and structural adjustment (austerity) for the state over time. The macroeconomic trend of monetary expansion combined with fiscal restraint manifests differently across space and time. In the United Kingdom, austerity has been very successful as a political project to transform the role of the state after an economic crash, but not at all successful as a public policy agenda to achieve stable economic growth through fiscal consolidation.

Austerity is how most citizens in the United Kingdom have experienced the economy since 2008 (Wren-Lewis, 2018). Analysis that begins at the scale of the household makes visible the power of austerity and, in particular, how choosing unequal distribution of gains (at the very top of the wealth distribution) and hardship (the remaining 95% of households) is justified through a political narrative about the economic hardship of debt. The common-sense logic is that fiscal consolidation after economic shock is necessary to repair the balance sheet. It is widely acknowledged that this technocratic framing masks the inherent political choice to impose austerity on public spending by erroneously suggesting austerity is equivalent to the retrenchment of private households (Blakeley, 2019). The widespread debates over the household fallacy made by proponents of austerity point to the real-world differences between the public and private household (Reinhart and Rogoff, 2011; King et al., 2012; Krugman, 2015). However, despite the logical fallacy of the household metaphor, it is politically powerful. The macroeconomic justification of austerity reinforces households' own experience of financial crisis. In other words, the austerity narrative reinforces how private households respond to economic shocks and retrenchment. It makes sense to people living under conditions in which the costs of financial crisis are being imposed and must be navigated to survive. The counter-narrative to austerity simply repeats the reality that nation-states are different from households—they create their own currency and can re-finance debt at will (unlike a private household). However, this narrative does not resonate at the level of common-sense economic metaphor.

Thinking through the geographical concept of network positions finance as distinct, but interconnected, spaces that unevenly distribute the gains and harms of austerity. These material connections become intuitively framed in terms of the household balance sheet to disrupt the discourses of complexity that hide the politics and power relations that make austerity possible (Christophers, 2015). Austerity can be differentiated by geographies of household finances. The geographical concentration of retail financial flows from households, the uneven distribution of services and income transfers across households, the re-distributional outcomes of quantitative easing integrate overlapping spatial perspectives to understand the unfolding of austerity in the post-2008 period. It is not enough to account for why households are integrated into financialization, what is also required is a demonstration of how household finances vary geographically, socio-culturally, and historically, but still form recognizable trends of inequality.

The household as a place of and for lived experience highlights the everyday practices through which people cope with the effects of austerity politics in ways that are messy and complex (Hall, 2019). Echoing Sarah Marie Hall's (2020: 1) rich empirical work, the household is one means 'to more fully consider the ways in which austerity can be encountered at and across a range of social spaces, with growing interest in how austerity politics play out in everyday personal lives'. Inter-generational differences (Hall, 2016; Horton, 2017) and the role of affect (Deville, 2015; Seigworth, 2016; Dawney et al., 2020) have become key means through which such households relate to finance in both the present and future. Debt-led austerity has transformed debt into a force that reaches into the intimacies of life and, in doing so, becomes a political formation to be acted against (Montgomerie and Tepe-Belfrage, 2016, 2017); an austere home also becomes a place for political struggle in which harmful financial relations are resisted and/or disavowed (Davey, 2019).

Conclusion

In this chapter, we have argued that the household is a key site from and through which to understand finance and financialization. Financial geography approaches have understood household as a scale, a node in a network, and a place. These geographies are often articulated in overlapping fashion in the works cited. Collectively, they understand the household as a distinct but interconnected, complex, and heterogeneous financial space. They foreground the unequal relations of power and agentic practices through which household finance is constituted, and the importance of geographical difference. Geographies of household finance make visible the spatial processes creating financial gains and hardship, inclusions and exclusions from credit/debt, and the power of creditor/debtor relations. In conclusion, we expand on these collective characteristics to underscore what a geographical approach has to offer broader intellectual and political engagements with finance.

Geographical approaches to household finance foreground practices of connection and disconnection. Households, in general, have long been excluded from finance and the knowledge production practices that underpin them. These exclusions often stem from and reinforce gender inequalities. Building on feminist traditions, geographical studies highlight how particular households in particular places become connected and disconnected from the financial practices of markets and/or states. For instance, while Langley (2008a) demonstrates how middle-class homes in the United Kingdom have become key nodes for financial markets, other studies in the United Kingdom demonstrate how poorer households are excluded from such networks and rely on different, often more expensive, financial products (Leyshon et al., 2004; Flaherty and Banks, 2013; Datta and Aznar, 2019). As Leyshon et al.'s (2004) study of doorstep lending in London—the purported heart of global finance—demonstrate, relationships of financial inclusion and exclusion are geographically nuanced, complex, and unevenly distributed across different households. Such geographies of dis/connection may not just be topographic either, as Tooker and Clarke's (2018) discussion of 'relational finance' emphasizes.

Second, geographies of household finance provide nuanced understandings of both power and resistance. Financial power is understood to cross and construct scales, or something that is distributed through networks. Both perspectives help us understand how finance is not only a transformative force, but also one that is contested through household practices. Montgomerie and Tepe-Belfrage (2019) focus on the methodological tool of the household debt audit, as a means of making visible the intersections of households and credit practices. This process invites people to care for debts, potentially in different ways: paying them down, diverting expenditures, defaulting, repudiating, cancelling, or paying them off altogether (see also Davey, 2019). Kear's (2016) study of microfinance in San Francisco, USA—which upsets common understandings linking microfinance with the Global South—also demonstrates how formalized Rotating Savings and Credit Associations enable financially excluded groups to exert strategic control over the calculation of their credit scores.

Finally, geographical approaches to household finance stress divergence and difference. In this chapter, we have cited studies that explore how both households and financial practices differ across time-space. However, geographical difference must also be understood as a resource through which other kinds of futures are made possible. Here, the work of Gibson-Graham (2014) on weak theory is vital for understanding how thinking through difference opens up imaginaries of different (better) economic, social, political, and ecological relations. As Deville and Seigworth (2015: 619) note:

> Debt seen as a generalized phenomenon, seemingly with the power to seep into 'everywhere' and affect 'everyone', occludes not just a plethora of quite distinct financial circumstances and cultural/national regulatory practices and proclivities, but also the innumerable ways in which different financial instruments are organized, encountered and come to resonate with daily life.

The household provides an excellent scale, node, and place from/through which to develop such an understanding. Geographical diversity means the ability to learn from elsewhere, and thus promises to make our strategies for transforming finance more robust.

References

Allen J. (2011). Topological twists: Power's shifting geographies. *Dialogues in Human Geography* 1: 283–298.

Allen J. & Pryke M. (2013). Financializing household water: Thames water, MEIF, and 'ring-fenced' politics. *Cambridge Journal of Regions, Economy and Society* 6 (3): 419–439.

Allon F. (2014). The feminisation of finance. *Australian Feminist Studies* 29 (79): 12–30.

Bakker I. (2007). Social reproduction and the constitution of a gendered political economy. *New Political Economy* 12 (4): 541–556.

Becker G. (1981). *A Treatise the Family*. Cambridge, MA: Harvard University Press.

Blakeley G. (2019). Theresa May's plan to bribe Labour MPs to back Brexit shows austerity was always a choice. *The New Statesmen*, January 31, 2019. Available at https://www.newstatesman.com/politics/economy/2019/01/theresa-may-s-plan-bribe-labour-mps-back-brexit-shows-austerity-was-always

Blyth M. (2013). *Austerity: The History of a Dangerous Idea*. Oxford: Oxford University Press.

Bourne C., Gilbert P., Haiven M. & Montgomerie J. (2018). Focus: Colonial debts, imperial insolvencies, extractive nostalgias. *Discover Society*, September 4, 2018. Available at https://discoversociety.org/2018/09/04/focus-colonial-debts-imperial-insolvencies-extractive-nostalgias/

Bryan D. (2010). The duality of labour and the financial crisis. *The Economic and Labour Relations Review* 20 (2): 49–59.

Christophers B. (2015). Geographies of finance II: Crisis, space and political-economic transformation. *Progress in Human Geography* 39 (2): 205–213.

Datta K. & Aznar C. (2019). The space-times of migration and debt: Re-positioning migrants' debt and credit practices and institutions in, and through, London. *Geoforum* 98: 300–308.

Davey R. (2019). Mise en scène: The make-believe space of over-indebted optimism *Geoforum* 98: 327–334.

Dawney L., Kirwan S. & Walker R. (forthcoming). The intimate spaces of debt: Love, freedom and entanglement in indebted lives. *Geoforum*.

Deville J. (2015). *Lived Economies of Default*. London: Routledge.

Deville J. & Seigworth G. (2015). Everyday debt and credit. *Cultural Studies* 29 (5–6): 615–629.

Doling J. & Ronald R. (2010). Property-based welfare and European homeowners: How would housing perform as a pension? *Journal of Housing and the Built Environment* 25 (2): 227–241.

Durst J. (2016). Juggling with debts, moneylenders and local petty monarchs: Banking the unbanked in 'Shanty-villages' in Hungary. *Review of Sociology* 25 (4): 30–57.

Elias J. & Gunawardana S. (Eds.) (2013). *The Global Political Economy of the Household in Asia*. London: Palgrave MacMillan.

Elias J. & Rai S. (2019). Feminist everyday political economy: Space, time, and violence. *Review of International Studies* 45 (2): 201–220.

Elson D. & Cagatay N. (2000). The social content of macroeconomic policies. *World Development* 28 (7): 1347–1364.

Elyachar J. (2002). Empowerment money: The World Bank, non-governmental organizations, and the value of culture in Egypt. *Public Culture* 14 (3): 493–513.

Engelen E., Ertürk I., Froud J., Johal S., Leaver A., Moran M. & Nilsson, A. (2011). *After the Great Complacence: Financial Crisis and the Politics of Reform*. Oxford: Oxford University Press.

Ehrenreich B. & Hochschild A. (2003). *Global Woman: Nannies, Maids, and Sex Workers in the New Economy*. New York: Macmillan.

Fichtner J. (2019). The rise of institutional investors. In P. Mader, D. Mertens & N. Van der Zwan (Eds.) *International Handbook of Financialization*. London: Routledge.

Fields D. (2015). Contesting the financialization of urban space: Community organizations and the struggle to preserve affordable rental housing in New York City. *Journal of Urban Affairs* 37 (2): 144–165.

Flaherty J. & Banks S. (2013). In whose interest? The dynamics of debt in poor households. *Journal of Poverty & Social Justice* 21 (3): 219–232.

Folbre N. (1986). Cleaning house: New perspectives on households and economic development. *Journal of Development Economics* 22 (1): 5–40.

French S., Leyshon A. & Wainwright T. (2011). Financializing space, spacing financialization. *Progress in Human Geography* 35: 798–819.

Froud J. & Williams K. (2002). Financialisation and the coupon pool. *Capital and Class* 78: 119–151.

de Goede M. (2005). *Virtue, Fortune, and Faith: A Genealogy of Finance*. Minnesota: University of Minnesota Press.

Gabor D. & Brooks S. (2017). The digital revolution in financial inclusion: International development in the Fintech Era. *New Political Economy* 22 (4): 423–436.

García-Lamarca M. & Kaika M. (2016). 'Mortgaged lives': The biopolitics of debt and housing financialisation. *Transactions of the Institute of British Geographers* 41 (3): 313–327.

Gibbons D. (2014). *Solving Britain's Personal Debt Crisis*. Cambridge: Searching Finance.

Gibson-Graham J.-K. (2014). Rethinking the economy with thick description and weak theory. *Cultural Anthropology* 55(S9): S147–S153.

Graham S. & Marvin S. (2001). *Splintering Urbanism*. London: Routledge.

Green J. & Lavery S. (2015). The regressive recovery: Distribution, inequality and state power in Britain's Post-Crisis Political Economy. *New Political Economy* 20 (6): 894–923.

Guérin I. (2015). Juggling with debt, social ties, and values: The everyday use of microcredit in rural South India. *Current Anthropology* 55 (S9): S40–S50.

Guermond V. & Samba Sylla N. (2018). When monetary coloniality meets 21st century finance: Development in The Franc Zone. *Discover Society*, September 4, 2018. https://discoversociety.org/2018/09/04/when-monetary-coloniality-meets-21st-century-finance-development-in-the-franc-zone/

Hall S.M. (2016). Everyday family experiences of the financial crisis: Getting by in the recent economic recession. *Journal of Economic Geography* 16 (2): 305–330.

Hall S.M. (2019). *Everyday Life in Austerity: Family, Friends and Intimate Relations*. London: Palgrave Macmillan.

Hall S.M. (2020). The personal is political: Feminist geographies of/in austerity. *Geoforum* (110): 242–251.

Han C. (2013a). *Life in Debt: Times of Care and Violence in Neoliberal Chile*. Berkeley: University of California Press.

Han C. (2013b). Suffering and pictures of anthropological inquiry: A response to comments on Life in debt. *HAU: Journal of Ethnographic Theory* 3 (1): 231–240.

Harker C. (2017). Debt space: Topologies, ecologies and Ramallah, Palestine. *Environment and Planning D: Society and Space* 35 (4): 600–619.

Harker C. (forthcoming). *Spacing Debt: Obligations, Violence and Endurance in Ramallah, Palestine*. Durham, NC: Duke University Press.

Harker C., Sayyad D. & Shebeitah R. (2019). The gender of debt and space: Notes from Ramallah-Al Bireh, Palestine. *Geoforum* 98: 277–285.

de Henau J. & Himmelweit S. (2013). Examining public policy from a gendered intra-household perspective: Changes in family-related policies in the UK, Australia and Germany since the mid-nineties. *Oñati Socio-Legal Series* 3 (7): 1222–1248.

Himmelweit S. (2002). Making visible the hidden economy: The case for gender-impact analysis of economic policy. *Feminist Economics* 8 (1): 49–70.

Horton J. (2017). Young people and debt: Getting on with austerities. *Area* 49 (3): 280–287.

Hoskyns C. & Rai S. (2007). Recasting the global political economy: Counting women's unpaid work. *New Political Economy* 12 (3): 297–317.

Iversen V. (2003). Intra-household inequality: A challenge for the capability approach? *Feminist Economics* 9 (2–3): 93–115.

James D. (2015). *Money from Nothing: Indebtedness and Aspiration in South Africa*. Stanford: Stanford University Press.

Joseph M. (2014). *Debt to Society: Accounting for Life under Capitalism*. Minneapolis: University of Minnesota Press.

Katz C. (2001). Vagabond capitalism and the necessity of social reproduction. *Antipode* 33 (4): 709–728.

Katz E. (1997). The intra-household economics of voice and exit. *Feminist Economics* 3 (3): 25–46.

Kar S. (2018). *Financialising Poverty: Labor and Risk in Indian Microfinance*. Stanford: Stanford University Press.

Kar S. & Schuster C. (2016). Comparative projects and the limits of choice: Ethnography and microfinance in India and Paraguay. *Journal of Cultural Economy* 9 (4): 347–363.

Kear M. (2016). Peer lending and the subsumption of the informal. *Journal of Cultural Economy* 9 (3): 261–276.

Kirwan S. (2019). On 'those who shout the loudest': Debt advice and the work of disrupting attachments. *Geoforum* 98: 318–326.

King L., Kitson M., Konzelmann S. & Wilkinson F. (2012). Making the same mistake again—or is this time different? *Cambridge Journal of Economics* 36: 1–15.

Krippner G. (2005). The financialization of the American economy. *Socio-Economic Review* 3 (2): 173–208.

Krugman P. (2015). The austerity delusion. *The Guardian*, April 29, 2015. Available at https://www.theguardian.com/business/ng-interactive/2015/apr/29/the-austerity-delusion

Lai K. (2017). Unpacking financial subjectivities: Intimacies, governance and socioeconomic practices in financialisation. *Environment and Planning D: Society and Space* 35 (5): 913–932.

Langley P. (2006). Securitising suburbia: The transformation of Anglo-American mortgage finance. *Competition & Change* 10 (3): 283–299.

Langley P. (2008a). *The Everyday Life of Global Finance: Saving and Borrowing in Anglo-America*. Oxford, UK: Oxford University Press.

Langley P. (2008b). Sub-prime mortgage lending: A cultural economy. *Economy and Society* 37 (4): 469–494.

Langley P. (forthcoming). *The folds of social finance: Making markets, remaking the social. Environment and Planning A: Economy and Space.*

Lazzarato M. (2012). *The Making of Indebted Man*. Los Angeles: Semiotext(e).

Leyshon A., Burton D., Knights D., Alferoff C. and Signoretta P. (2004). Towards an ecology of retail financial services: Understanding the persistence of door-to-door credit and insurance providers. *Environment and Planning A* 36 (4): 625–646.

Leyshon A. & Thrift N. (2007). The capitalization of almost everything: The future of finance and capitalism. *Theory, Culture & Society* 24 (7–8): 97–115.

Mader P. (2018). Contesting financial inclusion. *Development and Change* 49 (2): 461–483.

Marston S. (2000). The social construction of scale. *Progress in Human Geography* 24 (2): 219–242.

Marston S. (2008). *A long way from home: Domesticating the social production of scale*. In E. Sheppard & R. McMaster (Eds.) *Scale and Geographic Inquiry: Nature, Society, and Method*. New York: John Wiley & Sons, pp. 170–191.

Marston S., Jones J.P. & Woodward K. (2005). Human geography without scale. *Transactions of the Institute of British Geographers* 30: 416–432.

Massey D. (1994). *Space, Place and Gender*. Cambridge: Polity Press.

Massey D. (2005). *For Space*. London: Sage.

Mian A. & Sufi A. (2014). *House of Debt: How They (and You) Caused the Great Recession, and How We Can Prevent It from Happening Again*. Chicago: University of Chicago Press.

Montgomerie J. (2009). The pursuit of (past) happiness? Middle-class indebtedness and Anglo-American financialisation. *New Political Economy* 14 (1): 1–24.

Montgomerie J. (2013). America's debt safety-net. *Public Administration* 91 (4): 871–888.

Montgomerie and Tepe-Belfrage D. (2016). A feminist moral-political economy of uneven reform in austerity Britain: Fostering financial and parental literacy. *Globalizations* 13 (6): 890–905.

Montgomerie and Tepe-Belfrage D. (2017). Caring for debts: How the household economy exposes the limits of financialisation. *Critical Sociology* 43 (4–5): 653–668.

Montgomerie J. & Tepe-Belfrage D. (2019). Narrating the search for a methodology of the Household. Unpublished manuscript.

Moodie M. (2013). Microfinance and the gender of risk: The case of Kiva.org. *Signs: Journal of Women, Culture & Society* 38 (2): 279–302.

Peterson V.S. (2010). Global householding amid global crises. *Politics & Gender* 6 (2): 271–281.

Pósfai Z., Gál Z. & Nagy E. (2017). Financialization and inequalities: The uneven development of the housing market on the eastern periphery of Europe. In S. Fadda & P. Tridico (Eds.) *Inequality and Uneven Development in the Post-Crisis World*. London: Routledge, pp. 167–190.

Pratt G. (2004). *Working Feminism*. Edinburgh: Edinburgh University Press.

Pratt G. (2012). *Families Apart: Migrant Mothers and the Conflicts of Labor and Love*. Minnesota: University of Minnesota Press.

Rankin K. (2001). Governing development: Neoliberalism, microcredit, and rational economic woman. *Economy & Society* 30 (1): 18–37.

Reinhart C. & Rogoff K. (2011). From financial crash to debt crisis. *American Economic Review* 101 (5): 1676–1706.

Roberts A. (2013). Financing social reproduction: The gendered relations of debt and mortgage finance in twenty-first-century America. *New Political Economy* 18 (1): 21–42.

Roy A. (2009). The 21st-century metropolis: New geographies of theory. *Regional Studies* 43 (6): 819–830.

Roy A. (2012). Subjects of risk: Technologies of gender in the making of millennial modernity. *Public Culture* 24 (1): 131–155.

Runyan A. (2018). *Global Gender Issues in the New Millennium*. London: Routledge.

Ruwanpura K. (2007). Shifting theories: Partial perspectives on the household. *Cambridge Journal of Economics* 31 (4): 525–538.

Sassen S. (1991). *The Global City*. Princeton: Princeton University Press.

Seigworth G. (2016). Wearing the world like a debt garment: Interface, affect, and gesture. *Ephemera* 16 (4): 15–31.

Simone D. & Walks A. (2019). Immigration, race, mortgage lending, and the geography of debt in Canada's global cities. *Geoforum* 98: 286–299.

Soederberg S. (2014). *Debtfare States and the Poverty Industry: Money, Discipline and the Surplus Population*. London: Routledge.

Stanley L., Deville J. & Montgomerie J. (2016). Digital debt management: The everyday life of austerity. *New Formations* 87: 64–82.

Steans J. & Tepe D. (2010). Social reproduction in international political economy: Theoretical insights and international, transnational and local sitings. *Review of International Political Economy* 17 (5): 807–815.

Stenning A., Smith A., Rochovska A. & Swiatek D. (2010). *Domesticating Neoliberalism: Spaces of Economic Practice and Social Reproduction in Post-socialist Cities*. Oxford: Wiley-Blackwell.

Tooker L. & Clarke C. (2018). Experiments in relational finance: Harnessing the social in everyday debt and credit. *Theory, Culture & Society* 35 (3): 57–76.

True J. (2012). *The Political Economy of Violence against Women*. Oxford: Oxford University Press.

Van der Zwan N. (2014). Making sense of financialization. *Socio-Economic Review* 12 (1): 99–129.

Waring M. (1989). *If Women Counted: A New Feminist Economics*. London: Macmillan.

Waring M. (2015). *Counting for Nothing: What Men Value and What Women Are Worth*. University of Toronto Press.

Wren-Lewis S. (2018). *The Lies We Were Told: Politics, Economics, Austerity and Brexit*. Bristol: Bristol University Press.

Zelizer V. (1997). *The Social Meaning of Money*. Princeton: Princeton University Press.

15

IMPACT INVESTORS

The Ethical Financialization of Development, Society and Nature

Paul Langley

Introduction: 'A New Alternative'

Amidst the global financial crisis, Adair Turner sparked a media and political storm in the United Kingdom when he described aspects of financial innovation as 'socially useless'. As he put it:

> It is hard to distinguish between valuable financial innovation and non-valuable. Clearly, not all innovation should be treated in the same category as the innovation of either a new pharmaceutical drug or a new retail format. I think that some of it is socially useless activity.
>
> (Turner, 2009a)

At the time of his remarks, Turner was Chairman of the now defunct Financial Services Authority and, in effect, the chief financial regulator in the United Kingdom. Earlier that year, his official investigation into the crisis had reached a similar set of conclusions (Turner, 2009b). While Turner and many others were very publicly questioning the social value of financial innovation, representatives from major banks and financial institutions attended a series of meetings that coined the rubric of 'impact investment' (Barman, 2015; Oleksiak et al., 2015). Taking place in Bellagio, Italy, organized and funded by the Rockefeller Foundation, what these meetings sought to achieve was the distillation of a somewhat diverse and disparate set of developments that pre-dated the crisis. As the subsequent report on the meeting produced by staff from J.P. Morgan Global Research put it:

> In a world where government resources and charitable donations are insufficient to address the world's social problems, impact investing

> offers a new alternative for channelling large-scale private capital for social benefit. With increasing numbers of investors rejecting the notion that they face a binary choice between investing for maximum risk-adjusted returns or donating for social purpose, the impact investment market is now at a significant turning point as it enters the mainstream.
>
> (O'Donohoe et al., 2010: 5)

In contrast to the traits of financial innovation identified by Turner, then, this was a concerted effort to name and distinguish impact investment as a socially useful financial innovation for adoption by 'mainstream' investors.

O'Donohoe et al. (2010: 7) offer a definition of impact investments—'investments intended to create positive impact beyond financial return'—that is widely shared by business school academics, practitioners and advocates, and policy-makers alike (e.g., Balkin, 2015; Freireich and Fulton, 2009; G8 Social Impact Investment Taskforce, 2013; IFC, 2018; Oleksiak et al., 2015; Rodin and Brandenburg, 2014; UBS, 2018; World Economic Forum, 2013). The more-than-financial returns sought by impact investors tend to be public, collective and social, and/or environmental in character, with 'the term 'social'' often used 'to include social and environmental' (O'Donohoe et al., 2010: 5). Impact investment finances enterprises, projects, and initiatives that, in particular sites and settings in the Global South and North, seek to make an incremental impact on specific social problems, environmental issues, or aspects of sustainable development. Moreover, the techniques of impact investment typically entail setting and monitoring quantified targets for the more-than-financial returns that may be realized. Accordingly, impact investment techniques tend to amount to frameworks and tools for translating broad investment objectives into strategies, providing metrics, measures and data processes for identifying, managing, and reporting impact performance. Although these frameworks and tools are often proprietary to the investors that mobilize them (Barman, 2015), industry associations (e.g., the Global Impact Investment Network, GIIN) and not-for-profit organizations (e.g., B-Analytics) also provide guides, and standardized metrics and measures of impact.

Focusing on the development of impact investment since the late 2000s, this chapter is divided into four further sections. As briefly detailed in the next section, impact investment is highly diverse in terms of the investors that participate, the assets created, and the types and locations of the organizations and impacts that are financed. The vast majority of impact investors are based in North America and Europe, but greater than half of impact investments by total value are made in the Global South. Development finance institutions (DFIs), including multilateral development banks and bilateral agencies, are key impact investors in this respect, and governments and international organizations variously elicit and guarantee impact investments made in development programmes, social policies, and environmental projects. Globally, the aggregate value of impact investment is known to amount to at least US$230 billion (GIIN, 2018), and remains far from 'large-scale' in the context of capital markets where global stock markets alone are valued at close to US$100 trillion.

Human geographers and social scientists tend not to focus explicitly on impact investment but have, nonetheless, encountered it in the course of their research. As the review of this presently fragmented critical literature in the third section of the chapter will show, impact investment is variously implicated to a greater-or-lesser extent in financialization processes. In the 'financialization of development' (Mawdsley, 2018), for example, impact investment figures in the transformation of development assistance and associated emergence of 'development finance' (Mitchell and Sparke, 2016; Mitchell, 2017). It is also to the fore as development is equated with the provision of 'poverty finance' (Rankin, 2013), and investments are made in micro-credit institutions and, increasingly, in mobile payments and FinTech platforms, and in the name of 'financial inclusion' (Aitken, 2017; Gabor and Brooks, 2017; Mader, 2016; Maurer, 2015). The role of impact investment in poverty programmes is not limited to the Global South, however (Rosenman, 2017a). It also figures strongly in the 'financialization of the social' (Chiapello and Godefroy, 2017) in the Global North, where private investment is mobilized for behaviour-change social policies and in support of social economy organizations that provide for social services and social change (Andreu, 2018; Berndt and Wirth, 2018; Chiapello, 2015; Chiapello and Godefroy, 2017; Cooper, Graham, and Himick, 2016; Dowling, 2017; Kish and Leroy, 2015; Rosenman, 2017b). Moreover, while the techniques of impact investment are currently less material to the 'financialization of nature' (Ouma et al., 2018), there is a growing awareness among critical researchers that impact investment is one of the 'directions' taken by the 'growth of green finance' (Bigger and Dempsey, 2018: 30). This includes impact investing in initiatives and projects designed to enable mitigation and adaptation to climate change (Bracking, 2012; Christophers, 2018; Sullivan, 2018).

Bringing together and building on this existing critical research, this chapter will foreground impact investment because it signals and permeates throughout contemporary financialization processes wherein financial logics, techniques, and practices are harnessed to govern a host of developmental, social, and environmental problems. While impact investment is a novel and interesting feature of the present day global financial landscape, this alone is not why it is worthy of attention. Rather, a decade on from the global financial crisis that began in 2007, impact investment is a touchstone for renewed faith and confidence in financial innovation as 'powerful problem-solving machine' for global challenges that states are ostensibly unable to address in a new era of fiscal austerity (Palmer, 2015: *xviii*; see also, e.g., Keohane, 2016). Despite channelling relatively small-scale flows of private capital to date and achieving annual growth rates that are disappointing for its advocates, impact investment is the exemplification of a contemporary mode of neoliberal government that seeks to secure the future of human and more-than-human life through financial logics, techniques, and practices (Langley, 2019).

Conceptual and analytical questions remain, however, about what is actually constituted by 'financialization'. Its processes are certainly far from uniform or smooth, and also tend to be uneven and partial, and replete with frictions and tensions. As such, while existing research points out that the tangible consequence of impact investment is the advancement of financialization processes, it remains unclear exactly how impact investment itself serves to further financialization. The fourth section of this chapter will therefore seek to present a precise specification of the more-or-less discrete and ongoing ways in which impact investment furthers the financialization of development, society, and nature. To this end, taking a cultural economy perspective (Hall, 2011; Langley, 2015; Pryke and du Gay, 2007), it will focus on a set of processes that are already recognized as important to constituting financialization; that is, the making of financial subjectivities (e.g., Lai, 2017; Langley, 2008; Langley and Leyshon, 2012). What is at issue here is 'the co-constitutive relationship between the growing power of financial markets and new forms of financial subjectivity' (Hall, 2012: 406). Industry associations, 'how-to' books and guides, and training programmes summon up the impact investor as a distinctive financial subjectivity. With reference to these materials, the making of the impact investor will be held to be taking place amidst the operation of investment as a political technology and distinct financializing logic of government. The impact investor is shown to be figured in ways that are consistent with and run counter to the making of the mainstream investor: investors are financial subjects that act as the authoritative arbiters of capital allocation in return for legitimate returns, but the impact investor is also an ethical agent of change who has the potential to address global challenges through their distinctive financial techniques and practices.

Impact Investment: What, Who, Where?

'Impact investment' is an investment technique for targeting returns on capital that are also more-than-financial and measurable. It promises and brings into relation two sets of returns: 'a financial one for the investors and a social one for the public interest' (Chiapello and Godefroy, 2017: 158). Impact investment thereby diverges in important ways from 'the more mature field of socially responsible investments ('SRI'), which generally seek to minimize negative impact rather than proactively create positive social or environmental benefit' (O'Donohoe, Leijonhufvud, and Saltuk, 2010: 5). Investing for impact should not to be confused, then, with screening-out and divesting from so-called 'sin stocks' (e.g., tobacco, alcohol, arms, fossil fuels) (Hebb, 2013). Neither is it the same as the more positive variant of SRI that centres on assembling investment portfolios of enterprises that meet standards of corporate social responsibility

(CSR) (Authers, 2018). Impact investment is also very different from the forms of money and finance—for example, time banks, complementary currencies, credit unions, and local exchange trading schemes—that have previously been studied by human geographers and social scientists as 'alternatives' to capitalist financial markets (Fuller et al., 2010; Leyshon et al., 2003). Unlike these alternatives, impact investment does not feature participatory associational and organizational forms of sociality. As such, impact investment is not what we might call 'solidarity finance' (Langley, 2020). The 'impacts' of impact investment are 'social' because of *what* they are, and not because of *how* impact investment is organized.

The private investors that employ the techniques of impact investment are diverse and far from uniform (Rodin and Brandenburg, 2014: 17–32). The recent edition of the most authoritative industry survey of impact investment reports that, of 229 institutional respondents, most are for-profit fund managers (46%), followed by not-for-profit fund managers (13%), foundations (13%), banks (6%), pension funds or insurance companies (4%), DFIs (3%), and 'other' organizations (9%) such as non-government organizations (NGOs) and community development finance institutions (CDFIs) (GIIN, 2018: 1). Roughly one-third of impact investors are also what the GIIN (2018: iii) survey terms 'conventional investors', while two-thirds specialize in impact investment. The role of fund managers is particularly significant, especially given that they are intermediaries who practice impact investment on behalf of others, and sell their services and earn fees accordingly. Fund managers that practice impact investment techniques are typically specialist providers, although many large and mainstream institutions (e.g., BlackRock, Goldman Sachs, UBS) also offer impact investment funds.

Impact funds are marketed to investors through prospectuses and strategies that focus on a particular asset class, and they aggregate investments in the enterprises or projects of a specific kind of impact, sector, and/or geographic location. Consider, for example, ImpactAssets50 (https://www.impactassets.org/ia50_new/), a publicly available searchable database of 50 major impact investment funds produced by one of the leading intermediaries. In addition to basic information about asset class, each entry in the database includes a map that indicates the continents and regions where investments will be made, and is categorized according to its alignment with one of the United Nation's 2015 Sustainable Development Goals. Investors in funds are primarily the institutions that also make direct impact investments, and include DFIs, foundations, family offices, pension funds, and banks (GIIN, 2018: 31). In addition, it would seem that 'anyone can engage in this form of investing' (Rodin and Brandenburg, 2014: vi): a number of funds are marketed to retail investors (e.g., Calvert Impact Capital, Enterprise Community Partners, RSF Social Finance, Triodos Fair Share Fund, OikoCredit); and certain crowdfunding platforms (e.g., SeedTribe) now also make it possible to invest directly for impact in start-up and early-stage social enterprises (Walker, 2018).

A key legal, organizational, and strategic difference between impact investment institutions is their orientation to risk and return (Nicholls and Tomkinson, 2015). Across the impact investors who participated in the most recent GIIN (2018: x) survey, 64% pursue risk-adjusted market-rate returns alongside impact, 20% seek returns that are below but close to market-rate returns, and 16% prioritize impact alongside capital preservation. So-called 'blended finance' arrangements are also common for pooling and distributing impact investment risks, 'a strategy that combines capital with different levels of risk [i.e., different types of investors] in order to catalyse risk-adjusted, market-rate-seeking capital into impact investments' (GIIN, 2018: 19). As may be expected, those not pursuing risk-adjusted market rate returns are typically not-for-profit fund managers, some philanthropic foundations, NGOs, and CDFIs. Measured by value of assets under management (AUM), a number of US-based CDFIs are amongst the largest private impact investment institutions, most notably, the Reinvestment Fund and the Community Reinvestment Fund (Maverick, 2015).

The assets that are the objects of impact investment tend to be private debt instruments and private equity, with the former typically issued by relatively mature or so-called 'growth stage' companies, and the latter issued by seed- and venture-stage start-ups and social enterprises. Of the respondents to the GIIN (2018: 11) survey, 41% primarily invest in private debt, and company debts accounted for 74% of total AUM across all investors. While only 18% of impact investors primarily invest in private equity, there are nonetheless 'High numbers of investors' who 'allocate smaller amounts of capital into seed and venture-stage companies' (GIIN, 2018: 11). This is especially the case for managed funds that, focusing on private equity as an asset class, distribute investments to the start-ups and early-career firms that they aggregate into their portfolio. Only 14% of impact investors primarily invest in publicly traded equities, such that impact investment largely does not to feature the secondary trading and exchange of assets.

The impact types sought by investors and intermediaries vary considerably. Over half of the respondents to the GIIN (2018) survey target both social and environmental objectives, while a further 40% primarily target social impacts and only 6% primarily target environmental objectives. To achieve their objectives, the majority of respondents (76%) set specific impact targets for some or all of their investments (GIIN, 2018: xiii). Where specific targets are not set, this is often because the delivery of impact is felt to be embedded within the performance of the asset in question (e.g., a start-up enterprise with a designated social purpose). Across the broad categories of social and environmental impact, the range of sectors covered by impact investment techniques are considerable. The GIIN (2018: ix) survey, for example, uses 'sector codes' that include: arts and culture; conservation; education; energy; food and agriculture; healthcare; housing; information and communications technology; infrastructure; manufacturing; and, water, sanitation and hygiene (WASH). It also includes two further categories, microfinance services and financial services (excluding microfinance). The aggregate distribution of AUM across these sectors is uneven, however. According to GIIN (2018: xi), 19% of total AUM are presently allocated to financial services and a further 9% to microfinance, a feature of impact investment that we return to in the third section of the chapter. The next most popular sectoral destinations for impact investment, as measured as a share of total AUM, include energy (14%), housing (8%) and food and agriculture (6%). AUM allocated for each of the other sectors designated by GINN is 5% or less, with arts and culture registering below 1%.

The sectoral categories and breakdown of AUM provided by GIIN (2018) also provide a strong hint of the geographies of impact investment flows. Impact investments in housing, for example, are made almost entirely in the Global North, while investments in food and agriculture and in microfinance are made almost exclusively in what GIIN (2018) calls the 'emerging markets' of the Global South. Close to half of the institutions practising impact investment are headquartered in the United States and Canada, with a further 30% in Western, Northern, and Southern Europe (GIIN, 2018: x). Yet, 103 of 229 impact investors surveyed by GINN allocated greater than 75% of their assets under management to emerging markets, primarily sub-Saharan Africa, Latin America and the Caribbean, and South East Asia ((GIIN, 2018: ix). This should not obscure the practices of impact investors in the Global North who allocate capital either solely or primarily to the country and/or region in which they are based, especially in the United States and Canada, and Western Europe. Nonetheless, globally and in aggregate, over half (56%) of impact assets under management are located in emerging markets, and the breakdown of the highest shares of capital allocated by region in the categories used by GIIN (2018: x) are the United States and Canada (20%), Latin America and the Caribbean (16%), and sub-Saharan Africa (12%).

The sheer diversity of the impact investment landscape clearly makes it difficult to determine its scale precisely. For example, in the report that followed the Bellagio meetings highlighted at the outset of this chapter, O'Donohoe, Leijonhufvud, and Saltuk (2010: 6) shy away from providing an aggregate figure for the scale of impact investment. Instead, they forecast an impressive growth rate that, over the decade to 2020, will result in the total volume of capital invested reaching between US$400 billion and US$1 trillion. The GIIN (2018: 10) survey, meanwhile, provides an aggregate figure based on self-reporting by its respondents—226 respondents had US$ 228.1 billion worth of AUM in 2017. But this is cast as 'a figure which serves as the latest best-available 'floor' for the size of the impact investing market'. While referring to this figure as a 'floor' does suggest that the scale of impact investment may be somewhat larger—which it almost certainly is—it is nonetheless fair to conclude that impact investment remains relatively small in the context of global capital markets. To put the scale of impact investment into perspective, the floor figure for total AUM arrived at by GIIN (2018) is roughly equivalent, for example, to one-third of investments made globally in 2017 in oil and gas supplies (IEA, 2018). What is also especially notable about the scale of impact investment,

Table 15.1 Impact AUM by investor type

Organizations	*N*	*AUM (US$ million)*	*Percentage of total AUM*
DFI	7	102,923	45.0
Fund manager (for-profit)	106	67,494	30.0
Fund manager (not-for-profit)	30	4,385	2.0
Pension fund/insurance company	9	29,542	13.0
Bank/diversified financial institution	14	14,591	6.0
Foundation	30	6,036	3.0
Family office	6	469	0.2
Permanent investment company	4	148	0.1
Other	20	2,513	1.0

n = 226
Based on GIIN (2018, Table 9).

moreover, is the extent to which AUM are actually concentrated in the hands of a relatively small number of institutions (see Table 15.1). Put bluntly, close to half of assets with impact are held by the seven DFIs who responded to GIIN's (2018) survey, with just two unnamed DFIs accounting for 38% of total AUM (GIIN, 2018: 21). Impact investment is certainly diverse in terms of the kinds of investors that participate, the different assets involved, and the types and locations of the organizations and impacts that are capitalized. But a limited number of institutions manage particularly large pools of impact investment capital.

Financialization and Impact Investment

For business school academics, practitioners, advocates, and policy-makers, impact investment is broadly understood as an innovation that, in making it possible for financial markets to correct their own failings and address externalities, puts the inherently productive qualities of investment to work on global challenges. Consider, for example, the views of Mark Haefele (quoted in Walker, 2018), a former Harvard academic who is now global chief investment officer for the wealth management division at UBS, the Swiss bank that, amongst major mainstream financial institutions, is one of the leading champions of impact investment:

> If you look at the large demographic trends—a growing and ageing population, as well as greater urbanisation—all these factors play into the hands of impact investing because they create negative [effects]… Demands on healthcare, access to clean water, the need to deal with pollution and more green public transport—we can find solutions to these problems.

Human geographers and social scientists tend not to focus explicitly on impact investment, but nonetheless suggest a sharply different view of its consequences. This arises from their encounters with impact investment in the course of researching diverse and wider-ranging processes of financialization. Impact investment is thus commonly implicated by human geographers and social scientists in changes and transformations that, in the first instance, institute the power of financial logics and interests across new domains of life, extend the reach of financial regimes of valuation, and generate new opportunities for the extraction of financial value.

Consider, for example, how impact investment registers in existing research into the financialization of development. For Mawdsley (2018), financialization processes are engendering two main sets of changes currently under way in global development: first, the consolidation of 'development finance' and associated transformation of development assistance, such that aid is used to catalyse and leverage private investment; and, second, the provision and restructuring of microcredit programmes, such that they have become further integrated into global financial circuits. What is especially notable for us, moreover, is that Mawdsley (2018) points towards the presence of impact investment across each of these dimensions of the financialization of development.

First, and partly revealed by the prominence of DFIs in impact investment as noted above, impact investment informs the critique of developmental aid programmes and plays a constitutive role in the rise of development finance. As Katharyne Mitchell (2017; Mitchell and Sparke, 2016) highlights, the emergence of development finance can be traced to contemporary philanthropic institutions—such as the Gates Foundation and Omidyar Network—that were established on the back of money from the dot.com era and booming venture capital, digital technology, and real estate markets. While there are important continuities with the grant-making of early twentieth-century philanthropy—not least, concerns with cost-effectiveness, the privileging of incremental and technical solutions, and 'moral arguments about the rights of human beings to live educated, healthy, and productive lives' (Mitchell and Sparke, 2016: 726)—this new breed of institutions frame their own philanthropic practices as investments that seek to make positive and measurable impacts on global challenges. Indeed, while grant-making persists across longer-standing philanthropic foundations, it is increasingly supplemented with so-called 'mission' and 'programme' investments in organizations and projects deemed capable of making an impact and becoming economically sustainable over time.

The influence of impact investment in the consolidation of development finance is thus bound-up with the wider discourse and practices that, identifying the previous failings of both state-led and market-driven approaches to development, are championed by Bishop and Green (2008) as 'philanthro-capitalism'. As Mitchell (2017: 755) summarizes it:

> Philanthro-capitalism adopts the logic of finance capital and business management in the emphasis on return on investment (ROI), the leveraging of funds, evidence-based assessment, scalability, and targeted sites for investment. The programs funded under this rubric emphasize capacity building and the development of human capital. They are usually short-term, with numerous partners and easy exit strategies in the case of individual or program failure; these are generally measured by benchmarks mutually adopted by both donors and recipients.

Impact investing is the financial face of philanthro-capitalism. It contributes to galvanizing experimental and project-based public–private partnerships, bringing together philanthropic institutions, multilateral development banks, bilateral development agencies, NGOs, and so on through the structures of blended finance. While there is clearly a sense in which some DFIs—such as the IFC— have, in effect, been practising impact investment for close to three-quarters of a century (Walker, 2018), the influence of philanthropic institutions and the partnership model of development finance has instituted the adoption of impact investment in organizations such as the EIB, the United Kingdom's Department for International Development (DFID), and the U.S. Agency for International Development (USAID). Impact investment flourishes, then, as it contributes to development finance and benefits, more broadly, from philanthro-capitalist concerns with the so-called 'scalability' of projects and 'evidence-based' policy-making.

Second, impact investment contributes to the financialization of development because it features in what Rankin (2013) calls 'poverty finance'. As suggested by the relatively high volume of impact investments in microcredit and other financial services that was noted in the second section, specialist impact investors were initially to the fore when poverty alleviation was made a problem of access to loans for entrepreneurs, and such loans made by microcredit institutions and agents were securitized and assembled as an asset class for investors (Aitken, 2013; Mader, 2015). And, more recently, impact investors have again played an important role the emergence of 'financial inclusion' as a developmental priority, and what Mader (2016: 65) identifies, more precisely, as the 'new centrality of financial intermediation in poverty finance'. As he explains, the logic which equates financial inclusion with development holds that:

> poor people intermediate between their past and future incomes in order to meet their present and future needs, and *doing so alleviates their poverty*; and in the process, they provide capital for others, or they use the capital of others, and thereby facilitate a more efficient allocation of capital, which leads to *growth that alleviates their poverty.*
>
> (Mader, 2016: 68, original emphasis)

In contexts such as sub-Saharan Africa and large parts of Asia, Latin America and the Caribbean—where the majority of populations are 'unbanked' (Aitken, 2017)—the key intermediaries advancing financial inclusion are often FinTech platforms that provide access to payment and credit facilities via mobile telephones (Mader, 2016; Maurer, 2015). And, in a set of trends that broadly mirrors those in development finance discussed above, it would seem that philanthropic impact investors are core to the FinTech-led development-as-financial-inclusion agenda in poverty finance. For Gabor and Brooks (2017), it is possible to identify a 'fintech–philanthropy–development complex'. Figured through impact investment techniques, this promises to accelerate financial inclusion by aggregating and analysing data to better assess the creditworthiness of users while, at the same time, often assisting state projects that seek to render populations legible for taxation and other targeted interventions.

As existing critical social scientific research shows, moreover, the role of impact investment in poverty programmes is not limited to the Global South. As Rosenman (2017a) skilfully highlights, the parallels between poverty programmes in the Global South and those that address the problems of peripheral and 'left behind' places in the Global North are not limited to public–private partnerships, the promotion of entrepreneurial self-help, individual behaviour change, and so on. They also include the role played by impact investment and other forms of social finance, as 'Investors *mine* geographies of poverty for profitable opportunities' (Rosenman, 2017a: 7, emphasis added). As Rosenman (2017b: 2–3) summarizes, 'a new logic of poverty regulation…is securitized through the architecture of finance', 'predicated on the financial enclosure, or financialization, of previously-public or non-market welfare provision'.

Consistent with definitions of impact investment as 'financing methods intended for firms and organizations with a social purpose, whether they are for-profit (e.g. firms set up by social entrepreneurs) or more traditional non-profit organizations that provide social services (e.g. education, health, housing, etc.)' (Chiapello and Godefroy, 2017: 153), the significance of impact investment techniques for the financialization of social reproduction in the Global North largely relates to the financing of social economy organizations. As noted in the second section, this includes considerable investments by CDFIs, managed funds, and other institutions into education and health initiatives, and subsidized housing projects in deprived urban areas in the United States and Canada. As Rosenman (2017b) details for housing projects of this kind in the San Francisco Bay Area, the provision of subsidized housing is grounded in a self-help approach to poverty alleviation, and is based on the assumption that reduced housing costs will increase the capacity of individuals and families to spend their hard-earned cash in other ways and in support of improving their own lives—transportation, healthcare, and education, for example. State subsidies in the form of rental vouchers for tenants and tax breaks for housing developers are critical to making impactful housing projects of this kind into investable propositions.

Impact investment is also being mobilized in social policy-making, something that has received particular attention from social scientists (e.g., Andreu, 2018; Berndt and Wirth, 2018; Chiapello, 2015; Chiapello and Godefroy, 2017; Cooper, Graham, and Himick, 2016; Dowling, 2017; Kish and Leroy, 2015). In social policy-making, impact investment takes a specific asset form—namely, social impact bonds (SIBs)—that is also being experimented with in other domains as development impact bonds (DIBs) (Mawdsley, 2018) and environmental impact bonds (EIBs) (Christophers, 2018). The defining feature of SIBs—and, indeed, DIBs and EIBs—is that they structure an explicit link between the payment of financial returns to investors, on the one hand, and measurable impacts targeted by the project in question, on the other. Subject to the meeting of specified impact targets, then, investors are repaid and receive interest payments from the commissioning agency—that is, SIBs are a 'payments-for-success' instrument. While the specific organizational structures of SIBs vary considerably, impact investors typically enter into a contract via an intermediary with a social service company that is responsible for the organization and delivery of a time-limited project. Each project targets a particular population of individuals living in a particular place in order to 'impact' a specific problem, such as recidivism, homelessness, loneliness, education, or health. Projects are commissioned by cash-strapped public policy agencies because, in theory at least, they will result in medium-to-long term fiscal savings on social expenditures. The UK government is the self-proclaimed world-leader in SIBs, launching 45 SIBs between 2010 and June 2018, just less than half of all SIBs globally (Government Outcomes Lab, 2018).

There is not scope here for full discussion of the various debates over the effectiveness and consequences of SIBs (Berndt and Wirth, 2018; Fraser et al., 2018), but what is especially notable for us is how they are regarded by many critical social scientists as a particularly stark example of the financialization of society and social reproduction. Dowling (2017) provides perhaps the most strident expression of this view, stressing how SIBs in the United Kingdom serve the interests of finance capital as they open up new opportunities for value extraction. Kish and Leroy (2015) largely concur but, with reference to the application of SIBs in the context of racialized socio-spatial inequalities in the United States, also argue that 'contemporary social finance practices such as SIBs are inextricable from histories of race' (p. 630). They identify parallels and continuities, then, between the financing of the Atlantic slave trade and present day impactful social policy, not least because 'both required black bodies to be made available for investment' (Kish and Leroy, 2015: 630). Others, such as Chiapello (2015: 13), regard SIBs to be less an extension of the frontiers of financialized value extraction and more an example of the 'colonisation of nonfinancial activities by financialised valuations'. Not dissimilarly, as Cooper et al. (2016: 63) have it, SIBs are 'an attempt to marketize/financialize certain contemporary, intractable 'social problems" that 'rely on a vast array of accounting technologies'...and 'represent a powerful and potentially problematic use of accounting to enact government policy'.

Relative to their constitutive presence in the transformations under way in development agendas and the government of poverty and social reproduction, the techniques of impact investment are currently less material to the 'financialization of nature' (Ouma et al., 2018). The main exception here is the financialization of farming, wherein 'Agriculture is particularly attractive to impact investors due to its potential to make profit as well as foster food security and local development' (Kish and Fairbairn, 2018: 570). Human geographers and social scientists have also encountered impact investment in their research into rapidly proliferating green financial markets and practices, and, as Sullivan (2018) notes, there is also clearly a sense in which impact investment techniques initially developed for addressing developmental and social problems are presently being repurposed and redesigned for environmental concerns. A key driver here is change in the fund management industry, where the rise of index-tracking funds has significantly eroded fees such that "impact' investing looks like a gift to asset managers' (Authers, 2018).

Seeking to elucidate the 'socio-technical arrangement' of 'nature-based accumulation', Bracking (2012: 271) finds impact investment techniques to be at work as private equity funds partner up with DFIs and undertake valuations for various resource-based economies in Africa, including recent ventures into biodiversity, bio-fuels, carbon capture, and strategic minerals. As such, impact investment provides the 'calculative technologies employed to measure, place and value the 'environment'', and provides for 'an experiment in the financialization of environmental harm/care' (Bracking, 2012: 272–3). In a very different geographical context, meanwhile, Christophers (2018) shows that impact investment techniques are actually only gaining limited traction in the greening of water infrastructures. As part of the Clean Rivers Project for the waterways of the Potomac and Anacostia Rivers and for Rock Creek, DC Water issued the very first EIB in 2016 to capitalize the US capital city's sewerage infrastructure. But Christophers (2018) finds that of the total of US$575 million worth of municipal green bonds issued by DC Water to finance infrastructure investment to prevent untreated sewerage from flowing into the waterways (especially following heavy rainfall), only the US$25 million EIB actually requires DC Water to have an impact on water quality in order for investors (including Goldman Sachs) to receive returns.

There are indications, however, that the techniques of impact investment are at work across the green bond market broadly defined, a market that is widely hailed as a success story of the financialized governance of global climate change (Climate Bonds Initiative, 2017). Although returns on green bonds are not collateralized against future more-than-financial returns in the manner of EIBs, there is a growing trend for issues of green bonds (also known as 'climate bonds') to be accompanied by commitments to make specified and measurable impacts, and to report on performance (G20 Finance Study Group, 2016). This is significant, not least because rapid growth since the mid-2000s is often attributed by advocates and critical commentators alike to the flexibility of green bond issuance (Christophers, 2016; Keohane, 2016). Green bonds are issued in much the same way as 'plain vanilla' (or 'brown') bonds: they are issued against the full balance sheet and earnings potential of the corporations, banks, multilateral institutions, sovereign states, and municipalities that raise them. It is therefore not necessary for issuers fully to specify and measure the impacts of the earmarked green project to be funded, whether that is a renewable energy initiative, the retrofitting of residential and commercial buildings, or the transformation of industrial plant and processes to further energy efficiency, for example. Nonetheless, as part of a wider body of work that reveals the multiple ways in which value(s) for nature(s) are fabricated rather than found, Sullivan (2018) finds that attempts to conserve, restore, and rehabilitate terrestrial ecosystems (e.g., tropical forests) by raising debt in green bond markets increasingly entail the deployment of impact investment techniques.

Financial Subjects and Agents of Change

Because it encounters impact investment in the course of wider concerns with the financialization of development, society, and nature, existing research by human geographers and social scientists tends not to specify whether impact investment furthers these processes in ways that are distinctive and different from the operations of mainstream finance. An exception is a recent article by Kish and Fairbairn (2018) that, focusing on the financialization of agricultural farmland, examines how intermediaries and fund managers appeal to constituencies of mainstream and impact investors in quite different ways. They find that:

> Those promoting agricultural investment projects to mainstream investor audiences hew closely to the script of neoclassical economic rationality, in which the pursuit of profit contributes, almost incidentally, to the good of society.... these stories and their attendant claims to economic productivity are precisely how this group performs morality. For impact investors, on the other hand, explicitly moral, often highly emotive, storytelling is an essential aspect of value generation. Their solicitation of capital depends on their ability to persuade investors of the ethical framework guiding the entire sector.
>
> (Kish and Fairbairn, 2018: 571)

Kish and Fairbairn's (2018) intervention is important in several respects. It reminds us, first, that all market practices are 'moral projects' that articulate normative justifications (Fourcade and Healy, 2007). Relative to mainstream investment, the distinctive contribution of impact investment to processes of financialization therefore cannot be understood in the binary terms of immorality/morality. Mainstream investment that seeks to maximize risk-adjusted returns is itself a moral economy that rests on the purported collective benefits of individual utility maximization. Morality, then, is constitutive of both mainstream and impact investment, but plays out somewhat differently in each set of techniques and practices: 'for mainstream investors, producing economic value is a basis for moral claims-making, whereas for impact investors moral claims are a basis for producing economic value' (Kish and Fairbairn, 2018: 571).

Second, Kish and Fairbairn (2018) begin to show how a concern with the making of what they term 'ethical investor-subjects' can illuminate how impact investors articulate their 'moral claims' in ways that lead to a discrete contribution to financialization processes. Research into financial subjectivities is a key theme of the cultural economy of finance (Lai, 2017; Langley, 2008; Langley and Leyshon, 2012). Cultural economy research often focuses, however, on everyday financial subjectivities, including the emergence since the 1980s of the popular investor who variously seeks to secure their own future by building up and holding stakes (however meagre) in asset markets (Langley, 2008). But research into the subjectivity of the investor also extends beyond the general population, informed by an awareness that 'elites are not a geographically homogeneous, pre-existing cadre of actors', but are hailed as 'who a successful elite financier could or should be' (Hall, 2012: 407). This helps to explain the existence, then, of a wealth of work by industry associations, 'how-to' books and guides, and training programmes that all seek to summon up who the impact investor should be, despite the dominance of impact investment by institutional rather than retail investors.

One of the consequences of the up-take of impact investment techniques by mainstream investment institutions, for example, is what is known as 'the risk of 'impact washing', i.e. that some actors may be adopting the label without meaningful fidelity to impact' (GIIN, 2018: *iii*). This is a concern that pervades the impact investment industry (IFC, 2018). As Walker (2018) puts it in the introduction to the recent special report in the *Financial Times*, 'Impact investing has become one of the hottest strategies in fund management. But...not all those piling into the strategy are solely motivated by doing good'. At the time of writing in early 2019, the GIIN's attempt to maintain 'industry integrity' and to mitigate the risk of impact washing includes 'developing a set of principles...to strengthen the identity of impact investing' (GIIN, 2018: iii). This is being carried forward through a consultation with its members on a 'draft set of characteristics' that 'outlines a baseline of values and behaviors that investors apply with the portion of their assets used for impact investments' (see https://thegiin.org/characteristics). Such 'characteristics' seek, in effect, to define the traits and tendencies of the impact investor as a financial subjectivity. The characteristics are broken down into two main categories: 'The Impact Investor's Worldview' and 'The Actions Taken by Impact Investors'. The characteristics of the 'Worldview' is expressed by GIIN as follows:

We as impact investors hold as truths:

- Financial markets are central in driving solutions to critical threats facing the world and realizing opportunities to generate benefits for people and planet.

- Every investment, regardless of intention, contributes to short- and long-term positive and negative social and environmental effects.
- Impact investing has a role to play in generating solutions to these critical threats and realizing opportunities to create benefits in the pursuit of a just and sustainable world.
- Transformative change requires deliberate and coordinated action from each actor in the impact investing industry.

Meanwhile, the characteristics of the 'Actions' of the impact investor are more exhaustive, and are organized under four subheadings that concentrate, in turn, on investor intentions with regard to impact, decision-making on impact, the management of impact, and collaboration with the impact investment community. For GIIN, establishing the characteristics of the impact investor subject is supposed to be an inclusionary rather than exclusionary intervention, especially given that 'Implementation is a journey, and the GIIN embraces investors at all stages in that journey'. To this end, GIIN commits itself to producing 'resources that provide standards, guidance, or tools to support implementation' across each of the four 'Action' characteristics.

Such attempts to specify the traits and truths of the impact investor as a figure of the contemporary financial landscape clearly draw sustenance from much longer-standing processes that produce the mainstream investor, a financial subject who acts as the authoritative arbiter of capital allocation and legitimately receives returns of capital. It was in the United States, United Kingdom, and France during the eighteenth and nineteenth centuries that the investor first became differentiated from the gambler and speculator (de Goede, 2005; Preda, 2005). The gendered and masculine financial subject of the investor thus emerged as the bearer of a distinctive set of legally guaranteed liberal economic rights related to the allocation of capital, an individual who was also in possession of the kinds of calculative, technical, and scientific skills necessary for the rational pursuit of the maximization of returns as a universally valid set of financial goals. As Preda (2005: 155) puts it, this was a matter of investment becoming regarded as 'true speculation', "grounded in observation and study, conducted according to rules, useful and honest'. Cultural and juridical legacies that date from the emergence of the investor as a recognizable and legitimate economic figure continue to be at work, then, as the financial subjectivity of the impact investor is rounded-out in the present.

There are, moreover, important contemporary developments that undergird the making of the impact investor. Under the current mode of neoliberal government that seeks to secure the future of human and more-than-human life through financial logics, techniques, and practices (Langley, 2019), 'decisions about on what to innovate and how are to be taken by an investor rather than by a legislator' (Muniesa, 2017: 451). Investment and the viewpoint or 'gaze' of the investor has today become regarded as so essential to 'value creation' and to economic and social renewal that it operates as a 'political technology'; that is, 'the vector around which political power should organize' (Muniesa, 2017: 451). In this respect, investment is conflated with a particular understanding of 'finance' as 'the science of the optimal allocation of money, a form of knowledge that is in effect presented as an instrument against the irresponsible peril of dilapidation' (Muniesa, 2017: 448). Investment 'stands…as the viewpoint from which even the most pressing challenges of 'society' can be overcome (e.g. the ecological crisis)' (Muniesa, 2017: 451).

The summoning up of the financial subjectivity of the impact investor is thus taking place amidst the operation of investment as a political technology, a financializing logic of government that is somewhat distinct from the logics of speculation and indebtedness that have received considerably more attention from critical scholars (e.g., Konings, 2018; Lazzarato, 2012). Investment rests on processes of 'assetization' that turn things into 'assets' as '*capitalized* property' (Birch, 2017: 468, original emphasis; see also Muniesa et al., 2017; Ouma, 2016). And, for the investor, 'financial value amounts to a future return anticipated through a calculation of the cost of capital rather than to a 'price' given to the asset on the market' (Muniesa, 2017: 449). The key markers of the viability of state policy, corporate strategy, and household and individual creditworthiness therefore become whether it is possible to 'attract investors' and hold and sustain 'investor confidence'. In this respect, as Feher (2018) contends, the investor–investee relation has become crucial to contemporary capitalism.

The impact investor, however, is not merely a rational and calculative liberal economic subject who holds a legally guaranteed right to decide freely how capital should or should not be allocated, how much to charge for that capital, and so on. To be sure, the impact investor is an investor rather than a benefactor, proceeding on the basis of 'the conferral of benefits from investor to beneficiary, rather than a redistribution of resources' (Rosenman, 2017a: 7). Impact investment thereby performs 'a relation of assistance' at the same time that it also performs 'a relation of inequality' (Andreu, 2018: 275). What distinguishes the impact investor from the historical and presently privileged figure of the investor, then, is that the impact investor is an ethical financial subjectivity. As I have argued elsewhere by drawing on Foucault's reading of liberal ethics as 'the conscious practice of freedom' (Langley, 2010), ethical investors choose to accept responsibilities to others in addition to themselves. As such, impact investment does not feature normative condemnations of mainstream investment, or call for the use of sovereign regulation to prohibit, for example, investment in a new coal-fired power station that will contribute to global warming. The moral economy of mainstream investment is left intact, but is appended with a liberal ethics of investment.

Revealing in this regard is that, while some impact investors target below market returns and the preservation of capital alongside impacts of various kinds, the majority of impact investors retain market norms in pursuit of maximized risk-adjusted returns. Indeed, what appears to be innovative about impact investment is precisely that, in the oft-repeated parlance of practitioners, it is all about 'doing good' *and* 'doing well'. Accounts of what it means to be an impact investor thus tend to envisage an ethical terrain and set of practices that is somewhere in-between mainstream investment and philanthropic donation. The impact investor is, of course, free to decide how they themselves will choose to take up the 'opportunity to complement precious philanthropic capital and to promote market driven solutions', how they will occupy that space or 'middle way' (Rodin and Brandenburg, 2014: xv). This also includes discretion over how to perform their responsibilities to people and planet. The impact investor, in short, also decides and determines the social and environmental problems for which they wish to show responsibility and on which they wish to make an incremental impact. By way of illustration, consider how Hornsby and Blumberg (2013: 6–7) do not seek to prescribe the ethical outlook and choices of what they call *The Good Investor*:

> Different investors will have different areas of focus and, according to their own mission and priorities, different things they care more or less about. This naturally will be reflected in their treatment of impact, which consequently will vary from investor to investor in terms of the weight attributed to the various questions, and the level of detail entered into upon each of them.

As ethical subjects pursuing positive more-than-financial returns, impact investors do not necessarily have to give up on maximizing returns on their capital, or indeed on delivering returns on the capital that they manage on behalf of investors. Neither are they required to privilege particular issues and areas as they seek to make an impact.

For the impact investor, the challenge of doing good and doing well is thus often cast as finding an appropriate way to combine their "values' with their 'valuations', to 'embed their values in the allocation of their capital' (Rodin and Brandenburg, 2014: xiii; e.g., UBS, 2018). Put another way, for the impact investor, the category of 'value' operates in an inclusive manner to capture otherwise incompatible orders of worth. It provides a flexible placeholder where competing valuations and values not only coexist, but are ostensibly combined. As Jed Emerson (2003: 35) states when elaborating his influential concept of 'blended value' for impact investors, 'Value is often viewed in either economic or social terms', but 'true value is non-divisible, consisting of a blend of economic, social, and environmental components'. It follows that valuation is not a zero-sum relation between the collective social interest and narrow self-interest, wherein achieving greater social or environmental impact inevitably minimizes financial returns to capital (Emerson, 2003: 37–8). Rather, through blended value, equivalences between investor values and an array of collective and associational values are made possible. For investors, a singular financial 'bottom-line' becomes a 'double bottom-line' or, when environmental values and interests are added, a 'triple bottom-line'.

The commitment of the impact investor to incorporate their values into valuation processes is manifest in what Barman (2015) calls the 'value infrastructure' of impact investment; that is, the metrics and measures that enable the negotiation and calculation of impacts. As Bracking (2012: 271) argues, what is most significant here is not that these 'thin, partial and pseudo-mathematical methods' only provide for 'a dissociated, incomplete and partial valorization', but that they are 'performative' and 'assist in legitimizing' impact investment and its financializing consequences. Crucial in this respect is how value infrastructures make it possible for the impact investor to retain the relation between risk and return as the arbiter of capital allocation decisions and cost calculations. In mainstream finance, there is a positive relationship between financial risk and financial return. Higher expected returns are required to compensate investors for accepting higher risk, where 'risk' captures the probability that actual returns will differ from expected returns. Accordingly, for impact investors, 'impact risk' represents a calculation of the likelihood that an intended social return will be generated (Brandstetter and Lehner, 2015; Emerson, 2012; Nicholls and Tomkinson, 2015). It captures three components: probability (likelihood that the impact will be achieved), variance (variability in the impact expected from the investment), and uncertainty (unknown chance that endogenous or exogenous factors—e.g., economic, political, organizational factors—change the social returns) (Nicholls and Tomkinson, 2015). For example, an impact investment that targets and calculates a particularly thorny educational problem in a specific setting may have a high impact risk but, since it offers the potential for a significant and step-wise change, it is also likely to be calculated to have high impact returns.

Resting on the powerful agency of the investor and the world-making character of investment, impact investment ultimately entails a theory of change in which the ethical figure of the impact investor is the privileged agent. Through their valuations and investment decisions, impact investors appear to be capable of setting in train a host of progressive social and environmental transformations. Impact investors, in short, are assembled, at once, as both ethical financial subjects and political agents of change. At the outset of their guide for *The Good Investor*, for example, Hornsby and Blumberg (2013: 4) provide an explicit and succinct summary of this theory of change:

> All investments, besides making—and possibly losing—money, create change. The things an investment facilitates are an important part of what it really is, and how its performance can best be understood. Harnessing this force for change, and aligning it with the investor's greater sense of value, can be a powerful means to do good, and thereby, in the fullest sense of the words, to make good investments.

Other guides to impact investment are replete with similar statements that conjure up the impact investor as the one who will take advantage of the inherently positive capacities of investment as a 'force for change'. Balkin (2015), for example, places this in the context of the debates over capitalist finance that were engendered by the global financial crisis, debates that provided our entry point into impact investment in the Introduction of this chapter. For Balkin (2015), 'the corollary to the premise that finance has played a destructive role in the modern economic landscape' is that there is 'a limitless capacity to use the same set of resources to create a different outcome by following a different moral path' (2015: xvii). Moreover, as he continues, 'The power to effect positive change is infinitely greater in finance than it is in any other industry or sector, including government'. What is needed is more effort to 'rebalance the ethical compass and harness financial resources', such that 'we can improve the state of the world and generate positive social impact, correcting terminal mistakes of the past' Balkin (2015: xvii).

Conclusions

Consolidating since the late 2000s and in the wake of the global financial crisis, impact investment is a recently established domain of the contemporary global financial landscape. Setting out an agenda for geographical and social scientific research into impact investment, this chapter has suggested that careful consideration needs to be given to the specific ways in which impact investment furthers the financialization of development, society, and nature. Because impact investment has been variously encountered to date in research into financialization, rather than foregrounded and studied in its own right, its distinctive contribution to these processes is largely neglected. Impact investment is clearly not 'a new alternative' as its proponents claim, but neither is it simply another example of financial innovation that furthers processes of financialization. As the chapter has shown, the discrete contribution to the financialization of development, society, and nature that is prompted and promoted by impact investment comes sharply into focus once research considers the production of the impact investor as an ethical financial subject. As ethical financial subjects pursuing positive more-than-financial returns, impact investors can choose to seek maximized returns on their capital as they select the particular issues and areas on which they want to make an impact. They are responsible to themselves and to others, and their values are incorporated into investment valuations and calculations of risk/reward.

It would perhaps be tempting to dismiss the wider significance of impact investment, especially given that it remains relatively small-scale at present and that AUM are concentrated in a limited number of institutions that manage particularly large pools of impact capital. It is certainly not the case that—at this point in time, at least—the 'Fundamental norms governing the role and purpose of capital in society are changing, and impact investing is at the forefront driving this transformational shift' (GIIN, 2018: iii). However, impact investment's analytical and political significance is precisely that it extends and deepens the current mode of neoliberal government which, seeking to secure the future of human and more-than-human life through financial logics, techniques, and practices, institutes investment as a political technology. The impact investor is summoned up not only as a new and relatively progressive ethical financial market subject, but as a key change agent in the governance of social and environmental transformation. Dedicated and critical attention needs to be given to impact investment, then, because in the contemporary period it is the figure of the responsible, enlightened, and ethical impact investor who appears as the ostensible saviour of our age. The critical interrogation of the contingent and ambiguous character of impact investors serves not only to puncture the overblown promises of impact investment, but also contributes to broader questioning of the operation of investment as a political technology.

References

Aitken, R. (2013). The financialization of micro-credit. *Development and Change* 44(3), 473–499.

Aitken, R. (2017). All data is credit data: Constituting the unbanked. *Competition & Change* 21(4), 274–300.

Andreu, M. (2018). A responsibility to profit? Social impact bonds as a form of "humanitarian finance". *New Political Science* 40(4), 708–726.

Authers, J. (September 20, 2018). Impact investing – make good intentions pay. *Financial Times*. Available at: https://www.ft.com/content/6d55d61e-7570-11e8-bab2-43bd4ae655dd

Balkin, J. (2015). *Investing With Impact: Why Finance is a Force for Good*. Brookline, MA: Bibliomotion.

Barman, E.. (2015). Of principle and principal: Value plurality in the market of impact investing. *Valuation Studies* 3(1), 9–44.

Berndt, C. and Wirth, M. (2018). Market, metrics, morals: The Social Impact Bond as an emerging social policy instrument. *Geoforum* 90(2018), 27–35.

Bigger, P. and Dempsey, J. (2018). The ins and outs of neoliberal natures. *Environment and Planning C* 1(1–2), 25–43

Birch, K. (2017). Rethinking value in the bioeconomy: Finance, assetization, and the management of value. *Science, Technology and Human Values* 42(3), 460–490

Bishop, M. and Green, M. (2008). *Philanthrocapitalism: How the Rich Can Save the World and Why We Should Let Them*. London: A&C Black.

Bracking, S. (2012). How do investors value environmental harm/care? Private equity funds, development finance institutions and the partial financialization of nature-based industries. *Development and Change* 43(1), 271–293

Brandstetter, L. and Lehner, O. M. (2015). Impact investment portfolios: Including social risks and returns. *Entrepreneurship Research Journal* 5(2), 87–107

Chiapello, E. (2015). Financialisation of valuation. *Human Studies* 38(1), 13–35

Chiapello, E. and Godefroy, G. (2017). The dual function of judgment devices: Why does the plurality of market classifications matter? *Historical Social Research* 42(1), 152–188

Christophers, B. (2016). Risking value theory in the political economy of finance and nature. *Progress in Human Geography* 42(3), 330–349.

Christophers, B. (2018). *Risk Capital: Urban Political Ecology and Entanglements of Financial and Environmental Risk*. Washington, DC: Environment and Planning E Online. DOI: 10.1177/2514848618770369.

Climate Bonds Initiative. (2017). *Bonds and Climate Change: The State of the Market 2017*. Climate Bonds Initiative. Available at: https://www.climatebonds.net/files/files/CBI-SotM_2017-Bonds%26ClimateChange.pdf

Cooper, C., Graham, C., and Himick, D. (2016). Social impact bonds: The securitization of the homeless. *Accounting, Organizations and Society* 55(1), 63–82.

de Goede, M. (2005). *Virtue, Fortune and Faith: A Genealogy of Finance*. Minneapolis: University of Minnesota Press

Dowling, E. (2017). In the wake of austerity: Social impact bonds and the financialisation of the welfare state in Britain. *New Political Economy* 22(3), 294–310

Emerson, J. (2003). The blended value proposition: Integrating social and financial returns. *California Management Review* 45(4), 35–51.

Emerson, J. (2012). *Risk, return and impact: Understanding diversification and performance within an impact investing portfolio*. ImpactAssets Briefing #2. Available at: https://www.impactassets.org/files/downloads/ImpactAssets_IssueBrief_2-052611.pdf

Feher, M. (2018). *Rated Agency: Investee Politics in a Speculative Age*. New York: Zone Books

Fourcade, M. and Healy, K. (2007). Moral views of market society. *Annual Review of Sociology* 33(1), 285–311.

Fraser, A., Tan, S., Lagarde, M., and Mays, N. (2018). Narratives of promise, narratives of caution: A review of the literature on social impact bonds. *Social Policy Administration* 52(1), 4–28

Freireich, J. and Fulton, K. (2009). *Investing for Social & Environmental Impact: A Design for Catalyzing an Emerging Industry*. New York: Monitor Group.

Fuller, D., Jonas, A.E.G., and Lee, R. (eds.) (2010). *Interrogating Alterity: Alternative Economic and Political Spaces*. Farnham, Surry: Ashgate

G8 Social Impact Investment Taskforce. (2013). *Impact investment: The invisible heart of markets*. Available at: http://www.socialimpactinvestment.org/reports/Impact%20Investment%20Report%20FINAL[3].pdf

G20 Finance Study Group. (2016). *Green bonds: Country experiences, barriers and options*. Available at: http://unepinquiry.org/wp-content/uploads/2016/09/6_Green_Bonds_Country_Experiences_Barriers_and_Options.pdf

Gabor, D. and Brooks, S. (2017). The digital revolution in financial inclusion: International development in the fintech era. *New Political Economy* 22(4), 423-436

GIIN. (2018). *Annual Impact Investor Survey*. New York: Global Impact Investment Network.

Government Outcomes Lab. (2018). *An introduction to social impact bonds*. Available at: https://golab.bsg.ox.ac.uk/knowledge/basics/introduction-social-impact-bonds/pdf/

Hall, S. (2011). Geographies of money and finance I: Cultural economy, politics and place. *Progress in Human Geography* 35(2), 234–245.

Hall, S. (2012). Geographies of money and finance II: Financialization and financial subjects. *Progress in Human Geography* 36(3), 403–411

Hebb, T. (2013). Impact investing and responsible investing: What does it mean? *Journal of Sustainable Finance & Investment* 3(2), 71–74.

Hornsby, A. and Blumberg, G. (2013). *The Good Investor: A Book of Best Impact Practice*. London: Investing for Good

IEA (International Energy Agency). (July 2018). World Energy Investment Report 2018. Available at: https://www.iea.org/reports/world-energy-investment-2018

IFC. (2018). *Investing for impact: Operating principles for impact management*. Available at: https://www.ifc.org/wps/wcm/connect/Topics_Ext_Content/IFC_External_Corporate_Site/Impact-investing/Consultations/

Keohane, G.L. (2016). *Capital and the Common Good: How Innovative Finance is Tackling the World's Most Urgent Problems*. New York: Columbia University Press.

Kish, Z. and Fairbairn, M. (2018). Investing for profit, investing for impact: Moral performances in agricultural investment projects. *Environment and Planning A* 50(3), 569–588

Kish, Z. and Leroy, J. (2015). Bonded life. *Cultural Studies* 29(5–6), 630–651.

Konings, M. (2018). *Capital and Time: For a New Critique of Neoliberal Reason*. Stanford, CA: Stanford University Press

Langley, P. (2008). *The Everyday Life of Global Finance: Saving and Borrowing in Anglo-America*. Oxford: Oxford University Press

Langley, P. (2010). The ethical investor and embodied economies. In: Abdelal, R., Blyth, M. and Parson, C. (eds.), *Constructing the International Economy*. Ithaca, NY: Cornell University Press, 211-226.

Langley, P. (2015). *Liquidity Lost: The Governance of the Global Financial Crisis*. Oxford: Oxford University Press.

Langley, P. (2019). The financialization of life. In: Van der Zwan, N., Mertens, D. and Mader, P. (eds.), *International Handbook of Financialization*. Abingdon, Oxon: Routledge.

Langley, P. (2020). The folds of social finance: Making markets, remaking the social. *Environment and Planning A* 52(1), 130–147. Available at https://doi.org/10.1177/0308518X17752682

Langley, P. and Leyshon, A. (2012). Guest editors' introduction - Financial subjects: Culture and materiality. *Journal of Cultural Economy* 5(4), 369–373.

Lai, K.P.Y. (2017). Unpacking financial subjectivities: Intimacies, governance and socio-economic practices in financialisation. *Environment and Planning D* 35(5), 913–932

Lazzarato, M. (2012). *The Making of Indebted Man*. Los Angeles, CA: Semiotext(e)

Leyshon, A., Lee, R., and Williams, C. (eds.) (2003). *Alternative Economic Spaces*. London: Sage

Mader, P. (2015). *The Political Economy of Microfinance: Financialising Poverty*, London: Palgrave

Mader, P. (2016). Card crusaders, cash infidels and the Holy Grails of digital financial inclusion. *Behemoth* 9(2): 59–81

Maurer, B. (2015). Data-mining for development? Poverty, payment, and platform. In: Roy, A. and Crane, E.S (eds.) *Territories of Poverty: Rethinking North and South*. Athens, GA: University of Georgia Press, 126–143

Maverick, J.B. (September 1, 2015). *The top 5 impact investing firms*. Investopedia. Available at: https://www.investopedia.com/articles/active-trading/090115/top-5-impact-investing-firms.asp

Mawdsley, E. (2018). Development geography II: Financialization. *Progress in Human Geography* 42(2), 264–274

Mitchell, K. (2017). Metrics millennium: Social impact investing and the measurement of value. *Comparative European Politics* 15(5), 751–770.

Mitchell, K. and Sparke, M. (2016). The new Washington consensus: Millennial philanthropy and the making of global market subjects. *Antipode* 48(3), 724–749.

Muniesa, F. (2017). On the political vernaculars of value creation. *Science as Culture* 26(4), 445–454.

Muniesa, F. et al. (2017). *Capitalization: A Cultural Guide*. Paris: Presses des Mines.

Nicholls, A. and Tomkinson, E. (2015). Risk and return in social finance. In: Nicholls, A., Paton, R. and Emerson, J. (eds.) *Social Finance*, Oxford: Oxford University Press, 282–310

O'Donohoe, N., Leijonhufvud, C., Saltuk, Y., Bugg-Levine, A., and Brandenburg, M. (2010). *Impact Investments: An Emerging Asset Class*. New York: JPMorgan Chase & Co. Available at: https://www.jpmorganchase.com/corporate/socialfinance/document/impact_investments_nov2010.pdf

Oleksiak, A., Nicholls, A., and Emerson, J. (2015). Impact investing: A market in evolution. In: Nicholls, A., Paton, R. and Emerson, J. (eds.), *Social Finance*. Oxford: Oxford University Press, 207–251

Ouma, S. (2016). From financialization to operations of capital: Historicizing and disentangling the finance–farmland-nexus. *Geoforum* 72(2016), 82–93.

Ouma, S., Johnson, L., and Bigger, P. (2018). Rethinking the financialisation of 'nature'. *Environment and Planning A* 50(3), 500–511

Palmer, A. (2015). *Smart Money: How High-Stakes Financial Innovation is Reshaping Our World – For the Better*. New York: Basic Books

Preda, A. (2005). The investor as a cultural figure in global capitalism. In: Knorr Cetina, K. and Preda, A. (eds.) *The Sociology of Financial Markets*, Oxford: Oxford University Press, 141–162.

Pryke, M. and du Gay, P. (2007). Take an issue: Cultural economy and finance. *Economy and Society* 36(3), 339–354

Rankin, K.N. (2013). A critical geography of poverty finance. *Third World Quarterly* 34(4), 547–568.

Rodin, J. and Brandenburg, M. (2014). *The Power of Impact Investing: Putting Markets to Work for Profit and Global Good*. Philadelphia, PA: Wharton Digital Press.

Rosenman, E. (2017a) The geographies of social finance: Poverty regulation through the 'invisible heart' of markets. *Progress in Human Geography* 40(5), 610–628

Rosenman, E. (2017b) *The spaces of social finance : poverty regulation through the "invisible heart" of markets*. PhD Thesis, University of British Columbia. Available at: https://open.library.ubc.ca/cIRcle/collections/ubctheses/24/items/1.0354982

Sullivan, S. (2018). Bonding nature(s)? Funds, financiers and values at the impact investing edge in environmental conservation. In: Bracking, S., Fredriksen, A., Sullivan, S. and Woodhouse, P. (eds.) *Valuing Development, Environment and Conservation: Creating Values that Matter*. London: Routledge, 101–121

Turner, A. (August 27, 2009a). How to tame global finance. *Prospect Magazine*. Available at: https://www.prospectmagazine.co.uk/magazine/how-to-tame-global-finance

Turner, A. (2009b). *The Turner Review: A Regulatory Response to the Global Financial Crisis*. London: Financial Services Authority.

UBS Investor Watch. (2018). *Return on Values: Most sustainable investors expect better performance, bigger impact*. Global and UK insights: What's on investors' minds/2018, 2.

Walker, O. (September 20, 2018). *Special Report: Impact Investing – Impact investors shoot for clearer goals. Financial Times*. Available at: https://www.ft.com/content/fc7964f2-7474-11e8-bab2-43bd4ae655dd

World Economic Forum. (2013). *From the Margins to the Mainstream: Assessment of the Impact Investment Sector and Opportunities to Engage Mainstream Investors*. New York: World Economic Forum.

16

THE FOUNDATIONS OF DEVELOPMENT BANKING

A Critical Review

Aniket Shah

Introduction

This chapter presents a critical review of the topic of development banking. A review of development banking is required given both the persistence and prevalence of development banks as financial institutions and the lack of critical analysis of their effectiveness (Diamond, 1957; Martinez, 2017; Musacchio et al., 2017). The motivation for this chapter is to provide an analysis of the conceptual underpinnings of development banks in order for academics and policy-makers to achieve more critical assessments of the form, function, and effectiveness of development banks in their respective domains.

Development banks are noteworthy from the perspectives ofboth persistence and prevalence. With regard to persistence, development banks have existed since the early nineteenth century, when state-owned and state-capitalized financial institutions were formed throughout continental Europe to support the industrialization efforts of the continent (Diamond, 1957). Since this period, development banks have persisted and grown in highly diverse geographies. From the perspective of prevalence, there were over 500 development banks operating in the world as of 2019. The combined assets of the world's development banks are well over US$5 trillion dollars (Bruck, 1998; Musacchio et al., 2017). Development banks are a sizeable portion of the world's financial assets.

Despite the persistence and prevalence of development banks, there is little academic or policy knowledge regarding how these organizations operate and their impacts on economic and sustainable development outcomes. According to a recent World Bank survey: 'little is known about DBs [development banks]...Little is known about how DBs operate, what their policy mandates are, what financial services they offer, which type of clients they target, how they are regulated and supervised, what business models they have adopted, what governance framework they have, and what challenges they face' (Martinez and Vincente, 2012). I argue that one of the reasons that academics and policy-makers do not have a strong understanding of development banks is that they have not systematically interrogated the underlying conceptual foundations that led to the existence of development banks. This chapter seeks to present a critical assessment of the conceptual foundations of development banking in order to pave the way for future research and analysis of this topic.

The chapter is presented in three sections. First, I provide an overview of the topic of development banking, focusing on the wide divergences of definitions of what constitutes a development bank and the historical evolution of this financial institution. Second, I examine the conceptual underpinnings of development banks by investigating the theoretical and empirical debates surrounding four areas related to development banks: development, the state and market in economic affairs, institutions, and banking. Third, I end the chapter by articulating the implications of the review on how academics and policy-makers should approach the study of development banks.

Overview of Development Banking

The central topic of this paper is development banking. A defining element of development banks is their heterogeneity. Development banks range in their size, scope, spatial orientation, ownership structure, sources of capital, and uses of capital (Martinez, 2017). In this section, I provide an analysis of the definitions, historical evolution, and contemporary state of development banks.

Definition of Development Banks

No commonly accepted definition of a development bank exists. However, three definitions of development banks to which reference is commonly made are:

1) A development bank is a financial institution devoted primarily to stimulating the private sector of the economy (Diamond, 1957).
2) Development banks are government-sponsored financial institutions concerned primarily with the provision of long-term capital to industry (De Aghion, 1999).
3) A development bank is any type of financial institution that national government fully or partially owns or controls and has been given an explicit legal mandate to reach socioeconomic goals in a region, sector or market segment. (Martinez, 2017).

For the purposes of this paper, based on these three definitions, I define a development bank as a financial institution, directly owned by state actors, that has an explicit development mandate. By defining a development bank as such, I attempt to focus the subsequent research and inquiry in the following four ways: first, I will focus on development banks as *financial* institutions, thereby ensuring that the analysis focuses on the role of institutions providing financial capital, as opposed to other types of capital (social, human, and so on). Second, I will focus on banks that are under direct government ownership. This means that this chapter will not focus on other types of financial institutions, such as privately owned investment banks and impact investment firms, which may have a development orientation through their functioning but are not owned by state actors. Third, I will focus on institutions that are explicitly mandated for the pursuit of 'development'. The term, 'development', will be analysed further in this chapter and does not limit the research to bodies that are only financing private entities. Fourth, the definition that I offer makes no claim to the necessary spatial orientation of a bank to be considered a development bank.

Stages of Development Banking

To investigate the foundations of development banking, I argue that it is important to understand their role and evolution throughout economic history. I posit that there have been four eras of development banking in recent economic history.

The first era of development banking occurred in continental Europe as a catalyst for the Industrial Revolution. Continental Europe was the home for the first era of development banking while the region was playing 'catch up' with Great Britain's early efforts and progress towards industrialization. In 1822, the Societe Generale pour Favoriser l'Industrie Nationale was formed in Brussels as a financial institution aimed at supporting Belgian industry (Diamond, 1957). In 1852, France witnessed the inception of two of the most significant and foundational development banks in history—Credit Foncier, a mortgage bank focused on long-term agricultural loans and, subsequently, industrial development; and Credit Mobilier, which focused on utilities and industry (Cameron, 1961). Although these institutions did not survive for long—Credit Mobilier, for example, only lasted for 15 years—their model was imitated by other European nations, including Germany, Austria, the Netherlands, Italy, Switzerland, and Spain. These banks were mainly privately owned but had significant government connections, including, at times, initial capital from national governments. According to Diamond, these banks served as 'planners, entrepreneurs, financiers and managers', and served Europe's needs for large amounts of capital needs for industrial development (Diamond, 1957).

The second era of development banking was the creation of state-led development banks after World War I and World War II—once again, mainly in

Europe. After World War I, various countries in Europe—including Belgium, France, Finland, Poland and Hungary—created state-owned financial institutions focused on the 'problems and reorganization of existing enterprises' (Diamond, 1957: 8). Unlike the set of development banks created in the nineteenth century described above, these institutions were less focused on building and promoting new enterprises and more focused on rebuilding pre-existing enterprises. After World War II, many development banks were created at various spatial scales. In 1944, the International Bank for Reconstruction and Development (IBRD) was created as part of the Bretton Woods system to help reconstruct Europe and to finance anti-poverty work globally. In addition to the IBRD, large national development banks were formed in major economies, including the Development Bank of Japan (DBJ) in 1948, the Kreditanstalt fur Wiederaufbau (KfW) in Germany in 1948, and the Industrial and Commercial Finance Corporation in Great Britain in 1945, among others (Diamond, 1957).

The third era of development banking was during the period of decolonization in Asia, Africa, and Latin America during the 1950s and 1960s. It was during this period that many regional and sub-regional development banks were created— regional development banks included the Asian Development Bank, the African Development Bank, and the Inter-American Development Bank. This was a period that coincided with state-led development efforts, particularly in Asia (World Bank Group, 1993). Two major forces drove this period of development banking: the need for industrialization, and Cold War dynamics. Industrially led growth was seen broadly as the way forward for countries that were entering their post-colonial period. In addition, the United States and the Soviet Union had entered proxy wars around the Cold War and the regional development banks were possible tools with which the United States and its allies could achieve influence over Asia, Africa, and Latin America. This period of development banking was critical, as it witnessed the creation of the largest development banks still operating today (Engen and Prizzon, 2018).

The fourth era of development banking has been the era of development banking led by China through the creation of both national and global development banks by the Government of the People's Republic of China. The China Development Bank, created in 1994, has played an important role in China's own development trajectory, both domestically and internationally (Yuan, 2013). In 2014, the Government of the People's Republic of China also led the creation of two regional development banks—the Asian Infrastructure Investment Bank (AIIB) and the New Development Bank (NDB) (Shah, 2016).

Contemporary Status of Development Banking

In this section, I provide an overview of development banking operations through a spatial lens, providing a context for how development banks operate at the global and regional, national and sub-national levels.

At the global and regional levels, there areat least 25 development banks (Engen and Prizzon, 2018). These banks can be categorized within three sub-categories: global, regional, and sub-regional. Global/regional development banks refer to the set of financial institutions that have multiple nations as owners. At the national level, there is no consensus estimate regarding the number of national development banks that exist. There a loosely constructed global industry association exists called the World Federation of Development Finance Institutions (WFDFI), which is a federation consisting of five regional associations of development financing institutions: the African Association of Development Finance Institutions (AADFI), the Association of Development Financing Institutions in Asia and the Pacific (ADFIAP), the Association of National Development Finance Institutions in Member Countries of the Islamic Development Bank (ADFIMI), the Latin American Association of Development Financing Institutions (ALIDE), and the European Development Finance Institutions Association (EDFI). As of 2019, there are collectively 300 individual members of the constituent associations of the WFDFI, after removing development banks that are members of multiple associations and privately owned banks. Note, however, that this list is not comprehensive with regard to all national development banks operating globally, as the memberships of these associations is voluntary and there is no obligation for a national development bank to join. At the sub-national level, a growing number of financial institutions exists that have been developed to finance specific aspects of the broader sustainable development agenda. These institutions include state-, county-, and city-level development finance institutions that are owned by government actors at the sub-national level. There is no global association of sub-national development finance institutions. There are many financial institutions at city level that have an orientation toward development, including community development finance institutions (CDFIs), credit cooperatives, and microfinance institutions (MFIs). The CDFI network in the United States and United Kingdom consists of privately owned commercial banks that serve low-income communities (Benjamin, Rubin, and Zielenbach, 2004). Some MFIs are publicly owned and some are privately owned. For the purposes of this chapter, community-level development banks have been omitted from the scope of the research (Cull, Demirgüç-Kunt, and Morduch, 2009).

Conceptual Foundations of Development Banking

The purpose of this section is to situate development banks within four theoretical building blocks. First, development banks operate within a broader debate around the concept of 'development'. Second, development banks exist in the dynamics between the roles of the state versus the role of markets in economic affairs. Third, development banks can be understood as institutions, and therefore need to be placed in the context of the role of institutions in economic development. Fourth, development banks are banks, and therefore need to be examined through the perspective of the role of banks in a financial system.

Development

In this section, I analyse the concept of 'development' with regard to the broader topic of development banking. In doing so, I focus on three specific aspects of the topic: the evolution and definitions of the term 'development', the various contributors to development, and the evolution from economic development to sustainable development.

Development: Evolution and Definitions of the Concept

The concept of 'development' is used in many disciplines in both the physical and social sciences. The term 'development' is derived from the French term *developper*, the original meaning of which is, 'a gradual unfolding, a full working out or disclosure of something' (Develop, 2020) This etymology has an important parallel to contemporary discussions of development in the social science context, particularly the two concepts of 'gradualism' and 'unfolding'. With regard to 'gradualism', the original meaning of 'development' alludes to a slow pace of evolution. This observation is relevant to the significant debates in the twentieth century regarding the pace at which economic transitions and development should occur (Weitzman, 1993). With regard to 'unfolding', the original meaning of the term assumes that development is the exposure of what may already exist, as opposed to the creation of something new. This observation presaged a widespread belief that economic development is ultimately about the unfolding of human and societal capabilities (Sen, 1999).

Conceptually, economic development and economic growth have been linked, although it is important to note that the two concepts are not synonymous with one another (Lewis, 1955). Economic growth refers to a rise in income/output, either at the national level or the per capita level (Perkins et al., 2013). This is an objective arithmetic figure, although the questions as to how and why economies grow, and the best way to measure that growth are complex. (The methodology for measuring GDP is not consistent across geographies and many approaches have been criticized for not capturing the full economic output of a region (Lepenies, 2016). Economic development, however, refers to a broader set of outcomes, including improvements in health, education, inequality, social cohesion, and other aspects related to human welfare (Perkins et al., 2013). Although it is the case that economic growth can lead to, and is often associated with, economic development, it is also the case that economic development requires a broader lens of understanding with regard to how the income is produced, distributed, spent, and structured within an economy. Economic development is therefore related to the significance of the structure of an economy and a society (Perkins et al., 2013).

Today, no commonly accepted definition exists for the concept of development within the field of development economics. The general concept refers to the improving of living standards of individuals. There have been attempts to define the concept—such as Mydral's definition of development as, 'the movement upward of the entire social system' (Myrdal, 1974: 730)—but such definitions lead to many conceptual and empirical questions. For example, what is meant by 'upward'? What is meant by 'social system'? How do we measure a 'social system'? What about the role of the natural environment? The Human Development Index was created in 1975 to measure a country's broader development outcomes, as opposed to focusing only on economic growth, and was the result of a belief that measuring economic output (GDP) did not give a full picture of a country's development. The Human Development Index is a quantitative measure of life expectancy, education, and per capita income (UNDP, 2008, 2011).

Contributors to Development

Many outstanding questions remain regarding how development is achieved. The type of economic configurations and the policy interventions that optimally lead to development are the focus of both theoretical and empirical analysis. This section provides an overview of the most relevant axes of the debate.

From the middle of the twentieth century, economic growth models played an important role in identifying the need for increased national savings to support the increased level of investments for economic growth and development. The Harrod-Domar (Domar, 1946; Harrod, 1939) Model and its associated Two-Gap Model (Chenery, 1967) were particularly important in emphasizing the importance of increasing savings to fuel investments. The Harrod-Domar model posited that the growth rate of an economy was linked directly and linearly to its national savings and its capital–output ratio, which meant that the more a country saved, and therefore invested (since in a closed economy, savings and investment are equal), the more it can grow. Holis Chenery's Two-Gap model grew out of the Harrod-Domar framework, and posited that developing countries are limited by not only a gap in in their national savings, but also a gap in their foreign exchange, due to limited abilities to export. Both frameworks gave support to the notion that developing countries needed foreign aid to increase investments to grow. The Harrod-Domar and Two Gap models have been criticized by many development economists for being overly simplistic and empirically inaccurate (Easterly, 2001), but they played an important role in setting the debate and initial policy frameworks for development policy in the 1950s and onwards.

In the subsequent section, I lay out three important debates regarding contributors to development that are linked to our understanding of development banking. (I note that a major debate in economic development is on the respective roles of the state versus the markets. This topic is the subject of the proceeding section of this chapter).

The first major debate is with regard to the relative importance of geography versus institutions for economic development. The 'geography is destiny' thesis argues that the relative growth and development of one physical region compared to another can be explained by geographical factors, including the physical climate, its impact on the fertility of land, and the implications of this for the long-term stability of a region (Diamond, 2005). More recently, the geography-centered view of development has focused on issues such as the proximity of countries to trade routes, a country's natural resource, and the incidence of disease in certain geographies as statistically significant determinants of development (Bloom et al., 1998; Gallup, Sachs, and Mellinger, 1999). The 'institutions rule' thesis posits that variations in levels of economic development cannot be explained by geographical factors but, instead, are the results of certain political institutions as norms, specifically the level of inclusiveness of a society (Acemoglu and Robinson, 2020). This argument focuses on the long-term negative impacts of 'extractive' institutions, where elites of a society capture economic rents and disincentive entrepreneurship. This literature touches on the much broader debate on whether certain political systems, such as democracy, is conducive to economic development at certain stages of a country's evolution.

A second major debate is the role of foreign aid for low-income countries. Proponents of foreign aid for development argue that aid is necessary for two related, yet distinctly separate reasons: historical obligations and investment gaps. The historical obligations argument focuses on the notion that developing countries were systematically under-developed during the period of colonization and are therefore owed aid to support development now (Tharoor, 2018). The investment gap argument focuses on the notion that low-income countries do not have enough national savings to support national public investments in critical sectors such as health, education, and infrastructure—sectors that are generally considered public goods and that cannot easily be financed by private sources (Sachs, 2005). Critics of foreign aid focus on two major strands of argument regarding the ineffectiveness of aid to promote development. The first argument is that foreign aid, and the accompanying role of foreign experts, prevents local solutions to local problems; instead, this situation promotes solutions that are not feasible to local conditions (Easterly, 2006; Ramalingam, 2013). The second argument is that foreign aid is often tied to conditions that are harmful to local populations and supportive of authoritarian governments, which ultimately prevents human rights from being achieved (Easterly, 2013).

The third major debate focuses on the role of financial system development in promoting economic development. There are two critical questions within this topic of economic development: What are the 'right' financial system institutions and policies to support development? Is there an optimal size for a financial system for a specific level of development of a country? With regard to the first question, there are various perspectives for which financial institutions are needed, and the sequences in which they should they be created, to support growth and development in low-income countries (World Bank Group, 2020). One argument is that development requires a full array of financial institutions that can intermediate both national and international savings for domestic investments, and, to achieve this, governments need to play a major role in establishing domestic institutions and capital markets in the early stages of development. This argument is countered by a strand of literature in development economics that argues that although domestic capital markets are important for economic development, they should be liberalized to allow interest rates to reflect the domestic scarcity of capital (McKinnon, 1973). With regard to the second question, there is very strong empirical work that shows that, after a certain point, the size of a financial system can be deleterious to the growth prospects of a country (Rajan and Zingales, 1998; De Gregorio and Guidotti, 1995; Levine, 2006).

State and Market

In this section, I analyse the role of the state versus the role of the market for economic development and growth. This topic is one of the elemental aspects of modern economics and development studies, and has significant implications for the study and analysis of development banking. Given the breadth of this topic, I focus on two specific aspects of the broader topic that have direct relevance for the study of development banking: the broader debate about the role of state versus the role of markets in economic systems, and the concept and implementation of industrial policy.

Role of the State versus the Role of the Market in Economic Systems

The optimal role of the state in an economy has been a topic for debate for a considerable time. At a broad level, the proponents of a significant role of the state in economic affairs argue that there are inherent flaws in the ability of markets to allocate resources for the benefit of an economy and its citizens, and therefore state intervention is necessary. The shortcomings of the markets can lead to suboptimal outcomes on a variety of fronts, including allocation of resources to the poor (Sachs, 2005), allocation of resources to environmental protection (Sachs, 2015), and the allocation of capital for long-term and uncertain projects (De Aghion, 1999), among others. The state can be viewed as the provider of public goods (Samuelson, 1954)—goods that are non-rivalrous and non-excludable. Proponents of a significant role of the market in economic affairs argue that markets are unique in their ability to allocate scarce resources within a system efficiently and effectively. Proponent of free market systems argue that any interventions that distort the functioning of markets can lead to broader distortions in an economy (Friedman, 1962).

A useful analytical framework of the state versus the market debate is provided by the concepts of 'market failure' and 'government failure'. The term 'market failure' was first defined in 1958 by Francis Bator, who defined it as, 'the failure of a more or less idealized system of price-market institutions to sustain 'desirable' activities or to stop 'undesirable' activities. The desirability of an activity, in turn, is evaluated relative to the solution values of some explicit or implied maximum-welfare problem' (Bator, 1958) A market failure occurs when the functioning of market forces leads to outcomes that are not in line with the maximization of the welfare of a system. Various issues—including asymmetry of information, externalities, monopolistic behavior, among others—can create market failures. Market failures can then be corrected by government intervention. However, government intervention can also create a 'government failure', whereby a set of interventions by the state in a market has created inefficiencies itself (Krueger, 1990; Winston, 2006). Government failure can occur for a variety of reasons, including misaligned incentives of government workers, poor implementation, and the limits of public policy in changing behavior. The tension between market and government failures is at the core of the challenge of deciphering how and when a government should intervene in a market-based economy.

Proponents of market-oriented economies have conceded the role of the state in a few critical areas. Ibn Khaldun, a fourteenth-century scholar, was skeptical about the role of the government in economic affairs (Boulakia, 1971). He believed that government intervention in commercial activities would lead to poor outcomes, due to misaligned incentives of government bureaucrats compared to those of business leaders. Despite his skepticism, Khaldun conceded that the state should play a role in establishing laws that were supporting of commercial activities, as well as protecting trade routes and providing security. Adam Smith held a similar perspective to that of Khaldun. Not dismissing the role of the government entirely, Smith believed that the state should limit its activities to administering justice, securing property rights, and ensuring education and public works are financed through tax revenues that are not a burden on enterprise. Smith's views on the importance of government provision of public works for the support of commercial enterprise is an important point that is echoed by other market-oriented economic thinkers (Smith, 2000). Friedrich Hayek conceded that the state should create laws that respect the freedom of individuals and also suggested that the state should be involved in providing health insurance to individuals (Hayek and Hamowy, 2013).

During the early twentieth century, there was a significant challenge to the market-oriented economic philosophy of scholars such as Khaldun and Smith, both in economic thinking and practice. John Maynard Keynes made a significant contribution to the field by underscoring the important role of government spending during recessions (Keynes, 1936). Keynes argued that markets are not self-balancing in the short run, and that the government stimulating the aggregate demand of an economy can overcome periods of economic recession. Keynes' economic thinking was highly influential in the United States during the aftermath of the Great Depression. During this period, the Federal Government of the United States undertook a major public spending program known as the 'New Deal' in order to stimulate the economy, employ citizens, and kick start growth (Leuchtenburg, 2009). Keynesian economic thinking continued to have a significant influence throughout twentieth and twenty-first centuries as a justification for increased government involvement in economic affairs, both during periods of economic crisis and beyond.

There is a specific set of questions that pertain to the role of the state in financial markets. These questions arise out of the notion that financial markets are distinct from other economic markets—due to the existence of more market failures in financial markets, and the various feedback loops between financial systems and the real economy. The questions on the role of the state in financial markets focus on the following topics, among others: When should a government intervene in financial markets? How should the state regulate financial markets? Should the government direct credit to key economic sectors? These topics have been debated amongst financial scholars and economists for centuries. One important contribution is that of Joseph Stiglitz, who argues for a robust role of the state in solving financial market failures. He provides a six-part framework to guide government intervention in financial markets, which includes providing consumer protection, ensuring bank solvency, improving macroeconomic stability, ensuring competition, stimulating growth, and improving the allocation of resources (Stiglitz, 1994).

The topic of 'markets versus states' is complex, given the fact that there are hardly any real-life examples of a completely free market, or a completely state-driven economy. Effectively, all economic systems are mixed economies, in one-way or another, with the state being involved in some aspects of economic affairs and the market in others. For example, the United States, often heralded as a paragon of a 'free market' system, is home to significant government involvement in agriculture, banking, energy, and transportation, among other key sectors (Hacker and Pierson, 2016). On the other hand, North Korea, a country that is known for its autarkic system, is home to economic markets for the exchange of goods and services (Lankov, 2016). Countries exist on a spectrum of the relative influence of the state versus the market in different sectors specifically, and in the functioning of the economy generally. Recent empirical scholarship has demonstrated that the role of the state in capitalism is increasing globally and that 'state capitalism' manifests itself in different models of state ownership of industry, either directly through state-owned enterprises, or indirectly through national financial intermediaries such as sovereign wealth funds and development banks (Musachio and Lazzarini, 2014; Kurlantzick, 2016).

Industrial Policy

The dynamics of states versus markets becomes particularly relevant with regard to the process of industrialization and questions surrounding whether a government should play a role in supporting the industrialization efforts of a country and, if so, what that role should be—a question that is at the heart of industrial policy (Rodrik, 2004, 2015; Stiglitz, 2011). The topic of industrial policy is particularly relevant for the study of development banking, given the fact that the formation of development banks co-existed with preceding periods of industrialization.

Industrial policy is closely linked with the concept of import-substitution industrialization (ISI) (Dervis and Page, 1984). The strategy of ISI for economic development refers to policies that promote domestic production over foreign imports to drive industrialization. One of the clearest and most foundational articulations of an approach towards industrial policy is Alexander Hamilton's 1791 Report on Manufactures to the U.S. House of Representatives (Hamilton, 2001). In this document, Hamilton argued for the importance of a strong manufacturing sector for the country. Hamilton believed that the government needed to play an active role in ensuring that the manufacturing sector succeeded, through the placing of tariffs on imported goods and providing incentives for innovation.

The idea of a significant role of the state in industrialization is linked with economic models related to the 'Big Push' and broader topics of economic planning that became important during the second half of the twentieth century. Paul Rosenstein-Rodan developed the Big Push model in 1943 (Rosenstein-Rodan, 1944, 1961). In this model, Rosenstein-Rodan argued that economic growth required a network of activities to occur. He argued that no single firm could organize this larger network of activities by itself and that, therefore, government was needed to make major investments in various sectors at the same time so as to promote industrialization and, thereby, growth. The Big Push model towards development was closely linked with concepts and tools around economic planning that were developed in the 1960s and 1970s. Jan Tinbergen was a pioneer in the study of economic planning. His work contributed to tools and frameworks for long-term economic planning by central actors that used various economic tools for various economic outcomes (Chenery, 1984; Tinbergen, 1968). The Big Push model, as well as broader efforts in economic planning, had a significant influent on international aid and development efforts in Africa and Latin America in the second half of the twentieth century. Accordingly, these models have been criticized both empirically and theoretically for their ineffectiveness for economic development outcomes.

The analytical approach and evidence towards industrial policy and its implementation has benefited from China's approach to economic development and the lessons learned from this experience (Lin, 2012a). China's economic development efforts since 1979, when the country began opening its domestic economy to global market forces, has demonstrated the benefits and challenges that come from a significant role of the state in industrial policy and strategy. China's evolution from an agricultural economy to an industrial giant can be attributed, although to varying degrees, to the government's role in protecting and supporting industries so that, over time, they could compete globally (The China Development Bank and Renmin University of China, 2011; Yuan, 2013). There are many outstanding questions, however, about the long-term economic sustainability of this approach, as well as the unintended consequences of large state involvement in China's industrial evolution. These questions include, but are not limited to: Can the Chinese government afford to support uncompetitive industries in the future? Are the geopolitical costs of state support for industry worth the benefits? Will Chinese companies be able to compete globally without government support (Economy, 2018; Magnus, 2018).

The implementation of industrial policy has benefited from recent scholarship by academics and practitioners inspired by China's recent successes. Lin's work on 'new structural economics' outlines a systematic and quantitative methodology for states to support industry through sound industrial policy (Lin, 2011, 2012b). Lin's approach to industrial policy focuses on a six-step framework that focuses on government's identification and support of industries that are within the country's comparative advantage compared to other countries that may be further along in that same industry but have similar resource endowments.

Relatedly, the role of the state has been argued to be critical for advancements in technology in the latter half of the twentieth century. Many of the major technological breakthroughs of the twentieth century, including the Internet, telecommunications, lasers, and semiconductors were made possible due to resources provided by the US federal government for research in both public and private sector research laboratories (Hacker and Pierson, 2016). Recent work by Mariana Mazzucato has made the case for an 'entrepreneurial state', whereby the government should take an active leadership role in developing technologies and promoting industries that can provide solutions to challenges brought about by the need for sustainable development (Mazzucato, 2015). Mazzucato's prescriptions are based on her analysis of the commercial benefits for companies, such as Apple, that have been able to commercialize technologies that were initially financed and discovered by the state.

The topic of industrial policy has many critics (Pack and Saggi, 2006). There are two broad conceptual arguments against industrial policy: the inability of governments to pick winners, and the political influences that drive government investment decision. Within the first category, there remains significant skepticism that governments and their associated experts are able to pick winners—whether entire sectors or areas within a sector—more effectively than markets. This argument rests on the fact that government is not, and should not be, in the business of commerce—arguments that date back to the work of Ibn Khaldun in the fourteenth century. The second set of arguments against industrial policy refers to the political influences that drive government investments and support for sectors. This argument rests on the fact that the state is inextricably linked to politics. If the state is making investment decisions based on the political preferences of the ruling coalition, this could lead to poor long-term outcomes.

Institutions

In this section, I analyse the broader literature on the role of institutions and organizations in economic development. Specifically, I focus on two topics within this field: the relationship between institutions viewed as 'rules of the game' and institutions as 'organizations', institutional legitimacy, and design; and the spatial dimensions of financial institutions. This section borrows heavily from the recent theoretical and empirical work of economic geographers who have studied the role of institutions in long-term investing, including pension funds and sovereign wealth funds (Clark and Monk, 2010b; Clark, Dixon and Monk, 2013).

Institutions as Rules of the Game versus Organizations

There are two broad and related conceptualizations of institutions—one as 'rules of the game', the other as specific 'organizations' or structures that operate within a system. One commonly accepted view of institutions is as, 'rules of the game in a society or, more formally, are the humanly devised constraints that shape human interaction'. This perspective of institutions views the primary role of institutions as, 'reducing uncertainty by providing a structure to everyday life' (North, 1990: 7) Institutions, in this formulation, can be understood as both formal and informal 'rules' and laws, such as broader accepted norms within a society. In this formulation, institutions are formed to decrease uncertainty and the costs in economic and social exchange (Williamson, 1985).

The 'institutions as organizations' perspective can be understood through the two perspectives: as 'players in the game' (North, 1990), and as entities that were formed to decrease the transactions costs of economic exchange (Coase, 2012). The 'institutions as players in the game' perspective is important as it underlines an interaction between institutions as rules and institutions as organizations. North argued that organizations operate within the incentive structure that is created by institutions. He posited that organizations are formed to take advantage of the opportunities that present themselves through the institutional structure of a society and that, as organizations evolve to do so, they alter institutions. There is therefore, according to North (1990), a 'lock-in that comes from the symbiotic relationship between institutions and the organizations that have evolved as a consequence of the incentive structure provide by those institutions'. The second, related perspective of institutions as partnerships formed to decrease transactions costs of exchange was put forward by a foundational contribution by Ronald Coase (2012). He argued that firms are formed to decrease the total costs of transactions that would otherwise occur through markets. Coase's theoretical contributions served as a foundation for a significant amount of work in the institutional economics literature.

The study of the behavior and function of organizations was deepened significantly by the work of Herbert Simon and two related theoretical contributions he made to management science: the notion of bounded rationality and 'satisficing' (March and Simon, 1958). Simon's work on organizations arose from a belief that although organizations represent 'a major part of the environment', they had not been studied or examined in a systematic and theoretical way. Among Simon's many contributions to the study of organizations was the notion that there are cognitive limitations to humans who participate in organizations in terms of the time that they have to make a decision, the limitations of their own abilities' and the challenges of the decisions themselves. These limitations 'bind' the rationality of decision-making, and lead decision-makers to make decisions that 'satisfice' the conditions but are not the theoretically the optimal decision to be made. This insight about organizational behavior has been highly influential in understanding and guiding organizations' practices since the early 1970s.

Although there has been a significant amount of work done on the role of institutions in economic development, most of this work has looked at institutions through the first definition highlighted above—as 'rules of the game'. This literature is both historical and empirical in nature, and focuses on trying to understand the contribution of property rights and the rule of law in explaining the divergence of economic development and growth patterns between geographies. The roles of specific organizations and categories of organization in economic development has received much less attention. By understanding that institutions can be seen as both rules of the game as well as organizations, scholars can widen the lens of analysis of how socially created entities have an impact on the material well-being of individuals in development processes.

Institutional Legitimacy and Design

One important aspect of the topic of institutions is the question of whence its legitimacy is derived. The topic of institutional legitimacy is particularly relevant for institutions that have both financial and national objectives. Clark and Monk provide a two-part framework for how the legitimacy of an institution can be evaluated. First, institutions can be deemed legitimate, judged against 'societal norms including moral and political expectations as to proper roles and responsibilities' (Clark and Monk, 2010a). This perspective is normative in nature, and implies that the legitimacy of an institution is contingent on the prevailing set of 'societal norms' in a region. This approach has its challenges though: it presupposes that a country or region has a set of 'societal norms' that is either widely shared, or at least shared to a sufficient extent, to enable it to be used as the basis for judging legitimacy. The second approach towards understanding the legitimacy of an institution is to judge its progress in achieving whatever purpose the institution has set out for itself. This approach towards evaluating the legitimacy of an institution is functionalist in nature, but it presupposes that institutions have a clear purpose that is commonly understood and accepted by the various stakeholders of the institution itself. Despite having legitimacy, though, either for normative or functional reasons, financial institutions may react to short-term political considerations over their legitimate reasons (Roe, 2012).

Institutional and organizational design focuses on the process of creating and improving these entities. The topic of the design of organizations has two salient aspects: pragmatism versus 'truth-discovery', convergence versus path dependency.

First, there is a fundamental distinction between the design process and scientific inquiry, with designers focused on the questions relating to whether something will work and scientists focusing on the question of whether something is true (Dixon and Monk, 2011). The design-mentality for organizations makes historical empirical research challenging, given the constantly iterating and evolving nature of organizational design (Dunbar and Starbuck, 2006). Arising from this is an important philosophical question: Is there an 'optimal' design for an organization, such as a scientist may want to discover, or should the design of an organization merely reflect its response to its context and the purpose for which it is trying to find a solution? Institutions and organizations evolve not only for exogenous reasons, as a reaction to external events, but also for endogenous reasons, responding to the changing internal dynamics.

Second, there is a debate regarding how institutions and organizations respond to global market forces and, specifically, whether individual firms and organizations converge to a uniform set of behavior, or whether there is path dependency of institutional behavior based on local cultures, norms, and regulatory frameworks (Monk, 2008). The convergence argument is based on the belief that globalization and global market forces cause individual firms and organizations to exert a strong influence on individual firm strategy and behavior, thereby driving institutions to a converging set of practices (Gertler, 2001). The path-dependency argument is supported by the 'varieties of capitalism' framework, which argues that institutions do not converge and, instead, are a function of a specific 'variety of capitalism' that dictates their behavior and is the result of local variables (Hall and Thelen, 2009).

Two significant, recent breakthroughs in the study of institutional design are the 'best practice' frameworks for asset owners (Clark and Urwin, 2008) and for sovereign wealth funds (Dixon and Monk, 2011) that were recently developed by economic geographers (Gertler, 2001). These frameworks are noteworthy in two ways: methodological and functional. From a methodological perspective, the 'best practices' put forward are the result of individual case study research and are generalized. The generalized best practices find a strong balance between an appreciation of context-specificity and the need for some generalizable concepts. From a functional perspective, these frameworks are noteworthy for focusing both on principles as well as practices of institutions that are operating in these spaces. The focus on practice is a reminder that organizations are not static and evolve due to both internal and external forces.

Banking

In this section, I analyse the development banking literature. Specifically, I focus on the topic of development banking and the related conceptual questions of the role of banks as financial intermediaries, and the role of the government as direct and indirect owners of banks.

Government Interaction with the Banking Sector

Governments have a significant role in the banking sector. The amount of government intervention in the banking sector varies significantly by geography and sector. There are many ways in which governments interact with the banking sector. These mechanisms include, but are not limited to: regulation and supervision of the banking sector, provision of deposit insurance, and intervention during periods of financial crises and panics.

One aspect of the interaction between governments and the banking sector is the topic of whether governments should be the direct owners of banks. In 2002, a highly influential study on the impacts of government ownership of banks analysed the impacts of government ownership of banks using a unique data set comprised of government ownership of large banks in 92 countries (La Porta, Lopez-De-Silanes, and Shleifer, 2002). The paper framed the topic of the government of banks with the notion that government ownership of banks can be explained for 'developmental' reasons or 'political' reasons. By developmental reasons, government ownership of banks can be explained as having the goal of improving the state of development of a region; by political reasons, government ownership of banks can be explained by the desire of government to control finance and politicize resource allocation. The paper ultimately sided with the 'political view' of government ownership of banks and came to four conclusions: that government ownership of banks is large and pervasive;is particularly significant in developing countries; is associated with slower subsequent financial development; and is associated with lower subsequent growth of per capita income.

Critiques of the paper argue that, conceptually, lower growth rates could, in fact, prove a developmental function of government ownership of the banking sector (Rodrik, 2012). Empirical critiques find that higher state ownership in the banking sector is, indeed, associated with faster economic growth, with institutional factors and architecture serving an important role in explaining subsequent growth (Andrianova, Demetriades, and Shortland, 2008). In addition, the paper was written during a period of significant transition from government ownership to private ownership of banking industries globally, and the impacts of this transition on growth and development had still not been fully borne out in the data.

The concept of the interaction between politics and the banking sector was examined closely in an important contribution by Calomiris and Haber (2014) that identifies the underlying influence of politics throughout a banking system, and not only for banks that are under direct government ownership. The guiding questions for Calomiris and Haber were: Is a stable banking system is so critical for economic growth and stability? Why are there so many banking crises, particularly given the high level of supervision and regulation that exists in most major financial capitals in the world? The authors argued in this analysis that the answer to this conundrum is politics. They argued that the fragility of banking systems reflects the political institutions that exist in a country and the interaction between the following players in the system: the group in control of the government, bankers, minority shareholders, debtors, and depositors. The authors suggested that the ultimate function, and fragility, of a banking system depends on interactions and coalitions built between these actors. This political–economy approach to banking leads to an important and startling observation: 'that there are no fully private banking systems; rather, modern banking is best thought of as a partnership between the government and a group of bankers, a partnership that is shaped by the institutions that govern the distribution of power in the political system' (Calomiris and Haber, 2014).

Banks as Financial Intermediaries

The linkage between saving and investing can occur through various intermediaries, including banks and capital markets. The study of the organizations and institutions involved with financial intermediation can provide important insights into why financial intermediaries exist and how they function. Globally, banks are the most pervasive form of financial intermediary and a plurality of external finance for firms and households comes through the banking sector, particularly in developing countries. This sub-section benefits from an important review of the topic of financial intermediation undertaken by Gary Gorton and Andrew Winton (2002).

The first important discussion in the subject of financial intermediation is the reasons why financial intermediaries exist. This question is foundational because the link between saving and investment could otherwise occur due to those who want to invest contracting directly with those who require investment dollars, through capital markets, rather than through an organization or intermediary. This question is the subject of significant theoretical and empirical literature, and can be analysed from the perspectives of whether bank loans are different than bonds, and the specific roles banks play in the broader financial system.

With regard to the question of whether bank loans are different than bonds, there is both conceptual and empirical evidence that suggests that bank loans are, in fact, unique in their function of connecting savings and investment.

Mostly conceptual work by Fama suggested that bank loans are, in fact, unique compared to commercial loans. He observed that, since banks must hold reserves against their liabilities, banks could invest less than their total amount of liabilities. This is like a tax on the bank and therefore, if banks are not providing any special service or function, banks should be replaced by non-bank alternatives within a financial system. Given the fact that those who place deposits in banks are willing to bear this cost, Fama implied that there must be a uniqueness attributable to banks and their financial instruments. Empirical work on this has focused on event studies between firms and banks that show abnormal stock market reactions to bank loan agreements on firms compared to other sources of financing. This implies that banks perform a special role in intermediating savings for investments.

A critical defining characteristic of banks is their role as a delegated monitor. This argument was put forward by Douglas Diamond and has served as important conceptual pillar of the study of banks in financial intermediation (Diamond, 1984). Diamond posited that banks exist to 'monitor' borrowers—a function that is important for lenders, given the cost associated with this function. Diamond observed that there is fundamentally an information asymmetry between borrowers and lenders/investors, and that an intermediary can help solve this information asymmetry by monitoring the borrowers at a cost that is lower than lenders would incur were they to monitor the borrowers. Diamond further observed that the intermediary is, in itself, 'monitored' by the fact that if it is unsuccessful in monitoring borrowers, such intermediary would pay the costs through bankruptcy and poor financial performance. The 'delegated monitor' framework put forward by Diamond had a significant influence in further work on the role of banks in financial intermediation, with significant parallels and important insights into development banks.

Another important characteristic of banks is their role as producers of information (Gorton and Winton, 2002). Banks are able to produce information regarding the return dynamics of a specific project by investing their own capital in those projects. By investing the wealth of the bank (which, of course, is the wealth of the individuals and institutions who have put their capital into the bank), the bank is providing information to the broader market about specific projects that are otherwise private in nature. Institutional investors—in the form of pension funds, and insurance companies and their delegated asset managers—also serve a similar function. Although banks may be incentivized not to share this information with other banks, they can overcome this by creating coalitions (or syndicates) of lenders to projects and companies, thereby sharing the information that they are 'producing' about private opportunities with a larger group of institutions. However, there remains an important debate about whether banks are more efficient at producing information relating to specific markets than capital markets.

Specific circumstances complicate the study of banks as financial intermediaries. First, price data for banks is not as easily available as it is for the other securities markets; for example, stocks and bonds. It is not easy to discover the prices of individual assets (loans) that banks are trading at specific points in time, making empirical research on banks somewhat complicated. Second, banking is strongly linked to law and regulation, topics that cause the study of the banking sector to fall outside specific, narrow sectors of academia. Third, banking technologies have evolved considerably over recent decades, with new platforms and instruments calling into question which aspects of intermediation have remained constant, and which aspects of intermediation fundamentally different to require new frames of analysis.

Banks can play a critical role in the achievement of development outcomes. They are one of the main mechanisms through which financial savings are intermediated into investments, which include investments in areas such as infrastructure that can help development outcomes to be achieved (World Bank Group, 2018). In their role as delegated monitors and information producers, the banks help to transmit information regarding the creditworthiness and profitability of various projects that are being financed in an economy, providing a positive externality to other actors in the economic system.

Conclusion

In this chapter, I provided a critical review of the theoretical and empirical foundations of development banking. I presented an introduction to the topic of development banking and analysed four specific foundational pillars of the topic: the concept of development, the interaction between the state and the market in economic affairs, the role of institutions, and the importance of the banking sector.

I conclude that, although the existence of development banks rests on these four pillars, the pillars themselves are open to significant interpretation and a broad range of perspectives. With regard to the concept of development, there is no commonly accepted definition of development banks, despite their persistence in academic analysis and as policy instruments. Equally important is the fact that there is no commonly accepted understanding of what actions lead to the development of a region. With regard to the state versus market dynamic, although a certain broad understanding exists that both state and market are needed for an economy to function well, the exact balance of the two is heavily debated in theoretical and empirical economics and in political science. Industrial policy, which is one way that the state and market join forces for economic development, is the subject of significant debate regarding how government either accelerates or impedes economic activity. With regards to institutions, the optimal design of institutions for development sits between efforts to standardize best practice and efforts to find context-specific design solutions for particular institutions. Finally, with regard to the banking sector, I underscore how banks play a crucial role in the intermediation of financial savings for investment. I highlight that the banking sector is deeply intertwined with the state.

The complexities of the foundational elements of development banking underscore why the topic is relevant to the broader scope of financial geography in at least three important ways. First, financial geography is a field of study that is fundamentally supported by the importance of place and context for the analysis of finance. Second, development banks exist at different sizes and scales in various countries and regions. The existence of development banks in different geographies can be understood through historical, social, cultural, and political lenses, all of which provide critical insights into these institutions and all of which are elements of the broader sub-field of financial geography. Third, development banks have, arguably, played a demonstrably important role in the development, or lack thereof, in certain regions in the world. Financial geography, as a field of geography that examines the interaction of finance with social outcomes, is therefore a relevant and important lens through which development banks can be analysed.

References

Acemoglu, D. and Robinson, J. (2020). *Why Nations Fail: The Origins of Power, Prosperity and Power*. New York: Crown Publishing.

Andrianova, S., Demetriades, P. and Shortland, A. (2008). 'Government ownership of banks, institutions, and financial development', *Journal of Development Economics* 85(1–2): 218–252. doi: 10.1016/j.jdeveco.2006.08.002.

Bator, F. M. (1958). 'The anatomy of market failure', *The Quarterly Journal of Economics* 72(3): 351–379. doi: 10.2307/1882231.

Benjamin, L., Rubin, J. S. and Zielenbach, S. (2004). 'Community development financial institutions: Current issues and future prospects', *Journal of Urban Affairs* 26(2): 177–195. doi: 10.1111/j.0735-2166.2004.00196.x

Bloom, D. et al. (1998). 'Geography, demography, and economic growth in Africa', *Brookings Papers on Economic Activity* 2: 207–295. doi: 10.2307/2534695.

Boulakia, J. D. (1971). 'Ibn Khaldun: A Fourteenth-century economist', *Journal of Political Economy* 79(5): 1105–1118. doi: 10.1086/259818.

Bruck, N. (1998). 'The role of development banks in the twenty-first century', *Journal of Emerging Markets* 3: 39–68.

Calomiris, C. and Haber, S. (2014). *Fragile by Design: The Political Origins of Banking Crises and Scarce Credit*. Princeton, NJ: Princeton University Press.

Cameron, R. (1961). *France and the Economic Development of Europe*. Princeton, NJ: Princeton University Press.

Chenery, H. (1967). 'Foreign Assistance and Economic Development', in J. H. Adler (ed.), *Capital Movements and Economic Development*. London: Palgrave Macmillan. doi: 10.1007/978-1-349-15238-4_9.

Chenery, H. (1984). 'The evolution of development planning', *Journal of Policy Modeling* 6(2): 159–174. doi: 10.1016/0161-8938(84)90011-5.

Clark, G., Dixon, A. and Monk, A. (2013). *Sovereign Wealth Funds: Legitimacy, Governancce and Global Power*. Princeton, NJ: Princeton University Press.

Clark, G. and Monk, A. (2010a). 'Government of Singapore investment corporation (GIC): Insurer of last resort and bulwark of nation-state legitimacy', *Pacific Review* 23(4): 429–451. doi: 10.1080/09512748.2010.495997.

Clark, G. and Monk, A. (2010b). 'Sovereign wealth funds: form and function in the 21st century', *SSRN Electronic Journal*, 1–27. Available at: http://papers.ssrn.com/sol3/papers.cfm?abstract_id=1675091.

Clark, G. and Urwin, R. (2008). 'Best-practice pension fund governance', *Journal of Asset Management* 9: 2–21. doi: 10.1057/jam.2008.1.

Coase, R. (2012). 'The nature of the firm', in *The Economic Nature of the Firm: A Reader*, Third Edition. Cambridge, UK: Cambridge University Press. doi: 10.1017/CBO9780511817410.009.

Cull, R., Demirgüç-Kunt, A. and Morduch, J. (2009). 'Microfinance meets the market', *Contemporary Studies in Economic and Financial Analysis* 92. doi: 10.1108/S1569-3759(2009)0000092004.

De Aghion, B. A. (1999). 'Development banking', *Journal of Development Economics* 58(1): 83–100. doi: 10.1016/S0304-3878(98)00104-7.

De Gregorio, J. and Guidotti, P. (1995). 'Financial development and economic growth', *World Development* 23(3): 433–448. doi: 10.1016/0305-750X(94)00132-I.

De Luna-Martinez, J. and Vicente, C. L. (2012). *Global survey of development banks, Policy Research Working Paper Series* 5969. New York: World Bank.

De Luna-Martinez, J., Vicente, C. L., Arshad, A. Bin, Tatucu, R., and Song, J. (2018). *2017 Survey of National Development Banks* (English). Washington, DC: World Bank Group. http://documents.worldbank.org/curated/en/977821525438071799/2017-Survey-of-National-development-banks

de Martinez, J. L. (2017). *2017 Survey of National Development Banks.*

de Martinez, J. L. and Vincente, C. L. (2012). *Global Survey of Development Banks.*

Dervis, K. and Page, J. (1984). 'Industrial policy in developing countries', *Journal of Comparative Economics 8*. doi: 10.1016/0147-5967(84)90040-4.

Develop. (2020). Merriam Webster.

Diamond, D. (1984). 'Financial intermediation as delegated monitoring', *Review of Economic Studies*. doi: 10.2307/2297430.

Diamond, J. (2005). *Guns, Germs and Steel: The Fates of Human Societies*. New York: W.W. Norton & Company.

Diamond, W. (1957). *Development Banks*. Washington, DC: World Bank.

Dixon, A. and Monk, A. (2011). *The design and governance of sovereign wealth funds: Principles & practices for resource revenue management*. Available at SSRN. doi: 10.2139/ssrn.1951573.

Domar, E. D. (1946). 'Capital expansion, rate of growth, and employment', *Econometrica* 14(2): 137–147. doi: 10.2307/1905364.

Dunbar, R. and Starbuck, W. (2006). 'Learning to design organizations and learning from designing them', *Organization Science* 17(2): 171–312. doi: 10.1287/orsc.1060.0181.

Easterly, W. (2001). *The Elusive Quest for Growth: Economists' Adventures and Misadventures in the Tropics*. Cambridge: MIT Press.

Easterly, W. (2006). *The White Man's Burden: Why the West's Efforts to Aid the Rest Have Done So Much Ill and So Little Good*. New York: Penguin Press.

Easterly, W. (2013). *The Tyranny of Experts*. New York: Basic Books.

Economy, E. C. (2018). *The Third Revolution: Xi Jinping and the New Chinese State*. Oxford: Oxford University Press.

Engen, L. and Prizzon, A. (2018). *A Guide to Multilateral Development Banks*. www.odi.org/sites/odi.org.uk/files/resource-documents/12274.pdf.

Friedman, M. (1962). *Capitalism and Freedom*. Chicago, IL: University of Chicago Press.

Gallup, J. L., Sachs, J. and Mellinger, A. (1999). 'Geography and economic development', in *International Regional Science Review* 22(2): 179–232. doi: 10.1177/016001799761012334.

Gertler, M. (2001). 'Best practice? Geography, learning and the institutional limits to strong convergence', *Journal of Economic Geography* 1(1): 5–26. doi: 10.1093/jeg/1.1.5.

Gorton, G. and Winton, A. (2002). *Financial intermediation*, NEBR Working Paper Series. doi: 10.1162/00335530360535162.

Hacker, J. and Pierson, P. (2016). *American Amnesia: How the War on Government Led Us to Forget What Made America Prosper*. New York: Simon and Schuster.

Hall, P. and Thelen, K. (2009). 'Institutional change in varieties of capitalism', *Socio-Economic Review* 7(1): 7–34. doi: 10.1093/ser/mwn020

Hamilton, A. (2001). 'Report on the subject of manufactures', in *Hamilton Writings*. https://founders.archives.gov/documents/Hamilton/01-10-02-0001-0007

Harrod, R. (1939). 'An essay in dynamic theory', *The Economic Journal* 49(193) 14–33. doi: 10.2307/2225181.

Hayek, F. and Hamowy, R. (2013). *The Constitution of Liberty: The Definitive Edition*. London: Routledge. doi: 10.4324/9780203713662.

Keynes, J. M. (1936) *The General Theory of Employment Interest and Money, The Collected Writings of John Maynard Keynes*. New York: Harcourt Brace. doi: 10.2307/2143949.

Krueger, A. O. (1990). 'Government failures in development', *Journal of Economic Perspectives* 4(3), Summer: 9–23. doi: 10.1257/jep.4.3.9.

Kurlantzick, J. (2016). *State Capitalism: How the Return of Statism is Transforming the World*. Oxford: Oxford University Press.

Lankov, A. (2016). *The Resurgence of a Market Economy in North Korea*. Available at: https://carnegieendowment.org/files/CP_Lankov_Eng_web_final_pdf

La Porta, R., Lopez-De-Silanes, F. and Shleifer, A. (2002) 'Government ownership of banks', *Journal of Finance* 57(1): 265–301. doi: 10.1111/1540-6261.00422.

Lepenies, P. (2016). *The Power of a Single Number: A Political History of GDP*. New York: Columbia University Press.

Leuchtenburg, W. E. (2009). *Franklin D. Roosevelt and the New Deal*. New York: Harper Perennial.

Levine, R. (2006). 'Chapter 12 Finance and growth: Theory and evidence', *Handbook of Economic Growth*. Amsterdam: North Holland. doi: 10.1016/S1574-0684(05)01012-9.

Lewis, A. (1955). *The Theory of Economic Growth*. London: George Allen and Unwin LTD.

Lin, J. Y. (2011). 'New structural economics: A framework for rethinking development', *World Bank Research Observer* 26(2): 193–221. doi: 10.1093/wbro/lkr007.

Lin, J. Y. (2012a). *Demystifying the Chinese Economy*. New York: Cambridge University Press. doi: 10.1017/CBO9781139026666.

Lin, J. Y. (2012b). 'From flying geese to leading dragons: New opportunities and strategies for structural transformation in developing countries', *Global Policy* 3(4): 397–409. doi: 10.1111/j.1758-5899.2012.00172.x.

Magnus, G. (2018). *Red Flags: Why Xi's China Is In Jeopardy*. New Haven, CT: Yale University Press.

March, J. and Simon, H. (1958). *Organizations*. New York: John Wiley & Sons.

Mazzucato, M. (2015). *The Entpreneurial State: Debunking Public vsPrivate Sector Myths*. New York: PublicAffairs.

McKinnon, R. (1973). *Money and Capital in Economic Development*. Washington, DC: The Brookings Institution

Monk, A. (2008). Institutional change in the era of globalization: A comparison of corporate pension policies in Japan and the U.S. Available at: SSRN. doi: 10.2139/ssrn.1082887.

Musacchio, A. et al. (2017). *The role and impact of development banks: A review of their founding, focus and influence*. Available at: http://people.brandeis.edu/~aldom/papers/The%20Role%20and%20Impact%20of%20Development%20Banks%20-%203-9-2017.pdf.

Musachio, A. and Lazzarini, S. (2014). *Reinvesting State Capitalism: Leviathan in Business, Brazil and Beyond*. Cambridge: Harvard University Press.

Myrdal, G. (1974). 'What is development?', *Journal of Economic Issues*, 8(4), 729–736.

North, D. (1990). *Institutions, Institutional Change and Economic Performance*. Cambridge: Cambridge Press.

Pack, H. and Saggi, K. (2006). 'Is there a case for industrial policy? A critical survey', *World Bank Research Observer* 21(2), Fall: 267–297. doi: 10.1093/wbro/lkl001.

Perkins, D. et al. (2013). *Economics of Development*, 7th Edition. New York: W.W. Norton & Company.

Rajan, R. and Zingales, L. (1998). 'Financial dependence and growth', *American Economic Review*. doi: 10.3386/w5758.

Ramalingam, B. (2013). *Aid on the Edge of Chaos*. Oxford: Oxford University Press.

Rodrik, D. (2004). *Industrial policy for the twenty-first century*. Available at: SSRN. doi: 10.2139/ssrn.617544.

Rodrik, D. (2012). 'Why we learn nothing from regressing economic growth on policies', *Seoul Journal of Economics* 25(2): 137–151. doi: CBO9781107415324.004.

Rodrik, D. (2015). Normalizing industrial policy, *Commission on Growth and Development*, Working Paper 3. doi: 10.1007/s13398-014-0173-7.2.

Roe, M. (2012). 'Capital markets and financial politics: Preferences and institutions', in *The Oxford Handbook of Capitalism*. Oxford: Oxford University Press. doi: 10.1093/oxfordhb/9780195391176.013.0004.

Rosenstein-Rodan, P. (1944). 'The international development of economically backward areas', *International Affairs* 20(2), April: 157–165. doi: 10.2307/3018093.

Rosenstein-Rodan, P. (1961). 'International aid for underdeveloped countries', *The Review of Economics and Statistics* 43(2), May: 107–138. doi: 10.2307/1928662.

Sachs, J. (2005). *The End of Poverty: How We Can Make It Happen in Our Lifetime*. New York: The Penguin Press. doi: 10.1353/lag.2006.0020.

Sachs, J. (2015). *The Age of Sustainable Development*. New York: Columbia University Press.

Samuelson, P. (1954). 'The Pure Theory of Public Expenditure', *The Review of Economics and Statistics*, 36(4), 387–389.

Sen, A. (1999). *Development as Freedom*. New York: Random House.

Shah, A. (2016). 'Building a sustainable belt and road', *Horizons* 7: 212–222.

Smith, A. (2000). *The Wealth of Nations*. New York: Random House.

Stiglitz, J. (1994). *The Role of the State in Financial Markets*. Washington, DC: World Bank.

Stiglitz, J. (2011). 'Rethinking development economics', *World Bank Research Observer* 26(2), August: 230–236. doi: 10.1093/wbro/lkr011.

Tharoor, S. (2018). *Inglorious Empire: What the British Did to India*. New York: Scribe.

The China Development Bank and Renmin University of China. (2011). *Development Finance in China: Theory and Implementation*. Hong Kong: Enrich Professional Publishing.

Tinbergen, J. (1968). 'Wanted: A world development plan', *International Organization* 22(1): 417–431. doi: 10.1017/S002081830001362X.

UNDP. (2008). 'Calculating the human development indices', *Human Development*. doi: 10.1115/1.1731317.

UNDP. (2011). 'Human development index and its components', in *Human Development Report 2011: Sustainability and Equity – A Better Future for All*. New York: UNDP. Available at: http://hdr.undp.org/en/content/human-development-report-2011 doi: 10.1186/1471-2164-9-411.

Weitzman, M. L. (1993). 'Economic transition. Can theory help?', *European Economic Review* 37(2–3): 549–555. doi: 10.1016/0014-2921(93)90044-B.

Williamson, O. (1985). *The Economic Institutions of Capitalism*. New York: The Free Press.

Winston, C. (2006). *Government Failure versus Market Failure: Microeconomics Policy Research and Goernment Performance*. Washington, DC: AEI-Brookings Joing Center for Regulatory Studies.

World Bank Group. (1993). *The East Asian Miracle*. Washington, DC: World Bank Group.

World Bank Group. (2018). *Global Financial Development Report 2017/2018: Bankers without Borders*. Washington, DC: World Bank Group.

World Bank Group. (2020). *World Development Report 1989: Financial Systems and Development*. Washington, DC: World Bank Group.

Yuan, C. (2013). *Aligning State and Market: China's Approach to Development Finance*. Beijing: Foreign Languages Press.

PART IV

Intermediation

17

BANKS AND CREDIT

Lindsey Appleyard

Introduction

Mainstream financial institutions, or banks, are commercial enterprises, driven by profit to provide banking services for consumers and enterprises. Banking services can include transactional current accounts, credit facilities such as mortgages, credit cards, overdrafts, and loans. Full and fair access to these services is an essential part of everyday life in order to secure basic needs such as housing, employment, and affordable credit. Understanding how such institutions operate is important to ensure that banks are promoting financially inclusive and responsible lending practices for economic stability and growth without detrimental impacts on the economy or society. This chapter examines the academic contributions and policy impacts economic geographers have made to understanding the geographical processes inherent in banking operations and practices, and therefore shows why exploring banking and consumer credit is important.

The aim of this chapter is to examine the roles and relationships between banks and citizens through consumer credit. First, this chapter briefly outlines the contributions economic geographers have made to understanding banks and credit. Second, the neoliberalization and financialization of banking is contextualized to examine how the contemporary bank/consumer credit relationship has evolved as a result of banking liberalization, securitization, deregulation, and restructuring. Third, the chapter explores how financialization processes create market segmentation into prime, near-prime and subprime categories which therefore result in 'unequal social outcomes' through the concepts of financial inclusion/exclusion (Leyshon et al., 2008: 449). Here, financial exclusion is defined as:

> those processes that serve to prevent certain groups and individuals from gaining access to the financial system [and] although the criteria for exclusion may vary over time, the financial system has an inherent tendency to discriminate against poor and disadvantaged groups.
>
> (Leyshon and Thrift, 1997: 228)

Finally, the chapter identifies emerging research themes for financial geography, and sets priorities for policy-makers and practitioners surrounding consumer credit. This is to highlight the role of policy in securing consumer rights and reducing irresponsible lending practices by promoting and enforcing best practice. As such, the chapter poses normative questions to challenge the status quo of financialization, banking operations, processes, and outcomes to contribute to current debates and to set the research agenda for future economic geography research.

A Brief History of Banking and Credit in Economic Geography

Since the 1970s, geographers have taken an increasing interest in mainstream financial institutions, banking, and consumer credit as neoliberalization and financialization have driven mainstream banks to restructure their operations in the interests of profit to favour the bottom line for shareholders, rather than in the interests of the individual (Peck and Tickell, 2002). Geographers have explored mainstream banking through the lens of financial inequality over space; for example, through examining the redlining of communities that were considered too risky to serve (Dymski and Veitch, 1996; Harvey, 1973; Leyshon and Thrift, 1997, 1999); observing how mainstream financial institutions' may restrict access to particular products and services; and investigating how irresponsible lending practices disproportionately impact on particular communities, such as women and Black and Minority Ethnic communities (Aalbers, 2008; Appleyard et al., 2016; Brown et al., 2013; Joseph, 2014; Li et al., 2001; Whyly et al., 2009). More broadly, geographers have made a significant impact in exploring how financial services restructuring and withdrawal, banking operations, and practices have longer-term consequences on local and global economic stability (Leyshon and Thrift, 1997).

Since the 1990s, geographers have been at the forefront of research around banking and credit, particularly financial exclusion (Dymski and Veitch, 1996; Fuller and Jonas, 2002; Leyshon and Thrift, 1994, 1995). As the financial services sector restructured in response to the cycles of boom and bust in the 1980s and 1990s, the nature of financial exclusion changed over time. The interest in the subject widened to include academics beyond geography, as well as those outside of academia, such as policy-makers who have recognized the impact of financial exclusion on particular groups and communities, and the need to address the issue through different solutions (Affleck and Mellor, 2006;

FSA, 2000; HMT, 2004; Marshall, 2004). As a result, research around credit soon expanded to include diverse economies and alternative forms of finance such as microfinance, credit unions, and community development finance, which emerged in response to the recognition that mainstream banks were undergoing a 'flight-to-quality' to find more reliable and profitable markets, such as individuals with higher incomes and levels of wealth (Appleyard, 2011; Brown et al., 2013; Fuller and Jonas, 2002; Gibson-Graham, 2008; Leyshon and Thrift, 1997).

As with previous financial crises in the 1980s and 1990s, the 2008 Global Financial Crisis has acted as a catalyst to renew economic geographers' attention towards banks and personal finance due to the impact of the financial crisis on local communities and households. This is with the knowledge that consumers will have to bear the cost of the Global Financial Crisis through economic restructuring, changing labour markets, increased taxation, government austerity policies, and the diversification and cost of banking products and services in the post-financial crisis era (French et al., 2009). Going forward, one role of economic geography is to explore the 'post-crisis' landscape of money and finance alongside the limits to financialization (Christophers, 2015: 195).

Neoliberalism, Financialization and Banking

Neoliberalism is an ideology based on laissez faire 'political economic practices' whereby individuals assume responsibility and risk for their welfare (Harvey, 2007: 22). The neoliberal role of the state is to facilitate the free hand of the market and to provide the infrastructure to support the market through the privatization and retrenchment of public services (Peck and Tickell, 2002). Neoliberalism is therefore an economic and geographical process of restructuring at different geographical scales—for example, state, regional and community levels—to enable capitalist regimes of accumulation.

One distinct element of neoliberalism is financialization, which emerged as a mode of capitalist accumulation designed to increase the role of financial markets in:

> organizing social and economic life, a retrenchment of welfare-state provisions, and concomitantly, major new rounds of privatization of public assets.
>
> (Christophers, 2015: 183)

As a result of neoliberal government policies and deregulation of financial services from the 1970s onwards, financialization has become an increasingly important feature in society. Access to financial services has meant that credit is used as a tool for people to participate actively in everyday life; and as a 'safety net' in response to the retrenchment of the welfare state (Joseph, 2014; Leyshon et al., 2008; Montgomerie, 2013). Leyshon et al. (2008: 449) summarize that a process of:

> neo-liberalization has proceeded through new policies by which states have sought to gradually abrogate responsibility for many areas of social life that are now left to the market and to the agency of individuals and households.

Lee et al. (2009) suggest that the liberalization of financial markets has intensified financialization, embedding new communities and individuals within financial markets as a way of propping up the economy. Financialization therefore:

> connects hitherto relatively discrete and separate spatial circuits of finance, especially in linking the domestic realm of people, families, and households with the international financial system.
>
> (Pike and Pollard, 2010: 37)

However, the relationship between finance and individuals and communities is highly unequal, thereby creating uneven outcomes—which identifies financialization as a 'profoundly spatial phenomenon' and has an impact on everyday life (French et al., 2011: 800).

The financial inclusion of 1.7 billion people currently unbanked is a major initiative of the World Bank with the aim of 'reducing poverty' and increasing wealth (World Bank, 2019). The drive towards financial inclusion is also considered to stimulate economic development in developing economies through finance-led capitalism (Soederberg, 2013). Digital financial services via mobile phone applications in sub-Saharan Africa, Asia, the Caribbean, and Latin America have become popular ways to transfer money, and to access remittances and credit, particularly in rural areas (Aker and Mbiti, 2010; Gabor and Brooks, 2017). For some, mobile banking is considered to have had a positive economic benefit by disrupting traditional banking infrastructures and creating greater opportunity for access and inclusion (Aker and Mbiti, 2010). Yet, research has also demonstrated that the poorest citizens continue to experience significant barriers to access transactional bank accounts and affordable credit (Brown et al., 2013). Digital financial inclusion initiatives within developing economies obscures the fact that 'poverty is understood as a new frontier for profit-making and accumulation' (Gabor and Brooks, 2017: 424). Financial inclusion policies are considered to be a process of 'financial(ised) inclusion' (Gabor and Brooks, 2017: 425; Soederberg, 2013).

In advanced economies, access to credit can be an important way of smoothing income fluctuations when incomes are declining as a result of wage stagnation and the rising cost of living. Credit is considered a social policy tool whereby borrowing is seen as a temporary solution to 'fix' the problem

(Beggs et al., 2014; Gonzalez, 2015; Montgomerie, 2013). However, credit and debt is believed to discipline financial subjects (individuals) into employment to service financial commitments and to support the functioning of the capitalist system (Beggs et al., 2014). This has led to the financialization of daily life whereby individuals become responsible for managing their finances in the short and longer terms, rather than the welfare state cushioning poor outcomes acting as a safety net (Joseph, 2014; Martin, 2002). However, financial institutions aim to 'maximise' their customers 'financial potential'', which means that financial institutions do not always provide good financial outcomes for active investors, as the consumers carry the risks rather than the financial institution (Martin, 2002: 5).

Through financialization and the deregulation of credit markets, increased competition within the banking sector has seen a boom in consumer credit in the UK:

> transformations in consumer credit networks, gathering pace over the last three decades or so, have made it possible for the capital markets to nourish extended consumer borrowing.
>
> (Langley, 2008: 135)

Credit and debt are a key feature of the 'lived realities' of financialization (Christophers, 2015: 186). Alongside the reduction of the welfare state, risk has also become normalized, which essentially:

> communicates to every citizen that there is 'no free ride', meaning that all must take for themselves the responsibility for a safety net.
>
> (Martin, 2002: 109)

Martin (2002: 9) suggests that, in this process:

> Financialization promises a way to develop the self, when even the noblest of professions cannot emit a call that one can answer with a lifetime. It offers a highly elastic mode of self-mastery that channels doubt over uncertain identity into fruitful activity.

For example, accounting and risk management are part of our everyday lives (now recognized as a part of financial capability) which we need to manage not only within our financial lives, but also elsewhere—in matters such as housing, health, education, and retirement—as the state rolls back further from supporting its citizens. For the wealthy, it is relatively easy to protect themselves from risks through insurance and other means but, for people with low levels of wealth and income, financial precarity is part of everyday life. Even those with moderate levels of income and wealth are at risk of economic instability, so it is important to recognize that financial precarity and exclusion are likely to become an increasingly significant issue in the future.

The neoliberal shift away from the welfare state and employers' responsibilities towards individual financial responsibility is captured through the concept of 'financial citizenship' which is:

> a concept that recognizes the significance of the financial system to everyday life and confers a right and ability on individuals and households to participate fully in the economy and to accumulate wealth.
>
> (Leyshon, 2009: 153)

Therefore, concepts of responsibility and risk have been transferred to financial subjects away from the state, promoting the accumulation of assets (in the form of housing, pensions, investments) thereby making people "financialise' the future' by investing on the market for good financial outcomes and greater financial security (Allen and Pryke, 1999: 65; Joseph, 2014; Leyshon et al., 2008; Sherraden, 1991).

Securitization: Opening Up New Markets

Financial innovation is a key feature of liberalized, financialized (deregulated) financial economies such as that of the United Kingdom. While financial innovation can offer opportunities for economic growth, it often precedes economic crises and household indebtedness (Leyshon and Thrift, 1997; Mullineux, 2010). One example of this is securitization and the ability to access finance from global markets. The ability to securitize assets was a result of innovation in information communication technologies from the 1970s onwards (Leyshon and Thrift, 1997; Leyshon et al., 2008). Langley (2008: 283) defines securitization as the:

> practice of 'bundling' together a stream of future obligations arising from mortgage repayments to provide the basis for the issue of, and the payment of principal and interest on securities.

Securitized assets (loans made against an asset, believed to be increasing in value) were seen as less risky than unsecured loans such as credit cards, due to the higher risk of the loan not being repaid on time or in full. For example, mortgage loans were packaged as asset-backed securities (ABSs), and then repackaged as collateralized debt obligations (CDOs) and put into banks' special investment vehicles—in the process, creating a shadow banking system to obscure the risky nature of these loans (Mullineux, 2010: 251).

Securitization, therefore, had two main roles. First, the aim was to open up new markets to increase economic growth. For example, US and UK governments promoted home ownership from the late 1990s and credit conditions were easy, with little or no deposits required alongside the innovation of 100% mortgages and increasing loan-to-income ratios (Wainwright, 2009). Self-certification of income for mortgages also increased the number of 'non-standard' or subprime borrowers, particularly those with no income, no job, no assets (NINJA loans). Low interest or teaser rates, which featured low interest rates for an introductory period followed by higher interest rates, meant that mortgages soon became unaffordable and led to a national foreclosure crisis. The predatory nature of the US mortgage lending market meant that these products were unaffordable and inappropriate, and were a primary example of irresponsible lending. With the expectation that house prices would continue to rise, mortgage companies profited from the inflated interest rates once the teaser rates ended, even if the homes were foreclosed. As a result, the foreclosure crisis was inevitable. The US subprime housing crisis led to the 2008 Global Financial Crisis. Second, advances in information communication technologies enabled telephone- and internet-based banking, centralizing credit decision-making, thereby replacing the need for more expensive and time consuming face-to-face, in-branch relationship banking (Leyshon et al., 2008). Ultimately, financialization and information communication technologies facilitated securitization, which connected global financial markets with local communities by encouraging and rewarding irresponsible lending practices in mainstream financial institutions.

Mainstream banks aggressively lent in new, underserved, subprime markets characterized by financial exclusion (Whyly et al., 2009). For mainstream finance, this was a 'new' or 'emerging' market waiting to be financialized. Whyly et al. (2009: 351) explain that:

> Subprime lending and Wall Street securitization have replaced the abusive local loan sharks and slum landlords with entrepreneurial brokers and lenders pushing high-cost credit backed by mortgage companies, subsidiaries of large national banks and the entire array of investment bankers, bond traders, ratings analysts and yield-hungry investors. The agents may be different, but the exploitation remains.

The Global Financial Crisis was brought on by the exploitation of lower income communities by mainstream banks that lent irresponsibly in pursuit of profit. In this way, the Global Financial Crisis quickly became a personal financial crisis. When the crisis effected banks, they were bailed out at the expense of homeowners who lost their homes and may have also lost their jobs in the economic recession. The lack of oversight by banks on their operations and practices is a form of irresponsibility, particularly as the wellbeing of the state and its citizens has become so dependent on financial services (Crouch, 2009).

Banks: Deregulation and Restructuring

As commercial financial institutions, banks are driven by maximizing profit and mitigating risk for external shareholders. Building societies are mutually owned financial services providers that operate in much the same way as banks. However, building societies have no external shareholders, meaning that they are driven by their members. Government regulatory reform, such as the Financial Services Act 1986, saw the liberalization of the United Kingdom's financial services industry to make it more competitive in a global marketplace. The 1986 Building Societies Act enabled building societies to become publicly limited companies (PLCs) and to become more competitive (for building society legislation changes, see Marshall et al., 2012). This process of demutualization had a major impact on the type of products and services banks could provide to individuals (retail banking and insurance), also impacting local communities through bank branch withdrawal (Leyshon and Thrift, 1997).

Traditionally, banks relied on their high street branches for deposits. This has changed with the shift to providing digital services online, making branches less cost-effective and competitive. The rationalization of bank branches has been an ongoing process due to a number of factors: bank mergers between competitors have reduced the number of banks needed; changing bank operations and financial innovations such as online banking have meant that banks and customers can function 'at a distance' replacing traditional, face-to-face relationship banking services based on trust; and 'competitive pressures' have meant that banks are reducing their operating costs by offering services via telephone and by automating applications and processes via online banking (Edmonds, 2018; French et al., 2013; Makortoff, 2018). This led to major labour market restructuring with significant numbers of jobs lost in the 1980s and 1990s (Leyshon and Thrift, 1997).

Bank branch withdrawal has had a major influence on which geographical areas decline or prosper. Dymski and Veitch (1996) suggest that access to credit is dependent on the 'financial dynamics' within the financial system, as these are shaped by the geographies of income and wealth, and geographical access to the financial system. In the United Kingdom, as a result of mergers and the rationalization of branches, between 1989 and 2012, 40% of high street bank branches were closed (7,500 bank branches) (French et al., 2013). The closures have been predominantly in urban and less affluent areas of the United Kingdom. The geographical areas that have been relatively protected from closures are described as relatively affluent suburbs or small towns characterized as 'Middle England' (French et al., 2013: 1).

One example of the geographical impact of bank demutualization and demise is Northern Rock. Northern Rock demutualized in the 1980s and grew rapidly to become the United Kingdom's fifth-largest mortgage bank. By 2007, it employed over 6,000 staff, largely in the north-east region of the United Kingdom, and operated 77 branches that helped to regenerate a former industrial area (Marshall et al., 2012). Yet, in 2007, at the beginning of the Global Financial Crisis, Northern Rock was the first UK retail bank to experience a run on it since 1866, as a consequence of asking the government for financial support (Marshall et al., 2012). This marked the start of the credit crunch, which was where access to credit for households and businesses was restricted due to lack of liquidity in the financial marketplace. Both Northern Rock's growth and demise had a significant impact on the region, particularly around the regeneration and decline of local areas, jobs, and local infrastructure. The example of Northern Rock therefore reproduced the financial dynamics identified by Dymski and Veitch (1996).

The closure of bank branches is therefore considered to be 'an important exclusionary trend', changing the geographies and nature of banking whereby:

> Branch closures impose costs on local communities. Residents, especially those who live in rural areas, face additional transport costs to gain access to financial services. The closure of a branch may result in a loss of local employment opportunities and reduced income in the area. Shops and services may be forced into decline because they are dependent on the close proximity of financial institutions.
>
> (Marshall et al., 2003: 747)

In response to bank branch withdrawal, spaces of financial exclusion were substituted by a variety of secondary tier financial services and subprime financial institutions, such as pawnbrokers, payday lenders, and cheque cashing facilities (Appleyard, 2011; Dymski and Veitch, 1996). However, the geographies of bank branch withdrawal are part of a deeper process of neoliberalization. It just so happens that:

> The closure of branches is the most visible expression of processes of financial exclusion and inclusion that are part of an ongoing renegotiation of the contract between the citizen and the state.
>
> (Leyshon et al., 2008: 448)

Bank branch closures are therefore only one element of neoliberalization and financial exclusion. The social contract between the state and its citizens is for them to be financially active and included within the system; in employment or education (if working age and able); financially literate and financially capable of managing their finances, and responsible for their own welfare in terms of supporting themselves and their family—ideally through owning their own home; investing in a pension; holding appropriate insurance and savings for emergencies, such as during long-term illness; and so on. However, there are concerns that bank branch closures increase financial exclusion via a lack of access to financial services; there are many citizens that are digitally excluded or are unbanked.

The spatiality of access to mainstream consumer credit in the United Kingdom has been analysed by economic geographers in order to understand geographies of financial exclusion and to find appropriate solutions to address them (Henry et al., 2017). Personal lending data was captured between 2013 and 2014, and was voluntarily disclosed by seven UK banks at a postcode sector level. Henry et al. (2017) established that this form of data disclosure alone is insufficient to understand the variegated nature of financial inclusion and exclusion in the United Kingdom. It is interesting to note that the banks in question only provided data with the threat of government legislation to enact the equivalent of a US Community Reinvestment Act (CRA), which would effectively force them to lend in areas they did not currently serve (for further details on the CRA, see Appleyard, 2011; Henry et al., 2017; Marshall, 2004). Henry et al. (2017) advocate greater breadth to the data currently captured to understand the spatiality of the UK credit landscape.

Financial Exclusion and Financial Capability

In the United Kingdom, there are 1.3 million people (or 3% of the adult population) without a bank account that are classified as 'unbanked' (FCA, 2018). Young adults between the ages of 18 and 24 are less likely to hold a bank account than other age groups, and 20% of adults living in London do not hold a bank account. Mitton (2008: 1) suggests that there are particular groups that are vulnerable to financial exclusion including:

> housing association tenants; young people not in employment, education or training; those leaving care; lone parents and divorced people; disabled people, those with mental health problems and carers; people living in isolated or disadvantaged areas; prisoners, ex-offenders and families of prisoners; members of ethnic minorities; migrants; asylum seekers and refugees; homeless people; older people; women; people with a Post Office Card Account or basic bank account; people with low incomes.

Alongside financially excluded individuals, there is a group of people that can be defined as 'underbanked', as they perhaps own a bank account but do not use the full range of products and services on offer due to financial marginalization. In this way, banks operate under gendered and racialized norms of what constitutes a responsible financial subject as, for example, women are more likely to be employed part-time (Joseph, 2014). In the context of credit, Langley (2008: 134–5) defines:

> the making of financial subjects and financial self-disciplines more broadly plays on freedom and security as central features of (neo) liberal governmentality. In the consumer credit boom, then, prudence

> and thrift are displaced by new moral and calculative selfdisciplines of responsibly and entrepreneurially meeting, managing and manipulating ever-increasing outstanding obligations.

However, Langley (2008: 144) recognizes that such entrepreneurial behaviour is challenging for those on low incomes that are managing unstable incomes and for whom it is therefore more difficult to maintain 'the financial self-discipline of the responsible borrower'.

There is a spectrum of financial marginalization from financial inclusion to exclusion. Leyshon (2009: 155) and Kempson and Whyly (1999) define financial exclusion as a multidimensional process whereby individuals may experience one or a number of reasons for exclusion based on the following forms:

- *access exclusion*: for example, they do not have access to a local bank branch as they live in a rural area;
- *condition exclusion*: for example, customers do not fulfil all the criteria to access a product, such as permanent employment;
- *price exclusion*: for example, they are unable to access fair, affordable credit products;
- *marketing exclusion*: for example, banks target particular products to certain demographic groups, and;
- *self-exclusion*: for example, where customers do not apply for products, as they presume that they will be denied, or do not follow particular cultural norms that exclude them from taking out particular products, such as loans.

The multidimensional nature of financial exclusion suggests that there are particular socio-economic geographies of financial exclusion and that some are at greater risk of exclusion than others due to their income, where they live, and particular circumstances—such as employment status. Financial exclusion is a process and could be a short- or longer-term issue for individuals as incomes and circumstances change over the life course. Individuals, whether they are financially included or excluded, often have a lack of trust in the financial system. For example, if they have had negative experiences, if they have been mis-sold products (e.g. payment protection insurance, known as PPI), or if they have seen the demise of regional banks—such as in the case of Northern Rock.

Even if individuals are financially included, they could still be considered financially vulnerable. The Financial Conduct Authority (FCA, 2018) suggests that half of the UK population can be considered as financially vulnerable and lacking financial resilience, which suggests that increasing numbers of UK adults may be viewed as 'risky' customers. This financial vulnerability is due to a number of reasons: (i) high levels of indebtedness; (ii) a lack of savings for an emergency (e.g., 13% of UK adults have no cash savings and 32% have cash savings under £2,000); (iii) lack of financial capability and the ability to manage their finances; (iv) risk of experiencing a negative financial shock due to job loss, bereavement, or relationship breakdown, or a significant health issue (FCA, 2018). Appleyard et al. (2016: 311) suggest that greater understanding is needed around variegated forms of financial inclusion as many individuals experience such 'precarious-inclusion' due to the unequal ways financialization works over geographical space.

Government policies serve to individualize responsibility (and risk), rather than changing the financial systems and processes. This is illustrated by the OECD (2009) and the Money and Pensions Service (MAPS), which encourage and deliver programmes to individuals so that they may develop their financial capability to become financially responsible and financially secure. Financial capability is defined thus:

> Financial capability gives people the power and the confidence to make the most of their money and improve their lives. Financial capability is the ability to manage money well—both day-to-day and through significant life events like having a baby, getting divorced or moving home. Being financially capable means you have the resilience to handle times when life is financially difficult—like when you lose your job unexpectedly or you can't work due to illness. But financial capability is more than this. It's also an attitude, that is more than just living for today—it's having the confidence to put your money skills into practice, and understanding the value of doing so.
>
> (MAPS, 2019)

In this sense, financial capability is demonstrating the ability to make good financial decisions through having appropriate knowledge, skills, attitude, and behaviour. However, being able to enact this type of financial capability is also about income and wealth, as citizens need sufficient disposable income in order to save, invest, and so on.

Clearly, the concept of financial capability is correlated with income, wealth, and inclusion, so that individuals have both the capability and means to participate actively in the financial system and be a financially responsible citizen. But the issue of income and wealth is ignored by financial capability literature. Financial capability is another form of governance hat individualizes 'an economic problem…into a cultural one' (Beggs et al., 2014: 988). For example, earning a sufficient income to pay for household bills and actively saving has become normalized as a moral issue and an example of good financial citizenship, rather than a structural, neoliberal issue. Beggs et al. (2014) suggests that financial capability:

> is not just about household wellbeing or even household viability, but the overall stability of the [global] financial system.
>
> (Beggs et al., 2014: 982)

Financial citizenship supports the basic right of individuals to access affordable mainstream finance (Leyshon, 2009: 156). The term 'financial citizenship' goes beyond financial inclusion, which suggests that by merely 'being 'inside' the financial system should not be confused as a position of greater financial autonomy and freedom' (Kear, 2013: 11). Kear (2013) suggests that, while financial citizenship goes beyond the financial inclusion/exclusion binary, it does not fundamentally change the dynamics of the financial system. Instead, Kear (2013: 17) asserts that the goal of financial inclusion advocates should not be focused on scaling access to affordable credit and moderating risk pricing but, rather:

> more about politicizing the financial system's cultivation of tractably risky populations. Financial 'exclusion' needs to be reframed, not as a matter of social justice or basic rights, but as a problem of financial government—that is as a problem of conducting the conduct of risky populations without threatening the security and autonomy of financial markets.
>
> (Kear, 2013: 17)

As such, financial market segmentation needs to be examined in greater detail to ensure people are not included simply for their value to be extracted and exploited for market gain, just as the Global Financial Crisis powerfully demonstrated.

Credit Scoring: Prime and Subprime

Financialization has supported market segmentation, which is deepening financial inequalities (Aitken, 2017; Dymski, 2005). On the one hand, market stratification has opened up new markets for near-prime and subprime borrowers (Aitken, 2010; Appleyard et al., 2016). On the other hand, financially included individuals are able to access mainstream financial products and services to meet their everyday and long-term needs; for example, for insurance, pensions, or savings to protect themselves from financial shocks and provide for later life. To assess which products and services consumers can access and the cost of these products for prime and subprime individuals, banks increasingly operate 'at-a-distance' quickly and effectively through centralized systems for the quantitative calculation of customer risk, and the cost of these products and services. Applicants are assessed on their level of risk (e.g., of default on a loan, or the likelihood of claiming on an insurance product) using credit scoring, which is based on their credit history and demographic information (Wainwright, 2011). The advantage of credit scoring is to reduce the costs and time of assessing the financial capability of the customer and to overcome information asymmetries within the decision-making process (Stiglitz and Weiss, 1981). However, the credit scoring process can have a detrimental impact on an individual's ability to access affordable credit and services.

Credit scoring was developed in the 1950s as a decision-making tool to predict the risk of default on credit and the cost of that credit. Burton (2012: 111) summarizes that:

> Statistical modelling superseded traditional methods of assessing character and trustworthiness through personal knowledge and face-to-face interaction.

However, instead of trusting individuals on their ability to repay credit, 'risk-averse' banks have created:

> technologies that seek to remove the uncertainties of human behaviour by calculating risks…[in so doing] lending practices in financial institutions are directed towards the construction of socially responsible subjects.
>
> (Burton, 2012: 113)

In the process, the shift from relationship lending to credit scoring at-a-distance also widened access to credit (Burton, 2012). Leyshon et al. (2008: 136) suggests that:

> The statistical and predictive calculation of default risks through credit reporting and scoring has thus constituted the boom in consumer borrowing as rational, scientific and controlled.

Moreover, financial institutions have deepened the neoliberal project by infiltrating financialization into an individual's personal space.

Positive credit scores are associated with a 'normal' consumer who tends to be: employed full-time on a permanent basis, married, and an owner-occupier (with or without a mortgage) (Burton, 2012). Negative credit scoring is therefore based on whether individuals have experience of using (and repaying) credit, if they rent their home, are unemployed, employed part-time or on a contractual basis, have an irregular income, and are divorced. Credit scoring information therefore lacks context and builds only a partial picture of a consumer's credit history. This use of historical data questions as to whether an individual's history can also predict a person's future credit patterns as credit decisions are made in the present, but risk-based pricing of loans assesses the probability of default and is made on an individual's previous track record (Burton, 2012; Leyshon et al., 2008). Clearly, this data can discriminate against particular communities and can form geographical boundaries in which banks will not lend known as 'redlining' (Joseph, 2014).

Based on the positive or negative scores, the overall credit score has divided consumers into prime or subprime categories whereby:

> Prime customers—mainly middle and high income individuals—are actively pursued by retail financial services firms, and are the financially 'super-included', benefiting from intense competition between institutions for their business. Sub-prime customers, meanwhile, have low to moderate incomes and/or financial assets and are either excluded from mainstream financial marketing campaigns for new products or are denied access to services if they apply.
>
> (Leyshon et al., 2008: 463)

Prime customers are estimated to comprise 40% of the UK population, live predominantly in affluent areas that are well-served by financial institutions, and have access to a choice of low-cost products and services such as free, in credit banking (Leyshon et al., 2008). 'Near-prime' customers are thought to be a growing group who have reduced access to mainstream financial services (they may have access to a bank account, but limited access to mainstream credit).

Subprime customers are financially excluded in one or more ways, tending to rely on cash, rather than using electronic payments, but may have access to a basic bank account, and are more likely to be served by what can be termed non-prime, non-standard, or alternative financial services that are often high-cost and operate at the 'fringes' of the financial system (Leyshon et al., 2008). Subprime financial services mirror those of the mainstream at a higher cost including: cheque cashing, payday loans, rent-to-own products, guarantor loans, and home-collected credit. The subprime financial services industry effectively comprises a shadow, or secondary, financial services industry for those excluded from mainstream services. Global financial markets extend into every household across the world via mainstream and subprime products and services. For example:

> payday lending often re-circulates financial capital generated by mainstream global financial institutions [and is viewed as]...a local credit practice [but is also]...part of a much larger circuit of capital with global ambitions and reach.
>
> (Aitken, 2013: 387)

Subprime groups often pay a 'poverty premium' for banking services and credit (as well as other services such as utilities, etc.) as they often do not have a good credit score (Davies et al., 2016).

As part of the process of becoming responsible, calculative, and entrepreneurial, financial subjects are encouraged to know, understand, and build their credit score as part of their financial responsibilities—perhaps even taking out unwanted and risky products in order to increase the score so that they may transition to the financial mainstream in the future (Joseph, 2014; Rowlingson et al., 2016). This leaves people open to exploitation, as demonstrated by the US subprime housing crisis which was, for many people, a way of providing a stable home for their family (Joseph, 2014).

Inclusive credit scoring attempts to add value to traditional credit scoring models by making new forms of data available so that individuals can access affordable and fair sources of credit. These new forms of data sources include those from mobile phones, social media, psychometric testing, and rent payment history (Aitken, 2017; Henry and Morris, 2018). Inclusive credit scoring is designed not to lower the standards of lending but, rather, to add greater depth and context through alternative forms of data. However, there are concerns over how these alternative data and models may be used by lenders to extend consumer credit markets, even though these developments 'can clearly support fairer access and financial inclusion', the inclusive credit scoring process carries risk and does not necessarily guarantee 'positive financial outcomes' (Henry and Morris, 2018: iv). Alternative credit scoring could unwittingly lead to new forms of variegation and exclusion (Aitken, 2017).

Financial Ecologies

Understanding how financialization is variegating credit markets and 'the reproduction of the contemporary global financial system' is a pressing area of research for economic geographers (French et al., 2011: 812). One way this can be achieved is through exploring different groups through the financial spaces they inhabit over time and space. French et al. (2011: 812) outline how:

> The financial ecology approach…argues that like all systems the financial system is made up of smaller, constitutive ecologies. These consist of certain arrangements that emerge and that are more or less reproduceable over time. These processes unfold across space and evolve in relation to geographical difference so that distinctive ecologies of financial knowledge, practices and subjectivities emerge in different places. An ecological approach is not an alternative to a network approach, but constitutive of it, in that the topology of networks is uneven in their connectivity and material outcomes. Thus, some places are better connected to networks than others, while networks differ in their length and durability.

They go on to say:

> the financial ecology of the middle-class suburb can be seen as one of relative privilege, with deep and close connections to the financial system.
>
> (French et al., 2011: 813)

The middle-class, prime subject is part of a relatively safe, stable financial ecology that allowed financial markets to balance risk and extend into less privileged, subprime ecologies which 'appeared to offer a new and important temporal and spatial fix' for neoliberalism through the creation of new assets and forms of credit to a new market (French et al., 2011: 813).

However, with the hindsight of the Global Financial Crisis and the FCA's (2014) decision to regulate the UK payday loans or High-Cost, Short-Term Credit (HCSTC) market demonstrates that financialization has created:

> distinctive and highly socially and economically uneven 'financial ecologies'...characterised by spatially distinctive financial markets and institutions.
>
> (Leyshon et al., 2013: 3)

Understanding the financialization of individuals and households through financial practices, credit consumption, and indebtedness is an emerging area of research (Appleyard et al., 2016; Gonzalez, 2015; Hall, 2016; Langley, 2008). This body of work is breaking down the notion of 'homogenous financial subjects' through in-depth qualitative research with 'real households' in different 'social contexts' and the different degrees to which households become financialized (Gonzalez, 2015: 786). For example, Datta and Aznar (2019: 307) recognize that credit and indebtedness can be both 'enabling' and 'toxic', which creates:

> diverse debt ecologies which traverse multiple financial boundaries including formal/informal, social/economic and market/nonmarket practices.

Further research on the financialization of individuals and the household is critical to:

> consider the complex ways in which subjectivities are assembled in the interstices of other factors such as ethnicity, gender, age and, critically, location.
>
> (French et al., 2011: 808)

Therefore, financial market variegation and the 'precarious inclusion' of particular groups, such as those on low and moderate incomes, warrants further attention to examine 'the uneven ways in which financialization plays out over space' (Appleyard et al., 2016: 300). Clearly, economic geographers can make important contributions in demonstrating how financialization shapes spaces and places, and how subjects shape emerging and existing financial ecologies (Lai, 2016).

Conclusion

This chapter has explored the dynamics of the consumer credit landscape—and the broader role and relationship between the state, market, and individual—through concepts of financialization, financial exclusion/inclusion, financial subjects, and financial citizenship. Drawing on the money and finance literature within economic geography, this chapter has raised the questions: 'Who are banks for?' and 'What is their role in society?' Neoliberalization has driven financialization to segment financial markets into prime/near-prime/subprime spaces in order to extract value for profit. Financialization has effectively created a tiered financial services industry calculated by individuals' credit scores, which assess their level of risk by their income and wealth, demographic information, and employment status, which is an inherently biased process. This has been to the detriment of large sections of society.

Economic geographers have been at the forefront of research on the uneven geographies of finance and consumer credit since the 1970s, providing nuanced understandings of the consumer credit landscape and solutions that enable policy-makers to address financial exclusion. This chapter has demonstrated that money and finance have always had an important role in geography, but the legacy of the Global Financial Crisis and the new geographies of the financially excluded have created a new impetus for research in this field to contribute to debates beyond academia into policy and practice, in order to challenge the processes of financialization of everyday life (French et al., 2009). For example, while the number of citizens without a bank account has fallen globally, there are increasing numbers unable to access fair, affordable products and services due to increasing financial precarity within the labour market, housing system, and so on. In this context, financial exclusion is likely to remain a significant issue in the future.

As highlighted in this chapter, alternative and inclusive financial practices can challenge the hegemony of mainstream banks and banking practices (Dodd, 2012). However, as the example of inclusive credit scoring and subprime credit shows, this can serve both to open up new markets to exploit and to deepen exclusion. In the post-financial crisis era, questions remain around the ethical responsibility of banks, their role, and their duty to support financial inclusion alongside positive financial outcomes. Only further research into nuanced understandings of financial variegation, financial subjects, and the different financial ecologies that individuals inhabit over time and space is needed to provide the evidence base for policy to challenge the binaries of financial inclusion/exclusion for the benefit of the economy and society.

References

Aalbers, M. (2008). The financialization of home and the mortgage market crisis. *Competition and Change*, 12 (2), pp. 148–166.

Affleck, A. and Mellor, M. (2006). Community development finance: a neo-market solution to financial exclusion? *Journal of Social Policy*, 35 (2), pp. 303–319.

Aitken, R. (2010). Regul(ariz)ation of fringe credit: Payday lending and the borders of global financial practice. *Competition and Change*, 14 (2), pp. 80–99.

Aitken, R. (2013). Finding the edges of Payday lending. *Perspectives on Global Development and Technology*, 12 (3), pp. 377–409.

Aitken, R. (2017). 'All data is credit data': constituting the unbanked. *Competition and Change*, 21 (4), pp. 274–300.

Aker, J. C. and Mbiti, I. M. (2010). Mobile phones and economic development in Africa. *Journal of Economic Perspectives*, 24 (3), pp. 207–232.

Allen, J. and Pryke, M. (1999). Money cultures after Georg Simmel: mobility, movement and identity. *Environment and Planning D: Society and Space*, 17 (1), pp. 51–68.

Appleyard, L. (2011). Community development finance institutions (CDFIs): geographies of financial inclusion in the US and UK. *Geoforum*, 42 (2), pp. 250–258.

Appleyard, L., Rowlingson, K. and Gardner, J. (2016). Variegated financialization of subprime credit markets. *Competition and Change*, 20 (5), pp. 297–313.

Beggs, M., Bryan, D. and Rafferty, M. (2014). Shoplifters of the world unite! Law and culture in financialized times. *Cultural Studies*, 28 (5–6), pp. 976–996.

Brown, E., Castaneda, F., Cloke, J. and Taylor, P. (2013). Towards financial geographies of the unbanked: international financial markets, 'bancarizacion' and access to financial services in Latin America. *The Geographical Journal*, 179 (3), pp. 198–210.

Burton, D. (2012). Credit scoring, risk, and consumer lendingscapes in emerging markets. *Environment and Planning A*, 44 (1), pp. 111–124.

Christophers, B. (2015). The limits to financialization. *Dialogues in Human Geography*, 5 (2), pp. 183–200.

Crouch, C. (2009). Privatised Keynesianism: an unacknowledged policy regime. *The British Journal of Politics and International Relations*, 11 (3), pp. 382–399.

Datta, K. and Anzar, C. (2019). The space-times of migration and debt: Re-positioning migrants' debt and credit practices and institutions in, and through, London. *Geoforum*, 98 pp. 300–308.

Davies, S., Finney, A. and Hartfree, Y. (2016). *Paying to Be Poor: Uncovering the Scale and Nature of the Poverty Premium*. Bristol: Personal Finance Research Centre. Available at: https://www.bristol.ac.uk/media-library/sites/geography/pfrc/pfrc1615-poverty-premium-report.pdf [Accessed 4 June 2019].

Dodd, N. (2012). Simmel's perfect money: fiction, socialism and Utopia in the philosophy of money. *Theory, Culture & Society*, 29 (7/8), pp. 146–176.

Dymski, G. (2005). Financial globalization, social exclusion, and financial crisis. *International Review of Applied Economics*, 19 (4), pp. 439–457.

Dymski, G. and Veitch, J. M. (1996). Financial transformation and the metropolis: booms, busts, and banking in Los Angeles. *Environment and Planning A*, 28 (7), pp. 1233–1260.

Edmonds, T. (2018). *Bank Branch Closures*. House of Commons Briefing Paper Number 385, 19 October 2018. House of Commons Library. Available at: researchbriefings.files.parliament.uk/documents/SN00385/SN00385.pdf [Accessed 2 February 2019].

FCA. (2014). *Detailed Rules for the Price Cap on High-Cost Short-Term Credit Including Feedback on CP14/10 and Final Rules*. London: Financial Conduct Authority. Available at: https://www.fca.org.uk/publication/policy/ps14-16.pdf [Accessed 4 June 2019].

FCA. (2018). *The Financial Lives of Consumers across the UK: Key Findings from the FCA's Financial Lives Survey 2017*. London: Financial Conduct Authority. Available at: https://www.fca.org.uk/publication/research/financial-lives-consumers-across-uk.pdf [Accessed 4 June 2019].

French, S., Leyshon, A. and Thrift, N. (2009). A very geographical crisis: the making and breaking of the 2007–2008 financial crisis. *Cambridge Journal of Regions, Economy and Society*, 2 (2), pp. 287–302.

French, S., Leyshon, A. and Wainwright, T. (2011). Financializing space, spacing financialization. *Progress in Human Geography*, 35 (6), pp. 798–819.

French, S., Leyshon, A. and Meek, S. (2013). *The Changing Geography of British Bank and Building Society Branch Networks, 2003–2012* Available at: http://eprints.nottingham.ac.uk/2199/1/ChangingGeographyofBritishBank%26BuildingSocBranchNetworks2003-2012_FINAL.pdf [Accessed 4 June 2019].

FSA. (2000). *In or Out? Financial Exclusion: A Literature and Research Review*. Consumer Research 3. London: Financial Services Authority.

Fuller, D. and Jonas, A. E. G. (2002). Institutionalizing future geographies of financial inclusion: national legitimacy versus local autonomy in the British credit union movement. *Antipode*, 34 (1), pp. 85–110.

Gabor, D. and Brooks, S. (2017). The digital revolution in financial inclusion: international development in the fintech era. *New Political Economy*, 22 (4), pp. 423–436.

Gibson-Graham, J. K. (2008). Diverse economies: performative practices for 'other worlds'. *Progress in Human Geography*, 32 (5), pp. 613–632.

Gonzalez, F. (2015). Where are the consumers? *Cultural Studies*, 29 (5–6), pp. 781–806.

Hall, S. M. (2016). Everyday family experiences of the financial crisis: getting by in the recent economic recession. *Journal of Economic Geography*, 16 (2), pp. 305–330.

Harvey, D. (1973). *Social Justice and the City*. London: Edward Arnold.

Harvey, D. (2007). Neoliberalism as creative destruction. *The Annals of the American Academy of Political and Social Science*, 610 (March), pp. 22–44.

Henry, N., Pollard, J., Sissons, P., Ferreira, J. and Coombes, M. (2017). Banking on lending: data disclosure and geographies of UK personal lending markets. *Environment and Planning A*, 49 (9), pp. 2046–2064.

Henry, N. and Morris, J. (2018). *Scaling Up Affordable Lending: Inclusive Credit Scoring*. London: Responsible Finance, Oak Foundation and Coventry University. Available at: https://www.european-microfinance.org/sites/default/files/document/file/Inclusive-credit-scoring-Final.pdf [Accessed 6 June 2019].

HMT. (2004). *Promoting Financial Inclusion*. London: The Stationery Office.

Joseph, M. (2014). *Debt to Society: Accounting for Life under Capitalism*. Minneapolis, MN: University of Minnesota Press.

Kear, M. (2013). Governing Homo Subprimicus:Beyond Financial Citizenship, Exclusion, and Rights. *Antipode*, 45 (4), pp. 926–946.

Kempson, E. and Whyly, C. (1999). *Kept In or Opted Out? Understanding and Combating Financial Exclusion*. Bristol: Policy Press.

Lai, K. P.Y. (2016). Financial advisors, financial ecologies and the variegated financialisation of everyday investors. *Transactions of the Institute of British Geographers*, 41 (1), pp. 27–40.

Langley, P. (2008). Financialization and the consumer credit boom. *Competition and Change*, 12 (2), pp. 133–147.

Lee, R., Clark, G. L., Pollard, J. and Leyshon, A. (2009). The remit of financial geography—before and after the crisis. *Journal of Economic Geography*, 9 (5), pp. 723–747.

Leyshon, A. and Thrift, N. (1994). Access to financial services and financial infrastructure withdrawal: problems and policies. *Area*, 26 (3), pp. 268–275.

Leyshon, A. and Thrift, N. (1995). Geographies of financial exclusion: financial abandonment in Britain and the United States. *Transactions of the IBG*, 20 (3) pp. 312–341.

Leyshon, A. and Thrift, N. (1997). *Money/Space: Geographies of Monetary Transformation*. London: Routledge.

Leyshon, A. and Thrift, N. (1999). Lists come alive: electronic systems of knowledge and the rise of credit-scoring in retail banking. *Economy and Society*, 28 (3), pp. 434–466.

Leyshon, A., French, S. and Signoretta, P. (2008). Financial exclusion and the geography of bank and building society branch closure in Britain. *Transactions of the Institute of British Geographers*, 33 (4), pp. 447–465.

Leyshon, A. (2009). Financial exclusion. In: R. Kitchin and N. Thrift (eds.), *International Encyclopedia of Human Geography* (4th ed.). London: Elsevier. pp. 153–158.

Li, W., Zhou, Y., Dymski, G. and Chee, M. (2001). Banking on social capital in an era of globalization: Chinese ethnobanks in Los Angeles. *Environment and Planning A*, 33 (11), pp. 1923–1948.

Makortoff, K. (2018). UK banks urged to justify 'staggering' level of branch closures. *The Guardian*. Available at: https://www.theguardian.com/business/2018/nov/16/uk-bank-urged-justify-staggering-level-branch-closures-which-survey [Accessed 16 November 2018].

Marshall, J. N., Willis, R. and Richardson, R. (2003). Demutualization, strategic choice, and social responsibility. *Environment and Planning C*, 21 (5), pp. 735–760.

Marshall, J. N. (2004). Financial institutions in disadvantaged areas: a comparative analysis of policies encouraging financial inclusion in Britain and the United States. *Environment and Planning A*, 36 (2), pp. 241–261.

Marshall, N. J., Pike, A., Pollard, J. S., Tomaney, J., Dawley, S. and Gray, J. (2012). Placing the run on Northern Rock. *Journal of Economic Geography*, 12 (1), pp. 157–181.

Martin, R. (2002). *Financialization of Daily Life*. Philadelphia, PA: Temple University Press.

MAPS. (2019). What is financial capability? *Money and Pensions Service* [Online]. Available at: https://www.fincap.org.uk/en/articles/what-is-financial-capability [Accessed 6 June 2019].

Mitton, L. (2008). *Financial Inclusion in the UK: Review of Policy and Practice*. London: Joseph Rowntree Foundation. Available at: https://www.jrf.org.uk/sites/default/files/jrf/migrated/files/2234.pdf [Accessed 4 February 2019].

Montgomerie, J. (2013). America's debt safety net. *Public Administration*, 91 (4), pp. 871–888.

Mullineux, A. (2010). Financial innovation and social welfare. *Journal of Financial Regulation and Compliance*, 18 (3), pp. 243–256.

OECD. (2009). *Financial Education and the Crisis: Policy Paper and Guidance*. OECD International Network on Financial Education. Available at: https://www.oecd.org/finance/financial-education/50264221.pdf [Accessed 4 June 2019].

Peck, J. and Tickell, A. T. (2002). Neoliberalizing space. *Antipode*, 34 (3), pp. 380–404.

Pike, A. and Pollard, J. (2010). Economic geographies of financialization. *Economic Geography*, 86 (1), pp. 29–51.

Rowlingson, K., Appleyard, L. and Gardner, J. (2016). Payday lending in the UK: the regul(aris)ation of a necessary evil? *Journal of Social Policy*, 45 (3), pp. 527–543.

Sherraden, M. (1991). *Assets and the Poor: A New American Welfare Policy*. New York: Sharpe.

Soederberg, S. (2013). Universalising financial inclusion and the securitisation of development. *Third World Quarterly*, 34 (4), pp. 593–612.

Stiglitz, J. E. and Weiss, A. (1981). Credit rationing in markets with imperfect information. *American Economic Review*, 71 (3), pp. 393–410.

The World Bank. (2019). *Financial Inclusion*. Available at: https://www.worldbank.org/en/topic/financialinclusion/overview [Accessed 4 June 2019].

Wainwright, T. (2009). Laying the Foundations for a Crisis: mapping the historico-geographical construction of residential mortgage backed securitization in the UK. *International Journal of Urban and Regional Research*, 33 (2), pp. 372–388.

Wainwright, T. (2011). Elite knowledges: framing risk and the geographies of credit. *Environment and Planning A*, 43 (3), pp. 650–665.

Whyly, E., Moos, M., Hammel, D. and Kabahizi, E. (2009). Cartographies of race and class: mapping the class-monopoly rents of American subprime mortgage capital. *International Journal of Urban and Regional Research*, 33 (2), pp. 332–354.

18

INSURANCE, AND THE PROSPECTS OF INSURABILITY

Kate Booth

Introduction

Insurance is commonly understood as a benign financial tool in the distribution and management of risk. Premised on risk being calculable and risk information being singular, rational individuals or decision-making bodies pick up this tool (when they purchase insurance) and manage their risks accordingly. While this linear and universalizing logic resonates within some contemporary risk discourse, it lies in stark contrast to the complexity that is routinely described during government inquiries and inquests into insurance, insurers, and the financial sector more generally (e.g. Hayne, 2019).

Financial life—like social life—is complex, embodying more than is reducible to money and individual rational agency. As Johnson (2013a) observes, 'insurance is not a tangible product or service rendered at the time of payment, but rather an intangible promise of future financial exchange contingent upon the occurrence of an undesirable event' (2013a: 2674). As such, 'social work' is required for its existence and its maintenance, and for its uptake by individuals and other bodies. Geographers, amongst others, have been instrumental in unpacking the insurantial 'black-box' that has been created by the assumptions previously mentioned, and providing insight into its social and political dimensions. Specifically, geographers have contributed to providing more differentiated explanations for the form and function of insurance, and to exploring associated temporal and spatial variegations of affect, morality, and politics.

A review of this interdisciplinary research reveals a body of work small in breadth, but of considerable depth. It covers various scales from individuals, households, regions, and the globe; addresses issues of disasters, consumption, terrorism, climate change, life and death, and insurer sustainability; engages with processes of financialization, marketization, responsibilization, and individualization; and resonates concerns that cut across the social sciences—power, inequity, and inequality.

To do justice to this evolving and intricate research landscape, I have chosen to focus on three broad categories of insurance: self (e.g., health, life, retirement), property (e.g., home, contents, government assets), and climate (e.g., weather, crop yields, labor). This is not a comprehensive coverage of diversifying insurance types, some of which appear unresearched—or, at least, under-researched (e.g., pet insurance and agricultural insurance in developed countries). It does, however, allow insight into how insurance is co-producing the global economy, and constituting social and political relations, as well as agricultural, natural, and built environments.

Insurance is also becoming tied up in the everyday lives of households in ways that appear to be imbued with significant societal changes: 'As far as its… consumers are concerned; insurance is a promise—one that strikes at the heart of making the world liveable' (McFall, 2011: 665). Ideas of what constitutes a livable world for consumers as publics are on the move, and how households and insurance are co-produced is increasingly informing this sense of livability. This is not a straightforward, causal shift couched within discourses of responsibilization and privatization. As Collier (2014) observes in relation to the emergence of public flood insurance in the 1960s, the shift from liberalism to neoliberalism in the United States does not fit the simple narrative of a loss of 'mechanisms of security that socialized risk' (2014: 287) to be replaced by individuals responsible for their own security. Instead, and more complexly, 'neoliberalism modified the possible accommodations and articulations among risk, security, and responsibility' (Collier, 2014: 287). Insurance, as manifest within these accommodations and articulations, is reshaping social and political landscapes at multiple scales and in variegated ways.

A key theme in research exploring this social and political reshaping is how insurability is framed through calculations of risk and uncertainty. Ewald (1991: 198) observes:

> Insurance technology and actuarial science did not fall from the mathematical skies to incarnate themselves in institutions. They were built up gradually out of multiple practices which they reflected and rationalized, practices of which they were more effects than causes, and it would be wrong to imagine that they have now assumed a definite shape.

A complex ontological and epistemological landscape exists in which archival-statistical calculation plays but a partial role in defining insurability. Fire insurance in Australia, for example, was over 100 years behind life insurance in the uptake of actuarial calculations (O'Malley and Roberts, 2013), instead using a calculation of 'culminative dangerousness' based on a case-by-case assessment of each household's structural and moral risks by insurance salesmen. More recently, Collier (2008) and Lobo-Guerrero (2010) observe how epistemologies of catastrophe insurance are premised on modeling possible futures, instead of statistical-archival calculations based on past events:

> what we observe today is not a paralysis of frameworks of rational response to uncertain threats. Rather, we see the proliferation of such frameworks in multifarious emerging initiatives whose aim is to generate knowledge about uncertain future events and to link this knowledge to diverse mechanisms of mitigation.
>
> (Collier, 2008: 225–6)

Binary distinctions between a past of 'easy' risk calculation and a future of incalculable uncertainty are unwarranted. While rapid and global socio-ecological change has caused some to predict an 'acceleration towards non-insurability' (Bougen, 2003 cited in Sturm and Oh, 2010: 155), others identify how the insurance sector is innovating, adapting, and not only sustaining profitability but growing (e.g. Sturm and Oh, 2010). As Lobo-Guerrero maintains, 'insurers have an unrivalled potential to mobilize discourses of 'truth' and impose their ways of understanding and manage uncertainty at all levels of business around the globe' (Lobo-Guerrero, 2010: 240).

As I discuss below, a focus on insurability draws attention to the excess of insurability—how insurability co-produces other, possibly unforeseen arrangements. For example, as insurers work to grow insurance uptake and coverage through extensions of insurability, this acts to determine and maintain what is uninsurable. Thus, insurability necessitates non-insurability, and vice versa. It also acts, albeit inadvertently, to create spaces for the proliferation of contestation as other agencies renegotiate and reconfigure insurer ontologies and epistemologies of insurability. This co-produces a different manifestation of excess—schisms; contradictions; and limitations in, and resistance to insurer and financialized logics, as reflected in marketization more generally:

> the speeding up and extension of market arrangements inevitably leads to a proliferation of the social: that is, an intensification of… social and political contestation over the consequences of marketization, as framings of goods and agencies increasingly overflow.
>
> (Callon, 2007 cited in French and Kneale, 2012: 396)

Yet, the power and prowess of the insurance sector (as part and parcel of global financialized capitalism), can make it appear a natural given. It sits within the vision of a post-political world (e.g., Giddens, 2000) in which possibilities other than, or aside from, capitalism do not appear tenable, or even identifiable. Insurer and neoliberal-inclined government discourse on insurance resonate with logics that can appear complete and so normalized as to be commonsensical. As Mouffe (2005) describes, in the post-political there exists a given, naturalized state seemingly bereft of politics and history 'in which individuals liberated from collective ties can now dedicate themselves to cultivating a diversity of lifestyles, unhindered by antiquated attachments' (Mouffe, 2005: 1). Insurance, in this context, is perceived to act above and beyond politics, freeing individuals from dependency on family and friends, from the dictates and restrictions that can come with state welfare, and from land, culture, and tradition. Even providing freedom from the tyranny of a recalcitrant climate (Booth and Williams, 2014).

The fallacy of this imaginary is a central theme throughout geographic (and allied) research on insurance, as are the uneven power relations that exist between insurers and publics. However, less certain in this literature are pathways towards alternative politics. Financial researchers, including geographers, can play an important social role: intervening in policy debates and progressing equitable change (French et al., 2011; Hall, 2010). As I introduce below, there appears to be fruitful opportunities for this kind of contribution through describing and analysing multiple and spatially variegated excesses of insurability. This may be enabled by a Rancièrian approach to the political (e.g., Dikeç, 2005; Hallward, 2003; Rancière, 2001) that does more than make visible the multi-scalar and unequal distribution of power within insurance discourses and practices. This type of approach also provides a frame for understanding and progressing change—for seeing (and researching) how the schisms, contradictions, and limitations emergent through insurance discourses and practices could mobilize financial markets for improving the prospects of self, property, and climate.

Self

The options for insuring the self are diverse and diversifying. From life, health, and salary to death and the funeral, the fundamental risk of being mortal has engaged the prowess and innovative capacities of financiers since the mid-nineteenth century (Defert, 1991). These forms of insurance are often portrayed as providing individuals—and sometimes family members—with the capacity to bounce back, or at least sustain and secure lifestyles and livelihoods, in the advent of mishap or happenstance and into a comfortable retirement. They can appear as a form of social welfare and, indeed, are often represented as such. Yet, many of these forms of insurance emerged not from reforms implemented to address the plight of nineteenth-century workers but, rather, from the machinations of financiers, 'before later becoming a paradigm of social solutions to all cases of non-labour: first that of industrial accidents, then sickness and old age, and finally unemployment' (Defert, 1991: 211). With the more recent shift towards the (re)privatization of social welfare, this financialized heritage continues to resonate, albeit in new and novel ways.

McFall (2011: 665) notes in relation to early attempts by insurers to enroll nineteenth-century publics, 'insurance flourished because its proponents understood that even the most technical, most quantitative financial product, had also to engage the passions.' Contemporary insurance marketing continues to incite the senses, evoking feelings of fear, guilt, and hope (French and Kneale, 2009), and 'safety, belonging and respectability' (McFall, 2011: 680). The purchase of life insurance, for example, is presented as a foil to stirred up feelings of anxiety and failure; as promising 'peace of mind' (with a bonus of also acting a mechanism for saving) (Lobo-Guerrero, 2014).

Concerted effort is required to (re)produce enthusiasm through and for insurance. This includes engendering insurance with a *presence* in the here and now, and placing less emphasis on a more abstract sense of future contingency. The immediacy of affect and lifestyle facilitates such presence, doing the work—the social work—of prescribing what is and what is not common sense, and ensuring a form of enthusiasm for an otherwise distant benefit: 'insurance discourses and practices are always present-oriented and rather than preparing for 'the' future, they seek to shape the present to generate 'a' future' (Lobo-Guerrero, 2010: 246). Life insurance (or life assurance), for example, has explicitly mobilized lifestyle in the development and promulgation of new products. This involves the production of active financial subjects who are both investors and entrepreneurs, and carers of self: 'to call forth more active insurantial subjects, but also in the process to necessarily enliven insurance' (French and Kneale, 2009: 1032).

Yet, a life infused with emotions and passions is also a life exposed to uncertainty. Emotional and passion-driven behaviors disable the life-turned-capital premise on which life insurance products transform expectable life into an enabler of credit. Thus, life insurance also operates in constraining desire or, at the very least, in modulating it into normalized or 'domesticated' behavior (Lobo-Guerrero, 2014):

> By producing 'present(s)' insurers produce 'orders of the real'. Orders of the real are actualisations of imaginaries and are the materialisation of discourses and practices. When insurers perform an order of the real they are not only exercising specific forms of power but they are shaping reality for their stakeholders in insurantial terms.
>
> (Lobo-Guerrero, 2010: 246)

Insuring the self brings into being a moral ordering in which insurers define what is acceptable or not, and enroll a self-disciplining subject in the process. Having insurance becomes not so much a decision, its existence in one's life is self-evident, normalized, or 'domesticated' (Lehtonen, 2017a). As Langley (2006) observes, the evolution of pension insurance—in the United Kingdom and United States, at least—deployed and enacted a logic of individualization and, thus, co-produced individuals as 'entrepreneurial investor' subjects. Insurance was no longer about pooling and managing risk, it was, instead, normalized as a signifier of self-responsibility—of being a 'good' risk bearer:

> An assumed passive reliance on the state and/or on the employer to provide collective insurance for old age is deemed to be no longer sufficient. The investor is delineated discursively against an irrational counterpart, a subject who is necessarily mad, bad, and in danger of an insecure retirement during which his or her freedom will be seriously compromised.
>
> (Langley, 2006: 929)

In producing a particular understanding and associated reduction of 'life', this delineation and constraint renders life commodifiable (Lobo-Guerrero, 2014). This translation into capital relies on and produces an 'inside' that signifies insurability and an 'outside' that marks non-insurability. It also describes and prescribes moralities of the self; for example, calculations of moderate drinking co-produced by insurers and medical professionals. In rejecting claims from alcoholics and those who self-harm in other ways, 'the lives of those who are unable or unwilling to refashion their biosocial selves are devalued, excluded from the liberal way of life, and deemed uninsurable; that is, unworthy of securing' (Lobo-Guerrero, 2014: 22).

While this 'outside' or excess make insurance and insurability possible (Lobo-Guerrero, 2014), it also creates opportunities for new products that carry higher premiums, such as policies covering extreme sports. In this way, insurance acts to exclude certain types of risky behavior, while rendering others tolerable and profitable.

Thus, insurability is not only affective and normative, it is also more fuzzy and fluid than if it were co-produced purely through statistical-archival calculations and knowledge:

> even that warhouse of the trade, the mortality table, cannot be constructed from the data without a modicum of judgement and a good eye. Graphing the mortality figures yields an irregular scatter of points, not a smooth curve, from which the actuary extracts a mortality curve by 'graduation techniques'—i.e. by drawing a curve freehand through the cloud of points.
>
> (McFall, 2011: 670)

French and Kneale (2015: 17) describe the 'bricolage qualities of life insurance', where selves, agencies, and insurance products create certainty and security, and a sense of moral order (and profit). Yet, the activation and maintenance of this configuration also co-produces new distributions of affect and morality as selves, agencies, and insurance products exceed themselves.

As French and Kneale (2012) observe, commodifying or securing life necessitates the production of novel and specified forms of subject and subjectivity. However, for 'life lived carelessly', this also produces some innate contradictions and tensions: contemporary forms of life insurance 'foster new promises of security, [yet] new anxieties and uncertainties are simultaneously fashioned in their wake' (French and Kneale, 2012: 402). For example, contradicting government health initiatives in the United Kingdom, lower insurance premiums were awarded to those suffering ill health due to reduced life expectancy and the healthy were 'punished' for the likelihood of living longer. This was viewed by some as discriminatory against the rich, whose life expectancies are statistically longer, and an unfair penalization of the 'responsible and hardworking citizen-consumers of 'middle England'' (French and Kneale, 2012: 393).

Insurances of the self can also re-produce patterns of socio-economic advantage and disadvantage—sometimes contrary to government aspirations. In the United Kingdom, for example, pension insurance schemes have been mobilized by those with wealth to garner tax breaks and purchase investment properties (Langley, 2006). This may secure the future of these individuals, but also widens the gap between rich and poor. New divides also appear possible, with Lobo-Guerrero (2014) speculating that tensions could arise from determinations of insurability based on the human genome. This could produce a no-risk or low-risk population that feel no need to take out life or health insurance with only those at higher risk looking towards insurance, thus undercutting the horizontal, solidaristic sharing of risk on which insurance is based.

Property

While geographic (and allied) research into insurances of self exhibits a large footprint, the insurance of property has received surprisingly little attention beyond the fields of economics and finance (Johnson, 2013b). Yet, the small body of research that does exist addresses similar themes to those identified in relation to life insurance. Rather than the singularity apparent within statistical-archival knowledge, the insurance of property also manifests as a bricolage of affect, power, and morality that both enables specific forms of insurability and non-insurability, and, in exceeding associated containments, co-produces new terrains of insecurity, novel agencies, and perverse outcomes.

Ericson and Doyle (2004) observe that what has been accounted for and calculated as risk, has always included gaps and absences that have been 'filled' through 'non-scientific forms of knowledge that are intuitive, emotional, aesthetic, moral, and speculative' (Ericson and Doyle, 2004: 138). As introduced above, door-to-door insurance salesmen prior to the 1920s did not assess buildings in terms of risk based on statistical-archival probability, they were ascertaining 'cumulative dangerousness', including potential moral deviancy on behalf of householders (O'Malley and Roberts, 2014). It is not hard to image how being successful or unsuccessful in obtaining an insurance policy would then become, in part, a signifier of moral worth.

This co-production of insurance and householder subjectivity continues to resonate, with more recent research indicating a similar morality in relation to the types of people who do and do not have house and contents insurance, including some householders confidently predicting which neighbors are 'good insured-type people' (Booth and Harwood, 2016: 50). This morality sits within 'insurantial moments' in which householders move between speaking about insurance in terms of risk aversion, to its being a risk in and of itself stemming from the lack of trust in insurers (Tranter and Booth, 2019). At other times, if disaster were to strike, insurance provides an opportunity for imagining a fresh start and a better life. The affective terrain of house and contents insurance within places at high risk of wildfire includes uncertainty, anxiety, judgement, hope, and love for dependent family members (Booth and Harwood, 2016).

Booth and Harwood (2016) suggest that these everyday complexities co-produce house and contents underinsurance. In making decisions about insurance purchase and levels of coverage, householders make a range of trade-offs in relation to other daily concerns. As with life insurance, while this type of property insurance is normative and normalized, householders exert agency in what and how insurance works for them as part of everyday life. Everyday *presence* for householders can mean something different than how insurers and marketers mobilize affect—hope and lifestyle—in maintaining an enthusiasm for, and selling, insurance. Householders, in effect, create their own 'inside' and 'outside' of insurability. For example, a householder may identify a gifted piece of furniture as irreplaceable for sentimental reasons and thus deem it uninsurable, even if their insurer would cover it under contents insurance (Booth and Harwood, 2016).

Urban and housing trends appear to be changing patterns of householder-conceived insurability (Booth and Kendal, 2020). The rise in renting in countries such as Australia, the United Kingdom and the United States is contributing to more households doing without insurance—specifically, contents insurance. While this could be interpreted as 'underinsurance,' it also provides insights into how housing tenure contributes to ideas of insurability. If renting is only a temporary, transitional state for those looking to buy their first home and with few accumulated assets, then these assets may not be deemed worth insuring, or as insurable as a home full of belongings. However, in places where renting appears to be a new norm—long-term and asset-laden—then these historic ideas of householder insurability—of what's in and what's out—may be changing.

While existing within the powerful ontologies and epistemologies promulgated by insurers and insurance logics (Lobo-Guerrero, 2013), householders use and understand financial instruments, including insurance, in distinctly non-financial ways (Lehtonen, 2017a). Outcomes of property insurance can also speak to other forms of excess, revealing tensions between narratives of individual responsibilization, the power of the insurance sector, and government initiatives for climate change adaptation.

Historically, large-scale natural disasters were conceived as acts of God, rather than acts of self, and thus amendable to government intervention in victim-focused response and recovery (Collier, 2014). The financialized responsibilization of European flood-prone residents has shifted these (potential) victims towards active 'flood' consumers (O'Hare et al., 2015), though, as previously noted, this modifies, rather than transforms, relations between risk, security, and responsibility (Collier, 2014). In relying on flood insurance, households effectively cede power, as insurers become the de facto property owners, taking over responsibility for and controlling the nature of repairs (O'Hare et al., 2015). As the modus operandi for these insurance technologies is 'like-for-like'—replacing or returning properties to what existed before—the flood-prone nature of these buildings is retained with no room for incorporating new flood-adaptive technologies and resilient design: 'the transfer of risk… through the purchase of insurance may therefore partly shelter citizens from aspects of the responsibilization agenda' (O'Hare et al., 2015: 1182).

Insurance, in this context, is maladaptive in that it:

> serves to industrialise, commercialise and reproduce the consequences of risk rather than engendering any system transitions or adaptive behaviour…by consequence insurance catalyses a cycle of maladaptation, enabling individual recovery, but inhibiting adaption and sustaining exposure.
>
> (O'Hare et al., 2015: 1176)

It both fails to adapt, and perpetuates maladaptive building and urban responses in a changing climate.

However, in other contexts, the insurance of property is rapidly evolving and adapting in response to emerging configurations of uncertainty, with a recent rise in insurance-linked securities (Johnson, 2013b). Catastrophe bonds—specifically bonds 'whose rate of return depends on whether or not a pre-specified insurance loss trigger occurs within a certain time period' (Johnson, 2013b: 30)—are now a commonly recognized feature of natural disaster insurance. The Caribbean Catastrophic Risk Insurance Facility (CCRIF) is a prominent example. Instigated in 2007, this form of parametric insurance is regional in scope, and based on a public–private partnership covering 16 nation states throughout the Caribbean (Grove, 2012). Under this technology, payouts are triggered by meeting or exceeding a specified parameter, such as wind speed, rather than actual losses, thus expanding what is deemed insurable (hurricanes in the Caribbean had previously been deemed uninsurable). This insurance also stabilizes risk assets as a source of securitized returns:

> Such a process reorganizes disaster management around the imperatives of financial speculation, which imagines uncertain futures in a way that secures and make the present profitable…It does so through a process of appropriation and accumulation that transforms environmental insecurities into catastrophe risk that states leverage on financial markets to increase their adaptive capacity, or their ability to act within the socio-ecological emergency of a disaster.
>
> (Grove, 2012: 140)

The CCRIF was developed in response to the impact of Hurricane Ivan on Grenada in 2004. This hurricane caused damages up to double Grenada's GDP and temporally rendered this state non-existent. It brought to light that the lack of insurability was not only a potential issue for Caribbean nations and populations, but had broader security implications beyond the region vis-à-vis failed states, social disorder and emergent black economies (Grove, 2012). Rather than a disaster management and recovery mechanism, the CCRIF has emerged as a financialized security mechanism—as not so much about addressing vulnerabilities of populations and enabling adaptive capacity, but as a form of state security.

In places such as Haiti, where there are low levels of private insurance, payouts from the CCRIF flow to the state but bypass the people and places most impacted (Lobo-Guerrero, 2011). This security rationale also undermines other survival and adaptive capacities that non-insured populations could mobilize in the face of climate change and disaster events (Grove, 2012: 144). These populations must remain contained and constrained in the 'outside,' if the insured 'inside'—that is, undemocratic nation states—are to retain security. As Grove argues, this financialization of disaster management has a 'tendency to turn individuals affected by disasters into a faceless population of potential threats to state security' (Grove, 2012: 151) and act to marginalize the disadvantaged (Grove, 2010).

Another feature of catastrophe bonds is how, in effect, they link life and property insurances through loss triggers securitized through pension insurance payments (public pension funds). As Johnson (2013b: 30) describes, catastrophic risk is the asset, and pension plans the investor, with the co-joining of 'ontologically and geographically disparate orders' creating both flexibility and profit. Yet, the establishment of these new risk assets also comes with new fragilities as this biological, physical, and social 'intermingling' embodies a process of normatization in which social relations are 'coaxed' into orderings of truth that may upend the solidarity of insurance (Johnson, 2013b). Solidaristic insurance—whether private or through the 'insurers of last resort'—is commonly understood as inherently equitable (O'Hare et al., 2015), spreading risk equally across populations and risk types. However, catastrophe bonds and the like have the capacity to predetermine 'certain disaster anticipation logics and response pathways' (O'Hare et al., 2015: 1185), including co-producing 'haves' and 'have nots', and places that have and places that have not. As Bonizzi and Kaltenbrunner (2018) observe in relation to growing yet volatile insurance company and pension fund investment in emerging economies, this re-produces spatial patterns of financialized domination and subordination (Bonizzi et al., 2019).

Patterns of insurance-enabled exclusion and inclusion also resonate within the developed world, albeit in more muted forms. Tracking climate change impacts and insurer responses, Johnson (2015) predicts urban splintering:

> the selective coverage of vulnerable spaces containing high concentrations of insured value—where accordingly high premiums can be demanded from the wealthy—while the state underwrites those places and populations too unremunerative for private insurers.
>
> (Johnson, 2015: 2515)

Lower socio-economic communities appear routinely disadvantaged by insurance technologies that are not primarily developed in response to their needs (e.g., Nance, 2015; Booth and Tranter, 2018).

'Non-insurance' or 'underinsurance' is gaining new prominence in relation to climate change, but not in ways that question or disrupt the complex co-dependence of insurability and non-insurability. Insurance sector accounting and reporting is highlighting what appears to be an urgent and compelling issue—a startling gap between what is insured and what is insurable in the context of the rising impacts and costs of natural disasters (e.g., Lloyd's, 2018). 'Underinsurance' in this context is part of marketization (Callon, 2016). It is:

> a socio-technical device in pacifying and normalising new, and perhaps novel insurance 'goods' and markets. In rendering active and unbounded relations into discernible and passive goods—in this case, insurance—underinsurance is enacted as part of the conception, production and circulation of goods and markets.
>
> (Booth and Kendal, 2020)

Lobo-Guerrero (2010) describes the uninsured as a market, not a population or society, highlighting that 'splintered' urban places and populations are not of interest to insurers, but market opportunities are.

Climate

Along with catastrophe bonds, there has been a recent and rapid emergence of a collection of mechanisms termed 'climate insurance'—insurance against regional or local extreme weather events, rather than climate and climate change as risks per se (Müller et al., 2017). This includes nation-level insurance policies and index insurance (more accurately, derivatives). Index insurance is the creation of insurability through contracts premised on environmental indexes such as rainfall, wind speed, soil moisture, and crop yield (Johnson, 2013a), and much of this growth relates to microinsurance projects aimed at poor rural farmers in developing nations, and operating across Africa, southern Asia, and Central and South America. These are, by and large, driven by the discourse of climate change vulnerability within development agencies—from the United Nations to small non-profit aid groups—and, like the CCRIF, these are often formulated as public–private partnership projects. These are also frequently the first kind of insurance to ever be made available to small, low-yield and dispersed farmers.

From the perspective of insurers, index insurance is attractive as it removes the need of resource-intensive evaluation of ownership and losses, ameliorates the perceived risk of moral hazard, and addresses the problem of those at greater risk buying the most insurance and thus skewing the market. The promises associated with microinsurance include, 'its potential to decrease the vulnerability of poor rural households to climate shocks, crowd-in the provision of rural credit, and encourage more 'productive risk-taking' and input use by farmers' (Johnson, 2013a: 2663). In short, it facilitates the integration of small, subsistence farmers into larger-scale agricultural production. Whether these promises are forthcoming or not (whether they are even wholly desirable), there is an apparent equity in this kind of insurance innovation. In removing the need to prove ownership—or, indeed to 'own' anything—microinsurance appears to under-cut the idea that those who have are always those with access to security of subsistence (Johnson, 2013a).

Yet—and resonating with observations pertaining to insurances of self and property, and the excess of insurability—there are schisms and contradictions in these logics and promises. In decoupling actual loss from payouts, index insurance does not necessarily cover actual losses, and risks experienced by farmers and this re-organization of risk does not equate to risk mitigation (Johnson, 2013a). In fact, the socio-ecological impacts or side-effects of climate insurance appear to contradict the imperative of addressing climate change vulnerability, and appears at odds with the level of government and aid subsidies of this type of insurance—for agricultural insurance alone, estimated to be at least US$2 billion per annum globally (Müller et al., 2017). For example, negative impacts and new risks have been identified in relation to the replacement of drought-resistance subsistence crops with 'cash crops', the expansion of cultivation into ecologically sensitive areas, greater input of agrochemicals and associated environmental impacts (though this is debated and appears context specific), and the erosion of genetically sustainable forms of seed stock when insurance is bundled with the purchase of 'improved' seed (Müller et al., 2017). There is also speculation regarding how formal insurance may interact with informal insurance—that is, whether it strengthens or fragments networks of social support, and the emergence of unequal co-dependencies. Development discourses:

> frame the target subjects of insurance in three ways: as 'at risk' populations vulnerable to climate variability and/or climate change; as aspiring agricultural producers who should be encouraged to take prudent risks to scale up production; and as potential financial consumers who would prefer to transfer their production risks to a financial institution. Within this triangulation, the impacts of global climate change may be invoked as heralding the current or future disarticulation of smallholders from the 'traditional' or 'informal' risk-sharing and coping mechanisms on which they have historically depended—making their integration into formal risk transfer chains apparently all the more urgent.
>
> (Johnson, 2013a: 2667)

The dismantling of traditional knowledges and structures in this context appears problematic in terms of local survival and adaptative capacity, removing and fragmenting the very things that may enable sustainability (Johnson, 2013a; Lobo-Guerrero, 2010).

In addition, growing and developing enthusiasm for insurance in this context, as with insurances of self and property, relies on its *presence*. Johnson (2013a) observes, for example, how insurers hope for bad weather events that will trigger microinsurance so as to maintain the trust of farmers.

With developments in catastrophe bonds and index insurance, insurance companies appear to be on the front foot when it comes to climate change. Reinsurance companies, in particular, identify themselves as taking a quasi-governmental role in tackling climate-related challenges. Whilst openly identifying governments as failing on collective climate action, the biggest global reinsurer, Munich Re, represents itself as *the* repository for natural disaster data, an innovator of risk and climate solutions, and proactive in climate mitigation; as providing sound and reasonable leadership to manage and control the risk, and identify and develop opportunities (Lehtonen, 2017b).

This objectification of the climate through the logics of financialization and marketization (Lehtonen, 2017b), and more generally, this economization of uncertainty (Lehtonen and Van Hoyweghen, 2014) is a hallmark of contemporary capitalism premised on a logic that 'capital can be repaired and insurance provides a technology for doing so' (Lobo-Guerrero, 2010: 243–4). This produces particular geographies of uncertainty and security that mandate insurance as *the* technology of risk that enables participation in the political economy of risk management. When focused on 'underinsured' developing nations—often in conjunction with governments, and international aid and humanitarian agencies—this 'reinforces a rationality of governance that takes a Western liberal financial capitalist way of life as its reference' (Lobo-Guerrero, 2010: 250).

This rationality extends insurer concerns in relation to climate change beyond sector profitability and global financial system sustainability. Re-insurers need large-scale, destructive events to address issues of overaccumulation (Johnson, 2015). To put it simply, a big disaster payout is one of three mechanisms commonly deployed by insurers to address an oversupply of abundant and cheap reinsurance: with a disaster, 'objects in the built environment lose value, and as reinsurers' reserves are tapped to pay claims on these objects, capital is depleted and the ability to command rents grows' (Johnson, 2015: 2508). Hence, some of the costliest disaster events have been swiftly followed by soaring profits as capital is cycled in and out of built environments. There is uncertainty in future events, particularly in light of climate change, but there remains, for insurers, certainty (a form of stability and growth) in this uncertainty. While 'actual transactions in these markets remain relatively black boxed' (Johnson, 2015: 2505), it is incorrect to assume that insurer positioning and 'alarm' about climate change necessarily heralds declining insurability. It does, however, point towards new and novel manifestations of insurability, and, conjointly, new and novel excess.

Prospects of insurability

As introduced above, there has been considerable debate pertaining to the limits of insurability (Collier, 2008; Lobo-Guerrero, 2010). Some follow Ulrich Beck's (1992) idea that insurability is limited by the capacity of actuarial calculation, and others observe that insurability extends into managing and governing uncertainty (e.g., Collier, 2008; Ericson and Doyle, 2004; O'Hare et al., 2015). Broadly speaking, the former tends to invoke a focus on risk (i.e., Knight, 2006) and understands risk as 'a neologism of insurance'—anything that is insurable is a risk and vis versa; risk is 'calculable, it is collective, and it is capital' (Ewald, 1991: 201). The latter follows observations such as those by Ericson and Doyle (2004) in their examination of how the insurance industry addressed the 9/11 terrorism events: 'while the insurance industry is a central bulwark against uncertainty, insurers can also play a key role in fostering it' (Ericson and Doyle, 2004: 169).

Risk is not simply and benignly equated with calculability and capital, but is manifest within complexities of uncertainty that, when managed and governed, invariably create excess. As uncertainty is a 'correlate of discourses and practices of truth' (Lobo-Guerrero, 2013: 354) this, rather than risk per se, has led to critiques of power and engagement with affect. Risk, and power and affect are not unrelated (O'Malley, 2004), but it is the inflections of power and resonances of affect in the relationality implicit within uncertainty that informs much of the work on insurance in geography and allied fields—as reviewed above.

Also exemplified in this review of the insurances of self, property, and climate is that while insurance comes with the promise of translating uncertainties into calculable, knowable, and, thus, manageable risks, perverse outcomes or 'contradictions and discrepancies...exist between the promise of such new products and the excess of uncertainty' (French and Kneale, 2009: 1049). It is an excess of uncertainty—or, more specifically, an excess of insurability, and how this is progressively reconfigured by insurers and those purchasing insurance, and co-produced through changing environments—that appears a significant contributor to the prospects of insurability.

The excess of insurability can be mobilized as a source of fear, to build dependence on and maintain enthusiasm for insurance. As Lobo-Guerrero (2014) observes, being insured relies on a sense (or the risk) of not being insured; there must be something outside to maintain the validity of the inside:

> inside spaces are those where risks are deemed manageable and controllable through technologies of insurance. The outside, or the world of afuera, is the realm of uncontrollable risks and feral uncertainty. The role of insurance in providing cover for some, and not all, forms of circulation, including and excluding some lifestyles (e.g. smokers, heavy drinkers), contributes to creating spaces of governance where activities and behaviours are relatively 'secure'. In so doing, however, a space of insecure governance is simultaneously constituted either as its radical opposite or as a gradient of opposition to the order of the insured world where insurers would try to penetrate while seeking market opportunities.
>
> (Lobo-Guerrero, 2014: 310)

By way of example, Baldwin (2017) argues that climate or adaptive migrants are understood as positive and, importantly, productive contributors to resilience and markets. But only if they effectively access and participate in international labor markets *and* insure their movement—be this insurance that directly finances a move, or insurance that incentivizes movement to more habitable regions. This means that an adaptive migrant is also a financialized migrant, tied to and accessing global financial and information networks. For Baldwin (2017), this represents a problematic racialization that overflows normative categories of Black/White and us/them: it represents 'a form of power that seeks to purify and thus strengthen a population by removing from it those bodies deemed to be abnormal' (Baldwin, 2017: 132). This is mediated by the power of markets, rather than sovereign states, with those deemed abnormal moving to and (re)producing more precarious situations such as informal settlements within megacities. These people and populations are deemed risk failures—uninsurable, non-resilient, and maladaptive, despite multifarious registers of informal insurance, resilience, and adaptation required to sustain life in such situations (Baldwin, 2017). Here, shaping 'the present to generate 'a' future' (Lobo-Guerrero, 2010: 246) produces a future that is inhabited only by 'insured life', with 'non-insured life' disappeared through perpetual containment or extinction through adaption to 'insured life.'

The insurantial logics that underpin this mobilization and containment of excess can appear all-encompassing and all-powerful; prescribing and defining, rather than co-producing selves, properties, and climates. It can feel as though financialized capitalism 'is seemingly beyond the grasp of social agency and regulatory authority and is narrowly accountable only to its own webs of financial interests' (Pike and Pollard, 2010: 31). However, in its manifestation of schisms, contradictions, and limitations, the excess of insurability also creates spaces of contestation or resistance to these power structures and dynamics. These can appear insignificant and insufficient in relation to the multi-scalar and unequal power relations described above. These may also be interpreted as ultimately supporting or reproducing financial capitalist imperatives—in, perhaps, acting to create new market opportunities, or representing the social 'freedom' espoused in relation to processes such as marketization (Callon, 2016). To better understand how an alternative politics may emerge in relation to these and how progressive change may occur, it is useful to introduce an alternative understanding of politics than that employed within much insurance research—a Rancierian approach.

For Jacque Rancière, politics is not about relations of power and competition between, for example, insurers and consumers, or insurance logics and other ways of being and knowing. Rather, true politics—politics proper—is the disruption and displacement of subjects, objects, functions, and actions from well-established and familiar categories and places: 'Political struggle is not a conflict between well defined interest groups; it is an opposition of logics that count the parties and parts of the community in different ways' (Rancière, 2001: 19). For example, if prisoners were to demand more food and elect a prison director they thought could help them achieve this, this would not be political (Dikeç, 2005). Even if the prisoners succeed in securing more food, structurally nothing has changed. There has been no political moment, just a continuation of the status quo—prisoners are still prisoners, there is still a director in charge of the prison, and a goal still confines. In the prison, the naming and labeling of roles and the 'spatial organization provides the *given* on the basis of which problems are defined, solutions proposed' (Dikeç, 2005: 173). Recognizing and critiquing this given and acting within this given may provide invaluable insights and some change but does not, in and of itself, radically re-organize power. For Rancière, it does not amount to politics proper.

Rancière offers an ontological imagining: A 'police order' of naming and spatial distribution that maintains itself as the given by rendering itself 'sensible' and everything else 'insensible.' The former is visible and audible (thus, real, knowable, and valuable), and the latter is invisible and inaudible, or just noise (thus, *a*real and irrelevant in terms of knowability and value). The police order appears, in its certainty and prowess, to be the whole of things—it resonates a logic, or logics—that appear so complete and all-encompassing that all else dissipates into obscurity, is inherently deniable, or is instantaneously subsumed (Rancière, 2001). Possibilities other than a prison, for example, are just noise.

Politics proper is, when the whole is revealed through disruption, as only a part. The partition between what and who is visible and audible, and what and who is invisible and just noise is revealed as just that—a partition. Politics is thus, 'the making contentious of the givens of a particular situation' (Rancière,

2000: 125), and the moment of equality that this creates (Rancière, 2003). Following this, a new police order is established and politics ends (until the next time).

Thus, Rancièrian thought provides an opportunity to understand the seeming impenetrability and inevitability (the natural given) of insurantial logics as a 'whole', the sensibility of which appears to obliterate or marginalize all others. It also offers an imagining for how this could change and reassigns a focus on power within some insurance research towards the manifestation of schisms, contradictions, limitations, and, perhaps, resistance. This may, for example, be in how householders can use underinsurance as a form of adaptation to the demands of everyday life (Booth and Kendal, 2020), the undermining of government health initiatives as insurers offer cheaper life insurance premiums to those who will die younger from alcoholism (French and Kneale, 2015), or in Northern Kenya where 'sales agents claim that the rates of livestock insurance purchase in certain villages can be significantly affected by the seasonal weather predictions of respected diviners reading goat entrails' (Johnson, 2013a: 2677). None of these, in and of themselves, are politics proper—nothing fundamental changes, but they do point towards the cracks in the seemingly concrete nature of financialized logics and, thus, indicate the possibility of more equitable politics and change. In other words, Rancièrian thought provides an imagining in which the hegemony (Lobo-Guerrero, 2013) of insurance occupies contestable and contested space.

It is important to note critiques leveled at this kind of thesis. Some read Rancière (and others) as an 'overly ontologised theorizing' (Williams et al., 2014: 2804) that renders dissent, or attempts at dissent, as part and parcel of the 'police'—they are either recolonized by the 'whole', or interpreted as acting in support of the 'whole', albeit inadvertently. Dismissing minor or unsuccessful acts of dissent, thus, buys 'into a false dichotomy in which participation equals accommodative compromise, whilst resistance equals non-involvement with the state' (Williams et al., 2014: 2804). It also reduces critique of processes such as marketization to a 'tug-of-war' between assertions of freedom or tyranny (Callon, 2016). On one hand, marketization is understood to enable individuals to escape the constraints of a social life steeped in historical baggage, and, on the other, a perpetuation and reinforcement of structures of injustice and inequality. Both overlook nuances and complexities, in favor of two totalizing and oppositional accounts.

Paying greater attention to temporal and spatial variegations within the Rancièrian imaginary may address such critiques—that is, recognizing the 'whole' and dissent as non-essentialized, and thus never purely 'police' and purely 'resistance' (e.g., Gibson-Graham, 2006). Every hegemony comprises cracks, limitations, and contradictions. Each attempt at a politics proper always holds multiple possibilities of eventuality that are not predetermined. They are, however, very much co-produced within unequal distributions of power that will favor, rather than pre-determine, recolonization or repression. In this light, the growing body of research that explores the schisms, contradictions, and limitations of financialized capitalism signifies the possibility of political proper in financializing societies.

Geographers contribute important insights in this regard. As Pike and Pollard (2010: 36) note:

> dynamism, rapidity, and magnitude of change and innovation that are conjured up by financialization can appear, at least at first glance, to have generated economic activities that are disconnected from their geographic entanglements in space and place... The increasingly abstract nature of financial practices and discourses reinforces this sense of geographic detachment.

Resulting analytical habits can include an emphasis on the spatial, political, and functional *disconnections* of financial processes. Yet, as explored in this review of insurances of self, property, and climate, there is 'inescapable geographic construction, context, and rootedness of financial networks and practices' (Pike and Pollard, 2010: 38).

In this context, climate change is bringing together a range of insurance types in places that have traditionally appeared quite distinct; for example, catastrophe insurance and pension funds (e.g., Johnson, 2013b), and travel and labor insurances (e.g., Baldwin, 2017). Paying particular attention to the how these novel orderings are co-producing places and spaces in both developed and developing worlds appears an important direction of geographic insurance research. This includes a turn towards the spaces and places of the excess of insurability, and emergent politics proper.

Places, in all their diversity, are on the move, enabled by insurances of self, property, and climate into insured futures, and/or disabled by the same financialized logics into non-insured futures. A capacity for location or alignment within insurer-defined notions of insurability can support adaptive and sustained lives, and it can also produce maladaptive and perverse outcomes. Insurance can disable resilience in dismantling non-financialized structures and processes of sustenance and recovery (Johnson, 2013a). It can also be a risk in and of itself, manifest within an uneven distribution of power that repels, rather than compels, everyday enthusiasm for an otherwise normalized technology. Despite the ever-present affective promise of insurance (Johnson, 2013b; McFall, 2011) that seeks 'to shape the present to generate 'a' future' (Lobo-Guerrero, 2010: 246), insurer discourses and practices are reconfigured within everyday places and thus hold the possibility of producing *a*insurantial futures—livable *a*insurantial futures. With insurability understood, in part, as manifest within excess, the prospects of insurability lie with 'places within climates' and not, per se, with how insurers respond and adapt to climate uncertainty.

References

Baldwin, A. (2017). Resilience and race, or climate change and the uninsurable migrant: Towards an anthroporacial reading of 'race'. *Resilience*, 5 (2), pp. 129–143.

Beck, U. (1992). *Risk Society: Towards a New Modernity*. London: Sage.

Bonizzi, B. and Kaltenbrunner, A. (2018). Liability-driven investment and pension fund exposure to emerging markets: A Minskyan analysis. *Environment and Planning A: Economy and Space*, 51 (2), pp. 420–439.

Bonizzi, B., Kaltenbrunner, A. and Powell, J. (2019). *Subordinate Financialization in Emerging Capitalist Economies*. Greenwich papers in political economy No: GPERC69. Greenwich: Greenwich Political Economy Research Centre, University of Greenwich.

Booth, K. and Williams, S. (2014). A more-than-human political moment (and other natural catastrophes), *Space and Polity*, 18 (2) pp. 182–195.

Booth, K. and Harwood, A. (2016). Insurance as catastrophe: A geography of house and contents insurance in a bushfire prone area. *Geoforum*, 69, pp. 44–52.

Booth, K. and Tranter, B. (2018). When disaster strikes: Under-insurance in Australian households. *Urban Studies*, 55 (14), pp. 3135–3150.

Booth, K. and Kendal, D. (2020). Underinsurance as adaptation: Household agency in places of marketization and financialization. *Environment and Planning A: Economy and Space* 52(4): 728–746.

Bougen, P.D. (2003). Catastrophic risks. *Economy and Society*, 32 (2), pp. 253–574.

Callon, M. (2016). Revisiting marketization: From interface-markets to market-agencements. *Consumption Markets & Culture*, 19 (1), pp. 17–37.

Collier, S. (2008). Enacting catastrophe: Preparedness, insurance, budgetary rationalization. *Economy and Society*, 37 (2), pp. 224–250.

Collier, S. (2014). Neoliberalism and natural disaster: Insurance as political technology of catastrophe. *Journal of Cultural Economy*, 7 (3), pp. 273–290.

Defert, D. (1991). 'Popular life' and insurance technology. In: Burchell, G., Gordon, C. and Miller, P., eds., *The Foucault Effect: Studies in Governmentality*. Hertfordshire, UK: Harvester Wheatsheaf, pp. 211–233.

Dikeç, M. (2005). Space, politics, and the political. *Environment and Planning D: Society and Space*, 23, pp. 171–188.

Ericson, R. and Doyle, A. (2004). Catastrophic risk, insurance and terrorism. *Economy and Society*, 33 (2), pp. 135–173.

Ewald, F. (1991). Insurance and risk. In: Burchell, G., Gordon, C. and Miller, P., eds., *The Foucault Effect: Studies in Governmentality*. Hertfordshire, UK: Harvester Wheatsheaf, pp. 197–210.

French, S. and Kneale, J. (2009). Excessive financialization: Insuring lifestyles, enlivening subjects, and everyday spaces of biosocial excess. *Environment and Planning D: Society and Space*, 27, pp. 1030–1053.

French, S., Leyshon, A. and Wainwright, T. (2011). Financializing space, spacing financialization. *Progress in Human Geography*, 35 (6), pp. 798–819.

French, S. and Kneale, J. (2012). Speculating on careless lives. *Journal of Cultural Economy*, 5 (4), pp. 391–406.

French, S. and Kneale, J. (2015). Insuring biofinance: Alcohol, risk and the limits of life. *Economic Sociology*, 17 (1), pp. 16–24.

Gibson-Graham, J.K. (2006). *A Postcapitalist Politics*. Minnesota: University of Minnesota Press.

Giddens, A. (2000). *The Third Way and Its Critics*. Cambridge: Polity.

Grove, K. (2010). Insuring 'our common future?' Dangerous climate change and the biopolitics of environmental security. *Geopolitics*, 15 (3), pp. 536–563.

Grove, K. (2012). Preempting the next disaster: Catastrophe insurance and the financialization of disaster management. *Security Dialogue*, 43 (2), pp. 139–155.

Hall, S. (2010). Geographies of money and finance I: Cultural economy, politics and place. *Progress in Human Geography*, 35 (2), pp. 234–245.

Hallward, P. (2003). Politics and aesthetics: An interview. *Angelaki–Journal of the Theoretical Humanities*, 8, pp. 191–211.

Hayne, K.M. (2019). *Royal Commission into Misconduct in the Banking, Superannuation and Financial Services Industry*. Final report. Canberra: Commonwealth of Australia.

Johnson, L. (2013a). Index insurance and the articulation of risk-bearing subjects. *Environment and Planning A: Economy and Space*, 45, pp. 2663–2681.

Johnson, L. (2013b). Catastrophe bonds and financial risk: Securing capital and rule through contingency. *Geoforum*, 45, pp. 30–40.

Johnson, L. (2015). Catastrophic fixes: Cyclical devaluation and accumulation through climate change impacts. *Environment and Planning A: Economy and Society*, 47, pp. 2503–2521.

Knight, F.H. (2006). *Risk, uncertainty and profit: An unabridged republication of the 1957 edition*. Mineola, NY: Dover.

Langley, P. (2006). The making of investor subjects in Anglo-American pensions. *Environment and Planning D: Society and Space*, 24, pp. 919–934.

Lehtonen, T. (2017a). Domesticating insurance, financializing family lives: The case of private health insurance for children in Finland. *Cultural Studies*, 31 (5), pp. 685–711.

Lehtonen, T. (2017b). Objectifying climate change: Weather-related catastrophes as risks and opportunities for reinsurance. *Political Theory*, 45 (1), pp. 32–51.

Lehtonen, T. and Van Hoyweghen, I. (2014). Editorial: Insurance and the economization of uncertainty. *Journal of Cultural Economy*, 7 (4), pp. 532–540.

Lloyd's (2018). *A World at Risk: Closing the Insurance Gap*. Lloyd's: London.

Lobo-Guerrero, L. (2010). Insurance, climate change, and the creation of geographies of uncertainty in the Indian Ocean Region. *Journal of the Indian Ocean Region*, 6 (2), pp. 239–251.

Lobo-Guerrero, L. (2011). *Insuring Security: Biopolitics, Security and Risk*. Oxon, UK: Routledge.

Lobo-Guerrero, L. (2013). Uberrima Fides, Foucault and the security of uncertainty. *International Journal of the Semiotics of Law*, 26, pp. 23–37.

Lobo-Guerrero, L. (2014). The capitalisation of 'excess life' through life insurance. *Global Society*, 28 (3), pp. 300–316.

McFall, L. (2011). A 'good, average man': Calculation and the limits of statistics in enrolling insurance customers. *The Sociological Review*, 59 (4), pp. 661–684.

Mouffe, C. (2005). *On the Political*. Abingdon: Routledge.

Müller, B., Johnson, L. and Kreuer, D. (2017). Maladaptive outcomes of climate insurance in agriculture. *Global Environmental Change*, 46, pp. 23–33.

Nance, E. (2015). Exploring the impacts of flood insurance reform on vulnerable communities. *International Journal of Disaster Risk Reduction*, 13, pp. 20–36.

O'Hare, P., White, I. and Connelly, A. (2015). Insurance as maladaptation: Resilience and the 'business as usual' paradox. *Environment and Planning C: Government and Policy*, 34 (16), pp. 1175–1193.

O'Malley, P. (2004). *Risk, Uncertainty and Government*. London: Glass House Press.

O'Malley, P. and Roberts, A. (2013). Governmental conditions for the economization of uncertainty: Fire insurance, regulation and insurance actuarialism. *Journal of Cultural Economy*, 7 (3), pp. 253–272.

Pike, A. and Pollard, J. (2010). Economic geographies of financialization. *Economic Geography*, 86 (1), pp. 29–51.

Priest, S., Clark, M.J. and Treby, E.J. (2005). Flood insurance: The challenge of the uninsured. *Area*, 37 (3), pp. 295–302.

Rancière, J. (2000). Dissenting words: A conversation with Jacques Rancière (with Davis Panagia). *Diacritics*, 30, pp. 113–126.

Rancière, J. (2001). Ten theses on politics. *Theory and Event*, 5 (3). Available at: http://muse.jhu.edu/article/32639 [Accessed June 4, 2019].

Rancière, J. (2003). *Comments and responses. Theory and Event*, 6 (4). Available at: http://muse.jhu.edu/article/44787 [Accessed June 4, 2019].

Sturm, T. and Oh, E. (2010). Natural disasters as the end of the insurance industry? Scalar competitive strategies, alternative risk transfers, and the economic crisis. *Geoforum*, 41, pp. 154–163.

Tranter, B. and Booth, K. (2019) Geographies of trust: Socio-spatial variegations of trust in insurance. *Geoforum*. doi.org/10.1016/j.geoforum.2019.07.006

Williams, A., Goodwin, M. and Cloke, P. (2014). Neoliberalism, big society, and progressive localism. *Environment and Planning A: Economy and Space*, 46, pp. 2798–2815.

19

UNBUNDLING VALUE CHAINS IN FINANCE

Offshore Labor and the Geographies of Finance

Jana M. Kleibert

Introduction: Global Value Chains in/of Finance

The geographies of finance are intricately linked to international financial centers or 'global cities'. Employment in the financial services sector, today, is increasingly located at some distance to front offices in financial centers. Deutsche Bank, for instance, employs more staff in India (11,000) than in the United Kingdom (8,000) despite being not very active on the Indian retail market and the City of London being a key financial hub. The reason for these geographically stretched geographies of labor in financial services results from unbundling of financial and business service value chains through processes of outsourcing and offshoring.

Global value chains are complex organizationally and geographically stretched arrangements for the production of commodities. Over time, the reorganization of production has involved the outsourcing of non-core functions and in some cases even the entire production process. The downsizing of firms and the creation of 'fab-less' enterprises—enterprises that are no longer involved in the actual production facilities of their goods—has been an organizational strategy to increase shareholder value (Milberg and Winkler, 2013). Labor-intensive production steps in sectors such as apparel and electronics has been relocated geographically to lower-cost countries.

Technological advances—above all, in the field of information and communication technology, and the ensuing cost-reductions for transmitting data across distance—have enabled the unbundling of service activities that were previously *necessarily* produced at the sites of their consumption. Labor-intensive back-office tasks were first relocated towards places with lower real-estate and labor costs within countries, before being transferred across national borders.

The development of the entire industry or 'outsourcing complex' (Peck, 2017) is ripe with abbreviations: ITeS (information-technology enabled services), BPO (business process outsourcing), BPM (business process management), ITO (information technology outsourcing), KPO (knowledge process outsourcing), to name but a few (see also Massini and Miozzo, 2012). ITeS/BPO encompasses different functions, including customer-services, and, despite the prevalent use of the term 'outsourcing', it often includes firms operating fully-owned subsidiaries abroad, which are simply offshored and not outsourced.

Reliable figures on the size of the offshore services sector are difficult to establish. Gereffi and Fernandez-Stark (2010: 24) list estimates of global revenues between US$100 billion and US$160 billion, and the employment of 4.1 million in 2008, since which time these figures have continued to rise. The financial services industry is by far the sector that is responsible for the largest demand and uptake of ITeS offshoring. One-third of all offshore services activities are estimated to be inputs into financial services value chains (Gereffi and Fernandez-Stark, 2010: 28).

How has unbundling occurred in professional services sectors—in particular, financial services? How have global value chains of finance been re-configured organizationally and geographically? And what are the geographies of work in financial services resulting from offshoring of labor-intensive tasks? How does this (re)shape the geographies of labor in financial services?

Conceptualizing financial services in academic approaches of global value chains and global production networks (GPNs) is not straightforward. The first perspective conceptualizes services as *intermediaries* that occupy a supportive role in agricultural and industrial value chains. Coe et al. (2014) have made the case for integrating finance into global value chain analysis and have developed the term 'global financial networks', including not only financial services, but also advanced business services (ABS) more broadly, to highlight the critical role finance and financialization play in value generation and transfer in 'real economy' GPNs. Similarly, critical investigations of financialization have brought to light the offshoring of immaterial 'paper trails' of leading consumer electronics firms such as Apple Inc., which have established a complex value chain architecture of subsidiaries to minimize tax returns (Fernandez and Hendrikse, 2015: 13–15).

A second perspective has argued to understand (financial) services as value chains in and of themselves (Dörry, 2016; Kleibert, 2016). Coe and Yeung (2015: 24, emphasis in the original) have argued that business services should be analysed as value chains in their own right: 'GPN analysis is something that can and should be applied to *all* industries in the global economy. Most importantly, a plethora of business services, including finance, logistics, information technology services, human resource management' should be studied using a GPN heuristic.

Such a GPN approach, however, has to struggle with problems of central categories of analysis—most importantly, value. What constitutes value creation in financial services and how should value-added functions be mapped? To what extent can and should we even speak of wealth creation when the work of financial services might be better conceptualized as value extraction (Dörry, 2016; Seabrooke and Wigan, 2014)? To what extent is the rise of geographically spread and complex financial value chains a means of enabling the geographical transfer of value? The question of value creation and value extraction in the global economy are prominently discussed (Mazzucato, 2018). These discussions are at the heart of long-standing debates on the (un)productive role of finance in the global economy.

Global value chain and GPN approaches employ a networks-optic that is well-attuned to representations of financial *flows* through networks. If we look at the spatial patterns of financial geographies of labor, we are able to see the localized work embedded (and transferred) through these flows. The operation of finance requires a great deal of mundane grunt work that is conducted by people in particular places, increasingly at the global margins. Industrial geography tends to look at where production takes place, where value is created. Financial geography rarely engages with the geographies of employment in the sector, beyond elite workers based largely in 'global cities'. The paucity of studies that focus on geographies of labor is problematic, given the long-term shift of employment relocation and the fact that financial services are the most advanced sector driving the outsourcing and offshoring of services.

Governance and Geographies of Global Value Chains: Offshoring and Outsourcing

Considerable terminological confusion persists, essentially, around two dimensions of *ownership* ('make-or-buy' decision) of a task and its *location*, or the decision 'where' production or service-delivery takes place. In business lingo, the terms 'outsourcing' (decision to buy a service from a third-party provider) and 'offshoring' (decision to relocate the delivery of a task across a national border) have been adopted for these two key decisions which, together, constitute a matrix as shown in Figure 19.1.

The verbs indicate that it is a *dynamic process*, directed from the center of current operations of a firm ('onshore') and is evaluated from its relative position with regard to other places. Importantly, the arrows show the opportunity for reversal of earlier decisions through 'backsourcing' (sometimes also 'insourcing') or 're-shoring'. These terms, as well as the following more fine-grained differentiations, are not necessarily applied consistently in business and journalistic practice. 'Nearshoring' tends to signify closer geographical proximity than overseas offshoring—for instance, service centers in Central and Eastern Europe for Western European firms, but may also be employed within

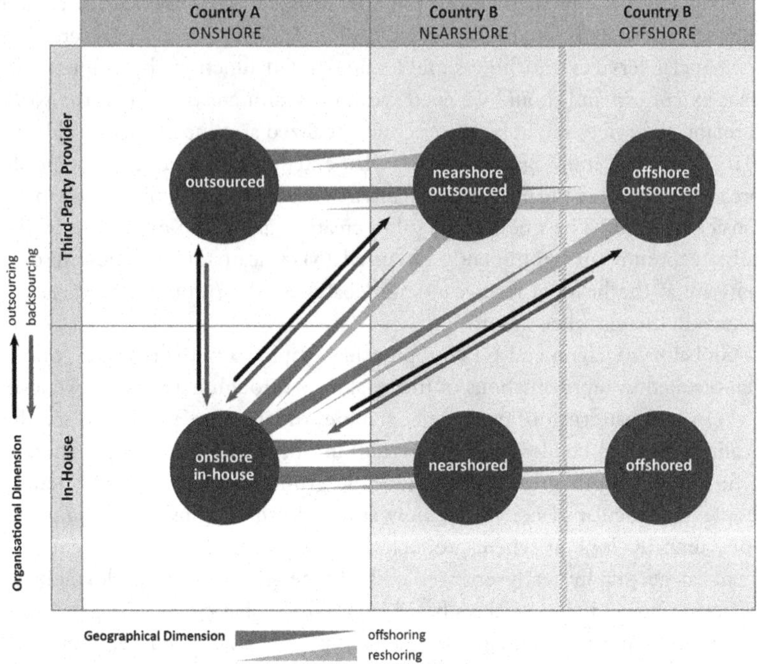

Figure 19.1 Governance and geographies of global value chains: dynamic dimensions

Source: Author.

a country—for instance, for relocating processes from New York to Florida. Rather than seeing places as abstractly, inherently being 'onshore', 'nearshore' or 'offshore', they can only be termed so *in relation to other places* as a result of concrete decisions to articulate them into global value chains. The vocabulary can be critiqued for the Eurocentric view inherent in the notions that tend unreflexively to see mainly Western locations as 'onshore', from where the rest of the world is constructed only in relation to the West and forms a largely undifferentiated 'offshore'.

When analysing business services and finance, in particular, the term 'offshore' can lead to further confusion with offshore finance or 'tax havens', which follow a very different rationale. Offshore finance is generally is driven by the avoidance of legal regulation and can be defined as 'the activity of booking and/or registering financial claims in a jurisdiction to avoid policy constraints in other jurisdictions' (Clark et al., 2015: 241), thus showing a close relationship to the development of tax havens. The term originally referred to the development of Eurocurrency markets, which accepted deposits in currencies foreign to the bank's branch location and operated outside of the jurisdiction of the issuing state (Clark et al., 2015: 240). In contrast, one of the main rationales driving the offshoring of (financial) services employment is cost reduction through labor arbitrage.

Historically, two transformations enabled the geographic relocation of the sector: first, the 'industrialization' of financial service sector employment enabled an unbundling of processes and, second, developments in information and communications technology (ICT) consequently made the relocation of activities possible. Leyshon and Thrift (1997) describe how, in the 1990s, the financial service sector in the United Kingdom, first, became segmented into a higher-paid core and a more precariously employed peripheral labor force and, second, corporate restructuring led to a *spatial specialization*: 'Information and communications technology makes it possible for banks to transfer the settlement function out of branches by shipping the cheques and other vouchers to central processing centres, where banks can reap considerable scale economies in the processing function as well as freeing much of the space and staff previously needed at branches to perform such tasks [...]. Such centres [...] introduce an industrial division into the banking sector. The processing division is integrated with, but necessarily apart from, the main operations of the bank. The industrial character of these operations is reflected not only in the nature of the work, which is highly automated, routinized and large scale, but also in the operation of shift systems and in their suburban locations in industrial or office parks' (Leyshon and Thrift, 1997: 212–13). The bifurcation of the sector was critically enabled through telecommunications infrastructures of 'teleports', which enabled access to satellites and fiber-optic networks from suburban office parks, and shaped the economic geographies of financial services beyond front office employment (Warf, 1989). The concept of a 'middle office' emerged only later; this serves as a link between front and back office, managing strategic activities, such as risk management or profit and loss calculation, and often being responsible for information technology.

The 2008 global financial crisis, led to the introduction of heightened regulation of the finance sector, obliging financial firms to increase the volume (and, thus, costs) of data reporting to regulatory authorities. Regulation thus creates tens of thousands of new compliance jobs, some of which can be outsourced and offshored, and has also sparked the advent of regulatory technology ('RegTech') for regulatory monitoring, reporting, and compliance (Arner et al., 2017).

The governance dimension of GPNs encompasses the 'make-or-buy' decision. Third-party suppliers handle the outsourced activities of firms. The contracts–service-license agreements–are often very dynamic and allow for changes in short-term 'trade in tasks' with different service providers. When the service activities are set up as own internal (cost) centers, these are generally referred to as *shared service centers* (the 'shared' element being that the center handles back-office functions for the entire corporation), *captives* (since they only cater to a single firm), or *centers of excellence*.

The governance of global value chains also refers to intra- and inter-firm relations, which are characterized by different levels of asymmetric power relations

(Gereffi et al., 2005). Analysing offshore service value chains, Fernandez-Stark et al. (2011) find multiple governance structures (including relational, modular, and market governance structures), that are dynamically changing over time. The power in GPNs typically rests with so-called 'lead firms'; in these cases, the buyers of offshore services either directly control their subsidiaries in captive relations, or can exert control over a range of different providers who compete against each other for service-license agreements over more standardized services. Some third-party providers of offshore services (including Indian firms such as TCS, Wipro, and Infosys) have become powerful multinational corporations, themselves coordinating office networks across multiple countries. With rising sophistication and complexity of tasks, mutual dependency of buyers and services suppliers grows, and the relationship shifts towards more 'relational' governance arrangements (Fernandez-Stark et al., 2011).

Large organizations with mature offshoring and outsourcing arrangements use combinations of geographic and organizational arrangements simultaneously, developing hybrid strategies of nearshoring and offshoring, with select processes outsourced to specialist providers. Benefits of multiple services locations are a reduction of business continuity risks in case one location is adversely affected; having offices in different time zones allows for easier around-the-clock customer service support and 'follow-the-sun' arrangements. The latter are, for instance, used in software development, whereby a project is transferred at the end of a day-shift to another site where the working day is just starting, and is again re-transferred to the first site at the start of a new working day.

On the downside, these complex, multi-sited offshoring and outsourcing arrangements tend to involve substantial coordination costs, which may reduce the cost-savings achieved through labor arbitrage. Moreover, services offshoring is particularly vulnerable to communication-related 'invisible costs', which are affected by interaction intensity and (cultural) distance (Stringfellow et al., 2008).

Territories of Finance beyond Global Cities and Offshore Jurisdictions

The territories of global finance are often viewed as hierarchical, and analyses often make a dualistic distinction between 'global cities', on the one hand, which have received the predominant share of attention, and 'tax havens' constituting offshore finance, on the other. In the territorial configurations of Coe et al.'s (2014: 764) schematic representations of the intersections between global production and financial networks, chartered territory are 'global cities' and 'offshore jurisdictions', with more generic 'regions' between them. Both the global cities and the offshore jurisdictions are part of networked arrangements and relational geographies. Global cities' power lies in their integration and orchestration of world city networks (see Sassen, 2001; Taylor, 2004) through which they shape global economic geographies of production. Offshore sites similarly function as an offshore 'system' in which the relations and flows between the different parts of the whole generate the importance of each particular place within them (see Bassens and van Meeteren, 2015; Shaxon, 2012).

The distinction between financial networks and offshore networks, however, has become increasingly porous. Keeping the two systems apart, which fundamentally rely for their operations on each other, is thus empirically and analytically difficult (Clark et al., 2015; Shaxon, 2012). The exposure of the 'Panama Papers' by investigative journalists have shown that offshore finance is not only about firms located in exotic, Southern, palm-fringed island states, but critically depends on financial firms based in London (the term 'London Papers' may have been more appropriate) and other places, which are usually mapped as part of the onshore financial system. Independent of the flawed binary distinction between offshore and onshore functions of places, both types of place perform crucial functions within networks and are, thus, critical sites for organizing global economic circuits of intermediation and value transfer (Bassens and van Meeteren, 2015).

In business practice, the term 'midshore' has been added to the problematic dichotomist vocabulary of onshore and offshore financial centers without, however, fully resolving the interdependent nature of both networks for the operation of globalized capitalism. An interrogation of places and their respective connections outward, their function as nodes in financial networks reveals the complex in-between positions of many international financial service hubs.

While disentangling the geographies of onshore and offshore finance, a crucial differentiation lies in the size of employment generated in each place. Whereas tax havens rely on providing infrastructure for letterbox companies, these typically require few staff. Two examples of such office buildings, reported in the *New York Times*, are Ugland House on the Cayman Islands (19,000 registered firms) and 1209 North Orange Street, Wilmington, Delaware (285,000 firms) (Landon and Landon, 2009; Wayne, 2012).

The viewpoint of the places of global finance as consisting of 'global cities' or 'offshore jurisdictions' ignores the function—and, indeed, specialization—of some of the more generic 'regions' for global financial networks. The contemporary geographies of advanced service firms is therefore simultaneously characterized by the centralization of key functions in a few cities and by decentralization of those tasks that do not require face-to-face interaction (Dicken, 2011: 394–6). The strong concentration of financial services and other advanced business services, including legal and consulting services, is found in international financial centers, such as London, New York and Tokyo (Sassen, 2001). Simultaneous to the operation of centralization forces, large-scale decentralization of financial services has shifted activities towards lower cost locations due to technological advancements enabling the uncoupling of front-office operations from those of the back office, first to office locations in the vicinity of the front offices, then towards lower cost locations within the same country, and, finally, also across state borders (UNCTAD, 2004).

The transfer of financial service employment does not simply entail dispersion towards lower-cost locations but, rather, a re-concentration within certain cities, which thus become places on the map of financial service flows. As Murphy (1998) wrote more than twenty years ago in his analysis of Dublin, which attracted primarily financial back-office services: 'Dublin, as a place, has entered the discourses of international finance' (Murphy, 1998: 163). Nevertheless, places such as Dublin do not tend to feature in geographers' analyses (which is focused on New York, London, and Tokyo, and select tax havens), although 'these 'peripheries' are worthy of our attention' (Murphy, 1998: 158). Much financial service employment takes place in what are implicitly constructed as peripheral places. More recently, Mumbai has been analysed as India's preeminent financial city and a regional financial center, simultaneously hosting large-scale offshore (financial and IT) service sector investments and employment (Lambregts et al., 2018).

Clearly, financial services sector employment in particular cities results from trends in both concentration and dispersion. Many places thus have a less than clear-cut position within global financial networks, and perform overlapping functions of international financial centers, offshore tax havens and back-office agglomerations. One way to get a clearer idea of their different roles is through an interrogation of the geographies of labor in financial services.

Offshore Labor and the Geographies of Finance

The major share of attention with respect to employment in financial services has been directed at the top-layer of managerial elites. Analyses have, for instance, focused on their concentration in international financial centers or 'global cities' and their reproduction through elite business schools (Beaverstock and Hall, 2012). Employment in international finance centers, such as the City of London, depends critically on highly skilled immigration (Hall, 2008). 'Elite labor' is a term that can be used for accountants, financial analysts, legal experts, and other top-level management of ABS firms (Hall, 2017). Following the financial crisis, popular representations and also revealing ethnographic research have aimed at shedding light on the world of high-paid, high-status bankers (Luyendijk, 2015). As fascinating as research on the elite segment of finance professionals is, a large share of financial service sector employment is not part of cosmopolitan, glamorous, at times scandalous, elite labor markets. At the medium and lower end of the financial services industry, 'white collar jobs' involve office clerks and customer-facing work, which are characterized by varying levels of labor-intensive routine work, technical skills, and/or emotional labor. Although exact figures are hard to establish, it is clear that the labor-intensive routine work of financial service firms constitutes a large share of overall employment.

When cost considerations—in particular, labor arbitrage—result in the offshoring of white-collar work from international financial centers to offshore destinations, the job profiles change. It is thus not an individual job that is relocated, but offshoring 'typically involve[s] job redesign, decomposition, and recomposition, new divisions of labor, and complex changes in the relationships within and between sending corporations, intermediaries, and service providers' (Peck, 2017: 5). Moreover, the tasks for the individual employee may become more skill-intensive, as the emotional labor usually involved in customer service work gets more complex in distanciated relations. Offshore service employment often involves undervalued and unrecognized emotional labor; for instance, that of projecting different (Western) identities to foreign customers (Bryson, 2007; Fabros, 2009).

The remainder of this chapter aims at shifting our gaze to processes beyond 'the established heartlands of global finance' (Hall, 2013: 290) to focus on places that elsewhere have been called the 'peripheries' (Murphy, 1998), the economic profiles of which nonetheless, in many cases, have been fundamentally transformed through large-scale employment in financial services.

Case Study
Deutsche Bank

Using Deutsche Bank as an illustrative case study, drawing on information from the bank's annual report, its website, and newspaper reports, is revealing of how these geographies operate in practice. According to its 2017 annual report, the financial service provider employs around 97,000 full-time equivalent staff in more than 70 countries (Deutsche Bank, 2018). The figure excludes all outsourced service delivery that is conducted through external suppliers and partners. Deutsche Banks' head office is located in Frankfurt am Main and most of its retail branches are located in Germany. Of the bank's staff, 43,000 are employed in Germany.

Through its subsidiary DBOI Global Services India, the bank employs 11,000 staff in India, with global centers in Pune, Mumbai, Bangalore, and Jaipur. The Philippines' Deutsche Knowledge Services employs 2,000 staff in its captive shared services center in Manila. Technology and operational support is delivered out of Deutsche Bank's TechCentre in Moscow by 1,250 staff and through the Deutsche Bank Global Technology Centre in Bucharest with 1,000 employees. In Dublin, 1,000 staff work for Deutsche Bank, including its subsidiary Deutsche Bank Service Centre. In the United Kingdom, back-office functions are also handled by 2,000 staff in Birmingham. In the United States, similarly, 1,800 staff work for Deutsche Bank in its office in Jacksonville, Florida. In Jacksonville, Deutsche Bank operates an entire trading floor.

These centers fulfil various roles, require different skill levels, and do not fit narrow conceptualizations of back-office work, but also include middle-office and (in some instances) front-office work. While most captive shared service centers are cost centers, many include activities that generate revenue. What emerges is a complex picture of geographically stretched value chains that encompass second-tier cities onshore, nearshore (e.g., Romania, Russia), and offshore (India, Philippines).

A simple addition of these figures shows that close to 20,000 employees (more than one-fifth of Deutsche Banks' total headcount) support the bank's global operations from 10 cities not usually on the map of financial geography: Pune, Mumbai, Bangalore, Jaipur, Manila, Moscow, Bucharest, Dublin, Birmingham, and Jacksonville. Thus, a considerable share of direct employment in the financial service firm is not in global international financial centers, offshore tax havens, or in the customer-facing markets of the Deutsch Bank, but is, instead, in lower-tiered cities that function as offshore service delivery hubs.

Offshore services (including business process outsourcing and knowledge process outsourcing) are not limited to financial services; however, the financial service industry is one the largest users of these services. Outsourcing and offshoring in the financial services industry pertains to low value-added and routine business processes, such as customer services and data processing, a range of mid-value IT related processes. Also, increasingly, more knowledge-intensive and high-value tasks require handling, such as market research, financial analysis and modelling, and the development of complex (trading) software (Currie et al., 2008; Deloitte, 2005; Dossani and Kenney, 2009). Having begun with traditional back-office work, outsourcing is increasingly encompassing middle-office and even front-office functions.

Financial institutions most commonly use business process outsourcing arrangements in the fields of private banking, asset management, and retail banking. *Private banking* requires services related to client and master data management; case, securities, loan, and trading processing; regulatory and client reporting; trading; credit scoring; anti-money laundering/'know your customer' and invoicing; and the reclaiming of tax. *Asset management* needs services involving valuation and accounting; custody and settlement; client servicing and reporting; treasury and cash management; and compliance and regulatory

Table 19.1 Offshore services destinations ranking

*Tholons ranking 2016**	*Top cities*	*Country*
1	Bangalore	India
2	Manila (NCR)[a]	Philippines
3	Mumbai	India
4	Delhi (NCR)	India
5	Chennai	India
6	Hyderabad	India
7	Cebu City	Philippines
8	Pune	India
9	Kraków	Poland
10	Dublin	Ireland

[a] National Capital Region

Source: Tholons (2016) ranking. Note that this is the last ranking for which city-level comparisons for services outsourcing were provided; since 2017, Tholons has published a ranking of Digital Nations and Super Cities based on different indicators that excludes China and Bangladesh.

reporting). *Retail banking* involves services related to procurement; payment; mortgages, and accounting (Deloitte, 2018: 118). This has increased the complexity of finance firms' production networks and has led to the establishment of offshore services centers in locations where cost–benefits (notably in the domain of labor), economies of scale (accrued from centralized or shared service provision), and access to specific kinds of skills are secured.

Table 19.1 shows that the top 10 cities for business process outsourcing are located in just two countries, India and the Philippines, followed by Poland and Ireland (Tholons, 2016).

In the following, the geographies of financial service sector employment are analysed through a discussion of the profiles of these relatively stable financial service employment 'hubs'.

Bangalore, Mumbai, Delhi, Hyderabad (India)

The most prominent case of service employment relocation has been India, which has become a much cited-case of becoming the 'back-office of the world', akin to China's role as the factory of the world, and much literature exists charting the successful development of its ITeS sector (see e.g., Dossani and Kenney, 2009; Parthasarathy, 2013). In 2018, the IT and ITeS sector in India employed 4.14 million workers and had total revenues of US$177 billion, of which US$136 billion were exports (NASSCOM, 2019). Despite claims of the reduced importance of physical location as a result of ICT developments, service sector employment in India is heavily concentrated in a few urban agglomerations, primarily Bangalore, Mumbai, Delhi (NCR), Hyderabad, and Pune. Financial services are largely located in Mumbai, India's financial center. Pune has more recently established itself as a hub for financial back-office operations, arguably benefiting from its proximity to Mumbai.

The types of activities conducted from India's offices vary but are predominantly linked to technical expertise and the strong IT sector. Offshoring of high-end, research related financial industry work is limited; however, certain tasks that depend less on face-to-face interaction can potentially be relocated. The main destination for financial service work are existing IT clusters, including Bangalore (Grote and Täuber, 2006). Goldman Sachs' offshore service operation in Bangalore is an example of the evolution and transformation. It grew from 300 staff in back-office functions in 2004 to about 5,000 across almost every division of the bank, including revenue-generating 'front office' roles (Hill, 2017). These activities take place in a fully-owned captive center of Goldman Sachs, while other functions, such as accounting, have been outsourced to third-party suppliers.

Mumbai stands out as a site for brownfield investments (Grote and Täuber, 2006) and its offshore (financial) services sector operates relatively disconnected from the 'onshore' financial functions of Mumbai for its region; while located within the city, offices are often in different parts of the city, and the labor markets for (global) back-office and front-office work are also segmented (Lambregts et al., 2018). However, Mumbai benefits from the offshore services sector through discursively raising its profile as a financial hub due to the larger firm base and labor force in financial services (Lambregts et al., 2018), as had occurred in Dublin previously (Murphy, 1998).

Manila, Cebu (Philippines)

Metro Manila (or the national capital region, NCR) is the Philippines' primary city and financial service capital. Particularly financial service firms, but also management consultancies, law firms, and other APS firms, have established an office in Metro Manila. JP Morgan Chase, for instance, employs more than 15,000 employees in the Philippine capital to deliver largely English-language voice-based services and to support back-office operations (Lim, 2018). Other financial institutions that operate shared service centers are Deutsche Bank, HSBC, ANZ, Citigroup, and Wells Fargo (see Kleibert, 2017). A second, much smaller hub for BPO employment is Cebu City. In total, the business process outsourcing sector employed 1.2 million employees and contributed more than US$21 billion to the Philippines' GDP in 2015, according to the business association IBPAP (Kleibert, 2017). The tasks handled from the Manila offices are back-office functions, including data processing, and are largely jobs that were formerly undertaken in front-offices, such as those involving customer-interaction via telecommunications infrastructure, including voice-based customer service (call centers) and non-voice based services (including through social media). Financial services—and, in particular, captive shared service centers—are operated from Manila. In general, however, a trend towards further dispersion to secondary cities in the Philippines, to Cebu and beyond, to so-called 'next-wave-cities', can be observed (Kleibert, 2014).

Employment in Philippine call centers, including for financial service firms, involves emotional labor and, in many instances, changing accents and identities (Fabros, 2009). Padios (2018) argues that the rise of offshore service sector employment presents a social and cultural predicament for the post-colonial nation, as it is deeply embedded in colonial histories, class relations, and national economic interests. Individually, many workers in the ITeS sector envision it as a stepping-stone for employment in other sectors of the Philippine economy or for overseas migration (Beerepoot and Hendriks, 2013).

Kraków (Poland)

The Polish city of Kraków is the only non-Asian city in the ranking in Table 19.1 and can be classified as a 'nearshoring' destination for European businesses. Financial service providers have also set up shared service centers in Kraków. For instance, HSBC and UBS operate a shared service center in the city. The total offshore services sector in Kraków is estimated to consist of 64,000 employees (ABSL, 2018). While the discourses around the attraction of highly skilled jobs and employment opportunities in offshore services suggest transformational potential, the actual contribution to regional economic development of the sector beyond (relatively high) direct wages appeared, at least initially, rather limited—for instance, with respect to linkages, or tax contributions (Micek et al., 2011). Nonetheless, given the strong growth of the global services sector in Kraków in recent years, the situation may have changed somewhat since 2010, calling for a renewed investigation into the regional development implications of the sector.

Based on these three examples, a few characteristics of the concentrated geographies of offshore financial service sector employment become apparent. Labor arbitrage is a key driver for unbundling and services offshoring in the finance industry. However, it is not simply cost reduction but, rather, questions of the availability of required skills in sufficient numbers (to enable scaling opportunities) that matter, in addition to stable and cost-efficient information and communications technologies (UNCTAD, 2004). Offshore service sector employment is thus particularly prevalent in post-colonial places with English language capabilities. Other languages spoken in the Global North offer opportunities for niche markets. Often, offshore service sector employment exists in places offering relatively limited alternative employment options and lacking strong manufacturing sectors, such as India and the Philippines.

A general herding behavior of firms and/or a performativity of rankings of 'top investment locations' may have exacerbated concentration of similar firms to invest in similar locations, thus contributing to the formation of offshore service hubs and concentrations in India and the Philippines, as well as Eastern European cities. The geographies of offshore service sector employment are thus concentrated, but by no means stable.

On the one hand, new players want to come into the market and replicate the successful examples of India, and, to a lesser extent, the Philippines. Business process outsourcing and offshore services sector development is high on the economic development agenda in many countries, particularly in Africa. High hopes are attached that the connectivity brought about by underwater fiber-optic broadband communication cables will help transform economies and lead to the rise of a 'Silicon Savannah' (Graham and Mann, 2013). The existing international market structures and governance arrangements of GPNs however, have proven difficult to access for Kenyan firms, which have, instead, turned towards the domestic economy for outsourcing contracts, including banks and insurance firms (Mann and Graham, 2016). The list of 'potential' new hubs in the making and competing for investments and contracts that consultancies propagate is long.

On the other hand, re-shoring of financial services activities has become an option for companies. To date, there is little empirical evidence for re-shoring of (financial) service activities, beyond anecdotal evidence of a few publicized cases of customer-facing call centers. These include the Spanish bank Santander's decision to re-shore several hundred jobs in customer support activities from India to the United Kingdom in 2011 due to quality concerns and the dissatisfaction of customers of having India-based agents answer their queries. In 2017, Vodafone has similarly re-shored 2,100 previously outsourced call center jobs from South Africa to the United Kingdom, also citing quality concerns as the main rationale, while continuing to operate its shared services facilities for IT in India (Fildes, 2017; Hill, 2017). Other drivers for re-shoring, amidst nationalistic and protectionist calls of governments in the Global North, are simply the failure to realize anticipated cost-reductions due to the 'hidden costs' of offshoring arrangements, including high transaction costs and a lack of control, combined with rising labor costs in many offshore destinations. In sum, however, existing empirical evidence does not point to a fully fledged reversal of services offshoring.

Future Outlook

'There is no final stage, no settled geography, and no moment of equilibrium in the continuously restructuring world wrought by global outsourcing. The intersecting calculi of cost, competition, techno-organizational capabilities, and geographical location are always in motion, their dynamic interactions making for a perpetually restless landscape' (Peck, 2017: 203). The outlined geographies of offshore work are fluid, dynamic, and subject to frequent review of performance of third-party providers, and the practice to have several firms providing the same services puts them in constant competition with each other and enables relatively fast switching between providers and locations. While captive shared service centers require higher sunk-cost investments, and are thus unlikely to disinvest in the short-term, up- or down-scaling of employment in these sites occurs as decisions to offshore or backshore particular tasks are taken. 'Dislocations', as Peck (2017) characterizes the shifting geographies of the outsourcing complex, is thus apt to characterize the geographies of much financial back-office work. At the same time, the geographies of back-office work analysed above, as hubs on the map, display relatively high stability. Academic research on the geographies of finance will require a new vocabulary to discuss the dynamics and roles of places within global financial networks beyond the problematic notion of the offshore.

How will global value chains of financial services shift in the future? First, automation will most likely have profound implications for employment geographies, and newspaper articles and analyses tend to take on alarmistic tones when referring to potential employment losses—in particular, at the lower-ends of repetitive, easily-codifiable tasks. Technological progress has always impacted what kinds of job can be delivered across distance and will undoubtedly do so in the future. The effects will be geographically differentiated and depend on the changing governance structures of financial services value chains and the extent of embeddedness of services in local economies.

Second, the looming decision of the United Kingdom to leave the European Union shows how important the geographies of regulation are for location choice in the financial services industry. Several large banks and other financial institutions are in the process of relocating financial service center jobs to other European financial hubs to have access to the internal European market. Financial services job relocations have been announced to several European cities, including Frankfurt, Paris, Dublin, and Luxembourg, thus leading to shifts in the relatively stable top tier of 'global cities'. Geopolitical shifts, uncertainties, and the risks inherent in operating global supply chains in an environment of increased protectionism will undoubtedly affect financial geographies, and will be an important research theme in the future. Relatedly, the question of whether 're-shoring' will have much of an impact and the rationales of (financial services) firms to relocate formerly offshored activities will require systematic research beyond anecdotal evidence.

Third, much is made of the disruption of the financial services sector through the rise of new financial technology (FinTech) (and, to a lesser extent, RegTech) firms. Online and smartphone-based banks are arguably more flexible in terms of where their staff is located than established retail banks. New FinTech startups, based in Berlin, London, or San Francisco, employ not only highly skilled technicians, marketers, and designers but, as they grow their consumer-base, have to establish large customer service employment centers. The Berlin-based startup bank N26, for instance, has moved to a larger office to accommodate employment growth in its customer services division, rising to several hundred staff in early 2018, a figure likely to grow as more customers are added globally. As the sector matures, questions of the potential savings of relocating certain tasks to lower-cost destinations will likely arise. Decisions on the outsourcing and offshoring of tasks, and thus the locations of employment, once again affect the geographies of work in financial services.

One avenue for further research on dynamic spatial restructuring processes is offered by the GPN approach. As Coe and Yeung (2019) outline in a review article, finance and labor have been two particularly fruitful fields of engagement with GPNs' 'constituent outsides'. To date, these have remained separate, but could offer an interesting opportunity for empirical and theoretical advancement for understanding socio-spatially variegated and uneven geographies of the globalizing economy. Future research may benefit from keeping the tension between place-based investigations and networked approaches. Taking a closer look at the relocation dynamics in financial services, analysed through careful investigations of the changing geographies of labor, may ground an analysis of networks and flows through its articulation in particular places.

References

ABSL (2018). *Business Services Sector in Poland*. Retrieved from: https://absl.pl/wp-content/uploads/2018/06/raport_absl_2018_EN_180527_epub.pdf [Accessed on 4 May 2019].

Arner, D. W., Barberis, J. and Buckey, R. P. (2017). FinTech, RegTech, and the reconceptualization of financial regulation. *Northwestern Journal of International Law and Business*, 37, pp. 371–414.

Bassens, D. and van Meeteren, M. (2015). World cities under conditions of financialized globalization: towards an augmented world city hypothesis. *Progress in Human Geography*, 39(6), pp. 752–775.

Beaverstock, J.V. and Hall, S. (2012). Competing for talent: global mobility, immigration and the City of London's labour market. *Cambridge Journal of Regions, Economy and Society*, 5(2), pp. 271–288.

Beerepoot, N. and Hendriks, M. (2013). Employability of offshore service sector workers in the Philippines: opportunities for upward labour mobility or dead-end jobs? *Work, Employment and Society*, 27(5), pp. 823–841.

Bryson, J. R. (2007). The 'second' global shift: the offshoring or global sourcing of corporate services and the rise of distanciated emotional labour. *Geografiska Annaler: Series B, Human Geography*, 89, pp. 31–43.

Clark, G. L., Lai, K. P.Y. and Wójcik, D. (2015). Editorial introduction to the special section: deconstructing offshore finance. *Economic Geography*, 91(3), pp. 237–249.

Coe, N. M., Lai, K. P.Y. and Wójcik, D. (2014). Integrating finance into global production networks. *Regional Studies*, 48(5), pp. 761–777.

Coe, N. M. and Yeung, H. W.-C. (2015). *Global Production Networks: Theorizing Economic Development in an Interconnected World*. Oxford: Oxford University Press.

Coe, N. M. and Yeung, H. W.-C. (2019). Global production networks: mapping recent conceptual developments. *Journal of Economic Geography*, 19(4), pp. 775–801.

Currie, W. L., Michell, V. and Abanishe, O. (2008). Knowledge process outsourcing in financial services: the vendor perspective. *European Management Journal*, 26(2), pp. 94–104.

Dicken, P. (2011). *Global Shift: Mapping the Changing Contours of the World Economy* (6th ed.). London: SAGE.

Deloitte (2005). *Global Financial Service Offshoring: Scaling the Heights*, London: Deloitte Touche Tohmatsu.

Deloitte (2018). Driving growth through business process outsourcing. *Inside Magazine*, Issue 18, June 2018. Luxembourg: MarCom, pp. 112–121.

Deutsche Bank (2018). *Annual Report 2017*. Retrieved from: https://annualreport.deutsche-bank.com/2017/ar/management-report/employees.html [Accessed on 4 May 2019].

Dörry, S. (2016). The geographies of industrialised finance: probing the global production networks of asset management. *Geography Compass*, 10(1), pp. 3–14.

Dossani, R. and Kenney, M. (2009). Service provision for the global economy: the evolving Indian experience. *Review of Policy Research*, 26(1–2), pp. 77–104.

Fabros, A. S. L. (2009). Global economy of signs and selves: a view of work regimes in call centers in the Philippines. *Sociologie du Travail*, 51(3), pp. 343–360.

Fernandez-Stark, K., Bamber, P. and Gereffi, G. (2011). The offshore services value chain: upgrading trajectories in developing countries. *International Journal Technological Learning, Innovation and Development*, 4(1–3), pp. 206–234.

Fildes, N. (2017). Vodafone to bring 2,100 call-centre jobs back to UK. *Financial Times*, 13 March. Retrieved from: https://www.ft.com/content/e822b784-071e-11e7-97d1-5e720a26771b [Accessed on 1 August 2019].

Gereffi, G. and Fernandez-Stark, K. (2010). *The Offshore Services Global Value Chain: Economic Upgrading and Workforce Development*, Durham, NC: Center on Globalization, Governance & Competitiveness (CGGC), Duke University.

Gereffi, G., Humphrey, J. and Sturgeon, T. (2005). The governance of global value chains. *Review of International Political Economy*, 12(1), pp. 78–104.

Graham, M. and Mann, L. (2013). Imagining a Silicon Valley: technological and conceptual connectivity in Kenya's BPO and software development sectors. *Electronic Journal of Information Systems in Developing Countries*, 56(2), pp. 1–19.

Grote, M. H. and Täube, F. A. (2006). Offshoring the financial services industry: implications for the evolution of Indian IT clusters. *Environment and Planning A*, 38(7), pp. 1287–1305.

Hall, S. (2008). Geographies of business education: MBA programmes, reflexive business schools and the cultural circuit of capital. *Transactions of the Institute of British Geographers*, 33(1), pp. 27–41.

Hall, S. (2013). Geographies of money and finance III: financial circuits and the 'real economy'. *Progress in Human Geography*, 37(2), pp. 285–292.

Hall, S. (2017). Elite labor. In: Richardson, D., Castree, N., Goodchild, M. F., Kobayashi, A., Liu, W. and Marston, R. A. (eds.), *International Encyclopedia of Geography: People, the Earth, Environment, and Technology*. Chichester, West Sussex: Wiley-Blackwell.

Hill, A. (2017). The new back office: inside Goldman Sachs' Bangalore hub. *Financial Times*, 13 April. Retrieved from: https://www.ft.com/content/6c1481ea-185d-11e7-9c35-0dd2cb31823a [Accessed on 18 January 2019].

Kleibert, J. M. (2014). Strategic coupling in 'next wave cities': local institutional actors and the offshore service sector in the Philippines. *Singapore Journal of Tropical Geography*, 35(2), pp. 245–260.

Kleibert, J. M. (2016). Pervasive but neglected: conceptualising services and global production networks. *Geography Compass*, 10(8), pp. 333–345.

Kleibert, J. M. (2017). On the global city map, but not in command? Probing Manila's position in the world city network. *Environment and Planning A*, 49(12), pp. 2897–2915.

Lambregts, B., Kleibert, J. M. and Beerepoot, N. (2018). The making of Mumbai as a global city: investigating the role of the offshore services sector. In: Hoyler, M., Parnreiter, C. and Watson, A. (eds.), *Global City Makers*. Cheltenham: Edward Elgar, pp. 124–150.

Landon, T. and Landon, T. Jr. (2009). Offshore haven considers a heresy: taxation. *New York Times*, April 10. Retrieved from: https://www.nytimes.com/2009/10/04/business/global/04cayman.html [Accessed on 30 April 2019].

Leyshon, A. and Thrift, N. (1997). *Money/Space: Geographies of Monetary Transformation*. London: Routledge.

Lim, J. C. (2018). JPMorgan Chase training BPO workers in higher-value skills. *Business World*, 15 April. Retrieved from: https://www.bworldonline.com/jpmorgan-chase-training-bpo-workers-in-higher-value-skills/ [Accessed on 4 May 2019].

Luyendijk, J. (2015). *Swimming with Sharks: My Journey into the World of the Bankers* (Vol. 4). London: Guardian Faber.

Mann, L. and Graham, M. (2016). The domestic turn: business process outsourcing and the growing automation of Kenyan organisations. *The Journal of Development Studies*, 52(4), pp. 530–548.

Massini, S. & Miozzo, M. (2012). Outsourcing and offshoring business services: challenges to theory, management and geography of innovation. *Regional Studies*, 46(9), pp. 1219–1242.

Mazzucato, M. (2018). *The Value of Everything: Making and Taking in the Global Economy*. London: Penguin.

Micek, G., DziaŁek, J. and Górecki, J. (2011). The discourse and realities of offshore business services to Kraków. *European Planning Studies*, 19(9), pp. 1651–1668.

Milberg, W. and Winkler, D. (2013). *Outsourcing Economics: Global Value Chains in Capitalist Development*. Cambridge: Cambridge University Press.

Murphy, L. (1998). Financial engine or glorified back office? Dublin's International Financial Services Centre going global. *Area*, 30(2), pp. 157–165.

NASSCOM (2019). *IT-BPM Industry: At a Glance*. Retrieved from: https://www.facebook.com/NASSCOMOfficial/photos/a.298423680268071/1917028615074228/?type=3&theater [Accessed on 4 May 2019].

Padios, J. M. (2018). *A Nation on the Line: Call Centers as Postcolonial Predicaments in the Philippines*. Durham, NC: Duke University Press.

Parthasarathy, B. (2013). The changing character of Indian offshore ICT services provision, 1985–2010. In: Bardhan, A., Kroll, C. A. and Jaffee, D. M. (eds.), *The Oxford Handbook of Offshoring and Global Employment*. Oxford: Oxford University Press, pp. 380–404.

Peck, J. (2017). *Offshore: Exploring the Worlds of Global Outsourcing*. Oxford: Oxford University Press.

Sassen, S. (2001). *The Global City: New York, London and Tokyo* (2nd ed.). Princeton, NJ: Princeton University Press.

Seabrooke, L. and Wigan, D. (2014). Global wealth chains in the international political economy. *Review of International Political Economy*, 21, pp. 257–263.

Shaxon, N. (2012). *Treasure Islands: Uncovering the Damage of Offshore Banking and Tax Havens*. Basingstoke: Palgrave Macmillan.

Stringfellow, A., Teagarden, M. B. and Nie, W. (2008). Invisible costs in offshoring services work. *Journal of Operations Management*, 26(2), pp. 164–179.

Taylor, P. J. (2004). *World City Network: A Global Urban Analysis*. London: Routledge.

Tholons (2016). *Tholons 2016 Top 100 Outsourcing Destinations*. Retrieved from: http://www.tholons.com/Tholonstop100/Tholons_Top_100_2016_Executive_Summary_and_Rankings.pdf [Accessed on 19 January 2019].

UNCTAD (2004). *World Investment Report 2004: The Shift Towards Services*. New York & Geneva: United Nations Conference on Trade and Development.

Wayne, L. (2012). How Delaware thrives as a corporate tax haven. *New York Times*, June 30. Retrieved from: https://nyti.ms/QD9kUW [Accessed on 30 April 2019].

Warf, B. (1989). Telecommunications and the globalization of financial services. *The Professional Geographer*, 41(3), pp. 257–271.

20

FINTECH

The Dis/Re-Intermediation of Finance?

Karen P.Y. Lai

Introduction

FinTech, a shorthand for 'financial technology' has been making waves in the headlines in recent years, particularly in terms of its potential to disrupt the landscape of not only banking, but also a range of financial institutions, intermediaries, technology, and e-commerce companies (*The Economist*, 2015; Langley and Leyshon, 2017b; Hendrikse et al., 2018). FinTech encompasses a new wave of companies that are developing products, systems, and platforms to change the way businesses and consumers make payments, lend, borrow, and invest. Operating at the intersections of financial services and technology sectors, technology-focused start-ups and new market entrants are creating new products and services that are currently provided by the traditional financial services industry. In doing so, FinTech is gaining significant momentum, and causing disruption to the traditional value chain and roles of conventional financial institutions. The most disrupted sectors—or, at least, those most frequently highlighted in the news—are payments and fund transfers, crowdfunding, and peer-to-peer lending. Between 2013 and 2014 alone, global investment in FinTech ventures tripled from US$4.05 billion to US$12.21 billion, outstripping the growth in overall venture capital investments (Accenture, 2015). While there are ongoing debates about whether the future of financial services would be characterized by ruptures (due to displacement or obsolescence) or redistribution (as existing players grow and enrich the market, or simply acquire new FinTech firms and technologies), FinTech is being actively promoted in a number of international financial centres (IFCs), such as New York, Luxembourg, Singapore, and Hong Kong, as presenting opportunities for capturing new market trends and developing new capabilities that would bolster their IFC status.

Amid the growing interest and enthusiasm about FinTech in the industry press and in consultancy reports, there is limited scholarly engagement with debates on how exactly FinTech is reshaping the intermediary functions of banks and financial institutions, and how it impacts firm strategies, organizational change, inter-firm relationships, and the underlying spatial dimensions of such evolving industrial landscapes and networks. This chapter examines the ways in which FinTech products and services are reshaping the intermediation function of banks, and the ways in financial institutions have engaged with FinTech firms in different ways, resulting in variegated forms of organizational change, inter-firm relationships, and changing production and financial networks.

The discussion focuses on the roles of banks as intermediaries between capital and production in providing financial products and services, and critically unpacks the positioning of banks as 'incumbents' in relation to FinTech firms as 'disruptors'. The cases of the Singaporean bank DBS and the British bank RBS exemplify the variegated ways in which banks are engaging with FinTech firms and technologies in order to meet specific organizational goals, or to mobilize business strategies in certain geographical markets. While it is difficult to conclude who may be the winners and losers in such a rapidly evolving landscape (especially since the banking industry is still in the early phase of FinTech engagement and collaboration), such an analysis critically evaluates the potential of FinTech firms in disintermediation, given the continuing dominance of banks in shaping the terms of engagement between banking and FinTech firms. An enquiry into the intermediary function of banks brings new insights into issues of power in economic processes and inter-firm relationships, in which financial ecologies serve as a framework for studying shifting configurations of economic actors across industry sectors and geographical scales. An ecologies approach emphasizes the fluidity and uncertainty of dynamic relationships between different actors, be they banking or technology firms, regulators or consumers, as they form distinctive groupings of business relationships, financial practices, and institutional networks that are further embedded in other configurations of wider technological or economic trends. The study of FinTech through financial ecologies is particularly well-suited to examining the intersection of banks and financial institutions with technology firms, and how they are, in turn, shaped by changing consumer expectations and regulatory environments. These have significant implications for how we study the nature of financial/non-financial firms, the changing roles of international financial centers, and the nature of inter-firm and inter-industry networks in global finance.

Incumbents and Disruptors

In one of the early reports on FinTech from the World Economic Forum (2015), payments, deposits and lending, and capital raising were already identified as the top sectors for disruption, in terms of changing the intermediary roles of banks in existing financial transactions or relationships. For business-to-consumer (B2C) and business-to-business (B2B) lending, the emergence of online platforms allows individuals and businesses to lend and borrow without necessarily going through traditional banking institutions. Innovations such as new data sources and big data analytics are changing the pricing of risks and lending processes, and lowering operating costs. More recently, the payments industry has also experienced a high level of disruption with the rise of blockchain technologies, new digital applications facilitating easier payments, and alternative processing networks, which could cut out intermediaries such as banks, clearing houses, and exchanges. Overall, disintermediation is seen as FinTech's most powerful potential impact on reshaping the financial services industry and financial networks.

Asset management and insurance are also feeling the pressure from FinTech innovations. For the insurance sector, new calculative technologies are changing the pricing and underwriting of risks, changing consumer behaviour, and generating new distribution and business models. The emergence of data analytics in the investment sector has enabled firms to target investors in new ways by delivering tailored products and automated investing through robo-advisors, which are digital platforms that provide automated, algorithm-driven financial planning services with little or no human supervision. Robo-advisors have gained recent popularity as consumers seek low-cost investment opportunities, with the ability to set up a customized, diverse portfolio and to access wealth management services previously reserved for the ultra-wealthy.

To examine how FinTech products and services are reshaping the intermediation function of banks and the ways in which banks have engaged with FinTech firms, this chapter takes an actor-focused approach in identifying key actors in the evolving FinTech ecosystem, which are grouped into five main types:

- *Banks* that have loans and deposit facilities, as well as a range of other financial service functions (such as credit, foreign exchange, money markets, and underwriting). These banks may be very large entities with a global customer base (such as HSBC, Citigroup, and Deutsche Bank), or medium-sized regional or local banks (such as Santander, Macquarie, and DBS). These banks are often seen as 'incumbents' in terms of their well-established hold on various segments of banking and finance, and their large customer base. Such banks are facing increasing competition from FinTech companies.
- *Non-bank financial institutions* such as insurance companies, venture capital firms, hedge funds, and asset managers who offer financial services but do not have a banking licence. While some of their key services are also being affected by FinTech applications (such as robo-advising and peer-to-peer lending), they tend to be seen as being less 'threatened' by FinTech companies compared to the position of banks.

- Big *technology companies* (also known as BigTech firm) that are active in the financial services segment but not exclusively so, such as Apple, Google, and Alibaba. They are seen as 'disruptors' entering into financial services provision as a non-financial company.
- *Start-ups* are usually small companies focused on a particular innovative technology or process that have the potential to change existing financial transactions or relationships. These are often fast-moving companies that are new to financial services and are commonly labelled as 'disruptors'. Companies include Stripe (mobile payments), Betterment (automated investing), Prosper (peer-to-peer lending), Moven (retail banking), and Lemonade (insurance).
- As *state entities*, regulators and government agencies work with financial institutions as well as technology firms in the revising or drafting of regulatory frameworks so as to ensure their relevance and effectiveness. Many of them are also taking on promotional roles in terms of industry communication and outreach activities to encourage research and investment in FinTech solutions. These regulatory and promotional policies may alter the scope of competiveness for incumbents and disruptors by, for instance, increasing the cost of compliance for some firms, or removing licensing requirements for certain types of financial services.

A key dimension of studying different types of actors relates to how FinTech may be reshaping the industry power and positions of incumbents (usually existing, large financial institutions) and disruptors (often small start-ups, or large technology firms moving into financial business segments), and the strategic response of incumbents in protecting their market share, or developing technological expertise themselves (through organic growth or acquisitions). Existing financial institutions, for instance, could leverage on their existing customer relationships and firm networks when developing new processes for predicting consumer needs, offer compelling value propositions, and generate new income streams. On the other hand, technology firms are placing significant pressure on the competitive landscape with lower costs, higher efficiency, and the ability to tailor products that better suit customer profiles and needs. Non-bank internet giants such as Ant Financial, JD.com, and Amazon Lending are increasingly encroaching on traditional banks' core businesses by extending loans to retail customers and small- and medium-sized enterprises (SMEs). These internet and technology firms often extend their edge in artificial intelligence (AI), data analytics, and the vast amounts of client data they have amassed through their technology services and internet platforms to service these borrowers, especially those previously been underserved by banks.

Amid these broader trends and expectations, however, there are different drivers in different geographical markets for FinTech developments. In developed markets such as the United States and Europe, where banks have well-established networks with corporate and retail customers, the advantages offered by FinTech come from the basis of improving efficiency, reducing transaction costs, and adding value to businesses and consumers. In developing economies, on the other hand, where large segments of the population are still unbanked, FinTech tends to be driven by other critical needs, such as financial inclusion and access to business working capital, building on an earlier history of micro-lending programmes (Duncombe and Boateng, 2009; Roy, 2010). This means the ways in which banks and technology firms engage with one another will differ across geographical markets, in terms of who may have greater leverage or advantages.

Integrating Banking and FinTech

In the contemporary marketplace, where consumers are used to quick and convenient access to a wide range of services, FinTech firms are placing considerable pressure on banks by offering financial products, such as business and personal loans, payments, mobile wallets, and investments in quicker and more flexible ways. In the lending space, for example, FinTech lenders have become particularly attractive to business and retail consumers due to much faster approval, a simpler transaction process, and greater flexibility around the types of documents and evidence required for application and reporting. Their mode of delivery through online and mobile platforms also appeals to a growing segment of consumers who have become used to such platform-based interfaces and who value the convenience of mobile financial applications that integrate with other lifestyle usage (e.g., retail payments, loyalty programmes, travel services). These are creating competitive pressures on banks to adjust to digitalization, data-driven modes of decision-making and changing consumer behaviour. However, setting up banks and technology firms as direct competitors in the FinTech ecosystem, as 'incumbents' versus 'disruptors', overly simplifies their position and power in different product segments, geographical markets, and industry networks. The relationships between banks and newer firms focused on technology are much more complex than those presented in consultancy reports and mainstream media. Many banks are engaging with FinTech firms and technologies in selective and variegated ways, ranging from creating wholly owned FinTech subsidiaries, to the selective licensing of FinTech products and platforms under the auspices of the banks. The use of application programming interfaces (APIs) offers a useful lens for examining the nature of banking–FinTech relationships.

APIs have been around since the 1960s, but have become a hot topic in an increasingly digital economy. At the very basic level, an API is an interface that software uses to access particular information or to connect to certain resources, such as data, servers, devices, and other applications, in order to perform certain tasks. While they used to be more limited to technical domains (such as computer coding and IT infrastructure), they have now become important for business growth and are increasingly used in sectors such as automotive and retail.

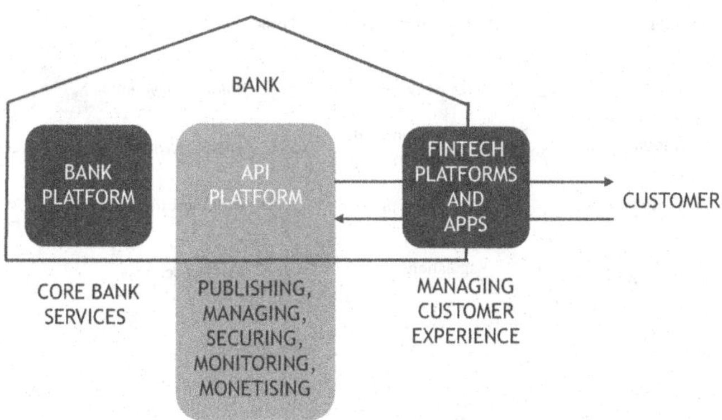

Figure 20.1 API connects banking services and FinTech applications to meet customer needs

Source: Author.

Within the automotive industry, for instance, APIs are used to embed efficiency data, driving statistics, route information, and real-time alerts onto dashboards. Some retailers are using APIs to set up multi-brand shopping platforms, track inventory, and help consumers locate stores. In banking and FinTech sectors, APIs are playing vital roles in connecting different organizations and technologies into broader ecosystems of information and resources (Figure 20.1). APIs underpin many types of financial product delivery, as they are a form of infrastructure technology that enables new forms of data packaging and analytics to 'speak' to one another between old legacy systems of banks and new offerings by FinTech companies. In a similar way to open-source software, APIs allow developers, applications, and websites to tap into databases and assets by acting like a universal converter plug to access a range of data and services. Figure 20.2 shows various functions offered by APIs in banking, ranging from traditional loans and lending, to digital payments, accounting, and fraud detection. Through combining or 'stacking' APIs, FinTech firms are able to tap into markets and consumers previously underserved by banks as they are able to bypass the legacy systems of banks to offer particular products or services directly to corporate or retail consumers.

Figure 20.2b shows some examples of FinTech firms that have made use of different APIs to offer different combinations of financial products and services. Stripe, for instance, is a technology company that has made significant inroads into the online payments sector in recent years. By stacking various APIs in machine learning, fraud detection, data analytics, payment systems, and tax management, Stripe is able to offer highly customized and cost-effective financial and business solutions to companies ranging from start-ups to large internet businesses such as Amazon, Google, Kickstarter, and Expedia. Under the Stripe umbrella, for example, Radar offers fraud detection through

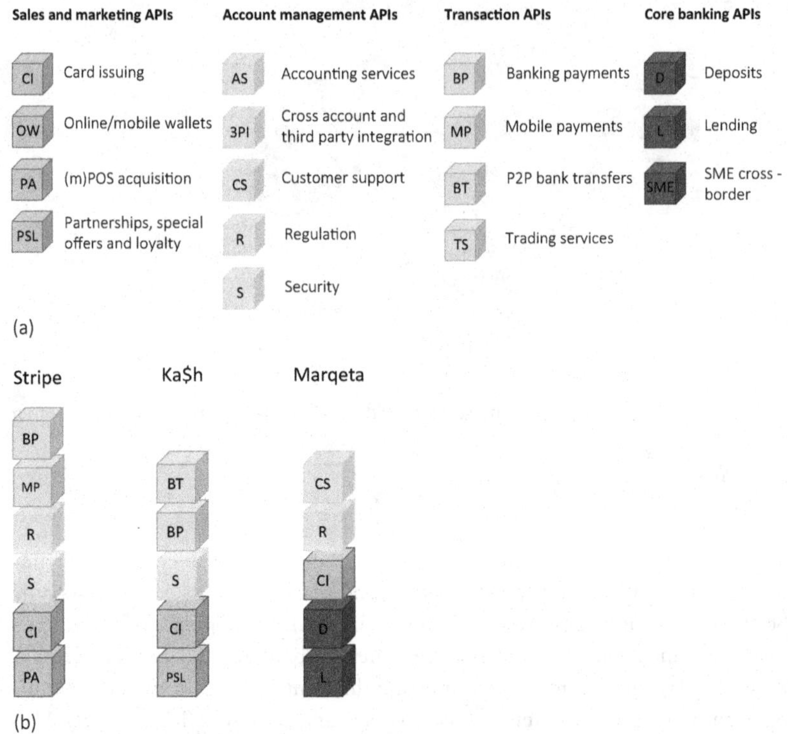

Figure 20.2 (a) Different types of API functions. (b) FinTech firms offer a range of financial products and services by stacking APIs

Source: Author.

machine learning across data points and transaction patterns; Sigma is a business analytics tool for corporate analysis, business management, and reporting requirements; Stripe Billing API integrate into existing websites, mobile apps, and customer relationship management (CRM) systems to offer customized subscription and pricing models; and Atlas is a tool for start-ups offering company incorporation, bank accounting opening, and tax advisory services. A key selling point of such FinTech companies is that they not only offer financial solutions (e.g., loans, mobile payments, invoicing, foreign exchange) but, through combining APIs, also offer a suite of customizable business solutions such as business analytics, accounting, customer relationship management, shipping, and data security. In doing so, they offer substantive value propositions to companies in moving their financial services needs away from traditional banks to FinTech companies, especially if the majority of their businesses are already based online and therefore require strong integration with online systems (whether for payments, loyalty programmes, data management, or cloud services).

Banks are certainly aware of the strengths of APIs and many are working at finding ways to open up or integrate their existing system to the wide library of APIs available. A key obstacle is the fact that most banks have old legacy systems for payments, customer data management, credit scoring, and so on, which are secure but also slow and difficult to integrate with new formats and demands that are increasingly driven by digital technologies and internet economies. Banking data, in dealing with 'matters as varied as account transactions, mortgage payments and fitness club subscriptions, is currently not easy to share with a third party in a format that computers can read for feeding into apps or for use by new banks getting off the ground' (Hussain, 2017). On the other hand, for FinTech firms and new challenger banks, while they exist as highly flexible platforms that offer plug-and-play capabilities through APIs, their functions can be limited if not connected to customer accounts and data, which many banks do still hold. Therefore, setting up banks and FinTech firms as direct competitors, as 'incumbents' versus 'disruptors', overly simplifies their roles and positions in the market.

In seeking to unpack the roles and practices of different banks and FinTech firms, trace the emergence of new relationships and networks, and examine broader shifts in the market for financial products and business services, the concept of financial ecologies could be a useful device. A financial ecologies approach recasts the financial system as a coalition of smaller constitutive ecologies, such that distinctive groupings of financial knowledge, practices, and subjectivities emerge in different places with uneven connectivity and material outcomes (Lai, 2016). Ecological networks capture the fluidity and emergence of socio-spatial relations, rather than resultant forms, which is well-suited for analysing tentative and emerging roles, networks, and structures in the FinTech space. Such configurations are constantly open to new elements, broken alliances, and reconstitutions. This financial ecologies approach is being taken up by some scholars to understand new financial logics and network behaviour, such as the crowdfunding economy (Langley and Leyshon, 2017a), how peer-to-peer lending reshapes entrepreneurial subjectivities (Carolan, 2019), and the investment philosophy and practices underpinning financial coaching and social finance (Loomis, 2018; Rosenman, 2019). Framing FinTech as ecologies can be particularly effective for capturing a certain 'stickiness' to relations and processes that could prove more stubborn to shifting than others, thereby preserving existing power relations amongst 'incumbents' and 'disruptors'. An ecologies approach also highlights the difficulty of predicting or steering mutations and new paths once they are set into motion, which then permits for greater scope of economic outcomes and possibilities in economic change.

For banks who seem to be facing an increasingly strong dis/re-intermediation challenge from FinTech firms, many of them are making different forms of investments in technology in terms of in-house infrastructure and technology-focused teams or departments, as well as engaging with FinTech firms to access or take over different assets and capabilities in areas such as blockchains,

AI, payments, and security. While almost no banks can now claim to ignore FinTech, their response and forms of engagement and investment in FinTech are quite varied and generally fall into four categories (Arnold, 2018): aggressive, acquisitions, partnerships, and diversification.

The first group of banks (sometimes called 'digital attackers') are *aggressive* in launching their own digital banks to enter new markets, or to defend their market share from new FinTech players. Examples include the digital savings and lending operation launched by Goldman Sachs (named Marcus) and Yolt, launched by Dutch bank ING, which are targeted at retail banking consumers.

The second approach is *acquisitions*, in which banks would buy or invest in a start-up. Spain's BBVA, for instance, is one of many banks that has acquired a string of FinTech companies in different countries, such as Simple (a web and mobile application) in the United States, Openpay (a payments platform) in Mexico, and Holvi (a banking and business management platform) in Finland.

The third group of banks have entered into *partnerships* with big technology companies. The partnership between JPMorgan Chase and Amazon, for example, brings together the biggest bank and largest e-commerce company in the United States and gives access to the huge database of Amazon Prime customers. In expanding its use of blockchain technologies, Standard Chartered has partnered with Alipay to launch a digital remittance service for cross-border payments.

A fourth group of banks are using FinTech for *diversification* and are moving into new markets as they face increasing pressure in their core payments and lending segments. Royal Bank of Canada, for instance, is aiming to become a more-than-banking firm by offering customers a more diverse range of services—such as company registration, cloud-based accounting software, and researching neighbourhoods when buying or selling a home—through a new digital platform that is integrated with other service partners. One particular area of concern common to all these four categories of banks is that of security and data protection. This is also an area where technology firms have been particularly important for banks and other financial institutions, as they could offer advanced data analytics and digital security solutions to control access, authenticate information, or detect fraudulent or suspicious transactions.

As seen in the above discussion, banks are taking the potential disruptive impacts of FinTech companies seriously by engaging with FinTech firms and technologies in various ways. This does not mean that FinTech firms are able to change or reconfigure business strategies and organizational networks of banks completely, as the former often do not have the customer base, brand name, and economies of scale of banks in order to utilize their technologies fully. The increasing use of APIs presents a good example of how banks and FinTech firms are partnering in changing the formulation and delivery of financial products and services. The next section presents two examples to illustrate how banks engage with FinTech in selective and varied ways in order to pursue particular goals, ranging from tentative partnerships and selective investments, to complete incorporation, or launching its own digital subsidiary bank. At the same time, these case studies also point to the unstable nature of such financial ecologies, as both banks and FinTech firms continually reassess their market position in light of new opportunities and challenges from new technologies and regulatory changes, such that these networks are always in flux and evolving over time.

Case Study 1
DBS—Geographical Expansion

DBS Bank was formerly known as the Development Bank of Singapore before it adopted its present soubriquet in 2003 to better reflect its changing role as a regional bank (Lai and Tan, 2016). The strategy for regional expansion into Asia was aligned with state developmental goals for Singaporean firms to develop a 'regional wing' to Singapore's economy and to create further growth opportunities for Singaporean firms in overseas markets (Lai and Daniels, 2017). The engagement of DBS with FinTech firms and technologies reflects this strategic interest of the bank to expand into new geographical markets in the region. This is done through the creation of a wholly owned subsidiary bank called DBS Digibank and an accelerator program called DBS Xchange (Figure 20.3).

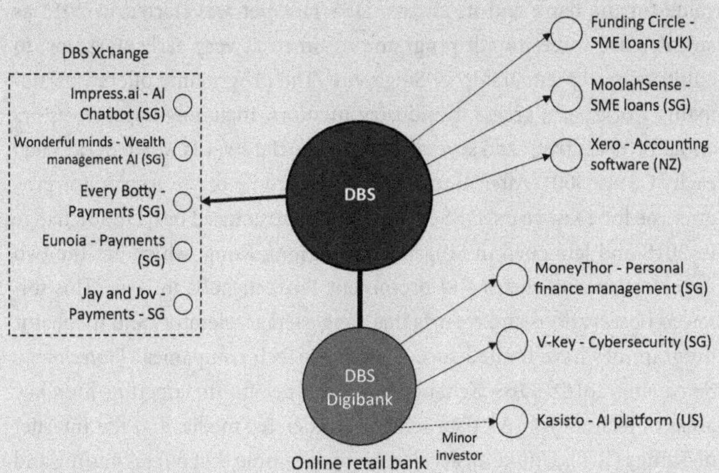

Figure 20.3 Financial ecologies of DBS, Digibank, DBS Xchange and other FinTech firms

Source: Author.

Digibank was set up in India and Indonesia to tap into the market potential of large unbanked populations in these two economies. It launched in India in April 2016 as India's only mobile bank with three key selling points enabled by FinTech. First, customer service is provided by an AI-driven Virtual Assistant (through partnership with US-based FinTech company Kasisto); second, it provides an financial management tool for customers (using Singapore-based MoneyThor); and third, it offers enhanced security in mobile authentication and transactions (through Singapore-based V-Key). In 2017, Digibank was launched in Indonesia with the same selling points, and also leveraging on a government biometric program that enabled accounts to be opened with a fingerprint for identity verification and enhanced security. DBS Digibank is only available in India and Indonesia, not in the home market of Singapore or elsewhere in the region. This points to the careful manner in which FinTech is being adopted for very specific goals of geographical expansion that are highly targeted to key market characteristics of those economies. In its home market in Singapore, and elsewhere in the region, DBS is engaging with other FinTech companies for SME loans and other services, such as in accounting.

Another key dimension of the DBS engagement with FinTech is through its accelerator programme, which has evolved over time with changing views about how investments in FinTech could provide better value for the bank and its clients. DBS Hotspot was started in 2015 as an intensive three-month programme, aimed at very early start-ups, to cultivate entrepreneurship in Singapore. The programme offered participants workspace; access to industry mentors, including angel investors and DBS executives; and several entrepreneurial awards worth SG$25,000 each (US$18,500). After monitoring the outcome of the accelerator programme for a few years, DBS Hotspot was restructured into DBS Xchange in 2018 and launched in Singapore and Hong Kong, which are the two largest financial centres and prominent FinTech hubs in Asia. This followed observations and reports that suggested accelerators and incubator programmes have limited success with FinTech companies (*Fintechnews Singapore*, 2018). DBS Xchange is more specific in targeting four key areas of technology: AI, data science, immersive media, and the Internet of Things (IoT). Unlike an accelerator programme that offers funding and more general mentorship, DBS Xchange operates more specifically as a matching service targeted at DBS internal units and the bank's corporate clients, to help them find the right FinTech solutions from the pool of companies in DBS Xchange. The evolution of DBS Hotspot into DBS Xchange demonstrates how a bank's strategy could change from being broad and tentative to becoming more selective and targeted as the bank identifies specific product segments, markets, and clients that could benefit from closer engagement with FinTech products and services, and from becoming aware of which forms of engagement may be more productive for different clients and business segments.

Case Study 2
RBS—Protecting Market Share

The Royal Bank of Scotland (RBS), based in the United Kingdom, is the retail banking arm of the Royal Bank of Scotland Group, which includes NatWest and Ulster Bank. At first glance, the engagement of RBS with FinTech firms appears to be broader and more substantive compared to DBS. However, a closer examination of its FinTech relationships and digital banking operations reveals the selective and tentative nature of such engagements. Rather than establishing a digital banking arm under its own brand name, RBS has set up three standalone digital banks in the United Kingdom, each with a different focus (Figure 20.4). Esme, launched in 2017, is a digital lending platform targeted at the SME customers of NatWest; Mettle, launched in 2018, provides current account services for small businesses and offers mobile phone-based means of managing invoices and expenses; Bó launched in November 2019 with the aim of becoming RBS/NatWest's digital consumer bank with a new mobile platform that offers savings and deposits products to retail customers. Although Mettle shares some staff with RBS, it operates independently in terms of forming partnerships and acquisitions with other FinTech firms. Esme and Mettle also benefit from being linked to RBS main banking systems for compliance needs, but they operate separate back offices, which are based on cloud computing and are therefore not tied to the bank's legacy IT system. 'The philosophy is one of facilitating front- and back-office experimentation, unencumbered by the legacy IT systems, and with a venture capital-like approach that drip-feeds funding to the projects' (O'Neill, 2018).

By setting up three digital banks with different specialization, RBS intended to experiment with new technologies and be agile in addressing

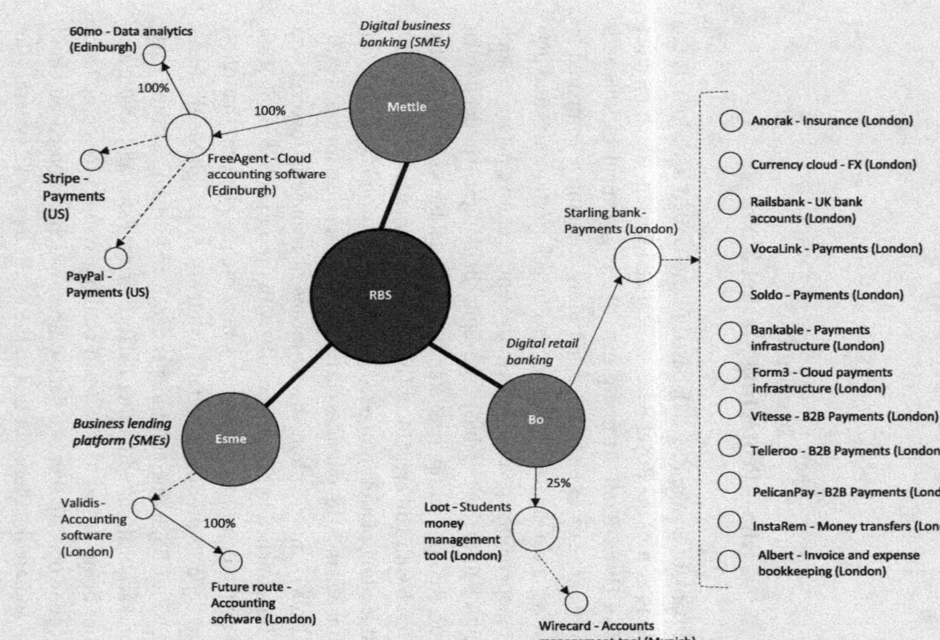

Figure 20.4 Financial ecologies of RBS and its digital banks, Mettle, Esme and Bo, with other FinTech firms

Source: Author.

consumer needs, while retaining control over its existing banking systems and databases. Without being encumbered by the bank's legacy systems, 'new features would be added [to Mettle] over time in response to customer priorities, with its new platform allowing it to develop and deploy new products more quickly than in the past' (Megaw, 2018). Having spent much of the 2010s recovering from the 2008 global financial crisis and focusing on bank restructuring after government bail-out, RBS has since prioritized technological investment after returning to profit. The overall plan is to digitize and restructure the bank with £1.5 billion committed over a two-year period. As it modernizes its existing IT system, which will take time, RBS is protecting its market share in the retail and SME banking sectors by experimenting with standalone digital banks like, such as Mettle.

This strategy of standalone digital banks also enables Mettle, Esme and Bó to have greater flexibility in engaging with various FinTech firms for new technologies and platforms that would improve financial services and the customer experience for their specific clientele (be they SMEs or retail banking clients). They are making direct acquisitions of other FinTech companies, such as Mettle's acquisition of FreeAgent (providing cloud-based accounting software, which, in turn, acquired the 60mo organization for data analytics and forecasting services). In addition, Bó has a 25% stake in Loot (a digital current account and money management app targeted at students and millennials), who is partnered with the payments giant Wirecard. These acquisitions and partnerships also point to the evolving nature of relationships between banks and FinTech firms, and also amongst FinTech firms themselves as they seek new rounds of investments, partnerships, and mergers & acquisitions in order to scale up operations, access more customers, or cash out (which is a priority of many start-up firms). Labels such as 'challenger banks' or 'disruptors' are quite fluid as competitive relationships could also evolve into partnerships. For example, although Bó is said to be pitched as a rival to a number of other UK challenger banks, including Monzo, Revolut, and Starling Bank, Bó itself also partners with Starling Bank in order to access a wide array of APIs to plug into (see Figure 20.4) and, in doing so, expand its suite of products and services.

While the case of RBS and the creation of standalone digital banks show how collaboration between banks and FinTech firms could result in new firm formation and organizational forms, it also illustrates some broader macro trends driven by FinTech in the form of new financial practices that are driven by user data and are based on mobile platforms. Instead of the batch processing and monthly updates familiar in traditional banks, the speed and accessibility introduced by FinTech firms has placed considerable pressure on banks to provide real-time updates, proactive alerts, and customized solutions, especially when consumers have become used to managing ever-more dimensions of their daily lives via digital apps and mobile platforms. Digital banks such as Mettle, Esme, and B6 are arguably better positioned to provide highly personalized and customized solutions similar to those many consumers already experience with technology-based firms such as Google and Amazon.

Conclusion

In examining the ways in which FinTech firms and services are reshaping the intermediation function of banks, and the ways in which financial institutions have engaged with FinTech firms, this chapter has questioned the positioning of banks as 'incumbents' in relation to FinTech firms as 'disruptors' in the financial services industry. While banks have well-established footholds on various segments of retail and corporate financial services and a large customer base, they are facing increasing competition from FinTech firms. The latter, consisting of both large technology firms as well as small start-ups, are seen as non-financial companies entering into financial services provision and as having competitive advantages through particularly innovative technologies, data analytics, or customer information from other sources. Be that as it may, setting up banks and FinTech firms as direct competitors, as 'incumbents' versus 'disruptors', overly simplifies their roles and positions in the rapidly changing financial services industry. So far, what we have mostly observed from the industry is the enrolment of FinTech products and services into existing bank offerings, as complementary products, rather than FinTech firms completely replacing or substituting existing financial services.

Banks are also transforming themselves by incorporating new technologies (often through partnerships with or acquisitions of FinTech firms) and creating separate digital finance entities. Such entities enable banks to experiment with new product offerings and systems management without being encumbered by existing banking legacy systems, which are very secure but difficult to collaborate with new platforms and technologies emerging from the FinTech space. As such, APIs are particularly useful and attractive channels through which banks and FinTech firms could draw on their respective advantages and overcome their own limitations, in order to reach more customers and improve overall financial services offerings. As open banking and open API requirements are implemented in the United Kingdom in 2018 and Australia in 2019, these are creating further opportunities to observe industry response, and providing the opportunity to observe whether different types of banks would be better positioned to benefit from such requirements.

Open banking requirements allow customers to compare the offerings and results of different financial providers more easily, and with open APIs customers can readily share their financial information with other providers, if they choose to do so, making it much easier to transfer accounts, manage payments, and conduct transactions when changing from one bank to other banks and non-bank institutions. On the one hand, smaller banks and cooperatives are seen, potentially, to benefit from open banking, as they are less encumbered with clunky legacy systems such as those operated by the big banks and are in a position to make use of APIs to offer a wider array of financial services to a broader range of customers. On the other hand, big banks have more resources to fund investments into new technologies and divisions, or to create new subsidiaries that could then later scale up new FinTech applications for greater market impact and returns. Banks are engaging with FinTech in various ways, ranging from aggressive launching of their own digital banks to more tentative partnerships and diversification into a broader range of business information and lifestyle services in order to meet changing consumer demands. The cases of DBS and RBS demonstrate how banks engage with FinTech in various forms in order to pursue particular goals, which could be about expansion into new products or geographical markets, or to protect existing markets from the encroachment of new challenger banks.

This chapter has highlighted the value of using a financial ecologies approach (Lai, 2016; Langley and Leyshon, 2017a) to analyse the changing roles and practices of different banks and FinTech firms, to trace the emergence of new relationships and networks, and to examine broader shifts in the market for financial products and business services. In the context of FinTech, the financial services industry can be studied as a coalition of smaller constitutive ecologies, with distinctive groupings of financial/technological knowledge and practices emerging in different places, with uneven connectivity and material outcomes. Such ecologies are constantly open to new elements, broken alliances, and reconstitutions. DBS, for instance, changed its FinTech strategy from an accelerator model (DBS Hotspot) to a more targeted 'matchmaking' service (DBS Xchange) based on the success rates of FinTech firms in its own accelerator programmes and elsewhere. Bó was intended to help RBS in its retail banking strategy by targeting retail banking customers with online current accounts and financial management tools. However, Loot (in which RBS has a 25% stake through Bó) subsequently went into administration after it failed to secure further financial backing. By the time of this book going to press, Bó itself had ceased operation in May 2020, due to technological problems and issues at RBS, such as coronavirus-related cost-cutting measures and internal politics (Woodford, 2020). These issues have raised questions regarding the effectiveness of the RBS strategy of developing its own digital banks to fend off FinTech rivals such as Monzo and Revolut (Megaw, 2019). Qualitative field research is needed to investigate the nature of such partnerships and investments, how key actors bargain in such relationships, and the ways in which expectations and outcomes are managed from the perspectives of banks and FinTech firms, as well as negotiations with state actors in reconfiguring spaces of finance in relation to technology in new regulatory frameworks. Taking a financial ecologies approach to examine the changing intermediary function of banks could bring new insights into issues of power in economic processes, and into the nature of inter-firm and inter-industry networks in global finance.

As seen in the above case studies, different market conditions and regulatory environments—such as whether there is a large segment of unbanked population, or whether a mature banking market means greater competition for digital challenger banks—present different opportunities and limitations for banks and FinTech firms in the provision of financial products and services. The partnerships and acquisitions of FinTech firms also seem to display a certain home market bias in terms of concentration in Singapore for DBS, and in London and Edinburgh by RBS. This chimes with a certain 'sticky' quality associated with financial ecologies, which could preserve existing relationships or processes, or could generate new momentum when new pathways are set in motion. Does that reflect certain spatial tendencies of knowledge and business networks in banking–FinTech relationships? While there has been a great deal written about the agglomeration of financial services and firms in financial centres, and of technology firms in science parks and high-tech clusters, how could FinTech change existing clusters and network patterns? These enquiries raise further questions for financial geographers interested in how FinTech might change existing understandings of the roles of banks and financial institutions, the nature of financial innovation, and key considerations for financial centre development in the future.

References

Arnold, M. (2018) 'Five ways banks are responding to the fintech threat", *Financial Times*, https://www.ft.com/content/d0ab6b84-c183-11e8-84cd-9e601db069b8 [Accessed 15 May 2019].

Carolan, M. (2019) "Capitalizing on financing ecologies: The world making properties of peer-to-peer lending through everyday entrepreneurship", *Geoforum*, 102: 17–26.

Duncombe, R. and Boateng, R. (2009) "Mobile phones and financial services in developing countries: A review of concepts, methods, issues, evidence and future research directions", *Third World Quarterly*, 30(7): 1237–1258.

Fintechnews Singapore (2018) "Accelerators aren't helping fintechs, so DBS banks on problem matchmaking instead", *Fintechnews Singapore*, http://fintechnews.sg/25396/ai/dbs-bank-startup-fintech-startup-xchange-match/ [Accessed 15 May 2019].

Hendrikse, R., Bassens, D. and Van Meeteren, M. (2018) 'The appleization of finance: Charting incumbent finance's embrace of FinTech", *Finance and Society*, 4(2): 159–180.

Hussain, N. Z. (2017) 'CYBG bets on fintech as open banking looms", *Reuters*, https://www.reuters.com/article/uk-cybg-results/cybg-bets-on-fintech-as-open-banking-looms-idUKKBN1DL0L2 [Accessed 15 May 2019].

Lai, K. P.Y. (2016) "Financial advisors, financial ecologies and the variegated financialisation of everyday investors", *Transactions of the Institute of British Geographers*, 41(1): 27–40.

Lai, K. P.Y. and Daniels, J. A. (2017) "Financialisation of Singaporean banks and the production of variegated financial capitalism", in Christophers, B., Leyshon, A. & Mann, G. (eds.) *Money and Finance after the Crisis: Critical Thinking for Uncertain Times*, Chichester, West Sussex: Wiley-Blackwell, pp. 217–244.

Lai, K. P.Y. and Tan, C. H. (2016) '"Neighbours first, bankers second": Mobilising financial citizenship in Singapore', *Geoforum*, 64: 65–77.

Langley, P. and Leyshon, A. (2017a) "Capitalizing on the crowd: The monetary and financial ecologies of crowdfunding", *Environment and Planning A: Economy and Space*, 49(5): 1019–1039.

Langley, P. and Leyshon, A. (2017b) "Platform capitalism: The intermediation and capitalization of digital economic circulation", *Finance and Society*, 3(1): 11–31.

Loomis, J. M. (2018) "Rescaling and reframing poverty: Financial coaching and the pedagogical spaces of financial inclusion in Boston, Massachusetts", *Geoforum*, 95: 143–152.

Megaw, N. (2018) "Royal Bank of Scotland to launch digital bank for SMEs", *Financial Times*, https://www.ft.com/content/fbb6d92c-e108-11e8-a6e5-792428919cee [Accessed 15 May 2019].

Megaw, N. (2019) "RBS-backed fintech Loot enters administration", *Financial Times*, https://www.ft.com/content/5ed36cce-7c99-11e9-81d2-f785092ab560 [Accessed 31 May 2019].

O'Neill, D. (2018) "RBS kicks off wave of digital bank offshoots", *Euromoney*, https://www.euromoney.com/article/b1bwpg6gc0zflw/rbs-kicks-off-wave-of-digital-bank-offshoots [Accessed 30 May 2019].

Rosenman, E. (2019) "The geographies of social finance: Poverty regulation through the "invisible heart" of markets", *Progress in Human Geography*, 43(1): 141–162.

Roy, A. (2010) *Poverty Capital: Microfinance and the Making of Development*, London: Routledge.

The Economist (2015) "The fintech revolution", *The Economist*, https://www.economist.com/leaders/2015/05/09/the-fintech-revolution [Accessed 15 May 2019].

Woodford, I. (2020) "The short history of RBS' failed digital bank Bó", *Sifted*, 1 May 2020, https://sifted.eu/articles/rbs-bo-close-decline/ [Accessed 11 September 2020].

PART V

Regulation and Governance

21
LEGAL FOUNDATIONS OF FINANCE

Katharina Pistor

Finance is about making investments in an unknown future in the hope and expectation of making some return on that investment. Financial assets are specific manifestations of a claim to receive some payoff at a future date, whether it is a debt instrument, or an 'I owe you' (IOU), or a share that promises participation in any profit the project generates.

In theory, the parties to a financial transaction may select the means of payment, whether it is made in gold, dollars, or bitcoins. They may also decide whether or not one or both parties have the right to transfer their part of the deal: the right to receive payments, or the obligation to pay. Borrowing and lending, owing and being owed, can be traced back at least 5,000 years (Graeber, 2011), but modern financial markets emerged only in the nineteenth century, when large-scale, anonymous markets linked investors and firms, buyers and sellers of securities from places far afield.

Moving from debt relations in relatively small, homogeneous settings, in which people know and trust each other ('credit' is derived from the Latin verb *credere*: 'to trust') to a financial system in which assets worth trillions of dollars are traded on a daily basis, however, requires an extra leap. The promises that people make to one another have to be enforceable against future holders of the assets, who often neither know the original parties to the agreement, nor wish to spend time investigating their credibility. They need to rely on the credibility of the commitments that are embodied in the assets in which they trade.

In what follows, I will argue that this leap reflects the transformation of simple agreements into binding contracts that are enforceable in a court of law and, finally, to assets that have strong self-executing features. It is a story that is rooted primarily in the institutions of private law, not public regulation. The basic 'toolkit' for transforming simple assets into financial assets that are fit for a huge, anonymous marketplace consists of contract, collateral, property, trust, corporate, and bankruptcy law (Pistor, 2019). Even the most sophisticated derivative instruments today can be broken down into these basic legal modules.

Finance is one of the most heavily regulated sectors in the economy, and public debates about finance often focus on public regulation, not private law. Nonetheless, public regulation is not foundational for finance in the same way as is the private law toolkit. It emerged in reaction to financial crises and has shaped financial systems in the aftermath of a crisis. Yet, subsequent financial innovation almost invariably will employ the same legal toolkit to reduce the costs that financial regulation tends to impose. In this way, financial regulation becomes the new focal point for financial innovation, but the innovations themselves are coded in private law, which market participants and their lawyers have at their disposal. While, in theory, the law is available to all, it takes legal expertise to turn a simple claim into a wealth-generating asset (Pistor, 2019). Access to lawyers and the accumulation of assets that enjoy special legal protection lies at the heart of inequality today. Further, the search for more wealth pushes lawyers and their clients to create new assets while externalizing the risks associated with them. In this way, they push the system towards another crisis, which will trigger another regulatory backlash. In this way, private law and public regulation become deeply imbricated in the construction of finance.

Two important implications follow. First, for financial relations to scale beyond where mutual monitoring or intermediation by agents who can mutually monitor each other is feasible, it requires formal law backed by coercive state powers. Second, large-scale, complex financial systems are coded in law even in the absence of regulation. Deregulation, or the scaling back of public law interventions, therefore does not create a law-free space. It only expands the scope for private actors to shape financial markets with the private law tools at their disposal. In short, law is *in* finance (Pistor, 2013a).

Finance's Legal Toolkit

This section gives a brief overview of the legal toolkit that is commonly used to forge financial assets. It includes contract law, property and collateral law, trust and corporate law, as well as bankruptcy law. Different legal systems have developed their own variants of these legal tools and not all can be found everywhere; trust law, for example, is a genuinely common law 'invention'. Still, for the purposes of showing how law is the stuff from which finance is made, these variations are not crucial.

At the most basic level, the legal toolkit enhances the probability that a given commitment will be enforced. This is what contract *law*, as opposed to private agreements, is all about. Parties can enter into any agreement, but not all agreements are enforceable in a court of law backed by the state's coercive powers. Law not only lends greater credibility to private agreements; it also ranks claims and ensures that the priority rights that are created with its help are respected by everyone, not only the original parties to the agreement. Law can also create legal shields that protect assets from all but the pool's own creditors, thereby effectively enhancing the durability of these assets. Finally, law can give asset holders the option to convert their assets into state money, the only asset that retains its nominal value even in times of crisis. None of these effects can be achieved by contracting alone; they require a third-party law enforcer.

The work of conferring priority, durability, universality, and convertibility onto different assets is done by core institutions of private law. Property and collateral laws do most of the work in ranking assets and creating priority rights. Bankruptcy law typically respects the priority rights that have been created outside bankruptcy, but it can also create priority rights itself. Trust and corporate law offer asset shielding devices, which enhance an asset's longevity or durability. Convertibility can be achieved by arming asset holders with the power to request cash payments from private or public counter-parties. Finally, universality comes with designing legal structures that will likely find the approval of a court of law. The expectation of actual enforcement is sufficient to give assets the stamp of approval that they are enforceable. Private parties can, of course, enter into all kinds of agreements without needing the law to help them. However, if they want to make credible commitments that are enforceable even among strangers, they need to ensure that their agreements meet the minimum requirements of an enforceable contract. Contracts must be specific about the obligations the parties owe to one another and these cannot violate fundamental principles of public policy in order to be enforceable. Some legal systems require more; English common law, for example, still requires a 'consideration'; that is, some token to be exchanged when the contract is entered into to make it binding.

Priority

Whenever there is more than a single claim to the same asset—or, in finance, to the same cash flow—the question arises as to who comes first. Even if there is enough to go around, the first-in-line claimants are more likely to get what they contracted for than those at the end of the line. In the event the debtor is insolvent—meaning that, by definition, her remaining assets are insufficient to satisfy all claimants—priority rights determine who gets anything at all, and who will leave empty-handed.

The most straightforward way to create a priority right is seniority. Whoever comes first, takes all, or at least as much as they need. Riparian water rights are often allocated in this way. It follows that when the river does not carry enough water for all, many will have no access to water whatsoever. Similarly, prior to the evolution of modern bankruptcy laws, the first creditor who reached the debtor would take everything, leaving little, if anything, for those who arrived later.

With the help of law, priority rules can be created that give even late arrivals a chance to fortify their claims. Whoever owns an asset that finds itself in the debtor's possession and is able to prove legal title, can pull it out immediately. And creditors who took the effort to secure their loans, have a right to separate the secured asset from the pool of the remaining assets and seek satisfaction from it. The unsecured creditors will have to make do with the leftovers.

This example illustrates the power of property law and of collateral law in structuring competing claims to the same asset. Holding a priority right over an asset is of value, because it increases the probability of enforcing a promise to future payment, even if legal protection cannot guarantee an asset's economic viability.

Not all priority rights that were created ex ante can be easily disentangled ex post. A prominent example is that of repos, especially when they were 're-hypothesized' (Ong and Yeung, 2010). A repo, or repurchase-agreement, is functionally identical with a secured interest in that it gives a creditor additional legal protection against a debtor. In a secured transaction, the debtor remains the owner of the secured assets, but transfers the right to seek satisfaction from the asset to the creditor, should they default on the loan. In repo transactions, the same debtor transfers full title to the creditor, who, in turn, promises to sell it back, once the money for the loan has been returned, whether it is overnight or a transaction of longer duration.

Interesting legal questions arise when the creditor (the purchaser of the first leg of the repurchase transactions) becomes insolvent before returning the asset under the second leg of the agreement. Black-letter law dictates that they own the asset and, therefore, it should be in the pool of assets available to all of their creditors. Functionally speaking, though, the repo was only meant to secure a loan, not to transfer title for good, but most legal systems will follow the functional approach.

The creditor who acquired a repo promising to sell it back to the debtor at an agreed time often obtained the legal right to use the asset just purchased in order to secure their own loans; that is, to sell the asset to yet another creditor. That creditor is now short on the asset that they have to return to the debtor. This does not matter much as long as the relevant assets are liquid; that is, widely available and with limited price fluctuation. Problems arise when liquidity dries up. Should the original creditor default before having closed the second leg of the transaction with the original debtor, the latter is left with an unsecured claim against him. Post-crisis, many counter-parties to repo transactions found themselves precisely in this situation.

Repos belong to a class of assets that also includes swaps and other directives that have been 'safe-harbored' from bankruptcy (Morrison and Riegel, 2005, Morrison et al., 2014). Most importantly, counter-parties to a repo transaction do not have to wait until all claims against the debtor have been collected and prioritized; they can net out their claims immediately, and they may even walk away with a surplus. Neither are they subject to rules that give receivers in bankruptcy the power to 'cherry-pick' the transactions that require a solvent party to perform, even when the likelihood is pretty low that they will ever receive the full portion of their claim against a debtor who finds himself in bankruptcy. These changes were meant to facilitate the development of repo and derivatives markets, which they surely did. Many creditors restructured simple loans as repo transactions to take advantage of the bankruptcy safe-harbor provisions. Creditors who failed to do so found themselves in the unenviable situation of having to yield to counter-parties to repo and derivatives transactions before they could recover from the assets that remained after they had completed the netting.

The example holds several important lessons: first, priority rights are forged not only in property or collateral law, but can also be created with similar effects in bankruptcy (and other) statutes. Second, market developments and legal change are closely intertwined. Assets that benefit from legal priority claims are more secure than assets that do not. Third, the validity of priority rights that were created outside bankruptcy stands and falls in the event of a default. Bankruptcy is therefore the acid test for priority claims. Finally, in the absence of legal rank orders of this kind, there could still be financial transactions—but not, however, financial markets on a global scale.

Durability

On face value, financial assets appear to be fickle: their prices rise and fall all the time, often within only fractions of a second. This seems to contradict the assertion that financial assets benefit from durability, an attribute created in law.

To see why durability is key for financial assets, it is important to recognize that all tradable financial assets represent claims against future cash flows from an asset base. For the claims to be viable, the underlying assets must be somewhat durable. The history of the business organization offers important clues for the centrality of legal durability in the evolution of finance.

Consider, first, the old trading companies back in the sixteenth century, the dominant form of business organizations prior to the invention of the corporate form. These old 'joint stock companies' were used for merchants to pool their stock for a joint business undertaking. On completing the project, such as a voyage to a marketplace, the gains were shared and the company was dissolved (Gelderblom, 2009). Trading in the shares of such companies was not common, and for a good reason: their life was short and their asset base was unlikely to generate wealth over time.

Creating a stable asset base was a major challenge in the evolution of the business corporation. Shareholders did not want to relinquish their right to pull out their funds whenever they wanted. When the Dutch East Indian Company (VOC) required shareholders to commit their funds for a 10-year period with no option to withdraw them earlier, this already marked a radical break from earlier practice of unwinding an enterprise at the end of each voyage. Yet, when the date of redemption finally approached, political motives forced a charter change: fearing that withdrawal of funds at this point may weaken, if not undermine, the competition of the VOC in East Asia with Portugal, the Estates General of the Netherlands negotiated a charter change: shareholders would no longer be able to withdraw their funds at all; they were locked in for good (Dari-Matiacci et al., 2016). This critical legal innovation fueled trading in the company's shares and allowed it to raise debt finance against its now very stable capital base.

Shareholder lock-in was a legal innovation that completed the legal separation of the corporation from its shareholders. The notion that incorporated entities enjoyed a separate legal personality dates back all the way to Roman law, where this legal device was used primarily for public foundations and other public purposes (Abatino et al., 2011). As a creature of law, a legal entity can be created for a fixed term, or indefinitely; it does not die a natural death but must be liquidated. And last, but not least, an incorporated entity owns its own assets and contracts in its own name. Shareholder lock-in and its sibling—entity shielding—ensured that neither the company's shareholders nor their personal creditors could put their hands on the assets of the firm; only the direct creditors of the corporation can do so (Hansmann et al., 2006). The assets of the corporation are thus well-protected to create wealth over time.

The 'common law trust' can be employed to similar ends (Morley, 2015). The trust rearranges property rights among three parties: a settlor, a trustee, and a beneficiary. The settlor transfers formal title to an asset to a trustee who manages the asset on behalf of the beneficiary. In the old days, the settlor would typically be a landowner who would transfer a piece of land to a trusted friend or relative to hold until his death and, thereupon, transfer it to his second-born son or to another relative. This scheme was often used to arbitrage around binding primogeniture inheritance rules.

Today, the trust is widely used in securitization and derivative structures. It separates the mortgage-backed loans in the 'special purpose vehicle' (SPV) from the assets of the bank. The investors who buy trust 'certificates' are the beneficiaries. They need not worry about the possibility of the bank defaulting at any time, because the trust ensures that the assets it holds are 'bankruptcy remote'. All the investors have to worry about is the quality of the assets in the trust.

In short, corporate and trust law can be used for the legal separation of assets from their previous owners and their creditors. Entirely new asset classes have been created along the way: corporate shares; corporate bonds, and variations thereof, such as preferred shares; convertible bonds; as well as freely transferable trust certificates. A durable asset base is the foundation for these assets and the markets in which they are traded.

Lastly, consider sovereign debt. Many economists have puzzled over the fact that anybody would ever lend to a sovereign, because debt is difficult to enforce against a sovereign. Who has the legal power to change unilaterally the underlying law under which the debt has been issued (Schwartz and Zurita, 1992)? At the same time, sovereign debt is often classified as low-risk, or even risk-free. This does not mean that sovereigns never default. Sovereigns that issue their debt in their own currency and under their own laws rarely do, because they can change the law or inflate the currency to reduce the debt burden. In comparison, sovereigns that issue debt under foreign currency can run out of foreign exchange reserves, which can force their hands. Even these sovereigns, however, cannot be liquidated. While creditors may have a hard time enforcing their claims against a sovereign, their debtor cannot simply disappear and, in all likelihood, will need more funding in the future. It is for this reason that sovereign debt markets are highly liquid and the debt of many sovereigns is considered safe.

Sovereignty is also key for difference between 'state money' and 'private money', or credit. Money is often described as an asset that combines three functions: it is a 'means of exchange, a unit of account, and a storage of value' (Ingham, 2004). Of greatest relevance for durability is money's role as a store of value; that is, its ability to hold its nominal value (Ricks, 2016). No privately issued asset has this capacity. The reason is that only sovereigns do not have a 'binding survival constraint' (Minsky, 1986). While private parties must make ends meet with the resources they have, sovereigns give themselves another lifeline by imposing taxes on their subjects, or by cutting social expenses and imposing austerity measures on them. Moreover, as indicated earlier, they can increase inflation, thereby lowering their debt burden. Another way of putting this is that private entities have a 'hard budget constraint', whereas the state, state-owned enterprises, and other entities the state deems to be too-big-to-fail, for example, have a 'soft budget constraint' (Kornai et al., 2003). Put differently, private entities must prove their ability to balance liabilities with assets and are forced to exit from the market; if they do not, states have the power to leverage the future productivity of their economy through taxes, fees, or long-term debt. Of course, the nominal value of a currency is of little help when its real value is declining rapidly, because it loses its value as means of exchanging it for food and shelter. Still, protecting the nominal value of an asset, such as a currency, is not trivial. It gives holders of private assets an option to lock in past gains before redeploying or consuming them. This is why, in times of crisis, a flight into hard currency—dollars, pounds, yen—is so common, and is correctly referred to as a 'flight into safety'.

Convertibility

Convertibility stands for the ability to swap one asset for another asset. Convertibility assumes the ability to transfer or assign a legal claim from one person to another. While largely taken for granted today, contractual obligations have not always been freely transferable. As long as contracts are conceived of as personal relations between two parties, not abstract legal commitments, substituting one contracting party for another amounted to a breach of that relationship. The expansion of commercial relations pushed for legal change. Notes found in Genova in the twelfth century suggest that private parties had found a way around the principle that contracts were not transferable: they simply stated that the debt could be paid to the creditor or 'your messenger'; that is, another person the creditor may assign (Rabinowitz, 1956).

The ability to assign an obligation in a legally valid fashion is only the first step in achieving convertibility, because a note-holder may accept not only legal tender (species or fiat money), but also goods, services, or another financial asset. As Hyman Minsky astutely remarked: anybody may issue an IOU, but not all will find takers (Minsky, 1986). The ability to find takers at all times determines the viability of financial assets over time, though not necessarily its short-term value. Not surprisingly, a great deal of creativity has been devoted to designing financial assets that enhance their convertibility into safe assets on demand.

A good example is the bill of exchange. It is a note that has been cloaked with 'negotiability' in legal jargon. A note can be enforced only against the original debtor; a bill can be cashed in against anybody who endorsed it (Rogers, 1995). As the bill gets passed on from one party to another, each adds their name, which creates the legal effect of an obligation to honor the bill and pay its value in species (gold or silver) when presented with the bill by any holder. The endorser may not require the holder to enforce against the original debtor first; neither can they argue that the goods they received from their seller were defective. They may not even raise the objection that the current holder of the bill may have stolen it. As long as the endorsement was valid, the endorser is obliged to pay.

These legal attributes make the bill a much safer financial asset than a simple note. It gives the current holder a put-option against any previous endorser to exchange the bill for the official currency. Not surprisingly, the bill of exchange sustained a complex payment system long before banks emerged and took over this function. It was used widely in long-distance trade that crossed the borders of states with different currencies.

The features of the bill of exchange are not self-enforcing. If a merchant were able to get relief from a local court for raising objections out of the merchant's contract with the seller of the goods that had been accepted in return for the bill, or if the merchant could claim that the holder of the bill obtained it in an illicit fashion, the effects of negotiability would be undermined. Though the bill of exchange emerged from private practice, it owes its spread and function as the cornerstone of a networked payment system in early modern Europe to the willingness of courts and city legislatures to recognize and enforce its key features (Kadens, 2011). Indeed, English common law developed a body of case law that specified the obligations of parties who had endorsed a bill, and major trading cities around Europe enacted statutes that endorsed the bills' key features.

Today, there is a bewildering array of financial assets that private parties may issue. They include notes, bills, corporate shares and bonds, securitized assets, and derivatives. The value of these assets is typically denominated in dollars or some other fiat currency. Students of money refer to this as the 'unit of account' function of money. There is, however, more to the denomination of assets in state money than just the need for a unit of account; it raises the expectation that the asset will, indeed, be convertible into state money at the end of the day. Holding state money is not very attractive in good times because it does not offer returns. In fact, inflation may erode its value. Unlike other assets, however, state money can hold its nominal value, a feature that is in high demand during bad times, as discussed earlier.

The question as to whether private money could replace state money as the means of final settlement has bedeviled alchemists, money theorists, and assets issuers alike. The latest version of creating private money that could replace state money is the introduction of cryptocurrencies (De Filippi and Wright, 2018). The first of its kind, Bitcoin, was designed as a means of payment that was protected by a digital, rather than the legal, code. By limiting the total amount of Bitcoin ever to be issued, using an immutable ledger, and requiring that transactions in Bitcoin are verified through a process called 'mining', Bitcoin would eliminate discretion, which is associated with state issued fiat money.

The major draw of Bitcoin was that it would solve the 'double-spending problem'—the ability of someone to spend money they did not have (Nakamoto, 2014). Buying and selling on credit, however, is a core feature of capitalist systems and Bitcoin soon became just another financial asset that was bought on credit. A key vulnerability of this system is convertibility: will the private asset be convertible into state money on demand without suffering a loss on the original claim—or, in financial jargon, a major haircut? When only a shadow of doubt is shed on prospective convertibility, investors have second thoughts about an asset, and when doubts spread, they will head for the exit. This is precisely what happened to Bitcoin in early 2019, and is bound to happen with other private cryptocurrencies. Convertibility requires an effective liquidity backstop, someone willing to accept a private asset in return for state-issued money.

Parties often contract for such a conversion with one another. Examples include the right to convert a bill of exchange into species, the ability to withdraw money from a bank account, and the right to make collateral calls paid in cash. Not all counter-parties to such claims, however, will be able to deliver at all times. Hoarding cash reserves will help, but only up to a point. Ultimately, only the entity that issues the coveted asset, and can issue more in whatever amounts are needed, can offer liquidity (Mehrling, 2011). And only entities that can manipulate their own survival constraint by imposing obligations on others can do so. Such entities are sovereign states.

The second best alternative to state money is private money that is issued by entities with access to liquidity backstopping by a state. Not surprisingly, the new generation of cryptocurrencies is issued not by start-ups but, rather, by major banks with access to central bank liquidity. J.P. Morgan Chase announced in February 2019 a new 'JPM Coin', a digital token that can be used to settle transactions between clients (Lee, 2019). J.P. Morgan Chase promises the holders of JPM Coin that they can always convert at par to the US dollar. This promise, however, is as empty as similar promises banks make to their depositors. Banks never retain cash reserves in amounts that would allow them to pay all their depositors on demand; this is why there is deposit insurance. To keep its promise, J.P. Morgan Chase will have to rely on its access to its reserves held in the Federal Reserve, to the discount window, or to any other liquidity facilities the Federal Reserve is willing to offer. The final word in protecting the par value of JPM Coin thus rests not with J.P. Morgan Chase, but with the Federal Reserve.

In sum, convertibility is a contingent attribute. Dressing up a claim in legal devices that enhance their enforceability makes such claims attractive to investors. This alone, however, is no guarantee that an asset can, indeed, be converted either at the desirable time or in the desirable amount. This depends on the willingness of others to buy and, in the final instance, on the ability of the asset's issuer to convert it into state money. It follows that not all monies are equal and that convertibility is not determined just by law. At the apex of this hierarchical system of money claims and counter-claims must be an entity with sufficient discretion to offer liquidity when none is owed, to protect an inherently unstable financial system from collapse (Pistor, 2013b). The critical policy question is how much discretion such an entity—that is, a state and its agents—should have, and for whose benefits such discretion should be used. Most countries that have delegated monetary policy to independent central banks authorize them to exercise substantial discretion in the event of an emergency. Determining who shall receive a lifeline from the central bank in the form of an emergency loan or liquidity support is, however, a political act with powerful distributional effects. The extensive use of these emergency powers in the context of the 2008 crisis has arguably undermined the aura of neutrality of many central banks.

Universality

The parties to a contract can agree on all kinds of matters. They can determine the quality of the goods, the price to be paid and the form of such payment, the time and place of delivery, and so forth. They can do all of this without ever talking to a lawyer or specifying their respective obligations in contract. They may simply trust each other's word and, when disputes arise, they may be able to solve it on their own, or with the help of a trusted arbiter. In short, contracting can and does occur outside the law, or only in its shadow (Charny, 1990).

Still, it does make a difference whether the law will recognize a deal as a legally enforceable contract. If it does not, parties have no recourse to coercive state enforcement as a last resort. Moreover, if a contract is recognized as legally binding, it can be enforced not only between the parties, but can also be protected against outside interference. In this way, even contract law exerts universal effects.

The power of the law is even more evident in cases where all the contracts in the world could not possibly create the desired outcome. Recall the example of the critical importance of creditors' priority rights in the event that their common debtor defaults. Typically, they have never met beforehand and have never negotiated who had a better claim, one that would prevail over others. Most likely, they have no idea who else has a claim against their debtor, or in what amounts. They may have tried to limit the debtor's rights to increase their debt burden contractually, but this gives them a claim against the debtor, not against the other creditors. In order to enforce a priority claim successfully, creditors must have perfected a secured interest in accordance with the law. Legal claims that invoke binding effects with regard to parties who did not participate in the deal require legal backing to be effective. This is the essence of 'universality'.

Establishing priority rights that withstand counter-claims, creating legal vessels with an infinite lifespan, and creating legally enforceable claims to convert private money against state money, all require state law and state enforcement, which lends these claims universality.

Often, the same legal institution may have features that can be contracted by all relevant parties and others that require state law to exert the desirable universal effect. There has been a long-standing debate in corporate law, for example, as to whether state law is needed at all for the creation of a modern corporation. If the corporation is nothing but a 'nexus of contracts', there may be no need for anything but contract law, which, as we have seen, can be left largely to the parties to the deal (Jensen and Meckling, 1976). Limited liability has been an early contender for the need for state intervention. Yet, while it may be cheaper to obtain limited liability by relying on the 'off-the-shelf' rules that corporate statutory law provides, it would be possible to limit shareholders' liability to their original contribution contractually (Easterbrook and Fischel, 1985). The corporation would simply have to include a provision in every contract that notifies its counter-party that shareholders bear no liability for the contractual obligation of the corporation. Importantly, though, this would not take care of tort creditors—third parties who were hurt by a product, or by an action of a corporation or its employees.

Corporate law, however, does more than just protect shareholders against the corporation's contractual liabilities. It also protects the corporation from the liabilities of its shareholders, and from the shareholders themselves. This feature of corporate law has been labeled 'asset partitioning' or 'asset shielding' (Hansmann and Kraakman, 2000). It gives full credence to the fact that, in law, the corporation is a person that is separate from its shareholders. It owns its own assets, contracts in its own name, sues and can be sued in its own name. This also means that the shareholders themselves and their own creditors are barred from seizing the corporation's assets. Combined with shareholder lock-in, asset shielding affords the corporation a solid capital base and thereby enhances its durability, as discussed earlier.

Critically, shielding the assets of the entity from the shareholders' creditors cannot be achieved by contract. This would require every shareholder of the corporation to clarify in their contracts with their personal creditors that the assets of the corporations in which they happen to be a shareholder will not stand in for their debt. This is highly impractical and would leave the corporate shield vulnerable to the creditors of shareholders who renege on their obligation to shield the corporation. To be effective, asset shielding must be universal and, to be universal, it must be backed by state law.

Finance on a Global Scale

Finance precedes the rise of the nation state and its laws; and, today, finance has become global, even in the absence of a global state and a global law. This creates the impression that, even if many aspects of finance today are coded in law, this is not essential for finance. In fact, modern finance theory has little room for law, and even the 'law and finance' literature treats law mostly as an add-on, not the essence from which finance is made (La Porta et al., 1998).

In the following section, I will discuss the promise and limits of finance without law, the changing landscape of financial systems after the rise of the nation states, and the institutional features that make global finance work today. I will argue that while there is room for finance without the state, the institutions that can sustain these relations are inherently limited in scope. Further, while it is true that state law is bounded by the territorial boundaries of the nation state, nothing prevents states from recognizing and enforcing foreign law, and thereby extending its reach.

Finance before the Nation State

Long-distance trade has been around for millennia. One of the hills on which the city of Rome was built—Monte Testaccio—is made up entirely of pottery, the broken amphorae that had been used to ship olive oil and other goods across the Mediterranean as early as the second century AD. Trade between ports that dotted the Mediterranean did not cease, even after the demise of the Roman Empire. Archives found in the synagogue of Fustat in old Cairo (the *geniza*) reveal dense trading networks in its Eastern parts in the eleventh century—before the rise of Genoa or Venice as major European trading hubs and the emergence of laws that governed the trade that was conducted in these cities (Greif, 2006). Further, trade along the Silk Road blossomed from the seventh to the ninth century, before it was replaced by the newly discovered sea routes that linked Europe to Asia, and before states loaded merchant ships up with canon, and endowed them with the power to engage in warfare and even rule other peoples overseas (Zhang and Elsner, 2017). Trade is, of course, based on exchange; while barter trade dominated along the Silk Road, in other settings, goods were exchanged for money, along long-distance trade routes often for private money, or notes, that were convertible into species.

Prior to the rise of nation states and legal systems that could be made to span the globe, long-distance trade was often mediated by a group of 'ethnically homogeneous middlemen' (Landa, 1981). They created a relational bridge of trust that outsiders could use to transact with strangers. Today, formal legal institutions perform a very similar function. They do not rely on personal relations among intermediaries but, rather, on a shared trust in legal institutions, or, more specifically, in the possibility of enforcing a claim in a court of law in a distant place, if necessary.

The abstract notion of 'ethnically homogenous middlemen' comprises many arrangements that differed from place to place. They include, for example, the Sogdian, merchants of Persian origin and tongue most of whom were Zoroastrians, a relatively small religious group who monopolized trade along the Silk Road; the Jewish Maghribi traders in the Mediterranean; and the Chinese diaspora in South East Asian trading networks. The dense networks of social ties among the middlemen could even be harnessed to trade with strangers. Because they knew and trusted one another, they also knew that they could trust outsiders whom one of them trusted.

The commitments group members made to one another varied, as did the services they provided to outsiders, such as brokerage, credit support, monitoring, and information sharing. The most detailed account for early informal trading networks exists for the Maghribi traders, because members of the network actively corresponded with one another, leaving a trace of letters that shows in impressive detail, how they overcame the information problem associated with long-distance trade in pre-modern times.

Avner Greif was the first to explore this treasure trove of information; he suggests that the Maghribi traders were a coalition (Greif, 1989). Membership was not open to just anyone, but had to be acquired. Once admitted, a member would have to follow the established rules, an *implicit* contract that required members to trade only with members of the coalition and to shun those who had cheated. Because merchants engaged each other as agents and shared information about each other with others, this commitment was enforceable and worked as an effective substitute for formal enforcement institutions. Courts existed at the time, but most of the disputes among the Maghribi traders never made it to court.

Whether informal contracting among strangers necessarily requires mediation by small, relatively homogeneous social groups, is debated in the literature. Lisa Bernstein, for example, has pointed out that the network among the Maghribi traders resembles a 'small world network', in which several merchants took a central position relative to other local traders, as well as with similarly situated merchants in distant places (Bernstein, 2019). This could suggest that the structure of the network and repeat interactions among the most central figures within it may have been equally important as the kinship ties or the coalition rules that define them.

Even if we assume that such networks can be created in the absence of ethnic or kinship ties, such networks are inherently limited in scope, as well. The trust that is generated among the central nodes of the network does not extend much beyond their own trusted counter-parties. Research on these early trading networks suggests that they had a difficult time penetrating the hinterlands of the major trading cities in which members of the network resided. Perhaps modern information technology will facilitate extensive networks of this kind that may even span the globe.

The rise of nation states with their national legal systems that were backed by coercive state enforcement offered different solutions to the conundrum of trading with strangers over long distances and under conditions of information scarcity and asymmetry. A new transport infrastructure, together with the standardization of law, helped integrate many local markets into a national market. National legal systems created their own boundaries, but their rise went hand-in-hand with the evolution of a set of rules that determined the conditions under which a local judge may enforce foreign law. These conflict-of-law rules are the glue that holds together our system of global finance today, as will be further discussed later in this chapter.

The Rise of National Financial Systems

The rising nation states increasingly turned finance into a nation-building project. The process of industrialization and urbanization required a vast amount of capital. Gerschenkron has famously divided countries into early and late developers (Gerschenkron, 1962). Early developers, such as England, had the luxury of accumulating capital over centuries, enough to fund the early stages of industrialization, and short-term funding could always be obtained from local merchant banks. In more backward countries, such as Germany and Italy, capital was much scarcer. The emergence of universal banks helped speed up the process. Finally, in backward countries, such as Russia, the state itself had to step in to foster the accumulation of capital and to jump start the process of industrialization.

While the historical accuracy of Gerschenkron's analysis remains disputed, the fact that the organization of national financial systems became part of the nation-building and industrialization project is not. The building of a national infrastructure, of roads and railways, required huge public outlays and the family-centered banking houses with operations across Europe helped finance it. With much of their capital now tied up in nation-building projects, peace became the order of the day in the nineteenth century. Polanyi famously went as far as to suggest that 'haute finance' played a key role in forging 'The

Hundred Years' Peace' between the end of the Vienna Congress in 1815 and the outbreak of World War I in 1914 (Polanyi, 1944).

Along with finance—in particular, debt finance—came financial turbulences that triggered national regulatory responses. Increased competition between financial intermediaries fostered greater risk-taking and, as a result, greater financial instability. Several major banking houses collapsed in mid-century, most famously, Overend & Gurney in England and Credit Mobilier in France, both in 1866 (Bignon et al., 2012; Cameron, 1953). They symbolized not only the lure of quick wealth, given the opportunities that industrialization and infrastructure development offered, but also finance's potentially destructive forces.

In response, nation states began to regulate finance much more heavily than they had ever done previously. England enacted the country's first banking law in response to Overend & Gurney's demise and, after having nationalized the Credit Mobilier, France imposed stricter regulations on similar banking ventures. Regulation, more than the financial practices that were regulated, helped forge distinct national banking systems throughout Europe (Cameron et al., 1967).

In the United States, the evolution of state-based and federal financial systems was tied to the struggle over the power of the federation relative to the states. In the early parts of the century, banks were formed first and foremost at the state level. States had relinquished their right to issue notes in return for the power to charter state banks, which helped fund state budgets (Sylla et al., 1987). Early attempts to charter a national bank were short-lived, as disputes over the federation's chartering power continued. Only the period of the civil war triggered robust efforts to create a set of federal banking institutions (Calomiris and Haber, 2014). State banks were first lured in with regulatory benefits that threatened, with punitive taxes, to swap their state for a federal charter. To retain their competitive edge, states allowed the creation of non-bank financial institutions, such as financial trusts, which competed head-on with the more strictly regulated federal banks, thus setting the stage for another crisis to come. And only in 1913 was a permanent central bank created, the Federal Reserve system.

The details of each country's banking history are less important than the fact that, at the end of the nineteenth century, every country had a financial system that bore distinct national features: a network of banks that traded and discounted financial assets with the Bank of England as its central node, as compared to a smaller number of universal banks with close industry ties in Germany, or the mix of federally- and state-chartered banks and other financial intermediaries in the United States. Two major world wars, several bouts of high or even hyper-inflation and depression deepened these national features, as they increased the dependence of states on their banks, and of banks on their states.

In the immediate aftermath of World War II, the Bretton Woods system, with its capital controls, kept a lid on transnational finance and thereby helped re-enforce the distinctiveness of national financial systems (Sylla, 2002). Only after this system was abandoned and several major crises accompanied the liberalization of global finance was a renewed attempt made to create a new governance structure for global banking in the 1980s under the auspices of the Bank for International Settlement (BIS). This governance structure takes national banking systems as a given and is built on domestic regulation supervision. The Basel Concordat and various Accords are designed to protect national financial systems from negative spill-over effects from financial crises elsewhere. Under the Basel Concordat, for example, each country assumes regulatory responsibility and a liquidity support function not only for the banks operating on its own territory, but also for the overseas branches of that bank (Pistor, 2010). Foreign subsidiaries, in contrast, were placed under the supervision of the host regulator. Further, the Basel Accords create standardized prudential regulation for globally active banks, which national legal systems promise to implement (Simmons, 2000). Neither the Concordat nor the Accords are legally binding, but they are backed by the threat that non-compliant banks may be barred from major financial markets. This new governance structure was hailed as an example of emergent global governance regimes. Yet, at the time even the first Basel Accord was adopted in 1989, global finance was already on the cusp of outgrowing a governance structure based on national supervision.

Global Finance's Domestic Laws

Looking back, it is clear that, by the time the first Basel Accord was adopted, a deep transformation of banking was already under way (Jones, 2000). In many ways, the emergent financial system of the late twentieth century bears greater resemblance to transnational finance *prior* to the rise of nation states. Major national banks are still with us and the global crisis of 2008 has prompted a revision of the regulatory framework for banks, giving us Basel III. Yet, the bulk of finance no longer takes place inside the entities we call banks but, rather, has been dispersed along chains of assets cloaked in the legal devices that give them priority, durability, convertibility, and universality. This system is often dubbed 'shadow banking', but it does not reside in the shadows, neither are there any shadow 'banks' (Pozsar et al., 2010). Many official banks are active participants in this system; they are arguably indispensable, because they provide the most direct channel to the central banks, the guarantors of liquidity in a system that depends on constant refinancing. Put differently, banking, or borrowing and lending for profit on a large scale, has altered its form. It used to be an in-house activity, but has been transformed, at least in part, into a market-based credit system.

The financial assets that have been created over the past several decades resemble an alphabet soup: ABS, RMBS, CDOs, CDSs, CLOs, ETFs, and so on. Closer inspection reveals that many of these assets have strikingly similar and familiar legal structures. Any asset type, including mortgages, student loans, and credit card receivables, can be turned into a securitized asset by following a standard recipe (Schwarcz, 1994). Intermediary A acquires a large number of claims, pools them, and sells them to Intermediary B. Intermediary B sponsors a 'special purpose vehicle' (SPV), which takes the legal form of a trust or, sometimes, a corporation. This ensures that the assets inside the SPV are shielded from the creditors of its sponsors; they are 'bankruptcy remote', in contemporary financial jargon, in the same way that corporate assets are bankruptcy remote in relation to the corporation's shareholders.

Next, the SPV issues certificates to its investors, who acquire claims to the future cash flows that the assets inside the SPV have generated. The claims reflect a pro rata share in all the assets in the pool on equal terms, or they may be *tranched*, or structured into claims with different characteristics. Buyers of senior tranches are first in line to receive any cash flows from the pool, junior investors are last in line, and investors of mezzanine tranches are somewhere in the middle. Any losses are distributed in the reverse order: juniors are the first to absorb them, and seniors the last. As should be expected, the legal rights the different tranches confer are reflected in the price investors pay, including the interest rate they will receive.

The identical legal structure can also be used for fashioning derivatives of the securitized assets, such as collateral debt obligations (CDOs), including their 'squared', 'cubed', or 'synthetic' forms (Bell and Dawson, 2002). The assets in the SPV that issues CDOs to investors are now securitized assets, typically lower mezzanine tranches from many different securitization schemes that were difficult to place with investors. By aggregating these assets, risk is diversified so that the senior tranches in the CDO structures were deemed 'safe', even though none of the assets in the pool had ever achieved similar ranking.

Placing assets behind a legal veil protects them from the creditors of their previous owners, and thus enhances their durability. Further, tranching these assets creates priority rights among investors in the same pool. Investors in derivatives, however, wanted more: they wanted priority rights in bankruptcy, should their counter-party in a subsequent transaction over these assets default. They could not create this priority right contractually, because other creditors (third parties) were implicated; legal change was required. The International Swaps and Derivatives Association (ISDA) successfully lobbied more than 50 legislatures around the globe to 'safe harbor' derivatives as well as repos from their mandatory bankruptcy codes (Morgan, 2008). As a result, counter-parties to derivatives transactions had the option to net out all their claims with the party in default before any other creditors could secure any assets to cover their claims. Bankruptcy safe harbors created new priority rights with universal effect.

Few financial assets give their holders an outright option to convert them, at any time, into cash (Brunnermeier, 2009). Shares that are redeemable at the option of the shareholders would be an example. Debt instruments are rarely made convertible unless certain conditions are triggered that are specified in advance in the debt covenants. Partial convertibility rights, however, are more common. They often take the form of margin or collateral calls that force the issuer of the asset to pay a cash amount to the counter-party, should the value of the assets decrease below a set threshold. Another way for providing cash liquidity to complex financial assets is for their sponsors, typically regulated banks with access to central banks liquidity support, to offer a credit line to the SPVs that hold them (May, 2014).

One may wonder how a financial system that is so dependent on domestic legal devices—including property, collateral, trust, and corporate and bankruptcy law—can give rise to a global system worth multi-trillions of dollars. After all, domestic law is bounded by the territory of the state that sponsors it. Internationally, states respect each other's prerogative to handle their internal affairs and, in return, commit not to extend the reach of their own laws extra-territorially. Yet, global trade in financial assets requires that the law that was used to code these assets travels with them. This is made possible by 'conflict-of-law-rules' (or 'international private law'), which form part of every domestic legal order. These rules stipulate when courts will apply and enforce foreign law to a dispute. 'Conflict-of-law-rules' determine whose country's laws shall govern a specific asset or transaction. Every country has its own rules and can, in principle, determine whether it wants to make it easy for private parties to opt into their laws, or to choose foreign law to govern their affairs, but still wish to enforce them in domestic courts. The more countries allow for easy opt-outs without taking away the option to use their courts to enforce transactions or property rights, the greater the power of private parties (and their lawyers) to pick and choose the laws that best serve their needs from a menu of legal options.

Most countries' 'conflict-of-law-rules' endorse private party autonomy at least for their contractual relations (Muir Watt, 2011). The principle of private party choice has also been extended to corporate and even property law. Many countries recognized a corporate entity, a legal creature, even if it were formed under the laws of a different state, as long as it was compliant with those rules. This is the case even if the corporate entity never conducted any business in its place of registration but only wanted to take advantage of its laws. Lastly, the place of incorporation also governs the assets such entities issue or manage, at least indirectly. Financial assets do not have a location, which is why the old rule—that the property law of the state where the asset is located governs—is inapplicable. Instead, many countries now use the place of issuance, or allow the parties to the account management contract to choose the law by which they wish to be governed (Crawford, 2003).

Free choice does not necessarily result in a coherent legal framework for global finance—potentially, the situation is just the opposite. In fact, two legal systems dominate the world of globally traded financial assets: English law and the laws of New York State (Pistor, 2019). This is also where the world's largest financial intermediaries and the 100 top global law firms are located. Finance may have become global, but its legal construction has remained remarkably parochial. The two central banks that provide the liquidity backstopping for global finance are the Federal Reserve and the Bank of England. As of 2013, they have entered into permanent currency swap lines with one another and with four other central banks serving Canada, the European Monetary Union, Japan, and Switzerland. Each of these central banks has the last say about when to swap private for state money, and they can draw on their swap lines with other central banks to ensure that entities within their borders that need foreign currency have access to it (Obstfeld et al., 2009).

Concluding Comments

Modern financial systems are coded in law. A simple promise to pay in the future, an IOU, is not easily scalable. A commitment that is enforceable—if necessary, with the help of the coercive powers of a state—can be more easily sold among strangers. The history of modern finance can therefore be described as a history of creating ever more fanciful claims that strangers will accept at face value, because they trust that what they are buying is not empty but, rather, a legally enforceable promise. While it is possible to substitute law to some extent with middlemen that serve as a human or relational bridge of trust among strangers, the size and scope of the social group that furnished these middlemen constrained the expansion of financial markets. In contrast, law is much more easily expanded. All it takes is a contract garnished with some additional protections, such as collateral or other priority rights, and enough countries willing to enforce these contracts even when they are governed by foreign law. Global finance is the product not of a global legal system or a global state; rather, it has been stitched together by domestic legal institutions that became portable once sufficient states committed to enforcing them. As a result, finance can easily transgress the territorial boundaries of nation states. It is bounded not by physical boundaries, but by invisible jurisdictional boundaries, which are much more malleable.

References

Abatino, B., Dari-Mattiacci, G., and Perotti, E. (2011). Depersonalization of Business in Ancient Rome. *Oxford Journal of Legal Studies.* Volume 31 (2), pp. 365–389. doi: 10.1093/ojls/gqr001.

Bell, I., and Dawson, P. (2002). Synthetic Securitization: Use of Derivative Technology for Credit Transfer. *Duke Journal of Comparative and International Law.* Volume 12, pp. 541–561.

Bernstein, L. (2019). Contract Governance in Small World Networks: The Case of the Maghribi Traders. *Northwestern University Law Review.* Volume 113 (5), p. 1009; University of Chicago Coase-Sandor Institute for Law & Economics Research Paper No. 880. Available at SSRN: https://ssrn.com/abstract=3278003 or http://dx.doi.org/10.2139/ssrn.3278003.

Bignon, V., Falndreau M., and Ugolini, S. (2012). Baghet for Beginners: The Making of Lender-of-Last-Resort Operations in the Mid-Nineteenth Century. *The Economic History Review*. Volume 65 (2), pp. 580–608.

Brunnermeier, M. K. (2009). Deciphering the Liquidity and Credit Crunch 2007–2008. *Journal of Economic Perspectives*. Volume 23 (1), pp. 77–100.

Calomiris, C. W., and Haber, S. H. (2014). *Fragile by Design: The Political Origins of Banking Crises and Scarce Credit*. Princeton, NJ: Princeton University Press.

Cameron, R., Crisp, O., Patrick, H. T., and Tilly, R. (1967). *Banking in the Early Stages of Industrialization*. New York/London/Toronto: Oxford University Press.

Cameron, R. E. (1953). The Crédit Mobilier and the Economic Development of Europe. *Journal of Political Economy*. Volume 61 (6), pp. 461–488. doi: 10.1086/257433.

Charny, D. (1990). Nonlegal Sanctions in Commercial Relationships. *Harvard Law Review*. Volume 104, pp. 375–467.

Crawford, B. (2003). The Hague 'PRIMA' Convention: Choice of Law to Govern Recognition of Dispositions of Book-Based Securities in Cross Border Transactions. *The Canadian Business Law Journal*. Volume 38 (2), pp. 157–206.

Dari-Matiacci, G., Gelderblom, O., Jonker, J., and Perotti, E. (2016). The Emergence of the Corporate Form. *Journal of Law, Economics and Organization*. Volume 33 (2), pp. 193–236.

De Filippi, P., and Wright, A. (2018). *Blockchain and the Law*. Cambridge, MA/London, England: Harvard University Press.

Easterbrook, F. H., and Fischel, D. R. (1985). Limited Liability and the Corporation. *University of Chicago Law Review*. Volume 52, pp. 89–117.

Gelderblom, O. (2009). The Organization of Long-Distance Trade in England and the Dutch Republic, 1550–1650. In: Gelderblom, O., ed., *The Political Economy of the Dutch Republic*. Aldershot: Ashgate, pp. 223–254.

Gerschenkron, A. (1962). *Economic Backwardness in Historical Perspective*. Cambridge, MA: Harvard University Press.

Graeber, D. (2011). *Debt: The First 5,000 Years*. Brooklyn, NY: Melvin House Publishing.

Greif, A. (1989). Reputation and Coalitions in Medieval Trade: Evidence on the Maghribi Traders. *Journal of Economic History*. Volume 59 (4), pp. 857–882.

Greif, A. (2006). *Institutions and the Path to the Modern Economy: Lessons from Medieval Trade (Political Economy of Institutions and Decisions)*. Cambridge: Cambridge University Press.

Hansmann, H., and Kraakman, R. (2000). The Essential Role of Organizational Law. *Yale Law Journal*. Volume 110 (3), pp. 387–475.

Hansmann, H., Kraakman, R., and Squire, R. (2006). Law and the Rise of the Firm. *Harvard Law Review*. Volume 119 (5), pp. 1333–1403.

Ingham, G. (2004). *The Nature of Money*. Cambridge: Polity Press.

Jensen, M. C., and Meckling, W. H. (1976). Theory of the Firm: Managerial Behavior, Agency Costs and Ownership Structure. *Journal of Financial Economics*. Volume 3 (4), pp. 305–360.

Jones, D. (2000). Emerging Problems with the Basel Capital Accord: Regulatory Capital Arbitrage and Related Issues. *Journal of Banking & Finance*. Volume 24 (1-2), pp. 35–58. doi: 10.1016/s0378-4266(99)00052-7.

Kadens, E. (2011). The Myth of the Customary Law Merchant. *Texas Law Review*. Volume 90, pp. 1153–1206.

Kornai, J., Maskin, E., and Gerard, R. (2003). Understanding the Soft Budget Constraint. *Journal of Economic Literature*. Volume 41 (4), pp. 1095–1136.

La Porta, R., Lopez-de-Silanes, F., Shleifer, A., and Vishny, R. W. (1998). Law and Finance. *Journal of Political Economy*. Volume 106 (6), pp. 1113–1155.

Landa, J. T. (1981). A Theory of the Ethnically Homogeneous Middleman Group: An Institutional Alternative to Contract Law. *Journal of Legal Studies*. Volume 10, pp. 349–362.

Lee, P. (2019, February 19). JPM coin Competes with the Federal Reserve as Much as with Ripple. Euromoney. Retrieved from: https://www.euromoney.com/article/b1d6gxdmgx4259/jpm-coin-competes-with-the-federal-reserve-as-much-as-with-ripple

May, A. D. (2014). Corporate Liquidity and the Contingent Nature of Bank Credit Lines: Evidence on the Costs and Consequences of Bank Default. *Journal of Corporate Finance*. Volume 29, pp. 410–429. doi: 10.1016/j.jcorpfin.2014.10.001.

Mehrling, P. (2011). *The New Lombard Street: How the Fed Became the Dealer of Last Resort*. Princeton, NJ: Princeton University Press.

Minsky, H. P. (1986). *Stabilizing an Unstable Economy*. New Haven, CT: Yale University Press.

Morgan, G. (2008). Market Formation and Governance in International Financial Markets: The Case of OTC Derivatives. *Human Relations*. Volume 61 (5), pp. 637–660. doi: 10.1177/0018726708091766.

Morley, J. (2015). The Common Law Corporation: The Power of the Trust in Anglo-American Business History. *Columbia Law Review*. Volume 116 (8), pp. 2145–2197.

Morrison, E. R., and Riegel, J. (2005). Financial Contracts and the New Bankruptcy Code: Insulating Markets from Bankrupt Debtors and Bankruptcy Judges. *American Bankruptcy Institute Law Review*. Volume 13 (2), pp. 641–664.

Morrison, E. R., Roe, M. J., and Sontchi, C. S. (2014). Rolling Back the Repo Safe Harbors. *Business Law Journal*. Volume 69, pp. 1016–1047.

Muir Watt, H. (2011). Private International Law beyond the Schism. *Transnational Legal Theory*. Volume 2 (3), pp. 347–428.

Nakamoto, S. (2014). *Bitcoin Manifesto: One CPU One Vote*. Antonio Tombolini.

Obstfeld, M., Shambaugh, J. C., and Taylor, A. M. (2009). Financial Instability, Reserves, and Central Bank Swap Lines in the Panic of 2008. *American Economic Review*. Volume 99 (2), pp. 480–486.

Ong, K. T. W., and Yeung, E. Y. C. (2010). Repos & Securities Lending: The Accounting Arbitrage and Their Role in the Global Financial Crisis. *Capital Markets Law Journal*. Volume 6 (1), pp. 92–103. doi: 10.1093/cmlj/kmq030.

Pistor, K. (2010). Host's Dilemma: Rethinking EU Banking Regulation in Light of the Global Crisis. In: Baum, H., Haar, B., Merkt, H., and Mülbert, P., eds., *Festschrif für Klaus J. Hopt*. Berlin: de Gruyter.

Pistor, K. (2013a). Law in Finance. *Journal of Comparative Economics*. Volume 41 (2), pp. 311–315.

Pistor, K. (2013b). A Legal Theory of Finance. *Journal of Comparative Economics*. Volume 41 (2), pp. 315–330.

Pistor, K. (2019). *The Code of Capital: How the Law Creates Wealth and Inequality*. Princeton, NJ: Princeton University Press.

Polanyi, K. (1944). *The Great Transformation: The Political and Economic Origins of Our Time*. Boston, MA: Beacon Press.

Pozsar, Z., Adrian, T., Ashcraft, A., and Boesky, H. (2010). Shadow Banking. Federal Reserve Bank of New York Staff Reports. Volume 458.

Rabinowitz, J. J. (1956). The Origin of the Negotiable Promissory Note. *University of Pennsylvania Law Review*. Volume 104 (7), pp. 927–939.

Ricks, M. (2016). *The Money Problem*. Chicago, IL: University of Chicago Press.

Rogers, J. S. (1995). *The Early History of the Law of Bills and Notes: A Study of the Origins of Anglo-American Commercial law, Cambridge Studies in English Legal History*. Cambridge: Cambridge University Press.

Schwarcz, S. L. (1994). The Alchemy of Asset Securitization. *Stanford Journal of Law, Business & Finance.* Volume 1 (1), pp. 133–155.

Schwartz, E., and Zurita, S. (1992). Sovereign Debt: Optimal Contract, Underinvestment, and Forgiveness. *Journal of Finance.* Volume 47 (3), pp. 981–1004.

Simmons, B. A. (2000). International Law and State Behavior: Commitment and Compliance in International Monetary Affairs. *American Political Science Review.* Volume 94 (4), pp. 819–835.

Sylla, R. (2002). The Breakdown of Bretton Woods and the Revival of Global Finance. *Jahrbuch für Wirtschaftsgeschichte.* Volume 2002 (1), pp. 81–88.

Sylla, R., Legler, J. B., and Wallis, J. J. (1987). Banks and State Public Finance in the New Republic: The United States, 1790–1860. *The Journal of Economic History.* Volume 47 (2), pp. 391–403.

Zhang, Y., and Elsner, W. (2017). A Social-Leverage Mechanism on the Silk Road: The Private Emergence of Institutions in Central Asia, from the 7th to the 9th Century. *Journal of Institutional Economics.* Volume 13 (2), pp. 379–400.

22
CENTRAL BANKS AND THE GOVERNANCE OF MONETARY SPACE

David S. Bieri

Introduction

From regional redistribution through mortgage markets to the monetary policy effects on local house price dynamics, the Great Financial Crisis (GFC) has been a powerful reminder that money and credit—always and everywhere—matter for the evolution of the space-economy. In addition to the spatially uneven impact of money and credit, the GFC has also demonstrated that the role of central banks is second-to-none in constituting the pivot points on which the global financial system hinges. It was the extreme measures by central banks—on their own, and in transnational coordination—that prevented the complete collapse of financial markets around the globe as interbank-funding came to a grinding halt and money markets began to seize up in the late 2000s.

With the financial system no longer capable of performing its core intermediation functions—liquidity, maturity, and credit transformation—central banks were forced to set in motion all the conventional levers of policy intervention, and, in the process, even invented new ones. While the unprecedented amounts of short-term liquidity injected into the system had averted the worst in the immediate aftermath of the Lehman Brothers collapse, policy rates were now near, or at, the zero lower bound. The conventional monetary policy approaches of the post-war period had become impotent, caught up in what Keynes had foreseen as a 'liquidity trap' wherein normal policy action was akin to 'pushing on a string'. Central banks, led by the Federal Reserve and its global monetary allies—the European Central Bank (ECB), the Bank of England (BoE), the Bank of Japan (BoJ), and the Swiss National Bank (SNB), collectively known as the C5—began to push the envelopes of their policy remits, testing new approaches and new instruments, ranging from special lending programs to the brute-force large-scale asset purchases that became known as 'quantitative easing' (QE).

These unconventional policy actions soon made clear that the GFC had precipitated central banking into a new evolutionary stage. A decade on, this 'new age of central banking' now appears firmly entrenched and largely normalized.[1] In addition to their time-tested role as lenders of last resort (LOLR), post-crisis central banks also began to act as 'dealers of last resort' (Mehrling, 2011) and, in doing so, they have been collapsing much of the post-crisis activity in financial markets onto their own balance sheets. Such crowding out of large swathes of trading volumes between private financial intermediaries meant that central banks had effectively become the 'only game in town' (El-Erian, 2016).

Indeed, the strategic use of central banks' balance sheet via these 'non-traditional actions' has given rise to some of the most striking facts of the post-crisis normal. For example, the combined assets of the 10 central banks with the largest growth in their foreign exchange reserves and balance sheets over the post-crisis decade currently amount to over US$17 trillion (Table 22.1). This is roughly the same as the total assets of the world's 10 largest, privately owned financial conglomerates.[2] By comparison—and in some ways a measure of the extreme financialization of the global economy—the combined assets of the world's 75 largest non-financial institutions is less than US$15 trillion.[3] Table 22.1 also reveals that the largest balance sheet growth was recorded by those central banks with the most active QE programs; that is, the Fed, BoE, BoJ, and ECB (and some of its member central banks)—a direct consequence of the balance sheet mechanics of their large-scale asset purchases. In fact, the combined assets of the C5 central banks currently account for almost 40% of the GDP of the advanced economies they represent.

Since economics is, as Michał Kalecki is famously said to have quipped, 'the science of confusing stocks with flows', it behooves us to quantify briefly the pure flow dimension of these extraordinary actions by central banks. Between 2007 and 2019, the cumulative QE related transaction volumes of these central banks reached a staggering US$197 trillion—an amount so vast that it would have been enough to acquire the total output of the world's largest economy in each year over that same period; that is, the combined flow of all goods and services produced in the United States since the GFC (see Figure 22.1).

However, unconventional policy actions and bloated balance sheets were not limited to the central banks of the core economies. Indeed, the policy activism of QE has led to broad-based policy concerns over a 'monetization of debt' and over the distributional effects of negative interest rate policies around the globe. And, as part of these concerns, the role of central bank independence (CBI)—one of the most sacred institutional policy arrangements of the post-war period—has come under close scrutiny again as board discontent with the growing inequalities of the post-crisis environment has fanned the flames of populism worldwide.[4]

But there were also fewer visible signs that, once they had saved the (financial) world, central bankers engineered a more subtle transformation of the international monetary system (IMS). First and foremost, perhaps, is an unprecedented

Table 22.1 Central Banks by Balance Sheet Growth (2006–17)

Institution	*Founded*	*CBI*	*Reserves*		*Balance sheet*		*Objectives*
			2017 (US$ million)	*Growth (%)*	*2017 (US$ million)*	*Growth (%)*	
Bank of England	1694	0.31	$136,469	8.9	$383,140	25.9	1
Federal Reserve System	1913	0.48	$124,447	6.1	$4,453,337	15.4	2
Bundesbank	1957	0.83	$67,569	3.6	$1,440,531	15.3	1
Banque de France	1800	0.83	$57,535	2.0	$878,446	15.1	1
Banca d'Italia	1893	0.83	$52,618	5.8	$792,723	14.6	1
People's Bank of China	1948	0.60	$3,131,117	11.3	$2,989,653	13.6	3
European Central Bank	1998	0.83	$61,382	4.4	$345,336	13.4	1
Saudi Arabian Monetary Authority	1952	0.55	$493,452	8.1	$620,493	12.9	1
Banco Central do Brasil	1964	0.46	$380,351	16.1	$960,270	11.9	4
Bank of Japan	1882	0.38	$1,230,743	3.4	$4,340,915	11.3	1

Sources: Author's calculations from IMF data and from Garriga (2016).

Notes: Sample selection criterion is largest balance sheet in absolute terms. Growth figures are annualized. Founded in 1668, the Sveriges Riksbank (Sweden's central bank) is the world's oldest central bank. CBI: Index of central bank independence (0 = no independence, 1 = fully independent) following Crowe and Meade (2008). Objectives: 1 = Price stability along with other objectives that do not seem to conflict with the former; 2 = Price stability along with other objectives of potentially conflicting goals (e.g., full employment); 3 = Price stability is the only goal; 4: Some goals appear in the charter but price stability is not one of them.

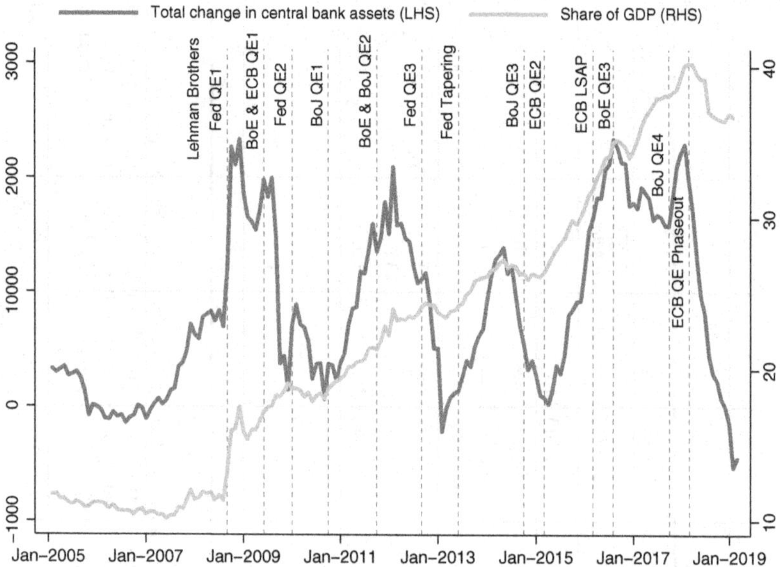

Figure 22.1 Quantitative easing and the evolution of C5 central bank balance sheets

Notes: Monthly changes of C5 central bank assets are averaged over a 12-month rolling window to smooth volatility due to operational characteristics that vary by institution.

Sources: Author's calculation from IMF and individual central bank data.

network of central bank lending facilities in the form of currency swaps lines that is anchored by the C5 and the Bank of Canada at its institutional core. This global swaps network now covers over 70 separate agreements involving over 50 central banks, thus establishing 'an elastic backstop of an international monetary system that remains very much a dollar system…for private foreign exchange operations' (Bernes et al., 2014: 3). On the periphery of this system, a further network of central bank swaps 'operates to economize on scarce reserves of the major currencies' (Mehrling, 2015: 311).

With central bankers being active on such a large scale and in such a globally coordinated manner, while facing so little democratic accountability, the specter of a technocratically governed IMS—a ghoul that most thought had died with the collapse of the Bretton Woods System during the 1970s—had risen once again. Wielding clubs of massive balance sheets and parading a new arsenal of unconventional monetary policy tools, the 'Lords of Finance' had staged an impressive return (cf. Ahamed, 2009). Their forceful display of control at the helm of the post-crisis IMS has infused the term 'unelected power' with new meaning and urgency. Indeed, this bold re-assertion of a resource-rich regulatory state has added a healthy dose of complexity to the all-too-simplistic narratives of hollowed-out government and austerity in the age of neoliberalism (Tucker, 2018). What began as a 'state of monetary-financial exception' has now matured into a 'new normal'. In short, in the decade after the GFC, central bankers have become more firmly established as the institutional apex of the modern monetary system than at any point in the post-war era.

In light of these developments, this chapter examines the evolving role and function of central banks in the post-crisis geography of money. One of the central perspectives taken here focuses on the fact that the IMS is at once *hierarchical in finance* and *hierarchical in power*, and that central banks play a pivotal role in this hierarchy. In fact, I argue that this role of central banks is best captured in the governance of what we will define as 'monetary space'; that is, an abstract economic space in the sense of François Perroux (1950a, b) that is spanned by financial markets, financial instruments, monetary-financial intermediaries, non-bank financial institutions, publicly sponsored intermediaries, and, of course, central banks. According to Perroux:

> [a] monetary space as defined by a *plan*...is formed by the relations which constitute the plan for the employment of money....Monetary space as a *field of forces*...is seen in terms of a 'network' of payments, or by means of the description of monetary flows....Monetary space as a *homogenous aggregate* suggests an almost perfect international currency market and an approximate unity in exchange rates.
>
> (Perroux, 1950b, pp. 97–9; emphasis in the original)

Expanding the Perrouxian perspective, this chapter takes a closer look at the different dimensions of monetary space and the role central banks are playing in the governance of each of these realms. Moreover, the crucial role that central banks fulfil as the institutional pinnacle in global monetary spaces is inherently hierarchical in an operational and functional sense. As such, this chapter argues that central banks critically shape three fundamental relationships among constituent economic elements in the Perrouxian system: (i) monetary space as defined by *a plan*; (ii) monetary space as a *field of forces*; and (iii) monetary space as a *homogeneous aggregate*.

This chapter also engages with the rapidly expanding post-crisis literature on the 'economic geography of money and finance', and argues that, despite an enthusiastic re-engagement with money and finance in the decade after the GFC, central banks and monetary space plays no more than a perfunctory role in this literature. Consequently, much of this rapidly expanding literature tends to remain singularly faithful to locational and agglomerational aspects of what Perroux (1950b) termed 'banal economic space' wherein the true monetary power of central banks is difficult to analyse. In doing so, the contemporary canon of geographical economists still enshrines the classical dichotomy, which moves the spheres of money beyond the microeconomic mechanics of analysing the realm of production. As such, the treatment of money in economic geography has only just begun to take the 'macro-effects of central banking' seriously (cf. Bieri, 2019a; Mann, 2010, 2012). This chapter hopes to contribute to a new research agenda that such an engagement would entail.

The remainder of this chapter is structured as follows. After an outline of some of the key elements of monetary space and central bank governance, I turn to a discussion of the different dimensions of monetary space in a Perrouxian sense, paying particular attention to constituent subspaces, namely 'currency space', 'regulatory space' and 'policy space'.

Central Banks and the Monetary Hierarchy

Given the dramatic changes to central banks' policy environment after the crisis, it is not only important to provide a larger contextualization of how these developments sit within the IMS, but also how the central bank—as the institutional top of the monetary hierarchy—is linked via its balance sheet to the rest of the monetary system. Indeed, the GFC has driven home the importance of financial flows and the composition of sectoral balance sheets for an understanding of real–financial linkages.[5]

As Minsky (2008) famously reminds us, the key to the flow of funds perspective is to look at all actors in the economy (households, firms, governments, including central banks, and the financial sector) as if they were banks. As such, each entity has a balance sheet of cash inflows and cash outflows, and each is bound by the 'survival constraint'; that is, the requirement that cash outflows not exceed cash inflows. The money flow economy then arises in aggregate from the interconnection of all balance sheets which, in turn, gives rise to the fundamental instability of a credit economy (Minsky, 1977, 1993). The money flow economy is the basis for a flow-of-funds accounting view which—as an analytical approach—provides a unique characterization of how financialization has progressively reshaped the modern macroeconomy through the process of financial globalization.

The process of financialization has thus completely intertwined the monetary system with the financial system such that we cannot talk about money without talking about finance. This raises the importance of several institutional hallmarks of the current system. At its core, there are the wholesale money markets as the central funding mechanism, with 'shadow banks'—that is, non-bank financial intermediaries that provide services similar to traditional commercial banks but that reside outside normal banking regulations—as key institutions that facilitate short-term funding of long-term lending. Given the importance of these flow-based changes to the relevance of the inner workings of the monetary-financial system, the need arises for refocusing the discussion in conceptual terms. The most important concepts in this regard are the (international) monetary hierarchy and the central bank's balance sheet.

Among one of the most central characteristics of the modern monetary system is its hybrid and hierarchical nature, at both the national and international levels. Its hybridity comes from the fact that it is part public (it involves 'outside money') and part private (it involves 'inside money'). 'Outside money' is either of a fiat nature or is backed by some asset that is in positive net supply within the private sector (e.g., gold), whereas 'inside money' is an asset backed by any form of private liability (credit) that circulates as a medium of exchange. While this analytical distinction was first introduced over half a century ago (Gurley and Shaw, 1960), it has only recently been augmented by work that explicitly emphasizes the hierarchical relationship between public and private liabilities that circulate as money (Bell, 2001; Mehrling, 2013).

With regard to this hierarchical nature, it is important to highlight that money is not only hierarchical in finance, but also hierarchical in power (e.g., in the Federal Reserve's ex post definition of what is adequate collateral and its inherent role as the 'market maker of last resort', Mehrling, 2011). In the context of the IMS, the hierarchy in power plays a particularly important role with regard to the uneven 'international moneyness' of different national currencies. Indeed, as Keynes has already contended, the monetary side of the (global) economy anything but neutral.[6] To the contrary, in part because of its hierarchy, episodes of international financial instability are—at their very core—the results of the varying degrees in 'international moneyness' that make currencies unequal (Terzi, 2005). In this regard, the GFC was no different.

The upper portion of Figure 22.2 illustrates the hierarchy of money at the national level, where money and credit are created by different financial institutions at separate levels of the hierarchy (left to right). For simplicity, we only show instruments discussed so far, leaving out government debt as the most important asset of the central bank (see lower portion of Figure 22.2, for a more complete characterization of a central bank balance sheet), loans as an asset of the banking system, and the entire 'shadow banking' system. Note that all of the instruments except gold (and FX reserves) appear as both assets and liabilities.[7] Because they are all forms of credit, they would all cancel out if we consolidated the three balance sheets into one in order to treat the economy as a single aggregate entity. Only gold and FX reserves would remain and only gold is an asset that is no one's liability—the very definition of 'outside money'. The monetary pyramid thus arises because of such credit-based linkages across sectoral balance sheets.

As we have seen, the central bank sits at the apex of the pyramid and connects the national system to the IMS. The hierarchy of money can thus be read both institutionally and, perhaps more importantly, in a functional manner; that is, in terms of what constitutes money and credit as an accepted means of settlement. A central feature of view is the fact that the distinctions between money and credit are not strict, and largely depend on the specific vantage point from within each layer of the system. At the top of the hierarchy, gold and deposits at the central bank are the 'ultimate money' because they are the ultimate means of international payment. To see why this is the case, we need to examine the monetary hierarchy 'in action' by discussing the mechanics of cross-border

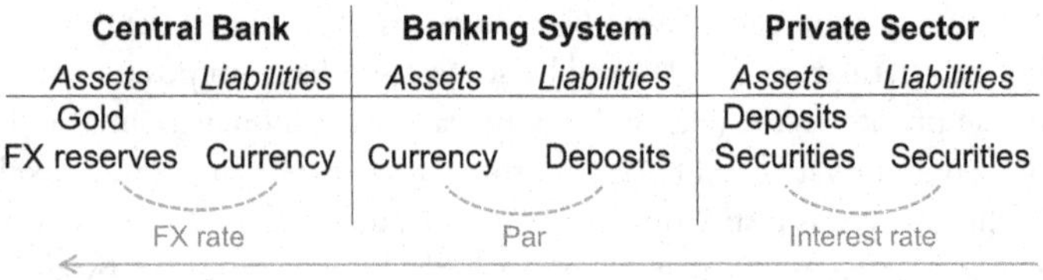

Central Bank		Banking System		Private Sector	
Assets	*Liabilities*	*Assets*	*Liabilities*	*Assets*	*Liabilities*
Gold				Deposits	
FX reserves	Currency	Currency	Deposits	Securities	Securities
FX rate		Par		Interest rate	

Central Bank

Assets	*Liabilities + capital*
Net international assets	Reserve money
Gold, SDR	*Currency in circulation*
Foreign exchange reserves	*Reserves of commercial banks*
Net domestic assets	Non-monetary liabilities
Cash	*Central bank securities*
Bank loans	*Others*
Securities (OMO)	Equity capital

Figure 22.2 Hierarchy of money and balance sheets

Notes: The relative prices that define the hierarchy of money are the FX rate ('price of currency' in terms of gold, or foreign currency; i.e., the FX rate can be thought of as a relative price of converting one currency into another or gold). Similarly, par can be thought of as the 'price of deposits' in terms of currency (i.e., the cost of converting a deposit into cash) and the interest rate as the 'price of securities' in terms of deposits or currency. OMO: open market operations.

Sources: Author's illustration, adapted from Bieri (2000), Caruana (2012), and Mehrling (2013).

payments that appear—to the naked eye, at least—simply to rely on transfers of bank deposits (or physical movements of cash). Before we do this, however, let us also consider the related fact that currencies, both international money and national money, are deemed a form of credit insofar as they are promises to pay gold or central bank (fiat) money. Similarly, further down the hierarchy, bank deposits are viewed as a form of private credit money—effectively, promises to pay currency on demand and thus twice removed from the promises to pay ultimate money. Private money in the form of debt obligations (IOUs) or securities is, then, a promise to pay currency or deposits over some specific time horizon.

A second crucial feature of this hierarchical view of money lies in the fact that, at each layer of the system, the 'moneyness of credit' depends how easy it is to convert a specific form of credit into the next higher form of money (e.g., deposits into currency, or currency into gold). In other words, what counts as money and what counts as credit depends on the layer of the hierarchy under consideration, and on what counts as the ultimate means of settlement. This brings us right back to how gold and central bank deposits, not bank deposits, act as 'ultimate money' for cross-border payments. A brief look at the 'credit mechanics' across the hierarchy of money should help to clarify this point.

Consider the payment flows in the case of Firm A, a German supplier of industrial robots located 50 km northwest of Munich, selling a new assembly system for say, €10 million, to Firm B, a large Spanish car manufacturer located 25 km northwest of Barcelona. On the surface, the money flow equivalent of this transaction appears to be a simple direct transfer of deposits from the Spanish bank account of Firm B to Firm A's account at its German correspondent bank. Behind the scenes, however, the hierarchical nature of money as outlined above implies that Firm B's commercial bank will see its reserve account at the Banco d'España (an asset on the commercial bank's balance sheet) reduced by €10 million, and it will see Firm B's deposits (a liability) reduced by €10 million. The receiving commercial bank in Germany will see corresponding increases in its reserve account at the Bundesbank and in its customers' deposits. Just as both commercial banks have balanced changes in assets and liabilities, so do both Eurozone central banks. The Banco d'España's reserve account liabilities decrease by €10 million, the Bundesbank's reserve account liabilities increase by €10 million, and the offsetting changes on the asset side of the Eurozone central banks' balance sheets occur through their respective accounts in TARGET2, the interbank settlement and payments system of the European Monetary Union (EMU).[8] Because the Banco d'España is effectively making a payment to the Bundesbank, its TARGET2 balance (an asset) falls by €10 million, and the Bundesbank's TARGET2 balance rises by €10 million. The ultimate settlement of this transaction thus happens in terms of 'central bank money', not 'commercial bank money'.[9]

As we have seen, then, the notion of monetary hybridity implies that the credit pyramid oscillates between a condition where money is 'scarce' and one where credit is 'elastic' (Mehrling, 2013). In this regard, one of Minsky's (2008) key insights was that the hierarchy of money shifts across the economic cycle through three distinct phases: hedge finance, speculative finance, and Ponzi schemes. Money and credit are thus fluctuating between states of elasticity and states of discipline. In this context, central banks determine the institutional plane within which the monetary-financial pendulum swings across monetary space.

Conceptualizing Monetary Space

As a next step, we must therefore engage in more detail with the conceptualization of monetary space as an analytical abstract. A central feature of such a move lies in distinguishing between physical and functional notions of space, a distinction that was first introduced to the analysis of the space-economy by Perroux's (1950a, b) re-theorization of economic space around a set of '(economic) plans', 'field forces', 'homogenous aggregates' and 'domination effects' between them. Such an abstraction primarily privileges 'spaces of flows' over the more conventional notion of 'spaces of places'. In many ways, such a reconfiguration of the spatial relations of money and finance can be read as being consistent with what Thrift and Olds (1996: 314) envisage—in the Perrouxian sense described above—as a 'transformative re-conceptualization of the remit of economic'. In this very spirit, Leyshon and Thrift (1997) and Martin (1999) provide the first broader conceptualizations of and engagements with monetary space as an analytical abstract. Similarly, French et al. (2011) suggest that research on financializaton has been insufficiently attentive to network- or flow-based notions of economic space. Yet, none of this work connects back to Perroux's pioneering inquiries.

In fact, of all abstract economic spaces, Perroux places particular emphasis on monetary space as a *field of forces* in terms of 'a 'network' (in the mathematical sense) of payments, or by means of the description of monetary flows. A center (or pole) has then to be chosen, from which one draws the 'network' of payments towards or from other centres; or from which emanate, and to which come, monetary flows. The most significant of these 'centres' are complex aggregates of monetary and financial organisms—the 'places'' (Perroux, 1950b: 98). In Perroux's analysis, monetary space is simultaneously delocalized, yet inherently hierarchical, operating at several levels of 'banal space' (i.e., at the regional, national, and global scales).[10]

As such, the discourses on the monetary geography are centered around what Cohen (1998) terms a 'flow-based model of currency relation', where networks and hierarchies form the primary units of analysis, all within a largely *de-territorialized spatial organization of monetary-financial relations*. Instead of dealing with money and central banking in what Perroux termed '*localized* banal space' (i.e., where space is simply the 'genomic relations between points, lines, surfaces, and volumes'), I want to conceptualize monetary space as a '*delocalized* space' in the abstract sense.

Thus, instead of using conventional definitions of space as the 'disequilibrating frictions' that give rise to agglomerational phenomena, economies of scale and other distance-based spatial effects, Perroux's abstract spaces are characterized by power relations and domination effects that impinge on 'the plan of units' and that regulate 'the relations of a homogenous aggregate relative to the unit'. And finally, Perrouxian spaces are economic force fields that both 'emanate from units' and 'act on units'; that is, these spaces are pinned down by 'centres (or poles or foci) from which centrifugal forces emanate and to which centripetal forces are attracted. Each centre being a centre of attraction and repulsion, has its proper field, which is set in the fields of other centres' (Perroux, 1950b: 95) In short, monetary space thus conceptualized is not the locus for financial localization effects between economic actors per se, but the money-based force fields and power-relations between economic actors. It is in this precise sense that I want to analyse the role of central banks in the governance of monetary space.

Specifically, we can now conceive of monetary space along three nested dimensions ('policy space', 'regulatory space', and 'currency space'), or subspaces, for each one of which the central bank acts as a key institutional pole. Figure 22.3 presents a schematic illustration of these monetary subspaces and the

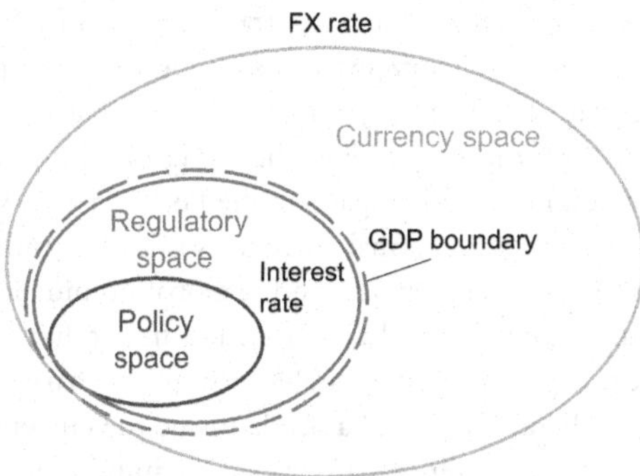

Figure 22.3 Dimensions of monetary space

Notes: Policy space ('defined by plan'), regulatory space ('defined by homogeneous aggregate') and currency space ('field of forces'). This synoptical approach to monetary space follows Perroux (1950b), where every set of relations constitutes an abstract space in the Perrouxian sense.

Source: Author's illustration.

relationship between them, particularly with regard to the policy instruments that are under the control of central banks. At the central core of monetary space, there is 'policy space' wherein the central bank regulates the economic relationship and economic 'plans between units' by regulating the intertemporal price of money; that is, interest rates. While the central banks have conventionally exerted *direct* control over interest rates via their short-term policy rates, the secular decline of the policy rate towards the zero lower bound in the wake of the GFC has demonstrated the importance of central banks *indirect* control over longer-term interest rates by affecting quantities, rather than prices, as was the case in QE policies. Policy space is thus spanned by the extent and nature of how the transmission mechanism of monetary policy acts on the plan of economic units. From the availability of interbank lending to the price of residential mortgages, central banks sit at the very center of this monetary subspace. As will be discussed, the rapid digitization of money on the back of distributed-ledger technology (DLT) is posing a new set of unprecedented challenges over the control of monetary space in general and over policy space, in particular.

'Regulatory space' forms an overlapping, but distinctly separate and more expansive, monetary space wherein central banks regulatory and supervisory activities can be thought of as regulating the economic relations of an aggregate 'relative to the units and to their structure, or relative to the relations between these units' (Perroux, 1950b: 96). Specifically, we could think of regulatory space as the structure of the regulatory system that in important ways influences the roles played by the various components of the monetary-financial system (financial instruments, financial markets, monetary and financial intermediaries) in promoting the inter-regional mobility of funds and, by extension, the mobility of funds among the various sectors of the space economy.[11] Rapid economic and financial globalization notwithstanding, central banks' control over the governance of both policy and regulatory space is still bound by the political boundaries of the nation state. In many ways, national central banks provide the most powerful national lever for leaning against the winds of economic globalization.

Lastly, then, we define 'currency space' as the Perrouxian monetary subspace that is spanned by competing national currencies in a constantly evolving 'field of forces' wherein national currencies vie for global dominance. Whether this is 'in one case, a dominant national currency, and in another, a currency dealt with by a number of places of comparable power and harmonizing policies' (Perroux, 1950b, p. 99), both central banks that issue the currency and financial centers within which the currencies are traded are important nodes that shape the global network of currency spaces. Figure 22.4 attempts to visualize such

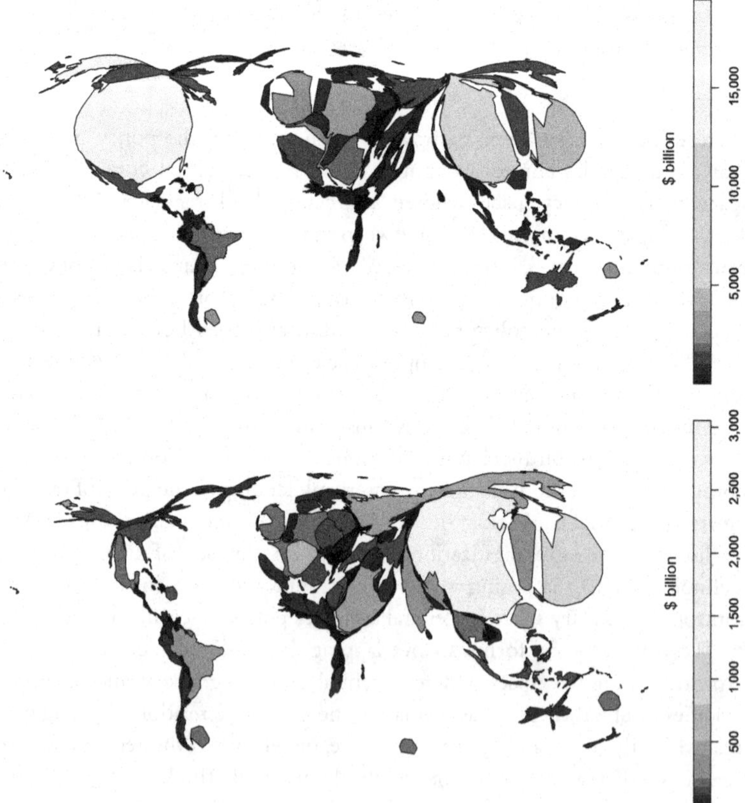

Figure 22.4 FX reserves and the shaping of currency space

Notes: The cartograms use GDP (top) and nominal foreign exchange reserves (bottom) as scaling variables.

Sources: Author's calculation from BIS and IMF data.

Table 22.2 Central Banks, Policy Instruments, and Monetary Space

Type of monetary space	*Character*	*Instruments*	*'Domination effect' (CB control)*
Policy space	'defined by a plan'	Monetary policy (interest rates, asset purchases)	High
Regulatory space	'defined by a homogenous aggregate'	National banking regulation, international supervisory standards (e.g., Basel Accords)	Medium
Currency space	'defined by a field of forces'	International currency competition, exchange rate arrangements (fixed, floating)	Low

Note: See text, for more details.

a force field-based version of global currency space in an semi-abstract sense, whereas Table 22.2 summarizes our conceptualization of aggregate monetary space along its most important dimensions.

For all their analytical distinctness, it is also clear that the three types of monetary spaces share large areas of mutual dependence and overlap (as is, indeed, implied in Figure 22.2). For example, in an open economy, policy-makers are often seen as constrained by the so-called 'monetary policy trilemma', which imposes stark trade-offs across the three monetary spaces, specifically exchange rate stability (currency space), monetary independence (policy space), and capital market openness (regulatory space). Specifically, the trilemma—which is sometimes also referred to as the 'impossible trinity'—implies that a country cannot simultaneously achieve a fixed exchange rate, independent monetary policy, and free capital flows. While it is mostly unchallenged that countries can still choose only two out of the three policy goals, increasing capital mobility appears to have changed the policy consensus about the relative weight given to each of them; namely, that the exchange rate needs to adjust more flexibly than in the past (see, e.g., Obstfeld, Stambaugh, and Taylor, 2010). The sharp rise in central bank holdings of foreign exchange reserves since the 1990s, however, seems to tell a very different story. In the context of the recent financial crisis, the trade-offs implied by the trilemma have once again risen to the very top of policy-makers' agendas; yet, in contrast to previous episodes of financial instability, burgeoning central bank reserves and the emergence of sovereign wealth funds are viewed as challenges to—rather than possible solutions for—a redesign of the architecture of the global financial system.

Moreover, across all monetary spaces, central banks exert varying levels of control over other economic actors within a given monetary space. This, in turn, gives rise to a multitude of what could be described as 'monetary domination effects', which we define by simply extending to our setting of monetary spaces Perroux's definition of a situation when 'unit A exercises on unit B an irreversible or partially irreversible influence' (Perroux, 1950a: 188). However, in each of the monetary spaces, the nature of the domination effect is a function of the central bank's power within that space. The strength of the domination effect of central banks is largest in the 'policy space' because of its tight control over monetary policy instruments, old and new. It is 'medium' in regulatory space due to the variegated nature of institutional regulatory and supervisory mechanisms, many of which often lie outside the direct control of the central bank. The strength of the domination effect is weakest in the 'currency space', which is largely due the hybrid nature of the global monetary-financial system. This implies that every central bank that issues an 'internationalized currency' shares its institutional control over the corresponding 'currency space' with internationally active private depository institutions that operate out of global financial centers such as London, Tokyo, or Zürich.[12] We will now turn our attention to how this two-tiered control over currency space in the eurodollar market has given rise to a new geography of money.

The New Geography of Money

Tracing out the evolution of monetary (sub)spaces in historical perspective, this section engages with the geographic shifts in the global structure and governance of various 'currency spaces' in general, and the changing nature of the IMS, in particular. Indeed, the history of modern capitalism has seen two versions of the IMS; first, the sterling era that lasted until World War I, and then the dollar era, which has been in effect since. From a functional perspective, these two eras were accompanied by the gradual evolution of the IMS from a commodity (gold)-based system into a credit system. In the context of our previous discussion about the hierarchical and hybrid nature of monetary space, the important point to appreciate here is that international money has typically been a 'promise to pay some *national money*, the issue of a specific reserve currency nation state. The key institutional mechanism for extending national into *international money* has been the growth of international financial centers (in London for sterling, in New York for dollars) to support the emerging globalization of trade, production and finance' (Bernes et al., 2014, p. 8, emphasis added).

Today, the undisputed international money is (still) the dollar—in particular, the eurodollar (i.e., dollar-denominated deposits of non-US banks that are held overseas by non-US customers and that are used to finance dollar loans and securities issued by other non-US customers). Eurodollars emerged with the Marshall Plan after World War II when vast amounts of dollar funds were circulating across war-torn Europe in the custody of foreign banks outside the direct control of US monetary authorities. Because they are held outside the United States, eurodollars are not subject to regulation by the Federal Reserve, including reserve requirements and deposit insurance, which added to their rapid growth in the post-war environment. At the same time, cost-push inflation and US budget deficits in the wake of the collapse of the Bretton Woods system further dampened the international attractiveness of the 'on-shore' dollar such that, by the early 1980s, eurodollars had overtaken certificates of deposit (CDs) issued by US banks as the primary private short-term money market instruments. As such, the singular role of the 'dollar space'—both onshore and offshore—remains a symbol and a source of strength for the US economy, despite the fact that the Federal Reserve actually only exerts very weak direct control over this part of its 'currency space'. To some, these are all developments that characterize the first stage of a 'new geography' of the post-Bretton Woods order (Cohen, 2003; Helleiner, 2010; Subacchi, 2010).

In the second stage of this geographic transformation, the IMS has seen the creation and rise of the euro as a reserve currency, and the unprecedented, politically engineered internationalization of the Chinese renminbi.[13] In fact, in the decade before the GFC, the 'new geography of money' reached its climax as currencies were becoming, at once, more de-territorialized in their international use ('currency internationalization') and were under more intense competitive pressure from foreign-issued currencies in their domestic use ('currency substitution'). In the setting of this new geography, states were developing new modes of monetary governance that increasingly mirrored the process of 'marketization' that was taking hold in other realms of economic governance. More and more, realms that were hitherto the traditional province of state power have become reliant on markets and private institutions.

Yet, for all its geopolitically convincing appeal, this multilateral transformation of the IMS may have, as Mehrling (2015) argues, less to do with changing international relations between states than it has to do with commercial relations—and, hence, payment systems and liquidity—between national financial systems. Nevertheless, it is clear that the commercial logic of this increase in currency competition was ultimately shaped by large historical-political shifts that were set in motion by the collapse of Bretton Woods, and then intensified by fall of the Berlin Wall, the creation of the EMU, and the rise of China (Clark, 2015; Helleiner, 1994).

Symptomatic for these developments in global currency trends was the slide of the hegemonic role of the US dollar as the reserve currency of choice. In 1973, the year when the Smithsonian Agreement officially rang in the post-Bretton Woods era, close to 80% of global foreign exchange reserves were denominated in dollars, and the rest mostly in pound sterling with some euro legacy currencies (i.e., the Deutsche mark and French franc). By the 1990s, after a decade of concerted currency interventions by the G7 central banks in the Plaza and Louvre Accords, the dollar's global share in official reserve portfolios had fallen to under 60%. But, since the beginning of the new millennium—when international reserves began their explosive growth, which has slowed down only recently—the dollar share in central bank reserves has

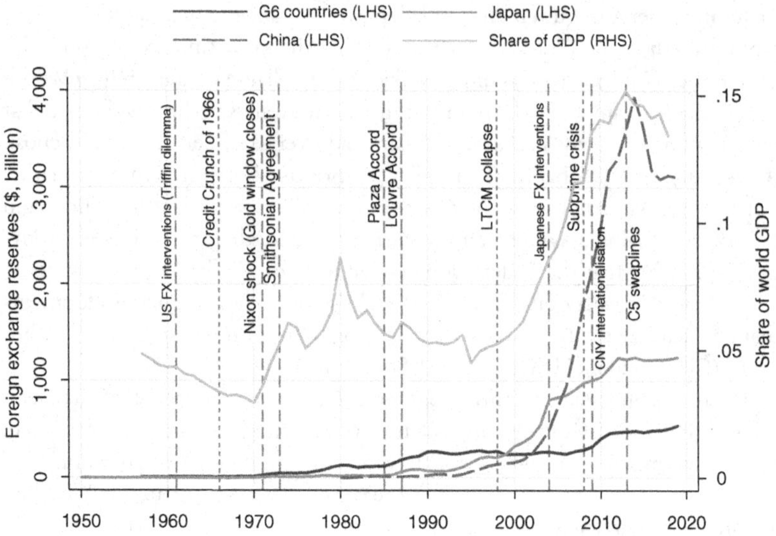

Figure 22.5 The IMS and the growth of global foreign exchange reserves

Notes: Vertical lines denote important events in the governance of the international monetary system (long dash) and financial crises (short dash).

Sources: Author's calculations from IMF and BIS data.

bounced back to around two-thirds of official holdings. Today, close to US$7.1 trillion of the approximately US$11.2 trillion of reserves are denominated in dollars. At US$2 trillion, the euro is a distant second, with yen and pound sterling sharing about half the balancing amounts. Figure 22.5 illustrates the transformative growth of global foreign exchange reserves across various post-war stages of the IMS.

And it is not only in foreign exchange reserve holdings that the dollar has been able to maintain its dominant position. While the years in the run-up to the GFC may have given the impression that the IMS was moving toward a multicurrency system with several poles, the crisis certainly has unambiguously reversed this trend, at least for now. As Figure 22.6 highlights, the evolution of 'international currency space' as measured by the force field of currency shares in foreign exchange market turnover shows the domination effect of the dollar anything but weakening. Indeed, even the most recent evidence on the size and structure of global foreign exchange markets—the 2019 BIS Triennial Survey—confirms that there still is only one true pole in the IMS: the US dollar. The euro is lagging behind considerably and the yen, pound sterling, and Swiss franc are, at best, niche players (Cohen and Benney, 2014). For much of the political importance of its arrival on the world stage as a convertible international currency a decade ago, the renmimbi's presence is barely noticeable

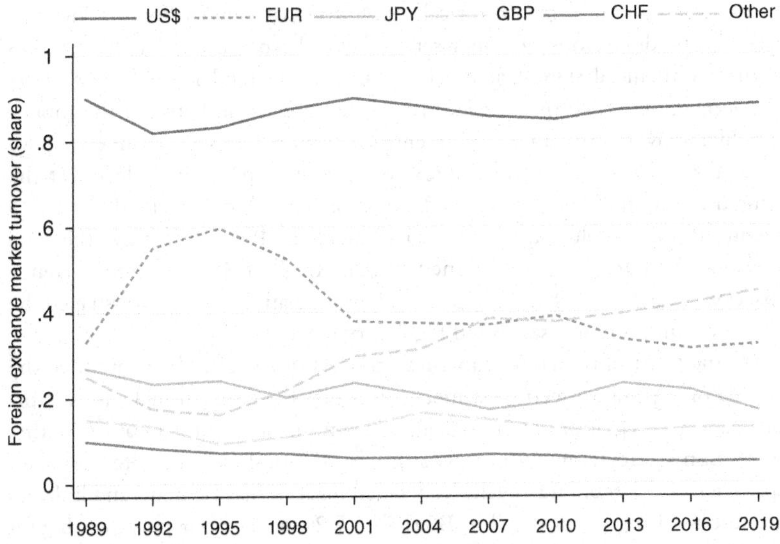

Figure 22.6 Currency shares in foreign exchange market turnover

Notes: As two currencies are involved in each transaction, the sum of shares in individual currencies will total 200%.

Source: Author's calculations from BIS Triennial Survey data (BIS2019b).

yet. In light of recent developments, the question remains under what circumstances the euro and the renmimbi may perhaps come to rival the dollar, and how such increased currency competition could affect global financial stability (e.g., Eichengreen et al., 2017; Kirshner, 2014).

At the same time, the financial crisis has also led to a certain amount of *re-territorialization* of the discourse on the spatial consequences of finance as regulatory responses to the crises—from bailouts to the creation of new regulatory arrangements—almost invariably took place within the institutional framework of nations. Yet, this re-territorialization is not simply a reversion to the realities of the 'old geography', with competing nation-states and clear urban hierarchies as the key spatial units of interest. Instead, it is an emergent new arrangement where globally dispersed creditors and debtors are the main actors (Bieri, 2009). Within this new geography, the traditional roles and interactions between borrowers and investors are being reconstituted with regard to both their spatial and their institutional organization. While the monetary and financial aspects of this new spatial order still assign states significant control over their 'regulatory space', the political governance of the Westphalian system has been replaced by a new geography of globalized currency relations (Cohen, 2007). And in this market-based arrangement, states only exert modest direct control over 'currency space'.

In tracing out the historical evolution of international 'currency spaces', our discussions of a hierarchy of globalized money that has the US monetary-financial system at its core immediately render visible this *monetary hierarchy-monetary space nexus*; that is, the connection between the monetary hierarchy and the different dimensions of monetary space. While we have focused on this nexus in the context of 'currency space', it is clear that the structure and function of 'policy and regulatory space' are also closely linked to the institutional evolution of its monetary hierarchy. Put differently, in the same way that the interplay between the hierarchy of the IMS maps into currency space, we could show that there is an analogous relationship that has shaped the evolution of US policy space and regulatory space.

At the heart of this connection lies a process that I refer elsewhere to as the 'regulatory-spatial dialectic'—a mechanism that operates through the vectors of financial integration, economic agglomeration, and suburbanization, setting in motion spatio-temporal processes that continuously reconstitute monetary space across the economic cycle. Its detailed institutional elements and linkages are discussed in greater detail in Bieri (2017, 2018). For our purposes, here it will suffice to remark that—analogous to the force fields that have shaped the historical trajectory of the IMS—the evolutionary interplay between markets, institutions, and the state initiate dialectical processes of adjustments and counter-adjustments with respect to monetary governance and financial regulation. In the following section, we will turn to the most current stage in this process: the radical transformation of monetary space through the inexorable rise of digital monies, both private and public.

The Digital Struggle over Monetary Space

The digitization of money has come to present one of the most unique challenges to central banks in their modern history. The rise of cryptocurrencies and the prospect of central bank digital currency (CBDC) are set to redefine the shape and forms of control over monetary space in unprecedented ways. This institutional disruption is perhaps at its most acute in policy space where crypto assets will transform the monetary transmission mechanism, possibly even undermining central banks' century-old monopoly of providing the official unit of account. In this section, I will argue that the very same lens of our spectrum of dominance effects introduced earlier will provide useful insights in analysing this new reality of *digital monetary space*. In fact, 'cryptocurrencies' writ large readily present a number of challenges along Perrouxian dimensions, particularly with regard to their impact on both 'policy space' and 'regulatory space'.

What is commonly referred to by the term 'cryptocurrencies' are new forms of financial instruments that often rely on distributed ledger technology (DLT) that most commonly runs on a public (permissionless) or private (permissioned) blockchain. Aside from all the 'tech' excitement that comes with the possibilities of disruption in the current 'FinTech moment', we therefore also need to examine the 'fin' element a little more closely.[14] In fact, financial regulators, such as the SEC, the Federal Reserve, or the OCC, prefer to use the term 'cryptoassets', because these DTL-based products—from BitCoin, Etherium to the rapidly expanding class of stable coins (including Facebook's prospective Libra)—are really a new class of financial instruments that are based on the issuance of private digital tokens either for general payment or wholesale purposes. The monetary space of privately issued cryptoassets is a fiercely competitive environment and, for all the promises of a grass-roots revolution, in many instances, it is not entirely clear what the value proposition of a number of these new 'monies' really is. Are many of them simply still the proverbial solution looking for a problem, and how should that then translate into intrinsic value? This is a very broad topic, well beyond the scope of this chapter, but, in the context of our discussion of monetary space, we can reduce it to the question of the extent to which digital money transforms the role of money in a system of finance-led capitalism.

With regard to the impact on 'policy space', privately issued cryptoassets that can be used for payment purposes fundamentally challenge the monetary hierarchy because they are—like gold—the ultimate 'outside money'. In other words, they are nobody's liability but, unlike gold, they can be produced at the 'push of a button'. Indeed, while many of the cryptoassets may pretend to be currencies and make varying claims about their 'moneyness', they invariably fail the basic textbook definitions of what constitutes sound money (unit of account, means of payment, store of value). Most would agree that they do not function as a unit of account. Their volatile valuations make them unsafe to rely on as a common means of payment and a stable store of value. They also defy lessons from theory and experiences. Most importantly, given their many fragilities, cryptocurrencies are unlikely to satisfy the requirement of trust to make them sustainable forms of money. Thus, while new technologies have the potential to improve economic well-being, this is not invariably the case (Carstens, 2018, 2019a, b). Indeed, concerns over the ability of this outside money to serve as a reliable unit of account have been illustrated in a very tangible manner in the context of the spectacular bursting of the BitCoin bubble which began in early 2018. While BitCoin is an incredibly important 'proof of concept' for blockchain technology applied to payments, economists agree that there is no reason why BitCoin should have an intrinsic value (Dwyer, 2015; Schilling and Uhlig, 2019). These issues aside, to some, algorithmic digital currencies still appear to be viable competitors to central bank fiat currency. And, as such, they thus fundamentally challenge central banks' control of 'policy space' and threaten an unprecedented flattening of the monetary hierarchy.

As a response to this potentially existential challenge, central banks themselves have started actively embracing the possibility of DLT-powered CBDC, which not only promises to improve central banks' payment and clearing operations, but would also allow them to cement, and even extend, the strength of their dominance effect in this monetary subspace. In fact, a sovereign digital currency could have profound implications for the banking system because it obviates the need for the public to keep deposits in fractional reserve commercial banks. The prospect of CBDC would thus radically tighten, but not flatten, the monetary hierarchy by narrowing the relationship between citizens and central banks (Raskin and Yermack, 2017; BIS, 2020). And, as a consequence, central banks' dominance over policy space could become even *stronger*! Indeed, recent evidence from a survey of over 60 central banks around the globe shows that, while most central banks are only at a conceptual stage with regard to CDBC, a handful of central banks are already poised to issue a digital currency in the short or medium term (Bartorini and Holden, 2019).

By contrast, the impact of cryptoassets on 'regulatory space' should be thought of as a potential *weakening* of the central banks' control over that specific monetary subspace. Specifically, there is the question of the extent to which these instruments can be forced to be part of the Perrouxian 'homogenous aggregate' by being pulled on this side of the regulatory perimeter—one of the most important challenges is to raise the bar of financial literacy such as to protect consumers. In the case of cryptoassets, this is particularly important because, on the one hand, these products are more often than not operating outside of the regulatory safety zone, and, on the other hand, because many of those products come associated with a new business models that have yet to demonstrate their viability at scale.

For all the laudable democratizing impetus that lies at the origin of many a new community-based digital token (e.g., Langley and Leyshon, 2017), it is not clear how these crypto efforts represent an improvement in local economic empowerment over their physical analogues, such as, for example, the Bristol pound, the Chiemgauer, or other forms of community-issued scrip. As financial regulators continue to tighten the leash on new DTL-based FinTech products, the cost of regulatory compliance will simply be too high for many of the crypto players to survive in the medium run. There is a good historical reason why banking and finance are among the most regulated industries (because they are risky and volatile) and why, in all advanced economies, the issuance of money is a state monopoly under the control of the central bank. Even in the United States. The 'Free Banking' experiment of the mid-1800s, where private banks were engaging in competitive currency issuance, eventually ended and the Federal Reserve was created in 1913 to become the only issuer of currency. This time will be no different.

In the realm of 'currency space', the impact of the digitization of money can readily be subsumed under the heading of the competitive field of forces that is spanned by 'currency internationalization' and 'currency substitution', as discussed above. In this new frontier in the realm of monetary space, the arrival of private token-based cryptocurrencies has opened up the century-old state monopoly on currency issuance to technology-enabled private sector challengers, thus leading to a potential further weakening of central bank governance in this realm.

In sum, we have seen that central banks have been at the very center of discussions and debates about the governance implications of digital money—above all, shielding their hierarchical power from blockchain-fueled disruptors. Table 22.3 summarizes the previous discussion of how to conceptualize the impact of the digitization of money on our three monetary subspaces. In particular, we can see that, in response to the digitization challenge of their control over monetary space, central banks are evaluating how to maintain, and even increase, their authority via the introduction of new digital central bank instruments. This could include such tools as general purpose central bank accounts to pin down policy space and CBDC, both in general purpose and wholesale form, to pin down control in currency space.

Somewhat paradoxically, then, in their quest to assert institutional control over digital monetary space, central banks have even been accelerating the race of digitizing currencies, pushing the boundaries further still by incubating small proofs of concepts for the use of blockchain-powered CBDC (cf. Cœré, 2018; CPMI, 2018; FSB, 2018).

Outlook

In addition to the financial fallout, the GFC also generated sizable dislocations of an intellectual nature, challenging the very core of economic orthodoxy about the self-correcting nature of markets, in general, and the efficiency of financial markets, in particular. As a result, the GFC has underlined the crucial role of central banks as institutional pivot points on which the global financial system hinges. Bolstered by their policy successes of mastering monetary stability via interest rate targeting, central bankers fully took on the mantle of policy high priests after the crisis, justifying with ease their very unorthodox policy interventions in the decade since the GFC. In any case, the crisis has impressively demonstrated that money and credit are certainly not neutral in the short and medium terms. On the one hand, the extraordinary intervention measures by central banks have created an action environment under historically unique interest rate conditions, whereby many of the monetary debates over the nature of the quantity theory that were long-believed to have been overcome have once more been brought to the fore. Above all, the QE policies of the C5 central banks have not only reinvented the central bank balance sheet as an instrument of monetary policy, but have also revitalized the dogmatic discussion over the nature of Quantity Theory (i.e., the relationship between money supply and prices) in its own right (e.g., Marcuzzo, 2017).

Against this background, this chapter examines the evolving role and function of central banks in the post-crisis geography of money. In particular, I turn to the pioneering work of François Perroux (1950a, b) on the analysis of economic spaces in order to argue that central banks form the institutional, operational, and functional apex in the inherent hierarchy of *global monetary spaces*. As such, central banks critically shape three fundamental relationships

Table 22.3 Control Over Digital Monetary Space

	Central bank control		*Private control*	
	Digital	*Physical*	*Digital*	*Physical*
Policy space	CB reserves, **CB accounts** (general purpose)			
Regulatory space	Bank deposits			
Currency space	**CBDC** (general purpose, wholesale)	Cash	Private digital tokens ('cryptocurrencies'), wholesale tokens	Precious metal coins, local currencies (e.g., Brixton Pound, Bristol Pound, Chiemgauer), US 'wild cat banks'

Notes: Bold entries denote new, digital central bank (CB) instruments. Following Bech and Garratt (2017), the digitization of money space can be conceptualized with regard to four key properties of money: in terms of issuer (central bank or not); form (digital or physical); accessibility (widely or restricted); and technology (account-based or token-based).

among constituent economic elements in the Perrouxian system. First, they exert strong control over what I call 'policy space'—that is, the part of monetary space wherein the central banks influence economic 'plans between units' by regulating the intertemporal price of money; in other words, interest rates. Second, central banks are active in 'regulatory space', which forms a related, but distinctly separate, monetary subspace wherein central banks' regulatory and supervisory activities can be thought of as regulating the economic relations of an aggregate 'relative to the units and to their structure'. Third, I define 'currency space' as the Perrouxian monetary subspace that is spanned by competing national currencies in a constantly evolving 'field of forces' wherein national currencies vie for global dominance.

One of the implications of this chapter is to call for a deeper engagement in the rapidly evolving literature on the 'economic geography of money and finance', with the topic of central banks, on the one hand, and—perhaps more importantly—with Perroux's conceptualization of monetary space, on the other hand. Indeed, the true scope of central banks' monetary power can only be rendered fully legible in abstract economic space. Therein lies an additional motivation for a re-engagement with the novel spatial thought of François Perroux. Instead of being shackled by a singularly faithful focus on locational and agglomerational aspects that operate within the limiting confines of 'banal economic space', the future potential of financial geography would be well-served were it to be infused with a healthy dose of abstract economic spaces that de-localize economic units and economic relations.

Acknowledgement

I am grateful to the editors, Janelle Knox-Hayes and Dariusz Wójcik, for detailed comments and guidance on earlier drafts, and to participants at the 2019 AAG Meetings for helpful discussions. The usual disclaimers apply. Ben Coleman provided diligent research assistance.

Notes

1 See BIS (2019a) and CGFS (2019), for recent supranational attempts to diffuse legitimacy issues from the use of 'unconventional monetary policy tools' and their possible adverse consequences on market functioning.

2 The world's four largest financial institutions are all Chinese state-owned banks (ICBC, China Construction Bank, Agricultural Bank of China, Bank of China) with combined assets of approximately US$14 trillion. The 10 largest privately owned financial institutions are Mitsubishi UFJ Financial (Japan), JPMorgan Chase (United States), HSBC Holdings (United Kingdom), Bank of America (United States), BNP Paribas (France), Citigroup (United States), Wells Fargo (United States), Sumitomo Mitsui Financial (Japan), Santander (Spain), and Allianz (Germany).

3 This figure includes Amazon, Disney, Facebook, Google, and Microsoft (US$0.9 trillion); Apple, IBM, Intel, Samsung, and Sony (US$1.1 trillion); BP, Chevron, ExxonMobile, Royal Dutch Shell, and Total (US$1.5 trillion); BMW, Daimler,

General Motors, Toyota and VW (US$1.8 trillion); Anheuser-Busch, Johnson & Johnson, Nestlé, Novartis, and Walmart (US$0.9 trillion).

4 Goodhart and Lastra (2018) examine the challenges to central bank independence in the light of the rise of populism. Draghi (2018), Economist (2018), and Fels (2016) provide additional discussions over the renewed conflict between central bank independence and more activist monetary policy.

5 See Bieri (2017), for a detailed discussion of the role of spatial flow-of-funds analysis in economic geography.

6 August Lösch's (1944, 1949) pioneering analysis of the hierarchy of international monetary-financial arrangements recognizes that money and credit are always and everywhere fundamentally hierarchical in nature, and that all money is credit money, even state money. See Bieri (2019b), for more detail on Lösch's monetary theory.

7 Securities appear as both assets and liabilities of the private sector because they are both IOUs issued by some firms (liability) that are used as investments (assets) by others. See Caruana (2012), for a detailed line item explanation of central banks' balance sheets.

8 In a strict accounting sense, TARGET2 is the ECB (cf. Lubik and Rhodes, 2012).

9 In the wake of the European sovereign debt crisis, large positive and negative TARGET2 balances have arisen, causing widespread concern over the stability of the Eurozone. Much like in our example, current TARGET2 balances show the Bundesbank as a large net creditor to the ECB, and central banks in the periphery nations (Portugal, Ireland, Italy, Greece, and Spain) as significant net debtors to the ECB. See Auer and Bogdanova (2017) and Bindseil and König (2012), for more details on the TARGET2 discussion.

10 Despite some similarities between August Lösch's (1944) notion of economic space and his own approach, Perroux insists that 'the generalization in terms of 'abstract spaces' is alien to [Lösch's] important contribution' (Perroux, 1950b: 94).

11 Cf. Bieri (2009), for more details on the geographies of regulation, and Bieri (2017), for more details on the nature of regulatory space.

12 See also He and McCauley (2012) and Avdjiev et al. (2016), for details on the process of currency internationalization, and Wójcik et al. (2018), for the role of international financial centers therein.

13 Conventionally, currency internationalization is viewed as the gradual process whereby market participants (residents and non-residents alike) begin to rely on a currency outside their home country denominating bank deposits, loans, and bonds, as well as invoicing trade and making exchanges against other currencies. In the case of the Chinese renminbi, this was not a slow historic process but, rather, one that was politically orchestrated (McCauley, 2011).

14 See Davidson et al. (2008) for a general discussion of blockchains as institutional innovation, and Bieri and Datz (2019), for a more detailed discussion of the 'disruptive potential' of FinTech to the monetary-financial system.

References

Ahamed, L. (2009): *Lords of Finance: The Bankers Who Broke the World*. New York: Penguin Books.

Auer, R. A. and Bogdanova, B. (2017): "What Is Driving the Renewed Increase of TARGET2 Balances?," *BIS Quarterly Review*, 22(1): 7–9.

Avdjiev, S., McCauley, R. N., and Shin, H. S. (2016): "Breaking Free of the Triple Coincidence in International Finance," *Economic Policy*, 31(87): 409–451.

Bartorini, C. and Holden, H. (2019): "*Proceeding with Caution: A Survey on Central Bank Digital Currency*," BIS Papers No. 101. Bank for International Settlements, Basel, Switzerland.

Bech, M. and Garratt, R. (2017): "Central Bank Cryptocurrencies," *BIS Quarterly Review*, 22(3): 55–70.

Bell, S. (2001): "The Role of the State and the Hierarchy of Money," *Cambridge Journal of Economics*, 25(2): 149–163.

Bernes, T. A., Jenkins, P., Mehrling, P., and Neilson, D. H. (2014): "*China's Engagement with an Evolving International Monetary System: A Payments Perspective.*" Waterloo, ON, and New York City: Centre for International Governance Innovation and the Institute for New Economic Thinking.

Bieri, D. S. (2000): "*Does a Central Bank's Balance Sheet Really Matter?*" Unpublished mimeograph, Basel, Switzerland.

Bieri, D. S. (2009): "Financial Stability, the Basel Process and the New Geography of Regulation," *Cambridge Journal of Regions, Economy and Society*, 2(2): 303–331.

Bieri, D. S. (2017): "Regulatory Space and the Flow of Funds across the Hierarchy of Money," in R. L. Martin and J. Pollard (Eds.), *Handbook of the Geographies of Money and Finance*, Research Handbooks in Geography Series, Chap. 16, pp. 373–414. Cheltenham, UK: Edward Elgar.

Bieri, D. S. (2018): "Conceptualizing Financial Resilience: The Challenge for Urban Theory," in J. Bohland, J. Harald, and D. Brosnan (Eds.), *The Disaster Resiliency Challenge: Transforming Theory to Action*, pp. 89–111. Springfield, IL: Charles Thomas Publishers.

Bieri, D. S. (2019a): "*After the Great Half-Century: Post-Crisis Economic Geography in Retrospect and Prospect*," Working Paper. School of Public & International Affairs, Virginia Tech, Blacksburg, VA.

Bieri, D. S. (2019b): "*Hamlet without the Prince? August Lösch and How Spatial Economics Abandoned Monetary Analysis*," Working Paper. School of Public & International Affairs, Virginia Tech, Blacksburg, VA.

Bieri, D. S. and Datz, G. (2019): "*Reaping the Digital Dividend: Disruption and Resilience in the Global Financial Sector*," Working Paper. School of Public & International Affairs, Virginia Tech, Blacksburg, VA.

Bindseil, U. and König, P. H. (2012): "TARGET2 and the European Sovereign Debt Crisis," *Kredit und Kapital*, 45(2): 135–174.

BIS. (2019a): "*Large Central Bank Balance Sheets and Market Functioning*," Markets Committee Papers No. 11. Markets Committee, Bank for International Settlements, Basel, Switzerland.

BIS. (2019b): "*Triennial Central Bank Survey: Foreign Exchange Turnover in April 2019.*" Bank for International Settlements, Basel, Switzerland.

BIS. (2020): *"Central Banks and Payments in the Digital Era.' BIS Annual Economic Report*, pp. 67–95. Bank for International Settlements, Basel, Switzerland.

Carstens, A. (2018, December 4): "*Big Tech in Finance and New Challenges for Public Policy*," Keynote Address delivered at *the FT Banking Summit*, London.

Carstens, A. (2019a, March 23): "*The Future of Money and Payments*," 2019 Whitaker Lecture, Central Bank of Ireland.

Carstens, A. (2019b, March 14): "*The New Role of Central Banks*," in *Financial Stability Institute's 20th Anniversary Conference*, Basel, Switzerland.

Caruana, J. (2012): "Why Central Bank Balance Sheets Matter," in *Are Central Bank Balance Sheets in Asia Too Large?*, BIS Paper No. 66. Bank for International Settlements, Basel, Switzerland.

CGFS. (2019): "*Unconventional Monetary Policy Tools: A Cross-country Analysis*," CGFS Papers No. 63. Committee on the Global Financial System, Bank for International Settlements, Basel, Switzerland.

Clark, G. L. (2015): "The Geography of the European Central Bank: Form, Functions and Legitimacy," *Journal of Economic Geography*, 15(5): 855–881.

Cœré, B. (2018): "The Future of Central Bank Money," Speech at *the International Center for Monetary and Banking Studies*, European Central Bank, Frankfurt.

Cohen, B. J. (1998): "Currency Competition and Hierarchy," in B. J. Cohen (Ed.), *The Geography of Money*, 1st edition, pp. 92–118. Ithaca, NY: Cornell University Press.

Cohen, B. J. (2007): "The New Geography of Money," in B. J. Cohen (Ed.), *Global Monetary Governance*, pp. 207–224. London: Routledge.

Cohen, B. J. and Benney, T. M. (2014): "What Does the International Currency System Really Look Like?," *Review of International Political Economy*, 21(5): 1017–1041.

CPMI. (2018): "*Central Bank Digital Currencies*," CPMI Papers No. 174. Committee on Payments and Market Infrastructures, Markets Committee, Bank for International Settlements, Basel, Switzerland.

Crowe, C. and Meade, E. E. (2008): "*Central Bank Independence and Transparency: Evolution and Effectiveness*," IMF Working Paper No. 08/116. International Monetary Fund, Washington, DC.

Davidson, S., di Filippi, P., and Potts, J. (2018): "Blockchains and the Economic Institutions of Capitalism," *Journal of Institutional Economics*, 14(1): 639–658.

Draghi, M. (2018): "*Central Bank Independence*," First Lamfalussy Lecture at the National Bank of Belgium, Brussels.

Dwyer, G. P. (2015): "The Economics of Bitcoin and Similar Private Digital Currencies," *Journal of Financial Stability*, 17(1): 81–91.

Economist. (2018, October 20): "*A Debate about Central-bank Independence Is Overdue*," Finance and Economics Section.

Eichengreen, B., Mehl, A., and Chitu, L. (2017): *How Global Currencies Work: Past, Present, and Future*. Princeton, NJ: Princeton University Press.

El-Erian, M. (2016): *The Only Game in Town: Central Banks, Instability, and Avoiding the Next Collapse*. New York: Random House.

Fels, J. (2016, May): "*The Downside of Central Bank Independence*," PIMCO Macro Perspectives.

French, S., Leyshon, A., and Wainwright, T. (2011). "Financializing Space, Spacing Financialization," *Progress in Human Geography*, 35(6): 798–819.

FSB. (2018): "*Crypto-Assets*," Report to the G20 on Work by the FSB and Standard-Setting Bodies, Financial Stability Board, Basel, Switzerland.

Garriga, A. C. (2016): "Central Bank Independence in the World: A New Data Set," *International Interactions*, 42(5): 849–868.

Goodhart, C. A. E. and Lastra, R. (2018): "Populism and Central Bank Independence," *Open Economies Review*, 29(1): 49–68.

Gurley, J. G. and Shaw, E. S. (1960): *Money in a Theory of Finance*. Washington, DC: Brookings Institution Press.

He, D. and McCauley, R. N. (2012): "Eurodollar Banking and Currency Internationalization," *BIS Quarterly Review*, 17(3): 33–46.

Helleiner, E. (1994): *States and the Reemergence of Global Finance: From Bretton Woods to the 1990s* , Ithaca, NY, and London: Cornell University Press.

Helleiner, E. (2010): "A Bretton Woods Moment? The 2007–2008 Crisis and the Future of Global Finance," *International Affairs*, 86(3): 619–636.

Kirshner, J. (2014): "Same as It Ever Was? Continuity and Change in the International Monetary System," *Review of International Political Economy*, 21(5): 1006–1017.

Langley, P. and Leyshon, A. (2017): "Platform Capitalism: The Intermediation and Capitalization of Digital Economic Circulation," *Finance and Society*, 3(1): 11–31.

Leyshon, A. and Thrift, N. (1997): *Money/Space: Geographies of Monetary Transformation*, London/New York: Routledge.

Lösch, A. (1944): *Die räumliche Ordnung der Wirtschaft*, 2nd edition. Jena: G. Fischer.

Lösch, A. (1949): "Theorie der Währung: Ein Fragment," *Weltwirtschaftliches Archiv*, 62: 35–88.

Lubik, T. A. and Rhodes, K. (2012): "TARGET2: Symptom, Not Cause, of Eurozone Woes," *Federal Reserve Bank of Richmond Economic Brief*, 5(8): 1–5.

McCauley, R. N. (2011): "Internationalizing the Renminbi and China's Financial Development Model," *Council on Foreign Relations Working Paper*, Washington, DC.

Mann, G. (2010): "Hobbes' Redoubt? Toward a Geography of Monetary Policy," *Progress in Human Geography*, 34(5): 601–625.

Mann, G. (2012): "Release the Hounds! The Marvelous Case of Political Economy," in T. J. Barnes, J. A. Peck, and E. Sheppard (Eds.), *The Wiley-Blackwell Companion to Economic Geography*, pp. 61–73. Chichester, UK: John Wiley & Sons, Inc.

Marcuzzo, M. C. (2017): "The "Cambridge" Critique of the Quantity Theory of Money: A Note on How Quantitative Easing Vindicates It," *Journal of Post Keynesian Economics*, 40(2): 260–271.

Martin, R. L. (1999): *Money and the Space Economy*. Chichester: John Wiley & Sons.

Mehrling, P. G. (2011): *The New Lombard Street: How the Fed Became the Dealer of Last Resort*. Princeton, NJ: Princeton University Press.

Mehrling, P. G. (2013): "The Inherent Hierarchy of Money," in *Social Fairness and Economics: Economic Essays in the Spirit of Duncan Foley Festschrift*, Routledge Frontier of Political Economy, pp. 394–404. New York: Routledge.

Mehrling, P. G. (2015): "Elasticity and Discipline in the Global Swap Network," *International Journal of Political Economy*, 44(4): 311–324.

Minsky, H. P. (1977): "The Financial Instability Hypothesis: An Interpretation of Keynes and an Alternative to "Standard" Theory," *Challenge*, 20(1): 20–27.

Minsky, H. P. (1993): "On the Non-Neutrality of Money," *Federal Reserve Bank of New York Quarterly Review*, 18(1): 77–82.

Minsky, H. P. (2008): *Stabilizing an Unstable Economy*. New York: McGraw Hill.

Obstfeld, M., Stambaugh, J. C., and Taylor, A. M. (2010): "Financial Stability, the Trilemma, and International Reserves," *American Economic Journal: Macroeconomics*, 2(1): 57–94.

Perroux, F. (1950a): "The Domination Effect and Modern Economic Theory," *Social Research*, 17(2): 188–206.

Perroux, F. (1950b): "Economic Space: Theory and Application," *Quarterly Journal of Economics*, 64(1): 89–104.

Raskin, M. and Yermack, D. (2017): "Digital Currencies, Decentralized Ledgers, and the Future of Central Banking," in P. Conti-Brown and R. Lastra (Eds.), *Research Handbook on Central Banking*, pp. 474–486. Cheltenham, UK: Edgar Elgar.

Schilling, L. and Uhlig, H. (2019): "Some Simple Bitcoin Economics," *Journal of Monetary Economics*, 107: 16–26.

Subacchi, P. (2010): "Who Is in Control of the International Monetary System?," *International Affairs*, 86(3): 665–680.

Terzi, A. (2005): "International Financial Instability in a World of Currencies Hierarchy," *Working Papers of the Istituto di Economia e Finanza*, Università Cattolica del Sacro Cuore, Dipartimenti e Istituti di Scienze Economiche (DISCE), Milan, Italy.

Thrift, N. and Olds, K. (1996): "Refiguring the Economic in Economic Geography," *Progress in Human Geography*, 20(3): 311–337.

Tucker, P. (2018): *Unelected Power: The Quest for Legitimacy in Central Banking and the Regulatory State*. Princeton, NJ: Princeton University Press.

Wójcik, D., Knight, E., and Pažitka, V. (2018): "What Turns Cities into International Financial Centres? Analysis of Cross-border Investment Banking 2000–2014," *Journal of Economic Geography*, 18(1): 1–33.

23

FINANCIAL GEOGRAPHY, IMBALANCES AND CRISES

Excavating the Spatial Dimensions of Asymmetric Power

Gary Dymski

> [F]inance is still poorly understood in economics and social sciences. Mainstream economists live in the Neverland where space does not matter to finance and finance matters little to economic development. The view of finance in economics became as detached from the social reality of finance, as some financial practices…became detached from society. Social scientists in turn neglected money and finance assuming it was taken care of by economists.
>
> (Dariusz Wójcik, What on earth is financial geography?, March 2017.)[1]

Introduction: Defining the 'Space' for Financial Geography

Dariusz Wójcik's foundational blog-post on the Fingeo website underlines two justifications for enabling financial geography as a distinct field of intellectual inquiry: first, the limitations of mainstream economics in incorporating space; second, the need for spatial analyses that better illuminate the 'social reality of finance' than have economists' models. These provocative assertions imply a bold claim: financial geography can fill important explanatory gaps in economists' accounts of financial phenomena with a spatial dimension. But precisely what intellectual hole is this new area of inquiry hoping to fill? We attempt to answer this question here, and thus to suggest the 'space' of financial geography, by exploring alternative approaches to cross-border financial imbalances and crises in the global economy.[2]

The passage cited above clearly refers to mainstream economists' models, not to that discipline's heterodoxy.[3] There are, to be sure, some overarching methodological critiques of mainstream economic models implicit in the above challenge. Mainstream models sacrifice detail for analytical elegance—they 'mistak[e] beauty for truth', as Krugman (2009) put it in a post-crisis reflection; and their empirical estimates use biased estimators to reach conclusions of dubious validity. Financial economists are among the worst offenders: the efficient-market hypothesis that constitutes the reference point for their analysis was already suspect before the Great Financial Crisis (Shiller, 2003), and certainly lost all credibility after it (Cassidy, 2010).

Certainly, these broad critiques ring true. Mainstream economists themselves have debated these points fiercely for years[4] and, in any case, they could return the favour by pointing out weak points in geographers' methods and models. The argument should be joined, instead, over the explanatory adequacy of mainstream economics' models of financial issues that undeniably have spatial dimensions.

This is the argument taken up here. It unfolds in two steps. The chapter, first, outlines two key components required to build a financial geography consistent with Wójcik's critique.[5] The first step is to avoid the practice, common in economic models, of discussing events distributed across space and time without confronting the fundamental challenges posed by space for social analysis. Drawing on the work of Lefebvre and Soja, we distinguish between the aspatial analysis that characterizes economists' forays into geography, and a spatial analysis capable of exploring the 'social realit[ies]' that, when recognized, expose the limits of 'detached' financial models. The second step is to recognize that hierarchical power is implicitly or explicitly an inescapable component of financial relations that unfold across spatial boundaries.

Cross-border problems at the global level—and, specifically, financial crises and current and capital account imbalances—are used here as a test-ground for evaluating the possible contributions of a financial geography. In undertaking this exploration, we may extend Wójcik's comment that economics is detached from the 'social reality of finance' to include its disengagement from the geo-political realities of finance, as well. Two books on the geography of global finance provide a point of departure for this discussion: *The Geography of Money* by Benjamin J. Cohen and *The Geography of Power* by Richard Peet. The important difference between these works for our purpose lies in their approaches to power. Peet lines up with Lefebvre and Soja, while Cohen conforms with economists' more limited conception.

The chapter goes on to set out iconic economic models of cross-border financial crises and current/capital account imbalances. These illustrate economists' use of their toolkit to explain spatial problems. This exercise highlights what these models permit economists to see, and what they invisibilize. The chapter then sketches out a more spatially aware approach to these two cross-border problems. This shows how financial geography can cover gaps left in economists' explanations with historically informed analyses that open up richer analyses of power and of the 'social reality of finance.

Spatial Analysis and Social Power

We begin by contrasting aspatial and spatial approaches to theoretical analysis. In a recent paper (Dymski and Kaltenbrunner, 2019), Annina Kaltenbrunner and I developed a contrast between aspatial and spatial analyses, along lines parallel to the difference between probabilistic risk and fundamental uncertainty in post-Keynesian economics. We then compared post-Keynesian writing that incorporates place without being spatial to work that has an analytical role for space. Our argument is that bringing 'real space' into Keynesian models that incorporate 'real time' opens a dimension of analysis as fundamental as that of time. When time is 'real', the unforecastable unknown itself affects human decisions in the present; when space is 'real', what can and cannot be done depends on factors beyond physical distance itself.

Paul Davidson, founder of the *Journal of Post Keynesian Economics*, provides an example of aspatial analysis in two of his foundational volumes. In his 1978 book, *Money and the Real World*, Davidson shows why liquidity preference in the face of irreducible uncertainty ('real time') provides a central, irreducible decisional problematic for firms and households. Economic policy-makers' responsibilities, then, include the provision of a stable macroeconomic environment that minimizes disturbances in beliefs—and in the confidence with which they are held; this avoids flights to safety that will erode aggregate demand. Space is not explicitly introduced in that volume. Davidson's next book, *International Money in the Real World* (1982), did incorporate place—specifically, transactions across national borders are linked by exchange rates; the same imperative to maintain stability so as to avoid flights to safety exists, only now it applies to exchange rates in addition to the other macroeconomic variables that policy-makers manage. Kaltenbrunner and I argue that while this brings in place, it is done in an aspatial way.

By contrast, post-Keynesian Sheila Dow (1987) discusses explicitly the ways the domestic banking system can exacerbate differences in the pace of bank lending and economic growth in core and peripheral regions of a national economy, due to credit starvation in the periphery in periods of financial stress. Dow's analysis is spatial because it shows how separation between two points in space has consequences that matter in institutional behaviour and in the outcomes for spatially separated economic agents. Her emphasis on core versus periphery rests on an unstated theory of power differentials. For our purpose, it is important to make these implicit power relations explicit. That is, economic units are disadvantaged in the periphery because of their spatial fixity in a region with fewer resources. Of course, cities and towns, as sites for social relations of production and reproduction, have determinate spatial locations embodying power differentials in wealth, income flows, and capital; but these differentials also apply to firms and households, no matter whether they are located in core or periphery areas, and either constrain or enable their mobility across space. The differential economic power of core and periphery follows as a consequence of the spatial architecture of her analysis: because space matters, differences in levels of financing, liquidity, and growth are linked to spatial location—differential power exists.

So, whereas aspatial analysis may encompass processes or social phenomena that occur across—'in'—space, spatial analysis recognizes that social relations are impacted by social processes that exist simultaneously and are interpenetrated at multiple scales. Here, 'scale' refers to the ordering of economic and social processes according to the extent of the physical realm over which they are defined. This physical realm has an implicit or explicit border, so that processes and entities are contained within it, are outside of it, or cross it. What these entities are depends on the purpose of the analysis. Consider the United States as a bordered space: it contains 50 states, or several geo-physical regions, or so many cities and towns, or megabanks, and so on. Each of the cities within the United States, in turn, has distinct components—neighbourhoods, business establishments, and so on.

From the viewpoint of spatial analysis, empirical tests or theoretical models of cause–effect linkages for any given spatial layer—such as the determinants of national income in a macro-econometric model, in the first case, or the impact of information asymmetries between borrowers and lenders, in the second case—are provisional and incomplete by definition. A spatial analysis of a phenomenon defined for a given spatial layer, by contrast, requires recognizing that phenomenon's spatial context: the social, political, and economic processes at larger spatial scales that may bind or enable its field of action; and the (smaller-scale) processes contained within its borders that contribute to its system state. Households are comprised of individual humans, neighbourhoods contain households, cities contain neighbourhoods, nations contain cities, and global regions contain nations.

No comprehensive model of a phenomenon at any spatial layer is possible: no depiction, no matter how minutely detailed, could capture more than a slice of the interlinkages at work. Constraining and enabling relations are not unidirectional—top-down—but can flow in both directions.[6] And these relations either reinforce or undermine power differentials. This flexible approach to the directions of causation or influence across spatial scales permits instances in which places or people at spatially 'lower' levels may influence 'higher' levels directly.[7]

The notion of spatial analysis set out here has been framed thus far using examples from post-Keynesian economics. Geographers will immediately note that the very conception of space introduced above is located somewhere between the polar representations of space introduced by Lefebvre (1991): at one extreme, the 'strictly geometrical meaning: the idea…of an empty space' (ibid.: 1); at the other, the 'production of space' (or 'social space') (ibid.: 67). Whereas Lefebvre emphasizes space as a site of social production and reproduction, constructed through 'spatial practices' (ibid.: 16–18), the notion of spatial layers mentioned above refers to the size of the physical realm under consideration, from globe to nation to region and city, to the street, or even the house or flat. The point is that these layers contain actors and objects connected by social relations—production processes, loan contracts, ownership claims, and so on—that create dense bonds and ties of 'upward' and 'downward' linkages—rights, obligations, options. The agents identified at any given spatial layer invariably interact with those at other layers. So, spatiality always has to be investigated in any analysis that attempts to push beyond the provisional. In this respect, spatial analysis here is akin to what Soja called 'thirdspace': the '*spatiality* of human life' together with its '*historicality* and *sociality*' (Soja, 1996: 3).

This brings us to the problematic of power.[8] Lefebvre (1991) argues that capital exerts power over the production of space and, indeed, is hegemonic over space. The interest here is in the fact of control, not in the mechanisms by which control is exerted. Control can extend not only over the action that is forced, but over beliefs about that action; as Soja notes:

> 'Hegemonic power…actively *produces and reproduces difference* as a key strategy to create and maintain modes of social and spatial division that are advantageous to its continued empowerment and authority.'
>
> (Soja, 1996: 87)

Economists' and Geographers' Approaches to Power[9]

To paraphrase Wójcik's blog-post, how do economists 'take care of' power, when they consider it? As Lukes and Hearn (2016: 17) put it, 'Economists—although they regularly deploy concepts such as market power and bargaining power—do so unreflectively'. Power involves mechanisms or situations that either shift the distribution of gains and losses between parties, or reduce or eliminate choice on the part of one party to a transaction. Suppose one party to a transaction is mobile, while the other is not; then, as Bowles (2006: 256) puts it, power accrues to the party on the 'short' side of the market.

A key difference between economists' and geographers' definitions of power is that the former view it through the lens of market transactions, whereas the latter view it through the lens of overall social dynamics (of which market transactions form just one part). Mainstream economists, in turn, are tightly bound by the shared convention wherein the preferred explanation is one that requires the fewest deviations from the assumptions required for Walrasian general equilibrium (Dymski, 2014). These economists view this as an Occam's Razor criterion: the simplest explanation is best. However, the point of reference for this criterion is precisely the Walrasian equilibrium—an imaginary state in which supply simultaneously equals demand in every market, because transactions are timelessly executed by fully rational agents operating with complete knowledge, facing zero transaction costs, and trading perfectly divisible goods.[10] This means that spatial analysis, as defined here, is inconsistent with efficient theorizing. Multi-scalar models are much too messy to resolve in any Walrasian way; they are to be avoided, not embraced.[11]

The Geography of Money versus the Geography of Power at the Global Level

These ideas about spatial analysis and power are proposed at a general level. But the subject matter of financial geography is more specific—the social relations surrounding money and finance. And, as noted above, our focus in the following two sections will be on global finance—financial relations at the level of nation-states and multilateral institutions.[12]

As it happens, two foundational texts focusing on the geography of global finance have been written. It will be instructive to compare the two. The older of the two books is Cohen's *The Geography of Money* (1998). In fairness, note that this author's field is international political economy, not geography. This said, this widely known book does contend with the geography of power. The author's stated aim is to achieve 'a new understanding of the spatial organization of currency relations'. Cohen implicitly defines the root of financial power as national governments' 'monopoly control over the issue and management of their own money' (Cohen, 1998: 4). He notes that a 'geography' is now necessary because the:

> currencies increasingly are employed outside their country of origin, penetrating other monetary spaces... [further] power has been redistributed not only between states but, even more important, from states to market forces.... [States'] role in monetary governance has been transformed from Wesphalian monopolist to something more akin to an industrial monopolist. Now authority must be shared with other market agents, in particular the users on the demand side of the market.
>
> (Cohen, 1998: 5)

Cohen's approach to power stays within the 'market power' conception of power favoured in mainstream economics. By contrast, Peet's *The Geography of Power*, which also emphasizes global political economy, takes a far different approach:

> With the term 'geography of power' I refer to the concentration of power in a few spaces that control a world of distant others. My

> argument is that a new kind of economic power system has arrived on the world scene. Power has increasingly been accumulated at the global level by governance institutions—the G7/G8, the European Union, the Bretton Woods Institutions and the United Nations.
>
> (Peet, 2013: 1)

Peet's subsequent discussion focuses, as do those of Lefebvre and Soja, on the fact of control, not mechanisms. He adds to his list as he elaborates on the structures of control: global finance capital, 'the influence of capital markets on the making of global development policy by government and governance institution' (Peet, 2013: 35), and the revolving door between Wall Street and government, among other factors.

Economic Models of Cross-Border Financial Crises and Global Imbalances

As mentioned, Walrasian general equilibrium constitutes the explanatory gold standard for economists. This status derives from the fact that it shows explicitly how decentralized market equilibrium can exist in a setting with rational agents operating with limited wealth endowments. While rarified assumptions are needed to establish a unique equilibrium, mainstream economists view a model as satisfactory to the extent that it identifies how any given outcome can be interpreted as the result of the rational behaviour of individual economic agents. A macroeconomic model describing the aggregated behaviour of economic agents in a given nation is deemed a satisfactory model if it is 'microfounded'—that is, if the economist building that model demonstrates how the claimed aggregate result follows from the rational choices of one or more individual agents in a representative market setting.[13] Behind the formidable mathematical constructions that serve as entry barriers, mainstream economists' criterion for a good model is that it efficiently tells a story about how rational behaviour lies behind observed economic outcomes.[14]

Until the 1980s, this was an unsolved problem in the models guiding economists' understanding of aggregate economic events and outcomes. The macroeconomic model in use since the 1950s, termed the 'neoclassical synthesis' by Paul Samuelson (1955: 255), was far from that standard: it incorporated aggregate variables into macro equilibria while microeconomic markets were simultaneously in persistent disequilibria (Tobin, 1972). As Olivier Blanchard (2017: 99) put it, this 'synthesis' 'suffered from the start from schizophrenia in its relation to microeconomics, which eventually led to a serious crisis from which it is only now re-emerging'.

Oil-price shocks in the 1970s generated price inflation and recession in advanced economies; the rising interest rates that accompanied it triggered disintermediation, leading large advanced economy banks to make loans to commodity rich developing economies, especially in Latin America. This was the death of the synthesis model. Robert Lucas and his associates played the Occam's Razor card: by imposing an assumption that all economic agents held rational expectations, one could 'formalize the economy as if markets were competitive and clearing instantaneously' (Blanchard, 2017: 104). 'New Classical' macroeconomics had arrived. It coincided with the election of Ronald Reagan as US President in 1980, an event that opened the doors to financial deregulation, to the end of inflation-indexed union wage contracts, and to widespread deindustrialization.

A Model of Cross-Border Financial Crisis

Meanwhile, renewed recession and even higher interest rates in the early 1980s led, first Mexico and then other Latin American nations' borrowers to default on their cross-border loans.[15] How, then, could economists explain this while conforming with the 'rational agent' requirement imposed by the macroeconomic reformation? One way to introduce an acceptable deviation from Walrasian equilibrium was to assume the existence of asymmetric information in factor markets. This set up a principal–agent problem between lenders and borrowers: lenders do not know how borrowers will perform once they receive loans, and thus face potential loss from this 'moral hazard'. This became the dominant explanation of the Latin American debt crisis: in the definitive formulation by Eaton, Gersovitz, and Stiglitz (1986), the borrower country, conceptualized as a unitary agent, compares the gains from repaying and from defaulting, and rationally defaults when the penalty for defaulting is set too low. While this model purports to explain loan defaults across space, it is aspatial—space plays no role. Further, instead of conceptualizing the diverse agents interacting at multiple spatial scales prior to default—the companies unable to pay, the governments stepping in, the workers shouldering the resulting higher public debt burden—the borrower is simply conceived as a unitary agent, a 'country'.

This specific model proved durable. Paul Krugman (1998) used this same framework to argue that the root cause of the East Asian crisis of 1997 was rampant moral hazard in Asia's state-controlled banking systems. This same model has been used to characterize the Greek crisis in the Eurozone (Ardagna and Caselli, 2014), as well as the subprime crisis (Calomiris and Haber, 2015).

A Model of the 2008 Crisis and the US Current-Account Deficit

Our second example is a more recent model, developed just after the Great Financial Crisis, which links it to the excessive riskiness of governments in developing economies to the US current account deficit. MIT economist Ricardo Caballero pioneered this model in 2008 and 2009, along with several co-authors. The abstract of a January 2009 NBER working paper with Arvind Krishnamurthy summarizes the principal argument:

> A key structural factor behind this [2008] crisis is the large demand for riskless assets from the rest of the world. In this paper we present a model to show how such demand not only triggered a sharp rise in U.S. asset prices, but also exposed the U.S. financial sector to a downturn by concentrating risk onto its balance sheet. In addition to highlighting the role of capital flows in facilitating the securitization boom, our analysis speaks to the broader issue of global imbalances....capital flows into the U.S. are mostly non-speculative and in search of safety. As a result, the U.S. sells riskless assets to foreigners, and in so doing, it raises the effective leverage of its financial institutions. In other words, as global imbalances rise, the U.S. increasingly specializes in holding its 'toxic waste.'
>
> (Caballero and Krishnamurthy, 2009: 1)

An extended Fall 2008 *Brookings Papers* version of this thesis put it more succinctly: 'The current financial crisis has its origins in global asset scarcity, which led to large capital flows toward the United States and to the creation of asset bubbles that eventually burst' (Caballero et al., 2009: 1). Kathryn Dominguez of the University of Michigan, commenting on this paper, put it more succinctly still: 'This ambitious paper...seeks to explain, in one model, all that is wrong in the global economy. The culprit is underdeveloped financial markets in emerging Asia and the oil producing countries. U.S. fiscal and monetary policies play no role' (Dominguez and Reinhart, 2009: 56). She goes on point out that the model has no banking and no financial sector.

As in the case of the moral-hazard model of debt crises, papers exploring 'safe assets' and their availability or shortage have proliferated. The *Web of Science* counts 302 total topic-word uses of this phrase in the period 1977–2019, of which 260 appear in 2009 or afterwards. Some economic research—especially by authors located in regulatory bodies—has pushed back against this 'shortage of safe asset' argument. BIS economist McCauley (2012: 281), for example, points out that developing economies end up 'supplying safe havens to global investors', as they are forced to draw down their reserves in crisis periods. And four Federal Reserve economists (Bertaut et al., 2012) have shown that European investors, not developing economies, accounted for the vast majority of cross-border asset-backed securities purchases in advance of the 2008 crisis. Nonetheless, Caballero and his co-authors have doubled down, arguing that 'the supply of safe assets has not kept up with global demand. The reason is straightforward: the collective growth rate of the advanced economies that produce safe assets has been lower than the world's growth rate' (Caballero et al., 2017).

Aspatiality in Mainstream Models of Global Processes

More examples of mainstream models of cross-border crises or processes could readily be found; but these two are sufficient to demonstrate the pattern.

First, the moral-hazard and safe-asset explanations rest on thinly specified models with incomplete representations of even the processes they are explaining. The moral-hazard model of the Latin American crisis denotes the borrower as the sovereign—a misrepresentation. The 'borrower' in this model, the sovereign nation, was not originally part of the credit-market transaction with the overseas lender. Financial structures within the borrower countries are ignored, as is the commodity-price decline. Krugman's model argues that crony-capitalism, the provision of credit on the basis of clientelism, explains the 1997 East Asian crisis. This ignores the social and cultural basis on which the successful model of Korea and other East Asian nations was built.[16] But all that is needed to make the moral-hazard argument is a binary principal–agent relationship: and this is justified by the Occam's Razor principal, combined with a willingness to ignore historical and institutional context. The safe-asset argument, in turn, ignores other processes that could explain the systematic inflow of capital into the United States, such as deindustrialization and financial deregulation in the 1980s.

Second, both models are aspatial. While they pertain to agents and instruments separated in space, space plays no role. And because of the aspatiality of the constructs, which places all parties within the model on an imaginary even playing field, power differentials are invisibilized. Third, the multi-scalar social and political context of the nation-states in question receives no attention. Economic dynamics at the regional and global scales larger than the borrower and safe-asset seeking nations are ignored, as are economic and social dynamics within these nations. The fact that cross-border constraints have to be met—and, indeed, are part and parcel of the flows highlighted in the 'search for safe assets' story—is ignored, as are the implications of those cross-border constraints for the net direction of flows (as McCauley's study points out).

An Excavation of Financial Power across Three Dimensions of Global Space

The reason to make space for financial geography in foundational discussions of the political economy of financial processes, outcomes, and systems is that there are different stories to be told than can be reached while working within the confines of models disciplined by concerns about Occam's Razor distancing from general equilibrium. In this section, we will sketch out the bare bones of a spatial analysis encompassing the two global scenarios covered in the preceding section on the occurrence and consequences of sovereign debt crises, and the driving forces of global imbalances. Instead of highlighting developing economy wealth-owners' search for safe assets, we focus attention on structural factors that have led developing-economy sovereign nations to endure financially fragile—risky—structural positions. And, instead of considering why those sovereigns are such reluctant payers, we consider structural pressures compromising their ability to pay.

This change of perspective requires that we shift our analytical focus from the nation-state level, highlighted in the models covered in the previous section, to the global architecture of power in finance. This change in perspective allows us to excavate the spatial logic of financial crises in the neoliberal era by delineating the structural connections between crises in the centres and peripheries of global finance. It also sheds light on the spatial expansion of financialization, and lets us trace the shortage of sovereign nations' 'safe assets' to the role of the United States as global consumer of last resort.

This shift represents, at least, a gesture towards replacing the economic models summarized in earlier with a financial geography. We will indicate the outline of a thicker, multi-scalar representation of the actors involved in contemporary cross-border financial dynamics. The point is to show how location in space affects the options and constraints of nation-states, firms, and households, and thus impacts their freedom of movement and their resources—that is, the multi-scalar shape of power. To organize this journey, we proceed by mapping three linked zones within global financial space. Paralleling the hierarchical ordering of central places in abstract space, this mapping identifies a hierarchical spatial ordering at the global level.

We first delineate the origin and shape of financial power at the global scale, deployed to establish rules of the game; then, we turn to nation-states inside or seeking to enter the global core; and, finally, we consider the situation of nation-states in the periphery. These are, to summarize crudely, zones of control, of dominance, and of submission. Our focus in every one of these spheres is to consider in what power consists—and how accessible forms of power differ.

The reader is advised that this story will not resolve, even if it were more fully elaborated, into one or more counter-models to set against mainstream economists' moral-hazard and safe-asset constructions. To deny that Walrasian general equilibrium is a relevant reference point for historically informed social analytics is not to embrace an alternative Occam's Razor measure. Social power, to pick one reference point, is multi-scalar; within any spatial scale, it is multi-dimensional; and it evolves capriciously through time. So, we have to track its footprints through space-time, without ever being confident that we can track it down.

Power in Finance at the Global Spatial Scale

At the core of the core of global finance, even years after the end of the Bretton Woods system, are the United States and its too-big-to-fail megabanks. This position was achieved via a series of radical policy measures that remade a regulated system that was losing customers to the money and bond markets by the end of the 1970s. Ending geographic segmentation and deregulating banking instruments and product-lines, together with an extended bank merger wave (Dymski, 1999), fed new capital into the financial system and bolstered the importance of the country's money-centre banks. The attempts by these large banks to replace lost customers by opening new markets, including Latin America and East Asia, led, first, to financial crisis (as noted above), but then to the emergence of too-big-to-fail megabanks in the United States from the mid-1980s onwards.

Then, and subsequently, the US Federal Reserve demonstrated the capacity and willingness to support its national-champion banks (the 11 banks declared to be too-big-to-fail in 1984 were consolidated into the 'big four' by 2004; and these were joined by Goldman and Morgan Stanley in 2008). The US Federal Reserve demonstrated its resolve in issuing US dollars as lender-of-last-resort in a series of financial panics from the 1980s onwards: backstopping the money-centre banks that had overlent to Latin America and to the 'oil patch' region of the United States; the 1987 stock-market crash; the Mexican Tesebono crisis of 1994–95; the 1997 East Asian financial crisis; the 1998 Long-Term Capital Management collapse and the 1998 Russian financial crisis; and the bursting of the IT bubble in 2000. Had there been any doubts about whether the US Federal Reserve could, by issuing its own currency as needed, satisfy 'flight to safety' impulses in a crisis-prone world, these were laid to rest.

From 1980 onwards, the current-account deficit grew, and the capital-account surplus along with it. The growing willingness of global markets to hold dollars, encouraged by the Federal Reserve's steady hand, facilitated the steady inflow of capital; this provided financing for the growing federal–government deficit, and consolidated the permanence of the systematic US current account deficit. One element of the macro-financial structure of the global economy in the neoliberal era was in place. It consists of the use by the United States of the 'exorbitant privilege' (Eichengreen, 2011) afforded it by the global dominance of the dollar to sustain and fund large budget and current account deficits. The Treasury liabilities emitted to support these imbalances are held by central banks the world over.

With this stable neoliberal structure came positional power—the ability to define the rules of the game.[17] Once the United States had done so, other countries hastened to deregulate their financial systems. US housing finance was reshaped from a bank-based to a market-based credit system, with mortgages bundled and securitized. Initially only 'plain vanilla' loans were securitized, supported primarily by publicly underwritten government-sponsored enterprises (GSEs). But, by the 1990s, private underwriting enabled the securitization of riskier loans, including subprime mortgages. Changes in the GSE's charters permitted them to buy and hold subprime paper, as well. An interconnected network of shadow banks centred around megabanks and investment banks (Wójcik, 2012) grew to originate, service, and hold these loans. Again, overseas capital flowed in to secure its share. The second element of this architecture of power was thus locked into place: the US–megabank-centred shadow banking system, which has transformed credit markets and either escaped, or challenged, regulatory oversight since the 1980s.

This was, then, the system being put in place when the Latin American crisis unfolded, and that was solidifying its gains when empirical evidence of a hunt for 'safe assets' could first be detected. The global economic consequences of this system are made devastatingly clear in Jane D'Arista's recent volume *All Fall Down* (2018). D'Arista shows that financial globalization creates a global pyramid, under the terms of which only the country at the top can stop panics when financial crises occur. She demonstrates, as suggested here, that problems of unchecked financial flows are reinforced by structural imbalances in current and capital accounts. Further, she shows that the persistent neoliberal era US current account deficit implies that developing-economies' holdings of US liabilities are supporting financialization globally, and increasing pressures that destabilize governments and increase the returns to global financial predation.

So, location in space (and time) matters, in terms of what vector of forces is at work, and with what effect, across the face of the inhabited planet. And, indeed, we may differentiate between different spaces and, in turn, agents' positions within those spaces. If one is not located at the centre of the system, it matters greatly for financial dynamics and differential power both whether one is located in the core or periphery and, in turn, where one is positioned, whether in the core or periphery.

Nation-States in the Global Financial Core

Beyond the hegemonic dollar, which nations are in the global financial core? Cohen observes that governments that maintain 'monetary monopoly' over payments systems accrue four powers: 'political symbolism, seignorage, macroeconomic management, and insulation from external influence' (1998: 119). Cohen's monetary monopoly, however, establishes only territorial integrity, not the viability of national finance beyond its own boundaries.

There are three possible projections of financial power outside a nation's own boundaries. The first is the ability to emit a currency that other nation-states willingly hold. The test of this lies in global currency reserve holdings. The International Monetary Fund (IMF) lists the holdings of only eight nations' currencies in its published registry; so this is a small club. Figure 23.1 shows the global holdings of the US dollar on its right-hand axis, and those of the next four global currencies by value held on the left-hand axis. Dollar holdings far exceed those of the Euro, which, in turn, vastly outstrip those of the UK pound and Japanese yen, with Chinese renminbi holdings even farther behind. Beyond the even smaller global reserve holdings of Canadian and Australian dollars, and of Swiss francs, this club has no other members.

The second power arises when a given nation's currency is used in contracts outside its own borders. An example arises when one nation's currency is used to finance investment outside its national borders. When this is done recurrently, this nation's legal practices and business service firms can shape the cross-border financial processes in which they participate. Kaltenbrunner and

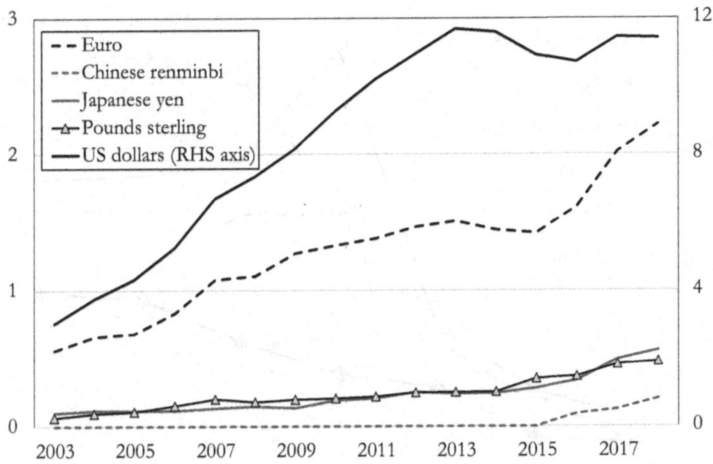

Figure 23.1 Reserve currency holdings, 2003–18, in US$ trillion

Source: International Monetary Fund.

Lysandrou (2017) show that virtually no nations' currencies now challenge the dominance of the US dollar in this regard. A third power is the capacity to provide third-party financial services to foreign buyers. The best example here is the City of London, whose foreign-currency and offshore bond markets are world leaders, almost a century after the British pound lost its central place in the global monetary system.

Projections of any of these three cross-border powers is sufficient to qualify a nation for the global financial core. Membership in the core entails two benefits. First, safety is guaranteed: nations in the core maintain very low reserves; they do not fear systematic speculative attack—speculators know their central banks can emit domestic money (reserves) at will, without reserve. Reserve totals are not publicly reported by the International Monetary Fund; but Howmuch.net reported in 2018 that, respectively, the United States, Germany, France, and the United Kingdom—home nations of aggressive, globally active megabanks that have attracted the close scrutiny of the Financial Stability Board—held reserves of US$44 billion, US$37 billion, US$40 billion, and US$123 billion. By contrast, Brazil held US$358 billion, Mexico US$170 billion, and Korea US$385 billion.[18] The second benefit to core nations is that, precisely because they are immune to speculative attack, they can host financial firms that can take stakes in other nations' systems and/or engage in zero-sum speculation with external parties. This can be considered offensive power. Figure 23.2 shows how the largest banks in six core countries have grown from being uniformly less than 20% of home nation GDP to multiples of that relative size.[19]

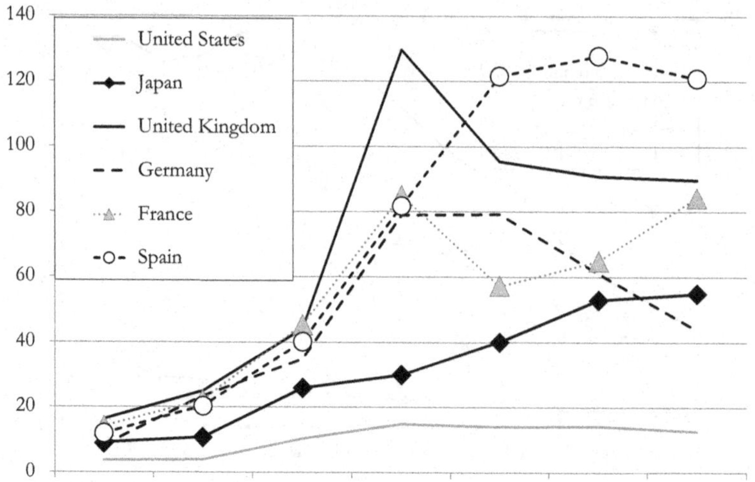

Figure 23.2 Assets of largest bank as percentage of home-nation GDP (measured in US$), selected years, 1989–2018

Key: This figure lists the size of the largest banking firm in each of the listed nations, as a percentage of those nations' GDP, for selected years.

Data sources: GDP–International Monetary Fund. Bank size: *Business Week* magazine (1989–2004), *Forbes* (2008–18).

Nation-States in the Global Financial Periphery

A nation is classified in the global financial periphery when it does not maintain 'monetary monopoly' over its own territory and/or when it lacks any of the three cross-border powers detailed above. To fail both the former and latter tests, of course, puts a nation in the deep core of the periphery. A nation that lacks any cross-border power but retains monetary monopoly is vulnerable to attack by financial firms based in nations in the financial core. Further, such a nation is more vulnerable to 'sudden stop' crises (Dymski, 2019), especially if it depends on a flow of financing from external lenders.

The asymmetric power of core nations in relation to peripheral nations—immunity from speculative attack—constitutes a severe danger for the latter. Countries whose currencies have begun to enter open global markets are under the greatest threat. To offset that disadvantage, a peripheral country may take action by enhancing its defensive power. Defensive power can take several forms. One is to impose inward capital controls. This move may be ruled out by prior action put in place after IMF intervention in the wake of a previous financial crisis. A second form of defensive power is the build-up of excess stocks of foreign-currency reserves.[20]

An examination of the cross-border accounts of many developing economies, including India and Brazil, reveals that, despite having current account

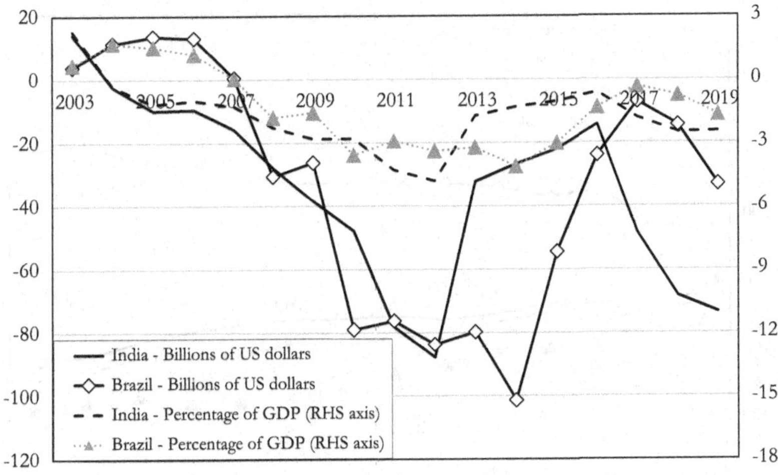

Figure 23.3 Two measures of current-account balance, 2003–19, India and Brazil

Source: International Monetary Fund.

deficits, these countries are overborrowing so as to build up their stocks of currency reserves. Protection from attack—the power to be left alone—is a key motive for many developing nations. To see this graphically, first, consider Figure 23.3, which shows that both countries' current account balances shifted from positive to negative in the global financial crisis period, recovering somewhat thereafter. The inescapable logic of cross-border balances is that a nation's current account deficits (resulting in net outflows of domestic currency chasing foreign goods and services) must be financed either by an inflow of foreigners' savings (such as foreign direct investment), or by spending down its stock of foreign reserves. The implication of Figure 23.3 is thus that foreign savings should be increasing or reserves declining, or both.

Figures 23.4 and 23.5 provide the evidence for the capital-flow side of this equation by summarizing the net investment position of these two countries in the same time frame. The net investment position is positive when a nation's wealth-owners' net purchases of foreign assets exceeds foreigners' purchases of domestic assets (and vice versa). So, the net investment position should be negative for both India (Figure 23.4) and Brazil (Figure 23.5). It is, in both cases, for three categories of net investment (portfolio, direct, and other). The anomaly is that, in both countries, reserve assets held rise systematically throughout the 2005–18 period depicted. As noted, reserves should remain constant, or be reduced when the current account balance is negative. But both countries have, to the contrary, amassed systematically more holdings of foreign currencies. They have, in effect, over-borrowed so as to protect themselves from speculation.

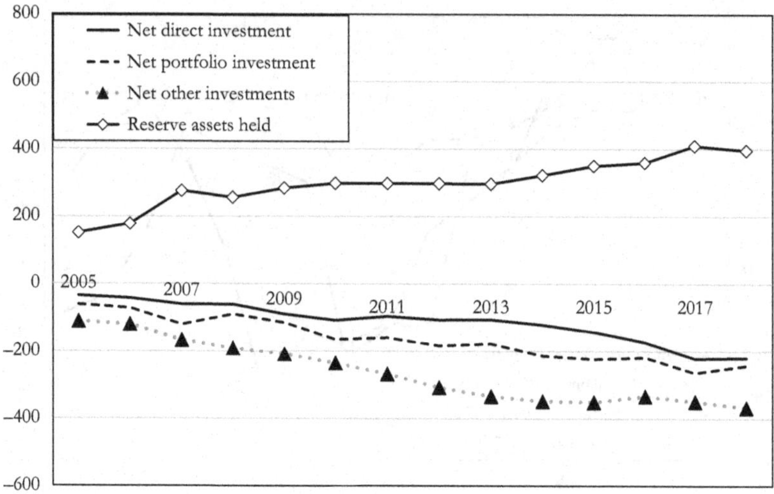

Figure 23.4 Net international investment position, India, 2005–18 (US$ billion)

Source: International Monetary Fund.

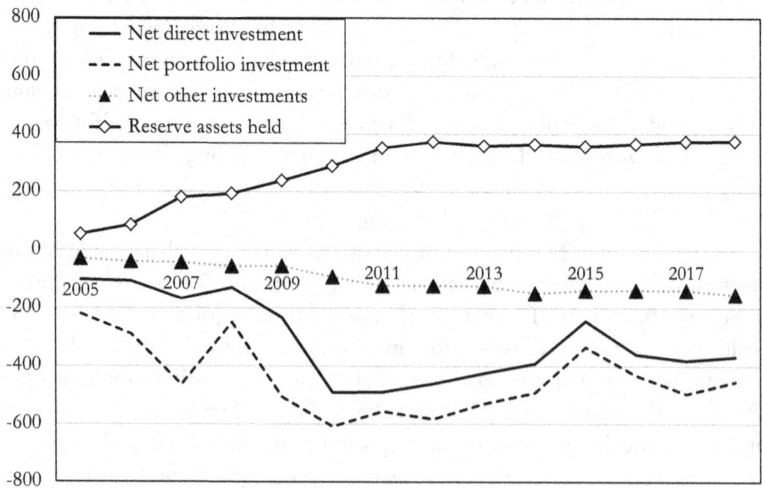

Figure 23.5 Net international investment position, Brazil, 2005–18 (US$ billion)

Source: International Monetary Fund.

Conclusion: The Consequences of Global Financial Asymmetries

This chapter has argued for the importance of establishing a financial geography that can offer counter-analyses to mainstream economists' aspatial models of spatial processes. Comparing economists' models of imbalances and crises with spatial analyses focused on asymmetrically distributed economic power illustrates why financial geography is needed. Economists' models are disciplined by their fealty to rational behaviour and to their own version of Occam's Razor. These pre-commitments make it difficult or impossible to introduce important institutional and historical elements into their models; as we have seen, this often leads to models that are descriptively wrong or partial, and that ignore history rather than heeding its lessons.

This pattern of ignoring history while prioritizing modelling conventions is especially consequential in the period after the 2008 crisis. Dymski (2018) has shown that, in the post-crisis period, austerity macroeconomic policies have been a key factor in reversing the overall current and capital account positions of advanced and developing nations. Before the crisis, the developing nations had a current account surplus, and advanced nations a current account deficit. This implies that developing nations' economic growth was supported, in part, by a systematic trade surplus with advanced nations. After the crisis, however, these positions have reversed: now, developing countries have an overall current account deficit, and advanced countries a surplus. This means developing countries, as a bloc, became systematically indebted to advanced countries after the crisis. The Euro area countries account for virtually all of the increase in the current account surplus of the advanced economies. While trade and capital flows between countries and global regions have many determinants, the Euro area's adoption of macroeconomic austerity as of mid-2009 is undoubtedly a major factor in this global reversal.

The failure of the 'safe assets' literature to examine the historical emergence of the US current account deficit (and its role in capital inflows 'seeking safe assets' there), or to undertake holistic evaluations of the links between macroeconomic flows and cross-border imbalances, has led to a profoundly mistaken understanding of what is driving these processes. Economists' models of developing-economy debt crises have failed even to acknowledge the interconnections between global commodity prices, growth, banking competition, and developing-country debt burdens.

In the absence of an effective counter-narrative, the consequences of global financial power go unremarked, even unseen. Financial geography can fill this gap. Spatialized representations of power can capture some of the key financial dynamics of our time. Space is not unitary, and does not follow one repeating pattern. The distribution of agents across space, in the context of centralized systems of control, allocation, and extraction, means that societies spread across space encompass tableaus of exploitation, at many different spatial scales—the local, the regional, the national, the global. Differentials of financial power and of the distribution of income flows and wealth are at work at each of these levels. These points are, in many cases, already well-known to geographers; however, they are absent in the narratives and models of economics that drive discussions of policy alternatives. Efforts to redress the imbalance of global spatial power must begin with efforts to rebalance the governing analyses of its drivers and consequences.

Notes

1 Accessed on 17 November 2019 at http://www.fingeo.net/what-on-earth -is-financial-geography/.

2 Sokol (2013) both synthesizes the emerging literature on financial geography and closely parallels Wójcik's statement in favour of a more grounded, relevant financial geography. See also Seo (2011).

3 Mainstream economic models use, as an analytical reference point, market equilibria in which all agents are fully rational—that is, they use all available information and resources to reach the highest feasible levels of utility. The term 'heterodox' refers to economic models that do not accept this criterion. Heterodox models, while diverse, uniformly reject the equilibria achieved by rational agents as an analytical standard; some prioritize the importance of economic class; others, irreducible uncertainty about the future; still others, institutional features of society, such as social conventions or power, that can radically restrict the realm of choice.

4 On theoretical models, see Tobin (1980) and Solow (2018); on econometric methods, see Leamer (1983) and Ziliak and McCloskey (2008).

5 The incompleteness of this chapter's references to literatures in geography and other social sciences should be acknowledged at the outset; it reflects the limits of the author's knowledge, not his intent.

6 This is a key point in the literature on global assemblages (Collier and Ong, 2005; Sassen, 2006).

7 One important example is the advocacy of region- and urban-led national economic policies; see Katz (2000), Katz and Bradley (2014), Acuto (2016), and Rapoport, Acuto, and Grcheva (2019).

8 See also Allen (2011).

9 In this section, and elsewhere in this paper, the term 'economics' or 'economists' implicitly refers to mainstream economics or economists; see footnote 2.

10 The classic exposition of this model is by Debreu (1959).

11 At the heart of the workhorse model of contemporary mainstream macroeconomics, the dynamic stochastic general-equilibrium model, is a rational, infinitely lived representative agent (Woodford, 2003).

12 At the subnational level, spatial analytics of the subprime crisis of 2008 were described in many papers consistent with the criteria suggested above for financial geography. Examples are Ashton (2009), Hernandez (2009), and Fields (2017).

13 See Rizvi (2013). Roger Farmer (1993, p. 1) summarized this transition as follows: 'the future of macroeconomics is as a branch of applied general equilibrium theory'.

14 McCloskey (1983) made this point long ago, and it remains valid. The new behavioural economics only reinforces this emphasis on locating the logic of transacting individual agents at the centre of every mainstream economic explanation.

15 Dymski (2019) provides a comprehensive review of international financial crises since 1980.
16 When Krugman wrote his paper in January 1998, he would have had access to two detailed studies of the success of the Korean growth model (Amsden, 1989; Kim, 1997) that would suggest very different stylized facts than those embedded in his moral-hazard model.
17 A nation can be considered fully hegemonic in financial terms when its currency establishes the level at which all other currencies in the global system exchange, and when its rules for financial-market activity set the standard for all other nations' rules. A country is partially hegemonic when it defines rules of financial market activity that other nations imitate or follow.
18 See https://www.visualcapitalist.com/countries-most-foreign-currency-reserves/ and https://www.howmuch.net. These sites were accessed on 12 February 2020.
19 The United States provides the sole exception here. But this is due to the large relative scale of the United States compared to the other economies in the global core. When measured in asset size, US banks are consistently the largest or near-largest in the world.
20 ECB (2006) defines such holdings as indicating a 'precautionary motive'; but this term is ambiguous, insofar as it could refer to a nation's need for currency because of its own miscalculations (as though one of its export goods' prices collapsed), or due to an external attack (or a sudden withdrawal of external lending).

References

Acuto, M. (2016). *Are Cities the New Global Leaders?* Oxford: Polity Press.

Allen, J. (2011). Topological twists. *Dialogues in Human Geography*, 1(3), pp. 283–298.

Amsden, A.H. (1989). *Asia's Next Giant: South Korea and Late Industrialization.* New York: Oxford University Press.

Ardagna, S. and Caselli, F. (2014). The political economy of the Greek debt crisis: A tale of two bailouts. *American Economic Journal: Macroeconomics*, 6(4), pp. 291–323. [online] Available at: https://personal.lse.ac.uk/casellif/papers/greece.pdf [Accessed November 30, 2019].

Ashton, P. (2009). An appetite for yield: The anatomy of the subprime mortgage crisis. *Environment and Planning A: Economy and Space*, 41(6), pp. 1420–1441.

Bertaut, C., DeMarco, L.P., Kamin, S., and Tryon, R. (2012). ABS inflows to the United States and the global financial crisis. *Journal of International Economics*, 88(2), pp. 219–234.

Blanchard, O. (2017). *Neoclassical Synthesis. New Palgrave Dictionary of Economics*. London: Palgrave-Macmillan.

Bowles, S. (2006). *Microeconomics: Behavior, Institutions, and Evolution*. Princeton, NJ: Princeton University Press.

Caballero, R.J. and Krishnamurthy, A. (2009). Global imbalances and financial fragility. *American Economic Review*, 99(2), pp. 584–588.

Caballero, R.J., Farhi, E., and Gourinchas, P.-O. (2009). Financial crash, commodity prices, and global imbalances. *Brookings Papers on Economic Activity*, 2008(2), pp. 1–55.

Caballero, R.J., Farhi, E., and Gourinchas, P.-O. (2017). The safe assets shortage conundrum. *Journal of Economic Perspectives*, 31(3), pp. 29–46. [online] Available at: https://escholarship.org/uc/item/8h3182xb [Accessed April 26, 2019].

Calomiris, C.W. and Haber, S. (2015). *Fragile by Design: The Political Origins of Banking Crises and Scarce Credit*. Princeton, NJ/Oxford: Princeton University Press.

Cassidy, J.C. (2010). *How Markets Fail: The Logic of Economic Calamities*. New York: Picador/Farrar, Straus and Giroux.

Cohen, B.J. (1998). *The Geography of Money*. Ithaca, NY/London: Cornell University Press.
Collier, S.J. and Ong, A. (2005). *Global Assemblages : Technology, Politics, and Ethics as Anthropological Problems*. Oxford: Blackwell Publishing.
D'arista, J.W. (2018). *All Fall Down: Debt, Deregulation and Financial Crises*. Cheltenham, UK: Edward Elgar Publishing.
Davidson, P. (1982). *International Money in the Real World*. New York: John Wiley & Sons.
Debreu, G. (1959). *Theory of Value: An Axiomatic Analysis of Economic Equilibrium*. London: Yale University Press.
Dominguez, K.M. and Reinhart, C.M. (2009). Comments and discussion. *Brookings Papers on Economic Activity*, 2008(2), pp. 56–60.
Dow, S.C. (1987). The treatment of money in regional economics. *Journal of Regional Science*, 27(1), pp. 13–24.
Dymski, G.A. (1999). *The Bank Merger Wave: The Economic Causes and Social Consequences of Financial Consolidation*. Armonk, NY, and London: M.E. Sharpe.
Dymski, G.A. (2014). The neoclassical sink and the heterodox spiral: Political divides and lines of communication in economics. *Review of Keynesian Economics*, 2(1), pp. 1–19.
Dymski, G.A. (2018). Developing economies, international financial integration, and sustainable development. *Paper delivered at the 2nd Session of the Debt and Development Conference of the United Nations Conference on Trade and Development*, Palais des Nations, Geneva, November 7–9, 2018.
Dymski, G.A. (2019). Post-war international debt crises and their transformation. In: J. Michie, ed., *Handbook of Globalization*. Cheltenham, UK: Edward Elgar, pp. 103–118.
Dymski, G.A. and Kaltenbrunner, A. (2019). Space in Post-Keynesian monetary economics: An exploration of the literature. In: B. Bonizzi, A. Kaltenbrunner, and R. Ramos, eds., *Emerging Economies and the Global Financial System: Post-Keynesian Analysis*. London: Routledge.
Eichengreen, B. (2011). *Exorbitant Privilege: The Rise and Fall of the Dollar and the Future of the International Monetary System*. New York: Oxford University.
European Central Bank (ECB). (2006). The accumulation of foreign reserves. *Occasional Paper Series*, 43, authored by an International Relations Committee Task Force. Frankfurt: European Central Bank.
Farmer, R.E.A. (1993). *The Macroeconomics of Self-Fulfilling Prophecies*. Cambridge, MA: MIT Press.
Fields, D. (2017). Constructing a new asset class: Property-led financial accumulation after the crisis. *Economic Geography*, 94(2), pp. 118–140.
Hernandez, J. (2009). Redlining revisited: Mortgage lending patterns in Sacramento 1930–2004. *International Journal of Urban and Regional Research*, 33(2), pp. 291–313. [online] Available at: https://www.linesbetweenus.org/sites/linesbetweenus.org/files/u5/redlining_revisited.pdf [Accessed February 8, 2019].
Kaltenbrunner, A. and Lysandrou, P. (2017). The US dollar's continuing hegemony as an international currency: A double-matrix analysis. *Development and Change*, 48(4), pp. 663–691.
Katz, B. (2000). *Reflections on Regionalism*. Washington, DC: Brookings Institution Press.
Katz, B. and Bradley, J. (2014). *The Metropolitan Revolution: How Cities and Metros Are Fixing Our Broken Politics and Fragile Economy*. Washington, DC: Brookings Institution Press.
Kim, E.M. (1997). *Big Business, Strong State: Collusion and Conflict in South Korean Development, 1961–1990*. Albany, NY: State University of New York Press.
Krugman, P. (1998). What Happened to Asia? Working Paper, MIT Department of Economics.
Krugman, P. (2009, September 2). How did economists get it so wrong? *New York Times* SM36-43.

Leamer, E. (1983). Lets take the con out of econometrics. *American Economic Review*, 73(1), pp. 31–43.

Lefebvre, H. (1991). *The Production of Space*. London: Blackwell.

Lukes, S. and Hearn, J. (2016). Power and economics. In: R. Skidelsky and N. Craig, eds., *Who Runs the Economy? The Role of Power in Economics*. London: Palgrave Macmillan, pp. 17–30.

McCauley, R.N. (2012). Risk-on/risk-off, capital flows, leverage, and safe assets. *Public Policy Review, Policy Research Institute, Ministry of Finance Japan*, 8(3), pp. 281–298.

McCloskey, D.N. (1983). The rhetoric of economics. *Journal of Economic Literature*, 21(2), pp. 481–517.

Peet, R. (2013). *The Geography of Power: Making Global Economic Policy*. London: Zed Books.

Rapoport, E., Acuto, M., and Grcheva, L. (2019). *Leading Cities: A Global Review of City Leadership*. London: Ucl Press.

Rizvi, A. (2013). On the microfoundations of macroeconomics. In: G. Harcourt and P. Kriesler, eds., *Oxford Handbook of Post-Keynesian Economics*, Volume 2: Critiques and Methodology. Oxford: Oxford University Press.

Samuelson, P.A. (1955). *Economics, an Introductory Analysis. Instructor's Manual and Answer Key to Student Workbook*. New York: McGraw-Hill.

Sassen, S. (2006). *Territory, Authority, Rights: From Medieval to Global Assemblages*. Princeton, NJ: Princeton University Press.

Seo, B. (2011). Geographies of Finance: Centers, Flows, and Relations. *Hitsosubashi Journal of Economics*, 52(1), pp. 69–86.

Shiller, R.J. (2003). From efficient markets theory to behavioral finance. *Journal of Economic Perspectives*, 17(1), pp. 83–104.

Soja, E.W. (1996). *Thirdspace: Journeys to Los Angeles and Other Real-and-Imagined Places*. Oxford: Blackwell.

Sokol, M. (2013). Towards a "newer" economic geography? Injecting finance and financialisation into economic geographies. *Cambridge Journal of Regions, Economy and Society*, 6(3), pp. 501–515.

Solow, R. (2018). A theory is a sometime thing. *Review of Keynesian Economics*, 6(4), pp. 421–424.

Tobin, J. (1972). Inflation and unemployment. *American Economic Review*, 62(1/2), pp. 460–463.

Tobin, J. (1980). Discussion. In: J. Kareken and N. Wallace, eds., *Models of Monetary Economics*. Minneapolis, MI: Federal Reserve Bank of Minneapolis, pp. 83–90.

Wójcik, D. (2012). The end of Investment Bank capitalism? An economic ceography of financial jobs and power. *Economic Geography*, 88(4), pp. 345–368.

Woodford, M. (2003). *Interest and Prices: Foundations of a Theory of Monetary Prices*. Princeton, NJ/Oxford: Princeton University Press.

Ziliak, S.T. and McCloskey, D.N. (2008). *The Cult of Statistical Significance: How the Standard Error Costs Us Jobs, Justice, and Lives*. Ann Arbor, MI: University of Michigan Press.

24

CREDIT RATING AGENCIES IN THE ERA OF NEOLIBERAL CAPITALISM

Stefanos Ioannou

Introduction

Credit rating agencies (CRAs) have emerged as a core financial institution in neoliberal capitalism. In assessing the creditworthiness of firms and governments around the globe, these agencies determine the cost and sustainability of debt financing, and shape the norms of corporate and public governance. Along with global megabanks, they are some of the most significant players hiding behind the otherwise amorphous veil of 'financial markets'. Furthermore, in their locational clustering in global financial centres—particularly New York City (NYC)—they provide a lucid manifestation of the influence of these centres on the economic fortunes of the rest of the world.

Despite an abundance of rating agencies around the world, there are three truly global CRAs. These are Standard & Poor's, Moody's, and Fitch. All three are owned by US conglomerates whose broader scope also involves ownership and administration of stock market indices, business data analytics, and media. Effectively, the three CRAs rate everything that can be rated, from simple bonds to complex financial products. For the greater part of this chapter, our discussion is centred around these three agencies.

There are various critiques that have been put forward against CRAs. Most notably, these include the well-documented conflict of interest between these agencies and the banks whose financial instruments they were rating in the build-up of the 2007/08 crisis; the identification of procyclical and culturally-biased behaviour; and their authoritative positioning regarding rated borrowers. The latter is a particularly important concern for public governance, as it connects with the degrees of freedom available to local and national governments for exercising social and economic policy.

The rest of this chapter proceeds as follows. In the next section, we outline the history and current landscape of the credit ratings market; we also provide some detailed commentary over selected stylized facts of the big-three CRAs. The chapter goes on to describe the main aspects of credit rating methodology, and then discusses the macroeconomic effects of sovereign ratings in detail and presents the geographical distribution of these ratings around the globe. Next, the chapter provides a thorough discussion over the lines of critique developed towards the CRAs. In the last section, we conclude and reflect on policy implications.

History and Current Landscape

The history of CRAs goes back more than one hundred years. In 1909, John Moody, founder of Moody's Investors Service (also known as Moody's), published the first catalogue of credit ratings for bonds of railroad companies in the United States (Sylla, 2002; White, 2013). As pointed out by Sylla and White, John Moody's focus on US railroads was not a coincidence but, rather, indicative of the fact that the US bond market was by far the largest at the time. Similarly, railroad companies were some of the largest in the United States and in a phase of rapid growth. In 1916, the Poor's Publishing Company entered the US ratings business, followed by the Standard Statistics Company in 1922 (the two merged in 1941 to form Standard & Poor's; hereafter S&P). Fitch published their first ratings in 1924, also in the United States.

Following the crisis of 1929, credit ratings gained in prominence. The early game-changer was the consideration of ratings in prudential banking regulation in the 1930s—particularly the 1936 prohibition of banks to invest in 'speculative-grade' bonds (White, 2013). In the subsequent decades, the use of ratings became even more widespread as regulators adopted them for setting capital requirements for insurance companies, pension funds, and investment banks. A further milestone was the designation of Nationally Recognized Statistical Rating Organizations (NRSROs) by the Securities and Exchanges Commission (SEC) in 1975 and, thus, the certification of a small group of CRAs.

Credit ratings were mostly a US business up until the 1970s. This changed with the collapse of the Bretton Woods system and the start of the era of financial globalization (Sylla, 2002). An increasing number of private corporations and sovereign states started moving away from traditional bank lending and became issuers of bonds in the international bond market. At the same time, the increase in geographical distance between investors and their investments amplified the need for standardized and trustworthy information. Subsequently, as with the earlier development in the United States, ratings came to be incorporated into domestic and global financial regulations.

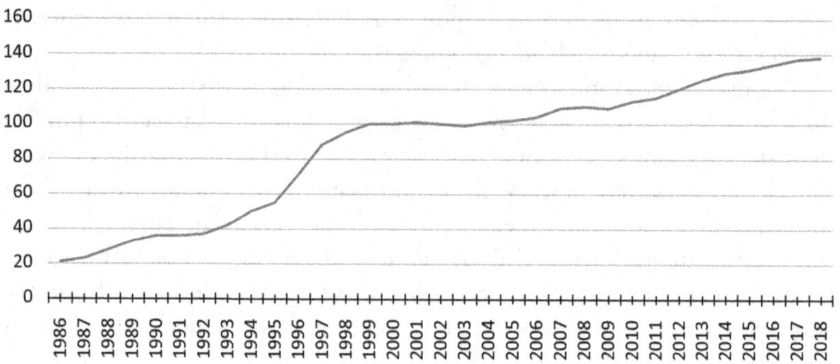

Figure 24.1 Number of countries rated by Moody's

Source: Moody's (2019c).

All these developments led to a substantial increase in the size and scope of CRAs. Sylla (2002: 24), for example, writes that S&P's group of industrial analysts grew from 30 people in 1980 to 800 in 1995, with its total staff amounting to 1,200 employees in that year. He also documents a similar surge for Moody's. Another illuminating aspect is the increase in the number of rated issuers. Figure 24.1 provides a glimpse of such evidence, with a focus on the number of countries rated by Moody's. As displayed in the Figure 24.1, whereas in 1986 there were 21 sovereign governments with a Moody's rating, by 2018 the number had risen to 138. The second half of the 1990s is the period with the steepest hike in rating subscriptions.

The IMF (2010) reports more than 70 CRAs around the world. Besides the United States, some indicative countries with their own rating agencies are Russia, Turkey, Colombia, India, and China. Many of those CRAs focus on domestic activities. In addition, some CRAs specialize in specific industries. A.M. Best, for example, is a US rating agency that specializes in insurance companies (SEC, 2018). Similarly, Wiserfunding is a European FinTech CRA specializing in rating small and medium-sized enterprises, usually unrated by the big CRAs.[1] Currently, 9 CRAs are officially recognized as NRSROs by the SEC in the United States.[2] Moreover, 27 agencies are registered in the European Union (ESMA, 2019).

Having said this, S&P, Moody's, and Fitch remain the three dominant and truly global CRAs. Practically, these agencies rate anything that can be rated, from simple bonds of private firms and the public sector, to structured financial instruments, such as asset backed securities. According to the most recent report of the SEC on NRSROs (SEC, 2018), their combined global share of revenues has been systematically close to 94%.[3] Of the total number of outstanding ratings across all sectors (around 2.1 million), 49% are issued by S&P (SEC, 2018). Moody's is the second largest issuer, with a share of 33%, and Fitch the third, with a share close to 14%.

To complete this sub-section, it is worth adding a few notes on China. As discussed in Kennedy (2019), China initiated the effort to build a modern financial system in the early 1990s. Part of that was also to establish its own CRAs. Five such CRAs are reported on IMF (2010) list. Nonetheless, these rating agencies have been largely unimportant in the eyes of foreign and Chinese investors (Kennedy, 2019; Wildau, 2018). There are two main reasons for this. First, as pointed out by Kennedy (2019), it is often the case that the economic interventions by the Chinese state implicitly guarantee the creditworthiness of domestic entities. Second, Chinese CRAs have openly been associated with concerns regarding corruption and moral hazard. The most notable example here is the case of Dagong, one of the biggest Chinese CRAs, which, in 2018, was accused of over-rating Chinese issuers. Dagong was subsequently suspended and taken over by a state-owned investment company (Hornby, 2019; Wildau, 2018).

Contemporary Characteristics of the Big-3

We provide here an overview of some indicative stylized facts for each of the big-three CRAs. Our focus is on the corporate ownership, office location, and revenues (with some variation depending on data availability).

To begin with, S&P (formally labelled 'S&P Global Ratings') is owned by S&P Global, the latter being previously known as McGraw-Hill Financial.[4] Outside the rating subsidiary, the parent company also owns a business analytics platform named S&P Global Market Intelligence and has a majority stake (about 70%) in S&P Dow Jones Indices, the operator of S&P500 and the Dow Jones Industrial Average. Until 2013, it was also the owner of the educational publisher McGraw-Hill. Of its current lines of activity, the ratings business is the most lucrative. In 2018, of a total gross revenue of US$6,258 million, ratings accounted for US$2,883 million (S&P, 2019). The market intelligence platform was the second largest business, with a gross revenue of US$1,833 million.

S&P Global's headquarters are in Lower Manhattan, NYC. The conglomerate has offices in 36 locations in 26 countries, mostly in cities classified as global financial centres (Yeandle and Wardle, 2019). Some of the other US cities where S&P Global's offices can be found are Chicago, Boston, and San Francisco (Table 24.1). Five offices are registered in the rest of the Americas (e.g., Buenos Aires, São Paulo) and nine in Europe (e.g., London, Paris). Another nine are located in Asia, with four in China and two in India. In total, S&P Global employs about 21,000 people.

Moody's Investors Service is owned by Moody's Corporation. The latter is also the owner of the analytics platform Bureau van Dijk (operator of the Orbis database). In 2018, Moody's Corporation registered a total revenue of US$4,442.7 million (Moody's, 2019a). As with S&P, the majority of these revenues came from its credit ratings operations (US$2,693.4 million). As reported in the company's annual statement, the most profitable category of ratings has

Table 24.1 Office locations of S&P, Moody's, and Fitch

	S&P	*Moody's*	*Fitch*
United States	New York City (HQ), Boston MA, Chicago IL, Dallas TX, San Francisco CA, Centennial CO, Charlottesville VA	New York City (HQ), Atlanta GA, Boston MA, Chicago IL, Dallas TX, San Francisco CA	New York City (HQ), Austin TX, Chicago IL, San Francisco CA
Europe	London, Paris, Frankfurt, Munich, Dublin, Milan, Warsaw, Madrid, Stockholm, Moscow	London, Paris, Frankfurt, Milan, Prague, Limassol, Warsaw, Madrid, Stockholm, Moscow	London (HQ), Paris, Frankfurt, Milan, Barcelona, Warsaw, Madrid, Stockholm, Moscow
Rest of the Americas	Toronto, Buenos Aires, Mexico City, São Paolo, Bogota	Toronto, Buenos Aires, Mexico City, São Paolo	Toronto, Buenos Aires, Mexico City, São Paolo, Bogotà, Lima, Monterrey, Montevideo, Rio de Janeiro, San José (Costa Rica), San Salvador (El Salvador), Santiago (Chile), Santo Domingo (Dominican Republic)
China	Beijing, Shanghai, Hong Kong	Beijing, Shanghai, Hong Kong	Beijing, Shanghai, Hong Kong
Rest of Asia & Middle East	Mumbai, Tokyo, Singapore, Seoul, Taiwan, Tel Aviv, Dubai	Mumbai, Tokyo, Singapore, Seoul, Bangalore, Gurgaon (India), Riyadh, Dubai	Mumbai, Tokyo, Singapore, Seoul, Taiwan, Jakarta, Colombo (Sri Lanka), Riyadh, Dubai
Africa	Johannesburg	Johannesburg	Johannesburg
Oceania	Sydney, Melbourne	Sydney	Sydney

Source: Author's elaboration, based on Moody's, Fitch, and https://craft.co websites (the latter used for S&P).

been that associated with corporate finance. On the other hand, ratings associated with the public sector (local and national governments, plus infrastructure) were the least lucrative.

Moody's has 33 offices listed on its website. The company's headquarter office is also in Lower Manhattan, NYC. As displayed in Table 24.1, 10 offices are registered in the Americas—six in the United States and four elsewhere (e.g., Buenos Aires, São Paulo, Mexico City). Like S&P, it also has nine offices in Europe. In addition to offices in large cities such as London, Paris, and Frankfurt, it also has an office in Limassol, Cyprus. Its presence in Asia is very similar to that of S&P. Its total employment level is 13,000 people, of whom about 4,000 are based in the United States.

Fitch was formerly co-owned by the French risk management company FIMALAC (Financière Marc de Lacharrière) and the US media giant the Hearst Corporation, until the latter became its sole owner in 2018. While the name Hearst may not sound familiar to the reader, some of its media outlets may do. Indicatively, Hearst is the publisher of a number of magazines, such as *Elle*, *Cosmopolitan*, *Harper's Bazaar*, and *Car and Driver*; it is also a stakeholder in numerous US television channels, including ESPN, and online media (e.g., BuzzFeed and Vice).

In contrast to the other two major CRAs, Fitch has dual headquarters, one in Lower Manhattan, NYC, and one in London's Canary Wharf. Another notable difference is that Fitch has a smaller presence in the United States (four offices are mentioned on its website) and more offices in the rest of the Americas (Table 24.1). In addition to the usual large financial centres, some of the Latin American cities with Fitch offices are Bogotá, Lima, Monterrey, and San José (Costa Rica). Furthermore, the company has eight offices in Europe and 11 in Asia. Of the Asian offices, four are in China, only one is in India, while an office is also based in Sri Lanka's Colombo. In total, Fitch's is present in 41 cities.[5]

Overall, the geography of the big-three office locations offers interesting lessons for research on financial centres. Chicago and San Francisco are the only US cities other than NYC where all three agencies have an office, highlighting the position of these cities as leading financial centres of the country. European geography underscores the role of Warsaw as a leading financial centre in Central and Eastern Europe, and Stockholm as a leading financial centre for the Nordic countries. Johannesburg is the only city on the African continent hosting big-three companies. Sydney, rather than Melbourne, is confirmed as the primary financial centre in Australia. There are intriguing absences as well, as none of the big-three CRAs has an office in Switzerland. There are also locations that clearly serve as back offices, rather than customer facing centres; for example, Bangalore and Gurgaon in India.

Credit Rating Methodology

Credit rating agencies see themselves as institutions that provide an opinion. In the words of S&P, for example, a rating is 'an educated opinion about an issuer's likelihood to meet its financial obligations in full and on time' (S&P, 2020). This opinion is typically summarized in an alpha-numerical score, ranging from triple-A (top creditworthiness) to single-C or D (effectively, junk or default). Table 24.2 provides a summary of those scores.

Table 24.2 Credit rating categories

	Credit quality	*S&P*		*Moody's*		*Fitch*	
		Long-term	*Short-term*	*Long-term*	*Short-term*	*Long-term*	*Short-term*
	Highest	AAA	A-1+	Aaa	P1	AAA	F1+
Investment grade	Very high	AA+		Aa1		AA+	
		AA		Aa2		AA	
		AA−		Aa3		AA−	
	High	A+	A-1	A1		A+	F1 or F1+
		A		A2		A	F1
		A−	A-2	A3	P1 or P2	A−	F2 or F1
	Good	BBB+		Baa1	P2	BBB+	F2
		BBB	A-3	Baa2	P2 or P3	BBB	F3 or F2
		BBB−		Baa3	P3	BBB−	F3
Speculative grade	Speculative	BB+	B	Ba1	Not prime	BB+	B
		BB		Ba2		BB	
		BB-		Ba3		BB-	
	Highly speculative	B+		B1		B+	
		B		B2		B	
		B−		B3		B−	
	Substantial credit risk	CCC+	C	Caa1		CCC+	C
		CCC		Caa2		CCC	
		CCC−		Caa3		CCC−	
	Very high level of credit risk	CC		Ca		CC	
	Exceptionally high levels of credit risk	C		C		C	
	Under regulatory supervision	R					
	Selective/ restricted default	SD				RD	RD
	Default	D				D	D

Source: Author's elaboration, based on S&P, Moody's, and Fitch websites.

The rating-making protocol is more or less similar across the three agencies. As listed in S&P (2020), there are eight steps involved in assembling a rating. First, the issuer requests a rating score and signs an engagement letter. Second, analysts review all relevant information, which they then discuss with management. They then propose a rating to a rating committee which reviews the recommendation and votes on it. Next, the rating is announced and accompanied by a press release in which the main elements of the rating's rationale are outlined. Thereafter, the rated borrower is monitored and the rating adjusted if and when necessary.

In their methodology reports, all three rating agencies emphasize that ratings are not just the output of a mathematical model; they are also informed by a qualitative judgement (Fitch, 2019; Moody's 2019b; S&P, 2017). This is an existential distinction for rating agencies, as it allows them to claim they do something more nuanced than simply gathering available information. It also enables them to preserve a sort of a 'black box' quality, or mystique, over their assessments. Moreover, it gives them space for manoeuvring as, at any point, they can refer to their ad hoc judgement to explain why a rating may diverge from the performance indicated by quantitative factors.

The emphasis on qualitative judgement is also useful for understanding the persistence of CRAs' influence, despite advances in information technology. In theory, one could assume that greater access to information, particularly data on borrowers, would make investors less dependent on credit rating scores. In this line of reasoning, the spread in the use of the internet in the 1990s, for example, should have contained the reliance on CRAs. The fact that recent history unfolded in precisely the opposite way shows that CRAs have been influential not in their supply of information, but in their supply of judgement.

The three CRAs typically draw a distinction between long- and short-term ratings, and between ratings for debt in foreign and domestic currency. They also make a distinction between issuer ratings and the ratings of specific debt instruments. Additionally, they provide forward-looking estimations of the rating changes to be expected in the future. In their vocabulary, the 'review/watch' notification reflects possible developments within the next 90 days, while the 'outlook' announcement providing a similar idea for a two-year horizon.

Sovereign Credit Ratings and Their Impacts

Sovereign ratings—the ratings of national governments—comprise a category that requires special attention. In the vast majority of cases, these ratings provide a ceiling and a point of reference for all other ratings in a country.[6] As such, they link directly with macroeconomic stability, particularly with movements in interest rates and cross-border capital flows. Along with ratings of lower layers of public governance, they also form the most politicized rating category.

In their prescriptions of sovereign ratings, all three CRAs unanimously claim to be paying attention not only to strict fiscal and economic indicators, but also to broader institutional and political variables. Fitch (2019), for example, indicates four analytical pillars: structural features, macroeconomic performance, public finances, and international finances. Examples of what are considered to be structural features are government quality, political stability, and business environment. Similarly, Moody's (2019b) indicate quality of institutions and governance as a separate category in their rating scorecard.

One of the early papers investigating the link between sovereign ratings and interest rates is Reisen and Maltzan (1999). With focus on developing economies, these authors argue that rating changes are most significant when synchronized by the three CRAs. Furthermore, they report an asymmetry between rating upgrades and downgrades, indicating the latter as the most impactful with regard to interest rate spreads. A similar finding comes out of Gande and Parsley (2004a), who suggest that rating downgrades are the most significant in transmitting across borders. More recently, Arezki et al. (2011) confirm the existence of cross-border spill-over effects of rating downgrades in the Eurozone. They also point out that such effects tend to become more systematic once the country's sovereign rating reaches the speculative range. Other studies with a focus on Europe are Afonso et al. (2011), De Santis (2012), Gibson et al. (2017), and Altdörfer et al. (2019).

A particularly interesting aspect pointed out in Gibson et al. (2017) is the occurrence of doom-loops between sovereign credit ratings, sovereign interest rates, and bank ratings. As discussed in their work, sovereign downgrades and hikes in interest rates in the countries of the European periphery (Greece, Italy, Ireland, Portugal, and Spain) led to the downgrading of banks within these countries. In turn, bank downgrades contributed to further sovereign downgrades and increases in interest rate spreads, therefore creating a self-reinforcing downward spiral.

Research has been undertaken into the impact of sovereign ratings on capital flows; these works include Gande and Parsley (2004b), Kim and Wu (2008), Ioannou (2017), Swamy and Narayanamurthy (2017), and Cai et al. (2018). Gande and Parsley (2004b), for example, expand their previous findings by showing how rating downgrades drive capital out of a country. Ioannou (2017) concentrates on the Eurozone and explores the significance of the qualitative component of sovereign ratings in affecting capital flows. Cai et al. (2018) show that sovereign ratings matter not only for importers, but also for exporters of capital. Whereas recipient countries with higher ratings tend to import more capital, countries with net outflows tend to export less capital when their ratings are high. An additional finding in Cai et al. (2018) is that the average rating of the broader region of a country, relative to others, is also significant.

Contemporary Geographical Distribution of Moody's Sovereign Ratings

We provide here a brief elaboration of the contemporary geographical distribution of Moody's sovereign ratings. Our choice to focus on Moody's is based on the wider availability of data, compared to that available for S&P and Fitch. Given the

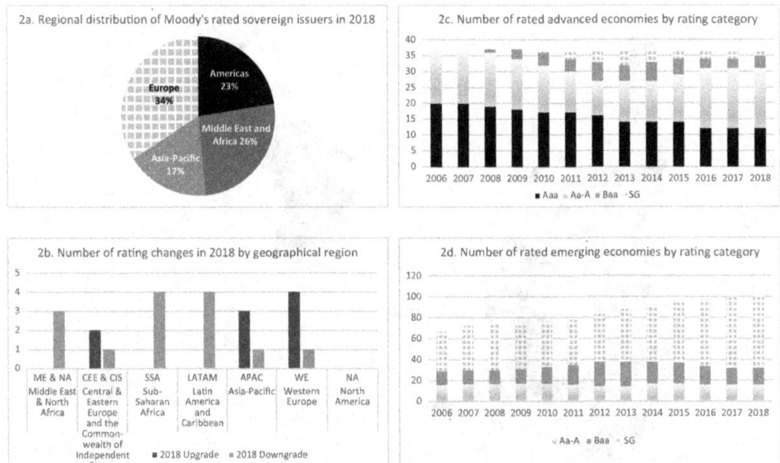

Figure 24.2 Breakdown of Moody's sovereign ratings by geographical region

Notes: 'SG' stands for speculative grade; Moody's separates between advanced and emerging economies based on the historical terminology of international bond indices.

Source: Moody's (2019c).

high similarity of sovereign rating methodologies between the three CRAs, however, we can also treat Moody's ratings as representative of the broader industry.

Figure 24.2 provides an overview of the distribution of sovereign ratings by region. Figure 24.2a shows that the largest number of rated governments are located in Europe. The region of Asia-Pacific, on the other hand, registers the smaller share of the pie (a limitation of the figure is that it does not account for the differences in size of the rated countries). Figure 24.2b registers the total number of rating upgrades and downgrades in each region for 2018. As can be seen, Europe is the continent with the greatest number of upgrades for that year. To some extent, this can be explained by the (still partial) recovery of many countries from the steep downgrades experienced during the Eurozone crisis.

Figure 24.2, panels c and d, expand on what was previously demonstrated in Figure 24.1. Reading the two graphs in conjunction, we see that the main driver in the increase of rated countries comes from emerging economies. In the case of advanced economies, we observe that, although investment grade is still the dominant category of rating scores, a relative decline has taken place in rating quality, with triple-A scores becoming a minority in the post-crisis period. An indicative example of this trend is the United Kingdom, where the triple-A score held by the British government since 1978 went down to Aa1 in 2013 and, subsequently, to Aa2 in 2017 (Moody's website). Moreover, Figure 24.2d shows that speculative grade (SG) still remains the dominant rating category in emerging countries. Strikingly, not a single emerging economy registers a triple-A score in any of the years for which data is available.

Figure 24.3 The world in the eyes of Moody's

Notes: The figure depicts sovereign ratings as of mid-December 2019; 'C scores' includes Caa1, Caa2, Caa3, Ca and C; unrated countries are intentionally left blank.

Source: https://countryeconomy.com/ratings (last accessed on 16 December 2019).

Figure 24.3 corroborates this picture by mapping the current (mid-December 2019) sovereign rating scores around the globe. As expected, some of the countries with the highest rating scores are the United States, Canada, Australia, and those in northern Europe. At the same time, China and Japan are the countries with the highest rating scores in Asia (both currently standing at A1); Chile and Peru, the countries with the highest scores in Latin America (A1 and A3, respectively); and the United Arab Emirates and Qatar, the countries with the highest ratings in the Middle East (Aa2 and Aa3, respectively). We have intentionally left entries for unrated territories blank so as to mark their relative inexistence in the universe of credit ratings.

Critiques towards Credit Rating Agencies

There are three major lines of critique of CRAs. One is the well-known critique associated with conflicts of interest and moral hazard, most notably with regard to the global financial crisis of 2007/08. The second is the critique associated with their performance (other than failures due to moral hazard), particularly with procyclicality and cultural biases in their judgement. Third, there is the critique that concentrates on the power of CRAs to dictate 'responsible' fiscal and economic policies to local and national governments.

The Moral Hazard Critique

The moral hazard critique is not only the most common issue raised against the CRAs, but also a critique broadly adopted across social sciences, endorsed even by mainstream economics. The argument, in broad strokes, is that the way in which ratings were attributed to complex financial instruments, such as mortgage-backed securities (MBSs) and collateralized debt obligations (CDOs)—with CRAs receiving an income fee from the issuers of the securities themselves—gave rise to conflicts of interest. Since CRAs' main source of income was obtained from issuers, the agencies had an incentive to be 'nice' by attributing inflated ratings to them and their products. The underlying conflicts of interest became evident when the value of these instruments collapsed in 2007/08. Subsequently, CRAs became one of the first players to be blamed for the mess.

As pointed out in White (2010, 2013), the 'issuer pays' scheme arose in the United States during the early 1970s, replacing the previous 'investor pays' model. White (2010) lists a number of reasons that can explain this shift. One scenario is that, in view of the widespread use of the photocopy machine, CRAs were afraid of free-riding behaviour on the part of the investors, who would now be in a position to photocopy and share rating manuals. Another view is that CRAs may have realized that, due to their incorporation into financial legislation, ratings became something like a 'blessing' for bond issuers. This would imply that issuers would be happy to pay something in order to ensure the acceptability of their papers.

White (2010) notices that, in comparison with the traditional bond rating activities of CRAs, there were now three main differences. First, the agencies themselves got actively involved in the design of the securities they rated by prescribing to the issuers what kind of mortgages and what size of tranches would earn favourable ratings. Second, the oligopolistic structure of the mortgage-related securities market gave issuers the power to threaten their rating agency that they could easily move to one of its competitors. Third, CRAs had no prior experience with the products they were asked to evaluate. As a result, CRAs failed to appreciate fully the correlations between the performances of the underlying assets in products such as MBSs.

Procyclicality and Cultural Bias

The procyclicality critique points out that credit ratings tend to be inflated in good times, and too low in bad times. To making an assessment, the typical approach is to estimate credit ratings based on a set of fundamental variables, and then contrast them with actual rating scores. Ferri, Liu, and Stiglitz (1999) is one of the first papers to follow such an approach, with a focus on the East Asian crisis. According to their account, CRAs not only failed to predict the crisis, but also formed excessively conservative expectations in its aftermath. As a result, they downgraded crisis hit countries more than their fundamentals would justify and, hence, made matters worse. From the point of view of those authors, one aspect that may explain this switch to conservatism could have been CRAs' incentive to recover from their failure and rebuild their reputations.

Ioannou (2016) provides a similar set of evidence in the context of the Eurozone crisis and the concomitant downgrading of the governments of peripheral European economies by the three CRAs. One way in which this work differs from Ferri et al. (1999) is in its interpretation as to what makes ratings procyclical. In particular, Ioannou (2016) associates CRAs' qualitative judgement with Keynes's notion of fundamental uncertainty; that is, the type of uncertainty related to events never repeated under identical circumstances (a point predominantly associated with long-term investment in Keynesian theory; see Keynes, 1936, 1937). Notably, this uncertainty cannot be dealt with by any mathematical model; neither it is a matter of data availability, as the data required does not exist a priori. To deal with these circumstances, people often use their spontaneous judgement,—what Keynes refers to as 'animal spirits'. In this context, Ioannou (2016) points out that a sovereign default is itself a non-uniform and non-repetitive event; hence, CRAs are also destined to use their spontaneous judgement—often involving excessive euphoria or pessimism. Procyclicality in ratings, therefore, is not (just) a result of false incentives, but a consequence of the fact that CRAs do not have access to the full set of knowledge required to produce an accurate rating.

With regard to cultural biases in credit ratings, Fuchs and Gehring (2017) is a cornerstone article. Utilizing a sample of 143 countries and nine CRAs (including the big-three and the Chinese Dagong), Fuchs and Gehring show that sovereign ratings tend to be biased on the basis of home country and culture. More specifically, CRAs tend to assign a rating that is, on average, one notch higher to their home country. Additionally, they tend to inflate ratings in countries that are close to theirs in terms of linguistic distance. A further finding of their paper is that CRAs tend to give higher ratings to economies in which home-country banks have large risk exposures (something that implies a tendency to protect the asset side of home banks' balance sheets).

Of more recent works, Yalta and Yalta (2018) examine potential regional biases of the big-three CRAs. Considering a sample of 99 countries, and separating the world into eight regions, plus the United States, these authors claim that, whereas there is, indeed, a strong home bias in favour of the United States, no specific bias exists against any other region. Altdörfer et al. (2019) spot an additional cultural bias for the ratings of Fitch. Based on the fact that Fitch has dual headquarters in NYC and London, and given its co-ownership by the French FIMALAC during the period of their coverage, Altdörfer and his colleagues flag the agency as being relatively more European than S&P and Moody's. Based on this presumption, they trace a positive skewness in Fitch's average Eurozone rating, compared to those of S&P and Moody's, particularly throughout the European crisis.

The Dimension of Political Power

Sylla (2002) is correct in arguing that credit rating agencies are not, by default, an intrinsic part of bond markets. After all, as noted in his account, the latter are three centuries older than CRAs. Historical context, therefore, matters greatly when appreciating the political and economic influence of those institutions.

It has been the social and economic transformations, broadly associated with neoliberalism, that have made CRAs important. Besides the aspects pointed out earlier (the rise in financial globalization, the attachment of CRAs in regulation, and the shift towards bond financing), a further dimension worth highlighting has been financial deregulation, not only across, but also within countries. The loosening of credit and interest rate controls, for example, were key developments in creating more volatile economic environments.[7] Given the corresponding increase in uncertainty, CRAs became influential in providing a sense of safety to investors. Their judgement as to what constitutes 'responsible' governance also became a driver for investment flows.

From the point of view of borrowers, these developments lifted CRAs to the status of financial market gatekeepers (Hackworth, 2002; Ioannou, 2016; Peck and Whiteside, 2016; Sinclair, 1994, 2005). In order to obtain and/ or maintain a favourable rating, and thus achieve affordable borrowing costs, public and private rated entities found themselves needing to comply with the agencies' views. In that way, borrowers were forced to adopt the conceptual framework of CRAs, limiting their range of choices to what was considered acceptable. Importantly, this constraint of choices did not just concern the exercise of 'getting the numbers right', but also encompassed the broader norms of governance (Sinclair, 1994).

In the sphere of public governance, CRAs' influence translated into an augmented pressure on local and national governments to apply fiscal conservatism (i.e. austerity) and privatize public assets (of course, this is not to deny the possibility of governments aiming to pursue such policies themselves). This pressure largely complemented the more 'visible' authority of other imperative institutions, such as the International Monetary Fund (IMF) and the World Bank. Perhaps the simplest way of demonstrating this pressure is by listing a series of examples.

At the level of urban governance, Hackworth (2002) discusses the examples of NYC in the 1970s, and Philadelphia and Detroit in the 1980s and the 1990s. As noted in his account, NYC is one of the first examples of fiscal restructuring led by the CRAs. Following a period of financial distress (partly due to increased welfare spending, and partly due to deindustrialization and population loss), Moody's downgraded the city into speculative status in 1975. Practically, this move pushed NYC out of the market and brought it close to bankruptcy. In the years that followed, a far-reaching fiscal restructuring programme was put in place, simultaneously cutting spending on health, housing, and other social services, while assisting the financial, insurance, and real estate sectors. In 1983, Moody's rewarded the city by lifting it into investment grade, despite NYC becoming one of the most polarized cities in the country.

Another example, discussed in Sinclair (2005), is that of Australian states' encounter with CRAs in the 1990s and early 2000s. In the Australian State of Victoria, for example, Moody's two-notch downgrade in October 1992 helped the newly elected conservative government to justify its stance on the public budget, and go ahead with cuts in education, health, and other programmes. Once these cuts were under way, S&P and Moody's unanimously announced rating upgrades.

Omstedt (2019) provides closer and more recent evidence of how local government officials interact with CRAs. As documented in his work, based on a set of semi-structured interviews in the state of New Jersey, municipal officials often see themselves in need of taking CRA analysts out in a 'dog and pony show', driving them around to show them the new shopping mall, train station, and so on (Omstedt, 2019: 620). According to another interviewee, CRAs are portrayed as 'another boss' to whom a municipal finance officer needs to report, next to the mayor, the city council, and the directors (Omstedt, 2019: 625).

National governments' positioning against CRAs is hardly any different from that which is experienced at the local level. Indicatively, two contemporary examples worth pointing out are CRAs' reaction to the election of an anti-austerity government in Greece in the first half of 2015, and their endorsement of Argentina's neoliberal reforms in 2016/17. In the Greek case, Moody's, fearing the government would jeopardize the implementation of the austerity programme imposed by Greece's Troika of creditors, announced its intention to downgrade Greece's rating, which was already close to junk status (Caa1), days after the new government had taken office (Moody's, 2015).[8]

Similarly, in 2016 Moody's expressed a highly positive assessment of the neoliberal reforms that had started being implemented in Argentina at the time (Moody's, 2016). Amongst others, these reforms included the floating of the Argentinian Peso, the lifting of cross-border capital controls, and fiscal cuts in energy and transportation subsidies. Note, for the record, that, soon after their implementation, the first two of these policies resulted in a crash of the currency and a bailout request to the IMF.[9]

Conclusions, Policy Implications and Directions for Future Research

This chapter discusses the positioning of credit rating agencies (CRAs) in the contemporary world of finance. Following their incorporation into financial regulation from the 1930s onwards, in the United States and elsewhere, and the globalization of finance, CRAs became intrinsically important for both investors and borrowers. Currently, the big-three CRAs—Standard & Poor's, Moody's, and Fitch—provide a full suite of ratings, from ratings of simple bonds of national and local governments, to ratings of complex financial instruments. While all three CRAs are US-owned, their presence and scope are global. Economically, these agencies have a significant impact on interest rates, capital flows, and banking stability. Politically, they exert an authoritative influence over local and national governments, bounding their policy choices and aiding the promotion of fiscal austerity and privatizations.

A reasonable question one could pose is what has been done to contain their influence? After all, not only critical scholars, but even mainstream economists agree that these agencies played a role in fuelling the 2007/08 crisis, and that there were serious conflicts of interest involved in their rating of asset-backed securities.

Mennillo and Sinclair (2019) provide a comprehensive survey of the post-crisis policy responses in the United States and in Europe. As pointed out by these authors, a common ground on both sides of the Atlantic has been the intention to detach ratings from regulation—though, in practice, these attempts have only materialized in part. Other initiatives have aimed at reducing conflicts of interest, boosting competition in the ratings market, and improving regulatory oversight (see, for instance, European Commission, 2013). In the case of Europe, attempts to enhance competition have also included the certification of FinTech CRAs. The idea of setting up a European rating agency was also discussed, though subsequently dismissed on the basis that it would cost a great deal of money and that it would put private CRAs at a comparative disadvantage (European Commission, 2013).

There are various reasons why none of these attempts for reform can achieve their target without a broader transformation of our financial systems. First, as pointed out by White (2013), amongst others, a switch from the issuer-pays model to one in which investors pay for ratings can be equally rigged with conflicts of interest. A major investor customer of an investor-pays CRA may have a large exposure to bonds of a certain kind and, hence, be unhappy to see them downgraded. Or, an investor may be interested in buying a specific set of bonds that may become cheaper if downgraded first. Second, the idea of promoting competition amongst CRAs is largely incompatible with the very raison d'être of rating agencies. As discussed in Mennillo and Sinclair (2019), a rating provides a centralized assessment of creditworthiness, a function that, by definition, can only be fulfilled in an oligopolistic market. Third, mere concentration on improving regulatory oversight can backfire. Mennillo and Sinclair (2019) point out that better oversight can easily increase, rather than reduce, reliance on ratings, since these will now be made in a more transparent and closely scrutinized environment and, hence, will be signalled as publicly approved. Fourth, the idea of setting up a European, or other, public rating agency can achieve very little if it is left up to investors to trust its judgement. Either because of an ideological belief in the incompetence of the public sector to operate transparently, or simply due to the lack of reputational capital, a public CRA can easily be ignored by the market. Additionally, inasmuch as such CRA would be administered by institutions committed to neoliberal governance themselves, such as the European Central Bank, its establishment would not go a long way in altering the policy constraints faced by borrowers.

With regards to future research, there are various ways in which financial geography could contribute to the topic. First, financial geographers are best-positioned to explore further the implications of CRAs at the level of cities and regions. Building on the existing, but so far limited literature, one idea would be to conduct more case studies and cross-sectional analyses. For example, are different localities—within and across countries—subordinated in the same way to the power of the rating agencies? If not, what are the factors that explain such variation? Does, for instance, the size of a locality matter for its rating score? Is there a bias of rating agencies in favour of cities described as leading financial centres? Do local characteristics matter at all, or are CRAs 'blinded' by the overarching country-level assessment of creditworthiness?

Second, the consideration of rating agencies can enrich the financial geography agenda on finance and advanced business services, often labelled as FABS (e.g., Wójcik, 2020). Like other FABS, such as legal, consulting and accounting firms, CRAs are a key component of contemporary financial systems, located predominantly in leading financial centres. One particularly interesting path for research could be to investigate whether and how other FABS firms serve the credit rating industry; and, vice-versa, the ways in which they utilize ratings in their operations.

Third, given the increasing interest of geographers in financial technology (e.g., Cojoianu et al., 2019), a further avenue for future research could be to explore the relationship between the FinTech sector and CRAs. For example, do FinTech firms use the rating scores of the big-three CRAs in their day-to-day activities? Do they aim to obtain a rating once growing in size, and, if yes, what impact would this make to their business model? What prospects do CRAs see for these firms, and how could the rise of FinTech affect the credit ratings of other financial institutions; for example, big banks?

Notes

1 See, for instance, Finextra, 'Wiserfunding to provide credit ratings for SMEs', *Finextra*, July 19, 2019.
2 See here for the full list: https://www.sec.gov/ocr/ocr-current-nrsros.html.
3 Ratio calculated on the basis of the CRAs recognized by the SEC. ESMA (2019) also provides figures very close to what reported here, on the basis of the 27 CRAs registered in the EU.
4 Throughout this chapter the sole mentioning of S&P refers to the ratings entity. The same applies to the names 'Moody's' and 'Fitch'.
5 We were unable to find a separate annual statement for Fitch, and hence any accurate information on its revenues and employment.
6 Some of the exceptions to this rule relate with countries with a high degree of regional autonomy. One such example is Moody's rating of the Basque Country in Spain, wherein the local government's credit rating was downgraded less severely than that of the federal government during the Eurozone crisis, and has thus been exceeding the latter by one notch since 2011 (*Source*: Moody's website).
7 For detailed evidence on financial reforms around the world see Abiad et al. (2008).
8 The word 'Troika' conventionally referring to the IMF, the European Commission and the European Central Bank. Greece is of course a special case, given that it had already been excluded from financial markets since 2009/10.
9 See, for example, Bronstein and Otaola, 'IMF studying Argentina request for early help as peso crashes', *Reuters*, August 29, 2018.

References

Abiad, A., Detragiache, E., and Tressel, T. (2008). A New Database of Financial Reforms. IMF Working Paper Series, Working Paper No. WP/08/266. Available at https://www.imf.org/en/Publications/WP/Issues/2016/12/31/A-New-Database-of-Financial-Reforms-22485 [accessed January 14, 2020].

Afonso, A., Furceri, D., and Gomes, P. (2011). Sovereign Credit Ratings and Financial Market Linkages: Application to European Data. ECB Working Paper Series, Working Paper No. 1347. Available at http://www.ecb.int/pub/pdf/scpwps/ecbwp1347.pdf [accessed January 14, 2020].

Altdörfer, M., De Las Salas Vega, C., Guettler, A., and Löffler, G. (2019). The Case for a European Rating Agency: Evidence from the Eurozone Sovereign Debt Crisis. *Journal of International Financial Markets, Institutions & Money*, 58(C), pp. 1–18.

Arezki, R., Candelon, B., and Sy, A. (2011). Sovereign Rating News and Financial Markets Spillovers: Evidence from the European Debt Crisis. IMF Working Paper No. 11/68. Available at http://www.imf.org/external/pubs/ft/wp/2011/wp1168.pdf [accessed January 14, 2020].

Cai, P., Gan, Q., and Kim, S.-J. (2018). Do Sovereign Credit Ratings Matter for Foreign Direct Investments? *Journal of International Financial Markets, Institutions & Money*, 55, pp. 50–64.

Cojoianu, T., Clark, G., Hoepner, A., Pažitka, V., and Wójcik, D. (2019). Fin vs. Tech: Determinants of Fintech Start-Up Emergence and Innovation in the Financial Services Incumbent Sector, SSRN Working Paper. Available at https://papers.ssrn.com/sol3/papers.cfm?abstract_id=3347755 [accessed January 14, 2020].

De Santis, R. (2012). The Euro Area Sovereign Debt Crisis: Safe Haven, Credit Rating Agencies and the Spread of the Fever from Greece, Ireland and Portugal. ECB Working Paper Series, Working Paper No. 1419. Available at http://www.ecb.europa.eu/pub/pdf/scpwps/ecbwp1419.pdf [accessed January 14, 2020].

European Commission. (2013, June 18). New Rules on Credit Rating Agencies (CRAs) Enter into Force—Frequently Asked Questions. European Commission Memo Item, No. MEMO/13/571. Brussels. Available at https://ec.europa.eu/commission/presscorner/detail/en/MEMO_13_571 [accessed January 14, 2020].

European Securities and Markets Authority. (2019, November 29). Report on CRA Market Share Calculation. ESMA33-9-340. Paris. Available at https://www.esma.europa.eu/sites/default/files/library/esma33-9-340_cra_market_share_calculation_2019.pdf [accessed January 14, 2020].

Ferri, G., Liu, L. G., and Stiglitz, J. (1999). The Procyclical Role of Rating Agencies: Evidence from the East Asian Crisis. *Economic Notes*, 28(3), pp. 335–355.

Fitch Ratings. (2019). Sovereign Rating Criteria: Master Criteria. Available at https://www.fitchratings.com/site/re/10072225 [accessed January 14, 2020].

Fuchs, A. and Gehring, K. (2017). The Home Bias in Sovereign Ratings. *Journal of the European Economic Association*, 15(6), pp. 1386–1423.

Gande, A. and Parsley, D. (2004a). News Spillovers in the Sovereign Debt Market. *Journal of Financial Economics*, 75(3), pp. 691–734.

Gande, A. and Parsley, D. (2004b). Sovereign Credit Ratings and International Portfolio Flows. Owen Graduate School of Management, Vanderbilt University. Available at http://www.imf.org/external/np/seminars/eng/2004/ecbimf/pdf/parsle.pdf [accessed January 14, 2020].

Gibson, H., Hall, S., and Tavlas, G. (2017). Self-Fulfilling Dynamics: The Interactions of Sovereign Spreads, Sovereign Ratings and Bank Ratings during the Euro Financial Crisis. *Journal of International Money and Finance*, 73(B), pp. 371–385.

Hackworth, J. (2002). Local Autonomy, Bond-Rating Agencies and Neoliberal Urbanism in The United States. *International Journal of Urban and Regional Research*, 26(4), pp. 707–725.

Hornby, L. (2019, April 19). China's Dagong Rating Agency Taken over by State-Owned Investor. *Financial Times*. Available at https://www.ft.com/content/7079c7aa-6265-11e9-b285-3acd5d43599e [accessed January 14, 2020].

IMF. (2010). Global Financial Stability Report: Sovereigns, Funding, and Systemic Liquidity. Washington DC: International Monetary Fund. Available at http://www.imf.org/external/pubs/ft/gfsr/2010/02/pdf/text.pdf [accessed January 14, 2020].

Ioannou, S. (2016). The Political Economy of Credit Rating Agencies: The Case of Sovereign Ratings. PhD thesis. University of Leeds, Leeds.

Ioannou, S. (2017). Credit Rating Downgrades and Sudden Stops of Capital Flows in the Eurozone. *Journal of International Commerce, Economics and Policy*, 8(3), 1–36.

Kennedy, S. (2019, August 8). In China's Credit Ratings, Democracies Pay a Price. *Foreign Policy*. Available at https://foreignpolicy.com/2019/08/08/976045-china-dagong-credit-creditratings-democracy/ [accessed January 14, 2020].

Keynes, J. M. (1973/1936). *The General Theory of Employment, Interest and Money*. Cambridge: Cambridge University Press.

Keynes, J. M. (1937). The General Theory of Employment. *The Quarterly Journal of Economics*, 51(2), pp. 209–223.

Kim, S. J. and Wu, E. (2008). Sovereign Credit Ratings, Capital Flows and Financial Sector Development in Emerging Markets. *Emerging Markets Review*, 9(1), pp. 17–39.

Mennillo, G. and Sinclair, T. (2019). A Hard Nut to Crack: Regulatory Failure Shows How Rating Really Works. *Competition & Change*, 23(3), pp. 266–286.

Moody's Investors Service. (2015, February 6). Rating Action: Moody's places Greece's Caa1 Government Bond Rating on Review for Downgrade. Moody's Investors Service. Available at moodys.com upon subscription [accessed January 14, 2020].

Moody's Investors Service. (2016, April 15). Rating Action: Moody's Upgrades Argentina's Issuer Rating to B3 with a Stable Outlook. Moody's Investors Service. Available at moodys.com upon subscription [accessed January 14, 2020].

Moody's Investors Service. (2019a). Annual Report 2018. Available at https://s21.q4cdn.com/431035000/files/doc_financials/annual/2018/MCO-2018-Annual-Report_FINAL.PDF [accessed January 14, 2020].

Moody's Investors Service. (2019b). Sovereign Ratings Methodology. Available at https://www.moodys.com/researchdocumentcontentpage.aspx?docid=PBC_1158631 [accessed January 14, 2020].

Moody's Investors Service. (2019c). Sovereign Default and Recovery Rates, 1983–2018. Available at https://www.moodys.com/researchdocumentcontentpage.aspx?docid=PBC_1164180 [accessed January 14, 2020].

Omstedt, M. (2019). Reading Risk: The Practices, Limits and Politics of Municipal Bond Rating. *Environment and Planning A: Economy and Space*, 52(3), pp. 611–631.

Peck, J. and Whiteside, H. (2016). Financializing Detroit. *Economic Geography*, 92(3), pp. 235–268.

Reisen, H. and Maltzan, J. (1999). Boom and Bust and Sovereign Ratings. *International Finance*, 2(2), pp. 273–293.

Securities and Exchange Commission. (2018, December). Annual Report on Nationally Recognized Statistical Rating Organizations. Washington DC. Available at https://www.sec.gov/2018-annual-report-on-nrsros.pdf [accessed January 14, 2020].

Sinclair, T. (1994). Passing Judgement: Credit Rating Processes as Regulatory Mechanisms of Governance in the Emerging World Order. *Review of International Political Economy*, 1(1), pp. 133–159.

Sinclair, T. (2005). *The New Masters of Capital: American Bond Rating Agencies and the Politics of Creditworthiness*. London: Cornell University Press.

Standard and Poor's. (2017). Sovereign Rating Methodology. Available at https://www.spratings.com/documents/20184/4432051/Sovereign+Rating+Methodology/5f8c852c-108d-46d2-add1-4c20c3304725 [accessed January 14, 2020].

Standard and Poor's. (2019). Powering the Markets of the Future: Annual Report 2018. Available at https://www.spglobal.com/_division_assets/images/annual-report/sp-global-2018-annual-report.pdf [accessed January 14, 2020].

Standard and Poor's. (2020). Understanding Ratings. [online] Available at https://www.spglobal.com/ratings/en/about/understanding-ratings [accessed January 14, 2020].

Swamy, V. and Narayanamurthy, V. (2017). What Drives the Capital Flows into BRICS Economies? *The World Economy*, 41(2), pp. 519–549.

Sylla, R. (2002). A Historical Primer on the Business of Credit Ratings, in Levich, R., Majnoni, G., and Reinhart, C. (eds.), *Ratings, Rating Agencies and the Global Financial System*. New York: Springer.

White, L. (2010). Markets: The Credit Rating Agencies. *Journal of Economic Perspectives*, 24(2), pp. 211–226.

White, L. (2013). Credit Rating Agencies: An Overview. *Annual Review of Financial Economics*, 5(1), pp. 93–122.

Wildau, G. (2018, August 17). China Suspends Major Credit Ratings Agency Dagong. *Financial Times*. Available at https://www.ft.com/content/1be968d4-a1ff-11e8-85da-eeb7a9ce36e4 [accessed January 14, 2020].

Wójcik, D. (2020). Financial and Business Services: A Guide for the Perplexed, in Knox-Hayes, J. and Wójcik, D. (eds.), *Routledge Handbook of Financial Geography*. London: Routledge.

Yalta, T. and Yalta, Y. (2018). Are Credit Rating Agencies Regionally Biased? *Economic Systems*, 42(4), pp. 682–694.

Yeandle, M. and Wardle, M. (2019, September). The Global Financial Centres Index 26. Financial Centre Futures, Long Finance Institute. Available at https://www.long-finance.net/media/documents/GFCI_26_Report_v1.0.pdf [accessed January 14, 2020].

25

OFFSHORE AND THE POLITICAL AND LEGAL GEOGRAPHY OF FINANCE

1066–2020 AD

Daniel Haberly

Introduction

Economic geographers have long defined themselves in opposition to the abstract theoretical universe of economics, rather emphasizing the specificity of economic activities in the 'real world'. To a large extent, this emphasis also characterizes the subfield of financial geography, which has tended to focus on the human and material apparatus of financial centres. This focus has allowed the field to provide key insights into the organization and operation of the world economy that have been overlooked by researchers in other fields. However, it also often led to less emphasis being paid to the abstract vehicles and constructs that constitute finance itself.

Crucially, the fact that these abstract constructs and vehicles do not inhabit the physical world does not mean that they do not have a geography. Rather, their geographic footprint defines what is broadly referred to as the 'offshore' financial system. A quick review of almost any international economics statistics underscores the rather alarming centrality of this system to the organization of the world economy. Roughly two-thirds of the world's stock of foreign direct investment (FDI), for example, is either in or from shell company jurisdictions where it is unlikely to have a local attachment to substantive activity[1]. However, notwithstanding a significant body of work in economic geography (e.g., Cobb, 1998; Dörry, 2014; Haberly and Wójcik, 2015; Hudson, 2000; Poon et al., 2019; Roberts, 1994; Töpfer and Hall, 2018; Wainwright, 2011; Warf, 2002), the offshore system continues to be mostly treated as a footnote in analyses of the world economy.

As will be demonstrated in this chapter, attempting to construct a model of the 'real' economy or financial system that simply ignores or strips away the 'fictions' of the offshore system is somewhat analogous to stripping away the operating system of a computer in order to try to get a clearer view of the hardware. In other words, rather than being regarded as some veil of illusions that obscures our view of the economy, the offshore system needs to be regarded as an integral and critical component of its operational fabric (Coe et al., 2014; Maurer, 2008; Palan et al., 2010; Seabrooke and Wigan, 2014). Furthermore, far from being some novel feature of the modern world, offshore has deep historical roots. Specially, as will be shown, the unbundling of the state as an institution into what can be described as onshore and offshore spheres has been, since the Middle Ages in Europe, a persistent outcome of fundamental political tensions that surround the role of the state in capitalism. Indeed, capitalism was in many respects born offshore, and offshore is where capital, to a large extent, continues to live.

Offshore as Space and Place: Jurisdictions, Facilities, and States

The definition of 'offshore' is notoriously difficult and contested. In approaching this task, however, the best starting point is arguably a problematization of the dual nature of capital as 'two ingredients: an asset, and a legal code' (Pistor, 2019: 2)—or, more specifically, 'assets placed on legal steroids' (Pistor, 2019: 11). These 'legal steroids' used to encode capital are built upwards from assets via tiers of increasingly abstract constructs (see also Chapter 5, this volume). Towards the bottom of this stack of constructs, it may be possible to speak of some direct geographic attachment to underlying assets; however, as one moves upwards to higher levels of abstraction, this attachment becomes increasingly tenuous, with the 'paper' legal geography of capital assuming an increasingly autonomous logic. It is this free-floating and autonomous legal geography of capital, in relation to the geography of underlying assets and activities, that defines offshore as a *space*.

Crucially, the geographic autonomy of this offshore legal space from the geography of the physical world does not allow capital to live an autonomous existence from the state (Palan, 1999). Rather, the substrate that supports this fluid legal geography of capital is the amorphous and malleable nature of the state itself as an 'imagined community' consisting of 'impersonal power' 'mediated by abstract concepts' (Piccioto, 1999: 45). It is this reality of the state itself as a 'legal fiction' (Piccioto, 1999) that defines offshore as a legal *place* of capital—that is, as a network of offshore jurisdictions.

The concept of an offshore jurisdiction is inherently relative, context-based, and subjective, and there is no consensus definition at the level of either concepts or specific places. However, the role of offshore jurisdictions as places—as well as of the offshore system as a legal-jurisdictional space—can arguably be best understood in terms of the impulse to liberate the legal realm in which capital resides *within the state*, from the realm of politics, such that the state's role as the provider of rule of law comes to operate primarily on behalf of, and in relation to, private contract and property, rather than public policy.

Above all, offshore jurisdictions, and the offshore system more broadly, are defined by the paradoxes that surround this impulse to liberate law from politics within the state. Indeed, the very existence of identifiably 'offshore' jurisdictions essentially stems from the fact that it is fundamentally impossible to disentangle law from political context; rather, this separation can, at most, be simulated, by embedding law in a specialized political structure. The specialized political structures in which offshore jurisdictions are embedded are constituted at two levels: offshore *facilities*, and offshore *states*.

Offshore facilities are special rules for designated 'foreign' or 'international' activities, which are defined to be largely removed from the remit of domestic political contestation. Typically, this involves constructing 'ring fences' to prevent the use of offshore facilities by residents, and/or for local activities (Shaxson, 2011). This logic of creating circumscribed institutional spaces for international commercial and financial activities, that are partially insulated from the local economy and politics, is quite ancient. During the Middle Ages and early Modern Era in Europe, long-distance commerce and finance were largely conducted through fairs established and administered by feudal or town authorities. The fairs were special jurisdictional platforms, within which merchants were granted their own separate system of private contractual law that the responsible local authority would enforce in relation to fair business. Above all, the jurisdiction of the fair was designed to attract the commercial and financial activity of foreigners, by freeing them from the discriminatory and protectionist measures pervading local laws (Edwards and Ogilvie, 2012; Kadens, 2004; Munro, 2001)—or, as one critic of fairs put it as late as the eighteenth century, '[granting] special privileges and franchises...to trade at particular places, whereas it is laden down elsewhere by dues and taxes' (quoted in Braudel, 1983: 93). More broadly, as Palan (1999: 19–20) puts it, offshore can be seen as a 'case of having your cake and eating it' from the standpoint of the state, wherein 'the more mobile economic sectors are provided with a separate regulatory space' while 'the state can carry on discharging its traditional roles as though nothing had happened'.

Via offshore facilities, any state can act as an offshore jurisdiction in relation to particular clients or activities. However, offshore services tend to be disproportionately provided—whether via offshore facilities, or via a jurisdiction's broader legal and regulatory framework—by what can be described as *offshore states*. Above all, the political architecture of the offshore state must hold the line against either tyrannical or mass-participatory democratic encroachments on a particular technocratic logic of public and private decision-making that operates on behalf of the international financial and commercial sector. Within this offshore state decision-making logic, the legislature and executive primarily act as an adjunct to the judiciary and to the legal and financial professions in defining—and where possible expanding—the parameters of *private* contractual law.

In practice, this is a delicate balancing act, as the offshore state ideally needs to be highly responsive to the needs of international financial and business groups, without being gratuitously corrupted in a manner that undermines the rule of law itself. Coe et al. (2014) describe the key interest group catered to by the contemporary offshore state as, broadly, the 'advanced business services' (ABS) or 'financial and business services' (FABS) complex, which encompasses major international law, accountancy, and consultancy firms, in addition to international financial services firms themselves—most importantly in investment/merchant banking (see also Wójcik, this volume). As shown in the remainder of the chapter, more or less the same conceptual framework can be applied historically to cases ranging from the role of Italian merchant banks in developing 'exchange fairs' throughout medieval and early modern Europe, to the role of corporate law firms and investment banks in establishing New Jersey and Delaware as incorporation platforms.

Like the offshore facility, the offshore state can be regarded as an ancient European institution. Specifically, its roots can be located in medieval 'free cities' characterized by systems of elite commercial and financial-interest dominated pseudo-democratic rule, that were able to operate largely outside of the parameters of the overarching feudal polities and societies within which they were embedded (Pirenne, 2014). The still extant medieval Corporation of London (i.e., 'City' proper)—where the government is mostly elected, in an evolution of the guild system, by the management of locally operating businesses in proportion to their employment (i.e., primarily by multinational financial services firms; see Shaxson, 2011)[2]—along with Hong Kong and Singapore, can be described as living examples of such a limited elite republic providing a political substrate for the operation of an offshore jurisdiction.

Notably, however, the overt limitation of democracy within offshore states is more the exception than the rule in the contemporary world. Rather, today one more often finds that the offshore state carves out formal or informal spaces of technocratic autonomy within a mass participatory democratic state apparatus. The most extreme example of this is the most durable and successful offshore jurisdiction, Switzerland, which arguably has the world's most democratic system of government. Counterintuitively, it seems that direct democracy in Switzerland—at the Federal and local levels—tends to foster a conservative, consensus-oriented approach to decision-making, led largely by stakeholders, experts, and bureaucrats, which is aimed largely at avoiding referenda (Papadopoulos, 2000). As described by Guex (2000), for example, Switzerland's watershed 1934 banking secrecy law was implemented in an uneasy compromise between the banking community and socialists, which was essentially predicated on the avoidance of public scrutiny or debate. In other contexts, one finds specialized spaces of technocratic offshore state autonomy from mass politics carved out within more conventional representative democracies. In matters of company law, for example, the Delaware legislature has a long tradition of rubber-stamping the annual updates developed by the Council of the Corporation Law Section of the Delaware State Bar Association (Strine, 2005). Meanwhile, in the decades after World War II, the broad regulatory discretion of the Bank of England allowed it to play a semi-autonomous technocratic role in promoting the development of the Eurodollar market in the United Kingdom and its overseas territories (Hampton, 1996; Shaxson 2011).

Arguably the most important precondition for the success and durability of an offshore state is relative smallness in terms of population and territory. Smallness engenders a greater potential for any given financial services 'hinterland' to generate per capita economic and fiscal spill-over (see Strine, 2005)—as well as a greater potential for the local economy to be structurally captured by the offshore sector (Christensen et al., 2016). Just as importantly, smallness facilitates the building of a tightly woven long-term political consensus around the offshore sector that marginalizes or coopts dissenting voices (Bullough, 2019; Christensen and Hampton, 1999; Shaxson, 2011). This is not to say that larger states cannot function as offshore jurisdictions. However, this is typically limited to providing relatively circumscribed offshore facilities, and/or various types of crude deregulation and tax cuts that are likely to be intrinsically lacking in long-term political credibility. In practice, the United Kingdom seems to be near—and possibly somewhat beyond—the maximum size limit for a polity to sustain politically something of the character of an offshore *state* in the contemporary world.

Crucially, offshore states are usually not fully sovereign or independent, but rather semi-sovereign statelets that operate under the formal or informal protection of some powerful patron—often in a nested hierarchy of offshore dependencies within offshore dependencies (Hampton, 1996). More broadly, it is the smallness of the states hosting offshore jurisdictions that conditions their fundamentally relational existence as the counterpart to the 'onshore' realm of complex and expansive political contestation. In this respect, the key paradox of offshore is that capital—in seeking to free itself from 'onshore' politics—concentrates its legal footprint within the jurisdiction of states that are too small to defend the political interests of the capital that they host or, in many cases, even themselves. The counterintuitive result is a centralization of political authority in the hands of whatever *onshore* state apparatus is in a position to protect, regulate, and exploit offshore activities.

The implications of this paradox are far from peripheral for the evolution of the capitalist system; rather, as will be shown, the partial bifurcation of the institution of the state into offshore and onshore realms has long played a critical role within the dialectical co-development of state and market in capitalism. By the same token, the role of offshore ultimately needs to be problematized within this broader story of the co-development of state and market, and it is on this that the remainder of the chapter is focused.

Offshore and the Double Movement: Market Institutionalization, Financial Innovation, and Social Protection

This role of offshore in mediating the dialectical relationship between state-making and market-making is defined by two key logics, each of which involves the state being counterintuitively consolidated via tendencies that superficially appear to constitute a retreat of its authority. The first is the Polanyian 'double movement', wherein the state mediates the tension between the political impulses towards commodification on the one hand, and social protection on the other. Here, the paradox, as observed by Polanyi (2001), is that processes of commodification and marketization that seek to take the state out of the economy invariably both entail and drive increased levels of state intervention—both to advance commodification, and to contain its socially disruptive fallout. Meanwhile, the second key dialectical logic of offshore-mediated state-building surrounds the development of the state as 'protection racket' as described by Tilly (1985) and North (1993). Here, the key paradox is that more resources can typically be extracted by the state, to feed the expansion of its military coercive capabilities, from a private sector that enjoys strong institutional protections from extraction than from a private sector that is subject to unrestricted 'mafia-like extortion' (North, 1993). Offshore jurisdictions play two critical mediating roles within these processes of dialectical state and market-making: (i) simultaneously intensifying *and* containing processes of commodification, and (ii) fortifying the legal foundations of private property protection.

With respect to the first, as described by Polanyi (2001), the politics of commodification are characterized by multiple layers of cognitive dissonance (see also Brenner et al., 2010). This involves the state actively constructing the supposedly 'natural' institution of the market, even while being continuously compelled, politically, to contain the socially disruptive forces unleashed by its own commodification agenda. For Polanyi (2001), the roots of this cognitive dissonance lay in the conflict between ideology and reality—and, specifically, in the impractical nature of the 'utopian project' of liberalism. However, political cognitive dissonance in relation to commodification is arguably also endemic, at a deeper level, to the nature of actually-existing states as messy, variegated institutional spaces. In this respect, far from unitary or well-bounded actors, states are invariably characterized by both profound fragmentation internally—between various factions and functions, and usually also geographic sub-units—as well as a vague and amorphous substantive-relational, even if not formal legal, definition of borders externally.

Most importantly, from the standpoint of offshore, the critical role that 'the state' plays in commodification does not always entail the sort of active or conscious policy agency described by Polanyi. Rather, it often simply involves the state acting as a conduit—via its provision and enforcement of the rule of law—for the private sector development of innovative contractual devices for the 'coding of capital' (Pistor, 2019). Indeed, this pattern of legal—as opposed to political—engagement with the state is especially attractive to private capital, as investments in creative legal engineering and litigation tend to earn a more predictable 'return', in the form of favourable state action, than investments in politics (Pistor, 2019). The architecture of offshore jurisdictions is essentially designed to maximize the return on this private legal investment in the state as a conduit for commodification. Importantly, the conceptualization of commodification here is somewhat different from that used by Polanyi. Rather than focusing on the role of the state as an imposer of market discipline on 'land, labour, and money', it emphasizes the role of the state as a facilitator of the private sector development of legal devices that render things and relationships—or particular cash flows and rights attached to them—progressively more fungible through market exchange (i.e., liquid). The distinction between 'commodification' and 'financial innovation' here is inherently ambiguous. Rather, what one sees is an integrated flow of legal-contractual construction whereby obligations and rights are bundled together and repackaged as successive layers of progressively more liquid legal vehicles.

Offshore jurisdictions maximize their utility as 'laboratories of financial innovation' (Le Marchant, 1999) by providing diverse and flexible 'toolboxes' of such legal vehicles (Haberly and Wójcik, 2017). To a large extent, such a toolbox can be provided via a legal system that maximizes, as a general principle, the scope for private contractual discretion, while minimizing the time, cost, and uncertainty of state-mediated private contractual dispute resolution. In this respect, what can be described as an 'onshore'–'offshore' legal bifurcation—with the former broadly emphasizing the role of law as a vehicle for the projection of state authority and reconciliation of diverse social considerations, and the latter emphasizing the role of law as a flexible realm of private contractual discretion backed by state authority—has deep historical roots. In Europe, these date back to the Middle Ages, when the development of trade and finance within a profoundly decommodified socio-economic order was facilitated by a specialized legal regime—the Law Merchant (Pirenne, 2014). This provided a speedy and predictable system of dispute resolution that was based primarily on equity (fairness), and free from feudal encumberments such as trial by ordeal or combat, or wagers of law (Kadens, 2004; Pirenne, 2014). It also recognized key legal vehicles and concepts (e.g., in various contexts, bills of exchange, partnerships, and bankruptcy) that otherwise lacked solid or consistent legal standing (Kadens, 2004; Munro, 2003; Pirenne, 2014).

Crucially, while the Law Merchant was largely rooted in mercantile custom, its operation, enforcement, and, to a large extent, content depended on specific legal forums backed by official authority. As a consequence, it existed as a heterogenous jurisdictional patchwork anchored and defined by the courts and laws of the cities and fairs (and their feudal patrons), or in some cases (e.g., England after Edward I) special commercial courts established by the monarch in selected cities (Edwards and Ogilvie, 2012; Kadens, 2004; Marsilio, 2010; Munro, 2001, 2003). In general, commercial and financial instruments, and the legal frameworks supporting them, were far more precociously developed in the leading Italian mercantile city-states than elsewhere. Indeed, Kadens (2015) argues that much of what is commonly described as universal medieval Law Merchant could be more accurately described as Italian commercial law.

During the seventeenth and eighteenth centuries, English courts came to affirm that 'Law Merchant' mercantile custom was a source of precedent for mainstream English Common Law (Baker, 1979). Simultaneously, and into the nineteenth century, older English common law vehicles—such as the medieval feudal device of the trust—were also gradually adapted for commercial use (Hansmann and Kraakman, 2006; Morley, 2016; Pistor, 2019). In a direct line of descent from this medieval legal lineage, most leading offshore jurisdictions today are current or former British colonies that have developed their own specialized variants of English common law and equity. The distinction between onshore and offshore here is complex; most international commercial activity is governed, at some level, by the law of New York or England proper, which has assumed an 'offshore' character in relation to transactions with little or no direct connection to either jurisdiction (Pistor, 2019; Potts, 2020). Meanwhile, more conventional 'offshore jurisdictions' fill various niches in relation to these global regimes.

Cayman Islands law firms, for example, advertise points of local law such as the absence of a general concept of 'substance over form', a 'creditor friendly' insolvency regime, and express statutory recognition of contractual subordination—which help to provide private actors with an exceptionally flexible legal regime in the context of complex financial innovations such as securitizations (Ashman and Bestwick, 2003; Deacon, 2004; Haberly and Wójcik, 2017; Moon, 2003). Meanwhile, the pervasive use of British Virgin Islands (BVI) vehicles by Chinese multinationals is reportedly driven partly by their preference for the fast and flexible local application of equity in the resolution of disputes (Maurer and Martin, 2012). The world's leading incorporation centre, Delaware, has actually preserved the old English separation between courts of Law and Chancery (equity), with the latter effectively operating as a parallel legal system that serves the incorporation sector (Strine, 2005). Notably, as discussed by Nougayrede (2019), many of the same features of offshore jurisdiction law that minimize transaction costs (e.g., minimal participation and liability of directors) can also structurally undermine transparency and accountability.

Crucially, even where there is a general acceptance of the primacy of private contract, the legal contractual 'toolbox' of offshore jurisdictions often needs to be expanded through statutory state action. This is particularly true for entities, with the legal basis for new entity categories or capabilities often being legislated on demand for particular clients or client groups. In such situations, as described by Shaxson (2011: 184), offshore jurisdictions act as 'fast and flexible private lawmaking machines' (see also Arsht, 1976; Hansmann, 2006). New Jersey, for example, essentially invented the modern shell company in 1888–89, when it granted the right to corporations ('holding companies') to own stock in other corporations, in response to lobbying by the 'trusts'. After New Jersey abandoned its liberal corporate legal and regulatory approach in 1913, Delaware became, and has subsequently remained, by far the most important jurisdiction in the world for the formation of shell entities (Arsht, 1976; Yablon, 2007). As described by Hansmann (2006: 3), this long-term success is largely rooted in Delaware's proactive approach to the continuous expansion of its 'menu' of entity types and capabilities, with Delaware LLCs, LLPs, and business trusts now granting 'nearly limitless contractual flexibility' constrained only by US federal regulation.

Light or absent taxation is also a key characteristic of offshore vehicles; however, this is arguably more of a corollary of the principle of maximal private contractual freedom and property protection, than the defining feature of offshore. Indeed, while tax avoidance or evasion is probably the most common contemporary use of offshore jurisdictions, what is more fundamentally important (e.g., as illustrated by US state-level vehicles) is that they afford tax neutrality or efficiency (Haberly and Wójcik, 2017). In other words, offshore jurisdictions ensure that little or no additional local taxation is levied on activities and structures, even when the purpose of these structures is not tax avoidance or evasion per se. A combination of tax flexibility and predictability is also characteristic of offshore jurisdictions, with many defining taxation on a quasi-contractual basis. In the Cayman Islands, for example, companies can receive a 'Tax Exemption Undertaking' binding the power of the government to raise taxes for 20–30 years, which is especially useful for long-term securitizations (Deacon, 2004). Similarly, one major attraction of entities in the Netherlands and Luxembourg is the ability to obtain advance tax rulings in relation to the future treatment of complex and often aggressively tax-avoiding structures (van Dijk, 2006; Vlcek, 2019).

The fact that the abstract legal geographic space inhabited by offshore vehicles pervades the 'real' geographic space of the assets and activities that they reference means that onshore economic institutional changes can often be mediated offshore. By the same token, however, it means that offshore jurisdictions are intrinsically subject to onshore state authority. In the Middle Ages, the merchants of both local and foreign cities depended on charters or other grants of rights to gain access to and privileges within particular territories, which, in turn, gave monarchs and other local authorities substantial leverage over these merchants and cities (e.g., to extract wartime loans, or reciprocal trading rights).[3] Today, offshore jurisdictions rely heavily on international tax, trade, and investment treaties, and are extremely vulnerable to even informal 'blacklisting' or 'grey listing'—or even the threat thereof (Eden and Kudrle, 2005; Sharman, 2009; Vlcek, 2007). Beyond this, onshore tax and regulatory authority in the contemporary world often has a pervasive extraterritorial reach—for example, as defined on the basis of either actor home state/nationality or instrument target market (Chang, 2003; Haberly and Wójcik, 2017; Herring, 2007). In the most extreme case, the United States has translated its gatekeeping role in relation to global dollar clearing via New York into expansive unilateral discretion to sanction or regulate financial activities and actors on a global basis (Economist, 2020; Emmenegger, 2015).

The pervasive, even if uneven influence of onshore state authority offshore is crucial in relation to the Polanyian 'double movement' of state-mediated commodification and social protection. For one thing, the fact that offshore jurisdictions can essentially only operate when permitted to do so by onshore states—or, at least, by some powerful onshore state patron—means that the processes of commodification they mediate are usually implicitly, if not explicitly, sanctioned by some onshore authority. Indeed, one often finds offshore jurisdictions being actively used or created by onshore states (or groups within them) to help push through liberalizing economic restructuring agendas. Paradoxically, part of what makes this offshore-mediated restructuring pathway so attractive, is the fact that it *at least appears to* partially contain the disruptive economic, social, and political consequences of restructuring—in other words, to simultaneously fulfil both impulses in the Polanyian double movement. This impulse to create confined jurisdictional spaces of controlled commodification can be seen in the very origins of capitalism within the free cities chartered by medieval rulers—whose walls simultaneously kept feudalism out and capitalism in (Pirenne, 2014). More or less the same logic can be seen—albeit deployed much more rapidly and coherently—in China's long-standing strategy of mediating marketization through multiple layers of offshore jurisdictions within (e.g., special economic zones and free trade zones), outside of (e.g., United Kingdom-dependent Caribbean incorporation centres), and astride (e.g., the Hong Kong capital market) its borders (Lim, 2019; Walter and Howie, 2011; Wójcik and Camilleri, 2015).

Importantly, the same intrinsic geographic co-location (from a functional standpoint) of onshore and offshore that allows the latter to be used to advance the economic restructuring agendas of the former invariably renders naïve any expectations that these agendas' disruptive effects can be contained offshore. Consequently, offshore-mediated commodification processes invariably provoke second-order 'counter-movements' by onshore state authority—even in cases where offshore-mediated commodification is deliberately set in motion by these same onshore states.

This is, above all, true with respect to credit instruments. Credit plays a critical role in the 'coding of capital' (Pistor, 2019), as it allows for illiquid assets and uncertain future cash flows (i.e., collateral) to be used to obtain current liquidity, while simultaneously allowing current liquidity to obtain the higher rates of return of illiquid assets and uncertain cash flows. The logic of this translation is so compelling that there is an inexorable impulse towards the private production of liquid credit money instruments backed by illiquid collateral (Ferri and Minsky, 1992). However, the build-up of debt also imprisons current activities within the accumulated dead weight of past decisions and contracts; where liquid credit money is backed by problematic collateral, this dead weight can drag the economy into a downward spiral and, ultimately, spark a collapse of the payments system. As has been widely observed (Ferri and Minsky, 1992; Pistor, 2019; Polanyi, 2001), any state confronted by this prospect invariably blinks and is forced to backstop the integrity of the credit system. Due to this, and the more broadly inequitable and disruptive social impacts of indebtedness, states have always tightly regulated credit. Ultimately, however, the impulse towards private 'minting of debt' is so overpowering that private actors invariably circumvent these constraints through subversive financial innovation—usually with the at least partial cooperation of the state itself (Ferri and Minsky, 1992; Pistor, 2019; Polanyi, 2001)

What can be described as offshore jurisdictional spaces have long played an important role in this dialectic of financial innovation and regulation. In some cases, this has simply involved allowing practices to be conducted outside the jurisdictional scope of 'onshore' regulations. Medieval and early modern usury laws, for example, were generally severely restrictive (see Munro, 2003), but also geographically uneven in letter and enforcement. In the original charter granted to the City of Geneva in 1387, for example, the Bishop of Geneva broke with mainstream canon law in permitting lending with interest (Innes, 1983). More recently, the post-World War II development of the Eurodollar market, as pioneered by the United Kingdom and its overseas territories, hinged on the decision of the Bank of England to decline to regulate (most importantly, with respect to capital controls, interest rate caps, and reserve requirements) the foreign (i.e., non-GBP) currency activities of foreign banks (Hampton, 1996; Shaxson, 2011).

Importantly, however, such overt enabling of jurisdictionally based regulatory avoidance is not the only mechanism whereby offshore jurisdictions can facilitate destabilizing financial innovation. Indeed, the fact that offshore jurisdictions are always located more or less within the scope of onshore authority means that their ability to enable direct regulatory escape is often limited, compared to their ability to facilitate financial innovation through more subtle and indirect means—which can be broadly summarized as the reduction of fiscal and legal 'frictions' to novel or complex financial transactions and structures (see Haberly and Wójcik, 2017). Historically, this role has been particularly importantly in relation to 'shadow banking'—that is, the conduct of banking functions through nominally non-bank forms that avoid regulation on a definitional, rather than jurisdictional, basis. The roots of what can be described as shadow banking, as well as the role of offshore jurisdictional spaces in facilitating it, are extremely old. In Europe, they can be dated to the late Middle Ages, when the rise of bills of exchange was largely driven by the fact that they could, if structured carefully as cross-currency transactions, allow lending to be compliant with—or, at least, not be flagrantly non-compliant with—the bans on usury promulgated by the Church and most governments (Munro, 2003). Bills of exchange also allowed merchant banks to partially circumvent the bans on deposit banking maintained by many governments (e.g., in England prior to the seventeenth century, or the Hapsburg-ruled Low Countries in the fifteenth century), as well as pervasive systems of capital and exchange controls (Munro, 2003).

Crucially, despite being technically (or at least plausibly) legal, the widespread international use of bills of exchange was hindered by various practical frictions—particularly regarding their legal enforceability in various forums, and their negotiability (i.e., transferability) in general (Boerner and Hatfield, 2017; Munro, 2003). The key devices that emerged to cut through these frictions were the exchange fairs, which were set up by major international (typically Italian, e.g., Genoese) banking houses in various locations throughout Europe (e.g., Champagne, Lyons, Geneva, Besancon, Piacenza). These provided what can be described as an 'offshore' platform—that is, the jurisdiction of the fair, with its own special court and rules designed by the major international banking houses/banking centres, but backed by some local feudal or town authority[4]—for the clearing, refinancing, and enforcement of international debt securities in multiple currencies, and the resolution of any disputes related to these (Boerner and Hatfield, 2017; Boyer-Xambeau et al., 2015; Braudel, 1983; Edwards and Ogilvie, 2012; Marsilio, 2010; Munro, 2001, 2003; Pezzolo and Tattara, 2006). Notably, the various currencies involved here were mostly only referenced as abstract units of account; as Boerner and Hatfield (2017: 2004) put it 'nothing was rarer than money at these clearing fairs'. As noted by Pezzolo and Tattara (2006), the exchange fairs were essentially forerunners of the offshore wholesale market, which were remote-controlled from the leading substantive banking centres, and which simultaneously facilitated the international raising and movement of capital and the avoidance of regulation.

One finds offshore jurisdictions playing a similarly subtle, facilitative role in the shadow banking activities implicated in the 2008 global financial crisis. Crucially, by this time, the logic of overt, territorial jurisdiction-based regulatory avoidance that characterized the post-World War II Euromarket had been largely rendered obsolete by post-1980 international regulatory reconfiguration. On the one hand, this involved a widespread international regulatory race to the bottom, wherein traditional areas of territorialized regulation (e.g., reserve requirements, or interest rate caps) were relaxed or eliminated (Roberts, 1994; Shaxson, 2011; Strange, 1994). However, it also involved a far-reaching process of international extraterritorial financial re-regulation—as defined, most importantly, by the Basel framework, which transferred primary prudential regulatory authority to the home states of financial institutions charged with overseeing their global capital supervision on a consolidated basis (Haberly and Wójcik, 2017; Herring, 2007; Kapstein, 1991).

Like the medieval Church's usury laws, the post-1980s international regime of (partially) harmonized and extraterritorialized prudential regulation encouraged the development of shadow banking instruments that were designed primarily to fall outside of the definitional, rather than the geographic territorial, scope of regulation (Gorton and Metrick, 2010; Pozsar et al., 2012). However, while these instruments were technically, or at least plausibly legal, from an onshore regulatory standpoint (at least in the United States), they involved complex transactions and structures that could, as a practical matter, generally only be implemented via the types of tax efficient, contractually flexible vehicles available offshore (Haberly and Wojcik, 2017). Notably, the onshore–offshore jurisdiction of Delaware could provide such vehicles for the purposes of most securitizations—and, in practice, was the most important site for the manufacture of toxic mortgage-backed securities. However, the most esoteric and complex vehicles seemed to have required the greater level of tax and legal flexibility afforded by offshore jurisdictions outside the United States (Haberly and Wojcik, 2017; Wainwright, 2011). Most structured investment vehicles (SIVs) and collateralized debt obligations (CDOs), for example, were domiciled in the Cayman Islands; meanwhile, the securities of these vehicles were typically listed on either the London Stock Exchange (for SIVs), or its offshoot market in Dublin (for CDOs) (Haberly and Wojcik, 2017; Palan et al., 2010).

The global financial crisis spawned by these vehicles—and the costly state clean-ups that followed—prompted a further tightening and extraterritorialization of financial regulation under Basel III, as well as additional national extraterritorial regulation (e.g., the US Volker Rule). The effectiveness of these new regulations is unclear, with the chairman of the Basel Committee citing the so-called 'behavioral responses' of banks as a major issue (Ingves, 2018). However, the basic role of offshore jurisdictions as flexible legal nodes within the evolving international system of credit and investment does not seem to be threatened. Indeed, as detailed in Haberly et al. (2019), what seem to be emerging as the new category of innovative, systemically important credit intermediaries are massive fund managers such as BlackRock, whose paper legal-geographic footprint is as strongly rooted in offshore jurisdictions (e.g., Delaware, the Cayman Islands, Ireland, and Luxembourg) as any major bank.

Offshore and State Power

As suggested by the discussion above, the net effect of the offshore-mediated double movement tends to be the migration of authority to whatever level of national or supranational 'onshore' authority is capable of providing oversight and protection to the offshore arena. This paradoxical tendency for the offshore–onshore unbundling of the state to drive a centralization of state authority, across progressively larger geographic scales, is even more pronounced in relation to the second key dialectical pathway of offshore-mediated state-making—namely the development of the capitalist state as 'protection racket' described by Tilly (1985). As Tilly sees it, building on North and Thomas (1973), the historical co-development of capitalism and the state proceeded through a chaotic Darwinian process, wherein the survival of political structures was determined, above all, by their success on the battlefield—or, as North (1993: 4) describes it, a 'kaleidoscope of endless warfare at every level'. Most importantly, states that struck a bargain of 'protection and justice' for revenue with capitalists were simply more successful, over the long run, at cultivating and mobilizing military resources than states that engaged in 'Mafia-like extortion' (North, 1993: 5). As time progressed, this bargain became progressively more solidly enshrined in legal institutions of private property protection, and political institutions of democratic representation—at least, for property holders.

The key paradox of the state's 'protection racket,' as described by North and Tilly, is that its power is ultimately strengthened—both in relation to competing centres of domestic power, and other states—by a weakening of the state's despotic power in relation to the rights of property holders in general, and financial creditors in particular. Notably, North, Tilly, and other commentators often acknowledge the role played by medieval city states and fairs as early incubators of this symbiotic yet contested relationship between state and capital. However, there is tendency to treat the messy, variegated political and legal landscape of the Middle Ages and early Modern Era as a transitional form in the development of a rather cartoonish Westphalian nation-state—as opposed to what has arguably remained, to a large extent, the persistent form of the actually-existing capitalist state system to the present day.

Most important in this respect, from the standpoint of the evolution of the capitalist system, is the long-term persistence of what can be described as onshore–offshore jurisdictional variegation. As in the context of the 'double movement', the historical reproduction of this can be described as a direct result of the generally inverse relationship between the geographic scale of a state, and the extent to which the realm of private legal contract and property can be insulated from complex political contestation. Paradoxically, this causes the legal footprint of capital to pool within small states that have only a limited ability to protect or assert the interests of this capital beyond their own borders—or, indeed, even defend themselves militarily. The result, in turn, is the inexorable emergence and reproduction of an offshore–onshore political umbilicus, wherein offshore pools of capital are continuously pulled back into, even as they seek to escape from, the 'protection rackets' of powerful onshore states. Ultimately, the effect of this is often to flip the role of offshore on its head, from that of a refuge from politics, to that of an arena for great power ambition freed from domestic legal or political accountability.

As noted by Wallerstein (2004), private capital is not only dependent on the state's role as a passive protector of property rights, but also on the state's role as an active mediator of the generation and allocation of monopoly rents—without which capital cannot earn more than a marginal return. The state's 'protection racket' relationship with capital can thus be described as a circuit of rent production via monopoly enforced by state coercive authority, on the one hand, and rent recycling into the sovereign balance sheet, on the other (see Arrighi, 1994). Crucially, in this respect, the fact that medieval and early modern monarchies not only tolerated, but also actively promoted the role of free cities and fairs as sites of commodification and financial engineering had nothing to do with 'liberal' ideology. Rather, it stemmed from their desire to harness these locales as nodes for liquid financial rent concentration (i.e., via the granting of various privileges and monopoly rights) and extraction (i.e., via more or less compulsory lending to the monarch or, in some cases, simply discretionary feudal levies; Pirenne, 2014).

During the later Middle Ages and early Modern Era, two regional trajectories of state–city relationship emerged. In the consolidating monarchies of western Europe, the major cities (e.g., London, Paris) remained substantially under the thumb of state authority and extraction. Meanwhile, within the slowly unravelling political structure of the Holy Roman Empire in central Europe, cities often obtained much higher levels of autonomy (Tilly, 1989). Many of these central European cities were able, either individually (e.g., Genoa, Florence, or Venice) or as confederacies (e.g., Switzerland or the Netherlands), to develop into independent powers in their own right—which came to exercise dominance, at various times, over major sections of the international credit and maritime trading systems. However, as described by Arrighi (1994) and Tilly (1989), each invariably found itself outgunned—literally—by the larger territorial states consolidating themselves in western Europe and, ultimately, came to be pulled into the orbit of—and, in turn, help to advance the further consolidation of—these powerful states.

Most of these city states—for example, Genoa, which developed a deeply symbiotic financial relationship (mediated through the Piacenza and Bescancon exchange fairs) with the Hapsburgs in the sixteenth and seventeenth centuries (Arrighi, 1994; Braudel, 1983)—would eventually be absorbed outright into the consolidating nation-states. However, this was not always the case; the historical development of the Swiss banking sector, for example, was strongly conditioned from the Middle Ages to the present day by its interaction with the 'protection rackets' of more powerful states. As described in the previous section, the history of Geneva as an offshore jurisdiction goes back more than six centuries, to the lax treatment of usury established by the original city charter. For a time, in the 1400s, Geneva came to host the leading exchange fair in Europe, with activity driven by the major Italian banking houses (Boyer-Xambeau et al., 2015; Marsilio, 2010). As in many modern offshore booking centres, there was minimal local participation in mediating the tremendous international flows of wealth sloshing through the fair (Innes, 1983). However, as with many other free cities of the era, Geneva's local feudal rulers (prior to Geneva's joining the Swiss confederacy, the Dukes of Savoy) used it as a captive credit facility, extracting forced loans from the city that it could only raise by, in turn, borrowing from the Italian bankers (Innes, 1983).

Geneva's position as the leading European 'offshore' market was unseated by the exchange fair in Lyons by the end of fifteenth century—marking the culmination of a strategy by the French Crown to draw in the major Italian banks through inducements such as the relaxation of exchange controls and usury laws in the city (Boyer-Xambeau et al., 2015). However, from the 1500s, the development of banking in Geneva came to be driven largely by influxes of wealthy Huguenot merchants (and capital) fleeing persecution in France itself, first, during French wars of religion in the 1500s and, again, after the issue of the Edict of Fountainebleau by Louis XIV in 1685 (Faith and Macleod, 1979). Ironically, having established Geneva as a refuge from the French Crown, the Huguenot merchants soon returned to the lucrative business of lending to it—even while constructing an elaborate pipeline for the illicit siphoning of capital out of France, largely via Lyons (Faith and Macleod, 1979). This relationship was never a comfortable one, with France meddling continuously in Genevan politics, and the inhabitants of protestant Geneva rioting in outrage over the bankers' support for Louis. In response, in 1702 the bankers publicly pledged to end their loans to Louis, even while continuing to lend to him in secret. Shortly thereafter, in 1713, banking secrecy was codified in Geneva by law (Faith and Macleod, 1979).

This close relationship between Genevan banks and the French Crown continued after the death of Louis XIV, with a Genevan banker, Jacques Necker, becoming finance minister to the ill-fated Louis XVI, who, in turn, assisted Geneva in putting down a popular rebellion (Louise, 2017; Venturi, 1991). Ironically, Geneva would benefit again from the revolution that ousted Louis XVI by absorbing a new wave of flight capital from the French nobility—with another Genevan, Jacques Mirabaud, becoming the 'official banker' to Napoleon following France's annexation of the city (Ugolini, 2018). A century later, the European political turmoil and tax hikes that followed World War I prompted yet another wave of capital flight to Switzerland/Geneva—with the Swiss government implementing statutory banking secrecy at the Federal level, in 1934, to thwart the efforts of the French and German governments to trace or tax these assets (Guex, 2000). However, within a few years, Switzerland would find itself strong-armed into financing the war effort of Germany and the other Axis powers. The Allies were aware of this collaboration—with the United States freezing Swiss assets during the war—and planned a major post-war assault on Swiss banking secrecy. Switzerland, however, was able to head-off this retaliation through a concerted programme of post-war lending to Britain and France, aimed largely at cultivating political goodwill towards its banking sector (Guex, 2000).

Notably, the history of Swiss banking may be the instance of offshore jurisdiction development that is the *least* entangled with onshore politics. Indeed, the contemporary offshore system is perhaps, above all, a creature of US politics—both domestic and international. At the centre of both the historical and contemporary US political relationship with the offshore world is the central role played by the latter in mediating the generation and circulation of monopoly rents by US corporations. Crucially, in the United States as in other contexts, the corporation has long been the most important device in capitalism for the generation and management of monopoly rents—and has thus always been at the centre of political contestation over these rents. Indeed, until the nineteenth century, the explicit granting of monopoly rights was invariably a central fixture of the charters that states used to create corporations—first, via the chartering (as corporations) of the medieval free cities themselves and, later, with the chartering of mercantilist era colonial trading and proto-central banking corporations (Roy, 1999). The understanding was that granting these monopoly rights would pull private capital into areas of strategic importance to the state, with the resulting monopoly profits being recycled back into the state's balance sheet—and thus military power—through some combination of lending, taxation, or direct state ownership (Quinn, 2008; Roy, 1999; Taviani, 2015). In the early eighteenth century, for example, the most important British corporation was the South Sea Company, which was essentially a sovereign debt securitization vehicle backed by monopoly trading rights in South America. In practice, these rights mostly provided cover for a massive illicit contraband trade that was mediated through British Caribbean island entrepôts and lubricated by international networks of bribery (Hunt, 2013; Quinn, 2008).

This model of state-directed corporate monopoly chartering was exported by Britain to its colonies in North America. There, following US independence, it came to be largely stripped of the British corporate military-fiscal and colonial-expansionist emphasis. Rather, the chartering of 'mixed'[5] corporations became the centrepiece of a paradigm of active US state-level developmentalism that relied on pulling private capital into designated areas of monopoly privilege (most importantly, in banking and infrastructure; Roy, 1999). Importantly, however, the fact that company law in the United States was a state-level affair, opened the door to dramatically different trajectories of corporate evolution in, and legal-regulatory competition between, different states. In the late 19th century, the consequences of this would become apparent with the rise of a new breed of sprawling, multi-state private-sector monopolies (Roy, 1999; Yablon, 2007). Crucially, unlike the earlier chartered corporate monopolies of US states, these were politically unsanctioned monopolies that quickly came under widespread and intense state-level regulatory assault (Collins, 2013; Yablon, 2007). Indeed, their very existence as sprawling multi-subsidiary business empires rested on shaky legal ground; while, by this time, free incorporation without a charter was widely available, corporations did not have a general right to own other corporations, meaning that 'trust'-based holding structures had to be cobbled together as a substitute (Navin and Sears, 1955; Yablon, 2007).

In 1888 and 1889, however, the trusts were granted safe harbour when New Jersey created the legal device of the holding company with the ability to own other corporations—via legislation that seems to have been 'actively drafted' by the trusts and their lawyers (Collins, 2013; Roy, 1999; Yablon, 2007). By the turn of the century, most large American firms had incorporated as

New Jersey holding companies, which were essentially the prototype for the modern offshore shell company (Palan et al., 2010; Yablon, 2007). Importantly, beyond simply defending themselves from state-level regulatory assault, incorporation allowed the trusts to list their shares formally on the New York Stock Exchange (Navin and Sears, 1955). The legal centralization of American corporate governance in New Jersey thus went hand-in-hand with the centralization of the capital market in New York—as well as the rise of the so-called 'money trust' investment bank network, led by JP Morgan, that managed the New York Stock Exchange listings and, in many cases, the corporate legal organization of the industrial trusts (De Long, 1992; Navin and Sears, 1955; Yablon, 2007).

Ultimately, the reprieve that New Jersey granted to the trusts would prove to be short-lived, as their very success at avoiding state-level regulation encouraged the consolidation of countervailing US federal regulatory authority. The Sherman Antitrust Act was passed in 1890, and seriously enforced after the turn of the century (Collins, 2013; Kovacic and Shapiro, 2000). Under the presidency of Woodrow Wilson—whose prior reforms as governor of New Jersey had prompted the flight of the state's incorporation business to Delaware, which essentially copied-and-pasted the business-friendly company laws of its neighbour (Mahoney, 1966)—the federal government further intensified its antitrust assault via the Clayton Act, and began a long-term expansion of its regulatory apparatus with the creation of the Federal Reserve system and the Federal Trade Commission (De Long, 1992; Kovacic and Shapiro, 2000).

This process reached its zenith in the New Deal and post-World War II era (De Long, 1992; Kovacic and Shapiro, 2000). However, while these reforms curtailed the worst excesses of unregulated industrial and Wall Street monopoly power, they did little to fundamentally weaken the oligopolistic organization of American business. Rather, their major long-term effect—as crystallized in the national military economic planning of World War II and the Cold War—was arguably to bring this concentration of corporate power into a closer political relationship with the federal government (Galbraith, 1967). Within this context, the offshore world came to play an even more important role in the operation of American business. Not only did Delaware remain the epicentre of American corporate governance—with just under two-thirds of Fortune 500 companies currently incorporated there (Palan et al., 2010)—but the federal government both passively and actively promoted the post-war US corporate development and use of overseas offshore facilities.

Crucially, American business found itself, after the war, in a position of overwhelming global monopolistic industrial, technological, and financial dominance. The federal government, in turn, worked with the corporate community to ensure that this monopoly power was channelled into maintaining the technological and industrial basis of US military supremacy, and into supporting the reconstruction and development of America's Cold War allies and client states. This meant providing these states with productive capital and alleviating the 'dollar shortage' hindering their ability to pay for imports (Gowa, 1985). To facilitate this, the federal government turned a blind eye to the proliferating US corporate use of tax haven 'base companies' in the 1940s and 1950s—most importantly, in Switzerland, Liechtenstein, and US satellite states such as Liberia, Panama, Venezuela, Cuba, and Haiti; and, to some extent, the Netherlands Antilles, Bahamas, and Luxembourg (Gibbons, 1956; Stevens, 1962)—as conduits for outward investment (Engel, 2001). Indeed, the Eisenhower administration advocated a further expansion of tax inducements to overseas investment by US corporations, including by proposing the extension of tax deferral to the income of their overseas branches, rather than only subsidiaries (Gowa, 1985).

The unconditional nature of the offshore subsidy to foreign investment ended as soon as the dollar shortage of the 1950s turned into a 'dollar glut' in the early 1960s, which threatened the international position of the dollar (Engel, 2001; Gowa, 1985). Indeed, it was primarily concerns over the US balance of payments that prompted the Kennedy administration to push successfully for the first Controlled Foreign Corporation (CFC) anti-offshore corporate tax avoidance rules in 1962 (Engel, 2001; Piccioto, 1992). As Kennedy bluntly put it 'since the post-war reconstruction of Japan and Europe has been completed, there are no longer foreign policy reasons for providing tax incentives for foreign investment in the economically advanced economies' (Committee on Ways and Means, 1961: 9). However, as the continued deterioration of the US balance of payments led the Kennedy and Johnson administrations to impose additional measures to stem outward investment—first, by taxing overseas lending, and then by imposing capital controls—they soon found themselves promoting another offshore device, the London Eurodollar market, as a platform for American multinational banks and industrial firms to transact with one another outside of US capital controls (Helleiner, 1994; Shaxson, 2011). Beyond reconciling the international banking needs of US firms with capital controls, the Eurodollar market was regarded, as Undersecretary of State for Economic Affairs Douglas Dillon put it, as 'quite a good way of convincing foreigners to keep their deposits in dollars' (quoted in Shaxson 2011: 100). The United States also encouraged the abuse of provisions of its Dutch tax treaty that allowed the Netherlands Antilles to be used as an 'IRS-engineered' (Papke, 2000) offshore conduit for US multinationals to issue Eurobonds to fund investment in the United States itself (Palan et al., 2010).

The offshore Eurodollar market was originally an obscure facility developed in London by British merchant banks in the 1950s—largely for the use of the governments of the Soviet bloc countries. However, it was quickly endorsed by the Bank of England as a mechanism that could help preserve the City's position as an international financial centre, without compromising the UK's Keynesian monetary policy (Helleiner, 1994; Shaxson, 2011). In the 1960s and early 1970s, the Eurodollar market grew by orders of magnitude as American banks and industrial corporations stampeded into it—both in the City of London itself, and in the subsidiary Eurodollar markets established by the Bank of England in UK colonial territories (e.g., in the Caribbean; Lissakers, 1977).

Its development was further boosted by the oil shocks of the 1970s, which caused dollar balances to pile up erratically in the offshore accounts of OPEC states, most importantly at the overseas branches of American banks (Kapstein, 1996; Lissakers, 1977; Spiro, 1999). Far from being 'recycled' by market forces, these funds rapidly became the target of an international political scramble in which various states and firms sought to appropriate the bonanza of rents being generated (Kapstein, 1996; Spiro, 1999; Wellons, 1987).

The United States was by far the most important player in this scramble (Spiro, 1999). This entailed negotiating arms sales and treasury purchase deals with the Saudis, Iranians, and other Gulf state allies—aimed at simultaneously bolstering security ties and funnelling petrodollar rents into the United States—while also enabling and encouraging US banks to intermediate offshore petrodollar deposits to strategically important developing world borrowers (Kapstein, 1996; Spiro, 1999; Wellons, 1987). Most of the total value of these loans was directed at just a few countries in Latin America, and East and Southeast Asia (e.g., Mexico, Brazil, South Korea, Venezuela; Spiro, 1999). As this level of lending concentration contravened US bank borrower risk concentration rules, it was necessary for the Office of the Comptroller of the Currency—as the Federal Deposit Insurance Corporation (1997: 204) described it, due to 'political pressure'—to deliberately open the floodgates of offshore petrodollar intermediation by first failing to enforce US risk concentration rules and, then, simply eliminating them for loans to developing countries (FDIC, 1997; Kapstein, 1996 ; Lissakers, 1977). More broadly, this lending rested on a foundation of basically overt moral hazard, wherein multilateral institutions and the United States were viewed (correctly) as ultimately standing behind the creditworthiness of strategically important developing world borrowers, as well as the major US banks that were lending to these states (Lissakers, 1977).

In fact, the politicization of the offshore Eurodollar market went far beyond development lending, to encompass tangled webs of covert Cold War strategic relationships and operations wherein the distinction between sanctioned and rogue activities was often far from clear. The best window onto this is provided by the Bank of Commerce and Credit International (BCCI). Founded in 1972 under the joint ownership of the ruler of Abu Dhabi and Bank of America, with principal operations in London and Karachi, BCCI was organized through a dual Luxembourg–Cayman Islands holding structure that was, as a US Congressional investigation led by Senator John Kerry described it, 'set up deliberately to avoid centralized regulatory review' (Kerry and Brown, 1992). BCCI's capital structure was largely fraudulent, and it was reportedly 'the drug dealers' favorite bank' in the 1980s (Kapstein, 1996: 164). However, it was also a key covert financial platform for the CIA and, more broadly was, as the Bank of England confidentially described it, 'banker to intelligence agencies for most major agencies of the world' (Kerry and Brown, 1992: 290). In this capacity, BCCI played a key role in affairs ranging from Iran-Contra, to the financing of the Pakistani nuclear weapons programme and Afghan Mujaheddin, and payments to the CIA-backed Narco-state regime of Manuel Noriega in Panama (Kerry and Brown, 1992; Passas, 1996). Ironically, BCCI's role as a platform for the covert activities of one arm of the US government (and other governments) would ultimately be stumbled onto by another arm of the government, US Customs (and ultimately Congress)—with the trigger for this attention being the explosive growth, in the 1980s, of the bank's US drug money laundering activities. The bank's legal defence was coordinated by former US Secretary of Defence Clark Clifford, who had previously facilitated BCCI's surreptitious entry into the United States via its secret purchase of Washington DC's largest bank: First American Bankshares—and which Clifford had in-turn been made chairman of by BCCI (Kapstein, 1996; Kerry and Brown, 1992).

The petrodollar rent recycling system had emerged during a period in which US business was under intensifying competitive assault from the reconstructed industries of US allies. Since the 1990s, however, a new generation of US technology firms has largely recaptured the position of global monopolistic dominance that US business enjoyed after World War II—and, in turn, generated new rents that have become the most important drivers of the latest wave of global offshore system expansion (Bryan et al., 2017). These firms are very much creatures of the US military industrial complex, with their technological roots lying primarily in defence research spending and contracts (Mazzucato, 2013). However, their global dominance in their respective market segments also rests heavily on indirect political support from the United States, provided both by means of its leading role in strengthening global intellectual property rights (e.g., via the WTO; Piccioto, 2002)—on which the business model of US tech firms fundamentally rests—and through its long-standing provision of an enormous de facto tax subsidy to these firms' overseas operations, via the failure to restrict their strategies of IP-linked offshore profit shifting.

The scale of IP-linked profit shifting by US technology and pharmaceuticals firms is vast, and appears to have become the single largest component of contemporary offshore corporate tax avoidance globally, not to mention a massive percentage of Ireland's GDP (Bryan et al., 2017; Krugman, 2017). It has also been more or less actively aided and abetted by the US federal government since 1996, when the Internal Revenue Service (IRS) largely sabotaged the US CFC anti-avoidance regime with its 'check-the-box' experiment—which was quickly protected by the Republican Congress when the IRS attempted to reverse it (Engels, 2001). Crucially, however, the offshore tax avoidance leeway granted to US firms has never been unconditional. Rather, the Federal Government has consistently sought to keep US firms on an extraterritorial leash from the standpoint of fiscal surveillance and policy prerogative, even while permitting them to engage in aggressive offshore strategies to avoid the taxes of *foreign* countries. Apart from a one-off tax holiday on repatriated offshore corporate earnings in 2003—which was granted as an explicit substitute for a US export-promotion tax break that the World Trade Organization ruled to be illegal (Andrews, 2003)—this has entailed ensuring that companies cannot actually escape from their deferred US tax backlogs. Indeed, the 2017 Tax Cuts and Jobs Acts (TCJA) imposed a deadline for the payment of historically accumulated deferred taxes (albeit at a new reduced rate; Barry, 2019). The United States has also repeatedly taken bi-partisan action to curtail offshore 'inversions' whereby corporations remove themselves from US tax jurisdiction altogether at the parent company level (Palan et al., 2010; Shaviro, 2016; Talley, 2014).

In fact, under both the Obama and Trump administrations, the United States has asserted an increasingly expansive extraterritorial umbrella of authority over the global tax haven system—both for corporations and for individuals. In this respect, the 2017 TCJA—despite often being mischaracterized as creating a 'territorial' corporate tax system—has actually expanded the scope of US CFC legislation, including through far-reaching provisions (Global Intangible Low-Taxed Income—GILTI)[6] that target 'intangible'-based profit shifting strategies (Barry, 2019; Davis, 2019; Kamin et al., 2019). Notably, the GILTI rules seem to do little to discourage (and may, in fact, encourage) offshore profit-shifting by US firms, even while bringing about a 'massive complexification' (Davis, 2019) of the already convoluted and intrusive US federal regime of worldwide corporate tax compliance (Barry, 2019; Kamin et al., 2019). Meanwhile, in the area of personal extraterritorial income taxation, the 2010 Foreign Account Tax Compliance Act (FATCA) has leveraged the threat of crippling US market access restrictions to force virtually all of the world's significant financial institutions (hundreds of thousands in total) to collect and report information to the IRS on the assets of US citizens (Bean and Wright, 2015). Notably, the United States itself has refused to join the new OECD multilateral automatic tax information exchange system (Common Reporting Standard)—with US state wealth management vehicles (e.g., South Dakotan perpetual trusts) apparently enjoying a boom in their international business as a result of the de facto status of the United States as the world's last great remaining secrecy jurisdiction (Bullough, 2019).

Perhaps the greatest irony of FATCA is the fact that the largest American offshore tax avoiders—that is, Silicon Valley technology firms—have already long-provided various agencies of the US security state with a vast semi-private apparatus of global surveillance. Indeed, the twenty-first century US offshore 'protection racket' can be said to operate through an interlocking high-tech mixture of financial, electronic, and—crucially—military offshore spaces, with the latter comprising an extra-legal arena of cyberwarfare, drone strikes, and secret renditions coordinated through information extracted from around the globe via the other two prongs of the offshore system.

As illustrated by cases from the South Sea Company to BCCI, such a structural inversion of the role of offshore from a zone of escape from state politics, to an arena for unrestrained state power projection, is far from novel.[7] Furthermore, the United States is far from alone in developing and exploiting such arrangements today—with its dominance over the global offshore system increasingly both emulated and challenged by rival powers. Ironically, the US Cold War 'victory' has proven to be especially destabilizing in this respect, as it unleashed processes of post-socialist economic restructuring that have been disproportionately mediated through, and in turn transformed, the global offshore system (Nougayrede, 2019). In the case of Russia, the idea of a state offshore 'protection racket' is not so much a metaphor, as a literal description of a globalized quasi-mafioso enterprise. This initially emerged from the use of the offshore system (particularly Cypriot holding companies and the City of London) as a repository for assets stolen from a weak Russian state in the 1990s (Markus, 2017; Nougayrede, 2014). Subsequently, it has become consolidated under the oversight of a strong Russian state that has incorporated the offshore empires of vassal oligarchs into its apparatus of domestic rule, and international geopolitical disruption, extortion, and expansionism (Markus, 2017).

In China, perhaps even more so than in Russia, the offshore system has, in many respects, come full circle back to its medieval role of providing a legal-institutional island of capitalism catalysing change within an (at least, initially) non-capitalist social order. Indeed, UK Caribbean territories such as the Cayman Islands, British Virgin Islands, and Bermuda have effectively become the 'Delawares' of China, with a high proportion of the country's largest firms incorporated in these jurisdictions to facilitate listings in New York and/or Hong Kong (Nougayrede, 2019; Sutherland and Ning, 2011). The massive state-owned enterprises and parastatal private sector internet technology firms that dominate this offshore 'round-trip' investment circuit are, in many respects, throwbacks to the state-chartered monopoly corporations of the mercantilist era, designed to pull private capital into the state's strategic priority areas (Wójcik and Camilleri, 2015). China has also consciously emulated a policy that the United States stumbled into accidentally; namely promoting an offshore market in its own currency (Lim, 2019; Töpfer and Hall, 2018; Walter and Howie, 2011).

Meanwhile, the transatlantic alliance between the United States and Europe has become increasingly strained in the area of offshore tax governance, as in other matters. Historically, this transatlantic relationship has been crucial for the United States, which has relied heavily on multilateral organizations such as the OECD, BIS, and FATF, with a strong (or dominant) European influence, as adjuncts to its ability to achieve its interests within the offshore system—including, in some cases, by deflecting other countries' efforts to combat US abuses of the system (Palan et al., 2010). Indeed, coordinated multilateral responses to offshore tax avoidance pre-date US hegemony, with efforts by the League of Nations in the 1920s and 1930s laying the groundwork for the post-World War II OECD-centred international tax regime (Palan et al., 2010; Piccioto, 1992). In recent years, a particularly acrimonious transatlantic rift has emerged over corporate taxation, with the offshore siphoning of profits out of European countries by US tech monopolies increasingly destabilizing the political foundations of the OECD tax regime. Indeed, the EU and its member states have taken increasingly aggressive action against US tech firm offshore profit-shifting (Lips, 2019)—with the European perception reportedly being that this profit-shifting has been engineered by the United States as a mercantilist export-promotion strategy (Shaviro, 2016). The United States has responded by simultaneously voicing support for the idea of a new OECD-brokered global tax compromise, and threatening retaliation against any European country that attempts to tax its tech firms, with the issue increasingly becoming embroiled within the broader transatlantic trade war (Alderman et al., 2020; Shaviro, 2016).

Ultimately, however, it is the United Kingdom—which, since World War II, has been the central hub in the global offshore system—that appears to be in the greatest danger of being politically dismembered by the tensions now propagating through the system. Historically, the United Kingdom has fostered the development of its offshore 'second empire' (Shaxson, 2011) by locating itself at the nexus of a multi-pronged web of post-colonial relationships, the transatlantic alliance, EU integration, and the economic restructuring and globalization of the former USSR and China (Haberly and Wójcik, 2015; Palan et al., 2010). However, as tensions between these states have intensified, the sustainability of this web of financial relationships has become questionable. The Trump administration has threatened, for example, a mass expulsion from the New York Stock Exchange of listed Chinese firms—most of which are incorporated in UK Caribbean territories (Alper and Lawder, 2019)—while Russia's gratuitous use of chemical weapons on British soil against its diaspora has called into question London's position as a politically 'safe' international platform for Russian business.

Meanwhile, the combination of Brexit and the deteriorating transatlantic alliance has jeopardized Britain's financial relationships with its allies, with the United Kingdom simultaneously antagonizing the EU with its plans for regulatory divergence (Fleming and Peel, 2020), and the United States with its planned tax assault on US technology companies (Elliott and Mason, 2020). Most problematically, the United Kingdom has arguably proven to be too large geographically to sustain its finance/London-centred development model from a regional distributional standpoint, threatening the domestic political stability on which the financial sector depends (Macleod and Jones, 2018; Rodríguez-Pose, 2017). Indeed, the United Kingdom's relationship with the offshore world increasingly resembles a politically volatile emerging market; in the lead-up to the latest election, British utilities placed their assets under offshore holding companies to ensure that shareholders would receive a fair price if expropriated by the state (BBC, 2019).

Offshore in Historical Perspective

As Maurer (2008: 160) puts it, 'Far from a marginal or exotic backwater of the global economy, offshore in many ways *is* the global economy.' The analysis in this chapter has pushed this line of argument one step further by demonstrating the need to conceptualize offshore and onshore as, in effect, the two faces of the state in capitalism. Notably, while the architecture of the offshore system, and the devices employed in it, have become increasingly sophisticated over time, the basic logic of the dialectical relationship between onshore and offshore has been remarkably stable over deep historical timescales. In this respect, far from being an expression of some 'new medievalism', offshore is arguably part of an old medievalism that never actually went away, apart from in the imagination of political theory. Indeed, the leading offshore jurisdictions are, to a large extent, a cast of living fossils (Haberly and Wójcik, 2015). The decaying remnants of European empires are the *newest* additions to this cast; meanwhile, its older members are simply medieval city states and principalities that have survived to the present day in either individual (e.g., Luxembourg, Liechstenstein, Monaco, Jersey, Guernsey, the Corporation of London) or confederated form (e.g., Switzerland). Celebrating its mere 120th anniversary, the incorporation business of Delaware is still in its youthful prime compared to an entity such as the Corporation of London, whose status as a special zone of freedom and privilege under the protection of the Crown is so ancient that people had already forgotten exactly when and how it arose by the time of the Norman conquest—with William simply affirming long-standing customary arrangements in the City's 1067 charter (Shaxson, 2011).

Importantly, the durability of the offshore system does not imply that is unreformable. This is illustrated most clearly by US state-level offshore jurisdictions, which have become caged within an elaborate system of federal level taxation and regulation, combined with state-level formulary apportionment-based corporate taxation.[8] Rather, it is precisely the reformability—and, more broadly, the adaptability—of the offshore system that has underpinned its historical durability. Most importantly, 'offshore' has been persistently reproduced as the structural counterpart to 'onshore' via a powerful convergent evolutionary logic that transcends any particular policies, by any particular states, at any particular time. On the one hand, this entails bottom-up, private-sector led processes of offshore development that seek to evade onshore state authority, invariably sparking countervailing onshore state action aimed at controlling the offshore system. On the other hand, it entails attempts by onshore states to employ the offshore system to advance their own political objectives, invariably unleashing forces beyond their control—and, in turn, setting in motion additional rounds of reactive onshore state re-regulation. Ultimately, it is unclear exactly how the offshore system will evolve under the influence of the geopolitical tensions now propagating through it. In some form, however, it is clearly with us to stay.

Notes

1 According to IMF data. Notably, this includes the world's most important *international* shell company hub, the Netherlands, but excludes its most important overall shell company hub, the US state of Delaware.
2 While the special political powers, rights, and privileges of the City are relatively limited today compared to the Middle Ages, they are far from non-existent (see Shaxson, 2011).
3 E.g., Hanseatic and Florentine merchants in fourteenth- and fifteenth-century England (Munro, 2014; Palais, 1959).
4 For example: 'in 1535, a Genoese senate act established that exchange fairs were to be held in Besançon, in the Free County, under the protection of the emperor Charles V' (Marsilio 2010: 8).
5 I.e., partially state-owned and/or controlled.
6 Global Intangible Low-Taxed Income.
7 Notably, this inversion both mirrors and is intertwined with the same basic paradox observed by Lessig (2006) for the state's relationship with cyberspace (see also Haberly et al., 2019).
8 In other words, US states unilaterally define the locally taxable income base of companies based on substantive factors (sales, assets, payroll, etc.), regardless of where they are incorporated or book their profits (Clausing 2016).

References

Alderman, L., Tankersley, J., and Swanson, A. (Jan. 21, 2020). France and U.S. move towards temporary truce in trade war. *The New York Times*. Available at: https://www.nytimes.com/2020/01/21/business/france-US-digital-tax.html [accessed Jan. 24 2020].

Alper, A., and Lawder, D. (Sept. 27, 2019). Trump considers delisting Chinese firms from U.S. markets: Sources. *Reuters*. Available at: https://www.reuters.com/article/us-usa-trade-china-limits/trump-considers-delisting-chinese-firms-from-u-s-markets-sources-idUSKBN1WC1VP [accessed Jan. 24 2020].

Andrews, E. L. (Oct. 2, 2003). Senate panel backs bill to give tax windfall to U.S. companies. *The New York Times*.

Arrighi, G. (1994). *The Long Twentieth Century: Money, Power, and the Origins of Our Times*. London: Verso.

Arsht, S. S. (1976). A history of Delaware corporation law. *Delaware Journal of Corporate Law*, 1(1), 1–22.

Ashman, I., and Bestwick, H. (2003). *Securitization in the Cayman Islands*. Walkers Attorneys at Law memo.

Baker, J. H. (1979). The Law Merchant and the Common Law before 1700. *The Cambridge Law Journal*, 38(2), 295–322.

Barry, F. (2019). Aggressive tax planning practices and inward-FDI implications for Ireland of the new US corporate tax regime. *Economic and Social Review*, 50(2), 325–340.

BBC. (Nov. 24, 2019). National Grid and SSE move offshore over Labour plans. *BBC*. Available online: https://www.bbc.co.uk/news/business-50536205 [accessed Jan. 22 2020].

Bean, B., and Wright, A. L. (2015). The U.S. Foreign Account Tax Compliance Act: American legal imperialism? *Journal of International & Comparative Law*, 21(2), 333–368.

Boerner, L., and Hatfield, J.W. (2017). The design of debt clearing markets: Clearinghouse mechanisms in pre-industrial Europe. *Journal of Political Economy*, 125(6), 1991–2037.

Boyer-Xambeau, M. T., Deleplace, G., and Gillard, L. (2015). *Private Money and Public Currencies: The Sixteenth Century Challenge*. London: Routledge.

Braudel, F. (1983). *The Wheels of Commerce: Civilization and Capitalism, 15th-18th Century: Volume II*. Berkley: University of California Press.

Brenner, N., Peck, J., and Theodore, N. (2010). Variegated neoliberalization: Geographies, modalities, pathways. *Global Networks*, 10(2), 182–222.

Bryan, D., Rafferty, M., and Wigan, D. (2017). Capital unchained: Finance, intangible assets and the double life of capital in the offshore world. *Review of International Political Economy*, 24(1), 56–86.

Bullough, O. (Nov. 14, 2019). The great American tax haven: Why the super-rich love South Dakota. *The Guardian*. Available online: https://www.theguardian.com/world/2019/nov/14/the-great-american-tax-haven-why-the-super-rich-love-south-dakota-trust-laws [accessed Jan 10 2020].

Chang, K. Y. (2003). Multinational enforcement of U.S. securities laws: The need for the clear and restrained scope of extraterritorial subject-matter jurisdiction. *Fordham Journal of Corporate & Financial Law*, 9(1), 89–125.

Christensen, J., Shaxson, N., and Wigan, D. (2016). The finance curse: Britain and the world economy. *The British Journal of Politics and International Relations*, 18(1), 255–269.

Christensen, J., and Hampton, M. P. (1999). A legislature for hire: The capture of the state in Jersey's offshore finance centre. In Hampton, M.P., Abbott, J.P. (eds), *Offshore Finance Centres and Tax Havens*. London: Palgrave Macmillan.

Clausing, K. (2016). The U.S. state experience under formulary apportionment: Are there lessons for international reform? *National Tax Journal*, 69(2), 353–386.

Cobb, S. C. (1998). Global finance and the growth of offshore financial centers: the Manx experience. *Geoforum*, 29, 7–21.

Coe, N. M., Lai, K. P.Y., and Wojcik, D. (2014). Integrating finance into global production networks. *Regional Studies*, 48, 761–777.

Collins, W. D. (2013). Trusts and the origins of anti-trust legislation. *Fordham Law Review*, 31(5), 2279–2348.

Committee on Ways and Means. (1961). *President's 1961 Tax Recommendations: Hearings before the Committee on Ways and Means, House of Representatives*. Washington, DC: U.S. Congress.

Davis, C. A. (2019). Is the tax cuts and jobs act GILTI of anti-simplification? *Virginia Tax Review*, 38(3), 315–396.

Deacon, J. (2004). *Global Securitisation and CDOs*. Hoboken, NJ: Wiley.

De Long, J. B. (1992). JP Morgan and his Money Trust. *Wilson Quarterly*, 16, 16–30.

Dörry, S. (2014). Strategic nodes in investment fund global production networks: The example of the financial centre Luxembourg. *Journal of Economic Geography*, 15(4), 797–814.

Economist. (Jan 18–24, 2020). American economic power: Spooked by sanctions. *Economist*.

Eden, L., and Kudrle, R. T. (2005). Tax havens: Renegade states in the international tax regime? *Law and Policy*, 27(1), 100–127.

Edwards, J., and Ogilvie, S. (2012). What lessons for economic development can we draw from the Champagne fairs? *Explorations in Economic History*, 49(2), 131–148.

Elliott, L., and Mason, R. (Jan. 22, 2020). UK to impose tax on tech giants but risks US tariffs on car exports. *The Guardian*. Available at: https://www.theguardian.com/business/2020/jan/22/uk-to-impose-tax-on-tech-giants-but-risks-us-tariffs-on-car-exports [accessed Jan. 24 2020].

Emmenegger, P. (2015). The long arm of US justice: US structural power and international banking. *Business and Politics*, 17(3), 473–493.

Engel, K. (2001). Tax neutrality to the left, international competitiveness to the right, stuck in the middle with Subpart-F. *Texas Law Review*, 79(6), 1525–1607.

Faith, N., and Macleod, A. (Nov. 1, 1979). The mysterious private banks of Geneva. *Euromoney*. Available online: https://www.euromoney.com/article/b1d06hwcxg-bq9y/the-mysterious-private-banks-of-geneva?copyrightInfo=true [accessed Jan 10 2020].

Federal Deposit Insurance Corporation (FDIC). (1997). *History of the Eighties: Lessons for the Future. Volume I: An Examination of the Banking Crises of the 1980s and Early 1990s.* Washington, DC: FDIC.

Ferri, P., and Minsky, H. P. (1992). Market processes and thwarting systems. *Structural Change and Economic Dynamics*, 3(1), 79–91.

Fleming, S., and Peel, M. (Jan. 19, 2020). Brussels alarmed by UK's vow to diverge from EU rules. *The Financial Times*. Available at: https://www.ft.com/content/cd70c1c0-3acd-11ea-a01a-bae547046735 [accessed Jan. 24 2020].

Galbraith, J. K. (1967). *The New Industrial State*. Princeton, NJ: Princeton University Press.

Gibbons, W. J. (1956). Tax effects of basing international business abroad. *Harvard Law Review*, 69(7), 1209–1249.

Gorton, G., and Metrick, A. (2010). Regulating the shadow banking system. Brookings Papers on Economic Activity 261. Available at: https://www.brookings.edu/wp-content/uploads/2010/09/2010b_bpea_gorton.pdf [accessed Jan. 21 2020].

Gowa, J. (1985). Subsidizing American corporate expansion abroad: Pitfalls in the analysis of public and private Power. *World Politics*, 37(2), 180–203.

Guex, S. (2000). The origins of the Swiss banking law and its repercussions for Swiss federal policy. *Business History Review*, 74, 237–266.

Haberly, D., and Wójcik, D. (2015). Regional blocks and imperial legacies: Mapping the global offshore FDI network. *Economic Geography*, 91(3), 251–280.

Haberly, D., and Wójcik, D. (2017). Culprits or bystanders? Offshore jurisdictions and the global financial crisis. *Journal of Financial Regulation*, 3(2), 233–261.

Haberly, D., MacDonald-Korth, D., Urban, M., and Wójcik, D. (2019). Asset management as a digital platform industry: A global financial network perspective. *Geoforum*, 106, 167–181.

Hansmann, H. (2006). Corporation and contract. *American Law and Economics Review*, 8(1), 1–19.

Hansmann, H., Kraakman, R., and Squire, R. (2006). Law and the rise of the firm. *Harvard Law Review*, 119(5), 1335–1403.

Hampton, M.P. (1996). *The Offshore Interface: Tax Havens in the Global Economy*. London: MacMillan.

Helleiner, E. (1994). *States and the Emergence of Global Finance: From Bretton Woods to the 1990s*. Ithaca: Cornell University Press.

Herring, R. (2007). Conflicts between home and host country prudential supervisors. In D. Evanoff, J. LaBrosse, G. Kaufman (eds.) *International Financial Instability: Global Banking and National Regulation*, 201–219. Singapore: World Scientific Publishing.

Hudson, A. (2000). Offshoreness, globalization and sovereignty: a postmodern geopolitical economy? *Transactions of the Institute of British Geographers*, 25, 269–283.

Hunt, N. (2013). Contraband, free ports, and British merchants in the Caribbean world, 1739–1772. *Diacronie Studi di Storia Contemporanea*, 13(1), 1–12.

Ingves, S. (Jan. 29, 2018). Basel III: Are we done now? Keynote speech by Mr Stefan Ingves, Chairman of the Basel Committee on Banking Supervision, *at the Institute for Law and Finance Conference*, Goethe University, Frankfurt am Main. Available at: https://www.bis.org/speeches/sp180129.htm [accessed Jan. 23 2020].

Innes, W. C. (1983). *Social Concern in Calvin's Geneva*. Eugene: Pickwick Publications.

Kadens, E. (2004). Order within law, variety within custom: The character of the medieval merchant law. *Chicago Journal of International Law*, 5(1), 39–66.

Kadens, E. (2015). The medieval Law Merchant: The tyranny of a construct. *Journal of Legal Analysis*, 7(2), 251–289.

Kamin, D., Gamage, D., Glogower, A., Kysar, R., Shanske, D., Avi-Yonah, R., Batchelder, L., Fleming, J., Hemel, D., Kane, M. (2019). The games they will play: Tax games, roadblocks, and glitches under the 2017 tax legislation. *Minnesota Law Review*, 103(3), 1439–1522.

Kapstein, E.B. (1991). Supervising international banks: Origins and implications of the Basel Accord. Essays in International Finance No. 185, December 1991. International Finance Section, Department of Economics, Princeton University. Available online: https://www.princeton.edu/~ies/IES_Essays/E185.pdf [accessed Jan. 21 2020].

Kapstein, E. B. (1996). *Governing the Global Economy: International Finance and the State*. Cambridge: Harvard University Press.

Kerry, J., and Brown, H. (1992). *The BCCI Affair: A Report to the Committee on Foreign Relations United States Senate*. Washington, DC: U.S. Government Printing Office.

Kovacic, W. E., and Shapiro, C. (2000). Anti-trust policy: A century of economic and legal thinking. *Journal of Economic Perspectives*, 14(1), 43–60.

Mahoney, J. F. (1966). Backsliding convert: Woodrow Wilson and the "Seven Sisters". *American Quarterly*, 18(1), 71–80.

Krugman, P. (Nov. 8, 2017). Leprechaun economics and neo-Lafferism. *The New York Times*. Available online: https://web.archive.org/web/20180430234132/https://krugman.blogs.nytimes.com/2017/11/08/leprechaun-economics-and-neo-lafferism/ [accessed Jan. 22 2020].

Le Marchant, C. M. (1999). Financial regulation and supervision offshore: Guernsey, a case study. In Hampton, M.P., Abbott, J.P. (eds.), *Offshore Finance Centres and Tax Havens*. London: Palgrave Macmillan.

Lessig, L. (2006). *Code, Version 2.0*. New York: Basic Books.

Lim, K. F. (2019). *On Shifting Foundations: State Rescaling, Policy Experimentation, and Economic Restructuring in Post-1949 China*. Oxford: Wiley.

Lips, W. (2019). The EU Commission's digital tax proposals and its cross-platform impact in the EU and the OECD. *Journal of European Integration*. doi: 10.1080/07036337.2019.1705800.

Lissakers, K. (1977). *International Debt, the Banks, and U.S. Foreign Policy: A Staff Report Prepared for the Use of the Subcommittee on Foreign Economic Policy of the Committee on Foreign Relations of the United States Senate*. Washington, DC: US Government Printing Office.

Louise, S. (2017). The small republic and the great power: Censorship between Geneva and France in the later eighteenth century. *Library (Land)*, 18(2), 191–217.

MacLeod, G., and Jones, M. (2018). Explaining "Brexit capital": Uneven development and the austerity state. *Space and Polity*, 22(2), 111–136.

Markus, S. (2017). Oligarchs and corruption in Putin's Russia: Of sand castles and geopolitical volunteering. *Georgetown Journal of International Affairs*, 18(2), 26–32

Marsilio, C. (2010). Four times a year for so many years. The Italian Exchange Fairs during the XVIth-XVIIth Century: Comparing Financial Institutions. *Bankhistorisches Archiv - Banking and Finance in Historical Perspective*, 36(2), 151–165.

Maurer. B. (2008). Re-regulating offshore finance? *Geography Compass*, 2(1), 155–175.

Maurer, B., and Martin, S. J. (2012). Accidents of equity and the aesthetics of Chinese offshore incorporation. *American Ethnologist*, 39(3), 527–544.

Mazzucato, M. (2013). *The Entrepreneurial State: Debunking Public vs. Private Sector Myths*. London: Anthem.

Morley, J. (2016). The common law corporation: The power of the trust in Anglo-American business history. *Columbia Law Review*, 116(8), 2145–2197.

Moon, A. (May 21, 2003). Cayman Islands Securitisation. *Mondaq*.

Munro, J. H. (2001). The "New Institutional Economics" and the changing fortunes of fairs in medieval and early modern Europe. *VSWG: Vierteljahrschrift für Sozial- und Wirtschaftsgeschichte*, 88(1), 1–47.

Munro, J. H. (2003). The medieval origins of the financial revolution: Usury, rentes, and negotiability. *The International History Review*, 25(3), 505–562.

Munro, J. H. (2014). The dual crises of the late-medieval Florentine cloth industry, 1320–1420. In A. L. Huang and C. Jahnke (eds.), *Textiles and the Medieval Economy: Production, Trade, and Consumption of Textiles, 8th-16th Centuries*. Oxford: Oxbow Books.

Navin, T. R., and Sears, M.V. (1955). The rise of a market for industrial securities, 1887–1902. *The Business History Review*, 29(2), 105–138.

North, D. C. (1993). The Paradox of the West. Working Paper. Available at: http://dlc.dlib.indiana.edu/dlc/bitstream/handle/10535/4158/9309005.pdf [accessed Jan. 21 2020].

North, D. C., and Thomas, R. P. (1973). *The Rise of the Western World: A New Economic History*. New York: Cambridge University Press.

Nougayrede, D. (2014). Outsourcing Law in Post-Soviet Russia. *Journal of Eurasian Law*, 3, 383–448

Nougayrede, D. (2019). After the Panama Papers: A private law critique of shell companies. *The International Lawyer*, 327–367.

Palais, H. (1959). England's first attempt to break the commercial monopoly of the Hanseatic league, 1377–1380. *The American Historical Review*, 64(4), 852–865.

Palan, R. (1999). Offshore and the structural enablement of sovereignty. In Hampton, M.P., Abbott, J.P. (eds), *Offshore Finance Centres and Tax Havens*. London: Palgrave Macmillan.

Palan, R., Murphy, R., and Chavagneux, C. (2010). *Tax Havens: How Globalization Really Works*. Ithaca: Cornell University Press.

Papadopoulos, Y. (2000). How does direct democracy matter? The impact of referendum votes on politics and policy-making. *West European Politics*, 24(2), 35–58.

Papke, L. E. (2000). One-way treaty with the world: The U.S. withholding tax and the Netherlands Antilles. *International Tax and Public Finance*, 7, 295–313.

Passas, N. (1996). The genesis of the BCCI scandal. *Journal of Law and Society*, 23(1), 57–72.

Pezzolo, L., and Tattara, G. (2006). Una fiera senza luogo. Was Bisenzone an offshore capital market in sixteenth-century Italy? Working Paper, Department of Economics, Ca' Foscari University of Venice No. 25/WP/2006.

Piccioto, S. (1992). *International Business Taxation: A Study in the Internationalization of Business Regulation*. London: Weidenfeld and Nicholson.

Piccioto, S. (1999). Offshore: The state as legal fiction. In Hampton, M.P., Abbott, J.P. (eds), *Offshore Finance Centres and Tax Havens*. London: Palgrave Macmillan.

Piccioto, S. (2002). Defending the public interest in TRIPs and the WTO. In P. Drahos and R. Mayne (eds.) *Global Intellectual Property Rights: Knowledge, Access, and Development*. New York: Palgrave Macmillan.

Pirenne, H. (2014). *Medieval Cities: Their Origins and the Revival of Trade* (Updated Edition). Princeton, NJ: Princeton University Press.

Pistor, K. (2019). *The Code of Capital: How the Law Creates Wealth and Inequality*. Princeton, NJ: Princeton University Press.

Polanyi, K. (2001). *The Great Transformation: The Political and Economic Origins of Our Time* (2nd Edition). Boston, MA: Beacon Press.

Poon, J.P.H., Tan, G.K.S., and Hamilton, T. (2019). Social power, offshore financial intermediaries and a network regulatory imaginary. *Political Geography*, 68, 55–65.

Potts, S. (2020). (Re-)writing markets: Law and contested payment geographies. *Environment and Planning A*, 52(1), 46–65

Pozsar, Z., Adrian, T., Ashcraft, A., and Boesky, H. (2012). Shadow banking. Federal Reserve Bank of New York Staff Reports No 458. Available at: https://www.newyorkfed.org/medialibrary/media/research/staff_reports/sr458.pdf [accessed Jan. 21 2010].

Quinn, S. (2008). Securitization of Sovereign Debt: Corporations as a Sovereign Debt Restructuring Mechanism in Britain, 1694 to 1750. Working Paper. Available on SSRN: https://papers.ssrn.com/sol3/papers.cfm?abstract_id=991941 [accessed Jan. 23 2020].

Roberts, S. (1994). Fictitious capital, fictitious spaces: The geography of offshore financial flows. In R. Martin, N. Thrift, and S. Corbridge (eds.), *Money, Power and Space*, 91–115. Oxford: Blackwell.

Rodríguez-Pose, A. (2017). The revenge of the places that don't matter (and what to do about it). *Cambridge Journal of Regions, Economy and Society*, 11(1), 189–209.

Roy, W. G. (1999). *Socializing Capital: The Rise of the Large Industrial Corporation in America.* Princeton, NJ: Princeton University Press.

Seabrooke, L., and Wigan, D. (2014). Global wealth chains in the international political economy. *Review of International Political Economy*, 21, 257–263.

Sharman, J. C. (2009). The bark is the bite: International organizations and blacklisting. *Review of International Political Economy*, 16(4), 573–596.

Shaviro, D. (2016). The U.S. Response to OECD-BEPS and the EU State Aid Cases. NYU Law and Economics Research Paper No. 16–27. Available at: https://papers.ssrn.com/sol3/papers.cfm?abstract_id=2791697 [accessed Jan. 24 2020].

Shaxson, N. (2011). *Treasure Islands: Tax Havens and the Men Who Stole the World.* London: Vintage.

Spiro, D. E. (1999). *The Hidden Hand of American Hegemony: Petrodollar Recycling and International Markets.* Ithaca: Cornell University Press.

Stevens, O. P. (1962). A current appraisal of foreign base companies. *Taxes*, 40(2), 117–120.

Strange, S. (1994). From Bretton Woods to the casino economy. In R Martin, N Thrift and S Corbridge (eds), *Money, Power and Space.* Oxford: Blackwell, 49–62.

Strine, L. E. (2005). The Delaware way: How we do corporation law and some of the new challenges we (and Europe) face. *Delaware Journal of Corporation Law*, 30(3), 673–696.

Sutherland, D., and Ning, L. (2011). Exploring "onward-journey" ODI strategies in China's private sector businesses. *Journal of Chinese Economic and Business Studies*, 9(1), 43–65.

Talley, E. L. (2014). Corporate inversions and the unbundling of regulatory competition. *Virginia Law Review*, 101, 1649–1751.

Taviani, C. (2015). An ancient scheme: The Mississippi Company, Machiavelli, and the Casa di San Giorgio (1407–1720). In E. Erikson (ed.), *Chartering Capitalism: Organizing Markets, States, and Publics.* Bingley: Emerald.

Tilly, C. (1985). War making and state making as organized crime. In Evans, P. B., Rueschemeyer, D., and Skocpol, T. (eds.), *Bringing the State Back In.* Cambridge: Cambridge University Press.

Tilly, C. (1989). Cities and States in Europe, 1000–1800. *Theory and Society*, 18(5), 563–584.

Töpfer, A. M., and Hall, S. (2018). London's rise as an offshore RMB financial centre: State–finance relations and selective institutional adaptation. *Regional Studies*, 52(8), 1053–1064.

Ugolini, S. (2018). The origins of Swiss wealth management? Genevan private banking, 1800–1840. *Financial History Review*, 25(2), 161–182.

Van Dijk, M., Weyzig, F., and Murphy, R. (2006). The Netherlands: A Tax Haven? Stichting Onderzoek Multinationale Ondernemingen (SOMO). Available online: https://www.somo.nl/nl/wp-content/uploads/sites/2/2006/11/A-tax-haven.pdf [accessed Jan 11 2020].

Venturi, F. (1991). *The End of the Old Regime in Europe, 1776–1789, Part I: The Great States of the West*. Princeton, NJ: Princeton University Press.

Vlcek, W. (2007). Why worry? The impact of the OECD harmful tax competition initiative on Caribbean offshore financial centres. *The Round Table: The Commonwealth Journal of International Affairs*, 96(390), 331–346.

Vlcek, W. (2019). Tax avoidance. In T. M. Shaw, L. C. Mahrenbach, R. Modi, and X. Yi-Chong (eds.), *The Palgrave Handbook of Contemporary International Political Economy*. London: Palgrave Macmillan.

Wainwright, T. (2011). Tax doesn't have to be taxing: London's "onshore" finance industry and the fiscal spaces of a global crisis. *Environment and Planning A*, 43(6), 1287–1304.

Wallerstein, I. (2004). *World-Systems Analysis: An Introduction*. Durham, NC: Duke University Press.

Wellons, P. A. (1987). *Passing the Buck: Banks, Governments, and Third World Debt*. Cambridge: Harvard Business School Press.

Walter, C. E., and Howie, F. J. T. (2011). *Red Capitalism: The Fragile Financial Foundations of China's Extraordinary Rise*. Singapore: John Wiley & Sons.

Warf, B. (2002). Tailored for Panama: offshore banking at the crossroads of the Americas. *Geografiska Annaler*, 84, 33–47.

Wójcik, D., and Camilleri, J. (2015). "Capitalist tools in socialist hands"? China Mobile in global financial networks. *Transactions of the Institute of British Geographers*, 40(4), 464–478.

Yablon, C. M. (2007). The historical race: Competition for corporate charters and the rise and decline of New Jersey: 1880–1910. *The Journal of Corporation Law*, 32, 323–380.

PART VI

Finance, Development and the Environment

26

FINANCE AND DEVELOPMENT IN SUB-SAHARAN AFRICA

Susan Newman

Introduction

The five decades since independence across sub-Saharan Africa (SSA) began in 1960 have seen dramatic shifts in the definition of economic development in the rhetoric, policy, and practice of African nations, international financial institutions (IFIs), and bilateral donors from the Global North. There has also been a significant redefinition of finance in relation to capital accumulation, and the role and functioning of national financial sectors.

Approaches to economic development that were prominent between the 1950s and 1970s stressed the role of finance as a servant to industrial development. The development of manufacturing with industrial policy was viewed as an imperative in order to transform newly independent economies—once characterized by capitalist enclaves and extractivist structures, and formed under colonialism—into integrated and diversified modern economies that promoted productivity enhancement and employment generation.

Since the 1980s, development policies have been underpinned by the logics of the Washington Consensus and by the neoclassical economics that informs the approach. Concerns of financial and industrial structure gave way to issues of efficiency of intermediation and growth, and the rejection of industrial policy. From the late 1990s, the market-centred logic has moved further towards a view that the achievement of a market-based financial system should be a goal of development in itself whereby 'financial development' is both the means and the end of 'financing development'.

The shift from 'financing development' to 'financial development' and, more recently, the promotion of private finance and private sector development in SSA, has taken place in the context of the profound restructuring of the global economy and capitalist accumulation in relation to finance. Financialization can be understood most broadly as the 'increasing power of the owners of money in the management of economic affairs' (Bracking, 2016: 1). The extension of power and influence over economic activities across SSA has occurred through different avenues, including development policies and financial sector development programmes that take on particular local characteristics due to the specificity of colonial histories and capitalist development.

This chapter traces broad changes in the role of finance in development policies, practices, and processes in SSA. It does so by assessing the relationship between finance and industrial development: (i) that is implied by different approaches to finance in development policy; (ii) in relation to the trends and changing patterns of external debt and financial flows on the continent; and (iii) in the historical development of economies in SSA. The cases of Tanzania and South Africa are presented to illustrate commonalities and differences in the ways in which financial sectors have developed owing to similarities and differences in their respective colonial experience, and the character of capitalist development after independence.

The Evolution of Finance in Development Policy

State Directed Finance for Modernization

Early approaches to late/catch-up industrialization stressed both the imperative for modernization of economies in the Global South and the need for adequate external financing due to the limited scope for taxation, and low or negligible domestic savings rates. The early independence period saw relatively generous flows of concessional lending in the form of overseas development assistance (ODA) from Western nations that reflected the influence of modernization theory in development thinking, the project of nation-building in post-colonial Africa, and the global political economy context of the Cold War. State intervention in directing finance for economic development was prevalent across much of SSA, variously involving the establishment of state-owned financial institutions channelling ODA, nationalization of commercial banks established during the colonial period, and/or establishment of government owned commercial banks.

State directed industrial development with external finance registered early success. For example, the average annual growth rate of manufacturing was 11% between 1948 and 1959 in the Democratic Republic of the Congo, and 5% between 1956 and 1963 in Kenya (Pearson, 1969). Moreover, manufacturing was relatively diversified in countries of the East African Union, Kenya, Uganda, and Tanzania (Pearson, 1969). However, gains made in the 1960s were rapidly eroded during the second half of the 1970s when OPEC oil price shocks resulted in unsustainably high import bills that triggered a wave of balance of payments crises across the so-called Third World.

The Washington Consensus and the Financial Development Agenda

With the rise of neoliberalism and the Washington Consensus, as the articulation of its related development approach, the debt crisis was interpreted by the World Bank as the result of poor policies, state capture by elites, and widespread corruption and rent-seeking in post-colonial SSA, as well as the more general misallocation of resources by developing country governments through 'financial repression' (McKinnon, 1973; World Bank, 1981). During the 1980s, heavy conditions were placed on the disbursement of development assistance by the World Bank that severely limited the role of the state in directing investment. Emphasis was placed on supporting the development of a market-based financial sector that could ensure the efficient allocation of capital.

Towards the end of the 1990s, the World Bank began actively promoting financial development as an end in itself. This strategic focus was premised on a growing literature that emphasized a long-run positive statistical relationship between financial development and growth, with the assumption that causality ran from the former to the latter (Levine, 1997; Demirgüç-Kunt, and Levine, 2004). Financial development involves the proliferation and growth of a range of financial institutions and markets (financial deepening), increased efficiency of intermediation, and improved and widened access to financial services. Theoretical justification for financial development through liberalization of interest rates, financial sector deregulation, and capital account liberalization was provided by the financial repression thesis of McKinnon (1973), which argued against policy interference in the allocation of credit. Financial development, it was argued, would bring about a more efficient allocation of capital, and higher rates of investment and returns in developing countries.

The Financialization of Development Policy

The current 'consensus' of the IFIs and Northern donors with respect to development finance has been comprehensively articulated in the agenda set by the Third Conference on Financing Development held in Addis Ababa in July 2015. In order to meet the Sustainable Development Goals (SDGs) set in the 2030 Agenda for Sustainable Development, an estimated US$600 billion and US$1.2 trillion per year in Africa would be required (UNCTAD, 2016). Focus has thus turned on the private sector as a critical source of finance for development. The focus on the private sector as a source of development finance is part of a longer-term reorientation of development policy that has been referred to as the 'private turn in development', which centres on the role of the private sector in development policy and practice. In relation to development finance, this has involved: (i) the promotion of ODA in facilitating private sector investment; (ii) the promotion of blended mechanisms for financing social and economic infrastructure, with public–private partnerships (PPP) playing a major role that was once the purview of public finance; and (iii) the extension of financial inclusion aimed at tackling poverty (Van Waeyenberge, 2015; Mawdsley, 2016; Bayliss and Van Waeyenberge, 2018; Lavinas, 2018). This process has resulted in increased alignment between financing development and financial development and a reduction in the role for aid as 'residual and auxiliary' (Van Waeyenberge, 2015: 6).

The private turn in development policy has been operating in the context of the rise of international private finance on a global scale. This has involved financial globalization as the quantitative increase in cross-border financial flows and increasing interconnectedness between countries through financial networks (Wójcik, 2018). Since the 1990s, dramatic changes have occurred in the ways in which countries on the continent have been networked into a global financial architecture. These changes relate to economic restructuring in the Global North and have become referred to as 'financialization'. Financialization as a process takes place at different levels of economic organization. At the level of corporate governance, financialization has been driven by the doctrine of maximizing 'shareholder value' and has manifested itself in corporate downsizing, shifts in corporate strategy to focus on 'core competencies', and the outsourcing of ancillary activities and low value-added portions of the production chain (e.g. to supplier firms in low-wage economies) (Milberg and Winkler, 2009; Lazonick, 2014). The rise of global value chains as the dominant way in which production is organized in the world economy since the 1990s has necessarily involved a greater role for finance. More finance is required to facilitate the trade in intermediate goods between suppliers and users of parts and part-finished products that operate at arms-length along transnational supply chains. Finance is required for the direct payment for goods and services, and insurance, as well as hedging against foreign exchange fluctuations and other price variations Finance has also played an increasingly important role in the corporate strategy of multinational firms. Non-financial multinational corporations have increased their investment in purely financial activities and increasingly use financial instruments to determine the distribution of income in their favour (Baud and Durand, 2012; Bargawi and Newman, 2017; Staritz et al., 2018).

Financialization has also been associated with the withdrawal of the welfare state in social provisioning, and the rise of private pension and insurance funds that seek increasing opportunities for investment, including in developing and emerging markets, to ensure returns for the 'ultimate human owners of assets' (Quentin and Campling, 2018: 38). In the 2000s, until the global financial crisis (GFC), a number of economies in SSA became attractive destinations for financial investment because of capital market liberalization and improved GDP growth rates in commodity exporting countries that had been fuelled by a decade-long commodity boom. This has seen greater integration of some African economies into international capital markets. There was a rush by investors towards commodities as equity returns plummeted in the wake of the GFC. Moreover, the context of low interest rates in the Global North since the GFC has improved the attractiveness of African economies to financial investors. The evolution of external debt in SSA (discussed in the next section) relates increasingly to the nature of the integration of African economies into the global financial system. This is visible in the changing maturity structure of the debt towards more short-term financial flows that reflect refinancing and hedging requirements of financial investors, rather than related to current account imbalances (Bonizzi et al., 2015).

Continued economic stagnation in the Global North, persistent low interest rates, and the financialization of social provisioning has seen the alignment of interests between individual and institutional investors, on the one hand, and development agencies in the Global North, on the other. Commitments to 0.7% of GNI for international aid, made in 2005 by the EU; the G8 Gleneagles summit; and the UN World Summit are not popular amongst electorates subjected to a decade of austerity policies and real wage stagnation. 'With dwindling traditional financing', IFIs and national development agencies grappled with the issue on how to meet 'the increasing financial needs of the continent' required to achieve the SDGs (UNCTAD, 2016: 92). The answer, as outlined above, has been the exploration of non-traditional sources of finance including PPPs, sovereign wealth funds, remittances and diaspora bonds, GDP-indexed and climate related bonds, and social impact bonds. These financing modalities satisfy the demand for new financial assets by investors in the Global North and turn the process of development itself into a financial asset. In relation to the rise in PPP advocacy by donor agencies, Bayliss and Van Waeyenberge (2018: 578) observed that this has been 'anchored almost entirely in arguments seeking to match a glut in global savings with the need to upscale public service provisioning in developing countries [that] has created an increasingly financialised approach to infrastructure, as a policy is framed in terms of investment opportunities for financial investors and institutional arrangements bearing on infrastructure provision are reconfigured to facilitate their entry into the sector.'

The financialization of development policy has been extended to the micro level in the deployment of financial inclusion promoted through digital financial technologies to tackle poverty (Mawdsley, 2016; Gabor and Brooks, 2017; Mader, 2018). Indeed, access to financial services features in at least 5 of the 17 SDGs. Rather than a consequence of structural issues related to economic underdevelopment, including high unemployment and underemployment, poverty has been redefined as the inability of individuals to mitigate risks. Access to appropriate formal financial services for the purposes of consumption smoothing and insurance thus lend themselves as obvious solutions to the problem of poverty. While the demonstrable outcomes of financial inclusion on poverty alleviation are scant, that financial inclusion generates economic growth and development more broadly is both assumed by protagonists of the policy approach and not evidenced in outcomes (Mader, 2018). It has been highlighted by numerous authors that the extension of financial development to financial inclusion readily serves the interests of private finance by extending markets to the previously unbanked and underbanked. The promotion of demonetarization through the extension of digital payments systems for social welfare is an example of how social policy agendas have been reconfigured to generate more financial assets for investors by collateralizing, securitizing, and capturing these government-to-citizen payments (Lavinas, 2018). Moreover, demonetarization and the inclusion of the poor into digital financial networks generate digital footprints that represent lucrative information for the marketing and extending of further financial products to the poor (Gabor and Brooks, 2017).

This section has discussed the evolution of finance and development policy from the early post-liberation period in SSA, when the role of (largely public) finance was framed in its service to state directed industrial development, to the relegation of the role of the state to ensure a stable macroeconomic environment in the context of liberalized trade and finance. Development finance gave way to financial development as an end in itself, with only a tenuous link to the financing of investment. Financial development in the form of the financial inclusion agenda has further distanced the development of finance from broader sustained processes of economic growth and development as development finance is increasingly equated with private finance.

International Capital Flows and Financial Development in Sub-Saharan Africa

External financing and external debt have been an enduring feature of capitalist development in SSA, from the limited and enclaved industrial development under colonial rule into the post-independence era of state-led industrialization and beyond (Figure 26.1). The issue of the financing gap between the extent to which domestic resources can be mobilized and the needs for rapid economic development has been central to the rhetoric, policy, and practice of development in SSA since liberation from colonial rule. This section examines the historical trends in external debt and, particularly, the changing composition of financial flows and creditors, highlighting both broad trends as well as key differences between countries. Moreover, we consider the implications of the changing composition of financial flows on structural transformation of economies in SSA.

Trends and Changing Composition of External Debt

The problem of external finance has not simply been one of ensuring adequate financial inflows to meet the gap between domestic savings mobilization and required investment for structural transformation of the economy. The sustainable maintenance of a significant debt burden has been a critical issue. In line with the post-war political consensus across the United States, United Kingdom and Western Europe, economic development in the newly

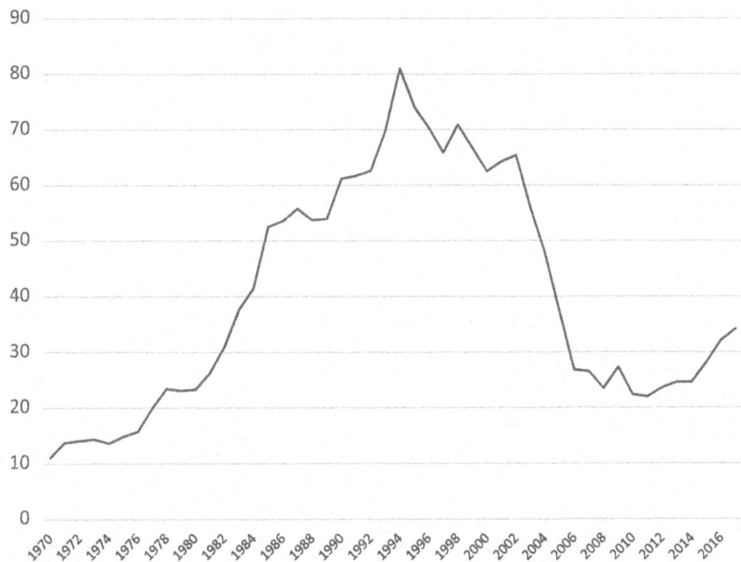

Figure 26.1 External debt stock as a percentage of SSA GDP 1970–2017

Source: World Debt Tables 2018.

independent nations of 1960s SSA was reliant on foreign inflows in the form of concessional lending by multilateral institutions—such as the precursor to the World Bank, the International Bank for Reconstruction and Development (IBRD)—as well as bilateral lending from former colonial rulers. Early approaches to late industrialization stressed both the imperative for the modernization of the economy, as well as the need for adequate financing for development. Modernization theorists, including Kaldor, emphasized the unique growth-pulling or growth-enhancing properties of manufacturing development. Structural transformation of the economy from traditional production and agriculture to a diversified and integrated manufacturing economy was therefore seen as imperative for catch-up development. in unleashing economic growth via growth pull effects (Tregenna, 2008). Drawing on the history of Germany's industrialization, Gerschenkron (1962) pointed out the importance of investment banks to the channelling of finance for industry based on long-term relationships between banks and firms. Many newly independent nations in SSA thus set about the development of domestic financial institutions that channelled finance for industrial development—in particular, manufacturing.

As a share of GDP, total external debt increased from just over 11% in 1970 to nearly 56% in 1987 at the height of the debt crisis (Figure 26.1). Throughout the 1970s, 80% of external debt was public and publicly guaranteed (PPG) debt (Figure 26.2). Bilateral and multilateral debt as a share of total PPG in the 1970s was, on average, respectively, 53% and 19% (Figure 26.3). The balance

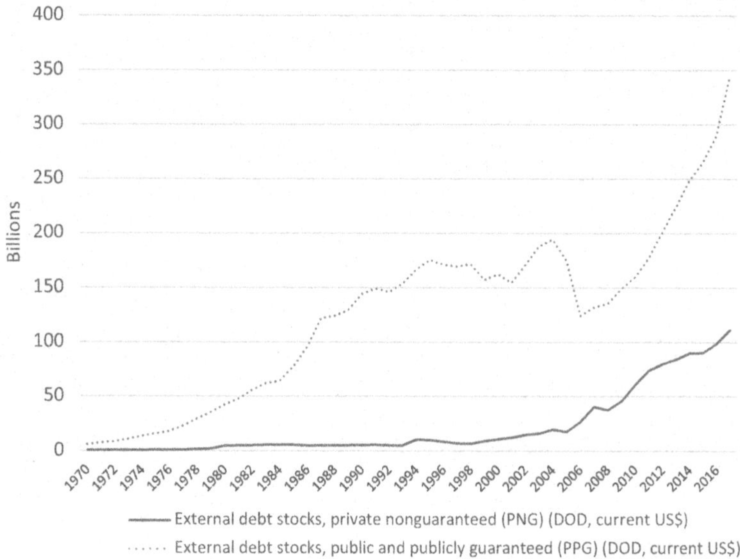

Figure 26.2 Type of external debt stock in SSA (current US$)

Source: World Debt Tables 2018.

of payments crises of the late 1970s and the 1980s saw an increasing role for multilateral institutions—namely, the IMF—in lending to SSA that was subject to the uptake of structural adjustment programmes (SAPs). Debt to GDP increased further during this period, reaching a historical peak of 81% in 1994 (Figure 26.1).

By the 1990s, conditional lending by the World Bank and a reoriented IMF towards development policy and practice saw these institutions taking on a greater share of lending. The share of multilateral debt in PPG in the 1990s and 2000s was, on average, respectively 31% and 37%. While external debt as a share of GDP had been falling for SSA as a whole from 1994 until 2011, there has been a dramatic shift in the composition of external debt. With greater borrowing by the private sector in SSA, which had been negligible prior to 1995,[1] the latter half of the 1990s saw year-on-year growth in private non-guaranteed (PNG) debt, which accelerated from the mid-2000s, contributing to the sharp increase in external debt from 2006 onwards (Figure 26.2). The accumulation of external debt has continued apace in SSA since the GFC and has been increasing as a share of GDP since 2011, reversing the downward trend between 2000 and 2010 related to debt relief programmes such as the Highly-Indebted Poor Countries (HIPC) initiatives and the Multilateral Debt Relief Initiative (MDRI) as part of the Millennium Development Goals (MDGs), for which many SSA countries qualified. (UNCTAD, 2016; IMF, 2017).

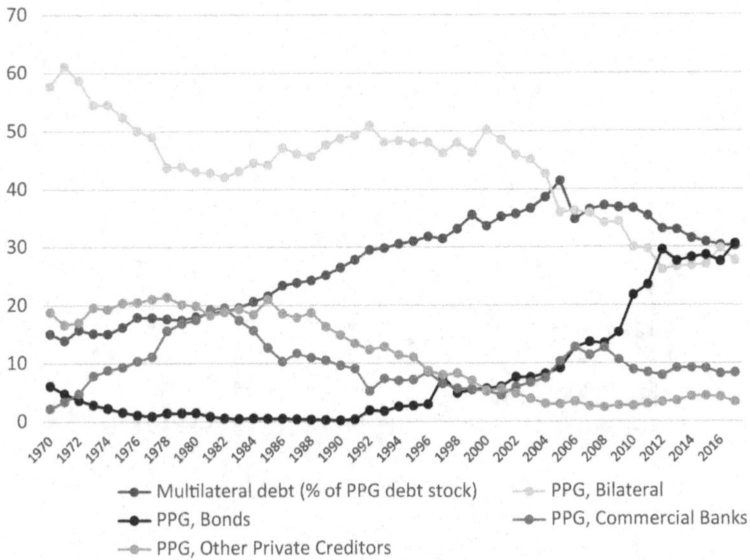

Figure 26.3 Creditor shares of total PPG debt stock in SSA

Note: Multilateral debt refers to that which is incurred through borrowing from international financial institutions such as the World Bank and the International Monetary Fund. Bilateral debt is debt incurred from borrowing and lending between individual nation states.

Source: World Debt Tables 2018.

Moreover, with the launch of the Addis Ababa Action Agenda in 2015 and its emphasis on the role of private finance, we have seen a major qualitative shift in external debt—namely, the increasing role of private creditors in PPG that has been on the rise since the global financial crash of 2007/08 (Figure 26.3). While commercial bank lending has continued to play a role in PPG lending, the issuance of sovereign bonds by some SSA countries has become an increasingly important source of external borrowing (UNCTAD, 2016).

Having presented aggregate trends and changes in the composition of external debt in SSA, the diversity across the countries of SSA cannot be overstated. Figure 26.4 compares the external debt stock, GNI, and external debt to GNI ratios across SSA countries. Angola's growing external debt stock reflects the rise of China's role in foreign aid and development cooperation in Africa since the 1990s (Mawdsley, 2007; Brautigam, 2011). This is evident in the rising share of bilateral lending in a number of SSA countries receiving substantial loans from China, including Angola, the Republic of Congo, the Democratic Republic of the Congo, Djibouti, and Zambia (Figures 26.6 and 26.7). The sectoral pattern of lending by China in Africa is concentrated in mining, transport, power, and communications, which are reflective of Chinese economic interests in the continent.

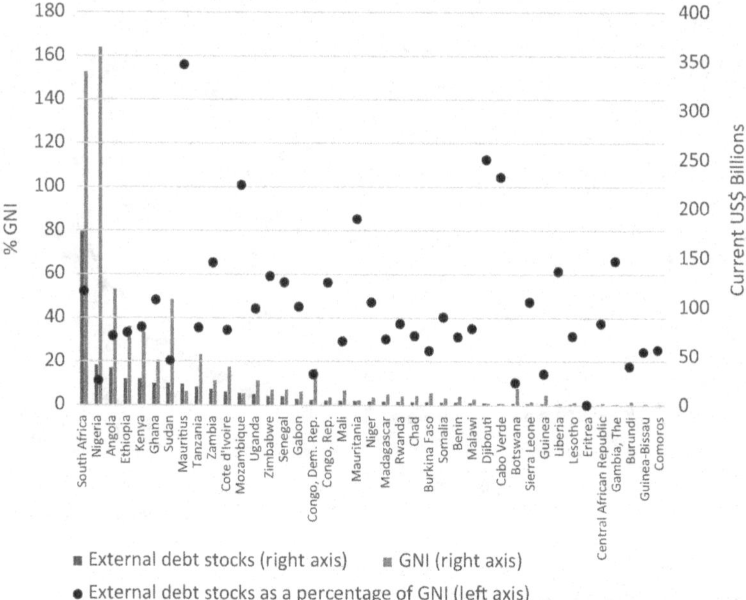

Figure 26.4 External debt stock and GNI across SSA countries in 2017

Source: World Debt Tables 2018.

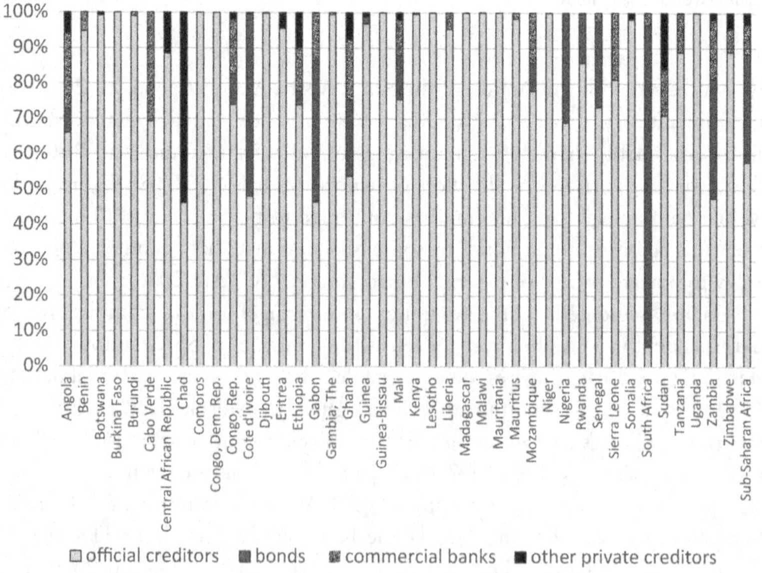

Figure 26.5 Composition of PPG debt stock by creditor, 2017

Note: Official creditors include international financial institutions and governments.

Source: World Debt Tables 2018.

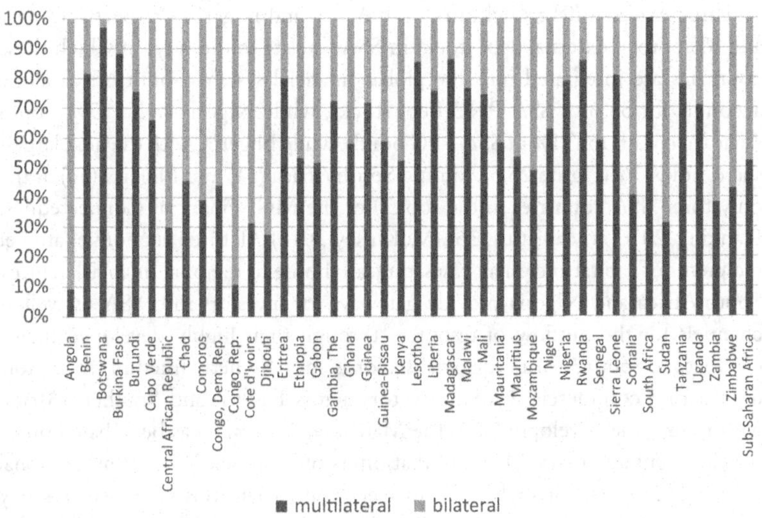

Figure 26.6 Composition of PPG debt stock owed to official creditors, 2017

Source: World Debt Tables 2018.

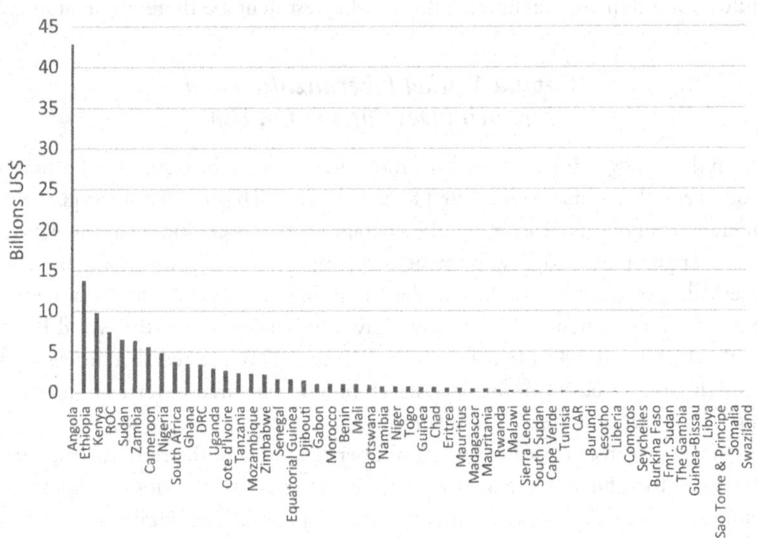

Figure 26.7 Sum of loans to countries in SSA from China between 2000 and 2017

Source: Johns Hopkins SAIS China-Africa Research Initiative.

Large external debt stocks in South Africa and Nigeria—respectively, 34% and 8% of total external debt stocks in SSA—relate to the ways in which these countries are integrated into the global financial system. South Africa alone accounts for 54% of SSA PNG debt stocks, while Nigeria holds 17%. South Africa accounts for 71% of SSA PPG bonds, while Nigeria, with the next largest share, holds 6% (Figure 26.5). Joining South Africa (31) and Nigeria (50) as the only three SSA countries in the top 50 of the MGI Financial Connectedness Ranking, 2016, is Mauritius (36) (McKinsey, 2017). All three economies are net recipients of capital and, in all cases, they are home to regional financial centres. South Africa and Nigeria provide gateways for investors into SSA, as well as channels for the outflow of resources through their highly developed financial sectors. South Africa's financial sector is strongly networked in the region, dominating commercial banking sectors across Eastern and Southern Africa. Meanwhile, the development of the Mauritian economy has been based on its development as a financial centre that offers offshore services for international financial investors. For a relatively small economy, Mauritius accounts for a very large share of PNG stock in SSA, at 13%, and has the highest external debt to GDP ratio of any country in SSA, which exceeds over 150%.

The rise of Mauritius to become a financial centre can be related to the rise of global wealth chains. Global wealth chains are routes through which owners of capital, such as multinational corporations, channel value created—for example, along global value chains—in order to avoid fiscal claims, legal obligations, or regulatory oversight; they therefore tend to exist in offshore jurisdictions and tax havens (Seabrooke and Wigan, 2014). The relationship between capital inflows and domestic credit extension and investment are therefore tenuous.

Capital Market Liberalization and Financial Development in SSA

From the 1980s, IFIs advocated for a more active role to be played by the 'politically neutral' and market-oriented financial sector. This role would require the liberalization of capital accounts, the liberalization of domestic financial sectors, the strengthening and development of private financial institutions, and the deepening of financial markets under the policy umbrella of 'financial development'. The influential McKinnon-Shaw thesis, taken on by the World Bank in the 1990s and 2000s (e.g. Levine and King, 1993) asserted that accelerated growth would stem from financial development measured in terms of increasing size, depth, and breadth of financial sectors.

In the first instance, capital account liberalization and the removal of policy measures to influence credit was expected to increase the nominal and real interest rates in SSA, so as to attract foreign capital inflows. Figure 26.8 shows that FDI inflows as a share of gross national income were volatile, but showed a positive overall trend from 1990 to 2002. While net-FDI inflows as a share of GNI have been in overall decline since 2002, they remain high by historical

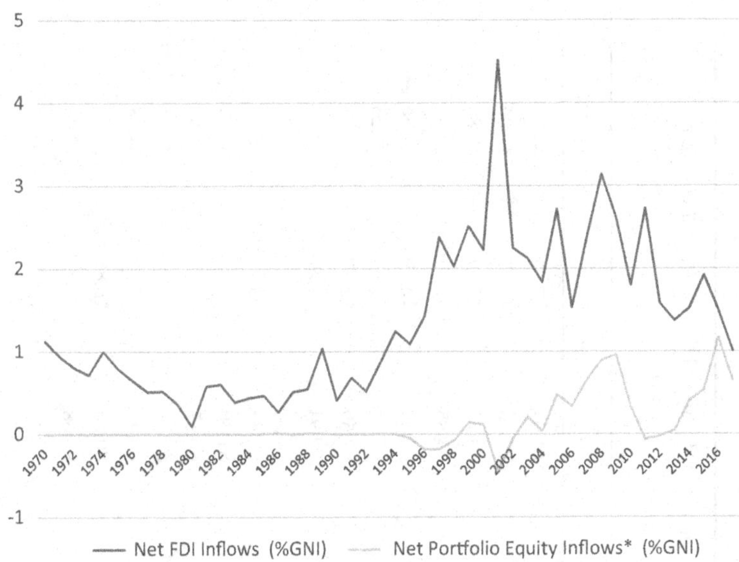

Figure 26.8 Net recorded capital flows to SSA

Source: World Debt Tables 2018.

comparisons. Net portfolio inflows have risen since 2002. Increases in portfolio inflows after 2010 have been attracted by high domestic interest rates in SSA compared with the persistently low interest rates in the post-GFC environment of the Global North. South Africa, with its highly developed financial markets, has been the destination of the bulk of flows.

Capital inflows have been associated with financial deepening/development and credit growth across SSA. As illustrated in Table 26.1, financial development occurred in most SSA countries between 2005 and 2015. In particular, there has been a significant expansion in domestic credit.

The expansion of credit has not had a commensurate effect on domestic investment. Rather, much of this credit has been extended to finance personal consumption in the context of limited state provisioning for welfare, often of imported products (see Newman, 2015, for an example of South Africa). Griffith-Jones and Karwowski (2013) showed how financial deepening has not promoted credit allocation to productive sectors in SSA. More recently, Karwowski (2018) analysed changing lending patterns in 12 SSA countries to find that financial deepening has tended to be extended towards the expansion of household consumption credit and low productivity tertiary sectors (such as personal services), with the share of credit financing manufacturing declining overtime. This pattern of credit extension is visible in the case of Tanzania (Figure 26.9).

The thesis of financial development has been increasingly challenged, including in the context of SSA (Stiglitz and Ocampo, 2008; Griffiths-Jones, 2016).

Table 26.1 Selected measures of financial development in SSA

	Private credit by deposit money banks and other financial institutions (%GDP)		*Domestic credit to the private sector (%GDP)*		*Bank credit to bank deposit (%)*		*Bank deposits to GDP (%)*	
	1995	*2015*	*1995*	*2015*	*1995*	*2015*	*1995*	*2015*
Angola	1.14	25.01	4.79	27.23	43.40	61.34	2.62	40.77
Benin	7.21	21.96	7.43	21.04	42.46	73.05	16.97	30.06
Botswana	12.20	32.54	11.89	33.77	69.44	79.59	17.57	40.88
Burkina Faso	6.42	27.68	6.79	27.67	53.11	93.85	12.08	29.50
Burundi	18.49	18.64	12.27	16.46	99.60	89.00	13.20	18.85
Cabo Verde	19.59	61.12	27.59	61.82	41.01	67.74	47.77	90.23
Cameroon	7.96	15.46	7.43	15.06	67.59	90.59	11.77	17.07
Central African Republic	3.81	12.85	4.16	12.54	86.73	102.91	4.39	12.49
Chad	3.18	8.38	3.85	8.32	103.04	98.89	3.09	8.47
Comoros	13.20	24.79	13.51	27.01	221.95	81.30	4.83	30.49
Congo, Dem. Rep.		5.73	1.06	6.29		60.57		9.47
Congo, Rep.	7.74	20.60	8.11	22.06	101.17	60.43	7.65	34.08
Côte d'Ivoire	17.21	20.40	18.50	22.01	101.88	80.88	16.89	25.23
Equatorial Guinea	3.36	14.44	4.80	14.17	63.98	84.68	5.25	17.06
Eritrea	15.02		17.10		19.35			

Ethiopia	7.94		9.20		36.18		16.42	
Gabon	6.73	14.83	7.92	14.52	69.61	74.48	9.67	19.91
Gambia, The	7.09		4.84		57.87		12.25	
Ghana	2.77	17.85	5.07	20.71	34.56	71.62	8.02	24.93
Guinea	3.20	9.72	4.96	10.96	103.23	57.91	3.10	16.79
Guinea-Bissau	2.18	10.05	8.68	8.12	77.59	59.75	2.81	16.81
Kenya	16.26	32.01	25.81	34.25	68.17	88.17	23.86	36.30
Lesotho	17.78	17.24	18.25	17.21	66.18	61.45	26.86	28.06
Liberia	147.90		2.85	20.64	39.58		373.72	
Madagascar	11.03	12.52	11.50	13.39	82.27	75.33	13.40	16.61
Malawi	3.81	10.41	5.86	12.26	49.60	57.50	6.96	18.11
Mali	6.61	20.76	9.76	23.55	72.73	95.68	9.09	21.70
Mauritania								
Mauritius	42.74	100.44	47.02	102.72	68.01	104.36	62.84	96.24
Mozambique	7.86	30.91	10.23	35.11	52.10	69.82	15.09	44.27
Namibia	43.99	55.99	43.79	63.82	119.33	98.21	36.87	51.24
Niger	6.63	14.26	4.47	13.86	76.31	101.01	8.68	14.12

(Continued)

Table 26.1 (Continued)

	Private credit by deposit money banks and other financial institutions (%GDP)		*Domestic credit to the private sector (%GDP)*		*Bank credit to bank deposit (%)*		*Bank deposits to GDP (%)*	
	1995	*2015*	*1995*	*2015*	*1995*	*2015*	*1995*	*2015*
Nigeria	6.27	14.04	10.05	14.21	93.64	79.38	6.70	17.69
Rwanda	8.41	20.03	8.41	21.13	63.40	112.91	13.27	17.74
São Tomé and Principe	4.46	25.32		27.59	42.56	73.61	10.47	34.40
Senegal	14.56	32.43	14.69	32.99	106.76	89.66	13.63	36.16
Seychelles	15.14	27.66	11.37	25.32	17.50	40.32	59.48	61.89
Sierra Leone	1.76	5.20	2.68	5.39	50.07	29.19	3.52	17.80
Somalia								
South Africa	107.06	145.87	116.00	147.61	124.71	111.00	43.18	59.52
South Sudan		1.89				10.46		18.04
Sudan	2.44	7.95	1.63	7.14	34.94	66.74	6.98	11.92
Swaziland	13.06	20.78	15.06	20.65	83.83	87.31	15.58	23.80
Tanzania	9.04	13.64	6.66	15.18	47.79	73.63	18.91	18.53
Togo	16.20	33.61	20.08	36.78	95.57	82.86	16.95	40.56
Uganda	3.89	13.59	4.59	15.60	52.81	79.64	7.36	16.25
Zambia	6.09253	16.9988	7.72021	19.7648	56.1107	69.8563	11.5147	19.2042
Zimbabwe	0.254518	22.7657	33.8378		102.534	82.0552	0.182697	27.7444

Source: World Bank Global Financial Development Database, 2018.

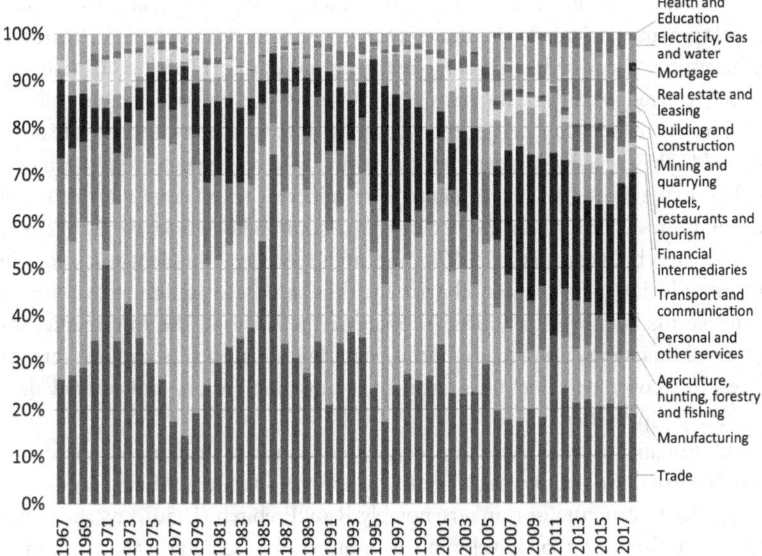

Figure 26.9 Distribution of total domestic credit by economic activity in Tanzania, 1967–2018

Source: Bank of Tanzania Quarterly Economic Bulletin 2019 and 2014.

The critique of financial development/capital market liberalization approach from the perspective of the 'financial systems' has stressed that financial institutions are not unproblematic intermediaries that channel funds from household savings to private investment. Rather, financial systems are imperfect and are influenced by institutional structures (Stiglitz and Ocampo, 2008). These authors have been particularly concerned with the destabilizing effect of volatile capital flows, their procyclicality and the impact of the global monetary cycle on domestic development,[2] and advocate for the development of suitable development finance institutions, such as industrial banks and countercyclical monetary and fiscal policies. While acknowledging variations across financial systems and the interaction between global and national systems, the financial systems approach is limited in its analysis of how financial systems developed in the first place within a national context, and how they have developed historically (Ashman and Fine, 2013).

Geda (2003) countered the ahistorical analysis of the African debt crisis offered by the World Bank (1981) by taking into account the historical specificities of post-independent economic development and changes in the global economy. Governments in SSA were striving for structural transformation of their economies from export enclaves for primary commodities into diversified and integrated modern capitalist economies. For this, government spending for social and economic development was necessary.

External borrowing in Africa complemented export income to finance development, particularly in infrastructure investment. Unfortunately, the levels of investment required to enact far-reaching and transformative industrial policy contracted with the debt crisis that was set off by an unpredictable collapse in non-oil commodity prices, their continued decline, and the first oil shock in 1974. These events saw external borrowing take on a greater role to finance public expenditure, as governments were reluctant to reverse levels of social expenditure. There was an expectation that commodity prices would recover. The period between the late 1970s and mid-1980s saw the debt stock soar in magnitude due to: (i) further oil price shocks that necessitated the expansion of external finance for oil imports; (ii) increased reliance on the Euromarket for external financing at worsening terms, including steep increases in real interest rates; (iii) continued decline in non-oil commodity prices and limited debt servicing capabilities.

Unsustainable debt levels thus originated from the structure of the economy, external shocks, and continued dependence on external financing (Geda, 2003). Early structuralist thinkers, notably Raul Prebisch (1950), saw the structural transformation of developing economies through the state promotion of manufacturing as imperative, given the observed long-run decline in the net barter terms of trade between primary commodities and manufactured products, and the dangers that this implied for continued commodity dependence. The relationship between commodity dependency and external debt has recently been stressed by UNCTAD (2016), who advocate for alternative sources of finance for necessary structural transformation, including a reorientation towards domestic resource mobilization.

Finance and Accumulation in SSA

The financial economics that underpins the financial development/capital market liberalization approach, and its critics in the form of proponents of the financial systems approach, understand the financial and the real as operating in different spheres and bridged by financial intermediaries. By contrast, Marx's political economy sees finance and industrial capital as integrated within the industrial circuit of capital and, therefore, analytically inseparable. '[T]he character of a financial system is not purely dependent upon the terms of its structural separation from industry and how they interact with one another. Nor are the intrinsic structures and functions of these two components invariant since there are different types and dynamics of industry as well as of finance' (Ashman and Fine, 2013: 155). Rather, the evolution and developments of national financial systems occur in relation to the character of capitalist accumulation, specific in space and time, that are built in relation to existing structures in a contested, frustrated, and co-constitutive manner. Moreover, the way that changes at the global level interact with local specificities will be the product of historical processes. This section outlines two cases to highlight the political economy of the development of national financial systems in Tanzania and South Africa in relation to specific national systems of accumulation.

·South Africa has the largest and most sophisticated financial sector on the continent. By many measures of financial development, South Africa has reached levels of financial depth and development that exceed those in the Global North. The finance, insurance, real estate, and business service sectors account for 20% of GDP.[3] In spite of this, South Africa has experienced very low levels of investment, deindustrialization and extreme levels of unemployment, and worsening inequality and poverty. Deindustrialization has also occurred in Tanzania since the 1980s and, while financial sector reforms have been undertaken since the 1990s, it still has one of the least developed financial sectors on the continent. In the remainder of this section, we outline the historical development of the financial sectors ofTanzania and South Africa from colonialism to the present day, paying particular attention of the role of finance in shaping the pace and character of economic development.

Colonial Development of Finance in East Africa

The British colonial monetary system in East Africa was 'designed in such a way as to enable the unimpeded creaming-off of surplus from the colony to the metropolitan country' (Loxley, 1972: 44). Commercial banking in the region originated in the commercial connection between British East Africa and British India in the late nineteenth century.The main role played by commercial banks during the colonial period was in the settlement of accounts for the colonial economy, rather than the mobilization of domestic resources for investment in domestic enterprise (Upadhyaya and Johnson, 2015).While the absence of exchange controls allowed the colonies to borrow cheaply in London, more was loaned and permanently remitted abroad than was ever received back (Upadhyaya and Johnson, 2015).The outflow of resources from the colonies was also managed by the legal requirement for colonial financial institutions—such as the Currency Board, Post Office Savings Bank, and various pension and trust funds—to invest their assets overseas. Other foreign-owned financial institutions, such as commercial banks, also chose to invest in familiar home markets, rather than lend within the colonies. Further, the free mobility of funds between parent banks in the metropolitan country and its branches in the colonies, at a fixed rate of exchange between the East African Shilling and British Pound, meant that commercial banks could fully determine the supply of credit and the interest rates, which they did in an arrangement akin to a cartel in Kenya (Johnson and Upadhyaya, 2015).[4]

Given the concentration of financial institutions and their predominant foreign and colonial ownership, commercial banks 'accounted for almost the entire surplus passing through financial intermediaries' in the region (Johnson and Upadhyaya, 2015: 44). In the rare cases where financial institutions acquired local assets, these tended to serve expatriate/settler communities and colonial interests—namely, short-term assets such as working credit and trade-financing, or long-term loans for buildings or luxury housing (Johnson and Upadhyaya, 2015: 44). Lending to indigenous Africans was heavily restricted both by law and by the range of assets that were acceptable as collateral for loans by foreign-owned banks (Loxley, 1972; Upadhyaya and Johnson, 2015). In Tanganyika, long-term loans were available to expatriate farmers for land purchase and improvement, and some expatriate banks set up special lending institutions that provided limited long-term funds for foreign-owned industry and agriculture (Loxley, 1972).

The late colonial period after World War II saw the extension of some of the social and economic goals of the post-war settlement in the West to the colonies. However, even the most modest budgets of colonial governments were met with the impossible challenge of finance owing to the structure of a monetary system that was geared towards the heavy draining of surplus and the aversion of banks to long-term lending. In 1956, the East African Currency Board was empowered to lend to East African governments, but this was mainly on a short-term basis[5] and thus inappropriate for long-term development finance. The colonial monetary system and the heavy restrictions that it placed on government budgets meant that there was no scope for any government influence on the allocation of resources between consumption and investment, or on the use to which scarce foreign exchange earnings could be put. The colonial monetary system thus perpetuated the dependence of the economies of East Africa on a narrow range of commodity exports, managed the long-term permanent outward transfer of resources, and placed tight limits on long-term investment necessary for economic transformation—separation of money and industrial capital in the system of accumulation in colonial East Africa.

Financial Development in Post-independence Tanzania

The early post-independence period also saw the establishment of a wide range of public sector financial institutions that extended beyond the critical role of the central bank, the Bank of Tanzania, with the objective of amassing domestic surplus and channelling this towards domestic investment, through the state development budget and new investment outlets. These included the National Cooperative Bank (NCB), the National Development Credit Agency, a National Provident Fund, and a National Housing Corporation that operated alongside eight expatriate commercial banks and two newly formed local banks (Tanzania Bank of Commerce and NCB) (Loxley, 1972; Bank of Tanzania, 1981). Wholesale nationalization of the banking sector took place immediately after the Arusha Declaration of 1967. All banks, with the exception of the NCB, merged to form the National Bank of Commerce (NBC), Tanzania's only commercial bank operation until reforms in the 1990s (Bank of Tanzania, 1981). These developments served to concentrate financial capital under state control and coordination, relieving the financial constraint to development, with the government mobilizing much greater quantities of local surplus than it had ever imagined. Critically, this diminished the role of foreign capital in influencing the patterns of accumulation. Ten years after independence, 'the government was in a position to exert considerable influence on resource allocation and income distribution purely through its budgetary activities' (Loxley, 1972: 48). These institutional developments also provided the basis for the tightly bound relationship between finance and industrial capital following the Arusha Declaration of 1971 and the nationalization of the modern industrial sector.

Overall, the monetary system saw greater refinement, with the development of new institutions for specific areas of credit specialization geared towards investment and accumulation. The relationship between finance and industrial capital was tied through policy in annual financial planning designed to meet the aggregate investment targets. Credit expansion to parastatal[6] organizations through the banking sector increased by 13% per annum between 1969 and 1973, and investment rates exceeded 20% of GDP (Loxley, 1972; Bank of Tanzania, 1981). The Bank of Tanzania played a direct role in investment decisions of parastatals and maintained tight controls over associated use of foreign exchange.

Fifteen years of economic planning proved insufficient to bring about the radical structural transformation of the economy from one based on colonial extractives to an integrated and diversified modern economy, leaving Tanzania structurally vulnerable to a debt spiral set off by unfavourable external conditions. Industrial policies between 1961 and 1967 drove rapid growth in industry, but little diversification from the agro-processing that had been established under colonialism. After 1967, the state took on a more active role in the process of industrialization so as to bring about 'a productive economic transition as well as the radical restructuring of economic power by limiting the expansion of domestic and international capital' (Gray, 2013: 188). This involved the nationalization of existing industries and the creation of new industrial parastatals. The extent and pattern of nationalization reflected the immediate priority to generate economic growth over the political need to promote indigenous capitalists, given the historical dominance of foreign capital in industry (Gray, 2013).

By the late 1970s, signs of weakness in the financial system began to show. Poor financial management of a number of parastatals led to substantial financial losses (Bank of Tanzania, 1981). Internal weaknesses were exacerbated by external shocks. While, to a degree, the Tanzanian economy was able to weather the first oil shock in 1974 due to increased foreign exchange revenue associated with the coffee price boom (1976–1979), the second and third OPEC oil shocks occurred at a time of non-oil commodity price decline. This led to a greater reliance on external debt to finance enlarged oil bills. Increased external borrowing also financed the maintenance of public expenditure. Contrary to the narrative of reckless borrowing of the Berg report, Tanzania was mainly borrowing for public infrastructure investment, with the expectation that coffee prices would recover. Debtor governments were also unable to predict the deteriorating terms of borrowing that would prevail as steep real interest rate hikes for foreign borrowing increased the debt service burden, while falling commodity prices limited debt servicing capabilities (Geda, 2003). By 1995, 77% of the total loans of the largest bank, the National Bank of Commerce, were non-performing loans (World Bank, 1995). Fifteen years after independence, Tanzania and many economies in SSA remained tied to the colonial legacy of commodity dependence.

Financial Liberalization and Deindustrialization in Tanzania

The debt crisis of the 1980s led the Tanzanian government to enter into a stand-by agreement with the IMF that involved the liberalization of the interest rate and elimination of price controls as policy conditions. Economic growth improved from 1991, driven by rising foreign and domestic investment, and an emerging gold mining sector. While manufacturing output did increase in this period, it was not of the scale required for structural transformation of the economy. Unemployment and poverty rates remained stubbornly high into the 2000s.

The second round of reforms, between 1996 and 2006, under the IMF's Poverty Reduction and Growth facility and the joint IMF-World Bank Financial Sector Assessment Program, saw much more comprehensive restructuring that included the privatization of most manufacturing and agricultural parastatals, as well as pervasive liberalization of the financial sector. The state banking system consisting of six state-owned banks that had allocated credit according to the National Credit Plans was opened up. In order to foster competition, Tanzanian policy-makers pursued a very liberal approach to bank licensing, and the period from 1996 saw the rapid expansion in the number of banks, particularly foreign-owned banks that, in 2015, numbered 29 out of 56 banks, with 12 community banks and 9 private domestic banks, with 6 state-owned banks remaining (IMF, 2017). Despite the proliferation of new banking institutions, the sector remains highly concentrated. In 2017, the four largest banks held 50% of all banking institution assets in Tanzania (Bank of Tanzania, 2017).

Despite wholesale liberalization, financial development has been modest. Credit extension as a proportion of GDP has seen very little growth and remains amongst the lowest in SSA (Table 26.1). The credit to deposit ratio did not increase between 1995 and 2005, but increased by 26 percentage points between 2005 and 2015, while credit to the private sector has remained low, at just 15% of GDP in 2015.[7] Moreover, the pattern of credit extension has not changed in a way that supports accelerated domestic capital accumulation and structural transformation of the economy. Figure 26.9 shows trends in the distribution of domestic credit extended by commercial banks according to economic activities between 1967 and 2018. Both manufacturing and agriculture have seen falling shares in credit received since 2000. By contrast, shares of credit going to low productivity, and personal and other services[8] has increased dramatically since 1995, reaching over 30% in 2018.

Financial liberalization and associated developments in the banking sector in the 2000s, together with privatization and liberalization of manufacturing and agriculture, has seen the delinking of finance from the development of production. The expansion in bank credit has not resulted in the commensurate expansion of lending to the private sector and productive investment in Tanzania has stagnated, thus fuelling the process of deindustrialization (Figure 26.9).

In accordance with changes in the financial development agenda of the World Bank and IMF, there has been a reorientation of policy from rapid and general liberalization to a more targeted approach aimed at addressing financial inclusion alongside the promotion of policy lending through development finance institutions, focusing on PPPs in the social and economic infrastructures. The rapid rise of mobile banking in Tanzania since 2008 has been one of the most dramatic changes to take place in the financial sector (Gray, 2017). It has expanded the reach and access to formal financial services populations and remote regions that had previously been excluded. The promotion of financial inclusion has also harnessed rural financial institutions that developed during the 1960s and 1970s as part of the promotion of cooperatives for agricultural production and marketing: the Savings and Credit Co-operative Societies (SACCOS). Of the 1,880 microfinance practitioners registered in the Microfinance Institutions Directory of the Bank of Tanzania, 1,620 are SACCOS. In Tanzania, cooperatives (including SACCOS) contribute about 40% to GDP, and employ 94.7% of school leavers every year, through the financing of small and medium-sized enterprises (SMEs), the majority of which are in rural regions and depend on the cooperatives for external financing (Bwana and Mwakujonga, 2013).

Financial sector reforms and the reorientation of financial development policy in Tanzania has culminated in a highly stratified financial system that continues to be dominated by a heavily concentrated banking sector that has rationed credit for productive activities in the private sector. This is, in part, because higher returns can be obtained from the purchase of low-risk government securities and because the reliance of smaller banks on large banks for funding has led to high lending rates (Gray, 2020). Large foreign owned banks, particularly those with ties to the former colonial banks—such as Barclays, Standard Charter, and Stanbic—specialize in the financing of export activities by foreign owned companies, mirroring the extractivist operations of colonial era financial institutions. Microfinance institutions, in the form of SACCOs, while small in terms of assets, have the closest ties to productive investment in rural areas. This begs the question on the possibilities for scaling up credit extension for the promotion of larger-scale productive activities beyond SMEs and microenterprises.

Development of the Financial System in South Africa from Colonialism to Apartheid

For South Africa, four distinct periods of financial development can be identified based on changes in the relationship between finance and industrial capital in processes of accumulation from British Colonialism up until the transition to democracy in 1994. The first phase mirrors that of other colonial subjects in SSA. As in East Africa, commercial banking in South Africa began with the establishment of London-based imperial banks in the Cape Colony. Indeed, a number of imperial banks that established first in South Africa, extended and expanded into other colonial markets—the Standard Bank of British South Africa. As in East Africa, these banks provided the mechanism for surplus extraction under colonial relations and were relatively unimportant in providing funds for accumulation in South Africa, while domestic lending was largely limited to loans to white farmers for agricultural purposes.

The second phase of financial development began with the discovery of diamonds in Kimberly and then gold in the Transvaal. Imperial banks benefited from the minerals revolution but were not central in the provision of funding in the booming mining sector. The geology of the Witwatersrand Basin meant that considerable capital was required in order to exploit the narrow gold seams deep underground. Large capital requirements informed the establishment of finance houses by mining companies to raise capital from overseas (Innes, 1984; Verhoef, 2009b). The control of the mining houses over the financial sector helped to establish the dominance of the mining conglomerates in the financial economy. By 1930, six mining groups with interests in the imperial banks dominated the mining sector. This process intertwined productive and finance capital in mining, and underpinned the pattern of capital accumulation and the emergence of the Minerals-Energy-Complex as (MEC) the historical system of accumulation in South Africa (Innes, 1984; Fine and Rustomjee, 1996; Ashman and Fine, 2013).

The third phase of financial development was driven by the project of Afrikaner Nationalism that had emerged in opposition to British Colonial rule in the wake of the Boer Wars. Economic depression between 1905 and 1909 presented the issue of poor (mostly Afrikaner) whites who had been forced to migrate to urban areas following the devastation of agriculture during the War. It was recognized that, while the Afrikaner Nationalist movement was amassing political power, economic power was in the hands of English capital tied to mining and connected industries. Command over finance was thus seen as key to the integration of Afrikaner capital into mining and secondary industry, where it had little representation. The Afrikaner national project relied on, and sought to increase, representation of Afrikaner capital within the structure of economic ownership and control, tying together finance and industrial capital in conglomerate ownership that had developed out of the mining revolution.

The South African Trust and Insurance Company and its subsidiary, The South African National Life Assurance Company (Sanlam), were formed in 1918 to establish South African insurance and life assurance companies serving Afrikaners, becoming the material basis for the rise to power of the Nationalist Party in 1948 (Verhoef, 2009a). Alongside the establishment of a people's savings bank (Volskas Bank), an investment company for the provision of capital for Afrikaner business was established with Sanlam as the Federal People's Investments Bank (FVB). FVB channelled Afrikaner savings and agricultural surplus into the development of an 'Afrikaner' industrial base that following the model of English-speaking capital in the development of mining (Ashman and Fine, 2013).

After coming into power in 1948, the Nationalist government set about the heavy promotion of Afrikaner finance and industrial capital through industrial policy based on the state's ability to extract and direct surpluses from mining activities that were dominated by English-speaking capital with historical links to Britain.[9] Industrial policies created state-owned sectors in electricity, as well as other linked industries that complemented the needs of mining conglomerates such as in synthetic chemicals, fuels, and basic metals processing. Industrial policies were supported by the formation of a number of financial institutions, including the Industrial Development Corporation, which funded state-owned heavy industry, and the National Finance Corporation, which was instrumental in the development of a long-term capital market (Fine and Rustomjee, 1996).

A process of competition, conflict, and compromise between English-speaking and Afrikaner capital saw the rapid growth of merchant banking from the late 1950s under conglomerate control. This reinforced the close connection between finance and industrial capital in the South African economy. The development of finance and industry around mining was not informed by a desire to promote structural transformation of the economy towards diversified and integrated economy as an end. Rather, industrial policy was shaped by the needs of Afrikaner capital to amass a material base that could rival English-speaking capital economically. South Africa's system of accumulation, the MEC, involved the development of a powerful and concentrated financial system with uniquely close ties and overlapping ownership structures with productive capital and strong state support (Ashman and Fine, 2013).

The fourth phase of financial development began with growing political and economic isolation following the Sharpeville massacre of 1960. Banking reforms were enacted in the early 1970s to reduce foreign control and the external vulnerability of the banking sector. The resulting acquisition of

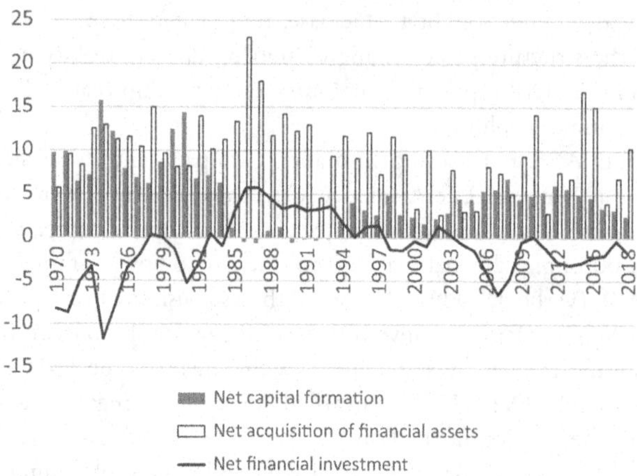

Figure 26.10 Net annual capital formation, acquisition of financial assets and financial investment by non-financial corporations in South Africa

Data Source: Quantec 2019.

Notes: Net annual formation is the sum of new fixed capital investments less expenditures to replace depreciating capital. Net acquisition of financial assets is the net amount of financial assets acquired within a specific period of time. For non-financial corporations, these assets usually comprise equity, loans, investment fund shares, currency, and deposits. Net financial investment is the difference between savings and all capital transactions. When this is greater than zero, firms are net lenders; when it is less than zero, firms are net borrowers. Between 1985 and 1994, firms in South Africa were reluctant to invest in the domestic economy, they therefore hoarded their savings and did not borrow from the financial sector to finance investment.

larger stakes by domestic capital and divestment by foreign banks meant that, for a short period, the banking sector was almost entirely domestically owned (Singleton and Verhoef, 2010). With the dual crises of debt and political legitimacy, the 1980s and early 1990s saw volatile and negative GDP growth rates underpinned by external economic sanctions and the reluctance of domestic capitalists to invest in illiquid fixed assets with growing political uncertainty.

Trapped by economic sanctions, domestic capital sought alternative avenues for investment through the financial sector. The period from the mid-1980s until the early 1990s saw persistently large financial surpluses as a share of GDP in the domestic economy that financed the acquisition of financial assets by non-financial corporations throughout the 1980s (Figure 26.10). This fuelled rapid expansion of the financial sector that was further supported by a series of financial sector deregulations that involved the abolition of specialized bank categories, removal of barriers against foreign entry into the sector, and the shift to international standards for capital requirements as prescribed by Basel (Verhoef, 2009b). This period saw the decoupling of finance from industrial capital (Newman, 2015).

Financialization of the South African Economy since 1994

Post-apartheid South Africa inherited a heavily skewed and highly concentrated economic structure. Democratic transition and the opening up of the South African economy saw the unleashing of previously trapped financial surpluses, and set in motion a different dynamic relationship between finance and industrial capital. South African capital rapidly internationalized through financial mechanisms that involved corporate unbundling, downsizing, and foreign listing of South African corporations (Chabane et al., 2006; Ashman et al., 2011a; Mohamed, 2016). Fuelled by the minerals boom in the decade preceding the global financial crisis, the South African economy experienced sizeable and sustained long-term capital outflows (Ashman et al., 2011b; Alami, 2018). With a liberalized capital account and a highly developed and profitable financial sector, South Africa was able to attract large volumes of portfolio and other short-term investment to ensure a capital account surplus to offset both the long-term expatriation of capital and the perennial current account deficit driven by deindustrialization since 1994. Figure 26.10 shows that net capital formation did recover after 1994, but was low compared to the 1970s as a percentage of GDP. Moreover, rising fixed investment was not matched by a commensurate decrease in the acquisition of financial assets by non-financial corporations (NFCs). Large NFCs listed on the Johannesburg Stock Exchange, for example, hoard cash and other liquid financial assets, rather than invest in productive activities (Karwowski, 2018). The post-apartheid period has been characterized by a financialized MEC (Ashman et al., 2011a; Ashman and Fine, 2013; Isaacs, 2018), in which a neoliberal macroeconomic policy framework dominates the policy realm, providing the conditions for the rapid expansion of finance and financialized accumulation, at the expense of productive investment and employment (Ashman et al., 2014; Newman, 2015).

In summary, financial development in South Africa since 1994 continues apace in relation to the prevailing MEC that has reconfigured the relationship between finance and industrial capital. The financialized MEC has reproduced the apartheid pattern of investment centred on MEC sectors in South Africa, and has extended its influence in the region as part of its own internationalization strategy (Carmody, 2002; Taylor, 2011).

Until relatively recently, development and growth of the South African financial sector has occurred in relative isolation from the population at large. Albeit uneven in character, proleterianization and the incorporation of South Africans into the world of corporate capitalism as consumers began earlier and has been more comprehensive than in other African countries (Hull and James, 2012). The first decade of independence saw a very rapid expansion in access to credit, fuelling consumption and growing indebtedness. In 2011, 37% of the population in South Africa still did not have a bank account (Finscope, 2011). The Marikana massacre of 16 August 2012 drew attention to the highly exploitative relations of debt that many in South Africa have been tied into, from informal loan sharks to formal banks offering unsecured lending (Bond, 2013). Such lending has been promoted within the financial inclusion agenda that sees access to financial services as the solution to poverty.

> As part of an attempt to bring all investors, consumers, savers and spenders within the ambit of a single economy, to regulate the activities of loan sharks and to make financial markets 'work for' the poor.
>
> (Hull and James, 2012: 3)

But, rather than contribute to productive investment in microenterprise, the context of high unemployment, worsening poverty, and inequality has meant that many borrowers have come to rely on high interest, unpayable loans for consumption (Gronbach, 2018). In spite of the indictment of usury lending in the wake of Marikana, the financial inclusion agenda presses ahead. Efforts have been made to promote financial inclusion via digital technologies, most notably in the transition from cash payments to electronic transfers for social grants. In 2012, the private financial service provider Cash Paymaster Services (CPS) was appointed by South Africa's Social Security Agency (SASSA). Given that close to one-quarter of the population rely on social grants as their main source of income, the programme brought a large portion of the unbanked population into formal financial networks and access to pro-poor financial products. Social grant recipients were issued with biometrically enabled smart cards with which they could withdraw money or make electronic payments. They also received free bank accounts with CPS banking partner Grindrod Bank.

Within just two years, the unbanked population fell from 37% to 25% in 2014, and further to 23% in 2015 (Finscope, 2015). By 2014, irregular, unauthorized, and undocumented debit deductions were widely reported. About half of these unauthorized deductions were traced back to other subsidiaries of Net1, the CPS parent company who were 'leveraging CPS' direct access to a large and promising market segment' (Gronbach, 2018: 6). In spite of growing complaints and attempts to outlaw these deductions, it took a Constitutional Court ruling, in 2014, that the award of the contract to CPS was itself invalid due to procedural flaws in the tender process, to prompt SASSA to seek a new payment solution (Gronbach, 2018: 6). To avoid the interruption of grant payments and the inevitable suffering that this would cause, the Constitutional Court extended the contract between SASSA and the CPS for six months beyond its original deadline. Moreover, financial services companies controlled by Net1 now own the biometric information and digital payments footprints of grant recipients whose accounts have effectively become 'conduits between the South African fiscus and the private financial empire that has taken shape around grant dispersement' (du Toit, 2017: 2).

The promotion of financial inclusion in South Africa has done little to affect poverty, and has opened up new avenues for furthering the indebtedness of the poor in facilitating the opening up of new markets for private finance in a process that has been referred to as the 'financialization of social policy' (Lavinas, 2018).

Conclusion

This chapter has explored the changing nature of finance and economic development in SSA since the early independence period to the present day. While closely integrated with industrial capital, the formal financial institutions developed to serve surplus extraction and expatriation from the colonies. Industrial development occurred in enclaves and excluded the majority of colonial populations from capitalist wage relations. Thus, newly independent African nations sought rapid industrialization through state directed investment with the promotion of finance as a servant to industry. Heavy reliance on external financing of investment good imports, the OPEC oil shocks, and declining commodity prices sunk many African economies into unsustainable levels of indebtedness. International financial institutions responded to this with the promotion of Washington Consensus policies. In the context of heavy promotion by the World Bank, financial development has occurred unevenly across SSA. Moreover, credit extension to productive sectors of the economy has not been forthcoming. Rather, rising indebtedness has emerged from the extension of credit for consumption. The extension of financial development to financial inclusion has further detached the development of finance from economic development in SSA. The financial inclusion agenda—by concealing the inherent unevenness in power relations between debtors and creditors, and the speculative tendencies involved in financial inclusion strategies—arguably promotes exploitation of the poor in the interests of private finance (Soederberg, 2013; Bracking, 2016).

The concrete forms taken by financial development and financialization are shaped by historical developments in capitalism from colonialism into independence. Albeit in very different ways, financial development in each of the case studies presented has been shaped by the historical emergence of capitalist relations during colonialism. Newly independent Tanzania sought to leverage the financial system for domestic investment and the development of industry. In South Africa, the development of finance was critical for the development of Afrikaner industrial interests in surplus producing sectors, and reinforced an economic structure skewed towards heavy industry linked to mining. In both cases, financial liberalization and financial development have led to the detachment of finance from industrial capital and suppressed diversification, and have promoted renewed extractivist economic systems based on the appropriation and expatriation of surplus. In Tanzania, as in many low-income countries in SSA, the financialization process has been accelerated and deepened 'in the name of 'development'' where '[f]oreign aid is being used to de-risk investment, 'escort' capital to 'frontier' markets, and carry out the mundane work of transforming objects into assets available to speculative flows' (Mawdsley, 2016: 264). By contrast, financialization in South Africa has been predominantly shaped by the internationalization strategy of previously trapped capital and, more recently, the extraction of surplus from the wider region through financial mechanisms in the name of South African-led regional development (Taylor, 2011).

Moving forward, finance for development policies needs to be informed by detailed historical analysis of the development of finance in particular space and time, as it is related to the processes and patterns of accumulation in specific locations and is in relation to regional and global dynamics. The task is to design financial architectures that support the integration of finance and industrial capital for accumulation that is broad-based, diversified, inclusive, and sustainable. An understanding of the political economy of finance and industry, how it has emerged, and its path dependence is critical to this endeavour.

Notes

1 The expansion of private borrowing from 1995 can largely be attributed to democratic transition in South Africa and South Africa's integration into the global economy.

2 Such authors emphasize that a focus on net flows will tend to downplay the destabilizing potential of global capital flows that can be several orders of magnitude greater.

3 The figure of 20% of GDP has been calculated from GDP statistics published by Statistics South Africa for 2018. Accessed from http://www.statssa.gov.za/publications/P0441/P04413rdQuarter2019.pdf, 17 December 2019.

4 Further, given that commercial bank advances were made up largely of their own resources and borrowing from the parent bank, there was very little competition for deposits and, hence, the interest rates on deposits as well as loans could be freely determined by the commercial banks (Upadhyaya and Johnson 2015).

5 It was argued that the need to preserve adequate liquidity and to develop Treasury Bill markets would have been undermined by excessive long-term lending (Loxley, 1972).

6 Following the Arusha Declaration of 1967, the vast majority of economic activities and social provisioning were organized under parastatals. For example, while the coffee sector was characterized by small-holder production, the marketing, processing, agricultural extension services, and exports were all managed by parastatal organizations in the service of national policy. After nationalization, parastatal organizations were also responsible for a significant share of industrial production.

7 According to Gray (2020), 'One reason for this was the availability of low-risk, highly lucrative government securities. The large banks dominated the government securities market, holding around 40% of these assets. With zero risk-weights and an interest rate of around 15% they had little incentive to extend credit to the private sector. Smaller banks, which did not operate so extensively in these markets, relied on being able to borrow from these larger banks, thus pushing up interest rates.'

8 Personal services include low productivity activities with limited linkages to the rest of the economy such has beauty salons, funeral services, and laundering.
9 The two main competing factions of capital post-1948 can be described as Afrikaner capital and English-speaking capital. The first is owned by Afrikaner nationalists who dominated in terms of political power, while English-speaking capital refers to capital that was owned and controlled by those with historical links to Britain that dominated in mining and industry.

References

Bonizzi, B., Laskaridis, C. and Toporowski, J. (2015). Developing countries' external debt and international financial integration. FESSUD: Working Paper Series, No 121.

Ashman, S. and Fine, B. (2013). Neo-liberalism, varieties of capitalism, and the shifting contours of South Africa's financial system. *Transformation: Critical Perspectives on Southern Africa*, 81(1), 144–178.

Ashman, S., Fine, B. and Newman, S. (2011a). The crisis in South Africa: Neoliberalism, financialization and uneven and combined development. *Socialist Register*, 47, 174–195.

Ashman, S., Fine, B. and Newman, S. (2011b). Amnesty International? The nature, scale and impact of capital flight from South Africa. *Journal of Southern African Studies*, 37(1), 7–25.

Bank of Tanzania. (1981). *Tanzania: Twenty Years of Independence (1961-1981): A Review of Political and Economic Performance*. Dar Es Salaam: Bank of Tanzania

Bank of Tanzania (2017). *Directorate of Banking Supervision: Annual Report*. Dar Es Salaam: Bank of Tanzania.

Bargawi, H.K. and Newman, S.A. (2017). From futures markets to the farm gate: A study of price formation along Tanzania's coffee commodity chain. *Economic Geography*, 93(2), 162–184.

Brautigam, D. 2011. *The Dragon's Gift: The Real Story of China in Africa*. Oxford: OUP.

Baud, C. and Durand, C. (2012). Financialization, globalization and the making of profits by leading retailers. *Socio-Economic Review*, 10(2), 241–266.

Bayliss, K. and Van Waeyenberge, E. (2018). Unpacking the public private partnership revival. *The Journal of Development Studies*, 54(4), 577–593.

Carmody, P. (2002). Between globalisation and (Post) Apartheid: The political economy of restructuring in South Africa. *Journal of Southern African Studies*, 28(2), 255–275.

Chabane, N., Roberts, S. and Goldstein, A. (2006). The changing face and strategies of big business in South Africa: More than a decade of political democracy. *Industrial and Corporate Change*, 15(3), 549–577.

Demirgüç-Kunt, A. and Levine, R. eds. (2004). *Financial Structure and Economic Growth: A Cross-country Comparison of Banks, Markets, and Development*. MIT Press.

Du Toit, A. (2017). The real risks behinf South Africa's social grant payment crisis. [online]. (Last updated 20 February 2017). Available at: https://theconversation.com/the-real-risks-behind-south-africas-social-grant-payment-crisis-73224 [Accessed 14 September 2019]

Fine, B. and Rustomjee, Z.Z.R. (1996). *The Political Economy of South Africa*. Johannesburg: Witwatersrand University Press.

Finscope. (2011). *Finscope South Africa 2011*. [online]. Available at: http://finmark.org.za/finscope-south-africa-2011 [Accessed 15 September 2019]

Finscope. (2015). Finscope South Africa 2015 Consumer Survey Brochure. [online]. Available at: http://finmark.org.za/finscope-south-africa-2015-consumer-survey-brochure [Accessed 15 September 2019]

Gabor, D. and Brooks, S. (2017). The digital revolution in financial inclusion: international development in the fintech era. *New Political Economy*, 22(4), 423–436.

Geda, A. (2003). The historical origin of African Debt Crisis. *Eastern Africa Social Science Research Review*, 19(1), 59–89.

Gerschenkron, A. (1962). *Economic Backwardness in Historical Perspective: A Book of Essays*. Cambridge, MA: Belknap Press of Harvard University Press.

Gray, H. (2020). Tanzania: From institutional hiatus to the return of policy-based lending. In: Jones et al. (eds) *Reluctant Regulators: The Politics of Banking Regulation in Low Income Countries*. Oxford: Oxford University Press.

Griffiths-Jones, S. (2016). Achieving financial stability and growth in Africa. In: P. Arestis and M. Sawyer (eds) *Financial Liberalisation*. Palgrave Macmillan, 133–175

Griffith-Jones, S. and Karwowski, E. (2013). Finance and growth in Sub-Saharan Africa: Policy and research challenges. In *Working Papers. Africa Task Force Meeting*, Yokohama and New York: JICA and Initiative for Policy Dialogue, 132–139.

Gronbach, L. (2018). *Financilising the Poor.* [online]. Available at: http://roape.net/2018/11/13/financialising-the-poor [Accessed 14 September 2019]

Hull, E., & James, D. (2012). Introduction: Popular economies in South Africa. *Africa*, 82(1), 1–19.

International Monetary Fund. (2017). East Africa Regional Technical Assistance Centre Mid-Year Report FY 2017. East AFRITAC.

Innes, D. (1984). *Anglo-American and the Rise of Modern South Africa*. Johannesburg: Ravan Press.

Karwowski, E. (2018). Changing lending patterns in Sub-Saharan Africa: Financial deepening or financialisation? Paper Presented at *Forum 2018: Finance and Industrial Development, TIPS Annual Forum*, 6 & 7 June 2018, Johannesburg

Lavinas, L. (2018). The collateralization of social policy under financialized capitalism. *Development and Change*, 49(2), 502–517.

Lazonick, W. (2014). Profits without prosperity. *Harvard Business Review*, 92(9), 46–55.

Lazonick, W. and O'Sullivan, M. (2000). Maximizing shareholder value: a new ideology for corporate governance. *Economy and Society*, 29(1), 13–35.

Levine, R. (1997). Financial development and economic growth: Views and agenda. *Journal of Economic Literature*, 35(June), 688–726.

Levine, R. (2001). International financial liberalization and economic growth. *Review of International Economics*, 9(4), 688–702.

Loxley, J. (1972). Financial planning and control in Tanzania. *Development and Change*, 3(3), 43–61.

Mader, P. (2018). Contesting financial inclusion. *Development and Change*, 49(2), 461–483.

Mawdsley, E. (2016). Development geography II: financialization. *Progress in Human Geography*, 42(2), 264–274.

Mawdsley, E. (2007). China and Africa: Emerging challenges to the geographies of power. *Geography Compass*, 1(3), 405–421.

McKinnon, R. I. (1973). *Money and Capital in Economic Development*. Washington, DC: Brookings Institution.

McKinsey Global Institute. (2017). *The New Dynamics of Financial Globalisation*. McKinsey & Company

Milberg, W. and Winkler, D. (2009). Financialisation and the dynamics of offshoring in the USA. *Cambridge Journal of Economics*, 34(2), 275–293.

Mohamed, S. (2016). Financialization of the South African economy. *Development*, 59(1–2), 137–142.

Newman, S. (2015). Financialisation and the financial and economic crisis: The case of South Africa. FESSUD: Working Paper Series, No 26.

Pearson, D. S. (1969). *Industrial Development in East Africa.* Oxford: Oxford University Press

Prebisch, R. (1950) *The Economic Development of Latin America and Its Principal Problems.* New York: United Nations Department of Economic Affairs, Economic Commission for Latin America (ECLA)

Quentin, D. and Campling, L. (2018). Global inequality chains: Integrating mechanisms of value distribution into analyses of global production. *Global Networks*, 18(1), 33–56.

Seabrooke, L. and Wigan, D. (2014). Global wealth chains in the international political economy. *Review of International Political Economy*, 21(1), 257-263.

Singleton, J. and Verhoef, G. (2010). Regulation, deregulation, and internationalisation in South African and New Zealand banking. *Business History*, 52(4), 536–563.

Soederberg, S. (2013). Universalising financial inclusion and the securitisation of development. *Third World Quarterly*, 34(4), 593–612

Staritz, C., Newman, S., Tröster, B. and Plank, L. (2018). Financialization and global commodity chains: Distributional implications for cotton in Sub-Saharan Africa. *Development and Change*, 49(3), 815–842.

Stiglitz, J. E. and Ocampo, J. A. (Eds.). (2008). *Capital Market Liberalization and Development.* Oxford: Oxford University Press.

Taylor, I. (2011). South African 'imperialism' in a region lacking regionalism: A critique. *Third World Quarterly*, 32(7), 1233–1253.

UNCTAD. (2016). *Economic Development in Africa: Debt Dynamics and Development Finance in Africa.* Geneva and New York: United Nations

Shaw, E. S. (1973). *Financial Deepening in Economic Development.* New York: Oxford University Press

Upadhyaya, R.& Johnson, S. (2015). Transformation of Kenya's Banking Sector 2002-2017. In: A. Heyer and M. King (eds), *Kenya's Financial Tranformation in the 21st Century.* Financial Sector Deepening Kenya. Nairobi: FSD Kenya

Van Waeyenberge, E. (2015). The private turn in development finance. FESSUD: Working Paper Series, 140.

Verhoef, G. (2009a). Savings for life to build the economy for the people: the emergence of Afrikaner corporate conglomerates in South Africa 1918-2000. *South African Journal of Economic History*, 24(1), 118–163.

Verhoef, G. (2009b). Concentration and competition: the changing landscape of the banking sector in South Africa 1970-2007. *South African Journal of Economic History*, 24(2), 157–197.

Wójcik, D. (2018). Rethinking global financial networks: China, politics, and complexity. *Dialogues in Human Geography*, 8(3), 272–275.

World Bank. (1981). *Accelerated Development in Sub-Saharan Africa: An Agenda for Action.* Washington, DC: World Bank.

World Bank. (1995). *Memorandum and Recommendation of the President of the International Development Association to the Executive Directors on a Proposed Credit in the Amount Equivalent to SDR 7.5 Million to the United Republic of Tanzania for a Financial Institutions Development Project.* Report No. P-6479-TA. Washington, DC: World Bank.

27

THE RENEWABLE ENERGY REVOLUTION

Risk, Investor and Financing Structures—with Case Studies from Germany and Kenya

Britta Klagge

Introduction: Some Facts and Figures

The massive political support for renewable energies since the late twentieth century has triggered a renewable energy revolution that—together with liberalization—has transformed energy sectors worldwide. As many countries strive to replace fossil fuel power and, in some cases, also nuclear power with renewable energies, the latter have developed rapidly since the turn of the millennium. Between 1990 and 2016, renewables increased their share in global power generation from 20% to 24%, mainly at the expense of nuclear power, whose share decreased from 17% to 10%, whereas fossil power generation increased its share slightly from 63% to 65% (IEA data).[1] Figures on the investment in annual power generation reveal an even clearer picture: Whereas, in 2005, renewable and fossil fuel power received similar investment amounts, their development diverged afterwards (Figure 27.1). Renewable power investment more than doubled between 2005 and 2018, with a steep increase until 2010, while investment in fossil fuel power has stagnated. And although total renewable power spending has been relatively stable since 2010 in terms of US dollars spent, investment activity is up by 55% since 2010 if adjusted for declines in cost (IEA, 2019: 53).

In 2017, investment in renewables already accounted for 67% of global investment into power generation, whereas fossil (30%) and nuclear (4%) had much smaller shares (IEA, 2018: 26). Geographically, China is leading investment into power generation in all three categories—fossil, nuclear and renewable—and was responsible for 29% of worldwide investment into power

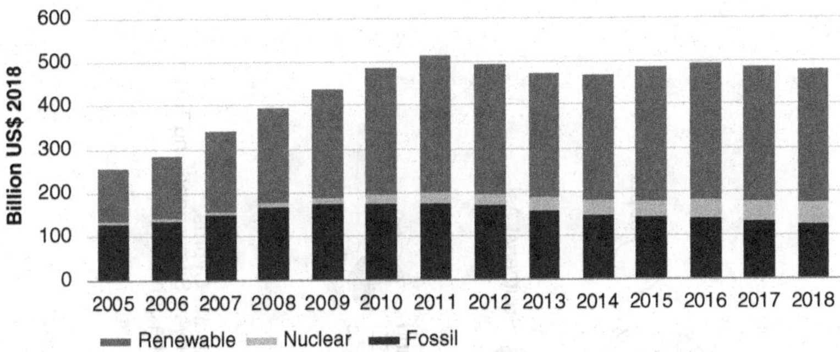

Figure 27.1 Global investment in power generation by technology, 2005–18

Source: The author; adapted from IEA (2019: 51).

generation in 2017 (Figure 27.2). It is followed by European OECD countries with 16% of overall power generation investment and the United States with 13%. Together, these three countries or regions accounted for 58% of the global total and an even higher share (69%) of renewable investment in 2017 (China: 33%, Europe: 22%, United States: 14%). This leaves fairly small shares for other countries and regions, of which many still have far more fossil than renewable investment (e.g., Russia, the Middle East, South East Asia, Australia and Africa).

The vast majority of renewable power generation investment in 2017 was in solar photovoltaics (PV), which dominate renewable investment in most world regions—most notably in China (45% of global solar PV investment), followed by the United States, Japan, and India (IEA, 2018: 14). Wind is the second largest renewable power investment target, with major investment sums in China, the United States, and, most importantly, Europe, where its share exceeds any other energy source including solar PV and fossil. Wind power generation and investment, especially in Europe, has, over the years, shifted from onshore to offshore (REN21, 2019) for a variety of reasons. Suitable sites for onshore wind farms are becoming scarce in some countries, partly due to problems of local acceptance; the challenge of connecting offshore farms to the grid has been successfully integrated into public support schemes; and last, but not least, offshore wind power generation has now become as mature as, and can be more reliable than, onshore wind.

Both solar PV and wind have developed dynamically in recent decades, not only in terms of investment and technology, but also regarding ownership and financing structures. Starting from small-scale, owner- and bank-financed operations, renewable power generation from wind and solar has become a large-scale business with access to capital market finance. In contrast, hydropower, which was the third most important renewable source in terms of investment in 2017, has been employed in large-scale facilities for many decades. Its growth, however, has slowed down: first, because many suitable sites for large-scale hydropower projects have already been used, and, second, the

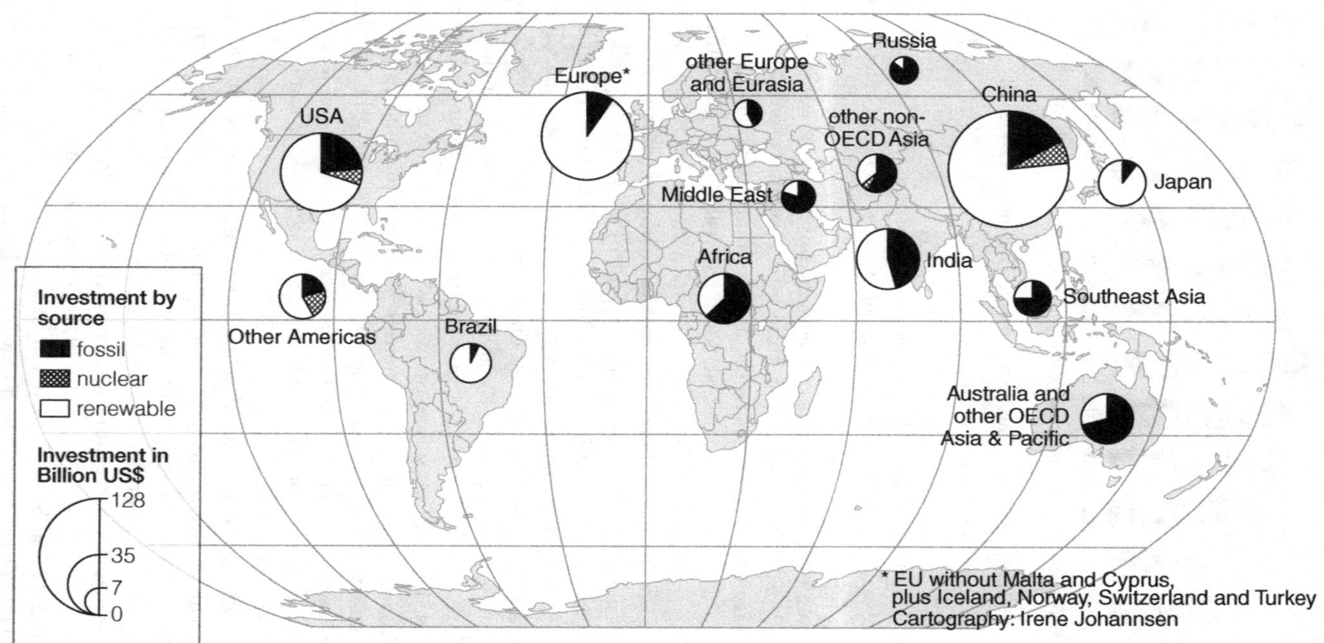

Figure 27.2 Map of global power generation investment by fuel and region, 2017 (US$ billion)

Source: The author; based on data from IEA (2018: 26, Table 1.1).

growing frequency of droughts has rendered hydropower unreliable in many world regions. Other renewables—such as biomass and geothermal—are so far, at least from a global perspective, much less important for power generation. Yet, there are geographical differences; Kenya, for example, is increasingly relying on geothermal power generation, as will be explained later.

The transition to renewable energies has been accompanied by great public and academic attention for their support, implementation, and resulting geographies (Bridge et al., 2013, 2018a), thus contrasting sharply with an earlier lack of interest for 'boring' power generation issues.[2] While this transition has become a much-discussed topic in geography and other academic fields, geographical research on the financing of renewable energies is still in its infancy. However, as this chapter shows, renewable energy finance is a worthwhile and rich topic for financial geography. This is not only due to the various scales and distinct geographies of renewable energy infrastructures, but is also related to their specific risk–return profiles, and the significant role of regulation and public policies.

The chapter argues that public actors and policies are vitally important for the transition to renewable energies with a deep impact on the mix of investor groups, and the variety of ownership and financing structures, in at least two respects. First, national government agencies have a profound impact through regulation and support schemes. Second, especially in the Global South, public investment into renewable energy projects is important not only in its own right, but also due to its facilitating and leveraging private investment, thereby playing a decisive role for globalizing the renewable energy revolution. Case studies from Germany and Kenya exemplify the twofold argument. The German case shows how strong public support policies can trigger a national renewable energy revolution, and makes Germany a model case for a successful transition to renewable power generation with a very diverse mix of investors and financing structures. Similarly, the examples from Kenya illustrate the importance of the national state for the development of renewable energy facilities, but also highlight the key role of international development finance institutions as (co-)investors in a Global South context. Before developing and substantiating the argument, the next section provides some historical background to the ongoing renewable energy revolution.

Transition of the Electricity Sector: Liberalization, Privatization and Climate Policies

The electricity mix in most countries has, for a considerable time, been dominated by fossil fuels (coal, oil, gas), nuclear energy and/or hydropower, with only minor shares for other renewables. These energy sources came along with large power plants, integrated into national grids with centralized load management systems. The electricity sector is therefore a prime example of a large technological system, whose development requires stable institutional conditions and consistent regulation (Hughes, 1983). Bridge et al. (2018b) even argue that the development of large-scale energy infrastructures is closely tied with 'the fate of the nation' (Bridge et al., 2018b). It is against this background that state actors and related utilities, mostly as a monopoly, were for a long time the major and dominant players—and financiers—in energy, and specifically electricity markets.

Financing energy infrastructures remained a domain of the state and monopolistic utilities until the late twentieth century. Mainly from the 1990s, energy sector liberalizations in many parts of the world encouraged and facilitated competition, large-scale privatizations and, thus, a greater role for private investment and public–private partnerships. This also applies to power generation, which, after unbundling of generation, transmission, and distribution, became attractive to a variety of players other than utilities as incumbent players (Bergek et al., 2013; Klagge and Brocke, 2013; Mazzucato and Semieniuk, 2018). These include citizens, farmers, cooperatives, institutional investors and other financial firms, firms from non-energy and non-financial sectors and, last but not least, independent power producers (IPPs). IPPs are firms that specialize in electricity generation, but are not a utility, and sell the generated electricity to utilities and/or end users. Their number has grown rapidly after, and where, electricity markets were liberalized. Thus, liberalization of energy markets has had a deep impact on actor and governance constellations in the power sector, and has facilitated the emergence of new ownership and financing structures.

While liberalization has been an important game changer, it has not diminished the role of policy, regulation, and, more generally, the state. How energy sectors are organized and who invests into what type of electricity generation is highly dependent on mostly national—and, in Europe, EU—regulations and energy policies. This is especially the case for the renewable energy revolution. Global, national, and local climate and renewable energy support policies have triggered a boom of renewable energies and are transforming energy sectors. Part of the associated investment has come from private sources. To understand why renewable energies have become attractive to a great variety of non-state and non-utility investors, we need to look at them from an investor perspective. For this, we first explain the risk structure of renewable energies, before we turn to how support policies help to overcome these risks.

Renewable Energy Investment: Challenging Risk–return Profile

One of the most profound challenges associated with attracting and incorporating non-state capital into renewable energy facilities is their specific risk–return profile (OECD, 2015; Wüstenhagen and Menichetti, 2012). This is mainly due to the long-term nature of renewable energy projects, where high up-front capital expenditures are facing very long payback periods of 20 or more years. Associated risks include political, legal, and regulatory risks, as well as macro-economic risks, which are often summarized as 'country risk'. Political, legal, and regulatory risks refer not only to state failure, or when (domestic) state actors change regulation or remuneration agreements, or—in a worst-case scenario—expropriate owners, but also to complex bureaucratic procedures, corruption, and policy uncertainty, whereas macro-economic risks comprise fluctuation of the interest rate, fluctuation of the exchange rate, and inflation. While all these risks are present throughout the project's lifetime, there are also specific risks in the project development and construction phase (pre-completion), and in the operational phase (post-completion).

Pre-completion risks are related to exploration and assessment of resources, the planning and construction of facilities, and technological failure. When exploration and the assessment of resources do not lead to a financially viable project, large sums of money can be lost, especially in the case of geothermal energy (see the example in Kenya later in this chapter). Planning and construction risks are about obtaining the necessary permits, licences and concessions—often including successful social and/or environmental impact assessments—and about choosing capable construction firms (often subcontractors) or personnel, as well as adequate technologies. The risk lies in (not) finalizing these various activities successfully and on schedule; that is, without delays and preferably without resistance from, or even sabotage by, local or other opponents.

Post-completion risks include operational, supply, and market risks. Operational risk is about malfunctioning, accidents, and other equipment related hazards; it is usually taken on by the facility operator, who is responsible for operation and maintenance (O&M). Supply risk refers to the availability and price of the necessary inputs, such as coal, oil, or gas in fossil fuel electricity generation, over the lifetime of the facility. In the case of renewable energy, supply risk varies with the renewable energy type and technology. For solar energy, it is mainly about solar radiation quantities; for wind power, about wind conditions; for bioenergy, about the provision—and price—of (suitable) biomass, and so on. The major difference with fossil fuels is that most inputs for renewable electricity are free, but dependent on local environmental conditions, whereas up-front investment costs are significantly higher for renewable energies, which makes them even more capital-intensive than fossil fuel power plants (Steffen, 2018). Market risk refers to the selling of generated electricity on the respective markets; that is, finding buyers and achieving a satisfactory price—again, for the whole lifetime of operation. In many cases, state-guaranteed feed-in-tariffs (FITs), or power purchase agreements (PPAs) with an offtaker, provide a guarantee for selling renewable electricity at a pre-specified price.

In developing a renewable power facility, and designing its ownership and financing structure, the various types of risk need to be considered, not least because different types of investors differ in their appetite for risk (Mazzucato and Semieniuk, 2018; Wüstenhagen and Menichetti, 2012). Particularly in large-scale projects with private participation, these problems usually are addressed by contractual risk allocation mechanisms, which transfer risks to specific shareholders or stakeholders. The latter can include specialized firms such as insurance companies, contractors and engineers, operators, and utilities as offtakers (OECD, 2014: 9). However, the higher the perceived risk of a technology (e.g., offshore versus onshore wind), or of an institutional context (e.g., country risk, Global South versus Global North), the more important and prevalent becomes public support, or even investment (Mazzucato and Semieniuk, 2018). The state or, more generally, public agencies can be part of, or support, a renewable power project in various ways, as will be elaborated in the next section.

Renewable Energy Support: The Large Role of Market-Oriented Risk Mitigation

Despite liberalization and privatization, (domestic) state actors remain important for power generation development. First, the state provides the regulatory framework through which private investors gain access to electricity markets in the first instance, often including stipulations to guarantee a certain scale and scope of renewable power generation; the state is also responsible for permits, licences, and concessions. Second, state actors, including public utilities, can participate in power generation as (partial) owners or shareholders, a provider of debt capital, an offtaker or guarantor of payment for generated electricity and/or as a supplier (e.g., of land). Third, the state can provide additional investment incentives through various renewable energy support policies to further mitigate the risks inherent in renewable energy projects, in order to make them attractive to non-state investors. Such policies can include tax incentives (e.g., tax breaks, tax credits, waiver of import taxes for equipment); investment grants; concessional loans or guarantees—for example, provided by state development or (green) investment banks (Geddes et al., 2018). Furthermore, in some countries state actors take responsibility for arranging supporting finance—for example, from international (bilateral or multilateral) development banks, export credit insurance or climate finance, which helps to leverage in private capital.

Most important and effective in the promotion of renewable energies are instruments that target the market risk of (not) selling the generated power. While investment support helps to overcome pre-completion risks by reducing project development and construction costs, market-oriented instruments are important in securing the revenue streams over the operational phase, which are needed for recovering investment costs and making profits. For renewable energies, there are three main policy instruments that target the market risk of renewable power generation: (1) feed-in-tariffs, (2) renewable energy quota and certificates, (3) auctions and tenders.

(1) **Feed-in-tariffs** (FITs), usually combined with guaranteed grid access, provide a fixed price for generated power over an extended period (20 years or so). Usually, the prices are technology-specific to reflect the cost

of generation of the respective source and technology. Typically, FITs are reduced stepwise over time in line with technology advancement and falling costs, so that later entrants have lower FITs, thus taking account of a lower overall generation cost. FITs provide long-term security to investors and have therefore become a very successful policy instrument, not only promoting investment in renewable energies, but also stimulating technology development, as for example in Germany, as will be discussed. Overall, FITs are an easy-to-handle and reliable support instrument that is independent from the scale of operations and thus attractive for both small- and large-scale investors (Nolden, 2013), setting them apart from quota and certificate systems, and from auctions and tenders.

(2) **Quota and certificate systems** have been introduced or discussed under different names, such as renewable obligations (ROs) in the United Kingdom, renewable portfolio standards (RPSs) in several US states, renewable energy certificates (REC) or tradable green certificates (TGC). They aim at utilities or other electricity suppliers and oblige them to supply a specified—increasing, over time—minimum proportion of their electricity from renewable sources. Quota for renewable energies are usually combined with certificates that are issued for power generated from renewable sources and then traded with suppliers. Suppliers need them to fulfil the quota regulation and are penalized in the event of non-compliance. Selling certificates creates additional revenue for renewable energy operators and thus supports the development of renewable energy facilities by covering the extra costs as compared with fossil fuel and nuclear power plants. Certificates are traded on specific (financial) markets, and, in an efficient market environment, their fluctuating price reflects the costs of investment in, and operation of, renewable electricity facilities. This is why quota and certificate systems are often promoted as safeguarding cost efficiency in renewable electricity generation more effectively than FITs, which need to be adapted in legislative procedures to reflect decreasing technology costs. However, due to the fluctuating price of certificates and the transaction costs associated with the certificate trading system, they provide a less reliable risk mitigator than FITs. They give an advantage to large and professional investors and 'tend [...] to favor market incumbents over new market entrants' (Toke and Lauber, 2007: 685).

(3) **Auctions and tenders** are competitive bidding processes initiated by state agents, where bidders offer to construct renewable power capacities and provide electricity at a certain price. The best bid, usually the lowest price per kWh, is the winner and is granted a power purchase agreement (PPA) that guarantees the stipulated price for a certain time period. If well-managed, this mechanism has the advantage of being flexible, transparent, effective, and (cost-)efficient, thus providing a greater certainty regarding both quantities and adequate prices than FITs (IRENA, 2015). However, aggressive bidding has led to cases where bidders have

> not lived up to their bids, and the promised capacities were never realized. Furthermore, transaction costs are quite high for both the organizing agency and the bidders. This advantages large professional investors over citizens, farmers, cooperatives, and other small-scale investors, who, in the event of a failed bid, often have difficulty recovering the high costs associated with bidding (securing land, permits, feasibility studies, etc.) through other bids and successful projects.

There has been a controversial debate about which instrument is best-suited to support the transition to renewable energies in a cost-efficient manner (Lipp, 2007; Toke and Lauber, 2007; Wüstenhagen and Menichetti, 2012). Different countries have applied different support schemes, and there have also been changes over time as a reaction to low expansion rates and/or high costs for the public and/or customers. The empirical evidence suggests that FITs are the best instrument with which to scale up renewable power generation rapidly, for which Germany is the model example—as opposed to the United Kingdom, where the introduction of ROs has only led to a very modest increase in renewable capacities and generation (Lipp, 2007; Toke and Lauber, 2007). Regarding cost efficiency and resulting electricity prices, the evidence is mixed. In the German case, for example, the rising consumer prices for electricity associated with the fast expansion of renewable electricity generation, together with grid capacity problems, led to a reorientation in renewable energy support from 2014 and a shift from FITs to auctions in 2017. This has been accompanied by a contentious debate about who can and should (be able to) invest in renewable electricity capacities.

The German Energy Transition: From FITs to Auctions

Germany is an example—and has become a model—for how the generous provision of FITs can accelerate the transition to renewable energy and generate a diverse mix of small- and large-scale renewable electricity investors. The foundation for this development was, together with the liberalization and unbundling of the energy sector in the 1990s, the German Renewable Energy Act (Erneuerbare Energien Gesetz—EEG, passed in 2000), which introduced FITs for all types of renewable electricity generation. The resulting boom of investment into renewable power facilities was, at first, mainly driven by citizens and farmers; that is, small-scale investors. Their investment was preceded by earlier engagement with, and for, renewable electricity facilities, particularly wind, which was motivated by environmental concerns and anti-nuclear protests since the 1980s.[3] While the EEG is often mentioned as the key driver of the German renewable energy revolution, one should not underestimate the importance of the country's decentralized banking system and the importance of the state development bank KfW (Geddes et al., 2018; Hall et al.,

2016). Local banks were important debt capital providers for projects by local firms, farmers, and citizens, often financially backed by the KfW. In addition to the direct provision of capital, the KfW played an important de-risking, educational, signalling and, last but not least, first-mover role, thereby helping to mobilize private capital into renewable energy projects at the start of the energy transition (Geddes et al., 2018).

The rise of renewable energies in Germany, which reached a share of almost 40% in the German power mix in 2018 (Figure 27.3), was accompanied by a decentralization of ownership in the electricity sector, with a decreasing role for utilities and a greater role for various other investor groups (Figure 27.4). Most utilities, the dominant players in the fossil and nuclear electricity markets, ignored, or even resisted, the Renewable Energy Act (EEG) for more than a decade. Until 2010, they were not only outstripped by small-scale investors, but also by strategic investors, particularly project developers. Even the financial sector provided more equity capital for renewable energy facilities than the four largest utilities, who used to own more than 80% of the power generation capacity in Germany. In 2009, their share of renewable power generation was still much lower than for Germany as a whole—with the vast majority coming from (traditional) hydropower and only miniscule shares of new renewables such as wind, solar PV, and bioenergy (Berkel, 2013; Greenpeace, 2011). Most utilities only started investment into renewable facilities at a larger scale after the Fukushima nuclear disaster in 2011, which prompted the conservative German government to shut down several nuclear power plants and pledge to close those remaining by the end of 2022.

The EEG was repeatedly amended to adapt FITs to the decreasing costs of renewable energy technologies and to solve emerging problems, such as the negative impact of biomass production on land and animal food prices, as well as the rising electricity prices for consumers. The rapid expansion of renewable energies continued but, from 2015 on, increasing electricity costs and bottlenecks in the national grid served as reason to start phasing out FITs and to shift to an auction system in 2017. This reorientation was accompanied by a highly controversial debate in which proponents of small-scale renewable generation protested against the hurdles that an auction system would pose to them, whereas others argued that an auction system would help to curb the increasing electricity price. While this debate is too complex to be laid out here in detail, it should be mentioned that the German energy transition not only resulted in an impressive rise in the share of renewable electricity but, at the same time, to an upsurge of electricity from brown coal/lignite. This was associated with an only modest decline of CO_2 emissions, which was far from enough to reach the government's declared emission targets (Umweltbundesamt, 2018). This development, and with it the rising costs for electricity, are mainly due to how FITs interact with the price-setting system at the European Power Exchange in Leipzig (EEX) and the malfunctioning EU emission trading system (ETS).[4]

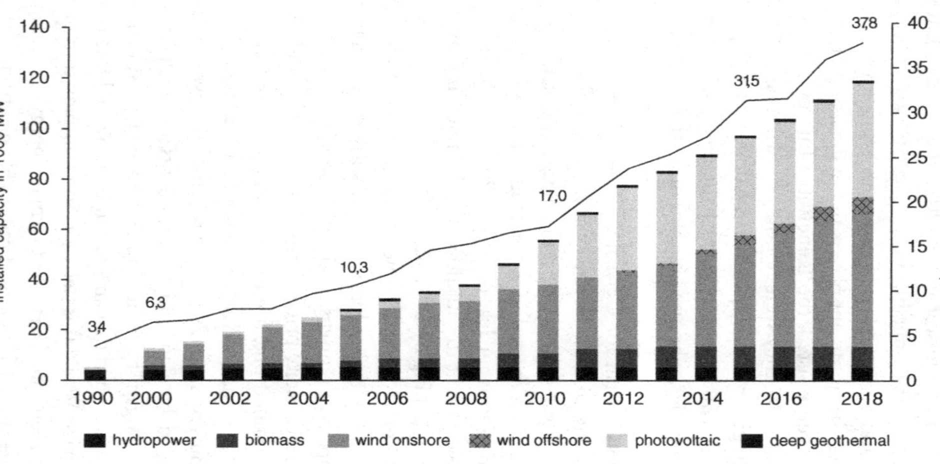

Figure 27.3 Development of installed renewable capacity in Germany and share of renewables in the German power mix, 1990, 2000–18

Source: The author; adapted from BMWi (2019).

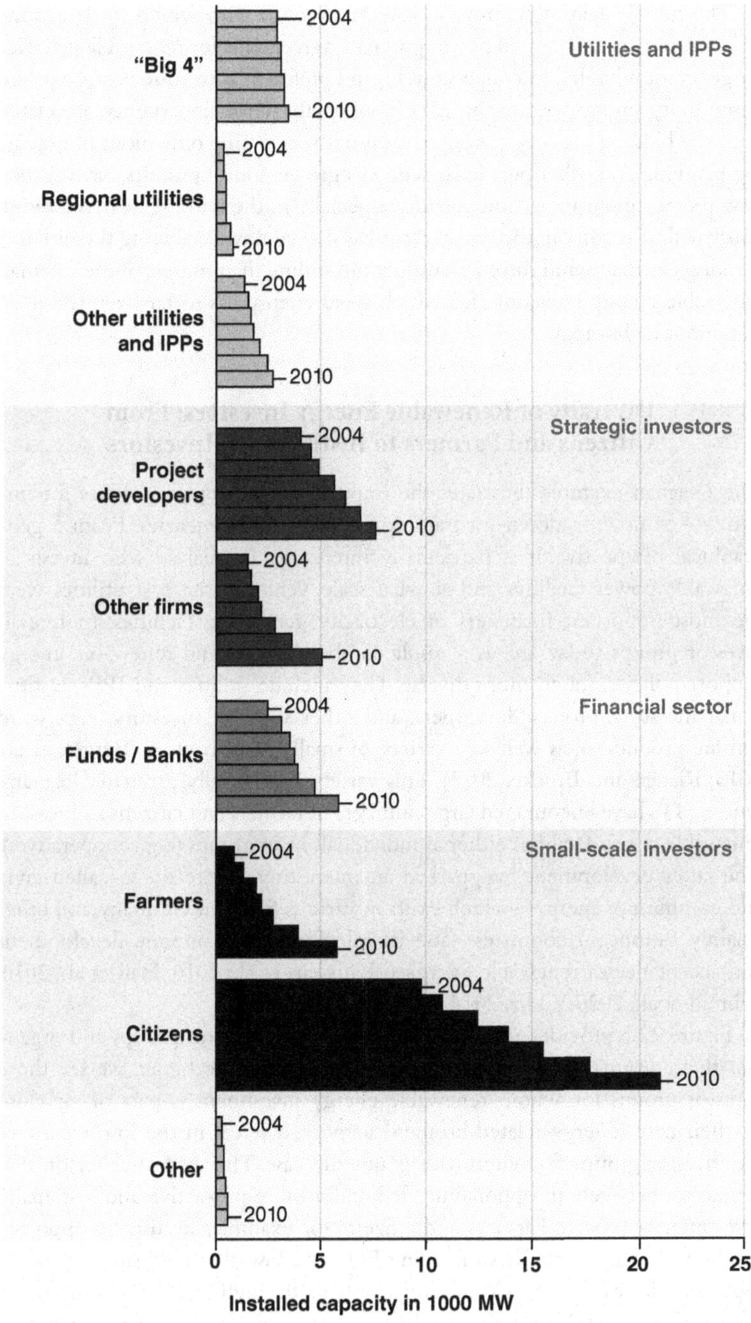

Figure 27.4 Renewable energy ownership structure, 2004–10

Source: The author; adapted from Trend: Research & KNI, 2011: 44).

The protest against auctions as sole mechanism with which to determine which investors are granted power purchase agreements for renewable electricity generation has led to concessions to, and preferential treatment of, civic and community energy organizations. However, the legal uncertainty associated with the bidding process, in conjunction with increasing difficulties in obtaining planning and other permissions due to growing local protests, have curbed new project applications and permits, especially in the wind sector. As a result, construction activity in the wind sector has slowed down, affecting the hitherto thriving German wind turbine industry and stifling the progress of the German renewable energy transition, for which wind energy has so far been the most important technology.

Diversity of Renewable Energy Investors: From Citizens and Farmers to Institutional Investors

The German example illustrates the importance of support policies for initiating—or slowing down—a transition to renewable energies. From a geographical perspective, it is particularly interesting to analyse who invests in renewable power facilities and at what scale. While in the past utilities were the most important financiers of electricity generating facilities, (potential) investor groups today are, as a result of liberalization and renewable energy support policies, much more diverse. They include utilities and IPPs, institutional investors, project developers, and other strategic investors (e.g., wind turbine producers), as well as a variety of small-scale investors (Bergek et al., 2013; Klagge and Brocke, 2013). This variety is especially great in Germany, where FITs have encouraged large numbers of farmers and citizens to invest in renewable power facilities either as individuals or in groups (e.g., cooperatives). The latter development has sparked an interesting debate on so-called civic and community energy—which exists in various forms in Germany and other (mainly European) countries—and its role for local economic development and acceptance of renewable energies (Bauwens et al., 2016; Hall et al., 2016; Schmid et al., 2020; Yildiz, 2014).

Figure 27.5 provides an overview of (potential) investor groups and organizes them around two criteria. In the upper part of the figure, we see those investor groups for whom renewable energy investment is part of, or close to, their core (energy-related business) activity, whereas in the lower part we see investor groups for whom this is not the case. The second criterion distinguishes between an opportunity-led and a more pro-active and systematic investment approach. Farmers and citizens, for example, are usually opportunity-led, with opportunities including FITs as a low-threshold support policy together with easy access to bank finance (e.g., through local banks) and ownership of, or access to, suitable land and other resources. For them, renewable power investment is (originally) not part of their core business activity or main income, although some farmers, in the course of the energy transition, have

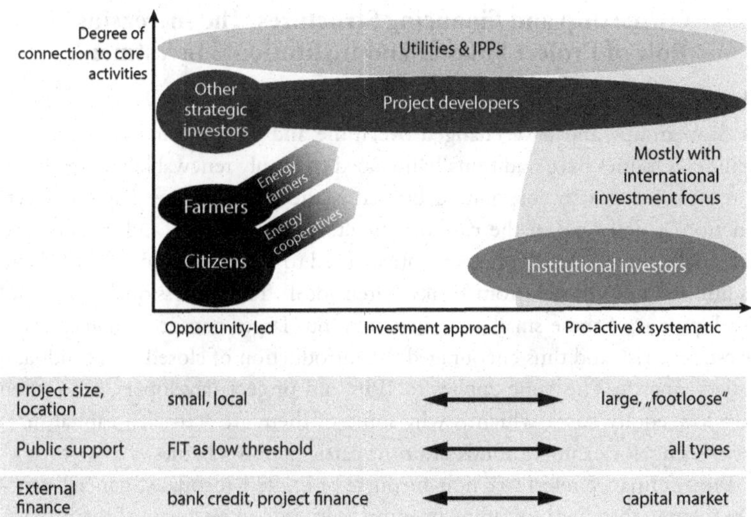

Figure 27.5 Investor groups and their business models

Source: The author.

specialized into so-called 'energy farmers', and some formerly small and local cooperatives have grown into larger businesses (Klagge and Meister, 2018).

Large financial investors share with small-scale investors for whom renewable energies are not part of their core activities. However, while the latter usually invest locally into small, self-governed facilities and are often driven by other than (only) financial motives, institutional investors are mainly interested in large and professionally managed projects with a promising risk–return profile. They pursue a pro-active investment approach and systematically search for projects nationally, or even internationally, that suit their investment philosophy and risk appetite. Renewable energy projects have become interesting for institutional investors because they generate steady revenue streams and have relatively low transaction costs, if large enough for generating economies of scale. Furthermore, they help to diversify their portfolios (Wüstenhagen and Menichetti, 2012), which became an important issue in the wake of the global financial crisis. However, many institutional investors shy away from bearing the pre-completion risks associated with the initial investment in large-scale renewable projects and prefer to invest in completed projects that are already generating revenue (Geddes et al., 2018; OECD, 2015). This fits well with the preferences of strategic investors such as project developers and technology suppliers, who are often main financiers in the project development and construction phase, and tend to sell their shares once the project is operational, in order to free up capital for investment in new projects (Baker, 2015: 154).

Ownership and Financing Structures: The Increasing Role of Project Finance and Institutional Investment

The financing structures and capital sources of renewable energy differ between investor groups, and have changed over time and with the increasing size of facilities. Utilities have traditionally financed (not only renewable) energy facilities on balance with corporate debt; that is, the assets on their balance sheets function as collateral in the case of default. At first, farmers and citizens, but also small entrepreneurs and cooperatives, used to rely on their own capital and traditional debt finance from banks (often local). The professionalization and development of these small-scale investors into larger consortia increased the investment risk and thus encouraged the introduction of closed-end funds and project finance. The same applies to IPPs and project developers, who often have low equity bases, which is why some of them are active on capital markets—using, for example, funds or profit participation schemes.

Project finance refers to a non-recourse or limited-recourse financial structure where repayment to capital investors is limited to revenues of the projects ('off balance'), thus limiting the risk for shareholders and thereby very suitable for the specific risk–return profile of renewable energy facilities. The contractual structure of project finance is usually through a special-purpose vehicle (SPV), with public and/or private shareholders and various other stakeholders. Besides protecting shareholders from project failure and the risk of bankruptcy, an additional argument for project finance is the clear contractual division of responsibilities among its shareholders and stakeholders, which helps to avoid agency conflicts (Steffen, 2018). On the downside, project finance is associated with significantly higher transaction costs than corporate finance, which is why it is mainly used in large-scale, high-risk projects and in projects with many different (types of) shareholders. This does, interestingly, include smaller low-risk projects in the civic or community energy sector in Germany (Steffen, 2018).

There is clear evidence that the use of project finance for financing renewable energies has increased both absolutely and relatively, but the illustrative figures differ. Steffen cites a 'remarkable share of 52% in 2015' (2018: 281) for new renewable energy plants based on data provided by UNEP. In contrast, according to the International Energy Agency (IEA), project finance reached a share of only 20% of global renewables generation investment in 2017, with on balance financing still dominating renewable energy investment (IEA, 2018: 121). Geographically, the shift to project finance is a global phenomenon, as in recent years, the 'perceived maturity and reliability of renewable technologies and better risk management of renewable projects has facilitated the expansion of off-balance sheet structures outside of the United States and Europe, with project finance rising in Asia, Latin America and Africa' (IEA, 2018: 16).

The rise of project finance is accompanied by an increasing role of institutional investment, although their relationship is somewhat unclear. Institutional investment also focuses on large-scale projects, but renewable power generation is still a fairly new field with a challenging risk–return profile for capital market actors. Therefore, institutional investors and especially pension funds were initially quite hesitant to invest in renewable energies (OECD, 2015). Meanwhile, with some experience and the maturing of renewable industries and institutional contexts, pension funds and other institutional investors have become more confident and now invest into renewable power facilities in various forms, direct or intermediated (e.g., through funds), and both equity and debt (Table 27.1). In the wake of the global financial crisis and supported by the fact that renewable asset performance is hardly correlated with traditional asset classes, renewable energies have even developed into a new asset class on financial markets and become susceptible to financialization (Baker, 2015; Klagge and Anz, 2014).

Geographically, and in terms of renewable energy sources, institutional and, particularly, pension fund investment is still very uneven—and more so than global power investment into renewable power production (cp. Figure 27.1). There is a stronger focus on wind projects, as well as a geographical investment bias towards European projects. This reflects the falling costs of wind energy, as well as the stable and renewable-friendly institutional contexts in Europe. In other parts of the world, which are perceived as more risky, institutional investors, as well as other private investors, engage either much more reluctantly, or not at all. The resulting funding gap for realizing renewable power projects in the Global South is often filled by (public) development finance, as the examples from Kenya illustrate. While direct public financing from international and domestic sources is much more important in Kenya than in Germany, there is a similarity regarding the key role of national-state regulation and support schemes.

Financing Renewable Energy in the Global South: Two Examples from Kenya

Renewable power investment in the Global South has increased significantly over recent decades, with China accounting for its bulk (REN21, 2019; cp. Figure 27.2). Whereas in China domestic public sector capital plays the dominant role (Mazzucato and Semieniuk, 2018; Ming et al., 2014), other countries are important destinations of international public capital, mainly in the form of development finance. Overall, in developing and emerging economies, the public sector—national and international—accounts for roughly two-thirds of investment financing for sustainable energy infrastructure, and only one-third comes from private sources (OECD, 2015: 31). This is the reverse of the picture in OECD countries, where only one-third is provided by public sector sources, such as various levels of government and national development banks, and two-thirds come from private sources.

Table 27.1 Summary of project investments by pension funds in sustainable energy (sample of 47)

	Number of cases	*Percentage of sample*
Investment type		
direct	28	60
intermediated	19	40
Debt vs. equity		
debt	33	70
equity	14	30
Year of investment		
2008	1	2
2009	2	4
2010	5	11
2011	6	13
2012	6	13
2013	19	40
2014	8	17
Sector		
Wind	31	66
Solar	11	23
Other	5	11
Project location by region		
Europe	28	60
United States and Canada	8	17
Africa	4	9
Asia	2	4
Latin America	2	4
Middle East	1	2
Australia	0	0
Global	2	4
Geographic flow of investment		
North–North	38*	81
South–South	7	15
North–South	2	4
South–North	0	0

Note: * The source has the number 39 here, but this is incompatible with both the total of 47 and the proportion of 81%. The number has therefore been changed to 38, which is in line with both the total and the percentage.

Source: Adapted from OECD (2015): 63–4, table 3.1.

The background for this disparity is differences in institutional settings and maturity of financial markets, resulting in lower trust and higher risk perceptions in most countries of the Global South. This includes not only political, legal, regulatory, and macro-economic (country) risks, but also construction and technology, as well as market risk; that is, the ability and willingness of domestic offtakers to pay for generated electricity according to FITs or PPAs. However, domestic public support and co-financing by bilateral and multilateral development banks increasingly attracts private investment to renewable power facilities in institutionally stable contexts in the Global South, for which the Lake Turkana Wind Park (LTWP) in the marginal and arid north of the Kenya provides a good example (Figure 27.6).

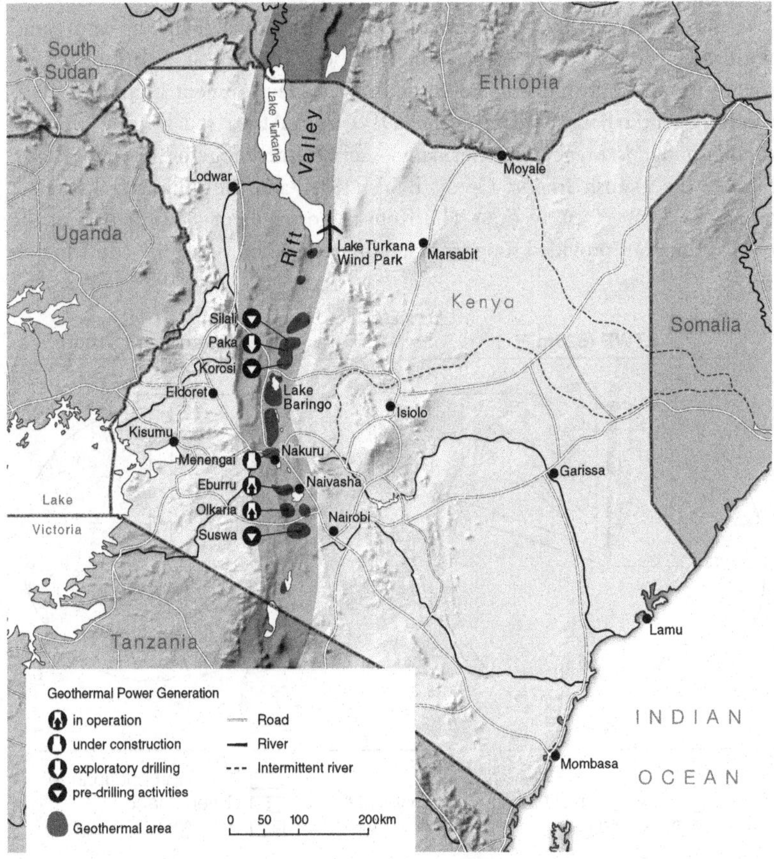

Figure 27.6 Map of Kenya showing the Lake Turkana Wind Power project (LTWP) and geothermal power generation areas

Source: The author; based on Browne (2015); Mangi (2017); Interview information (2019).

The LTWP was developed by an international consortium of private and public firms and institutions from 2006, and started feeding electricity into the national grid in late 2018 (Kamau, 2018).[5] With 365 turbines and a generation capacity of over 300 MW, LTWP is the largest wind park in Africa—and the largest private investment in Kenya's history at the time, with total project financing of €623 million (LTWP, 2014). Private shareholders included project development firms based in Europe (the Netherlands and the United Kingdom) and Kenya; the Danish turbine producer (and provider) Vestas; and, with a very small share, a Kenyan GIS firm; together, this accounted for 14% of total financing. Public shareholders in the consortium were three government established development finance institutions (DFIs) from Scandinavian countries (Denmark, Norway, and Finland) who were jointly responsible for 6% (Figure 27.7).

Debt capital for LTWP made up 80% of the total financing and came, with the small exception of the Dutch Triodos Bank (1%), from public sector institutions only. This included the African Development Bank (AfDB) as the lead debt arranger, various other DFIs from Africa and Europe (the EU, the Netherlands, France, and Germany)—all DFI debt together accounting for 55%—, the Danish Export Credit Bank (19%), and the multilateral Interact Climate Change Facility (5%). The Kenyan government was not part of the consortium, but provided support by taking responsibility for the construction

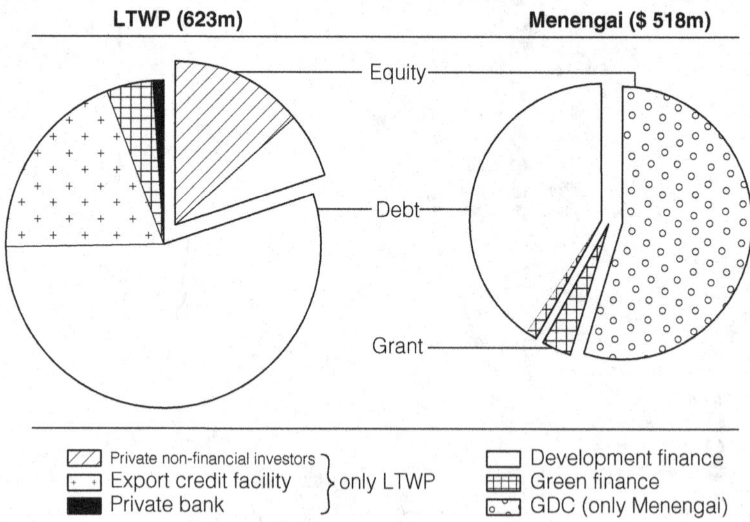

Figure 27.7 Shares of equity, debt and grant financings of the Lake Turkana Wind Park (LTWP) and Menengai geothermal project (Phase 1; assessment, exploration and drilling)

Source: The author; from Klagge and Nweke-Eze (2020).

Table 27.2 Grid-connected power production by sources in Kenya, 1995, 2005, 2015 (GWh and % of total)

	1995		*2005*		*2015*	
Energy sources		%		%		%
Oil	416	10.2	1,645	28.3	1,206	12.4
Biofuels	122	3.0	131	2.3	122	1.3
Hydro	3,163	77.3	3,026	52.0	3,787	39.1
Geothermal	390	9.5	1,003	17.2	4,479	46.2
Solar PV			13	0.2	37	0.4
Wind					57	0.6
Total	4,091		5,818		9,688	

Source: IEA data from www.iea.org/statistics.

of the high-voltage transmission line of more than 400km that was required to connect the LTWP with the national grid, and by facilitating a 20-year PPA with the national utility (Eberhard et al., 2016: 113).[6]

The LTWP expanded Kenya's power generation capacity substantially, accounting for approximately 17% (LTWP, 2018), but the most important initiative for increasing power generation in Kenya is the further development of the country's rich geothermal resources in the Rift Valley (cp. Figure 27.6). Geothermal resources in Kenya have been harnessed for electricity generation since the early 1980s and, in 2014, geothermal surpassed hydropower in terms of grid-connected power production (Eberhard et al., 2016: 107; cp. Table 27.2). To fast track the exploitation of geothermal energy, the government of Kenya incorporated the Geothermal Development Corporation (GDC) as an SPV in 2004. The stated aim for the GDC was to realize a geothermal capacity of 5,000 MW by the year 2030. The background for this ambitious goal—in 2013, total installed power generation capacity in Kenya was still below 2000 MW (Eberhard et al., 2016)—is the aspiration of becoming a middle-income country by 2030, as envisioned and elaborated in the Kenyan 'Vision 2030' document (GoK, 2007).

The establishment of the GDC as a parastatal agency is due to the fact that geothermal energy entails a high (pre-completion) exploration risk, which is specific to this technology. It includes the risks of high and hard-to-calculate drilling costs, and of not hitting steam or of achieving less capacity than anticipated, which makes these activities too risky and therefore unattractive to private investors. Supported by loans and grants from foreign donors, development partners and (public) green finance, the GDC covers the very high up-front costs for drilling and assessment of geothermal resources in several new sites in the Rift Valley and, together with other state agencies, for establishing the necessary ancillary infrastructures (roads, water provision, grid connection, etc.).[7] Eventually, in the event of sufficient resource potential, the GDC sells the generated steam to the national power generation company KenGen or, as in Menengai, to private IPPs (Kiplagat et al., 2011). It is only then that private investors become involved, whereas the much riskier assessment, exploration, and drilling are financed solely by domestic and international public sector sources, as illustrated by the first phase of the Menengai project (Figure 27.7).

Overall, the Kenyan case illustrates the complexities of renewable energy deployment and financing in a sub-Saharan African context. Aiming at a rapid increase in power generation to enable the envisaged economic and social development of Vision 2030, the Kenyan state is dependent on private and international investment. The high up-front financing requirements of large-scale geothermal and other renewable energy projects far exceed Kenya's public finances, which is why private participation and international development finance are actively solicited through supporting policies, frameworks, and infrastructures. Climate finance plays a supportive role and, together with state and DFI investment, helps to mitigate risk and leverage private investment. Also important are the Kenyan state's efforts to reduce investors' perception of country risk and to provide a stable and reliable institutional context that honours its obligations (e.g., PPAs, grid-connection commitments) even when this poses a challenge to the country's already high debt burden.

Summary and Conclusion

Financing the renewable energy revolution is a complex and challenging endeavour. It is geographically uneven, not only in terms of investment sums and generated capacities, but also with respect to energy sources, investor groups, ownership, and financing structures. State and public sector agencies play a vital role as regulators, capital investors, and providers of investment incentives to mitigate the multifarious and geographically uneven risks.

The risk structure of renewable energy investments is multi-layered; there is considerable significance in terms of the temporal dimension and project- and context-related risks, thereby accounting for its geographical complexity. At the national context level, differences in country risk—which include detrimental political, legal, regulatory, and macro-economic developments—explain some of the distinctions, especially between the Global North and the Global South. The importance of stable institutional conditions for (not only renewable) energy infrastructures and investments is reinforced by their long-term nature, which is key for understanding the specific risk–return profile at the project level.

In the highly capital-intensive project development and construction phase, pre-completion risks related to resources, permits, management, and technology tend to scare off risk-averse investors. In the operational phase, the main post-completion risk is about generating a constant stream of revenues to pay off the high initial investment costs. How this market risk is assessed by investors depends on national energy market structures and their support policies. As a successful investment depends on the long-term performance of a renewable power plant, country and market risk are probably the most important factors in the investment decision.

The complex risk structure of renewable energy investments, together with their relative novelty, provide multifarious challenges to investors, which explains why public actors and policies are vitally important. Renewable energy transitions started around 2000 and were initiated by different types of support scheme. They coincided with, or were preceded by, liberalizations of energy markets, which facilitated the emergence of more diverse actor constellations with various new entrants to the energy sector. These range from small-scale investors such as citizens and farmers to independent power producers, project developers, and other strategic investors to institutional investors, thereby side-lining utilities to some extent. Renewable energy support policies, especially those aiming at the mitigation of market risk (FITs, quota and certificate systems, auctions and tenders), can play a decisive role in providing opportunities for the engagement of specific investor groups, thereby significantly shaping national renewable energy transitions, their actor constellations, and geographies, as shown by the examples of Germany and Kenya.

With the advancement and upscaling of renewable energy technologies, the scale of projects is growing and, concomitantly, the financial needs to realize individual projects. Particularly large-scale facilities are increasingly financed through project finance, which limits the risk for shareholders and corresponds well with the specific risk–return profile of renewable energy facilities. Their high up-front investment costs and long pay-back periods fit well with the investment preferences of many institutional investors, especially pension funds. Nonetheless, such investors were initially, as some still are, quite hesitant to invest in renewable energies, due to the challenging overall risk–return profile and their unfamiliarity with renewable energies. Yet, with growing experience, and maturity of the sector and its technologies, this has started to change.

Though still low, institutional investment into renewable energies is increasing; and renewable energy has now even become a new asset class. However, institutional investment in renewable energy is concentrated, both in terms of technology—with wind leading and solar PV gaining in importance—and geographically, mainly in the pioneer markets in the Global North. The flipside of this is the, as yet, much larger role of public investment in renewable power facilities in the Global South. While in the Global North national development banks often play a key role as investor or support agency, renewable energy investment in Africa and other parts of the Global South is, to a large degree, contingent on international development finance, as the two Kenyan examples illustrate, with green or climate finance playing a supportive role.

While the ongoing renewable energy investments and transitions are a good start, the power sector is still very far from becoming sustainable. To further advance renewable energy transitions worldwide, and thereby contribute to global climate policy, much more investment is needed. While public investment will remain important, particularly in the Global South, a rapid transition will require (considerably more) private capital. Due to the specific risk–return profile of renewable power and strong dependency on state regulation, stable institutional conditions and active public support policies have so far been, and continue to be, important in attracting both private and international public capital. Designing effective, and hopefully efficient, energy support policies together with conducive institutional conditions is a challenge for both national governments and international organizations, for which there is no single solution. Rather, renewable energy policies have to accommodate different geographical and institutional environments and, at the same time, attract large amounts of capital from a broad variety of investors—possibly reaching from local stakeholders to national to large international investors, and including both public and private capital providers—in order to fast track the global renewable energy revolution.

Acknowledgements

Research for this chapter was supported by the Deutsche Forschungsgemeinschaft (DFG, German Research Foundation) through funding for the project 'Energy futures' as part of the collaborative research centre 'Future Rural Africa' (Project-ID 328966760—TRR 228), and by the Swiss National Science Foundation (SNSF) through funding for the project 'Collective financing of renewable energy projects' (Project no. 407140_153800).

Notes

1 Data available on www.iea.org/statistics
2 However, this view excludes the highly controversial public debates about, and protests against, nuclear energy since the 1970s in some European countries and the United States.
3 There was an earlier support scheme for renewable power generation in 1991–2000, but it was smaller in scope and financially less attractive. While not leading to a large boom, it still provided an opportunity to gain experience with renewable power production and its technologies (for a detailed account, see Jacobsson and Lauber, 2006).
4 More specifically, marginal cost pricing and the resulting merit order effect in combination with low prices for emission certificates favour, first, renewables with almost no operating costs, and then cheap high-emission lignite, thus leading to very low wholesale prices. The difference between low wholesale prices and relatively high FITs paid to producers is added to the consumer prices through a so-called EEG levy, which has been increasing with the growing share of renewables in the German power mix.
5 Since the mid-1990s, the Kenyan government has established the necessary institutional conditions in the Kenyan power sector and, under the influence of the

World Bank, restructured and liberalized its energy sector (Eberhard et al., 2016). This 'neoliberal energy transition' (Newell and Phillips, 2016: 39) resulted in the current hybrid market structure, which is dominated by publicly owned or publicly dominated companies, but in which private investment and investors are playing an increasingly large role (Eberhard et al., 2016; Kiplagat et al., 2011).

6 Further details on the development and financing of the project, as well as on its environmental, social, and economic dimensions and related CSR measures, are provided in Danwatch (2016), Enns (2016), Klagge and Nweke-Eze (2020), and Schilling et al. (2018).

7 Furthermore, the GDC deals with legal issues regarding land (access) rights and Environmental and Social Impact Assessment (ESIA) Licences, and establishes community-engagement frameworks, all of which can cause conflict and thus pose risks to the realization of geothermal projects (Mariita, 2002).

References

Baker, L. (2015). The evolving role of finance in South Africa's renewable energy sector. *Geoforum*. 64, 146–156.

Bauwens, T., Gotchev, B. and Holstenkamp, L. (2016). What drives the development of community energy in Europe? The case of wind power cooperatives. *Energy Research & Social Science*. 13, 136–147.

Bergek, A., Mignon, I. and Sundberg, G. (2013). Who invests in renewable electricity production? Empirical evidence and suggestions for further research. *Energy Policy*. 56, 568–581.

Berkel, M. (2013). Die Großen Vier. In: *Bundeszentrale für Politische Bildung*, ed., Dossier Energiepolitik. 1.3.2013. [online]. Available at: https://www.bpb.de/politik/wirtschaft/energiepolitik/152780/die-grossen-vier [Accessed: 30 September 2019].

BMWi – Bundesministerium für Wirtschaft und Energie. (2019). *Entwicklung der erneuerbaren Energien in Deutschland im Jahr 2018. Grafiken und Diagramme unter Verwendung aktueller Daten der Arbeitsgruppe Erneuerbare Energien-Statistik (AGEE-Stat). Stand: Februar 2019*. [online]. Available at: https://www.erneuerbare-energien.de/EE/Navigation/DE/Service/Erneuerbare_Energien_in_Zahlen/Entwicklung/entwicklung-der-erneuerbaren-energien-in-deutschland.html [Accessed: 30 September 2019].

Bridge, G., Bouzarovski, S., Bradshaw, M., and Eyre, N. (2013). Geographies of energy transition: Space, place and the low-carbon economy. *Energy Policy*. 53, 331–340.

Bridge, G., Barr, S., Bouzarovski, S., Bradshaw, M., Brown, E., Bulkeley, H., and Walker, G. (2018a). *Energy and Society. A Critical Perspective*. London/New York: Routledge.

Bridge, G., Özkaynak, B., and Turhan, E. (2018b). Energy infrastructure and the fate of the nation: Introduction to special issue. *Energy Research & Social Science*. 41, 1–11.

Browne, A. J. (2015). *LAPSSET : The History and Politics of an Eastern African Megaproject*. London: Rift Valley Institute Report.

Danwatch. (2016). A people in the way of progress - Part 3. [online]. Available at: https://medium.com/@Danwatch/a-people-in-the-way-of-progress-part-3-b01c3be0caee [Accessed: 30 September 2019].

Eberhard, A., Gratwick, K., Morella, E., and Antmann, P. (2016). *Independent Power Projects in Sub-Saharan Africa: Lessons from Five Key Countries*. Washington, DC: World Bank Group.

Enns, C. (2016). Experiments in governance and citizenship in Kenya's resource frontier. PhD dissertation. University of Waterloo. [online]. Available at: https://pdfs.semanticscholar.org/f128/a6dfcdbf19df60b08283b50165fb0d44dcf1.pdf [Accessed: 30 August 2019].

Geddes, A., Schmidt, T. S., and Steffen, B. (2018). The multiple roles of state investment banks in low-carbon energy finance: An analysis of Australia, the UK and Germany. *Energy Policy.* 115, 158–170.

GoK – Government of Kenya. (2007). *Kenya Vision 2030.* [online]. Available at: http://www.vision2030.go.ke/home/ [Accessed: 12 January 2019].

Greenpeace. (2011). Investitionen der vier großen Energiekonzerne in Erneuerbare Energien. *Stand 2009, Planungen und Ziele 2020 – Kapazitäten, Stromerzeugung und Investitionen von E.ON, RWE, Vattenfall und EnBW.* Hamburg: Greenpeace. [online]. Available at: https://www.greenpeace.de/presse/publikationen/investitionen-der-vier-grossen-energiekonzerne-erneuerbare-energien [Accessed: 30 September 2019].

Hall, S., Foxon, T. J., and Bolton, R. (2016). Financing the civic energy sector: How financial institutions affect ownership models in Germany and the United Kingdom. *Energy Research & Social Science.* 12, 5–15.

Hughes, T. P. (1983). *Networks of Power: Electrification in Western Society, 1880-1930.* Baltimore, MD: The John Hopkins University Press.

IEA – International Energy Agency. (2018). *World Energy Investment 2018.* Paris: IEA.

IEA – International Energy Agency. (2019). *World Energy Investment 2019.* Paris: IEA.

IRENA – International Renewable Energy Agency. (2015). *Renewable Energy Auctions: A Guide to Design.* Abu Dhabi: IRENA. [online]. Available at: https://www.irena.org/publications/2015/Jun/Renewable-Energy-Auctions-A-Guide-to-Design [accessed: 30 September 2019].

Jacobsson, S. and Lauber, V. (2006). The politics and policy of energy system transformation—explaining the German diffusion of renewable energy technology. *Energy Policy.* 34, 256–276

Kamau, M. (2018). Payback time: Wind power firm faces fine for delayed supplies. Standard Digital. [online]. Available at: https://www.standardmedia.co.ke/article/2001297554/payback-time-wind-power-firm-faces-fine-for-delayed-supplies [Accessed: 30 September 2019].

Kiplagat, J. K., Wang, R. Z., and Li, T. X. (2011). Renewable energy in Kenya: Resource potential and status of exploitation. *Renewable and Sustainable Energy Reviews.* 15 (6), 2960–2973.

Klagge, B. and Anz, J. (2014). Finanzialisierung der Windenergienutzung in Deutschland? Entwicklungen im Spannungsfeld von Finanzsektor und Energiepolitik. In: Heires, M. and Nölke, A., eds., *Politische Ökonomie der Finanzialisierung.* Heidelberg: Springer VS, 241–257.

Klagge, B. and Brocke, T. (2013). Energiewende vor Ort: dezentrale Stromerzeugung und die Rolle von Stadtwerken und Regionalversorgern. *Geographische Rundschau.* 65 (1), 12–18.

Klagge, B. and Meister, T. (2018). Energy cooperatives in Germany – an example of successful alternative economies? *Local Environment.* 23 (7), 697–716.

Klagge, B. and Nweke-Eze, C. (2020): Financing large-scale renewable-energy projects in Kenya. Investor types, international connections, and financialization. *Geografiska Annaler: Series B, Human Geography.* 102 (1), 61–83.

Lipp, J. (2007). Lessons for effective renewable electricity policy from Denmark, Germany and the United Kingdom. *Energy Policy.* 35, 5481–5495.

LWTP – Lake Turkana Wind Power Ltd. (2014). LTWP signs financing documents with AfDB and other lenders. [online]. Available at: https://ltwp.co.ke/ltwp-signs-financing-documents-with-afdb-and-other-lenders/ [Accessed: 30 September 2019].

LTWP. (2018). Providing reliable, low cost energy to Kenya. [online]. Available at: https://ltwp.co.ke/ [Accessed: 30 September 2019].

Mangi, M. P. (November 9–29, 2017). Geothermal exploration in Kenya – Status report and updates. Paper Presented at *Sustainable Development Goals (SDG) Short Course II on Exploration and Development of Geothermal Resources*, Lake Bogoria and Naivasha, Kenya. [online]. Available at: https://orkustofnun.is/gogn/unu-gtp-sc/UNU-GTP-SC-25-0701.pdf [Accessed: 30 September 2019].

Mariita, N. O. (2002). The impact of large-scale renewable energy development on the poor: environmental and socio-economic impact of a geothermal power plant on a poor rural community in Kenya. *Energy Policy.* 30, 1119–1128.

Mazzucato, M. and Semieniuk, G. (2018). Financing renewable energy: Who is financing what and why it matters. *Technological Forecasting and Social Change.* 127, 8–22.

Ming, Z., Ximei, L., Yulong, L., and Lilin, P. (2014). Review of renewable energy investment and financing in China: Status, mode, issues and countermeasures. *Renewable and Sustainable Energy Reviews.* 31, 23–37.

Newell, P. and Phillips, J. (2016). Neoliberal energy transitions in the South: Kenyan experiences. *Geoforum.* 74, 39–48.

Nolden, C. (2013). Governing community energy—Feed-in tariffs and the development of community wind energy schemes in the United Kingdom and Germany. *Energy Policy.* 63, 543–552.

OECD – Organisation for Economic Co-operation and Development. (2014). *Private Financing and Government Support to Promote Long-term Investments in Infrastructure.* Paris: OECD Publishing.

OECD – Organisation for Economic Co-operation and Development. (2015). *Mapping Channels to Mobilise Institutional Investment in Sustainable Energy.* Paris: OECD Publishing.

REN21. (2019). *Renewables 2019. Global Status Report.* Paris: REN21 Secretariat c/o UN Environment

Schilling, J., Locham, R., and Scheffran, J. (2018). A local to global perspective on oil and wind exploitation, resource governance and conflict in Northern Kenya. *Conflict, Security & Development.* 18 (6), 571–600.

Schmid, B., Meister, T., Klagge, B., and Seidl, I. (2020). Energy cooperatives and municipalities in local energy governance arrangements in Switzerland and Germany. *Journal of Environment & Development.* In print.

Steffen, B. (2018). The importance of project finance for renewable energy projects. *Energy Economics.* 69, 280–294.

Toke, D. and Lauber, V. (2007). Anglo-Saxon and German approaches to neoliberalism and environmental policy: The case of financing renewable energy. *Geoforum.* 38 (4), 677–687.

Trend: Research Institute and KNI - Klaus Novy Institute. (2011). *Marktakteure Erneuerbare Energien - Anlagen in der Stromerzeugung.* [online]. Available at: https://sverigesradio.se/diverse/appdata/isidor/files/3345/12617.pdf [Accessed: 30 September 2019].

Umweltbundesamt. (2018). Entwicklung der spezifischen Kohlendioxid-Emissionen des deutschen Strommix in den Jahren 1990–2017. [online]. Available at: https://www.umweltbundesamt.de/sites/default/files/medien/1410/publikationen/2018-05-04_climate-change_11-2018_strommix-2018_0.pdf [Accessed: 30 September 2019].

Wüstenhagen, R. and Menichetti, E. (2012). Strategic choices for renewable energy investment: Conceptual framework and opportunities for further research. *Energy Policy.* 40, 1–10.

Yildiz, Ö. (2014). Financing renewable energy infrastructures via financial citizen participation – The case of Germany. *Renewable Energy.* 68, 677–685.

28

FINANCE AND CLIMATE CHANGE

Patrick Bigger and Wim Carton

Introduction

An examination of the links between the financial economy and a rapidly warming atmosphere is more pressing than ever. In October 2018, the Intergovernmental Panel on Climate Change (IPCC) released a report vividly demonstrating the short- and medium-term risks posed by climate change, warning that we need to achieve 'rapid, far-reaching , and unprecedented changes in *all aspects of society*' to avoid dangerous climate change (IPCC, 2018, emphasis added). The IPCC does not typically use language of this urgency, but it is not as though these outcomes were unpredictable, or, indeed, that no action has been taken on climate. In this chapter, we explore how finance and climate change are entangled in 'climate changed capitalism' (Bryant, 2019). We show how financial practices are inexorably bound up in a variety of carbon economies, from finance's role in facilitating the production and consumption of fossil fuels, to the financial mechanisms that have been trialled to rein in emissions, to the ways that activists are pressuring investors to divest from carbon intensive industries.

There has been widespread experimentation for climate governance in both the private and public sectors since the late 1990s but, even as these experiments dabbled at the edges of the carbon economy, global emissions and proven fossil fuel reserves continued to grow. We discuss some of these climate policy experiments in this chapter but, critically, this period coincided with what may come to be considered the high-water mark of neoliberalization. Mechanisms for regulating greenhouse gas emissions such as emissions trading markets, feed-in tariffs, and renewable energy credits mostly cleaved to prevailing elite attitudes that markets were the most efficient mechanism for achieving desirable outcomes (Bryant, 2019; Felli, 2015). But no matter the source or form they take, financial flows meant to reduce emissions or adapt to climate change are dwarfed by 'brown' finance; the market capitalization of Exxon Mobil was five times the value of all greenhouse gas (GHG) emissions markets in 2016 (Bigger et al., 2018) . While there has been some movement towards problematizing continued financial support for fossil fuels and other climate-polluting industries, many private and public actors continue to invest in both carbon-intensive activities *and* low-carbon initiatives. The two can go hand-in-hand, and often do (Newell et al., 2009).

To explore the landscape of heterogeneous financial links to the atmosphere, the chapter has four sections. The first three are oriented around key entanglements of finance and climate change, both as causes of, and responses to, the crisis. The fourth section concludes the chapter by suggesting that we need a robust political response to the staggering inequities bound up in the conjunction of global warming and financialization. It is only by denaturalizing the causes and ongoing impediments to meaningful decarbonization or transformative adaptation that the worst outcomes of global warming can be averted.

The first section describes how the financial sector is an indispensable component of the vast global furnace for extracting and burning fossil fuels. That indispensability cuts both ways: fossil fuel assets are structurally important for the 'normal' function of capital markets (Labban, 2010) as much as capital markets facilitate discovery, extraction, distribution, and consumption of those fuels (Labban, 2008). The second section explores financial markets or mechanisms designed explicitly to ameliorate some aspect of climate change. The critical point here is that market mechanisms have a poor record of spurring decarbonization and as an accumulation strategy. In the third section, we discuss state- and industry-defined capital market regulations that are meant to steer investment into more climate-safe sectors while also stabilizing entire classes of capital and the financial system more generally. Following Christophers (2017), we demonstrate that regulation through pricing and disclosure relies overwhelmingly on the rational decision-making of asset owners. We argue that market logics and practices have inexcusably delayed vital actions to curb emissions, putting marginalized people, ecosystems, and entire countries at dire risk. We are sceptical that the same socio-economic institutions that precipitated the climate crisis are the ones that can solve it. Assigning monetary values to emissions and associated detriments may be rhetorically powerful, but cannot be the totality of responses to climate change (Bryant, 2019).

The Financial Foundations of Climate Change

The role of financiers in facilitating the extraction and consumption of fossil fuels is a good place to start unpacking climate changed capitalism. Only 100 fossil fuel-producing companies are responsible for 71% of total emissions since the industrial revolution (Griffin, 2017). Many of these companies continue to form a structurally important pillar of financial markets, so a rapid move to decarbonization has significant ramifications for the portfolios of investors, not to mention the fortunes of politicians in fossil fuel producing and consuming countries. As a result, fossil fuel production and consumption comprise a massively state-subsidized exercise involving staggering sums of money, particularly when compared with the money circulating in financial mechanisms designated for environmental protection. In 2017, states subsidized fossil fuel production and consumption between US$373 billion to US$617 billion even as the need for drastic cuts to combustion grew (OECD, 2018). Meanwhile, the largest five publicly traded oil and gas producers banked profits of over US$50 billion in 2017 (Olson and Kent, 2017), demonstrating public subsidization of investors and environmental degradation.

Paradoxically, some of the countries that are most vociferous about climate action are, simultaneously, some of the biggest subsidizers. For example, the Trudeau government in Canada made international headlines for rebuking the US withdrawal from the Paris Agreement, while simultaneously proposing to nationalize a major pipeline that would facilitate the export of tar sands oil, a subsidy of CAN $4.5 billion. This is not only the case in the capitalist heartland. Throughout the first decade of the 2000s, 'pink tide' governments in Latin America, notably in Ecuador and Bolivia, made headlines for new commitments to environmental protection even as they facilitated the extraction and export of fossil fuels (de Frietas et al., 2015).

The biggest reason for the ongoing subsidization of fossil fuels, as well as the difficulties of switching to clean alternatives, lies in the vast sums of capital tied up in fossil fuel assets—a financial lock-in that accompanies infrastructural lock-in (Erickson et al., 2015). These assets include the sprawling infrastructures already built for the extraction, refining, distribution, and consumption of fossil fuels, as well as the future profit anticipated from exploiting known oil and gas reserves. These virtual returns to investors are not insubstantial, and the threat that they may be regulated away through strong climate action is reflected in the term 'stranded assets' (Carbon Tracker Initiative, 2013). Despite growing concern about climate change among some investors, the scale of assets that will need to be stranded is still growing. Since the Paris Agreement in 2015, world proven oil reserves have *risen* by 3% to 1.67 trillion barrels—enough to meet current demand for 50 years (Xu and Bell, 2018). If we are to avoid civilization-threatening climate change, almost all of this carbon will need to be left in the ground (McGlade and Ekins, 2015), a feat unlikely to be accomplished through painlessly gradual drawdown.

Similar dynamics prevail in sectors of the economy responsible for non-fossil fuel GHG emissions. Nearly one-quarter of anthropogenic emissions originate in agriculture, forestry, and other forms of land use. For the most part, these emissions are due to deforestation, an expanding livestock sector, soil carbon losses, and fertilizer-intensive nutrient management regimes (Smith and Bustamante, 2014). As with fossil fuels, significant financial interests underpin these land-based emissions. While the focus in climate policy circles is often on the (contested and commonly simplified) connections between deforestation/land degradation and resource use by the rural poor (Hajdu and Fischer, 2017; Leach and Scoones, 2015), agricultural investments and global commodity networks play a major role. For example, Curtis et al. (2018) attributes 27% of global forest loss between 2001 and 2015 to commodity production, and 26% to large-scale forestry, with the remainder shared almost equally between small-scale agriculture and wildfires. These ratios have remained fairly constant, indicating that the voluntary actions pledged by implicated corporations have so far yielded no meaningful results. Research by Austin et al. (2017), focusing on roughly the same period concludes that in South America and Southeast Asia, where close to 80% of tropical deforestation occurs, there is a clear trend towards medium to (very) large forest clearings, suggesting an increasing importance of industrial, commodity-oriented deforestation drivers.

Commodity and investment chains related to deforestation are notoriously opaque, but one estimate puts their value at the US$941 billion per year (CDP, 2017, p. 6). This is almost certainly an underestimate, given that disclosure is voluntary and often partial (Newell et al., 2009). Indeed, entire industries are implicated in the problem. Infamous examples include the palm oil industry, a key driver of deforestation in both Indonesia and Malaysia, and the cattle/soybean complex that is driving forest loss in the Brazilian Amazon (Goldstein, 2016). Commodity production in these sectors is largely dependent on financing in the form of loans, bonds, or equity (Forests and Finance, 2018), with major financial actors such as BlackRock and Vanguard known to hold stakes in companies directly tied to deforestation (Galaz et al., 2018). The meat and dairy sector, meanwhile, is a concern even aside from its links to deforestation, being the single largest source of agricultural GHG emissions. At a time when calls for steep reductions in the consumption of animal products are growing (Springmann et al., 2018), the sector is expanding in newly industrialized and developing countries (Thornton, 2010). As with fossil fuels, significant subsidies continue to be poured into this sector. The EU alone spends about €30 billion per year—equivalent to nearly one-fifth of its total budget—supporting European meat and dairy production (Greenpeace, 2019). As with fossil fuels, one could legitimately speak of a meat and dairy lock-in, raising the possibility of significant stranded assets if emission reduction goals are to be met.

The Financialization of Climate Policy

Having reviewed some key aspects of finance's contribution to climate change, we move to consider how financiers have been enrolled to scale back global emissions. From the start of negotiations on global climate policy leading to the 1997 Kyoto Protocol, keeping emissions in check was framed by key parties as primarily an exercise in economic (and especially financial) management, rather than environmental management (Lane, 2012). It is more accurate to say that climate policy was not financialized; it has always been financial. Drawing on its experience using market mechanisms for regulating acid rain pollutants in the 1980s, the United States pushed European negotiators to include emissions trading as the cornerstone of global climate policy on threat of withdrawing from the pact. The Europeans eventually agreed; the United States withdrew from the Protocol anyway.

GHG emissions trading is operational through 17 supranational, national, and subnational markets (ICAP, 2018) covering 15% of global emissions. In this section, we examine the political economy of emissions markets and other 'market-mechanisms' ostensibly related to climate action. While we focus on emissions markets of varying types, it is worth remembering that 'market-mechanism' encompasses policy tools ranging from feed-in tariffs to renewable fuel credits to agricultural subsidies (Bigger, 2017). Climate action has meanwhile largely been reduced to a question of financing, as illustrated in an endless parade of supranational reports on sundry 'financing gaps', implying that what is lacking in climate action is, above all, sufficient investment. This myopia neglects the wider social, political, and economic changes required for immediate and sustained decarbonization.

Emissions Markets

Nowhere is the mobilization of finance to curb emissions clearer than in quixotic efforts to 'put a price on carbon'. But what price? One consequence of the ossification of neoclassical dogma in the North Atlantic in the late twentieth century was a rejection of environmental regulation that 'picked winners and losers'. Neoclassical economists and policy-makers assigned this responsibility to markets (Carton, 2018). The overarching logic of emissions markets is straight-forward: emissions need to be reduced and markets are the most efficient way of determining from whence those reductions should come. In theory, the role of the state is reduced to defining the legal, tradable representations of the right to pollute, and then those rights can be traded amongst firms or financiers. Offset markets take this even further, with private or supranational organizations defining and regulating tradeable credits, and exchange occurring across different jurisdictions. The desired result in both cases is flexibility for polluters and the prioritization of low-cost emission reductions.

Regulatory Jurisdictional Markets

Jurisdictional (or 'cap-and-trade') markets are the *sine qua non* of neoliberal, financialized climate management, blending command-and-control environmental regulation (cap) with financial transactions whose efficiency turns on the rational behaviour of investors (trade). Until the rapid growth of green bonds in the mid-2010s, regulatory emissions markets were the biggest monetary flows ostensibly targeted at reducing greenhouse gas emissions. These markets were greeted with enthusiasm throughout the early 2000s by both policy-makers and financiers. Richard Sandor, known as 'the father of futures' for his work in developing interest rate derivatives in the 1970s, proclaimed in 2010 that, 'carbon... will be unambiguously the largest commodity in the world' (in Erlich, 2010). It seems this prognostication was wildly optimistic. While major banks opened environmental trading desks in the early 2000s to trade representations of greenhouse gases (Knox-Hayes and Levy, 2011), most were closed in the wake of the financial crisis and in response to the poor performance of emissions permits driven by a lack of regulatory ambition, policy uncertainty, and the failure of the United States to adopt a comprehensive carbon trading system following the 2008 election (Böhm, 2013).

Despite the failure of markets to achieve the scale—both environmental and financial—envisioned by their champions, cap and trade markets remain the highest profile experiment in environmental governance through marketization. The largest and longest established regulatory market is the European Union Emissions Trading System (EU ETS). Comprised of the EU-28 countries plus Norway, Iceland, and Lichtenstein, the system aimed to reduce bloc-wide emissions to 20% below 1990 levels by 2020. This goal has already been met, but it is uncertain how much of these emissions reductions are attributable to carbon trading and, further, whether these emissions have truly been eliminated, or whether they have been displaced elsewhere (Bryant, 2019). Beyond environmental concerns, the financial performance of the market has fallen far short of expectations, both those of proponents such as Sandor, and those of critics such Neil Smith (2006) who warned that emissions markets were poised to signal the real subsumption of nature by capital (Bigger et al., 2018).

The design of the EU ETS was an unwieldy, protracted, and, above all, political matter (Bailey, 2010). In the EU ETS, regulators settled on mandatory market participation by the 11,000 most polluting industrial installations. These polluters are initially given their emissions allowances for free but, for every ton of GHGs emitted, they are obligated to surrender a corresponding allowance. The number of allowances available was to be gradually reduced, inducing polluters either to cut their emissions, or to buy permits from installations that were able to reduce theirs more cheaply—thus emissions would fall at the lowest economy-wide cost. Controversy swirled from the beginning of the programme, largely around fundamental questions such as how the cap was to be set; how regulated polluters would be allocated their initial permits, which they would then be allowed to swap; and what the role of non-regulated (speculative) market participants should be (Bryant, 2019). Each of these questions has critical implications for the operation of regulatory emissions trading programmes and they have been rehearsed in every subsequent market.

The EU ETS faced setbacks almost from the day it launched, setbacks that have been present in virtually every carbon market that has been implemented. First and foremost, permit prices have generally been low but, when they rise, markets usually become intolerably volatile. This presents problems for regulators, financiers, and regulated industry. For regulators, low prices undermine one of the key justifications for the use of market mechanisms—that market-derived prices force industries (and, ultimately, consumers) to internalize the environmental costs of fossil fuel combustion. After the extent of overallocation became clear and the financial crisis began to bite, EU carbon prices settled near €15 per ton from 2008 to 2012, only to bounce between €5 to €10 per ton from 2012 to 2018 (Morison and Hodges, 2018). While prices have begun to rise again with recent regulatory reform, current estimates put the social cost of carbon, or the monetary damages created by the emissions of each additional ton of greenhouse gases, between €155 and €705 per ton (Ricke et al., 2018), and this number is unable to account for those climate change losses that are less amenable to economic valuation, such as biodiversity loss and loss of traditional ways of living. Even in its narrowly economistic reading, the management of greenhouse gases through emissions trading has been incapable of internalizing the costs of climate change because the attendant political costs are perceived as too severe (CEO, 2015).

Two causes for persistently low prices in the EU ETS and in other emissions markets merit explanation here; one internal to market design, the other external. Internally, regulations are generally under-ambitious and regulatory design has been deferential to major polluters because of the outsized importance of industries such as electricity generation, oil refining, and steel making to the extant economy, stifling demand. The cap is simply too high. Externally, the 2008 financial crisis and its lingering impacts highlights the entanglement between financial markets for environmental governance, and financial markets more broadly. The financial crisis led to reduced industrial output among regulated entities, creating a glut of permits. Polluters thus not only had no need to buy additional permits, but also could flood markets with excess permits that simultaneously subsidized dirty production and reduced the costs of polluting for other industries with a less generous allocation (Reyes, 2011a).

Low prices are not the only factor that led financiers to withdraw from the EU ETS. Low prices are not in-and-of-themselves a problem for speculators. Instead, the inability to predict price movements limits intertemporal arbitrage opportunities, or opportunities to use emissions permits to hedge against price movements in other markets, especially fossil fuels. This is true not only in the EU ETS, but in most environmental credit trading programmes (Bigger, 2017). Seemingly stochastic uncertainties arise from the regulatory nature of these markets. Carbon markets are 'in vivo experiments' (Callon, 2009) where market rules are never fully settled. These rule changes can include the quantity and types of offsets allowed (discussed in the next section), or trading restrictions to combat the use of carbon credits for money laundering—a problem that plagued the EU ETS for years (Williams, 2013). When coupled with overgenerous allocation to protect industry that deprives markets of liquidity by obviating industry needs to go to market to purchase additional permits, financiers have found carbon market speculation a poor proposition.

Offset Markets

The logic of conceiving of all GHG emissions as intrinsically fungible that gave the world jurisdictional carbon markets also produced carbon offsetting. When governments finally managed to agree on the Kyoto Protocol in 1997, it was in no small part because of the inclusion of three so-called 'flexible mechanisms'. One of these, the Clean Development Mechanism (CDM), established an international market in carbon offsets that industrialized countries could use to meet their emission reduction commitments (Spash, 2010). As with emissions trading, the general idea behind this mechanism is centred around a cost-reduction exercise that takes advantage of geographically differentiated costs and opportunities for emission reductions. Since emission reductions in the Global South tend to be more 'efficient' than equivalent reductions in the Global North, there is a clear economic advantage to outsourcing some of the industrialized world's mitigation commitments. Thus, under the CDM interested parties are able to register emission-reduction projects in the Global South with a centralized CDM secretariat. On approval, these projects gain the right to sell carbon offset credits, predominantly to buyers in the Global North who use them *in lieu* of domestic emission cuts, as part of their regulatory obligations (as in the EU). An important rationale for this mechanism was the supposed added benefit of financing sustainable development in the Global South, promising to deliver benefits including biodiversity conservation, renewable energy, infrastructure development, and new employment opportunities for local communities (Olsen, 2007).

In fact, the CDM has been marred by significant, seemingly fatal problems. First, despite ambitions of driving investment for sustainable development in the Global South, the demonstrated outcomes of the CDM have been underwhelming, to say the least (Disch, 2010). Carbon credit funding frequently ends up in the coffers of large corporations, often with unclear benefits, or distinctly negative impacts, for poor communities (Edstedt and Carton, 2018; Wittman et al., 2015). Financial flows have been highly uneven, as most of the money went to China and India, rather than least-developed countries (CDM, 2016). Second, the so-called 'additionality' of CDM projects has been scandalous. To guarantee that offsets contribute to real climate change mitigation, projects need to demonstrate that they produce emission reductions that would not have occurred without CDM project funding. This involves the articulation of counterfactual scenarios, in which there is ample room for unduly optimistic, or outright fraudulent interpretations of, existing trends. In practice, additionality is impossible to guarantee. This has led to widespread integrity concerns with claimed offsets. A study commissioned by the European Commission concluded that 85% of CDM projects, corresponding to 73% of all issued CDM credits for 2013–20, are unlikely to be additional, with 7% of credits highly likely to be so (Cames et al., 2016). In essence, this renders the claimed offsets invalid, as there was no environmental benefit.

The CDM has also long been dominated by rather questionable project types that do little to incentivize a sustainable development transition. This is especially true of industrial gas projects that focused on the destruction of HFC-23 and N_2O, GHGs hundreds or thousands of times more potent than CO_2. In the spirit of market efficiency, the CDM creates equivalence between a wide range of economic practices and different greenhouse gas emissions. Given their enormous global warming potential, and the low cost with which these industrial gases can be avoided, this meant that HFC-23 and N_2O projects, mainly in China and India, long constituted the majority of CDM carbon credits. At the prevailing credit prices of the CDM's first few years, these projects proved phenomenally profitable (Bryant et al., 2015), to the extent that their inclusion in the CDM was feared to create perverse incentives to continue, or even expand, HFC23-emitting production processes with the sole purpose of then destroying those emissions to bring in valuable CDM funding (Schneider, 2011). This vividly illustrates the limits of GHG and international fungibility that is at the heart of offset markets.

The CDM witnessed other forms of rent-seeking as well, especially in its first few years. Michaelowa (2012) documents how a number of companies sprang up in the Global North to buy up cheap forward contracts for offsets, which they then sold on at a premium to buyers in the EU ETS. Speculation on offset prices was made possible by banking purchased credits forward. Many of these actors were left exposed when offset prices nosedived around 2011, largely in line with prices in the EU ETS. Prices have remained at rock-bottom rates ever since, mostly due to faltering demand. From a high of around US$20 per ton of CO2e in 2008, offsets traded at around US$0.3 in December 2018. In parallel, and reflecting the uncertainty of the CDM in the post-Kyoto period, registration of new CDM projects increased to a record high at the end of 2012, and then promptly fell to a record low in 2013, from which they never recovered (CDM, 2018). This drop in offset prices marked the end of significant rent-extraction from the CDM.

Aside from regulatory offset markets, there has also long been a voluntary carbon market (VCM) that targets consumers seeking to reduce individual emissions and businesses wanting to adopt (or project) a 'greener' profile. The diversity of actors operating in this sector is perhaps even broader than in the CDM, ranging from NGOs to venture capitalists, carbon brokers, certification and verification bodies, small-scale entrepreneurs, government departments, aid organizations, and so on. Indeed, despite the eventual failure of the CDM, a sizeable sub-industry was constituted for the creation and circulation of financial representations of GHGs (Knox-Hayes, 2009). This is represented in the sprawling diversity of project types and designs that typify this market from payments for ecosystem services such as afforestation or avoided deforestations (Osborne and Shapiro-Garza, 2018) to more traditional development projects that provide financing for renewable energy technologies (Karhunmaa, 2016), or the distribution of energy-efficient cooking stoves (Wang and Corson, 2015).

As with the CDM, though, the VCM has fallen far short of expectations on the financial transfers it would represent. In the early days of carbon markets, there was no limit to the optimism about the future of offsets. A 2009 prognosis by McKinsey, for example, expected offsets to make up a significant proportion of a 'US$800 billion and possibly as much as $2 trillion' global carbon market by 2020 (Hoffman and Twining, 2009). With the benefit of hindsight, this appears as a pipedream. The value of traded offsets on the VCM plummeted after 2008, dropping from its record high of US$790 million that year to a (current) record low of US$191 million in 2016 (Hamrick and Gallant, 2017). Lack of demand and low prices for offset permits is meanwhile emerging as an important driver of project failure and one more obstacle on the road to promised socio-economic co-benefits (Otto, 2018).

In spite of common descriptions of 'zombie' carbon markets (cf. Reyes, 2011b), the offsetting idea has failed to die completely, always clinging to hopes of a brighter future. The latest manifestation of this is CORSIA, the proposed carbon offsetting scheme for the airline industry, which—depending on implementation—could create significant new demand for offsets. The offsetting logic also continues to infuse new sectors of marketable natures, from 'blue carbon' (marine carbon sinks like sea grasses) to 'soil carbon' (agricultural land conservation). This seemingly endless parade of new mechanisms and project types points up the extent to which the proponents of mitigation-through-markets have recast all facets of the natural world composed of carbon as tradeable financial representations—what Büscher calls 'liquid nature' (2013).

(Self)Regulation through Extant Financial Markets

Considering the failure of tradeable emissions permits and credits to reduce global emissions, and widespread unwillingness of major polluting countries to implement carbon taxes, robust feed-in tariffs, or command-and-control regulations for climate action, some financiers, and even financial regulators, have turned to markets to facilitate decarbonization in other ways. In this section, we discuss environmentally inflected financial practices, ranging from data sharing to new products, that have aimed to facilitate decarbonization or transition. In turn, we discuss emissions reporting, green bonds, and property (re)insurance. While this comprises a diverse set of practices, the unifying feature is the faith that market-derived price signals coupled with assurances of corporate environmental responsibility will lead to better environmental outcomes (see Christophers, 2017).

Reporting refers to a suite of data disclosure activities ostensibly linked to mitigating the environmental risks posed by uncontrolled emissions. In the first instance, disclosure is aimed at mitigating financial risks posed by more stringent regulations imposed on companies, or the material losses faced by companies such as insurers, and, in turn, financial risks to investors and lenders. The argument holds that better data will allow market participants and regulators to accurately assess risks and then act accordingly. Mark Carney, Governor of the Bank of England and head of the Taskforce on Climate Financial Disclosure, summed up the rationale for pursuing regulation-through-disclosure in a speech to central bankers in 2018, saying, '[t]hat financial institutions have come out so strongly in support of enhanced disclosure reflects their recognition that there is a correlation between managing climate risk and long-term value creation as well as their belief in the power of markets'. Carney himself uncovers a central problematic with this approach to decarbonization in the same speech, noting that:

> too rapid a movement towards a low-carbon economy could materially damage financial stability. A wholesale reassessment of prospects, as climate-related risks are re-evaluated, could destabilise markets, spark a pro-cyclical crystallisation of losses and lead to a persistent tightening of financial conditions: a climate Minsky moment.

This gives us an indication that climate governance through financial regulation is, above all, a gradualist approach, and one that virtually no climate scientist would endorse based on the urgency of the problem. It is a perfect illustration of what Swyngedouw (2011: 264) identifies as a post-political approach to global warming, an initiative to 'change so nothing really has to change'.

The other problematic that goes unsaid by Carney, but that has been unpacked by Christophers (2018), is that decarbonization through investment strategy assumes that investors are rational and will make good decisions with proper information. This is unambiguously not the case, as evidenced most forcefully by the Global Financial Crisis. The roots of the crisis lay, in large part, in the widespread deregulation of investment practice in favour of voluntary reporting and faith in auditing. If this form of non-regulation regulation contributed to the 'Minsky Moment' of 2008, then it is entirely possible that emergency environmental regulations or the crystallization of massive insurance losses brought on by extreme weather events could produce a climate Minsky Moment, but not the one envisioned in Carney's quote.

While mandatory reporting of exposure to climate risks (both physical and financial) is becoming pervasive across Global North jurisdictions, the impetus for reporting began as a voluntary CSR exercise. The Global Reporting Initiative was launched in 1997, followed by the Carbon Disclosure Project in 2002, and now comprises around 400 different standards for businesses to report the sundry environmental impacts they create and environmental risks they face (Christophers et al., 2018). These initiatives, while fragmented and piecemeal, cover wide-ranging climate-damaging activities, not simply direct GHG emissions, or portfolio exposure to fossil fuels. For example, disclosure organizations are increasingly framing the involvement of companies and investors in deforestation-dependent activities as an investment risk, for 'operational', 'reputational', and 'regulatory' reasons (CDP, 2017). And yet their preferred solution, such as voluntary 'zero-deforestation' commitments, have failed to make a significant dent in deforestation (Curtis et al., 2018).

Green Debt

While reporting is a high-visibility mechanism for self-regulation, reporting also includes ascendant financial products linked to climate action, particularly green bonds. Green bonds are identical to other forms of tradeable institutional debt, except that they contain a promise that the issuer will use the proceeds for expenditures that contribute in some way to a low carbon economy (Tripathy, 2017). In other words, without necessarily identifying the specific projects to which proceeds of the bond are flowing, the green label alerts markets to the fact that issuers have considered the sustainability dimensions of their operations and value sustainability enough to go through internal processes to flag it. The amorphousness is by design. Proponents of green bonds and market service providers such as indexes have been quick to propagate an array of taxonomies and definitions for what constitutes greenness in an effort to demonstrate to regulators that markets are capable of self-regulation without putting off potential issuers. At present, 'green bond' is not a legal category; it is purely a marketing strategy that coheres to various market self-regulatory and CSR practices, such as indexing criteria by stock exchanges, or signatory status for various non-binding industry accords. This means that the bar for transforming regular debt, be it municipal, corporate, or supranational, into 'green' debt is relatively low.

This low bar is a key factor to the growth in labelled green debt over the last decade. Following labelled green debt's invention by the European Investment Bank in 2007, issuance grew to nearly $200 billion in 2018, dwarfing most other pools of capital designated for environmentally beneficial projects. Initially the province of multilateral development banks, issuance began to pick up in 2014 when US and European municipalities began to put green labels on infrastructure bonds to pay for water and public transportation projects. At this point, corporate issuers started coming to market, including Apple's US$1 billion issuance earmarked to pay for its new, renewable energy powered corporate headquarters. The newest market entrants have been sovereign issuers, from Poland to Nigeria.

The ramp-up of green bond issuance has been dramatic, but it consistently falls short of proponents' expectations. From 2017 to 2019, the Climate Bonds Initiative (CBI), a key vector for promoting green bonds, has seen actual issuance of labelled green bonds fall 40–50% short of projections, which cumulatively sums to significantly reduced expectations over time. While these projections should be understood as aspirationally performative rather than actual market projection, they make the CBI's stated goal of US$1 trillion in issuance in 2020 appear unlikely. This is significant not only because less money is going into explicitly climate delineated projects than proponents thought possible, but because it indicates slower growth into what is probably the easiest form of green finance available, given self-identified criteria and the size of the global debt market. Finally, high projected growth may also provide cover to governments to make fewer direct climate investments based on the premise that the private sector is already scaling up (Bracking, 2015).

Insurance

Insurance at both the retail and reinsurance levels is the financial product that we could reasonably expect to have already been reshaped most dramatically by climate change. As climate change creates more, and more intense, extreme weather events, insured losses have risen significantly (Johnson, 2010). The tipping point for reinsurers was 2005, when a series of Atlantic hurricanes ravaged coastal US cities, including New Orleans. Insured losses topped US$180 billion that year, an increase of US$119 billion in 2004, itself the costliest hurricane season at the time (Johnson, 2010). These escalating losses prompted reinsurers to re-evaluate their climatic and financial models (Johnson, 2013). Even as the logics of risk and the ever-increasing hazards brought on by climate change unsettle the core business of property insurance, and even life insurance (Johnson, 2013), insurers are also substantial investors. But, by and large, insurers have done little to decarbonize their portfolio, contributing to the risks to which they are simultaneously attempting to adapt (Scott, 2018).

Beginning in the 1990s, insurance was tipped to be a driver for decarbonization and adaptation since its business model fundamentally turns on rendering risks predictable, pricing those risks, and ensuring that incoming revenue in the form of premiums exceeded expected pay-outs over the foreseeable future (Ericson et al., 2003). The trouble is, 'the foreseeable future' is becoming shorter for many specific geographies or scales. While insurance is clearly among the most climate-inflected financial sectors, there remains a curious paucity of empirical work on the operation of retail insurance, particularly in cities that will inevitably be reshaped by climate change (c.f. Taylor, 2020). This is particularly true in places such as Miami, Guangzhou, and Jakarta, which are facing risk of inundation by sea level rise and subsidence, but whose risks are both stochastic and non-stochastic. Storms may periodically and, indeed catastrophically, impact these cities, but the long-term trend is submersion. Thus, insurance models will need to be dramatically reshaped, since insurance is a technology of probabilities, not inevitability (Christophers et al., 2018).

One way that reinsurers have already attempted to produce new revenue streams considering increased unpredictability and losses in core insurance markets is the introduction of catastrophe bonds. 'Cat bonds' are insurance-linked securities that allow investors, often pension and hedge funds, to speculate on the potential for low-probability, high-impact events such as hurricanes or earthquakes. The funds are held in escrow by reinsurance firms. If a catastrophic event 'triggers' the bond, insurers can use the cash to cover losses; if no catastrophe occurs over the duration of the contract, investors claim back their principal, plus an often generous coupon. Investors such as pension funds are attracted to cat bonds because nature-based investments offer returns uncorrelated with other markets (Johnson, 2013; Ouma et al., 2018). Thus, while other financial incursions for managing the climate aim to produce nature as an accumulation strategy through familiar processes of rent capture and the operation of markets (regardless of their success), catastrophe bonds and other insurance linked securities aim to produce returns through contingency (Johnson, 2013).

Conclusion: Repoliticizing Climate Action

Broad swathes of climate scientists, geographers, the general public, and even economists recognize that markets—and financial markets, in particular—have had their shot at reducing emissions and failed spectacularly. Emissions trading has done very little to reduce emissions and, even where it has, it is has created regressive social outcomes (Bryant, 2019); carbon offsetting has often been even worse (Cames et al., 2016; Wittman et al., 2015). Insurers have talked a big game about driving investment decisions and facilitating climate adaptation, and yet coastal cities remain woefully underprepared for sea level rise, and new luxury skyscrapers continue to be built on vulnerable coastlines (Taylor and Weinkle, 2020; perhaps most damningly, market valuations of carbon majors remain high as vast new reserves of oil and gas are found and technology for extracting those fuels continues to improve (LuxResearch, 2013).

In other words, the mainstays of contemporary climate policy—the prioritization of economic efficiency; the pursuit of voluntary commitments; and the accommodation, rather than confrontation, of corporate interests—have been toothless in the face of the continued profits that can be accumulated by ignoring, delaying or 'gradualizing' necessary mitigation and adaptation efforts. Yet, despite these failures, the powers-that-be seem determined to continue this path. Under the Paris Agreement, governments are establishing the successor to the CDM. While the exact architecture of this new 'sustainable development mechanism' remains unclear for now, the disputes and controversies that are occurring in the negotiations—including on whether or not 'junk credits' from the CDM can be carried over to the new mechanism—suggest there are plenty of ways in which a future market mechanism may perpetuate past failures.

This is not to say that there are no progressive tendencies to be uncovered in the way the climate/finance nexus is taking shape. For example, climate divestment movements have been increasingly effective at taking data available through disclosure initiatives and pressuring shareholders with public service commitments, such as universities and pension funds, to divest from companies with damaging environmental records. Starting around 2010 and popularized primarily through the activist network 350.org, the divestment movement has convinced over 1,000 institutions with more than US$8 trillion in investments to divest from fossil fuels, partially or in full. This includes high-profile institutions such as the Rockefeller Foundation, the City of New York, and the government of Ireland (Fossil Free, 2019). While still marginal in the context of total investment flows, the divestment campaign has helped change the conversation on finance and climate change. Perhaps the best indicator of its success is the fact that a number of large fund managers, including Blackrock, have felt compelled to set up portfolios that explicitly exclude fossil fuel companies (Ayling and Gunningham, 2017).

As a way of undermining the fossil fuel industry's financial foundations, divestment is a blunt, largely ineffective instrument (Parenti, 2012). But this was never the campaign's immediate ambition. From the beginning, Fossil Free pursued a moral argument against fossil fuel investment, thereby seeking to 'culturally marginalize the fossil fuel industry, making it harder for them to exert political influence and gum up the gears of needed climate legislation' (Rowe et al., 2016: 2). The movement's real merit, and where it has booked successes, lies in eroding fossil capital's social licence to operate—in turn, making regulation more likely. This has been helped by the wider proliferation of concerns over stranded assets, which is now articulated by a diverse group of international and financial institutions, including the International Energy Agency. Finally, some investors are jumping ship on purely financial grounds. When the Norwegian wealth fund recently announced the partial divestment of its US$1 trillion in (oil money) funds, its concerns were neither focused on the morality of continued fossil fuel investments, nor on the immediate risk of stranded assets but, rather, on maximizing profits and minimizing the risks to the Norwegian economy of a major drop in oil and gas prices (Boyd, 2018).

We are encouraged by the growth and success of the climate divestment movement, but ultimately divestment will not be sufficient. We suggest it is high time to relocate the primary centre of action on climate and finance from markets to the public sphere. Indeed, we are beginning to see serious movements in some countries for unprecedented state action to invest in decarbonization, climate adaptation, and large-scale social restructurings that are broadly in line with a low-carbon world. These new initiatives aim to take the power of climate regulation away from market mechanisms or voluntary compliance schemes, while radically scaling up public spending, treating the climate and associated environmental concerns as public goods, to be managed by the public.

The most visible example currently is in the United States, where a bill to pursue a Green New Deal (GND) was released with much fanfare in early 2019. Whether the GND will come to fruition or die an unceremonious death—as have all previous US federal climate laws—remains to be seen. However, there are robust discussions building across the world about the role of governments in not only regulating emissions, but in recentring investment for a green economy towards the state. Due to years of inaction, vast swathes of the built environment will need to be remade. If policy-makers had taken climate change seriously in 2000, the costs of infrastructural renewal would have had a more modest price tag—emissions would have needed to fall by 2% per year, achievable through smaller-scale investments (Le Quéré et al., 2018). Instead, without a 5% per year fall, we are now staring down the barrel of unchecked climate calamity that will disproportionately impact the most vulnerable and those least responsible for emissions that are driving climate change (Le Quéré et al., 2018).

The ambitious form of the GND, which is now being mooted in jurisdictions from Denmark to South Africa, entails the massive scale up of public sector investments in decarbonization and adaptation. As public coffers the world over have been ravaged by a 40-year tax-strike among the asset-owning class, the most intense battles are likely to be fought over how investments that can deliver radically revamped energy, transportation, and water infrastructure can be publicly financed. Investments that do not cleave to narrow cost–benefit logics will be needed globally if a just transition to a low-emissions, high-temperature world is to be achieved. That said, even the most ambitious version of the GND will need to move beyond a mere focus on investments, if climate change is to be kept in check. Keeping temperatures within a habitable range is not just a matter of massive infrastructural development, but also of devaluing and decommissioning the climate-wrecking infrastructure and financial assets that are in place now. Investment and planned devaluation must go hand-in-hand to bring about a rapid transition, and, if done correctly, can serve to reinforce each other. There is no hiding that this will involve trade-offs and confrontations, requiring regulators to take up battles with vested interests, rather than perpetuate the weak, compromising approach of recent decades. The need for far-reaching political change illustrates that climate policy is ultimately irreducible to a question of finance.

Clearly, this is a tall order. But the choice we face is not between transition or no transition—we are already locked into continued planetary changes for at least the next century (Zickfeld and Herrington 2015). Instead, the choice is between a just transition and a transition that produces a hideous eco-apartheid. If this sounds polemical or out of place in a discussion of finance and climate change, it bears remembering that it is precisely the owners of capital who will be able to shield themselves from climate change impacts. Given the degree to which financial capitalism has been predicated on investments that cook the earth and dodges tax in a way that leaves less money available for state action, leaving climate policy to markets, we think that coming to grips with the actual realities we are facing should be framed in the strongest terms possible. What we have tried to demonstrate in this chapter is that not only is it unconscionable that investment strategy and financial market regulation be the drivers of our response to climate change, it also is also an impossible situation if we are to find a planet more or less as habitable in 30 years as it is now.

References

Austin, K. G., González-Roglich, M., Schaffer-Smith, D., Schwantes, A. M., & Swenson, J. J. (2017). Trends in size of tropical deforestation events signal increasing dominance of industrial-scale drivers. *Environmental Research Letters, 12*(7), 079601. doi:10.1088/1748-9326/aa7760.

Ayling, J., & Gunningham, N. (2017). *Non-state governance and climate policy: The fossil fuel divestment movement*, 3062. doi:10.1080/14693062.2015.1094729.

Bailey, I. (2007). Neoliberalism, climate governance and the scalar politics of EU emissions trading. *Area, 39*(4), 431–442. doi:10.1111/j.1475-4762.2007.00770.x.

Bailey, I. (2010). The EU emissions trading scheme. *Wiley Interdisciplinary Reviews: Climate Change, 1*(January/February), 144–153. doi:10.1002/wcc.017.

Bigger, P. (2017). Measurement and the circulation of risk in green bonds. *Journal of Environmental Investing, 8*(1), 273–287.

Bigger, P. (2018). Hybridity, possibility: Degrees of marketization in tradeable permit systems. *Environment and Planning A: Economy and Space, 50*(3), 512–530.

Bigger, P., Dempsey, J., Asiyanbi, A. P., Kay, K., Lave, R., Mansfield, B., … Simon, G. L. (2018). Reflecting on neoliberal natures: an exchange. *Environment and Planning E: Nature and Space, 1*(1–2), 2514848618776864. doi:10.1177/2514848618776864.

Böhm, S. (2013, April). Why are carbon markets failing? *The Guardian*. Available at: https://www.theguardian.com/sustainable-business/blog/why-are-carbon-markets-failing. Accessed 19 March 2019.

Boyd, J. (2018). Debate over Norwegian oil fund divestment of fossil fuels continues. *Investment Europe*. Available at: https://www.investmenteurope.net/investmenteurope/news/3724075/debate-norwegian-oil-fund-divestment-fossil-fuels-continues

Bracking, S. (2015). Performativity in the Green Economy: how far does climate finance create a fictive economy?. *Third World Quarterly, 36*(12), 2337–2357.

Bryant, G. (2019). *Carbon Markets in a Climate-Changing Capitalism*. Cambridge, UK: Cambridge University Press.

Bryant, G., Dabhi, S., & Böhm, S. (2015). "Fixing" the climate crisis: capital, states, and carbon offsetting in India. *Environment and Planning A, 47*(10), 2047–2063. doi:10.1068/a130213p

Büscher, B. (2013). Nature on the Move I: The value and circulation of liquid nature and the emergence of fictitious conservation. *New Proposals: Journal of Marxism and Interdisciplinary Inquiry, 6*(1–2), 20–36. Available at: http://ojs.library.ubc.ca/index.php/newproposals/article/view/183690

Callon, M. (2009). Civilizing markets: Carbon trading between in vitro and in vivo experiments. *Accounting, Organizations and Society, 34*(3–4), 535–548. doi:10.1016/j.aos.2008.04.003

Cames, M., Harthan, R. O., Füssler, J., Lazarus, M., Lee, C. M., Erickson, P., & Spalding-Fecher, R. (2016). *How additional is the clean development mechanism?* Available at: https://ec.europa.eu/clima/sites/clima/files/ets/docs/clean_dev_mechanism_en.pdf

Carbon Tracker Initiative. (2013). *Unburnable Carbon 2013: Wasted capital and stranded assets, 40*. Available at: http://www.lse.ac.uk/GranthamInstitute/publications/Policy/docs/PB-unburnable-carbon-2013-wasted-capital-stranded-assets.pdf

Carton, W. (2018). Environmental economics. In N. Castree, M. Hulme, & J. Proctor (Eds.), *Companion to environmental studies* (pp. 281–285). Oxon/New York: Routledge.

CDM. (2016). *Distribution of expected CERs from registered projects by host party*. Retrieved February 14, 2016, from https://cdm.unfccc.int/Statistics/Public/files/201601/ExpRed_reg_byHost.png

CDM. (2018). *CDM insights*. Retrieved December 20, 2018, from https://cdm.unfccc.int/Statistics/Public/CDMinsights/index.html

CDP. (2017). *From risk to revenue: The investment opportunity in addressing corporate deforestation.* Available at: https://6fefcbb86e61af1b2fc4-c70d8ead6ced550b4d987d7c03fcdd1d.ssl.cf3.rackcdn.com/cms/reports/documents/000/002/860/original/CDP-2017-forests-report.pdf?1511199969

Christophers, B. (2017). Climate change and financial instability: Risk disclosure and the problematics of neoliberal governance, *Annals of the American Association of Geographers, 107*(5), 1108–1112.

Christophers, B., Bigger, P., & Johnson, L. (2018). Stretching scales? Risk and sociality in climate finance. *Environment and Planning A: Economy and Space*, 0308518X18819004.

Corporate Europe Observatory. (2015). *EU emissions trading: 5 reasons to scrap the ETS.* Available at: https://corporateeurope.org/environment/2015/10/eu-emissions-trading-5-reasons-scrap-ets. Last accessed 1 February 2019.

Curtis, P. G., Slay, C. M., Harris, N. L., Tyukavina, A., & Hansen, M. C. (2018). Classifying drivers of global forest loss. *Science, 361*(6407), 1108–1111. doi:10.1126/science.aau3445

de Freitas, C., Marston, A. J., & Bakker, K. (2015). Not-quite-neoliberal natures in Latin America: An introduction. *Geoforum, 64*, 239-245.

Dempsey, J., & Suarez, D. C. (2016). Arrested development? The promises and paradoxes of "Selling Nature to Save It". *Annals of the American Association of Geographers*, 1–19. doi:10.1080/24694452.2016.1140018

Disch, D. (2010). A comparative analysis of the "development dividend" of clean development mechanism projects in six host countries. *Climate and Development, 2*(1), 50–64. doi:10.3763/cdev.2010.0034

Edstedt, K., & Carton, W. (2018). The benefits that (only) capital can see? Resource access and degradation in industrial carbon forestry, lessons from the CDM in Uganda. *Geoforum, 97*, 315–323. doi:10.1016/j.geoforum.2018.09.030

Erlich, N. (2010, April 26). Carbon Could Be No. 1 Commodity: Exchange Chief. *CNBC.* Available at: https://www.cnbc.com/id/36782147. Accessed 19 March 2019.

Erickson, P., Kartha, S., Lazarus, M., & Tempest, K. (2015). Assessing carbon lock-in. *Environmental Research Letters, 10*(8), 084023.

Ericson, R., Doyle, A. and Barry, D. (2003). *Insurance as Governance.* Toronto: University of Toronto Press.

Felli, R. (2015). Environment, not planning: the neoliberal depoliticisation of environmental policy by means of emissions trading. *Environmental Politics, 24*(5), 641–660. doi:10.1080/09644016.2015.1051323

Forests and Finance. (2018). *Is your money destroying rainforests?* Available at: http://forestsandfinance.org/wp-content/uploads/2018/10/Forests-Finance-Brochure.pdf

Fossil Free. (2019). 1000+ Divestment Commitments. Available at: https://gofossilfree.org/divestment/commitments/

Galaz, V., Crona, B., Dauriach, A., Scholtens, B., & Steffen, W. (2018). Finance and the Earth system – Exploring the links between financial actors and non-linear changes in the climate system. *Global Environmental Change, 53*(November), 296–302. doi:10.1016/j.gloenvcha.2018.09.008

Goldstein, J. E. (2016). Knowing the subterranean: Land grabbing, oil palm, and divergent expertise in Indonesia's peat soil. *Environment and Planning A: Economy and Space, 48*(4), 754-770.

Greenpeace. (2019). *Feeding the Problem: the dangerous intensification of animal farming in Europe.* Available at: https://storage.googleapis.com/planet4-eu-unit-stateless/2019/02/83254ee1-190212-feeding-the-problem-dangerous-intensification-of-animal-farming-in-europe.pdf

Griffin, P (2017). *The carbon major database.* Available at: https://b8f65cb373b1b7b-15feb-c70d8ead6ced550b4d987d7c03fcdd1d.ssl.cf3.rackcdn.com/cms/reports/

documents/000/002/327/original/Carbon-Majors-Report-2017.pdf?1499691240. Accessed 19 March 2019.

Hajdu, F., & Fischer, K. (2017). Problems, causes and solutions in the forest carbon discourse: a framework for analysing degradation narratives. *Climate and Development, 9*(6), 537–547. doi:10.1080/17565529.2016.1174663

Hamrick, K., & Gallant, M. (2017). *Unlocking potential - State of the voluntary carbon markets 2017*. Available at: https://www.forest-trends.org/wp-content/uploads/2017/07/doc_5591.pdf

Hoffman, N., & Twining, J. (2009). Profiting from the low-carbon economy. *McKinsey&Company Financial Services*. Retrieved December 23, 2018, from https://www.mckinsey.com/industries/financial-services/our-insights/profiting-from-the-low-carbon-economy

ICAP. (2018). Emissions Trading Worldwide: International Carbon Action Partnership (ICAP) Status Report 2018, 108. Available at: https://icapcarbonaction.com/en/?option=com_attach&task=download&id=447

Intergovernmental Panel on Climate Change (IPCC). (2018). Summary for Policymakers of IPCC Special Report on Global Warming of 1.5°C approved by governments. Retrieved February 10, 2019, from https://www.ipcc.ch/2018/10/08/summary-for-policymakers-of-ipcc-special-report-on-global-warming-of-1-5c-approved-by-governments/

Johnson, L. (2010). Climate change and the risk industry: the multiplication of fear and value. *Global Political Ecology*, 185–202.

Johnson, L. (2013). Catastrophe bonds and financial risk: Securing capital and rule through contingency. *Geoforum, 45*, 30–40. doi:10.1016/j.geoforum.2012.04.003

Karhunmaa, K. (2016). Opening up storylines of co-benefits in voluntary carbon markets: An analysis of household energy technology projects in developing countries. *Energy Research and Social Science, 14*, 71–79. doi:10.1016/j.erss.2016.01.011

Knox-Hayes, J. (2009). The developing carbon financial service industry: expertise, adaptation and complementarity in London and New York. *Journal of Economic Geography, 9*(6), 749–777.

Knox-Hayes, J. and Levy, D.L., 2011. The politics of carbon disclosure as climate governance. *Strategic Organization, 9*(1), 91–99.

Klein, N. (2014). *This Changes Everything: Capitalism vs. the Climate*. London: Allen Lane.

Labban, M. (2008). *Space, Oil and Capital*. Routledge.

Labban, M. (2010). Oil in parallax: Scarcity, markets, and the financialization of accumulation. *Geoforum, 41*(4), 541–552.

Lane, R. (2012). The promiscuous history of market efficiency: The development of early emissions trading systems. *Environmental Politics, 21*(4), 583–603. doi:10.1080/09644016.2012.688355

Le Quéré, C. et al. (2018). Global carbon budget 2018. *Earth System Science Data, 10*, 1–54.

Leach, M., & Scoones, I. (2015). Carbon Conflicts and Forest Landscapes in Africa. New York: Routledge.

Lohmann, L. (2011). Financialization, commodification and carbon: the contradictions of neoliberal climate policy. In L. Panitch, G. Albo, & V. Chibber (Eds.), *Socialist Register 2012: The crisis and the left* (pp. 85–107). London: Merlin Press.

LuxResearch (2013). Evaluating New EOR Technologies in Oil Industry Megaprojects. Boston, MA: LuxResearch.

McAfee, K. (1999). Selling nature to save it? Biodiversity and green developmentalism. *Environment and Planning D: Society and Space, 17*(2), 133–154.

McGlade, C., & Ekins, P. (2015). The geographical distribution of fossil fuels unused when limiting global warming to 2 °C. *Nature, 517*(7533), 187–190. doi:10.1038/nature14016

Michaelowa, A. (2012). *Strengths and weaknesses of the CDM in comparison with new and emerging market mechanisms*. Available at: http://www.cdmpolicydialogue.org/research/1030_strengths.pdf

Morison, R and Hodges, J. (August 23, 2018). Carbon Reaches 10-Year High, Pushing Up European Power Prices. *Bloomberg*. Available at: https://www.bloomberg.com/news/articles/2018-08-23/carbon-reaching-20-euros-a-ton-in-europe-raises-price-for-power. Last accessed 19 March 2019.

Newell, P., Jenner, N., & Baker, L. (2009). *Governing clean development: A framework for analysis*, *27*(6), 717–739.

OECD. (2018). *OECD companion to the inventory of support measures for fossil fuels 2018*. Paris. Available at: https://dx.doi.org/10.1787/9789264286061-en

Olsen, K. H. (2007). The clean development mechanism's contribution to sustainable development: A review of the literature. *Climatic Change*, *84*(1), 59–73. doi:10.1007/s10584-007-9267-y

Olson, B and S. Kent (2017, October 27). Profits jump at Exxon, Chevron, BP, Total, Shell. *Marketwatch*. Accessed 19 March 2019.

Osborne, T., & Shapiro-Garza, E. (2018). Embedding carbon markets: Complicating commodification of ecosystem services in Mexico's Forests. *Annals of the American Association of Geographers*, *108*(1), 88–105. doi:10.1080/24694452.2017.1343657

Otto, J. (2018). Precarious participation: Assessing inequality and risk in the carbon credit commodity chain. *Annals of the American Association of Geographers*, 1–15. doi: 10.1080/24694452.2018.1490167

Ouma, S., Johnson, L., & Bigger, P. (2018). Rethinking the financialization of "nature". *Environment and Planning A: Economy and Space*, *50*(3), 500–511.

Parenti, C. (2012, November 29). Problems with the math: Is 350's carbon divestment campaign complete? *Huffington Post*. Available at: https://www.huffingtonpost.com/christian-parenti/carbon-divestment-_b_2213124.html

Reyes, O. (2011a). Zombie carbon and sectoral market mechanisms. *Capitalism Nature Socialism*, *22*(November), 37–41. doi:10.1080/10455752.2011.617508

Reyes, O. (2011b). EU Emissions Trading System: failing at the third attempt. *Corporate Europe Observatory and Carbon Trade Watch, Barcelona.*

Ricke, K., Drouet, L., Caldeira, K., & Tavoni, M. (2018). Country-level social cost of carbon. *Nature Climate Change*, *8*(10), 895.

Rowe, J., Dempsey, J., & Gibbs, P. (2016). The power of fossil fuel divestment (and its Secret). In W. K. Carroll & K. Sarker (Eds.), *A World to Win: Contemporary Social Movements and Counter-Hegemony*. ARP Books.

Schneider, L. R. (2011). Perverse incentives under the CDM: An evaluation of HFC-23 destruction projects. *Climate Policy*, *11*(2), 851–864. doi:10.3763/cpol.2010.0096

Scott, M. (2018, May 31). Insurers will be hard-hit by climate change but they're not investing in the low-carbon economy. *Forbes*. Available at: https://www.forbes.com/sites/mikescott/2018/05/31/insurers-in-the-front-line-of-the-fight-against-climate-change-shoot-themselves-in-the-foot/#5cce82d40fab. Accssed 19 March 2019.

Smith, N. (2006). Nature as accumulation strategy. In L. Panitch & C. Leys (Eds.), *Socialist Register 2007: Coming to terms with nature* (pp. 16–36). London: Merlin Press.

Smith, P., & Bustamante, M. (2014). Agriculture, forestry and other land use. *Climate Change 2014: Mitigation of climate change*. doi:10.1104/pp.900074

Spash, C. L. (2010). The brave new world of carbon trading. *New Political Economy*, *15*(2), 169–195.

Springmann, M., Clark, M., Mason-D'croz, D., Wiebe, K., Bodirsky, B. L., Lassaletta, L., … Willett, W. (2018). Options for keeping the food system within environmental limits. *Nature*, *562*, 519–525. doi:10.1038/s41586-018-0594-0

Swyngedouw, E. (2011). Depoliticized environments: The end of nature, climate change and the post-political condition. *Royal Institute of Philosophy Supplement*, *69*, 253–274.

Taylor, Z. J. (2020). The real estate risk fix: Residential insurance-linked securitization in the Florida metropolis. *Environment and Planning A: Economy and Space*, 0308518X19896579.

Taylor, Z. J., & Weinkle, J. L. (2020). The riskscapes of re/insurance. *Cambridge Journal of Regions, Economy and Society*. Available at https://doi.org/10.1093/cjres/rsaa015.

Thornton, P. K. (2010). Livestock production: recent trends, future prospects. *Philosophical Transactions of the Royal Society B: Biological Sciences*, *365*(1554), 2853–2867.

Tripathy, A. (2017). Translating to risk: The legibility of climate change and nature in the green bond market. *Economic Anthropology*, *4*(2), 239-250.

Wang, Y., & Corson, C. (2015). The making of a "charismatic" carbon credit: Clean cookstoves and "uncooperative" women in western Kenya. *Environment and Planning A*, *47*(10), 2064–2079.

Williams, C. C. (2013). A burning desire: The need for anti-money laundering regulations in carbon emissions trading schemes to combat emerging criminal typologies. *Journal of Money Laundering Control*, *16*(4), 298-320.

Wittman, H. K., Powell, L. J., & Corbera, E. (2015). Financing the agrarian transition? The Clean Development Mechanism and agricultural change in Latin America. *Environment and Planning A*, *47*(10), 2031–2046.

Xu, C. and L. Bell (2018, March 12). Worldwide oil, natural gas reserves exhibit marginal increases. *Oil and Gas Journal*. Available at: https://www.ogj.com/articles/print/volume-116/issue-12/special-report-worldwide-report/worldwide-oil-natural-gas-reserves-exhibit-marginal-increases.html. Accessed 19 March 2019.

Zickfeld, K., & Herrington, T. (2015). The time lag between a carbon dioxide emission and maximum warming increases with the size of the emission. *Environmental Research Letters*, *10*(3), 031001.

29

ENVIRONMENTAL SUSTAINABILITY AND FINANCE

Janelle Knox-Hayes, Jungwoo Chun, and Priyanka deSouza

Introduction

This chapter speaks to the issue of environmental sustainability and finance, or sustainable development and value creation in economic, environmental, and social terms. Sustainable finance seeks to improve economic efficiency, prosperity, and economic competitiveness both today and in the long-term, while contributing to protecting and restoring ecological systems, and enhancing cultural diversity and social well-being. This chapter additionally situates sustainable finance as an issue of appropriate valuation and sustained use of resources across time. The nature of sustainable finance is examined through case studies of Louisiana and Norway. Finance is designed to extend the reach of resources, and to mobilize them across space and time to maximize their development potential. Critical to the issue of sustainability is the question of how and where value is generated in space and time. For resources economies, this is a question of finding ways to bring the scale and rate of socio-economic production into alignment with the scale and rate of natural systems of production. Critical to this process is an understanding of how economies generate value through socio-economic as well as socio-natural circuits of capital, as well as within circuits in time.

At the Southeastern tip of the United States, Louisiana is one of the richest ecosystems in the world. Fed by the Mississippi River at its confluence with the Gulf of Mexico, the delta comprises an area measuring three million acres that stretches from Vermillion Bay in the west to Chandeleur Islands in the east. Part of the American Mediterranean Sea and the Louisiana coastal plain, it is one of the largest areas of coastal wetlands in the United States and has an extremely diverse ecological landscape, consisting of a number of habitats from fresh and saline marshlands to bottomland hardwood forests and maritime forests. The coastal area is the nation's largest drainage basin, which historically brought rich sediments to the delta, supplying the marshlands and attendant ecosystem with nutrients. As a consequence of its geographic and geological position, it is a site of productive resource economies. In the 1800s, Louisiana was a lush site of timber, sulfur, rice, salt, and fur production. In the 1900s, Louisiana became a leading producer of petroleum products, the legacy of millennia of its rich vegetation deposits.

Today, Louisiana produces 20% of the country's oil supply and 10% of the US natural gas supply. Sitting at the mouth of the Mississippi River, Louisiana has the five largest ports in the nation, sending and receiving over US$100 billion per year in agricultural goods, machinery, and other products including chemicals, coal, timber, and steel. It is estimated that Louisiana's river ports supply around 270,000 jobs and bring over US$32.9 billion annually to the state's economy. Commercial and recreational fisheries are additionally economically, culturally, and historically important for the Louisiana coast. Louisiana has the second largest commercial fishery in the United States by weight. The Mississippi River Delta contains seven of the top 50 seafood landing ports in the United States, and provides 33% of the nation's seafood harvest. Commercial fishing is a US$2.4 billion industry in the Gulf of Mexico, with about 75% of the fish landed coming through Louisiana ports. Given the historic and current wealth of its natural resources, Louisiana should be one of the wealthiest states in the United States, and yet Louisiana consistently ranks at the bottom of human development indexes. It is emblematic of the resource curse, or the paradox of the plenty, that regions with an abundance of natural resources (fossil fuels, minerals, etc.) tend to have less economic growth, less democracy, and worse development outcomes than countries with fewer natural resources (Zebrowski and Leach, 2014). As this chapter demonstrates, the curse is a problem of the financial mis-valuation and mismanagement of resources.

Half a world away, Norway exists in a different geographic context but shares a similarly rich resource base. The territory of Norway comprises the western and northernmost portions of the Scandinavian Peninsula, with an extensive and impressive coastline, facing the North Atlantic Ocean and the Barents Sea. The rugged coastline is broken by huge fjords and thousands of islands. With the Gulf Stream passing directly offshore from the northern areas of the Atlantic Coast, the maritime influence dominates Norway's mild climate, and produces a coastline rich in marine flora and fauna. Norway's coast is, for example, home to more than 20,000 species of algae, and more than 4,500 species of fresh and saltwater invertebrates (NOU, 2004). As a consequence Norway's economy has historically been similar to Louisiana with a series of resource intensive industries including agriculture, fishing, hunting, timber, and ship-building. In the twentieth century, Norway discovered and developed its capacity to produce petroleum, particularly offshore, and successfully built a series of parallel petroleum supporting industries.

Today, export revenues from oil and gas have risen to almost 50% of total exports and constitute more than 20% of Norway's GDP (Statistics Norway, 2009). Norway is the fifth-largest oil exporter and third-largest gas exporter in the world. As a consequence, Norway is one of the wealthiest nations in the world, measured both as GDP per capita and in capital stock. Yet, this growth has not come at the cost of human development. Norway regularly ranks at the top of the United Nations Human Development Index.

Part of Norway's success stems from its ability to maintain a strong diversity of industries. For example, Norway has maintained its fishery industries, and today is the world's second-largest exporter of fish. The government carefully manages resources through a combination of state ownership and control of licensing of exploration and production of oil fields. In 1995, the government established the sovereign wealth fund Government Pension Fund—Global supported by oil revenues, including taxes, dividends, sales revenues, and licensing fees. The Government Pension Fund controlled assets have surpassed US$1 trillion. In contradiction to the resource curse, Norway's huge stocks of natural resources combined with a skilled labor force and the adoption of new technology have made it prosperous.

The cases of Louisiana and Norway sit at the heart of debates about the sustainability of finance. They suggest a way to understand the resource curse from the standpoint of the management of resource value. This is a question of how and where value exists, but also of how different forms of value are accrued and managed. The paradox of the plenty suggests that capital that is not both created and embedded in place cannot foster a sustainable economy. Capital is not just a process of exchange but a process of value creation; not just the nature of the resource, but the means through which resources create value in conjunction with social environmental systems in space and time. The resource curse tends to occur with highly liquid (in both space and time) assets, such as petroleum. These assets lend themselves to economies that produce private gain through social cost.

The phenomenon of the creation of liquid financial wealth at the expense of social and ecological costs is evident in Louisiana, which has suffered any number of social and ecological catastrophes, both acute and chronic, as a consequence of the extractive industries that have destroyed marshland, reengineered riparian dynamics, and which directly lead to land subsidence and sea level rise. In contrast, through financial management, economic restructuring and social programming, Norway has managed to escape the resource curse, by carefully diversifying the nature of the value created from petroleum resources, and diverting it to other economic sectors. There still remains some question about the viability of such a system and whether it is simply exporting its ecological crises through the generation of climate change. Nevertheless, Norway demonstrates the principles of successful financial management of resources. Norway has particularly accomplished the generation of long-term, collective, rather than private, wealth.

The chapter proceeds with an examination of the relationship of finance to the resources of an economy. In the next section, we examine the relationship between socio-economic and social-natural circuits of capital. Subsequently, the chapter examines the spatial and temporal nature of value, and considers the importance of balancing types and temporalities of value within an economy. In the fourth section, we examine in detail the case of Louisiana, and how and why the financialization of the petroleum economy has had such devastating effects on the state. In particular, we examine the nature of social cost at private gain. In the subsequent section, we contrast Louisiana with the case of Norway, which has built incredible present and long-term social and economic value from its management of petroleum resources. In particular, we examine the ways in which the sovereign wealth fund is managed to divert resources across industries and into the future for collective gain. The final section concludes with the implications of sustainable finance, and suggests ways in which regions can work to build more successful policies of economic management.

Socio-Economic and Socio-Environmental Circuits of Capital

In examining the economies of Louisiana and Norway, it is important to distill the underlying function of social and ecological systems in the generation of these economies. The sources of value and the nature of crises are long-debated topics within economic geography and related disciplines (see, e.g., Mol and Spaargaren, 2000; Kettell, 2006). In the classical and Marxist traditions, value is believed to stem from the productivity of labor. Surplus accumulation accrues from the transformation of commodities according to the formula M-C-M': money transformed into commodities transformed (through the labor of the proletariat) into surplus value (Marx, 1867). Thus, the wealth of capitalism is built through social labor. However, Marxist thinking on value also asserts a relationship to natural resources through concepts such as the metabolic rift—the idea that increasing the productivity of large-scale agriculture and industry ultimately leads to a decline of the long-term fertility and productivity of the soil (Foster, 1999). In this vein, Jared Diamond (2005) explores the specific socio-environmental contingencies under which various productive forms have evolved. Civilizations must either learn to balance the use of the natural environment in their productive activities, or experience systematic collapse (Diamond and Ordunio, 2005).

Environmental historians such as William Cronon (1990, 1993) take issue with the over-emphasis on labor in neo-Marxist conceptions of the production of value and seek, instead, to integrate both the natural environment and cultures of ecological interaction into the understanding of production and consumption decisions at various points in time. Cronon (1993), in particular, highlights the ways societies make production decisions based on both the ecology of the environment in which they live, as well as culturally driven perceptions of society: environment relations.

The distinction between socio-economic and socio-environmental systems is spatial. Space here does not refer specifically to place but, rather, to a frame of reference from which relationships between subjects and objects can be understood (Lefebvre, 1991). Socio-economic space references socio-material relationships, particularly relationships that are built around economic transactions—for example, a laborer paid a wage for performing a service, such as operating a well, or working in a petrochemical plant, is a relationship that can be framed from the standpoint of socio-economic space. As examined later, in the cases of both Louisiana and Norway, the nature of the micro contracts that structure the relationship of laborers to the value they create, or even the connection of land to the value of its extracted minerals, is significant in the macro-economic outcomes they produce.

Socio-environmental space refers to the relationship between humans and environmental resources—for example, the dredging of canals or the consumption of petroleum energy are relationships that can be framed from the standpoint of socio-environmental space. These relationships are about physical materiality, and the consumption and use of physical resources (Bansal and Knox-Hayes, 2013). The nature of the valuation of these socio-environmental relationships, both in terms of extracted commodities and externalities (the pollution of wetlands and food resources), is also significant in the macro-economic outcomes they produce. To fully understand the nature of the circulation of capital—how, when, and where it exists—as well as the consequences the circulation of capital generates, it is important to understand the nature of the value of capital and, in particular, its spatial and temporal connotation.

Spatial and Temporal Dynamics of Value

The Nature of Value in an Economy

Contemporary definitions of value within economics are derived from a common understanding of two primary forms of value: use value and exchange value. Use value is objective, in the sense that it is value that is fixed in space and time. It is embedded in both the object and the activity that uses it. The spatial and temporal dimensions of use value can be identified on a Cartesian grid and located in a specific frame of time. It is perhaps these characteristics that led Marx to refer to use value as 'singular' (Harvey, 1982; Marx, 1867). Exchange, in contrast, is a process of liberating or moving value in space and time. It is a collaborative or intersubjective value, rather than a singular experience of value. The very purpose and nature of exchange is to move value. An exchange contract for petroleum can represent the value of petroleum in multiple cities and on different time horizons—for instance, a petroleum futures contract may guarantee a future price for a certain quantity of petroleum. The contract can even be used as capital, exchanged for other sources of financial value. But the contract does not guarantee the production of petroleum, neither does it relay the consequences of its production. In this regard, exchange value is potential value, rather than realized value, because it is subject to judgment and future use (Ramsay, 2005).

Within the dynamics of exchange, there is an issue of the temporal movement of value that arises from systems of financialization. Finance serves to move capital not only in space, but also in time. Financialization is the process of reducing value that is exchanged (whether tangible, intangible, future, or present) into financial instruments or derivatives of financial instruments (Krippner, 2010). Financialization is also a process of accelerating the rate and profit accumulation from the exchange of financial instruments (Epstein, 2005; Krippner, 2005).

The exchange of these financial instruments accelerates the rate at which economic transactions occur (Harvey, 1990; Castells, 1996; Leyshon and Thrift, 2007) because financial capital can be used to represent future value that does not yet objectively exist (Bryan and Rafferty, 2006). In the process of representing future value, finance can create demand to accelerate the rate of production that underlies commodity exchange. In other words, by accelerating the rate at which future value is represented, finance creates demand to accelerate the rate at which value is actually produced. Consider the example of the petroleum economy.

The Impact of Finance on the US Petro-Economy

Since the end of World War II, petroleum has become essential to virtually every aspect of modern life. As the *New York Times* put it: 'Oil oozes through your life, showing up in everything from asphalt to milk shakes or drugs to plastics to fertilizers. Oil is capacious, the lifeblood of civic freedoms and political liberties that most Americans have come to take for granted: unlimited personal mobility, cheap food, the prospect of property ownership in the suburbs' (Clifford, 2011). Modern economic systems rely on constant economic growth, with direct increases in rates of production and consumption to avoid and overcome crises of capital. The period between 1945 and 1973 is often referred to as the 'golden age of capitalism', or the 'postwar economic boom'. It was a period of worldwide economic expansion, in which US GDP alone increased from US$228 billion in 1945 to just under US$1.7 trillion in 1975.[1] Rapid growth was sustained by a low oil price of less than US$20 per barrel, which saw consumption climb by an average annual rate of 4.5%, well in excess of the growth of real GDP.

The period of growth came to an abrupt halt in 1973 when the Organization of Arab Petroleum Exporting Countries proclaimed an oil embargo, targeted at the United States and their allies, and drove the price of oil up by nearly 400%. The embargo caused an oil crisis with many short and long-term effects on global politics and the global economy. During the crisis in 1973, the United States sought new methods of diversification of risk capital (Watts, 2011).

Building on reforms to float the dollar in 1971 and to deregulate the financial system, the financial service industry developed new financialized petroleum products linking growth to volatility of the oil markets. Following a second oil crisis in 1979 in the wake of the Iranian Revolution, the price of crude oil more than doubled to US$39.50 per barrel.

In the aftermath of the oil crises, a group of energy and futures companies in the United States founded the first contract for oil futures on the International Petroleum Exchange (IPE) in 1981 (Watts, 2011). The futures contract served as a means to insure against market volatility and to mitigate the risks of further oil price shocks. Derivatives instrumentalize risk in such a way as to promote financial accumulation without a linear relationship to the processes of wealth creation. The contract operates by extending the value of petroleum into the future based on conditions in the present. Since 1980, the oil market has experienced continuous growth. And yet, the extension of value of crude oil into the future with derivatives contracts such as the future, swap, and option has also created tremendous volatility in the price of oil.

The consequence of the financialization of petroleum is that the wealth generated from the resource is situated within exchange value, and further dislocated from the source and consequence of its production. The oil crises created predictable shocks in the oil markets as a consequence of global political upheaval amongst producing states. Since the 1980s, the volatility of price reflects conditions of financial market exchange, with an estimated 60% of the oil futures market generated by speculators (Moors, 2011). In the 1970s, before the advent of futures, most oil produced was traded via long-term contracts. Since the beginning of the 1990s, oil exchange has been dominated by investment banks and other intermediaries, rather than end users, which contributes to the unprecedented price volatility. Oil became an asset class similar to equities and bonds, with the volume of unregulated over-the-counter commodity transactions growing enormously since 2000 (Dicker, 2011). As demonstrated by Dicker (2011), the rise of the commodity index funds and exchange traded funds, financialization, and electronic access to oil markets has not only increased volatility, but also given the oil commodities market a massive boost.

The volatility has reduced the planning horizon, the so-called 'vega problem', or the inability to determine the genuine value of crude oil based on its market price. The vega problem is particularly cumbersome for developing states that heavily rely on petroleum for the function of their economies (Moors, 2011). The increasing inability to determine the genuine value of crude oil based on its market price leads, in particular, to an inability to plan, predict, and compensate economies (Watts, 2011). Governments allocate budgets to subsidizing fuel, which exposes them to budgetary risks with environmental costs, and crowds out funding for education, health, and other investments in development. In sum, and as will be explored in the case of Louisiana, financial innovation generated greater profit for oil markets, rather than the capacity to nurture socio-environmental systems. Part of the problem has been the inability to account for social and ecological externalities. Another part of the problem has been a failure to consider the genuine connotation of value in the future.

A Typology of Value Reconsidered

The matrix in Figure 29.1 represents a typology of value that accounts for spatial and temporal dynamics. The vertical axis divides space into socio-economic and socio-environmental relations. The horizontal axis divides time into present (realized economy) and future (potential economy). Four distinct types of value are identified: use; exchange; derived (e.g., derivatives such as petroleum options); and external (the value of externalities, or value outside present use and exchange) (Knox-Hayes, 2016: 228).

Returning to the consideration of a commodity such as a barrel of oil, the barrel can be used in various forms—WTI grade crude oil, heating oil, gasoline, and natural gas—to generate use value, such as heating a home (lower-left quadrant). It can also first be exchanged in units of 1,000 barrels (upper-left quadrant) and then consumed to generate use value—sold to a petrochemical company and used to generate plastic. Derived value (upper-right quadrant) is the value derived from the exchange of the commodity in the future a contract to sell 1,000 barrels of oil at a certain price at a set time, for example. It could

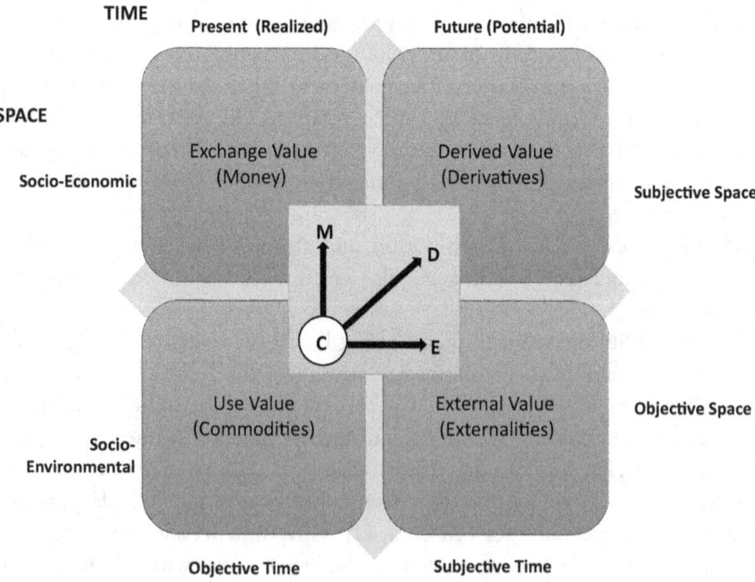

Figure 29.1 A spatial and temporal typology of value

also be converted to external value, due to a high carbon tax it could be left in the ground, and generate a positive externality of avoided greenhouse gas emissions. The negative externality of the production of petroleum may be the value of depleted marshland, or chemical runoff from the extraction and refinement of the barrel of oil. Derived value leverages an underlying commodity to create future, potential exchange value. External value leverages an underlying commodity to create future, potential use value. Whereas use and exchange are temporally singular—an item can be either used or exchanged—derived and external values present multiple alternatives for use and exchange because they both reflect subjective time frames.

The subjective nature of derived and external value creates concerns for the accounting of financial value and, particularly, for the ways in which financial value becomes represented in present time. This can be seen through the price volatility experienced in the petroleum markets after the introduction of petroleum derivatives in the 1980s, as well as the boom in the value of petroleum derivatives. Modern economic systems recognize all types of value as commensurate through pricing, regardless of qualifications of how, when, and where value actually exists. A crude oil option may generate a quantitatively similar price to a barrel of oil, but the quality of value contained within the two, as well as the consequence of their value, is considerably different. The barrel of oil can be put to use. The crude oil option merely provides the opportunity for a potentially advantageous economic transaction in the future. This is not to say a financial option is without value but, rather, that its value is qualitatively different from the value of a commodity itself.

Similarly, external value can recognize a range of potential future use outcomes that result from the production and consumption of the underlying commodity. Negative externalities (costs) from the production of petroleum include the destruction of coastal marshlands, the subsidence of land, and runoff into watercourses. Positive externalities (benefits) can be accrued by the decision not to extract petroleum, such as the preservation of coastal marshlands. The key to the creation of external value is the idea that the ultimate objective is not only the generation of value from resources, but the sustained generation of value across time. This supports the argument that the benefits of petroleum production (energy now) should not be weighed against the external effects (emissions of the greenhouse gases that generate climate change), and the present and future costs.

Use—particularly sustained use across time—is critical to the valuation of environmental resources. Valuing resources based exclusively on price, singularly in time, does not appropriately account for the value of resources. The goal of external value is not only to borrow value from the future (as with derivatives), but to shape present consumption so as to return value to the future. The case of Louisiana is emblematic of the failure of an economy to sustain value types and to return value to the future.

The Case of Louisiana: Private Gain at Social Cost

Louisiana is an iconic example that shows how the resource curse can be more prevalent with a highly liquid asset across space and time. Coastal Louisiana provides support to about one-third of crude oil and one-fifth of natural gas in the United States (Hemmerling et al., 2016). Despite hosting an oil and gas industry with annual revenues of more than US$70 billion, Louisiana ranks 47th out of 50 states in per capita income and tied for 2nd place in the percentage of people living under the poverty level as of 2010 (Zebrowski and Leach, 2014). Moreover, a majority of coastal communities and residents live in the 'sacrifice zone', suffering severely from negative health, and social and environmental impacts from the petroleum industry during production, manufacturing, and transportation (Colten, 2012). These negative externalities are detrimental to the embedded value systems in the region, the people and the local economy internalizing the socio-environmental costs in face of private (and external) gains.

During the 1920s, oil emerged on the back of extractive industries such as forestry, furs, rice, and salt. The growth of onshore infrastructure in the region began in the first decade of the twentieth century, during a time where environmental regulation was almost nonexistent (Colten, 2012). The trend of rentier economy continued with the use of wetland leases, which allowed companies to build massive network of canals, roads, platforms, and wells (Watts, 2011). Louisiana's petrochemical industry grew exponentially between 1940 and 1970 to meet demand for gasoline from the growing automobile fleet (Zebrowski and Leach, 2014). The number of refineries rose from 25 in 1947 to 57 in 1977 (Colten, 2012). The production process includes not only extraction of oil and gas, but also processing, refining, and transporting (mainly through pipelines). In addition to oil and gas produced on or within three nautical miles of land, millions of barrels of oil enter and exit the state each year through the Louisiana Offshore Oil Port (LOOP) (Zebrowski & Leach, 2014). Nearly 34% of all workers in Louisiana are employed in oil-associated industries, including oil and gas production, construction, manufacturing, and transportation, to be found mainly in coastal parishes (Hemmerling et al., 2016).

One of the most obvious consequences from the resource curse in Louisiana is the dramatic loss of coastal wetlands in the area. Louisiana is one of the richest ecosystems in the world, fed by the Mississippi River Delta. With deep geological temporal history, the region is rich in minerals and has a range of biodiversity and nutrients covered by marshes, aquatic vegetation, and mudflats (Ko et al., 2004). The coastal wetlands contain about 37% of all estuarine marshes in the United States providing irreplaceable ecosystem services, including sustaining water use and quality, fisheries production, carbon sequestration, and surge reduction (Hemmerling et al., 2016). With extensive petroleum extraction activities in the Delta, the wetland area decreased by about 25% (Ko et al., 2004). Pervasive hydrologic change and dramatically increased subsidence are the two main causes for such net loss in the wetland area (Ko et al., 2004). On average, between 1985 and 2010, rapid subsidence and land loss reached about 42.9 km^2 per year (Hemmerling et al., 2016), which has led to increased plant death, and loss of biodiversity and geological value (Ko et al., 2004). Due to a large number of river levees up the Mississippi River; the delta is being blocked from being replenished by sediment, which has caused the land to sink; canal dredging for oil and gas drilling; and sea level rise, the southern coast of Louisiana is rapidly eroding. Louisiana estimates that, by mid-century, 28,000 homes will have to be moved or bought out due to flood risk (Coastal Protection and Restoration Authority of Louisiana, 2017).

Even though residents, citizens groups, and communities acknowledge the socio-environmental costs imposed by the petro-chemical industry, the private sector has promoted self-regulation as a best practice that would minimize personal, social, and environmental damage (Colten, 2012). The brunt of the impacts of such economic activity are felt in the lower Mississippi Delta, which has been termed the 'sacrifice zone' to acknowledge its deliberate degradation for the pursuit of economic gain (Colten, 2012). The 'sacrifice zone' is symbolic of an economy that derives private gain from social cost. The majority of gains from petroleum exploitation do not remain internally for the communities and residents who, single-handedly, face the costs. The cashflow is, instead, controlled by the most mobile sector of the workforce, including holders of mineral rights, owners of development companies, and a small number of the highest paid workers who actually reside in California and New York (Zebrowski and Leach, 2014). The liquid capital of the petro-economy is easily exported to other regions in the form of capital or derivatives, and yet the serious social and environmental consequences remain.

As Cohen (2012) contends: 'Environmental degradation in the lower Mississippi River industrial complex was not the result of a coordinated assault; rather it reflected negligent behavior by industries and government authorities'. The industry frequently fails to live up to safety and pollution control standards. The cost to local communities is borne both through destruction of marshland and other habitats, as well as in the diminishing and damage of other valuable resource stocks such as timber, wildlife, and fisheries from chemical wastes and pollution. This pattern is comparable between onshore and offshore operations, which can particularly be seen after the catastrophic Deepwater Horizon incident, in which a failed BP rig leaked 5 million barrels of oil into the Gulf of Mexico, affecting 35% of Louisiana's coast (Watts, 2011). Pollution has generated severe health impacts. Chemical pollution in Louisiana has triggered cancers, neurological disorders, and genetic damage, with a corridor of the state where petro-chemicals are refined nicknamed 'cancer alley' due to the rates of cancer being so high (Zebrowski and Leach, 2014). According to the Centers for Disease Control (CDC), the death rate from cancer is significantly higher in Louisiana (196.2 deaths out of 100,000) as compared to the national average (178.1 deaths out of 100,000) (Zebrowski and Leach, 2014).

The effects of pollution and other negative externalities have been felt across Louisiana's industries. While not employing as many as those in the oil and gas sector, Louisiana's fisheries industry remains a vital source of income for the coastal residents. Nationwide, Louisiana's fisheries accounted for almost 21% of all commercial fish and shellfish transactions in 2010 (Hemmerling et al., 2016). Yet, a series of catastrophic events—including the Deepwater Horizon spill and the slow-moving flood of polluted water in the river delta—has decimated some of the most productive fishing grounds (Kistner, 2019). The estimated brown shrimp catch in Louisiana was, for example, down by about 80% in 2019 (Kistner, 2019). The failure of Louisiana's government both to redistribute value to other industries and protect the local environment has also hurt the tourism industry; coastal recreation business, including recreational fishing, represents an essential source of jobs and earnings for many coastal communities (Hemmerling et al., 2016). The economic impact of recreational fishing exceeds US$757 million annually and supports thousands of jobs (Hemmerling et al., 2016). These other crucial sectors represent fundamental economic, social, and cultural values. Those who gain from the extractive industry show little effort to sustain or protect these values.

Although a number of lawsuits are pending for damages to parishes in the state through coastal erosion, oil companies have not had to pay for the externalities of their activities, or to compensate the communities for the incalculable socio-economic losses (Zebrowski and Leach, 2014). With limited regulation, the five largest oil companies, Exxon Mobil, BP, Shell, Chevron, and ConocoPhilips reported combined profits of US$140 billion in 2011 alone (Zebrowski and Leach, 2014). These funds have not been reinvested into the region, either in terms of social benefits and productivity of the workforce, or in efforts to restore ecosystem services in the Mississippi Delta. Instead, following conventional logics of finance, the wealth and capital of these companies is reinvested into their own stocks (Zebrowski and Leach, 2014). The major value accrued from Louisiana's petro-economy is exchange value or derived value. It is not used to diversify industries, support social programming, or to replenish natural reserves. Consequently, Louisiana faces an unsustainable local economy.

The case of Louisiana demonstrates how poor value management can generate a resource curse with severe social and ecological impacts. Although blessed with rich reserves of petroleum, the state has failed to provide opportunities for the sustenance of socio-environmental value over time. Instead, communities within the state have faced irreparable health, social, and environmental damages as private companies have accrued hundreds of billions of dollars in revenue with lax state regulations and tax treatments (Zebrowski and Leach, 2014). The State Office of Conservation has done little to force the oil companies to clean up the waste and protect the embedded resource value of the marshlands, timber, and fisheries.

To be successful, an economy must balance the types, ratios, and impacts of the values which it creates. The case of Norway provides a solid counterpoint to the example of Louisiana. Norway's institutions serve to enhance socio-ecological value over time. The Norwegian government has specifically worked to build long-term wealth from its petro-economy following a process of value diversification and sustained use.

The Norwegian Oil Experience: Value across Space and Time

When oil was discovered off the continental shelf of Norway in 1969, the Norwegian government, acutely aware of the finite nature of petroleum, quickly enacted legislation to manage the new-found resource in a manner that would provide Norwegians with long-term wealth, and benefit the entire society. The Norwegian government understood the need to create a competitive advantage that surpassed their capacity as simply a commodities exporter. They also sought to protect other industries. In 1972, the government founded the Norwegian Petroleum Directorate (a precursor of Statoil ASA), which operated as an integrated petroleum company owned by the state to create the greatest possible value for society from the oil and gas activities by means of prudent resource management.

The Norwegian government channels its oil revenues through the Government Pension Fund Global (GPFG), which it set up in 1990. Today, the GPFG is the largest sovereign wealth fund in the world—worth in excess of US$1 trillion, or about US$195,000 per Norwegian citizen—and is a powerful player in global markets. The Norwegian parliament established the status and powers of the GPFG. The Fund's mandate is to maximize international purchasing power, for acceptable levels of risk.

The Fund is managed by Norges Bank Investment Management (NBIM) with a goal of broad diversification (the creation of a variety of value propositions) and long-term investments to secure sustainable economic, environmental, and social objectives. To this end, it is also governed by a Council on Ethics, which considers risk exposures and ethical challenges in making recommendations on where and how NBIM should invest the Fund. Indeed, the Fund has fostered a benign reputation through its emphasis on ethical investments, and has inspired the creation of the Santiago principles, which specify international best practices for the operation of sovereign wealth funds (Clark and Monk, 2010). The Fund's broad strategy of managing Norway's petroleum wealth operates to diversify and sustain the four types of value discussed in the typology earlier. In effect, this allows Norway to operate a traditional circuit of capital, generating commerce and financial value from the operation of the petroleum economy; however, in tandem, the Norwegian government has built a parallel circuit of value that utilizes the petroleum wealth to return value to the broader economy, including social welfare programs and ecological programs, and to secure collective gain for the long term.

When Norway first discovered oil, it was feared that the economy would succumb to Dutch disease; that is, that resource wealth would distort the economy, discounting the value of agriculture and industry, as well as the benefits of education for long-term human capital and social development. In other words, it was feared that Dutch disease could result in the weakening of internationally exposed industries, and generate substantial restructuring costs and unemployment. Norway avoided Dutch disease by investing the GPFG outside Norway. In effect, the Fund serves as a long-term savings vehicle to secure the income from a non-renewable resource by diversifying into a broad portfolio of international securities. The initial allocation of NOK 2 billion (US$0.4 billion) in 1996 to the Fund was restricted to investment in government bonds. However, in 1998, the investment universe was widened to allow a 40% allocation to foreign equities. Thereafter, there were further innovations to the strategy in the form of inclusion of new asset classes and an increase in the equity allocations to 60% (Chambers et al., 2012). The fund is invested in government bonds so that it provides support to the Norwegian government and the domestic economy. However, the diversification into foreign equities protects against inflation of the Norwegian currency and, as a consequence, protects other exporting industries, such as fisheries.

GPFG assets are not earmarked for any specific purpose. The Norwegian parliament established the status and powers of the GPFG. No single person or organization has claims over it. Unlike most other funds, the GPFG does not have a CEO or independent board of trustees controlling it. Transfers from the fund can only be made to the state budget and, from there, funds flow into the Norwegian economy. Additionally, transfers are made only from the oil-adjusted budget deficit. The intention is that, over time, withdrawals correspond to the Fund's anticipated long-term annualized real return rate of approximately 4%. The Fund thus instils fiscal discipline into the government budget and reduces the risk of hyperinflation. In good economic conditions, when tax revenues are high, less than 4% of the Fund is spent; during bad times, more than 4% is spent to offset losses. A long-term commitment to the Fund helps in restraining overspending (Dimson and Ilmanen, 2011).

Aside from sound fiscal management of the revenue generated from the petro-economy, Norway has built and sustained a dual economy, one that relies not only on petroleum products, but also domestic sustainable green industries such as fisheries and forestry. The cooperation between government and industry has a long history. In order to protect the manufacturing sector after the discovery of oil, the government coordinated incomes to prevent a dramatic increase in wages in the oil and gas sector. As a consequence, other sectors—such as fishing—remained a priority (Larsen, 2006). Industrial policy sought to stimulate learning-by-doing and to maintain diverse industrial activities. In addition, oil revenues were channeled into education and into research and development to improve the efficiency and capacity of the extractive technologies and of the workforce deploying these technologies.

The oil sector has a much higher capital intensity than other industrial sectors. This capital intensity has important technology and knowledge spillover effects. The Norwegian government took advantage of this spillover by building a dual economy of highly skilled industries comprising petroleum core products and petroleum industrial supply firms. Petroleum supply firms (supplying both equipment and technical capacity) now constitute the second-largest industry in Norway. In this regard, Norway was able to leverage its petro-economy to support the growth across the country of diverse highly skilled industries that would have a lower environmental impact.

The GPFG is tasked with maximizing utility not only for the current generation, but also future generations. In the late 1990s, Norwegian civil society introduced another facet of how the Fund would protect the welfare of future generations, by introducing the notion of investment ethics. What will the external value of the fund be and how will it be used to support Norwegian social values? (Reiche, 2010). Specifically, in 2001 the Norwegian government introduced a socially responsible investment (SRI) mandate to the GPFG. They then established a three-year trial Environment Fund within the larger Petroleum Fund for investing in companies in emerging economies that met environmental performance criteria. At the same time, the GPFG was designated as a sovereign wealth fund, with the potential for its decisions to be attributed to Norway as a matter of state responsibility. Its first ethical screenings were guided by an Advisory Commission on International Law appointed by the Ministry of Finance in 2001. In 2002, Norway moved to develop regulations to create a normatively and procedurally clear approach to ethical investment by the Fund. The ethics committee decided to use 'exclusion' as a means for the Fund to avoid complicity in problematic activities (Richardson, 2011).

The GPFG's current ethical guidelines were adopted in 2010, following a major review in 2009 of the legal mandate and practices of the Council of Ethics. The review was conducted by the Ministry of Finance and concluded that the ethical guidelines were generally robust, but recommended that additional engagements with companies under scrutiny be excluded from GPFG investment. For example, the review recommended that tobacco production be singled out as a new criterion for investment exclusion. Among other things, it also recommended more attention to climate change.

Consequently, in 2010, the Ministry of Finance issued two standards that the ethics committee must take into consideration. Guideline I consists of factors such as the probability of future violation of ethical norms, the degree to which norms are violated, and whether the company can be expected to reduce the risk of future violations in a reasonable time frame. Guideline II, which is directed at the work of the Norges Bank, obliges the Bank to integrate good governance, environmental and social issues in its investments, and to contribute actively to good international standards in responsible management and active ownership (Richardson, 2011).

As a consequence of institutions of wealth management such as the GPFG in Norway, as well as the country's broader socio-environmental approach, Norway has thrived in recent decades. It has one of the highest per capita income levels in the world, and continually ranks at the top of indices of social and environmental well-being. For example, life expectancy at birth in Norway is 83 years, three years higher than the OECD average of 80 years. The level of atmospheric pollution is considerably lower than the OECD average of 13.9 $\mu g/m^3$ (OECD, 2020). The Norwegian sovereign wealth fund is widely considered to be one of the most transparent and well-governed institutions. Nevertheless, the Fund illustrates a false dichotomy between the economy and ethics. Human rights, the environment, and climate change are bundled together as the responsibility of the Council on Ethics. NBIM has the job of ensuring financial returns for the welfare of future generations of Norwegians. Although it has been recommended that the Fund invest in unlisted renewable energy infrastructure, the Ministry of Finance has recommended the rejection of this proposal, despite the prospect of very strong returns (Richardson, 2011). The Ministry has, instead, argued that the Fund's focus should be on the economic security of future generations, and it should not be used as a tool for foreign or climate policy.

Staying within planetary boundaries is a prerequisite for long-term return on investments. This is not a question of ethics over economics but, rather, the fact that economic returns—like everything else, in the long run—are dependent on stable living conditions on Earth. Although the Norwegian sovereign wealth fund is an example par excellence in the management of revenues from non-renewable fossil fuel resources, the money from the Fund is still derived from the burning of oil and gas. The emissions from these fuels are contributing to climate change, on an ever-warming planet. In order to move from this paradigm of weak sustainability to one of strong sustainability, countries such as Norway must consider increasing investments in renewable energy. Additionally, while Norway demonstrates the potential of balancing value types and securing long-term wealth from a highly liquid resource often associated with the 'resource curse', there is an argument to be made that the ultimate objective of sustainable finance should be to generate an economy from a sustainable resource.

Conclusion

The divergent cases of the petro-economies in Louisiana and Norway demonstrate the ways in which economies must distribute value across space and time to achieve the successful management of a highly liquid resource such as petroleum. Sustainable finance requires a systematic consideration of the nature and means of producing value; it is not just about the quantity of value produced, but rather the forms of value that are generated. In particular, the spatial and temporal connections of an economy to a host of indicators of social and environmental well-being must be considered.

In the case of Louisiana, as in other resource curse examples, petroleum has been rapidly extracted to maximize exchange and derived value in the short term without considering local effects. Little care has been taken with regard to the social and environmental safety of the processes of extraction and refinement. The considerable negative externalities—pollution of waterways, destruction of marsh, subsidence of land, loss of domestic industries, severe health impacts—have been left to the local communities. The profits of petroleum transacted through the state of Louisiana are not an accurate representation of the full range of costs. Communities, particularly in Louisiana's 'sacrifice zone' have been impoverished. Fundamentally, the government not only failed to instill institutions and policies that would balance the distribution (exchange, derived, but also use and external) of value generated from the tremendous petroleum reserves, but also failed to ensure that these would serve the people of Louisiana over the long term.

Sustainable finance requires policies and institutions that spread wealth over a time-horizon that is almost always long-term. The case of Norway demonstrates the potential of sustainable finance to overcome the resource curse and secure the wealth of a highly liquid asset for the long term. In the first instance, the bulk of revenues from petroleum extraction are paid into Norway's GPFG. The sovereign wealth fund is controlled by the government for public benefit and is invested in assets such as bonds to guarantee long-term returns that also benefit the Norwegian economy. The fund is otherwise invested outside the country to stabilize the national currency and to protect other exporting industries. Policies ensure that some of the value of the Fund is returned to work for enhancement, research, and development. This creates a range of opportunities for employment, but also ensures the creation of less environmentally detrimental industries in Norway. Additionally, the government actively enforces strong safety protections for workers and the natural environment. The effect of these policies is to ensure that the types of value generated from petro-economy are balanced across use, exchange, external, and derived formats. Critically, such a balance ensures wealth is not rapidly exhausted by a few private entities but, rather, preserved for public benefit for generations to come.

While there are undoubtedly advantages to financialization and the ability to mobilize value across space and time, there are also dangers to finance, particularly in the way it represents the natural world. Finance transforms physical processes into compressed virtual representations. The exchange value inherent in finance loses connections to the material processes and the external consequences that have been borne by value generation in the first place. To be meaningful, value must be useful; it must be connected to material impact, which is inevitably embedded in space and time. To be made more effective, the systems of environmental finance, and perhaps even finance, must be made to account for spatial and temporal scale. There are a number of ways in which this could be envisioned, including having instruments that have geographic limits on the extent to which they can be traded. Additionally, there could be temporal restrictions placed on the exchange of environmental instruments such that their rate of turnover is slowed to better represent the underlying physical processes of the natural environment valued by the instruments. It may even be possible to imagine a system through which property rights could be transformed such that instruments of environmental finance could have fixed use but flexible exchange parameters. In such an instance, the instruments would allow for the generation of exchange value, but guarantee a specific type and quality of use value to the natural environment. In any event, to better accommodate the function of environmental systems, economies must seek to entrain the spatial and temporal scale of production and reproduction between the socio-economic and the socio-environmental worlds. This requires a more careful accounting of the values economies produce, and the ways these serve or hinder a range of social and environmental goals.

To this end, the case of Norway presents a particular paradox. The country has been incredibly successful in managing the petro-economy, and yet its sustainability is, at best, weak due to its being built on a resource that is inherently unsustainable. Petroleum is appealing because modern economies are built on the logic of growth and require exponential increases in energy use to modernize and develop. As a readily available and cheap source of energy, petroleum is an incredibly liquid financial asset. It is, for this reason, also difficult for most governments to manage properly. The logic of rapid extraction and exchange by private actors who do not pay the social costs of the resource has led to the social and ecological devastation of a number of communities. Norway succeeded in managing petroleum to generate long-term wealth because it is a nation state built on strong social institutions and protections. Nevertheless, it is, at best, exporting some of the negative externalities of petroleum production and consumption, including the generation of greenhouse gas emissions.

Climate change is a multifaceted problem that signals the dangers of current economic activities and of the increasing disconnect between socio-economic and environmental productivity (Newell and Paterson, 2010). Human systems have become over-productive, undermining the spatial and temporal regenerative requirements of environmental systems. To be meaningful, sustainable finance must counter the ecological waste and destruction of economic systems that are designed only to extract and never to return value. Sustainable finance requires that, instead, governments pursue economies that are beneficial not just in the distribution of wealth they create, but also in the nature of the resources they harness. In this regard, a country such as Iceland, which has built considerable socio-economic wealth from renewable energy, might serve as a better example.

Note

1 Countries GDP 1975: GDP annual comparison, CountryEconomy.com

References

Bansal, P. and Knox-Hayes, J. (2013). The time and space of materiality in organizations and the natural environment. *Organization & Environment*. doi: 10.1177/1086026612475069.

Barker, E. (1952). *Aristotle: Politics*. London: Oxford University Press.

Bryan, D. and Rafferty, M. (2006). *Capitalism with Derivatives*. New York: Palgrave Macmillan.

Bumpus, A.G. (2011). The matter of carbon: understanding the materiality of tCO_2e in Carbon offsets. *Antipode*, 43(3), 612–638.

Castells, M. (1996). *The Rise of the Network Society*. Oxford: Blackwell.

Chambers, D., Dimson, E., and Ilmanen, A. (2012). The Norway model. *The Journal of Portfolio Management*, 38(2), 67–81.

Christophers, B. (2010). On voodoo economics: Theorising relations of property, value and contemporary capitalism. *Transactions of the Institute of British Geographers*, 35(1), 94–108.

Clark, G.L. and Monk, A.H. (2010). The legitimacy and governance of Norway's sovereign wealth fund: The ethics of global investment. *Environment and Planning A*, 42(7), 1723–1738.

Clark, G.L. and Monk, A.H. (2013). Financial institutions, information, and investing-at-a-distance. *Environment and Planning A*, 45(6), 1318–1336.

Clifford, S. (2011, June 25). Oil oozes through your life. *New York Times*.

Coastal Protection and Restoration Authority of Louisiana. (2017). Louisiana's comprehensive master plan for a sustainable coast. Baton Rouge, LA: Coastal Protections and Restoration Authority Members.

Colten, C.E. (2012). An incomplete solution: Oil and water in Louisiana. *The Journal of American History*, 99(1), 91–99.

Cronon, W. (1990). Modes of prophecy and production: Placing nature in history. *The Journal of American History*, 76(4), 1122–1131.

Cronon, W. (1993). The uses of environmental history. *Environmental History Review*, 17(3), 1–22.

Daly, H.E. (1992). Allocation, distribution, and scale: Towards an economics that is efficient, just, and sustainable. *Ecological Economics*, 6(3), 185–193.

de Soto, H. (2000). *The Mystery of Capital: Why Capitalism Triumphs in the West and Fails Everywhere Else*. New York: Basic Books.

Diamond, J. (2005). *Collapse: How Societies Choose to Fail or Succeed*. London: Penguin.

Diamond, J. and Ordunio, D. (2005). *Guns, Germs, and Steel*, National Geographic Magazine. New York: W.W. Norton.

Dicker, D. (2011). *Oil's Endless Bid*. Hoboken, NJ: John Wiley.

Ellerman, A.D., Joskow, P.L., Harrison, D., and Pew Center on Global Climate Change. (2003). *Emissions Trading in the US: Experience, Lessons, and Considerations for Greenhouse Gases*. Arlington, VA: Pew Center for Global Climate Change.

Epstein, G.A. (2005). *Financialization and the World Economy*. Cheltenham, UK/ Northampton, MA: Edward Elgar Publishing.

Foster, J.B. (1999). Marx's theory of metabolic rift: Classical foundations for environmental sociology: 1. *American Journal of Sociology*, 105(2), 366–405.

Frankel, J.A. (2010). The natural resource curse: A survey (No. w15836). National Bureau of Economic Research.

Goodland, R.J.A., Daly, H.E., and El Serafy, S. (2009). The urgent need for rapid transition to global environmental sustainability. *Environmental Conservation*, 20(4), 297–309.

Harvey, D. (1982). *The Limits to Capital*. Chicago, IL: University of Chicago Press.

Harvey, D. (1990). *The Condition of Postmodernity*. Oxford: Blackwell.

Hayek, F.A. (1931). *Prices and Production*. New York: Augustus Kelly.

Hayek, F.A. (2014). *The Road to Serfdom: Text and Documents: The Definitive Edition*. London: Routledge.

Hemmerling, S.A., Carruthers, T.J.B., Hijuelos, A.C., Riley, S., and Bienn, H.C. (2016). Trends in oil and gas infrastructure, ecosystem function, and socioeconomic well-being in coastal Louisiana. WISR-001-2016. The Water Institute of the Gulf, 20pp.

Holden, S. (2013). Avoiding the resource curse the case Norway. *Energy Policy*, 63, 870–876.

Kettell, S. (2006). Circuits of capital and overproduction: A Marxist analysis of the present world economic crisis. *Review of Radical Political Economics*, 38(1), 24–44.

Keynes, J.M. (1937). The general theory of employment. *The Quarterly Journal of Economics*, 209–223.

Kistner, R. (2019). There's an environmental disaster unfolding in the Gulf of Mexico. Huffpost, accessed at https://www.huffpost.com/entry/mississippi-louisiana-gulf-coast-environmental-disaster_n_5d262c42e4b0583e482b28ed?x5g9.

Knight, E.R.W. (2008). The economic geography of carbon market trading: How legal regimes and environmental performance influence share performance under a carbon market. SSRN Working Papers. Retrieved on October 20, 2016 from http://ssrn.com/abstract=1302982.

Knox-Hayes, J. (2016). *The Cultures of Markets: The Political Economy of Climate Governance*. Oxford: Oxford University Press.

Ko, J.-Y., Day, J., Barras, J., Morton, R., Johnston, J., Kemp, G., Clairain, E., and Theriot, R. (January 2004). Impacts of oil and gas activities on coastal wetland loss in the Mississippi delta.

Kossoy, A., Oppermann, K., Platonova-Oquab, A., Suphachalasai, S., Höhne, N., Klein, N., and Wu, Q. (2014). State and trends of carbon pricing 2014. World Bank. Retrieved on October 20, 2016 from https://wdronline.worldbank.com/handle/10986/18415.

Krippner, G. (2005). The financialization of the American economy. *Socio-Economic Review*, 3(2), 173–208.

Krippner, G.R. (2010). The political economy of financial exuberance. *Research in the Sociology of Organizations*, 30, 141–173.

Larsen, E.R. (2006). Escaping the resource curse and the Dutch disease? When and why Norway caught up with and forged ahead of its neighbors. *American Journal of Economics and Sociology*, 65(3), 605–640.

Lefebvre, H. (1991). *The Production of Space*. Oxford: Blackwell.

Leyshon, A. and Thrift, N. (2007). The capitalization of almost everything: The future of finance and capitalism. *Theory, Culture & Society*, 24(7–8), 97.

Lohmann, L. (2005). Marketing and making carbon dumps: Commodification, calculation and counterfactuals in climate change mitigation. *Science as Culture*, 14(3), 203–235.

Lohmann, L. (2009). Toward a different debate in environmental accounting: The cases of carbon and cost–benefit. *Accounting, Organizations and Society*, 34(3–4), 499–534.

Lotay, J.S. (2009). Subprime carbon: Fashioning an appropriate regulatory and legislative response to the emerging us carbon market to avoid a repeat of history in carbon structured finance and derivative instruments. *Houson Journal of International Law*, 32, 459.

MacKenzie, D. (2009). *Material Markets: How Economic Agents Are Constructed*. Oxford: Oxford University Press.

Marx, K. (1867). *Capital*, volume I. Harmondsworth: Penguin/New Left Review.

Marx, K. (1993). *Grundrisse*. London: Penguin.

Marx, K. and Nicolaus, M. (1973). *Grundrisse: Foundations of the Critique of Political Economy*. Harmondsworth: Penguin in Association with New Left Review.

Mason, C.F. and Plantinga, A.J. (2013). The additionality problem with offsets: Optimal contracts for carbon sequestration in forests. *Journal of Environmental Economics and Management*, 66(1), 1–14.

Michaelowa, A. (2004). CDM incentives in industrialized countries—The long and winding road. *International Review for Environmental Strategies*, 5(1), 217–231.

Michaelowa, A. and Michaelowa, K. (2007). Climate or development: Is ODA diverted from its original purpose? *Climatic Change*, 84(1), 5–21.

Mol, A.P.J. and Spaargaren, G. (2000). Ecological modernisation theory in debate: A review. *Environmental Politics*, 9(1), 17–49.

Moors, K. (2011). *The Vega Factor: Oil Volatility and the Next Global Crisis*. Hoboken, NJ: John Wiley & Sons.

Newell, P. and Paterson, M. (2010). *Climate Capitalism: Global Warming and the Transformation of the Global Economy*. Cambridge: Cambridge University Press.

NOU. (2004). Regjeringen.no. Archived from the original on May 11, 2008. Retrieved May 30, 2010.

OECD. (2020). Better life index. Available at: http://www.oecdbetterlifeindex.org/countries/norway/, Last accessed February 8, 2020.

O'Neill, J. (2007). *Markets, Deliberation and Environment*. London: Routledge.

Plambeck, E.L. (2012). Reducing greenhouse gas emissions through operations and supply chain management. *Energy Economics*, 34, S64–S74.

Ramsay, J. (2005). The real meaning of value in trading relationships. *International Journal of Operations and Production Management*, 25(6), 549–565.

Reiche, D. (2010). Sovereign wealth funds as a new instrument of climate protection policy? A case study of Norway as a pioneer of ethical guidelines for investment policy. *Energy*, 35(9), 3569–3577.

Reinhart, C.M. and Rogoff, K.S. (2008). Is the 2007 US sub-prime financial crisis so different? An international historical comparison. *American Economic Review*, 98(2), 339–344.

Richardson, B.J. (2011). Sovereign wealth funds and the quest for sustainability: Insights from Norway and New Zealand. *Nordic Journal of Commercial Law*, 2, 1–27.

Smith, A. (1776). *The Wealth of Nations* (E. Cannan, ed., 1937 edition). New York: Modern Library.

Statistics Norway. (2009, March 15). Secondary industries. This is Norway, p. 40. Retrieved March 24, 2013.

Thrift, N. (2005). *Knowing Capitalism*. New York: Sage Publications.

Zebrowski, E. and Leach, M.Z. (2014). *Hydrocarbon Hucksters: Lessons from Louisiana on Oil, Politics, and Environmental Justice*. Jackson, MS: University Press of Mississippi.

Index

Printed in the United States
by Baker & Taylor Publisher Services

Printed in the United States
by Baker & Taylor Publisher Services